nth
Edition

Publisher's Note

Paragraphs in this supplement update and replace in their entirety those published in the Ninth edition mainwork of Williams on Wills. To highlight specifically those points which have changed, a note is provided at the beginning of each reprinted paragraph to indicate what the changes are. The exception to this is in Volume 2, Part G, the statutes, where it will be clear from the annotations what are the new amendments.

Williams on Wills

Fourth (Cumulative) Supplement to Ninth Edition

Consultant Editor

FRANCIS BARLOW
MA (OXON)
One of Her Majesty's Counsel, a Bencher of Lincoln's Inn
10 Old Square, Lincoln's Inn, London WC2A 3SU

Editors

CHRISTOPHER SHERRIN
LLM PHD
Emeritus Professor of Law, Department of Professional Legal Education,
University of Hong Kong

RICHARD WALLINGTON
MA (CANTAB)
Barrister, a Bencher of Lincoln's Inn
10 Old Square, Lincoln's Inn, London WC2A 3SU

SUSANNAH L MEADWAY
MA (OXON)
of the Middle Temple and Lincoln's Inn, Barrister
10 Old Square, Lincoln's Inn, London WC2A 3SU

MICHAEL WATERWORTH
MA (CANTAB)
of Lincoln's Inn, Barrister
10 Old Square, Lincoln's Inn, London WC2A 3SU

LexisNexis®

Members of the LexisNexis Group worldwide

United Kingdom	LexisNexis, a Division of Reed Elsevier (UK) Ltd, Lexis House, 30 Farringdon Street, London, EC4A 4HH, and London House, 20–22 East London Street, Edinburgh EH7 4BQ
Australia	LexisNexis Butterworths, Chatswood, New South Wales
Austria	LexisNexis Verlag ARD Orac GmbH & Co KG, Vienna
Benelux	LexisNexis Benelux, Amsterdam
Canada	LexisNexis Canada, Markham, Ontario
China	LexisNexis China, Beijing and Shanghai
France	LexisNexis SA, Paris
Germany	LexisNexis Deutschland GmbH, Munster
Hong Kong	LexisNexis Hong Kong, Hong Kong
India	LexisNexis India, New Delhi
Italy	Giuffrè Editore, Milan
Japan	LexisNexis Japan, Tokyo
Malaysia	Malayan Law Journal Sdn Bhd, Kuala Lumpur
New Zealand	LexisNexis NZ Ltd, Wellington
Poland	Wydawnictwo Prawnicze LexisNexis Sp, Warsaw
Singapore	LexisNexis Singapore, Singapore
South Africa	LexisNexis Butterworths, Durban
USA	LexisNexis, Dayton, Ohio

Published by LexisNexis

A CIP Catalogue record for this book is available from the British Library.

ISBN 978 1 4057 8262 3

Typeset by Columns Design Ltd, Reading, England
Printed and bound in Great Britain by CPI Group (UK) Ltd, Croydon, CR0 4YY

Visit LexisNexis at www.lexisnexis.co.uk

Preface

Since the 3rd Supplement went to press the main non-tax legislative changes have been the Trusts (Capital and Income) Act 2013 and the Marriage (Same Sex Couples) Act 2013. The Trusts (Capital and Income) Act 2013 means that it is no longer necessary to exclude the Apportionment Act 1870 or the rules of equitable apportionment (see para **[214.2A]** below). We have therefore, in the administration trusts in Volume 2 Part C (complete wills), removed the subclause excluding the apportionment rules. This change in the law removes an unnecessary technicality from will drafting, and reduces the amount that needs to be explained to testators. The text of the Act is reproduced below at para **[246.202]** ff.

The Marriage (Same Sex Couples) Act 2013 has the relevance to wills that words such as 'husband', 'wife', 'spouse', 'widow', and 'widower' appearing in, for example, the definition of the class of beneficiaries under a discretionary trust, will take on a wider meaning, though not in wills made before the Act comes into force (see Sch 4, para 1 of the Act, reproduced at para **[245.158]** below, for this exception). This Act is not yet in force, and there may be further legislation by statutory instrument concerning same-sex marriage which affects the law of wills. A particular issue is whether anything will be done to preserve against revocation wills which have been made in expectation of forming a civil partnership where the civil partnership is subsequently converted into marriage. The relevant parts of the Act are reproduced below at para **[245.149]** ff.

As regards tax, particularly inheritance tax (IHT), HMRC have been hard at work on legislative change, with the product of much of their labours enacted in FA 2013. The change most directly relevant to will preparation is the change in the conditions which any newly created will trust for disabled persons or bereaved minors must satisfy in order to qualify for privileged tax status in respect of IHT, income tax or CGT. The new rules are more restrictive as to the income trusts possible, more relaxed as to the presence of statutory or express powers of advancement, and the IHT rules on the one hand and the income tax and CGT rules on the other hand have been harmonised. Volume 2, Part C4, complete forms of will providing for someone with a disability, is reprinted in full in this Supplement, with both the notes and the forms revised to describe and take account of the new rules. Notes and forms relating to trusts for minor children, for example, paras **[200.108]–[200.110]**, **[217.1]**, **[217.4]** and **[217.9]**, have also been revised to take account of the new rules.

Other IHT changes in FA 2013 which do not directly affect the drafting of wills, but which anyone advising on testamentary dispositions needs to be aware of, include the restrictions on the deductibility of debts which have financed the acquisition maintenance or improvement of excluded property or property entitled to business, agricultural, or woodlands relief (FA 2013, Sch 36), and the changes to the rules concerning gifts between spouses where the donor is domiciled in the UK and the donee is domiciled outside the UK (FA 2013, ss 177 and 178). See, eg paras **[200.78]**, **[200.85]**, **[205.10A]**, **[233.12A]**, **[236.3] and [236.4].**

Connoisseurs of the law of succession will be pleased to hear that there are two exciting developments in the offing. One is the Inheritance and Trustees' Powers Bill, which has reached Second Reading stage in the House of Lords, and which will carry into law the uncontroversial parts of the Law Commission's recommendations in their recent report on intestacy and family provision. It will also amend Trustee Act 1925, ss 31 and 32 so that the standard form amendments to these, which are routinely included in wills, will be written into the legislation, thus enabling a further simplification of the standard forms of will. The other impending development is that the Supreme Court is to hear an appeal in the memorable case of *Marley v Rawlings* [2013] Ch 271 (CA), where a husband and wife signed each other's wills, and where the High Court and the Court of Appeal refused rectification. Apart from the interest of the legal issues, it also has the interest that it will be the first time the court of last resort will have considered the law of wills for a very long time, possibly the first since *Wintle v Nye* [1959] 1 WLR 284.

If you have any comments on this work or suggestions for its improvement, please do not hesitate to get in touch. In the preparation of this Supplement we have been particularly grateful to Mr Vincent Oakley, solicitor, of Wolverhampton, for his helpful suggestions.

This Supplement is based on materials to hand as at 1 October 2013.

November 2013

The Editors

Contents

VOLUME 1 – THE LAW OF WILLS

Part L Construction of wills: particular rules relating to persons

Part M Construction of wills: particular rules relating to beneficial interests

Table of abbreviations

Abbreviation	Full Title
AA 1976	Adoption Act 1976
AA 1984	Anatomy Act 1984
ACA 2002	Adoption and Children Act 2002
AEA 1925	Administration of Estates Act 1925
AJA 1982	Administration of Justice Act 1982
CA 1985	Companies Act 1985
CCA 1984	County Courts Act 1984
CDPA 1988	Copyright, Designs and Patents Act 1988
ChA 1989	Children Act 1989
CLSA 1990	Courts and Legal Services Act 1990
CPA 2004	Civil Partnership Act 2004
EDP(FRLS)A 2011	Estates of Deceased Persons (Forfeiture Rule and Law of Succession) Act 2011
FA 1984	Finance Act 1984
FA 2002	Finance Act 2002
FA 2003	Finance Act 2003
FA 2004	Finance Act 2004
FA 2005	Finance Act 2005
FA 2006	Finance Act 2006
FA 2008	Finance Act 2008
FA 2013	Finance Act 2013
FAA 1976	Fatal Accidents Act 1976
FoA 1982	Forfeiture Act 1982
FLRA 1969	Family Law Reform Act 1969
FLRA 1987	Family Law Reform Act 1987
FPA 1966	Family Provision Act 1966
GRA 2004	Gender Recognition Act 2004
HA 1996	Housing Act 1996
HFEA 1990	Human Fertilisation and Embryology Act 1990
HFEA 2008	Human Fertilisation and Embryology Act 2008
HRA 1998	Human Rights Act 1998
HTA 1961	Human Tissue Act 1961
HTA 2004	Human Tissue Act 2004
IA 1978	Interpretation Act 1978
ICTA 1988	Income and Corporation Taxes Act 1988
IEA 1952	Intestates' Estates Act 1952

I(PFD)A 1975	Inheritance (Provision for Family and Dependants) Act 1975
IHTA 1984	Inheritance Tax Act 1984
ITA 2007	Income Tax Act 2007
ITTOIA 2005	Income Tax (Trading and Other Income) Act 2005
LA 1976	Legitimacy Act 1976
LLPA 2000	Limited Liability Partnerships Act 2000.
LP(MP)A 1989	Law of Property (Miscellaneous Provisions) Act 1989
LRA 2002	Land Registration Act 2002
LR(S)A 1995	Law Reform (Succession) Act 1995
M(SSC)A 2013	Marriage (Same Sex Couples) Act 2013
MCA 2005	Mental Capacity Act 2005
MeHA 1983	Mental Health Act 1983
MFPA 1984	Matrimonial and Family Proceedings Act 1984
MGACA 1972	Museums and Galleries Admissions Charges Act 1972
MGA 1992	Museum and Galleries Act 1992
MHA 1959	Mental Health Act 1959
PAA 1964	Perpetuities and Accumulations Act 1964
PAA 2009	Perpetuities and Accumulations Act 2009
PLMA 1964	Public Libraries and Museums Act 1964
RA 1977	Rent Act 1977
SL(R)A 1981	Statute Law (Repeals) Act 1981
TA 1925	Trustee Act 1925
TCGA 1992	Taxation of Chargeable Gains Act 1992
TLATA 1996	Trusts of Land and Appointment of Trustees Act 1996
TrA 2000	Trustee Act 2000
WA 1837	Wills Act 1837
WA 1968	Wills Act 1968

VOLUME 1

The law of wills

PART A

Nature of wills

CHAPTER 1

Nature of a will

[1.14]

[Updated in footnote 4 for *Feltham v Bouskell* [2013] EWHC 1952 (Ch), [2013] WTLR 1363.]

Liability for preparation of a will. A solicitor instructed by his client to carry out a transaction to confer a benefit on an identified third party, such as making a will in favour of that person, owes a duty of care to that third party to use proper care in carrying out instructions.[1] This duty extends in law to an intended beneficiary who is reasonably foreseeably deprived of his intended legacy as a result of the solicitor's negligence in circumstances in which there was no confidential or fiduciary relationship and neither the testator nor his estate has a remedy against the solicitor.[2] A solicitor, when preparing a will, owes a duty of care to an intended beneficiary to ensure that effect is given to the testator's testamentary intentions so that the beneficiary receives what the testator intended he should receive.[3] A solicitor instructed to draw up a will must ensure that the will is presented for execution by the client within a reasonable time.[4] The Court of Appeal has held that a solicitor who is instructed to prepare a will for a client is liable in damages to a disappointed beneficiary when the client dies before the will has been prepared or signed.[5] It has been held that a solicitor could owe a duty of care to a beneficiary named in a will in respect of advice given to a testator.[6] But a solicitor who had acted for a testator in preparing his will owed no duty of care to a beneficiary under that will when acting in a subsequent transaction for the testator which adversely affected the value of an asset which formed part of the beneficiary's potential interest under the will.[7] If the mistake in the will is one that is capable of being cured by rectification of the will, that remedy must be pursued before a negligence action against the draftsman will be entertained.[8]

1 *Ross v Caunters* [1980] Ch 297, [1979] 3 All ER 580. Solicitor liable in negligence for failing to warn testator that attestation by beneficiary's spouse would invalidate the testamentary gift to that beneficiary. A solicitor who had failed to check that the testator's will was signed was held liable in negligence to a beneficiary who had been deprived of the benefit of the testator's estate; in *Humblestone v Martin Tolhurst Partnership* [2004] EWHC 151 (Ch). See *Watts v Public Trustee for Western Australia* [1980] WAR 97; *Seale v Perry* [1982] VR 193; *Whittingham v Crease & Co* (1978) 88 DLR (3d) 353; *Sutherland v Public Trustee* [1980] 2 NZLR 536; *Allied Finance and Investments Ltd v Haddow & Co* [1983] NZLR 22, NZCA.

2 *White v Jones* [1995] 1 All ER 691, HL, affirming [1993] 3 All ER 481, CA; solicitor liable in negligence for delay that effectively deprived the beneficiaries of their legacies. The general tortious cases of *Headley Byrne & Co Ltd v Heller & Partners* [1963] 2 All ER 575 and *Caparo Industries plc v Dickman* [1990] 2 AC 605,[1990] 1 All ER 568, amongst others, followed. See also *Esterhuizen v Allied Dunbar Assurance plc* [1998] 2 FLR 668 and *Ryan v Public Trustee* [2000] 1 NZLR 700.

3 *Carr-Glynn v Frearsons (a firm)* [1999] Ch 326 [1998] 4 All ER 225, CA; reversing Lloyd J [1997] 2 All ER 614 (failing to ensure testatrix severed her joint tenancy in property disposed by will), applying *White v Jones* [1995] 2 AC 207, [1995] 1 All ER 691; *Humblestone v Martin Tolhurst Partnership* [2004] EWHC 151 (Ch). The duty was owed notwithstanding that the testator's estate might also have a remedy against the solicitor for breach of duty, since the duties owed by the solicitor to the testator and to the beneficiary were complementary, and extended to ensuring that the relevant property formed part of the testator's estate: *White v Jones* above at p 710.

4 *Gartside v Sheffield, Young and Ellis* [1983] NZLR 37 (NZCA), solicitor instructed by elderly testatrix in poor health to draw up a will. Seven days later she died, the solicitors having failed to present the new will to her for execution. Probate of a previous will granted. Solicitors held to be liable to person who would have been a beneficiary under the new will. Similarly in *White v Jones* [1995] 2 AC 207, [1995] 1 All ER 691. In *Feltham v Bouskell* [2013] EWHC 1952 (Ch), [2013] WTLR 1363 a solicitor was found liable for failing to prepare a will where there were doubts about the testamentary capacity of the testatrix. The judge said that in such a situation the solicitor must either refuse the instructions and make the position clear to the client, or take steps to satisfy himself as to his client's mental capacity promptly.

5 *White v Jones* [1995] 2 AC 207, [1995] 1 All ER 691. See also *Murphy v Brentwood District Council* [1991] 1 AC 398, [1990] 2 All ER 908 and *Smith v Claremont Haynes & Co* (1991) Times, 3 September.

6 *Kecskemeti v Rubens Rabin & Co* (1992) Times, 31 December.

7 *Clarke v Bruce Lance & Co (a firm)* [1988] 1 All ER 364, [1988] 1 WLR 881, CA.

8 *Walker v Geo H Medlicott & Son (a firm)* [1999] 1 All ER685; the plaintiff must seek to mitigate his (alleged) loss by bringing proceedings for rectification of the will under the Administration of Justice Act 1982, s 20 (if appropriate) and to exhaust that remedy before bringing proceedings for negligence against the solicitor. It will be appreciated that rectification will only be an appropriate remedy in certain circumstances; see Chapter 6; thus the mistakes of the solicitors in *Ross v Caunters* [1980] Ch 297, [1979] 3 All ER 580 and *White v Jones* [1995] 2 AC 207, [1995] 1 All ER 691 would not be susceptible to rectification.

[1.15]

[Updated in footnotes 3 and 11 for *Vallee v Birchwood* [2013] EWHC 1449 (Ch), [2013] WTLR 931.]

Donatio mortis causa. Property may also pass on death under a *donatio mortis causa* which has been described[1] as a singular form of gift, which is of an amphibious nature, being a gift which is neither entirely inter vivos nor testamentary. It is an act inter vivos by which the donee is to have the absolute title to the subject of the gift, not at once, but if the donor dies. If the donor dies the title becomes absolute, not under, but as against, the executor. In order to make the gift valid it must be made so as to take complete effect on the donor's death.[2] The essentials of a *donatio mortis causa* are that it is a gift made in contemplation of,[3] and conditional on,[4] death, and that before death the deceased should have either handed over the subject matter of the gift[5] or some essential indicia of title to the gift.[6] A valid *donatio mortis causa* cannot be revoked by will.[7]

Where a testatrix wished to give certain jewellery to a donee, some of which was in safe deposits, there was held to be sufficient delivery by the handing over of the key to the trunk, in which was the key to one safe deposit, which in turn contained the key to the other safe deposits. The fact that the key alone was not sufficient to gain entry to the safe deposits (a signed authority and a password being also required) was irrelevant.[8] Similarly handing over a post office savings bank book, a trustee savings bank book, and deposit pass books of two joint stock banks was held to be a sufficient delivery.[9] It has now been decided by the Court of Appeal that real property, a house in this case, can be the subject of a valid *donatio mortis causa*.[10] It was thought that the title deeds are the essential *indicia* of title to unregistered land and that the handing over of the deeds could amount to a parting with the dominion over the land.[11] Nourse LJ commented:

> 'Let it be agreed that the doctrine is anomalous. Anomalies do not justify anomalous exceptions. If due account is taken of the present state of the law in regard to mortgages and choses in action, it is apparent that to make a distinction in the case of land would be to make just such an exception. A *donatio mortis causa* of land is neither more nor less anomalous than any other. Every such gift is a circumvention of the Wills Act. Why should the additional statutory formalities for the creation and transmission of interests in land be regarded as some greater obstacle? The only step which has to be taken is to extend the application of the implied or constructive trust arising on the donor's death from the conditional to the absolute estate.'[12]

1 Per Buckley J in *Re Beaumont, Beaumont v Ewbank* [1902] 1 Ch 889 at 892. Such gifts should be distinguished from wills since, for example, the subject-matter of a *donatio mortis causa* does not vest in the personal representatives on the deceased's death, but passes retroactively to the donee. But see the Inheritance (Provision for Family and Dependants) Act 1975, s 8(2); Chapter 105.

2 Per Buckley J in *Re Beaumont, Beaumont v Ewbank* [1902] 1 Ch 889 at 892–893. In *Re Beaumont, Beaumont v Ewbank* [1902] 1 Ch 889 the gift of a cheque drawn by the deceased was held not to be a good *donatio mortis causa* because a person's cheque is not property; it is only a revocable order such that if the banker acts on it the donee will have the money to which it relates, following *Hewitt v Kaye* (1868) LR 6 Eq 198; and *Re Beak's Estate, Beak v Beak* (1872) LR 13 Eq 489.

3 *Re Craven's Estate, Lloyds Bank Ltd v Cockburn* [1937] Ch 423 at 426 (the donor must contemplate death in the near future; what may be called death for some reason believed to be impending); *Wilkes v Allington* [1931] 2 Ch 104 (immaterial that death occurs from different cause); *Re Dudman, Dudman v Dudman* [1925] Ch 553 (but not contemplation of suicide); *Vallee v Birchwood* [2013] EWHC 1449 (Ch), [2013] WTLR 931 (evidence of a terminal illness is not necessary and a subjective contemplation of the possibility of death in the near future suffices).

4 *Gardner v Parker* (1818) 3 Madd 184 (can be implied); *Treasury Solicitor v Lewis* [1900] 2 Ch 812; *Re Ward, Ward v Warwick* [1946] 2 All ER 206.

5 *Re Craven's Estate, Lloyds Bank Ltd v Cockburn* [1937] Ch 423 at 427.

6 *Sen v Headley* [1991] Ch 425, [1991] 2 All ER 636, CA; reversing Mummery J [1990] Ch 728, [1990] 1 All ER 898; *Birch v Treasury Solicitor* [1951] Ch 298, [1950] 2 All ER 1198 (a post office savings bank book held to be sufficient even though all the terms of the contract between the saver and the bank were not included). The giving of a power of attorney was not alone sufficient: *Re Craven's Estate, Lloyds Bank Ltd v Cockburn* [1937] Ch 423. The following have been held good subjects of donation as amounting to *indicia* of title: a promissory note payable to the deceased's order but not indorsed (*Veal v Veal* (1859) 27 Beav 303); bills of exchange in favour of the deceased on his order (*Rankin v Weguelin* (1832) 27 Beav 309); bills of exchange payable to order and which had not been indorsed (*Re Mead, Austin v Mead* (1880) 15 Ch D 651); a cheque drawn payable to the donor's order and not indorsed (*Clement v Cheeseman* (1884) 27 Ch D 631); a banker's deposit note (*Re Dillon, Duffin v Duffin* (1890) 44 Ch D 76). But not the deceased's own cheque: *Re Beaumont, Beaumont v Ewbank* [1902] 1 Ch 889.

7 *Jones v Selby* (1710) Prec Ch 300.

8 *Re Lillingston, Pembery v Pembery* [1952] 2 All ER 184, following *Re Wasserberg* [1915] 1 Ch 195 at 202, 205; and *Delgoffe v Fader* [1939] Ch 922 at 927. See also *Ward v Turner* (1752) 2 Ves Sen 431; compare *Re Johnson, Sandy v Reilly* (1905) 92 LT 357 at 358. In *Woodard v Woodard* [1995] 3 All ER 980 the handing over the keys to a car was thought to

be a sufficient parting with the dominion in the car to constitute a valid donatio mortis causa; *Re Craven's Estate, Lloyds Bank Ltd v Cockburn* [1937] Ch 423 and *Sen v Headley* [1991] 2 All ER 636 followed.

9 *Birch v Treasury Solicitor* [1951] Ch 298, [1950] 2 All ER 1198, applying *Re Dillon, Duffin v Duffin* (1890) 44 Ch D 76 (banker's deposit note), and *Moore v Darton* (1851) 4 De G & Sm 517 (debt), distinguishing *Delgoffe v Fader* [1939] Ch 922 and *Reddel v Dobree* (1839) 10 Sim 244 (cash box not fully handed over).

10 *Sen v Headley* [1991] Ch 425, [1991] 2 All ER 636, CA; reversing Mummery J [1990] Ch 728, [1990] 1 All ER 898. Followed in *Vallee v Birchwood* [2013] EWHC 1449 (Ch), [2013] WTLR 931. The nearest previous authority was that of Lord Eldon's in *Duffield v Elwes* (1827) 1 Bli NS 497, HL where it was held that there could be a *donatio* of a gift of money secured by a mortgage of land, by delivery of the mortgage deed.

11 Analogous to the handing over of the savings bank books in *Birch v Treasury Solicitor* [1951] Ch 298, [1950] 2 All ER 1198, CA. In *Vallee v Birchwood* [2013] EWHC 1449 (Ch), [2013] WTLR 931 the delivery of the deeds and keys to a house in which the donor continued to reside until his death five months later was held sufficient.

12 *Sen v Headley* [1991] 2 All ER 636 at 647. It was noted that both *Re Dillon, Duffin v Duffin* (1890) 44 ChD 76, CA and *Birch v Treasury Solicitor* [1950] 2 All ER 1198 had extended the doctrine. The essential requirements for the application of the doctrine, noted above, were affirmed.

CHAPTER 2

Joint and mutual wills

[2.3]

[Name corrected in footnote 2.]

Mutual wills. In England a joint will is practically never executed at the present time, but what are called mutual wills, where two or more persons each agree to execute a separate will conferring, with or without other provisions,[1] usually, reciprocal benefits on each other, have become more common in recent times.[2]

Mutual wills embrace the twin concepts of an agreement by the two parties to make such wills and the enforcement of that agreement after the death of the first to die by means of a constructive trust. Such wills can lead to difficulties in the proof of the agreement and to uncertainties and complexities relating to the nature, scope and effect of the trust imposed on the estate of the second to die. These difficulties centre on questions such as whether the trust is constructive or implied; whether the trust is fixed or floating; when the trust is imposed, ie at the death of the first to die, or the death of the second to die; and what property is affected by the trust, ie all the joint property or only the property inherited by the second to die from the first to die. Depending on the answer to these questions, problems can arise as to the powers of the survivor to deal or dispose of the joint property or his own property, after the death of the first to die. The will of the survivor will remain revocable but the property will none the less still be affected by the trust imposed to give effect to the agreement. Mutual wills can thus have the effect of restricting the freedom of the survivor to effectively deal with both his own property and the property inherited from the first to die. For these reasons professional advisors often advise that mutual wills are not recommended. The High Court of Australia has held that the estate of a testator was available to satisfy a family provision claim even though the estate was bound by a mutual will agreement.[3]

1 The origin of the doctrine of mutual wills is the decision of Lord Camden LC in *Dufour v Pereira* (1769) 1 Dick 419; see Morritt J in *Re Dale* [1993] 4 All ER 129 at 133 where the authorities are reviewed. The usual form of mutual wills includes reciprocal benefits given to each party, which may be either absolute interests in each other's property (*Stone v Hoskins* [1905] P 194) with alternative provisions in case of lapse (*Re Oldham, Hadwen v Myles* [1925] Ch 75; *Re Heys' Estate, Walker v Gaskill* [1914] P 192 at 196; *Re Cleaver, Cleaver v Insley* [1981] 2 All ER 1018, [1981] 1 WLR 939) or life interests with the same ultimate disposition on the death of the survivor (*Gray v Perpetual Trustee Co Ltd* [1928] AC 391; *Re Hagger, Freeman v Arscott* [1930] 2 Ch 190). The other provisions are usually pecuniary legacies or specific gifts of a personal nature and these will generally be outside the mutual provisions or the provisions intended to be irrevocable where an agreement as to

revocability is made. Though perhaps the most common case of mutual wills is that of husband and wife, they can also be made by persons having common interests, such as unmarried brothers or sisters or persons engaged to be married.

2 For recent illustrations see *Re Cleaver, Cleaver v Insley* [1981] 2 All ER 1018, *Re Dale* [1993] 4 All ER 129, *Re Goodchild* [1996] 1 All ER 670; affd [1997] 3 All ER 63, CA, and *Healey v Brown* [2002] WTLR 849. To the contrary, the Law Reform Committee 22nd Report on The Making and Revocation of Wills (1980) (Cmnd 7902) paras 3.50–3.52 thought that mutually binding wills were 'extremely rare' and created a number of problems, but they did not recommend their abolition; see Carnwath J in *Re Goodchild* [1996] 1 All ER 670 at 677.

3 *Barns v Barns* [2005] WTLR 1093, not following *Schaefer v Schuhmann* [1972] AC 572, PC; see para **[105.49]** below.

[2.5]

**[Updated in footnote 1 for *Fry v Densham-Smith* [2010] EWCA Civ 1410, [2011] WTLR 389, CA.
Updated in footnote 7 and in the text for *Olins v Walters* [2009] Ch 212.]**

Agreements relating to mutual wills. In order for the doctrine of mutual wills to apply there has to be, what amounts to, a contract at law between the two testators that both wills will be irrevocable and will remain unaltered.[1] A mere mutual desire that both wills should remain unaltered could not, in the absence of an express agreement, of itself prevent the survivor from departing from the arrangement.[2] Such agreements vary according to the circumstances of particular cases and the wishes of the parties. The wills may be executed upon an agreement that they shall not be revoked or altered.[3] On the other hand, they may be made in pursuance of an agreement that they shall be freely revocable by any party.[4] In a modern case such wills and the accompanying agreement were construed so that as to one part of the residuary estate revocation was allowed, but not as to the other part.[5] In some cases no agreement at all is made, or at least none is proved.[6]

The 'irreducible core' of the doctrine has been described as a contract between two testators, T1 and T2, that in return for T1 agreeing to make a will in form X and not to revoke it without notice to T2, then T2 will make a will in form Y and agree not to revoke it without notice to T1. If such facts are established then upon the death of T1 equity will impose upon T2 a form of constructive trust (shaped by the exact terms of the contract that T1 and T2 have made.) The constructive trust is imposed because T1 has made a disposition of property on the faith of T2's promise to make a will in form Y, and with the object of preventing T1 from being defrauded.[7]

1 *Re Goodchild* [1997] 3 All ER 63, CA; affirming Carnwath J [1996] 1 All ER 670; applying *Gray v Perpetual Trustee Co Ltd* [1928] All ER Rep 758 at 762 and *Re Dale, Proctor v Dale* [1993] 4 All ER 129 at 133. In *Re Goodchild* the absence of proof of such an agreement meant that the mutual wills were not established. See also *Fry v Densham-Smith* [2010] EWCA Civ 1410, [2011] WTLR 389.

2 *Re Goodchild* [1997] 3 All ER 63.

3 Such an agreement was held proved in *Stone v Hoskins* [1905] P 194. In *Re Oldham, Hadwen v Myles* [1925] Ch 75, it was only proved that the parties agreed to make mutual wills and nothing was proved as to any agreement to revoke.

4 This is commonly evidenced by making the gift to the other 'absolutely and beneficially and without any sort of trust or obligation'. It may also be evidenced by a recital that the will, though made as a mutual will, is made without any agreement that it or any of its provisions shall be irrevocable and that the intention is that either party shall have full liberty to revoke or alter all or any of the provisions of his or her will. This clearly leaves it open to the survivor to revoke his will and make other provisions, which, indeed, may often be necessary in altered circumstances, such as remarriage, or the marriage of some children

while others remain unmarried. It is apprehended that an agreement not to revoke leaves the testator free to dispose of his property during his lifetime (see para **[2.3]**, above, n 1), and this is clearly so where there is no such agreement. Where the agreement is in special terms (see eg *Re Green, Lindner v Green* [1951] Ch 148, [1950] 2 All ER 913, more fully discussed in n 5, below) it may be that the terms of the agreement prevent his disposing of his own property or property coming from the first to die or some other specified source. If the agreement relates to specific property, the right of disposition is fettered as to that property, but, if the agreement has been ignored, it may be that only a remedy in damages is available against the estate of the testator so ignoring it: see Chapter 3.

5 *Re Green, Lindner v Green* [1950] 2 All ER 913. In this case the survivor remarried and made a new will giving the whole of the residue to his second wife. Certain property which by his former will he had disposed of as property belonging to his first wife was held to be taken by the personal representatives upon trust to give effect to the first will. Certain legatees were given pecuniary legacies under both wills but not of identical amounts. As these legacies had in the first will been given out of property notionally regarded as the first wife's property, the legatees were entitled to take under both wills. Apparently the legacies under the first will were in the special circumstances of the case subject to abatement.

6 *Re Oldham, Hadwen v Myles* [1925] Ch 75; *Gray v Perpetual Trustee Co Ltd* [1928] AC 391; *Garioch's Trustees v Garioch's Executors* 1917 SC 404. In such case the will may be revoked by one of the parties by a holograph will: *Saxby v Saxby Executors* 1952 SC 352.

7 *Olins v Walters* [2009] Ch 212 at [38].

[2.6]

[Updated in footnote 2 for *Fry v Densham-Smith* [2010] EWCA Civ 1410, [2011] WTLR 389, CA. Updated in footnotes 2, 5 and 9 and the text for *Charles v Fraser* [2010] EWHC 2124 (Ch), [2010] WTLR 1505. References to *Healey v Brown* [2002] WTLR 849, and *Olins v Walters* [2009] Ch 212 added in footnote 4. Updated reference to the Law of Property (Miscellaneous Provisions) Act 1989, in footnote 4.]

Proof of agreement. The agreement may be incorporated in the will by recital or otherwise,[1] or it may be proved outside the will.[2] It may be oral or in writing,[3] but it would seem that in so far as such agreement affects a disposition of land, it must be in writing.[4] The mere simultaneity of the wills and the similarity of their terms are not enough taken by themselves to establish the necessary agreement,[5] which must be established by clear and satisfactory evidence on the balance of probabilities.[6] Proof of the precise terms of the agreement is essential, for any subsequent limitation of the powers of disposition of any party is dependent upon the precise restriction being proved to have been agreed between the parties.[7] The key issue in the proof of mutual wills is that each of the parties has agreed with the other not to alter his or her testamentary dispositions on the death of the first to die.[8] Given the difficulties which can arise in proving mutual wills, it has been said that it is the plain duty of a solicitor faced with two testators wishing to make reciprocal wills, to ascertain their intentions as to revocation, to advise as to the effect of making mutual wills and to ensure that any agreement they wish to make is clearly and accurately recorded[9].

1 *Re Hagger, Freeman v Arscott* [1930] 2 Ch 190. This is certainly the better course because, if any question arises, it may well arise many years after the execution of the will and evidence of an oral agreement may be either unobtainable or it may be difficult to establish its precise terms. See *Re Ohorodnyk* (1980) 102 DLR (3d) 576 on proof of the agreement.

2 *Re Heys' Estate, Walker v Gaskill* [1914] P 192 at 194, and *Charles v Fraser* [2010] EWHC 2124 (Ch), [2010] WTLR 1505, where evidence was given that two sisters had spoken freely about 'the will' saying they had decided that the surviving sister was to have their money for her care and it would then be distributed between friends and relatives. See also *Fry v Densham-Smith* [2010] EWCA Civ 1410, [2011] WTLR 389.

3 See *Stone v Hoskins* [1905] P 194; *Re Oldham, Hadwen v Myles* [1925] Ch 75; *Gray v Perpetual Trustee Co Ltd* [1928] AC 391.

4 It would seem that this must be so since 1989 by virtue of the Law of Property (Miscellaneous Provisions) Act 1989, s 2; see *Healey v Brown* [2002] WTLR 849, but see also *Olins v Walters* [2008] EWCA Civ 782, [2009] Ch 212, both cases referred to in footnote 2 of para **[2.8]** below. In the latter case it was held that the formalities of the Law of Property (Miscellaneous Provisions) Act 1989, s 2 did not have to be met where the property effected by the mutual will agreement was directed by the will to be converted into money. Whereas the lack of a written agreement may prevent the doctrine of mutual wills applying to impose a constructive trust on land belonging throughout to the survivor of testators making mutual wills, it may not prevent a constructive trust being imposed by means of the doctrine of secret trusts on land coming to the survivor from the first-to-die: see *Healey v Brown* [2002] WTLR 849. As to cases before that Act, see *Humphreys v Green* (1882) 10 QBD 148. It seems there is no distinction between the law applicable to an ordinary agreement not to revoke a will and a mutual agreement not to revoke a mutual will; indeed, it was said in *Dufour v Pereira* (1769) 1 Dick 419, as reported in 2 Hargrave Juridicial Arguments 304 at 309, that 'there is no difference between promising to make a will in such a form and making a will with a promise not to revoke it', and this has been cited with approval in *Stone v Hoskins* [1905] P 194 at 196, 197; *Re Oldham* [1925] Ch 75 at 84, and in *Gray v Perpetual Trustee Co Ltd* [1928] AC 391 at 399.

5 *Gray v Perpetual Trustee Co Ltd* [1928] AC 391 at 399–400 per Viscount Haldane; *Dufour v Pereira* (1769) 1 Dick 419, cited with approval by Nourse J in *Re Cleaver, Cleaver v Insley* [1981] 2 All ER 1018 at 1022. See also *Re Oldham, Hadwen v Myles* [1925] Ch 75 at 87; *Re Skippen, Hodgson v Armstrong and MacInnes* [1947] 1 DLR 858; *Re Gillespie* (1969) 3 DLR (3d) 317. But see *Charles v Fraser* [2010] EWHC 2124 (Ch), [2010] WTLR 1505 where identical and intricate provisions dividing two estates between the same friends and relatives were held to be indicative of mutual wills.

6 Per Nourse J in *Re Cleaver, Cleaver v Insley* [1981] 2 All ER 1018 at 1024, applying *Birmingham v Renfrew* (1937) 57 CLR 666; clear and satisfactory evidence of the agreement was found in *Re Cleaver, Cleaver v Insley* [1981] 2 All ER 1018. See *Re Goodchild* [1997] 3 All ER 63 where these points were emphasised by Leggatt LJ at 67–72: a 'common understanding' will not suffice, 'clear and satisfactory evidence' is required. The crucial difference between *Re Cleaver* and *Re Goodchild* was that in the former case there was specific evidence as to the testator's mutual intentions at the time the wills were made, whereas in the latter case there was not: *Re Goodchild* [1997] 3 All ER 63 at 71c. Similarly in *Birch v Curtis* [2002] EWHC 1158 (Ch), [2002] 2 FLR 847, where it was emphasised that the doctrine of mutual wills derived from a contract between the parties making the wills, the crucial ingredient being the contracting out of the right to revoke the wills. And in *Lewis v Cotton* [2001] WTLR 1117 it was held that a contention that wills were mutual required very careful scrutiny and proof beyond a balance of probabilities; the contention failed in that case.

7 This seems to follow from the decision in *Re Oldham*, where it was held that an agreement to make mutual wills was proved but there was no proof of an agreement not to revoke such wills. In *Re Green, Lindner v Green* [1951] Ch 148, [1950] 2 All ER 913, the agreement was set out in the wills which were in identical terms *mutatis mutandis*. At the time of making the wills the parties had little property but were entitled in reversion to a substantial estate given to them in equal shares or to the survivor as the case might be. The wife died and the husband succeeded to the whole of her estate, then the reversionary interest fell in. The husband remarried, made a subsequent will and later died. It was held that the effect of the mutual wills was that the wife's moiety was impressed with a trust binding on the testator, while the testator's moiety remained at his free disposition; *Dufour v Pereira* (1769) 1 Dick 419 applied; *Re Oldham, Hadwen v Myles* [1925] Ch 75, distinguished. See also *Re Grisor* (1980) 101 DLR (3d) 728. See also para **[2.8]**, n 1.

The principle has been extended to the case where the agreement is that if one party makes a change in his will, the other will make a corresponding change and the court will compel him to do so: *Re Fox* [1951] 3 DLR 337.

8 *Estate of Brynelsen v Verdeck* (2001–02) 4 ITELR 857 (BC CA). In this case there was no evidence that the parties had bound themselves in that way and thus the essential foundation of mutual wills was absent; *Dufour v Pereira* (1769) 1 Dick 419 and Lord *Walpole v Orford* (1797) 3 Ves 402, applied. A similar result was reached in *Osborne v Estate of Osborne (2001–02)* 4 ITELR 804 (Vic CA). The mere making of similar or identical wills

was not sufficient to prove that they were mutual wills. Mutual wills were the result of an arrangement or contract which obliged the survivor not to dispose of his estate in any way other than that agreed with the deceased. In this case there was no evidence, other than the making of the wills, that the parties intended to bind each other for the lifetime of the survivor; *Birmingham v Renfrew* (1936) 57 CLR 666 applied.

9 See *Charles v Fraser* [2010] EWHC 2124 (Ch), [2010] WTLR 1505 at [66].

[2.8]

[Updated in footnote 2 for *Olins v Walters* [2009] Ch 212. Revised generally in footnote 2. Updated in footnote 10 for *Shovelar v Lane* [2011] 4 All ER 669, CA.]

Effect of first to die abiding by agreement. Where the first to die has left his will unaltered and unrevoked in pursuance of the agreement, the survivor is bound by the agreement, and, though it is not strictly true to say that he cannot alter or revoke his will, the court, if asked, will ultimately refuse to give effect to such alteration or revocation.[1] The agreement is enforced by means of a constructive trust. Nourse J has stated the position as follows:[2]

> 'The principle of all these cases[3] is that a court of equity will not permit a person to whom property is transferred by way of gift but on the faith of an agreement or clear understanding that it is to be dealt with in a particular way for the benefit of a third person, to deal with that property inconsistently with that agreement or understanding. If he attempts to do so after having received the benefit of the gift equity will intervene by imposing a constructive trust on the property which is the subject matter of the agreement or understanding.'[4]

In a more recent case the principles were expressed as follows. The doctrine of mutual wills is to the effect that where two individuals have agreed as to the disposal of their property and have executed mutual wills in pursuance of the agreement, on the death of the first (T1) the property of the survivor (T2), the subject matter of the agreement, is held on an implied trust for the beneficiary named in the wills. The survivor may thereafter alter his will, because a will is inherently revocable, but if he does so his personal representatives will take the property subject to the trust.[5]

The agreement or understanding must be such as to impose on the donee a legally binding obligation to deal with the property in the particular way and certainty as to the subject matter of the trust and the persons intended to benefit under it must be present.[6] Giving effect to such a mutual will is an indirect process because probate must be granted of a testator's last will. If, therefore, the survivor has revoked the mutual will by making a new will, it is the new will which is admitted to probate.[7] If he has altered the will by duly executing a codicil, the codicil must be admitted to probate with the will.[8] It is, however, open to those benefiting under the mutual will to apply to a court of construction,[9] and then in a proper case an order will be made upon the personal representatives to hold the estate upon trust to give effect to the provisions of the mutual will.[10] Where the trusts are for the survivor for life with absolute remainders over, the remainders vest on the first death and the remainderman's interest does not lapse where he survives the first deceased but dies before the death of the second.[11] The parties might intend that the mutual wills should only affect those assets which are in existence before the death of the first party to the agreement.[12]

1 *Re Heys' Estate, Walker v Gaskill* [1914] P 192 at 200. The doctrine is not confined to cases in which the surviving testator receives a benefit under the will of the first to die but extends to cases where both testators leave their estates to beneficiaries other than themselves: *Re Dale, Proctor v Dale* [1994] Ch 31, [1993] 4 All ER 129.

2 In *Re Cleaver, Cleaver v Insley* [1981] 2 All ER 1018 at 1024; see also Clauson J in *Re Hagger, Freeman v Arscott* [1930] 2 Ch 190 at 195, on the authority of Lord Camden in *Dufour v Pereira* (1769) 1 Dick 419. See also *Re Dale, Proctor v Dale* [1993] 4 All ER 129, where the fraud giving rise to a constructive trust approach was followed. In *Healey v Brown* [2002] WTLR 849, A and F were joint tenants of the matrimonial home. They had made mutual non-revocable wills under which the survivor would receive the entirety of the other's estate with an ultimate gift of the matrimonial home to H on the death of the survivor. A died first and F became entitled to the whole of the matrimonial home. Subsequently, by inter vivos gift, F transferred the matrimonial home from his sole name to the joint names of himself and B, so that when F died the matrimonial home passed by survivorship to B. H claimed that B held the matrimonial home on trust for H in accordance with the scheme of the mutual wills. It was held that the disposition of the property by F had been intended to defeat H's legitimate expectations under the mutual wills and, since F had accepted A's share of the property on the basis of the mutual wills agreement, it was unconscionable for B to retain it, and a constructive trust was imposed in respect of A's one half undivided share on B in favour of H; *Yaxley v Gotts* [2000] Ch 162 referred to and *Lloyds Bank plc v Rosset* [1991] 1 AC 107, distinguished. It was held that the trust only affected A's half share and not the original interest of F, because the declarations contained in the mutual wills of A and F had no legal effect as a contract for the disposition of land because they failed to satisfy the requirements of LP(MP)A 1989, s 2 and therefore the doctrine of mutual wills did not apply; *Goodchild v Goodchild* [1997] 1 WLR 1216 applied. In *Olins v Walters* [2007] EWHC 3060 Norris J (at first instance) held that a direction by the testatrix to her executors to convert her estate, and after directing them to pay her testamentary and funeral expenses, debts and taxes, to dispose of the residue so realised does not require any formalities and is not within the rule applied in *Healey v Brown*. *Olins v Walters* was upheld on appeal ([2009] Ch 212).

3 *Birmingham v Renfrew* (1936) 57 CLR 666; *Ottaway v Norman* [1972] Ch 698, [1971] 3 All ER 1325.

4 Nourse J equated mutual wills with analogous situations such as secret trusts, in which a court of equity will intervene to impose a constructive trust, referring to *Ottaway v Norman* [1971] 3 All ER 1325, and *Re Pearson Fund Trusts* (21 October 1977, unreported).

5 Per Morritt J in *Re Dale, Proctor v Dale* [1993] 4 All ER 129 at 132. The judge continued: 'The basic doctrine is not in dispute. The dispute is as to the circumstances in which the doctrine applies.' In *Re Goodchild* [1996] 1 All ER 670, Carnwath J referred to the trust as a 'floating trust'; see affirmed [1997] 3 All ER 63, CA but mutual wills were not made out: see para **[2.4]** above.

6 *Re Goodchild*, n 5 above. It was held in *Re Dale, Proctor v Dale* [1993] 4 All ER 129, that the doctrine will apply not only where the parties each take a benefit but also where both leave their property to particular beneficiaries.

7 *Hobson v Blackburn and Blackburn* (1822) 1 Add 274; *Re Heys' Estate, Walker v Gaskill* [1914] P 192. In the case of *Re O'Connor's Estate* [1942] 1 All ER 546, it was part of the agreement to make separate wills after the execution of the joint will and one testatrix dying very shortly after the other, the court made a grant of the joint will and ignored the separate will of the second to die as conditional on her predeceasing the first to die.

8 See n 7, above.

9 That is the Chancery Division of the High Court.

10 *Stone v Hoskins* [1905] P 194; *Re Hagger, Freeman v Arscott* [1930] 2 Ch 190; *Re Green, Lindner v Green* [1951] Ch 148, [1950] 2 All ER 913 as in *Re Cleaver, Clever v Insley* [1981] 2 All ER 1018, [1981] 1 WLR 939. Since an action in respect of mutual wills is not a probate action but a Chancery action for a declaration of constructive trust, any rule in probate actions that costs do not fall on an unsuccessful challenger to probate of a will does not apply: see *Shovelar v Lane* [2011] EWCA Civ 802, [2011] 4 All ER 669.

11 *Re Hagger, Freeman v Arscott* [1930] 2 Ch 190.

12 *Re Gillespie* (1969) 3 DLR (3d) 317.

CHAPTER 3

Contracts relating to wills

[3.1]

[Name corrected in footnote 1.]

General statement. Although a will is by its nature always revocable, yet a testator may bind himself personally as to the contents of his will and may bind his assets so that his personal representative, whether he dies testate or intestate, must give effect to such agreement at the expense of the beneficiaries under the will or intestacy. There must, however, in any such case, be a binding agreement by the testator to dispose of his property in a certain way, and this involves two certainties. It must be shown that there was an agreement in law and not a mere statement of intention or a mere representation. It must also be shown with certainty what the subject-matter of the gift by the will was to be. Further, if the agreement relates to real property it must comply with the formalities prescribed by the Law of Property (Miscellaneous Provisions) Act 1989 s 2.[1] It can be noted that apart from contract it may be possible to base a claim against a deceased person's estate on the principles of constructive trust[2] or proprietary estoppel.[3]

1 *Healey v Brown* [2002] WTLR 849. For a case in which a pre-1989 Act agreement by a testator to leave a freehold property by will was held to be enforceable on the basis that a document signed by the testator constituted a sufficient memorandum within the LPA 1925, s 40(1) see *Irani v Irani* [2006] EWHC 1811 (Ch), [2006] WTLR 1561.

2 See para **[2.8]** above.

3 See *Re Basham* [1987] 1 All ER 405, [1986] 1 WLR 1498 which indicates an alternative approach to a claim to a house, based on proprietary estoppel. Similarly in *Gillett v Holt* [2000] 2 All ER 289, CA (reversing [1998] 3 All ER 917) the deceased made repeated inter vivos assurances to the plaintiff that in return for his work on the deceased's farm he would leave him the farm in his will. The deceased did not do so. The court allowed the plaintiff's claim to an equity in the farm, under the doctrine of proprietary estoppel arising from reliance on the latter's assurances causing the plaintiff detriment. See further discussed in Chapter 43.

[3.6]

[Updated in the text and in footnote 10 for the Contracts (Rights of Third Parties) Act 1999.]

Enforcement. The promisee's rights do not arise under the will; they arise contractually and exist independently of the will.[1] If the contract is to devise or bequeath specific property then the agreement is enforceable by way of damages for its breach[2] and the remedy by way of damages may be claimed immediately the covenantor has put it out of his power to perform his obligation, even during his life.[3] If the promisee can intervene before a purchaser for value without notice obtains an interest in the property he can obtain a declaration of his right to have it left to him by will and an injunction to restrain the testator from disposing of it in breach of contract.[4] If the property is land he could also register the contract or a caution against the title.[5] It may also be enforced by specific performance where there is valuable consideration and the other circumstances are such that the court will specifically enforce it,[6] but when this remedy is granted the court does not set aside a will not in accordance with the contract, but orders the personal representatives or possibly the devisees to convey the property according to the contract or otherwise to give effect to it.[7] The agreement may also be given effect to upon the principle that the law imposes an obligation upon the estate to compensate a person who has rendered services to the deceased based upon the principle of unjust enrichment.[8] In such proceedings, the statute of limitations runs from the death of the deceased.[9] Where a contract is made on or after 11 November 1999 it may be that a person who is not a party but who stands to benefit under it may be able to enforce it under the Contracts (Rights of Third Parties) Act 1999. If he can, then there is available to him any remedy that would have been available to him in an action for breach of contract if he had been a party to the contract.[10]

1 *Coffill v Stamp Duties Comr* (1920) SRNSW 278; *Re Syme* [1933] VLR 282; *Re Richardson's Estate* (1935) 29 Tas LR 149, followed and approved in *Schaefer v Schuhmann* [1972] 1 All ER 621 at 629–631, overruling *Dillon v Public Trustee of New Zealand* [1941] AC 294, [1941] 2 All ER 284.

2 *Hammersley v De Biel* (1845) 12 Cl & Fin 45; *Synge v Synge* [1894] 1 QB 466, CA.

3 *Synge v Synge* [1894] 1 QB 466, CA (covenant to leave specific realty, which the covenantor sold in his lifetime). If the testator sells the property during his lifetime the promisee can treat the sale as a repudiation of the contract and recover damages at law which will be assessed subject to a reduction for the acceleration of the benefit, and also if the benefit of the contract is personal to the promisee, subject to a deduction for the contingency of his failing to survive the promisor: *Schaefer v Schuhmann* [1972] 1 All ER 621 at 628.

4 *Synge v Synge* [1894] 1 QB 466, CA; *Schaefer v Schuhmann* [1972] 1 All ER 621 at 628.

5 *Schaefer v Schuhmann* [1972] 1 All ER 621 at 628.

6 *Goilmere v Battison* (1682) 1 Vern 48; *Dufour v Pereira* (1769) 1 Dick 419; *Coverdale v Eastwood* (1872) LR 15 Eq 121.

7 *Schaefer v Schuhmann* [1972] 1 All ER 621 at 636. The will is a valid will of which probate must be granted and the court granting probate is not concerned with the contract. The contract, therefore, can be enforced only in the administration of the estate, ie by order upon the personal representatives to convey the property so as to give effect to the contract and not to the gift in the will.

8 See *Balkwill v Smith* (1957) 21 WWR 474 (agreement to provide maintenance in consideration of being compensated by gift by will); *Deglman v Guaranty Co of Canada* [1954] SCR 725.

9 See n 8, above.

10 Contracts (Rights of Third Parties) Act 1999, s 1(5).

PART B

Capacity and disposing intent

CHAPTER 4

Testamentary capacity

VI. SOUND DISPOSING MIND

[4.9]

[Updated in footnotes 2 and 3 for *Re Perrins, Perrins v Holland* [2009] WTLR 1399, [2009] EWHC 2029 (Ch).
Updated in footnotes 2 and 3 for *Perrins v Holland* [2011] Ch 270, CA.
Updated in footnotes 2 to 4 and in the text for *Scammell v Farmer* [2008] WTLR 1261.]

Mental Capacity Act 2005 The test for mental capacity, whether to make a will or do any other act, has previously been established by a series of judicial decisions, the most significant of which are noted in the following paragraphs. The Mental Capacity Act 2005, sections 1 to 4 of which were brought into force on 1 April 2007,[1] puts the test for mental capacity on a statutory footing. The Act is not retrospective and is of no consequence in considering the validity of wills made prior to 1 April 2007.[2] The Act was intended to be a codification of the existing law and it does not purport to deal with all areas in which mental capacity may be relevant. There is some doubt as to whether the Mental Capacity Act 2005 has any relevance to wills made outside the statutory jurisdiction[3] and it is plain[4] that, in the case of wills, the existing authorities discussed in the remainder of this section will continue to be relevant.

Nonetheless, the Mental Capacity Act 2005 and the Code of Practice under it, provide a new definition of capacity and judges might use the new statutory definition to develop common law rules in particular cases. Medical experts are expected to find the statutory definition easier to use and may ignore the existing rules. The Mental Capacity Act 2005 provides that the starting point should be that there is a presumption of capacity: s 1(2); this reflects the common law presumption.

Lack of capacity is catered for in s 2 by reference to a 'functional' approach which is 'decision specific'. The section provides that:

> 'For the purposes of this Act, a person lacks capacity in relation to a Matter if at the material time he is unable to make a decision for himself in relation to the matter because of an impairment of, or a disturbance in the functioning of, the mind or brain. It does not matter whether the impairment or disturbance is permanent or temporary.'

The provisions which, in reality, provide the test for capacity are to be found in s 3(1) which provides that:

> 'For the purposes of section 2, a person is unable to make a decision for himself if he is unable—

(a) to understand the information relevant to the decision,
(b) to retain that information,
(c) to use or weigh that information as part of the process of making the decision or
(d) to communicate his decision (whether by talking, using sign language or any other means).'[5]

That is qualified by the remainder of s 3 so that:

'(2) A person is not to be regarded as unable to understand the information relevant to a decision if he is able to understand an explanation of it given to him in a way that is appropriate to his circumstances (using simple language, visual aids or any other means).

(3) The fact that a person is able to retain the information relevant to a decision for a short period only does not prevent him from being regarded as able to make the decision.

(4) The information relevant to a decision includes information about the reasonably foreseeable consequences of—
(a) deciding one way or another, or
(b) failing to make the decision.'[6]

As these new rules are adopted and applied in wills cases there should be less reliance on the previous case law tests of testamentary capacity as embodied in such time–honoured cases as *Banks v Goodfellow*.[7]

1 SI 2007/563. The remainder of the Act came into force on 1 October 2007 (SI 2007/1897).

2 *Scammell v Farmer* [2008] WTLR 1261 at [21] to [30]; *Re Perrins, Perrins v Holland* [2009] WTLR 1399, [2009] EWHC 2029 (Ch), at [40]. *Perrins v Holland* was upheld on appeal ([2010] EWCA Civ 840, [2011] Ch 270).

3 For doubts as to the application of the Mental Capacity Act 2005 to the making of wills see *Scammell v Farmer* [2008] WTLR 1261 at [26], although Lewison J seems to have accepted (albeit obiter) that it was applicable to wills made after the Act, see *Re Perrins, Perrins v Holland* [2009] WTLR 1399, [2009] EWHC 2029 (Ch), at [40]. *Perrins v Holland* was upheld on appeal ([2010] EWCA Civ 840, [2011] Ch 270) although no mention was made of this obiter acceptance. The Code of Practice provides (at para 4.32) that: 'The Act makes clear that the definition of "lack of capacity" and the two-stage test for capacity set out in the Act are "for the purposes of this Act". This means that the definition and test are to be used in situations covered by this Act.' For statutory wills see para **[4.21]** below.

4 See paras 4.31 to 4.33 of the Code of Practice and, in particular para 4.33: 'The Act's new definition of capacity is in line with the existing common law tests, and the Act does not replace them'.

5 The Code of Practice explains that the Mental Capacity Act 2005, s 3 sets out the test for assessing whether a person is unable to make a decision for him/herself and therefore lacks capacity. This is a 'functional' test, focussing on how the decision is made rather than the outcome of it and is primarily aimed at inter vivos decisions. The Act says that a person is unable to make a decision if he is unable to satisfy any of the tests at (a) to (d) above.

6 Only time will tell the extent to which these new provisions will affect the nature of the test to ascertain mental capacity in the context of probate claims and the peculiar nature of certain rules peculiar to probate claims, such as the rule in *Parker v Felgate* (1883) 8 PD 171, see para **[4.10]** below.

7 (1870) LR 5 QB 549, see para **[4.11]** below.

[4.10]

[Updated in footnote 2 for *Re Perrins, Perrins v Holland* [2009] WTLR 1399, [2009] EWHC 2029 (Ch).
Updated in footnote 2 for *Perrins v Holland* [2011] Ch 270, CA.
Updated in footnote 5 for *Re Baker, Baker v Baker* [2008] WTLR 565.]

The relevant time. It must be shown that the testator was of sound disposing mind at the time when the will or codicil was made.[1] The law requires that there should be sound disposing mind both at the time when the instructions for the will are given and when the will is executed, but it would appear that if the will is shown to have been drawn in accordance with instructions given while the testator was of sound disposing mind, it is sufficient that, when he executes it, he appreciates that he is being asked to execute as his will a document drawn in pursuance of those instructions though he is unable to follow all its provisions.[2] Supervening insanity will not revoke the will[3] nor will a recovery validate a will or codicil made during absence of testamentary capacity.[4] A will has been admitted to probate although a codicil made shortly after has been refused on the ground of want of sound disposing mind at the time of its execution.[5]

1 *Arthur v Bokenham* (1708) 11 Mod Rep 148; *Palmer and Brown v Dent* (1850) 2 Rob Eccl 284 (where a later will made while not of sound mind was rejected). This paragraph and others in the 7th edition, of *Williams on Wills*, were cited extensively and applied in *Re Wilkes dec'd, Wilkes v Wilkes* [2006] WTLR 1097 in which it was held by the Deputy Judge (Terence Etherton QC), upholding the will under challenge, that allegations of incapacity, want of knowledge and approval and undue influence had not been made out.

2 *Perera v Perera* [1901] AC 354; *Kenny v Wilson* (1911) 11 SRNSW 460; *Wilkie v Wilkie* (1915) 17 WALR 156; *Thomas v Jones* [1928] P 162; *Battan Singh v Amirchand* [1948] AC 161, [1948] 1 All ER 152. This is so even though the testator is unable to remember the instructions previously given and his signature was affixed by another person on his behalf: *Parker v Felgate* (1883) 8 PD 171. This case was applied in *Clancy v Clancy* [2003] EWHC 1885 (Ch), where a testatrix had testamentary capacity when she gave instructions for her will to be drafted and the will was properly drafted in accordance with those instructions and executed by the testatrix, the will was held to be valid if the testatrix understood that she was signing a will which she believed gave effect to her earlier instructions, even if there was some doubt as to her capacity at that time. See also *Re Perrins, Perrins v Holland* [2010] EWCA Civ 840, [2011] Ch 270, where a will was upheld where the testator was found to have testamentary capacity when he gave instructions for it in April 2000, although not when he executed it in September 2001.

See *Re Flynn, Flynn v Flynn* [1982] 1 All ER 882, [1982] 1 WLR 310, per Slade J at 890, 891 and *Re Rodziszewski's Estate* (1982) 29 SASR 256. As to cases where testator is too ill to sign, see para **[11.21]** below. *Forse and Hembling's Case* (1588) 4 Co Rep 60 b at 61 b; *Warn v Swift* (1832) 1 LJ Ch 203 (incapacity developing shortly after execution); *Re Crandon's Goods* (1901) 84 LT 330. Since any testamentary disposition must be made while the testator is of sound disposing mind, supervening insanity will ex hypothesi prevent his varying any will made while sane, and since the same sound disposing mind is required for revocation (see Chapter 18, para **[18.4]** below) it also prevents any revocation of a will made while sane.

3 *Arthur v Bokenham* (1708) 11 Mod Rep 148 at 157; *Public Trustee v Prisk* (1896) 14 NZLR 306.

4 *Brouncker v Brouncker* (1812) 2 Phillim 57.

5 *Harwood v Baker* (1840) 3 Moo PCC 282; *Banks v Goodfellow* (1870) LR 5 QB 549 at 569; *Re Sever's Will* (1887) 13 VLR 572; *Boreham v Prince Henry Hospital* (1955) 29 ALJ 179. See also *Baker Estate v Myhre* [1995] 6 WWR 410 and *Webb v Webb Estate* [1995] 6 WWR 52. There is a simple statement of the essentials in a very early case; *Re Marquess Winchester's Case* (1598) 6 Co Rep 23a, in these words:

> 'It is not sufficient that the testator be of memory when he makes his will to answer familiar and unusual questions, but he ought to have a disposing memory, so that he is able to make a disposition of his lands with understanding and reason.'

The equivalent paragraph in the eighth edition was approved in *Re Baker, Baker v Baker* [2008] WTLR 565.

[4.11]

[Updated in footnotes 2 and 7 for *Blackman v Man* [2008] WTLR 389 and *Schrader v Schrader* [2013] EWHC 466 (Ch), [2013] WTLR 701; in the text and footnote 3 for *Sharp v Adam* [2006] WTLR 1059 (CA); in footnote 7 for *Ledger v Wooton* [2008] WTLR 235, *Re Barker-Benfield, Hansen v Barker-Benfield* [2006] WTLR 1141 and *Scammell v Farmer* [2008] WTLR 1261; in footnote 10 for *Key v Key* [2010] EWHC 408 (Ch), [2010] WTLR 623 and *Re Wilson* [2013] EWHC 499 (Ch), [2013] WTLR 899.
Updated in footnote 7 for *Cowderoy v Cranfield* [2011] EWHC 1616 (Ch), [2011] WTLR 1742, *Hawes v Burgess* [2013] WTLR 453 (CA), and *Wharton v Bancroft* [2011] EWHC 3250 (Ch), [2012] WTLR 705.]

Criterion of sound disposing mind. At common law[1] sound testamentary capacity means that four things must exist at one and the same time:

(i) The testator must understand that he is giving his property to one or more objects of his regard;
(ii) he must understand and recollect the extent of his property;[2]
(iii) he must also understand the nature and extent of the claims upon him both of those whom he is including in his will and those whom he is excluding from his will;
(iv) no insane delusion shall influence his will in disposing of his property and bring about a disposal of it which, if the mind had been sound, would not have been made.[3]

The testator must realise that he is signing a will and his mind and will must accompany the physical act of execution.[4] It is said that perversion of moral feeling does not constitute unsoundness of mind in this respect,[5] but this is really a matter of degree.[6] The criterion to be applied has been thus stated by Cockburn CJ, in *Banks v Goodfellow*:[7]

> 'It is essential to the exercise of such a power that a testator shall understand the nature of the act and its effects; shall understand the extent of the property of which he is disposing; shall be able to comprehend and appreciate the claims to which he ought to give effect; and with a view to the latter object, that no disorder of the mind shall poison his affections, pervert his sense of right, or prevent the exercise of his natural faculties—that no insane delusion shall influence his will in disposing of his property and bring about a disposal of it which, if the mind had been sound, would not have been made.'

The mere fact that the testator was eccentric or was subject to one or more delusions is not of itself sufficient.[8] It must be shown that the delusion had, or was calculated to have, an influence on testamentary dispositions.[9] Further it has been said, without in any way detracting from the authority of *Banks v Goodfellow*, that it must be recognised that psychiatric medicine has come a long way since 1870 in recognising an ever widening range of circumstances now regarded as sufficient at least to give rise to a risk of mental disorder, sufficient to deprive a patient of the power of rational decision making.[10] A will has been held good subject to the deletion of a clause affected by a delusion.[11]

1 See para **[4.9]** above.

2 But precise knowledge of the value of property is not necessary: *Blackman v Man* [2008] WTLR 389 and *Schrader v Schrader* [2013] EWHC 466 (Ch), [2013] WTLR 701.

3 *Sharp v Adam* [2006] WTLR 1059 (CA) at [68]. For a statement of the essentials by the Supreme Court of Canada, see *Re Poirier Estate, Leger v Poirier* [1944] 3 DLR 1.

4 *Langlais v Langley* [1952] 1 SCR 28.

5 *Frere v Peacocke* (1846) 1 Rob Eccl 442 at 456.

6 *Sutton v Sadler* (1857) 3 CBNS 87; *Burdett v Thompson* (1873) LR 3 P & D 72n.

7 LR 5 QB 549 at 565; applied in *Wood v Smith* [1993] Ch 90, [1991] 2 All ER 939, affirmed on this point by Court of Appeal [1993] Ch 90, [1992] 3 All ER 556, where capacity was lacking. In *Richards v Allan* [2001] WTLR 1031 the testatrix's condition was described as having moments of lucidity interspersed between periods of confusion. She was found to have been confused earlier in the day the will was executed and she was subsequently admitted to hospital having been found in a collapsed state and observed there to be confused. The testatrix was found to lack capacity and knowledge and the will was held to be invalid. *Banks v Goodfellow* and other cases were cited in *McClintock v Calderwood* [2005] EWHC 836 (Ch), [2005] All ER (D) 356 (Apr) where an allegation that the testator lacked testamentary capacity was held not to have been made out. In *Sharp v Adam* [2006] WTLR 1059 the Court of Appeal upheld the decision of the Deputy Judge (Nicholas Strauss QC) ([2005] EWHC 1086 (Ch)) that a testator paralysed by advanced multiple sclerosis was held to lack the capacity to make a will because he was not capable of making a rational judgment. See also *Westendorp v Warwick* [2006] EWHC 915 (Ch); *Re Laxston dec'd* [2006] WTLR 1567; *Turner v Turner* [2007] All ER (D) 238 (May); *Rutland v Rutland* [2007] All ER (D) 326 (Mar); *Blackman v Man* [2008] WTLR 389; *Ledger v Wooton* [2008] WTLR 235; *Re Barker-Benfield, Hansen v Barker-Benfield* [2006] WTLR 1141; *Scammell v Farmer* [2008] WTLR 1261; *Cowderoy v Cranfield* [2011] EWHC 1616 (Ch), [2011] WTLR 1742; *Wharton v Bancroft* [2011] EWHC 3250 (Ch), [2012] WTLR 705; *Schrader v Schrader* [2013] EWHC 466 (Ch), [2013] WTLR 701; and *Hawes v Burgess* [2013] EWCA Civ 74, [2013] WTLR 453 (CA).

The corresponding paragraph in the seventh edition of *Williams on Wills* was cited in its entirety and applied in *Re Wilkes dec'd, Wilkes v Wilkes* [2006] WTLR 1097; see also the Note to para **[4.9]**. See para **[11.10]** below on the formalities aspect of this case. See also *Brown v Pourau* [1995] 1 NZLR 352 where a number of points relating to capacity are set out, *Banton v Banton* (1998) 164 DLR (4th) 176 (lacked capacity) and *Longmuir v Holland* (2000) 192 DLR (4th) 62 (will invalid on grounds of incapacity).

8 *Banks v Goodfellow* (1870) LR 5 QB 549; *Murfelt v Smith* (1887) 12 PD 116. It had been laid down at one time that a mind unsound on one subject could not be called sound on any subject (*Waring v Waring* (1848) 6 Moo PCC 341) and that proof of such unsoundness of mind on one subject, though quite irrelevant to any testamentary disposition, completely negatived testamentary capacity, but this doctrine has long been not only departed from but definitely overruled.

9 *Boughton v Knight* (1873) LR 3 P & D 64; *Smee v Smee* (1879) 5 PD 84; *Montreal Trust Co v McKay* (1957) 21 WWR 611. This passage of the text was cited with approval by White J in *O'Connell v Shortland* (1989) 51 SASR 337, at 350, 351, where despite the near approach of death and no medical evidence of the testator's capacity at the time, the testator was held to have capacity.

10 See *Key v Key* [2010] EWHC 408 (Ch), [2013] WTLR 623, where the testator had made the will in dispute a week after the unexpected loss of his wife after 65 years of marriage. It was found, on the basis of psychiatric evidence, that he had been so devastated by his wife's death that he lacked testamentary capacity. See also *Re Wilson* [2013] EWHC 499 (Ch), [2013] WTLR 899 where the testatrix was found to have an affective disorder brought about by her deep grief at the death of her brother.

11 *Re Bohrmann's Estate, Caesar and Watmough v Bohrmann* [1938] 1 All ER 27 l. There are two old decisions in which part of a will was admitted to probate: *Billinghurst v Vickers* (1810) 1 Phillim 187; *Wood v Wood* (1811) 1 Phillim 357.

[4.12]

[Amended for provisions of the Mental Health Act 2007 brought into force on 3 November 2008.]

Mental disorder. The law relating to persons suffering from mental disorders is now governed by the Mental Health Act 1983 (MeHA 1983) as heavily amended by the Mental Health Act 2007.[1]

Under the Mental Health Act 2007 there is only one definition of 'mental disorder' meaning any disorder or disability of the mind and the term 'mentally disordered' is to be construed accordingly.[2] Dependence on alcohol or drugs is not considered to be a disorder or disability of the mind for these purposes.[3] A person with a learning disability[4] is not to be considered by reason of that disability to be suffering from mental disorder unless that disability is associated with abnormally aggressive or seriously irresponsible conduct on his part.[5]

The provisions of the Mental Health Acts govern the classification and treatment of persons suffering from mental disorders but, since 1 October 2007, they no longer govern the management of property', which is now subject to the provisions of the Mental Capacity Act 2005.[6]

However, simply because a person is deemed to be suffering from mental disorder within the meaning of the MeHA 1983, or even that he is detained pursuant to the powers contained in the MeHA 1983, does not necessarily mean that he is incompetent to make a will. Each case must, it seems, be considered with reference to the general definitions noted above; and medical and psychiatric evidence will be important.[7]

1 The MeHA 1983 came into force on 30 September 1983 repealing and consolidating the previous legislation, notably the Mental Health Act 1959. MeHA 1983 is substantially amended by Mental Health Act 2007 and the definitions referred to here have been amended by Mental Health Act 2007 with effect from 3 November 2008: Mental Health Act 2007 (Commencement No 7 and Transitional Provisions) Order 2008 (SI 2008/1900).

2 MeHA 1983, s 1(2), which derives from the Mental Health (Amendment) Act 1982, ss 1, 2. This is now amended by Mental Health Act 2007 which replaces the four categories of mental disorder previously identified by MeHA 1983. These were:

'mental disorder' which means mental illness, arrested or incomplete development of mind, psychopathic disorder and any other disorder or disability of mind and 'mentally disordered' shall be construed accordingly;

'severe mental impairment' which means a state of arrested or incomplete development of mind which includes severe impairment of intelligence and social functioning and is associated with abnormally aggressive or seriously irresponsible conduct on the part of the person concerned and 'severely mentally impaired' shall be construed accordingly;

'mental impairment' which means a state of arrested or incomplete development of mind (not amounting to severe mental impairment) which includes significant impairment of intelligence and social functioning and is associated with abnormally aggressive or seriously irresponsible conduct on the part of the person concerned and 'mentally impaired' shall be construed accordingly; and

'psychopathic disorder' which means a persistent disorder or disability of mind (whether or not including significant impairment of intelligence) which results in abnormally aggressive or seriously irresponsible conduct on the part of the person concerned.

3 Mental Health Act 1983, s 1(3).

4 The term 'learning disability' means a state of arrested or incomplete development of the mind which includes significant impairment of intelligence and social functioning: MEHA 1983, s 1(4).

5 It is expressly provided by MeHA 1983, s 1(2A)–(2B), that a person shall not be deemed to be suffering from any form of mental disorder as described above, by reason only of

promiscuity or other immoral conduct, sexual deviancy or dependence on alcohol or drugs. Under Mental Health Act 2007 the references to promiscuity, immoral conduct and sexual deviancy have been removed.

6 Mental Capacity Act 2005, ss 16 to 18 came into force on 1 October 2007 (SI 2007/1897) and, from that date, the repeal of MeHA 1983, ss 96 and 97 took effect. See the power to make wills for mentally disordered persons: Mental Capacity Act 2005, ss 16 and 18(1), Sch 2, paras 1–4, paras **[4.21]–[4.23]** below.

7 This passage of the text was cited with approval by White J in *O'Connell v Shortland* (1989) 51 SASR 337.

[4.13]

[Updated in the text and at footnote 11 for *Hawes v Burgess* [2013] EWCA Civ 74, [2013] WTLR 453 (CA) and in the text and at footnote 12 for *Schrader v Schrader* [2013] EWHC 466 (Ch), [2013] WTLR 701.]

Presumption of sound disposing mind. It is presumed that the testator was sane at the time when he made his will[1] but, if the question of his sanity is contested, the onus is on the person propounding the will to prove that the testator was of sound disposing mind at the time when he made his will.[2] While there must be a vigilant examination of all the evidence, if the court feels there is no doubt substantial enough to defeat a grant of probate, the grant must be made. Complete proof of capacity or even proof beyond reasonable doubt is not essential.[3] A will not irrational on its face,[4] duly executed, is admitted to probate without proof of competence unless such competence is contested.[5] The law presumes that a state of things shown to exist continues to exist unless the contrary is proved and thus a testator, when there is no suggestion of insanity, is presumed to have remained sane[6] and, on the other hand, if there is evidence of insanity at a time prior to the making of the will, the person propounding the will must prove competence at the relevant time.[7]

In the latter case the presumption in the first instance is against sanity especially where the will contains dispositions which are prima facie not such as an ordinary testator would make.[8] Such presumption as there is, is always affected by the provisions of the will itself. If these are such as a sane person would make, and, still more, if the will is drawn by the testator himself, the will can be held valid.[9] If the dispositions are irrational, the presumption is against the will.[10]

Although no presumption probably arises, it has been said that it is a very strong thing for a judge to find that a testatrix did not have mental capacity when her will had been prepared by an experienced and independent solicitor following a meeting.[11] Further, the absence of any express explanation for a change in testamentary disposition is not sufficient to call a testatrix's testamentary capacity into question.[12]

1 *Wellesley v Vere* (1841) 2 Curt 917.

2 *Re Flynn, Flynn v Flynn* [1982] 1 All ER 882 at 890. See also *Sutton v Sadler* (1857) 3 CBNS 87, where the fundamental proposition is stated that a party propounding a will is bound to show that the testator was of sound disposing mind, but it is agreed that, if there is no evidence of incompetence the will must be found for. This last proposition was upheld in *Turner v Penny* (1843) 1 LTOS 412 (where there was a plea of insanity but no evidence). See *Chambers and Yatman v Queen's Proctor* (1840) 2 Curt 415 (will found for where there had been previous delusions and testator committed suicide on the day following the execution of the will). Where the will is sought to be proved in solemn form, the onus is still on the person propounding it although there has been a grant in common form: *Robins v National Trust Co* [1927] AC 515. Contrast, *In the estate of Parsons, Borman v Lel* [2002] WTLR 237

(propounder had discharged the burden of proof of capacity), with *Brown v Deacy* [2002] WTLR 781 (propounder had not). See also *Royal Trust Co v Ford* (1971) 20 DLR (3d) 348 and *Re Schwartz* (1970) 10 DLR (3d) 15; on appeal (1971) 20 DLR (3d) 313; *Vout v Hay* (1995) 125 DLR (4th) 431.

3 *Worth v Clasohm* (1952) 86 CLR 439. This passage of the text was cited with approval by White J in *O'Connell v Shortland* (1989) 51 SASR 337.

4 As to the weight to be given to the nature of the dispositions, see *Levy v Lindo* (1817) 3 Mer 81 (reasonable will by person found to be insane); *Re Watt's Goods* (1837) 1 Curt 594 (a similar case); *Nichols and Freeman v Binns* (1858) 1 Sw & Tr 239; *Evans v Knight and Moore* (1822) 1 Add 229 (slight evidence needed to support reasonable dispositions); *Re Sample's Estate* [1955] 3 DLR 199 (gifts to friends rather than to nephews); *Re Breidenbach Estate, Yaerger v Breidenbach* (1956) 19 WWRNS 109 (gifts to strangers in blood insufficient in itself).

5 *Sutton v Sadler* (1857) 3 CBNS 87.

6 *Chambers and Yatman v Queen's Proctor* (1840) 2 Curt 415.

7 *Smee v Smee* (1879) 5 PD 84; *Groom v Thomas* (1829) 2 Hag Ecc 433; *Banks v Goodfellow* (1870) LR 5 QB 549; *Guerin v Guerin* [1962] SCR 550.

8 *Harwood v Baker* (1840) 3 Moo PCC 282 at 291; *Re Davis* (1963) 40 DLR (2d) 801.

9 *Cartwright v Cartwright* (1793) 1 Phillim 90 at 100; *Rutherford v Maule* (1832) 4 Hag Ecc 213 at 226; *Clarke v Leare and Scarwell* (1791) cited in 1 Phillim at 119; *Symes v Green* (1859) 1 Sw & Tr 401. This passage of the text was cited with approval by White J in *O'Connell v Shortland* (1989) 51 SASR 337.

10 See cases cited in nn 2 and 3, above, but mere foolishness or eccentricity of a disposition is not sufficient; see para **[4.18]** below.

11 *Hawes v Burgess* [2013] EWCA Civ 74, [2013] WTLR 453 (CA).

12 *Schrader v Schrader* [2013] EWHC 466 (Ch), [2013] WTLR 701.

[4.15]

[Updated in footnote 5 for *Walters v Smee* [2008] EWHC 2029 (Ch), [2009] WTLR 521.]

Delusions. A delusion is a belief in the existence of something which no rational person could believe and, at the same time, it must be shown to be impossible to reason the patient out of the belief.[1] To avoid a will, the delusion must be such as to influence the testator in making the particular disposition made.[2] The existence of a delusion is quite compatible with the retention of the general powers and faculties of the mind.[3] It is a question of fact whether the delusion affects the disposition, and, even where the delusion is connected with the subject-matter of the disposition, it is not a necessary conclusion that the delusion affected it.[4] A parent may take a harsh view of the character and conduct of his children or relations without being subject to such a delusion as will avoid a will, but there is a point where such a view ceases to be a harsh unreasonable judgment and must be held to proceed from some mental defect.[5] For the will to stand the testator's mind must not be dominated by an insane delusion so as to overmaster his judgment to such an extent that he is incapable of disposing of his property reasonably and properly or of taking a rational view of the matters to be considered in making a will.[6] The well-trusted legal decision, that best of all guides on this question,[7] is the following statement of Cockburn CJ in *Banks v Goodfellow*:[8]

> 'Here, then, we have the measure of the degree of mental power which should be insisted on. If the human instincts and affections, or the moral sense, become perverted by mental disease; if insane suspicion, or aversion, take the place of natural affection; if the reason and judgment are lost, and the mind becomes a prey to insane delusions calculated to

interfere with and disturb its functions, and to lead to a testamentary disposition, due only to their baneful influence—in such a case it is obvious that the condition of the testamentary power fails, and that a will made under such circumstances ought not to stand.'

It cannot be said that there are people who are not suffering from delusional insanity but are incapable of making a will.[9] A testator may be stated by medical evidence to have recovered from delusions, and yet the will be pronounced against on the ground that the onus of proof has not been discharged, even where the dispositions are probable.[10] The court may grant probate of will and codicil with the deletion of one clause from the codicil which has been affected by a delusion.[11] A pretended delusion assumed for the purpose of deception will not invalidate a will.[12]

1 *Dew v Clark and Clark* (1826) 3 Add 79. This paragraph was cited with approval by White J in *O'Connell v Shortland* (1989) 51 SASR 337 at 351.

2 *Jenkins v Morris* (1880) 14 Ch D 674; *Frere v Peacocke* (1846) 1 Rob Eccl 442; *Smith v Tebbitt* (1867) LR 1 P & D 398; *Boughton v Knight* (1873) LR 3 P & D 64; *Smee v Smee* (1879) 5 PD 84; *Murfett v Smith* (1887) 12 PD 116; *Pare v Cusson* (1921) 60 DLR 105; *O'Neil v Royal Trust Co and McClure* [1946] 4 DLR 545.

3 *Boughton v Knight* (1873) LR 3 P & D 64; *Banks v Goodfellow* (1870) LR 5 QB 549; *Beal v Henri* [1951] 1 DLR 260; but a will has been found against even where it was sensible on the face of it and contained no trace of any reference to or connection with the testator's then subject of delusion: *Symes v Green* (1859) 1 Sw & Tr 401; *Smith v Tebbitt* (1867) LR 1 P&D 398.

4 *Jenkins v Morris* (1880) 14 Ch D 674; *Smith v Tebbitt* (1867) LR 1 P&D 398, and see *Greenwood v Greenwood* (1790) 3 Curt App 1; *Dew v Clark and Clark* (1826) 3 Add 79; *Fowlis v Davidson* (1848) 6 Notes of Cases 461.

5 *Boughton v Knight* (1873) LR 3 P & D 64; *Thamer v Jundt* [1912] 4 DLR 753; *Royal Trust Co v Ford* (1971) 20 DLR (3d) 348; *Walters v Smee* [2009] WTLR 521; [2008] EWHC 2029 (Ch).

6 *Banks v Goodfellow* (1870) LR 5 QB 549; *Hope v Campbell* [1899] AC 1; *Re Walker's Estate, Watson v Treasury Solicitor* (1912) 28 TLR 466; *Re Belliss, Polson v Parrott* (1929) 141 LT 245; *Ballantyne v Evans* (1886) 13 R (Ct of Sess) 652; *Sivewright v Sivewright's Trustees* 1920 SC (HL) 63; *Re Mitchell's Estate (Man)* [1924] 1 DLR 1039; *Re Onofrichuk, Onofrichuk v Onofrichuk* [1974] 2 WWR 469.

7 Per Langton J in *Re Bohrmann's Estate, Caesar and Watmough v Bohrmann* [1938] 1 All ER 271 at 278. The decision in *Re Bohrmann's Estate* was not followed in *Woodhead v Perpetual Trustee Co Ltd* (1981) 11 NSWLR 267.

8 (1870) LR 5 QB 549 at 565.

9 *Re Bohrmann's Estate* [1938] 1 All ER 271 at 279.

10 *Johnson v Blane* (1848) 6 Notes of Cases 442.

11 *Re Bohrmann's Estate, Caesar and Watmough v Bohrmann* [1938] 1 All ER 271. This is a singular decision which should, perhaps, be treated with caution.

12 *Ditchburn v Fearn* (1842) 6 Jur 201.

[4.17]

[A reference to *Blackman v Man* [2008] WTLR 389 has been added to footnote 1.]

Senile decay and illness. Unsoundness of mind may be occasioned by physical infirmity or advancing years as distinguished from mental derangement and the resulting defect of intelligence may be a cause of incapacity, but the intelligence must be reduced to such an extent that the proposed testator does not appreciate the testamentary act in all its bearings.[1] In particular, the instructions for the will may have been given when the testator was of far better understanding than when the will was actually executed, and in these cases the will is generally pronounced for.[2] Where it is shown that the testator was incapable of reading the will and it is not read over to him, it is generally rejected but the criterion in such cases is whether he was really aware of the contents.[3] A will has been found for where the testatrix could only answer the drawer by means of nods and pressure of the hand in answer to questions as to her intentions,[4] but where the testatrix had suffered from delusions, the dispositions being probable and made when her medical attendant stated that she had recovered from her delusions, it was held that the onus of showing capacity had not been discharged.[5] The infirmity of the testator will strengthen certain presumptions which arise against the will in any case, e g where the will is contrary to the previously expressed intentions of the testator as to his testamentary dispositions[6] or where the will is drawn by the propounder and is wholly or largely in his favour.[7] Old age, or the near approach of death at any age, lend strength to suggestions that the testator had no proper knowledge of the contents of the will,[8] or that there was undue influence,[9] or the suspicion arising from the fact that the will is largely in favour of the person drawing or procuring it.[10] A desirable safeguard in such circumstances is for the will to be witnessed by a medical practitioner who satisfies himself as to the capacity and understanding of the testator and makes a record of his examinations and findings.[11] This has been described as the 'golden rule'.[12] although that is not, of itself a touchstone of validity, but only a means of minimising disputes.[13] It has been said that the grand criterion by which to judge whether the mind is injured or destroyed is to ascertain the state of the memory, for without memory the mind cannot act.[14]

1 *Banks v Goodfellow* (1870) LR 5 QB 549 at 566; *Emes v Emes* (1865) 11 Gr 325 (there must be some evidence of mental incapacity); *Re Munn, Hopkins v Warren* [1943] SASR 304; *Re Smith's Estate* [1945] 3 WWR 216; *Re Schwartz* (1970) 10 DLR (3d) 15; on appeal (1971) 20 DLR (3d) 313. In *Tchilingirian v Ouzounian* [2003] EWHC 1220 (Ch) the testatrix was found to be showing signs of confusion and dementia in everyday matters prior to making the challenged wills. It was held that she lacked mental capacity. Further there was even less evidence that she knew and approved the contents of the wills. The corresponding paragraph in the 7th edition of *Williams on Wills* was cited in its entirety and applied in *Re Wilkes dec'd, Wilkes v Wilkes* [2006] WTLR 1097. See also *Blackman v Man* [2008] WTLR 389.

2 *Parker v Felgate* (1883) 8 PD 171; *Perera v Perera* [1901] AC 354; *Thomas v Jones* [1928] P 162; *Re Wallace's Estate, Solicitor of the Duchy of Cornwall v Batten* [1952] 2 TLR 925; *Re Flynn, Flynn v Flynn* [1982] 1 All ER 882, [1982] 1 WLR 310.

3 *Mitchell v Thomas* (1847) 6 Moo PCC 137; *Durnell v Corfield* (1844) 1 Rob Eccl 51. For a case where the will was read over to the testatrix but was not admitted to probate, see *Tyrrell v Painton* [1894] P 151. See also *Fulton v Andrew* (1875) LR 7 HL 448; *Re Martin, MacGregor v Ryan* (1965) 53 DLR (2d) 126. For a case where the will was not read over but admitted to probate, see *Re Wallace's Estate, Solicitor of the Duchy of Cornwall v Batten* [1952] 2 TLR 925.

4 *Re Holtham's Estate, Gillett v Rogers* (1913) 108 LT 732. See also *Re Souch* [1938] 1 DLR 563 (loss of power of speech and writing due to epileptic fit).

5 *Johnson v Blane* (1848) 6 Notes of Cases 442; *Batten Singh v Amirchand* [1948] AC 161, [1948] 1 All ER 152 (testator stating he had no relations when in fact he had nephews); *Re Morrison's Estate* [1953] 3 DLR 274 (changes in dispositions made on advice of solicitor); *Re Nightingale, Green v Nightingale (No 2)* (1974) 119 Sol Jo 189 (testator suffering from cancer made a second will shortly before he died excluding his son, who was the principal beneficiary under the first will, from benefiting. This exclusion was prompted by a belief founded on fanciful evidence that the son was trying to kill him. Held, executors had failed to discharge onus of proof of capacity and first will pronounced for).

6 *Harwood v Baker* (1840) 3 Moo PCC 282.

7 *Reece v Pressey* (1856) 2 Jur NS 380; *Mackenzie v Handasyde* (1829) 2 Hag Ecc 211.
8 *Durnell v Corfield* (1844) 1 Rob Eccl 51.
9 *Ashwell v Lomi* (1850) LR 2 P & D 477.
10 See cases cited in n 3.
11 *Re Simpson, Schaniel v Simpson* (1977) 121 Sol Jo 224; *Kenward v Adams* [1975] CLY 3591, and *Buckenham v Dickinson* [1997] CLY 4733; see para **[4.21]** below.
12 See n 11.
13 *Cattermole v Prisk* [2006] 1 FLR 693.
14 *Murphy v Lamphier* (1914) 20 DLR 906.

[4.20]

[Updated in footnote 1 for *Re Baker, Baker v Baker* [2008] WTLR 565, in footnote 14 for *Williams v Wilmot* [2012] EWHC 2211 (Ch), [2012] WTLR 1635, and in footnote 16 and in the text for *Blackman v Man* [2008] WTLR 389 and *Hawes v Burgess* [2013] EWCA Civ 74, [2013] WTLR 453 (CA).]

Evidence of sound disposing mind. Both oral and documentary evidence is admissible to show that the testator was of sound disposing mind at the relevant time.[1] All statements made by him at the time of making the will or preparatory thereto are admissible to prove that he knew the character of the act he was undertaking.[2] The fact that the will is in his own handwriting is strongly in favour of his capacity.[3] The evidence of an attesting witness, since it must impeach his own act of attestation, is admissible but in general requires corroboration.[4] Evidence of the manner in which the act of making the will was performed is admissible, and also evidence of its accord with natural affection and moral duty, and its conformity to past and subsequent declarations of intention.[5] Evidence of conduct before and after the actual making of the will is admissible,[6] but it carries little weight where there is satisfactory evidence of sound disposing mind at the actual time of making the will,[7] and its importance varies with the nature of the mental disease from which the testator is alleged to be suffering.[8] Generally, evidence of the general habits and course of life is of a greater weight than that of particular acts.[9] It has been doubted whether the fact that unsoundness of mind has existed or exists in the testator's family is admissible.[10] The treatment of the testator by his friends and relations is admissible as for or against them, but not as against third parties, such evidence being admissible to introduce what the testator did with regard to it but not otherwise.[11] General reputation that a person is suffering from unsoundness of mind is not admissible.[12] The evidence of a medical witness who has attended the testator is admissible but such a witness cannot be asked to give his opinion as to the existence of facts which he has not himself observed.[13] The evidence of experts, however, has been held not to outweigh that of eye-witnesses who had opportunities for observation and knowledge of the testatrix[14] but a scientific witness who did not see the testator may be asked his opinion upon the facts proved in evidence[15] but the court should be wary of placing too much reliance on the evidence of medical experts who did not have the opportunity of seeing the deceased.[16]

1 *Wheeler and Batsford v Alderson* (1831) 3 Hag Ecc 574; *Jenkins v Morris* (1880) 14 Ch D 674; *Bannatyne v Bannatyne* (1852) 2 Rob Eccl 472; *Snook v Watts* (1848) 11 Beav 105. Subsequent letters are admissible but of little value: *Bootle v Blundell* (1815) 19 Ves 494. This paragraph of the text was cited with approval by White J in *O'Connell v Shortland* (1989) 51 SASR 337 at 353. The corresponding paragraph in the 7th edition of *Williams on*

Wills was cited extensively and applied in *Re Wilkes dec'd, Wilkes v Wilkes* [2006] WTLR 1097. The equivalent paragraph in the eighth edition was approved in *Re Baker, Baker v Baker* [2008] WTLR 565.

2 *Hall v Warren* (1804) 9 Ves 605 at 610; *Levy v Lindo* (1817) 3 Mer 81; *Filmer v Gott* (1774) 4 Bro Parl Cas 230; *Fane v Duke of Devonshire* (1718) 6 Bro Parl Cas 137; *Wheeler and Batsford v Alderson* (1831) 3 Hag Ecc 574; *Butlin v Barry* (1837) 1 Curt 614 at 629; *Durling and Parker v Loveland* (1839) 2 Curt 225.

3 *Cartwright v Cartwright* (1793) 1 Phillim 90 at 100; *Rutherford v Maule* (1832) 4 Hag Ecc 213 at 216; *Clarke v Leare and Scarwell* (1791), cited in 1 Phillim at 119.

4 *Bootle v Blundell* (1815) 19 Ves 494 at 504; *Howard v Braithwaite* (1812) 1 Ves & B 202; *Kinleside v Harrison* (1818) 2 Phillim 449 at 499; *Young v Richards* (1839) 2 Curt 371; *Pennant v Kingscote* (1843) 3 Curt 642.

5 *Wrench v Murray* (1843) 3 Curt 623; *Boughton v Knight* (1873) LR 3 P & D 64; *Arbery v Ashe* (1828) 1 Hag Ecc 214; *Brouncker v Brouncker* (1812) 2 Phillim 57; *Evans v Knight and Moore* (1822) 1 Add 229; *Brydges v King* (1828) 1 Hag Ecc 256. But a change in dispositions may be accounted for: *Williams v Goude* (1828) 1 Hag Ecc 577. In *King v Farley* (1828) 1 Hag Ecc 502, there was a change of dispositions and a subsequent reversion to the former dispositions.

6 *Rodd v Lewis* (1755) 2 Lee 176; *Re Watts' Goods* (1837) 1 Curt 594; *Beavan v M'Donnell* (1854) 10 Exch 184.

7 *Ferguson v Borrett* (1859) 1 F & F 613; *Prinsep and East India Co v Dyce Sombre* (1856) 10 Moo PCC 232.

8 *Mudway v Croft* (1843) 3 Curt 671.

9 *Snook v Watts* (1848) 11 Beav 105; *Smith v Tebbitt* (1867) LR 1 P & D 398; *Boughton v Knight* (1873) LR 3 P & D 64 at 75.

10 *M'Adam v Walker* (1813) 1 Dow 148; *Doe d Mather v Whitefoot* (1838) 8 C & P 270.

11 *Re Windham* (1862) 4 De G F & J 53; *Wright v Doe d Tatham* (1834) 1 Ad & El 3; *Wheeler and Batsford v Alderson* (1831) 3 Hag Ecc 574; *Bannatyne v Bannatyne* (1852) 2 Rob Eccl 472.

12 *Greenslade v Dare* (1855) 20 Beav 284.

13 *Doe d Bainbrigge v Bainbrigge* (1850) 16 LTOS 245; *Martin v Johnston* (1858) 1 F & F 122; *Lovatt v Tribe* (1862) 3 F & F 9 (evidence of medical men who gave certificates on which person confined. Such medical men should give the grounds on which they base their certificates). As to the advisability of having a medical man at hand to hear a person critically ill approve the contents of a will, see *Re Johnson's Estate* [1946] 3 WWR 424.

14 *O'Neil v Royal Trust Co and McClure* [1946] 4 DLR 545; *Boughton v Knight* (1873) LR 3 P&D 64. The evidence of an experienced private client solicitor who attended to the registration of the testatrix's enduring power of attorney shortly before she made her disputed will with other solicitors was considered important in *Williams v Wilmot* [2012] EWHC 2211 (Ch), [2012] WTLR 1635.

15 *Papijans v Gudowski* [1963] Tas SR 183; *Re Schwartz* (1970) 10 DLR (3d) 15; on appeal (1971) 20 DLR (3d) 313.

16 *Blackman v Man* [2008] WTLR 389 and *Hawes v Burgess* [2013] EWCA Civ 74, [2013] WTLR 453 (CA).

[4.21]

[Revised generally as a result of *Scammell v Farmer* [2008] WTLR 1261 and the light it sheds on previous decisions.
Updated in footnote 3 for *Feltham v Bouskell* [2013] EWHC 1952 (Ch), [2013] WTLR 1363.
Updated in footnote 10 for *Key v Key* [2010] EWHC 408 (Ch).]

Solicitor's duty. It has been suggested that a solicitor taking instructions for a will or supervising the execution of a will, has a duty to satisfy himself that the client has testamentary capacity.[1] The extent of such duty as might exist is limited. A duty is owed to the testator to procure a legally effective will in favour of the beneficiaries of the last will but not to beneficiaries taking under an earlier will who suffered a loss (costs) in successfully arguing that the later will was not valid.[2] A solicitor who hesitates because of unfounded doubts about a testator's capacity will breach his duty to the testator and potentially incur liabilities to the intended beneficiaries of the will that is not made as a result.[3]

Where capacity is in doubt it might be useful for the solicitor to record his or her impressions of the testator's state of mind, at the time.[4] It has been suggested that solicitors should follow the 'golden rule' that when a solicitor is drawing up a will for an aged testator or one who has been seriously ill it should be witnessed or approved by a medical practitioner, who ought to record his examination of the testator and his findings.[5] Other precautions were that if there was an earlier will it should be examined and any proposed alterations should be discussed with the testator[6] and solicitors should at least ask the testator open questions such as 'why, what, who or when' to establish that the testator can hear and understand the provisions of a will which was being read aloud.[7] It has also been said that it is desirable that an elderly, infirm testator should be seen by a solicitor who knows him.[8] This so-called 'golden rule' contains prudent guidance for solicitors and does not purport to lay down the law,[9] it only provides guidance as to how disputes may be avoided but is not a touchstone of validity or a substitute for established tests of capacity or knowledge and approval.[10]

1 *Murphy v Lamphier* (1914) 31 OLR 287; affd 32 OLR 19; *Re Carvell Estate* (1977) 21 NBR (2d) 642; *Re Worrell* (1970) 8 DLR (3d) 36.

2 See *Worby v Rosser* [2000] PNLR 140, *Corbett v Bond Pearce* [2001] PNLR 739. Two New Zealand decisions shed further light on the extent of a solicitor's duty in respect of the liability for the unrecovered costs of Probate Claims. These concerned a Mr. Hooker who made a series of wills between 1990 and 1992. In a probate action the last two wills (made in 1992) were held invalid for want of capacity but the last 1991 will was upheld. The costs of the probate action were substantial and both the beneficiary and executor of the 1991 will brought claims against the solicitor who prepared the 1992 wills. In *Knox v Till* [2002] WTLR 1147, the beneficiary under the 1991 will had alleged that the solicitor had a duty to ensure that the testator had testamentary capacity and, thus, to refuse to act for the testator in 1992. The New Zealand Court of Appeal had little difficulty in holding that the solicitor owed no duty of care to the beneficiary of the 1991 will because the overriding duty was to carry out the testator's instructions and he could not go behind the testator's back to establish capacity; the question of capacity was outside the solicitor's expertise; and there was a conflict between different beneficial interests. In *Public Trustee v Till* [2002] WTLR 1169 the Public Trustee sought to recover the estate's costs of the probate action. This claim also failed, principally because there was nothing in the circumstances when the testator instructed the solicitor that would have alerted a reasonably competent solicitor to the testator's lack of capacity.

3 See, for example, *Ryan v Public Trustee* [2000] 1 NZLR 700. In *Feltham v Bouskell* [2013] EWHC 1952 (Ch), [2013] WTLR 1363 a solicitor was found liable in negligence for failing to prepare a will where there were doubts about the testamentary capacity of the testatrix. The judge said that in such a situation the solicitor must either refuse the instructions and make the position clear to the client, or take steps to satisfy himself as to his client's mental capacity promptly.

4 *Maw v Dickey* (1974) 52 DLR (3d) 178 at 190–191; *Ross v Caunters* [1980] Ch 297, [1979] 3 All ER 580; *Whittingham v Crease & Co* (1978) 88 DLR (3d) 353; *Orles and Kruger v R* (1958) 38 Sask LR 38.

5 *Kenward v Adams* [1975] CLY 3591 followed in *Re Simpson* (1977) 121 Sol Jo 224. For a summary of the cases see *Scammell v Farmer* [2008] WTLR 1261 at [117] to [124].

6 *Kenward v Adams* [1975] CLY 3591; *Hoff v Atherton* [2005] WTLR 99 at [49].

7 *Buckenham v Dickenson* [2000] WTLR 1083 (testator very old, partially blind and deaf, held not to have capacity).

8 *Re Belliss, Polson v Parrott* (1929) 141 LT 245 per Lord Merrivale P.

9 *Hoff v Atherton* [2005] WTLR 99 at [49] per Peter Gibson LJ.

10 *Cattermole v Prisk* [2006] 1 FLR 693 at 699. In that case the will of an elderly and infirm testatrix was upheld despite the failure to observe the rule. Contrast *Westendorp v Warwick* [2006] EWHC 915 (Ch), [2006] All ER (D) 248 (Apr) and *Key v Key* [2010] WTLR 623, [2010] EWHC 408.

[4.21A]

[This is a new paragraph.]

Costs in probate disputes. The normal rule (apart from the special position of executors) is that costs should follow the event so that the losing party pays the costs of the winning party.[1] The importance of this general rule cannot be overstated. Unless an unsuccessful party can make out an alternative case he should expect to pay the successful party's costs. There are three exceptions to the general rule as to costs in probate claims. One of these (Defendant's notice to cross-examine only) is expressly acknowledged in the Civil Procedure Rules.[2] The other two are of common law origin. They are:

(a) When the facts reasonably required investigation, the unsuccessful party might sometimes be entitled to his costs out of the estate or be left to bear his own costs but is not ordered to pay another party's costs.[3]
(b) When the deceased or those interested in residue have been the cause of the litigation, the costs of those who unsuccessfully opposed probate may be ordered to be paid out of the estate.[4]

The application of the exceptions is less likely (but not impossible) when coercion ('undue influence') has been alleged unsuccessfully.[5]

1 CPR 44.3(1), (2)(a).
2 At CPR 57.5(5).
3 *Spiers v English* [1907] P 122 at 123 per Sir Gorell Barnes P; *Wylde v Culver* [2006] 1 WLR 2674; *Kostic v Chaplin* [2007] EWHC 2909 (Ch), where the older authorities are thoroughly discussed.
4 *Kostic v Chaplin* [2007] EWHC 2909 (Ch); *Spiers v English* [1907] P 122; *Re Cutcliffe's Estate* [1959] P 6; *Hoff v Atherton* [2005] WTLR 99; *Broughton v Knight* [1873] LR 3 P7 D 64; *Twist v Tye* [1902] P 92.
5 *Spiers v English* [1907] P 122; *Re Cutcliffe's Estate* [1959] P 6; *Re Fuld (No 3)* [1968] P 675.

VII. POWER TO MAKE WILLS FOR MENTALLY DISORDERED PERSONS

[4.22]

[Updated in the text and footnotes 3, 5 and 6 for *Re P* [2009] EWHC 163 (Ch). Updated in footnote 5 for *Re M, ITW v Z* [2009] EWHC 2525 (Fam), [2009] WTLR.]

The jurisdiction. The Mental Health Act 1959 (MHA 1959) conferred in s 102 a wide general power on the court with respect to the property and affairs of a mentally disordered person ('a patient') to do all such things as appear necessary or expedient in order to provide maintenance for the patient or his or her family, or otherwise for administering the patient's affairs. Without prejudice to this general provision s 103(1) conferred specific powers to manage and deal with the patient's property in the patient's name; and to make settlements and gifts of the patient's property.[1]

However, the MHA 1959 did not confer the power to make a will for the patient a deficiency which was remedied by the Administration of Justice Act 1969, s 17, which added a new provision, as paragraph (dd), to this effect to the MHA 1959, s 103(1). This new power was considered in a number of reported decisions[2] and guidelines relating to the law and practice were laid down by Vice-Chancellor Megarry in *Re D(J)*.[3] The MHA 1959 was repealed and the legislation consolidated in the Mental Health Act 1983, the relevant parts of which are themselves repealed by the Mental Capacity Act 2005 with effect from 1 October 2007 and the jurisdiction is now to be found in the Mental Capacity Act 2005, ss 16, 18(1) and Sch 2, paras 1–4.[4] The former practice as laid down in *Re D(J)* was reconsidered by Lewison J in *Re P*[5] in the light of the Mental Capacity Act 2005 and it is clear that a new regime[6] is in place.

Under the Mental Capacity Act 2005, if a person (referred to as 'P') lacks capacity in relation to a matter or matters concerning P's property and affairs,[7] the court may, by making an order, make the decision or decisions on P's behalf in relation to the matter or matters.[8] The powers as respects P's property and affairs extend in particular to the execution for P of a will[9] although no will may be made under subsection (1)(i) at a time when P has not reached 18.[10] The jurisdiction can only be exercised where the judge has reason to believe that the patient is incapable of making a valid will for himself.[11] It will be appreciated that it is possible for a person subject to the Court of Protection to have capacity to make a personal will and in such cases that should be done subject to guidance and advice.

The will may make any provision (whether by disposing of property or exercising a power or otherwise) which could be made by a will executed by P if he had capacity to make it.[12]

The details relating to the formalities governing the exercise of this jurisdiction are to be found now in the Mental Capacity Act 2005 Sch 2.[13] This provides that the will must state that it is signed by P acting by the authorised person, should be signed by the authorised person with the name of P and with his own name, in the presence of two or more witnesses present at the same time, and these witnesses attest and subscribe in the usual way and the will is then authenticated with the official seal of the Court of Protection.[14] Where these formalities are complied with then it is provided that the will shall have the same effect for all purposes as if the patient were capable of making a valid will and the will had been executed by him in the manner required by the Wills Act 1837 (WA 1837).[15]

However, this does not apply to the will in so far as it disposes of immovable property outside England and Wales, or in so far as it relates to any other property or matter if, when the will is executed P is domiciled outside England and Wales, and, under the law of P's domicile, any question of his testamentary capacity would fall to be determined in accordance with the law of a place outside England and Wales.[16].

With the exception, of course, of s 9, the WA 1837 applies to such wills.[17] The will so made, often referred to as a 'statutory will' (although judicial will would seem more apt) becomes the patient's will for all purposes and thus precludes the Court of Protection from jurisdiction to make a different distribution.[18]

1 It was this power to make settlements for the patient which was invoked in *Re L(WJG)* [1966] Ch 135, [1965] 3 All ER 865, to provide, in effect, a substitute for a will; an inter vivos settlement was ordered by the court on behalf of a 68-year-old bachelor patient, who would otherwise have died intestate with assets of over £130,000.
2 See *Re HMF* [1976] Ch 33, [1975] 2 All ER 795, and *Re Davey* [1980] 3 All ER 342, [1981] 1 WLR 164.
3 [1982] Ch 237, [1982] 2 All ER 37. In *Re R (Execution of Statutory Will)* [2003] WTLR 1051 Ferris J emphasised that, in exercising its powers under MHA 1983, the Court of Protection should be satisfied that such decisions reflected the intention of the patient. In that case a statutory will made on the application of a nephew whereby he was given a substantial legacy to the disadvantage of his brother, was set aside on appeal. Following *Re P* [2009] EWHC 163 (Ch), that approach is no longer justified.
4 Mental Capacity Act 2007 came into force on 1 October 2007: SI 2007/1897.
5 [2010] Ch 33. See also *Re M, ITW v Z* [2009] EWHC 2525 (Fam), [2009] WTLR.
6 See para **[4.23]** below.
7 Section 16(1)(b) of the Mental Capacity Act 2005.
8 Mental Capacity Act 2005, s 16(2)(a).
9 Mental Capacity Act 2005, s 18(1)(i).
10 Mental Capacity Act 2005, s 18(1)(ii).
11 Thus in many cases the court will require a report from one of the Lord Chancellor's visitors as to this and such further medical evidence as the Master may direct; *Practice Direction* [1983] 3 All ER 255.
12 Mental Capacity Act 2005, Sch 2, para 2.
13 Mental Capacity Act 2005, Sch 2, para 4.
14 Mental Capacity Act 2005, Sch 2, para 4(1).
15 Mental Capacity Act 2005, Sch 2, para 4(3).
16 Mental Capacity Act 2005, Sch 2, para 4(4)–(5)
17 Mental Capacity Act 2005, Sch 2, para 4.
18 This can be achieved by revoking the statutory will and making a new will in its place–which is impossible if (as in *Re Davey* [1980] 3 All ER 342, [1981] 1 WLR 164; see Fox J at 349) the patient were then dead since it is not possible to make a will for, or to revoke the will of, a deceased person.

[4.23]

[Updated in the text and footnotes 5 to 9 for *Re P* [2009] EWHC 163 (Ch), [2009] All ER (D) 160 (Feb) and MCA 2005.
Updated in footote 2 for *NT v FS* [2013] EWHC 684 (CP), [2013] WTLR 867.
Updated in footnote 7 for *Re M, ITW v Z* [2009] EWHC 2525 (Fam), [2009] WTLR.
Updated in footnote 10 and in the text for *Re D (Statutory Will)* [2012] Ch 57. Updated in footnote 11 and in the text for *Re JC* [2012] WTLR 1213.]

Guidelines governing the exercise of the jurisdiction. Under MeHA 1983 all statutory will applications were decided in accordance with the guidance laid down by the Vice-Chancellor in *Re D(J)*.[1] The continuity of these guidelines assisted not only the masters concerned with making the order but more importantly the patient's relatives and their legal advisers in formulating a set of agreed proposals that could form the basis of the application. The crucial consideration under the approach adopted in *Re D(J)* was that the court would regard the disposition of the estate subjectively from the patient's point of view and would, so to speak sit in his armchair and make for him a will that he or she was likely to have made.[2] This meant that it was to be assumed that the patient was having a brief lucid interval at the time when the will is made and that, during the lucid interval the patient had a full knowledge of the past and a full realisation that as soon as the will was executed he or she would relapse into the actual mental state that previously existed with the prognosis as it actually was. These two propositions although recognised to be somewhat curious assumptions were consistent with the accepted practice regarding making of settlements for the patient under MeHA 1983.[3] The court would assume, thirdly, that during the hypothetical lucid interval the patient was to be envisaged as being advised by a competent solicitor. Finally, the patient was assumed to take a fairly broad view of any claims upon his bounty and the court would not be concerned with examinations analogous to a profit and loss account. Although, recognised by the Vice-Chancellor not to be either exhaustive or precise these principles for factors did provide useful guidance on the judicial attitude to the power vested in them.[4]

Under the Mental Capacity Act 2005 the counter-factual assumptions concerning a brief lucid interval with complete knowledge of the past and the substituted judgment of the court are not part of the test which requires the court to act in the best interests of the patient.[5] The Mental Capacity Act 2005 does not require the counter-factual assumption that P is not mentally disordered. The facts must be taken as they are. It is not therefore necessary to go through the mental gymnastics of imagining that P has a brief lucid interval and then relapses into his former state. The goal of the enquiry is not what P 'might be expected' to have done; but what is in P's best interests. This is more akin to the 'balance sheet' approach than to the 'substituted judgment' approach. The code of practice[6] makes this clear in that it points out that the test of best interests was one that was worked out by the courts mainly in decisions relating to the provision of medical care. The previous guidance was concerned with deciding what P would have wanted if he were not mentally disordered. But the Mental Capacity Act 2005 requires the decision maker to consider P's present wishes and feelings, which ex hypothesi are wishes and feelings entertained by a person who lacks mental capacity in relation to the decision being made on his behalf. The same structured decision making process applies to all decisions to be made on P's behalf, whether great or small, whereas the previous guidance was specific to the making of a will, gift or settlement. Moreover, it is a decision making process which must be followed, not only by the court, but by anyone who takes decisions on P's behalf. In making his decision the decision maker must consider 'all relevant circumstances'. The Act expressly directs the decision maker to take a number of steps before reaching a decision. These include encouraging P to participate in the decision. He must also 'consider' P's past and present wishes, and his beliefs and values and must 'take into account' the views of third parties as to what would be in P's best interests.[7] In reaching a decision a third party decision maker will, if appropriate, take legal or other advice. The other advice may be medical, financial, or advice of any other kind. The court will, of course, act according to the law, and be assumed to have sufficient knowledge of the law (either before or after assistance from advocates) to make whatever decision it is called upon to make. But there is, no need (as envisaged by *Re D(J)*) to assume (a) that P has taken legal advice (which he has not) and then (b) to attempt to decide what P would have done with that advice if he had had capacity (which he does not). If P's wishes have been formed without having taken legal advice in circumstances where a person with capacity would have taken legal advice, that may be a reason for giving them less weight than might otherwise have been the case.[8] Furthermore, in deciding what provision should be made in a will to be executed on P's behalf and which, ex hypothesi, will only have effect after he is dead, the court is entitled to take into account, in assessing what is in P's best interests, how he will be remembered after his death; for many people it may be in their best interests that they be remembered with affection by their family and as having done 'the right thing' by their will.[9] This was an important factor in *Re D (Statutory Will)*[10] where a daughter made an application for a statutory will in circumstances where her half brother and sister had used a forged enduring power to take substantial amounts from their mother's estate. The application was for a will treating the three children equally, and was made on the basis that two previous wills which favoured the half brother and sister might be invalid on account of the mother's lack of capacity following her stroke. On two separate occasions the application had been rejected on the grounds that the Court of Protection was not the appropriate forum for a dispute as to the validity of wills during the lifetime of the testator. However, on a reapplication, Judge Hodge QC accepted that the best interests of the testator dictated that all concerns about her true testamentary wishes should be set to rest by ordering the execution of a statutory will, 'rather than leaving her estate to be eroded by the costs of litigation after her death, and her memory to be tainted by the bitterness of a contested probate dispute between her children (which may extend to members of the next generation).' It may not though be an important factor where the testator has spent his lifetime doing 'the wrong thing'.[11]

1 [1982] Ch 237, [1982] 2 All ER 37. Although expressed with reference to the jurisdiction in the MHA 1959 the comments are equally applicable to the consolidating MeHA 1983.

2 See Sir Robert Megarry, VC, [1982] Ch 237, [1982] 2 All ER 37 at 43; disagreeing with the previous remarks of Fox J in *Re Davey* [1980] 3 All ER 342 at 348, [1981] 1 WLR 164. It should be noted that the making of a statutory will by the court does not preclude an application under the Inheritance (Provision for Family and Dependants) Act 1975 (I(PFD)A 1975) and as Fox J emphasised in *Re Davey*, any objective unfairness can be remedied by an application under that Act. However, on the other hand it is not helpful for the court to make a totally unreasonable will consistent perhaps with the arbitrary prejudices of the patient when sane, if that will inevitably gives rise to an immediate application under the I(PFD)A 1975 on the death. It is inevitable perhaps that the court will try to effect … the will which the actual patient, *acting reasonably*, would have made …' per Sir Robert Megarry VC, [1982] Ch 237, [1982] 2 All ER 37 at 43. When deciding what provision to make for an individual with a strong moral claim on the testator the Court of Protection will not speculate on what that individual might achieve on an application under the I(PFD)A 1975, see *NT v FS* [2013] EWHC 684 (CP), [2013] WTLR 867.

3 See Cross J in *Re WJGL* [1965] 3 All ER 865 at 871–872.

4 Sir Robert Megarry VC, [1982] Ch 237, [1982] 2 All ER 37 at p 43.

5 MCA 2005, s 1(5).

6 At paragraph 5.1.

7 *Re P* [2010] Ch 33 at [38] per Lewison J. See also *Re M, ITW v Z* [2009] WTLR, [2009] EWHC 2525 (Fam).

8 [2010] Ch 33 at [43].

9 [2010] Ch 33 at [44].

10 [2010] EWHC 2159 (Ch), [2012] Ch 57.

11 *Re JC* [2012] WTLR 1213 at [54]. In this case Senior Judge Denzil Lush refused to make a statutory will for a patient in favour of all four of his biological children, one of whom had been adopted at birth so would not take if the patient died intestate. That child had by conscious decision never contacted or met her biological father which the judge considered a 'factor of magnetic importance' in refusing the application. A statutory will was made though in favour of the other three children who would take on an intestacy to enable them to direct the devolution of their share of their father's estate if they predeceased him.

[4.24]

[Updated in the text and footnote 1 for *Re P* [2009] EWHC 163 (Ch), [2009] All ER (D) 160 (Feb).
Updated in the text and in footnote 5 for *Re D* (*Statutory Will*) [2012] Ch 57.]

Illustrations of the exercise of the jurisdiction. Aside from *Re P*,[1] the power has been invoked to remedy an injustice caused by effect of ademption on a specific devise[2] or an emergency or salvage jurisdiction to avoid an undesirable intestacy.[3] The court has exercised the jurisdiction to make a will for a person who had been mentally disabled since birth and who had inherited a substantial estate. The will made provision for such persons and purposes for whom/which the patient might have been expected to provide if she had not been mentally disordered on the assumption that she would have been a normal decent person who would have acted in accordance with contemporary standards of morality.[4] It has also been exercised where there was an uncertainty about the validity of a recent will, the terms of which departed from those of an earlier, apparently valid, will, and the execution of a statutory will would set to rest all concerns about the testatrix's true testamentary wishes.[5]

1 *Re P* [2009] EWHC 163 (Ch), [2009] All ER (D) 160 (Feb).

2 See *Re D(J)* [1982] Ch 237, [1982] 2 All ER 37 which was concerned with an elderly woman patient whose mental condition had deteriorated to such an extent that her affairs were made subject to the control of the Court of Protection. Whilst of full capacity the patient had devised the house in which she lived to one of her daughters and the residue of her estate to her five children in equal shares. Subsequently, the patient moved in with the daughter and remained with her, selling her own house and thus adeeming the devise. The patient purchased a new house near to her daughter but never lived in that house but remained with her daughter and her husband. The daughter (and another daughter who had been appointed to be patient's receiver) applied to the Court of Protection under the MHA 1959, s 103(1)(dd) for the execution of a codicil to the original will specifically devising the new house to the daughter in place of the adeemed legacy of the old house and contents. The patient's new house was then sold for £22,000 and her estate was likely to be valued at about £50,000. The daughter was, no doubt, now looking for a legacy equal to the sale price of the house but the deputy master was less generous, ordering the execution of a will giving her a legacy of £10,000 with an equal share with the other children in the residue. The daughter appealed to the Vice-Chancellor, who decided that he did have a power of review, and ordered a new will which increased the legacy to £15,000.

3 A striking illustration is provided by *Re Davey* [1980] 3 All ER 342, [1981] 1 WLR 164, where a 92-year-old woman described as suffering from senile mental deterioration to a degree which rendered her incapable of properly managing her affairs, went through a ceremony of marriage with a much younger male employee of the nursing home in which she resided. That marriage, though voidable, had the effect of revoking an earlier will which the woman had made in favour of her two nephews who were her nearest relatives (see *Re Roberts, Roberts v Roberts* [1978] 3 All ER 225, [1978] 1 WLR 653, CA and Chapter 17). Her affairs were made subject to the Court of Protection and the Official Solicitor applied to the court for an order for the execution under the MHA 1959, s 103(1)(dd) of a will for the woman in the same terms as the earlier will that had been revoked by the marriage. The matter was regarded as one of great urgency (which, in fact, proved to be the case since the woman died six days later) and the will was made by the deputy master without notice being given to the other party to the marriage or to the beneficiaries under the earlier will. The court (Fox J) decided that, in the circumstances, this was an acceptable procedure since although normally notice should be given to parties adversely affected by the exercise of the jurisdiction, the urgency of the matter precluded that course in this case. The judge thought that any delay might result in an undesirable intestacy and that any unfairness to the other party to the marriage could be remedied by an application by him to the court, during the patient's lifetime, for a new statutory will, or, after her death, for provision out of her estate under the Inheritance (Provision for Family and Dependants) Act 1975. See also the

Administration of Justice Act 1982, s 49 which facilitates the presentation of petitions for matrimonial relief on behalf of the patient and thus might provide an alternative, although more protracted, solution to cases like *Re Davey* [1980] 3 All ER 342, [1981] 1 WLR 164.

4 *Re C (a patient)* [1991] 3 All ER 866. On that basis it was thought that the patient would have felt a moral obligation to show recognition to the community and to her family since she had spent the whole of her life in the care of the community, as embodied in the national health service, the hospital and voluntary mental health charities, and had derived her fortune from being a child of a family. *Inter vivos* gifts of £100,000 to charity and £400,000 to her family were made, with a will drawn leaving her estate equally between charity and the family. The difficulty in such a case where the patient has been disabled since birth is that there is no subjective indication of her wishes. See also *Re S* [1997] 1 FLR 96 where inter vivos dispositions under the MeHA 1983, s 95, and a statutory will under the MeHA 1983, s 103, were made for a mental patient. See also *Re R (Execution of Statutory Will)* [2003] WTLR 1051.

5 *Re D (Statutory Will)* [2010] EWHC 2159 (Ch), [2012] Ch 57: see para **[4.23]** above.

CHAPTER 5

Knowledge and approval

I. KNOWLEDGE AND APPROVAL

[5.1]

[Updated in footnote 1 for *Re Baker, Baker v Baker* [2008] WTLR 565 and in footnote 2 for *Boudh v Boudh* [2008] WTLR 411.
Updated in footnotes 4 and 12 for *Perrins v Holland* [2011] Ch 270, CA. Updated in footnote 7 for *Gill v Woodall* [2011] Ch 380, CA.]

Knowledge and approval. Before a paper is entitled to probate[1] the court must be satisfied that the testator knew and approved of the contents at the time he signed it.[2] It has been said[3] that this rule is evidential rather than substantive and that in the ordinary case proof of testamentary capacity and due execution suffices to establish knowledge and approval,[4] but that in certain circumstances the court requires further affirmative evidence.[5] It was at one time thought that the fact that the will had been duly read over to a capable testator on the occasion of its execution, or that its contents had been brought to his notice in any other way, should when coupled with his execution thereof, be held conclusive evidence that he approved as well as knew the contents thereof.[6] However, the better view now seems to be that such a circumstance raises but a prima facie presumption of knowledge and approval.[7] In *Fuller v Strum*[8] the proposition that a testator can have knowledge and approval of part of his will but not of another part was affirmed. An obvious example would be where a person preparing a will for another fraudulently included wording in the will which was contrary to the testator's instructions but which were not noticed by the testator when the will was executed. The court has always had power to omit words from a will which were inserted per incuriam, quite apart from the more recently conferred jurisdiction to rectify wills under s 20 of AJA 1982.[9]

In some cases where the testator employs an expert draftsman to provide the appropriate wording to give effect in law to the testator's intentions, the testator has to accept the phraseology selected by the draftsman without himself really understanding its esoteric meaning and in such a case he adopts it and knowledge and approval is imputed to him.[10] This principle is carried further by the so-called rule in *Parker v Felgate*[11] to the effect that a will which has been prepared in accordance with previous instructions given when the testator fully understands the contents and effect thereof is valid, notwithstanding that at the time of execution the testator does not in fact have that understanding.[12]

1 The paragraph in the 7th edition of *Williams on Wills* corresponding with para **[5.1]** of the current edition was cited in its entirety and applied in *Re Wilkes dec'd, Wilkes v Wilkes* [2006] WTLR 1097. The equivalent paragraph in the eighth edition was approved in *Re Baker, Baker v Baker* [2008] WTLR 565.

2 *Guardhouse v Blackburn* (1866) LR 1 P & D 109 at 116; *Barry v Butlin* (1838) 2 Moo PCC 480; *Wintle v Nye* [1959] 1 All ER 552, [1959] 1 WLR 284; *Re Morris, Lloyds Bank Ltd v Peake* [1971] P 62, [1970] 1 All ER 1057; *Boudh v Boudh* [2008] WTLR 411.

3 *Re Fuld's Estate (No 3), Hartley v Fuld* [1968] P 675 at 697, [1965] 3 All ER 776 at 781.

4 As to the presumption of the execution see Chapter 13. There is though a clear distinction is to be drawn between testamentary capacity and knowledge and approval: testamentary capacity includes the ability to make choices, whereas knowledge and approval requires no more than the ability to understand and approve choices that have already been made: see *Re Perrins, Perrins v Holland* [2010] EWCA Civ 840, [2011] Ch 270 at [64].

5 *Barry v Butlin* (1838) 2 Moo PCC 480, at 490; *Re Ireland* (1963) 147 DLR (3d) 480 at 482. Where a major beneficiary gave instructions to a solicitor to draft a will for an elderly aunt with failing eyesight it was held that a suspicion was raised which had to be removed before the will could be admitted to probate: *Re Hall* (1988) 50 DLR (4th) 51. *Tyrrell v Painton* [1894] P 151, CA; *Fulton v Andrew* (1875) LR 7 HL 448 and *Barry v Butlin* (1838) 2 Moo PCC 480 referred to.

6 Per Lord Penzance in *Guardhouse v Blackburn* (1866) LR 1 P & D 109; *Atter v Atkinson* (1869) LR 1 P & D 665; *Harter v Harter* (1873) LR 3 P & D 11 at 22.

7 *Re Morris, Lloyds Bank Ltd v Peake* [1971] P 62, [1970] 1 All ER 1057, tracing the progressive erosion of the rule; *Fulton v Andrew* (1875) LR 7 HL 448 at 449, 460, 461, 469; *Martell v Consett Iron Co Ltd* [1955] Ch 363 at 414, [1955] 1 All ER 481 at 498; *Gregson v Taylor* [1917] P 256 at 261; *Crerar v Crerar* (1956) unreported, see 106 Law Journal 694. See also *Re Ticehurst, Midland Bank Executor and Trustee Co v Hankinson* (1973) Times, 6 March; *Re Schwartz* (1971) 20 DLR (3d) 313 (change of solicitor not a suspicious circumstance that could lead to inference that the testator might not have known and approved of the contents of the will); and *Re Fenwick* [1972] VR 646. In *Gill v Woodall* [2010] EWCA Civ 1430, [2011] Ch 380, it was said that the fact that a will had been properly executed after being prepared by a solicitor and read over to the testatrix raised a very strong presumption that it represented the testatrix's intentions at the moment she had executed the will; that the presumption was reinforced by policy considerations in support of the fundamental principle of testamentary freedom and the evidential difficulties presented by the fact that the testatrix could not be directly examined. But in the very unusual circumstances of that case, in particular the severity of the testatrix's anxiety disorder, the will, having been properly executed, prepared by a solicitor and read to the testatrix, was found invalid for want of knowledge and approval.

8 [2001] EWCA Civ 1879, [2002] 2 All ER 87. See also *Lau Hau Chu v Ip Kam* [2006] HKLR 100.

9 *Re Morris, Lloyds Bank Ltd v Peake* [1971] P 62, [1970] 1 All ER 1057. There are few case law authorities where part of a will was pronounced for and part against but two such cases are *Re Austin's Estate* (1929) 73 Sol Jo 545 and *Fulton v Andrew* (1875) LR 7 HL 448 (*Fuller v Strum* also contains some helpful statements on the evidence needed to prove knowledge and approval).

10 *Rhodes v Rhodes* (1882) 7 App Cas 192 at 199, 200; *Re Morris, Lloyds Bank Ltd v Peake* [1971] P 62, [1970] 1 All ER 1057 at 79 and 1066 (respectively). But see *Re Ticehurst, Midland Bank Executor and Trustee Co v Hankinson* (1973) Times, 6 March.

11 (1883) 8 PD 171.

12 See also, *Perera v Perera* [1901] AC 354; *Thomas v Jones* [1928] P 162; *Re Wallaces' Estate, Solicitor of the Duchy of Cornwall v Batten* [1952] 2 TLR 925; *Re Flynn, Flynn v Flynn* [1982] 1 All ER 882 at 890, 891; and *Perrins v Holland* [2010] EWCA Civ 840, [2011] Ch 270.

[Updated in footnote 3 for *Re Bates, Bates v Wheildon* [2008] WTLR 1705 and *Blackman v Man* [2008] WTLR 389.
Updated in the text and in footnote 4 for *Cowderoy v Cranfield* [2011] EWHC 1616 (Ch), [2011] WTLR 1742. Updated in the text and in footnote 5 for *Singellos, Singellos v Singellos* [2010] EWHC 2353 (Ch).]

[5.2]

When evidence required. The cases when affirmative evidence of knowledge and approval of the contents of a will will be required include the following: testators who are deaf and dumb,[1] or blind,[2] and when the person who prepared the will received a benefit under the will.[3] Generally, affirmative evidence of knowledge and approval of the contents of a will will be required in cases which 'excite suspicion' on the part of the court.[4] But it has been said that whether circumstances are such as to arouse the suspicion of the court is a question of fact in each case, and should not be reduced to some tick-box exercise, it being important that the suspiciousness or otherwise of the features identified as arousing suspicion is judged in the light of the full background of the relationships between the relevant parties.[5]

1 The question is a matter of fact in each case, see *Dickenson v Blisset* (1754) 1 Dick 268; *Re Harper* (1843) 6 Man & G 732; *Re Owston's Goods* (1862) 2 Sw & Tr 461; *Re Geale's Goods* (1864) 3 Sw & Tr 431; *Re Biddulph's Trusts, Re Poole's Trusts* (1852) 5 De G & Sm 469; *Re Souch* [1938] 1 DLR 563; *Re Sellwood's Estates, Heynes v Sellwood* (1964) 108 Sol Jo 523. The paragraph in the 7th edition of *Williams on Wills* corresponding with para **[5.2]** of the current edition, was cited in its entirety and applied in *Re Wilkes dec'd, Wilkes v Wilkes* [2006] WTLR 1097.

2 To establish the will of a testator wholly blind, or so nearly as to be incapable of discerning writing, it must be shown to the satisfaction of the court that the will was read over to him in the presence of the witnesses or that he was otherwise acquainted with its contents: *Fincham v Edwards* (1842) 3 Curt 63; affd 4 Moo PCC 198; *Re Axford* (1860) 1 Sw & Tr 540; *Re Sellwood* (1964) 108 Sol Jo 523. See also *Re Hall* (1988) 50 DLR (4th) 51.

3 *Barry v Butlin* (1838) 2 Moo PCC 480; *Fulton v Andrew* (1875) LR 7 HL 448; *Wintle v Nye* [1959] 1 All ER 552; *Re Stott, Klouda v Lloyds Bank Ltd* [1980] 1 All ER 259; See also *Tchilingirian v Ouzounian* [2003] EWHC 1220 (Ch) applying *Fulton v Andrew* (1875) LR 7 HL 448 and *Re Loxton dec'd* [2006] WTLR 1567. Suspicion was not aroused in *Re Bates, Bates v Wheildon* [2008] WTLR 1705 or in *Blackman v Man* [2008] WTLR 389.

4 *Cowderoy v Cranfield* [2011] EWHC 1616 (Ch), [2011] WTLR 1742.

5 See *Singellos, Singellos v Singellos* [2010] EWHC 2353 (Ch) at [91], [2011] Ch 324.

[5.3]

[Updated in footnote 1 for *Re Baker, Baker v Baker* [2008] WTLR 565, in footnote 4 for *Re Bates, Bates v Wheildon* [2008] WTLR 1705 and *Blackman v Man* [2008] WTLR 389, and in footnote 5 for *Boudh v Boudh* [2008] WTLR 411, *Williams v Wilmot* [2012] EWHC 2211 (Ch), [2012] WTLR 1635, *Hawes v Burgess* [2013] EWCA Civ 74, [2013] WTLR 453 (CA), and *Paynter v Hinch* [2013] EWHC 529, [2013] WTLR 529.]

The evidence in support of the plea. The Court of appeal in *Fuller v Strum*[1] set out the law relating to proof of knowledge and approval of the contents of a will. First, the *onus probandi* lies in every case upon the party propounding a will and he must satisfy the Court that the instrument so propounded is the last will of a free and capable testator; *Barry v Butlin*.[2] Second, proof of testamentary capacity of the deceased and the due execution of the will, without more, will give rise to a proper inference of knowledge and approval; *Fuller v Strum*.[3] Third, where the circumstances are such as to arouse the suspicion of the court the propounder must prove affirmatively that knowledge and approval so as to satisfy the court that the will represents the wishes of the deceased; *Fuller v Strum*[4] and *Wintle v Nye*.[5] Fourth, the standard of proof required in relation to knowledge and approval in a probate case is the civil standard – that is, the court must be satisfied, on a balance of probability, that the contents of the will do truly represent the testator's intentions; *Fuller v Strum*.[6] It is possible for the court to infer knowledge and approval from the circumstances. The extent of the evidential burden depends on how grave a suspicion is aroused by the circumstances in which the will was made.

It has been said that where a question is raised concerning knowledge and approval of the contents of a will the circumstances which are held to excite the suspicions of the court must be circumstances attending or at least relevant to, the preparation and execution of the will itself,[7] but it is accepted that the allegations could also be relevant to the testamentary capacity of the deceased or to a plea of undue influence.[8] It is open to a party alleging want of knowledge and approval to cross-examine the person propounding the will on matters which may result in establishing fraud or undue influence on the part of such person, even though fraud or undue influence are not pleaded.[9] Further there is authority to the effect that the failure or deliberate omission of a party, who had raised a plea of want of knowledge and approval in a probate action, also to plead undue influence, does not preclude such a party from introducing in support of his plea matters of fact which would also, at least in a broad sense, be relevant in support of a plea of undue influence.[10] However the defence of want of knowledge and approval is not to be used 'as a screen behind which one man is to be at liberty to charge another with fraud or dishonesty without assuming the responsibility for that charge in plain terms'.[11]

1 [2001] EWCA Civ 1879, [2002] 2 All ER 87, [2002] 1 WLR 1097, where the Court of Appeal upheld the validity of the whole will albeit that it was somewhat eccentric and home made. *Fuller v Strum* was referred to in *Re Good (decd), Carapeto v Good; Brennan v Good* [2002] EWHC 640 (Ch), where it was held that the burden of proof that the testatrix knew and approved the contents of her will had been discharged. The testatrix was described as a highly intelligent woman who had received legal advice prior to the execution of her will and there was no evidence that she had been coerced into making her will. *Fuller v Strum* was also referred to in *Shuck v Loveridge* [2005] EWHC 72 (allegation of want of knowledge and approval not made out). See also *Hoff v Atherton* [2004] EWCA Civ 1554, [2005] WTLR 99, CA, *Reynolds v Reynolds* [2005] EWHC 6 (Ch), *In the Estate of Sherrington Deceased, Sherrington v Sherrington* [2005] EWCA Civ 326, [2005] WTLR 587, CA.; *Re Johnson's Estate* [2006] All ER (D) (Oct) 146. and *Franks v Sinclair* [2006] EWHC 3365 (Ch). *Fuller v Strum* was applied in *Re Rowinska dec'd, Wyniczenko v Plucinska-Surowka* [2006] WTLR 487 in which the Deputy Judge (Judge Behrens) rejected, on the balance of probability, an allegation of forgery even though there was a real possibility that the will was forged, but held in the light of the suspicious circumstances surrounding the will that the propounder had not shown that the testatrix had known and approved its contents. The equivalent paragraph in the eighth edition was approved in *Re Baker, Baker v Baker* [2008] WTLR 565.

2 (1838) 2 Moo PCC 480, at pp 482–483.

3 [2001] EWCA Civ 1879, [2002] 2 All ER 87, [2002] 1 WLR 1097.

4 Ibid, see Peter Gibson LJ at p 1107; p 96. Suspicion was not aroused in *Re Bates, Bates v Wheildon* [2008] WTLR 1705 or in *Blackman v Man* [2008] WTLR 389.

5 [1959] 1 All ER 552, [1959] 1 WLR 284. See also *Boudh v Boudh* [2008] WTLR 411 where the suspicion was not removed, and *Williams v Wilmot* [2012] EWHC 2211 (Ch), [2012] WTLR 1635. In *Hawes v Burgess* [2013] EWCA Civ 74, [2013] WTLR 453 (CA), the suspicion of the court was aroused, and not removed, when there was no reason why a testatrix should have cut her son out of her will and her daughter had been involved in making arrangements for the new will. In *Paynter v Hinch* [2013] EWHC 529, [2013] WTLR 529, the suspicions of the court were not aroused by the instruction of a will-writing firm, the inclusion of an incorrect date of birth in the will, or the fact that the simple will was not read over to the testatrix.

6 *Fuller v Strum*, per Chadwick LJ, at p 1120; p 109.

7 Per Willmer J in *Re R* [1951] P 10, [1950] 2 All ER 117 where allegations irrelevant to the plea of want of knowledge and approval were struck out.

8 Per Willmer J in *Re R* [1951] P 10, [1950] 2 All ER 117; see Slade J in *Re Stott, Klouda v Lloyds Bank Ltd* [1980] 1 All ER 259 at 262.

9 See Lord Simonds in *Wintle v Nye* [1959] 1 All ER 552 at 560; Slade J in *Re Stott, Klouda v Lloyds Bank Ltd* [1980] 1 All ER 259 at 264.

10 Scarman J in *Re Fuld's Estate, Hartley v Fuld (No 3)* [1965] 3 All ER 776 at 783. Thus in *Re Stott, Klouda v Lloyds Bank Ltd* [1980] 1 All ER 259, there was an attempt to strike out many of the allegations pleaded in support of a defence of want of knowledge and approval as contravening RSC Ord 76, r 9(3) in that the allegations would also be relevant in support of a plea of undue influence which the defendant had not pleaded. The attempt failed because the judge thought that there will often be an inevitable overlap between evidence in support of want of knowledge and approval and evidence in support of undue influence.

11 Willmer J in *Re R* [1950] 2 All ER 117 at 123. The risk as to costs of a party opposing a will is reduced if he puts his opponent to proof of knowledge and approval instead of making positive allegations of fraud or undue influence which he himself has the burden of proving.

III. UNDUE INFLUENCE AND FRAUD

[5.9]

[Updated in footnote 1 for *Gudavadze v Kay* [2012] EWHC 1683 (Ch), [2012] WTLR 1755. Updated in footnote 3 for *Hubbard v Scott* [2011] EWHC 2750 (Ch), [2012] WTLR 40. Updated in footnote 4 for *Schrader v Schrader* [2013] EWHC 466 (Ch), [2013] WTLR 701. Updated in footnote 5 for *Wharton v Bancroft* [2011] EWHC 3250 (Ch), [2012] WTLR 705.]

Undue influence and fraud. Fraud and undue influence are really questions of knowledge and approval rather than of testamentary capacity since what has first to be proved is not the lack of capacity of the testator, but the acts of others whereby the testator has been induced to make dispositions which he did not really intend to make. Although undue influence is not impossible in the case of a testator of sound health and understanding, it is far more common in the case of a testator of weak or impaired mental capacity or in failing health. A gift obtained by undue influence or fraud is liable to be set aside upon proof of the undue influence or fraud.[1] Undue influence means coercion to make a will in particular terms.[2] The principle has thus been stated by Sir J P Wilde in *Hall v Hall*:[3]

> 'Persuasion is not unlawful, but pressure of whatever character if so exerted as to overpower the volition without convincing the judgment of the testator, will constitute undue influence, though no force is either used or threatened.'

The proof of motive and opportunity for the exercise of such influence is required but the existence of such coupled with the fact that the person who has such motive and opportunity has benefited by the will to the exclusion of others is not sufficient proof of undue influence. There must be positive proof of coercion overpowering the volition of the testator.[4] The mere proof of the relationship of parent and child, husband and wife, doctor and patient, solicitor and client, confessor and penitent, guardian and ward, or tutor and pupil does not raise a presumption of undue influence sufficient to vitiate a will[5] and although coupled with, for example, the execution of the will in secrecy, such relationship will help the inference, yet there is never in the case of a will a presumption of undue influence.[6] There is no presumption of undue influence, which must be proved by the person who sets up that allegation. The onus of proof resting upon a party propounding a will where circumstances of suspicion are disclosed does not extend to the disproof of an allegation of undue influence or fraud, the burden of establishing which always rests upon the parties setting it up.[7] The person who affirms the validity of the will must show that there was no force or coercion depriving the testator of his judgment and free action[8] and that what the testator did was what he desired to do.[9] The act of the testator in making the will or gift must be inconsistent with any hypothesis of undue influence.[10] Exaggerated description of the conduct of a proposed beneficiary is insufficient.[11] Where the testator is influenced by immoral considerations, there is no undue influence provided the will expresses his wishes.[12] Much less influence will induce a person of weak mental capacity or in a weak state of health to do any act and in such cases the court will the more readily find undue influence[13] and where a legatee for a large amount or one where a fiduciary relationship is found to exist between the testator and the beneficiary propounds a will prepared by himself more than ordinary proof of the authenticity of the will is called for[14] and this is so where the will is signed by a mark instead of the testator's usual signature.[15]

Undue influence has been found to be exercised by a person who was dead at the date of the execution of the will,[16] and, in a rare case, exercised on a person other than the testator.[17] Undue influence exerted for the benefit of someone other than the person exerting the influence is equally subject to the rules concerning undue influence as influence exerted by someone for his own benefit.[18] The party setting up a case of undue influence must give the particulars of the acts alleged in exercise of it with necessary dates[19] but not the means of the persons present.[20] Evidence of a statement of the party exerting the undue influence though not made in the presence of the testator is admissible.[21] A plea of undue influence ought never to be put forward unless the person who pleads it has reasonable grounds to support it.[22]

1 *Wingrove v Wingrove* (1885) 11 PD 81. The onus of proof is upon the party asserting undue influence or fraud: *Hutley v Grimstone* (1879) 5 PD 24; *Craig v Lamoureux* [1920] AC 349; *Re Hodgins* (1978) 85 DLR (3d) 705; *Maw v Dickey* (1974) 52 DLR (3d) 178; *Winter v Crichton* (1991) 23 NSWLR 116; *Baker Estate v Myhre* [1995] 6 WWR 410; *Robertson v Smith* [1998] 4 VR 144. The paragraph in the 7th edition of *Williams on Wills* corresponding with para **[5.9]** of the current edition was cited extensively and applied in *Re Wilkes dec'd, Wilkes v Wilkes* [2006] WTLR 1097. This paragraph of the text was referred to by the Hong Kong Court of Final Appeal in *Nina Kung (alias Nina TH Wang) v Wang Din Shin* (2006), FACV No 12 of 2004, where an allegation that a will had been forged was rejected. See *Supple v Pender* [2007] EWHC 829 (Ch) where a will was held to have been forged and *Gudavadze v Kay* [2012] EWHC 1683 (Ch), [2012] WTLR 1755, where Sales J held by way of summary judgment that the propounder of certain alleged testamentary documents had no real prospects of success since the evidence indicated they were forgeries.

2 *Williams v Goude* (1828) 1 Hag Ecc 577; *Wingrove v Wingrove* (1885) 11 PD 81; *Hall v Hall* (1868) LR 1 P & D 481.

3 LR 1 P & D 481 at 482. See also *Hubbard v Scott* [2011] EWHC 2750 (Ch), [2012] WTLR 40 at [52]: 'Persuasion without more is not coercion' per Proudman J. In this case undue influence was not proved when the testator left his whole estate to his cleaner. It was found that he was elderly, lonely, had become fond of her, and there was no one else to whom he wished to leave his estate.

4 *Craig v Lamoureux* [1920] AC 349; *Pocock v Pocock* [1952] OR 155; *Re Montone* [1955] OWN 799; *Banton v Banton* (1998) 164 DLR (4th) 176 (onus of proving wife exercised undue influence over husband satisfied). It will though be a common feature of a large number of undue influence cases that there is no direct evidence of the application of undue influence; it is of its nature that it goes on when no-one is looking, see *Schrader v Schrader* [2013] EWHC 466 (Ch), [2013] WTLR 701, where undue influence was inferred from a

number of factors including the testatrix's vulnerability, her dependence on her son who had a forceful and physical personality and who was filled with hatred for his brother.

5 These relationships raise a presumption of undue influence in the case of contracts, but, in the case of a will, these relationships (or most of them) are naturally the source and reason of the testator's bounty and no such presumption is made. See *Parfitt v Lawless* (1872) LR 2 P & D 462; *Nye v Sewell* (1894) 15 NSWLR 18; and *Wharton v Bancroft* [2011] EWHC 3250 (Ch), [2012] WTLR 705 where a deathbed will in favour of a woman the testator had treated as his wife for 32 years and whom he had just chosen to marry was held not to have been procured by undue influence. For cases on inter vivos gifts see, *In Jennings v Cairns, sub nom In the Estate of Davidge* [2003] EWCA Civ 1935, [2004] WTLR 361; *In the Estate of Rochelle, Padgham v Rochelle* [2002] 38 LS 36; *Hammond v Osborn* [2002] EWCA Civ 885, [2002] WTLR 1125, and *In the Estate of Morris (decd), Special Trustees for Great Ormond Street Hospital for Children v Rushin* [2001] WTLR 1137. See also *Re Loxton dec'd* [2006] WTLR 1567. Gifts to executors and trustees as such tend to excite any suspicion. However, in *Re Howell* [1955] OWN 85, a will prepared by a parish priest leaving nearly all the estate to the priest's church was held to be obtained by undue influence.

6 *Wheeler and Batsford v Alderson* (1831) 3 Hag Ecc 574; *Wyatt v Ingram* (1832) 3 Hag Ecc 466; *Walker v Smith* (1861) 20 Beav 394; *Croft v Day* (1838) 1 Curt 782; *Tuckwell v Cornick* (1844) 2 LTOS 336; *Wintle v Nye* [1959] 1 All ER 552, [1959] 1 WLR 284; *Fulton v Andrew* (1875) LR 7 HL 448 at 462, all cases where the solicitor largely benefited under the will; *Barry v Butlin* (1838) 2 Moo PCC 480, a similar case where the will was found for; see also *Re Fuld's Estate (No 3), Hartley v Fuld* [1968] P 675, [1965] 3 All ER 776; *Tilley v Berg and Berg (No 2)* [1945] 4 DLR 179 (where a solicitor was sole beneficiary, but the will was drawn by another solicitor it was held that there was no evidence of fraud or undue influence); *Greville v Tylee* (1851) 7 Moo PCC 320 (medical attendant); *Ashwell v Lomi* (1850) LR 2 PD 477 (medical attendant); *Re Stott, Klouda v Lloyds Bank Ltd* [1980] 1 All ER 259, [1980] 1 WLR 246 (manageress of nursing home); *Parfitt v Lawless* (1872) LR 2 P & D 462 (confessor); *Aimers v Taylor* (1897) 15 NZLR 530; *Eady v Waring* (1974) 43 DLR (3d) 667; *Goldsworthy v Thompson* (1974) 46 DLR (3d) 237; and *Re Bailey* (1974) 47 DLR (3d) 670.

7 *Boyse v Rossborough, Boyse v Colclough* (1857) 6 HL Cas 2; *Low v Guthrie* [1909] AC 278; *Tyrrell v Painton* [1894] P 151; *Re R* [1951] P 10, [1950] 2 All ER 117 (the circumstances which are held to excite the suspicions of the court must be circumstances attending, or at least relevant to, the preparation and execution of the will itself); *Craig v Lamoureux* [1920] AC 349; *Riach v Ferris* [1934] 1 DLR 118; *Re Kaufman, Anderson and Houge v Walkey and Mason* (1961) 27 DLR (2d) 178; *Vout v Hay* (1995) 125 DLR (4th) 431.

8 *Williams v Goude* (1828) 1 Hag Ecc 577; *Earl Sefton v Hopwood* (1855) 1 F & F 578; *Lovett v Lovett* (1857) 1 F & F 581 (where it is said that gratitude, affection and esteem do not give rise to undue influence); *Leach v Smith* (1859) 23 JP 168.

9 *Wingrove v Wingrove* (1885) 11 PD 81.

10 *Boyce v Rossborough, Boyse v Colclough* (1857) 6 HL Cas 2; *Re Boyd's Will, Miller v Farr* (1872) 3 VR 46.

11 *Browning v Budd* (1849) 6 Moo PCC 430.

12 *Wingrove v Wingrove* (1885) 11 PD 81.

13 *Hampson v Guy* (1891) 64 LT 778; See *Re Edwards (decd), Edwards v Edwards* [2007] All ER (D) (May) 46, [2007] WTLR 1397, where undue influence was proved.

14 This passage was cited with approval in *Ma Shiu-lim's Estate, Ma Po-chim v Ma Lok-shan* [1992] 2 HKLR 286 at 290, where it was held that although there were well-founded suspicions surrounding the preparation and execution of a will there was no case of actual coercion in which pressure was made to bear on or was otherwise exercised, to overpower the volition of the deceased in making the will, and thus no undue influence.

15 *Donnelly v Broughton* [1891] AC 435.

16 *Radford v Risdon* (1912) 28 TLR 342.

17 *Chennells v Bruce* (1939) 55 TLR 422.

18 See *Naidoo v Naidu* (2000) Times, 1 November and *Huguenin v Baseley* (1807) 14 Ves 273 at 289.

19 CPR PD 16.8.

20 *Re Earl of Shrewsbury's Estate, McLeod v Earl of Shrewsbury* [1922] P 112; but to the contrary *Jackson v Hillas* (1869) 18 WR 216.

21 *Radford v Risdon* (1912) 28 TLR 342. The question is one of fact and an appellant court will not reverse concurrent findings of the courts below: *Laramée v Ferron* (1909) 41 SCR 391.

22 Per Slade J in *Re Stott, Klouda v Lloyds Bank Ltd* [1980] 1 All ER 259 at 264, where it was alleged, unsuccessfully, that what was in effect being raised was a plea of undue influence under cover of a plea of want of knowledge and approval; see also *Re Fuld's Estates, Hartley v Fuld (No 3)* [1968] P 675 at 722, [1965] 3 All ER 776 at 783; and *Re R* [1951] P 10 at 19, [1950] 2 All ER 117 at 123.

CHAPTER 6

Rectification

[6.1]

[Updated in the text and in footnote 11 for *Marley v Rawlings* [2013] Ch 271 (CA).]

Rectification. Although the law of probate permits the court to omit words from a will in certain circumstances,[1] the general equitable doctrine of rectification was not previously available as a remedy in the law of wills.[2] Although it is beyond the scope of this work to consider rectification in detail one or two important characteristics can be noted.[3] Rectification is an equitable discretionary remedy[4] primarily available to remedy mistakes in written instruments recording the terms of contracts.[5] The remedy is however generally available and has always been applicable to unilateral documents such as voluntary settlements.[6] Wills, have hitherto, been one of the very few types of document which could not be rectified. The point was expressed by Templeman J in *Re Reynette-James, Wightman v Reynette-James*.[7]

> 'Any document other than a will could be rectified by inserting the words which the secretary omitted, but in this respect the court is enslaved by the Wills Act 1837. Words may be struck out but no fresh words may be inserted. …'[8]

The Administration of Justice Act 1982 (AJA 1982)[9] has now conferred a limited power to rectify wills to remedy two types of mistake; first, those caused by clerical errors, and secondly those arising from a failure to understand the testator's instructions. The power to rectify applies only to the wills of testators who die on or after 1 January 1983.[10] It cannot be exercised unless the will is formally valid, so cannot be exercised to make a document comply with the requirements of the Wills Act 1837, s 9.[11]

1 See previous Chapter for illustrations.

2 The reason for the exclusion has always been somewhat obscure since analogous unilateral documents such as voluntary settlements could be rectified, see, for example, *Re Butlin's Settlement Trusts, Butlin v Butlin* [1976] Ch 251, [1976] 2 All ER 483. The true explanation seemed to relate to the strict formal requirements for the execution of wills for it could be said that words varied or added by the court could not properly have been executed in accordance with the formalities. However, this is hardly convincing and modern cases such as *Re Morris, Lloyds Bank Ltd v Peake* [1971] P 62, [1970] 1 All ER 1057 and *Re Reynette-James, Wightman v Reynette-James* [1975] 3 All ER 1037, [1976] 1 WLR 161, had illustrated the necessity for a change in the law, at least in so far as patent clerical errors (of the sort apparent in those two cases) are concerned. In *Re Jensen* [1992] 2 NZLR 506 a judge rectified a codicil even though there was no statutory power in the jurisdiction to do so: '… the time has come to review that assumption' commented Fisher J at 511.

3 See Law Reform Committee's 19th Report on the Interpretation of Wills, 1973 Cmnd 5301.
4 *Whiteside v Whiteside* [1950] Ch 65, [1949] 2 All ER 913.
5 *Joscelyne v Nissen* [1970] 2 QB 86, [1970] 1 All ER 1213, CA, a useful modern case where the remedy is considered.
6 *Re Butlin's Settlement Trusts, Butlin v Butlin* [1976] Ch 251, [1976] 2 All ER 483, where it was decided that the court had power to rectify a voluntary settlement notwithstanding that the mistake had arisen not in omitting, or using, words intended or not intended to be included, but in ascribing the wrong interpretation to words intended to be used; applying *Lackersteen v Lackersteen* (1860) 30 LJ Ch 5; *Jervis v Howle and Talke Colliery Co Ltd* [1937] Ch 67, [1936] 3 All ER 193; *Whiteside v Whiteside* [1950] Ch 65, [1949] 2 All ER 913; and *Joscelyne v Nissen* [1970] 2 QB 86, [1970] 1 All ER 1213, CA. Rectification ordered, after some hesitation, despite the opposition of one trustee.
7 *Re Reynette-James, Wightman v Reynette-James* [1975] 3 All ER 1037, [1976] 1 WLR 161, words accidentally omitted changing sense of clause; clause omitted although mistake clear.
8 Referring to *Re Schott's Goods* [1901] P 190; *Re Horrocks, Taylor v Kershaw* [1939] P 198, [1939] 1 All ER 579; *Re Boehm's Goods* [1891] P 247.
9 Administration of Justice Act 1982, s 20; (Vol 2, Part G, para **[244.98]**) following the recommendations of the Law Reform Committee's 19th Report on the Interpretation of Wills, 1973 Cmnd 5301. For a general discussion of the jurisdiction under s 20, see Mummery LJ's judgment in *Walker v Geo H Medlicott & Son (a firm)* [1999] 1 All ER 685 at 699–670 where the previous cases are reviewed.
10 Administration of Justice Act 1982, ss 73(6)(c) and 76(11); and the provision applies only to England and Wales, s 77(1). For statutory provisions in other jurisdictions, see, for example, *Re Hess* [1992] 1 Qd R 176.
11 *Marley v Rawlings* [2013] Ch 271 (CA). In this case a husband and wife had made mirror wills leaving their estate to the survivor, or if the other failed to survive, to their putative son. Each though signed the will of the other. An application to rectify the survivor's would-be will was rejected because it did not comply with the Wills Act 1837, s 9 so there was no will no rectify.

[6.2]

[Updated in footnote 2 for *Boswell v Lawson* [2011] EWCA Civ 452, [2011] WTLR 931.
Updated in footnotes 3 and 4 and in the text for *Pengelly v Pengelly* [2008] Ch 375.
Updated in footnote 4 for *Austin v Woodward* [2011] EWHC 2458 (Ch), [2012] WTLR 559, *Lines v Porter* [2011] EWHC 2310 (Ch), [2012] WTLR 629 and *Joshi v Mahida* [2013] EWHC 486 (Ch), [2013] WTLR 859.
Updated in footnote 5 for *Kell v Jones* [2013] WTLR 507.]

Clerical errors. The Administration of Justice Act 1982, s 20[1] provides as follows:

> 'If a court is satisfied that a will is so expressed that it fails to carry out the testator's intentions[2], in consequence—
>
> (a) of a clerical error … it may order that the will shall be rectified so as to carry out his intentions.'

It has been stated that the term 'clerical error' means an inadvertent error made in the process of recording the intended words of the testator in drafting or in the transcription of his will. Thus where a solicitor failed to include a clause in a later will which was intended to mirror a clause in an earlier will which it replaced, it was held to be an error made in the process of recording the intended words of the testatrix. The will was rectified to include the omitted clause.[3] The introduction of a clause which is inconsistent with the testator's instructions in circumstances in which the draftsman has not applied his mind to its significance or effect is also a 'clerical error' for the purposes of this provision[4] but the introduction of words to which the draftsman has applied his mind with a proper understanding of his instruction but which (perhaps through failure properly to understand the law) do not achieve the objective which he and the testator intended is not.[5]

This provision seems apt to cover cases such as *Re Morris*,[6] where it will be recalled the codicil as written revoked 'clause 7 of the will' whereas the admitted intention had been to revoke 'clause 7(iv) of the will'. The omission of the Roman numeral (iv) was accepted on all sides as a clerical error, and such a case would now be simply resolved by the addition of the missing number, or words as the case might be. In many of these cases the error will be that of the draftsman, typist or amanuensis but the section is not so limited.[7]

1 See Vol 2, Part G, para **[244.98]**.
2 It is a prerequisite of the relief that the will should have failed to carry out the testator's intentions, so that where it is found on the evidence that the will has not so failed, rectification will not be available: see *Boswell v Lawson* [2011] EWCA Civ 452, [2011] WTLR 931.
3 *Wordingham v Royal Exchange Trust Co Ltd* [1992] Ch 412, [1992] 3 All ER 204. In *Wu Man Shan v Registrar of Probate* [2006] 2 HKC 106 a will was rectified under corresponding Hong Kong legislation where the mistake was regarded as clerical and trivial.
4 *Re Segelman* [1996] Ch 171, [1995] 3 All ER 676 at 686 (in which the offending clause was deleted). An order for rectification was granted in *Wong v Wong,* sub nom *Re Munday (dec'd)* [2003] WTLR 1161, to correct an obvious clerical error. Rectification was ordered in *Re Vautier's Estate* (2000–01) 3 ITELR 566 to give effect to the testator's intention in the circumstances described in the note to para **[5.7]** above. See also *Bush v Jouliac* [2006] EWHC 363 (Ch) (failure to omit WA 1837, s 33); *Hobart v Hobart* [2007] WTLR 1213; *Re Craig (decd), Price v Craig* [2006] EWHC 2561 (Ch); *Clarke v Brothwood* [2007] WTLR 329; *Pengelly v Pengelly* [2008] Ch 375; and *Joshi v Mahida* [2013] EWHC 486 (Ch), [2013] WTLR 859, in all of which cases, a will was rectified to correct a clerical error. In *Austin v Woodward* [2011] EWHC 2458 (Ch), [2012] WTLR 559, an error had been introduced by the testatrix's solicitors when the testatrix was updating her will by using the text of new precedents without considering the consequences of a gift to the claimant. It was held that this was a clerical error and the will was rectified. The use of a standard precedent without advertence to its significance or effect also resulted in rectification in *Lines v Porter* [2011] EWHC 2310 (Ch), [2012] WTLR 629 where it had not been intended that a widower's life interest be cut down on his remarriage or cohabitation, but the solicitor used a standard precedent which provided for this.
5 *Re Segelman* [1996] Ch 171 at 184–185; *Pengelly v Pengelly* [2008] Ch 375 at [23]–[24]; and *Kell v Jones* [2013] WTLR 507.
6 [1971] P 62, [1970] 1 All ER 1057.
7 The Law Reform Committee 19th Report on the Interpretation of Wills (1973, cmnd 5301), para 19, saw no difference in principle between a slip made by the testator himself, his solicitor or the typist: and there is nothing in the wording in s 20 to introduce such a distinction. This view has been confirmed, obiter, by Nicholls J in *Re Williams, Wiles v Madgin* [1985] 1 All ER 964 at 969.

[6.3]

[Updated in footnote 3 for *Sprackling v Sprackling* [2009] WTLR 897, [2008] EWHC 2696 (Ch) and *Kell v Jones* [2013] WTLR 507.]

Failure to understand the testator's instructions. The second situation where the AJA 1982, s 20(1)[1] introduces a power of rectification is as follows:

> 'If a court is satisfied that a will is so expressed that it fails to carry out the testator's intentions, in consequence—
> (a) …
> (b) of a failure to understand his instructions,

it may order that the will shall be rectified so as to carry out his intentions.'

It will be noticed that this provision is confined to cases where a draftsman fails to understand instructions and thus has a limited scope. The section does not cover the more common type of mistake, ie cases where the testator (and possibly his solicitor as well) fails to understand the legal effect of the words actually used, and thus produces the wrong result although using the intended expression; where in effect, all concerned may know what the testator wants but fail to use the right technique to achieve it.[2]

But where it can be established first, that the will fails to embody the testator's instructions, and secondly, what those instructions were, then it is now open to the court to rectify the will so as to make it embody them.[3] An example of such a case is where for instance, the testator has instructed his solicitor to draw his will in such a way as to leave certain property to X; the solicitor failing to understand what is wanted draws the will in such a way as to leave the property to Y, and the testator, not appreciating the mistake executes the will. Such a will could be rectified under the power in section 20.

It is apparent from the wording, '... a failure to understand his instructions ...', that the power of rectification in this second context is available only where there has been the intervention of another person. This will typically be where the testator has instructed another to draft his will, whether that person be a solicitor or a lay person, or where the testator dictates his will to an amanuensis. Thus this power would not be available in the much more common cases where mistakes occur, where a lay testator writes out his whole will using inappropriate or unsatisfactory language.

Further in order for the remedy to be available it must be established not only that the will fails to carry out the testator's instructions but also what those instructions were.[4] This will be a matter of proof and there is no guidance in the section as to the admissibility of the evidence in support. Section 21, which provides for the admissibility of extrinsic evidence as an aid in a will's interpretation, does not assist here, but clearly extrinsic evidence must be admitted to aid rectification since by definition the instructions for a will are not to be found within the will.[5]

1 See Vol 2, Part G, para **[244.96]**.

2 Rectification in such circumstances is sometimes possible in relation to eg settlements: see *Re Butlin's Settlement Trusts, Butlin v Butlin* [1976] Ch 251, [1976] 2 All ER 483. But the Law Reform Committee did not think the power of rectification appropriate to wills in such cases, op cit, para 20.

3 Law Reform Committee, 19th Report on the Interpretation of Wills (1973, cmnd 5301), para 21. See *Sprackling v Sprackling* [2008] EWHC 2696 (Ch), [2009] WTLR 897 where a will was rectified for a failure to understand the testator's instructions as to the property to form part of a devise. In *Kell v Jones* [2013] WTLR 507 great weight was placed on the solicitor's evidence as an experienced wills solicitor whose sole purpose was to ascertain those testamentary intentions.

4 See *Walker v Geo H Medlicott & Son (a firm)* [1999] 1 All ER 685 where the plaintiff failed to prove by convincing evidence that the testatrix had instructed the solicitor defendants to include in her will a gift of a house to the plaintiff as alleged. But an application failed in *In the Estate of Grattan (Robin Francis), Grattan v McNaughton* [2001] WTLR 1305 because the evidence was insufficient to show that the testator's will had failed to carry out his instructions; *Walker v Geo H Medlicott & Son* [1999] 1 WLR 727 applied. See also *Goodman v Goodman* [2006] EWHC 1757 (Ch), [2006] WTLR 1807 and *Sprackling v Sprackling* [2008] All ER (D) 55 (Nov), in both of which rectification was ordered on the ground of failure to

understand the testator's instructions, and *Racal Group Services Ltd v Ashmore* [1995] STC 1151, CA, upholding Vinelott J [1994] STC 416, a case concerning a claim to rectify a deed of covenant, for the circumstances in which rectification for tax reasons may be obtained.

5 The Law Reform Committee (n 3, above, para 28–30) considered the question and concluded that although the standard of proof should be high, there should be no rigid restrictions on the nature of the evidence admissible (or on its weight) on a claim of rectification of a will (n 3 above, para 65). In the absence of anything in the section to the contrary this is probably the position.

[6.5]

[Updated in footnote 1 for *Price v Craig* [2006] WTLR 1873, *Pengelly v Pengelly* [2008] Ch 375 and *Hobart v Hobart* [2007] WTLR 1213.]

Supplementary. An application for rectification must be made within six months of the date when representation is first taken out (except with the permission of the court).[1] In computing this period certain limited grants (settled land, trust property etc) are left out of account.[2] There is an express provision protecting personal representatives in that they will not be liable for any distribution of the estate, after the six months' period has elapsed, … 'on the ground that they ought to have taken into account the possibility that the court might permit the making of an application for an order under this section after the end of that period'.[3] However, this is without prejudice to the power of the court to recover any part of the estate so distributed.[4]

1 AJA 1982, s 20(2); Vol 2, Part G, para **[244.98]**. In *Price v Craig* [2006] WTLR 1873 the necessary permission was given in a case where the problem requiring rectification had not come to light until after the end of the six month period, and no one had been prejudiced by the delay. In similar circumstances permission was readily granted: *Pengelly v Pengelly* [2008] Ch 375. Permission was also granted after six months in *Hobart v Hobart* [2007] WTLR 1213.

2 AJA 1982, s 20(4).

3 AJA 1982, s 20(3).

4 AJA 1982, s 20(3).

PART C

What dispositions may be made

CHAPTER 7

What may be disposed of by will

[7.3]

[Updated in the text and footnote 5 for *Re Woolnough, Perkins v Borden* [2002] WTLR 595 and *Carr v Isard* [2007] WTLR 409.]

Joint tenancy. Property held under a joint tenancy survives to the surviving joint tenant or joint tenants and one of two or more joint tenants has no power to dispose of his interest by will.[1] The rule is applicable to both legal and equitable joint tenancies and a purely legal joint tenancy (ie where the joint tenant has no beneficial interest and which must be a trust estate) is also governed by the rule that a testator cannot now dispose of a trust estate.[2] A joint tenancy may be severed during the lifetime of the joint tenant,[3] but he cannot sever it by any disposition made by his will.[4] Instructions given by joint owners of property to make wills in terms inconsistent with the continuation of a joint tenancy may be capable of effecting severance by mutual agreement[5] but severance in such a case occurs at the point when the wills are made and is not the result of the operation of the will taking effect on death. Since, however, the will speaks from the death of the testator and he is expressly empowered to devise or bequeath any real or personal estate 'which he shall be entitled to, either at law or in equity, at the time of his death', it is clear that, if there is a severance during the testator's lifetime, a gift in his will made before severance will pass the severed interest in the property and of course a gift made after severance will pass that interest. If there is no severance but the testator by the death of the other joint tenant or tenants becomes the sole survivor, the will can pass the whole interest in the property.[6]

1 *Swift d Neale v Roberts* (1764) 1 Wm Bl 476; *Low v Carter* (1839) 1 Beav 426; *Turner v A-G* (1876) 10 IR Eq 386; *Renouf's Trustees v Haining* 1919 2 SLT 15. The matter is now settled so far as England and Wales is concerned by the Administration of Estates Act 1925, s 3(4), which provides that the interest of a deceased person under a joint tenancy where another tenant survives the deceased is an interest ceasing on his death. It can be noted that by the Trusts of Land and Appointment of Trustees Act 1996, Sch 2, para 4, trusts for sale of land, whether created before or after 1 January 1997, now become trusts of land; statutory trusts for co-owners under Law of Property Act 1925, s 34 (tenants in common) and s 36 (joint tenants) cease to be trusts for sale and become trusts of land.

2 See n 1.

3 Severance would be effected by an assignment of the joint tenant's interest: *Partriche v Powlet* (1740) 2 Atk 54; *Daly v Aldworth* (1863) 15 I Ch R 69; or by a mortgage or charge of his share: *Re Pollard's Estate* (1863) 3 De G J & Sm 541; or by the bankruptcy of the joint tenant: *Re Butler's Trusts, Hughes v Anderson* (1888) 38 Ch D 286; or by a notice in writing given to the other joint tenant or tenants under the Law of Property Act 1925, s 36(2) (as amended by the Trusts of Land and Appointment of Trustees Act 1996, Sch 2, para 4). See *Nielson-Jones v Fedden* [1975] Ch 222, [1974] 3 All ER 38; *Burgess v Rawnsley* [1975]

Ch 429, [1975] 3 All ER 142, CA; and *Harris v Goddard* [1983] 3 All ER 242, [1983] 1 WLR 1203, CA; *Goodman v Gallant* [1986] Fam 106, [1986] 1 All ER 311, CA.

4 2 Cru Dig tit 18 Joint Tenancy, c 2, s 19; but an agreement to devise his share in a mutual will followed by a will carrying out the agreement severs the joint tenancy: *Re Hey's Estate, Walker v Gaskill* [1914] P 192.

5 See *Re Woolnough, Perkins v Borden* [2002] WTLR 595, a decision of Master Moncaster in which the wills were found to have severed the joint tenancy. For this to happen, however, the wills should be 'unequivocably inconsistent with the continuation of the joint tenancy' and made in the presence and with the knowledge (and probably with the mutual agreement) of both joint tenants since 'It will not suffice to rely on an intention with respect to the particular share, declared only behind the backs of the other persons interested' (*Williams v Hensman* (1861) 1 J & Hem 546). See *Carr v Isard* [2007] WTLR 409. Severance in this fashion is more readily inferred in the case of mutual wills, see para **[2.4]** n 6 above.

6 *Re Horton, Lloyd v Hatchett* [1920] 2 Ch 1; *Re Russell, Russell v Chell* (1882) 19 Ch D 432; and see Wills Act 1837, s 24; Vol 2, Part G, para **[244.26]**. Possibly it is necessary that the wording of the gift shall not be such as can only refer to a share in the property.

[7.22]

[Revised generally in the text and in footnote 1. Updated in the text and in footnote 3 for *Re Smith, Smith v Smith* [2001] 3 All ER 552.]

Interest given under will of another. In the case of a testator who died before 1 January 1983, he could devise an interest given to him under the will of another, even where such other person survived him, if the Wills Act 1837, s 33 applied to prevent lapse.[1] A testator may bequeath specific assets comprised in the unadministered estate of a deceased person.[2] A putative beneficiary under the will or intestacy of a living person has no interest in the deceased's estate which can be the subject of a disclaimer and so a purported inter vivos disclaimer by such a beneficiary has no effect.[3]

1 *Re Scott* [1901] 1 KB 228; *Johnson v Johnson* (1843) 3 Hare 157; *Winter v Winter* (1846) 5 Hare 306, in which cases the gift was saved by WA 1837, s 33 which deemed the other person to have died immediately after the testator so that the gift would pass in accordance with the terms of the testator's will. See paras **[47.12]–[47.14]** below for WA 1837, s 33 as it applied to deaths before 1 January 1983. For deaths on or after 1 January 1983 lapse is not prevented by deeming the testator to have survived, but by effecting a substitution in favour of his issue: see paras **[47.15]–[47.20]** below.

2 *Re Leigh's Will Trusts* [1970] Ch 277.

3 *Re Smith, Smith v Smith* [2001] 3 All ER 552, [2001] 1 WLR 1937, even if the disclaimer was made by deed.

[7.33]

**[Updated in footnote 2 for *Lewisham Hospital NHS Trust v Hamuth* [2007] WTLR 309 and *Hartshorne v Gardner* [2008] 2 FLR 1681, and *Burrows v HM Coroner for Preston* [2008] 2 FLR 1225 and in footnote 6 for *Ghai v Newcastle City Council* (*Ramgharia Gurdwara, Hitchin and another intervening*) [2009] EWHC 978 (Admin), [2009] All ER (D) 68 (May) and in footnotes 4, 6, 12 and 13 for the Cremation (England and Wales) Regulations 2008.
Updated in footnote 6 for *R* (*on the appn of Ghai*) *v Newcastle City Council* [2010] EWCA Civ 59, [2010] All ER (D) 106 (Feb).]**

Funeral and burial wishes. A binding disposition of the dead body of the testator cannot be made by will so as to oust the executors' or administrators' rights and duties as to its disposal[1] but statutes have allowed some qualification of this position. In the event of a dispute the court may give directions for the disposal of the body.[2]

Cremation is not unlawful at common law unless it is done so as to create a nuisance or to prevent the coroner holding an inquest.[3] A direction, therefore, for cremation is valid apart from the statute[4] and, although under the statute and the regulations made thereunder it is not necessary that written directions for cremation should be given, it is not unlawful to cremate the body of a person who has left written directions to the contrary,[5] and cremation must take place in a recognised crematorium.[6] Although it is a common practice for such directions to be included in a will, it is not the most convenient method of giving such directions as the will may not be found or not be opened before the funeral.

The testator can if he so desires give directions as to funeral[7] or the erection of tombstone or other monument[8] and provide for the maintenance of his grave.[9] He may, where he desires to be cremated, arrange for the disposal of his ashes. These may be buried or scattered on consecrated ground[10] or under a church even after it has been closed for burial subject to a faculty from the ordinary.[11] A fortiori they may be scattered or kept in an urn in any unconsecrated place. In the absence of a direction by the testator, the person who applies for cremation may arrange for such disposal[12] and, in the absence of any such direction, they will be decently interred in a burial ground or land adjoining the crematorium or scattered thereon.[13]

1 *Williams v Williams* (1882) 20 Ch D 659. The doubt expressed in this case as to the legality of cremation has been departed from; see cases in n 3, below: *Hunter v Hunter* [1930] 4 DLR 255.

2 As in *Lewisham Hospital NHS Trust v Hamuth* [2007] WTLR 309 in which the relatives of the deceased could not agree as to how to dispose of his body and the hospital, being in lawful custody of the corpse, sought directions as to the appropriate means for the disposal by cremation. See also *Hartshorne v Gardner* [2008] 2 FLR 1681 and *Burrows v HM Coroner for Preston* [2008] 2 FLR 1225 where it was held that the wishes of the deceased and what family life he enjoyed must now (in the light of decisions on the European Human Rights Convention) be taken into account in deciding which of more than one claimant should have control of the disposal of his body.

3 *R v Price* (1884) 12 QBD 247; *R v Stephenson* (1884) 13 QBD 331.

4 Cremation Act 1902; Cremation (England and Wales) Regulations 2008, SI 2008/2841, in force with effect from 1 January 2009 and replacing the Cremation Regulations 1930, SR & O 1930/1016, as amended by the Cremation Regulations 1965, SI 1965/1146. The procedure relating to cremation was slightly amended by the Cremation Act 1952.

5 Formerly there was such a prohibition by virtue of reg 4 of the Cremation Regulations 1930, but this regulation was revoked by the Cremation Regulations 1965, SI 1965/1146.

6 Cremation (England and Wales) Regulations 2008, SI 2008/2841, reg 13, replacing, with effect from 1 January 2009, the Cremation Regulations 1930, SR & O 1930/1016, reg 3. 'Crematorium' means any building fitted with appliances for the purpose of burning human remains, and includes everything incidental or ancillary thereto: Cremation Act 1902, s 2. A structure is a 'building' within this meaning if it is relatively permanent and substantial, and can normally be described as a building, and a structure enabling Hindu cremation by traditional fire, rather than by using electricity, and enabling sunlight to shine directly on the body while it was being cremated, could be a building within the Act, see *R (on the appn of Ghai) v Newcastle City Council* [2010] EWCA Civ 59, [2010] All ER (D) 106 (Feb).

7 Such directions are in general better given in a separate writing to be opened immediately on death; but, if the testator desires any specific arrangement which is likely to increase the funeral expenses beyond what is reasonable for a person of his rank, he should also include them in his will with an authority to pay out of his estate all such expenses as the proper carrying out of such directions shall entail and the executor's decision as to what is reasonable and proper in accordance with the direction should be made conclusive on all parties; see *Re Read, Galloway v Harris* (1892) 36 Sol Jo 626. Where an executrix was directed to spend £300 on the funeral and grave, it was held she was entitled to spend that sum or any smaller sum she thought proper: *Re Pearce* [1946] SASR 118.

8 See *Re Dean, Cooper-Dean v Stevens* (1889) 41 Ch D 552. It would appear that the cost of a monument is not funeral expenses (*Hart v Griffith-Jones* [1948] 2 All ER 729); but as to a tombstone, see *Goldstein v Salvation Army Assurance Society* [1917] 2 KB 291, where the question is said to be one of fact.
9 See para **[9.29]** below.
10 *Re Dixon* [1892] P 386.
11 *Re Kerr* [1894] P 284.
12 Cremation (England and Wales) Regulations 2008, SI 2008/2841, reg 30, replacing, with effect from 1 January 2009, the Cremation Regulations 1930, SR & O 1930/1016, reg 16.
13 Cremation (England and Wales) Regulations 2008, SI 2008/2841, reg 30, replacing, with effect from 1 January 2009, the Cremation Regulations 1930, SR & O 1930/1016, reg 16.

CHAPTER 9

Who may benefit under a will

III. UNLAWFUL KILLINGS: RULE OF PUBLIC POLICY

[9.13]

[Updated in footnote 3 for the Estates of Deceased Persons (Forfeiture Rule and Law of Succession) Act 2011 ('EDP(FRLS)A 2011').]

Introduction. The rule of public policy which precludes a person who has unlawfully killed another from acquiring a benefit in consequence of the killing has been modified in respect of deaths on or after 13 October 1982 by the Forfeiture Act 1982 ('FoA 1982'). The FoA 1982 enables the court to grant relief in some cases from the consequences of the rule.[1] The rule is a wholly judge-made creation but the FoA 1982 gives statutory recognition to it by stating that the 'forfeiture rule' means 'the rule of public policy which in certain circumstances precludes a person who has unlawfully killed another person from acquiring a benefit in consequence of the killing'.[2] A useful modern judicial statement of the rule is as follows:[3]

> 'Under this rule, so far as relevant, a person who murders another cannot take, or enforce, any right or benefits resulting from his crime. The rule applies to rights and benefits arising under the victim's intestacy, just as much as it does to rights and benefits arising under the victim's will.'

This quotation refers to murder because that was what had happened in the case the judge was considering, but the rule applies to other forms of unlawful killing: see para **[9.15]**. The case law principles will be considered initially in the next paragraph.

1 See para **[9.20]** below.

2 FoA 1982, s 1(1). Generally speaking, however, no person is of so unmeritorious a character that he is debarred from benefiting under a will (*Thellusson v Woodford* (1799) 4 Ves 227 at 312, 329) and the disqualification of the slayer of the testator must be taken as an exception made to that general rule by reason of public policy (*Re Hall's Estate, Hall v Knight and Baxter* [1914] P 1).

3 See Blackburne J in *Re DWS, Re EHS, TWGS v JMG* [2000] 2 All ER 83 at 86; affd [2001] 1 All ER 97, CA. This statement is not affected by the fact that the decision in *Re DWS* has been reversed with effect from 1 February 2012 by the EDF(FRLS)A 2011, as recommended by the Law Commission Report '*The Forfeiture Rule and the Law of Succession*', Consultative Paper No 172 and Report No 295; see para **[9.17]** below.

[9.17]

[Updated for the Estates of Deceased Persons (Forfeiture Rule and Law of Succession) Act 2011 ('EDP(FRLS)A 2011').]

Effect of the incapacity. It has been stated that where the rule applies, the interest of the killer passes as if there has been a 'lapse', and in other cases it has been said that the name of the wrongdoer must be treated as 'struck out'.[1]

The property bequeathed to the killer under the will does not pass to the Crown as bona vacantia but passes to the other beneficiaries under the will in accordance with the plain construction of the will.[2] However, as a matter of general law, which remains relevant in some circumstances (see below), the property does not pass as if the killer had predeceased the deceased.[3] Thus, on the intestacy of someone dying before 1 February 2012, if the killer was disqualified from benefiting under the rule of public policy, the killer's son could not take as issue under the statutory trusts as if the killer had predeceased the deceased,[4] but the next class of intestate beneficiary was entitled to take.[5] In *Re DWS, Re EHS, TWGS v JMG,*[6] it was held that the effect of disqualification of a son from inheriting his parents' estates on intestacy, was that the estates passed, not to his innocent son (the grandchild), but to (the executor of) a sister. The reason was that on a strict construction of AEA 1925, ss 46 and 47, the grandson could only take by substitution if his parent had predeceased the intestate, which had not occurred. The decision was considered by the Law Commission, *'The Forfeiture Rule and the Law of Succession'*, Consultation Paper No 172 and Report No 295, which gave rise to EDP(FRLS)A 2011, which reverses the effect of *Re DWS*.

In relation to the estates of persons dying on or after 1 February 2012[7], EDP(FRLS)A 2011 amends the intestacy rules as follows. If someone is prevented from taking on an intestacy by the forfeiture rule he is treated, for the purposes of those rules, as having predeceased the intestate[8]. This is without prejudice to the court's powers to relieve from the forfeiture[9]. It reverses the effect of *Re DWS* and will enable issue of the intestate whose parent has killed the intestate to inherit from the intestate.

EDP(FRLS)A 2011 also amends WA 1837. If someone is prevented by the forfeiture rule from taking under a will he is treated as having predeceased the testator for the purposes of WA 1837[10], again in relation to deaths on or after 1 February 2012[11]. This is subject to a contrary intention expressed in the will[12], and without prejudice to the court's powers to relieve from the forfeiture[13].

It should be noted that the provision concerning wills falls short of providing that the testator's will has effect for all purposes as if the killer had predeceased the testator. It goes no further than providing that for the purposes of WA 1837 the killer is treated as having predeceased the testator[14]. Accordingly, the statutory substitution of issue under WA 1837, s 33 (see para **[47.15]**) will operate as if the killer had predeceased the testator, but an express substitution clause in a will which substitutes other beneficiaries for a primary beneficiary in the event of the latter predeceasing the testator, will not so operate. This was not the Law Commission's intention[15].

1 Per Vaisey J in *Re Callaway, Callaway v Treasury Solicitor* [1956] Ch 559 at 563, [1956] 2 All ER 451 at 453.

2 *Re Callaway, Callaway v Treasury Solicitor* [1956] Ch 559 at 563, [1956] 2 All ER 451. Thus in *Re Callaway*, where the whole estate had been given to a son and a daughter and the daughter murdered the mother, the whole estate passed to the son. See also *Re Sigsworth, Bedford v Bedford* [1935] Ch 89, 104 LJ Ch 46; *Cleaver v Mutual Reserve Fund Life Association* [1892] 1 QB 147; *Re Peacock, Midland Bank Executor and Trustee Co Ltd v Peacock* [1957] 2 All ER 98; *Hunter's Executors, Petitioners* 1992 SLT 1141; and *Re Jones, Jones v Midland Bank Trust Co Ltd* [1997] 3 FCR 697.

3 *Re DWS, Re EHS, TWGS v JMG* [2000] 2 All ER 83; affd [2001] Ch 568, [2001] 1 All ER 97; applying *Re Sinclair, Lloyds Bank plc v Imperial Cancer Research Fund* [1985] Ch 446, [1985] 1 All ER 1066, a case on the effect of failure of a gift to a spouse by reason of divorce under the Wills Act 1837, s 18A. See also *Re Scott, Widdows v Friends of the Clergy Corpn* [1975] 2 All ER 1033, a case on the effect of a disclaimer under intestacy. It can be noted that the reasoning in *Re DWS* is different from that in *Re Scott*, which could lead to a different conclusion in certain situations; see para **[46.1]**, n 1 and para **[48.8]**, n 5, where the point is explained. See also *Re Robertson's Estate, Marsden v Marsden* (1963) 107 Sol Jo 318.

4 As set out in the Administration of Estates Act 1925, ss 46 and 47.

5 *Re DWS, Re EHS, TWGS v JMG* [2000] 2 All ER 83; affd [2001] Ch 568, [2001] 1 All ER 97.

6 [2000] 2 All ER 83; affd [2001] Ch 568, [2001] 1 All ER 97. The son of the murderer was held not to be entitled but the deceased's sister's estate, being the next class of intestate beneficiary entitled under the Administration of Estates Act 1925, was held to be entitled. The decision has been criticised: see R Kerridge, *Visiting the Sins of the Fathers on their Children* (2001) 117 LQR 371, and R Wallington, *Unlawful Killings, Disclaimer and the Intestacy Rules* [2001] NLJ 919.

7 EDP(FRLS)A 2011, s 4(2), (4), and EDP(FRLS)A 2011 (Commencement) Order 2011, SI 2011/2913.

8 AEA 1925, s 46A(1), (2) (see para **[244.35A]**), inserted by EDP(FRLS)A 2011, s 1(2).

9 AEA 1925, s 46A(3) (see para **[244.35A]**), inserted by EDP(FRLS)A 2011, s 1(2). For relief from forfeiture see **[9.20]**.

10 WA 1837, s 33A(1), (2) (see para **[244.35A]**), inserted by EDP(FRLS)A 2011, s 2(2).

11 EDP(FRLS)A 2011, s 4(2), (4), and the EDP(FRLS)A 2011 (Commencement) Order 2011, SI 2011/2913.

12 WA 1837, s 33A(2) (see para **[244.35A]**), inserted by EDP(FRLS)A 2011, s 2(2).

13 WA 1837, s 33A(3) (see para **[244.35A]**), inserted by EDP(FRLS)A 2011, s 2(2).

14 Contrast the more general provisions in relation to divorce and civil partnership in WA 1837, ss 18A and 18C (see paras **[244.18]** and **[244.20]**).

15 The recommendation in the Law Commission's *'The Forfeiture Rule and the Law of Succession'*, Report No 295, was that where a person forfeits a benefit under a will through having killed the testator, the will should be applied as if the killer had died immediately before the testator, unless the will contains a provision to the contrary (see paras 4.11 and 5.3 of the Report). The draft Bill annexed to the Report contains the more limited provision which is now WA 1837, s 33A(2), but with a note on it which shows that the authors of the Report thought that it would apply to a substitution clause contained in a will. The more limited effect of s 33A(2) therefore seems to arise from a drafting error or a misunderstanding of the scope of WA 1837.

VI. CHILD BORN AS A RESULT OF FERTILISATION TECHNIQUES

[9.27]

[Updated for Human Fertilisation and Embryology Act 2008.]

Status of such children. The status of children born as a result of artificial insemination or other fertilisation techniques ('assisted reproduction') is governed by the Human Fertilisation and Embryology Act 1990 (HFEA 1990) or the Human Fertilisation and Embryology Act 2008 (HFEA 2008). HFEA 1990 applies where the placing in the woman of embryos or sperm and eggs, or the artificial insemination, occurred before 6 April 2009, and HFEA 2008 applies where it occurred on or after that date. The provisions of the HFEA 1990 and HFEA 2008 are discussed in Chapter 74.

XVI. DISCRIMINATION

[9.38]

[Updated in the text for the Equality Act 2010.]

Apart from statute, it would seem that a trust which discriminated against potential beneficiaries on the grounds of colour[1] or religion[2] was not void as being contrary to public policy. Acts of discrimination against sections of the community are now governed by the Equality Act 2010. The relevant provisions of this Act are discussed post in the context of charitable gifts.[3]

1 *Re Dominion Students' Hall Trust* [1947] Ch 183.
2 *Re Lysaght, Hill v Royal College of Surgeons of England* [1966] Ch 191, [1965] 2 All ER 888.
3 See Chapter 102.

XX. INSOLVENT BENEFICIARIES

[9.46]

[This is a new paragraph.]

Capacity to receive. There is no objection to an insolvent person being a beneficiary under a will, but a bankrupt's estate vests in the trustee in bankruptcy immediately upon his appointment.[1] A bankrupt's estate comprises all property belonging to or vested in the bankrupt at the commencement of the bankruptcy.[2] Property for this purpose includes money, goods, things in action, land and every description of property wherever situated and also obligations and every description of interest, whether present or future or vested or contingent, arising out of or incidental to, property.[3] A specific or pecuniary legatee's entitlement to a legacy is within this definition of property[4] and so vests in the trustee in bankruptcy. The same is true of residuary legatees: even if a residuary legatee's right is limited to a right to compel due administration of the estate, the legatee nevertheless still has an immediate 'interest', being the right to receive the assets comprising residue as and when the administration of the estate is complete, which vests in the trustee in bankruptcy.[5] It follows that the date of vesting in the trustee is the later to occur of the bankruptcy or the death of the testator, provided that the latter occurs before the bankrupt's discharge.

1 Insolvency Act 1986, s 306(1).
2 IA 1986, s 283(1).
3 IA 1986, s 436.
4 *Lord Sudeley v Attorney-General* [1897] AC 1.
5 *Re Hemming, Raymond Saul & Co (a firm) v Holden* [2009] Ch 313; *Official Receiver in Bankruptcy v Schultz* (1990) 170 CLR 306 (concerning the Australian Bankruptcy Act 1966).

PART D

Form of will and execution

CHAPTER 11

Signature

[11.11]

[Updated in the text and in footnote 6 for *Marley v Rawlings* [2013] Ch 271 (CA).]

The intention. The 'intention' in the section refers to the act of signing not to the presence on the document of the testator's signature.[1] Thus it will not suffice where the testator signed the document as an earlier will and then made alterations to it, in effect making a new will, to argue that his earlier signature was intended to give effect to the later will.[2] It cannot be said that when the testator signed the earlier will he was intending to give effect to the later will.[3] In contrast the Court of Appeal,[4] reversing the first instance decision, has held where the deceased signed his name at the top of the paper before he had written out the dispositive provisions, that this could be sufficient because the testator intended his name as his signature.[5] But the signature has to be to the document containing the testamentary provisions intended by the testator, not to some other document containing similar testamentary provisions, albeit that the testator thought that the document he signed contained the testamentary provisions he intended.[6] Examples of circumstances where the testator's intention in relation to his signature is problematic are the 'envelope cases', i e cases where the testator has enclosed the will in an envelope and has signed the envelope. In the most recent of these[7] the testatrix had signed her will, at the top, and had also written her name on the envelope in which the will was enclosed. The court held that on the facts, the testatrix had not intended her name on the envelope to be a signature to her will, since she had already signed it, but was more in the nature of a label or identification.[8] However the signature on the will was invalid since it was at the top and not the bottom, and thus the will was invalid. Under the new provisions the attitude to the signature on the envelope would be the same but the signature on the will might now be acceptable.[9]

The new WA 1837, s 9 requires that it should 'appear' that the testator intended by his signature to give effect to the will. In most cases the intention (or lack of it) will appear from the will or alleged will itself, but the section does not require that it should appear from the will. It is thought that extrinsic evidence will be admissible to show the testator's intention, just as it was admissible under the previous law, and as it normally is admissible to show matters relevant to the validity of a will.[10]

The intention to give effect to the will, will govern those cases where the will is written on several sheets and the testator only signs one; such cases[11] were generously treated under the old law, and it is thought will be unaffected by the new provisions. Similarly where there is an interpolation or interlineation in the will.[12]

1 *Re White, Barker v Gribble* [1991] Ch 1, per Ferris J at 6.
2 *Re White, Barker v Gribble* [1991] Ch 1.
3 *Re White, Barker v Gribble* [1991] Ch 1. Probate was granted of the earlier, not the later will.
4 *Wood v Smith* [1993] Ch 90, [1992] 3 All ER 556, CA; reversing on the formalities point [1991] 2 All ER 939. The will was held to be invalid due to lack of testamentary capacity of the deceased at the time of execution. This 'practical' approach was followed in *Weatherhill v Pearce* [1995] 2 All ER 492.
5 See n 4 above.
6 *Marley v Rawlings* [2013] Ch 271 (CA). In this case a husband and wife had made mirror wills leaving their estate to the survivor, or if the other failed to survive, to their putative son. Each though signed the will of the other so that the Wills Act 1837, s 9(b) was not satisfied. Whereas each testator may have intended to give effect to 'a' will, they did not intend, by their signatures, to give effect to the actual documents they executed.
7 *Re Beadle, Mayes v Beadle* [1974] 1 All ER 493, [1974] 1 WLR 417.
8 See also *Re Bean's Estate* [1944] P 83, [1944] 2 All ER 348 and contrast *Re Mann's Goods* [1942] P 146, [1942] 2 All ER 193.
9 Provided, of course, it is correctly attested, which it was not in *Re Beadle, Mayes v Beadle* [1974] 1 All ER 493, [1974] 1 WLR 417.
10 See Chapter 57.
11 See para **[11.4]**, n 1.
12 See para **[11.3]**, n 3.

IV. FORM OF SIGNATURE

[11.16]

[Updated in footnote 1 for *Lim v Thompson* [2009] EWHC 3341 (Ch), [2010] WTLR 661.]

Stamp. Signature by a stamp has been accepted.[1]

1 *Jenkins v Gaisford and Thring, Re Jenkins' Goods* (1863) 3 Sw & Tr 93 (where an aged person had a stamp made of his signature). A photocopied signature is not a signature, see *Lim v Thompson* [2009] EWHC 3341 (Ch), [2010] WTLR 661.

[11.21]

[Updated in the text and in footnotes 5 and 6 for *Barrett v Bem* [2012] EWCA Civ 52, [2012] 2 All ER 920.]

Signature on testator's behalf. When the signature is written by another on behalf of the testator it must be made in his presence and by his direction.[1] The person so signing may be one of the attesting witnesses.[2] The person so signing on the testator's behalf may sign his own name so long as it is expressly stated to be on behalf of the testator.[3] The testator must in some way indicate to the witnesses that the signature has been put there at his request and this may be evidenced by his conduct.[4] But some positive and discernible communication is required in order to amount to a valid direction by a testator to another person to sign a will on his behalf. The communication may be non-verbal, but there has to be more than passive acquiescence in someone else's actions; a direction may not be given by negative conduct.[5] There is no statutory requirement that the person who signs on behalf of a testator should not be a beneficiary of the will, but it has been said that it is plainly undesirable that beneficiaries should be permitted to execute a will in their own favour in any capacity and Parliament should consider changing the law to ensure that this could not happen in the future.[6]

1 WA 1837, s 9, as substituted by the AJA 1982, s 17; see Vol 2, Part G, para **[244.7]**, which makes no change in this respect. *Re Kevil's Goods* (1873) IR 8 Eq 244.
2 *Re Bailey's Goods* (1838) 1 Curt 914; *Smith v Harris* (1845) 1 Rob Eccl 262; *Re Ullersperger's Goods* (1841) 6 Jur 156.
3 *Re Clark's Goods* (1839) 2 Curt 239; *Smith v Harris* (1845) 1 Rob Eccl 262; *Jenkins v Gaisford and Thring, Re Jenkins' Goods* (1863) 3 Sw & Tr 93; *Re Blair's Goods* (1848) 6 Notes of Cases 528; *Re Deeley and Green* [1930] 1 DLR 603 (signature by notary in own name); *Re Fiszhaut Estate* (1966) 56 DLR (2d) 381.
4 *Re Marshall's Goods* (1866) 13 LT 643. The testator may by subsequent declarations show that the signature was on his behalf: *Re Elcock's Goods* (1869) 20 LT 757. All that is required is mere consent to the signature being appended and no instructions in writing are necessary: *Parker v Felgate* (1883) 8 PD 171; *Parker v Parker* (1841) Milw 541. For a case where the testatrix was incapable of speech or writing, see *Re Holtman's Estate, Gillett v Rogers* (1913) 108 LT 732.
5 *Barrett v Bem* [2012] EWCA Civ 52, [2012] 2 All ER 920. In this case when a testator had tried and failed hours before his death to sign his will personally, the sole legatee had stepped in to assist, but this was not at his direction, and his lack of protest or objection could not amount to an implicit direction to her to sign.
6 *Barrett v Bem* [2012] EWCA Civ 52, [2012] 2 All ER 920 at [39] per Lewison LJ.

[11.24]

[Text and footnote 7 removed to para [12.13].]

Sufficiency of acknowledgment. The testator must sign his will or acknowledge his signature in the presence of two or more witnesses present at the same time.[1] It is not sufficient for the testator to acknowledge his signature to each witness in turn; the acknowledgment must be made in the joint presence of the witnesses.[2] Nor is it sufficient to commence a signature in the presence of both witnesses, one of whom then departs to return when the testator's and the other witness's signature are on the will.[3] The acknowledgment may be by gesture[4] or made in answer to a question[5] but the witnesses must at the time of the acknowledgment see, or have the opportunity of seeing, the signature of the testator, and if what takes place involves an acknowledgment by the testator that the signature is his, that is enough.[6] The signature to be acknowledged may be made either by the testator or by another for him;[7] but it must be a signature and it is not enough that the name of the testator is pencilled to show where the signature should be.[8]

1 Wills Act 1837, s 9 as substituted by the AJA 1982, which makes no change in this respect. It is the signature and not the will which has to be acknowledged: *Re Shewchuk* (1968) 1 DLR (3d) 288. No express declaration of acknowledgment is necessary to satisfy the WA 1837, s 9(c): *Weatherhill v Pearce* [1995] 2 All ER 492, [1995] 1 WLR 592.
2 *Re Groffman, Groffman and Block v Groffman* [1969] 2 All ER 108, [1969] 1 WLR 733.
3 *Re Colling, Lawson v von Winckler* [1972] 3 All ER 729, [1972] 1 WLR 1440 (the part of the name that had been subscribed before the witness departed was neither the name itself nor some mark intended to represent the name).
4 *Re Davies' Goods* (1850) 2 Rob Eccl 337; *Re Owston's Goods* (1862) 2 Sw & Tr 461 (testator deaf and dumb). Going over testator's own signature with a dry pen may be an acknowledgment or a re-execution: *Lewis v Lewis* [1908] P 1.
5 *Kelly v Keatinge* (1871) IR 5 Eq 174; in *Re Groffman, Groffman and Block v Groffman* [1969] 2 All ER 108, [1969] 1 WLR 733, the signed will was in the testator's inside coat pocket and it was held that gesturing towards that pocket was not a sufficient acknowledgment since the witnesses could not see the signature.
6 *Re Gunstan's Goods, Blake v Blake* (1882) 7 PD 102; *O'Meagher v O'Meagher* (1883) 11 LR Ir 117; *Clery v Barry* (1887) 21 LR Ir 152; *Daintree v Butcher and Fasulo* (1888) 13 PD 102 (document not stated to be a will); *Whiting v Turner* (1903) 89 LT 71; *Re Swift's Goods* (1900) 17 TLR 16, and see *Brown v Skirrow* [1902] P 3; *Re Groffman, Groffman and Block v Groffman* [1969] 2 All ER 108, [1969] 1 WLR 733; *Re Colling, Lawson v von Winckler* [1972]

3 All ER 729, [1972] 1 WLR 1440. See *Re White, Barker v Gribble* [1990] 3 All ER 1, at 7 where *Daintree v Butcher and Fasulo* (1888) 13 PD 102, was referred to.

7 *Re Regan's Goods* (1838) 1 Curt 908; *Parker v Parker* (1841) Milw 541. It is not enough that the witnesses see the signature written if they are not present when the testator directs the signature to be made: *Burke v Moore, Re Moore's Goods* (1875) IR 9 Eq 609.

8 *Reeves v Grainger* (1908) 52 Sol Jo 355. Nor, in a case where the signature was not written by the testator, was it enough where the testator affixed a seal and said that the document was his act and deed: *Re Summers' Goods* (1850) 2 Rob Eccl 295.

[11.26]

[Updated in footnote 2 for *Re Rawlinson* [2010] EWHC 1269 (Ch), [2010] WTLR 1443.]

Acknowledgment by production of signed will. The production of a will by the testator with his signature upon it, and a request by him, or by someone for him in his presence,[1] to the witness to attest it, is a sufficient acknowledgment of the signature.[2] Where the witnesses are familiar with the signature of the testator, it is sufficient if they see the will.[3] There need not be positive evidence from the attesting witnesses that the testator's signature was on the will when they signed it,[4] but the mere calling in of witnesses, who had no opportunity of seeing the testator's signature, without giving them any explanation of the instrument they were signing, is not an acknowledgment.[5] It is not, however, absolutely necessary that the witnesses should know that the instrument is a will provided they are told that it is a document requiring attestation by two witnesses.[6] On the re-execution of a will acknowledgment of the original signature is sufficient.[7]

1 *Inglesant v Inglesant* (1874) LR 3 P & D 172; *Re Bishop's Goods* (1882) 46 JP 392. It seems that the testator must be aware of the request of the third party: *Morritt v Douglas* (1872) LR 3 P & D 1; *White v Tunnicliffe* (1897) 13 TLR 469.

2 *Ilott v Genge* (1842) 3 Curt 160; *Gaze v Gaze* (1843) 3 Curt 451; *Keigwin v Keigwin* (1843) 3 Curt 607; *Leech v Bates* (1849) 1 Rob Eccl 714; *Wright v Sanderson* (1884) 9 PD 149; *Daintree v Butcher and Fasulo* (1888) 13 PD 102; *Lewis v Lewis,* above; *Weatherhill v Pearce* [1995] 2 All ER 492, [1995] 1 WLR 592; *Re Rawlinson* [2010] EWHC 1269 (Ch), [2010] WTLR 1443.

3 *Re Gibson* [1953] NZLR 122.

4 *Blake v Knight* (1843) 3 Curt 547.

5 *Ilott v Genge* (1842) 3 Curt 160; *Gaze v Gaze* (1843) 3 Curt 451; *Keigwin v Keigwin* (1843) 3 Curt 607; *Re Rees' Goods* (1865) 34 LJPM & A 56; *Fischer v Popham* (1875) LR 3 P & D 246; *Wright v Sanderson* (1884) 9 PD 149; *Daintree v Butcher and Fasulo* (1888) 13 PD 102; *Patterson v Benbow* (1889) 7 NZLR 673. This is especially so where there is no evidence that the testator's signature was on the will at the time: *Re Swinford's Goods* (1869) LR 1 P & D 630; *Pearson v Pearson* (1871) LR 2 P & D 451.

6 *Daintree v Butcher and Fasulo* (1888) 13 PD 102.

7 *Re Dewell's Goods* (1853) 1 Ecc & Ad 103.

CHAPTER 12

Attestation

II. MODE OF ATTESTATION

[12.3]

[Updated in footnote 5 for *Re Wilson* [2013] EWHC 499 (Ch), [2013] WTLR 899.]

Signature in presence of both witnesses. The signature of the testator must be made or acknowledged in the presence of two witnesses,[1] and such witnesses must attest and sign the will,[2] or acknowledge a prior signature,[3] in the presence of the testator.[4] Both attesting witnesses must be present at the same time[5] and both witnesses must attest and sign,[6] or acknowledge,[7] after the testator's signature has been made or acknowledged in their presence.[8] Each witness should be able to say that he knows of his own knowledge that the testator had signed the document.[9] There is no sufficient acknowledgment unless the witnesses either saw or had the opportunity of seeing the signature,[10] even though the testator should expressly declare that the paper to be attested is his will or should state that his signature is inside the will.[11] A blind person cannot be a witness.[12]

1 The presence of one witness is not enough: *Re Garner's Goods* (1861) 25 JP 183; *Re Swift's Goods* (1900) 17 TLR 16; *Brown v Skirrow* [1902] P 3 (a second witness near but not really cognisant of the signing); *Re Groffman, Groffman and Block v Groffman* [1969] 2 All ER 108, [1969] 1 WLR 733 (witnesses called in one after the other). For a case where the execution was seen by neither witness, see *Ilott v Genge* (1842) 3 Curt 160; *Re Hammond's Goods* (1863) 3 Sw & Tr 90 (no evidence of any writing on paper when witnesses signed); *Re Trinder's Goods* (1844) 3 Notes of Cases 275 (witnesses saw only blank space where they signed); *Hudson v Parker* (1844) 1 Rob Eccl 14 (will and testator's signature purposely concealed); *Shaw v Neville* (1855) 2 Ecc & Ad 203 (perfect signature and attestation clause, but attesting witnesses saw nothing whatever except the space where they wrote); *Re Pearsons' Goods* (1864) 33 LJPM & A 177 (a similar case).

2 In the case of testators who die before 1 January 1983; WA 1837, s 9; see Vol 2, Part G, para **[244.6]**.

3 As an additional alternative in the case of testators who die on or after 1 January 1983; WA 1837, s 9 as substituted by the Administration of Justice Act 1982, s 17; see Vol 2, Part G, para **[244.7]**.

4 WA 1837, s 9, as substituted by the AJA 1982, s 17. *Hudson v Parker* (1844) 1 Rob Eccl 14; *Betts v Gannell* (1903) 19 TLR 304. As to what amounts to a signature, see, above, and as to what amounts to an acknowledgment of signature, see above. As to documents which cannot take effect as wills for want of attestation, see *Re Hughes* (1888) 59 LT 586; *Re Williams, Williams v Ball* [1917] 1 Ch 1.

5 *Wyatt v Berry* [1893] P 5; *Hindmarsh v Charlton* (1861) 8 HL Cas 160; *Re Morgan's Will* [1950] VLR 335; *Re Groffman, Groffman and Block v Groffman* [1969] 2 All ER 108, [1969] 1 WLR 733. If only one is present on the first occasion, then the signature of the testator must be acknowledged and both sign on the second occasion: *Re Allen's Goods* (1839) 2 Curt 331; *Moore v King* (1842) 3 Curt 243. But where there was a proper attestation on the

first occasion but, one of the witnesses being an executor, it was wrongly supposed to be invalid, and it was amended by erasing his name and adding another, the will was held good, as it had been properly attested on the first occasion and the subsequent actions would not invalidate it: *Re Hannam's Goods* (1850) 7 Notes of Cases 437. Where the second witness came within view of the document while the first witness was completing his signature, it was held that such witness came too late to validate the execution: *Re Linley, McDonnell v Linley* (1949) 207 LT Jo 372, CA. In *Gray v Richards Butler* [2001] WTLR 625, the will on which the professional executor relied to justify the retention of his firm's charges had been held invalid in previous proceedings because the witnesses had not witnessed it at the same time. In *Re Wilson* [2013] EWHC 499 (Ch), [2013] WTLR 899 there was conflicting evidence as to where the witnesses were precisely, but the judge concluded that the individual overseeing the execution would have ensured the formalities were properly adhered to.

6 See n 1, above.

7 See n 4, above.

8 *Moore v King* (1842) 3 Curt 243; *Cooper v Bockett* (1843) 3 Curt 648; *Hindmarsh v Charlton* (1861) 8 HL Cas 160; *Wyatt v Berry* [1893] P 5; *Brown v Skirrow* [1902] P 3 at 7; *Re Davies' Estate* [1951] 1 All ER 920; *Re Groffman, Groffman and Block v Groffman* [1969] 2 All ER 108, [1969] 1 WLR 733; *Hudson v Bower* (1968) 67 WWR 564, 1 DLR (3d) 288; *Re Colling, Lawson v von Winckler* [1972] 3 All ER 729 [1972] 1 WLR 1440; see para **[12.5]**, n 3.

9 *Brown v Skirrow* [1902] P 3 at 5; but it is not necessary that an attesting witness should know that the document signed is a will: *Re Benjamin's Estate* (1934) 150 LT 417.

10 *Re Gunstan's Goods, Blake v Blake* (1882) 7 PD 102; it is sufficient if the witnesses see the testator write what the court presumes to be the signature: *Smith v Smith* (1866) LR 1 P & D 143.

11 See cases cited in n 6, para **[11.24]** above.

12 *Re Gibson's Estate* [1949] P 434, [1949] 2 All ER 90.

[12.4]

[Updated in footnote 1 for *Olins v Walters* [2007] EWHC 3060 (Ch), [2007] All ER (D) 291 (Dec).]

Witness must attest the will. It is essential that the witnesses in signing should attest the will and not merely some alteration to it.[1]

1 *Re White, Barker v Gribble* [1990] 3 All ER 1 at 7. *In the Estate of Sherrington Deceased, Sherrington v Sherrington* [2005] EWCA Civ 326, [2005] WTLR 587. Where a will was validly executed in 1981 and alterations were made to it in 1984 which the witnesses signed, it was held that they did not attest the document as the 1984 will but merely as alterations to the 1981 will. Applying *Re Martin's Goods* (1849) 1 Rob Eccl 712 and *Re Shearn's Goods* (1880) 50 LJ P 15. See also *Olins v Walters* [2007] EWHC 3060 (Ch), [2007] All ER (D) 291 (Dec) where a question arose as to whether a will made in 1988 and a codicil made in 1998 had been properly witnessed. Norris J (at [32]–[40]) held that attestation was good despite one of the witnesses giving evidence to the contrary. For commentary as to the presumption of due execution where a witness has a recollection contrary to the attestation clause see Chapter 13 below.

[12.6]

[Updated in footnote 1 for *Re Rawlinson* [2010] EWHC 1269 (Ch), [2010] WTLR 1443.]

Attestation in presence of testator. It is not necessary that the testator should actually see the witnesses sign, it is sufficient if he might have seen them if he cared to look.[1] The witnesses may be in an adjoining room, but only in such part of that room as is visible by the testator.[2] The testator must be mentally capable of recognising the act of attestation, and conscious of the transaction in which the witnesses are engaged and, if the testator becomes insensible before the witnesses sign, the attestation is insufficient.[3]

1 *Tod v Winchelsea (Earl)* (1826) 2 C & P 488; *Jenner v Ffinch* (1879) 5 PD 106; *Carter v Seaton* (1901) 85 LT 76: *Re Rawlinson* [2010] EWHC 1269 (Ch), [2010] WTLR 1443. But where the testator is incapable of turning to see the witnesses sign, even if he cares to do so, the attestation is bad: *Tribe v Tribe* (1849) 1 Rob Eccl 775; *Re Wozciechowiecz Estate* [1931] 4 DLR 585.

2 *Re Trimnell's Goods* (1865) 11 Jur NS 248; *Re Piercy's Goods* (1845) 1 Rob Eccl 278 (testator might have seen, but was blind). For cases where the will was rejected because the position in the adjoining room was not visible by the testator, see *Re Killick's Goods* (1864) 3 Sw & Tr 578 (where testatrix might have seen by raising herself but there was no evidence that she did so); *Carter v Seaton* (1901) 85 LT 76 (impossible to see); *Betts v Gannell* (1903) 19 TLR 304 (impossible to see); *Jenner v Ffinch* (1879) 5 PD 106 (testator unaware witnesses were signing); *Norton v Bazett* (1856) Dea & Sw 259 (testator could have seen by shifting position but evidence that he did not); *Winchilsea v Wauchope* (1827) 3 Russ 441 (where seeing possible, presumption in favour of will if no evidence).

3 *Right v Price* (1779) 1 Doug KB 241. Where testator blind, see *Re Piercy's Goods* (1845) 1 Rob Eccl 278. A testator may be losing his facilities, yet they may be sufficient to validate the execution: *Re Chalcraft's Goods, Chalcraft v Giles* [1948] P 222, [1948] 1 All ER 700.

[12.13]

[Text and footnote 7 added from para [11.24].]

Acknowledgment by witness. The AJA 1982 includes an additional alternative to the requirement that each witness 'attests and signs the will', namely, 'or acknowledges his signature'.[1] This change applies to the wills of testators who die on or after 1 January 1983.[2] This power will enable wills which are incorrectly attested because of the order of signing to be remedied by the witness acknowledging a prior signature after the testator has signed or acknowledged,[3] although a re-signing is preferable.[4] The section makes it clear, by providing for signature or acknowledgment in the alternative that one witness can sign and the other acknowledge.[5] It is thought that so far as the sufficiency of an act of acknowledgment is concerned, the position would be analogous to the rules governing a testator's acknowledgment.[6] It has been held that a witness sufficiently acknowledged her signature by protesting throughout the transaction as to her signature's validity.[7]

1 Wills Act 1837, s 9, as substituted by the AJA 1982, s 17; see Vol 2, Part G, para **[244.7]**.

2 AJA 1982, s 73(6); s 76(11).

3 See para **[12.12]** above; and *Re Colling, Lawson v von Winckler* [1972] 3 All ER 729.

4 For the reasons given in para **[12.5]**, n 3.

5 The wording of the provision was expressly changed in order to make this clear.

6 See para **[11.24]** above. Where there has been a subsequent addition to the will it is possible for this to be authenticated by the testator and witnesses collectively acknowledging their prior signatures; however, for obvious reasons, this is not recommended and it is better to re-sign in full.

7 *Couser v Couser* [1996] 3 All ER 256, applying *Brown v Skirrow* [1902] P 3 and *Casson v Dade* (1781) 1 Bro CC 99.

IV. INTENTION TO ATTEST

[12.14]

[Updated in footnote 4 for *Re Rawlinson* [2010] EWHC 1269 (Ch), [2010] WTLR 1443.]

General rule. Apart from the subscription of the signature, it must be shown that the signatures were added to the document with the intention of attesting the testator's signature.[1] Whether a person signed as an attesting witness is a question of fact depending on the circumstances of each case and is to be determined without regard to what the consequences might be.[2] In the absence of any evidence the intention to attest might be presumed.[3] The Court of Appeal has reaffirmed the principle that a witness to a will must intend to witness the testator's signature or the will; though it is not necessary that he should know that the document is a will.[4] Where a presumption of due execution arises from the existence of a regular attestation clause and the presence of the signatures of the testator and the witnesses, 'the strongest evidence' will be required to demonstrate that a witness did not intend to witness the testator's signature or the will.[5]

1 *Re Wilson's Goods* (1866) LR 1 P & D 269; *Re Sharman's Goods* (1869) LR 1 P & D 661; *Re Streatley's Goods* [1891] P 172; *Re Beadle, Mayes v Beadle* [1974] 1 All ER 493, [1974] 1 WLR 417.

2 *Re Bravda's Estate* [1968] 2 All ER 217, [1968] 1 WLR 479.

3 *Re Bravda's Estate* [1968] 2 All ER 217, [1968] 1 WLR 479. See Presumption of Due Execution, Chapter 13.

4 *In the Estate of Sherrington Deceased, Sherrington v Sherrington* [2005] EWCA Civ 326, [2005] WTLR 587. Nor is it necessary that he should know the requirements of the Wills Act 1837: see *Re Rawlinson* [2010] EWHC 1269 (Ch), [2010] WTLR 1443.

5 Ibid.

CHAPTER 13

Presumption of due execution

[13.1]

[Updated in footnote 2 for *Re Morgan, Griffin v Wood* [2008] WTLR 73.
Updated in footnote 2 for *Singh v Ahluwalia* [2012] EWCA Civ 1635, [2013] WTLR 331 (CA).]

The presumption. If a will, on the face of it, appears to be duly executed, the presumption is in favour of due execution, applying the principle *omnia præsumuntur rite esse acta.*[1] The force of the presumption varies with the circumstances. If the will is entirely regular in form, it is very strong, but if the form is irregular and unusual the maxim does not apply with the same force.[2] If the witnesses are entirely ignorant of the details of the execution the presumption is the same.[3] If they profess to remember and state that the will was not duly executed, and this negative evidence is not rebutted by showing that the witnesses are not to be credited, or, taking their statement of the facts, that their memories are defective, the will must be pronounced against.[4] The court does not require direct affirmative evidence of due execution.[5]

1 *Re Musgrove's Estate, Davis v Mayhew* [1927] P 264, CA; *Byles v Cox* (1896) 74 LT 222; *Re Ferreira* [1927] VLR 90; *Re Denning, Harnett v Elliott* [1958] 2 All ER 1, [1958] 1 WLR 462; *Chester v Baston* (1980) 118 DLR (3d) 323. It is said in an Irish case that it is only where witnesses or persons present at the execution of the will are dead or cannot give evidence or their evidence is unreliable, that the doctrine can be called in: *Rolleston v Sinclair* [1924] 2 IR 157. When the deceased had lived alone leaving a will, wholly in the deceased's handwriting and witnessed apparently by two witnesses of whom nothing was known, the maxim was not applied to establish the will: *Re Robertson's Estate* [1964] NSWR 1087; *Re Sims, Sims v Faulkner* (1972) 116 Sol Jo 356.

2 *Re Bercovitz's Estate, Canning v Enever* [1962] 1 All ER 552, [1962] 1 WLR 321; *Re Lucas* [1966] VR 267; *Re Haverland* (1975) 55 DLR (3d) 122. This passage of the text was applied in *Re Young* [1969] NZLR 454 at 458. In *In the Estate of Sherrington Deceased, Sherrington v Sherrington* [2005] EWCA Civ 326, [2005] WTLR 587, the Court of Appeal held that where the testator's and witnesses' signatures appear in the right places and there is an attestation clause, very strong evidence indeed is needed before it is possible for the court to find that the will was not duly executed. Similarly *Briscoe v Green* [2006] All ER (D) 182 (Jul), where the presumption was applied and *Re Morgan, Griffin v Wood* [2008] WTLR 73 where summary judgment was granted on appeal on the strength of the presumption. But see *Re Papillon (decd), Murrin v Matthews* [2008] WTLR 269, [2006] All ER (D) 297 (Dec), where the will was pronounced against, and also *Singh v Ahluwalia* [2012] EWCA Civ 1635, [2013] WTLR 331 (CA).

3 *Re Moriaty's Will* [1956] VLR 400.

4 *Burgoyne v Showler* (1844) 1 Rob Eccl 5; *Keating v Brooks* (1845) 4 Notes of Cases 253; *Brenchley v Still* (1850) 2 Rob Eccl 162; *Re Amos* [1954] 2 DLR 574 (where the will was found in irregular order of pages). For cases where the evidence of the two attesting witnesses was not accepted, see *Bailey v Frowan* (1871) 19 WR 511; *Dayman v Dayman* (1894) 71 LT 699; *Re Collins* [1955] OWN 603.

5 *Gregory v Queen's Proctor* (1846) 4 Notes of Cases 620; *Blake v Knight* (1843) 3 Curt 547; *Leech v Bates* (1849) 1 Rob Eccl 714. It has been suggested that a solicitor who has taken instructions for a will should furnish a statement of evidence to any one interested in challenging or upholding the will; 56 Law Society's Gazette 619.

[13.2]

[Updated in footnote 3 for *Olins v Walters* [2007] EWHC 3060 (Ch) and *Re Morgan, Griffin v Wood* [2008] WTLR 73.
Updated in the text and in footnote 4 for *Re Rawlinson* [2010] EWHC 1269 (Ch), [2010] WTLR 1443.]

Attestation clause. Where there is a proper attestation clause, even though the witnesses have no recollection of having witnessed the will, the presumption applies.[1] In the absence of such a clause a will which on the face of it is duly executed is accepted, although no evidence is forthcoming.[2] Where there is such a clause, the court requires the strongest evidence before deciding that the will was not duly executed.[3] It has been said obiter that the presumption of due execution cannot apply when it is common ground that the attestation clause is wrong.[4]

1 *Lloyd v Roberts* (1858) 12 Moo PCC 158; *Wright v Sanderson* (1884) 9 PD 149; *Wright v Rogers* (1869) LR 1 P & D 678; *Woodhouse v Balfour* (1887) 13 PD 2 (witnesses having no recollection of having seen the paper before); *Vinnicombe v Butler* (1864) 3 Sw & Tr 580; *Harris v Knight* (1890) 15 PD 170, CA. Where the attestation does not say that the signature was made by the direction of the testator, the omission may be passed over in cases where everything is otherwise in order: *Re Cooper's Goods* (1847) 5 Notes of Cases 618.

2 *Re Peverett's Goods* [1902] P 205; *Clarke v Clarke* (1879) 5 LR Ir 47; *Re Malins' Goods* (1887) 19 LR Ir 231; *Vinnicombe v Butler* (1864) 3 Sw & Tr 580; *Re Rees' Goods* (1865) 34 LJPM & A 56; *Scarff v Scarff* [1927] 1 IR 13; *Re Griffiths* [1955] NZLR 127; *Re Laxer* (1963) 37 DLR (2d) 192; *Re Strong's Estate, Strong v Hadden* [1915] P 211. In *Re Denning, Harnett v Elliott* [1958] 2 All ER 1, [1958] 1 WLR 462, there were only two signatures on the back of a single sheet will.

3 See *Sherrington v Sherrington* [2005] EWCA Civ 326, [2005] WTLR 587; *Wright v Rogers* (1869) LR 1 P & D 678; *Whitting v Turner* (1903) 89 LT 71; *O'Meagher v O'Meagher* (1883) 11 LR Ir 117; *Goodisson v Goodisson* [1913] 1 IR 31, 218; *Dubourdieu v Patterson* (1919) 54 ILT 23. The decision in *Re Swinford's Goods* (1869) LR 1 P & D 630, seems out of line with the general run of the cases. Where it was suggested that the signature was a traced forgery the court accepted the positive evidence of the witnesses: *Re Kryskiw* [1954] OWN 717. In *Channon v Perkins (a firm)* [2006] WTLR 425, the Court of Appeal held, following *Sherrington v Sherrington,* that where a will had a regular attestation clause and appeared on its face to have been duly signed by the testator and the witnesses, the fact that the witnesses had, in one case, no recollection of signing the will and, in the other, no very precise recollection of signing the will was not, in the absence of any positive evidence of a specific failure to comply with the formalities, sufficient to rebut the presumption of due execution. See also *Briscoe v Green* [2006] All ER (D) 182 (Jul) in which it was held, following *Sherrington v Sherrington* and *Channon v Perkins*, that the strongest evidence would be required to show that a will had not been properly executed where it appeared on its face to have been properly executed and there was no question but that the will represented the testator's intentions. See also *Olins v Walters* [2007] EWHC 3060 (Ch) and *Re Morgan, Griffin v Wood* [2008] WTLR 73.

4 *Re Rawlinson* [2010] EWHC 1269 (Ch), [2010] WTLR 1443 at [137].

[13.3]

[Updated in footnote 6 and in the text for *Channon v Perkins (a firm)* [2006] WTLR 425 and *Olins v Walters* [2007] EWHC 3060 (Ch), [2007] All ER (D) 291 (Dec).]

Evidence rebutting presumption. This must be positive and reliable[1] and the court must not give undue weight to the circumstances on which the presumption is founded and on the other hand must not lose sight of them.[2] The burden of proving due execution, whether by presumption or by positive evidence rests on the propounder.[3] The direct evidence of both attesting witnesses unless discounted rebuts the presumption[4] and the evidence of one of the witnesses has been held to do so[5] but even an apparently positive recollection of contradicting the attestation clause must be treated with caution.[6]

1 *Glover v Smith* (1886) 57 LT 60; *Wyatt v Berry* [1893] P 5; *Pilkington v Gray* [1899] AC 401, DC; *Re Moore's Goods* [1901] P 44.

2 *Cooper v Bockett* (1846) 4 Moo PCC 419 at 439; *Re Bladen* [1952] VLR 82 (presumption applied in spite of conflicting evidence); *Re Gramp* [1952] SASR 12 (presumption rebutted).

3 *Brenchley v Still* (1850) 2 Rob Eccl 162; *Clery v Barry* (1887) 21 LR Ir 152; *Loftus v Harris* (1914) 19 DLR 670.

4 *Croft v Croft* (1865) 4 Sw & Tr 10; *Glover v Smith* (1886) 57 LT 60; *Pennant v Kingscote* (1843) 3 Curt 642; *Re Michnik Estate* [1945] 4 DLR 521. See *Dayman v Dayman* (1894) 71 LT 699; *Neal v Denston* (1932) 147 LT 460, for cases where the evidence was discounted. Since the reason for the provisions of the Wills Act 1837, s 9, was the prevention of fraud, evidence is admissible to show that the two attesting witnesses are wrong: *Re Vere-Wardale* [1949] P 395, [1949] 2 All ER 250.

5 *Cregeen v Willoughby* (1860) 24 JP 408; *Noding v Alliston* (1850) 14 Jur 904. To the contrary: *Keating v Brooks* (1845) 4 Notes of Cases 253 (where the presumption prevailed although one witness said her signature was forged); *Re Thomas' Goods* (1859) 1 Sw & Tr 255 (incomplete recollection); *Wright v Rogers* (1869) LR 1 P & D 678 (perfect attestation clause rebutted only by strongest evidence). See also *Reeves v Grainger* (1908) 52 Sol Jo 355 (execution by illiterate testator: evidence of clerk writing testator's name as guide where signature should be, in ignorance of the fact that testator was too illiterate to sign); *Pattie v Fry* (1911) 30 NZLR 581; *Re Irwin* [1920] NZLR 440. The will was held good where one witness would not deny proper execution: *Re Johnson* [1953] 4 DLR 777.

6 See *Channon v Perkins (a firm)* [2006] WTLR 425 at [8]: 'Oral testimony as to the way in which a document was executed many years ago is not likely to be inherently particularly reliable on, one suspects, most occasions. As anyone who has been involved in contested factual disputes will know, people can, entirely honestly and doing their very best, completely misremember or wholly forget facts and events that took place not very long ago, and the longer ago something may have taken place, the less accurate their recollection is likely to be.' In *Olins v Walters* [2007] EWHC 3060 (Ch), [2007] All ER (D) 291 (Dec) Norris J found (at [32]–[40]) that a witness's express recollection contradicting the attestation clause was nonetheless unreliable.

CHAPTER 16

Wills of soldiers, sailors and airmen

[16.3]

[Updated in the text and in footnotes 11 and 13 for *Re Servoz-Gavin; Ayling v Summer* [2009] EWHC 3168 (Ch), [2010] 1 All ER 410.]

Mariner or seaman. The privilege to make an informal will extends to 'any mariner or seaman being at sea'.[1] In these circumstances there is no requirement of actual military service and the privilege is of wide scope. In a fairly recent case[2] it has been said that the privilege can be invoked if the following conditions are satisfied. First, it has to be shown that the testator was serving, or employed, in, or by, the Royal Navy[3] or the Merchant Navy,[4] on service of whatever nature, that could be regarded as sea-service.[5] It matters not whether the person be a man or a woman.[6] Secondly, the testator must be 'on maritime service' in the sense that the testator either, (a) is already (that is at the time of signing the document in question or making the nuncupative will) in post as a ship's officer[7] or (b) is already a member of a particular ship's company serving in that ship[8] or on shore leave,[9] or on long leave ashore[10] or (c) being employed by owners of a fleet of ships and having been discharged from one such, is already under orders to join another ship in that fleet.[11] But the privilege will not apply to the will of a seaman made whilst on shore on leave, at a time when he is not a member of the compliment of a particular ship and when he has not yet received orders to join a ship.[12] In a more recent case, it has been decided that the privilege extends to merchant seaman serving with foreign vessels and not just British-registered ships.[13]

1 WA 1837, s 11.

2 Per Judge Finlay QC in *Re Rapley's Estate, Rapley v Rapley* [1983] 3 All ER 248, [1983] 1 WLR 1069; but see Havers J in *Re Newland's Estate* [1952] P 71 at 75, [1952] 1 All ER 841 at 843 who doubted whether any principle of universal application could be extracted from the cases.

3 *Re M'Murdo's Goods* (1868) LR 1 P & D 540 (mate in HMS Excellent); *Re Lay's Goods* (1840) 2 Curt 375 (mate in HMS Calliope).

4 *Re Newland's Estate* [1952] P 71 at 75, [1952] 1 All ER 841 (apprentice); *Re Wilson's Estate, Wilson v Coleclough* [1952] P 92, [1952] 1 All ER 852 (chief officer); *Re Hayes's Goods* (1839) 2 Curt 338 (purser).

5 Per Judge Finlay QC in *Re Rapley's Estate, Rapley v Rapley* [1983] 3 All ER 248 at 251, [1983] 1 WLR 1069 at 1071; see for example, *Re Hale's Goods* [1915] 2 IR 362 (female typist on Lusitania); *Re Saunders's Goods* (1865) LR 1 P & D 16 (naval surgeon); *Re Stanley's Goods* [1916] P 192 (female nurse) but not the will of an admiral living ashore, *Euston v Seymour* (1802) cited in 2 Curt 339, 340, nor of a canal pilot, *Re Barnes' Goods, Hodson v Barnes* (1926) 96 LJP 26, nor of the captain of a cross-Channel ferry, *Barnard v Birch* [1919] 2 IR 404.

6 *Re Rapley's Estate, Rapley v Rapley* [1983] 3 All ER 248, [1983] 1 WLR 1069.
7 *Re M'Murdo's Goods* (1868) LR 1 P & D 540; *Re Lay's Goods* (1840) 2 Curt 375.
8 *Re Patterson's Goods* (1898) 79 LT 123.
9 *Re Lay's Goods* (1840) 2 Curt 375.
10 *Re Newland's Estate* [1952] P 71 at 75, [1952] 1 All ER 841.
11 *Re Hale's Goods* [1915] 2 IR 362; *Re Wilson's Estate, Wilson v Coleclough* [1952] P 92, [1952] 1 All ER 852. It seems that it is sufficient for a testator to be under orders to join a particular ship, and not necessarily already be in the employ of the owners: *Re Servoz-Gavin; Ayling v Summer* [2009] EWHC 3168 (Ch), [2010] 1 All ER 410.
12 *Re Rapley's Estate, Rapley v Rapley* [1983] 3 All ER 248, [1983] 1 WLR 1069; distinguishing, *Re Hale's Goods* [1915] 2 IR 362; *Re Newland's Estate* [1952] P 71 at 75, [1952] 1 All ER 841 and *Re Wilson's Estate, Wilson v Coleclough* [1952] P 92, [1952] 1 All ER 852 where the deceased was under orders to join another ship. The mere contemplation of another voyage will not suffice.
13 *Re Servoz-Gavin; Ayling v Summer* [2009] EWHC 3168 (Ch), [2010] 1 All ER 410.

PART E

Revocation, republication and revival of wills

CHAPTER 17

Revocation by marriage or civil partnership

III. WILLS MADE ON OR AFTER 1 JANUARY 1983

[17.6]

[Updated in footnote 6 for *Court v Despallieres* [2009] EWHC 3340 (Ch), [2010] WTLR 437.]

Wills in expectation of marriage or civil partnership. In the case of wills made on or after 1 January 1983[1] the AJA 1982 repeals the Law of Property Act 1925, s 177[2] and substitutes a new provision governing wills made before marriage, or now, before the formation of a civil partnership.[3] The legislation covers two situations. First, WA 1837, s 18(3)[4] provides:

> 'where it appears from a will that at the time it was made the testator was expecting to be married to a particular person and that he intended that the will should not be revoked by the marriage, the will shall not be revoked by his marriage to that person.'

This provision refers to an intention with respect to the will and provides that the whole will is not to be revoked. The second situation relates to the more difficult case (and the more commonly met situation with home-made wills) where the intention relates only to a disposition or to a part of the will. Such a case is provided for by WA 1837, s 18(4)[5] as follows:

> 'where it appears from a will that at the time it was made the testator was expecting to be married to a particular person and that he intended that a disposition in the will should not be revoked by his marriage to that person—
>
> (a) that disposition shall take effect notwithstanding the marriage; and
>
> (b) any other disposition in the will shall take effect also unless it appears from the will that the testator intended the disposition to be revoked by the marriage.'

It will be noticed that both subsections embody the dual tests of the expectation of marriage to a particular person, and the intention that the will, or the disposition, should not be revoked by the marriage to that person.[6] Three points can be made; first, both the expectation and the intention are subjective to the testator; it is what he thought which is crucial not an objective view of the circumstances. Second, it is submitted that this subjective expectation and intention must appear from the will, ie the evidence in support of each must be intrinsic not extrinsic. Third, that both the expectation and the intention must be present at the time the will is made.[7]

The effect of the latter provision is that an expectation and intention in any clause of the will, will not only save that disposition but will also tend to preserve the whole will.[8] The effect of subsection (4)(b) set out above is to reverse the burden of proof; previously it was necessary to find positive evidence supporting the non-revocation of the will; now the will will only be revoked if there is positive evidence in favour of revocation. Since in most cases there will be no indication either way in the clauses of the will other than the gift to eg the fiancé, the effect will be to preserve the whole will. Thus an express indication of expectation of marriage in one part of the will tends to colour the whole; a change surely to be welcomed as not only tending to preserve rather than revoke wills, but also as being most likely to be consistent with most testators' intentions.

WA 1837, s 18B[9] provides, in what are for practical purposes identical terms to s 18, for revocation of a will if the testator forms a civil partnership, subject to the same exceptions for wills made in expectation of forming a civil partnership. The Marriage (Same Sex Couples) Act 2013[10] (M(SSC)A 2013), s 9 provides for conversion of civil partnerships into marriage. It is to be hoped that the power to make consequential amendments to UK legislation in M(SSC)A 2013, s 17 will be exercised to ensure that conversion of a civil partnership into marriage does not revoke a will which was made in expectation of forming the preceding civil partnership.

1 AJA 1982, s 73(7); s 76(11).
2 AJA 1982, s 75(1) and Sch 9, Pt 1.
3 As to civil partnerships, see para **[17.3]** above.
4 As substituted by the AJA 1982, s 18(1); see Vol 2, Part G, para **[244.16]**.
5 The provisions are based on the recommendations of the Law Reform Committee, 22nd Report on The Making and Revocation of Wills, 1980 (Cmnd 7902). See paras 3.13–3.18.
6 The proof of these matters will therefore be found in the inclusion of express statements of expectation and intention and in professionally drawn wills such as an introductory clause should be included in appropriate cases; see Volume 2. A general statement in a will that it was intended to survive marriage, civil partnership or adoption, made two months before the testator formed a civil partnership did not satisfy the tests because it did not show that the testator expected to form a civil partnership, let alone with a particular person, see *Court v Despallieres* [2009] EWHC 3340 (Ch), [2010] WTLR 437.
7 Strictly WA 1837, s 18(3) and (4), as substituted by the AJA 1982, s 18(3) and (4).
8 Thus if the facts of *Re Coleman, Coleman v Coleman* [1976] Ch 1, [1975] 1 All ER 675, were to recur in a post-1982 will, the whole will would be likely to be held to survive the marriage. This is because the word 'fiancé' would probably suffice to indicate the required expectation and intention; see the cases in para **[17.4]**, n 7.
9 Inserted by CPA 2004, s 71, Sch 4, paras 1 and 2, with effect from 5 December 2005.
10 Not in force at time of writing. See Vol 2, Part G, paras **[245.149]** ff.

CHAPTER 18

Voluntary revocation

IV. LATER WILL OR CODICIL

[18.10]

[Updated in footnote 4 for *Curati v Perdoni* [2012] EWCA Civ 1381 [2013] WTLR 63, (CA).]

Subsequent inconsistent will. A later unambiguous will dealing with all the testator's property revokes all earlier wills whether or not it contains a clause of revocation.[1] A later will covering practically the same ground as an earlier one must be taken as in substitution for it, and probate of the later one only is granted.[2] This may be so where the whole ground is not completely covered, if the language shows an intention on the part of the testator to dispose of his property in a manner different from that in the earlier will.[3] The mere fact of making a subsequent disposition does not, however, work a total revocation of an earlier disposition, unless the later one expressly or in effect revokes the former, or the two are incapable of standing together.[4] A later inconsistent disposition not valid in itself does not revoke an earlier disposition;[5] but a codicil altering and confirming a first will may thereby revive that will and revoke a will made after the first will but before the last codicil.[6] The fact that a document has been admitted to probate even after consideration of the construction of that and other testamentary instruments does not prevent a court of construction from coming to the conclusion that the document has no operative effect.[7]

1 *Re Palmer's Goods, Palmer v Peat* (1889) 58 LJP 44; *Cadell v Wilcocks* [1898] P 21; *Re Bryan's Estate* [1907] P 125 (residue left undisposed of); *Re Fitzsimmons* [1939] 2 DLR 50.

2 *Henfrey v Henfrey* (1842) 4 Moo PCC 29; *Dempsey v Lawson* (1877) 2 PD 98; *Re Turnour's Goods* (1886) 56 LT 671; *Re Palmer's Goods, Palmer v Peat* (1889) 58 LJP 44; *O'Leary v Douglass* (1878) 3 LR Ir 323; *M'Ara v M'Cay* (1889) 23 LR Ir 138; *Cadell v Wilcocks,* above; *Chichester v Quatrefages* [1895] P 186 (two codicils, one a virtual repetition of the other).

3 *Dempsey v Lawson* (1877) 2 PD 98; *Re Bryan's Estate* [1907] P 125.

4 *Lemage v Goodban* (1865) LR 1 P & D 57; *Re Petchell's Goods* (1874) LR 3 P & D 153; *Re Summers' Goods* (1901) 84 LT 271 (one treated as codicil of the other); *Townsend v Moore* [1905] P 66; *Simpson v Foxon* [1907] P 54; *Reeves v Reeves* [1909] 2 IR 521; *Re Bund, Cruikshank v Willis* [1929] 2 Ch 455; *Busteed v Eager* (1834) Milw 345; *Clarke v Clarke* 1925 SC 431 (English and Scottish wills); *Re Allen Estate* [1935] 1 WWR 584 (one will dealing with Canadian property, later will excepting such property, but revocation upheld); *Re Owens Estate* (1956) 2 DLR (2d) 144 (second will bequeathing only certain personal chattels and with revocation clause struck out but not initialled); *Re Mitchell Estate, Bradshaw v Pidgeon* (1954) 33 MPR 359 (two holograph wills with no revocation clause); *Curati v Perdoni* [2012] EWCA Civ 1381, [2013] WTLR 63, (CA). The same rule applies to a codicil: *Pilsworth v Mosse* (1862) 14 I Ch R 163; *O'Leary v Douglass* (1878) 3 LR Ir 323; *Re Wray* [1951] Ch 425, [1951] 1 All ER 375; *Re Spensley's Will Trusts* [1952] Ch 886, [1952]

2 All ER 49, and a codicil may be revoked by a similar disposition in a later codicil: *Re Buckley* [1952] VLR 107, where the second codicil repeated the disposition but made it conditional on the general residuary beneficiary under the will predeceasing the testator and if both should perish in the same disaster.

5 *Re Fleetwood, Sidgreaves v Brewer* (1880) 15 Ch D 594; *Duguid v Fraser* (1886) 31 Ch D 449; *Morley v Rennoldson* [1895] 1 Ch 449; *Vencatanarayana Pillay v Subammal* (1915) 32 TLR 118; *Ward v Van der Loeff* [1924] AC 653; *Alexander v Kirkpatrick* (1874) LR 2 Sc & Div 397; *Re Gardner* [1935] 1 DLR 308; *Baker v Story* (1874) 31 LT 631, was not followed in *Ward v Van der Loeff* [1924] AC 653, and in *Re Robinson, Lamb v Robinson* [1930] 2 Ch 332 (where it is said that the rule that a second will will revoke an earlier one though it is ineffective to confer any gift, if such failure is due to the incapacity of the devisee or legatee and not to any infirmity in the will itself, is no longer acceptable).

6 *Re Baker, Baker v Baker* [1929] 1 Ch 668; followed in *Re Pearson, Rowling v Crowther* [1963] 3 All ER 763, [1963] 1 WLR 1358; *Re Alford's Estate* (1939) 83 Sol Jo 566; but in *Goldie v Adam* [1938] P 85, [1938] 1 All ER 586, it was held that where there are no words of revival an earlier will was not revived, see Chapter 21, below.

7 *Re Hawksley's Settlement, Black v Tidy* [1934] Ch 384 at 396; approved in *Re Resch's Will Trusts, Le Cras v Perpetual Trustee Co Ltd* [1969] 1 AC 514, [1967] 3 All ER 915.

[18.12]

[Updated in footnote 2 for *Re Ciebrant* [2008] EWHC 1268 (Ch), [2009] WTLR 69.]

Lost will. Where a testamentary document has been lost or destroyed in such a way as not to effect a revocation[1] probate may be granted of the contents thereof upon proof of such contents and due execution and attestation of the instrument.[2] Where the person setting up an alleged will cannot produce any copy or draft of any written evidence of its contents, he must prove all these matters so as to remove all reasonable (but not all possible) doubt on these points.[3] The evidence of a solicitor that he had made the will and that it was not informal establishes due execution and attestation.[4] The contents may be proved from the instructions given to the solicitor[5] or by the evidence of a witness, although he is an interested party, but his evidence must be unimpeached.[6] An alleged draft will be considered side by side with the oral evidence.[7] There has been doubt about the admission of declarations made by the testator after the making of the will,[8] but almost certainly for the reason that evidence of such declarations would be hearsay[9] if that is the reason, such evidence will now be admissible under Civil Evidence Act 1968, s 1, or the replacement of it now going through Parliament. The fullest enquiries must be made in any such case.[10]

1 As to the position where the loss effects a revocation, see para **[18.28]** below.

2 *Brown v Brown* (1858) 8 E & B 876; *Sugden v Lord St Leonards* (1876) 1 PD 154, 238, CA; *Allan v Morrison* [1900] AC 604, PC; *Re Crandon's Goods* (1901) 84 LT 330; *Re Spain* (1915) 31 TLR 435 (where the testator, attesting witnesses and the will were lost in an explosion); *Re Phibbs' Estate* [1917] P 93; *Re Queen Marie of Roumania* (1950) 94 Sol Jo 673; *Re Davies, Panton v Jones* [1978] CLY 3095; *Re Ciebrant* [2008] EWHC 1268 (Ch), [2009] WTLR 69.

3 *Harris v Knight* (1890) 15 PD 170 at 179; *Re Wipperman's Estate* [1953] 1 All ER 764 at 766; *Re MacGillivray's Estate* [1946] 2 All ER 301. As to the contents of the affidavit to lead to probate of a lost will, see *Tristram and Coote's Probate Practice* (30th edn) LexisNexis Butterworths. For a case where the evidence was insufficient, see *Re Plunkett* [1965] VR 118.

4 *Re Hannah* [1954] NZLR 836.

5 *Fincham v Edwards* (1842) 3 Curt 63; on appeal 4 Moo PCC 198.

6 *Sugden v Lord St Leonards* (1876) 1 PD 154, 238, CA; applied in *Nicholls v Hudson* [2006] EWHC 3006 (Ch). See also *Jersey Society for the Prevention of Cruelty to Animals v Rees (2001–02)* 4 ITELR 294, where, notwithstanding the presumption that a will lost in the possession of the testator had been destroyed by him with an intention to revoke, there was

held to be sufficient evidence on the facts of the case to rebut the presumption. For recent cases in which the presumption was held to have been rebutted, see *Rowe v Clarke* [2006] EWHC 1292 (Ch), [2006] WTLR 347 and *Nicholls v Hudson* [2006] EWHC 3006 (Ch). See also *Re Yelland, Broadbent v Francis* (1975) 119 Sol Jo 562 (will proved by daughter's recollection of contents).

7 *Burls v Burls* (1868) LR 1 P & D 472 at 474; *Re Webb Smith v Johnston* [1964] 2 All ER 91, [1964] 1 WLR 509 (a draft will was admitted because the inclusion of a proper attestation clause led to the presumption that the will had been duly executed).

8 *Atkinson v Morris* [1897] P 40; but they were admitted in *Sugden v Lord St Leonards* (1876) 1 PD 154, 238, CA.

9 This seems clear from *Atkinson v Morris* [1897] P 40, but *Barkwell v Barkwell* [1928] P 91 at 97 seems to suggest that the rule is based on the requirement of Wills Act 1837, s 9 that a will must be in writing.

10 See *Re Ferguson-Smith Estate* (1954) 13 WWR NS 387; on appeal (1955) 15 WWR 237, Sask CA.

[18.14]

[Updated in footnote 4 for *Curati v Perdoni* [2012] EWCA Civ 1381, [2013] WTLR 63 (CA).]

Partly inconsistent wills. Where there are several testamentary instruments which are not wholly inconsistent, they are read together to constitute the last will of the testator[1] for any number of documents whatever their date or form can be so admitted to probate.[2] The prior disposition is not to be disturbed further than is absolutely necessary to give effect to the later one.[3] The presumption against implied revocation is greater where the testator has used words showing an intention only to alter the dispositions in certain specific respects.[4] The general rule is that a revocation by subsequent will or codicil shall operate only so far as is necessary to effectuate the intention of the testator.[5] Therefore, an apparent inconsistency in the testamentary instruments may be rebutted by oral evidence that the testator did not intend revocation[6] or by extrinsic evidence of the surrounding circumstances.[7] It is incumbent upon those who contend that a gift in one testamentary instrument is not to take effect by reason of some subsequent instrument, to show that the intention to revoke is as clear and free from doubt as the original intention to give.[8] Extrinsic evidence, including evidence of the testator's intention, is admissible if the relevant wording is ambiguous on its face, or extrinsic evidence, other than evidence of intention, shows the wording to be ambiguous in the light of surrounding circumstances.[9]

1 *Re Budd's Goods* (1862) 3 Sw & Tr 196; *Birks v Birks* (1865) 4 Sw & Tr 23; *Lemage v Goodban* (1865) LR 1 P & D 57; *Re Fenwick's Goods* (1867) LR 1 P & D 319; *Re Griffith's Goods* (1872) LR 2 P & D 457; *Re Petchell's Goods* (1874) LR 3 P & D 153; *Re Hartley's Goods* (1880) 50 LJP 1; *Re Hodgkinson's Goods* [1893] P 339; *Reeves v Reeves* [1909] 2 IR 521.

2 *Lemage v Goodban* (1865) LR 1 P & D 57; *Townsend v Moore* [1905] P 66.

3 *Farrer v St Catharine's College, Cambridge* (1873) LR 16 Eq 19; *Young v Hassard* (1841) 1 Dr & War 638; *Wallace v Seymour* (1872) 20 WR 634.

4 *Follett v Pettman* (1883) 23 Ch D 337; *Curati v Perdoni* [2012] EWCA Civ 1381, [2013] WTLR 63 (CA).

5 *Doe d Evers v Ward* (1852) 18 QB 197. The question is what disposition the testator intended, not what papers did he desire to be admitted to probate: *Dempsey v Lawson* (1877) 2 PD 98 at 107.

6 *Busteed v Eager* (1834) Milw 345; *Fawcett v Jones, Coldrington and Pulteney* (1810) 3 Phillim 434 at 478.

7 *Jenner v Ffinch* (1879) 5 PD 106; *Paton v Ormerod* [1892] P 247; *Re Brian's Estate* [1974] 2 NSWLR 231; *Re Bryan's Estate* [1907] P 125.

8 *Follett v Pettman* (1883) 23 Ch D 337; *Doe d Hearle v Hicks* (1832) 8 Bing 475; approved in *Re Resch's Will Trusts, Le Cras v Perpetual Trustee Co Ltd* [1967] 3 All ER 915 at 925.
9 See the AJA 1982, s 21: Vol 2, Part G, para **[244.99]**. See also *Thorne v Rooke* (1841) 2 Curt 799. See full discussion on admission of extrinsic evidence, Chapter 57.

V. BY DESTRUCTION

[18.29]

[Updated in footnote 1 for *Cheung So Lan v Yim Yin Ming* [2009] HKCU 117, [2010] WTLR 971.
Updated in footnote 2 for *Nicholls v Hudson* [2006] EWHC 3006 (Ch), [2007] WTLR 341, [2006] All ER (D) 60 (Oct); and in footnote 3 for *Wren v Wren* [2006] EWHC 2243 (Ch), [2007] WTLR 531, [2006] All ER (D) 30 (Sep).
Updated in footnote 7 and in the text for *Nicholls v Hudson* [2006] EWHC 3006 (Ch), [2007] WTLR 341, [2006] All ER (D) 60 (Oct).
Also updated in footnote 8 and in the text for *Re Zielinski, Korab-Karpinski v Lucas-Gardiner* [2007] WTLR 1655.]

Rebuttal of presumption. The presumption may, however, be rebutted by evidence, but the evidence must be clear and satisfactory.[1] Recent declarations by a testator of satisfaction at having settled his affairs,[2] or of goodwill towards the persons benefited by the will, or of adherence to the will and to the contents of the will itself,[3] may be used for this purpose. A declaration by the testator of adherence to a will may be answered by his declarations to a contrary effect.[4] The presumption may, it seems, also be rebutted by a consideration of the contents of the will itself,[5] or by showing that the testator had no opportunity of destroying the will, or that it had been lost or destroyed without his privity or consent.[6] Other factors which might go towards rebutting the presumption would be the testator's lack of efficiency and methodology which may explain the loss of the will,[7] or the testator's inclination to instruct solicitors to carry out acts of legal significance making it unlikely a revocation would have been made without such intervention.[8]

1 *Eckersley v Platt* (1866) LR 1 P & D 281; *Battyll v Lyles and Phillips* (1858) 4 Jur NS 718; *Eaton (Norris Estate) v Heyman* [1946] 4 DLR 441; *Cheung So Lan v Yim Yin Ming* [2009] HKCU 117, [2010] WTLR 971.
2 *Whiteley v King* (1864) 17 CBNS 756; *Nicholls v Hudson* [2006] EWHC 3006 (Ch), [2007] WTLR 341, [2006] All ER (D) 60 (Oct).
3 *Keen v Keen* (1873) LR 3 P & D 105; *Patten v Poulton* (1858) 1 Sw & Tr 55; *Re Mackenzie's Estate* [1909] P 305. See also *Sugden v Lord St Leonards* (1876) 1 PD 154; *Unwin v Unwin* (1914) 20 BCR 77; *Public Trustee v Kells* (1904) 23 NZLR 605; *Re Matt Estate* (1954) 11 WWRNS 28; *Re Boyd's Will, ex p Whelan* [1959] SRNSW 369 (where the testator was asked shortly before his decease as to the whereabouts of the will and said it was in a bag beside his bed and there appeared to be no one who could benefit other than the named beneficiary); *Brown v Woolley* (1959) 27 WWR 425; *Re Keluga Estate* (1956) 64 Man R 138; *Wren v Wren* [2006] EWHC 2243 (Ch), [2007] WTLR 531, [2006] All ER (D) 30 (Sep).
4 *Keen v Keen* (1873) LR 3 P & D 105; *Re Sykes, Drake v Sykes* (1907) 23 TLR 747. But it seems that oral declarations of destruction are not admissible: *Atkinson v Morris* [1897] P 40.
5 *Sugden v Lord St Leonards* (1876) 1 PD 154, where the contents of a codicil and the testator's papers were also given weight. In *Re Witham* [1938] 3 DLR 142, the cutting out was so carefully done and an intelligible will left properly executed that the resulting will was admitted.
6 *Finch v Finch* (1867) LR 1 P & D 371.
7 *Nicholls v Hudson* [2006] EWHC 3006 (Ch), [2007] WTLR 341, [2006] All ER (D) 60 (Oct).
8 *Re Zielinski, Korab-Karpinski v Lucas-Gardiner* [2007] WTLR 1655.

PART F

Wills with foreign element

CHAPTER 23

Form of wills where foreign property or domicile is involved

[23.1]

[Reference to EU Regulation No 650/2012 added.]

General statement. Where a will is made in England by a testator domiciled in England at the date of his death, all matters, other than disposition of immovables (ie generally speaking land) situated outside England, will be governed by English law. In other cases questions of locality and domicile may arise and these questions are of importance because England law persists in applying different rules of succession to movables, which are governed by the law of domicile (*lex domicilii*) and to immovables, which are governed by the law of the country in which they are situate (*lex situs*). The meaning of these terms is thus crucial to an understanding of the rules of private international law governing succession. It is beyond the scope of this work to consider these concepts in detail[1] but some brief reference can be made. For the possibility that the English law of succession might be applied to immovable property in EU states subject to EU Regulation No 650/2012 in relation to deaths on or after 17 August 2015, see para **[24.2]**.

1 For full accounts see the specialist works, Cheshire and North, *Private International Law* (13th edn); and Dicey, Morris and Collins, *The Conflict of Laws* (14th edn).

VI. PREPARATION OF THE WILL

[23.18]

[Reference to EU Regulation No 650/2012 added.]

Foreign testator. If the intending testator has a foreign domicile then, in accordance with the rules above, any will of movable property should be made according to the law of the person's domicile. In most cases English practitioners will not feel competent to undertake this task and the client will be referred to a lawyer in the country of his domicile or a foreign lawyer will be appointed as agent for this purpose. If the intending testator has an English domicile but immovable property situated in a foreign jurisdiction then the English will should clearly be confined to movable property and immovable property situated in England and Wales.[1] This is subject to the point that if the immovable property is in an EU state which is subject to EU Regulation No 650/2012, the testator can elect to have English succession law apply to it, provided that he is a British citizen and survives at least until 17 August 2015: see para **[24.2]**. Otherwise a separate will or wills should be prepared by a foreign lawyer restricted to the immovable property situated within that jurisdiction. If there is evidence that such an intending testator previously made a will or wills then care must be exercised to ensure that the previous will or wills, are correctly revoked according to the rules set out above. Advice will need to be sought where foreign elements are involved, as to the effect on the will of the rules of essential validity and construction which might be applicable to the will.

1 *Re Osoba, Osoba v Osoba* [1978] 1 WLR 791 at 796.

CHAPTER 24

Wills with a foreign element: essential validity and construction and exercise of powers of appointment

[24.2]

[EU Regulation No 650/2012 noted.]

Rules applicable. The essential validity of a will of movables, or of a gift of movables is governed by the law of the testator's domicile at the time of his death.[1] The essential validity of a will of immovables or of a gift of immovables, is governed by the law of the country where the immovables are situated, the *lex situs*.[2] It is the domicile at the time of death, not at the time of the will, which is applicable, so that a change of domicile after the will is made can affect the essential validity of the dispositions contained in the will.[3]

For deaths on or after 17 August 2015, EU Regulation No 650/2012[4] will apply in all EU states except the UK, Republic of Ireland and Denmark. Although it will not apply to the UK, it will be able to affect succession to the property of UK citizens who have property in EU states to which the Regulation applies. The Regulation contains conflict of laws rules which will determine the applicable law of succession. The basic principle is that the applicable law will be that of the territory of the deceased's habitual residence at death, but subject to a right to choose the law of some other territory of which the testator is a citizen at the time of making the will[5]. Where such a choice is made, there will be no renvoi[6]. Accordingly, where a British citizen owns immovable property in an EU state subject to the Regulation, it will be possible for him to elect for English law to apply to the succession to his estate, with the consequence that English domestic succession law is applied by the courts of the territory in which the immovable property is located. The English courts are likely to do the same[7]. A UK citizen owning such immovable property, hoping to die after 16 August 2015, and not wanting the compulsory inheritance laws of the state in which the immovable property is located to apply, should therefore make a will choosing English law in a manner effective under Article 22 of the Regulation[8].

1 See Dicey and Morris, *The Conflict of Laws* (12th edn), p 1034 citing *Whicker v Hume* (1858) 7 HL Cas 124; *Thornton v Curling* (1824) 8 Sim 310; *Campbell v Beaufoy* (1859) John 320; *Macdonald v Macdonald* (1872) LR 14 Eq 60; *Re Groos, Groos v Groos* [1915] 1 Ch 572; *Re Annesley, Davidson v Annesley* [1926] Ch 692; *Re Ross, Ross v Waterfield* [1930] 1 Ch 377; *Re Priest, Belfield v Duncan* [1944] Ch 58; *Philipson-Stow v IRC* [1961] AC 727,

[1960] 3 All ER 814; *Re Levick's Will Trusts, Ffennell v IRC* [1963] 1 All ER 95, [1963] 1 WLR 311; *Haque v Haque* (1962) 108 CLR 230; and *Re Adams, Bank of Ireland Trustee Co Ltd v Adams, Hutchings and Parker* [1967] IR 424. See also *Re Berger* [1990] Ch 118, [1989] 1 All ER 591.

2 See Dicey and Morris, *The Conflict of Laws* (12th edn), p 1037 citing *Earl Nelson v Lord Bridport* (1846) 8 Beav 547; *Freke v Lord Carbery* (1873) LR 16 Eq 461; *Duncan v Lawson* (1889) 41 Ch D 394; *Re Moses, Moses v Valentine* [1908] 2 Ch 235; *Re Hoyles, Row v Jagg* [1911] 1 Ch 179; *Re Miller, Bailie v Miller* [1914] 1 Ch 511; *Re Ross, Ross v Waterfield* [1930] 1 Ch 377 and *Haque v Haque* (1962) 108 CLR 230.

3 *Re Groos, Groos v Groos* [1915] 1 Ch 572.

4 Selected extracts are set out at para **[248.1]** ff.

5 See Articles 20, 21, and 22, set out at paras **[248.7]–[248.9]**.

6 See Article 34 set out at paras **[248.18]–[248.9]**.

7 *Re Ross, Ross v Waterfield* [1930] 1 Ch 377.

8 See **[201.5A]**, and Form B1.7A at para **[201.12A]** for a choice of law clause.

II. CONSTRUCTION

[24.6]

[Updated for new reference to *Dellar v Zivy* [2007] EWHC 2266, [2008] WTLR 17, [2007] All ER (D) 121 (Oct).]

Law governing construction. As a general rule, wills of movables must be construed with reference to the law of the place which was the domicile of the testator at his death.[1] Where, however, there appears on the face of the will an intention that it should be construed by reference to some other law, that law will govern the construction.[2] For example, where technical expressions peculiar to a foreign law are used, that law and not the law of the domicile may determine the construction,[3] but the presence of a few such technical expressions may not by itself be a sufficient indication of the testator's intention to induce the court to construe the will with reference to the law to which such expressions belong,[4] and where it is shown that no technical rules of construction are applied to words by the law of the domicile, no reference to that law is necessary, and the will must be construed according to English rules of construction.[5] The construction of a will is not altered by reason of any change in the testator's domicile after the execution of the will.[6]

1 *Nisbett v Murray* (1799) 5 Ves 149; *Bradford v Young* (1884) 26 Ch D 656; on appeal (1885) 29 Ch D 617, CA; *Re Price, Tomlin v Latter* [1900] 1 Ch 442; *Re Lewal's Settlement Trusts, Gould v Lewal* [1918] 2 Ch 391; *Re Levick's Will Trusts, Ffennell v IRC* [1963] 1 All ER 95, [1963] 1 WLR 311; *Re Lord Cable, Garratt v Waters* [1976] 3 All ER 417, [1977] 1 WLR 7 and *Curati v Perdoni* [2012] EWCA Civ 1381, [2013] WTLR 63 (CA). Where a testator domiciled in Quebec made a will in English form it was to be construed according to the law of Quebec and the English rule that the later of two incompatible clauses is to prevail could not be applied: *Bayer v Montreal Trust Co* [1953] Que SC 89. In a gift of personalty to a person or his heirs, the persons taking under the words 'heirs' must be determined by the law of the domicle of the testator: *Re Collishaw* [1953] 3 DLR 829; *Re Cunnington, Healing v Webb* [1924] 1 Ch 68. But see *Dellar v Zivy* [2007] EWHC 2266, [2008] WTLR 17, [2007] All ER (D) 121, in which it was held that the will in English form of a Frenchman who had moved to England, but who the judge was not prepared to assume on a summary application had acquired a domicile of choice in England, was to be construed in accordance with English law.

2 *Re Price, Tomlin v Latter* [1900] 1 Ch 442.

3 *Studd v Cook* (1883) 8 App Cas 577; *Re Cliff's Trusts* [1892] 2 Ch 229; *Re Cunnington, Healing v Webb* [1924] 1 Ch 68 (where the rule was not applied); *Re Allen's Estate, Prescott v Allen and Beaumont* [1945] 2 All ER 264 (reference to English law).

4 *Bradford v Young* (1884) 26 Ch D 656.
5 *Bernal v Bernal* (1838) 3 My & Cr 559. As to translations of foreign will, see para **[57.7]** below.
6 Wills Act 1963, s 4; see Vol 2, Part G, para **[244.80]**.

PART G

Executors, trustees and guardians

CHAPTER 25

Executors

[25.1]

[Updated in footnote 8 for *Khan v Crossland* [2012] WTLR 842.]

Appointment of executor.[1] An executor is the person appointed by the will to administer the property of the testator and to carry into effect the provisions of the will.[2] The ordinary method of appointing an executor is for the testator to name in his will a specific person to be his executor. The clause or provision appointing the executor or executors must be in the body of the will and a direction beneath the testator's signature has been held to be ineffective.[3] If any question arises as to the identity of a person so named, the court can have regard to extrinsic evidence to resolve such a question.[4] This could include evidence of intention to resolve but not to create the ambiguity if latent.[5] Where the description can be regarded as a patent ambiguity, as being applicable in all its parts to two or more persons, then extrinsic evidence, including evidence of intention can be adduced.[6] Where there is a person exactly answering the name and description, the court will not admit evidence to show that some other person was intended.[7] The court has power where, by reason of the insolvency of the estate of the deceased or of any other special circumstances, it appears necessary or expedient, to pass over the executor named in the will and grant letters of administration with the will annexed to such person as the court thinks expedient.[8] Thus the court, acting under this provision, has passed over the testator's widow, who had been convicted of his manslaughter and sentenced to life imprisonment, and made a grant to his daughters.[9] There may be such uncertainty as to the person intended that the appointment is entirely void on the ground of uncertainty.[10] A corporation may be named as executor. A testator may authorise another to nominate an executor of his will, and effect will be given to such nomination;[11] and the person to nominate may nominate himself.[12] The number of executors is limited to four in relation to any one part of the estate.[13]

The expression 'executor de son tort' (although it should perhaps more properly be an administrator de son tort) is applied to a person who takes possession of, or intermeddles with, any of the deceased's assets as if he were an executor or administrator but without taking out any grant of probate or letters of administration.[14]

1 See *Tristram and Coote's Probate Practice* (30th edn) LexisNexis Butterworths, Chapter 4. The Non-Contentious Probate Rules 1987 (SI 1987/2024) replaced the 1954 Rules with effect from 1 January 1988. The new rules reflect changes in the law and practice over the past thirty years and include a provision to ensure that executors not joining in an

application for a grant of probate are nevertheless notified of the application: SI 1987/2024, r 27. There is also a provision for the grant of administration to a person acting as attorney under a registered enduring power of attorney: SI 1987/2024, r 35. Provision is no longer made requiring a guarantee as a condition of granting letters of administration.

See *Practice Direction* [1988] 1 All ER 192, [1988] 1 WLR 195; notice of application where power reserved.

2 A personal representative is not the agent of the deceased; he derives his powers not on the authority given to him by the deceased but on the authority given to him by law to stand in the place of the deceased: *Rickless v United Artists Corpn* [1988] QB 40, [1987] 1 All ER 679.

3 *Re Woods' Goods* (1868) LR 1 P & D 556; *Re Dallow's Goods* (1866) LR 1 P & D 189.

4 See the Administration of Justice Act 1982 (AJA 1982), s 21, fully discussed in Chapter 57. For pre-AJA 1982 case law see: *Grant v Grant* (1869) LR 2 P & D 8; *Re De Rosaz's Goods* (1877) 2 PD 66; *Re Twohill's Goods* (1879) 3 LR Ir 21; *Re Brake's Goods* (1881) 6 PD 217.

5 AJA 1982, s 21. For pre-AJA 1982 case law see *Re Twohill's Goods* (1879) 3 LR Ir 21; *Re Chappell's Goods* [1894] P 98.

6 AJA 1982, s 21 For pre-AJA 1982 case law see: *Re Ashton's Goods* [1892] P 83; *Re Hubbuck's Estate* [1905] P 129.

7 *Re Peel's Goods* (1870) LR 2 P & D 46.

8 Supreme Court of Judicature (Consolidation) Act 1925, s 162; see now the Supreme Court Act 1981, s 116. See for example, *Re Clore, IRC v Stype Instruments (Jersey) Ltd* [1982] Ch 456, [1982] 3 All ER 419; *Re Mathew* [1984] 2 All ER 396, [1984] 1 WLR 1011; *Khan v Crossland* [2012] WTLR 842.

9 *Re S's Estate* [1968] P 302, [1967] 2 All ER 150.

10 *Re Baylis' Goods* (1862) 2 Sw & Tr 613; *Re Blackwell's Goods* (1877) 2 PD 72. The court will not accept a shifting appointment, as the manager for the time being of a company: *Re Were's Will* (1886) 12 VLR 271.

11 *Re Cringan's Goods* (1828) 1 Hag Ecc 548; *Re Deichman's Goods* (1842) 3 Curt 123. This power is unaffected by the Wills Act 1837; *Jackson and Gill v Paulet* (1851) 2 Rob Eccl 344; *Bradley v Saunders* (1906) Cout 380; *Re Hadden's Will* (1879) 5 VLR 91; *Re Macgregor's Will* (1901) 1 SRNSW 50; *Re Cleghorn* [1931] 2 DLR 865.

12 *Re Ryder's Goods* (1861) 2 Sw & Tr 127.

13 There is no actual limitation on the number who may be appointed but probate will not be granted to more than four in respect of any one part of the estate: Supreme Court Act 1981, s 114. Where four general and one literary executors were appointed, it was held under the Supreme Court of Judicature (Consolidation) Act 1925, s 160(1) that the grant could only go to four and one must renounce: *Re Holland's Estate* [1936] 3 All ER 13. In view of the change in wording in the Supreme Court Act 1981, s 114, this decision is now obsolete.

14 See most recently *James v Williams* [1999] 3 All ER 309 where the authorities are discussed. It is interesting to note that on the facts of that case the court found a constructive trust so that the intermeddler became a trustee. See also *Pollard v Jackson* (1993) 67 P & CR 327.

[25.17]

[Updated in footnote 2 for *Re Loftus, Green v Gaul* [2005] EWHC 406 (Ch), [2005] WTLR 1325; and *Alkin v Raymond* [2010] WTLR 1117. Updated in footnotes 3 and 4 and in the text for *Kershaw v Micklethwaite* [2010] EWHC 506 (Ch), [2011] WTLR 413; and *Dobson v Heyman* [2007] EWHC 3503 (Ch), [2010] WTLR 1151.

Updated in the text and in footnote 5 for *Goodman v Goodman* [2013] EWHC 758 (Ch), [2013] WTLR 1181.]

Substitution or removal of personal representative. In addition to the Trustee Act 1925 powers, the Administration of Justice Act 1985,[1] confers power on the High Court to appoint a person to act as personal representative in place of the existing personal representative or to remove one or more but not all of the personal representatives. The Judicial Trustees Act 1896, s 1 provides a similar power. The powers under AJA 1985, s 50 and Judicial Trustees Act 1896, s 1 can be invoked for example, where there has been excessive dilatoriness in winding up the estate, or there has been positive misconduct by the executor such as to endanger the trust property, or to show want of honesty, or a want of proper capacity to execute the duties, or a want of reasonable fidelity.[2] An executor will not be removed merely because of hostility between the executor and beneficiaries; however, hostility should be taken into account where it might obstruct the administration of the estate.[3] In deciding whether to remove an executor, the fact that the testator has chosen him may be relevant because he will have made that choice with full knowledge of the characteristics and personalities involved.[4] Where a claim to remove a personal representative is brought by a person entitled to an interest in the estate under a mutual wills agreement, where the testator's last will is in breach of the agreement and the claimant is not a beneficiary under that will, the claim can be brought under Judicial Trustees Act 1896, s 1, but not under AJA 1985, s 50.[5] An executor may be removed under AJA 1985, s 50 even before probate has been granted since he derives his title as personal representative from the will, and so from the date of the testator's death.[6]

1 Administration of Justice Act 1985, s 50.
2 See *Letterstedt v Broers* (1884) 9 App Cas 371 at 386, held to be the relevant statement of principle as to the criteria for removal by the court for misconduct of a personal representative or trustee in *Thomas and Agnes Carvel Foundation v Carvel [2007] EWHC 1314* (Ch), 4 All ER 81; [2007] WTLR 1297. In *Re Loftus, Green v Gaul* [2005] EWHC 406 (Ch), [2005] WTLR 1325 an executor beneficiary who had converted estate property to her own use, claiming she had done so as a result of a compromise agreement between herself and the other beneficiaries which the court found had not been made, was removed. In *Alkin v Raymond* [2010] WTLR 1117 executors were removed when they had rendered an invoice from a building company owned by one of them to the testator, backdated to before the date of his death and not in accordance with normal industry standard, or any custom and usage of the construction industry.
3 *Letterstedt v Broers* (1884) 9 App Cas 371; *Kershaw v Micklethwaite* [2010] EWHC 506 (Ch), [2011] WTLR 413. In *Dobson v Heyman* [2007] EWHC 3503 (Ch), [2010] WTLR 1151 the sole executor of a small estate was replaced when the beneficiaries were reluctant to accept his account of dealings with the estate.
4 *Kershaw v Micklethwaite* [2010] EWHC 506 (Ch), [2011] WTLR 413.
5 *Thomas and Agnes Carvel Foundation v Carvel* [2007] EWHC 1314, 4 All ER 81, [2007] WTLR 1297. This is because only personal representatives or persons beneficially interested under the will or intestacy of the deceased can claim under AJA 1985, s 50.
6 *Goodman v Goodman* [2013] EWHC 758 (Ch), [2013] WTLR 1181 (cf *Thomas and Agnes Carvel Foundation v Carvel* [2007] EWHC 1314 (Ch), 4 All ER 81; [2007] WTLR 1297 at para [21]).

CHAPTER 28

Appointment of guardians

I. APPOINTMENT OF GUARDIANS ON OR AFTER 14 OCTOBER 1991

[28.2]

[Updated in the text and footnotes 11–15 for Human Fertilisation and Embryology Act 2008.]

Who may appoint guardians—parental responsibility. The Children Act 1989, s 5 gives the power to appoint a guardian to the parent or parents with parental responsibility for a child, and to a guardian of a child.[1] Parental responsibility means all the rights, duties, powers, responsibilities and authority which by law a parent of a child has in relation to the child and his property, and includes the rights, powers and duties which a guardian of the child's estate appointed before the ChA 1989 came into force would have had in relation to the child.[2]

Both parents of a legitimate child[3] have equal parental responsibility for him.[4] In the case of an illegitimate child the mother has parental responsibility,[5] and in the case of a child whose birth is registered before 1 December 2003 the father only acquires it if there is an order of the relevant court that he shall have it or it is conferred by a parental responsibility agreement between him and the mother,[6] or he marries the mother. A parental responsibility agreement only has effect if it is in the form prescribed by regulations made by the Lord Chancellor,[7] and once made it can only be terminated by an order of the court,[8] ie the mother cannot revoke it at will. The Adoption and Children Act 2002, (ACA 2002), ss 111 and 112 have added to the possible ways of attaining parental responsibility for a child. Section 111 amends ChA 1989, s 4 so as to cause the father of an illegitimate child who is registered as the father on the birth certificate to have parental responsibility by virtue of the registration.[9] ACA 2002, s 112 adds a new s 4A to ChA 1989 which enables the parent or parents having parental responsibility for a child to confer by agreement parental responsibility for the child on a step-parent of the child, where the step-parent is the spouse or civil partner of the parent or of one of them. It also empowers the court to make an order conferring parental responsibility on a step-parent.[10]

The Human Fertilisation and Embryology Act 2008 (HFEA 2008) makes parallel provision for a child of a same sex female couple, where the child is born as a result of either artificial insemination or other form of treatment regulated under HFEA 1990 and 2008 and carried out on or after 6 April 2009.[11] If the couple are in a civil partnership[12] at any time between the treatment and the birth of the child, the one who is not the mother has parental responsibility for the child.[13] If not, but the one who is not the mother gave her consent to the treatment in such manner as to make her a parent of the child,[14] she will have parental responsibility for the child if her name appears on the birth certificate, there is a parental responsibility agreement with the mother, she and the mother form a civil partnership after the birth of the child, or there is a court order conferring parental responsibility on her.[15]

A guardian of a child whose appointment has taken effect also has parental responsibility for that child,[16] but power is expressly conferred on a guardian to appoint someone else to take his place in the event of his death, independently of the provisions about parental responsibility.[17] It is arguable that this power of a guardian to appoint his successor may be exercised by someone who has been appointed a guardian before that appointment has taken effect,[18] but on balance it is thought that such an argument is incorrect.[19] The court also has power to appoint a guardian.[20] There are no further categories of persons empowered to appoint guardians.[21]

1 ChA 1989, s 5(3) and (4).
2 ChA 1989, s 3(1) and (2).
3 This includes a child legitimated by the subsequent marriage of his parents, an adopted child, and a child otherwise treated in law as legitimate: see the Family Law Reform Act 1987, s 1(2) and (3) (Vol 2, Part G, para **[245.70]**) and ChA 1989, ss 2(1) and (3).
4 ChA 1989, s 2(1), (4) and (5).
5 ChA 1989, s 2(2)(a).
6 ChA 1989, s 4(1). Where an order made under Family Law Reform Act 1987, s 4(1) giving a father parental rights and duties in relation to a child was in force immediately before 14 October 1991 it has effect from then as an order under ChA 1989, s 4 giving the father parental responsibility, and an order in force immediately before that date under previous legislation giving the father custody or care and control has effect under the Children Act 1989 from then as an order conferring parental responsibility on him: ChA 1989, Sch 14, paras 4 and 6(2) and (4).
7 ChA 1989, s 4(2). For the prescribed form see the Parental Responsibility Agreement Regulations 1991, SI 1991/1478 as amended by SI 1994/3157. The ChA 1989, s 4(2) also requires such an agreement to be recorded in the prescribed manner if the relevant regulations so require; SI 1991/1478 requires recording of a parental responsibility agreement in the Principal Registry of the Family Division of the High Court as a precondition of it taking effect.
8 ChA 1989, s 4(3).
9 It came into force on 1 December 2003 (SI 2003/3079), and does not apply in relation to registrations which occurred before that date (see s 111(7)).
10 It came into force on 30 December 2005 (SI 2005/2213).
11 See HFEA 2008, ss 42 and 43, and paras **[74.5]**, **[74.6]** below.
12 Under the Civil Partnership Act 2004, in force from 5 December 2005.
13 HFEA 2008, ss 42, 43, FLRA 1987 s 1(2)(ba) and (bb) inserted by HFEA 2008, Sch 6, para 24, and Children Act 1989, s 2(1A) inserted by HFEA 2008, Sch 6, para 26.
14 See HFEA 2008, ss 43, 44.
15 Children Act 1989, s 4ZA inserted by HFEA 2008, Sch 6, para 27, Legitimacy Act 1976, s 2A inserted by HFEA 2008, Sch 6, para 16, FLRA 1987, s 1(2) and (3), and ChA 1989, s 2(1A) inserted by HFEA 2008, Sch 6, para 26.
16 ChA 1989, s 5(6).
17 See ChA 1989, s 5(4).
18 Because the reference in ChA 1989, s 5(8), to s 5(4) of that Act would appear to have no function if it is only a guardian whose appointment has taken effect who can appoint another guardian.
19 The wording of the power in ChA 1989, s 5(4) 'a guardian of a child may appoint … to take his place as the child's guardian in the event of his death' suggests it is a power only

exercisable after a guardian has taken up the office. Also a guardian is not really a guardian until his appointment has taken effect, and an appointment of a guardian is always revocable during the life of the appointor.

20 ChA 1989, s 5(1) and (2).

21 In particular, a person who is not the child's parent and in whose favour a residence order is made has parental responsibility but does not have power to appoint a guardian: see the ChA 1989, s 12(2) and (3)(c).

PART H

Contents of wills

CHAPTER 29

Appropriation

II. STATUTORY POWER

[29.17]

[Updated in footnote 5 for *Hughes v Bourne* [2012] EWHC 2232 (Ch), [2012] WTLR 1333.]

The Administration of Estates Act 1925[1] gives certain statutory powers of appropriation to personal representatives which, of course, includes administrators as well as executors to whom the common law powers are in general restricted.[2] The statutory power extends to any part of the real or personal estate,[3] including things in action, of the deceased in the actual condition or state of investment thereof at the time of the appropriation[4] in or towards satisfaction of any legacy bequeathed by the deceased, or of any other interest or share in his property, whether settled or not,[5] as to the personal representative may seem just and reasonable, according to the respective rights of the persons interested in the property of the deceased. This general power is subject to the following provisos: (i) no appropriation can be made under this section so as to affect prejudicially any specific devise or bequest; (ii) an appropriation of property, whether or not being an investment authorised by law or by the will, if any, of the deceased for the investment of money subject to the trust, cannot (save as hereinafter mentioned) be made under the section except with the following consents; (a) when made for the benefit of a person absolutely and beneficially entitled in possession, the consent of that person; (b) when made in respect of a settled legacy share or interest,[6] the consent of either the trustee thereof, if any (not being also the personal representative), or the person who may for the time being be entitled to the income (if the person whose consent is so required is a minor[7] or incapable through mental disorder, the consent shall be given on his behalf by his parent, testamentary or other guardian, receiver, or if, in the case of a minor there is no such parent or guardian, by the court on the application of his next friend); (iii) no consent (save of such trustee as aforesaid) shall be required on behalf of a person who may come into existence after the time of appropriation, or who cannot be found or ascertained at the time;[8] (iv) if no receiver of a person incapable through mental disorder has been appointed, then, if the appropriation is of an investment authorised by law or by the will, if any, of the deceased for the investment of money subject to the trust, no consent shall be required on his or her behalf; (v) if, independently of the personal representative, there is no trustee of a settled legacy, share or interest, and no person of full age and capacity entitled to the income thereof, no consent shall be necessary to an appropriation in respect of such legacy, share or interest, provided that the appropriation is of an investment authorised as aforesaid. Any property duly appropriated under these powers is thereafter to be treated as an authorised investment, and may be retained or dealt with accordingly.

As to the right of a surviving spouse or civil partner to appropriate the matrimonial home on intestacy in satisfaction or part satisfaction of his or her interest, see para **[104.5]** below.

1 Administration of Estates Act 1925, s 41. Subsection (6) has been amended with effect from 1 January 1997 by the Trusts of Land and Appointment of Trustees Act 1996, s 25(1), Sch 3, para 6(3).

2 Before 1926 administrators had little need of a power of appropriation since the interests of the next of kin were immediately vested and either the next of kin being *sui juris* could agree to divide the estate in specie or it had to be turned into money and the proceeds divided between them. As to the nature of the interests of the next of kin, see *Cooper v Cooper* (1874) LR 7 HL 53, and *Vanneck v Benham* [1917] 1 Ch 60. In the case of gifts by will, as in all other cases, where all the persons entitled to the property in question are *sui juris*, of full age, and have not encumbered their interests or rendered them subject to subsidiary trusts, they can deal with such property (whether it is the whole estate or any part of it) as they desire. This, however, is the right of the parties as owning all the beneficial interests in the property and is more in the nature of a partition than an appropriation, but it is an absolute right of such parties and does not require the support of any power to partition or to appropriate.

3 The common law power applied to real estate only where it was held upon trust for sale—now upon trust of land.

4 Compare the cases relating to common law appropriation, para **[29.1]** ff.

5 The common law power to appropriate to settled shares or legacies is narrower than that in the cases of an immediately vested interest. It has been held that the statutory power authorises an appropriation to settled shares not just where the trusts are in respect of proportionate shares of a fund, but also where they are in respect of proportionate shares of the income of a fund: see *Hughes v Bourne* [2012] EWHC 2232 (Ch), [2012] WTLR 1333, notwithstanding *Re Freeston's Charity* [1979] 1 All ER 51, [1978] 1 WLR 741.

6 A settled legacy, share or interest includes any legacy share or interest to which a person is not absolutely entitled in possession at the date of the appropriation, and also an annuity.

7 Under 18: Family Law Reform Act 1969, s 1.

8 No appropriation can be made at common law where a legatee cannot be found: see para **[29.1]**, n 7, above. But when acting under the statutory power the personal representative must have regard to the interests of persons not in existence or who cannot be found and of all persons whose consent is required, but these matters will not concern purchasers of the appropriated property; Administration of Estates Act 1925, s 41(5) and (7), the substance of which is set out in the text at para **[29.23]** below.

CHAPTER 30

Legacies

VI. TO EMPLOYEES

[30.23]

[Updated in the text and at footnote 6 for *Creasey v Sole* [2013] EWHC 1410 (Ch), [2013] WTLR 931.]

Description. Where the donees are described by their employment and not by name the persons taking are prima facie those filling the character at the date of the will, and it is not essential that the employment should continue until the date of the death of the testator;[1] but, if it appears from the will that the donees are a class to be ascertained in accordance with the ordinary rules,[2] the will may by its terms require the donees to fill the particular character required at the date of the will,[3] or at the death of the testator,[4] or for some specified length of time.[5] Most of the authorities on legacies to employees are old cases concerning domestic servants. Such gifts will obviously be less common in modern wills, but the construction adopted in these cases can be noted shortly as providing some general guidance. There is though a recent reported decision concerning a gift of a farming business to such of the testator's children 'who may be working either as employee or partner fulltime in such business at date of the death of myself or my wife (whichever shall last happen)'.[6]

1 *Parker v Marchant* (1842) 1 Y & C Ch Cas 290 at 299 (the circumstance that the description is by employment and not by name does not import continuance of employment); *Re Miller, Galloway v Miller* (1913) 135 LT Jo 10. For precedents, see Vol 2, paras **[210.57]** to **[210.62]**.

2 *Re Marcus, Marcus v Marcus* (1887) 56 LJ Ch 830 (office and warehouse employees to receive six months' full salary held to refer to employees at time of death). As to rules for determining classes, see Chapter 66, post, but in this connection the class will almost certainly be ascertained at the date of the death.

3 *Parker v Marchant* (1842) 1 Y & C Ch Cas 290; *Re Strombeck Estate* (1956) 2 DLR (2d) 109. See *Jones v Henley* (1685) 2 Rep Ch 361 (where the will on its construction was held to refer to servants at the date of the will who continued to be such until the date of the testator's death).

4 *Re Marcus, Marcus v Marcus* (1887) 56 LJ Ch 830; *Re Bell, Wright v Scrivener* (1914) 58 Sol Jo 517.

5 *Re Sharland, Kemp v Rozey* [1896] 1 Ch 517 (servant in employ for over ten years; servant who had been employed for the requisite period, but left before the date of the will held entitled); *Re Miller, Galloway v Miller* (1913) 135 LT Jo 10 ('at least three years'; apprenticeship for five years but salaried for less than three years).

6 *Creasey v Sole* [2013] EWHC 1410 (Ch), [2013] WTLR 931 (see **[30.26]** below).

[30.26]

[Updated in the text and at footnote 5 for *Creasey v Sole* [2013] EWHC 1410 (Ch), [2013] WTLR 931.]

Employed. The usual meaning of 'employed' is well understood, but a person may be affected by changes in the nature of a business. Where the testator secretly formed a partnership but continued to run the business himself, it was held that there was no break in the employment.[1] On the other hand, where the employees were required to be in the service of a limited company for a stated period before the death of the testator, service with the testator before the formation of the company (though substantially the same business) did not count[2] and interruption by service in the armed forces of the Crown prevented any aggregation of service before enlistment and after discharge.[3] 'A period of five years' does not necessarily mean a continuous period of five years and not an aggregate of shorter periods amounting to five years.[4] Where a testator made a gift of his share of a farm and farming business to such of his children 'who may be working either as employee or partner fulltime in [the testator's and his wife's] business at date of the death of myself or my wife (whichever shall last happen)', it was said that the words 'employee' and 'partner' were legal terms with a fairly clear meaning describing legal concepts, and a son who worked for the majority of his time in his own farming business, while giving part-time assistance to his parents in their business in return for being allowed to use the farmland for his, was held not to qualify.[5]

1 *Re Howell's Trusts, Barclays Bank Ltd v Simmons* [1937] 3 All ER 647. See also *Ryan v Smith* (1972) 22 DLR (3d) 1 (condition that beneficiaries be employees of business).
2 *Re Marryat, Westminster Bank Ltd v Hobcroft* [1948] Ch 298, [1948] 1 All ER 796.
3 *Re Marryat, Westminster Bank Ltd v Hobcroft* [1948] Ch 298, [1948] 1 All ER 796. The basis of this decision is that there was no agreement with the company for the continuation of the employment.
4 *Re Bedford* [1951] Ch 905, [1951] 1 All ER 1093, but see *Re Marryat, Westminster Bank Ltd v Hobcroft* [1948] Ch 298, [1948] 1 All ER 796, to the contrary. See also *Re Hartley's Trusts* (1878) 47 LJ Ch 610; *Re Silverston, Westminster Bank Ltd v Kohler* [1949] Ch 270, [1949] 1 All ER 641; *Re King, Jackson v A-G* [1917] 2 Ch 420.
5 *Creasey v Sole* [2013] EWHC 1410 (Ch), [2013] WTLR 931.

CHAPTER 32

Interest and income on legacies

III. GENERAL AND DEMONSTRATIVE LEGACIES

[32.4]

[Updated in the text and in footnote 1 for a change in the rate of interest on general legacies with effect from 1 February 2009. Also updated in footnotes 1 and 2 for *Re Allen, Lewis v Vincent* [2008] WTLR 1691.]

When no time fixed for payment. Where no special time is fixed for the payment of a general legacy, it carries interest at the basic rate payable for the time being on funds in court, currently 2 per cent per annum with effect from 1 February 2009[1] from the expiration of one year after the testator's death,[2] although expressly made payable out of a particular fund which does not fall in until after a longer period.[3]

1 This rate of interest is that applicable where an account of legacies is directed by the court, and is set by the Civil Procedure Rules, Part 40, *Practice Direction– Accounts, Inquiries etc*, para 15 as the basic rate for funds in court. The rate was previously 4 per cent with effect from 1 February 2002. Prior to this it had been 6 per cent, RSC Ord 44, r 10; SI 1982/1111; see also CCR 1981 Ord 23, r 2; substituted for the previous 5 per cent with effect from 1 October 1983 by RSC (Amendment No 2) Order 1983, SI 1983/1181. Other relevant rates of interest are 6 per cent now payable on statutory legacies: (Intestate Succession (Interest and Capitalisation) Order 1983, SI 1983/1374); previously the rate was 7 per cent, after 1977; and 4 per cent, after 1952. All these rates of interest are liable to change by statutory instrument and should be checked to ascertain the prevailing rate at any particular time. CPR 40 PD 15 provides as an alternative to the court funds rate of interest 'such other rate as the court shall direct', so it may be that in a particular case executors could apply to the court for a different rate of interest to apply; see *Re Allen, Lewis v Vincent* [2008] WTLR 1691 where executors successfully applied to the High Court of New Zealand to pay interest on a legacy at a lower rate equivalent to the interest actually earned when the legatee had caused much of the delay in the administration and payment of her legacy.

2 *Re Lord's Estate, Lord v Lord* (1867) 2 Ch App 782 at 789; *Webster v Hale* (1803) 8 Ves 410 (direction in will to pay as soon as possible), but see para **[32.5]**, n 5, where legacy is immediately payable; *Bourke v Ricketts* (1804) 10 Ves 330 (legacy in currency of Jamaica where testator resided); *Wood v Penoyre* (1807) 13 Ves 325 (payment out of mortgage debt when recovered); *Marquis of Hertford v Lord Lowther* (1846) 9 Beav 266 (delay in payment); *Re Barr* [1947] 3 DLR 784. As to directions which do not amount to a direction for payment at a special time, see *Re Yates, Throckmorton v Pike* (1907) 96 LT 758; *Re Whiteley, Whiteley v Bishop of London* (1909) 101 LT 508; *Walford v Walford* [1912] AC 658. See, further, as to legacy payable at a future date, para **[32.10]** below. It has been held in New Zealand that there is no discretion in the court to change the period: *Re Allen, Lewis v Vincent* [2008] WTLR 1691.The interest is payable out of the residuary personal estate: *Greene v Flood* (1885) 15 LR Ir 450, and is subject to deduction of income tax at the current rate: *Hamilton v Linaker* [1923] 1 IR 104.

3 *Walford v Walford* [1912] AC 658.

VI. GENERAL POINTS

[32.31]

[Updated in the text and in footnote 2 for a change in the rate of interest on general legacies with effect from 1 February 2009.]

Rate of interest. The rate of interest set by the court is now governed by the Civil Procedure Rules.[1] It is the basic rate on funds in court unless the court orders otherwise. This rate is currently 2 per cent with effect from 1 February 2009.[2] Interest is not allowed at a higher rate, even though the residuary estate has been producing interest at a higher rate.[3]

1 CPR Part 40, *Practice Direction–Accounts, Inquiries etc*, para 15.
2 The rate had previously been 4 per cent which was substituted for the previous 6 per cent with effect from 1 February 2002; see para **[32.4]**, n 1 above.
3 *Re Campbell, Campbell v Campbell* [1893] 3 Ch 468.

CHAPTER 34

Conditions generally

V. PUBLIC POLICY

[34.12]

[Updated in footnote 4 for the Equality Act 2010.]

Conditions against public policy. A condition is against public policy if it is in the interest of the state that it should not be performed.[1] What is contrary to public policy has varied from time to time, and many conditions are now upheld which in former days would have been declared to be contrary to the policy of the law. The rule remains, but its application varies with the principles which for the time being guide public opinion.[2] The prevalent judicial-attitude to questions of public policy in testamentary gifts was stated by Lord Simon in *Blathwayt v Lord Cawley,*[3] as follows:

> 'I must not be taken thereby to be implying that it is for courts of law to embark on an independent and unfettered appraisal of what they think is required by public policy on any issue. Courts are concerned with public policy only in so far as it has been manifested by parliamentary sanction or embodied in rules of law having binding judicial force. As to such rules of law your Lordships have the same powers to declare, to bind and to lose as in regard to any other judicial precedent. Rules of law expressing principles of public policy therefore fall to be treated with the same respect and circumspection, the same common sense and regard for changing circumstances, as any other rules of law.'

In that case the court also emphasised the balancing rule of public policy that a testator should be free, subject to the rights of his surviving spouse and children, to dispose of his property as he pleases.[4]

The following conditions attached to a gift in a will have been held to be contrary to public policy and void: a condition inciting the beneficiary to commit a crime[5] or to do any act prohibited by law;[6] a condition requiring the beneficiary to exert his influence in any political matter, such as obtaining a title;[7] a condition tending to induce the future separation of husband and wife;[8] an unreasonable restraint of marriage,[9] or of trade or industry;[10] a condition forbidding service for the defence of the realm,[11] or any other public duty;[12] a condition tending to deprive a parent of the control of children;[13] a condition which requires a change of religion during infancy;[14] a condition which will operate beyond the limit imposed by the rule against perpetuities;[15] a gift for the mother of the largest number of children born during a certain period;[16] extravagant, wasteful or futile directions.[17]

1 *Cooke v Turner* (1846) 15 M & W 727.
2 *Evanturel v Evanturel* (1874) LR 6 PC 1 at 29. See Lord Wilberforce in *Blathwayt v Lord Cawley* [1975] 3 All ER 625 at 636 (forfeiture clause if the person entitled 'be or become Roman Catholic'; not void for public policy despite the Race Relations Act 1968; public policy does not require that testators may not prefer one branch of the family to another on religious grounds). See also *AN v Barclays Private Bank & Trust (Cayman) Limited* [2007] WTLR 565, referred to in para **[34.11]**, n 3 above.
3 [1975] 3 All ER 625 at 637.
4 See Lord Wilberforce, [1975] 3 All ER 625 at 636, and Lord Frazer of Tulleybelton, [1975] 3 All ER 625 at 650. The rights of other 'dependants' under the Inheritance (Provision for Family and Dependants) Act 1975 would also now have to be considered; see Chapter 105. It may be noted that Lord Wilberforce said at [1975] 3 All ER 625 at 636: 'I do not doubt that conceptions of public policy should move with the times and that widely accepted treaties and statutes may point the direction in which such conceptions, as applied by the courts, ought to move. It may well be that conditions such as this are, or at least are becoming, inconsistent with standards now widely accepted.' It is unclear whether public policy, as manifested in legislation such as the Human Rights Act 1998 and the Equality Act 2010, has now moved so far that conditions which may have been upheld in the past would not now be upheld.
5 *Mitchel v Reynolds* (1711) 1 P Wms 181 at 189; *Earl of Shrewsbury v Hope–Scott* (1859) 6 Jur NS 452 at 456.
6 *Mitchel v Reynolds* (1711) 1 P Wms 181; *Re Piper, Dodd v Piper* [1946] 2 All ER 503.
7 *Earl of Kingston v Pierepont* (1681) 1 Vern 5; *Egerton v Earl of Brownlow* (1853) 4 HL Cas 1; *Re Wallace, Champion v Wallace* [1920] 2 Ch 274 (where it was held that a condition to acquire the title of baronet was not against public policy since the title involved no duties other than those of every good citizen). A condition that if a person should not succeed to a peerage the lands should go over has been held valid in Scotland: *Earl of Caithness v Sinclair* 1912 SC 79, and a similar gift was held good in Ireland where the condition was: 'if the House of Lords will allow his right' to be Viscount N: *Earl of Fingal v Blake* (1829) 2 Mol 50.
8 See para **[35.35]** below.
9 See para **[35.1]** below.
10 Though restraint of trade or industry has been one of the most discussed topics in connection with public policy, there appears to be no English decision on the point so far as a condition in a will is concerned apart from references in the judgments in *Cooke v Turner* (1846) 15 M & W 727 at 736, and *Egerton v Earl of Brownlow* (1853) 4 HL Cas 1 at 18, 144, 241. This note was referred to in *Re Cowley* [1971] NZLR 468 at 472, where it was stated to be doubtful as to how far, if at all, the requirements of public policy could invalidate conditions in wills tending to restrict the freedom of trade of a beneficiary: referring to *Cooke v Turner* (1846) 15 M & W 727; *Egerton v Earl of Brownlow* (1853) 4 HL Cas 1: *Permanent Trustee Co v Dougall* (1931) 34 SRNSW 83; and *Esso Petroleum Co Ltd v Harper's Garage (Stourport) Ltd* [1968] AC 269, [1967] 1 All ER 699. In *Re Cowley*, it was held that a provision tending to encourage grandsons to become farmers was not contrary to public policy in New Zealand.
11 See Chapter 35.
12 See Chapter 35.
13 See Chapter 35.
14 See Chapter 35.
15 See Chapter 94.
16 *Re Millar* [1938] 2 DLR 164.
17 *Sutherland's Trustee v Verschoyle* 1968 SLT 43 (trust fund for maintenance of unimportant art collection).

CHAPTER 35

Particular conditions

[35.2]

[Updated in footnote 1 for the Equality Act 2010.]

General restraint of marriage. Although it has been said that all general restraints upon marriage are void by the law and practice of the courts of this country, as being against the policy of the law,[1] yet the better view is that a condition subsequent in a will in restraint of the marriage of a single person is not absolutely but only prima facie void; and, if the intention of the testator is to promote, not celibacy, but some other lawful object, the condition may be valid.[2] A distinction has in this connection been taken between a condition precedent and a condition subsequent.[3] Where a gift of a certain duration is abridged by a condition subsequent in restraint of marriage, the condition is prima facie void and the original gift remains,[4] but property may be given to a person until she marries and when she marries then over and such a condition is valid.[5] A condition of this nature will be supported if the intention of the testator is to protect or to provide for a child of his even though the child be illegitimate.[6] The condition may also be personal to the donee herself as a provision that she marry only a man able to provide for her or to induce the donee to remain single for the benefit of her children.[7] In these cases, however, there is also a distinction between gifts of realty and personalty. In the case of gifts of real estate or legacies charged on real estate, an intention to restrain marriage is not shown by a gift on marriage,[8] but in the case of legacies payable out of personalty or the proceeds of sale of realty such a provision does show an intention to restrain marriage and is consequently void.[9] A distinction must be drawn between a condition against marriage or requiring marriage with a particular person[10] or one of a particular class of persons[11] and gifts where the words relating to marriage merely describe the interest to be taken by the donee.[12] There is no objection to gift to endure so long as the donee remains unmarried for marriage may be made the ground of a gift commencing or ceasing.[13] In such a case the words constitute not a condition but a limitation.[14]

It seems that a general restraint of marriage, subject as above stated, being against public policy, such a condition is void both in gifts of real and personal estate[15] even where the condition is a condition precedent.[16] The better view appears to be that such a condition is not within the in terrorem doctrine (ie it is invalid even if there is a gift over on failure to satisfy the condition).[17]

1 *Godfrey v Hughes* (1847) 1 Rob Eccl 593, but even in this case it was agreed that a gift until marriage is good. It may be, however, that such a condition is always void in the case of a gift of an entailed interest because it is of the nature of the interest that the donee shall marry and have issue: see *Anon* (1574) Jenk 243; but the condition is void for repugnancy rather than illegality. But the fact that different gifts are made on the death of a person married and on his death unmarried may not be a restraint on marriage at all: *Re Fentem, Cockerton v Fentem* [1950] 2 All ER 1073. It is not clear whether similar principles would apply to restraints against forming a civil partnership, but they probably would in the light of the Human Rights Act 1998 and the Equality Act 2010. As to restraint on remarriage, see para **[35.8]** below.

2 *Jones v Jones* (1876) 1 QBD 279; *Carrodus v Carrodus* [1913] VLR 1; *Re Haythornwaite's Estate* [1930] 3 DLR 235. In *Re Fentem, Cockerton v Fentem* [1950] 2 All ER 1073, after a life interest to a son, it was provided that, if he had not married, the gift was to become absolute, but, if he had married, there was a gift over to a servant for life, then for charity. It was held that the testatrix had not meant to prevent the son from marrying but merely that, after his death, the property should be dealt with in a particular way and the condition was valid. Where restrictions on persons allowed to reside on the property excluded a husband or issue, the gift was in restraint of marriage and void: *Re Snadden's Will* [1962] VR 571. A condition against remarriage where the testator knew the beneficiary was a spinster may be construed as a condition against marriage: *Re Fowler* [1963] VR 639.

3 *Morley v Rennoldson* (1843) 2 Hare 570.

4 *Morley v Rennoldson* (1843) 2 Hare 570; *Lloyd v Lloyd* (1852) 2 Sim NS 255. As to condition against remarriage of widow, see para **[35.8]** below.

5 *Morley v Rennoldson* (1843) 2 Hare 570; *Godfrey v Hughes* (1847) 1 Rob Eccl 593; *Webb v Grace* (1848) 2 Ph 701.

6 *Potter v Richards* (1855) 24 LJ Ch 488; *Re Hewett, Eldridge v Iles* [1918] 1 Ch 458.

7 *Re Greene, Greene v Kirkwood* [1895] 1 IR 130 at 142; *Re Moore's Trusts, Lewis v Moore* (1906) 96 LT 44. See also *Long v Dennis* (1767) 4 Burr 2052 (not to marry without portion or consent: held condition performed by having portion only without consent).

8 *Jones v Jones* (1876) 1 QBD 279.

9 *Lloyd v Lloyd* (1852) 2 Sim NS 255; *Morley v Rennoldson* (1843) 2 Hare 570; *Bellairs v Bellairs* (1874) LR 18 Eq 510 (mixed fund); *Re Bellamy, Pickard v Holroyd* (1883) 48 LT 212; *Ree Wright, Mott v Issott* [1907] 1 Ch 231.

10 See para **[35.7]** below.

11 See para **[35.4]** below.

12 As in the case of gifts ceasing on remarriage.

13 *Morley v Rennoldson* (1843) 2 Hare 570; *Godfrey v Hughes* (1847) 1 Rob Eccl 593; *Webb v Grace* (1848) 2 Ph 701; *Re Davies, Davies v Public Trustee* [1954] NZLR 520 (gift to daughter so long as she remained unmarried, gift over on marriage: gift to daughter valid: the gift over was vested and took effect in possession on marriage or death of the daughter); *Crown Trust Co v McKenzie* (1958) 66 Man R 294. A person given a gift for life or until remarriage has the ordinary powers of a life tenant and no power to commit waste: *Fullarton v Humble* (1958) 42 MPR 118.

14 *Webb v Grace* (1848) 2 Ph 701; *Heath v Lewis* (1853) 3 De GM & G 954; *Potter v Richards* (1855) 24 LJ Ch 488; *Evans v Rosser (or Rossall)* (1864) 2 Hem & M 190.

15 There seems to be no precise authority on this point.

16 *Keily v Monck* (1795) 3 Ridg Parl Rep 205; *Scott v Tyler* (1788) 2 Bro CC 431; *Younge v Furse* (1857) 8 De GM & G 756.

17 It has been held that these conditions are within the rule in *Marples v Bainbridge* (1816) 1 Madd 590, and *Bellairs v Bellairs* (1874) LR 18 Eq 510, but the better view seems to be that where these conditions are within the rules as stated above, they are to promote celibacy and are against public policy and void on that account. They are not rendered valid by a gift over: *Morley v Rennoldson* (1843) 2 Hare 570; *Lloyd v Lloyd* (1852) 2 Sim NS 255.

[35.4]

[Updated for the Marriage (Same Sex Couples) Act 2013 ('M(SSC)A 2013')]

Condition against marriage with a particular class of persons. These conditions have in general been upheld as being only in partial restraint of marriage, but the condition must not be so framed as to amount in effect to a general restraint of marriage.[1] Thus a condition against marriage with a Scotsman[2], or with a domestic servant[3] or against a person marrying beneath her have been held good.[4] Where the prohibition was against marriage with a New Zealand native it was held that there was not sufficient evidence to prove that the person in question was not a New Zealand native.[5] Where the condition was against marriage with a blood relation, it was held that, since a person could never be certain that he was marrying someone to whom a common ancestor could not be traced, the condition was of a nature as would lead to a total prohibition of marriage and was void though in terms only a partial restraint was imposed.[6] A partial restraint must not be joined with a further condition relating to cohabitation.[7]

The M(SSC)A 2013 gives rise to the question whether a condition against same sex marriage would be held invalid. On the one hand the donee might argue that because he or she is of an exclusively homosexual sexual orientation, the condition represents for him or her a general restraint of marriage which should be void (see para **[35.2]** above). On the other hand, the M(SSC)A 2013 makes allowance for conscientious objections, particularly religious objections, to same sex marriage. Accordingly, it could be argued, it should be permissible for a testator to have such objections and to give effect to them by imposing a condition in restraint of same sex marriage.

1 *Keily v Monck* (1795) 3 Ridg Parl Rep 205 (persons not seised of freehold of £500 yearly value); but cf *Long v Dennis* (1767) 4 Burr 2052 (marriage without a competent fortune, which seems to have been thought partial and valid).
2 *Perrin v Lyon* (1807) 9 East 170.
3 *Jenner v Turner* (1880) 16 Ch D 188.
4 *Re Greene, Greene v Kirkwood* [1895] 1 IR 130.
5 *Armitage v Armitage* (1868) 16 WR 643.
6 *Re Lanyon, Lanyon v Lanyon* [1927] 2 Ch 264; but a condition against marriage with a cousin german has been held good: *Welply v Cormick* (1864) 16 I Ch R 74.
7 *Poole v Bott* (1853) 11 Hare 33 at 39 (condition against marrying or illegally cohabiting with certain cousins and requiring beneficiaries to enter into bond not to do so: the execution of the bonds could not be insisted on and beneficiaries were entitled to their interests).

[35.23]

[Updated in footnote 4 for the Equality Act 2010.]

Separation of husband and wife. A gift subject to a woman making a house her permanent home and ceasing on her voluntary ceasing to do so is not valid either as being against public policy or as being uncertain, but in the case of a married woman the gift would not be defeated if she, at the injunction of her husband, made some other house the matrimonial home, because the cesser would not then be voluntary.[1] Indeed, in such a case the condition operates only while she is capable of residing, ie while she is a spinster.[2] A condition that a married woman should cease to reside at her husband's place of business has been held void for this reason.[3] Apart from this, however, a clause designed to separate persons other than husband and wife or parent and child is not illegal.[4]

1 *Re Wilkinson, Page v Public Trustee* [1926] Ch 842. As to the husband's right to say where a matrimonial home shall be, see *Mansey v Mansey* [1940] P 139, [1940] 2 All ER 424; and as to agreements to change it, see *King v King* [1942] P 1, [1941] 2 All ER 103.
2 *Re Wright, Mott v Issott* [1907] 1 Ch 231.

3 *Wilkinson v Wilkinson* (1871) LR 12 Eq 604. See para **[35.35]** below.
4 See *Ridgway v Woodhouse* (1844) 7 Beav 437 (clause designed to separate wife and her sister). See footnote 4 to para **[34.12]** above.

[35.30]

[Updated in footnote 2 for the Equality Act 2010.]

Roman Catholics. A forfeiture clause to operate should a beneficiary 'be or become a Roman Catholic' has recently been held to be not void for uncertainty, and the court after reviewing the cases concluded that the balance of authority was strongly in favour of validity.[1] Nor, despite the Race Relations Act 1968, was the clause void for public policy.[2] A condition against entering a convent or associating with Roman Catholics is good and, on entry into a Roman Catholic convent, the interest of the legatee ceases as from the time of entry,[3] but where the gift is absolute in the first instance, a condition cutting down the gift on embracing a religious life has been held repugnant to the absolute gift and void.[4] A condition against joining a religious society to which the legatee would be under an obligation to give his or her property is good, but where the society requires only that its members shall give to the society the income of their property and leaves them free to dispose of the capital there is no breach.[5] A condition not to become or marry a Roman Catholic is good, but this condition may upon its proper construction be confined to breaches before the death of the testator.[6] A gift to grandchildren who were Roman Catholics and not married to Protestants has been upheld as sufficiently certain,[7] and a condition not to marry a Roman Catholic or the child of Roman Catholic parents or parent or a scholar of a Roman Catholic school or institution was held sufficiently certain and a condition precedent.[8] Conditions requiring a child to be educated in the Roman Catholic faith or requiring a child not to be educated in a Roman Catholic school have been held bad as a fetter on the parent's right to choose the education he thinks best for a child.[9] However to say that any condition is void which in any way might affect or influence the way in which a child is brought up, or in which parental duties are exercised is to state the rule too widely.[10] A condition requiring a minor to be or become or cease to be a Roman Catholic does not in general become operative until he attains the age of 18,[11] but on attaining full age the condition has been held good.[12]

1 *Blathwayt v Lord Cawley* [1975] 3 All ER 625 at 635, distinguishing *Clayton v Ramsden* [1943] AC 320, [1943] 1 All ER 16.
2 *Blathwayt v Lord Cawley* [1975] 3 All ER 625 at 635, distinguishing *Clayton v Ramsden* [1943] AC 320, [1943] 1 All ER 16. See now the Equality Act 2010 which consolidates the race relations legislation, and see footnote 4 to para **[34.12]** above..
3 *Re Dickson's Trust, ex p Dickson* (1850) 1 Sim NS 37; *Wainwright v Miller* [1897] 2 Ch 255. Entering a convent means taking final vows and no forfeiture is incurred by becoming a novice or a postulant, still less by being a boarder in a convent school: *Re Madore Estate* [1936] NLR 215; *Maguire v Boylan* (1870) 5 IR Eq 90.
4 *Re Thompson, Griffith v Thompson* (1896) 44 WR 582.
5 *Re Bell, Bell v Agnew* (1931) 47 TLR 401.
6 *Re Wright, Public Trustee v Wright* (1937) 158 LT 368; *Re Morrison's Will Trusts, Walsingham v Blathwayt* [1940] Ch 102, [1939] 4 All ER 332. Where the ban was on those who 'will have become or become a Roman Catholic or marry or shall have married a Roman Catholic', it applied only to those who became or married Roman Catholics before the testator's death: *Re Wright, Public Trustee v Wright* (1937) 158 LT 368. Cf *Saywell v*

Saywell (1932) 32 SRNSW 155. The marriage may, on the construction of the whole will, be confined to marriage during infancy: *Duggan v Kelly* (1848) 10 I Eq R 473; *Re McKenna, Higgins v Bank of Ireland* [1947] IR 277. In *Re Morrison's Will Trusts, Walsingham v Blathwayt* [1940] Ch 102, [1939] 4 All ER 332, the will expressly provided that the condition was to apply during the lifetime of the testatrix and after her death and it was decided that on the life tenant becoming a Roman Catholic, not only her interest ceased, but that of a child of hers who had become a Roman Catholic and also those of two other children who had not become Roman Catholics. In *Re Evans, Hewitt v Edwards* [1940] Ch 629, any child or grandchild who at any time became a convert to the Roman Catholic religion was ipso facto to forfeit the right to any income or capital of the estate. The words ipso facto showed that the person forfeiting must have a right at the time of becoming a Roman Catholic; the clause applied only after the death of the testator and the beneficiaries having been baptised in that church before the testator's death did not forfeit their interests under the will. Such a condition has, however, been held to operate to restrain parents from doing their duty in the matter of religious instruction of their children and on that ground to be void: *Re Borwick, Borwick v Borwick* [1933] Ch 657; and see *Re AT St George, Perpetual Trustee Co Ltd v St George* [1964] NSWR 587. In *Re Orr* [1940] SASR 395, this condition was held void for uncertainty, and such a condition may now be subject to the decision in *Clayton v Ramsden* [1943] AC 320; and see *Re Borwick, Borwick v Borwick,* above. In *Grayson v Grayson* [1922] St R Qd 155, and *Re Found, Semmens v Loveday* [1924] SASR 301, such a condition had been held good, and in the last case it was held immaterial that the wife had changed her religion after marriage. A condition against ceasing to practise the Roman Catholic religion has been held uncertain: *Burke and O'Reilly v Burke and Quail* [1951] IR 216.

7 *Re Kearney* [1957] VLR 56.

8 *Re Whiting* [1957] VLR 400.

9 *Re Borwick, Borwick v Borwick* [1933] Ch 657; *Re Tegg, Public Trustee v Bryant* [1936] 2 All ER 878; *National Trustees, Executors and Agency Co Ltd v Keast* (1896) 22 VLR 447; *Birtwhistle v Myers* (1899) 25 VLR 306. As to a condition requiring a child to be educated for the priesthood, see *Re Regan* (1957) 8 DLR (2d) 541.

10 *Blathwayt v Lord Cawley* [1975] 3 All ER 625 at 637.

11 *Re May, Eggar v May* [1917] 2 Ch 126; *Patton v Toronto General Trusts Corpn* [1930] AC 629.

12 *Re May, Eggar v May* [1932] 1 Ch 99.

[35.31]

[Updated in footnote 2 for the Equality Act 2010.]

Jewish religion. A condition that a beneficiary should be of the Jewish faith and married to an 'approved wife', who was to be of Jewish blood and worship according to the Jewish faith, has been upheld.[1] A condition against marriage out of the Jewish religion is not void as against public policy,[2] but may be void for uncertainty[3] or as contravening the rule against perpetuities.[4] Where a beneficiary was to forfeit the benefit on marriage with a person not of Jewish parentage and of the Jewish faith it was held that this was only one condition of forfeiture and not two alternative conditions, and the whole would be void if one limb of the condition was void; in this case both limbs were void for uncertainty.[5] Where a daughter was married to a Jew and was not to take until she ceased to be the wife of a Jew, the condition was held void.[6]

1 *Re Tuck's Settlement Trusts, Public Trustee v Tuck* [1978] 1 All ER 1047; the relevant clause is set out above at para **[35.8]**, n 2. See also *Re Tepper's Will Trusts, Kramer v Ruda* [1987] Ch 358, [1987] 1 All ER 970, discussed para **[35.29]** above.

2 *Hodgson v Halford* (1879) 11 Ch 959; *Re Moss, Fox v Moss* [1919] VLR 192. It is, however, a condition in terrorem and in the absence of a gift over is ineffective: *Re Berens* (1888) 5 TLR 473. See footnote 4 to para **[34.12]** above.

3 *Re Blaiberg, Blaiberg and Public Trustee v De Andia Yrarrazaval and Blaiberg* [1940] Ch 385, [1940] 1 All ER 632; *Clayton v Ramsden* [1943] AC 320, [1943] 1 All ER 16; *Re Donn, Donn*

v Moses [1944] Ch 8, [1943] 2 All ER 564; *Re Moss's Trusts, Moss v Allen* [1945] 1 All ER 207; *Re Tarnpolsk, Barclays Bank Ltd v Hyer* [1958] 3 All ER 479; *Re Krawitz's Will Trusts, Krawitz v Crawford* [1959] 3 All ER 793; *Re Selby's Will Trusts, Donn v Selby* [1965] 3 All ER 386 (where the condition was held valid); *Re Solomon, Solomon v Solomon* [1946] ALR 195; *Perpetual Trustee Co Ltd v Wansey* (1945) 46 SRNSW 226; *Re Abraham's Will Trusts, Caplan v Abrahams* [1969] 1 Ch 463, [1967] 2 All ER 1175 (condition precedent as to marriage to a person professing the Jewish faith is sufficiently certain).

4 See para **[35.52]**, n 4.

5 *Clayton v Ramsden* [1943] AC 320, [1943] 1 All ER 16. But see now *Re Tuck's Settlement Trusts, Public Trustee v Tuck* [1978] 1 All ER 1047; and *Blathwayt v Lord Cawley* [1975] 3 All ER 625.

6 *Re Hurshman* (1956) 6 DLR 615.

[35.32]

[Updated in footnote 3 for the Equality Act 2010.]

Church of England. A condition to conform to and be members of the Church of England is not void for uncertainty.[1] A condition to be a member of the Church of England and an adherent to the doctrine of that church is not void for uncertainty where it is a qualification or limitation or condition precedent and, where it is a condition precedent, it is open to the beneficiary to prove that he is a member of that church and to prove his adherence to the doctrine of that church.[2] Where a will provided for payment of legacies at twenty-five years and that they should not be paid until the legatees had been confirmed as members of the Church of England, and included a gift over in the case of legatees who attained twenty-five without having been so confirmed, it was held that the condition was a condition precedent, and, even if it were a condition subsequent, it was not against public policy or void as being impossible of performance.[3] A condition that certain legacies for Church of England missions should be void if a particular person was employed by or held Holy Orders in the Church of England has been held valid and not against public policy.[4]

1 *Re Mills' Will Trusts, Yorkshire Insurance Co Ltd v Coward* [1967] 2 All ER 193, [1967] 1 WLR 837 (proviso that if a grandchild should not be a 'member of the Church of England or of some Church abroad professing the same tenets' then share to be forfeited; held, the description was not void for uncertainty since the tenets of the Church of England, being part of the law of England by virtue of the Act of Uniformity 1662, were not uncertain. The Methodist Church of Australia was not within this definition. But see *Re Tegg, Public Trustee v Bryant* [1936] 2 All ER 878, where a similar condition was void for uncertainty since it was open to grave doubts whether any particular act or omission in the future would bring about a forfeiture; *Clavering v Ellison* (1859) 7 HL Cas 707 (educated in England and in the Protestant faith according to the rites of the Church of England, but in this case it was only held that the condition was to be construed strictly).

2 *Re Allen, Faith v Allen* [1953] Ch 810, [1953] 2 All ER 898; *Re Mills' Will Trusts, Yorkshire Insurance Co Ltd v Coward* [1967] 2 All ER 193, [1967] 1 WLR 837. See also *Re Cowley* [1971] NZLR 468.

3 *Re Forbes, Harrison v Commis* [1928] 3 DLR 22. In this case it was also held that a legatee who was so confirmed at the age of thirty-one had not substantially complied with the condition. See footnote 4 to para **[34.12]** above.

4 *Re Rice, Turner v Rice* [1920] VLR 44.

[35.33]

[Updated in footnote 5 for the Equality Act 2010.]

Protestant faith. A condition that children shall be brought up in the Protestant faith is void both as being uncertain and as interfering with the duty of the parent to bring children up in such religion as he deems best for their moral and spiritual welfare.[1] A condition precedent that a minor shall be educated in the Protestant faith and power given to trustees of the will to determine in their absolute discretion whether or not that is so does not prevent the trustees contributing to the cost of such education during the contingency of the gift, for it is still possible that the condition might be fulfilled.[2] Where the condition is a condition precedent and has not been complied with, it is immaterial to inquire whether or not it is a valid condition.[3] A condition that a legatee should marry a Protestant wife, the daughter of Protestant parents, has been held good,[4] but this might now perhaps be held uncertain.[5] 'Protestant' means a church or sect separated from the Roman Communion in the sixteenth century or the subsequent offshoots of any such sect which professes Christianity.[6]

1 *Clavering v Ellison* (1859) 7 HL Cas 707; *Re Cross, Law v Cross* [1938] VLR 221; *Perpetual Trustee Co v Hogg* (1936) 36 SRNSW 61.
2 *Re Mercer* [1953] OWN 765.
3 *Re Going* [1951] 2 DLR 136.
4 *Re Knox's Goods* (1889) 23 LR Ir 542; *Mainwaring v Mainwaring* (1923) 23 SRNSW 531.
5 See *Clayton v Ramsden* [1943] AC 320. In Australia a condition for forfeiture on marrying anyone not of the Protestant religion or following any religion other than the Protestant religion has been held to be two independent conditions. The first was held certain and valid but the second is uncertain and void: *Re Winzar* (1953) 55 WALR 35. Also see now the Human Rights Act 1998 and the Equality Act 2010.
6 *Re Winzar* (1953) 55 WALR 35.

[35.34]

[Updated in footnote 1 for the Equality Act 2010.]

Conditions as to solemnisation of marriage. A condition that marriages of legatees should be solemnised according to the rites of any church recognised by the local law has been held a valid condition,[1] and so was a condition forbidding marriage contrary to the order and established rules of the people called Quakers.[2]

1 *Renaud v Lamothe* (1902) 32 SCR 357. This will also directed that the children of any such marriage should be educated according to the teachings of such church and this condition was held good, but at the present time this condition would probably be held invalid as against the rights of parents in this respect. See footnote 4 to para **[34.12]** above.
2 *Haughton v Haughton* (1824) 1 Mol 611.

[35.36]

[Typo in text corrected.]

Generally invalid. Conditions tending to the separation of parent and child are invalid as against public policy.[1] Where a testator whose daughter was living separate from her husband restricted the benefit to such of the daughter's children as should reside with her, the condition was unenforceable and the children were entitled in any event.[2] Similarly a condition not to live with or be under the control of a father is void.[3] Conditions requiring either parents or children to reside in a certain place or country may, if they entail such separation, be void.[4] It is unlikely that conditions would be void under this head as hindering or preventing the parent in the choice or supervision of the child's education. Thus a bequest for the benefit of a child to help with paying his school fees payable on condition of his going to a particular school, would be upheld.[5] Likewise a bequest on condition of his not going to a particular type of school, ought not to be contrary to public policy.[6] The same approach would apply to a requirement that a child be educated in a religious denominational school.[7] In special circumstances a condition that a father should not interfere with the education of his children was enforced.[8]

1 *Re Sandbrook, Noel v Sandbrook* [1912] 2 Ch 471; *Re Ellis, Perpetual Trustee Co Ltd v Ellis* (1929) 29 SRNSW 470; but a condition that an adult child shall not live with her mother has been held good: *McDonald v Trustees, Executors and Agency Co Ltd* (1902) 28 VLR 442.
2 *Re Morgan, Dowson v Davey* (1910) 26 TLR 398.
3 *Re Sandbrook, Noel v Sandbrook* [1912] 2 Ch 471; *Re Piper, Dodd v Piper* [1946] 2 All ER 503 (where the father was already divorced).
4 *Re Boulter, Capital and Counties Bank v Boulter* [1922] 1 Ch 75.
5 *Blathwayt v Lord Cawley* [1976] AC 397, [1975] 3 All ER 625, per Lord Cross at 644, and Lord Fraser at 650.
6 *Blathwayt v Lord Cawley* [1976] AC 397, [1975] 3 All ER 625, per Lord Cross at 644, and Lord Fraser at 650.
7 *Blathwayt v Lord Cawley* [1976] AC 397, [1975] 3 All ER 625, not following *Re Borwick, Borwick v Borwick* [1933] Ch 657; and *Re Tegg, Public Trustee v Bryant* [1936] 2 All ER 878.
8 *Colston v Morris* (1821) Jac 257n. It appeared that the parents were separated and the father a man of small means compared with the mother. The legacy was given by the grandfather and the trustees of the will were appointed guardians of the infant.

VIII. NOT TO DISPUTE WILL

[35.38]

[Reference to *Nathan v Leonard* [2003] 4 All ER 198 updated in footnote 3 and updated in text and footnote 10 for *Creasey v Sole* [2013] EWHC 1410 (Ch), [2013] WTLR 931.]

Beneficiary's rights protected. A condition not to dispute a will is not void for uncertainty, nor as being contrary to good morals or public policy, nor prohibited by any positive law,[1] but, on the other hand, it is not broken if the proceedings taken by the legatee are necessary for the protection of his rights.[2]Where a claim was brought under the Inheritance (Provision for Family and Dependants) Act 1975 it was held that such a condition was not void because, although the claim could amount to a contest or disagreement with the will, the claim would still be before the courts.[3] Proceedings for the revocation of probate are a breach[4] and so presumably are frivolous proceedings.[5] Such a condition is a condition in terrorem and in the case of personalty is void unless there is a gift over.[6]

Where, however, the clause attempts to oust the jurisdiction of the court, it is both repugnant and contrary to public policy.[7] Thus a clause making the trustees' decision final and binding upon all questions of doubt arising in the execution of the trusts of the will is invalid,[8] and so was a clause which made the trustees' decision final as to the identity of a beneficiary.[9] However, provisions giving the executors a discretion to determine specific matters which could give rise to uncertainty, such as whether a condition has been fulfilled, or the boundaries of parts of the land, may, by analogy with provisions for expert determination in contracts, be valid.[10]

1 *Evanturel v Evanturel* (1874) LR 6 PC 1; *Cooke v Turner* (1846) 15 M & W 727; *Stevenson v Abington* (1863) 9 LT 74.
2 *Powell v Morgan* (1688) 2 Vern 90; *Rhodes v Muswell Hill Land Co* (1861) 29 Beav 560; *Warbrick v Varley (No 2)* (1861) 30 Beav 347; *Phillips v Phillips* [1877] WN 260; *Wallace v Wallace* (1898) 24 VLR 859; *Re Kent* (1982) 139 DLR (3d) 318.
3 *Nathan v Leonard* [2002] EWHC 1701 (Ch), [2003] 4 All ER 198, [2003] 1 WLR 827. In fact the condition was held void for uncertainty in that case.
4 *Stevenson v Abington* (1863) 9 LT 74.
5 *Nutt v Burrell* (1724) Cas temp King 1; *Adams v Adams* [1892] 1 Ch 369. This was a gift of an annuity with a proviso for cesser if the annuitant should in any way intermeddle or interfere or attempt to intermeddle or interfere in the management of the estate. The annuitant brought a frivolous action against the trustees for a receiver. This was an attempt to interfere and caused the annuity to cease, but an action in defence of the annuity, it was said, would not have been within the proviso.
6 *Morris v Burroughs* (1737) 1 Atk 399; *Lloyd and Jobson v Spillet* (1741) 2 Atk 148; *Warbrick v Varley (No 2)* (1861) 30 Beav 347; *Re Gaynor's Will* [1960] VLR 640 (where an application made under the Family Maintenance Acts was held to be in order as the condition was void). As to conditions in terrorem, see para **[34.13]** above.
7 *Re Raven* [1915] 1 Ch 673; *Re Wynn* [1952] Ch 271, [1952] 1 All ER 341.
8 *Re Wynn* [1952] Ch 271, [1952] 1 All ER 341.
9 *Re Raven* [1915] 1 Ch 673.
10 Where the executors had a discretion to withhold a gift if they were satisfied that a hospital had been taken over by the state or a local authority, their decision was held to be final so long as it was arrived at reasonably and honestly; *Dundee General Hospital v Walker* [1952] 1 All ER 896, HL. In *Re Tuck's Settlement Trusts* [1978] Ch 49, [1978] 1 All ER 104, CA, Lord Denning MR, unsupported by the other two judges, expressed the view that *Re Wynn* and *Re Raven* need to be reconsidered in the light of *Dundee General Hospital v Walker*. See also the remarks of Morgan J in *Creasey v Sole* [2013] EWHC 1410 (Ch), [2013] WTLR 931 at paras 65 and 66.

[35.40]

[Updated in the text and in footnote 12 for *Howard v Howard-Lawson* [2012] 3 All ER 60.]

Assumption of name. If the condition does not state the method by which the name is to be assumed, a voluntary assumption of the name is sufficient.[1] There seems to have been some difference of opinion as to whether a minor can voluntarily change his name.[2] A minor can change his name by deed poll but, if the minor is not of the age of 16 years, the deed poll must be signed by the guardian on behalf of the minor. After his sixteenth birthday the minor can himself sign or the guardian can sign on his behalf, but if the minor signs, the guardian should witness the signature in order to show his consent.[3] A Christian name, it has been said, cannot be changed by deed poll.[4] If the condition requires the devisee to take the new name for himself and his heirs it has been said that a grant from the Queen or an Act of Parliament is necessary,[5] though changes by deed poll in practice adopt the name for the person executing the deed poll and his minor children (who need not be named in the deed) and, where they are named and execute the deed also for his adult children,[6] the condition as generally drafted requires the beneficiary to 'take and use' the name and this means that the use of the name is to be continued and a discontinuance involves a forfeiture.'[7] A direction for use 'upon all occasions' is not void for uncertainty;[8] nor is such a clause contrary to public policy merely because it is so drawn as to impose an obligation of change of name on a husband to whom a woman is married or whom she may thereafter marry.[9] The beneficiary is not now usually directed as to how he is to acquire the new name[10] and then all methods of acquiring the new name are open to him.[11] Where a name and arms clause required the name to be assumed and the arms to be applied for within one year it was held that the obligation to assume the name was not an independent obligation when the heir decided to seek a Royal Licence to take both the arms and the name, so that where the application for a Royal Licence was made but not granted within the year, there was no 'refusal' or 'neglect' to take up the name for the purposes of the forfeiture provision.[12]

1 *Doe d Luscombe v Yates* (1822) 5 B & Ald 544; *Davies v Lowndes* (1835) 1 Bing NC 597; *Earl of Cowley v Countess of Cowley* [1901] AC 450; *Re Earl of Midleton's Will Trusts, Whitehead v Earl of Midleton* [1969] 1 Ch 600, [1967] 2 All ER 834 (gift of income to the person who shall succeed to a peerage on the death of the present holder is ineffective since that person cannot be ascertained until such death); *Blathwayt v Lord Cawley* [1976] AC 397, [1975] 3 All ER 625 (where the requirement was 'either with or without his or her own proper surname'). But see *Littras v Littras* [1995] 2 VR 283, where a names clause was regarded as anachronistic and as infringing the right of an individual to use the surname of his own choosing.

2 See *Re Talbot* [1932] IR 714.

3 This is believed to be the practice of the Enrolment Office of the High Court.

4 *Re Parrott, Cox v Parrott* [1946] Ch 183, [1946] 1 All ER 321. But a Christian name may be changed by Act of Parliament or at confirmation, and an additional name may be added on adoption. It is submitted, however, that this principle must be limited to baptismal names. First names of persons other than Christians may, it is submitted, be changed in the same manner as surnames, and where the only change is to anglicise a foreign form of the Christian names there seems to be no objection to it. There is also no authority to say that a new name cannot be obtained at common law by use. In general it is intended, though not generally so stated, that the change of name shall be effected by deed poll.

5 *Gulliver d Corrie v Ashby* (1766) 4 Burr 1929 at 1940.

6 Where adult children so execute the deed; it must be stamped with an additional 50p stamp for each adult child so executing.

7 *Re Drax, Dunsany v Sawbridge* (1906) 75 LJ Ch 317; *Blagrove v Bradshaw* (1858) 4 Drew 230. The condition usually makes provision for the beneficiary to be excused from taking the name when he would thereby forfeit some other property.

8 *Re Neeld, Carpenter v Inigo-Jones* [1962] Ch 643, [1962] 2 All ER 335; overruling *Re Lewis' Will Trust, Whitelaw v Beaumont* [1951] WN 591; *Re Bouverie, Bouverie v Marshall* [1952] Ch 400, [1952] 1 All ER 408; *Re Wood's Will Trusts, Wood v Donnelly* [1952] Ch 406, [1952] 1 All ER 740; and *Re Kersey, Alington v Alington* [1952] WN 541.

9 *Re Neeld, Carpenter v Inigo-Jones* [1962] Ch 643, [1962] 2 All ER 335, overruling *Re Fry, Reynolds v Denne* [1945] Ch 348, [1945] 2 All ER 205; and *Re Kersey, Alington v Alington* [1952] WN 541, approving *Re Lewis' Will Trust, Whitelaw v Beaumont* [1951] WN 591.

10 The usual form is 'to use and bear the name and arms of'. In *Re Parrott, Cox v Parrott* [1946] Ch 183, [1946] 1 All ER 321, the beneficiary was directed 'by deed poll' to assume the name, but this, it is thought, is unusual; and it is thought that the older form 'apply for and endeavour to obtain a licence from the Crown to take use and bear' the specific name and arms is not now used. The arms, however, cannot be borne without proper authority; see para **[35.42]** below.

11 *Davies v Lowndes* (1835) 1 Bing NC 597 (the name may be acquired by use).

12 *Howard v Howard-Lawson* [2012] 3 All ER 60.

CHAPTER 36

Secret trusts

I. GIFT IN WILL ABSOLUTE

[36.2]

[Updated in the text to footnotes 7 and 9 and in footnotes 6, 7 and 9 for *Kasperbauer v Griffith* [2000] WTLR 333, CA. Also updated in footnote 7 for *Margulies v Margulies* [2008] WTLR 1871, CA.]

Where gift in terms absolute. The law requires every testamentary disposition to be duly executed and attested as a will or codicil,[1] but this requirement of the law is not carried to the length at which it would enable an apparent donee to act fraudulently. Therefore, where a testator makes, or leaves unrevoked, a disposition on the faith of a promise, whether express or tacit, on the part of the donee that he will carry out the testator's intentions with respect thereto,[2] equity will admit evidence[3] as to the testator's intentions and the communication thereof to the donee and his acquiescence therein, and will compel the donee, as being a trustee, to carry out the testator's intentions,[4] unless they are such as are prohibited by law.[5] Thus the essential elements of a secret trust are: the intention of the testator to subject the primary donee to an obligation in favour of the secondary donee; the communication of that intention to the primary donee; and the acceptance of that obligation by the primary donee either expressly or by acquiescence.[6] The obligation must satisfy the traditional requirement of three certainties for a trust, namely language in imperative form, certainty of subject-matter and certainty of objects or beneficiaries.[7] The method by which the primary donee is to carry out the obligation, whether by making a will in favour of the secondary donee or by some form of inter vivos transfer, is immaterial.[8] It is open to the testator or the legatee accepting the gift to change his mind before the gift takes effect on the death.[9]

1 Wills Act 1837, s 9; as substituted by the Administration of Justice Act 1982, s 17; Vol 2, Part G, para **[244.7]**.

2 Though the language used sometimes seems to point to a basis of implied contract, this doctrine has always been explained as the prevention of an act of fraud on the part of the apparent beneficiary. The word 'fraud' in this connection must not be construed in the *Derry v Peek* (1889) 14 App Cas 337 sense, but as something which equity will prevent as being unconscionable. Cf the case of *Tharp v Tharp* [1916] 1 Ch 142, where a testator was induced to revoke a codicil and thus revive a power of appointment upon an undertaking that the power would be exercised in a certain way and the same equitable doctrine was applied to enforce the power being exercised in that way. The case, however, went to appeal and was settled on terms, [1916] 2 Ch 205.

3 If a will contains a gift which is in terms absolute, clear evidence is needed before the court will assume that the testator did not mean what he said but intended that the gift should be

held by the beneficiary subject to a secret trust. The standard of proof is perhaps analogous to that which the court requires before it will rectify a written instrument; per Brightman J in *Ottaway v Norman* [1972] Ch 698 at 712, [1971] 3 All ER 1325 at 1333.

4 *Wallgrave v Tebbs* (1855) 2 K & J 313; *McCormick v Grogan* (1869) LR 4 HL 82; *Moss v Cooper* (1861) 1 John & H 352; *Jones v Badley* (1868) 3 Ch App 362; *McDonald v Moran* (1938) 12 MPR 424; *MacMillan v Kennedy* [1942] 3 DLR 170; *Re Pugh's Will Trusts, Marten v Pugh* [1967] 3 All ER 337, [1967] 1 WLR 1262; it is easier to infer an intention that a sole trustee should take beneficially than that two or more trustees should do so, but that indication is not sufficient alone. Where a deceased spouse has bequeathed property to a surviving spouse and it is sought to prove a secret trust in favour of a particular person, the surviving spouse can be compelled to give evidence as to communications made between the spouses during the marriage: *Shenton v Tyler* [1939] Ch 620, [1939] 1 All ER 827, and see para **[36.13]** below.

5 Most of the cases turn upon gifts or charities being illegal under the Mortmain Acts: *Muckleston v Brown* (1801) 6 Ves 52; *Stickland v Aldridge* (1804) 9 Ves 516; *Russell v Jackson* (1852) 10 Hare 204; *Springett v Jenings* (1871) 6 Ch App 333; *Tee v Ferris* (1856) 2 K & J 357; *Rowbothan v Dunnett* (1878) 8 Ch D 430. As to the effect of a trust being illegal, see n 2, para **[36.4]** below, and text thereto. The Mortmain Acts have now been repealed by the Charities Act 1960, s 38.

6 *Ottaway v Norman* [1972] Ch 698, [1971] 3 All ER 1325; *Kasperbauer v Griffith* [2000] WTLR 333 (CA).

7 *Kasperbauer v Griffith* [2000] WTLR 333 (CA); *Margulies v Margulies* [2008] WTLR 1871 (CA). If there is any question as to what part of the property is affected by the trust, the onus is on the donee to show what part is not affected by it: *Russell v Jackson* (1852) 10 Hare 204.

8 *Ottaway v Norman* [1972] Ch 698, [1971] 3 All ER 1325 (primary donee's executor obliged to hold a bungalow on trust for secondary donee in accordance with the terms of a secret trust that the primary donee would, on his death, devise the bungalow to the secondary donee).

9 *Kasperbauer v Griffith* [2000] WTLR 333, CA.

[36.5]

[Updated in footnote 7 for a change in the rate of interest on general legacies with effect from 1 February 2009.]

Effect of failure of trusts. If the secret trust is illegal, the apparent beneficiary holds the property on trust for those who would have taken if the gift had not been contained in the will.[1] Where, however, the trust is not illegal, but fails because, though not void in law, it cannot take effect,[2] or because it is not communicated to the donee,[3] or because it is not assented to by the donee during the lifetime of the testator,[4] the donee takes the gift absolutely and free from the trust.[5] If, therefore, in any such circumstances the donee does in fact apply the gift to the object indicated by the testator, he does so as a voluntary gift from himself.[6] Where the trusts fail as to part of the gift or where they relate in the first instance to part only of the gift the donee takes absolutely subject to the performance of the trusts, the benefits under the trusts being treated as legacies carrying interest after the expiration of one year from the testator's death.[7]

If there is any question as to what part of the property is affected by the trust, the onus is on the donee to show what part is not affected by it.[8]

1 That is to say it falls into residue or passes on intestacy according to the circumstances: see Chapter 48.

2 *Russell v Jackson* (1852) 10 Hare 204.

3 *Carter v Green* (1857) 3 K & J 591.

4 *Podmore v Gunning* (1836) 7 Sim 644; *Jones v Badley* (1868) 3 Ch App 362.

5 *Russell v Jackson* (1852) 10 Hare 204; *Re Gardom, Le Page v A-G* [1914] 1 Ch 662 at 672; revsd sub nom *Le Page v Gardom* (1915) 84 LJ Ch 749.
6 *Lomax v Ripley* (1855) 3 Sm & G 48 at 78; *Geddis v Semple* [1903] 1 IR 73.
7 *Irvine v Sullivan* (1869) LR 8 Eq 673; RSC Ord 44, r 10; SI 1982/1111; the current rate of interest set by the court is 2 per cent with effect from 1 February 2009, substituted for the previous rate of 4 per cent: Civil Procedure Rules, Part 40, *Practice Direction– Accounts, Inquiries etc*, para 15, see para **[32.4]**, n 1.
8 *Russell v Jackson* (1852) 10 Hare 204; *Re Huxtable, Huxtable v Crawfurd* [1902] 2 Ch 793.

CHAPTER 38

Residuary gifts

II. WHAT AMOUNTS TO A GIFT OF RESIDUE

[38.10]

[Updated at footnote 1 for *Day v Harris* [2013] EWCA Civ 191, [2013] WTLR 591 (CA).]

Ejusdem generis rule. Under this rule general words following particular words are restricted to articles or property of the same kind as those already enumerated or mentioned. The rule in general is subject to two important qualifications which restrict its general application and to one which restricts its application in the particular case of wills. In general, the particular words must, for the rule to apply, have some common characteristic which constitutes them a class or genus and then the rule applies to sweep in all other things of the same class, for the real purpose of the rule is to guard against accidental omissions.[1] The other general qualification, much less important, is that, if the particular words exhaust the whole class, there is nothing upon which the rule can operate and the general words then must refer to some larger class.[2] In the case of wills, the rule is commonly overridden by the presumption that, if a person makes a will, he does not intend to die intestate as to any part of his property, and, therefore, the will must be construed so as to prevent that result.[3] For this reason where general words occur in a clause in the nature of a residuary gift, the rule is not generally applied because the general words are often used for the very purpose of preventing the bequest from being so restricted.[4] This consideration, however, is not applied where the general words would in the wider meaning carry a residuary estate which is dealt with by another clause in the will;[5] nor where there is an intention to deal with a particular portion of the estate or property referred to as being in a particular locality.[6] From the general statement of the rule it applies only where the general words followed the specific enumeration, and it has been generally held not to apply where the general words precede the particular enumeration, so that, if the general words are such as would pass the residuary estate, they have that effect.[7] Again the testator may by express exception from a general description show that he intends to include that class of property in the gift, and, if that class of property is beyond a construction according to the ejusdem generis rule, the testator thus shows that the rule is not to apply. Then the disposition must be taken to carry all which has not been expressly excluded.[8]

1 *Lambourn v McLellan* [1903] 2 Ch 268; *Re Turner, Arnold v Blades* (1891) 36 Sol Jo 28. Where it is shown that there is no class or genus, the general words receive the widest interpretation; see, for example: *National Association of Local Government Officers v Bolton*

Corpn [1943] AC 166, [1942] 2 All ER 425. Where there is only one particular word followed by general words, it has been said that the rule does not apply: see *Arnold v Arnold* (1834) 2 My & K 365; *Swinfen v Swinfen (No 4)* (1860) 29 Beav 207; *Campbell v M'Grain* (1875) IR 9 Eq 397 at 400; though this principle was not applied in *Northey v Paxton* (1888) 60 LT 30 (all household furniture and effects in residence held not to include jewellery), and there is no rule that general words cannot be so cut down: *Northey v Paxton* (1888) 60 LT 30; *Re O'Brien, O'Brien v O'Brien* [1906] 1 IR 649 at 653. The principle has been applied to investment clauses: see *Edwards v Thompson* (1868) 38 LJ Ch 65, and *Re Castlehow, Lamonby v Carter* [1903] 1 Ch 352 (companies restricted to English companies); but see *Re Stanley, Tennant v Stanley* [1906] 1 Ch 131, where the context showed that no restriction was intended. The following are examples of general words: 'etc': see para **[38.11]** below; 'other things': *Trafford v Berrige* (1729) 1 Eq Cas Abr 201; *Re Smith's Goods* (1864) 3 Sw & Tr 589; *Stuart v Marquis of Bute* (1813) 1 Dow 73; 'all other societies': *Marks v Solomons* (1850) 2 H & Tw 323; 'other articles of a like nature': *Stone v Parker* (1860) 1 Drew & Sm 212; 'other articles': *Dutton v Hockenhull* (1874) 22 WR 701; 'all other goods of whatever kind': *Wrench v Jutting* (1841) 3 Beav 521. The general words may be restricted by one of themselves to a particular class of property: thus the words 'all other my personal estate property chattels and effects whatsoever and wheresoever to which I am now seised possessed or entitled to or may hereafter acquire and can hereby dispose of', despite their generality in some respects, were restricted by the word 'personal' occurring in them and realty did not pass under them: *Jones v Robinson* (1878) 3 CPD 344, and cf *Lampheir v Despard* (1842) 2 Dr & War 59. In *Re Resch's Will Trusts. Le Cras v Perpetual Trustee Co Ltd, Far West Children's Health Scheme v Perpetual Trustee Co Ltd* [1969] 1 AC 514, [1967] 3 All ER 915, PC, it was held that a gift to a boy of 'my cameras projectors films and other photographic appliances and my watches (other than my calendar watch) chain studs and other personal jewellery' did not include the valuable jewellery which the testator had inherited from his deceased wife, since the words 'other personal jewellery' should be construed ejusdem generis with the description that preceded them. By way of contrast, in *Day v Harris* [2013] EWCA Civ 191, [2013] WTLR 591 (CA), a gift of 'my household goods and possessions … including any manuscripts scores and musical literary or other written material', was not limited to manuscripts and scores within the house of the testator, Sir Malcolm Arnold, but included those on deposit at the Royal College of Music.

2 *Fenwick v Schmalz* (1868) LR 3 CP 313 at 315.

3 *Bridges v Bridges* (1729) 2 Eq Cas Abr 330; *Chalmers v Stroil* (1813) 2 Ves & B 222; *Re Kendall's Trusts* (1851) 14 Beav 608; *Gibbs v Lawrence* (1860) 30 LJ Ch 170; *Dean v Gibson* (1867) LR 3 Eq 713 (cases of enumeration of particulars, 'viz', 'consisting of' and the like), applied in *Re Johnston* (1970) 7 DLR (3d) 256; *Shepherd v Nottidge* (1862) 2 John & H 766; *Re Parrott, Parrott v Parrott* (1885) 53 LT 12.

4 *Parker v Marchant* (1842) 1 Y & C Ch Cas 290; *Everall v Browne* (1853) 1 Sm & G 368; *Harris v James* (1864) 12 WR 509; *Hodgson v Jex* (1876) 2 Ch D 122; *Re Parrott, Parrott v Parrott* (1885) 53 LT 12.

5 *Woolcomb v Woolcomb* (1731) 3 P Wms 112; *Mullins v Smith* (1860) 1 Drew & Sm 204; *Smith v Davis* (1866) 35 LJ Ch 874; *Campbell v M'Grain* (1875) IR 9 Eq 397; *Hutchinson v Rough* (1879) 40 LT 289; *Re Miller, Daniel v Daniel* (1889) 61 LT 365; *MacPhail v Phillips* [1904] 1 IR 155; *Trustees, Executors and Agency Co Ltd v Ramsey* (1920) 27 CLR 279. Similarly, it may appear from other parts of the will that the clause is not intended to be a residuary gift: see *Rawlings v Jennings* (1806) 13 Ves 39; *Re Curling's Goods* [1928] IR 521; or the same may appear from a codicil: *Sutton v Sharp* (1826) 1 Russ 146; or where the residuary property cannot be required for a particular purpose to which the will would, construing it as a residuary gift, require it to be put: *Borton v Dunbar* (1860) 2 De GF & J 338.

6 *Gibbs v Lawrence* (1860) 30 LJ Ch 170.

7 *Re Kendall's Trust* (1851) 14 Beav 608; *Fisher v Hepburn* (1851) 14 Beav 626; *Drake v Martin* (1856) 23 Beav 89; *Nugee v Chapman (No 2)* (1860) 29 Beav 290; *Dean v Gibson* (1867) LR 3 Eq 713; *Re Maberly's Settlement Trusts* (1871) 24 LT 262; *King v George* (1877) 5 Ch D 627; *Re Fleetwood, Sidgreaves v Brewer* (1880) 15 Ch D 594; *Re Roberts, Kiff v Roberts* (1886) 55 LT 498; *Re Duffell, Equity Trustees, Executors and Agency Co Ltd v Duffell* [1926] VLR 489; *Tighe v Featherstonhaugh* (1883) 13 LR IR 401; *Re Recknell, White v Carter* [1936] 2 All ER 36. But the subsequent particular words may be a qualifying and defining

statement substituted for the antecedent generality, when the gift will be confined to the particular words: *Sutton v Sharp* (1826) 1 Russ 146 (where the subsequent words were in a codicil); *Re Fletcher* (1914) 19 DLR 624.

8 *Hotham v Sutton* (1808) 15 Ves 319 ('other effects, money excepted': the gift included all property except money); but see *Cross v Wilks* (1866) 35 Beav 562 ('effects' controlled by the rule and real estate excluded).

V. WHERE THE RESIDUARY ESTATE IS SETTLED–DEATHS BEFORE 1 OCTOBER 2013

[38.16A]

The former presumptions as to apportionment. Prior to 1 October 2013 when the Trusts (Capital and Income) Act 2013[1] was brought into force,[2] it was presumed under s 2 of the Apportionment Act 1870 that as between successive beneficial interests income was to be apportioned on a time basis and certain equitable rules of apportionment adjusting the interests of capital and income were also presumed to apply. The statutory presumption as to the time apportionment of income and the equitable rules of apportionment known as the rule in *Howe v Dartmouth* (in both its branches), the rule in *Re Earl of Chesterfield's Trusts* and the rule in *Allhusen v Whittell* have been disapplied by s 1 of the 2013 Act in relation to any 'new trust', i e any trust created or arising on or after 1 October 2013 (the day on which s 1 was brought into force), including a trust created or arising under a power conferred before that day: s 1(4). Since a will takes effect only on the testator's death, the disapplication of these presumptions will apply in relation to the will of any person dying on or after 1 October 2013. The disapplication of the presumptions referred to above is subject to any contrary intention: s 1(5). The law as stated in paras **[38.17]** to **[38.28]** below continues to apply in relation to trusts created or arising prior to 1 October 2013.

The 2013 Act does not disapply all rules of equitable apportionment. The rules in *Re Bird* and *Re Atkinson* which apply when a debt or security comprised in a settled fund or estate is insufficient to discharge the principal and arrears of interest due (as to which see in para **[38.28]** below) are not disapplied by the Act and continue to apply.

1 For the text of the relevant parts of the Act, see Volume 2, paras **[246.202]** ff.

2 Sections 1 to 3 of the Act were brought into force on 1 October 2013 by the Trusts (Capital and Income) Act 2013 (Commencement No 1) Order 2013 (SI 2013/676).

[38.28]

[Updated for *Re Atkinson, Barbers' Company v Grose-Smith* [1904] 2 Ch 160, CA]

Other rights of tenant for life of residue. Where funds are set aside to answer legacies or annuities, the tenant for life of residue is entitled to the income of them which is not otherwise disposed of or by law payable to those entitled to the fund.[1] Where trustees enter into possession of mortgaged property being part of the residue, the tenant for life is entitled to so much of the rents as is equal to the interest on the mortgage and, if the rents be less, he is entitled to have this made up on a sale of the property, but without interest on arrears of income.[2] Where an authorised investment has in breach of trust been sold and the proceeds of sale invested in an unauthorised investment, then under the rule in *Re Bird* the whole transaction is reopened whether or not the tenant for life has been a party to the breach of trust.[3] In the more usual case where an authorised debt or security proves insufficient to discharge the principal and arrears of interest, then under the rule in *Re Atkinson* the sum realised on the sale of the security at a loss is apportioned between the life tenant and remainderman in the proportions which the amount due for arrears of interest bears to the amount due in respect of the capital debt.[3a] Payments due to the estate such as annual sums payable under an insurance policy for some years after the death of the testator or on the failure of a trust for accumulation are not income to which the tenant for life is entitled but capital which must be invested.[4] Where the reversion on a lease is purchased under compulsory powers, the tenant for life is entitled to the income from the invested compensation moneys up to the amount of the rent until the time when the lease would have expired, and from that date he is entitled to the whole income and the income from any accumulations in the earlier period.[5] Where the lease is purchased compulsorily, the tenant for life is entitled to such an annuity, to be fixed by an actuary, as would exhaust the compensation in the number of years of the unexpired part of the term whether that be greater or less than the rent.[6] Where a sum charged on freeholds and leaseholds is not raised until the leaseholds have decreased in value, an adjustment has been made,[7] but no adjustment is made where debts are directed to be paid out of income but are in fact paid out of capital.[8] Where sums are paid under a scheme of arrangement in respect of debentures the interest on which has not been paid for some time, an apportionment is made.[9] Where sums are received by the trustees of a will and the person paying those sums describes them as capital or income, the trustees must inquire into the source of those sums to establish their true nature.[10]

1 *Crawley v Crawley* (1835) 7 Sim 427; *Fullerton v Martin* (1860) 1 Drew & Sm 31; *Re Whithead, Peacock v Lucas* [1894] 1 Ch 678; *Re Fenwick's Will Trusts, Fenwick v Stewart* [1936] Ch 720, [1936] 2 All ER 1096.

2 *Re Moore, Moore v Johnson* (1885) 54 LJ Ch 432; *Re Walker's Settlement Trusts, Watson v Walker* [1936] Ch 280 (debentures). The latter case shows the method of apportionment where the amount realised is insufficient to meet capital and interest.

3 *Re Bird, Re Evans, Dodd v Evans* [1901] 1 Ch 916.

3a *Re Atkinson, Barbers' Company v Grose-Smith* [1904] 2 Ch 160, CA.

4 *Re Fisher, Harris v Fisher* [1943] Ch 377, [1943] 2 All ER 615; and see para **[38.17]**, n 4, above.

5 *Re Wootton's Estate* (1866) LR 1 Eq 589; *Re Mette's Estate* (1868) LR 7 Eq 72; *Re Wilkes' Estate* (1881) 16 Ch D 597; *Cottrell v Cottrell* (1885) 28 Ch D 628.

6 *Re Phillips' Trusts* (1868) LR 6 Eq 250; *Askew v Woodhead* (1880) 14 Ch D 27.

7 *Blake v O'Reily* [1895] 1 IR 479.

8 *Tewert v Lawson* (1874) LR 18 Eq 490; *Norton v Johnstone* (1885) 30 Ch D 649, and see *Re Brandon, Samuels v Brandon* (1932) 49 TLR 48.

9 *Re Morris's Will Trusts, Public Trustee v Morris* [1960] 3 All ER 548, [1960] 1 WLR 1210; and see *Re Pennington, Pennington v Pennington* [1914] 1 Ch 203.

10 *Re Whitehead's Will Trusts, Public Trustee v White* [1959] Ch 579, [1959] 2 All ER 497.

VI. WHERE THE RESIDUARY ESTATE IS SETTLED–DEATHS ON OR AFTER 1 OCTOBER 2013

[38.29]
The presumption as to apportionment of income on a time basis and the so-called rules in *Howe v Earl of Dartmouth, Re Earl of Chesterfield's Trusts* and *Allhusen v Whittell* (see paras **[38.17]** ff above) are frequently excluded as being administratively inconvenient. This is now no longer necessary in relation to the estates of persons dying on or after 1 October 2013 as, in the absence of a contrary intention, all the foregoing presumptions are disapplied by s 1 of the Trusts (Capital and Income) Act 2013[1] which was brought into force on that date.[2]

The rules in *Re Bird* and *Re Atkinson* (which apply when a debt or security comprised in a settled fund or estate is insufficient to discharge the principal and arrears of interest due)[3] are not disapplied by s 1.

1 The relevant provisions of this Act are set out in Volume 2 at paras **[246.200]** ff.
2 By the Trusts (Capital and Income) Act 2013 (Commencement No 1) Order 2013 (SI 2013/676).
3 See para **[38.28]** above as to these rules.

PART I

Failure of gifts

CHAPTER 41

Ademption

I. GENERAL PRINCIPLES

[41.2]

[Updated in footnote 3 for *Re Clements Estate* [2007] WTLR 1717.]

Change in nature of property. Where a change has occurred in the nature of the specific property given, even though effected by Act of Parliament, ademption follows,[1] unless the change is a change in name or form only, and the property exists as substantially the same thing although in a different shape.[2] Whether the property exists substantially the same at the death of the testator is a question of fact.[3]

1 *Frewen v Frewen* (1875) 10 Ch App 610 (advowson affected by Irish Church Act 1869); *Re Slater, Slater v Slater* [1907] 1 Ch 665 (water company acquired by Metropolitan Water Board); *Re Lane, Luard v Lane* (1880) 14 Ch D 856 (debentures into debenture stock).

2 *Oakes v Oakes* (1852) 9 Hare 666; *Re Pilkington's Trusts* (1865) 6 New Rep 246; *Humphreys v Humphreys* (1789) 2 Cox Eq Cas 184; *Re Dorman* [1994] 1 All ER 804.

3 *Re Bridle* (1879) 4 CPD 336 at 341; *Re Slater, Slater v Slater* [1906] 2 Ch 480 at 484 (where the effect of the Wills Act 1837, s 24 (Vol 2, Part G, para **[244.26]**), which makes the will speak and take effect as if executed immediately before the death, is considered, and the description of a particular thing as 'my ring' is contrasted with a generic description of property, in this case 'the interest arising from money invested in the Lambeth Waterworks Co', the latter company having before the death of the testator been taken over by the Metropolitan Water Board: it was held that there was an ademption); *Re Jameson, King v Winn* [1908] 2 Ch 111 at 115 (where on an amalgamation of banks there was held to be no ademption). See also *Re Sikes, Moxon v Crossley* [1927] 1 Ch 364, and *Re Wilson* [1958] Qd R 559; and *Re Puczka Estate* (1970) 10 DLR (3d) 339. In *Re Clements Estate* [2007] WTLR 1717, the Supreme Court of Nova Scotia found that there was no ademption of a gift of a house when it was partly destroyed in a fire which killed the testator because the evidence showed that the substantial damage had occurred only after his death when title to the house had already passed to his personal representatives.

II. PARTICULAR CASES

[41.12]

[Updated in the text and in footnotes 1, 2, 3 and 6 for the Mental Capacity Act 2005.]

Disposals under the Mental Capacity Act 2005 or the Mental Health Act 1983. Where the property of a person lacking capacity ('P') has been disposed[1] of by a deputy or by the Court of Protection exercising its powers under the Mental Capacity Act 2005, and under P's will or intestacy[2] another person would have taken an interest in the property but for the disposal, and on P's death any property belonging to P's estate represents the property disposed of, the other person takes the same interest if and so far as circumstances allow in the property representing the property disposed of.[3] Similarly, where any property of a person of unsound mind has been disposed[4] of pursuant to the powers under the Mental Health Act 1983, and under that person's will or intestacy,[5] any other person would have taken an interest in the property but for the disposal, he shall take the same interest, if and so far as circumstances allow, in any property belonging to the estate of the deceased which represents the property disposed of.[6]

1 Disposal of property means sale, exchange, charging of or other dealing, otherwise than by will, with property other than money, the removal of property from one place to another; the application of money in acquiring property; or the transfer of money from one account to another, see the Mental Capacity Act 2005, Sch 2, para 8(5).
2 Or by any gift perfected or nomination taking effect on his death.
3 Mental Capacity Act 2005, Sch 2, para 8(1) with effect from 1 October 2007: see SI 2007/1897, art 2(1)(a), (d).
4 Disposal of property means sale, exchange, charging or other dealing, otherwise than by will.
5 Or by any gift perfected or nomination taking effect on his death.
6 Mental Health Act 1983, s 101 (reproducing the Mental Health Act 1959, s 107, which itself embodied previous legislation), repealed by the Mental Capacity Act 2005, s 66(1)(a) with effect from 1 October 2007: see SI 2007/1897, art 2(1)(c), (d); for transitional provisions see the Mental Capacity Act 2005, s 66(4), Sch 5, Pt I.

CHAPTER 42

Election

[42.1]

[Updated for *Scarfe v Matthews* [2012] WTLR 1579.]

Statement of the doctrine. It has already been pointed out that a testator cannot, except in the proper exercise of a power of appointment,[1] dispose of property not vested in him at the time of his death or for any greater interest than is so vested in him.[2] Normally, therefore, a gift by the testator to a donee of property in which he has no interest fails altogether, but in the special case where the true owner of the property so given also receives a benefit under the same will, such owner is put to his election whether he will give up such benefit or will give effect to the disposition by the testator which has failed.[3] Thus, if the testator gives to A property which in fact belongs to B and by the same will makes a gift to B, then B will not be allowed to take such gift unless he undertakes to give effect to the gift to A or, in the usual phrase, he is prepared to carry into effect the whole of the testator's dispositions.[4] He is put to his election to take under the will or against it and, if he elects to take under the will, he will be ordered to convey his own property to the beneficiary under the will[5] or give effect to a provision in the will which is contrary to his own interests under a prior contract or settlement.[6] On the other hand he may elect to take against the will, ie he will keep his own property, but, if he does so, he must either give up his benefit under the will, or, since this would hardly be fair where there is great disparity between the value of the two gifts, the owner of the property which the testator has wrongly disposed of is given the opportunity of retaining his gift under the will provided he compensates the beneficiary by giving him the value of the property of which he is disappointed.[7] Where the gift of the property not belonging to the testator fails, because the beneficiary is unable to take, that gift falls into residue, and the residuary legatee profits by the election, and takes either the property wrongly disposed of or the compensation.[8]

The theoretical basis for the doctrine has changed over time. It has gone from being thought of as a matter of an irrebuttable presumption of the testator's intention[9], to being a matter of the application of a general equitable principle that one cannot at the same time take under and against an instrument[10].

1 In the case of property subject to a power of appointment, the property is usually vested in trustees and the exercise of a power of appointment varies the trusts upon which they hold the property. Where the trusts thus become absolute interests, the beneficiaries are entitled

to demand a transfer of the property from the trustees. In such cases, therefore, a testator can properly dispose of property not vested in him at the time of his death.

2 See para **[7.30]** above.

3 *Dillon v Parker* (1818) 1 Swan 359 at 394; *Blake v Bunbury* (1792) 1 Ves 514 at 523. See *Jay v Jay* [1924] 1 KB 826 (limitation of action). In a case of mutual wills of husband and wife, the doctrine does not apply so as to prevent the surviving spouse taking a benefit under the will of the deceased spouse and also making a new will, in the absence of a definite agreement to the contrary: *Gray v Perpetual Trustee Co Ltd* [1928] AC 391.

4 *Re Brooksbank, Beauclerk v James* (1886) 34 Ch D 160. The gift under the will must be bounty. A legacy in discharge of a statute-barred debt is bounty: *Re Fletcher's Settlement Trusts, Medley v Fletcher* [1936] 2 All ER 236.

5 *Blake v Bunbury* (1792) 1 Ves 514 at 527; *Gretton v Hayward* (1819) 1 Swan 409. For a discussion of the doctrine that a person cannot both 'approbate and reprobate', see *Lissenden v CAV Bosch Ltd* [1940] AC 412, [1940] 1 All ER 425.

6 *Re Fletcher's Settlement Trusts, Medley v Fletcher* [1936] 2 All ER 236, where under a settlement a settlor covenanted to take out a policy for £2,000 payable on his death to the trustees and to bequeath to the trustees all his copyrights. By his will he bequeathed £2,000 to the trustees in satisfaction of his obligation to effect a policy for that sum contained in the settlement (but the obligation under the covenant in the settlement was then statute-barred) and gave his copyrights to his widow. It was held that, if the trustees took the £2,000, they must allow the widow to take the benefit of the gift of the copyrights.

7 *Re Gordon's Will Trusts, National Westminster Bank Ltd v Gordon* [1978] 2 All ER 969 at 973, per Buckley LJ; *Brown v Gregson* [1920] AC 860 at 868–870, per Viscount Haldane; *Gretton v Haward* (1819) 1 Swan 409; *Pickersgill v Rodger* (1876) 5 Ch D 163; *Re Macartney, Macfarlane v Macartney* [1918] 1 Ch 300. If the property wrongly given by the testator is such that it cannot be assigned, as heirlooms or foreign property which cannot be made subject to the trusts of the will, the owner of such property is not put to his election, but can retain his gift under the will without assigning the property or giving compensation: *Re Lord Chesham, Cavendish v Dacre* (1886) 31 Ch D 466; *Brown v Gregson* [1920] AC 860. Property brought into the estate by reason of an election to take under the will is liable to contribute to the payment of debts: *Re Williams, Cunliffe v Williams* [1915] 1 Ch 450.

8 *Re Brooksbank, Beauclerk v James* (1886) 34 Ch D 160.

9 *Noys v Mordaunt* (1706) 2 Vern 581; *Herne v Herne* (1706) 2 Vern 555.

10 *Cooper v Cooper* (1874) LR 7 HL 53 at 67; *Re Lord Chesham* (1886) 31 Ch D 466 at 473; and see the summary of the history of this aspect of the doctrine in *Scarfe v Matthews* [2012] WTLR 1579 at [32] and [33] of the judgment.

[42.3]

[Updated for *Scarfe v Matthews* [2012] WTLR 1579.]

Doctrine not dependent on testator's knowledge that he has no title. There is authority for the proposition that the application of the doctrine does not depend on whether or not the testator knows he has no title to the property he purports to dispose of[1]. However, these authorities belong to the period when the doctrine of election was thought to be based on the presumed intention of the testator, and now that the doctrine is based on equitable principle rather than presumed intention[2] it is possible that the testator's knowledge could be relevant to the question whether the terms of the will show an intention to exclude the doctrine from applying[3]. In practice the application of the doctrine of election usually arises from a mistake, though not necessarily a mistake as to the ownership of the property disposed of. In *Scarfe v Matthews*[4] the deceased knew that his children could claim compulsory heirship rights under French law to immovable property which he wanted to give by his will to his partner, but he did not realise that they might claim that they were entitled to obtain payment from his estate of the

French inheritance tax on their compulsory inheritance under a clause in his will directing payment of taxes out of his estate (the doctrine of election was held to apply).

Where, however, the testator has shown that he meant election to be confined to a particular property, it will not extend to other property.[5] The principle is equally applicable where he is in error as to his power of disposition and thinks that he is disposing of his own property.[6] The court does not consider whether, had he realised the property was not his own, he would have made a different disposition, but takes the will as it is and insists on the beneficiaries giving effect to it.[7]

1 *Welby v Welby* (1813) 2 V and B 187; *Green v Green* (1816) 19 Ves Jun 665.
2 See para **[42.1]** and *Cooper v Cooper* (1874) LR 7 HL 53 at 67.
3 *Scarfe v Matthews* [2012] WTLR 1579 at [37]–[44] of the judgment.
4 [2012] WTLR 1579.
5 *East v Cook* (1750) 2 Ves Sen 30. See also the interpretation of this case in *Wilkinson v Dent* (1871) 6 Ch App 339 at 341–342.
6 *Swan v Holmes* (1854) 19 Beav 471; *Woolaston v King* (1869) LR 8 Eq 165.
7 *Whistler v Webster* (1794) 2 Ves 367; *Thellusson v Woodford* (1806) 13 Ves 209.

[42.5]

[Updated in footnote 5 for *Frear v Frear* [2008] EWCA Civ 1320, [2009] WTLR 221.]

Intention to dispose of particular property. To raise a case of election under a will upon the ground that the testator has attempted to dispose of property over which he had no disposing power, it must be clearly shown that the testator intended to dispose of the particular property;[1] and this intention must appear on the face of the will, either by express words or by necessary conclusion from the circumstances disclosed by the will.[2] The presumption is that a testator intends to dispose only of his own property;[3] and general words will not be construed so as to include other property,[4] nor will oral evidence be admitted to show that the testator believed such other property to be his own so as to allow it to be comprised in general words.[5] Similarly, where a testator has a limited interest in property, and purports to dispose of the property itself, the presumption is that he intends to dispose only of his limited interest;[6] and, if it is sought to carry the disposition further, it must be shown that he intended to dispose of more than that interest. But for this purpose positive declaration is not necessary. Regard may be had to the context of the will, and to the inaptitude of the testamentary limitations if applied to the testator's actual interest.[7] But a devise of an estate which is subject to incumbrances does not by itself import an intention to devise it free from incumbrances, so as to put incumbrancers who take under the will to their election.[8] Where it appears from a recital that a testator has disposed of his own property under an erroneous belief as to the interests in other property of certain beneficiaries under his will, giving less to some on the footing that they would be compensated by their interests in the other property, such a recital is not equivalent to a disposition of such other property, so as to raise a case of election against the persons who unduly benefit under the will.[9]

1 *Lord Rancliffe v Lady Parkyns* (1818) 6 Dow 149; *Wintour v Clifton* (1856) 8 De GM & G 641.

2 *Blake v Bunbury* (1792) 4 Bro CC 21; *Minchin v Gabbett* [1896] 1 IR 1; and see *Re Sullivan, Sullivan v Sullivan* [1917] 1 IR 38; *Re Goodwin* (1905) 5 SRNSW 576; *Re Dicey, Julian v Dicey* [1957] Ch 145, [1956] 3 All ER 696 (omission of numbers of houses but identity otherwise proved). In *Re Edwards, Macadam v Wright* [1958] Ch 168, [1957] 2 All ER 495, the property was specifically mentioned as part of the residue but here it was held that the doctrine of ademption applied and no case for election arose.

3 *Pickersgill v Rodger* (1876) 5 Ch D 163; *Cosby v Ashtown* (1859) 10 I Ch R 219; *Thornton v Thornton* (1861) 11 I Ch R 474.

4 *Miller v Thurgood* (1864) 33 Beav 496; *Re Bidwell's Settlement Trusts* (1862) 1 New Rep 176.

5 *Dummer v Pitcher* (1833) 2 My & K 262; *Clementson v Gandy* (1836) 1 Keen 309; *Galvin v Devereux* [1903] 1 IR 185. It has been said that evidence is admissible where the devise or bequest is specific: *Graham v Clark (Dorland Estate) and Dorland* [1949] 3 DLR 539. Parol evidence may be admissible under AJA 1982, s 21 to show what the testator intended to dispose of: see *Frear v Frear* [2008] EWCA Civ 1320, [2009] WTLR 221.

6 *Dummer v Pitcher* (1833) 2 My & K 262; *Howells v Jenkins* (1863) 1 De GJ & Sm 617; *Henry v Henry* (1872) 6 IR Eq 286. If the testator has only a life interest and the intention on the face of the will is to dispose of his interest (if any), there is no case of election; *Galvin v Devereux* [1903] 1 IR 185. Where a testator disposed of the residue of his property and the will was governed by English law, it was the residue according to English law, and as this included property of his wife to which community of goods applied, the wife must elect: *Re Allen's Estate, Prescott v Allen* [1945] 2 All ER 264.

7 *Wintour v Clifton* (1856) 8 De GM & G 641; *Usticke v Peters* (1858) 4 K & J 437. A bequest to a third person of stock standing in the joint names of the testator and his wife, where benefits are conferred on the wife by the will, puts the wife to her election (*Grosvenor v Durston* (1858) 25 Beav 97). Where a testator agreed to settle property on his niece and then left her a legacy on condition that she gave up her claim to a settlement, she was put to her election: *Central Trust and Safe Deposit Co v Snider* [1916] 1 AC 266.

8 *Stephens v Stephens* (1857) 1 De G & J 62; *Henry v Henry* (1872) 6 IR Eq 286. A devise inconsistent with the continuance of the incumbrance will put the incumbrancers to their election if they are beneficiaries under the will: *Blake v Bunbury* (1972) 1 Ves 514, and cf *Sadlier v Butler* (1867) IR 1 Eq 415; *Re Williams, Cunliffe v Williams* [1915] 1 Ch 450.

9 *Box v Barrett* (1866) LR 3 Eq 244. There is no case for election where a testator, erroneously reciting that a hotchpot clause will apply, refrains from appointing the unappointed residue of a fund: *Langslow v Langslow* (1856) 21 Beav 552.

CHAPTER 43

Estoppel

I. PROPRIETARY ESTOPPEL

[43.1]

[Updated in footnote 1 for *Suggitt v Suggitt* [2012] EWCA Civ 1140, [2012] WTLR 1607, (CA); *Bradbury v Taylor* [2012] EWCA Civ 1208, [2013] WTLR 29, (CA); and *Creasey v Sole* [2013] EWHC 1410 (Ch), [2013] WTLR 931.
Updated in footnote 3 for *Re Baker, Baker v Baker* [2008] WTLR 565. Updated in the text to footnotes 6 and 7 and in footnotes 1, 5, 6 and 7 for *Thorner v Major* [2009] UKHL 18. Updated in footnote 7 for *MacDonald v Frost* [2009] EWHC 2276 (Ch), [2009] WTLR 1815.]

General principles. It is beyond the scope of this text to set out in detail the principles relating to proprietary estoppel as they have been developed in the modern law. But it can be noted that the doctrine can operate to affect a testamentary gift of property which is claimed by another relying on proprietary estoppel. The principles of proprietary estoppel are founded on representation, reliance and detriment[1] and can be stated in broad terms as follows. Where one person (A) has acted to his detriment on the faith of a belief which was known to and encouraged by another person (B) that he has or is going to be given a right in or over B's property, B cannot insist on his strict legal rights if to do so would be inconsistent with A' s belief.[2] This has been applied to a situation where a claimant worked on the testator's farm for forty years (for allegedly less than full remuneration) on the reliance of repeated assurances by the testator that he would leave the claimant the bulk of his estate including the farm, by his will on his death.[3] The testator made a new will excluding the claimant entirely from inheriting. The claimant succeeded in an action against the estate, claiming an equity in the testator's property under the doctrine of proprietary estoppel, arising from reliance in the testator's assurances causing him detriment.[4] The doctrine has also been applied in favour of claimants in cases of intestacy.[5] In a recent House of Lords decision, the claimant had worked at his father's cousin's farm without any remuneration for 29 years. Although the assurances relied upon in that case were somewhat oblique, the House of Lords said that what amounts to sufficient clarity is hugely dependent on context, and that in the context of two taciturn and undemonstrative countrymen, the assurances in question were sufficient.[6] It is a necessary element of proprietary estoppel that the assurances given to the claimant should relate to identified property owned (or, perhaps, about to be owned) by the deceased.[7]

1 See, for example, *Plimmer v Mayor of Wellington* (1884) 9 App Cas 699, at 714; *Crabb v Arun District Council* [1975] 3 All ER 865 at 880; *Greasley v Cooke* [1980] 3 All ER 710 and *Grant v Edwards* [1986] Ch 638, [1986] 2 All ER 426. For the application of these same

principles in the case of testamentary dispositions, see *Thorner v Major* [2009] 3 All ER 945, para [29]. In this case, although four of the Law Lords applied the conventional proprietary estoppel analysis, Lord Scott expressed the view that in the case of testamentary dispositions a constructive trust analysis is more appropriate than the proprietary estoppel analysis, with proprietary estoppel confined to cases where the representation is unconditional, and the principles of remedial constructive trusts applying to cases where the representations are of future benefits, and subject to qualification on account of unforeseen future events. Other recent decisions concerning estoppel in the context of testamentary dispositions are *Suggitt v Suggitt* [2012] EWCA Civ 1140, [2012] WTLR 1607, (CA); *Bradbury v Taylor* [2012] EWCA Civ 1208, [2013] WTLR 29, (CA); and *Creasey v Sole* [2013] EWHC 1410 (Ch), [2013] WTLR 931 (where the claim failed).

2 Per Balcombe LJ in *Wayling v Jones* (1993) 69 P & CR 170 at p 172, citing Mr Nugee's statement of principle in *Re Basham* [1987] 1 All ER 405 at 410.

3 *Gillett v Holt* [2001] Ch 210, [2000] 2 All ER 289, Court of Appeal reversing Carnwath J at first instance [1998] 3 All ER 917 who had rejected the claim. This was a case where the facts supporting an estoppel were strong; it is not every promise or assurance of inheritance which will give rise to a successful claim under this head. See also *Jennings v Rice* [2001] WTLR 871 affd; [2002] EWCA Civ 159, [2002] WTLR 367, a claim against a deceased estate based on inter vivos promises made by the deceased to the claimant, succeeded in part on the basis of proprietary estoppel. A claim based on proprietary estoppel failed in *Ottey v Grundy (Andreae's Executor)* [2002] EWCA Civ 1176, [2003] WTLR 1253, applying *Wayling v Jones* [1995] 2 FLR 1029 and *Re Baker, Baker v Baker* [2008] WTLR 565.

4 *Re Basham* [1987] 1 All ER 405, was applied and *Taylor v Dickens* [1998] 3 FCR 455 not followed. See also *Layton v Martin* [1986] 2 FLR 227 and *Jones v Watkins* [1987] CA Transcript 1200.

5 *Thorner v Major* [2009] 3 All ER 945; *Re Basham* [1987] 1 All ER 405 (the claimant worked for many years, without payment, for her stepfather in the expectation of inheriting his estate; the stepfather died intestate. It was held that since her expectation had been encouraged by the deceased and she had acted to her detriment in reliance on that belief, she was entitled to the estate).

6 *Thorner v Major* [2009] 3 All ER 945, para [56]. The relevant assurances included the deceased handing to the claimant a bonus notice, relating to two policies on the deceased's life with a then value of about £20,000, saying 'That's for my death duties'.

7 *Thorner v Major* [2009] 3 All ER 945, para [61]. In that case, it was found that the common understanding was that the deceased's assurance to the claimant related to whatever the farm consisted of at the deceased's death. No decided view was given as to whether *Re Basham* [1986] 1 WLR 1498 was correctly decided so far as it extended to the deceased's residuary estate, although it was pointed out that the deputy judge had there relied largely on authorities about mutual wills, which are arguably a special case. For a case where a claim for proprietary estoppel failed because it was found that the deceased had made no express assurances or promises to the claimants, see *MacDonald v Frost* [2009] EWHC 2276 (Ch), [2009] WTLR 1815.

CHAPTER 44

Satisfaction

[44.4]

[Updated in footnote 4 for *Re Frost* [2013] EWHC 435 (Ch), [2013] WTLR 674.]

Both gifts must be in nature of portions. The presumptions of satisfaction of both portions by legacies and legacies by portions, only arise when the two gifts are in the nature of portions.[1] A portion is a sum of money given to a child by way of advancement, on marriage or for the purpose of establishing him in business,[2] or to pay for education[3] and in general it is only such a gift which will operate as a satisfaction of a prior gift.[4] Though it has been said that where a large sum has been given and nothing is known as to the circumstances, it will be treated as raising the presumption of satisfaction,[5] it has also been held that where the inference from the will is that the gift is mere bounty, the burden is on those setting up satisfaction to prove it.[6] It follows that gifts of small sums,[7] or payments of an annuity during the lifetime of the testator,[8] will not raise the presumption. Moreover, in the case of ademption the gift must be subsequent to the date of the will.[9]

1 *Re Lacon, Lacon v Lacon* [1891] 2 Ch 482 at 498, per Bowen LJ. There is no presumption of satisfaction where two portions are derived from different estates: *Douglas v Willes* (1849) 7 Hare 318 at 328. But a sum appointed under a special power may be a portion within the presumption of satisfaction: *Montague v Montague* (1852) 15 Beav 565; *Re Peel's Settlement, Biddulph v Peel* [1911] 2 Ch 165. See *Re Ashton, Ingram v Papillon* [1897] 2 Ch 574 at 579; *Re Newton King* [1953] NZLR 245.

2 *Taylor v Taylor* (1875) LR 20 Eq 155 at 158, per Jessel MR: see *Schofield v Heap* (1858) 27 Beav 93; *Re Lacon, Lacon v Lacon* [1891] 2 Ch 482, CA; *Re Watney, Watney v Gold* (1911) 56 Sol Jo 109; *Barry v Harding* (1844) 7 I Eq R 313. And it must be a benefit provided by the settlor, not merely a liability which he has incurred to the child—for example, by breach of trust: *Crichton v Crichton* [1895] 2 Ch 853 at 859.

3 See *Re Cameron, Phillips v Cameron* [1999] Ch 386r, [1999] 2 All ER 924, where provisions (in effect) by a grandmother to pay for the education of a grandchild were held to be portions benefiting the child's parent, ie the donor's son. See further discussed in para **[44.3]**, nn 3 and 4, above.

4 *Re Scott, Langton v Scott* [1903] 1 Ch 1. Formerly, money provided by a father to pay his son's debts was treated as an advance: *Boyd v Boyd* (1867) LR 4 Eq 305; *Re Blockley, Blockley v Blockley* (1885) 29 Ch D 250; but the view of Jessel MR in *Taylor v Taylor* (1875) LR 20 Eq 155, has prevailed, and the provision of sums for such a purpose does not raise a presumption of satisfaction: *Re Scott, Langton v Scott* [1903] 1 Ch 1. In *Re George's Will Trusts, Barclay's Bank Ltd v George* [1949] Ch 154, [1948] 2 All ER 1004, a gift of farming stock which had been valued in money and the taking over of the lease of the farm was held to be in the nature of a portion. In *Re Frost* [2013] EWHC 435 (Ch), [2013] WTLR 674, cash payments by a testator to his two daughters were found not to be portions but payments in return for their past and future care for him.

5 *Leighton v Leighton* (1874) LR 18 Eq 458 at 468; *Re Scott, Langton v Scott* [1903] 1 Ch 1 at 13, 16. And where a testator becomes of unsound mind after directing by his will advances

out of surplus income to be brought into hotchpot, the court has a discretion as to enforcing this requirement: *Re Merrall, Greener v Merrall* [1924] 1 Ch 45.

6 *Re Livesey's Settlement Trusts, Livesey v Livesey* [1953] 2 All ER 723, [1953] 1 WLR 1114 (gifts of mortgage debts substantial in amount accompanied by other gifts held not to be a satisfaction unless facts were proved to show that intention).

7 *Schofield v Heap* (1858) 27 Beav 93; *Watson v Watson* (1864) 33 Beav 574; *Re Peacock's Estate* (1872) LR 14 Eq 236 at 240. The court has never added up small sums in order to show that if the child claims those sums as well as the larger provision made for him by the parent, he would be taking a double portion: *Suisse v Lowther* (1843) 2 Hare 424 at 434, per Wigram V-C. As to evidence whether a cheque is given as a gift or a loan, see *Re England, England v Garnett* (1912) 134 LT Jo 29.

8 See *Hatfield v Minet* (1878) 8 Ch D 136, CA.

9 Gifts made before the date of the will cannot operate as a satisfaction (*Re Peacock's Estate* (1872) LR 14 Eq 236; *Taylor v Cartwright* (1872) LR 14 Eq 167 at 176; *Leighton v Leighton* (1874) LR 18 Eq 458) unless so agreed by the donee; *Upton v Prince* (1735) Cas temp Talb 71.

CHAPTER 46

Disclaimer of gift

[46.1]

[Updated for the Estates of Deceased Persons (Forfeiture Rule and Law of Succession) Act 2011 ('EDP(FRLS)A 2011').]

How disclaimer made. Disclaimer[1] may be made in the case of a person *sui juris* by informal acts as well as by deed,[2] and this was so even though the gift conferred a legal estate upon the donee,[3] but now the donee can obtain the legal estate only by the assent of the personal representative.[4] Where the gift is subject to burdens or requires the performance of conditions, the disclaimer relieves the donee from those burdens and conditions.[5] The disclaimer affects only the interest of the donee and does not affect any other right or interest given by the will, eg a charge on the property or a trust.[6] A beneficiary who is one of the objects of a discretionary power under which trustees may or may not decide to make a gift in his favour, has a right to renounce his interest.[7] A putative beneficiary under the will or intestacy of a living person has no interest in the deceased's estate which can be the subject of a disclaimer and so a purported inter vivos disclaimer by such a beneficiary has no effect.[8]

1 The disclaimer here dealt with is the disclaimer of a gift by will; see *Townson v Tickell* (1819) 3 B & Ald 31 at 36; and Ventris J in *Thompson v Leach* (1690) 2 Vent 198; see also *Perpetual Executors and Trustees Association of Australia Ltd v Probate Duties Comr* [1981] VR 91 at 101, where this Chapter is referred to. As to disclaimer by trustees: see Chapter 27. As to renunciation by executors, see Chapter 25. It now seems to be settled by the decision in *Re Scott, Widdows v Friends of the Clergy Corpn* [1975] 2 All ER 1033, [1975] 1 WLR 1260 (where the point was assumed and not argued; see Goodhart 40 Conv 292) that an interest acquired on intestacy can be disclaimed at least up to the time of making of the assent (see J L Pinkerton 42 Conv 213). It was also stated in *Re Scott* that if an interest on intestacy is disclaimed the property will not pass to the Crown as bona vacantia but will pass to the other persons entitled on intestacy as if the disclaimer had not survived; *Re Scott, Widdows v Friends of the Clergy Corpn* [1975] 2 All ER 1033, [1975] 1 WLR 1260. However, the reasoning in *Re DWS, Re EHS, TWGS v JMG* [2000] 2 All ER 83; affirmed [2001] 1 All ER 97, CA (although not overruling *Re Scott*) cast doubts on this: see paras **[46.5]** and **[48.8]**. However, in relation to the estates of persons dying on or after 1 February 2012 (SI 2011/2913), the intestacy rules are amended so that a disclaiming beneficiary is deemed to predecease the intestate: AEA 1925, s 46A(1)(a) and (2), inserted by EDP(FRLS)A 2011, s 1(2) (set out in para **[244.62A]**). *Re Scott, Widdows v Friends of the Clergy Corpn* [1975] 2 All ER 1033, [1975] 1 WLR 1260 was applied in *Re Simmons Estate* (1990) 56 SASR 1 where the text, 6th Edition, Vol 2, p 1342, was applied.

2 *Townson v Tickell* (1819) 3 B & Ald 31; *Begbie v Crook* (1835) 2 Bing NC 70; *Re Birchall, Birchall v Ashton* (1889) 40 Ch D 436; *Re Clout and Frewer's Contract* [1924] 2 Ch 230; *Re Moss* (1977) 77 DLR (3d) 314. A deed is certainly advisable as evidence of the disclaimer, especially where the gift is to a trustee, though the matter might now be satisfactorily completed by an assent in writing to the person becoming entitled on disclaimer by the

donee, supported by the curtain provision of AEA 1925, s 36(7). Disclaimer by informal acts is more readily presumed where it is to the manifest disadvantage of the beneficiary to retain the gift and will not be readily presumed where it is to his advantage to retain it: *Harris v Watkins* (1856) 2 K & J 473.

3 See the cases cited in n 2. Disclaimers are excepted from conveyances of land which must be by deed: Law of Property Act 1925, s 52(2). Where a deed, purporting to be a disclaimer, disclaimed a share held in joint tenancy, it was held that the deed was not a disclaimer but a release: *Re Schar, Midland Bank Executor and Trustee Co Ltd v Damer* [1951] Ch 280, [1950] 2 All ER 1069.

4 AEA 1925, s 36(4); but this would not be so where the personal representative was the same person as the donee or as the trustee.

5 *Silcock v Roynon* (1843) 2 Y & C Ch Cas 376; *Manson v Ross* (1884) 1 BCR (pt 2) 49 (disclaimer of partly paid-up shares).

6 *Wilson v Wilson* (1847) 1 De G & Sm 152; *Mallott v Wilson* [1903] 2 Ch 494 at 501.

7 *Re Gulbenkian's Settlement Trusts (No 2), Stevens v Maun* [1970] Ch 408, [1969] 2 All ER 1173.

8 *Re Smith, Smith v Smith* [2001] 3 All ER 552, even if the disclaimer was made by deed.

[46.5]

[Updated in footnote 2 for the Estates of Deceased Persons (Forfeiture Rule and Law of Succession) Act 2011 ('EDP(FRLS)A 2011').]

Effect of disclaimer. A disclaimer does not act positively as an assignment or disposition of property, but acts negatively by preventing the property from vesting at all.[1] Thus Walton J commented in *Re Scott, Widdows v Friends of the Clergy Corpn.*[2]

> 'The effect of a disclaimer is not to throw the property onto the scrap heap, but to refuse to accept it in the first place, leaving the ownership with the people or the interest or the estate, or whatever, from which it was derived in the first place.'

In many cases the effect of a disclaimer will be to accelerate a subsequent interest, and this is dealt with later.[3]

1 *Townson v Tickell* (1819) 3 B & Ald 31; see *Re Jung* (1979) 99 DLR (3d) 65.

2 [1975] 2 All ER 1033 at 1045. But see also *Re DWS, Re EHS, TWGS v JMG* [2000] 2 All ER 83; affirmed [2001] 1 All ER 97, where (in a different context) the court held the next available class under intestacy was entitled to take; but the conclusion in *Re DWS* is based on different reasoning to that in *Re Scott*; see para **[48.8]**. The decisions in *Re Scott* and *Re DWS* have been superseded for deaths on or after 1 February 2012 by EDP-(FRLS)A 2011, which provides for the property to pass as if the disqualified person had predeceased the intestate: see para **[48.8]**. See also *Re Stratton's Deed of Disclaimer* [1958] Ch 42, [1957] 2 All ER 594; *Re Parsons* [1942] Ch 335; *Sembaliuk v Sembaliuk* (1985) 15 DLR (4th) 303.

3 See Chapter 48, below.

CHAPTER 47

Lapse

IV. STATUTORY EXCEPTIONS FROM LAPSE

[47.15]

[Updated for the Estates of Deceased Persons (Forfeiture Rule and Law of Succession) Act 2011 ('EDP(FRLS)A 2011') and *Rainbird v Smith* [2012] EWHC 4176 (Ch), [2013] WTLR 1609.]

The substituted WA 1837, s 33. The Administration of Justice Act 1982[1] has substituted a new provision for the Wills Act 1837, s 33 applicable to the wills of testators who die on or after 1 January 1983.[2] The section applies to both gifts to individual children[3] and to gifts to classes of children.[4] In the case of the former the section applies where: first, the will contains a devise or bequest to a child or remoter descendant of the testator; secondly, the intended beneficiary dies before the testator leaving issue; and thirdly, issue of the intended beneficiary are living at the testator's death. In these cases it is provided that ... the devise or bequest shall take effect as a devise or bequest to the issue living at the testator's death'.[5] In this way, in contrast to the effect of the original s 33, the provision effects a simple and true substitution in favour of issue, per stirpes, unless a contrary intention appears by the will.[6] The old s 33 did not apply to a class gift since in such a case the share of a deceased member of the class did not lapse, but accrued to the other members of the class. In the case of a gift to children as a class this had the effect of benefiting the brothers and sisters of the deceased child even if he or she left issue. The new s 33 contains an important extension of the previous law in an attempt to remedy this situation. Where a will contains a gift to the testator's children (or remoter descendants) as a class, and a member of the class dies before the testator leaving issue who are living at the testator's death, then it is provided that the gifts, '... shall take effect as if the class included the issue of its deceased member living at the testator's death'. Again, this construction can be excluded if a contrary intention appears by the will.[7]

Where the section operates, the substituted issue take through all degrees per stirpes in equal shares if more than one, and in the usual way, they take the gift or share which their parent would have taken. Such issue do not take whose parent is living at the testator's death and so capable of taking[8], subject to the point that if the parent was living then but is disqualified from taking, by reason of having killed the testator unlawfully or having disclaimed, he or she is treated for the purposes of s 33 as having predeceased the testator.[9]

1 AJA 1982, s 19. See Vol 2, Part G, para **[244.36]**.

2 AJA 1982, ss 73(6), 76(11).
3 WA 1837, s 33(1).
4 Wills Act 1837, s 33(2). It is possible that the new provision would apply to gifts to persons as joint tenants because of the absence of any reference to the exclusion of interests ceasing on death (which the old s 33 contained and thus excluded gifts to joint tenants). However, it could be argued that a gift to joint tenants discloses a contrary intention within the section.
5 It will be noticed that in contrast to the previous formulation the new WA 1837, s 33 contains no reference to 'lapse'; see Michael Wheeler QC in *Re Sinclair, Lloyd's Bank plc v Imperial Cancer Research Fund* [1984] 3 All ER 362 and 365.
6 Contrast the effect of the old WA 1837, s 33, noted at para **[47.11]** above. Cases such as *Re Basioli, McGahey v Depaoli* [1953] Ch 367, [1953] 1 All ER 301 would now be decided differently if the facts were to recur with reference to a post-1982 death.
7 AJA 1982, s 19; new WA 1837, s 33(2); Vol 2, Part G, para **[244.36]**. It has been held that a provision in a will in favour of children aged 21 alive at the testator's death and who survived for one month afterwards did not exclude the operation of WA 1837, s 33(2) in relation to a child who predeceased him leaving a surviving child: *Ling v Ling* [2002] WTLR 553, [2001] All ER (D) 322 (Nov). A grandchild was thus held entitled to succeed to his parent's share provided he satisfied the same contingencies. However, *Ling v Ling* was not followed in *Rainbird v Smith* [2012] EWHC 4176 (Ch), [2013] WTLR 1609, where it was held that there was an intention contrary to s 33 applying where there was a gift to the testator's daughters as should survive the testator if more than one in equal shares (one of the daughters having predeceased the testator).
8 AJA 1982, s 19; new WA 1837, s 33(3).
9 WA 1837 s 33A, inserted by EDP(FRLS)A 2011 s 2 for deaths on or after 1 February 2012. See also paras **[9.17]** and **[48.8]**, and para **[244.35A]** for the text of s 33A.

[47.18]

[Updated for *Rainbird v Smith* [2012] EWHC 4176 (Ch), [2013] WTLR 1609.]

Contingent gifts. The application and effect of the new WA 1837, s 33 on contingent gifts is not clear. The first problem is whether the new WA 1837, s 33 applies at all where the gifts to a child or children or other descendant or descendants of the testator is contingent, and the second problem is, assuming the section does apply, whether the interests of the persons who take by statutory substitution are subject to the same contingency. If a gift to a specific child or descendant is contingent on the child or descendant surviving the testator (or surviving him by a specified period), that will usually be combined with there being some other gift of the same subject-matter which will take effect if he does not so survive. If so, that would seem to be an expression of a contrary intention excluding the operation of the new WA 1837, s 33(1), although the contrary might be arguable if the alternative gift were a general gift of residue (where there was no specific reference to it taking effect on the failure of the gift to the child or descendant). However, it has now been held in *Rainbird v Smith*[1] that an intention contrary to s 33 applying was shown where the gift was to such of the testator's daughters as should survive the testator if more than one in equal shares.

If a gift to a specific child or descendant is contingent on attaining a specified age and the child or descendant attains that age and dies before the testator, it seems that (in the absence of express provision in the will for what is to happen in that event, or the gift being expressed to be contingent on surviving the testator[2]) the new WA 1837, s 33(1) will apply just as the former s 33 did.[3] The former s 33 did not apply where the child or descendant died before the testator without having attained the age on the attaining of which the gift was contingent,[4] but that was because of the presence of wording (the exception from the effect of the section for any estate or interest determinable at or before the death of the child or issue and the provision that a gift within the section 'shall not lapse') in the old s 33 which is not repeated in the new version. It seems that the new WA 1837, s 33 may well apply in these circumstances if there is no provision in the will to take effect if the child or descendant fails to attain the age which is the age upon attaining which the gift is contingent, even though there would be no such substitution if he died without attaining a vested interest after the death of the testator.[5]

As regards the second problem mentioned above, it would seem that in the case of a gift to a specific child or descendant there is nothing explicit in s 33(1) to import into the statutory substitutional gift any contingency to which the primary gift was subject, though in *Ling v Ling*[6] it was held that the substituted beneficiary under s 33 was subject to the same contingency (attaining the age of 21) as his parent who predeceased the testator would have been subject.

1 [2012] EWHC 4176 (Ch), [2013] WTLR 1609.
2 The decision in *Rainbird v Smith* (2012) 156 Sol Jo (no 22) 31 (25 May 2012) implies that the inclusion of such a contingency shows an intention to exclude WA 1837 from applying.
3 See *Re Wilson, Lothian v Wilson* (1920) 89 LJ Ch 216.
4 See *Re Wolson, Wolson v Jackson* [1939] Ch 780, [1939] 3 All ER 852.
5 In the case of a class gift it is arguable that the new WA 1837, s 33 will not apply to anyone who dies without fulfilling any contingency to which the gift is expressly subject. The point here is that a gift to, for example, such of the testator's children as shall survive him and attain the age of 21 years, is arguably a gift to a class which consists of the testator's children who survive him and attain 21, not one which consists of the testator's children. If that is right, the WA 1837, s 33(2) will not apply where a child predeceases the testator without having attained 21 but leaving issue, because he was not 'a member of the class' within the meaning of paragraph (b) of s 33(2). This construction would mean that s 33(2) does not apply to most class gifts, and it is probably not a result which was intended. It would seem particularly contrary to what was intended if s 33 is excluded where the only contingency to which a gift was expressly subject was surviving the testator, but less so in relation to a contingency such as surviving to a specified age. However, it has been held that the contingency of surviving the testator is enough to exclude s 33 from operating, in *Rainbird v Smith* [2012] EWHC 4176 (Ch), [2013] WTLR 1609.
6 [2002] WTLR 553, [2001] All ER (D) 322 (Nov).

[47.19]

[Updated for *Rainbird v Smith* [2012] EWHC 4176 (Ch), [2013] WTLR 1609.]

Professional practice and substitutional gifts. It is suggested that the WA 1837, s 33 does not obviate the desirability of including express substitutional clauses in wills, particularly in the case of class gifts. Such a clause can clarify the uncertainties and difficulties relating to contingent gifts noted above in para **[47.18]** and illustrated by *Rainbird v Smith*[1]. Further s 33 only applies to issue and in all other gifts, e g to brothers, an express clause will be required. It is a requirement of the application of s 33 that the issue should predecease the testator and the section does not apply where the child survives the testator but dies before satisfying a condition or contingency. Finally it will usually be regarded as preferable to have the clause of substitution within the will rather than contained in an extraneous statutory provision which not all personal representatives or beneficiaries will be aware of. Where there is an express substitution clause or other gift intended to have effect on failure of a primary gift to issue of the testator, it can save argument later if there is an express exclusion of WA 1837, s 33.

1 [2012] EWHC 4176 (Ch), [2013] WTLR 1609. See paras **[47.15]**, **[47.18]**.

CHAPTER 48

Failure of gift

II. EFFECT OF FAILURE OF A GIFT

[48.4]

[Updated in footnote 7 for the Estates of Deceased Persons (Forfeiture Rule and Law of Succession) Act 2011 ('EDP(FRLS)A 2011').]

Effect on subject of gift. A general residuary gift includes all interests, not themselves interests in the general residue, which are otherwise undisposed of or which fail in any manner, unless the testator provides otherwise and, therefore, upon the failure of a gift, the subject-matter thereof falls into residue.[1] There may be a particular residuary gift, or a gift of the residue of a particular description of property, a specific part of which is the subject of a prior gift, and it may appear that on the failure of such latter gift the subject-matter is to fall into the particular residue.[2] Where the interest which fails is an interest in the general residue, such interest will pass as on an intestacy.[3] Where the failure of the beneficial interests leads to a total intestacy, the executor does not take beneficially, but in the absence of persons entitled by relationship under the provisions of AEA 1925,[4] the Crown takes the property, both real and personal.[5] In order to prevent an intestacy the will should include a comprehensive substitutional gift or gift over to cover the possibility of failure of the gift of residue.[6] The gift over will be strictly construed and must in terms comprehend the cause of the failure of the residuary gift, so that if it is merely expressed in terms of 'predecease' and the donee does not predecease but the gift fails for other reasons, the gift over will not take effect and there will be an intestacy.[7]

1 As to residuary gifts, see Chapter 38. A specific legacy passes on disclaimer under the residuary gift: *Re Backhouse, Westminster Bank Ltd v Shaftesbury Society and Ragged School Union* [1931] WN 168. As to failure due to the rule against perpetuities, see Chapter 94; as to failure due to lapse, see Chapters 47 and 48.

2 See *Malcolm v Taylor* (1832) 2 Russ & M 416; *De Trafford v Tempest* (1856) 21 Beav 564; *Burke Irwin's Trust, Barrett v Barrett* [1918] 1 IR 350.

3 *Kelley v A-G* [1917] 1 IR 183; *Hughes v McNaull* [1923] 1 IR 78; *Re Watson* [1927] 4 DLR 626.

4 AEA 1925, s 46; see Vol 2, Part G, para **[244.62]**; see discussion in Chapter 104.

5 Administration of Estates Act 1925, s 46(1)(vi).

6 For suitable clauses see Vol 2, Forms B19.5 and B19.6 at paras **[219.18]**, **[219.19]** and Part C passim.

7 *Re Sinclair* [1985] Ch 446 (gift of residue failed by reason of divorce; gift over on former spouse predeceasing testator failed); but note the effect of the 1995 amendment, see Chapter 47, para **[47.2]** above. Applied in *Re Jones, Jones v Midland Bank Trust Co Ltd* [1997] 3 FCR 697 (gift of residue failed by reason of the forfeiture rule; gift over on death of

forfeiting donee failed)). See also *Re DWS* [2001] Ch 568, CA, reversed as regards disclaimer of interests on intestacy under the estates of persons dying on or after 1 February 2012 by EDP(FRLS)A 2011. See, further, para **[48.8]**.

[48.8]

[Updated for the Estates of Deceased Persons (Forfeiture Rule and Law of Succession) Act 2011 ('EDP(FRLS)A 2011').]

Acceleration or substitution on disclaimer. The effect of a disclaimer is in general to accelerate the next interest in remainder[1] but where such next interest is not capable of taking at the time of the disclaimer (eg being an unborn person) the next remainder takes the income until the happening of the contingency even though that remainder be an absolute interest.[2] If the interests are vested subject to defeasance, they are given effect subject to the defeasance.[3] Where a testatrix appointed a fund to her mother but, if the mother predeceased her, she appointed part of the fund but left the rest unappointed, and the mother disclaimed all interest under the will and the appointment, the disclaimer did not accelerate the subsequent gifts of the appointment since they were contingent on the mother predeceasing the testatrix. The result being an intestacy, the mother took under the intestacy despite the disclaimer.[4] As a matter of general law, apart from EDP-(FRLS)A 2011 (see below), in the event of a disclaimer of an interest in a deceased person's estate, the will or the intestacy rules (as the case may be) do not have effect as if the person disclaiming had predeceased the testator or intestate[5]. It is a matter of the construction of the will what disposition takes effect following a disclaimer of an interest given by that will: a substitutional provision which is contingent on the disclaiming beneficiary predeceasing the testator will not have effect, but one which is contingent on the primary gift failing for any reason, or the primary beneficiary failing to attain a vested interest, will have effect.

In relation to the estates of persons dying on or after 1 February 2012[6], there is statutory intervention in the form of EDP(FRLS)A 2011. A person who disclaims an interest under an intestacy is treated for the purposes of the intestacy rules as having predeceased the intestate[7]. A person who disclaims an interest under a will is treated for the purposes of WA 1837 as having predeceased the testator[8]. This is subject to any contrary intention expressed in the will[9]. The provision in EDP(FRLS)A 2011 concerning wills is a narrower provision than that relating to intestacy[10]. It means that the statutory substitution of issue under WA 1837, s 33 (see para **[47.15]**) will operate as if the disclaiming beneficiary had predeceased the testator, but an express substitution clause in a will which substitutes other beneficiaries for a primary beneficiary in the event of the latter predeceasing the testator will not so operate.

1 *Re Scott, Scott v Scott* [1911] 2 Ch 374 at 377; *Re Hodge* [1943] Ch 300, [1943] 2 All ER 304; *Re Jacques* (1985) 16 DLR (4th) 472 (doctrine of acceleration should not be applied to defeat the testator's intention). As to acceleration upon disclaimer in the case of a settlement, see *Re Young's Settlement Trusts* [1959] 2 All ER 74, and *Re Penton's Settlements, Humphreys v Birch Reynardson* [1968] 1 All ER 36, [1968] 1 WLR 248.

2 *Re Willis, Crossman v Kirkaldy* [1917] 1 Ch 365; *Re Hatfield, Hatfield v Hatfield* [958] Ch 469, [1957] 2 All ER 261. As to the effect of a widow repudiating a gift under the will and electing to take her ius relictae, see *Muirhead v Muirhead v Crellin* (1890) 15 App Cas 289.

3 *Re Taylor, Lloyds Bank Ltd v Jones* [1957] 3 All ER 56, [1957] 1 WLR 1043 (where two remaindermen took equally subject to losing their share on death during the lifetime of the person disclaiming).
4 *Re Speedy, Guardian Trust and Executors Co of New Zealand Ltd v Speedy* [1964] NZLR 961.
5 As regards wills, see *Re Sinclair* [1985] Ch 446 (gift of residue failed by reason of divorce; gift over on former spouse predeceasing testator failed as the former spouse survived the testator), and as regards intestacy see *Re DWS, Re EHS, TWGS v JMG* [2000] 2 All ER 83; affd [2001] 1 All ER 97, CA, arguably overruling *Re Scott, Widdows v Friends of the Clergy Corpn* [1975] 2 All ER 1033 at 1045 on this point. In *Re DWS* the court applied AEA 1925, ss 46 and 47 literally, so that a person could not take where he belongs to a category in relation to which s 46 or s 47 provides that its members only take in the event of a prior category (which includes the person who has disclaimed his interest or murdered the intestate) not surviving the intestate. But a person could do so where he belongs to a category in relation to which s 46 or s 47 provides that its members take in the event of the members of the prior category 'not attaining a vested interest'. *Re DWS* concerns someone who was prevented from taking because he had murdered the testator, but the same reasoning would have applied to a disclaimer. The effect is reversed in relation to the intestacy rules by EDP(FRLS)A 2011, for which see below.
6 EDP(FRLS)A 2011, s 4(2), (4), and EDP(FRLS)A 2011 (Commencement) Order 2011, SI 2011/2913.
7 AEA 1925, s 46A(1), (2) (see para **[244.62A]**), inserted by EDP(FRLS)A 2011, s 1(2).
8 WA 1837, s 33A(1), (2) (see para **[244.35A]**), inserted by EDP(FRLS)A 2011, s 2(2).
9 WA 1837, s 33A(2) (see para **[244.35A]**), inserted by EDP(FRLS)A 2011, s 2(2).
10 The Law Commission Report No 295 on which EDP(FRLS)A 2011 is based recommends that wills should have effect as if a disclaiming beneficiary under the will has predeceased the testator. See paras 4.28 and 5.5 of the Report. The narrower provision contained in WA 1837, s 33A(2) may have arisen in error: see para **[9.17]** footnote 15.

[48.11]

[Updated for the Estates of Deceased Persons (Forfeiture Rule and Law of Succession) Act 2011 ('EDP(FRLS)A 2011').]

Acceleration on forfeiture. Where the forfeiture declares the forfeited interest to be utterly void and that interest is an estate tail, the accelerated interest is determined on the birth of a child to the donee in tail.[1] Where the forfeiture arose on bankruptcy there was no acceleration where the interest was to cease as if the beneficiary was then 'actually dead' but the income passed as on an intestacy.[2] For the effect of forfeiture of a gift by reason of unlawful killing of the deceased, and the provisions of EDP(FRLS)A 2011, see para **[9.17]**.

1 *Blathwayt v Lord Cawley* [1976] AC 397, [1975] 3 All ER 625; overruling Wynn-Perry J's earlier conclusion in *Re Blathwayt's Will Trusts, Blathwayt v Blathwayt* [1950] 1 All ER 582. This concerns forfeiture of an interest, in the event of becoming a Roman Catholic, under an express provision in a will.
2 *Re Cooper, Townend v Townend* (1917) 86 LJ Ch 507, and see *Craven v Brady* (1869) 4 Ch App 296 (where the forfeiture was brought about by a second marriage).

[48.13]

[Updated for Perpetuities and Accumulations Act 2009.]

Acceleration on gift being void for remoteness. By the Perpetuities and Accumulations Acts of 1964 and 2009, a disposition is not to be treated as void for remoteness by reason only that the interest disposed of is ulterior to or dependent on an interest under a disposition which is so void, and the vesting of an interest is not prevented from being accelerated on the failure of a prior interest by reason only that the failure arises because of remoteness.[1] Where these statutes do not apply there is no acceleration.[2]

1 PAA 1964, s 6; PAA 2009, s 9. These overrule the decisions in *Re Hubbard's Will Trusts, Marston v Angier* [1963] Ch 275, [1962] 2 All ER 917, and *Re Buckton's Declaration of Trust, Public Trustee v Midland Bank Executor and Trustee Co Ltd* [1964] Ch 497, [1964] 2 All ER 487; though it may be that the second part of the sections was recognised in *Re Coleman, Public Trustee v Coleman* [1936] Ch 528, [1936] 2 All ER 225. For an account of the rule against perpetuities and remoteness generally see Chapter 94.

2 *Re Buckton's Declaration of Trust, Public Trustee v Midland Bank Executor and Trustee Co Ltd* [1964] Ch 497, [1964] 2 All ER 487. These statutory provisions do not apply to dispositions made before PAA 1964 became law on 16 July 1964.

[48.15]

[Updated in footnote 1 for Perpetuities and Accumulations Act 2009.]

Contingent gifts over. Where a gift is liable to fail upon a contingent event[1] and is followed by a gift over then, upon the contingency happening, the prior gift is divested, although, owing to lapse or some rule of law, the gift over fails to take effect according to its tenor in favour of the donee;[2] and the residuary donee or the person entitled on intestacy takes, as the case may be. The entire contingency suspending the vesting of the gift over must occur in such cases.[3] It is otherwise, however, where the gift over is a substitutionary gift to children. In such a case there is a partial divesting sufficient to let in the remaindermen;[4] as is the case where it is to be inferred that the testator intended divesting not to take place unless the gift over is effective, or where the gift over is void for uncertainty.[5] Where the contingency on which the prior gift is to fail may happen in two ways, and there is a gift over only if it happens in one way, there will be an implied gift over if it happens in the other way, provided that in the circumstances this is in accordance with the intention of the testator.[6]

1 The contingency must be such as the law allows as a condition precedent to the vesting of the gift over. Thus, prior to the Perpetuities and Accumulations Act 1964, s 6—that is to say, in an instrument taking effect before 16 July 1964—it could not be void as a perpetuity. If it is, the prior gift is not divested. The prior limitation may be invalid as offending the perpetuity rule and then the ultimate trust is valid if it is not dependent on the earlier limitation: *Re Hay* [1932] NI 215; *Re Canning's Will Trusts, Skues v Lyon* [1936] Ch 309; *Re Coleman, Public Trustee v Coleman* [1936] Ch 528, [1936] 2 All ER 225; *Re Allan's Will Trusts, Curtis v Nalder* [1958] 1 All ER 401, [1958] 1 WLR 220. For the extent to which the PAA 2009 s 1(3) preserves the rule against perpetuities to estates or interests under trusts subject to a condition precedent in relation to instruments taking effect on or after 6 April 2010 (other than wills made before that date and exercises of special powers where the power was created before that date) see para **[94.40A]**.

2 *Doe d Blomfield v Eyre* (1848) 5 CB 713 (gift over rendered ineffective by invalid apportionment under power); *Robinson v Wood* (1858) 27 LJ Ch 726 (gift to charity void); *O'Mahoney v Burdett* (1874) LR 7 HL 388 (lapse); *Re Bold, Banks v Hartland* (1926) 95 LJ Ch 201 (gift over on death without issue living at his death: failure of gift over did not indefeasibly vest prior gift, which must in any case fail on death without issue); *Re White* [1965] VR 250 (gift over to take effect on death without issue). Where the gift over infringes the perpetuity rule, a prior absolute gift is not divested: *Re Pratt's Settlement Trusts, McCullum v Phipps-Hornby* [1943] Ch 356, [1943] 2 All ER 458.

3 For example, a combined contingency of the coming into existence of a class and death without children of life tenant: *Jackson v Noble* (1838) 2 Keen 590; or a gift over on a contingent event (which happens) to the survivor of a number of persons. If no survivor exists the prior gift is not divested: *Jones v Davies* (1880) 28 WR 455; *Re Deacon's Trusts, Deacon v Deacon* (1906) 95 LT 701.

4 *Re Rooke's Will Trusts, Taylor v Rooke* [1953] Ch 716, [1953] 2 All ER 110, applying dictum in *Hurst v Hurst* (1882) 21 Ch D 278 at 293, and distinguishing *Doe d Blomfield v Eyre* (1848) 5 CB 713. A share of residue was given after the death of the tenant for life to certain relatives or their respective issue. One relative survived the testator but predeceased the tenant for life. That relative was a spinster. The gift to issue was treated as substitutionary and therefore failed but the vested gift in the spinster remained and her personal representatives were entitled to her share.

5 *Re Archer* (1907) 14 OLR 374 at 377, citing *O'Mahoney v Burdett* (1874) LR 7 HL 388 at 407.

6 *Re Fox's Estate, Dawes v Druitt* [1937] 4 All ER 664; *Re Graham, Graham v Graham* [1929] 2 Ch 127; *Re Riggall, Wildash v Riggall* [1949] WN 491.

PART J

Construction of wills: general principles

CHAPTER 49

Functions of the court of construction

[49.8]

[Updated at footnote 2 for *Creasey v Sole* [2013] EWHC 1410 (Ch), [2013] WTLR 931.]

Attempts to oust the jurisdiction of the court. The jurisdiction of the court is not ousted by the fact that the will is in a foreign language, or has to be construed by foreign rules of construction;[1] or by direction of the testator that all questions of construction are to be decided by the trustees or by arbitration;[2] and a direction that a beneficiary seeking to have the will construed by the court shall lose his benefits under the will is inoperative.[3] The question of what conditions of this nature may be valid is considered elsewhere.[4]

1 *Di Sora v Phillipps* (1863) 10 HL Cas 624; *Re Bonnefoi, Surrey v Perrin* [1912] P 233.

2 *Re Wynn* [1952] Ch 271, [1952] 1 All ER 341 (decision of trustee to bind all persons – not valid); *Massy v Rogers* (1883) 11 LR Ir 409; *Price v Dewhurst* (1837) 8 Sim 279 (decision of an executor set aside as fraudulent); *Re Walton's Estate* (1856) 8 De GM & G 173; *Re Bronson* [1958] OR 367; *Re Raven, Spencer v National Association for the Prevention of Consumption and other Forms of Tuberculosis* [1915] 1 Ch 673 (direction that identity of legatees be decided by trustees whose decision was to be final held contrary to public policy and void for repugnancy). However, it was held in Australia that acts done in good faith under a determination by the tribunal set up by the testator were valid it seems, not only to protect the executors or trustees, but for all purposes *(Thompson's Will, Brahe v Mason* [1910] VLR 251 at 255), and in *Re Tuck's Settlement Trusts, Public Trustee v Tuck* [1978] Ch 49, [1978] 1 All ER 104, CA, Lord Denning MR, unsupported by the other two judges, expressed the view that *Re Wynn* and *Re Raven* need to be reconsidered in the light of *Dundee General Hospital v Walker* [1952] 1 All ER 896, where the executors had a discretion to withhold a gift if they were satisfied that a hospital had been taken over by the state or a local authority, and their decision was held to be final so long as it was arrived at reasonably and honestly. See also para **[35.38]** above and *Creasey v Sole* [2013] EWHC 1410 (Ch), [2013] WTLR 931 at paras 65 and 66. An alternative to attempting to limit the jurisdiction of the court or to forfeit the interests of beneficiaries who dispute the will is to relieve trustees from liability if they act upon the opinion of counsel: see, eg, Form 21.13 in Volume 2, para **[221.18]**.

3 *Rhodes v Muswell Hill Land Co* (1861) 29 Beav 560 at 604; *Massy v Rogers* (1883) 11 LR Ir 409. The persons claiming under the testator may agree upon arbitration: *Ridout v Pain* (1747) 3 Atk 486.

4 See para **[35.38]** above.

CHAPTER 50

General principles of construction

I. INTRODUCTION

[50.1]

[Updated in footnote 11 for *Parkinson v Fawdon* [2010] WTLR 79, [2009] EWHC 1953 (Ch); *RSPCA v Sharp* [2010] EWCA Civ 1474, [2011] STC 553; *Scarfe v Matthews* [2012] 35 LS Gaz R 20, [2012] WTLR 1579; and *Spurling v Broadhurst* [2012] EWHC 2883 (Ch), [2012] WTLR 1825.]

The modern approach to the construction of legal documents. The House of Lords decisions, and in particular the judgments of Lord Hoffmann, in *Mannai Investment Co Ltd v Eagle Star Life Assurance Co Ltd*[1] and *Investors' Compensation Scheme Ltd v West Bromwich Building Society,*[2] mark a fundamental change in the approach to the construction of legal documents. They concern the construction of commercial agreements but they affect the approach to the construction of legal documents generally. In *Mannai* Lord Hoffmann specifically referred disparagingly,[3] to the former (ie before AJA 1982, s 21) rule confining the admissibility of extrinsic evidence of intention in construing wills to cases of latent ambiguity and in *Investors Compensation*[4] to 'all the old intellectual baggage of 'legal' interpretation'.

The principles as they apply to wills may be briefly stated as follows:

(1) Interpretation is the ascertainment of the meaning which a document would convey to a reasonable person having all the background knowledge which would have been available at the time the will was made.[5]

(2) The admissible background knowledge includes 'absolutely anything which would have affected the way in which the language of the will would have been understood by a reasonable man'.[6]

(3) The law excludes from the admissible background declarations of subjective intent[7] (but in the case of a will, made by one party not two, subjective intent can in certain circumstances be looked at).[8]

(4) The meaning which a will would convey to a reasonable man is not the same thing as the meaning of its words. The meaning of words is a matter of dictionaries and grammars; the meaning of the will is what having regard to the relevant background the testator would reasonably have been understood to mean; the background may not merely enable the reasonable man to choose between the possible meanings of words which are ambiguous but even to conclude that the testator must, for whatever reason, have used the wrong words or syntax.[9]

(5) The 'rule' that words should be given their 'natural and ordinary meaning' reflects the common sense proposition that we do not easily accept people have made linguistic mistakes, particularly in formal documents; on the other hand, if one would nevertheless conclude from the background that something must have gone wrong with the language, the law does not require judges to attribute to the testator that which he plainly could not have had.[10]

Some of the more technical rules formerly applied in the construction of wills may need to be re-examined in the light of the new approach, or at any rate disregarded where there are grounds for thinking that the testator wanted something different.[11] It remains appropriate to retain the accumulated learning of centuries on the construction of wills. This is partly because it is not yet clear to what extent it is to be jettisoned. There is also the point that many problems of construction arise because of facts or circumstances unknown to or unforeseen by the testator and the testator's professional advisers, with the consequence that the testator formed no intention as to what should happen. In these circumstances the received rules of construction retain their utility.

1 [1997] AC 749.
2 [1998] 1 All ER 98, [1998] 1 WLR 896.
3 At pp 776–777.
4 At 912.
5 *Investors' Compensation Scheme v West Bromwich Building Society* [1998] 1 All ER 98, [1998] 1 WLR 896.
6 *Investors' Compensation Scheme v West Bromwich Building Society* ([1998] 1 WLR 896 at 912–913), provided that it is relevant (*Bank of Credit and Commerce International SA v Ali* [2001] UKHL 8, [2002] 1 AC 251).
7 *Investors' Compensation Scheme v West Bromwich Building Society* [1998] 1 All ER 98, [1998] 1 WLR 896.
8 See para **[57.23]** below.
9 *Investors' Compensation Scheme v West Bromwich Building Society* [1998] 1 All ER 98, [1998] 1 WLR 896.
10 *Investors' Compensation Scheme v West Bromwich Building Society* [1998] 1 All ER 98, [1998] 1 WLR 896.
11 For an example of the more modern approach to construction in the context of wills, in which *Mannai* was referred to, see *Blech v Blech* [2002] WTLR 483. *Thomas v Kent* [2007] WTLR 177 is another recent case in which the strict traditional rule of construction was held to be displaced by what was inferred to be the testator's intention. Though *Mannai* was not referred to in *Parkinson v Fawdon* [2010] WTLR 79, [2009] EWHC 1953 (Ch) the construction process there was in accordance with the modern approach. See also *RSPCA v Sharp* [2010] EWCA Civ 1474, [2011] STC 553 where Lord Neuberger MR acknowledged that the court's approach to the interpretation of wills is, in practice, very similar to its approach to the interpretation of contracts, although he noted at [32] that one obvious difference between a bilateral document such as a contract and a unilateral document such as a will, is that parties negotiating a contract may well be consciously content to include an obscurely drafted provision, on the basis that it represents an acceptable compromise, which enables overall agreement to be reached, whereas, save in a most exceptional case, which it is hard to conceive, a person making a will has no interest in obscurity. See, further, *Scarfe v Matthews* [2012] 35 LS Gaz R 20, [2012] WTLR 1579 at [19]–[27] of the judgment and *Spurling v Broadhurst* [2012] EWHC 2883 (Ch), [2012] WTLR 1825.

II. IN GENERAL

[50.2]

[Updated in footnote 10 for *RSPCA v Sharp* [2010] EWCA Civ 1474, [2011] STC 553.]

Intention collected from whole will. It has already been stated that the first principle of construction is to give effect to the intention of the testator as expressed in the words of the will.[1] The intention is collected from the whole will[2] with such evidence as the rules already stated allow[3] and the meaning of the will and every part of it is determined according to that intention.[4] A will is construed in the same way as any other document subject to this, that, if the intention is shown, the mode of expression of that intention and the form and language of the will are unimportant.[5] The want of technical words which are necessary in some instruments for the purpose of giving expression to the intention,[6] or any inaccuracy in grammar[7] or any want or inaccuracy in punctuation marks is immaterial so long as the intention is clear.[8] In all such cases a benevolent construction is adopted.[9] Consideration is given to the fact whether the will is drafted by a skilled lawyer or by the testator himself.[10]

1 *Roberts v Roberts* (1613) 2 Bulst 123 (the intention of the testator is plainly collected out of the very words of the will); *Lowen v Cocks* (1627) Het 63; *Bowen v Lewis* (1884) 9 App Cas 890; *Beaudry v Barbeau* [1900] AC 569; *Re Ackland Trust* [1944] 2 WWR 56; *Ng Chi-fong v Hui Ho Pui-fun* [1987] HKLR 462 at 485, applying Lord Halsbury LC in *Leader v Duffy* (1888) 13 App Cas 294. See also *Mardulyn v Lee Yee Hung* [1992] 2 HKC 164 at 171 and 174, where the text is referred to and *Re Golan Estate* [1996] 2 WWR 614. See also *Gibson Estate v Ashbury College Inc* (1999) 179 DLR (4th) 557 at 562. The rule first applied to a will is to give words their ordinary meaning: see *Roddy v Fitzgerald* (1858) 6 HL Cas 823 at 876; *Gorringe v Mahlstedt* [1907] AC 225 at 227, but see paras **[50.11]** and **[50.12]** below.

2 *Baddeley v Leppingwell* (1764) 3 Burr 1533; *Thellusson v Woodford* (1799) 4 Ves 227 at 329; *Martin v Lee* (1861) 14 Moo PCC 142 at 153; *Crumpe v Crumpe* [1900] AC 127; *Marchuk v Marchuk* (1965) 52 WWR 652; *Re Welsh* (1980) 111 DLR (3d) 390; *Re Huffman* (1979) 101 DLR (3d) 365.

3 *Stanley v Stanley* (1862) 2 John & H 491; *Re Cozens, Miles v Wilson* [1903] 1 Ch 138. Although the will may be plain and unambiguous on the face of it, yet extrinsic circumstances may show the words are not to have their ordinary meaning: *Crook v Whitley* (1857) 7 De GM & G 490 at 495 (a gift to children where there were only grandchildren); *Re Shaw, Shaw v Shaw* [1955] QSR 284 (all surrounding circumstances to be kept in mind); and although the words of the will are plain and can be given full effect to, a consideration of the whole will may lead the court to insert a word which it is clear the testator has omitted. Thus where the will said 'all the nephews and nieces of my late sister L', the court upon a consideration of the whole will and evidence of the state of the family inferred that the word 'children' had been omitted and the clause was intended to read 'all my nephews and nieces children of my late sister L': *Re Birkin, Heald v Millership* [1949] 1 All ER 1045. See also *Re Smith, Veasey v Smith* [1948] Ch 49, [1947] 2 All ER 708, but in *Re Hurring* [1950] NZLR 948, the court refused to construe the words 'grandnieces and grandnephews' otherwise than literally although there were no such at the date of the will nor of the death but there were many nieces and nephews. As to insertion of words, see para **[52.3]** below.

4 The intention, when legitimately proved, is competent not only to fix the sense of ambiguous words, but to control the sense even of clear words and to supply the place of express words, in cases of difficulty or ambiguity: *Re Haygarth, Wickham v Haygarth* [1913] 2 Ch 9 at 15, citing *Hawkins on Wills* (2nd edn) p 6; *Re Patterson, Dunlop v Greer* [1899] 1 IR 324. It has been said, however, that nothing is more fallacious than first endeavouring to find the intention of the testator and then to construe the words of the will with reference to the supposed intention: *Taaffe v Conmee* (1862) 10 HL Cas 64 at 85; see similarly *Ng Chi-fong v Hui Ho Pui-fun* [1987] HKLR 462, per Rhind J, at 485 (cited in para **[51.1]**, n 1, below) where the text is referred to.

5 *Ralph v Carrick* (1879) 11 Ch D 873 at 876; *Cave v Cave* (1762) 2 Eden 139 at 144; *Hull v Carpenter* [1920] NZLR 361.

6 *Ralph v Carrick* (1879) 11 Ch D 873; *Taylor v Shaw, Re Jones* (1920) 89 LJPC 124.

7 *Re Norman's Trust* (1853) 3 De GM & G 965; *Eden v Wilson* (1852) 4 HL Cas 257 at 284; *Hall v Warren* (1861) 9 HL Cas 420 at 427. The ordinary meaning must not be departed from upon a mere suggestion of false grammar: *Gorringe v Mahlstedt* [1907] AC 225 at 227.

8 *Gordon v Gordon* (1871) LR 5 HL 254 at 276; *Gauntlett v Carter* (1853) 17 Beav 586; *Re Campbell, M'Cabe v Campbell* [1918] 1 IR 429.

9 *Jones v Price* (1841) 11 Sim 557 at 565; *Lang v Pugh* (1842) 1 Y & C Ch Cas 718 at 725; *Edgeworth v Edgeworth* (1869) LR 4 HL 35 at 41; *Re Speakman, Unsworth v Speakman* (1876) 4 Ch D 620 at 625.

10 *Richards v Davids* (1862) 13 CBNS 69; affd (1863) 13 CBNS 861; *Re Dayrell, Hastie v Dayrell* [1904] 2 Ch 496; *Blathwayt v Lord Cawley* [1976] AC 397, [1975] 3 All ER 625. This guides the court as to the force to be given to technical words: *Thellusson v Lord Rendelsham* (1859) 7 HL Cas 429 at 486. In a home-made will words may be given a popular sense rather than a legal sense: *Forth v Chapman* (1720) 1 P Wms 663 at 666; *Re Taylor, Taylor v Tweedie* [1923] 1 Ch 99 at 105. The principles of construction are, however, the same in all cases: *Weale v Ollive (No 2)* (1863) 32 Beav 421 at 423; but technically rules of construction will not be strictly applied in the case of a home-made will: *Re Crocombe* [1949] SASR 302. In *RSPCA v Sharp* [2010] EWCA Civ 1474, [2011] STC 553, it was relevant in construing a clause in a will making a gift by reference to the maximum amount upon which inheritance tax would not be payable that the will had been drawn up by solicitors who it might be assumed had some familiarity with the way in which inheritance tax operated. Where a will is professionally drafted by a solicitor he is to be assumed to be competent, and although solicitors do obviously make mistakes, there needs to be something in the language of the document or its admissible background to justify that inference. See further para **[50.7]**, n 3, below.

III. SCOPE OR PURPOSE OF WILL CONSIDERED IN DOUBTFUL CASES

[50.5]

[Updated in the text and in footnote 6 for *RSPCA v Sharp* [2010] EWCA Civ 1474, [2011] STC 553.]

Inferences from the scope of the will. The court makes any reasonable inference from a particular passage, comparing that inference with what is apparent in other parts of the will.[1] This power of inference, however, is limited; a general intention not carried out by appropriate words in the will itself cannot give the court the right to place the words there for the testator,[2] and a priori reasoning upon what the testator would naturally intend cannot be allowed to weigh against the proper construction of the words used.[3] The court cannot conjecture what the testator would have said if a particular state of things had been presented to his mind which it is apparent, from the language he had used, had not occurred to him and for which it cannot be supposed that he intended to make any provision.[4] Where, however, the words are conflicting, the court attempts to reconcile successive provisions without unduly straining the language and to make the whole consistent with the apparent general intention of the testator.[5] Since a will is to be construed as a whole, clear words are required before one construes one clause as being subject or subordinate to another, simply because it is later in the will than the other clause.[6]

1 *Law Union and Crown Insurance Co v Hill* [1902] AC 263 at 265; *Jenkins v Hughes* (1860) 8 HL Cas 571 at 588.

2 *Hunter v A-G* [1899] AC 309 at 315, 317; *Re Evans, Public Trustee v Evans* [1920] 2 Ch 304.
3 *Coltsmann v Coltsmann* (1868) LR 3 HL 121 at 130.
4 *Martin v Holgate* (1866) LR 1 HL 175 at 186; *Inderwick v Tatchell* [1903] AC 120 at 122.
5 *Re Bedson's Trusts* (1885) 28 Ch D 523 at 525; *Taylor v Sturrock* [1900] AC 225 at 232; *Shields v Shields* [1910] 1 IR 116 at 120. As to inconsistencies, see Chapter 52.
6 Per Lord Neuberger MR in *RSPCA v Sharp* [2010] EWCA Civ 1474, [2011] STC 553 at [37].

IV. WORDS GIVEN THEIR USUAL MEANING

[50.6]

[Updated in footnote 2 for *Public Trustee v Butler* [2012] EWHC 858 (Ch), [2012] WTLR 1043.]

Grammatical and ordinary meaning. It is a general rule applicable to all kinds of documents[1] that the words used in it are in the first place to be given ordinary grammatical meaning;[2] but, despite all that has been said as to the universality of the rule,[3] it is by no means a hard and fast rule which is subject to no exception.[4] As has already been stated even the ordinary meaning of words give way to some different or modified meaning required by the context[5] or by a consideration of the whole will.[6] Where a word has two proper and recognised meanings, this rule, if it applies to all, must be greatly modified, and in such cases the meaning of the words in a particular passage must be decided by the context and the surrounding circumstances.[7] A word will not, however, be given an artificial, secondary or technical meaning unless it is shown that it cannot without propriety receive its ordinary meaning.[8]

1 *Re Levy, ex p Walton* (1881) 17 Ch D 746 at 751; *Caledonian Rly Co v North British Rly Co* (1881) 6 App Cas 114 at 131; *Spencer v Metropolitan Board of Works* (1882) 22 Ch D 142 at 148. See generally the House of Lords judgments in *Perrin v Morgan* [1943] AC 399.
2 *Thellusson v Woodford* (1799) 4 Ves 227 at 329, adopted in *Villar v Sir Walter Gilbey* [1907] AC 139 at 147. The rule has been enunciated in a very large number of cases; see for example *Hamilton v Ritchie* [1894] AC 310 at 313; *Higgins v Dawson* [1902] AC 1 at 12; *Gorringe v Mahlstedt* [1907] AC 225 at 227; *Tarbutt v Nicholson* (1920) 89 LJPC 127; *Lynch v Johnson* (1878) 4 VLR 263; *Crawford v Broddy* (1896) 26 SCR 345; *De Robeck v Lord Cloncurry* (1871) IR 5 Eq 588; *Church Property Trustees v Public Trustee* (1907) 27 NZLR 354; *Re Stalker's Executor's, Petitioners* 1977 SLT (Notes) 4: *Re Rowland, Smith v Russell* [1963] Ch 1 (contrast the approach of Lord Denning MR in a dissenting judgment at 9, 10). In *Public Trustee v Butler* [2012] EWHC 858 (Ch), [2012] WTLR 1043, the Chancellor found that where in a holograph will the language used was good, the handwriting educated and the content characteristic of one accustomed to managing property, the presumption would be that the testator used the words in their normal meaning.
3 There is the well-known dictum of Kindersley V-C in *Re Crawford's Trusts* (1854) 2 Drew 230 ('a rule of universal application, which admits of no exception, and which ought never under any circumstances to be departed from'). The dictum in *Gether v Capper* (1855) 24 LJCP 69 at 71, is perhaps nearer the truth: 'The most general of rules; a rule of great utility.' The rule applies to all wills: *Smith v Butcher* (1878) 10 Ch D 113 at 116.
4 *Hamilton v Ritchie* [1894] AC 310 at 313 (unless the context of the instruments shows that he intended to use the words with some other than the conventional meaning); *Gordon v Gordon* (1871) LR 5 HL 254 at 271 (to the same effect). In practice, the rule is entirely subservient to the context of the will: *Seale-Hayne v Jodrell* (1891) AC 304 at 306.
5 See para **[50.4]** above.
6 See para **[50.2]** above.
7 See *Cave v Horsell* [1912] 3 KB 533 at 543, 544.

8 *Walker v Tipping* (1852) 9 Hare 800; *Crook v Whiteley* (1857) 7 De GM & G 490; *Lowther v Bentinck* (1874) LR 19 Eq 166; *Re Jackson's Will* (1879) 13 Ch D 189; *Re Benn, Benn v Benn* (1885) 29 Ch D 839; *Re Bennett, Henderson v Bennett* (1903) 21 NZLR 113.

[50.15]

[Updated in text and at footnote 3 for *Sammut v Manzi* [2008] UKPC 58, [2009] WTLR 1051 and *Spurling v Broadhurst* [2012] EWHC 2883 (Ch), [2012] WTLR 1825.]

Regard to punctuation. Different views have been taken as to the importance of punctuation. It has been said that it is to be disregarded[1] but the modern view seems to be in favour of having regard to punctuation marks.[2] Their significance though depends upon the context and are likely to be more important in the case of a manuscript will than in one produced on a word processor.[3]

1 *Sandford v Raikes* (1816) 1 Mer 646; *Gordon v Gordon* (1871) LR 5 HL 254; *Re Campbell, M'Cabe v Campbell* [1918] 1 IR 429.

2 See Wood V-C in *Oppenheim v Henry* (1853), as reported in a note to *Walker v Tipping* (1852) 9 Hare 800, 803; Sir John Romilly MR in *Gauntlett v Carter* (1853) 17 Beav 586 at 589, 590; Knight Bruce LJ, note to *Manning v Purcell* (1855) 24 LJ Ch 522, 523; Lord Finlay LC in *Houston v Burns* [1918] AC 337 at 342; and Roxburgh J in *Re Jeffrey* [1948] 2 All ER 131 at 131. See also *Re Patton* (1971) 19 DLR (3d) 497 (mark not considered as a period); *Re Steel, Public Trustee v Christian Aid Society* [1979] Ch 218, [1978] 2 All ER 1026.

3 See *Sammut v Manzi* [2008] UKPC 58, [2009] WTLR 1051 and *Spurling v Broadhurst* [2012] EWHC 2883 (Ch), [2012] WTLR 1825.

CHAPTER 53

Uncertainty

[53.6]

[Updated in footnote 3 for *Public Trustee v Butler* [2012] EWHC 858 (Ch), [2012] WTLR 1043.]

Uncertainty as to the persons to whom a fund may be appointed. In considering this matter there are two quite different kinds of powers: (a) a power in the nature of a trust or coupled with a duty usually called a fiduciary power, and (b) powers not of this nature. The simplest example of a power in the nature of a trust is one where the fund or property is given to named or a class of beneficiaries and the power is to decide only in what shares they are to take.[1] In such cases the intention to benefit the class is mandatory and in cases of default the beneficiaries can compel the trustees to execute the trust, by an application to the court if necessary. The court adopts the principle as to trusts that it will not permit the trustee's negligence, accident or other circumstances to disappoint the interests of those for whose benefit he is called upon to execute it.[2] Once that proposition is established, then it follows that since the court might be required to execute the trust it is essential that the beneficiaries should be known, in the sense of its being possible to draw up a definitive and complete list of all the persons within the class of beneficiaries.[3] If in the case of a fixed, as opposed to a discretionary, trust it is not possible to ascertain the beneficiaries at the date of the document declaring the donor's intentions (in the case of a will, his death) in any case with that precision, then the trust fails for uncertainty.[4] However, the position with regard to powers is quite different: the court (except in the case of a mala fide exercise) has little interest in the exercise of a power, and if it is not exercised the fund goes to those entitled in default under the settlement, or on a resulting trust, as the case may be. The only duty on which the court could insist is that the trustees should consider exercising the power and in particular consider a request from a person within the ambit of the power that the power should be exercised in his favour.[5] Further, since the court might be required to assess the validity of any proposed appointment, to prevent an invalid appointment, it is necessary that the court should be able to say with certainty, whether any particular person is, or is not, within the permissible class of objects, and this is the degree of certainty of the objects necessary for a power of appointment.[6] This rule is equally applicable to special and intermediate or hybrid powers of appointment.[7]

This rule, previously only applicable to powers, has now been held to be also applicable to discretionary trusts, so that such a trust is valid if it can be said with certainty that any given individual is or is not a member of the class.[8] Thus a discretionary trust exercisable in favour of employees and former employees of a company and their relatives and dependants was upheld notwithstanding the argument that the class was so large and arbitrary that the trustees could not reasonably estimate the membership or know how to set about instituting inquiries which would reveal the membership.[9]

1 *Brown v Higgs* (1801) 8 Ves 561; *IRC v Broadway Cottages Trust* [1955] Ch 20, [1954] 3 All ER 120.

2 Per Lord Eldon in *Brown v Higgs* (1801) 8 Ves 561.

3 *Re Ogden, Brydon v Samuel* [1933] Ch 678, [1933] All ER Rep 720 (associations in the United Kingdom having liberal principles); *IRC v Broadway Cottages Trust* [1955] Ch 20, [1954] 3 All ER 120; *Re Sayer Trust, MacGregor v Sayer* [1957] Ch 423, [1956] 3 All ER 600 (employees, their children and dependent relatives). In *Re Eden, Ellis v Crampton* [1957] 2 All ER 430 (employees employed or previously employed by a company at a certain date), and in *Re Hain's Settlement, Tooth v Hain* [1961] 1 All ER 848, [1961] 1 WLR 440 (past, present and future employees of a company) it was held that the whole range of beneficiaries was ascertainable or at least it was not proved that it was not ascertainable. In *Public Trustee v Butler* [2012] EWHC 858 (Ch), [2012] WTLR 1043 a power to benefit promising relatives whose names appeared on a list was held void for uncertainty when no list was found.

4 *Re Saxone Shoe Co, Ltd's Trust Deed, Re Abbott's Will Trusts, Abbott v Pearson* [1962] 2 All ER 904, [1962] 1 WLR 943 (where the expression 'employees or dependants' was held to be too vague). See also cases cited in n 3 and *Re Leek, Darwen v Leek* [1967] Ch 1061, [1961] 2 All ER 1160 (wife, children or other issue or such persons as had a 'moral claim' on deceased); *Re Wootton's Will Trusts, Trotter v Duffin* [1968] 2 All ER 618, [1968] 1 WLR 681 (trust for such other organisation or body not being registered as a charity but in the opinion of the trustees having charitable objects).

5 *Re Manisty's Settlement, Manisty v Manisty* [1974] Ch 17, [1973] 2 All ER 1203; see also *Re Hay's Settlement Trusts* [1981] 3 All ER 786, [1981] 1 WLR 202 where Sir Robert Megarry V-C stated the duties of trustees in exercising a hybrid power under four heads; *Re Manisty's Settlement* and the *Baden* trust deed cases, applied; see also *Turner v Turner* [1984] Ch 100, [1983] 2 All ER 745.

6 *Re Gulbenkian's Settlement Trusts, Hacobian v Maun* [1968] Ch 126, [1967] 3 All ER 15, CA; affd sub nom *Re Gulbenkian's Settlement Trusts, Whishaw v Stevens* [1970] AC 508, [1968] 3 All ER 785, HL (power to appoint to 'persons by or with whom G may be residing'); *Re Gestetner, Barnett v Blumka* [1953] Ch 672, [1953] 1 All ER 1150 (settlor's relatives and employees and their wives or widows); *Re Coates, Ramsden v Coates* [1955] Ch 495, [1955] 1 All ER 26 (friends nominated by the widow); *Re Sayer Trust, MacGregor v Sayer* [1957] Ch 423, [1956] 3 All ER 600; *Re Gibbard, Public Trustee v Davis* [1966] 1 All ER 273 (any of my old friends—not uncertain); *Re Barlow's Will Trusts* [1979] 1 All ER 296, [1979] 1 WLR 278; *Re Manisty's Settlement, Manisty v Manisty* [1974] Ch 17, [1973] 2 All ER 1203.

7 *Re Manisty's Settlement, Manisty v Manisty* [1974] Ch 17, [1973] 2 All ER 1203.

8 *McPhail v Doulton* [1971] AC 424, [1970] 2 All ER 228, HL, overruling, at least with respect to discretionary trusts, *IRC v Broadway Cottages Trust* [1955] Ch 20, [1954] 3 All ER 120. In the case of a trust power, if the trustees do not exercise it, the court will do so in the manner best calculated to give effect to the settlor's or testator's intentions. See *Re Locker's Settlement Trusts, Meachem v Sachs* [1978] 1 All ER 216, [1977] 1 WLR 1323 (court directed discretionary trustees to repair their failure and to distribute the retained fund in shares according to the trustees' discretion) dictum of Lord Wilberforce in *McPhail v Doulton* [1971] AC 424 at 457, [1970] 2 All ER 228 at 247, applied. See also *Blausten v IRC* [1972] Ch 256, [1972] 1 All ER 41, which was not followed in *Re Hay's Settlement Trusts* [1981] 3 All ER 786, [1981] 1 WLR 202.

9 *Re Baden's Deed Trusts (No 2), Baden v Smith* [1973] Ch 9, [1972] 2 All ER 1304, applied in *Re Manisty's Settlement, Manisty v Manisty* [1974] Ch 17, [1973] 2 All ER 1203.

[53.7]

[Updated for Perpetuities and Accumulations Act 2009.]

Uncertainty and the perpetuity rule. Mere difficulty in ascertaining the class does not amount to uncertainty. Under the PAA 2009, s 5(1) the perpetuity period is now 125 years for all dispositions which take effect on or after 6 April 2010 and are subject to the rule against perpetuities, other than wills made before that date. There is now no other period.[1] Under the previous law, the formula for avoiding the perpetuity rule by reference to the survivor of all descendants now living of a sovereign has been held to be not void for uncertainty.[2] There are, however, limits to the amount of uncertainty and a trust 'for the longest period allowed by law that is to say, until the period of twenty-one years from the death of the last survivor of all persons living at my death' is void for uncertainty.[3] It has been said that the trust is still valid although the whole of the fund will be spent in ascertaining the possible beneficiaries.[4]

1 See the PAA 2009, ss 5(1), 15(1)(a) (Vol 2, Part G, para **[246.179]**).
2 *Re Villar, Public Trustee v Villar* [1929] 1 Ch 243.
3 *Re Moore, Prior to Moore* [1901] 1 Ch 936.
4 *Re Eden, Ellis v Crampton* [1957] 2 All ER 430 at 435.

CHAPTER 54

Context and meaning of words

[54.5]

[Updated in footnote 6 for *Public Trustee v Butler* [2012] EWHC 858 (Ch), [2012] WTLR 1043.]

How far presumed to have same meaning. The force of the context may give different meanings to the same word when used in different parts of the same will, and the court does not, merely because a word bears a special meaning in one clause, necessarily give to it the same meaning in another clause of that will, in itself clear, and not connected with the first clause.[1] In all cases the context must be considered.[2] There is a presumption, however, that a word used in one part of a will with some clear and definite meaning is intended to mean the same thing in another part of the will, where its meaning is not clear.[3] Having regard, however, to the rule that the words of a will must be construed with reference to the subject-matter,[4] a different meaning may be given to the same word when used with reference to real and personal property in a will, even in the same sentence.[5] If the presumption is that where a word is used in one part of a will it is intended to mean the same thing in another part of the will, the converse may be that where different words are used, it is intended that they mean different things.[6]

1 *Dalzell v Welch* (1828) 2 Sim 319 ('issue'); *Carter v Bentall* (1840) 2 Beav 551 ('issue'); *Head v Randall* (1843) 2 Y & C Ch Cas 231 ('issue'); *Williams v Teale* (1847) 6 Hare 239 at 250 ('issue'); *Neathway v Reed* (1853) 3 De GM & G 18 at 22 ('surviving'); *Gill v Barrett* (1860) 29 Beav 372 ('then').

2 *Doe d Stopford v Stopford* (1804) 5 East 501; *Right d Compton v Compton* (1808) 9 East 267; *Carter v Bentall* (1840) 2 Beav 551; *Neathway v Reed* (1853) 3 De GM & G 18.

3 *Re Birks, Kenyon v Birks* [1900] 1 Ch 417 at 418; *Edwards v Edwards* (1849) 12 Beav 97 ('issue'); *Rhodes v Rhodes* (1859) 27 Beav 413 ('issue'); *Re Buckle, Williams v Marson* [1894] 1 Ch 286 ('deductions'); *Ridgeway v Munkittrick* (1841) 1 Dr & War 84; *Edyvean v Archer, Re Brooke* [1903] AC 379 at 384; *Leeming v Sherratt* (1842) 2 Hare 14 ('survivors'). The rule, however, is not one of universal application: *Re Hickey, Beddoes v Hodgson* (1917) 86 LJ Ch 385; *Edyvean v Archer, Re Brooke,* above; *Clifford v Koe* (1880) 5 App Cas 447. Where a word is used inaccurately in one place, it will not necessarily mean the same when used in another: *Re Ridge, Hancock v Dutton* (1933) 149 LT 266.

4 *Williams v Jeckyl* (1755) 2 Ves Sen 681 at 683.

5 *Forth v Chapman* (1720) 1 P Wms 663 at 667; *Doe d Chattaway v Smith* (1816) 5 M & S 126 at 132. At one time the words 'without leaving issue' were, in the case of real property, given a meaning different from that given to them in case of personal property, but since the Wills Act 1837, s 29, Vol 2, Part G, para **[244.29]**, came into force the same meaning has to be given to them in each case; see Chapter 98.

6 In *Public Trustee v Butler* [2012] EWHC 858 (Ch), [2012] WTLR 1043 it was held that the testator must have meant different things by his uses of the words 'devote' and 'empower'.

CHAPTER 57

Evidence admissible in a court of construction – extrinsic evidence

VI. THE ADMISSIBILITY OF EXTRINSIC EVIDENCE: POST-1982 DEATHS

[57.25]

[Updated in footnote 1 for *Esson v Esson* [2009] EWHC 1953 (Ch), [2010] WTLR 187 and *Spurling v Broadhurst* [2012] EWHC 2883 (Ch), [2012] WTLR 1825.]

'The language used in any part of it is ambiguous on the face of it' (para (b)). This resembles the category of 'patent ambiguity' in the existing law, where evidence of surrounding circumstances, but not direct evidence of the testator's intention, was admissible. Examples are a gift of 'one thousand pounds (£10,000)' and a gift to 'the son of A' where the will itself shows that A has several sons. The effect of the section is that direct evidence of the testator's intention will now be admissible in this type of case. This change in the law is clearly capable of making a considerable difference to the outcome in many cases. Evidence of surrounding circumstances alone will often be incapable of resolving ambiguities of this kind in circumstances where direct evidence of the testator's intention can do so. Thus such evidence may assist to show which of two or more meanings a testator was attaching to a particular word or phrase, such as 'my effects' or 'my money'.[1] But the section cannot assist where the alleged meaning is one which the word or phrase cannot bear; in carrying out a process of construction the court cannot declare that meaning to be the meaning of the word or phrase. Such a conclusion, varying or contradicting the language used would amount to rewriting the will which can only be done under the limited powers of rectification provided by the AJA 1982, s 20.[2]

1 See Nicholls J in *Re Williams, Wiles v Madgin* [1985] 1 All ER 964 at 969. In *Esson v Esson* [2010] WTLR 187, [2009] EWHC 1953 (Ch) extrinsic evidence was admitted under AJA 1982, s 21(1)(b) to explain whether an ambiguous provision was a condition or an explanation for a gift. In *Spurling v Broadhurst* [2012] EWHC 2883 (Ch), [2012] WTLR 1825, extrinsic evidence was admitted to resolve an ambiguity as to the shares in which the legatees took a residuary estate.

2 See Nicholls J in *Re Williams, Wiles v Madgin* [1985] 1 All ER 964 at 969. In that case the will listed twenty-five names in three separate groups with no indication as to the purpose of the grouping. The question arose as to whether a letter written by the testatrix to her solicitors referring to the division in the will could be admitted in evidence to assist in the construction. It was held that the will was ambiguous on the face of it and that the letter could be admitted under the AJA 1982, s 21(1)(b) but that in fact the letter provided no assistance in the construction of the will. Nicholls J then construed the will without

reference to the letter and came to the somewhat surprising decision that the estate should be divided equally between the twenty-five named persons. It is interesting that Nicholls J took a rather broad view of what constitutes an ambiguity for the purpose of the section. The alternative would have been to say that the provision in the will was 'meaningless' within the AJA 1982, s 21(1)(a) and to admit the letter as an aid to construction under that paragraph. A similarly liberal approach was adopted in *Re Benham's Will Trusts, Lockhart v Harker, Read and The Royal National Lifeboat Institution* [1955] STC 210.

[57.26]

[Updated in the text and footnote 4 for *Frear v Frear* [2009] WTLR 231.]

'Evidence, other than evidence of the testator's intention, shows that the language used in any part of it is ambiguous in the light of surrounding circumstances' (para (c)). There was already a rule permitting the admission of extrinsic evidence, including evidence of intention, in cases of latent ambiguities or equivocations before AJA 1982, s 21. The principle was expressed as follows: 'where the object of a testator's bounty, or the subject of disposition is described in terms which are applicable indifferently to more than one person or thing, evidence is admissible to prove which of the persons or things so described was intended by the testator'.[1] The case law illustrations of this principle are well known. Thus in *Re Jackson, Beattie v Murphy*,[2] the testator made a disposition to 'my nephew Arthur Murphy' and since this name was applicable to more than one legitimate nephew, evidence was admitted, which in fact established that it was an illegitimate nephew of that name who was intended. Similarly when the testator simply devises his house to a beneficiary and he owns more than one.

It is thought that para (c) has the effect of admitting evidence of the testator's intention in a wider class of cases than the latent ambiguity rule did. The conditions which had to be fulfilled for the latent ambiguity rule to apply[3] were more stringent. For example, it did not apply if the ambiguity could be resolved by the application of a rule of construction, or by the construction of the will as a whole, or from evidence of surrounding circumstances other than the testator's intention. It is thought that none of these restrictions would apply in relation to para (c), and that in general evidence of the testator's intention is no longer a last resort to be used only when all other methods of interpretation have failed (although it still cannot be admitted to show that there is an ambiguity if none is apparent from the will itself or the surrounding circumstances). Also, para (c) is not restricted, as the latent ambiguity rule apparently was, to ambiguity in descriptions (usually of persons or property), although other kinds of latent ambiguity in wills must be unusual. An indication that para (c) does permit evidence of intention to be admitted in a wider class of cases than under the traditional latent ambiguity rule, although in the absence of specific argument on the point, appears in *Frear v Frear*,[4] where evidence showing that the testatrix, who was the sole legal owner of a house, owned only a beneficial share of the same, was held admissible to show that the language disposing of her residuary estate was ambiguous.

It will be noticed that evidence of the testatrix's intention is not admissible to establish the ambiguity, but only to resolve an ambiguity that has been established by factual evidence.[5]

1 Wigram, *An Examination of the Rules of Law, Respecting the Admission of Extrinsic Evidence in Aid of the Interpretation of Wills*, 5th edn (1914), Proposition VII, p 110. See para **[57.22]** above.
2 [1933] Ch 237.
3 See para **[57.22]** above.
4 [2008] EWCA Civ 1320, [2009] WTLR 231, para [38].
5 Following the majority of the Law Reform Committee, 19th Report on the Interpretation of Wills (1973, Cmnd 5301).

PART L

Construction of wills: particular rules relating to persons

CHAPTER 66

Class gifts – rules of convenience

II. PRESUMPTION AND EVIDENCE AS TO FUTURE PARENTHOOD – WHEN WOMAN PAST CHILD-BEARING

[66.3]

[Updated in text and footnote 5 for Perpetuities and Accumulations Act 2009.]

Although the law has always been averse to assuming for perpetuity purposes that a woman was past child-bearing or to fixing a date at which it can be said that a woman was no longer able to become the mother of children,[1] the Court of Chancery would in a clear case give trustees or others engaged in the administration of an estate permission to distribute on the footing that a woman was past child-bearing[2] and it has in practice been assumed that a woman who has attained 54 is past child-bearing.[3] However, it is now possible, by the application of techniques developed for the treatment of infertility, for a woman well over the age of 54 to bear a child, and the existing case law on the assumptions which the court will make must be treated with caution. Under the rule against perpetuities no presumption was ever made at common law. Now by the Perpetuities and Accumulations Act 1964, s 2 the rule was modernised, but this amendment only applied where the question arises in proceedings regarding the application of the rule against perpetuities in an instrument taking effect after 15 July 1964.[4] There is no corresponding presumption under PAA 2009 because of the adoption of a fixed term of years as the perpetuity period.[5]

1 *Re Dawson, Johnston v Hill* (1888) 39 Ch D 155; *Ward v Van der Loeff* [1924] AC 653. In *Re Blake, Berry v Geen* [1938] 2 All ER 362 at 367, Lord Maugham LC said: 'I do not think it necessary ... to express any opinion as to the decision in *Re Deloitte, Griffiths v Deloitte* [1926] Ch 56. That authority, which turned on the refusal of the court to presume a woman aged 65 to be past child-bearing for the purposes of the case, might require consideration in this House at some future time and I think it better to leave open the question which it involves'. And see *Figgs v Clarke* [1997] STC 247.

2 Danckwerts J said in *IRC v Bernstein* [1960] Ch 444 at 454, [1960] 1 All ER 697 at 702; 'It is quite true that the Court of Chancery as a practical matter and as a matter of administration, on being satisfied by reason of age or for medical reasons that a woman is past the age of child-bearing, will allow the distribution of a fund, thus exonerating the trustees of a will or settlement from what otherwise might be a breach of trust'.

3 The cases for and against this presumption are collected in 22 English and Empire Digest (Reissue), pp 190–192. It would seem that apart from special reasons, the relevant age was 54. The Perpetuities and Accumulations Act 1964, s 2: see Vol 2, Part G, para **[246.65]**, fixes the age of 55. The matters to be taken into consideration have been thus stated by Wilberforce J in *Re Westminster Bank Ltd's Declaration of Trust* [1963] 2 All ER 400n at 401: 'I think that the courts would now be rather cautious in accepting [the decided cases] as laying down any sort of rule as to any particular age. It seems to me that at this time one

must take into account the physiological changes in human beings as a result of improvements in health and also the different circumstances of family planning. Moreover, it should be borne in mind that more accurate medical evidence is nowadays available, and ought to be put before the court.' See also *Re Whichelow, Bradshaw v Orpen* [1953] 2 All ER 1558, [1954] 1 WLR 5.

4 In the case of a will the testator must have died after 15 July 1964 and before 6 April 2010. See Vol 2, Part G, para **[246.65]** for the Perpetuities and Accumulations Act 1964, s 2.

5 Under the PAA 2009, s 5(1) the perpetuity period is now 125 years for all dispositions which take effect on or after 6 April 2010 and are subject to the rule against perpetuities, other than wills made before that date. There is now no other period. See Vol 2, Part G, para **[246.179]**; and Chapter 94.

CHAPTER 72

Illegitimacy of donees

[72.1]

[Updated in footnote 4 for *Re Erskine 1948 Trust; Gregg v Pigott* [2012] EWHC 732 (Ch), [2012] 3 All ER 532.]

Introduction. The position with regard to the entitlement of illegitimate donees has been affected by the Family Law Reform Act 1969 (FLRA 1969),[1] in respect of dispositions made on or after 1 January 1970[2] and by the Family Law Reform Act 1987 (FLRA 1987), with effect from 4 April 1988.[3] It is necessary to consider the position, first, with reference to the traditional common law rules which apply to the construction of gifts in dispositions made before 1 January 1970 and to dispositions made after that date which manifest an intention to exclude the 1969 Act provisions; second, with reference to the position under the FLRA 1969, which continues to apply to wills made between 1 January 1970 and 4 April 1988, even though the testator dies after the latter date. Third, wills made after 4 April 1988 will be governed by the FLRA 1987. For this purpose it is provided that a will or codicil executed before that date is not to be treated for the purposes of the FLRA 1987, as made on or after that date by reason only that the will or codicil is confirmed by a codicil executed on or after that date. The failure until 1970 to legislate to give illegitimate children the same property rights as legitimate children may turn out to be a breach of the European Human Rights Convention.[4]

1 FLRA 1969, s 15. See Vol 2, Part G, para **[245.39]**.

2 Notwithstanding any rule of law, a disposition made by will or codicil executed before this date shall not be treated for the purposes of the section as made on or after that date by reason only that the will or codicil is confirmed by a codicil executed on or after that date; FLRA 1969, s 15(8).

3 Vol 2, Part G, paras **[245.69]** ff. Again a will executed before that date is not to be treated as made after that date by reason of a codicil: s 19(7), Vol 2, Part G, para **[245.72]**.

4 See *Pla and Puncernau v Andorra* [2004] 2 FCR 630, ECtHR. For most kinds of case this may be a matter justiciable only in the European Court of Human Rights as a breach of the Convention. The problem for anyone asking the English courts to apply the Convention to pre-1970 dispositions is that the Human Rights Act 1998 does not usually apply to rights arising or failing to arise before it came into force: see *Wilson v First County Trust Ltd* [2003] UKHL 40, [2004] 1 AC 816, HL. It has been held though, by a first instance judge, that this rule is not absolute: see *Re Erskine 1948 Trust; Gregg v Pigott* [2012] EWHC 732 (Ch), [2012] 3 All ER 532. In that case, in the special circumstances before him, the judge considered he was able to apply the European Human Rights Convention retrospectively so as to construe a trust for statutory next of kin, who were prima facie to be ascertained in accordance with the law in 1948 when adopted children would not have been included, as including adopted children. The meaning of statutory next of kin being a matter of statutory construction, and statutory next of kin of a living person having a mere spes

successionis rather than an equitable interest in remainder, were important special circumstances which enabled the judge to find as he did, and there is doubt as to whether the result would be the same in relation to equitable interests in remainder under a pre-1970 instrument.

[72.10]

[Updated in footnote 2 for *Re Erskine 1948 Trust; Gregg v Pigott* [2012] EWHC 732 (Ch), [2012] 3 All ER 532.]

Illegitimate children included. In any disposition[1] made on or after 1 January 1970 and before 4 April 1988, any express or implied reference to the child or children of any person shall (unless the contrary intention appears) be construed as (or as including) a reference to any illegitimate child of that person and any reference to a person or persons related in some other manner to another person shall (again unless the contrary appears) be construed as (or as including) a reference to anyone who would be so related if he, or some person through whom the relationship is deduced, had been born legitimate.[2] But this applies only where the reference in question is to a beneficiary under the disposition[3] or, for the purpose of designating a beneficiary, to someone else to or through whom that person is related. The construction of the word 'heir' or 'heirs' is unaffected.[4] Special provisions apply to property limited to devolve with a dignity or title of honour.[5] A post-1970 disposition in favour of illegitimate children not in being when the disposition is made is no longer in danger of being held void as contrary to public policy.[6] In relation to dispositions coming into force on or after 4 April 1988 the 1969 Act is replaced by the Family Law Reform Act 1987.[7]

1 Widely defined in the FLRA 1969, s 15(8). See Vol 2, Part G, para **[245.39]**.
2 FLRA 1969, s 15. See Vol 2, Part G, para **[245.39]**. For a case where the will had been made in 1936, see *Re Upton's Estate, Upton v National Westminster Bank* [2004] EWHC 1962 (Ch), [2004] WTLR 1339, in which the will came into operation well before FLRA 1969 or FLRA 1987 or AA 1976 came into force and the argument that this was a breach of the European Human Rights Convention was rejected. See though *Re Erskine 1948 Trust; Gregg v Pigott* [2012] EWHC 732 (Ch), [2012] 3 All ER 532 where a first instance judge applied the European Human Rights Convention retrospectively so as to construe a trust for statutory next of kin, who were prima facie to be ascertained in accordance with the law in 1948 when adopted children would not have been included, as including adopted children. See, further, para **[72.1]** footnote 4.
3 It seems therefore that a gift to 'my children' would include illegitimate children, but an appointment of 'my children as executors and trustees', would not.
4 FLRA 1969, s 15(2).
5 FLRA 1969, s 15(5).
6 FLRA 1969, s 15(7).
7 Vol 2, Part G, paras **[245.69]** ff. See para **[72.14]** below.

IV. LEGITIMATION

[72.18]

[Updated in the text and footnote 2 for Human Fertilisation and Embryology Act 2008.]

Human Fertilisation and Embryology Acts of 1990 and 2008 (HFEA 1990 and HFEA 2008). The HFEA 1990, ss 27–29 came into force on 1 August 1991 and make provision for who is treated as father and mother of a child produced by means (such as artificial insemination or in vitro fertilisation) regulated by the Act, and HFEA 2008, ss 33–53 replaced those sections of HFEA 1990 with effect from 6 April 2009.[1] The Legitimacy Act 1976 can therefore apply where an unmarried couple have had fertility treatment which results in a child of which the man is by virtue of one or other HFEA treated as the father, and they marry each other after the birth of the child. Further, the Legitimacy Act 1976 is amended by HFEA 2008 so as to apply to cases where a child is born to a same sex female couple where the one who is not the mother is treated by HFEA 2008 as a parent of the child, and they are not civil partners at any time between the treatment and the birth but form a civil partnership after the birth.[2] It is likely that this provision will be amended to cover cases where same sex couples have a child and then marry in a manner recognised under the Marriage (Same Sex Couples) Act 2013 after it comes into force.[3]

1 See **[74.3]** ff below.
2 See LA 1976, ss 2A and 3(2), inserted by HFEA 2008, Sch 6, paras 16, 17, and having effect in relation to assisted reproduction treatment carried out on or after 6 April 2009 (HFEA 2008, ss 43 and 57(1), SI 2009/479). See Volume 2, para **[245.45A]**.
3 See **[80.10]** and paras **[245.149]** ff.

CHAPTER 74

Gifts to children

[74.3]

[Updated for Human Fertilisation and Embryology Act 2008.]

Child born as a result of fertilisation techniques. The Human Fertilisation and Embryology Act 2008 (HFEA 2008),[1] ss 33–53, replacing the narrower corresponding provisions of the Human Fertilisation and Embryology Act 1990 (HFEA 1990)[2] with effect from 6 April 2009,[3] contains provisions identifying the persons who are to be treated as the mother and the father of a child born as a result of *in vitro* fertilisation or artificial insemination and governing the status of any such child. The HFEA 1990 applies to children born as a result of treatment carried out between 1 August 1991 and 5 April 2009. The HFEA 1990 and HFEA 2008 contain consequential provisions modifying the intestacy rules and the rules governing the construction of written instruments, including wills. Where a parental order has been made under HFEA 1990, s 30[4] or HFEA 2008, s 54[4a] in favour of persons who provided gametes in relation to a child carried by a surrogate mother, the adoption legislation applies subject to amendments made for the purpose by statutory instrument.[5]

1 Vol 2, Part G, paras **[245.111]** ff.
2 Vol 2, Part G, paras **[245.82]** ff.
3 SI 2009/479, art 6.
4 Vol 2, Part G, para **[245.88]**.
4a Vol 2, Part G, para **[245.133]**.
5 The power to do this is in HFEA 1990, ss 30(9) and 45(1) and (3), and has been exercised by the Parental Orders (Human Fertilisation and Embryology) Regulations 1994, SI 1994/2767, which came into force on 1 November 1994. HFEA 1990, s 30 has been replaced by the wider provisions of HFEA 2008, ss 54 and 55 and the Human Fertilisation and Embryology (Parental Orders) Regulations 2010, SI 2010/985 (Vol 2, Part G, paras **[245.142]** ff) with effect from 6 April 2010.

[74.4]

[Updated in the text and footnote 3 for Human Fertilisation and Embryology Act 2008.]

Child born as a result of artificial insemination before 1 August 1991. The Family Law Reform Act 1987 (FLRA 1987) anticipated the provisions of HFEA 1990 and 2008 with regard to children born as a result of artificial insemination on or after 4 April 1988. The FLRA 1987, s 27 provides that where on, or after, 4 April 1988[0] a child was born in England and Wales as the result of artificial insemination of a woman who was at the time of the insemination a party to a subsisting marriage and was artificially inseminated with the semen of some person other than the other party to that marriage, unless it is proved to the satisfaction of any court by which the matter has to be determined that the other party to that marriage did not consent to the insemination, the child should be treated in law as the child of the parties to that marriage and shall not be treated as the child of any person other than the parties to that marriage.[1] The effect of this provision would appear to be that the child is to be treated as the legitimate child of the parties to the marriage for succession purposes. It has been held in Tasmania that a child being the product of his father's semen and his mother's ovum, implanted in the mother's womb subsequent to the death of his father is upon birth entitled to a right of inheritance afforded by law.[2] This would not now be the case in England, as the relevant statutory provision is that the father is such a child's father for the purposes of the name of the father on the birth certificate and no other purpose.[3]

0 The commencement date for FLRA 1987, s 27 fixed by SI 1988/425.
1 FLRA 1987, s 27(1); Vol 2, Part G, para **[245.74]**. The provision does not apply to unmarried couples, so that such a child would not be treated as the child of the male cohabitant.
2 *In the Estate of K* (1996) 5 Tas R 365.
3 See HFEA 1990, s 29(3A)–(3D) (inserted by the Human Fertilisation and Embryology (Deceased Fathers) Act 2003) and HFEA 2008, ss 39(3), 41(2). See para **[74.5]** below.

[74.5]

[Updated for Human Fertilisation and Embryology Act 2008.]

Human Fertilisation and Embryology Acts of 2008 and 1990. The relevant provisions are HFEA 2008, ss 33–53,[1] replacing HFEA 1990, ss 27–29.[2] HFEA 1990, ss 27–29 were brought into force on 1 August 1991 and have effect only in relation to children born as a consequence of in vitro fertilisation or artificial insemination carried out on or after that date and before 6 April 2009. HFEA 2008, ss 33–53 have effect in relation to children born as a consequence of in vitro fertilisation or artificial insemination carried out on or after 6 April 2009.[3]

HFEA 2008, s 33(1) and HFEA 1990, s 27(1), define the 'mother' of a child for the purposes of those Acts as follows:

> 'The woman who is carrying or has carried a child as a result of the placing in her of an embryo or of sperm and eggs, and no other woman, is to be treated as the mother of the child'.[4]

This means that for the purposes of the HFEA 2008 and HFEA 1990 a woman may be treated as the mother of a child with whom she is not genetically connected.

The HFEA 2008, ss 35–37 (relating to treatment on or after 6 April 2009) and HFEA 1990, s 28 (treatment before 6 April 2009), define the 'father' for the purposes of these respective Acts. The provisions of these two Acts are for practical purposes the same where the woman is married at the time of the placing in her of an embryo or of sperm and eggs or of her artificial insemination. HFEA 2008, s 35(1) and HFEA 1990, s 28(2) provide that if

(a) at the time of the placing in her of the sperm and eggs or of her insemination, the woman was a party to a marriage, and
(b) the creation of the embryo carried by her was not brought about with the sperm of the other party to the marriage, then that other party is to be treated as the father of the child unless it is shown that he did not consent.

In the case of an unmarried couple where the treatment does not use the man's sperm (and he is alive at the time of the treatment), there is parallel provision for the man to be treated as the father (HFEA 2008, ss 36 and 37, HFEA 1990, s 28(3)). There is a difference between the two sets of provisions in that under HFEA 1990, s 28(3) he is treated as the father if the treatment services were provided for the woman and the man together, whereas under HFEA 2008, ss 36 and 37 he is treated as the father if both he and the woman have given the person responsible for the treatment a written notice of their consent and not withdrawn or varied it before the treatment was carried out. These provisions mean that for the purposes of the HFEA 1990 and HFEA 2008 a man may be treated as the father of a child with whom he is not genetically connected. Indeed the child might not be genetically connected with the woman either.

An innovation of HFEA 2008 is ss 42–45, relating to treatment occurring on or after 6 April 2009. These are provisions, parallel to the provisions outlined above, for any woman who at the time of having the treatment has a civil partner who has consented to the treatment, and for any woman who is not married and not in a civil partnership at the time of having the treatment where she and another woman have given the appropriate written notices of consent to the provider of the treatment. In these cases the civil partner of the mother or consenting other woman is treated as a parent of the child.

There are also provisions in HFEA 2008 and HFEA 1990 for fathers, civil partners, etc, who have died before the treatment was carried out to qualify for appearing on the birth certificate as the father or parent of the child,[5] but in such cases such a person is not treated as father or parent for any other purpose.[6]

The provisions mentioned in the preceding two paragraphs will be extended to same sex female married couples when the amendments to ss 42 and 46 of HFEA 2008 made by the Marriage (Same Sex Couples) Act 2013[6a] come into force.[6b]

The effect of these provisions for inheritance is set out in HFEA 1990, s 29 and HFEA 2008, s 48. Where by virtue of HFEA 1990, ss 27 or 28 or by virtue of HFEA 2008, ss 33, 35, 36, 42, or 43 a person is to be treated as the mother, father or (under HFEA 2008, ss 42 or 43) parent of a child, that person is to be treated in law as the mother, father or parent, as the case may be, of the child for all purposes.[7] Any provider of the genetic material for the treatment is expressly excluded from being the father, mother or parent.[8] Neither set of provisions says in terms that a child born to a married couple where the husband is treated as the father is to be treated as the legitimate child of that marriage, but this must surely follow from the principle established by the HFEA 1990 and 2008 that each party to the marriage is to be treated in law as the child's parent. This view is impliedly confirmed by the saving contained in HFEA 1990, s 27(5) and HFEA 2008, s 38(5) for any child who would be treated as the legitimate child of the parties at common law (eg a child born in wedlock as a consequence of the prescribed medical techniques carried out before the marriage with the consent of a man other than the husband), and by HFEA 2008, s 48(6). The latter provision is that where a child is born to a woman who is in a civil partnership at any point between the date of the treatment and the birth of the child, and the non-child bearing civil partner is treated as a parent of the child under HFEA 2008, s 42 or 43, the child is the legitimate child of his or her parents.

It also follows that where the person who is a child's father by virtue of HFEA 1990 or HFEA 2008 marries the child's mother after the birth of the child, the child will be legitimated under the Legitimacy Act 1976.[9] Where a child is born as a result of treatment under HFEA 2008 on or after 6 April 2009, and by virtue of HFEA 2008, s 43 a woman other than the mother is a parent of that child, and the mother and other parent form a civil partnership after the birth of the child, the child will become legitimate under the Legitimacy Act 1976.[10]

1 Vol 2, Part G, paras **[245.111]** ff.
2 Vol 2, Part G, paras **[245.82]** ff.
3 The commencement date fixed by SI 2009/479. See also HFEA 2008, s 57(1).
4 This includes cases where the procedure was carried out abroad (HFEA 1990, s 27(3), HFEA 2008, s 33(3)) and is subject to the possibility of adoption (HFEA 1990, s 27(2), HFEA 2008, s 33(2)).
5 HFEA 2008, ss 39, 40, 46; HFEA 1990, s 28(5A)–(5I) (inserted by the Human Fertilisation and Embryology (Deceased Fathers) Act 2003).
6 See HFEA 2008, ss 39(3), 41(2), 46(4), and HFEA 1990, s 29(3A)–(3D) (inserted by the Human Fertilisation and Embryology (Deceased Fathers) Act 2003).
6a By the Marriage (Same Sex Couples) Act 2013, s 17(4), Sch 7, paras 37, 40 and 41.
6b No date has been appointed for the coming into force of these amendments.
7 HFEA 1990, s 29(1), HFEA 2008, s 48(1). An exception is made for devolution of dignities or titles of honour and property limited to devolve with them: HFEA 1990, s 29(4), HFEA 2008, s 48(7).
8 HFEA 1990, ss 27(1), 28(4), 29(2); HFEA 2008, ss 33(1), 38(1), 41, 45, 47, 48(2).
9 For legitimation under the Legitimacy Act 1976 see paras **[72.15]**, **[72.16]** and **[72.18]** above.
10 Legitimacy Act 1976, ss 2A and 3(2), inserted by HFEA 2008, Sch 6 paras 16, 17.

[74.6]

[Updated for Human Fertilisation and Embryology Act 2008.]

The construction of wills—retrospective effect of HFEAs. The HFEA 1990, s 29(3) provides that where s 29(1) of it applies, and HFEA 2008, s 48(5) provides that where (inter alia) s 48(1) of it applies, 'references to any relationship between two people in any enactment, deed or other instrument or document (*whenever passed or made*) are to be read accordingly' (emphasis supplied).[1] Further, HFEA 2008, s 53(1), (2) provide in cases where a child has by virtue of the Act a female parent in addition to his or her mother, references to the child's father in any enactment, deed or other instrument or document, whenever made, are to that additional parent. The retrospective effect of the HFEA 1990, s 29(3) and HFEA 2008, s 48(5) is thought to be unique.[1a] In the past a statutory provision modifying the rules of construction affecting references to children and issue have been limited in their operation to deaths occurring or instruments made after the commencement of the provision. HFEA 1990, s 29(3) and HFEA 2008, s 48(5) represent significant departures from this practice. The effect of this is that, for example, a child born to a married couple as a result of fertility treatment effected on or after 1 August 1991 could be a beneficiary under a settlement or will which came into force before 1970 which created continuing trusts for issue of an ancestor of one the persons treated as the child's parents, even though the will or settlement does not contain any provisions modifying the rules of construction affecting references to children and issue, and although an illegitimate child conceived naturally would not be.[2] Further, a child born to a woman in a civil partnership as a result of fertility treatment effected on or after 6 April 2009 could be a beneficiary under such a settlement or will.[3]

As regards the rules of intestacy the HFEA 1990, s 29(3) and HFEA 2008, s 48(5) will in practice operate only prospectively, as the next of kin of a deceased person are all identified at the date of his death.[4]

1 Vol 2, Part G, paras **[245.87]** and **[245.127]**. See also para **[74.5]** above.
1a This approach seems to have been anticipated by s 27(1) of the Family Law Reform Act 1987: see para **[74.4]** above.
2 Because the provisions of the FLRA 1969 are not retrospectively applied to wills executed before 1 January 1990, whereas the provisions of the HFEA 1990 and HFEA 2008 are. An example will illustrate the point. Suppose that in 1993 an illegitimate child is born to a granddaughter of a testator who died before 1970, such a child, though genetically connected with the settlor or testator, will not be eligible to benefit as a member of the class of issue of the testator benefited by his will. On the other hand if that granddaughter is married and in 1993 has a child with her husband's consent in consequence of the implantation of another woman's egg, that child would by force of the HFEA 1990 be eligible to benefit as the granddaughter's legitimate child and so as the testator's issue, even though not genetically connected with the testator.
3 Such a child is treated as legitimate by virtue of HFEA 2008, s 48(6).
4 As does the Family Law Reform Act 1987, s 27 relating to children born as a result of artificial insemination.

[74.7]

[Updated for Human Fertilisation and Embryology Act 2008.]

Modifying or excluding the Acts. HFEA 1990 and HFEA 2008 do not expressly contain a provision stating that the effects of them can be excluded by a contrary intention expressed in the will. But it is thought that the provisions can be excluded by express wording in a will, if that is thought to be desirable, as a matter of the testamentary freedom of a testator to select his beneficiaries. A simple statement that the will should be construed as if the HFEA 1990 and HFEA 2008 had not been enacted should suffice.

CHAPTER 75

Adopted children

[75.1]

[Updated in footnote 6 for *Re Erskine 1948 Trust; Gregg v Pigott* [2012] EWHC 732 (Ch), [2012] 3 All ER 532.]

The position under previous Adoption Acts. Before 1 January 1950,[1] adoption, whether under an order of the court or otherwise, gave the adopted child no right to share in the property of the members of the adopting family, but, on the other hand, it did not deprive the child of any of its rights to share in the property of its original family to which it would have been entitled apart from the adoption.[2] This applied to all dispositions of property and to the rights upon intestacy.[3] This position was reversed by the Adoption of Children Act 1949 which provided that adopted persons were to be regarded as the children of the adopters, and of no other persons, for the purposes of intestacies[4]. However, an adopted person was only treated as a child of the adopter in relation to wills and settlements where the will or settlement was made *after* the adoption had taken place.[5] This basic provision was re-enacted in 1958, and again in 1975 with effect from 1 January 1976. The important change was made as from the latter date that an adopted person was treated as a child of the adopter, in relation to wills of persons dying and settlements made on or after 1 January 1976, even where the adoption was subsequent to the will or settlement. The earlier legislation continues to be printed in Vol 2, Part G, because it remains relevant to the devolution of property devolving under wills and settlements made at earlier dates. The failure until 1976 to legislate to give adopted children the same property rights as legitimate children may turn out to be a breach of the European Human Rights Convention.[6] The governing legislative provisions can be stated thus:

(i) deaths on or after 1 January 1950: Adoption Act 1950;[7]
(ii) deaths on or after 1 April 1959: Adoption Act 1958;[8]
(iii) deaths on or after 1 January 1976: Children Act 1975;[9]
(iv) deaths on or after 1 January 1988: Adoption Act 1976 (AA 1976),[10]
(v) deaths on or after 30 December 2005: Adoption and Children Act 2002 (ACA 2002).[11]

This discussion will refer to the ACA 2002[11] provisions which very largely, in so far as they are relevant to wills, reproduce the provisions of the previous CA 1975 and the AA 1976. Thus the current rules mostly date from 1 January 1976, and relate to settlements made and the wills of persons dying on or after that date. The position under the earlier Adoption Acts is described in more detail in previous editions of this text. AA 1976 also applies, subject to amendments made for the purpose by statutory instrument, where a parental order has been made under HFEA 1990, s 30 in favour of persons who provided gametes in relation to a child carried by a surrogate mother.[12]

1 The date when the Adoption of Children Act 1949 came into force.

2 Adoption of Children Act 1926, s 5(2), repealed by the Adoption of Children Act 1949; Vol 2, Part G, para **[245.4]**.

3 Adoption of Children Act 1926, s 5(2), repealed by the Adoption of Children Act 1949. Disposition includes assurance inter vivos as well as by will or codicil: Adoption of Children Act 1926, s 5(4); Vol 2, Part G, para **[245.4]**.

4 Adoption of Children Act 1949 s 9(2), re-enacted as Adoption Act 1950, s 13(1),vol 2, Part G, para **[245.18]**.

5 Adoption of Children Act 1949, ss 9, 10. See Adoption Act 1950, ss 13, 14, which re-enacted ss 9, 10 of the 1949 Act, in Vol 2, Part G, paras **[245.18]** and **[245.19]**.

6 See *Pla and Puncernau v Andorra* [2004] 2 FCR 630, ECtHR. For most kinds of case this may be a matter justiciable only in the European Court of Human Rights as a breach of the Convention. The problem for anyone asking the English courts to apply the Convention to pre-1976 dispositions is that the Human Rights Act 1998 does not usually apply to rights arising or failing to arise before it came into force: see *Wilson v First County Trust Ltd* [2003] UKHL 40, [2004] 1 AC 816. It has been held though, by a first instance judge, that this rule is not absolute: see *Re Erskine 1948 Trust; Gregg v Pigott* [2012] EWHC 732 (Ch), [2012] 3 All ER 532. In that case, in the special circumstances before him, the judge considered he was able to apply the European Human Rights Convention retrospectively so as to construe a trust for statutory next of kin, who were prima facie to be ascertained in accordance with the law in 1948 when adopted children would not have been included, as including adopted children. The meaning of statutory next of kin being a matter of statutory construction, and statutory next of kin of a living person having a mere spes successionis rather than an equitable interest in remainder, were important special circumstances which enabled the judge to find as he did, and there is doubt as to whether the result would be the same in relation to equitable interests in remainder under a pre-1976 instrument.

7 Adoption Act 1950, ss 13, 14, Sch 5, para 4, proviso; see Vol 2, Part G, paras **[245.18]** and **[245.19]**; which replaced the Adoption of Children Act 1949 with effect from the same commencement date.

8 Adoption Act 1958, ss 16, 17; see Vol 2, Part G, paras **[245.26]** and **[245.27]**; which repealed the Adoption Act 1950.

9 The provisions were contained in the Children Act 1975, which were replaced by the Adoption Act 1976; Vol 2, Part G, paras **[245.43]** ff. The provisions of the Children Act 1975 applied from 1 January 1976 but were repealed with retrospective effect by the same provisions in the Adoption Act 1976, from 1 January 1976. See the Children Act 1975 and the Adoption Act 1976 (Commencement No 2) Order 1987, SI 1987/1242 which brought the latter Act into force on 1 January 1988.

10 See Vol 2, Part G, paras **[245.91]** ff, replacing the Children Act 1975.

11 See Vol 2, Part G, paras **[245.91]** ff. The Act restates and amends the law relating to adoption and makes further amendments to the law relating to children. It received the royal assent on 7 November 2002, and the provisions concerning the property and succession rights of adopted children came into force on 30 December 2005 (SI 2005/2213) in relation to adoptions occurring on or after that date. With effect from 30 December 2005, it also repeals the whole of AA 1976, apart from Part IV and para 6 of Sch 2 (which regulate the property and succession rights of adopted children), and replaces these provisions with the corresponding provisions of the 2002 Act.

12 For HFEA 1990, s 30 see Vol 2, Part G, para **[245.30]**. The power to apply the adoption legislation subject to amendments is in HFEA 1990, ss 30(9) and 45(1) and (3), and has been exercised by the Parental Orders (Human Fertilisation and Embryology) Regulations 1994, SI 1994/2767 which came into force on 1 November 1994. It applies AA 1976 subject to the amendments there set out, and has continued to do so since 30 December 2005 despite the replacement of AA 1976 by ACA 2002; the latter Act amended

SI 1994/2767 so as to refer to AA 1976 as it stood immediately before the commencement of ACA 2002. HFEA 1990, s 30 is to be replaced by the wider provisions of HFEA 2008, ss 54 and 55, but no commencement order has yet been made for the latter provisions.

[75.4]

[Updated in text and footnote 14 for Perpetuities and Accumulations Act 2009.]

Wills. For the purposes of the ACA 2002 the death of the testator is the date at which a will or codicil is to be regarded as made.[1] The new provisions reproduce the established law in so far as unless there is a contrary intention, an express or implied reference in the will to a child or children will include a reference to the adopted child.[2] This presumably extends to persons claiming through adopted children, eg a gift to a class of grandchildren will include children who are the issue of adopted children, and adopted children of natural children of the donor.[3] If there is a gift to children with a substitutional gift to grandchildren, then again an adopted 'grandchild' will presumably be able to take his deceased parents' share.[4] But wills can present more difficult problems where, for example, the disposition depends on the date of birth of a child, as where the gift is to a class 'living' at a certain time. To meet these problems the ACA 2002 provides that the disposition shall be construed as if the adopted child had been born on the date of the adoption,[5] thus giving the child an artificial date of birth. If two or more children had been adopted on the same date, then they will be deemed to have been born on that date in the order of their actual births.[6] Thus, if there is a gift to the children of A 'living at my death, or born afterwards'[7] or, 'born within twenty-one years of my death', adopted children will qualify or not, depending not on their actual date of birth but on the date of adoption. Similar constructions will apply where the gift is a class gift,[8] to which the class closing rules apply.[9] When the first member of the class attains a vested interest and closes the class, those children then in existence will take, which in the case of adopted children, must mean those children then adopted.[10] Children then born and subsequently adopted would not take. The provisions of the ACA 2002 also apply to a conditional bequest eg 'to A for life, until he has a child, and then to his child or children'. The adoption of a child would satisfy the condition and the child would be deemed to have been born on the date of the adoption.[11] The effect of AA 1976, s 42 and the definition of an existing instrument in s 72(1) providing that the rules concerning property and succession rights do not apply to instruments made before 1 January 1976 is reproduced in the ACA 2002.[12]

So far as perpetuities are concerned in relation to wills made before 6 April 2010 the effect of the provision would seem to be that a 'parent' of the class of beneficiaries would only be a life in being for the purposes of the PAA 1964, s 3, if he was adopted at the date when the instrument takes effect.[13] Thus, if the gift was to 'A's grandchildren to attain 21' and A had two existing natural born children at the date of the gift, they would be lives in being under s 3(5)(c). If subsequently he adopted a third child who was alive at the date of the instrument containing the gift but not then adopted, presumably he could not be a life in being for the purposes of the PAA 1964. For wills made on or after 6 April 2010 the perpetuity period is now 125 years and there is now no other period.[14]

1 ACA 2002, s 73(4). Vol 2, Part G, para **[245.99]**, reproducing AA 1976, s 46.
2 ACA 2002, s 67(1); reproducing AA Act 1976, s 39.
3 ACA 2002, s 68(2) provides that 'parent' or any other term not qualified by the word 'adoptive' can be treated as including an adoptive relative. This section reproduces AA 1976, s 42.
4 ACA 2002, s 68. Presumably adopted children would rank as 'issue' for the purposes of the Wills Act 1837, s 33.
5 ACA 2002, s 69(2)(a).
6 ACA 2002, s 69(2)(b). These are rules of construction which will yield to a contrary intention.
7 ACA 2002, s 69(3), example 1. Likewise a gift to children of A 'living at my death or born afterwards before any one of such children for the time being in existence attains a vested interest and who attain the age of 21'; s 69(3), Example 2.
8 See paras **[66.19]**–**[66.21]** above.
9 See Chapter 66.
10 ACA 2002, s 69(2), Example 3. Presumably if the adopted child is the first member to attain a vested interest, he will close the class which might result in the class being closed earlier than the testator anticipated.
11 ACA 2002, s 69(3), Example 4.
12 ACA 2002, Sch 4, para 17. In relation to wills that means the wills of testators dying before 1 January 1976; AA 1976, s 46(3), ACA 2002, s 73(4). This is illustrated by *Re Upton's Estate, Upton v National Westminster Bank* [2004] WTLR 1339, for which see para **[72.10]** above.
13 In order to be a life in being under the Perpetuities and Accumulations Act 1964, a person must be 'in being and ascertainable at the commencement of the perpetuity period', s 3(4)(a).
14 PAA 2009, s 5(1). See Vol 2, Part G, para **[246.179]**; and Chapter 94.

[75.9]

[Updated in text and footnote 4 for Perpetuities and Accumulations Act 2009.]

Protection of trustee and personal representative. The ACA 2002 contains useful provisions to protect trustees and personal representatives. A trustee or personal representative is not under a duty, by virtue of the law relating to trusts or the administrations of estates to enquire, before distributing any property, whether any adoption has been effected or revoked, if that fact could affect entitlement to the property.[1] Furthermore such a person is not liable for any conveyance or distribution of the property made without regard to any such fact if he has not received notice of the fact before the conveyance or distribution.[2] However, this does not prejudice the right of any person to follow the property or any property representing it, into the hands of another person, other than a purchaser who has received it.[3] The ACA 2002 also contains a provision relating to future parenthood analogous to the PAA 1964 presumptions.[4] To protect trustees and personal representatives it is provided that where it is necessary to determine for the purposes of a disposition of property affected by an instrument whether a woman can have a child it shall be presumed that once a woman has attained the age of 55 years, she will not adopt a child after execution of the instrument and notwithstanding the provisions of the ACA 2002, if she does so, that child is not to be treated as her child or as the child of her spouse (if any) for the purposes of the instrument.[5]

1 ACA 2002, s 72(1); Vol 2, Part G, para **[245.98]**, reproducing AA 1976, s 45.
2 ACA 2002 s 72(2).
3 ACA 2002, s 72(3).

4 See Chapter 94. These presumptions are not reproduced in PAA 2009 because of the adoption of a fixed term of years as the perpetuity period.
5 ACA 2002, s 69(5).

CHAPTER 77

Gifts to next of kin

[77.2]

[Updated in footnote 2 for *Re Erskine 1948 Trust; Gregg v Pigott* [2012] EWHC 732 (Ch), [2012] 3 All ER 532.]

Reference to rules of distribution. If the will describes the donees by reference to the statutory rules for the distribution of the estate of an intestate, either expressly or impliedly,[1] the distribution may be under the former law or under the new law. References to any Statutes of Distribution in a will coming into operation after 1925 are to be construed as references to the new rules of distribution; and references in such a will to the statutory next of kin are to be construed, unless the context otherwise requires, as referring to the persons who would take beneficially under those rules; and trusts declared in a will which come into operation before 1926 by reference to the old Statutes of Distribution are to be construed as references to the earlier Acts.[2] Hence, in general, the old law applies where the trust is created by the will of a testator who died before 1926,[3] even though the event which brings the trust into effect occurs after 1925;[4] and also where the will, although coming into operation after 1925, declares trusts by reference to a settlement made before 1926.[5] Prima facie,[6] a wife[7] or husband[8] were not included in the next of kin, either apart from the Statutes of Distribution or under them, but where the donees were the persons who by virtue of the statute would be entitled to the testator's property, the widow was included,[9] but there is no such distinction for the purposes of the new rules of distribution.[10]

1 The following are cases of implied reference: *Garrick v Lord Camden* (1807) 14 Ves 372 ('as if I had died intestate'); *Edwards v Saloway* (1848) 2 Ph 625 ('as in case of intestacy'). For distribution to be made according to the statute, there must be a distinct indication to that effect in the will: *Halton v Foster* (1868) 3 Ch App 505 (where it was held that a reference to 'death unmarried' contained no such implication). In one case a reference to the Statutes of Distribution was treated as equivalent to 'by law' and the heir was held entitled to realty: *Re Hughes, Loddiges v Jones* [1916] 1 Ch 493.

2 Administration of Estates Act 1925, s 50(1), (2); Vol 2, Part G, para **[244.67]**. This section should now be read in the light of the Law Reform (Succession) Act 1995, s 1(4) (minor amendment). References to the AEA 1925, s 50(1) in wills or codicils coming into operation on or after 4 April 1988 will be construed subject to the provisions of the Family Law Reform Act 1987, ss 1 and 18; see Chapter 72, para **[72.14]** above. In the case of a settlement made in 1948 which provided for distribution to the life tenant's statutory next of kin on her death, which death occurred in 2010, it was held that 'statutory next of kin' had the statutory definition under the Administration of Estates Act 1925, s 50(1) as the persons who would qualify under the intestacy provisions in the 1925 Act itself. Those provisions were to be construed in accordance with the law at the date the settlement was made, rather than at the date of the life tenant's death, meaning that (had the judge not found that the

European Convention of Human Rights applied) the life tenant's sister's adopted children would have been excluded since in 1948 adopted children had no rights under an intestacy: *Re Erskine 1948 Trust; Gregg v Pigott* [2012] EWHC 732 (Ch), [2012] 3 All ER 532. See Vol 2, Part G, paras **[245.70]** and **[245.71]**.

3 *Edwards v Saloway* (1848) 2 Ph 625; *Bullock v Downes* (1860) 9 HL Cas 1; *Nichols v Haviland* (1855) 1 K & J 504; *Re Hughes, Loddiges v Jones* [1916] 1 Ch 493.

4 *Re Sutcliffe, Sutcliffe v Robershaw* [1929] 1 Ch 123 (where the testator died in 1875 and the property was on the death of a life tenant to be held in trust for the next of kin under the statute at his decease if he had then died intestate); *Re Sutton, Evans v Oliver* [1934] Ch 209 ('if I were to die immediately after the death of my wife intestate'; wife died in 1933 but old law applied where will came into operation before 1926); *Re Jackson, Holiday v Jackson* (1943) 113 LJ Ch 78 (similar case).

5 *Re Walsh, Public Trustee v Walsh* [1936] 1 All ER 327; *Re Hooper's Settlement, Phillips v Lake* [1943] Ch 116, [1943] 1 All ER 173 (a reference to the statute by itself is not a sufficient indication of a contrary intention: it required some such words as 'for the time being in force', either express or implied, to show a contrary intention).

6 But the context may justify her inclusion: *Re Collins' Trust* [1877] WN 87.

7 *Garrick v Lord Camden* (1807) 14 Ves 372 at 385; *Lee v Lee* (1860) 1 Drew & Sm 85; *Re Parry, Leak v Scott* (1888) 4 TLR 696; *Re Fitzgerald* (1889) 58 LJ Ch 662; *Re Gray's Settlement, Akers v Sears* [1896] 2 Ch 802; *Queensland Trustees Ltd v Robertson* [1911] St R Qd 172; *Re Richardson* [1956] QSR 485. But see *Re Gilligan's Goods* [1950] P 32, [1949] 2 All ER 401, 'next of kin under the statute of distributions' in (original) s 18, Wills Act 1837; see Vol 2, Part G, para **[244.15]**, held to include a widow.

8 *Milne v Gilbart* (1852) 2 De GM & G 715; *Walker v Cusin* [1917] 1 IR 63.

9 *Martin v Glover* (1844) 1 Coll 269; *Jenkins v Gower* (1846) 2 Coll 537. But the widow might be excluded by the class of the next of kin being ascertained at a date later than the death of the testator and his widow: see *Godkin v Murphy* (1843) 2 Y & C Ch Cas 351, but this case was doubted in *Jenkins v Gower* and see *Starr v Newberry* (1857) 23 Beav 436; *Lee v Lee* (1860) 1 Drew & Sm 85.

10 Administration of Estates Act 1925, s 50(1); see Vol 2, Part G, para **[244.65]**.

[77.3]

[Updated in the text and in footnote 7 for *Re Erskine 1948 Trust; Gregg v Pigott* [2012] EWHC 732 (Ch), [2012] 3 All ER 532.]

Ascertainment of class. Whatever may be the time of distribution, where there is a gift to the next of kin of a testator, without more, the class prima facie has to be ascertained as at the death of the testator,[1] and where there is a gift to the next of kin of any other person, the class prima facie has to be ascertained at that person's death if he survived the testator,[2] and, if not, at the testator's death.[3] This prima facie rule can be displaced by the terms of the will. Thus where a will made it clear that the testator did not intend 'next of kin' to include his two daughters, who were his sole next of kin at the date of the will and at his death, the class of next of kin was to be ascertained at the death of the survivor of his two daughters.[4] In a gift to a class of next of kin of the testator, or his nearest relatives, or similar class, living at a future period of distribution, the entire class is ascertained at the death of the testator, but only those take who survive the period of distribution.[5] It is always possible for the testator to say that the class is to be ascertained at some later time, e g he may give property after the death of a tenant for life to the persons who shall then be his next of kin, and then, apart from any reference to the Statutes of Distribution, the class is to be ascertained at the death of the tenant for life in accordance with the express words of the will.[6] Although the class may be ascertained at a date later than the testator's death, they are ascertained in accordance with the law as it stood at the testator's death, so that if the law at the testator's death excluded certain persons, such as adopted or illegitimate children, from being next of kin, those persons are prima facie not included.[7]

1 *Wharton v Barker* (1858) 4 K & J 483; *Bird v Luckie* (1850) 8 Hare 301 (where the sole next of kin took a prior life interest); *Gorbell v Davison* (1854) 18 Beav 556 (where two of the next of kin had prior life interests); *Lee v Lee* (1860) 1 Drew & Sm 85 (one of the next of kin had a prior life interest); *Re Ford, Patten v Sparks* (1895) 72 LT 5 (where the life tenants were restricted from alienating their interests); *Re Maher, Maher v Toppin* [1909] 1 IR 70. In all cases the class had to be ascertained at the death of the testator. See also *Re Blyth, Trustees, Executor and Agency Co Ltd v Malcolm* [1925] VLR 633; *Re Maine, Union Trustee Co of Australia Ltd v Maine* [1927] VLR 82; *Re Jermyn* [1965] VR 376; *Re Campbell* [1928] 4 DLR 797; *Re Wright* [1955] 5 DLR 213; *Re Richardson* [1956] QSR 485.

2 *Gundry v Pinniger* (1852) 1 De GM & G 502; *Wharton v Barker* (1858) 4 K & J 483; *Jacobs v Jacobs* (1853) 16 Beav 557; *Re Goldie* [1952] NZLR 928; *Coles v Blakeley* [1955] SCR 508. See *Re Gansloser's Will Trusts* [1952] Ch 30, [1951] 2 All ER 936, where a contrary conclusion was reached on the construction of the will; see also *Re Bourke's Will Trusts, Barclays Bank Trust Co Ltd v Canada Permanent Trust Co* [1980] 1 All ER 219, [1980] 1 WLR 539; *Re Johnston* (1982) 138 DLR (3d) 392; and *Re Verdonk* (1979) 106 DLR (3d) 450, at 457 where this sentence is cited.

3 *Philps v Evans* (1850) 4 De G & Sm 188; *Wharton v Barker* (1858) 4 K & J 483; *Re Philps' Will* (1868) LR 7 Eq 151; *Rees v Fraser* (1879) 26 Gr 233. For a case of contrary intention, see *Re Rees, Williams v Davies* (1890) 44 Ch D 484 (where a widow gave her personal estate to 'such persons as would have become entitled to my husband's personal estate had he died intestate and without leaving any widow him surviving': the persons entitled had to be ascertained at the death of the husband and the share of any who died in the widow's lifetime lapsed), and *Trustees etc Co Ltd v Engelbert* (1951) 51 SRNSW 244 (the persons who upon the deaths of the wife and daughter are entitled as the testator's next of kin according to the law relating to intestate's estates: class ascertained at death of survivor of wife and daughter).

4 *Re Clanchy's Will Trusts, Lynch v Edwards* [1970] 2 All ER 489, distinguishing *Re Winn, Brook v Whitton* [1910] 1 Ch 278, below; *Re Tuckett's Will Trusts, Williams v National Provincial Bank* (1967) 111 Sol Jo 811 (next of kin ascertained after the life tenant's death).

5 *Spink v Lewis* (1791) 3 Bro CC 355; *Re Nash, Prall v Bevan* (1894) 71 LT 5; *Re Winn, Brook v Whitton* [1910] 1 Ch 278 (next of kin living at the time of the trust failing). In every case of a gift 'to my next of kin' or 'my nearest relations' or any gift of that kind, the prima facie rule is, and it is not only a rule but the natural meaning of the words, that the class is to be ascertained at the death of the testator. When the testator dies, certain people answer the description of his relatives, or his next of kin, or his nearest in blood, or any of those expressions, and it is difficult to see, where he is contemplating a class some of whom may die before a certain time and others may survive that time, at what other time the class is to be ascertained than at the testator's death. Thus the most natural construction is that the gift is a gift to the next of kin to be ascertained at the testator's death, but that any one of the class so ascertained, in order to take under the gift, must survive the time stated in the will: *Re Winn, Brook v Whitton* [1910] 1 Ch 278 at 286; *Re McRae, McDonald v Creer* (1928) 28 SRNSW 447. This rule is not affected by the fact that the gift comprises the proceeds of sale of realty as well as personal property: *Cusack v Rood* (1876) 24 WR 391.

6 *Re Winn, Brook v Whitton* [1910] 1 Ch 278; *National Trustee Co Ltd v Fleury* [1965] SCR 817 (property given to a person for life who was the sole next of kin at his death and then for his next of kin); *Re Butler* (1965) 50 DLR (2d) 210; *Re Treble* (1966) 56 DLR (2d) 402; but, if there is a reference to the Statutes of Distribution, see the cases in para **[77.4]**, n 1.

7 See *Re Erskine 1948 Trust; Gregg v Pigott* [2012] EWHC 732 (Ch), [2012] 3 All ER 532. This case concerned a lifetime settlement but the principle would seem to be the same. It was held that the class of next of kin of the life tenant who died in 2010, though to be ascertained at her death, was to be ascertained in accordance with the law as it stood at the date the settlement was made in 1948. Therefore, the life tenant's sister's adopted children would not have taken as next of kin if the judge had not decided that the European Human Rights Convention applied retrospectively to include them.

[77.4]

[Updated in footnote 4 for *Re Erskine 1948 Trust; Gregg v Pigott* [2012] EWHC 732 (Ch), [2012] 3 All ER 532.]

Ascertainment of class described by reference to Statutes of Distribution. Where the gift was to the testator's next of kin entitled by virtue of the Statutes of Distribution, even though they were to be so entitled at some future time,[1] the class was prima facie ascertained as at the death of the testator.[2] The context, however, might require them to be ascertained as if the testator had died at some other period.[3] The same rules apply to the ascertainment of persons entitled under the new rules of distribution.[4]

1 *Re Winn, Brook v Whitton* [1910] 1 Ch 278. The ordinary rule which would have ascertained the class at the time referred to is rebutted, because of the necessity for every person who claims under the gift to prove his title by virtue of the statute.

2 *Bullock v Downes* (1860) 9 HL Cas 1 (in such cases the word 'then' is treated as referring only to the time when the persons entitled would come into possession of what had been bequeathed to them); *Mortimore v Mortimore* (1879) 4 App Cas 448; *Re Wilson, Wilson v Batchelor* [1907] 1 Ch 450 (a case where the tenant for life was the sole next of kin).

3 *Wharton v Barker* (1858) 4 K & J 483; *Clowes v Hilliard* (1876) 4 Ch D 413; *Sturge and Great Western Rly Co* (1881) 19 Ch D 444 (in such cases the class is said to be an artificial class); *Re McFee, McFee v Toner* (1910) 103 LT 210 (gift of annuity with a gift of accumulations of income on cesser of annuity); *Re Helsby, Neate v Bozie* (1914) 84 LJ Ch 682 (class to be ascertained at death of daughter of testatrix); *Re Mellish, Day v Withers* [1916] 1 Ch 562 (class to be ascertained after expiration of two life interests and to the next of kin of the first life tenant); *Hutchinson v National Refuges for Homeless and Destitute Children* [1920] AC 795 (class to be ascertained on failure of trusts); *Re Krawitz's Will Trusts, Krawitz v Crawford* [1959] 3 All ER 793, [1959] 1 WLR 1192 (a similar case).

4 *Re Bridgen, Chaytor v Edwin* [1938] Ch 205, [1937] 4 All ER 342. See footnote 7 to para **[77.3]** above.

CHAPTER 80

Gifts to 'wife' and 'husband'

I. 'WIFE'

[80.1]

[Updated in footnote 1a for Marriage (Same Sex Couples) Act 2013.]

When wife by subsequent marriage included.[1a] Where the donee is described as the wife of a person, and that person is married at the date of the will, then, in the absence of a context to the contrary, the wife existing at the date of the will is prima facie the person to take, and not any subsequent wife.[1] The fact that the interest conferred is only during widowhood, after a life interest to the husband,[2] or that it is expressed to be given for the support of the wife and her husband and his children,[3] does not of itself show any contrary intention. The context or the circumstances may show that the description, 'wife', is intended to include a subsequent wife,[4] a person not married to the testator or other person whose wife she is said to be,[5] or a betrothed woman.[6] Where a person is not married at the date of the will, prima facie the donee is the first person to answer the description in the will.[7]

1a This paragraph will need to be read in the light of the Marriage (Same Sex Couples) Act 2013 and regulations to be made thereunder when they are brought into force: see para **[80.10]** below and for the text of the relevant parts of the Act see Vol 2, Part G, paras **[245.149]** ff.

1 *Garratt v Niblock* (1830) 1 Russ & M 629; *Re Drew, Drew v Drew* [1899] 1 Ch 336 at 339; *Re Coley, Hollinshead v Coley* [1903] 2 Ch 102; *Re D'Oyley, Swayne v D'Oyley* (1921) 152 LT Jo 259. In *Marks v Marks* (1908) 40 SCR 210, the gift was held to be in favour of a mistress with whom he was living at the date of the will rather than a former wife. In this case it was assumed that the former wife had been validly married to the testator. Where a remainder was defeasible if a son was born to a life tenant, defeasance was held to occur on the birth of a son by any wife for the time being; but 'son' meant son and not grandson or more remoter issue: *Re Jennings* (1954) 33 UPR 230. See also *Re Devling* [1955] VLR 238; *Re Bassett* [1961] VR 51 (later wife not known to testator); *Re Herlichka* (1969) 3 DLR (3d) 700 (wife benefited rather than mistress).

2 *Re Coley, Hollinshead v Coley* [1903] 2 Ch 102 at 104.

3 On this there is some conflict of authority: *Boreham v Bignall* (1850) 8 Hare 131, which supports the text was followed in *Re Burrow's Trusts* (1864) 10 LT 184, and *Firth v Fielden* (1874) 22 WR 622, but not followed in *Re Lyne's Trust* (1869) LR 8 Eq 65. The last case was followed in *Re Lory* (1891) 7 TLR 419, but has since been departed from in *Re Griffiths' Policy* [1903] 1 Ch 739; *Re Coley, Hollinshead v Coley* [1903] 2 Ch 102.

4 In both *Longworth v Bellamy* (1871) 40 LJ Ch 513; and *Re Drew, Drew v Drew* [1899] 1 Ch 336, a discretionary trust, after a determinable life interest, for the benefit of the donee, his wife and children was held sufficient to rebut the prima facie meaning that wife was confined to the wife living at the date of the will. Where the donee was not married at the date of the will, a second wife has been included: *Peppin v Bickford* (1797) 3 Ves 570. In

Re Hardyman, Teesdale v McClintock [1925] Ch 287, the testator made a codicil after the second marriage and it was held that the codicil brought the will down to its date. There is a rule that where the person is not married at the date of the will, the first person to answer the description takes: *Re Hickman's Will Trust, Hickman v Hickman* [1948] Ch 624, [1948] 2 All ER 303; and cf *Radford v Willis* (1871) 7 Ch App 7; *Blount v Crozier* [1917] 1 IR 461. As to effect of divorce, see para **[80.3]** below.

5 A partner to an invalid marriage has been held to be described by the word 'wife': see below. For cases where a mistress has been referred to as 'wife' see *Re Davenport's Trust* (1852) 1 Sm & G 126 (gift void); *Turner v Brittain* (1863) 3 New Rep 21 (gift held good); *Re Lowe, Danily v Platt* (1892) 61 LJ Ch 415 (gifts held good except for illegitimate child born after date of will); *Anderson v Berkeley* [1902] 1 Ch 936 (gift held good); *Re Brown, Golding v Brady* (1910) 26 TLR 257 (gift held good); *Re Gale, Gale v Gale* [1941] Ch 209, [1941] 1 All ER 329 (gift bad because given to 'widow'); *Re Lynch, Lynch v Lynch* [1943] 1 All ER 168 (gift upheld because testator had provided his own dictionary).

6 Applied in *Re Brechin* (1973) 38 DLR (3d) 305. See also *Schloss v Stiebel* (1833) 6 Sim 1 (where the will recited the intended marriage); *Re Brown, Golding v Brady* (1910) 26 TLR 257 (a mistress).

7 See cases cited in n 5.

[80.2]

[Updated in footnote 1a for Marriage (Same Sex Couples) Act 2013.]

Wife during 'widowhood'.[1a] If the gift is to the wife, who is accurately so described, expressly 'during widowhood' the latter words form a condition as to the beginning and ending of her interest, so that the effect of a subsequent divorce before the gift takes effect is that she is disentitled to the gift, since she does not then become a widow.[1] If she is not accurately so described, that is where the marriage is for some reason invalid, the words 'until death or remarriage' may be read 'until death or marriage subsequent to the death of the testator'[2] and a similar construction may be put upon the word 'widowhood'.[3] A gift to a wife 'so long as she remains my widow' gives a determinable life interest and not a determinable fee simple.[4] It is a matter for future court decision whether an interest given during widowhood will be terminated by the widow entering into a civil partnership under Civil Partnership Act 2004.[5]

1a This paragraph will need to be read in the light of the Marriage (Same Sex Couples) Act 2013 and regulations to be made thereunder when they are brought into force: see para **[80.10]** below and for the text of the relevant parts of the Act see Vol 2, Part G, paras **[245.149]** ff.

1 *Re Boddington, Boddington v Clairat* (1884) 25 Ch D 685; *Re Kettlewell, Jones v Kettlewell* (1907) 98 LT 23.

2 *Re Wagstaff, Wagstaff v Jalland* [1908] 1 Ch 162; *Re Smalley, Smalley v Scotton* [1929] 2 Ch 112 ('to my wife EAS', where the marriage was bigamous); *Re McInerney* [1966] VR 263.

3 *Re Hammond, Burniston v White* [1911] 2 Ch 342; but see para **[80.6]** below, for cases where there has been no marriage; and see below under 'widow'.

4 *Re Dietrich* (1963) 36 DLR (2d) 17.

5 See para **[80.9]** below.

[80.3]

[Updated in footnote 1a for Marriage (Same Sex Couples) Act 2013.]

Effect of divorce.[1a] A decree absolute of dissolution of marriage finally dissolves the marriage and the parties cannot thereafter be properly described as 'husband', 'wife' or 'widow';[1] but where a testatrix described herself as the wife of V and left her estate to the said husband, V, the husband took although the testatrix subsequently divorced him.[2] Where a power of appointment is given to appoint a life or less interest to any wife who may survive the appointor, a wife who is divorced from the appointor cannot take under an appointment because she is not a wife who survives the appointer.[3] The effect of the new provision enacted as the Wills Act 1837, s 18A by the Administration of Justice Act 1982[4] has been noted above.[5] As originally enacted the section provides that where, after a testator has made a will, a decree of a court dissolves or annuls his marriage or declares it void then … any devise or bequest to the former spouse shall lapse',[6] and the will takes effect as if any appointment of the former spouse as an executor or as the executor and trustee of the will were omitted.[7] In relation to the wills of testators dying on or after 1 January 1996, s 18A deems for these purposes the former spouse to have died when the marriage was dissolved or annulled.[8] These provisions are subject to a contrary intention appearing by the will.[9] Presumably similar principles would apply to the termination of a civil partnership.[10]

1a This paragraph will need to be read in the light of the Marriage (Same Sex Couples) Act 2013 and regulations to be made thereunder when they are brought into force: see para **[80.10]** below and for the text of the relevant parts of the Act see Vol 2, Part G, paras **[245.149]** ff.

1 *Re Morrieson, Hitchins v Morrieson* (1888) 40 Ch D 30; *Re Slaughter Trustees Corpn Ltd v Slaughter* [1945] Ch 355, [1945] 2 All ER 214; *Re Newcombe, Cresswell v Newcombe* [1938] NZLR 98; and see the settlement cases, *Bosworthick v Clegg* (1929) 45 TLR 438; *Re Williams' Settlement, Greenwell v Humphries* [1929] 2 Ch 361. A wife remains a wife until the decree absolute and if the husband dies the day before the decree is made absolute the decree absolute is a nullity and the wife is properly described as his widow: *Re Seaford* [1968] P 53, [1968] 1 All ER 482, CA; see also *Re Kindl* (1982) 140 DLR (3d) 92. But the word may possibly be held upon the context to be a sufficient description: see *N v M* (1885) 1 TLR 523; *Bullmore v Wynter* (1883) 22 Ch D 619. In *Re Devling* [1955] VLR 238, the testator after divorce executed a codicil appointing a new executor but otherwise confirmed his will and it was held that divorced wife took; in *Couper's Judicial Factor v Valentine* 1976 SLT 83 a divorced wife took under a gift 'to my wife, Mrs DC'.

2 *Re Vine* [1955] VLR 200.

3 *Re Allan, Allan v Midland Bank Executor and Trustee Co Ltd* [1954] Ch 295, [1954] 1 All ER 646. A power was given to appoint by deed executed in contemplation of marriage or by will or codicil a life or less interest in a settled fund to any wife who may survive the appointor. Upon its proper construction the condition of being a wife and also that of being a wife surviving the appointor applied both to exercise by deed and by will.

4 See Vol 2, Part G, para **[244.18]**.

5 See Chapter 47, para **[47.2]** above.

6 Wills Act 1837, s 18A(1)(b); see *Re Sinclair, Lloyds Bank plc v Imperial Cancer Research Fund* [1985] Ch 446, [1985] 1 All ER 1066, CA.

7 Wills Act 1837, s 18A(1)(a). This wording applies to wills of testators dying before 1 January 1996: see next note.

8 Wills Act 1837, s 18A is so amended by Law Reform (Succession) Act 1995, s 3 for deaths on or after 1 January 1996.

9 Wills Act 1837, s 18A(3). And without prejudice to the right of such a spouse to apply for financial provision under the Inheritance (Provision for Family and Dependants) Act 1975. See Chapter 105.

10 See Civil Partnership Act 2004.

[80.4]

[Updated in footnote 1a for Marriage (Same Sex Couples) Act 2013.]

Widow.[1a] Widow prima facie means the surviving wife (ie legal wife) until death or remarriage. Therefore, a wife who is divorced cannot become a widow,[1] but there are cases where a person not legally married has been held sufficiently described as 'widow'.[2] Widowhood normally ends on remarriage, but if the remarriage should be annulled the widowhood does not cease on such remarriage or at least she is a widow after the decree absolute of annulment.[3] Where, after the date of the will, the testator's own marriage was declared null and void, the wife was held not to be entitled to any annuity payable 'so long as she shall continue my widow'.[4] It has been said that a 'spinster mistress' cannot become a widow.[5]

1a This paragraph will need to be read in the light of the Marriage (Same Sex Couples) Act 2013 and regulations to be made thereunder when they are brought into force: see para **[80.10]** below and for the text of the relevant parts of the Act see Vol 2, Part G, paras **[245.149]** ff.

1 *Re Williams' Settlement, Greenwell v Humphries* [1929] 2 Ch 361; *Bosworthick v Clegg* (1929) 45 TLR 438; and *Re Seaford, Seaford v Seifert* [1968] P 53, [1968] 1 All ER 482, CA.

2 *Re Wagstaff, Wagstaff v Jalland* [1908] 1 Ch 162; *Re Hammond, Burniston v White* [1911] 2 Ch 342. Compare *Re Lynch, Lynch v Lynch* [1943] 1 All ER 168.

3 *Re Dewhirst, Flower v Dewhirst* [1948] Ch 198, [1948] 1 All ER 147; *Re Eaves, Eaves v Eaves* [1940] Ch 109, [1939] 4 All ER 260; followed in *Re d'Altroy's Will Trusts, Crane v Lowman* [1968] 1 All ER 181, [1968] 1 WLR 120; compared *Re Rodwell, Midgley v Rumbold* [1970] Ch 726, [1969] 3 All ER 1363. But a transaction which has been carried into execution on the assumption of the validity of the marriage either immediately before the marriage and in expectation of it or during the marriage and before the decree of nullity, cannot be set aside: *Re Eaves, Eaves v Eaves*.

4 *Re Boddington, Boddington v Clairat* (1884) 25 Ch D 685. But it seems that the principle that widowhood is not ended by a remarriage which is subsequently annulled no longer applies if the nullity decree is granted on or after 1 August 1971, on the ground that the marriage is voidable: the Matrimonial Causes Act 1973, s 16.

5 *Re Gale, Gale v Gale* [1941] Ch 209, [1941] 1 All ER 329; *Re Lynch, Lynch v Lynch* [1943] 1 All ER 168 (in this case the judge held that the testator had made his own dictionary and upheld the gifts).

[80.5]

[Updated in text and footnote 2 for Perpetuities and Accumulations Act 2009.]

Surviving spouse. In the case of a will made before 6 April 2010, where a disposition is limited to the time of the death of the survivor of a person and his or her spouse (that person being a person in being at the commencement of the perpetuity period) and that time has not arrived at the end of the perpetuity period, this disposition is treated for all purposes as if limited to the time immediately before the end of the perpetuity period, if so doing would prevent it from being void for remoteness. As far as such wills are concerned this provision only applies where a person in being at the testator's death marries a person then unborn.[1] For wills made on or after 6 April 2010 the perpetuity period is now 125 years and there is now no other period.[2] Accordingly, there is no corresponding provision under PAA 2009.

1 Perpetuities and Accumulations Act 1964, s 5; see Vol 2, Part G, para **[246.78]**.

2 PAA 2009, s 5(1). See Vol 2, Part G, para **[246.179]**; and Chapter 94.

[80.6]

[Updated in footnote 1a for Marriage (Same Sex Couples) Act 2013.]

Partner in invalid marriage.[1a] The circumstances may show that the word 'wife' refers to a partner in an invalid marriage whether or not the parties know of the invalidity.[1] The fact that the description is false does not affect the validity of the gift, so long as the testator is not deceived for the purpose of obtaining the gift.[2]

1a This paragraph will need to be read in the light of the Marriage (Same Sex Couples) Act 2013 and regulations to be made thereunder when they are brought into force: see para **[80.10]** below and for the text of the relevant parts of the Act see Vol 2, Part G, paras **[245.149]** ff.

1 *Re Wagstaff, Wagstaff v Jalland* [1908] 1 Ch 162 (where the parties were aware of the invalidity); *Re Hammond, Burniston v White* [1911] 2 Ch 342 (where the parties, though they were aware of the remote possibility of the invalidity, thought the marriage valid and it was not found to be invalid until some years after the testator's death); *Re Smalley, Smalley v Scotton,* above (where the invalidity was known, but the reputed wife was in effect named); *Doe d Gains v Rouse* (1848) 5 CB 422 (a similar case); *Pratt v Mathew* (1856) 22 Beav 328 (marriage with deceased wife's sister then invalid: 'wife' could not refer to future wife because a future marriage would have revoked the will). See now as to voidable marriages, Matrimonial Causes Act 1973, s 16.

2 *Giles v Giles* (1836) 1 Keen 685; *Turner v Brittain* (1863) 3 New Rep 21 (gift to mistress of testator's son, whom testator believed to be married to him: legacy valid because deception of testator not for purpose of obtaining the legacy); *Anderson v Berkley* [1902] 1 Ch 936 (a similar case where it was said that the court could not speculate on the motive of the testator in making the gift. The donee was named); *Re Petts* (1859) 27 Beav 576 (wife assumed that former husband dead at time of marriage to testator upon not very satisfactory evidence, but gift held valid because evidence showed fraud on her part); *Re Posner, Posner v Miller* [1953] P 277, [1953] 1 All ER 1123 (gift to my wife R P is good although it is shown that the beneficiary is not the legal wife if the gift is not obtained by fraud on the part of the beneficiary). But in *Wilkinson v Joughin* (1866) LR 2 Eq 319, a wife knowing her husband was still alive married testator without disclosing that fact. A gift in these circumstances was held to have been obtained by fraud of the legatee and void.

II. 'HUSBAND'

[80.7]

[Updated in heading and footnote 1a to take account of the Marriage (Same Sex Couples) Act 2013.]

Husband.[1a] Generally speaking the decisions on the description of 'wife' apply mutatis mutandis in the case of 'husband'. In general, therefore, 'husband' means the husband at the date of the will and not an after-taken husband.[1] Where the person whose husband is referred to in the will is unmarried at the date of the will, the first husband she takes is the person referred to and he takes the gift for the interest given.[2] A divorced husband cannot be a surviving husband.[3]

1a This paragraph will need to be read in the light of the Marriage (Same Sex Couples) Act 2013 and regulations to be made thereunder when they are brought into force: see para **[80.10]** below and for the text of the relevant parts of the Act see Vol 2, Part G, paras **[245.149]** ff.

1 *Franks v Brooker* (1860) 27 Beav 635 (but in this case, there was a gift to five daughters (the wives of persons the testator named) and afterwards to their respective husbands, so that as the husbands were named, the context made the reference one to a named person); *Re Bryan's Trust, ex p Darnborough* (1851) 2 Sim NS 103.

2 *Radford v Willis* (1871) 7 Ch App 7; *Blount v Crozier* [1917] 1 IR 461: and cf *Re Hickman's Will Trusts, Hickman v Hickman* [1948] Ch 624, [1948] 2 All ER 303 (wife of grandson).

3 *Bosworthwick v Clegg* (1929) 45 TLR 438; *Bullmore v Wynter* (1883) 22 Ch D 619, to the contrary, was decided on the context and in so far as it states a general principle was dissented from in *Re Morrieson, Hitchens v Morrieson* (1888) 40 Ch D 30.

III. INHERITANCE TAX

[80.8]

[Updated in text and footnote 1 to take account of inheritance tax exemption for civil partners.]

The exemption for gifts to spouses. A transfer of value between spouses and civil partners is ordinarily exempt from inheritance tax to the extent of the value of property which thereby becomes comprised in the spouse's estate, or, where no property becomes so comprised to the extent that the spouse's estate is thereby increased.[1] The exemption is subject to an upper limit on the cumulative total of exempt transfers where the transferor is domiciled in the UK and the transferee is not. See, further, Volume 2, Part A, paras **[200.84]** and **[200.85]**.

1 See IHTA 1984, s 18 as amended (with effect from 5 December 2005) by FA 2005,s 103 and Tax and Civil Partnership Regulations 2005, SI 2005/3229, reg 7.

IV. CIVIL PARTNERSHIP

[80.9]

[Updated in text and footnote 2 for Marriage (Same Sex Couples) Act 2013.]

The Civil Partnership Act 2004[1] introduces an equivalent status to marriage for persons of the same sex and amends provisions relating to wills, administration of estates and family provision so that they apply in relation to civil partnerships as they apply in relation to marriage. It is possible that some of the rules of construction set out in this Chapter will be applicable by analogy to references in wills to civil partners. When brought into force the Marriage (Same Sex Couples) Act 2013 will permit the conversion of civil partnerships into marriages with retrospective effect.[2]

1 Section 71, Sch 4; Vol 2, Part G, paras **[244.132]** and **[244.133]**.
2 See para **[80.10]** below and, for the text of the relevant parts of the Act, see Vol 2, Part G, paras **[245.149]** ff.

V. SAME SEX MARRIAGE

[80.10]

At common law marriage is defined as 'the voluntary union for life of one man and one woman, to the exclusion of all others'.[1] A purported marriage between a man and another man is accordingly void at common law.[2] The position has been fundamentally altered by the Marriage (Same Sex Couples) Act 2013[3] which legalises same sex marriages and permits the conversion of civil partnerships into marriages with retrospective effect. Section 11 enacts the general principle that same sex marriages are to be treated in law as equivalent to opposite sex marriages. Section 17 of the Act confers powers, not yet exercised, to make appropriate consequential provision which will doubtless provide rules for the construction of wills and other instruments giving effect to this principle. The preceding paragraphs of this chapter will need to be read in the light of the Act and the regulations to be made thereunder when they are brought into force.

1 See *Hyde v Hyde and Woodmansee* (1866) LR 1 P & D 130 at 133 per Lord Penzance.
2 *Corbett v Corbett (otherwise Ashley)* [1971] P 83 at 105–106.
3 The relevant parts of the Act are printed in Vol 2, Part G, paras **[245.149]** ff.

PART M

Construction of wills: particular rules relating to beneficial interests

CHAPTER 82

Quantity of interest given

I. IN GENERAL

[82.3]

[Updated in footnote 1.]

Intention of testator governs construction. The intention of the testator as shown by the context of the whole will must in every case govern the construction and may cut down an apparent absolute interest to a life interest[1] or make it subject to defeasance;[2] and a life interest may, on the other hand, be extended to an absolute interest[3] or may be reduced to an interest until marriage or remarriage or other event.[4] An absolute interest is not cut down to a life interest unless the contingency cutting it down happens,[5] and an absolute interest subject to an executory gift over on a contingency remains absolute if the contingency does not happen.[6]

1 *Sherratt v Bentley* (1834) 2 My & K 149 (where the latter part of the will was held to prevail). The following were gifts to one person without any words showing what interest he or she is to take followed by a gift over after his or her death: *Joslin v Hammond* (1834) 3 My & K 110; *Hayes v Hayes* (1836) 1 Keen 97; *Re Bagshaw's Trusts* (1877) 46 LJ Ch 567 (where the gift in question was of personalty, but was accompanied by a gift of realty to the same person (the wife) for life); *Re Russell* (1885) 52 LT 559; *Re Sanford, Sanford v Sanford* [1901] 1 Ch 939 (a complicated will and codicil, but held that there were no words of limitation in the gift to the wife); *In the Estate of Last* [1958] P 134.

The following were gifts either in terms absolute or with limitations which would normally give an absolute interest followed by a gift after the death of the donee: *Morrall v Sutton* (1842) 5 Beav 100; *Johnston v Antrobus* (1856) 21 Beav 556; *Re Lupton's Estate* [1905] P 321; *Re Houghton, Houghton v Brown* (1884) 53 LJ Ch 1018 (an unlimited gift of rents). Where there is a gift to A for life, with remainder to B with remainder to C, B takes only a life interest: *Earl of Lonsdale v Countess of Berchtoldt* (1854) Kay 646.

2 *Bird v Webster* (1853) 1 Drew 338 (gift of personalty to persons and 'their descendants'. This gave an estate tail, but, being personalty, that became an absolute interest).

3 A gift of personal estate for life and afterwards to the donee's executors and administrators gives an absolute interest: *Re Brooks, Public Trustee v White* [1928] Ch 214. As to gift with a superadded power, see para **[83.8]** below. As to unlimited gifts of income, see Chapter 62.

4 *Meeds v Wood* (1854) 19 Beav 215 (to A for life and if she should marry to B: B takes on marriage of A or on death of A, if she does not marry. B's interest is vested independently of A's marriage); *Lancaster v Varty* (1826) 5 LJOS Ch 41 (remarriage). On the other hand where there is a gift to a widow until remarriage with a gift over to A when he attains twenty-three, the widow, whether or not she re-marries, takes the property until A attains twenty-three: *Doe d Dean of Westminster v Freeman* (1786) 1 Term Rep 389; *Re Cabburn, Gage v Rutland* (1882) 46 LT 848.

5 *Re Watson, Clume-Seymour v Brand* [1930] 2 Ch 344.

6 *Watkins v Weston* (1863) 3 De GJ & Sm 434; *Re Bourke's Trusts* (1891) 27 LR Ir 573; *Parnell v Boyd* [1896] 2 IR 571; *Re Lady Monck's Will, Monck v Crocker* [1900] 1 IR 56; but

see *Re Cohen's Will Trusts, Cullen v Westminster Bank Ltd* [1936] 1 All ER 103 (gift subject to the provisions and directions hereinafter contained).

CHAPTER 87

Distribution per capita and per stirpes

[87.1]

[Updated in footnote 1 for *Sammut v Manzi* [2009] WTLR 1051, [2008] UKPC 58 and *Spurling v Broadhurst* [2012] EWHC 2883 (Ch), [2012] WTLR 1825.]

Usually per capita. In a gift to a number of donees (for example, to the children of several persons), whether taking as a class or combination of classes or not, the distribution between them may be intended to be made per capita, in which case each donee takes a share equal in amount to the share of each other donee, or per stirpes, in which case each family or stock takes an equal share with every other family or stock, and such share is then subdivided equally between the members of such family or stock. Prima facie the distribution is made per capita and not per stirpes.[1] A number of words and expressions indicating the taking of equal shares have been said to show an intention that the division shall be per capita.[2] The following are examples of these expressions: 'equally';[3] 'share and share alike';[4] 'in equal shares';[5] 'equally divided';[6] 'divide';[7] 'for and equally between';[8] 'evenly distributed';[9] 'divided between'.[10] The prima facie rule is applicable, subject to a contrary intention appearing in the will,[11] to a number of class gifts;[12] gifts to a combination of classes;[13] gifts to a number of named persons taking as individuals together with a class;[14] and a gift to a number of persons taking as individuals and not as a class.[15] The rule is applied although the bequest is to persons who, under the statutory rule of distribution on the testator's intestacy, would take per stirpes,[16] and the fact that the persons taking are living relatives of the testator and the children of deceased relatives of the same relationship does not ordinarily take the case out of the rule.[17] Where the new Wills Act 1837, s 33 (substituted by the Administration of Justice Act 1982)[18] applies, the substituted class take per stirpes.[19] The word 'between' although originally referring to two, has been extended to more than two.[20]

1 *Re Alcock, Bonser v Alcock* [1945] Ch 264, [1945] 1 All ER 613 (the prima facie rule of distribution is per capita); *Re Jeffrey, Welch v Jeffrey* [1948] 2 All ER 131; *Re Adams Estate* [1957] OWN 568. See *Re Verdonk* (1979) 106 DLR (3d) 450; *Haidl v Sacher* (1979) 106 DLR (3d) 360. See *King v Perpetual Trustee Co Ltd* (1955) 94 CLR 70, where the authorities are discussed. There may be an express proviso that the distribution is to be per stirpes and not per capita; *Re Cockle's Will Trusts* [1967] Ch 690, [1967] 1 All ER 391, though this will not always be conclusive and the context may show that the words per stirpes are superfluous; *Sammut v Manzi* [2009] WTLR 1051, [2008] UKPC 58. In *Spurling v Broadhurst* [2012] EWHC 2883 (Ch), [2012] WTLR 1825 a per capita distribution was found, not through the application of any general rule, but through the process of construction of the will having regard to admissible extrinsic evidence.

2 *Mattison v Tanfield* (1840) 3 Beav 131 (the cases seem to show that the word 'equally' or the words 'share and share alike' would have the effect of making the division per capita).

3 *Butler v Stratton* (1791) 3 Bro CC 367; *Mattison v Tanfield* (1840) 3 Beav 131: *Rickabe v Garwood* (1845) 8 Beav 579; *Dugdale v Dugdale* (1849) 11 Beav 402; *Pattison v Pattison* (1855) 19 Beav 638; *Mason v Baker* (1856) 2 K & J 567; *Weldon v Hoyland* (1862) 4 De GF & J 564; *Re Jeffrey, Welch v Jeffrey* [1948] 2 All ER 131, *Houghton v Bell* (1892) 23 SCR 498; *Re Davies* (1913) 10 DLR 164.

4 *Phillips v Garth* (1790) 3 Bro CC 64; *Paine v Wagner* (1841) 12 Sim 184; *Abbay v Howe* (1847) 1 De G & Sm 470; *Boughten v Farrer* (1855) 3 WR 495; *Mitchison v Buckton* (1875) 32 LT 11; *Re Bossi* [1897] 5 BCR 446; *Anderson v Bell* (1883) 8 AR 531; *Re Baulderstone* [1928] SALR 262.

5 *Pearce v Edmeades* (1838) 3 Y & C Ex 246; *Cunningham v Murray* (1847) 1 De G & Sm 366; *Baker v Baker* (1847) 6 Hare 269; *Rook v A-G* (1862) 31 Beav 313; *Payne v Webb* (1874) LR 19 Eq 26; *Re Taylor, Taylor v Ley* (1885) 52 LT 839; *Kekewich v Barker* (1903) 88 LT 130; *Re Jones, Harris v Jones* [1910] VLR 306; *Re McKinnon* (1966) 55 DLR (2d) 20.

6 *Abrey v Newman* (1853) 16 Beav 431; *Re Fox* (1865) 35 Beav 163; *Swabey v Goldie* (1875) 1 Ch D 380; *Re Stone, Baker v Stone* [1895] 2 Ch 196; *Re Alcock, Bonser v Alcock* [1945] Ch 264, [1945] 1 All ER 613; *Re Foster's Will Trusts, Smith v Foster* (1967) 111 Sol Jo 685.

7 *Amson v Harris* (1854) 19 Beav 210.

8 *Re Richards, Davies v Edwards* [1910] 2 Ch 74.

9 *Re Foster* [1946] Ch 135, [1946] 1 All ER 333.

10 *Re Cossentine, Philp v Wesleyan Preachers' Association* [1933] Ch 119: *Cunningham's Trustees v Blackwell* 1909 SC 219; *Campbell's Trustee v Welsh* 1952 SC 343; *Equity, Trustees, Executors and Agency Co v Green* (1895) 21 VLR 618; but see *Re Heather* (1958) 13 DLR (2d) 587 (between my husband and my two sisters: husband took half).

11 The prima facie rule is very easily displaced: *Re Hall, Parker v Knight* [1948] Ch 437, and is displaced where the donees are of different generations and there is a reason arising from friendship or obligation for a stirpital distribution: *Re Birkett, Holland v Duncan* [1950] Ch 330, [1950] 1 All ER 316; *Canada Permanent Trust Co v Share* (1958) 25 WWR 638.

12 The following are examples of the class gifts held to be within the rule: to the children of A and B: *Weld v Bradbury* (1715) 2 Vern 705; descendants of A and B: *Lady Lincoln v Pelham* (1804) 10 Ves 166; nephews and nieces and issue of deceased nephews and nieces: *Tomlin v Hatfield* (1841) 12 Sim 167; parents and children 'to be classed together': *Pattison v Pattison* (1885) 19 Beav 638; children of brother and of sister equally: *Mason v Baker* (1856) 2 K & J 567; children of A and B for their education in equal shares: *Armitage v Williams* (1859) 27 Beav 346; testator's and his wife's next of kin in equal shares: *Rook v A-G* (1862) 31 Beav 313; issue of a deceased person equally to be divided between them: *Weldon v Hoyland* (1862) 4 De GF & J 564; to be equally divided between the children of the aforesaid share and share alike: *Re Stone, Baker v Stone* [1895] 2 Ch 196.

13 The following are examples of such combinations of classes: children and grandchildren: *Northey v Strange* (1716) 1 P Wms 340; the families of A and B: *Barnes v Patch* (1803) 8 Ves 604; testator's next of kin both maternal and paternal: *Dugdale v Dugdale* (1849) 11 Beav 402; children and issue: *Cancellor v Cancellor* (1862) 2 Drew & Sm 194; surviving brothers and sisters and their children: *Re Fox's Will* (1865) 35 Beav 163; see also *Re Hughes* [1968] VR 28.

14 In a case where such persons took as a single class, see *Kekewich v Barker* (1903) 88 LT 130. For cases where they were not made a single class, see *Paine v Wagner* (1841) 12 Sim 184; *Rickabe v Garwood* (1845) 8 Beav 579; *Cunningham v Murray* (1847) 1 De G & Sm 366; *Baker v Baker* (1847) 6 Hare 269; *Amson v Harris* (1854) 19 Beav 210; *Tyndale v Wilkinson* (1856) 23 Beav 74; *Re Harper, Plowman v Harper* [1914] 1 Ch 70; *Re Gill* [1959] Qd R 373.

15 *Cooke v Bowen* (1840) 4 Y & C Ex 244 (five nephews and nieces two shares each and their children one share each: children including all living at testator's death and those born in the lifetime of tenant for life and all took per capita, each nephew and niece (all of whom survived testator) taking a double share).

16 *Lady Lincoln v Pelham* (1804) 10 Ves 166 at 176.

17 *Blackler v Webb* (1726) 2 P Wms 383; *Amson v Harris* (1854) 19 Beav 210; *Payne v Webb* (1874) LR 19 Eq 26; *Evans v Turner* (1904) 23 NZLR 825.

18 Administration of Justice Act 1982, s 19; see Vol 2, Part G, para **[244.36]**; see Chapter 47.

19 Wills Act 1837, s 33(3), as substituted, which applies to deaths on or after 1 January 1983: Administration of Justice Act 1982, s 73(6); s 76(11).

20 *Re Cossentine, Philp v Wesleyan Preachers' Association* [1933] Ch 119; following *Re Harper, Plowman v Harper* [1914] 1 Ch 70, and distinguishing *Re Walbran, Milner v Walbran* [1906] 1 Ch 64; and see *Re Hall, Parker v Knight* [1948] Ch 437; *Cobban's Trustees v Cobban* 1915 SC 82; *Re McNeil Estate* (1959) 43 MPR 357.

CHAPTER 92

Option to purchase

[92.6]

[Updated for Perpetuities and Accumulations Act 2009.]

Perpetuities and Accumulations Act 1964 (PAA 1964) and options to purchase. By the PAA 1964, s 9[1] in the case of an option to acquire for valuable consideration the perpetuity period is 21 years and the law under which a period of 80 years or less could be prescribed did not apply in such a case nor did the period of life in being and 21 years. This did not apply to a right of pre-emption given to a public or local authority in respect of land used for religious purposes where the right becomes exercisable only on the land ceasing to be used for such purposes. By virtue of the PAA 1964, s 3(3) (applying to wills made before 6 April 2010) any exercise of the right within 21 years is valid although the provision giving the right does not limit it within that period, but in no case can the option be exercised after a period of 21 years from its creation.

For wills made on or after 6 April 2010, the perpetuity period is 125 years (and there is no other period): see the Perpetuities and Accumulations Act 2009, ss 5(1), 15(1)(a) (Ch [94] and Vol 2, Part G, para **[246.179]**). Following the coming into force of the PAA 2009 it is uncertain whether or to what extent the rule against perpetuities applies to testamentary options, whatever the nature of the property. Insofar as the rule applies the period is 125 years although there will still be 'wait and see' under the PAA 2009, s 7 (see Ch [94] and Vol 2, Part G, para **[246.181]**).

1 Vol 2, Part G, paras **[246.74]** ff.

CHAPTER 94

Perpetuities

[All paras of Chapter 94 updated for PAA 2009.]

PERPETUITIES

[94.A1]

Overview. There are now three different regimes for perpetuities, depending on the date of the disposition: common law, relating to dispositions before 16 July 1964; Perpetuities and Accumulations Act 1964 ('PAA 1964')[1] relating to dispositions made on or after 16 July 1964 and before 6 April 2010[2]; and Perpetuities and Accumulations Act 2009 ('PAA 2009')[3] relating to dispositions made on or after 6 April 2010[4]. For this purpose dispositions should be understood as meaning the date of death of the testator in the case of dispositions by will[5], save that PAA 1964 rather than PAA 2009 applies to a will made before 6 April 2010 of a person who dies on or after that date[6]. This is subject to the possibility that the will may be republished by a codicil made on or after 6 April 2010.[7] It seems likely that such republication, unless a contrary intention is expressed in the codicil, would have the effect of causing PAA 2009 to apply to the will. The main continuing importance of the pre 6 April 2010 law for the legal draftsman is for the exercise of special powers of appointment and similar special powers, because as a general rule the relevant perpetuity law is that which applies to the disposition creating the power. This is subject to the possibility in the case of a power created by a will made before 6 April 2010 of someone dying on or after date that PAA 2009 will apply to an exercise of the power[8].

1 Printed in Vol 2, Part G, paras **[246.74]** ff.
2 PAA 1964, s 15(5), and (5A) inserted by PAA 2009, s 16.
3 Printed in Vol 2, Part G, paras **[246.174]** ff.
4 PAA 2009 s 15(1) and Perpetuities and Accumulations Act 2009 (Commencement) Order 2010, SI 2010/37.
5 PAA 1964, s 15(1), PAA 2009, s 20(6).
6 PAA 1964, s 15(5A), inserted by PAA 2009, s 16, and PAA 2009, s 15(1).
7 For republication see para **[22.3]**. Note that PAA 2009, s 20(7) provides that in the Act a reference to a will include a reference to a codicil.
8 See PAA 2009, s 15(1) and para **[94.50]**.

I. PERIOD ALLOWED

[94.6]

The new statutory periods. The perpetuity period stated in the above paragraphs continued to apply to instruments made after the commencement of PAA 1964 and before the commencement of PAA 2009, but a new alternative type of period was added bythe PAA 1964, s 1[1], being such number of years not exceeding 80 as is specified in that behalf in the instrument. Thus a testator could provide in his will that for the purposes of the will the perpetuity period should be 80 years or some shorter period which the testator might prefer.[2] As the principal reason for this enactment was to provide a certain period instead of the rather uncertain period known as the 'royal lives' period, testators did not often choosea period much less than 80 years since the reason for choosing a 'royal lives' period was to ensure as long a perpetuity period as possible. This as stated above was purely an additional provision and, in the case of an ordinary will, the limit was still in general the attaining of the age of 21 years by grandchildren of the testator or the creator of the power.

PAA 2009 s 5(1)[3] took the more radical step of providing that for all dispositions which take effect on or after 6 April 2010 and are subject to the rule against perpetuities, other than wills made before that date, the perpetuity period is 125 years. There is no choice in the matter and the period does not have to be specified in the instrument.[4]

In the case of a special power of appointment, the already existing distinction between the creation of the power and its exercise was retained by the PAA 1964, s 1(2), and the PAA 2009 s 6(2), that is to say that the exercise of a special power must be 'read back' into the instrument creating it. Thus, under PAA 1964, assuming a period of 80 years was chosen, the instrument creating the special power could specify that as the perpetuity period, but in construing the instrument exercising the power, the period of 80 years must be reckoned from the date of the disposition creating the power and not from the date of the instrument exercising it. Under PAA 2009 the 125-year perpetuity period starts from the date of the disposition creating the power.[5]

1 Vol 2, Part G, paras **[246.74]** ff.
2 See *Re Green's Will Trusts, Fitzgerald-Hart v A-G* [1985] 3 All ER 455 where it was held that a period of 43 11/12 years had been specified within the Perpetuities and Accumulations Act 1964, s 1(1), since the disposition had unambiguously identified and made clear a period from the date of the testator's death, 1 February 1970 to 1 January 2020.
3 Vol 2, Part G, paras **[246.174]** ff.
4 PAA 2009, s 5(2).
5 PAA 2009, s 6(2).

[94.7]

Rule directed to the vesting of interests. The rule is directed to ensure that interests shall vest within the period allowed by the rule, and if an interest is immediately vested or must necessarily vest within the period allowed, its validity cannot be questioned so far as this rule is concerned.[1] An interest becomes vested[2] when, first, the person or persons or corporation or body of persons to whom or to which it is limited is or are ascertained and in existence and capable of taking,[3] secondly, the quantum of the interest is ascertained, and thirdly, all other events have happened to enable the interest to come into possession at once, subject to the determination at any time of the prior interests. Where property is to be accumulated, it is sufficient if within the period there is a person in existence entitled to take the property whatever its value or amount[4] if the limitation is vested in other respects; but where the direction for accumulation is a condition precedent to the interest, and that accumulation may extend beyond the legal limits and cannot be stopped and the fund disposed of by the beneficiary, the direction is void.[5] That the rule relates to the vesting of interests remains the case under PAA 2009.

1 *Oddie v Brown* (1859) 4 De G & J 179 at 196; *Redington v Browne* (1893) 32 LR Ir 347.
2 As to vesting of interests, see Chapter 93.
3 That the donee is himself under disability is ignored in questions of perpetuity: *Re Earl of Stamford and Warrington, Payne v Grey* [1912] 1 Ch 343 at 355; *Ferrand v Wilson* (1845) 4 Hare 344.
4 *Oddie v Brown* (1859) 4 De G & J 179; *Re Swain, Monckton v Hands* [1905] 1 Ch 669.
5 *Curtis v Lukin* (1842) 5 Beav 147 at 154; *Smith v Cunninghame* (1884) 13 LR Ir 480.

[94.8A]

Uncertainty as to when a perpetuity period ends. Under the PAA 2009, s 12[1] there is provision for cases where there is uncertainty, in an instrument which took effect before 6 April 2010 (and a will made before that date of someone dying after it)[2], as to when a perpetuity period based on lives in being will come to an end. If the trustees believe that it is difficult or not reasonably practicable for them to ascertain whether the lives have ended and therefore whether the perpetuity period has ended, and they execute a deed stating that they so believe and that the PAA 2009, s 12(2) is to apply to the instrument, the perpetuity period irrevocably becomes 100 years from the date when the instrument took effect. However, this provision cannot apply if the terms of the trust were exhausted before 6 April 2010, or before that day the trust property had become held on trust for charitable purposes by way of a final disposition of the property.[3]

1 Vol 2, Part G, para **[246.186].**
2 See PAA 2009, s 15(2): Vol 2, Part G, para **[246.189]**.
3 PAA 2009, s 15(3).

II. APPLICATION OF THE RULE: THE COMMON LAW RULES

[94.15]

[Updated in footnote 1 for *Pengelly v Pengelly* [2008] Ch 375.]

'As far as the law admits'. These and similar words have no effect in a will except in the case of executory trusts.[1] Where the gift is direct and unambiguous these words have no effect whatever, but as stated above, where the will is ambiguous, and these words are present, they aid the court to choose a construction which will render the will operative rather than void.[2] In one case an appointment on the trusts of a previous instrument or such of them as were 'capable of taking effect' took effect with the trusts excluded which would have been void under the rule.[3] Executory trusts, though subject to the rule in common with other trusts,[4] are executed by the court in such a way as to preclude the objection arising from the rule and are moulded so as to carry out the intention of the testator so far as the rules of law admit.[5] Provisions which offend against the rule are omitted,[6] modified,[7] or confined within the rule,[8] unless the creator of the trust has specifically or by necessary implication directed the inclusion of such provisions,[9] or the trust is wholly incapable of being executed so as to avoid the objection arising from the rule.[10] It follows, therefore, that in the case of executory trusts the court will in the ordinary way be prepared to give effect to a direction by a testator that the provisions of his will are to take effect only so far as the law allows or will admit. Where property is settled or directed to be settled in a particular course of succession, so far as the rules of law will admit, or with other words to the same effect, then, according to the intention shown, the qualification may refer to the quality of the property, to which the course of succession may be inapt (as in the case of personal property settled to follow real estate)—this being the ordinary sense of the words in such a case[11]—or to the length of time that the property is to be tied up, having regard to the rule against perpetuities. In the first case, no executory trust is necessarily created, nor are the interests deemed to be settled to the limits of time allowed by the rule.[12] In the second case, if the intention is that the property is to be tied up as long as possible, then an executory trust may be created, but such trust must be executed by prolonging the settlement, not to the farthest limit possible in any event under the rules, but to that convenient limit which will enable the primary purpose of the instrument to be carried out.[13] In such a case the court inclines to give life interests only to all persons, becoming entitled under the limitations, who are in existence at the date of the death of the testator creating the limitations.[14]

1 *Christie v Gosling* (1866) LR 1 HL 279; *Re Viscount Exmouth, Viscount Exmouth v Praed* (1883) 23 Ch D 158; *Portman v Viscount Portman* [1922] 2 AC 473; *Pengelly v Pengelly* [2008] Ch 375.

2 See cases cited in n 1; and *Re Vaux, Nicholson v Vaux* [1939] Ch 465, [1938] 4 All ER 297 (power to trustees to deal with capital and income as they think best within limits prescribed by law); *Re Craig* [1955] VLR 196 (where land was not to be sold until such time or times as the law directs. Held to be a direction that the sale must take place at the end of the perpetuity period).

3 *Re Finch and Chew's Contract* [1903] 2 Ch 486.

4 *Duke of Marlborough v Earl Godolphin* (1759) 1 Eden 404; *Blackburn v Stables* (1814) 2 Ves & B 367.

5 *Christie v Gosling* (1866) LR 1 HL 279; *Re Beresford-Hope, Aldenham v Beresford-Hope* [1917] 1 Ch 287.

6 *Miles v Harford* (1879) 12 Ch D 691; distinguished in *Re Flavel's Will Trusts, Coleman v Flavel* [1969] 2 All ER 232, [1969] 1 WLR 444.

7 *Lord Dorchester v Earl Effingham* (1813) 10 Sim 587n: *Woolmore v Burrows* (1827) 1 Sim 512.

8 *Bankes v Le Despencer* (1840) 10 Sim 576; *Lyddon v Ellison* (1854) 19 Beav 565; *Shelley v Shelley* (1868) LR 6 Eq 540.

9 *Sackville-West v Viscount Holmesdale* (1870) LR 4 HL 543; compare *IRC v Williams* [1969] 3 All ER 614 ('upon such trusts as shall not impinge the rule against perpetuities'). See also *Re Earl of Coventry's Indentures, Smith v Earl of Coventry* [1974] Ch 77, [1973] 3 All ER 1, where the words 'due regard being had to the law relating to perpetuities' were ineffective to save a void appointment, since the purpose of the words was merely to remind the trustees to think carefully before exercising the powers conferred on them, rather than to cut down the period during which the power could be exercised.

10 *Tregonwell v Sydenham* (1815) 3 Dow 194.

11 *Countess of Lincoln v Duke of Newcastle* (1806) 12 Ves 218; *Christie v Gosling* (1866) LR 1 HL 279.

12 *Lord Deerhurst v Duke of St Albans* (1820) 5 Madd 232; *Re Hill, Hill v Hill* [1902] 1 Ch 807.

13 *Williams v Teale* (1847) 6 Hare 239; *Shelley v Shelley* (1868) LR 6 Eq 540; *Re Beresford-Hope, Aldenham v Beresford-Hope* [1917] 1 Ch 287; *Pole v Pole* [1924] 1 Ch 156.

14 *Woolmore v Burrows* (1827) 1 Sim 512 at 526; *Bankes v Le Despencer* (1840) 10 Sim 576; *Williams v Teale* (1847) 6 Hare 239.

III. THE PERPETUITIES AND ACCUMULATIONS ACTS 1964 AND 2009

[94.16]

The statutory law. The common law rules discussed above were considerably modified by the provisions of PAA 1964,[1] which governs dispositions in instruments taking effect on or after 16 July 1964 and before 6 April 2010 (and also wills made before that date which take effect after it). The rules were even more considerably modified for dispositions taking effect on or after 6 April 2010 (apart from wills made before that date) by PAA 2009[2]. The common law rules however remain important since many of the provisions of these Acts are only applicable if the disposition would otherwise be void at common law, and because the former law can still apply to the exercise of special powers.

1 See Vol 2, Part G, paras **[246.74]** ff.
2 See Vol 2, Part G, paras **[246.174]** ff.

[94.17]

Wait and see. The most striking change introduced by the PAA 1964 and continued by PAA 2009 is the abrogation of the common law rule that possible, rather than actual events, should be considered, by the introduction of a 'wait and see' rule. Where a disposition would be void at common law on the ground that the interest disposed of might not become vested until too remote a time, then the disposition shall be treated until such time (if any) as it becomes established that the vesting must occur, if at all, after the end of the perpetuity period,[1] as if the disposition were not subject to the rule against perpetuities. In other words one can wait and see whether the interest does in fact vest within the period, rather than conjecturing at the outset the most adverse possibilities. Where the wait and see provisions of PAA 1964 are applicable the perpetuity period is either the statutory number of years, by virtue of the PAA 1964, s 1, or alternatively the duration of statutory lives in being as specified in s 3(5), plus 21 years.[2] Where the wait and see provisions of PAA 2009 are applicable the perpetuity period is the period of 125 years.[3] A beneficial consequence of the adoption of the single 125 year perpetuity period by PAA 2009 is that it much simplified the operation of the 'wait and see rule', so that the complexities of the PAA 1964, s 3(4) and (5) for determining what are the relevant lives in being for the purposes of wait and see could be discarded.

1 PAA 1964, s 3(1); see Vol 2, Part G, para **[246.76]**. PAA 2009, s 7(1), (2); see Vol 2, Part G para **[246.181]**.
2 PAA 1964, s 3(4). Before the PAA 1964 a limitation to a class who should be living at the death of a husband or his widow whichever should last happen, was subject to the 'unborn widow trap' and was void at common law; see *Re Frost, Frost v Frost* (1889) 43 Ch D 246; *Re Garnham, Taylor v Baker* [1916] 2 Ch 413. The PAA 1964, s 5 specifically validates such gifts.
3 PAA 2009, s 5; Vol 2, Part G, para **[246.179]**.

[94.18]

Presumptions and evidence as to future parenthood. The PAA 1964 seeks to remove some of the anomalies of the common law refusal to recognise de facto limits as to the age of parenthood in relation to dispositions to which it applies. The PAA 1964 introduces presumptions to the effect that a male can have a child at the age of 14 years or over, but not under that age, and that a female can have a child at the age of twelve years or over, but not under that age or over the age of 55 years; but in the case of a living person evidence may be given to show that he or she will not be able to have a child at the time in question.[1] There is no corresponding provision under PAA 2009 because of the adoption of a fixed term of years as the perpetuity period.

1 PAA 1964, s 2; Vol 2, Part G, para **[246.75]**. These presumptions are equally applicable to adoption and legitimation: PAA 1964, s 2(4).

[94.19]

Reduction of age. PAA 1964 provides in relation to the dispositions to which it applies that limitation by reference to the attainment by any person or persons of a specified age exceeding 21 years, where it is or becomes apparent that the disposition would be void for remoteness but it would not be so if the age specified had been 21, is to be treated for all purposes as if it had been limited to the age nearest to that age which would, if specified instead, have prevented it from being void.[1] Thus where the age specified is 25 years and the disposition would be valid if limited to 23 years, the age need only be reduced to 23 years and it is not necessary to reduce it to 21 years. Where different ages are specified in respect of different persons each age may be reduced so far as necessary to prevent remoteness.[2] Where the inclusion of potential members of class or unborn persons would under the disposition be void for remoteness, such members or persons are to be excluded.[3] Where this becomes apparent at the time the disposition is made or afterwards such members are to be excluded unless their exclusion would exhaust the class.[4] The operation of this section does not affect anything done by way of advancement or application of intermediate income before it becomes clear that the disposition is void for remoteness.[5] This is another feature of PAA 1964 which is not repeated in PAA 2009, because of the latter's introduction of a perpetuity period of a fixed term of years.

1 PAA 1964, s 4(1); Vol 2, Part G, para **[246.77]**. This section applies to dispositions taking effect after 16 July 1964. In the case of wills of a testator dying after 1925, the Law of Property Act 1925, s 163 provided for the reduction of excessive ages to 21, where to do so would validate the gift for perpetuities. It was repealed by the PAA 1964, s 4(6) but may still be applicable to exercises of special powers created by pre-PAA 1964 dispositions: see the PAA 1964, s 15(5).
2 PAA 1964, s 4(2).
3 PAA 1964, s 4(3).
4 PAA 1964, s 4(4).
5 PAA 1964, s 4(5).

[94.20]

Condition relating to death of surviving spouse. This has already been considered.[1]

1 See para **[80.5]**.

IV. CLASS GIFTS

[94.22]
The PAA 1964 and PAA 2009. The common law rule that 'the vice of remoteness affects the class as a whole, if it may affect an unascertained number of its members'[1] has been abrogated in relation to dispositions on or after 16 July 1964. The PAA 1964 and PAA 2009 enable the class in such circumstances to be split; where there is a gift to a class some members of which are ascertained within the perpetuity period but where other members of the class will not be ascertained within the period, the Act enables the gift to the void members to be severed and those takers excluded, leaving the gift to the unobjectionable class to take effect.[2] This is only resorted to if the gift is not saved by wait and see. It is necessary to approach class gifts in the following way; first, to ascertain whether the gift is void at common law—if it is then see if it saved by 'wait and see'; secondly, in a case where PAA 1964 applies, the relevance of the age reduction provisions and the presumptions as to future parenthood should be considered; thirdly, or secondly in a PAA 2009 case, if the gift is still invalid, the offending members of the class should be excluded. At each stage the application of the class closing rules (see Chapter 66) should be considered.

1 Per Lord Selborne LC in *Pearks v Moseley* (1880) 5 App Cas 714 at 723.
2 PAA 1964, s 4(4); see Vol 2, Part G, para **[246.77]**; PAA 2009, s 8; see Vol 2, Part G, para **[246.182]**.

V. EFFECT OF GIFT BEING VOID UNDER THE RULE

[94.32]
Statutory variation. By PAA 1964, s 6, and PAA 2009, s 9, a disposition is not treated as void for remoteness by reason only that the interest disposed of is ulterior to or dependent upon an interest under a disposition which is so void, and the vesting of an interest shall not be prevented from being accelerated on the failure of a prior interest by reason only that the failure arises because of remoteness.

VI. INTERESTS SUBJECT TO THE RULE

[94.33]
Interests in real estate. The following have been held subject to the perpetuity rule: executory devises;[1] springing and shifting uses;[2] legal contingent remainders[3] and certain rights of re-entry on breach of a condition subsequent.[4] Legal remainders in land have since 1925 taken effect as equitable interests if previously valid as legal interests.[5] A legal contingent remainder where the particular estate was limited to a person or persons in being, might be valid whatever the contingency on which it depended, though it might be invalid as an executory devise.[6] In such a case the nature of the remainder afforded a guarantee against remoteness, because the remainder, unless ready to take effect *eo instanti* on the determination of the particular estate, could never take effect at all as a remainder.[7] Where such a remainder was

limited by will, however, there was a doubt whether the effect of the Land Transfer Act 1897, was to provide a sufficient estate in the personal representative to save it from the doctrine of abeyance of the seisin.[8] By statute (now repealed) a legal remainder, limited on a contingency not too remote under the rule, which would, therefore, be valid if limited as an executory devise, might take effect notwithstanding the determination of the particular estate before the contingent vested.[9] In relation to dispositions on or after 6 April 2009 the rule against perpetuities is confined to trust or similar interests.[10]

1 *Thellusson v Woodward* (1805) 11 Ves 112; *Cadell v Palmer* (1833) 1 Cl & Fin 372.
2 *Blandford v Thackerell* (1793) 2 Ves 238; *Savill Bros Ltd v Bethell* [1902] 2 Ch 523; *Re Ramadge's Settlement, Hamiton v Ramadge* [1919] 1 IR 205.
3 *Re Frost, Frost v Frost* (1889) 43 Ch D 246; *Re Ashforth, Sibley v Ashforth* [1905] 1 Ch 535.
4 See para **[94.34]** below.
5 Law of Property Act 1925, s 1.
6 *Jack d Westby v Fetherstone* (1829) 2 Hud & B 320; *Doe d Winter v Perratt* (1843) 9 Cl & Fin 606; *Cole v Sewell* (1848) 2 HL Cas 186; *Symes v Symes* [1896] 1 Ch 272.
7 This rule did not apply where the determination was caused by forfeiture surrender or merger.
8 See *Re Robson, Douglass v Douglass* [1916] 1 Ch 116. Though saved from failure for this reason, the limitation may yet be too remote: *Re Finch, Abbiss v Burney* (1880) 17 Ch D 211.
9 Contingent Remainders Act 1877, s 1.
10 PAA 2009, s 1. See para **[94.40A]**.

[94.35]
Personal property. Executory limitations of personal property are subject to the rule.[1]

1 *Maddox v Staines* (1727) 2 P Wms 421. PAA 2009, s 1(5).

[94.36]
Equitable interests. Equitable interests of all kinds, including contingent remainders of equitable interests, were subject to the rule. The mode of creation of the interest, whether by will or otherwise, was immaterial.[1] However, the PAA 2009, s 1 provides for the rule to apply only to interests under trusts in relation to instruments to which it applies.[2]

1 *London and South Western Rly Co v Gomm* (1882) 20 Ch D 562.
2 See para **[94.40A]**.

[94.38]
Trusts for indefinite duration. The rule does not affect validly created trusts lasting a possibly indefinite period where the interests are vested and the beneficiaries may, apart from disability, put an end to the trust,[1] but an indefinite trust where the interests may not be vested within the perpetuity period, and the trust is therefore not determinable, is subject to the rule.[2] A discretionary trust of the income of a fund for the maintenance of a class of persons, some unborn, which may possibly last longer than the period is void[3] if not saved by statutory wait and see. On the other hand, a trust of income which is not discretionary for the maintenance of the children of a living person, in equal shares, where the interest of each child is fixed, is not void even though the trust may terminate after the period.[4] A gift rendering capital inalienable for an indefinite period is caught by the rule.[5]

1 See para **[95.12]** below.
2 *Mainwaring v Baxter* (1800) 5 Ves 458; *Thomson v Shakespear* (1860) 1 De GF & J 399; *Smith v Cunninghame* (1884) 13 LR Ir 480; *Trustees, Executors and Agency Co v Bush* (1908) 28 NZLR 117.
3 *Re Blew, Blew v Gunner* [1906] 1 Ch 624, not following *Re Wise, Jackson v Parrott* [1896] 1 Ch 281; *Re Watson, Cox v Watson* (1892) 27 LJNC 174; *Re Hyne* [1958] Qd R 431.
4 *Gooding v Read* (1853) 4 De GM & G 510; *Williams v Papworth* [1900] AC 563.
5 *Re Wightwick's Will Trusts* [1950] Ch 260, [1950] 1 All ER 689 (gift of income of fund until vivisection shall be made a punishable offence void as tending to a perpetuity, and as it could not be postulated when the gift would determine a gift over to a charity also failed. See also *Re Mander* [1950] Ch 547, [1950] 2 All ER 191 (gift to be retained until a candidate for priesthood comes forward); *Re Jones* [1950] 2 All ER 239 (capital sums to be paid when realisation of estate possible).

[94.40]
Possibilities of reverter, conditions subsequent, exceptions and reservations. In the case of a possibility of reverter on the determination of a determinable fee simple or a possibility of a resulting trust on the determination of any other determinable interest in property, the rule shall apply in relation to the provision causing the interest to be determinable as it would apply if that provision were expressed in the form of a condition subsequent giving rise, on the breach thereof, to a right of re-entry or an equivalent right in the case of property other than land and where the provision falls to be treated as void for remoteness the determinable interest shall become an absolute interest.[1] Where a disposition is subject to any such provision, or to any such condition subsequent or to any exception or reservation, the disposition shall be treated for the purposes of PAA1964 as including a separate disposition of any rights arising by virtue of the provision, condition subsequent, exception or reservation.[2]

1 PAA 1964, ss 12(1); Vol 2, Part G, para **[246.85]**. PAA 2009, ss 1(2), (4), (7) and 10; Vol 2, Part G, paras **[246.175]** and **[246.184]** makes similar provision.
2 PAA 1964, s 12(2).

[94.40A]
What the rule against perpetuities applies to—instruments taking effect on or after 6 April 2010, other than wills made before than date and exercises of special powers where the power was created before that date. In relation to such instruments[1] PAA 2009 confines the rule against perpetuities to applying to successive estates or interests under trusts, estates or interests under trusts subject to a condition precedent, rights of re-entry or the like in the event of a condition subsequent being broken, successive interests under the doctrine of executory bequests, and powers of appointment.[2] Successive trust interests or estate for this purpose include any estate or interest which arises under a right of reverter on the determination of a determinable fee simple, or which arises under a resulting trust on the determination of a determinable interest.[3] There are exceptions for property moving between charities and interests or rights arising under certain pension schemes.[4] The main point of this is that it takes out of the rule against perpetuities various interests arising from commercial transactions and dispositions of land such as future easements and land options. There is a question as to whether a testamentary option is still within the perpetuity rule. This is not a question of great practical importance because 125 years ought to be enough for a

testamentary option even if the rule against perpetuities does apply. It should be noted that the 21 year compulsory perpetuity period for land options under the PAA 1964, s 9 is not repeated by PAA 2009 and has no application to instruments to which PAA 2009 applies.

1 See the PAA 2009, s 15(1) (Vol 2, Part G, para **[246.189]**) for the instruments to which PAA 2009, s 1 relates.
2 PAA 2009, s 1(1)–(6), Vol 2, Part G, para **[246.175]**.
3 PAA 2009, s 1(7).
4 PAA 2009, ss 1(8) and 2.

VII. POWERS OF APPOINTMENT AND THE RULE AGAINST PERPETUITIES

[94.41]
Remoteness. If there is no statutory wait and see under PAA 1964 or 2009, objections to the validity of a power of appointment in its creation are based on the contention either that the persons to exercise it or the time fixed for its exercise or the objects or the subject-matter of the power may not be ascertained within the time allowed by the perpetuity rule.[1] Such an objection, if well founded, is fatal to the power from the time of its creation and it can never be effectively exercised.[2] Objection based on the rule may also be taken to the disposition exercising the power, but even if such objection is found to be valid, its effect can be only that the particular disposition is void. The perpetuity period must in the case of a special power of appointment always be reckoned from the creation of the power, but in the case of a general power the period for ascertaining the validity of an exercise of the power is reckoned from the time of its exercise and not from the time of its creation.[3]

1 That is, the interest must vest in interest within a life or lives in being and twenty-one years and a possible period of gestation afterwards, or if it so expressly stated, within a period of not more than 80 years: PAA 1964, s 1 (see Vol 2, Part G, para **[246.74]**) unless the power is created by an instrument taking effect on or after 6 April 2010 other than a will made before that date, in which case the interest must vest within 125 years from the creation of the power. This, so far as concerns wills of persons dying after 15 July 1964, is modified by the wait and see rule.
2 The exercise of a power of appointment by will is ambulatory, until the death of the testator, and events which happen between the date of the will and the death of the testator, though in a sense subsequent, are not subsequent for this purpose.
3 See para **[94.43]** below.

[94.42]
Perpetuities and Accumulations Acts of 1964 and 2009. The application of PAA 1964 and PAA 2009 to powers of appointment is largely consistent with these rules.[1] If a special power is created by an instrument taking effect before 15 July 1964, then the common law perpetuity rules will be applicable to determine the validity of both the creation and the exercise of the power. But if the power is created by an instrument taking effect after that date then the provisions of PAA 1964 or PAA 2009 as the case may be will be applicable to both the creation and the exercise of the power. In the case of a will, taking effect here means the death of the testator. The dividing line between PAA 1964 and PAA 2009 powers of appointment created by will is

complicated and is discussed in para **[94.50]**). The exercise of a general power, however, will be subject to the provisions of the PAA 1964 if it is exercised in an instrument taking effect after 15 July 1964, or the PAA 2009 is exercised in an instrument taking effect on or after 6 April 2010 (other than a will made before that date), even if created at an earlier date. If a general power is exercised before 16 July 1964, it will be governed by the common law rules. It is accordingly necessary to differentiate between the common law rules and the provisions of the PAA 1964 and PAA 2009, and the former will be stated first.

1 PAA 1964, s 15(5); see Vol 2, Part G, para **[246.88]**. PAA 2009, s 15(1); see Vol 2, Part G, para **[246.189]**.

(*b*) *Perpetuities and Accumulations Acts 1964 and 2009*

[94.50]

Application of the PAA 1964 and PAA 2009. For the purpose of the PAA 1964 a 'disposition' includes the conferring of a power of appointment and any other disposition of an interest in or right over property, and a power of appointment includes any discretionary power to transfer a beneficial interest in property without the furnishing of valuable consideration.[1] PAA 1964 applies to both the creation and the exercise of special powers of appointment, if the power was created by a disposition taking effect on or after 16 July 1964 and before 6 April 2010.[2] It also applies at least to the creation of a special power of appointment if it is created by a will made before that date of someone dying after it.[3] It governs general powers to the extent that the creation or exercise of the power is between those dates. PAA 2009 is worded in terms of instruments rather than dispositions but the effect is similar in most but not all contexts. It applies to instruments taking effect on or after 6 April 2010, other than exercises of special powers where the power was created by an instrument taking effect before that day, and wills made before that day.[4] In the case of wills, taking effect is defined for this purpose as the death of the testator.[5] Accordingly, it appears that PAA 2009 will apply to an *exercise* of a special power of appointment created by a will made before 6 April 2010, where the testator dies on or after that date (the perpetuity period running from the date of the testator's death). The statutory wording is clear, but this is contrary to a property lawyer's instinctive feeling that the exercise of a special power of appointment is governed by the perpetuity (and accumulations) rules applicable to the disposition creating the power. Another point to bear in mind in this context is that a pre-6 April 2010 will of someone dying on or after that date may be subject to PAA 2010 by virtue of republication by a codicil made on or after that date: see para **[94.A1]**.

1 PAA 1964, s 15(2); see Vol 2, Part G, para **[246.88]**.
2 PAA 1964, s 15(5), and (5A) inserted by PAA 2009, s 16. See also paras **[94.A1]** and **[94.42]** above.
3 PAA 1964, s 15(5A) inserted by PAA 2009, s 16.
4 PAA 2009, s 15(1); see Vol 2, Part G, para **[246.189]**.
5 PAA 2009, s 20(6); see Vol 2, Part G, para **[246.194]**.

[94.51]
Fixed perpetuity period. Where the creation of the special power is governed by PAA 1964, the alternative fixed perpetuity period, not exceeding 80 years, provided for by the PAA 1964 can be specified in the instrument creating a power of appointment, in which case it will govern both the creation and the exercise of the power.[1] But if not so specified it cannot be invoked for the exercise of a special power.[2] Where the creation of the special power is governed by PAA 2009[3], the fixed perpetuity period of 125 years running from the creation of the power will apply.[4] It also appears that in the case of a special power created by a will made before 6 April 2010 of someone dying after that date, that in relation to an exercise of the power the perpetuity period will be 125 years from the date of death of the testator, even though this is not the case for the will itself.[5]

1 See para **[94.6]** above.
2 PAA 1964, s 1(2); see Vol 2, Part G, para **[246.74]**.
3 See para **[94.50]** above.
4 PAA 2009, ss 5, 6(2); see Vol 2, Part G, paras **[246.179], [246.180]**.
5 See para **[94.50]** above.

[94.52]
Special power. For the purposes of the PAA 1964 a power of appointment shall be treated as special unless, firstly, in the instrument creating the power it is expressed to be exercisable by one person only, and secondly, it could, at all times during its currency when that person is of full age and capacity, be exercised by him so as immediately to transfer to himself the whole of the interest governed by the power without the consent of any other person or compliance with any other condition,[1] not being a formal condition relating only to the mode of exercising the power: provided that for the purpose of applying the perpetuity rule to an appointment made under a power of appointment exercisable by will only the power shall be treated as general if it would have been so treated had it been exercisable by deed.[2] The definition in PAA 2009 is differently and more elaborately worded but produces the same result in most contexts. Where the power is exercisable otherwise than by will (whether or not also exercisable by will), the power is a special power unless the instrument creating it expresses it to be exercisable by one person only, and at all times during its currency when that person is of full age and capacity it could be exercised by that person so as immediately to transfer to that person the whole of the interest governed by the power without the consent of any other person or compliance with any other condition other than formal one.[3] If the power is exercisable by will (whether or not also exercisable otherwise than by will) the power is a special power unless the instrument creating it expresses it to be exercisable by one person only, and that person could exercise it so as to transfer to that person's personal representatives the whole of the estate or interest to which it relates.[4] If it counts as a special power under one but not both of these categorisations, it is a special power.[5]

1 Thus a 'joint' power of appointment would for the purposes of this section be special: *Re Earl of Coventry's Indentures, Smith v Earl of Coventry* [1974] Ch 77, [1973] 3 All ER 1.
2 PAA 1964, s 7; see Vol 2, Part G, para **[246.80]**.
3 PAA 2009, s 11(1), (2); see Vol 2, Part G, para **[246.185]**.

4 PAA 2009, s 11(3), (4).
5 PAA 2009, s 11(5), (6).

[94.53]
Wait and see. Under the PAA 1964, s 3, and PAA 2009, s 7,where a disposition may be void as not becoming vested until too remote a time, it is to be treated as valid until it is established that the vesting must occur, if at all, at a time beyond the perpetuity period. That is, under PAA 1964, beyond the ordinary period of a life in being and 21 years or the special period of 80 years or less if the instrument creating the power so provides. Under PAA 2009 it is the period of 125 years from the instrument creating the power taking effect. So long as it can be so treated as valid, provisions as to advancement and application of intermediate income and so forth can be exercised and will be binding on all parties provided they are exercised before it becomes clear that the interest cannot vest within the perpetuity period.[1]

Where, in the case of a general power, the power might become exercisable within the perpetuity period, it is to be treated as valid until such time as it is certain that it cannot be exercised within the perpetuity period.[2]

Any power option or other right is to be treated as not subject to the rule against perpetuities in the case of any exercise thereof within the perpetuity period and is to be treated as invalid on the ground of perpetuity only if and so far as the power or right is not fully exercised within that period.[3]

Certain limitations are put upon the rule.[4] These concern only cases where, under PAA 1964, the period is for a life and 21 years and not those where the testator has specified a definite number of years (80 or less) as the perpetuity period, nor options to acquire an interest in land, nor where PAA 2009 applies. These limitations concern the lives that are to be taken into account in determining the perpetuity period.

The limitations put on wait and see under PAA 1964 where no perpetuity period for a fixed number of years has been specified, are as follows. Where the person making the disposition is alive at the commencement of the perpetuity period, only the duration of his or her life is to be considered. Where there is a disposition to a person or in his favour then the life or lives to be considered are: (i) any members or potential member of a class; (ii) where conditions have to be satisfied, any person satisfying some and likely to satisfy the remainder afterwards; (iii) in the case of a special power exercisable in favour of a class any member or potential member; (iv) where the special power is exercisable in favour of one person only, that person or, if the person has to satisfy conditions, any person satisfying some of the conditions and likely to satisfy the remainder afterwards. Cases (i) to (iv) above include a person having a child or grandchild or whose children or grandchildren if subsequently born would by virtue of descent fall within these sub-paragraphs. Where a disposition is limited to take effect on the failure or determination of a prior interest, the life to be considered is the life of the person given such prior interest.[5]

1 PAA 1964, s 3(1); see Vol 2, Part G, para **[246.76]**. PAA 2009, s 7(2) ; see Vol 2, Part G, para **[246.181]**.
2 PAA 1964, s 3(2). PAA 2009, s 7(5), (6).
3 PAA 1964, s 3(3). PAA 2009, s 7(3), and (4).
4 PAA 1964, s 3(4).
5 PAA 1964, s 3(5).

CHAPTER 95

Accumulations

[95.A1]

[Updated for PAA 2009.]

Perpetuities and Accumulations Act 2009. All the restrictions on accumulation for less than a perpetuity period which are described in paragraphs **[95.1]** ff are abolished for instruments to which PAA 2009 applies.[1] These are instruments taking effect on or after 6 April 2010 other than exercises a special powers of appointment where the power was created by an instrument taking effect before that date, and wills made before that date.[2] Newly defined restrictions for charitable trusts are introduced, however. One of these is relevant to the drafting of wills, namely that a power or trust to accumulate income of property held on trust for charitable purposes is only permitted for a maximum period of 21 years, but the period in question can start at any time, and is not restricted to commencing at the death of the testator.[3]

1 PAA 2009, s 13; Vol 2, Part G, para **[246.187]**.

2 PAA 2009, s 15(1) Vol 2, Part G, para **[246.189]**. See also paras **[94.A1]** and **[94.50]** for more details of the instruments to which PAA 2009 applies. The possibility discussed in **[94.50]** that the Act might apply to an exercise of a special power of appointment created by a will made before 6 April 2010 of someone dying on or after that date has more immediate relevance to accumulations than it does to perpetuities.

3 PAA 2009, s 14(2), (3) Vol 2, Part G, para **[246.188]**. See s 14(6) for what happens if there is a trust or power in excess of the permitted period. The alternative permitted period is the lifetime of the settlor, which is clearly not relevant to a charitable trust in a will.

PART N

Charities

CHAPTER 102

Charities: gifts for charitable purposes

I. CHARITABLE PURPOSES

[102.2]

[Updated in the text and in the footnotes for the Charities Act 2011.]

Charity. A charity is now defined as any institution, whether incorporated or not, including a trust or undertaking, which is established for charitable purposes only and falls to be subject to the control of the High Court[1] in the exercise of its jurisdiction with respect to charities.[2] There is provision for the registration of charities[3] and any registered charity is by the Charities Act 2011 (CA 2011), s 37(1) for all purposes other than rectification of the register, a charity.[4] Neither the Charities Act 1960 nor the CA 1993, defined charitable purposes. With effect from 1 April 2008, the Charities Act 2006 (CA 2006) and now since 14 March 2012 the Charities Act 2011 (CA 2011) does so, although in a non-exhaustive way which remains dependent in various ways on the pre-existing law.[5]

1 Considered in *Construction Industry Training Board v A-G* [1973] Ch 173, [1972] 2 All ER 1339.

2 CA 2011, ss 1(1), 9(3) (replacing CA 2006, ss 1(1), 78(5), which in turn replaced the similarly-worded CA 1993, s 96(1)). This definition of 'charity' does not apply for the purposes of an enactment if a different definition of that term applies for those purposes by virtue of that or any other enactment: CA 2011, s 1(2) (replacing CA 2006, s 1(2)).

3 CA 2011, ss 29–38 (replacing CA 1993, ss 3–3B).

4 Replacing CA 1993, s 37 (which in turn replaced Charities Act 1960, s 5(1)). *Wynn v Skegness UDC* [1966] 3 All ER 336, [1967] 1 WLR 52; *Finch v Poplar Borough Council* (1967) 66 LGR 324. If an institution is registered under the Charities Act 1960, and so conclusively presumed to be a charity by virtue of s 5(1), and its purposes are shown to have been the same for a certain period prior to registration, it will be presumed to have been a charitable institution during that period also; *Re Murawski's Will Trusts, Lloyds Bank Ltd v Royal Society for the Prevention of Cruelty to Animals* [1971] 2 All ER 328, [1971] 1 WLR 707. See also *Construction Industry Training Board v A-G* [1973] Ch 173, [1972] 2 All ER 1339; and *Childs v A-G* [1973] 2 All ER 108, [1973] 1 WLR 497.

5 Charities Act 2011 is a consolidating Act repealing and replacing many of the provisions of the Charities Act 2006. For the position under the CA 2011, see para **[102.3]** below.

[102.3]

**[Updated in the text and in the footnotes for the Charities Act 2011.
Updated in the footnotes for *Independent Schools Council v Charity Commission for England and Wales* [2011] UKUT 421 (TCC), [2012] 1 All ER 127 and at footnote 16 for *HMAG v Charity Commission* [2012] WTLR 977.]**

Meaning of 'Charitable Purposes' since 1 April 2008. CA 2006, ss 1–3 (which came into force in this respect on 1 April 2008)[1] included for the first time a statutory definition of 'Charitable Purposes'. These sections have now been replaced by CA 2011, ss 1–3 with effect from 14 March 2012,[2] and these sections include the same definition of 'Charitable Purposes'.

'Charitable purpose' is now defined as a purpose which falls within any of 13 different descriptions and is for the public benefit.[3] The descriptions of purposes which are capable of being charitable purposes are:[4]

(a) the prevention or relief of poverty;
(b) the advancement of education;[5]
(c) the advancement of religion (including a religion which involves a belief in more than one god and a religion which does not involve a belief in a god);[6]
(d) the advancement of health (including the prevention or relief of sickness, disease or human suffering) or the saving of lives;[7]
(e) the advancement of citizenship or community development (including rural or urban regeneration and the promotion of civic responsibility, volunteering, the voluntary sector or the effectiveness or efficiency of charities);[8]
(f) the advancement of the arts, culture, heritage or science;
(g) the advancement of amateur sport (meaning games which promote health by involving physical or mental skill or exertion);[9]
(h) the advancement of human rights, conflict resolution or reconciliation or the promotion of religious or racial harmony or equality and diversity;
(i) the advancement of environmental protection or improvement;
(j) the relief of those in need by reason of youth, age, ill-health, disability, financial hardship or other disadvantage (including the provision of accommodation or care to such persons);[10]
(k) the advancement of animal welfare;
(l) the promotion of the efficiency of the armed forces of the Crown, or of the efficiency of the police, fire and rescue services (under Part 2 of the Fire and Rescue Services Act 2004) or ambulance services;[11]
(m) any other purposes not within the previous categories but recognised as charitable under charity law as it was before this definition came into force or by virtue of CA 2011, s 5 (recreational and similar trusts, etc);[12] any purposes that may reasonably be regarded as analogous to, or within the spirit of, any purposes falling within any of the previous categories; and any purposes that may reasonably be regarded as analogous to, or within the spirit of, any purposes which have been recognised under charity law as falling within the above.[13]

Any reference in any enactment or document (in whatever terms and whenever made) is to be construed in accordance with these definitions unless the context otherwise requires.[14]

A purpose must also be for the public benefit if it is to be a charitable purpose. Public benefit means the public benefit as that term is understood for the purposes of the law relating to charities in England and Wales.[15] A purpose is not presumed to be for the public benefit because it falls into one of the 13 categories set out above.[16]

The Act provides for guidance as to the operation of the public benefit requirement to be issued by the Charity Commission.[17]

It will be apparent from the above that the pre-existing law remains relevant, both to category (m) and to the general requirement of public benefit. The main differences made to the law by this definition is that a more detailed and up-to-date list of specific categories of charitable purposes is provided, and that the former presumption, that the advancement of education, advancement of religion or relief of poverty were ipso facto for the public benefit, is abolished.

1 SI 2008/945.
2 CA 2011, ss 344, 335, Sch 10.
3 CA 2011, s 2(1) (replacing CA 2006, s 2(1)). See *Independent Schools Council v Charity Commission for England and Wales* [2012] 1 All ER 127 at [82], that in deciding whether a particular purpose is a charitable purpose it must fall within one of the 13 descriptions, and be for the public benefit which is ascertained according to what the position would have been prior to CA 2006.
4 CA 2011, s 3(1) (replacing CA 2006, s 2(2)).
5 See *Independent Schools Council v Charity Commission for England and Wales* [2011] UKUT 421 (TCC), [2012] 1 All ER 127 as to the additional requirement of public benefit if the advancement of education is to be a charitable purpose. The Upper Tax Tribunal there said that in the context of a fee-paying school, it was for the charity trustees of the school to address and assess how their obligation to satisfy the public benefit test might best be fulfilled in the context of their own particular circumstances. Trustees needed to consider not only payment of fees and provision of benefits but also the general question of access and how to treat all their potential beneficiaries fairly. Any school would need to consider whether the provision of some of its facilities could be justified as either part of or properly ancillary to the advancement of education.
6 CA 2011, s 3(1)(c) and 3(2)(a) (replacing CA 2006, s 2(2)(c) and 2(3)(a)).
7 CA 2011, s 3(1)(d) and 3(2)(b) (replacing CA 2006, s 2(2)(d) and 2(3)(b)).
8 CA 2011, s 3(1)(e) and 3(2)(c) (replacing CA 2006, s 2(2)(e) and 2(3)(c)).
9 CA 2011, s 3(1)(g) and 3(2)(d) (replacing CA 2006, s 2(2)(g) and 2(3)(d)).
10 CA 2011, s 3(1)(j) and 3(2)(e) (replacing CA 2006, s 2(2)(j) and 2(3)(e)).
11 CA 2011, s 3(1)(l) and 3(2)(f) (replacing CA 2006, s 2(2)(l) and 2(3)(f)).
12 Previously Recreational Charities Act 1958, s 1, as amended by CA 2006, s 5 with effect from 1 April 2010, see SI 2009/841.
13 CA 2011, s 3(1)(m) (replacing CA 2006, s 2(4)).
14 CA 2011, s 2(2), (3) (replacing CA 2006, s 2(6), (7)).
15 CA 2011, s 4(3) (replacing CA 2006, s 3(3). See *Independent Schools Council v Charity Commission for England and Wales* [2011] UKUT 421 (TCC), [2012] 1 All ER 127 at [82], that whether a particular purpose is for the public benefit is ascertained according to what the position would have been prior to CA 2006.
16 CA 2011, s 4(2) (replacing CA 2006, s 3(2)). See *Independent Schools Council v Charity Commission for England and Wales* [2011] UKUT 421 (TCC), [2012] 1 All ER 127 as to the additional requirement of public benefit if the advancement of education is to be a charitable purpose and *HMAG v Charity Commission* [2012] WTLR 977 as to the additional requirement of public benefit if the prevention or relief of poverty is to be a charitable purpose.
17 CA 2011, s 17 (replacing CA 2006, s 4). See the Charity Commission's 'Charities and Public Benefit' (2008) and 'Analysis of the Law underpinning Charities and Public Benefit' (2008). The first mentioned guidance together with two more specific pieces of guidance, 'Public Benefit and Fee-Charging' (2008) and 'The Advancement of Education for the Public Benefit' (2008) were subject to successful challenges in judicial review proceedings in *Independent Schools Council v Charity Commission for England and Wales* [2011] UKUT 421 (TCC), [2012] 1 All ER 127.

[102.4]

[Updated in the title and in footnote 1 for the Charities Act 2011.]

General nature of charitable purposes before 1 April 2008. The words have a special legal meaning which is much narrower in its scope than that popularly given to them.[1] Whilst all the purposes which are in law charitable would be within the popular meaning of the word, there are many things which are included in their popular significance which are not within their legal meaning. The purposes are strictly those mentioned in the preamble of a statute of the reign of Elizabeth I[2] or analogous to them,[3] but many there mentioned have little significance in the modern world and a more recent definition groups them under the following four heads, namely: (i) relief of poverty; (ii) advancement of education; (iii) advancement of religion; and (iv) other purposes beneficial to the community, not falling within the preceding heads.[4] A purpose regarded in one age as charitable may in another, by a change in social habits and needs, be regarded differently.[5] It is no objection that the persons to be benefited are resident outside the jurisdiction provided the other conditions relating to charitable gifts are satisfied.[6] A gift on charitable trusts is good although it is subject to a proviso which is void as infringing the perpetuity rule.[7]

1 See Sachs LJ in *Incorporated Council of Law Reporting for England and Wales v A-G* [1972] Ch 73 at 90, [1971] 3 All ER 1029 at 1038–1039; and Lord Hailsham LC in *IRC v McMullen* [1980] 1 All ER 884 at 890. Where however the intention is to set up a charitable trust and where there is an ambiguity, a benign construction should be given if possible. This is reflected in the breadth of Charities Act 2011, s 3(1)(m) (replacing Charities Act 2006, s 2(4)).

2 Stat 43 Eliz I, c 4. Though this statute has been repealed, the preamble has been expressly preserved for the purpose of defining charitable purposes; *Scottish Burial Reform and Cremation Society Ltd v Glasgow City Corpn* [1968] AC 138, [1967] 3 All ER 215, HL, per Lord Upjohn at 151; at 221. The Scots Law, however, gives a wider meaning to 'charity': *Blair v Duncan* [1902] AC 37; *Verge v Somerville* [1924] AC 496 at 502.

3 Usually referred to as the 'spirit and intendment' of the statute, alternatively as 'the equity of the statute': see *Incorporated Council of Law Reporting for England and Wales v A-G* [1972] Ch 73, [1971] 3 All ER 1029, per Russell LJ at 88; at 1035–36, and Sachs LJ at 1037. 'The purposes in question to be charitable must be shown to be for the benefit of the public or the community, in a sense or manner within the intendment of the preamble to the statute', per Lord Wilberforce in *Scottish Burial Reform and Cremation Society Ltd v Glasgow Corpn* [1968] AC 138, [1967] 3 All ER 215 at 223. The courts have endeavoured to keep the law as to charities moving according as new social needs arise or old ones become obsolete or satisfied; ibid and Lord Hailsham LC in *IRC v McMullen* [1980] 1 All ER 884 at 890, 891.

4 *Income Tax Special Purposes Comrs v Pemsel* [1891] AC 531. But it should be noted that this formulation, firstly, is a classification of convenience, so that there may be purposes which do not fit neatly into one or other of the headings. Secondly, that the words used must not be given the force of a statute to be construed. Thirdly, even prior to Charities Act 2006, that the law of charities is a moving subject which may well have evolved even since 1891; per Lord Wilberforce in *Scottish Burial Reform and Cremation Society Ltd v Glasgow Corpn* [1968] AC 138 at 154, [1967] 3 All ER 215 at 223; see cases referred to by Slade J in *McGovern v A-G* [1981] 3 All ER 493 at 503. The fourth heading has been described as a 'portmanteau' which is incapable of further definition per Lord Upjohn in *Scottish Burial Reform and Cremation Society Ltd v Glasgow Corpn* [1968] AC 138 at 150, [1967] 3 All ER 215 at 220.

5 *National Anti-Vivisection Society v IRC* [1948] AC 31 at 74, [1947] 2 All ER 217 at 238.

6 *Re Robinson, Besant v German Reich* [1931] 2 Ch 122; *Re Masoud* [1961] OR 583.

7 *George Drexler Ofrex Foundation Trustees v IRC* [1966] Ch 675, [1965] 3 All ER 529.

[102.5]

[Updated in the text and in footnote 8 for the Charities Act 2011.]

Relief of the aged. At one time it was said to be doubtful whether a gift for the aged was charitable unless there was an element of poverty[1] but more recent decisions have favoured the view that poverty is not essential, and that the words 'aged impotent and poor' in the preamble to the Elizabeth Act are to be construed disjunctively.[2] Further, essential to the charitable purpose is that it should relieve aged, impotent and poor people.[3] The word 'relief' implies that the persons in question have a need attributable to their condition as aged, impotent or poor persons which requires alleviating and which those persons could not alleviate, or would find difficulty in alleviating, themselves from their own resources.[4] Thus a trust to provide dwellings for aged persons was held to be charitable notwithstanding that they operated by way of bargain rather than by way of bounty; that the benefits could not be withdrawn once provided even if the beneficiary subsequently ceased to qualify and even though it was possible for the beneficiary to make a profit on his or her capital contribution.[5] A trust for persons not under 50 years of age is a good charitable gift for the benefit of 'aged' persons,[6] and also a gift for the 'oldest respectable inhabitants' of a district.[7] A gift for the relief of those in need by reason of age is charitable (if for the public benefit) under the new statutory law.[8]

1 *Re Lucas, Rhys v A-G* [1922] 2 Ch 52, [1922] All ER Rep 317; *A-G v Haberdashers' Co* (1834) 1 My & K 420 at 428.

2 *Joseph Rowntree Memorial Trust Housing Association Ltd v A-G* [1983] 1 All ER 288, referring to *Re Robinson, Davis v Robinson* [1951] Ch 198 [1950] 2 All ER 1148; *Re Bradbury, Needham v Reekie* [1950] 2 All ER 1150n; *Re Glyn's Will Trusts* [1950] 2 All ER 1150n; *Re Lewis, Public Trustee v Allen* [1955] Ch 104, [1954] 3 All ER 257 and *Re Cottam's Will Trusts, Midland Bank Executor and Trustee Co Ltd v Huddersfield Corpn* [1955] 3 All ER 704, [1955] 1 WLR 1299, which support the view that it is a sufficient charitable purpose to benefit the aged, or the impotent, without more. But Peter Gibson J in the *Rowntree* case preferred the approach adopted in *Re Neal, Barclays Bank Ltd v Neal* (1966) 110 Sol Jo 549 and in *Re Resch's Will Trusts, Le Cras v Perpetual Trustee Co Ltd* [1969] 1 AC 514, [1967] 3 All ER 915 that there must be a need which is to be relieved by the charitable gift, such need being attributable to the aged or impotent conditions of the person to be benefited. See also *Re Finkle* (1977) 82 DLR (3d) 445; *Re Bingham, Public Trustee v New Plymouth Council for Social Services Inc* [1951] NZLR 491; *McGovern v A-G* [1981] 3 All ER 493 at 503.

3 *Joseph Rowntree Memorial Trust Housing Association Ltd v A-G* [1983] 1 All ER 288 at 295.

4 *Joseph Rowntree Memorial Trust Housing Association Ltd v A-G* [1983] 1 All ER 288 at 295.

5 *Joseph Rowntree Memorial Trust Housing Association Ltd v A-G* [1983] 1 All ER 288 at 295, referring to *Re Cottam's Will Trusts, Midland Bank Executor and Trustee Co Ltd v Huddersfield Corpn* [1955] 3 All ER 704, [1955] 1 WLR 1299, and *Re Resch's Will Trusts, Le Cras v Perpetual Trustee Co Ltd* [1969] 1 AC 514, [1967] 3 All ER 915, and to cases on fee paying schools, such as *Abbey Malvern Wells Ltd v Ministry of Local Government and Planning* [1951] Ch 728, [1951] 2 All ER 154. See also *Re Estlin, Prichard v Thomas* (1903) 72 LJ Ch 687 (gift for the provision of homes of rest for lady teachers at a rent).

6 *Re Wall, Pomeroy v Willway* (1889) 42 Ch D 510; *Re Dudgeon, Truman v Pope* (1896) 74 LT 613 (where the age was 60). But in *Re Martin* (1977) 121 Sol Jo 828, a trust to create a home for old people with a right for either or both of the testator's daughters to reside there was held not to be a valid charitable trust.

7 *Re Lucas, Rhys v A-G* [1922] 2 Ch 52, [1922] All ER Rep 317.

8 Charities Act 2011, s 3(1)(j) (replacing Charities Act 2006 s 2(2)(j)).

[102.6]

[Updated in the text and in footnote 6 for the Charities Act 2011.]

Relief of the impotent. A gift for the relief of the impotent without any reference to poverty is a good charitable gift.[1] A gift for the blind is a good charitable gift under this heading[2] and so are gifts for disabled or wounded members of the forces[3] and for a home of rest for those in need of it[4] and a nursing home for those of moderate means although they might have to pay some part of the expense.[5] A gift for the advancement of health is charitable (if for the public benefit) under the new statutory law.[6]

1 *Re Roadley, Iveson v Wakefield* [1930] 1 Ch 524; *Re Elliot, Raven v Nicholson* (1910) 102 LT 528; *Re Fraser, Yeates v Fraser* (1883) 22 Ch D 827.
2 *Re Elliot, Raven v Nicholson* (1910) 102 LT 528; *Re Lewis, Public Trustee v Allen* [1955] Ch 104, [1954] 3 All ER 257.
3 *Re Hillier, Dauncey v Finch* [1944] 1 All ER 480; *Re Simmonds* [1933] NZLR Supp 172; *Re Robinson, Besant v German Reich* [1931] 2 Ch 122 (disabled soldiers of former enemy); *Muir v Open Brethren* (1956) 96 CLR 166.
4 *Re Estlin, Prichard v Thomas* (1903) 72 LJ Ch 687; *Re James, Grenfell v Hamilton* [1932] 2 Ch 25, [1932] All ER Rep 452; *Re Chaplin, Neame v A-G* [1933] Ch 115.
5 *Re Clarke, Bracey v Royal National Lifeboat Institution* [1923] 2 Ch 407.
6 Charities Act 2011, s 3(1)(d) (replacing Charities Act 2006, s 2(2)(d)).

[102.7]

[Updated in the text and in footnote 17 for the Charities Act 2011.]

Relief of poverty. 'Poor' is a relative term and is not confined to the destitute.[1] While the relief to the poor must be given by way of bounty and not by way of bargain,[2] it is not an absolute objection that the beneficiaries are required to contribute some part of the cost of the benefits.[3] The gift to the poor may be general and indefinite[4] or confined to the inhabitants of some particular place[5] or some particular religious sect[6] or the members of a regiment[7] or some particular section or class of the public.[8] A common form of charity is provision for the victims of a particular disaster.[9] A gift for such poor persons as the executor should consider deserving of assistance has been upheld as a good charitable gift.[10] The relief of poverty is still charitable although it is effected indirectly.[11] Thus, the establishment, maintenance, and support of institutions or funds for the relief of various forms of poverty or distress is charitable,[12] and this includes gifts to religious communities having for their object the relief of the sick and poor.[13] A gift for the working classes generally or restricted to a particular district is not charitable,[14] nor for members of a trade union.[15] A gift for the provision of religious services and instruction and for the social and physical training and recreation for persons of insufficient means otherwise to enjoy the advantages provided is not charitable.[16] A gift for the relief of poverty is charitable (if for the public benefit) under the new statutory law.[17]

1 *Mary Clark Home (Trustees) v Anderson* [1904] 2 KB 645; *Re Estlin, Prichard v Thomas* (1903) 72 LJ Ch 687; *Re Gardom, Le Page v A-G* [1914] 1 Ch 662; *Shaw v Halifax Corpn* [1915] 2 KB 170; *Re Clarke, Bracey v Royal National Lifeboat Institution* [1923] 2 Ch 407; *Re De Carteret, Forster v De Carteret* [1933] Ch 103, [1932] All ER Rep 355; *Jones v Executive Officers of T Eaton Co Ltd* (1973) 35 DLR (3d) 97 (trust for the benefit of 'needy or deserving' members of a club held to be charitable; 'poverty' is a relative term which extends to include those of moderate means). In *Re Drummond, Ashworth v Drummond* [1914] 2 Ch 90, persons earning a weekly wage of fifteen shillings were held not to be poor within the meaning of the statute but no doubt regard must now be had to the change in the cost of living. 'Eleemosynary charity' covers all charities directed to the relief of individual distress whether due to age, poverty, sickness or other similar afflictions: *Re Armitage, Ellam v Norwich Corpn* [1972] Ch 438, [1972] 1 All ER 708.
2 *IRC v Society for Relief of Widows and Orphans of Medical Men* (1926) 136 LT 60 at 65.
3 *Re Estlin, Prichard v Thomas* (1903) 72 LJ Ch 687; *Re Clarke, Bracey v Royal National Lifeboat Institution* [1923] 2 Ch 407; *Re Chaplin, Neame v A-G* [1933] Ch 115; *A-G v*

M'Carthy (1885) 12 VLR 535; *Re Monk, Giffen v Wedd* [1927] 2 Ch 197, [1927] All ER Rep 157; *Re Cottam's Will Trusts* [1955] 3 All ER 704; *Re Payling's Will Trusts, Armstrong v Payling* [1969] 3 All ER 698, [1969] 1 WLR 1595; *Joseph Rowntree Memorial Trust Housing Association Ltd v A-G* [1983] Ch 159, [1983] 1 All ER 288.

4 *A-G v Matthews* (1676) 2 Lev 167; *Nash v Morley* (1842) 5 Beav 177; *Re Darling, Farquhar v Darling* [1896] 1 Ch 50.

5 *A-G v Exeter Corpn* (1826) 2 Russ 45; (1827) 3 Russ 395; *A-G v Bovill* (1840) 1 Ph 762; *A-G v Blizard* (1855) 21 Beav 233; *Dillon v Reilly* (1873) IR 10 Eq 152; *Re Roadley, Iveson v Wakefield* [1930] 1 Ch 524 (poor of a parish); *Re Robinson, Davis v Robinson* [1951] Ch 198, [1950] 2 All ER 1148 (poor of parish over 65); *Re Lucas, Rhys v A-G* [1922] 2 Ch 52 (poor of a town); *Re Lousada, Bacon v Bacon* (1887) 82 LT Jo 358 ('London poor'); *Re Lambeth Charities* (1853) 22 LJ Ch 959; *Re St Alphage, London Wall* (1888) 59 LT 614; *Bristow v Bristow* (1842) 5 Beav 289 (on a particular estate); but see *Browne v King* (1885) 17 LR Ir 488 (poor tenantry not charitable); *Bruce v Deer Presbytery* (1867) LR 1 Sc & Div 96 (poor of a presbytery).

6 *Re Wall, Pomeroy v Willway* (1889) 42 Ch D 510 (Unitarians); *A-G v Mathieson* [1907] 2 Ch 383 (Jews); *A-G v Wansay* (1808) 15 Ves 231 (Presbyterians); *Income Tax Special Purposes Comrs v Pemsel* [1891] AC 531 (Moravians); *A-G v Shore* (1843) 11 Sim 592 (Unitarians); *A-G v Lawes* (1849) 8 Hare 32 (Irvingite ministers persecuted or in poverty); *Dawson v Small* (1874) LR 18 Eq 114 (Methodists); *Canada Permanent Trust Co v MacFarlane* (1972) 27 DLR (3d) 480 (Protestant homes or institutions for the care and welfare of children).

7 *Re Donald, Moore v Somerset* [1909] 2 Ch 410.

8 *A-G v Power* (1809) 1 Ball & B 145; *Re Estlin, Prichard v Thomas* (1903) 72 LJ Ch 687; *Mary Clarke Home (Trustees) v Anderson* [1904] 2 KB 645; *Re Gardom, Le Page v A-G* [1914] 1 Ch 662; *Shaw v Halifax Corpn* [1915] 2 KB 170; *Re Campbell* [1930] NZLR 713 (all charities for poor gentlewomen); *Re Young, Young v Young* [1951] Ch 344, [1950] 2 All ER 1245 (distressed gentlefolk); *Re Clarke, Bracey v Royal National Lifeboat Institution* [1923] 2 Ch 407 (persons of moderate means); *Re De Carteret, Forster v De Carteret* [1933] Ch 103, [1932] All ER Rep 355 (persons of limited means); *Re Central Employment Bureau for Women and Students' Careers Association* [1942] 1 All ER 232 (persons not self-supporting); *A-G v Pearce* (1740) 2 Atk 87 (housekeepers); *Re White's Trusts* (1886) 33 Ch D 449 (tradesmen); *Thompson v Thompson* (1844) 1 Coll 381 at 395 (unsuccessful literary men); in *Re Payling's Will Trusts, Armstrong v Payling* [1969] 3 All ER 698, [1969] 1 WLR 1595 (rent-free accommodation for the aged); *Reeve v A-G* (1843) 3 Hare 191; *Loscombe v Wintringham* (1850) 13 Beav 87 (servants); *Re Gosling, Gosling v Smith* (1900) 48 WR 300 (old clerk of a firm); *Re Rayner, Cloutman v Regnant* (1920) 89 LJ Ch 369 (poor or incapacitated employees); *Gibson v South American Stores (Gath and Chaves) Ltd* [1950] Ch 177 [1949] 2 All ER 985 (necessitous employees of a limited company and their dependants): *Re Drummond, Ashworth v Drummond* [1914] 2 Ch 90, [1914–15] All ER Rep 223 (contributions to the holiday expenses of employees not charitable); *Re Coulthurst, Coutts & Co v Coulthurst* [1951] Ch 661, [1951] 1 All ER 774 (dependants of bank officers); *Milne's Executors v Aberdeen University Court* (1905) 7 F 642 (poor struggling youths of merit); *Barclay v Maskelyne* (1858) 32 LTOS 205 (poor emigrants); *Re Tree, Idle v Tree* [1945] Ch 325, [1945] 2 All ER 65 (persons descending from residents in a particular borough in a particular year desirous of emigrating); *Re Wedge* (1968) 67 DLR (2d) 433 (needy displaced family of European origin); *Re Morrison, Wakefield v Falmouth* (1967) 111 Sol Jo 758 (relief of refugees); *A-G v Vint* (1850) 3 De G & Sm 704 (inmates of a workhouse); *Waldo v Caley* (1809) 16 Ves 206; *Re Friends of the Clergy's Charter, Friends of the Clergy v A-G* [1921] 1 Ch 409 (widows and orphans of poor clergymen); *Powell v A-G* (1817) 3 Mer 48 (seamen of a particular port); *Russell v Kellett* (1855) 3 Sm & G 264 (widows and orphans of a particular parish); *Weir v Crum-Brown* [1908] AC 162 (indigent bachelors and widowers interested in science). As to poor relations, and poor employees, see paras **[102.13]** and **[102.14]** below.

9 *Pease v Pattinson* (1886) 32 Ch D 154; *Re Hartley Colliery Accident Relief Fund, Plummer v Jordan* (1908) 102 LT 165n; *Cross v Lloyd-Greame* (1909) 102 LT 163; *Re North Devon and West Somerset Relief Fund Trusts, Hylton v Wright* [1953] 2 All ER 1032, [1953] 1 WLR 1250; *Re Gillingham Bus Disaster Fund* [1958] Ch 300, [1958] 1 All ER 37.

10 *Brett v A-G* [1945] IR 526; *Re Angell Estate* (1955) 16 WWR 342; *Re Ward's Estate* [1957] SASR 125.

11 *A-G v Minshull* (1798) 4 Ves 11; *A-G for Northern Ireland v Forde* [1932] NI 1; *Re Dean's Will Trusts, Cowan v St Mary's Hospital, Paddington, Board of Governors* [1950] 1 All ER 882.

12 *Biscoe v Jackson* (1887) 35 Ch D 460 (soup kitchens); *Re Welsh Hospital (Netley) Fund, Thomas v A-G* [1921] 1 Ch 655 (hospital); *Re Clarke, Bracey v Royal National Lifeboat Institution,* above (nursing home); *IRC v Roberts Marine Mansions Trustees* (1926) 43 TLR 270 (seaside boarding-house for business people needing rest); *IRC v Peeblesshire Nursing Association* 1927 SC 215 (nursing association); *Harbin v Masterman* (1871) LR 12 Eq 559 (asylum); *Re Whiteley, Bishop of London v Whiteley* [1910] 1 Ch 600 (alm-houses); *Re Estlin, Prichard v Thomas* (1903) 72 LJ Ch 687, and *Re James, Grenfell v Hamilton* [1932] 2 Ch 25 (homes for teachers); *Rolls v Miller* (1884) 27 Ch D 71 (homes for working girls); *Hall v Derby Sanitary Authority* (1885) 16 QBD 163 (orphanages); *Re Lacy, Royal General Theatrical Fund Association v Kydd* [1899] 2 Ch 149 (homes for impoverished actors); *Re Bernstein's Will Trusts, National Westminster Bank Ltd v Board of Governors of the United Liverpool Hospital* (1971) 115 Sol Jo 808 (extra comforts for the nursing staff); in *Re Niyazi's Will Trusts* [1978] 3 All ER 785, [1978] 1 WLR 910, it was held that a gift for a working men's hostel in Famagusta was charitable as being for the relief of poverty in a place where housing was in short supply. A gift of income for the general benefit and welfare of children in a children's home established by a local authority under the (then) Children Act 1948, s 15 has been held to be not charitable as it may be applied to non-charitable purposes: *Re Cole, Westminster Bank Ltd v Moore* [1958] Ch 877, [1958] 3 All ER 102.

13 *Cocks v Manners* (1871) LR 12 Eq 574; *Re Delany, Conoley v Quick* [1902] 2 Ch 642. A gift to establish a sanatorium or hospital is charitable: *Kytherian Association of Queensland v Sklavos* (1958) 101 CLR 56.

14 *Re Sanders' Will Trusts, Public Trustee v McLaren* [1954] Ch 265, [1954] 1 All ER 667.

15 *Re Mead's Trust Deed* [1961] 2 All ER 836, [1961] 1 WLR 1244 (where an element of self-help loomed large).

16 *Baddeley v IRC* [1953] Ch 504, [1953] 2 All ER 233; affd on this point in the House of Lords [1955] AC 572, [1955] 1 All ER 525.

17 Charities Act 2011, s 3(1)(a) (replacing Charities Act 2006, s 2(2)(a)).

[102.8]

[Updated in footnotes 12 and 18 for *Independent Schools Council v Charity Commission for England and Wales* [2011] UKUT 421 (TCC), [2012] 1 All ER 127.
Updated in footnote 18 and in the text for the Charities Act 2011.]

Education. The phrase 'advancement of education'[1] has consistently been taken to be an enlargement of the phrase 'advancement of learning' and the latter is included in the former.[2] An extended view of the meaning of education has been taken in a recent House of Lords decision consistent with modern concepts of what is educationally valuable so that the provision of sporting facilities limited to students at universities and schools was held to be charitable.[3] Charitable gifts for the purposes of education include the establishment and support of educational institutions of all kinds,[4] gifts to learned societies,[5] gifts for the education of special classes of persons,[6] and instruction in special subjects.[7] The institution and maintenance of a library for the study of a learned subject or a science, is within the phrase whatever be the age of those frequenting it.[8] Likewise, the provision of books forming the raw material for that study.[9] A students' union existing to further the educational purposes of a school of learning which is charitable has been held to be charitable,[10] notwithstanding the personal benefit conferred on the union members.[11] These trusts, however, must benefit a section of the public and be of public nature.[12] A trust for the promotion of the religious social and physical well-being of persons by the provision of facilities for religious services and instruction and for social and physical training and recreation is not a trust for education.[13] Nor does a trust for the mere promotion of a particular sport or sports qualify as charity under this head[14] but a gift to a particular educational establishment for the purpose of improving the sporting facilities available to the pupils there does so qualify,[15] and likewise the provisions of facilities in schools and universities generally.[16] But an overriding trust for charitable purposes is good though there is a non-charitable proviso which is void as infringing the perpetuity rule.[17] A gift for the advancement of education is charitable (if for the public benefit) under the new statutory law.[18]

1 As used by Lord Macnaghten in *Income Tax Special Purposes Comrs v Pemsel* [1891] AC 531.

2 Per Sachs LJ in *Incorporated Council of Law Reporting for England and Wales v A-G* [1972] Ch 73 at 92, [1971] 3 All ER 1029 at 1040.

3 *IRC v McMullen* [1981] AC 1, [1980] 1 All ER 884, where the Education Act 1944 was referred to. See also Dillon J in *Barralet v A-G* [1980] 3 All ER 918 at 927 who pointed out that the authorities show that the term 'education' is to be construed very widely, adopting Buckley LJ's view that this head … should be regarded as extending to the improvement of a useful branch of human knowledge and its public dissemination', *Re Hopkins' Will Trusts, Naish v Francis Bacon Society Inc* [1965] Ch 669 at 680, [1964] 3 All ER 46 at 52. In *Re Koeppler's Will Trusts, Barclays Bank Trust Co Ltd v Slack* [1984] Ch 243, [1984] 2 All ER 111, Peter Gibson J at 122 referred to 'the broad and evolving concept of education in the law of charity'.

4 Colleges: *Walsh v Gladstone* (1843) 1 Ph 290; *Aberdeen University v Irvine* (1868) LR 1 Sc & Div 289; *Wallis v New Zealand Solicitor-General* [1903] AC 173; schools: *Re Gilchrist Educational Trust* [1895] 1 Ch 367; *Smith v Kerr* [1902] 1 Ch 774; *Re Hawkins, Walrond v Newton* (1906) 22 TLR 521; *Brighton College v Marriott* [1926] AC 192; *Re Woodhams, Lloyds Bank Ltd v London College of Music* [1981] 1 All ER 202, [1981] 1 WLR 493 (music colleges); professorships: *Yates v University College, London* (1875) LR 7 HL 438; *Re Buckland, Buckland v Bennett* (1887) 22 LJNC 7; fellowship: *Jesus College Case* (1615) Duke on Charitable Uses ed Bridgman, 363; lectureship: *A-G v Cambridge Margaret and Regius Professors* (1682) 1 Vern 55; *Re Freeston's Charity, Sylvester v University College Oxford* [1978] 1 All ER 481, [1978] 1 WLR 120; affd [1979] 1 All ER 51, CA (alteration of beneficial interests); scholarships: *University College of North Wales v Taylor* [1908] P 140; *Re Williams, Taylor v University of Wales* (1908) 24 TLR 716; *Wilson v Toronto General Trustees Corpn* [1954] 3 DLR 136; educational bursary: *Re Evans* [1957] SR Qd 345; prizes: *Farrer v St Catherine College, Cambridge* (1873) LR 16 Eq 19; schoolmaster's house: *Sills v Warner* (1896) 27 OR 266; British School of Egyptian Archaeology where it was held no bar that a contributor was entitled to certain printed books: *Re British School of Egyptian Archaeology, Murray v Public Trustee* [1954] 1 All ER 887. Now that secondary education must be provided free of charge a bequest to assist pupils to obtain such education is void as incapable of performance: *Re Mackenzie, Moir v Angus County Council* [1962] 2 All ER 890, [1962] 1 WLR 880; distinguished in *Re Leitch* [1965] VR 204 (a scholarship is not limited to money to assist scholars financially to continue their education); *Construction Industry Training Board v A-G* [1973] Ch 173, [1972] 2 All ER 1339 (Industrial Training Board); *Re Koeppler's Will Trusts, Barclays Bank Trust Co Ltd v Slack* [1986] Ch 423, [1985] 2 All ER 869 (conference centre; but the mere organisation and conduct of conferences albeit dealing with topics of public interest, would not necessarily constitute a charitable activity. Charitable as advancement of education here).

5 *Beaumont v Oliveira* (1869) 4 Ch App 309; *Royal Society of London and Thompson* (1881) 17 Ch D 407; *Thomas v Howell* (1874) LR 18 Eq 198; *Re Lopes, Bence-Jones v Zoological Society of London* [1931] 2 Ch 130; *Re Bland-Sutton's Will Trusts, National Provincial Bank Ltd v Middlesex Hospital Medical School Council* [1951] Ch 70, [1950] 2 All ER 466.

6 Testator's descendants: *A-G v Sidney Sussex College* (1865) 34 Beav 654; *Re Lavelle, Concannon v A-G* [1914] 1 IR 194; daughters of missionaries: *German v Chapman* (1877) 7 Ch D 271; persons of particular religious faith: *Income Tax Special Purposes Comrs v Pemsel* [1891] AC 531; *Walsh v Gladstone* (1843) 1 Ph 290; *Carbery v Cox* (1852) 3 I Ch R 231n; *Re Michel's Trust* (1860) 28 Beav 39; *Re Doering* [1949] 1 DLR 267; children of employees of a company: *Re Rayner, Cloutman v Regnart* (1920) 89 LJ Ch 369, but this case

was disapproved in *Oppenheim v Tobacco Securities Trust Co Ltd* [1951] AC 297, [1951] 1 All ER 31, but not compulsory training of employees of a company: *Re Leverhulme, Cooper v Leverhulme* [1943] 2 All ER 143; *Davies v Perpetual Trustee Co Ltd* [1959] AC 439, [1959] 2 All ER 128 (education of Presbyterians, descendants of those settled in New South Wales hailing from or born in Northern Ireland).

7 *A-G v Flood* (1816) Hayes & Jo App xxi at p xxxviii (Irish language); *Re Berridge, Berridge v Turner* (1890) 63 LT 470 (economics); *Re Allsop, Gell v Carver* (1884) 1 TLR 4 (art); *IRC v Glasgow Musical Festival Association* 1926 SC 920 (music); *Re Shakespeare Memorial Trust, Earl of Lytton v A-G* [1923] 2 Ch 398 (drama); *Yates v University College, London* (1873) 8 Ch App 454 (archaeology); *A-G v Stepney* (1804) 10 Ves 22; *Scottish Woollen Technical College v IRC* 1926 SC 934; *Royal North Shore Hospital of Sydney v A-G for New South Wales* (1938) 60 CLR 396. A gift to the Simplified Spelling Society has been held not charitable: *Hunter (Sir GB) (1922) C Trusts (Trustees) v IRC (1929) 45 TLR 344.* See also *Re Dupree's Deed Trusts, Daley v Lloyds Bank* [1945] Ch 16, [1944] 2 All ER 443 (chess tournaments and prizes); *Re Hopkinson, Lloyds Bank Ltd v Baker* [1949] 1 All ER 346; *Re Shaw's Will Trusts* [1952] Ch 163, [1952] 1 All ER 49 (teaching, promotion, and encouragement of appreciation of the fine arts, and also of self-control, elocution, oratory, deportment, and the arts of personal contact, social intercourse and public, private, professional and business life—held a charitable trust); *Re Ogden, Taylor v Sharp* (1909) 25 TLR 382 (trust for art students, held not charitable); *Re Koettgen's Will Trusts, Westminster Bank Ltd v Family Welfare Association Trustees Ltd* [1954] Ch 252, [1954] 1 All ER 581 (higher commercial education giving preference to employees of a company and members of their families); *Re Webber, Barclays Bank Ltd v Webber* [1954] 3 All ER 712 (Boy Scouts); *Re Hopkins' Will Trusts, Naish v Francis Bacon Society Inc* [1965] Ch 669, [1964] 3 All ER 46 (trust to help find the Bacon-Shakespeare manuscripts); *Baldry v Feintuck* [1972] 2 All ER 81, [1972] 1 WLR 552 (educational purposes can include research, discussion, debate and reaching a corporate conclusion on social and economic problems): *Re Koeppler's Will Trusts, Barclays Bank Trust Co Ltd v Slack* [1986] Ch 423, [1985] 2 All ER 869 (conferences for the formation of informal international public opinion and the promotion of greater co-operation in Europe and the West; held by the Court of Appeal to be exclusively for the advancement of education and charitable); *Barralet v A-G* [1980] 3 All ER 918, [1980] 1 WLR 1565 (dissemination of ethical principles: educational). A foundation whose primary purpose was to educate people with the object of persuading them to accept the views of 'Henry George', which included the view that taxation should only be levied on land values, was accepted as charitable under the Australian Charitable Trusts Act 1993: *A-G of New South Wales v Henry George Foundation Ltd (2002–03)* 5 ITELR 568 (NSW). A trust was held to have satisfied the educational purpose in Income Tax *Special Purposes Comms v Pemsel* [1891] AC 531 by being limited to that which would advance the children in their future lives: *Re Carapiet's Trusts, Manoogian (Armenian Patriarch of Jerusalem v Sonsino; His Beatitude Archbishop Torkom Mangoonian, Arminian Patriarch of Jerusalem) v Sonsino* [2002] EWHC 1304 (Ch). See also *Rowland v Vancouver College Ltd: St Thomas More Collegiate Ltd v Burnell, etc (2000–03)* 3 ITELR 182 (BC).

8 *A-G v Marchant* (1866) LR 3 Eq 424 (Trinity College Oxford library); *Re Mason* [1971] NZLR 714 (Law Society's library in some respects charitable); *Carne v Long* (1860) 2 De GF & J 75 (library for the benefit of subscribers not charitable).

9 *Incorporated Council of Law Reporting for England and Wales v A-G* [1972] Ch 73 at 93, [1971] 3 All ER 1029 at 1040, per Sachs LJ. Accordingly, the publication of the law reports is charitable because their virtually exclusive purpose is to further the study of law.

10 *London Hospital Medical College v IRC* [1976] 2 All ER 113 applying *Re Mariette, Mariette v Aldenham School Governing Body* [1915] 2 Ch 284; *Re Coxen, McCallum v Coxen* [1948] Ch 747, [1948] 2 All ER 492; *Neville Estates Ltd v Madden* [1962] Ch 832, [1961] 3 All ER 769; in *Baldry v Feintuck* [1972] 2 All ER 81, [1972] 1 WLR 552, the point was conceded; *A-G v Ross* [1985] 3 All ER 334.

11 The union was held to further educational purposes of the college, rather than existing for the benefit of its members: Brightman J [1976] 2 All ER 113 at 120; distinguishing *IRC v Glasgow City Police Athletic Association* [1953] AC 380, [1953] 1 All ER 747; applying *IRC v Yorkshire Agricultural Society* [1928] 1 KB 611, [1927] All ER Rep 536.

12 *Re Compton* [1945] Ch 123, [1945] 1 All ER 198; *Oppenheim v Tobacco Securities Trust Co Ltd* [1951] AC 297, [1951] 1 All ER 31; *Re Mead's Trust Deed* [1961] 2 All ER 836, [1961] 1 WLR 1244. But see now *Dingle v Turner* [1972] AC 601, [1972] 1 All ER 878, HL; see para **[102.14]** below. In *Re Shaw's Will Trusts* [1952] Ch 163, [1952] 1 All ER 49, it is said

that where trusts are not only educational, but are educational in the sense that they benefit the public, no evidence of benefit to the community is required; applied in *Re Macdonald* (1971) 18 DLR (3d) 521 (part of residue 'to be used in collecting of historical objects for showing and presentation'). In *Independent Schools Council v Charity Commission for England and Wales* [2011] UKUT 421 (TCC), [2012] 1 All ER 127 the judges reviewed the cases decided before the Charities Act 2006 and found that in the context of educational charities, public benefit included two aspects; the first aspect was that the nature of the purpose itself had to be such as to be a benefit to the community; the second aspect was that those who could benefit from the carrying out of the purpose had to be sufficiently numerous, and identified in such manner, as to constitute a section of the public.

13 *IRC v Baddeley* [1955] AC 572, [1955] 1 All ER 525 (and such trusts were not exclusively for religious purposes).

14 *Re Nottage, Jones v Palmer* [1895] 2 Ch 649.

15 *Re Mariette, Mariette v Aldenham School Governing Body* [1915] 2 Ch 284.

16 *IRC v McMullen* [1981] AC 1, [1980] 1 All ER 884.

17 *George Drexler Ofrex Foundation (Trustees) v IRC* [1966] Ch 675, [1965] 3 All ER 529.

18 Charities Act 2011, s 3(1)(b) (replacing Charities Act 2006, s 2(2)(b)). See *Independent Schools Council v Charity Commission for England and Wales* [2011] UKUT 421 (TCC), [2012] 1 All ER 127.

[102.9]

[Updated in the text and in footnotes 2 and 16 for the Charities Act 2011.]

Religious purposes. The words 'advancement of religion' mean the promotion of spiritual teaching in a wide sense and the maintenance of the doctrines on which it rests and of the observances that serve to promote and manifest it,[1] but the gift must tend directly or indirectly to the instruction or edification of the public.[2] It has been said that a trust for the purpose of any kind of monotheistic theism would be a good charitable trust.[3] Religion is concerned with man's relations with God and the two essential attributes of religion are faith and worship; faith in a god and worship of that god.[4] Such gifts will include gifts for the saying of masses,[5] for missionary purposes,[6] provision and support of the clergy,[7] building or repair of buildings used for religious purposes[8] and graveyards[9] and burial places.[10] Such gifts when in general terms must, however, be confined to religious purposes and are not charitable where they include social or other non-charitable purposes.[11] The fact that a religious community opens its doors to those of all creeds and to those who have no creed, does not prevent its being a valid charity.[12] They may, however, include a gift for the choir;[13] for the organ and organist,[14] or for the provision of religious books.[15] A gift for the advancement of religion (including multi-theistic faiths and those which hold to no god) is charitable (if for the public benefit) under the new statutory law.[16]

1 *Keren Kayemeth Le Jisroel Ltd v IRC* [1931] 2 KB 465 at 477, CA; affd [1932] AC 650, HL. See *Re Brooks* (1969) 4 DLR (3d) 694 ('the work of the Lord') and *Re Barker's Will Trusts, Barker v Crouch* (1948) 64 TLR 273 ('for God's work'); *Re Le Cren Clarke, Funnell v Stewart* [1996] 1 All ER 715 (faith healing).

2 *Cocks v Manners* (1871) LR 12 Eq 574 at 585; *Re Delany, Conoley v Quick* [1902] 2 Ch 642 at 648; *Re Williams, Public Trustee v Williams* [1927] 2 Ch 283 at 287; *Gilmour v Coats* [1949] AC 426, [1949] 1 All ER 848; see *Holmes v A-G* (1981) Times, 12 February. In *Re Church of Scientology (England and Wales)* [2005] WTLR 1151, the Charity Commission declined to register the Church of Scientology as a charity on the grounds: (a) that scientology was not a religion for the purposes of English charity law which requires not merely a belief in a supreme being (a requirement which scientology satisfied) but also worship of that being (a requirement which it did not satisfy); and (b) that scientology was not an organisation established to promote the moral or spiritual welfare or improvement of the community and did not therefore fall into the residual category of organisations

established for the public benefit. Under the new statutory law the objection at (a) may be difficult to sustain but the overriding requirement of public benefit may still justify an objection as at (b).

3 Per Lord Parker of Waddington in *Bowman v Secular Society Ltd* [1917] AC 406 at 448–450.

4 Per Dillon J in *Barralet v A-G* [1980] 3 All ER 918 at 924; thus a society for the dissemination of ethical principles and cultivation of rational belief was not for religious purposes since ethics are concerned with man's relation with man, referring to *United Grand Lodge of Ancient Free and Accepted Masons of England v Holborn Borough Council* [1957] 3 All ER 281, [1957] 1 WLR 1080 (freemasonry not charitable as religious purposes).

5 *Re Hetherington* [1990] Ch 1, [1989] 2 All ER 129. *Re Caus, Lindeboom v Camille* [1934] Ch 162 followed, *Bourne v Keane* [1919] AC 815, and *Gilmour v Coats* [1949] AC 426, and other cases cited under this heading in the text, considered. The Vice-Chancellor Sir Nicholas Browne-Wilkinson considered that a gift for the saying of masses was prima facie charitable as being for a religious purpose. The necessary public benefit was found in the fact that the masses were to be celebrated in public and that the gift would contribute to the stipends of priests.

6 The term 'missionary' purposes is ambiguous and may comprise non-charitable objects: *Re Rees* [1920] 2 Ch 59; *Scott v Browrigg* (1881) 9 LR Ir 246; *A-G v Becher* [1910] 2 IR 251. See also for cases where purposes were charitable: *Dunne v Duignan* [1908] 1 IR 228; *Allan's Executors v Allan* 1908 SC 807.

7 *Dundee Magistrates v Dundee Presbytery* (1861) 4 Macq 228; *Pennington v Buckley* (1848) 6 Hare 451; *Re Maguire* (1870) LR 9 Eq 632; *Re Macnamara, Hewitt v Jeans* (1911) 104 LT 771; *Re Williams, Public Trustee v Williams* [1927] 2 Ch 283. See also *A-G v Parker* (1747) 1 Ves Sen 43 (pension for a perpetual curate); *Re Manuel* [1958] OWN 194 (gift to minister good though church acceded to another denomination); *Touchet and Touchet v Blais* (1963) 40 DLR (2d) 961 (gift to named bishop 'for his works as would aid French Canadians in his Diocese'); *Re Clark, Horwell v Dent* [1961] NZLR 635 (a gift of an annuity to the wife of the minister for the time being of a specified church is not a charitable gift and is void as infringing the perpetuity rule).

8 *Re Church Estate Charity, Wandsworth* (1871) 6 Ch App 296; *A-G v Dartmouth Corpn* (1883) 48 LT 933; *Re St Alphage, London Wall* (1888) 59 LT 614; *Re Manser, A-G v Lucas* [1905] 1 Ch 68; *Re Williams, James v Williams* (1910) 26 TLR 307; *Maguire v A-G* [1943] IR 238 (founding a convent); *Re Beresford* (1966) 57 DLR (2d) 380 (gift to 'build a church edifice of luxurious and beautiful appearance', sufficient general intention to devote to charity and could be used to renovate the crypt of a church for use as a church hall).

9 *Re Vaughan, Vaughan v Thomas* (1886) 33 Ch D 187; *Re Douglas, Douglas v Simpson* [1905] 1 Ch 279; *A-G v Blizard* (1855) 21 Beav 233.

10 *Re Manser, A-G v Lucas* [1905] 1 Ch 68.

11 *Oxford Group v IRC* [1949] 2 All ER 537 (expenditure on subsidiary purposes), and see *Re Morton Estate, Summerfield and London and Western Trusts Co Ltd v Phillips* [1941] WWR 310; *Munster and Leinster Bank v A-G* [1940] IR 19 (Catholic Young Men's Society); *Re Lloyd* [1958] VLR 523. If the social activities are merely ancillary to the religious purposes they do not prevent the gift being charitable: *Neville Estates Ltd v Madden* [1962] Ch 832, [1961] 3 All ER 769.

12 *Re Banfield, Lloyds Bank Ltd v Smith* [1968] 2 All ER 276, [1968] 1 WLR 846 (community received and assisted those members of the public who needed help for a variety of reasons, e g drug addiction, drink, having been in prison or loneliness; and members went out to offer help where required). Alternatively, if the community was not a religious charity, the gift was valid as being for a public purpose within the fourth heading in *Pemsel's Case*.

13 *Re Royce, Turner v Wormald* [1940] Ch 514, [1940] 2 All ER 291.

14 *Carbery v Cox* (1852) 3 I Ch R 231n.

15 *Re Anderson* [1943] 4 DLR 268.

16 Charities Act 2011, s 3(1)(c) and 3(2)(a) (replacing Charities Act 2006, s 2(2)(c) and 2(3)(a)).

[102.10]

[Updated in footnotes 2 and 4 and in the text for the Charities Act 2011.
Updated in footnote 3 for *Re Harding, Gibbs v Harding* [2008] Ch 235.
Updated in the footnote 5 for *Independent Schools Council v Charity Commission for England and Wales* [2011] UKUT 421 (TCC), [2012] 1 All ER 127.]

Purposes beneficial to the community. While all charitable gifts must be for the benefit of the public as distinct from private individuals,[1] the gifts now to be considered are essentially for the benefit of the general public. Under CA 2011 (previously CA 2006) all charities must satisfy the public benefit test described here if their purposes are to be charitable purposes.[2] It is not enough that the trust should be for the public benefit, it must also be beneficial in a way which the law regards as a charitable trust.[3] Until CA 2006 came into force[4] the question whether the purposes were for the benefit of the general public did not need to be considered where the gift was exclusively for the relief of poverty, for educational or religious purposes or for purposes analogous to those purposes, but the ambit of the purposes must not have been so wide as to include purposes which the law considers as not charitable.[5] The question of the public nature of the trusts arises when the primary class of eligible persons is ascertained. If this primary class is sufficiently wide, the fact that the trustees are bound to give priority to a narrower class does not destroy the essential public and charitable nature of the trust,[6] but where the class is confined not only to a particular area but also to be selected from within it by reference to a particular creed it is not charitable.[7] The question whether or not the potential beneficiaries of a trust can fairly be said to constitute a section of the public is a question of degree and cannot be by itself decisive of the question whether the trust is a charity: much will depend on the purpose of the trust.[8] These gifts which are extremely various in their nature may for convenience be classified as follows: gifts encouraging patriotism or national feeling;[9] gifts for public works;[10] gifts for public instruction or recreation;[11] gifts promoting the efficiency of the Army;[12] gifts for the improvement of agriculture;[13] gifts for the protection of animals;[14] gifts for the care of the sick;[15] gifts for the spread of certain principles;[16] gifts to foster promote and increase public interest in dramatic art[17] or music.[18] The question whether the promulgation of a particular doctrine or principle is for the benefit of the public is to be answered by the court on the evidence before it.[19] A gift of this nature is none the less charitable if it benefits only a section of the public[20] or a particular locality or the inhabitants of a particular locality[21] but not members of a particular creed in a particular locality.[22]

1 *Peggs v Lamb* [1994] Ch 172, [1994] 2 All ER 15; citing *Williams' Trustees v IRC* [1947] AC 447, [1947] 1 All ER 513.

2 CA 2006, ss 2(1)(b) and 3, in force from 1 April 2008 (SI 2008/945), replaced by CA 2011, ss 2(1)(b) and 4, from 14 March 2012. See also the Charity Commission's 'Charities and Public Benefit' (2008) and 'Analysis of the Law underpinning Charities and Public Benefit' (2008).

3 The importance of this aspect of charitable gifts came before the courts in *Re Compton, Powell v Compton* [1945] Ch 123, [1945] 1 All ER 198, and has been much discussed since that decision; see *Re Tree, Idle v Tree* [1945] Ch 325, [1945] 2 All ER 65; *Re Hobourn Aero Components Ltd's Air Raid Distress Fund, Ryan v Forrest* [1946] Ch 194, [1946] 1 All ER 501; *National Anti-Vivisection Society v IRC* [1948] AC 31, [1947] 2 All ER 217; *Gibson v South American Stores (Gath and Chaves) Ltd* [1950] Ch 177, [1949] 2 All ER 985;

Oppenheim v Tobacco Securities Trust Co Ltd [1951] AC 297, [1951] 1 All ER 31; *Keren Kayemeth Le Jisroel Ltd v IRC* [1932] AC 650; *Williams' Trustees v IRC* [1947] AC 447, [1947] 1 All ER 513; *Re Scarisbrick* [1951] Ch 622, [1951] 1 All ER 822 (poor relations); *IRC v Glasgow City Police Athletic Association* [1953] AC 380, [1953] 1 All ER 747 (to encourage athletic sports connected with city police force not charitable); *Incorporated Council of Law Reporting for England and Wales v A-G* [1972] Ch 73, [1971] 3 All ER 1029; the publication of the Law Reports is a purpose beneficial to the community). See also *Scottish Burial Reform and Cremation Society Ltd v Glasgow City Corpn* [1968] AC 138, [1967] 3 All ER 215, HL. However, since the court leans in favour of making a testator's testamentary dispositions effective, it may lean in favour of finding a gift to the inhabitants of a locality, without a specified purpose, a valid charitable gift, see *Re Harding, Gibbs v Harding* [2007] EWHC 3 (Ch), [2008] Ch 235, [2007] 1 All ER 747.

4 CA 2006 placed a public benefit requirement on all charitable purposes, including those which would have been charitable under the pre-existing law without the need to satisfy such a test: CA 2006, s 2(1)(b), in force from 1 April 2008 (SI 2008/945). See now CA 2011, s 2(1)(b) which has replaced it from 14 March 2012,

5 *IRC v Baddeley* [1955] AC 572, [1955] 1 All ER 525. The question whether a trust set up by a will was charitable because it was of public benefit stood or fell by the law and character of the objects of the trust at the date of the testator's death: *Re Bushnell, Lloyds Bank Ltd v Murray* [1975] 1 All ER 721, [1975] 1 WLR 1596, distinguishing *Scottish Burial Reform and Cremation Society Ltd v Glasgow City Corpn* [1968] AC 138, [1967] 3 All ER 215, HL. But see now *Independent Schools Council v Charity Commission for England and Wales* [2011] UKUT 421 (TCC), [2012] 1 All ER 127 where after a review of the pre-2006 Act cases the judges said there was no presumption that purposes relating to the relief of poverty, the advancement of education or the advancement of religion had a quality of being beneficial to the community which was sufficient to make them charitable, while an institution seeking to bring a purpose of another kind into the charitable fold had positively to show that the purpose was sufficiently beneficial to the community for it to be recognised as charitable. In practice, a judge would start with a predisposition that an educational gift, for example, was for the benefit of the community, but he would look at the terms of the trust critically, and if it appeared to him that the trust might not have the requisite element, his predisposition would be displaced so that evidence would be needed to establish public benefit. But if there was nothing to cause the judge to doubt his predisposition, he would be satisfied that the public element was present; that would not be because of a presumption, but because the terms of the trust would speak for themselves, enabling the judge to conclude, as a matter of fact, that the purpose was for the public benefit.

6 *Re Koettgen's Will Trust, Westminster Bank Ltd v Family Welfare Association Trustees Ltd* [1954] Ch 252, [1954] 1 All ER 581 (trust for commercial education generally with a preference for employees of a company and members of their families).

7 *IRC v Baddeley* [1955] AC 572, [1955] 1 All ER 525.

8 Per Lord Cross in *Dingle v Turner* [1972] AC 601 at 624, [1972] 1 All ER 878 at 889, 'sections of the public' include, for example, the ratepayers in the Royal Boroughs of Kensington and Chelsea, the blind; applied in *Re Denison* (1974) 42 DLR (3d) 652; the descendants of Gladstone and the employees of a small company are a private class: *Davies v Perpetual Trustee Co Ltd* [1959] AC 439, [1959] 2 All ER 128.

9 *Re Smith, Public Trustee v Smith* [1932] 1 Ch 153 (gift 'to my country England'); *Nightingale v Goulbourn* (1848) 2 Ph 594 (gift for benefit of country to be applied by the Chancellor of the Exchequer); *A-G v Bushby* (1857) 24 Beav 299 (for relief of taxes); *Thellusson v Woodford* (1805) 11 Ves 112 (for reduction of National Debt); *Newland v A-G* (1809) 3 Mer 684 (same); *Ashton v Lord Langdale* (1851) 4 De G & Sm 402 (same); *Re Bell, Ballarat Trustees, Executors and Agency Co Ltd* [1943] VLR 103 (person rendering in any year the greatest benefit to humanity); *Re Strakosch, Temperley v A-G* [1949] Ch 529, [1949] 2 All ER 6 (strengthen unity of mother country with South Africa: not charitable); *Re Spensley's Will Trusts, Barclays Bank Ltd v Staughton* [1954] Ch 233, [1954] 1 All ER 178 (residence of High Commissioner: not charitable); *Re Elgar* [1957] NZLR 556 (patriotism); *Gray Estate v Yule* (1990) 73 DLR (4th) 162, gift to 'the German people' held charitable.

10 *A-G v Day* [1900] 1 Ch 31 (repair of highways); *Forbes v Forbes* (1854) 18 Beav 552 (building bridges); *Wilson v Barnes* (1886) 38 Ch D 507 (protection of coast); *Jones v Williams* (1767) Amb 651 (provision of water); *A-G v Eastlake* (1853) 11 Hare 205 (provision of public lighting); *Re Spence, Barclays Bank Ltd v Stockton-on-Tees Corpn* [1938] Ch 96, [1937] 3 All ER 684 (public hall for borough); *Re Bones, Goltz v Ballarat Trustees, Executors and*

Agency Co Ltd [1930] VLR 346 (improvement of city); *Re Knowles* [1938] 3 DLR 178 (beautifying a street); *Re Bobier* [1949] 4 DLR 288 (hospital); *Re List, List v Prime* [1949] NZLR 78 (convalescent home for children); *Public Trustee v Nolan* (1943) 43 SRNSW 169 (to erect carillon: not charitable); *Re Wokingham Fire Brigade Trusts* [1951] Ch 373, [1951] 1 All ER 454 (provision of fire brigade); *Re Mair* [1964] VR 529 (gift of public park: charitable); *Scottish Burial Reform and Cremation Society Ltd v Glasgow City Corpn* [1968] AC 138, [1967] 3 All ER 215, HL (provision of crematorium and promotion of cremation).

11 *Re Scowcroft, Ormrod v Wilkinson* [1898] 2 Ch 638 (public library); *Re Holburne, Coates v Mackillop* (1885) 53 LT 212 (museum); *Re Scowcroft, Ormrod v Wilkinson* (reading-room); *Harrison v Southampton Corpn* (1854) 2 Sm & G 387 (botanical garden and observatory); *Re Jacobs, Westminster Bank v Chinn* (1970) 114 Sol Jo 515 (planting of a grove of trees in Israel); *Shillington v Portadown Urban Council* [1911] 1 IR 247 (recreation); *Re Hadden, Public Trustee v More* [1932] 1 Ch 133 (public recreation); *Taylor v Taylor* (1910) 10 CLR 218 (scientific research); *Re Vernon Estate, Boyle v Battye* [1948] 2 WWR 46 (community hall). A gift for the encouragement of mere sport is not charitable: *Re Jacques* (1967) 63 DLR (2d) 673 (residue to be distributed 'to finance some community project', possibly swimming pool: held, not charitable); *Re Gray, Todd v Taylor* [1925] Ch 362 (regimental sports: charitable); *Baddeley v IRC* [1953] 2 All ER 233 at 251; *Re Morgan, Cecil-Williams v A-G* [1955] 2 All ER 632 (public recreation ground); *Kearins v Kearins* [1957] SRNSW 286; *Alexandra Park Trustees v Haringey London Borough* (1967) 66 LGR 306 (public park and sports ground); *Royal College of Surgeons of England v National Provincial Bank Ltd* [1952] 1 All ER 984 (promotion of surgery); *Royal College of Nursing for England and Wales v St Marylebone Corpn* [1959] 3 All ER 663 (promotion of nursing); *General Nursing Council v St Marylebone Borough Council* [1959] 1 All ER 325 (regulation of nursing profession not charitable); *Re Lysaght, Hill v Royal College of Surgeons of England* [1966] Ch 191, [1965] 2 All ER 888 (gift for medical studentship: not void because Roman Catholics and Jews excluded there being a general charitable intent); *Re Pinion, Westminster Bank Ltd v Pinion* [1965] Ch 85 at 98, [1964] 1 All ER 890 (gift of studio paintings and old furniture to form exhibition not charitable where the few pieces of any educational value were not sufficient to make the whole charitable and the collection was directed by the will to be kept intact); *Incorporated Council of Law Reporting for England and Wales v A-G* [1972] Ch 73, [1971] 3 All ER 1029 (publication of Law Reports).

12 *Re Lord Stratheden and Campbell, Alt v Lord Stratheden and Campbell* [1894] 3 Ch 265 (volunteer corps); *Re Stephens, Giles v Stephens* (1892) 8 TLR 792 (teaching shooting); *Re Good, Harrington v Watts* [1905] 2 Ch 60, and *Re Donald, Moore v Somerset* [1909] 2 Ch 410 (officer's mess); *Re Gray, Todd v Taylor* [1925] Ch 362 (regimental fund for sport); *Re Barker, Sherrington v St Paul's Cathedral (Dean and Chapter)* (1909) 25 TLR 753 (prize for cadets); *Re Driffill, Harvey v Chamberlain* [1950] Ch 92, [1949] 2 All ER 933 (defence from air attack). A gift for training boys to become officers in the Navy or the mercantile marine is charitable: *Re Corbyn, Midland Bank Executor and Trustee Co Ltd v A-G* [1941] Ch 400, [1941] 2 All ER 160. See also *Whitmore v Regina Branch of Canadian Legion of British Empire Service League* [1940] 3 WWR 359 (returned soldiers); *Re Elgar* [1957] NZLR 556; *Re Gillespie* [1965] VR 402 (gift for any organisation for ex-members of forces, the choice is to be in the discretion of the trustee. Restriction to protestant members of British descent).

13 *IRC v Yorkshire Agricultural Society* [1928] 1 KB 611; *Re Pleasants, Pleasants v A-G* (1923) 39 TLR 675; *London University of Yarrow* (1857) 1 De G & J 72. As to gift to promote natural history, see *Re Benham* [1939] SASR 450. A gift of residue to found a bank for the purpose of granting loans to assist planters and agriculturalists at a low rate of interest, but compatible with the proper operation of the bank is not a valid charitable trust because the loans might not be applied by the planters or agriculturalists for agricultural purposes and restrictive words are not to be imported into a trust which without them is invalid: *Hadaway v Hadaway* [1955] 1 WLR 16.

14 See para **[102.13]** below.

15 *Re Resch's Will Trusts, Le Cras v Perpetual Trustee Co Ltd, Far West Children's Health Scheme v Perpetual Trustee Co Ltd* [1969] 1 AC 514, [1967] 3 All ER 915 (gift to a private hospital which charged fees, poor sometimes treated without payment). A gift for the purpose of a hospital is prima facie a good charitable trust; it is not a condition of validity of a trust for the relief of the sick that it should be limited to the poor sick; if a bequest is made on trusts requiring it to be applied for a particular purpose which is charitable, it is immaterial that some of the general purposes of the recipient body may not be charitable.

See also *Re Adams, Gee v Barnet Group Hospital Management Committee* [1968] Ch 80, [1967] 3 All ER 285; *Re Smith's Will Trusts, Barclays Bank Ltd v Merchantile Bank Ltd* [1962] 2 All ER 563, [1962] 1 WLR 763.

16 *Re Scowcroft, Ormrod v Wilkinson* [1898] 2 Ch 638 (Conservative principles combined with mental and moral improvement); *Re Hood, Public Trustee v Hood* [1931] 1 Ch 240 (Christian principles); *Re Price, Midland Bank Exor and Trustee Co Ltd v Harwood* [1943] Ch 422, [1943] 2 All ER 505 (teaching of Steiner); and see *Barralet v A-G* [1980] 3 All ER 918, [1980] 1 WLR 1565 (whole of society's objects were for the mental and moral improvement of man and thus for purposes beneficial to the community). But the trust must not be political; see *McGovern v A-G* [1982] Ch 321, [1981] 3 All ER 493, and next section. *Re Trusts of Arthur McDougall Fund* [1956] 3 All ER 867 (advancement of education or other charitable purposes connected with the art and science of government is charitable and not invalidated by the fact that the trustees must be members of the Proportional Representation Society); *Re Shaw, Public Trustee v Day* [1957] 1 All ER 745 (reform of alphabet); *Re Davis, Watts v Davis and Westralian Farmers Co-operative Ltd* [1965] WAR 25 (a gift to the directors of the company to apply the income in perpetuity for the expansion of co-operation and the co-operative movement held invalid); *Re Shapiro* (1980) 107 DLR (3d) 133.

17 *Associated Artists Ltd v IRC* [1956] 2 All ER 583, [1956] 1 WLR 752.

18 *Royal Choral Society v IRC* [1943] 2 All ER 101; *Re Levien, Lloyds Bank Ltd v Worshipful of Musicians* [1955] 3 All ER 35; *Re Delius' Will Trusts, Emanuel v Rosen* [1957] Ch 299, [1957] 1 All ER 854.

19 *Re Hummeltenberg, Beatty v London Spiritualistic Alliance Ltd* [1923] 1 Ch 237; *Re Grove-Grady, Plowden v Lawrence* [1929] 1 Ch 557; *National Anti-Vivisection Society v IRC* [1948] AC 31, [1947] 2 All ER 217, disapproving *Re Foveaux, Cross v London Anti-Vivisection Society* [1895] 2 Ch 501, where it was stated that where the merits of a particular object are controversial the court stands neutral.

20 *Re Hummeltenberg, Beatty v London Spiritualistic Alliance Ltd* [1923] 1 Ch 237. The part of the public to be benefited must be substantial enough to give it a public character: *Shaw v Halifax Corpn* [1915] 2 KB 170; *Hall v Derby Borough Urban Sanitary Authority* (1885) 16 QBD 163, and may be a class of the inhabitants of a particular locality: *Mitford v Reynolds* (1842) 1 Ph 185 (native inhabitants of Dacca); *Re Norwich Town Close Estate Charity* (1888) 40 Ch D 298 (freemen of a borough); *Re Mellody, Brandwood v Haden* [1918] 1 Ch 228 (schoolchildren of a town); *Re Koetten's Will Trusts, Westminster Bank Ltd v Family Welfare Association Trustees Ltd* [1954] Ch 252, [1954] 1 All ER 581 (employees of a company). A gift to a parish council is not necessarily charitable and where the object was described as 'some useful memorial' of the testator it was held not charitable and too uncertain to be enforced: *Re Endacott, Corpe v Endacott* [1960] Ch 232, [1959] 3 All ER 562.

21 *A-G v Earl Lonsdale* (1827) 1 Sim 105 (county); *A-G v Dartmouth Corpn* (1883) 48 LT 933 (town); *Re St Nicholas Acons (Parish)* (1889) 60 LT 532 (parish); *Schellenberger v Trustees etc Co* (1952) 86 CLR 454 (gift to add to the beauty and advancement of a town); *Goodman v Saltash Corpn* (1882) 7 App Cas 633; *Peggs v Lamb* [1994] Ch 172, [1994] 2 All ER 15.

22 *IRC v Baddeley* [1955] AC 572, [1955] 1 All ER 525; *Re Lipinski's Will Trusts, Gosschalk v Levy* [1976] Ch 235, [1977] 1 All ER 33 (trust for the Hull Judeans (Maccabi) Association, founded as a cricket club and subsequently provided social, cultural and sporting activities for Jewish youths who were members, held not charitable because essentially a sports club for the benefit of its members).

[102.12]

[Updated in the text and in the footnotes for the Charities Act 2011.]

Recreational charities. The Charities Act 2011 (CA 2011) (which consolidates the provisions of the Recreational Charities Act 1958 (RCA 1958)) provides that it shall be, and be deemed always to have been charitable, to provide, or assist in the provision of, facilities for recreation or other leisure-time occupation, if the facilities are provided in the interests of social welfare.[1] There must be some deprivation, although not necessarily financial deprivation, which falls to be alleviated[2] and the facilities have to be provided with the object of improving the conditions of life for the persons for whom the facilities are primarily intended, and either those persons have need of such facilities by reason of their youth,[3] age, infirmity or disablement, poverty or social and economic circumstances,[4] or the facilities are to be available to the members or female members of the public at large.[5] It is not necessary that the persons for whom the facilities were primarily provided be confined to those who had need of them by one of these forms of social deprivation.[6] It is sufficient if the facilities are provided with the object of improving the conditions of life for members of the community generally.[7] The object of the RCA 1958 (now consolidated in CA 2011) was to give statutory recognition to the charitable nature of the trusts and institutions in question, without enlarging the definition of charity or encroaching on the existing authorities. In particular it is specifically provided that it is charitable to provide or assist in the provision of facilities at village halls, community centres and women's institutes, and to provide and maintain grounds and buildings to be used for purposes of recreation or leisure-time occupation, including the provision of facilities for those purposes by the organising of any activity.[8] The provision of a holiday centre for North Derbyshire miners and their families in need of a change of air, has been held to be within the RCA 1958 (now CA 2011, s 5).[9] Under CA 2011, trusts for the advancement of amateur sport (if for public benefit) are charitable.[10]

1 CA 2011, s 5(1) (replacing RCA 1958), s 1(1)). See also *IRC v McMullen* [1979] 1 All ER 588, CA; revd [1981] AC 1, [1980] 1 All ER 884, HL, but without reference to the Court of Appeal's comments on the RCA 1958.

2 *IRC v McMullen* [1978] 1 All ER 230 at 241, per Walton J, who did not think the Football Association Youth Trust satisfied this condition since it was impossible for the court to say that, as a class, pupils at schools and universities were 'deprived' (affd [1979] 1 All ER 588; revsd, [1981] AC 1, [1980] 1 All ER 884, HL).

3 However, Walton J in *IRC v McMullen,* see n 3 above, did think that notwithstanding the presence of many mature students it would be possible to regard the trust as intended primarily to benefit the young.

4 CA 2011, s 5(3)(b)(i) (replacing RCA 1958, s 1(2)(b)(ii)).

5 CA 2011, s 5(3)(b)(ii) (replacing RCA 1958, s 1(2)(b)(ii)).

6 The RCA 1958 (now consolidated in CA 2011) was prompted by the House of Lords decision in *IRC v Baddeley* [1955] AC 572, [1955] 1 All ER 525, HL, where it was held that a trust for the promotion of the moral, social and physical well-being of persons, resident in a particular area, by the provision of facilities for moral, social and physical training and recreation and by promoting and encouraging all forms of such activities as were calculated to contribute to the health and well-being of such persons, was not charitable. It is doubtful whether the provisions of the Act would in fact have validated this very wide trust: *Guild v IRC* [1992] 2 AC 310, [1992] 2 All ER 10, HL.

7 *IRC v Baddeley* [1955] AC 572, [1955] 1 All ER 525, HL, dictum of Bridge LJ in *IRC v McMullen* [1979] 1 All ER 588, CA at 597–598 approved; dictum of Walton J in *IRC v McMullen* [1978] 1 All ER 230 at 241, disapproved. It was held that a gift of residue left 'to the Town Council of North Berwick for the use in connection with the Sports Centre in North Berwick or some similar purpose in connection with sport' was charitable as within s 1 of the 1958 Act. The House thought that a benignant approach should be adopted to the Act which favoured finding the gift charitable, rather than void. Dicta by Lord Loreburn LC in *Weir v Crum-Brown* [1908] AC 162 at 16; and of Lord Hailsham LC in *IRC v McMullen* [1980] 1 All ER 884 at 890 applied.

8 CA 2011, s 5(4) (replacing RCA 1958, s 1(3)); see *IRC v McMullen,* see n 3 above.

9 *Wynn v Skegness UDC* [1966] 3 All ER 336, [1967] 1 WLR 52. Compare the pre-Act case of *IRC v Glasgow City Police Athletic Association* [1953] AC 380, [1953] 1 All ER 747, HL (provision of recreation facilities for members of a police force not charitable); distinguished in *London Hospital Medical College v IRC* [1976] 2 All ER 113, [1976] 1 WLR 613

(students union held charitable on grounds of education; no decision on RCA 1958). See also *Bath and North East Somerset Council v A-G* [2002] EWHC 1623 (Ch), [2002] WTLR 1257.

10 CA 2011, s 3(1)(g) (replacing CA 2006, s 2(2)(g)).

[102.13]

[Updated in the text and in footnote 4 for the Charities Act 2011.]

Benefit to animals. A trust for the benefit of animals is charitable not upon the ground that it benefits the animals, but upon the ground that it produces some benefit to mankind, that is, it is calculated to develop the finer side of human nature.[1] The objects of such a trust are not charitable even though for the benefit of animals if, on balance, the object is detrimental to the public benefit, as, for example, hindering medical research.[2] On these principles trusts for the prevention of cruelty to animals have been upheld.[3] Under the new statutory law, trusts for the advancement of animal welfare (if for public benefit) are charitable.[4]

1 *Re Grove-Grady, Plowden v Lawrence* [1929] 1 Ch 557; *National Anti-Vivisection Society v IRC* [1948] AC 31, [1947] 2 All ER 217; *Re Moss, Hobrough v Harvey* [1949] 1 All ER 495; *Re Weaver* [1963] VR 257; *Re Salterthwaite's Will Trusts* [1966] 1 All ER 919, [1966] 1 WLR 277.

2 *National Anti-Vivisection Society v IRC* [1948] AC 31, [1947] 2 All ER 217.

3 *Re Murawski's Will Trusts, Lloyds Bank v Royal Society for the Prevention of Cruelty to Animals* [1971] 2 All ER 328, [1971] 1 WLR 707; *Re Wedgwood, Allen v Wedgwood* [1915] 1 Ch 113; *Re Grove-Grady, Plowden v Lawrence* [1929] 1 Ch 557; *Re Joy, Purday v Johnson* (1888) 60 LT 175; *Re Dean, Cooper-Dean v Stevens* (1889) 41 Ch D 552; *Re Moss, Hobrough v Harvey* [1949] 1 All ER 495; followed in *Re Green's Will Trusts, Fitzgerald-Hart v A-G* [1985] 3 All ER 455 (gift to trustees to set up foundation for rescue, maintenance and benefit of cruelly treated animals). Many of the cases are discussed in the House of Lords decision in *National Anti-Vivisection Society v IRC* [1948] AC 31, [1947] 2 All ER 217.

4 Charities Act 2011, s 3(1)(j) (replacing Charities Act 2006, s 2(2)(k)). The requirement of public benefit is in keeping with the principles justifying the charitable status of these trusts discussed in this paragraph.

[102.14]

[Updated in the text and in footnote 5 for the Charities Act 2011.]

Poor relations. Perpetual trusts for the benefit of poor relations are charitable[1] unless confined to statutory next of kin and such trusts are so confined unless a contrary intention appears from the will.[2] Poor relations who become rich must not participate[3] and a trust for poorest relations must not benefit persons in fact rich.[4] A trust for poor relations is not charitable under the new statutory law if it is not also for the public benefit.[5]

1 *A-G v Price* (1810) 17 Ves 371; *Bernal v Bernal* (1838) 3 My & Cr 559; *A-G v Duke of Northumberland* (1877) 7 Ch D 745; *Mahon v Savage* (1803) 1 Sch & Lef 111; *Re Compton, Powell v Compton* [1945] Ch 123, [1945] 1 All ER 198; *Re Cohn* [1952] 3 DLR 833; *Re McEnery, O'Connell v A-G* [1941] IR 323 (where trust was held invalid); *Re Scarisbrick, Cockshott v Public Trustee* [1951] Ch 622, [1951] 1 All ER 822; in this field the distinction between a public or charitable trust and a private trust depends on whether as a matter of construction the gift was for the relief of poverty amongst a particular description of poor people or was merely a gift to particular poor persons, the relief of poverty among them being the motive of the gift. The fact that the gift took the form of a perpetual trust would no doubt indicate that the intention of the donor could not have been to confer private benefits on particular people whose possible necessities he had in mind; but the fact that the capital of the gift was to be distributed at once did not necessarily show that the gift was a private trust. See *Dingle v Turner* [1972] AC 601 at 617, [1972] 1 All ER 878 at 883. *Re*

Scarisbrick, Cockshott v Public Trustee [1951] Ch 622, [1951] 1 All ER 822 ('in needy circumstances') was followed in *Re Cohen, Cowan v Cohen* [1973] 1 All ER 889, [1973] 1 WLR 415 ('relations of mine whom my trustees shall consider to be in special need', held to be charitable and not confined to persons living at the death of the testatrix); *Re Mills* (1981) 27 SASR 200. See also *Re Segelman* [1995] 3 All ER 676 at 687–692 (gift of fund on trusts for a period of 21 years for the assistance of 'the poor and needy' members of a class consisting of six named persons and their issue held to be charitable).

2 *Carr v Bedford* (1678) 2 Rep Ch 146.

3 *Mahon v Savage* (1803) 1 Sch & Lef 111.

4 *A-G v Duke of Northumberland* (1877) 7 Ch D 745.

5 Charities Act 2011, s 2(1)(b) (replacing Charities Act 2006, s 2(1)(b)).

[102.15]

[Updated in the text and in footnote 4 for the Charities Act 2011.]

Poor employees. The 'poor relations' cases, although of long-standing are an anomalous exception to the general requirement of public benefit and the courts seemed reluctant to extend the exception to include trusts for other groups.[1] However, it has now been decided that 'poor employees' and 'poor members' trusts are a natural development from the 'poor relations' cases and enjoy a similar exemption from the requirement of public benefit.[2] But a trust to wind up the fund applying any surplus for such a purpose and in such a manner for the benefit of employees or ex-employees as the trustees think most appropriate in the circumstances then existing is too vague and uncertain as it is impossible to ascertain the class entitled to benefit.[3] A trust for poor employees is not charitable under the new statutory law if it is not also for the public benefit.[4]

1 *Re Compton, Powell v Compton* [1945] Ch 123, [1945] 1 All ER 198; *Oppenheim v Tobacco Securities Trusts Co Ltd* [1951] AC 297, [1951] 1 All ER 31; *Re Hobourn Aero Components Ltd's Air Raid Distress Fund, Ryan v Forrest* [1946] Ch 194, [1946] 1 All ER 501; *Re Cox, Baker v National Trust Co Ltd* [1955] AC 627, [1955] 2 All ER 550; *Davies v Perpetual Trustee Co Ltd* [1959] AC 439, [1959] 2 All ER 128.

2 *Dingle v Turner* [1972] AC 601, [1972] 1 All ER 878, applying *Re Gosling, Gosling v Smith* (1900) 48 WR 300, and *Gibson v South American Stores (Gath and Chaves) Ltd* [1950] Ch 177, [1949] 2 All ER 985. See also *Re Scarisbrick, Cockshott v Public Trustee* [1951] Ch 622, [1951] 1 All ER 822; and *Re Young's Will Trusts, Westminster Bank Ltd v Sterling* [1955] 3 All ER 689.

3 *Re Sayer Trust, MacGregor v Sayer* [1957] Ch 423, [1956] 3 All ER 600.

4 Charities Act 2011, s 2(1)(b) (replacing Charities Act 2006, s 2(1)(b)).

[102.16]

[Updated in the text and in footnote 2 for the Charities Act 2011.]

Poor members. Funds held on trust for the relief of poverty among members of a voluntary association have been held charitable, the funds in each case, being derived in part from subscriptions made by the members and in part from donations or bequests by well-wishers.[1] As with the previous two categories, a trust for poor members is not charitable under the new statutory law if it is not also for the public benefit.[2]

1 *Spiller v Maude* (1881) 32 Ch D 158n; *Pease v Pattinson* (1886) 32 Ch D 154, [1886–1890] All ER Rep 507; *Re Buck, Bruty v Mackey* [1896] 2 Ch 727, [1895–99] All ER Rep 366. It does not appear to have been argued in these cases that the fact that the benefits were

confined to persons who were linked by the common tie of membership of an association prevented the trusts from being charitable, see *Dingle v Turner* [1972] AC 601 at 617, [1972] 1 All ER 878 at 883.

2 Charities Act 2011, s 2(1)(b) (replacing Charities Act 2006, s 2(1)(b)).

III. RULE AGAINST PERPETUITIES

[102.28]

[Updated in the text and in footnote 2 for the Perpetuities and Accumulations Act 2009.]

Accumulations. There are statutory restrictions on accumulations[1] applicable to charity funds directed to be accumulated,[2] and the ordinary rule applies that a charity absolutely entitled can stop the accumulation and require immediate payment of the fund.[3] Where there is a general charitable intention, the transgression of this rule will not defeat the gift and a scheme will be directed.[4]

1 See Chapter 95.

2 See the Perpetuities and Accumulations Act 2009, s 14. For earlier law, see *Martin v Margham* (1844) 14 Sim 230; *Re Swain, Monckton v Hands* [1905] 1 Ch 669.

3 *Wharton v Masterman* [1895] AC 186; *Re Travis, Frost v Greatorex* [1900] 2 Ch 541. The direction, however, should prima facie be carried out by the trustees: *Re Knapp, Spreckley v A-G* [1929] 1 Ch 341 at 344.

4 *Re Monk, Giffen v Wedd* [1927] 2 Ch 197; *Re Bradwell's Will Trusts, Goode v Board of Trustees for Methodist Church Purposes* [1952] Ch 575, [1952] 2 All ER 286; *Re Burns Estate* (1960) 25 DLR (2d) 427; *Jewish Home for Aged of British Columbia v Toronto General Trusts Corpn* [1961] SCR 465.

CHAPTER 103

Charitable gifts; construction and cy-près

I. CONSTRUCTION OF CHARITABLE GIFTS

[103.1]

[Updated in footnote 2 for *Harwood v Harwood* [2005] EWHC 3019 (Ch).]

General charitable intention. Where a clear intention is expressed that a fund or other property shall be applied to charity, it is immaterial that the objects are not defined.[1] The general intention will be carried into effect, if necessary by means of a scheme, notwithstanding that the particular objects are not stated.[2] The principle is that the court treats charity as the substance and the particular disposition as the mode of the gift,[3] and draws a distinction between the charitable intention, which must be clear, and the mode of executing it, which, though vague and indefinite, does not affect the validity of the gift. The existence of such a general intention is a matter of construction, and is not dependent on the issue of any particular words,[4] but is deemed to exist wherever a testator intended the subject-matter of the gift to be applied in charity, notwithstanding the failure of the particular object or mode of application indicated.[5] The distinction to be drawn is between, on the one hand, the case where the scheme prescribed by the will can be regarded as the mode by which a general charitable purpose is to be effected, in which case the mode is not the substance of the gift, and, on the other, the case where no part of the scheme in the will can be disregarded as inessential without frustrating the testator's intention.[6] A declaration to give the whole estate to charity will prevail although only part is specifically given to charity,[7] and precatory recommendations in favour of particular charities do not prevent partial applications in other ways.[8] A charitable intention is not inferred from the fact that the trustees are a charitable society and given a wide discretion.[9] A gift to trustees to apply it in any manner in their absolute discretion in furtherance of the testator's 'general charitable intention' is not sufficient to validate an intention or purpose which is not in itself charitable in law.[10] A gift to a legatee 'for the charitable purposes agreed between us' does not imply a general charitable intention, but only an intention limited to the purposes agreed[11] and evidence is admissible to show that the purposes are, but not to limit the amount of the gift.[12] The rule of general charitable intention is applicable where the testator has neither specified the objects nor the particular way of carrying out his intention as in bequests for charitable purposes generally[13] or in relief of poverty[14] or for advancement of education[15] or religion[16] generally. It also applies where the testator states the class of objects to be benefited but does not prescribe the particular way in which his intention is to be carried out, as in gifts to the poor of a particular place,[17] or the clergy of a particular sect.[18] Effect is given to gifts where the testator omits the names of the charities he wishes to benefit,[19] or the gift is for the benefit of such charities as he shall direct and he makes no direction.[20]

1 *Moggridge v Thackwell* (1803) 7 Ves 36; *Re White, White v White* [1893] 2 Ch 41; *Re Forester, Jervis v Forester* (1897) 13 TLR 555; *Re Pyne, Lilley v A-G* [1903] 1 Ch 83; *Re Gott, Glazebrook v Leeds University* [1944] Ch 193, [1944] 1 All ER 293 (charitable trust cannot fail for uncertainty so long as there is a general or specific charitable intention).

2 *Re Gott, Glazebrook v Leeds University* [1944] Ch 193, [1944] 1 All ER 293; *Harwood v Harwood* [2005] EWHC 3019 (Ch) (on the failure of a testator's trust to establish a museum, the court found a general charitable intention to devote his residuary estate to educational purposes, probably in the field of museums, and so a scheme was directed).

3 *Lyons Corpn v Advocate General of Bengal* (1876) 1 App Cas 91 at 113; *Re Spence's Will Trusts, Ogden v Shackleton* [1979] Ch 483, [1978] 3 All ER 92, per Megarry V-C at 101, '... the court is nevertheless able to see a clear general charitable intention underlying the particular mode of carrying it out that the testator has laid down', applying *Biscoe v Jackson* (1887) 35 Ch D 460.

4 *Mills v Farmer* (1815) 1 Mer 55 at 95.

5 *Clark v Taylor* (1853) 1 Drew 642 at 644.

6 *Re Woodhams, Lloyds Bank Ltd v London College of Music* [1981] 1 All ER 202, [1981] 1 WLR 493; referring to *Mills v Farmer* (1815) 19 Ves 483; *Re Rymer, Rymer v Stanfield* [1895] 1 Ch 19; *Re Wilson, Twentyman v Simpson* [1913] 1 Ch 314; *Re Willis, Shaw v Willis* [1921] 1 Ch 44; *A-G for New South Wales v Perpetual Trustee Co Ltd* (1940) 63 CLR 209; and *Re Lysaght, Hill v Royal College of Surgeons of England* [1966] Ch 191, [1965] 2 All ER 888, applied. A useful test was formulated by Vinelott J in *Re Woodhams*, above (at pp 210 and 501), as follows: 'one way of approaching the question whether a prescribed scheme or project which has proved impracticable is the only way of furthering a desirable purpose that the testator or settlor contemplated or intended is to ask whether a modification of that scheme or project, which would enable it to be carried into effect at the relevant time, is one which would frustrate the intention of the testator or settlor as disclosed by the will or trust instrument interpreted in the light of any admissible evidence of surrounding circumstances'. In the case the testator had bequeathed gifts of residue to music colleges for music scholarships for orphans from named charitable homes. There were in fact adequate public grants available for the musical education of such orphans and thus the gift was regarded as impractical in its stated form. A *cy-près* scheme was directed. See also *Re Machin* (1980) 101 DLR (3d) 438; *Re Jung* (1980) 99 DLR (3d) 65.

7 *Beverley Corpn v A-G* (1857) 6 HL Cas 310 at 318.

8 *Moggridge v Thackwell* (1803) 7 Ves 36.

9 *Re Freeman, Shilton v Freeman* [1908] 1 Ch 720. A gift to a charitable society is construed as a gift for the purposes of the society: *Re White, White v White* [1893] 2 Ch 41.

10 *Re Sanders' Will Trusts, Public Trustee v McLaren* [1954] Ch 265, [1954] 1 All ER 667.

11 *Re Huxtable, Huxtable v Crawfurd* [1902] 2 Ch 793.

12 *Blackwell v Blackwell* [1929] AC 318.

13 *Miller v Rowan* (1837) 5 Cl & Fin 99 at 109.

14 *A-G v Rance* (1728) cited in (1762) Amb at 422.

15 *Whicker v Hume* (1858) 7 HL Cas 124.

16 *Re White, White v White* [1893] 2 Ch 41 at 52.

17 *A-G v Wilkinson* (1839) 1 Beav 370.

18 *A-G v Gladstone* (1842) 13 Sim 7.

19 *Re White, White v White* [1893] 2 Ch 41.

20 *Pocock v A-G* (1876) 3 Ch D 342; *Re Pyne, Lilley v A-G* [1903] 1 Ch 83.

[103.3]

[Updated in footnote 5 and in the text for the Charities Act 2011.
Updated in footnote 10 for *Kings v Bultitude* [2010] EWHC 1795 (Ch), [2010] WTLR 1581.
Updated in footnote 17 and in the text for *Phillips v RSPB* [2012] EWHC 618 (Ch), [2012] WTLR 897.]

Charity wrongly named or having ceased to exist. A charitable gift does not fail because the institution cannot be identified[1] or has never existed;[2] but it must be clear from the description of the institution that the testator intended to benefit a charitable purpose.[3] A gift to an institution which has ceased to exist in the testator's lifetime, whether before or after the date of the will, lapses[4], unless it is saved by the registered merger provisions of Charities Act 2011,[5] or a general intention can be shown.[6] There is no lapse where the institution has not wholly ceased to exist;[7] nor where there has merely been a change of name,[8] nor where the institution is named merely as the channel for carrying out the charitable intention.[9] A gift to an institution carried on by the testator which ceased at his death is construed as a gift for the purposes of that institution[10] and similarly a gift to an institution properly described for purposes which have ceased to be exercised by that institution by reason of a profession ceasing to adopt a method of practice is good and possibly subject to a trust to apply to such purposes as far as possible.[11] If the charity ceases to exist after the death of the testator but before payment, the gift still takes effect.[12] Where the premises of the charity were before the execution of the will closed down on the expiration of the lease under which they were held but the charity was continued by a scheme, it was held that a gift by way of addition to the endowment of the charity and not merely for the upkeep of the particular premises of the charity did not fail.[13] Where the testator's intention was to benefit the charity generally the gift was not affected by the fact that he had referred to the address at which it was carried on at the date of his will, although the work at that address had been closed down before his death and transferred elsewhere.[14] A gift to a hospital does not lapse where its specified work is transferred to a general hospital and its funds are to be applied to such special work in the general hospital,[15] but where the hospital closed down and its work was carried on by the Australian Red Cross, the gift could not be treated as a gift to that society because the will said that the receipt of the treasurer of the hospital was to be a sufficient discharge.[16] Where a charity ceased to exist in circumstances where, although its assets were transferred to other bodies, its activities ceased to be carried on by any other body, it was held that a provision in the will for a transferee body to take the gift did not carry the gift to any of the transferees since none of them continued the activities of the charity.[17]

1 *Gibson v Coleman* (1868) 18 LT 236; *Re Kilvert's Trusts* (1871) 7 Ch App 170. As to the jurisdiction of the court to order a scheme in such a case, see para **[103.19]** below.

2 *Re Davis, Hannen v Hillyer* [1902] 1 Ch 876 at 884; *Re Clergy Society* (1856) 2 K & J 615; *Daly v A-G* (1860) 11 I Ch R 41; *Re Geary's Trusts* (1890) 25 LR Ir 171; *Re Mann, Hardy v A-G* [1903] 1 Ch 232; *Re Songest, Mayger v Forces Help Society and Lord Roberts Workshops* [1956] 2 All ER 765.

3 *Re Parkes, Cottrell v Parkes* (1909) 25 TLR 523. From *Re Bailey, Bailey v Working Ladies Guild* (1931) 75 Sol Jo 415, it might appear that the court requires only that there shall be no evidence to contradict the charitable intention shown by the name given by the testator to a society which has never existed. See also *Re Forshaw, Wallace v Middlesex Hospital* (1934)

51 TLR 97; *Re Nesbitt's Will Trusts* [1953] 1 All ER 936; *Re Kerr* [1957] QSR 292. In *Re Goldschmidt* [1957] 1 All ER 513, the gift was given to an institution not capable of identification and, the ultimate gift being to a charity, it passed under the ultimate gift. See also *Re Jacobsen* (1977) 80 DLR (3d) 122.

4 It is more difficult to find a general charitable intention where the gift is to a body which existed at the date of the will but ceased to exist before the testator died than it is to find the intention when the body never did exist: per Megarry V-C in *Re Spence's Will Trusts, Ogden v Shackleton* [1978] 3 All ER 92 at 100; *Re Ovey, Broadbent v Barrow* (1885) 29 Ch D 560 (ceasing to exist before date of will); *Re Rymer, Rymer v Stanfield* [1895] 1 Ch 19 (ceasing after date of will); *Re Joy, Purday v Johnson* (1888) 60 LT 175; *Makeown v Ardagh* (1876) IR 10 Eq 445; *Re Tharp, Longrigg v People's Dispensary for Sick Animals of the Poor Inc* [1942] 2 All ER 358; revsd on another point [1943] 1 All ER 257 (there is a lapse where the gift is to the particular society and not for the particular purpose); *Re Lucas, Sheard v Mellor* [1948] Ch 175 [1947] 2 All ER 773; *Re Stemson's Will Trusts, Carpenter v Treasury Solicitor* [1970] Ch 16, [1969] 2 All ER 517; *Re Rowell, Public Trustee v Bailey* (1982) 31 SASR 36.

5 CA 2011, ss 305–314 (replacing CA 1993, ss 75C–75F). See para **[103.9]** below.

6 *Clark v Taylor* (1853) 1 Drew 642; *Marsh v A-G* (1860) 2 John & H 61. It is difficult to find a general intention where the testator has taken care to identify the particular charity: *Re Harwood, Coleman v Innes* [1936] Ch 285; applied in *Re Spence, Ogden v Shackleton* [1979] Ch 483, [1978] 3 All ER 92 (a gift for the benefit of patients at a specified home; at the date of the will there were such patients but at the death of the testatrix there was no longer any home, or any patients there, or any possibility of them, held gift failed), distinguishing *Re Finger's Will Trusts, Turner v Ministry of Health* [1972] Ch 286, [1971] 3 All ER 1050. See also *Re Broadbent* [2001] 28 LS Gaz R 44.

7 *Re Waring, Hayward v A-G* [1907] 1 Ch 166 (school closed on weekdays, but used on Sundays); *Re Bradfield* (1892) 8 TLR 696 (closing of branch); *Re Faraker, Faraker v Durell* [1912] 2 Ch 488; *Re Scott Estate* (1957) 11 DLR (2d) 223 (cesser in named town but continuing elsewhere); applied in *Re Roberts, Stenton v Hardy* [1963] 1 All ER 674 (gift for the purposes of an institution not so correlated with the physical premises where the institution was located that it failed when those premises ceased to exist); *St Dunstan's University v Canada Permanent Trust Co* (1976) 67 DLR (3d) 480; *Re Bezpalko* (1980) 106 DLR (3d) 290; *Re Machin* (1980) 101 DLR (3d) 438.

8 *Re Donald, Moore v Somerset* [1909] 2 Ch 410; *Re Magrath, Histed v Queen's University of Belfast* [1913] 2 Ch 331; *Re Gray, Todd v Taylor* [1925] Ch 362; *Re Gordon* (1965) 52 DLR (2d) 197.

9 *Marsh v A-G* (1860) 2 John & H 61; *Re Ovey, Broadbent v Barrow* (1885) 29 Ch D 560 at 565; *Loscombe v Wintringham* (1850) 13 Beav 87; *Re Watt, Hicks v Hill* [1932] 2 Ch 243n.

10 *Re Mann, Hardy v A-G* [1903] 1 Ch 232; *Re Webster, Pearson v Webster* [1912] 1 Ch 106. But see *Kings v Bultitude* [2010] EWHC 1795 (Ch), [2010] WTLR 1581 where a testatrix's gift to an institution which came to an end on her death, since her activities were essential to its existence, failed, the evidence pointing to an intention on her part to make the gift dependent on the continued existence of the institution, and no general charitable intention being found.

11 *Sydney Homoeopathic Hospital v Turner* [1959] ALR 782.

12 *Re Slevin, Slevin v Hepburn* [1891] 2 Ch 236; *Re Wright, Blizard v Lockhart* [1954] 2 All ER 98 (where the purpose became impracticable after the testator's death); *Re Morrison, Wakefield v Falmouth* (1967) 111 Sol Jo 758; *Re Hunter* (1973) 34 DLR (3d) 602.

13 *Re Lucas, Sheard v Mellor* [1948] Ch 424, [1948] 2 All ER 22; distinguished in *Re Spence's Will Trusts, Ogden v Shackleton* [1978] 3 All ER 92, where, having regard to the fact that the testatrix had provided for the gift to be for the benefit of the patients of a specified home, the gift could not be added to the association's general endowment but was to be restricted by way of the scheme, to being used for the benefit of the patients for the time being of the specified home.

14 *Re Hutchinson's Will Trusts, Gibbons v Nottingham Area No 1, Hospital Management Committee* [1953] Ch 387, [1953] 1 All ER 996; *Re Abbott* (1974) 45 DLR (3d) 478; *Re MacAulay* (1971) 18 DLR (3d) 726; and *Re Boyd* (1969) 6 DLR (3d) 110.

15 *Re Boyd* (1969) 6 DLR (3d) 110.

16 *Re Slatter's Will Trusts, Turner v Turner* [1964] Ch 512, [1964] 2 All ER 469.

17 *Phillips v RSPB* [2012] EWHC 618 (Ch), [2012] WTLR 897.

[103.4]

[Updated in footnote 1 for the Charities Act 2011.
Updated in footnote 2 for *Phillips v RSPB* [2012] EWHC 618 (Ch), [2012] WTLR 897.]

Charity companies. Although traditionally charities are created as trusts, it is also possible for a charity to be constituted as a registered company.[1] A bequest to an incorporated body including a company charity prima facie, takes effect simply as a gift to that body beneficially as part of its general funds and without imposition of any trust.[2] If the body is incorporated for exclusively charitable purposes so that none of its funds could be used otherwise than for charitable purposes, then a change in the charity's mechanical aspect will not involve the charity ceasing to exist. In such case the law regards the charity, an abstract conception distinct from the institutional mechanism provided for holding and administering the fund of the charity, as the legatee, and so long as the charity as so conceived continues to exist the bequest will not lapse.[3] However it is possible for a testator or donor to introduce positive or express words in the gift to a charity company, importing a trust. In these circumstances, the charity company becomes a trustee of the gift made on trust and does not hold the fund representing the gift as part of its general property.[4] If such a charity company wishes to change or add to its purposes then the assets held on trust can only be altered by a *cy-près* scheme and those of the assets which form corporate property can only be varied by a change in the memorandum of association.[5]

1 Charities Act 2011, ss 1(1), 9(3).

2 Per Buckley J in *Re Vernon's Will Trusts, Lloyds Bank Ltd v Group 20, Hospital Management Committee,* noted [1972] Ch 300n at 303, [1971] 3 All ER 1061n at 1064; followed in *Re Finger's Will Trusts, Turner v Ministry of Health* [1972] Ch 286, [1971] 3 All ER 1050 (gift to a corporate body failed since there was no context in the will from which to imply a trust for carrying on of the work of the body; however it was possible to find a general charitable intention and the gift was applied *cy-près*). Considered in *Re ARMS (Multiple Sclerosis Research) Ltd, Alleyne v Attorney General* [1997] 2 All ER 679 where it was held that it could not be implied from the fact that the bequest was made to a company established for charitable purposes that the testator intended the company to take as trustee for charitable purposes. See also *Phillips v RSPB* [2012] EWHC 618 (Ch), [2012] WTLR 897 where the judge rejected the notion that a gift to an incorporated charity for its general purposes was impressed with a charitable purpose trust. Nevertheless, since the company was wound up after, rather than before the testatrix's death, the judge was able to apply the gift *cy-prés.*

3 Per Buckley J in *Re Vernon's Will Trusts*, see n 2 above, applying *Re Faraker, Faraker v Durell* [1912] 2 Ch 488, [1911–13] All ER Rep 488; and *Re Lucas, Sheard v Mellor* [1948] Ch 175, [1947] 2 All ER 773; revsd [1948] Ch 424, [1947] 2 All ER 773. Thus in *Re Vernon's Will Trusts, Lloyds Bank Ltd v Group 20, Hospital Management Committee,* noted [1972] Ch 300, [1971] 3 All ER 1061, a gift to a corporate body which was affected by the National Health Service Act 1946, and subsequently dissolved before the testatrix's death, did not fail but took effect in favour of the work of the charity as it was then being carried on; applied in *Liverpool and District Hospital for Diseases of the Heart v A-G* [1981] Ch 193, [1981] 1 All ER 994 (surplus assets of a charitable company applied *cy-près*).

4 Per Buckley J in *Re Vernon's Will Trusts*, see n 2 above. See the Report of the Charity Commissioners for England and Wales 1971, paras 22–30. A similar situation can arise also from the particular words used in an appeal made to the public for funds and expressed to be for particular purposes of the charity company.

5 Report of the Charity Commissioners for England and Wales 1971, para 28. It is obviously important that both alterations should have the same effect so that the purposes for which all the charity's assets may be applied will have been changed in the same way.

[103.5]

[Updated in the text and in footnote 2 for the Charities Act 2011.]

Unincorporated bodies. Every bequest to an unincorporated charity by name without more must take effect as a gift for a charitable purpose.[1] If the named charity ceases to exist in the testator's lifetime the gift will only fail if it is not preserved by the merger provisions of CA 2011[2] and the testator's intention is to make the gift dependent on the named charitable organisation being available at the time when the gift took effect to serve as the instrument for applying the subject matter of the gift to the charitable purposes for which it is by inference given.[3] But usually since the gift is per se a purpose trust, then if the work is still being carried on, effect will be given to it by way of a scheme, notwithstanding the disappearance of the donee in the lifetime of the testator.[4]

1 Per Buckley J in *Re Vernon's Will Trusts, Lloyds Bank Ltd v Group 20 Hospital Management Committee,* noted [1972] Ch 300n at 303, [1971] All ER 1061n at 1064; followed in *Re Finger's Will Trusts, Turner v Ministry of Health* [1972] Ch 286, [1971] 3 All ER 1050; and in *Re Morrison, Wakefield v Falmouth* (1967) 111 Sol Jo 758. This is because no individual or aggregate of individuals would claim to take such a bequest beneficially.

2 CA 2011, ss 305–314 (replacing CA 1993, ss 75C–75F). See para **[103.9]** below.

3 Per Buckley J in *Re Vernon's Will Trusts*, see n 1 above; see also *Re Ovey, Broadbent v Barrow* (1885) 29 Ch D 560; *Re Meyers, London Life Association v St George's Hospital* [1951] Ch 534, [1951] 1 All ER 538. Thus, in *Re Finger's Will Trusts, Turner v Ministry of Health* [1972] Ch 286, [1971] 3 All ER 1050, a gift to an unincorporated charity was a purpose trust for the work of the body which did not fail because there was no indication in the will to make that body of the essence of the gift and the work of the body had, since its dissolution, been carried on by the Secretary of State for Social Services; the gift was therefore valid and a scheme for its administration was settled; distinguishing *Re Harwood, Coleman v Innes* [1936] Ch 285, [1935] All ER Rep 918.

4 Per Goff J in *Re Finger's Will Trusts, Turner v Ministry of Health* [1972] Ch 286 at 295, [1971] 3 All ER 1050 at 1057.

[103.6]

[Updated in the text and in footnote 1 for the Charities Act 2011.]

Failure of particular intention. Where the intention is to benefit some particular charitable institution, or to accomplish some particular charitable purpose, then if circumstances render the carrying out impossible, and the gift is not preserved by the merger provisions of CA 2011,[1] then the gift fails and no *cy-près*[2] application is possible.[3] Where subscriptions are made and no intention can be inferred that the money should be returned on failure of the purpose, the funds are applied *cy-près*[4] but where return is possible such subscriptions must be returned though in some cases return is impossible.[5]

1 CA 2011, ss 305–314 (replacing CA 1993, ss 75C–75F). See para **[103.9]** below.

2 See para **[103.19]** below.

3 *Re Wilson, Twentyman v Simpson* [1913] 1 Ch 314; *Re Packe, Sanders v A-G* [1918] 1 Ch 437; *Re Stanford, Cambridge University v A-G* [1924] 1 Ch 73; *Re Blunt's Trusts, Wigan v Clinch* [1904] 2 Ch 767; *Re University of London Medical Sciences Institute Fund, Fowler v A-G* [1909] 2 Ch 1; *Re Good's Will Trusts, Oliver v Batten* [1950] 2 All ER 653; *Re Gwilym* [1952] VLR 282. But see *Re Hardy, Nelson v A-G* [1933] NI 150.

4 *Re Hillier, Hillier v A-G* [1954] 2 All ER 59.

5 *Re Ulverston and District New Hospital Building Trusts, Birkett v Barrow and Furness Hospital Management Committee* [1956] Ch 622, [1956] 3 All ER 164; *Re Gillingham Bus Disaster Fund, Bowman v Official Solicitor* [1958] Ch 300, [1958] 1 All ER 37. But see *Re West Sussex Constabulary's Widows, Children and Benevolent* (1930) *Fund Trusts, Barnett v*

Ketteringham [1971] Ch 1, [1970] 1 All ER 544 (amalgamation of police force so that original purpose of benevolent fund could not be carried out. It was held that money contributed by members of the fund and money obtained through entertainments, raffles, sweepstakes and collecting boxes, was bona vacantia; money contributed by members of the public by donation and legacies, was held on resulting trusts for the donors and their estates).

[103.9]

[Updated in the text and in the footnotes for the Charities Act 2011.
Updated in the text and in footnotes 7 and 10 for *Berry v IBS-STL (UK) Ltd* [2012] EWHC 666 (Ch), [2012] WTLR 1421.]

Amalgamation of institutions. Before the commencement of CA 1993, ss 75C–75F, now CA 2011, ss 305–314, amalgamation of institutions often did not affect the validity of a gift to one of them, which would be paid to the amalgamated institutions;[1] but the amalgamated institution might be put upon an undertaking to apply the gift for the purposes within the scope of the institution named in the will.[2] Where there were gifts to each of the amalgamated societies, the two legacies would be paid to the amalgamated institution[3] and where the gift was to the society and not expressed to be for its purposes, the gift could be applied by way of scheme or otherwise.[4] Although the objects of an amalgamated society are not identical with those of the named society yet if the general purposes of the named society were identifiable charitable purposes, then the bequest might be applied to those purposes by scheme or otherwise.[5] However, the problems which can be caused by charitable institutions merging with others or ceasing to operate and transferring funds to other charities are avoided where charities have merged and registered the merger in accordance with CA 2011, ss 305–314.[6] If this has been done, a gift which is expressed to be in favour of a charity which joined in the merger[7], and which takes effect after the date of the registration of the merger (typically this will be a gift in the will of someone dying after such registration), takes effect in favour of the resulting merged institution unless it is an 'excluded gift'.[8] It is an excluded gift for this purpose where the merged institution has not taken over the permanent endowment of a constituent charity, and the gift is intended to be held on the same trusts as some or all of that permanent endowment.[9] Where a testatrix gave her residuary estate to such of six named charities as were in existence at the date of her death, and one had merged before her death, it was held that since that named charity did not exist at her death, there was no gift to it, and so no gift to be transmuted by the statutory fiat into a gift to the new merged entity.[10]

1 *Re Adams, Harle v Adams* (1888) 4 TLR 757; *Re Faraker, Faraker v Durell* [1912] 2 Ch 488; *Re Pritt, Morton v National Church League* (1915) 85 LJ Ch 166; *Re Kappele* [1955] 1 DLR 29 (where the testator had executed several codicils after the amalgamation).

2 *Re Marchant, Weaver v Royal Society for the Prevention of Cruelty to Animals* (1910) 54 Sol Jo 425. It should be noted that in the case here cited the amalgamation took place 10 years before the date of the will. Most cases refer to amalgamations subsequent to the date of the will.

3 *Re Joy, Purday v Johnson* (1888) 60 LT 175. The fact that a dissolved society answers the testator's description better than an existing society does not prevent the latter taking so long as it sufficiently answers the description: *Coldwell v Holme* (1854) 2 Sm & G 31; *Re Magrath, Histed v Queen's University of Belfast* [1913] 2 Ch 331 (defunct institution reconstituted).

4 *Re Dawson's Will Trusts, National Provincial Bank Ltd v National Council of YMCA Inc* [1957] 1 All ER 177, [1957] 1 WLR 391.
5 *Re Roberts, Stenton v Hardy* [1963] 1 All ER 674, [1963] 1 WLR 406. See also *Re Bateman* 1972 SLT (Notes) 78.
6 Replacing CA 1993, ss 75C–75F.
7 For these purposes a gift includes not just a pecuniary legacy and a specific gift, but also a gift of residue or share of residue where a donee or a trustee is interposed with the obligation of conferring the benefit using the money (or property) provided by the benefactor: see *Berry v IBS-STL (UK) Ltd* [2012] EWHC 666 (Ch) at [8], [2012] WTLR 1421.
8 CA 2011, s 311(2) (replacing CA 1993, s 75F(2)).
9 CA 2011, ss 306(2), (3) and 311(3) (replacing CA 1993, ss 75C(5) and 75F(3)).
10 See *Berry v IBS-STL (UK) Ltd* [2012] EWHC 666 (Ch), [2012] WTLR 1421.

[103.11]

[Updated in footnote 1 for *Christian Brothers in Western Australia Inc v AG of Western Australia* [2007] WTLR 1375.]

Illegality or impossibility of purpose. Where a general charitable intention is expressed but the mode of carrying it out is illegal or impracticable, the intention is executed *cy-près*,[1] but if some of the purposes or some of the modes of application are illegal or impossible, the trust must be carried out for the purposes or in the modes not open to objection.[2] An immediate gift to charity is good although its application may not of necessity take effect within any reasonable limit of time, or may never take effect at all except on the occurrence of events in their essence contingent and uncertain.[3] Thus, bequests for building when the necessary sites have been obtained,[4] to endow a bishopric in case a bishop should be appointed,[5] to endow a church if erected,[6] or a bequest postponed until a licence in mortmain is obtained,[7] have been upheld. Where a gift is void as illegal or impossible, a secondary bequest for endowment of the charity also fails[8] unless there is a direction for its alternative application.[9] A gift to establish a charity on property not devoted to charity and of which the testator has no power to dispose, is void ab initio.[10] A gift with a total prohibition of sale or mortgage is valid in the case of a charity.[11]

1 *A-G v Vint* (1850) 3 De G & Sm 704 (legacy to provide intoxicating liquor); *Chamberlayne v Brockett* (1872) 8 Ch App 206 (legacy dependent on land being provided for almshouses); *Biscoe v Jackson* (1887) 35 Ch D 460 (violation of Mortmain Acts); *Bunting v Marriott* (1854) 19 Beav 163 (reduction of debt on chapel which was already paid off); *Re Wright, Blizard v Lockhart* [1954] Ch 347, [1954] 2 All ER 98 (founding a convalescent home); *Re Woodhams, Lloyds Bank Ltd v London College of Music* [1981] 1 All ER 202, [1981] 1 WLR 493, (music scholarship for orphans from named charitable homes already adequately provided for, applied *cy-près* by deleting restriction); *Re J W Laing Trust, Stewards' Co Ltd v A-G* [1984] Ch 143, [1984] 1 All ER 50; *Christian Brothers in Western Australia Inc v AG of Western Australia* [2007] WTLR 1375 (land devised for young men to establish farms was insufficient to support even one family).
2 *Hunter v A-G* [1899] AC 309 at 324; *Sinnett v Herbert* (1872) 7 Ch App 232; *Re Douglas, Obert v Barrow* (1887) 35 Ch D 472. 'If at any time it proves impracticable' includes an initial failure of the purpose: *Re Adams, Gee v Barnet Group Hospital Management Committee* [1968] Ch 80, [1967] 3 All ER 285, CA. If, however, the gift is repugnant to the Mortmain Act, it fails entirely: *Girdlestone v Creed* (1853) 10 Hare 480.
3 *Wallis v New Zealand Solicitor-General* [1903] AC 173; *Re Monk, Giffen v Wedd* [1927] 2 Ch 197; *Re Swan, Monkton v Hands* [1905] 1 Ch 669; *Re Pearse, Genn v Pearse* [1955] 1 DLR 801.
4 *Chamberlayne v Brockett* (1872) 8 Ch App 206 (almshouses); *Henshaw v Atkinson* (1818) 3 Madd 306 (school).

5 *A-G v Bishop of Chester* (1785) 1 Bro CC 444; *Society for Propagation of the Gospel v A-G* (1826) 3 Russ 142.
6 *Sinnett v Herbert* (1872) 7 Ch App 232.
7 *Abbott v Fraser* (1874) LR 6 PC 96.
8 *Edwards v Hall* (1853) 11 Hare 1; *Cramp v Playfoot* (1858) 4 K & J 479; *Re Taylor, Martin v Freeman* (1888) 58 LT 538; *Re Packe, Sanders v A-G* [1918] 1 Ch 437. But, if the principal gift is good and the secondary gift is void, the former stands: *A-G v Stepney* (1804) 10 Ves 22; *Blandford v Thackerell* (1793) 2 Ves 238.
9 *Faversham Corpn v Ryder* (1854) 5 De GM & G 350; *Dunn v Bownas* (1855) 1 K & J 596.
10 *A-G v Earl of Lonsdale* (1827) 1 Sim 105; *Hoare v Hoare* (1886) 56 LT 147; *Thomson v Shakespear* (1860) 1 De GF & J 399.
11 *Re Clark, Horwell v Dent* [1961] NZLR 635 following *Caldell v Fleming* [1927] NZLR 145.

[103.12]

[Updated in footnote 6 for *Re Harding, Gibbs v Harding* [2008] Ch 235.
Updated in the text and in the footnotes for the Equality Act 2010.]

Discrimination. Acts of discrimination against sections of the community[1] are now governed by the Equality Act 2010. This Act has replaced piecemeal legislation such as the Race Relations Act 1976 and the Sex Discrimination Act 1975 to provide a single code making it unlawful to discriminate against any person on the grounds of any 'protected characteristic', namely age (including retirement age), disability, gender reassignment, marriage and civil partnership, pregnancy and maternity, race, religion or belief, sex, and sexual orientation.[2] For the purposes of the Equality Act 2010, a person directly discriminates against another if because of a protected characteristic, such as race or sex, he treats that other less favourably than he treats or would treat others.[3] Further, he indirectly discriminates where he applies to another person a provision, criterion or practice which is discriminatory in relation to that other person's relevant protected characteristic.[4] The Act expressly refers to charities[5] and to a 'charitable instrument', which means an instrument establishing or governing a charity, including an instrument made or having effect before the commencement of the Act.[6] The Act differentiates between discrimination on the grounds of colour and discrimination on other grounds. A provision which is contained in a charitable instrument which provides for conferring benefits on persons of a class defined by reference to colour has effect for all purposes as if it provided for conferring the like benefits, (a) on persons of the class which results if the restriction by reference to colour is disregarded or, (b) where the original class is defined by reference to colour only, on persons generally.[7] Where though a charitable instrument provides for conferring benefits on persons sharing a protected characteristic (other than colour) then the Act is not contravened if it is a proportionate means of achieving a legitimate aim, or for the purpose of preventing or compensating for a disadvantage linked to the protected characteristic.[8] Thus charitable trusts which discriminate on the grounds of colour will be affected by the legislation but not trusts which discriminate in favour of a class defined otherwise than by reference to colour if it comes within specific exceptions.

1 For examples of discriminatory trusts before the anti-discriminatory legislation, see *Re Dominion Students' Hall Trusts* [1947] Ch 183 (colour bar); and *Re Lysaght, Hill v Royal College of Surgeons of England* [1966] Ch 191, [1965] 2 All ER 888 (exclusion of Roman Catholic or Jewish students from benefit).
2 Equality Act 2010, s 4. This came into force on 1 October 2010 by virtue of SI 2010/2317.

3 Equality Act 2010, s 13.
4 Equality Act 2010, s 19.
5 Equality Act 2010, ss 193–194. The Race Relations Act 1976, s 34 (repealed on 1 October 2010) and the Sex Discrimination Act 1975, s 43 (repealed on 1 October 2010) also so referred.
6 Equality Act 2010, s 194(4).
7 Equality Act 2010, s 193(4). In *Re Harding, Gibbs v Harding* [2008] Ch 235, [2007] 1 All ER 747, a gift to the Diocese of Westminster to hold in trust for the black community of Hackney, Haringey, Islington and Tower Hamlets took effect in accordance with RRA 1976, s 34(1) (the predecessor to Equality Act 2010, s 193(4)) as a gift to the Roman Catholic Diocese of Westminster on charitable trusts.
8 Equality Act 2010, ss 193(1), (2) and 194(2).

II. THE *CY-PRÈS* DOCTRINE

[103.18]

[Updated in footnote 1 for *Phillips v RSPB* [2012] EWHC 618 (Ch), [2012] WTLR 897. Updated in footnote 12 for the Charities Act 2011.]

Inherent jurisdiction. Where a clear charitable intention is expressed, it will not be permitted to fail because the mode, if specified, cannot be executed, but the law will, by directing a scheme to be prepared, substitute another mode *cy-près*,[1] that is, as near as possible to the mode specified by the testator[2] but it seems to be always in the discretion of the court whether or not in all the circumstances of the case it will order a scheme.[3] There can be no application *cy-près* until it is clear that the mode specified by the donor cannot be carried out,[4] and that the donor had a general charitable intention,[5] where the particular mode of application was the essence of the testator's intention[6] or where the gift is for a limited time and purpose which fails.[7] A condition or requirement attached to the gift can be removed by an approved scheme where it is shown to be impractical or manifestly undesirable.[8] The *cy-près* doctrine may be applied in the case of a charitable gift which has failed where the residue is given to charity,[9] even if there is a gift over to a second charity[10] but the gift over will be allowed to take effect where any possible scheme will not give effect to the testator's wishes.[11] Trustees cannot on their own authority apply the doctrine of *cy-près*. They must apply to and obtain the direction of the court.[12]

1 *Re Woodhams, Lloyds Bank Ltd v London College of Music* [1981] 1 All ER 202, [1981] 1 WLR 493 (particular charitable purpose expressed in will impractical; *cy-près* scheme settled). *Moggridge v Thackwell* (1803) 7 Ves 36 at 69; *Chamberlayne v Brockett* (1872) 8 Ch App 206; *Re Mitchner* [1922] St R Qd 39; *Re Mulcahy, Butler v Meagher* [1931] IR 239. In *Phillips v RSPB* [2012] EWHC 618 (Ch), [2012] WTLR 897 a *cy-prés* scheme was directed when an incorporated charity which was to receive a gift was dissolved following the testatrix's death.
2 *Re Avenon's Charity, A-G v Pelly* (1912) 106 LT 295.
3 *Re Hanbey's Will Trusts, Cutlers' Co v Christ's Hospital, London* [1956] Ch 264, [1955] 3 All ER 874.
4 *Re Weir Hospital* [1910] 2 Ch 124 at 132. This must be determined as at the testator's death; *Re Slevin, Slevin v Hepburn* [1891] 2 Ch 236, and *Re Wright, Blizard v Lockhart* [1954] Ch 347, [1954] 2 All ER 98.
5 *Biscoe v Jackson* (1887) 35 Ch D 460 at 465.
6 *Re Wilson, Twentyman v Simpson* [1913] 1 Ch 314 at 321; *Re Monk, Giffen v Wedd* [1927] 2 Ch 197 at 211; *Re Good's Will Trusts, Oliver v Batten* [1950] 2 All ER 653. As to

subscriptions, see *Re Hillier, Hillier v A-G* [1954] 2 All ER 59; *Re Gillingham Bus Disaster Fund, Bowman v Official Solicitor* [1958] Ch 300, [1958] 1 All ER 37.

7 *Re Cooper's Conveyance Trusts, Crewdson v Bagot* [1956] 3 All ER 28, [1956] 1 WLR 1096.

8 *Re Robinson, Wright v Tugwell* [1923] 2 Ch 332; *Re Dominion Students' Hall Trusts, Dominion Students' Hall Trust v A-G* [1947] Ch 183; *Re Lysaght, Hill v Royal College of Surgeons* [1966] Ch 191, [1965] 2 All ER 888; *Re J W Laing Trust, Stewards Co Ltd v A-G* [1984] Ch 143, [1984] 1 All ER 50.

9 *Lyons Corpn v Advocate-General of Bengal* (1876) 1 App Cas 91 at 115.

10 *Re Cunningham, Dulcken v Cunningham* [1914] 1 Ch 427.

11 *Re Hanbey's Will Trusts, Cutlers' Co v Christ's Hospital, London* [1956] Ch 264, [1955] 3 All ER 874.

12 *A-G v Coopers' Co* (1812) 19 Ves 187; *Re Campden Charities* (1881) 18 Ch D 310; *Cross v Lloyd–Greame* (1909) 102 LT 163. See Charities Act 2011, s 67 (replacing Charities Act 1993, s 16) and as to the duty of trustees to apply for a scheme, see Charities Act 2011, s 61 (replacing Charities Act 1993, s 13(5)): see para **[103.19]** below.

[103.19]

[Updated in the title and in the footnotes for the Charities Act 2011.]

Extended statutory powers of applying property *cy-près*. The circumstances in which the original purposes of a charitable gift can be altered to allow the property given or part of it to be applied *cy-près* are as follows.[1] (a) Where the original purposes, in whole or in part, (i) have been as far as may be fulfilled, or (ii) cannot be carried out, or not according to the directions given and to the spirit of the gift; or (b) where the original purposes provide a use for part only of the property available by virtue of the gift; or (c) where the property available by virtue of the gift and other property applicable for similar purposes can be more effectively used in conjunction, and to that end can suitably, regard being had to the spirit of the gift, be made applicable to common purposes; or (d) where the original purposes were laid down by reference to an area which then was but has since ceased to be a unit for some other purpose, or by reference to a class of persons or to an area which has for any reason since ceased to be suitable, regard being had to the spirit of the gift, or to be practical in administering the gift;[2] or (e) where the original purposes, in whole or in part, have, since they were laid down, (i) been adequately provided for by other means; or (ii) ceased, as being useless or harmful to the community or for other reasons, to be in law charitable; or (iii) ceased in any other way to provide a suitable and effective method of using the property available by virtue of the gift,[3] regard being had to the spirit of the gift. The above do not affect the conditions which must be satisfied in order that property given for charitable purposes may be applied *cy-près*, except in so far as those conditions require a failure of the original purposes. References to the original purposes of a gift are construed, where the application of the property given has been altered or regulated by a scheme or otherwise, as referring to the purposes for which the property is for the time being applicable.[4] Without prejudice to the above power to make schemes, the court may by scheme made under the court's jurisdiction with respect to charities, in any case where the purposes for which the property is held are laid down by reference to any local area, provide for enlarging that area.[5] A trust for charitable purposes places a trustee under a duty, where the case permits and requires the property or some part of it to be applied *cy-près*, to secure its effective use for charity by taking steps to enable it to be so applied.[6]

1 Charities Act 2011 (CA 2011), s 62, (replacing Charities Act 1993 (CA 1993), s 13, which came into force on 1 August 1993).
2 *Peggs v Lamb* [1994] Ch 172, [1994] 2 All ER 15, class enlarged from the freemen of the borough of Huntingdon, to the inhabitants as a whole.
3 *Re Lepton's Charity, Ambler v Thomas* [1972] Ch 276, [1971] 1 All ER 799 (direction in 1715 to pay £3 per annum; income now £791; scheme to pay £100 per annum approved); but see *Re J W Laing Trust, Stewards' Co Ltd v A-G* [1984] Ch 143, [1984] 1 All ER 50 (direction that fund be distributed within ten years of the settlor's death not part of the 'original purpose' of the gift within the meaning of the CA 2011, s 62(1) (replacing CA 1993, s 13(1)) and thus not within jurisdiction conferred by CA 2011, s 62(1)(e)(iii) (replacing CA 2011, s 13(1)(e)(iii)); condition removed under inherent jurisdiction.
4 CA 2011, s 62 (replacing CA 1993, s 13).
5 CA 2011, s 62 (replacing CA 1993, s 13).
6 CA 2011, s 62 (replacing CA 1993, s 13).

[103.20]

[Updated in the footnotes for the Charities Act 2011.]

Application *cy-près* of gifts of donors unknown or disclaiming. Property given for specific charitable purposes which fail is applicable *cy-près* as if given for charitable purposes generally, where it belongs – (a) to a donor who, after (i) the prescribed advertisements and inquiries have been published and made, and (ii) the prescribed period beginning with the publication of these advertisements has expired, cannot be identified or cannot be found; or (b) to a donor who has executed a disclaimer in the prescribed form of his right to have the property returned.[1] Where the prescribed advertisements and inquiries have been published and made by or on behalf of trustees with respect to any such property, the trustees shall not be liable to any person in respect of the property if no claim by him to be interested in it is received by them before the expiry of the period mentioned in the subsection above.[2] Property is conclusively presumed (without any advertisement or inquiry) to belong to donors who cannot be identified, in so far as it consists – (a) of the proceeds of cash collections made by means of collecting boxes or by other means not adapted for distinguishing one gift from another; or (b) of the proceeds of any lottery, competition, entertainment, sale or similar money-raising activity, after allowing for property given to provide prizes or articles for sale or otherwise to enable the activity to be undertaken. The court may by order direct that property shall be treated (without any advertisement or inquiry) as belonging to donors who cannot be identified, where it appears to the court either – (a) that it would be unreasonable, having regard to the amounts likely to be returned to the donors, to incur expense with a view to returning the property; or (b) that it would be unreasonable, having regard to the nature, circumstances and amounts of the gifts, and to the lapse of time since the gifts were made, for the donors to expect the property to be returned.[3] Where property is thus applied *cy-près* the donor is deemed to have parted with all his interest at the time when the gift was made; but where property is so applied as belonging to donors who cannot be identified or cannot be found, and is not applied as above – (a) the scheme shall specify the total amount of that property; and (b) the donor of any part of that amount shall be entitled, if he makes a claim not later than six months after the date on which the scheme is made, to recover from the charity for which the property is applied a sum equal to that part, less any expenses properly incurred by the charity trustees after that date in connection with claims relating to his gift; and (c) the scheme may include directions as to the provision to be made for meeting any such claim.[4]

Charitable purposes are deemed to 'fail' where any difficulty in applying property to those purposes makes that property or the part not applicable *cy-près*, available to be returned to the donors.[5]

1 CA 2011, ss 63–65 (replacing CA 1993, s 14).
2 CA 2011, s 63(2) (replacing CA 1993, s 14(2)).
3 CA 2011, s 64(1), (2) (replacing CA 1993, s 14(3), (4)). For the pre-statutory position see *Re Hillier, Hillier v A-G* [1954] 2 All ER 59; *Re North Devon and West Somerset Relief Fund Trusts, Hylton v Wright* [1953] 2 All ER 1032, [1953] 1 WLR 1260; *Re Gillingham Bus Disaster Fund* [1958] Ch 300, [1958] 1 All ER 37; affd [1959] Ch 62, [1958] 2 All ER 749, CA.
4 CA 2011, s 63(3), (4), (5) (replacing CA 1993, s 14(5).
5 CA 2011, s 66(1) (replacing CA 1993, s 14(7)).

[103.21]

[Updated in the text and in the footnotes for the Charities Act 2011.]

Application of *cy-près* of gifts made in response to certain solicitations. The Charities Act 2011, ss 65–66[1] provides rules governing the application of property *cy-près* which had been given for a specific charitable purpose and in response to a solicitation as defined.[2]

1 Replacing CA 1993, s 14A (which was added to CA 1993 by CA 2006, s 17).
2 CA 2011, 65(2) (replacing CA 1993, s 14A(2)).

[103.22]

[Updated in the text and in the footnotes for the Charities Act 2011.]

***Cy-près* schemes.** The Charities Act 2011, s 67 [1] governs *cy-près* schemes. The powers of the court or the Commission to make schemes for the application of property *cy-près* shall be exercised in accordance with the new section.[2]

1 Replacing CA 1993, s 14B.
2 See CA 2011, s 67(1)–(6) (replacing CA 1993, s 14B(1)–(6)).

[103.23]

[Updated in the text and in the footnotes for the Charities Act 2011.]

Charities Acts 1993, 2006 and 2011. The regulatory provisions of the Charities Act 1993 (CA 1993) were greatly added to and strengthened by the Charities Act 2006, and are now consolidated in the Charities Act 2011 (CA 2011). These mainly administrative and regulatory aspects of the law are beyond the scope of this text to discuss in detail. They reflect the increased size and activities of the charitable sector and the problems that had become apparent as charities had become more involved with the mainstream of social welfare provision. The new statutory law strengthens the supervisory role of the Charity Commissioners, and includes measures to control the activities of professional fund raisers and for the control of public charitable collections. It recognises the changed significance and characteristics of modern charities and has modernised, enlarged and strengthened the administrative supervision of charities by providing a new comprehensive regime for the regulation of charities. The role, function and responsibilities of the Charity Commissioners and the Charity Appeal Tribunal have been addressed and expanded.

It can be noted that CA 2011, ss 267–274 deal with the problems posed by small charities.[1] These sections apply to a charity if (a) its gross income in its last financial year did not exceed GBP 10,000; (b) it does not hold any designated land; and (c) it is not a company or other body corporate.[2] In such cases the charity trustees may resolve that all the property of the charity should be transferred to another charity or charities.[3]

1 Replacing CA 1993, s 74.
2 CA 2011, s 267(1) (replacing CA 1993, s 74(1)).
3 CA 2011, s 268(1) (replacing CA 1993, s 74(2)).

PART O

Intestacy

CHAPTER 104

Intestacy

I. TOTAL INTESTACY

[104.2]

[Updated for the increases in the fixed net sum from 1 February 2009.]

Entitlement: the spouse or civil partner. The succession to real and personal estate on intestacy is governed by the table of distribution in the Administration of Estates Act 1925 (AEA 1925), s 46.[1] The original wording of section 46 referred to 'a husband or wife', but with effect from 5 December 2005 the Civil Partnership Act 2004 has substituted the word 'spouse' and added 'or civil partner' throughout the section.[2] In the case of the death of a person intestate on or after 1 January 1996 all the rights of the intestate's spouse or civil partner are contingent on the spouse or civil partner surviving the intestate by 28 days.[3] There is no such contingency where the death occurs before that date. Where the intestate leaves a spouse or civil partner[4] and no issue, no parent or brother or sister of the whole blood or issue of a brother or sister of the whole blood, then the residuary estate is held in trust for the surviving spouse or civil partner absolutely.[5] Where the intestate leaves a spouse or civil partner and issue then the surviving spouse or civil partner takes the personal chattels absolutely;[6] a fixed net sum, currently (in relation to deaths on or after 1 February 2009) of £250,000,[7] and subject thereto the residuary estate is held as to one-half upon trust for the surviving spouse or civil partner and subject thereto on the statutory trusts for the issue of the intestate;[8]and as to the other half, on the statutory trusts for the issue of the intestate.[9] Where the intestate leaves a spouse or civil partner, no issue, but either a parent, or a brother or sister of the whole blood or issue of a brother or sister of the whole blood, then the surviving spouse or civil partner takes the personal chattels absolutely;[10] a fixed net sum, currently (in relation to deaths on or after 1 February 2009) of £450,000[11] and subject thereto the residuary estate is held as to one-half in trust for the surviving spouse or civil partner absolutely:[12] and as to the other half, where the intestate leaves one or both parents then in trust for the parent absolutely or, as the case may be, for the two parents in equal shares absolutely;[13]or where the intestate leaves no parent, on the statutory trusts for the brothers and sisters of the whole blood of the intestate.[14]

1 As amended in the case of deaths on or after 1 January 1953 by the Intestates' Estates Act 1952; in the case of deaths on or after 1 January 1967 by the Family Provision Act 1966; in the case of deaths on or after 1 January 1970 by the Family Law Reform Act 1969 and in the case of deaths on or after 1 January 1996 by the Law Reform (Succession) Act 1995. In

the case of deaths on or after 5 December 2005, by the Civil Partnership Act 2004. See Vol 2, Part G, paras **[244.62]** ff. The amount of the fixed net sum or statutory legacy has been progressively increased subsequent to 1967 by statutory instrument; see para **[104.5]** below.

2 Civil Partnership Act 2004, ss 71 and 263(2); Sch 4, para 7. See para **[104.3]** below.

3 AEA 1925, s 46(2A) inserted by Law Reform (Succession) Act 1995, s 1(1) and printed in Vol 2, Part G, para **[244.62]**.

4 Civil Partnership Act 2004, ss 71 and 263(2); Sch 4, para 7. The presumption in the Law of Property Act 1925, s 184 does not apply so that in a commorientes situation neither party is presumed to have survived the other; AEA 1925, s 46(3): see Vol 2, Part G, para **[244.62]**. In relation to deaths on or after 1 January 1996 this provision is largely superseded by the 28-day survivorship contingency (see above).

5 AEA 1925, s 46(1)(i)(1).

6 See para **[104.4]** below.

7 See para **[104.5]** below; see *Re Collens, Royal Bank of Canada (London) Ltd v Krogh* [1986] Ch 505, [1986] 1 All ER 611 concerning the entitlement of the spouse to the statutory legacy where he/she was also entitled to movable property in another jurisdiction.

8 See para **[104.5]** below.

9 AEA 1925, s 46(1)(i), (2).

10 See para **[104.4]** below.

11 See para **[104.5]** below.

12 AEA 1925, s 46(1)(i), (3)(a).

13 AEA 1925, s 46(1)(i), (3)(b)(i).

14 AEA 1925, s 46(1)(i), (3)(b)(ii).

[104.5]

[Updated for the increases in the fixed net sum from 1 February 2009.]

The fixed net sum. The amount to which the spouse or civil partner is entitled as a fixed net sum was initially fixed in 1925 as £1,000.[1] The Intestate's Estates Act 1952 increased the amount to £5,000, where there were issue surviving, and to £20,000, where there were no issue but specified relatives, with effect from 1 January 1953.[2] The Family Provision Act 1966 increased the amounts further, to £8,750 and to £30,000 respectively, with effect from 1 January 1967 and provided that henceforth the amounts should be increased by statutory instrument.[3] This has been done on six subsequent occasions of which the first five are: in the case of deaths on or after 1 July 1972 the entitlement was to £15,000 and £40,000 respectively;[4] in the case of deaths on or after 15 March 1977, the entitlement was to £25,000 and to £55,000 respectively;[5] in respect of deaths on or after 1 March 1981 the entitlement was to £40,000 and to £85,000 respectively;[6] in respect of deaths on or after 1 June 1987 to £75,000 and £125,000 respectively;[7] in respect of deaths on or after 1 December 1993, £125,000 and £200,000 respectively.[8] The current figures, in respect of deaths on or after 1 February 2009, are £250,000 and £450,000 respectively.[9] The absolute entitlement (in effect) to the statutory legacy (or the fixed net sum as it is more properly called) is often used to effect an appropriation of the matrimonial home under the Intestates' Estates Act 1952, Second Schedule, and the fixed net sum has been increased from time to time since 1981.[10] The sum carries interest at 6 per cent per annum from the date of death.[11]

1 AEA 1925, s 46(1)(i). In all cases, which was itself an increase on the £500 entitlement under the Intestates' Estates Act 1890.

2 AEA 1925, s 1(2).

3 Family Provision Act 1966, s 1.

4 Family Provision (Intestate Succession) Order 1972, SI 1972/96.

5 Family Provision (Intestate Succession) Order 1977, SI 1977/415.
6 Family Provision (Intestate Succession) Order 1981, SI 1981/255.
7 Family Provision (Intestate Succession) Order 1987, SI 1987/799.
8 Family Provision (Intestate Succession) Order 1993, SI 1993/2906.
9 Family Provision (Intestate Succession) Order 2009, SI 2009/135.
10 As to possible double entitlement where a foreign domicile is involved see *Re Collens, Royal Bank of Canada (London) v Krogh* [1986] Ch 505, [1986] 1 All ER 611 applying *Re Rea, Rea v Rea* [1902] 1 IR 451 and *Re Ralston* [1906] VLR 689.
11 Intestate Succession (Interest and Capitalisation) Order 1983 (Amendment) Order 1983, SI 1983/1374 with effect from 1 October 1983. The rate was previously 7 per cent with effect from 15 September 1977, SI 1977/1491; and before that date it was 4 per cent per annum, Intestate's Estates Act 1952, reducing the original rate of 5 per cent in the AEA 1925, in respect of deaths on or after 1 January 1953.

[104.6]

[Updated in footnote 1 for the new capitalisation tables effective on 1 February 2009.]

Redemption and appropriation. Where the surviving spouse or civil partner is entitled to a life interest in part of the residuary estate, he or she may elect to have the life interest purchased or redeemed by the personal representatives and thus receive the capitalised value instead.[1] The Intestates' Estates Act 1952[2] conferred a right on the surviving spouse to require the personal representatives to appropriate[3] the matrimonial home in or towards satisfaction of any absolute interest in the intestacy.[4] The right has now been extended to registered civil partners.[5]

1 AEA 1925, s 47A, added by the Intestates' Estates Act 1952, s 2(b) (see Vol 2, Part G, para **[244.64]**). For the method of ascertaining the capital value, see Intestate Succession (Interest and Capitalisation) Order 1977, SI 1977/1491, as amended, with effect from 1 February 2009, by Intestate Succession (Interest and Capitalisation) (Amendment) Order 2008. See Vol 2, Part G, para **[244.90]** ff. The amendments made by the latter Order, which allow for changes in government stocks, interest rates, and expectation of life since the previous Order was made, are not restricted to applying in relation to deaths on or after 1 February 2009, and apparently will apply to any redemption of a life interest which is elected for on or after that date.
2 See s 5 of and the Second Schedule to the Intestates' Estates Act 1952 as amended (see Vol 2, Part G, paras **[244.73]**, **[244.75]**).
3 In exercise of the power in the Administration of Estates Act 1925, s 41.
4 See *Re Phelps, Wells v Phelps* [1980] Ch 275, [1979] 3 All ER 373; *Robinson v Collins* [1975] 1 All ER 321, sub nom *Re Collins, Robinson v Collins* [1975] 1 WLR 309.
5 AEA 1952, s 5 and Sch 2 (rights of surviving spouse as respects the matrimonial home) have been amended by CPA 2004, Sch 4, para 13 (see Vol 2, Part G, paras **[244.73]**, **[244.75]**), to include civil partner (with spouse) and civil partnership (with marriage or matrimonial).

[104.7]

[Updated in the text and footnote 9 for Human Fertilisation and Embryology Act 2008.]

Entitlement of issue. Where the intestate leaves a surviving spouse or civil partner and issue then the spouse or civil partner has the primary entitlement as set out above.[1] Subject to the spouse's or civil partner's entitlement to the personal chattels, and to the fixed net sum, and to a life interest in one-half of the residuary estate, the estate is held on the statutory trusts for the issue.[2] In the case of one-half of the estate this is an interest in remainder after the spouse's or civil partner's life interest; in the case of the other half it is an immediate interest.[3] Where the intestate leaves issue but no spouse or civil partner, the residuary estate is held on the statutory trusts for the issue of the intestate.[4]

Leaving issue means leaving issue who attain an absolute vested interest.[5] Issue means children and grandchildren and more remote descendants,[6] and includes legitimated, adopted and illegitimate persons[7] and children en ventre sa mère at the death.[8] It also includes any person who counts as a descendant by having the deceased or a descendant of the deceased as a parent by virtue of the Human Fertilisation and Embryology Act 1990 or 2008.[9]

1 See para **[104.3]** above.
2 AEA 1925, s 46(1)(i), (2).
3 But possibly contingent, see para **[104.12]** below.
4 AEA 1925, s 46(1)(ii).
5 AEA 1925, s 47(2)(c).
6 See Chapter 76.
7 Legitimacy Act 1976, s 5(2); Adoption Act 1976, s 46(4); Adoption and Children Act 2002 ss 67, 68; and Family Law Reform Act 1987, ss 1 and 18 (replacing the more restricted provisions of Family Law Reform Act 1969, s 14), all of which are printed in Vol 2, Part G, para **[245.1]** ff. See Chapters 72 and 75.
8 AEA 1925, s 55(2), printed at Vol 2, Part G, para **[246.67]**. It is not possible in this section to discuss the meaning of issue for the purposes of intestate succession in any greater detail; see Chapter 76.
9 See paras **[74.3]**, **[74.5]** above.

[104.8]

[Updated in the text and footnotes 4, 5, 9 and 12 for the Estates of Deceased Persons (Forfeiture Rule and Law of Succession) Act 2011 ('EDP(FRLS)A 2011').]

The statutory trusts. Issue take on intestacy on the statutory trusts, which are defined in the AEA 1925, s 47. These trusts are not discussed in detail in this section but one or two points can be noted. First, children take in equal shares;[1] secondly, they take vested interests when they attain the age of eighteen years or marry or form a civil partnership under that age;[2] thirdly, issue take per stirpes, through all degrees, 'the share which their parent would have taken if living at the death of the intestate, and so that no issue shall take whose parent is living at the death of the intestate and so capable of taking'.[3] However, in relation to the estates of persons dying on or after 1 February 2012[4], if a person 'P' who is issue of the intestate is living at the intestate's death, and then dies under the age of 18 unmarried and not having formed a civil partnership, but leaving issue, P is treated as having died immediately before the intestate[5], with the consequence that his or her issue are enabled to share under the statutory trusts. The statutory powers of maintenance and advancement apply.[6] In relation to deaths before 1 January 1996 children must account for any inter vivos advancements in order to achieve equality of total shares between the class of children.[7] This requirement is abolished in relation to deaths on or after that date.[8]

In relation to the estates of persons dying on or after 1 February 2012[9], if any issue are disqualified from taking because he or she has unlawfully killed the intestate[10] or has disclaimed the interest[11], he or she is treated as having predeceased the intestate[12].

1 AEA 1925, s 47(1)(i).
2 AEA 1925, s 47(1)(i), as amended by the Family Law Reform Act 1969, s 3(2), in the case of deaths on or after 1 January 1970 (in the case of deaths before that date issue took a vested interest at the age of 21 years.
3 AEA 1925, s 47(1)(i).

4 EDP(FRLS)A 2011, s 4(2), (4), and EDP(FRLS)A 2011 (Commencement) Order 2011, SI 2011/2913.
5 AEA 1925, s 47(4B)–(4D) (see para **[244.63]**), inserted by EDP(FRLS)A 2011, s 3.
6 AEA 1925, s 47(1)(ii).
7 AEA 1925, s 47(1)(iii); grandchildren taking their parents' share must account for any advancements received by that child, but do not account for benefits made to them.
8 Law Reform (Succession) Act 1995, s 1(2)(a).
9 EDP(FRLS)A 2011, s 4(2), (4), and EDP(FRLS)A 2011 (Commencement) Order 2011, SI 2011/2913.
10 See para **[9.13]** ff.
11 See para **[46.1]** ff.
12 AEA 1925, s 46A (see para **[244.62A]**) and s 47(1)(i) and (4A) (see para **[244.63]**), amended or inserted by EDP(FRLS)A 2011, s 1.

[104.9]

[Updated in footnotes 2 and 3 for Human Fertilisation and Embryology Act 2008. Updated in footnotes 8 and 9 and in the text for the Estates of Deceased Persons (Forfeiture Rule and Law of Succession) Act 2011 ('EDP(FRLS)A 2011').]

Entitlement of other relatives. It has been seen above that a parent or parents, or brother or sister of the whole blood or issue of a brother or sister of the whole blood, have some entitlement where there is also a surviving spouse.[1] In other cases the entitlement of relatives other than the spouse and issue is set out in the order prescribed by the AEA 1925, s 46(1).[2]

If the intestate leaves no spouse or civil partner and no issue but both parents, then the residuary estate of the intestate is held in trust for the father[3] and mother in equal shares absolutely.

If the intestate leaves no spouse or civil partner no issue but one parent, then the residuary estate of the intestate is held in trust for the surviving father[4] or mother absolutely.

If the intestate leaves no spouse or civil partner and no issue and no parents, then the residuary estate of the intestate is held in trust for the following persons living at the death of the intestate, and in the following order and manner, namely:

First, on the statutory trusts for the brothers and sisters of the whole blood of the intestate; but if no person takes an absolutely vested interest under such trusts; then

Secondly, on the statutory trusts for the brothers and sisters of the half blood of the intestate; but if no person takes an absolutely vested interest under such trusts; then

Thirdly, for the grandparents of the intestate and, if more than one survive the intestate, in equal shares; but if there is no member of this class; then

Fourthly, on the statutory trusts for the uncles and aunts of the intestate (being brothers or sisters of the whole blood of a parent of the intestate[5] but if no person takes an absolutely vested interest under such trusts; then

Fifthly, on the statutory trusts for the uncles and aunts of the intestate (being brothers or sisters of the half blood of a parent of the intestate).

If the person or persons who are prima facie entitled in priority fail to take by reason of disclaimer,[6] or the public policy rule,[7] the persons entitled are the next class of qualifying relatives, who, in relation to deaths on or after 1 February 2012[8], qualify on the basis that the person disqualified is treated as having predeceased the intestate[9].

1 AEA 1925, s 46(1)(i), (3).
2 References to parents, brothers, sisters, etc have to be read subject to the adoption and legitimation legislation, the Family Law Reform Act 1987, ss 1, 18(1) in the case of deaths on or after 4 April 1988, and subject to HFEA 1990 and 2008 in relation to children born as a result of assisted reproduction techniques within either Act. See Chapters 72 and 75, and para **[74.3]** ff above.
3 There is a rebuttable presumption that the father of an illegitimate person (or any person claiming through the father) predeceased him: Family Law Reform Act 1987, s 18(2): see Vol 2, Part G, para **[245.71]**. The same applies to a female second parent of a child by virtue of HFEA 2008, s 43: see FLRA 1987, s 18(2A) inserted by HFEA 2008, Sch 6, para 25. For HFEA 2008, s 43 see para **[74.5]** above.
4 See n 3, above.
5 In *Re Patrick's Estate, Patrick v De Zeeuw* [2000] NI 506 a paternal uncle and a maternal aunt of the deceased intestate had married each other and had issue, and had not survived the intestate. It was held that the issue were entitled to claim shares under both stirpes.
6 See para **[46.1]** ff.
7 See para **[9.13]** ff.
8 EDP(FRLS)A 2011, s 4(2), (4), and EDP(FRLS)A 2011 (Commencement) Order 2011, SI 2011/2913.
9 AEA 1925, s 46A (see para **[244.62A]**), inserted by EDP(FRLS)A 2011, s 1. This reverses the effect of *Re DWS, Re EHS, TWGS v JMG* [2000] 2 All ER 83; affd [2001] 1 All ER 97. The latter decision held that the disqualified person is not treated as if he predeceased the intestate. EDP(FRLS)A 2011 gives effect to the recommendations of the Law Commission Report, No 295, 'The Forfeiture Rule and the Law of Succession' to deal with the anomaly in the intestacy rules revealed by the *Re DWS* decision. See also paras **[9.17]** and **[48.8]**.

PART P

Family provision

CHAPTER 105

Family provision

I. THE JURISDICTION

[105.5]

[Updated in footnote 6 for *Re Baker, Baker v Baker* [2008] WTLR 581.]

Time for application. Applications under the I(PFD)A 1975 should be made before the end of the period of six months from the date on which representation in regard to the estate of the deceased is first taken out.[1] The six-month period was also applicable under the Inheritance (Family Provision) Act 1938 and some of the decisions on that Act might still assist under the I(PFD)A 1975. Thus it was decided that the six-month period ran from the date of the grant of probate in common form and that no further period was initiated by a subsequent grant in solemn form.[2] If a grant of administration was revoked and a grant of probate made, the period ran from the date of the grant of probate.[3] Provided the originating summons was issued within six months, it was immaterial that it was not served within that time.[4] The court had power to order provision to be made as from a future date and could direct that the summons should stand over until a given date with liberty to all parties to apply in the meantime if circumstances should so require.[5]

An application should not be made before a grant of probate has been obtained and may be struck out as premature[6] but if a grant is obtained before the hearing and no objection on the ground of irregularity has been made before that time the application will be heard.[7]

The court has, however, power to permit applications to be made after six months.[8] The circumstances in which the court will permit an application for financial provision under the I(PFD)A 1975, to be made out of time, were considered in *Re Salmon*.[9] In that case permission to apply out of time under the I(PFD)A 1975, s 4 was refused for the following reasons; first, the delay was substantial and was wholly the applicant's fault; second, there had been no negotiations with, and no warning to, the executor during the six-month period;[10] third, almost all the estate had been distributed;[11] fourth, the applicant probably had a remedy in negligence against her solicitors;[12] fifth, it would in the circumstances have been unjust to the beneficiaries to grant the extension.

A similar application was also dismissed in *Re Dennis*,[13] where the court thought that a crucial factor in such cases was whether the applicant was able to satisfy the court that he had an arguable case that he was entitled to reasonable financial provision out of the estate.

1 I(PFD)A 1975, s 4; which must mean time begins to run from the date on which effective or valid representation was first taken out; *Re Freeman* [1984] 3 All ER 906, [1980] 1 WLR 1419 (probate revoked and letters of administration granted). In *Re Johnson* [1987] CLY 3882 it was held that time ran under the I(PFD)A 1975, s 4, not from the date of a limited grant, but from the date of the general grant.

2 *Re Miller, Miller v de Courcey* [1968] 3 All ER 844, [1969] 1 WLR 583.

3 *Re Bidie, Bidie v General Accident, Fire and Life Assurance Corpn Ltd* [1949] Ch 121, [1948] 2 All ER 995.

4 *Re Chittenden, Chittenden v Doe* [1970] 3 All ER 562, [1970] 1 WLR 1618.

5 *Re Franks, Franks v Franks* [1948] Ch 62, [1947] 2 All ER 638.

6 *Re McBroom* [1992] 2 FLR 49: the presence of some person entitled to administer the estate of the deceased was necessary. Cf. *Re Searle, Searle v Siems* [1949] Ch 73, [1948] 2 All ER 426, a decision under the Inheritance (Family Provision) Act 1938 (repealed): where a grant of representation had been obtained before trial, the objection was merely procedural and could not be taken at trial. The position is unsatisfactory: *Re Searle* was not cited in *Re McBroom* and see *Re Dawkins, Dawkins v Judd* [1986] 2 FLR 360: final order made before grant of representation taken out. In *Re Baker, Baker v Baker* [2008] WTLR 581 in which an I(PFD)A 1975 claim was made in conjunction with a probate claim, the judge, having found that the deceased died intestate so that the claimant had the right to apply for a grant of letters of administration, ruled, with the agreement of the parties, on the question of the I(PFD)A 1975 before the grant of representation had been obtained.

7 *Re Searle, Searle v Siems* [1949] Ch 73, [1948] 2 All ER 426.

8 Recognised as a power of the court in the I(PFD)A 1975, s 4.

9 *Re Salmon, Coard v National Westminster Bank Ltd* [1981] Ch 167, [1980] 3 All ER 532. For cases on the Inheritance (Family Provision) Act 1938, s 2(1A) see the seventh edition of this work.

10 See also *Re Ruttie, Ruttie v Saul* [1969] 3 All ER 1633, [1970] 1 WLR 89; *Re McNare, McNare v McNare* [1964] 3 All ER 373, [1964] 1 WLR 1255. An extension was granted where the delay was caused by the expectation that the executors would commence proceedings for the construction of the will and that the result of those proceedings might be materially to affect the provision to be made: *Re Bone, Bone v Midland Bank Ltd* [1955] 2 All ER 555, [1955] 1 WLR 703.

11 Distribution alone may not defeat an application if the beneficiaries have not changed their position: *Re Salmon* [1981] Ch 167 at 176C-D, [1980] 3 All ER 532 at 538a; *Re Longley, Longley and Longley v Longley* [1981] CLY 2885.

12 *See Re Gonin, Gonin v Garmeson* [1979] Ch 16, [1977] 2 All ER 720; *Re C* [1995] 2 FLR 24. A prospective claim in negligence against the claimant's own solicitors is not to be totally ignored but is not a factor of any great importance and does not counterbalance other important factors: *Adams v Adams* (12 November 1993, unreported), CA. A solicitor's ignorance of the limited time in which application might be made was not a circumstance which would justify an extension: *Re Greaves, Greaves v Greaves* [1954] 2 All ER 109, [1954] 1 WLR 760.

13 *Re Dennis, Dennis v Lloyds Bank Ltd* [1981] 2 All ER 140. See also *Re Longley* [1981] CLY 2885 and *Re Gonin, Gonin v Garmeson* [1979] Ch 16, sub nom *Re Gonin, Gonin v Garmeson* [1977] 2 All ER 720 (where the delay was 2.5 years and permission was refused since the vital dates were under the control of the plaintiff). Extensions were granted in *Stock v Brown* [1994] 2 FCR 1125 (delay of 5.5 years but applicant had no independent advice and there was no prejudice to other beneficiaries); *Re W (a minor)* [1995] 2 FCR 689 (child would otherwise suffer); *Re C* [1995] 2 FLR 24; (delay of 18 months, substantial estate and very strong claim); *Re W (a minor)* [1995] 2 FCR 689; *Re Abram* [1996] 2 FLR 379 (six months late) and in *Re B* [2000] 1 All ER 665 (court of appeal followed exercise of discretion by master and judge).

II. THE APPLICANTS

[105.9]

[Updated in footnote 10 for *P v G* [2004] EWHC 2944 (Fam), [2006] 1 FLR 431 and *Iqbal v Ahmed* [2011] EWCA Civ 900, [2011] WTLR 2010 (CA). Also updated at the end of footnote 10 more generally. Updated in footnote 12 for *P v E* [2007] WTLR 691. Also updated in footnote 13 for *Re Baker, Baker v Baker* [2008] 2 FLR 1956 and *Aston v Aston* [2007] WTLR 1349. Updated in footnote 14 for *Lilleyman v Lilleyman* [2012] EWHC 821 (Ch), [2012] WTLR 1033. Updated in footnote 15 for *Hope v Knight* [2010] EWHC 3443 (Ch), [2011] WTLR 583.]

The spouse. The specified class of persons who have locus standi to apply under the I(PFD)A 1975 includes the spouse of the deceased, formerly 'the wife or husband of the deceased'.[1] The applicant would thus have to prove that he or she was the deceased's spouse under a subsisting marriage at the date of the death. A judicially separated spouse can apply under this heading but provision is limited to maintenance.[2] Also included is a person who, in good faith, entered into a void marriage with the deceased, unless either the marriage of the deceased and that person was dissolved or annulled during the lifetime of the deceased, or that person has during the lifetime of the deceased entered into a later marriage.[3] Likewise, a party to a voidable marriage which has not been annulled before the death of the party is included.[4] In *Re Sehota, Surjit Kaur v Gian Kaur*,[5] the deceased had contracted two marriages at a time when all parties concerned had had Indian domiciles of origin and both marriages were valid under Indian law. The deceased had left the whole of his residuary estate to his second wife and it was held that the first wife was entitled to claim under the I(PFD)A 1975 despite the fact that the marriage was polygamous.

The I(PFD)A 1975 made an important change in the law so far as the standard of provision for a spouse is concerned. The Inheritance (Family Provision) Act 1938 set the standard of 'reasonable provision for the maintenance' of the applicant, whereas in divorce proceedings the court is not limited to any such standard.[6]

The Law Commission[7] recommended that the surviving spouse should have a claim upon the family assets at least equivalent to that of a divorced spouse. Accordingly, the I(PFD)A 1975, s 1(2)(a) provides:

> 'In this Act "reasonable financial provision"—
>
> (a) in the case of an application made by virtue of subsection (1)(a) above by the husband or wife of the deceased (except where the marriage with the deceased was the subject of a decree of judicial separation and at the date of death the decree was in force and the separation was continuing), means such financial provision as it would be reasonable in all the circumstances of the case for a husband or wife to receive, whether or not that provision is required for his or her maintenance.'

The court is instructed to have regard to what provision would have been awarded in divorce proceedings,[8] but this is not to be regarded as the sole criterion. The overriding consideration is what is reasonable in the circumstances.[9] Further it has been pointed out in a later case that the amount that might be awarded under the Matrimonial Causes Act 1973 is not analogous to the position on death, since an award under the former would have to take into account the husband's likely future needs.[10] Nevertheless this stated requirement of the Act in determining the level of provision for a surviving spouse, has been applied by the Court of Appeal. The intention of the Act was that the acceptable minimum posthumous provision for a surviving spouse should correspond as closely as possible to the inchoate rights enjoyed by that spouse during the deceased's lifetime under matrimonial law.[11] A successful application was made by a widow (competing against adult children) in *Singer v Isaac*.[12] The case raised several interesting points. In determining the amount of the award, the court had regard to the applicant's age, the length of the marriage and her contribution to it. An important factor was the divorce standard which was referred to, to determine the amount of the award.[13]

The Court of Appeal in *Cunliffe v Fielden*[14] has set out the approach to be adopted in relation to a claim for provision by a wife where the marriage had been very short.

In the case of stale marriages, if there is a principle to be derived from the cases it is that where the parties to the marriage have drawn a line under their financial relations there is little prospect of any significant award being made in favour of the surviving spouse.[15]

1 I(PFD)A 1975, s 1(1)(a). As amended by the Civil Partnership Act 2004, s 71, Sch 4, para 15.
2 I(PFD)A 1975, s 1(2)(a).
3 I(PFD)A 1975, s 25(4).
4 Law Com no 62, p 8.
5 *Re Sehota Surjit Kaur v Gian Kaur* [1978] 3 All ER 385, [1978] 1 WLR 1506.
6 Matrimonial Causes Act 1973, ss 23–25, and see *Wachtel v Wachtel* [1973] Fam 72, [1973] 1 All ER 829.
7 Law Com no 61, p 8.
8 I(PFD)A 1975, s 3(2). *White v White* [2001] 1 AC 596, [2001] 1 All ER 1, [2000] 2 FLR 981 has a significant impact on provision for spouses and may lead to more or less equal provision on death as in the case of divorce in the longer term.
9 *Re Besterman* [1984] Ch 458, [1984] 2 All ER 656 where, in the case of a very large estate where the testator's only obligation was to his widow who was wholly blameless and incapable of supporting herself, reasonable financial provision required that she should have access to a sufficient lump sum to ensure beyond any reasonable doubt that she was relieved of any anxiety for the future; capital sum of £378,000 awarded. But see now *Cunliffe v Fielden* [2005] EWCA Civ 1508, [2006] Ch 361, [2006] 2 All ER 115, where a different approach, based on the so-called divorce standard, was adopted.
10 *Re Bunning, Bunning v Salmon* [1984] Ch 480, [1984] 3 All ER 1, wife not limited to the amount she might have received under the Matrimonial Causes Act 1973 but given a lump sum award giving her roughly half the spouse's total assets; see now *White v White* [2001] 1 AC 596, [2001] 1 All ER 1, [2000] 2 FLR 981. See also *Re Rowlands* [1984] Fam Law 280 (small award); *Stead v Stead* [1985] Fam Law 154; *Rajabally v Rajabally* [1987] 2 FLR 390; *Davis v Davis* [1993] 1 FLR 54. See also *Re Krubert* [1997] Ch 97 where the approach in *Re Besterman* [1984] Ch 458, [1984] 2 All ER 656 which minimised the relevance of the 'divorce standard' was preferred to the approach in *Moody v Stevenson* [1992] Ch 486, sub nom *Re Moody, Moody v Stevenson* [1992] 2 All ER 524 which emphasised the relevance of the 'divorce standard', and see *P v G* [2004] EWHC 2944 (Fam), [2006] 1 FLR 431 where Black J said: 'The difference between divorce, where there are two surviving spouses to provide for, and death where there is only one, will not infrequently be reflected in greater provision under the Inheritance Act than would have been made on divorce even where the estate is large'. See now the Court of Appeal decision in *Cunliffe v Fielden* [2005] EWCA Civ 1508, [2006] Ch 361, [2006] 2 All ER 115 that there is no presumption of equal division of assets. Since a deceased spouse who leaves a widow is entitled to bequeath his estate to whomsoever he pleases, and his only statutory obligation is to make reasonable financial provision

for his widow, the concept of equality of division may bear little relation to such provision, depending on the value of the estate. See also *Iqbal v Ahmed* [2011] EWCA Civ 900, [2011] WTLR 2010.

11 *Moody v Stevenson* [1992] Ch 486, sub nom *Re Moody, Moody v Stevenson* [1992] 2 All ER 524 (widower awarded a settlement of the matrimonial home to enable him to continue living in the house as long as he was willing and able to do so).

12 [2001] WTLR 1045. See also *P v E* [2007] WTLR 691.

13 Reasonable provision had to be determined objectively, see para **[105.23]** below. The two adult children had not established a particular need to be provided for to the detriment of the widow; considering *Re Krubert (decd)* [1997] Ch 97. A successful application was made by a widow in *Stephanides v Cohen* [2002] EWHC (Fam) 1869, [2002] WTLR 1373 for further provision out of her deceased husband's estate competing against a 37-year-old son. The estate was worth £643,500; the widow had been left £25,000; with the rest of the assets going to the son. The Court took into consideration the relative merits of the widow and the son based on the conduct of each in relation to the deceased, under s 3(1)(g) of the Act. The widow had been a good and loyal wife whereas the son, who had a history of drug dependency, had not been a good son. The Court awarded the widow some 55 per cent of the estate leaving the son with 45 per cent. A widow, competing against stepchildren, succeeded in a claim under the Act in *In the Estate of Grattan (Robin Francis), Grattan v McNaughton* [2001] WTLR 1305, as did a widow competing against her children in *Re Baker, Baker v Baker* [2008] 2 FLR 1956. The 'divorce fiction' was considered to play a large part in *Aston v Aston* [2007] WTLR 1349 because the marriage of the deceased and the claimant had effectively come to an end some years before the death.

14 [2005] EWCA Civ 1508, [2006] Ch 361, [2006] 2 All ER 115. See also *Lilleyman v Lilleyman* [2012] EWHC 821 (Ch), [2012] WTLR 1033 where the widow of a two-year marriage (and four-year co-habitation) argued that reasonable provision for her was not merely provision to meet her reasonable needs, but an award of £1.5 million from her late husband's £6 million estate, She was awarded £500,000.

15 See *Re Rowlands* [1984] 5 FLR 813 (the applicant widow awarded only £3,000 out of an estate of £100,000 where there had been 43 years of separation in a marriage of 62 years). This can be contrasted with *Bheekun v Williams* [1999] 2 FLR 229 which involved a 37-year marriage for the second half of which the deceased had lived elsewhere. In that case divorce proceedings had begun and a decree nisi was obtained in 1990 (three years before the death) but never made absolute. The widow was awarded £70,000 out of an estate of £159,000 which award was upheld by the Court of Appeal. In *Parish v Sharman* [2001] WTLR 593 no award was made for a spouse of 33 years who had been separated for 11 years. A decree nisi was obtained in 1985 (at the time of the separation) but never made absolute. No award was made in part because Mrs Parish was probably better off than her late husband and, more particularly, because it was quite clear that the parties to the marriage had decided to let sleeping dogs lie at the time of the separation. It was also clear that the trial judge found Mrs Parish's evidence to be unreliable if not dishonest. *Barrass v Harding* [2001] 1 FLR 138 is another ostensibly harsh case concerning a couple who married in 1939 but who divorced in 1964. Agreement was reached as to the settlement of their financial affairs and Mrs Barrass' claim for Family Provision following her former husband's death failed. There was no ongoing relationship and no continuing moral claim even though the estate was of very substantial value. A similar case is *Hope v Knight* [2010] EWHC 3443 (Ch), [2011] WTLR 583 where a widow was refused provision when she and the deceased had entered into a separation agreement 19 years before his death. Although the agreement was not in terms expressed to be in full and final settlement of all financial claims, the evidence showed that that was what had been intended, and the deceased's obligations towards his widow had more than been satisfied by the capital provision that he had made in the past. The judge held further that if the marriage had ended by divorce on the date of the deceased's death, any claim by the widow for further provision in the matrimonial court would have been defeated by the delay since the separation agreement, so that the divorce yardstick did not assist her claim on his death.

[105.14]

[Updated in footnote 4 for *Lindop v Agus* [2009] EWHC 1795 (Ch), [2009] WTLR 1175. Updated in footnote 8 for *Negus v Bahouse* [2008] 1 FLR 381 and *Cattle v Evans* [2011] EWHC 945 (Ch), [2011] WTLR 2010.]

Applications by cohabitees – different sex couples – deaths on or after 1 January 1996. A new category of applicant has been added, in relation to persons dying on or after 1 January 1996, by the Law Reform (Succession) Act 1995.[1] A person is within this category of claimant if he or she is not the spouse or un-remarried former spouse of the deceased and, during the whole of the period of two years preceding the deceased's death, he or she lived in the same household as the deceased and as the husband or wife of the deceased.[2]

The 'living as husband and wife' formula can be found in a number of other statutes,[3] and there is some case law on it.[4] A question which could arise in practice, particularly where the applicant and the deceased were elderly, is whether sexual intercourse must be proved (i) at some stage in the history of the relationship or (ii) during the two years preceding the deceased's death, for the applicant to qualify as falling in this category. It is submitted that the presence or absence of sexual relations will be an important but not decisive factor,[5] along with other factors.[6] It may be an unusual case (eg where there was physical incapacity) where an applicant is held to fall into this category and there is no history of a sexual relationship at all. That there should have been sexual intercourse during the two years before the deceased's death is probably not a requirement if there was a previous history of sexual relations. For example, if the applicant and the deceased had had a sexual relationship, but sexual intercourse had ceased more than two years before the deceased's death as a result of age or illness, they could still be regarded as living together as husband and wife during the two years preceding the deceased's death.[7] The standard of provision for persons falling into this category is 'maintenance' rather than 'what it is reasonable for a husband or wife to receive'.[8]

In assessing whether a claimant could satisfy the requirements of ss 1(1)(ba), (1A) and 3(2A) of I(PFD)A 1975 the court will have regard to the general arrangements for maintenance subsisting at the time of death. The words 'immediately before the death of the deceased' should not be construed literally but rather the settled state of affairs during the relationship should be regarded. Accordingly it was held in *Gully v Dix, Re Dix (decd)*,[9] that the claimant's three-month absence immediately before the death, in the context of a 27-year cohabitation, was, on the facts, an abnormal situation and should not prevent a successful claim. By contrast, in *Churchill v Roach*[10] the parties had started living in the same household less than two years before the deceased's death, and the claimant did not fall into this category.[11]

Where it is not certain that an applicant was living with the deceased as his or her wife or husband, the case may be put in the alternative that the applicant qualifies for an order for provision under the I(PFD)A 1975 as someone who was wholly or partly maintained by the deceased[12] (if there is evidence to support such a claim), and it will be necessary to rely on the latter ground where the applicant and the deceased were together for less than two years preceding the deceased's death (or the applicant is of the same sex as or a sibling of the deceased).

1 See the I(PFD)A 1975, ss 1(1)(ba), (1A) and 3(2A), as inserted by Law Reform (Succession) Act 1995, s 2, and printed in Vol 2, Part G, paras **[247.2]** and **[247.4]**. This new category of cohabitee applicants was introduced on the recommendations of the Law Commission, *Distribution on Intestacy* (Law Com no 187), to deal with the problems of proving dependence which sometimes arose in claims by cohabitees. For the problems which had arisen see para **[105.18]** below.

2 I(PFD)A 1975, s 1(1)(ba), (1A). See *Re Watson* [1999] 1 FLR 878, the test of living in the same household is objective. In *Witkowska v Kaminski* [2006] EWHC 1940 (Ch), [2006] 3 FCR 250 the claimant, a Polish national and an illegal overstayer in the United Kingdom, was awarded provision under s 1(1)(ba) and 1(1)(e) of the 1975 Act on the basis of her maintenance requirements in Poland rather than in the United Kingdom. Art 12 of the EC Treaty (Nice) had no application to the substantive law of succession, whether by will or on intestacy or by force of the jurisdiction conferred by the 1975 Act, and that the claimant's claim that the award discriminated against her under Art 12 failed.

3 Eg Fatal Accidents Act 1976, s 1(3)(b) (which was added to that Act for the first time by Administration of Justice Act 1982, s 3); Social Security Contributions and Benefits Act 1992, s 137, definition of 'unmarried couple'; Housing Act 1985, s 113; Domestic Violence and Matrimonial Proceedings Act 1976, s 1(2).

4 See the first case reported on the I(PFD)A 1975, s 1(1A), *Re Watson* [1999] 1 FLR 878; the correct approach is to ask whether a reasonable person with normal perceptions would regard them as having lived together as man and wife bearing in mind the multifarious nature of marital relations. For a recent case see *Lindop v Agus* [2009] EWHC 1795 (Ch), [2009] WTLR 1175. For cases on other statutes see *Adeoso v Adeoso* [1981] 1 All ER 107 (a case on Domestic Violence and Matrimonial Proceedings Act 1976, s 1); *Crake v Supplementary Benefits Commission* [1982] 1 All ER 498; *Westminster City Council v Peart* (1991) 24 HLR 389 (a case on the Housing Act 1985, s 113(1)).

5 The test as to whether a person was living in the same household as the deceased as the husband or wife of the deceased is objective and should not ignore the multifarious nature of marital relationships: See *Re Watson* [1999] 1 FLR 878 *per* Neuberger J.

6 For a summary of the practice in social security cases see *Crake v Supplementary Benefits Commission* [1982] 1 All ER 498 at 505f–h. See also *Thomas v Thomas* [1948] 2 KB 294 at 297; *Re Watson* [1999] 1 FLR 878 and the Housing Act case of *Nutting v Southern Housing Group* [2004] EWHC 2982 (Ch), [2005] 1 FLR 1066.

7 See the remarks in *Crake v Supplementary Benefits Commission* [1982] 1 All ER 498 at 502g–h.

8 The I(PFD)A 1975, s 1(2)(b) applies. See para **[105.9]** above, and contrast the provision for spouses discussed in para **[105.9]** above. 'Maintenance' is maintenance in the context of the lifestyle of the claimant with the deceased, see *Negus v Bahouse* [2008] 1 FLR 381. But see *Cattle v Evans* [2011] EWHC 945 (Ch), [2011] WTLR 2010 where a co-habitee was awarded a right to live in a property to be purchased by the estate for the rest of her life, but it was to be smaller and less expensive than the one in which she and the deceased had lived together.

9 [2004] EWCA Civ 139, [2004] FCR 453. *Jelley v Iliffe* [1981] Fam 128 (discussed in paras **[105.18]**, **[105.19]**, **[105.22]** and **[105.29]**, below, applied.

10 [2002] EWHC 3230 (Ch), [2003] WTLR 779.

11 See *Kotke v Safferini* [2005] EWCA Civ 221, [2005] 1 FCR 642, on the same words in FAA 1976, where two people maintaining separate houses but planning to live together were held not to be living in the same household.

12 Ie that he or she falls within the I(PFD)A 1975, s 1(1)(e). See para **[105.19]** below.

[105.15]

[Updated in footnote 3 and in the text for *Baynes v Hedger* [2008] 2 FLR 1805.]

Applications by cohabitees – same-sex couples. The Civil Partnership Act 2004[1] has added a new sub-s (1B) to s 1 I(PFD)A 1975 which is in similar terms to sub-s (1A) and which applies to a person who has cohabited with the deceased in the same household 'as a civil partner of the deceased', with effect from the commencement date of the Civil Partnership Act 2004, 5 December 2005.[2] It is not possible to establish that two persons have lived together as civil partners unless their relationship as a couple is an acknowledged one.[3]

1 Section 71, Sch 4, para 15.
2 See the House of Lords decision in the Housing Act case of *Ghaidan v Godin-Mendoza* [2004] UKHL 30, [2004] 2 AC 557 a same-sex couple can, since the coming into force of HRA 1998, be said to be living together as husband and wife, contrary to the decision in *Fitzpatrick v Stirling Housing Association* [2001] 1 AC 27. See also the decision of Master Bowles in *Saunders v Garrett* [2005] WTLR 749.
3 *Baynes v Hedger* [2008] 2 FLR 1805. (Lewison J's dismissal of the co-habitee's claim in this case was not appealed against, as was his dismissal of the dependent's claim, so the part of his judgement considering the co-habitation claim was not considered by the Court of Appeal in *Baynes v Hedger* [2009] EWCA Civ 374, [2009] All ER (D) 50 (May)).

[105.16]

[Updated in footnote 9 for *Ilott v Mitson* [2011] 2 FCR 1, CA, and *Hope v Knight* [2010] EWHC 3443 (Ch), [2011] WTLR 583.
Updated in footnote 13 and in the text for *Challinor v Challinor* [2009] EWHC (Ch), [2009] WTLR 1051.]

Applications by children. Under the Inheritance (Family Provision) Act 1938 children of the deceased who could apply for provision were limited to unmarried and disabled daughters and minor and disabled sons. The definition of 'son' and 'daughter' included both adopted and illegitimate children as well as posthumous children of the deceased. The I(PFD)A 1975 refers simply to 'a child of the deceased'.[1] This removes the age limit and any distinction between married and unmarried children and the relevance of any disability, so far as locus standi is concerned. 'Child' includes an illegitimate child and a child en ventre sa mère at the time of the death of the deceased.[2] The standard of provision for children is limited to 'such financial provision as it would be reasonable in all the circumstances of the case for the applicant to receive for his maintenance'.[3] What is proper 'maintenance' depends on all the facts and circumstances of the case[4] but it has been said that it connotes only payments which would directly or indirectly enable the applicant to discharge the recurring costs of his living expenses.[5]

The element of mere obligation has been referred to as a criterion for determining whether a child should succeed in an application; however, whether the child is an adult or a minor,[6] in no case is there an invariable prerequisite that the child must show that the deceased had a moral obligation[7] to maintain him or that there is some other special circumstance which entitled him to seek provision.[8]

In the case of adult children whilst it is not necessary to show that the deceased had such a moral obligation to maintain the applicant, an adult child who is in employment, with an earning capacity for the foreseeable future is unlikely to succeed in his application without some special circumstance such as a moral obligation.[9]

Three further points[10] relevant to applications by children: first, a child who may have been qualified to apply for family provision ceases to be so qualified if he is subsequently adopted by another person before the application is made.[11] Second, in considering a claim under the I(PFD)A 1975 the court may take into account the wishes of the deceased expressed before death including any indications of his intentions in an invalid will. Third, it has been suggested that any receipts of social security benefits by the applicant are to be disregarded in considering the applicant's financial resources,[12], although this is not invariably the case and in a case where a child suffering from Down's Syndrome had been cared for by social services for 20 years it was not part of the case that provision should be made from the estate to fund the child's care privately.[13]

1 I(PFD)A 1975, s 1(1)(c).
2 I(PFD)A 1975, s 25(1).
3 I(PFD)A 1975, s 1(2)(b).
4 *Re Coventry,* [1980] Ch 461, [1979] 3 All ER 815 where an able-bodied 46-year-old son did not succeed in an application. The mere fact that it would have been reasonable for the deceased to make some provision was not sufficient; the applicant had to establish a moral claim to be maintained over and above the claim of a blood relationship. Not following *Re Christie, Christie v Keeble* [1979] Ch 168, [1979] 1 All ER 546. *Re Coventry* was followed in *Re Jennings* [1994] Ch 286, [1994] 3 All ER 27 in which the deceased's failure to support his son during his infancy was not of itself sufficient to justify an award. Likewise in *Garland v Morris* [2007] EWHC 2 (Ch), [2007] All ER (D) 11 (Jan) where an adult daughter failed to prove that it had been unreasonable for the deceased to make no provision for her. See also *Harlow v National Westminster Bank* (3 January 1994, unreported), Fam D. But a successful claim was made by an adult son against his father's estate in *Re Goodchild* [1997] 3 All ER 63 where the award was justified on the basis of 'exceptional circumstances' arising from the fact that his parents had made similar (though not mutual) wills under which the son was the ultimate beneficiary of the joint estate, a consideration which was held to give rise to a 'moral obligation' to the son. For other successful applications by adult children see *Re Abram* [1996] 2 FLR 379; *Re Pearce* [1998] 2 FLR 705; *Myers v Myers* [2004] EWHC 1944 (Fam), [2005] WTLR 851 and *Re Gold deceased, Gold v Curtis* [2005] WTLR 673.
5 *Re Dennis, Dennis v Lloyds Bank Ltd* [1981] 2 All ER 140 where an adult son failed in an application for payment of tax out of the father's estate. The application was also out of time, see para **[105.5]** above.
6 Minor children have a strong claim for financial provision: *Re C* [1995] 2 FLR 24.
7 *Re Coventry, Coventry v Coventry* [1980] Ch 461, [1979] 3 All ER 815, CA, (adult son failed to show moral obligation); *Re Dennis, Dennis v Lloyds Bank Ltd* [1981] 2 All ER 140, 124 Sol Jo 885 (desire for payment of capital sum to creditors was not an application for maintenance, application by adult son failed); *Re Callaghan* [1985] Fam 1, [1984] 3 All ER 790 (adult stepson awarded £15,000 out of estate of £31,000); *Re Leach, Leach v Lindeman* [1986] Ch 226, [1985] 2 All ER 754 (adult stepdaughter who never lived in the deceased's household and was never maintained by the deceased awarded half of the net estate); *Re Debenham* [1986] 1 FLR 404, adult epileptic daughter received an award of £3,000 capital plus a periodical payments order of £4,500; *Williams v Johns* [1988] 2 FLR 475 (a physically fit, 43 year-old adoptive daughter who was capable of maintaining herself was unable to show that the deceased had any obligation to maintain her. The applicant had nor cared for and, in the past, had caused shame and distress to the deceased); *Re Jennings* [1994] Ch 286, [1994] 3 All ER 27, CA, (application by adult son failed: mere blood relationship did not give rise to an enduring moral obligation); *Re Goodchild* [1997] 3 All ER 63, [1997] 1 WLR 1216, CA, (adult son's application was successful because of moral obligation imposed on deceased by his former wife's mistaken belief that wills were mutually binding); *Re Hancock* [1998] 2 FLR 346, CA, (an adult daughter with no earning capacity who had left home at 19 to live with a man who now had no resources save his pension and disability benefits awarded periodical payments of £3000 per annum); *Re Pearce* [1998] 2 FLR 705, CA (an adult son who worked on his father's farm between the ages of 6 and 16 and left only because the deceased could not afford to pay him was awarded a tax-free legacy of £85,000 out of an estate of £285,000); *Espinosa v Bourke* [1999] 1 FLR 747, CA (55-year-old daughter, long out of employment, in financial need and with doubtful earning capacity did not have to show moral obligation. The deceased was under an obligation arising from his promise to leave his wife's portfolio of shares to the daughter).
8 See: *Re Pearce* [1998] 2 FLR 705 at 710 per Nourse LJ and the cases referred to above.; *Re Hancock* [1998] 2 FLR 346, CA; *Espinosa v Bourke* [1999] 1 FLR 747 at 755 per

Butler-Sloss LJ; *Re Watson* [1999] 1 FLR 878; cf *Re Coventry, Coventry v Coventry* [1980] Ch 461, [1979] 3 All ER 815, CA; *Re Jennings* [1994] Ch 286, [1994] 3 All ER 27, CA.

9 *Re Hancock* [1998] 2 FLR 346 at 351F per Butler-Sloss LJ; *Re Pearce* [1998] 2 FLR 705 at 710 per Nourse LJ; *Espinosa v Bourke* [1999] 1 FLR 747 at 755 per Butler-Sloss LJ. Following the decision in *Re Hancock*, above, the moral obligation requirement derived from *Re Coventry, Coventry v Coventry* [1980] Ch 461, [1979] 3 All ER 815, CA, is of less rigid application but in many of the successful cases since *Re Coventry* the applicant has been able to rely on a moral obligation such as a promise made by the deceased to another. See, for example: *Re Goodchild; Espinosa v Bourke* (above). *Ilott v Mitson* [2011] 2 FCR 1, CA, contains a useful review of the authorities. The older decisions are more eclectic and may not now be terribly reliable. For a recent case, see *Hope v Knight* [2010] EWHC 3443 (Ch), [2011] WTLR 583 where a claim by an adult daughter who suffered from depression and an obsessive compulsive disorder was refused.

10 *Re Collins* [1990] Fam 56, [1990] 2 All ER 47.

11 This is consistent with the view taken in *Whyte v Ticehurst* [1986] Fam 64, [1986] 2 All ER 158, that the claim is neither an indefeasible right nor an interest expectant.

12 This is consistent with the view taken in *Re E, E v E* [1966] 2 All ER 44, [1966] 1 WLR 709, on a comparable point under the Inheritance (Family Provision) Act 1938.

13 *Challinor v Challinor* [2009] WTLR 1051, [2009] EWHC (Ch).

[105.18]

[Updated in footnotes 3 and 7 for *Baynes v Hedger* [2009] EWCA Civ 374, [2009] All ER (D) 50 (May).]

Applications by other dependants. The most important extension made by the I(PFD)A 1975 to the categories of applicants who can make applications for provision is the class of applicants defined by s 1(1)(e) as follows 'any person (not being a person included in the foregoing paragraphs of this subsection) who immediately before the death of the deceased was being maintained, either wholly or partly, by the deceased'. The importance of this category is now much reduced following the introduction of a separate category of cohabitees (who need not prove dependence). This category is further defined in s 1(3) to the effect that 'a person shall be treated as being maintained by the deceased either wholly or partly as the case may be, if the deceased, otherwise than for full valuable consideration, was making a substantial contribution in money or money's worth towards the reasonable needs of that person'. The I(PFD)A 1975, s 3(4) provides that 'without prejudice to the generality of paragraph (g) of subsection (1) above, where an application for an order under s 2 of this Act is made by virtue of section 1(1)(e) of this Act, the court shall, in addition to the matters specifically mentioned in paragraphs (a) to (f) of that subsection, have regard to the extent to which and the basis upon which the deceased assumed responsibility for the maintenance of the applicant and to the length of time for which the deceased discharged that responsibility'. These provisions have been fully considered in a number of decisions which provide useful guidance on the applications under paragraph (e).

The first case is the decision of Sir Robert Megarry V-C in *Re Beaumont, Martin v Midland Bank Trust Co Ltd.*[1] The plaintiff, a man who had lived with the deceased as man and wife for 36 years, applied for financial provision out of her estate as a dependant under the I(PFD)A 1975. Sir Robert Megarry V-C, decided that s 1(1)(e) was qualified by both ss 1(3) and 3(4) and that the plaintiff could only claim under that paragraph if he satisfied three conditions. First, it was necessary to show that he was being maintained 'immediately before' the death of the deceased with reference to the degree of maintenance normally and habitually existing under the arrangement. Second, the substantial contributions made towards the reasonable needs of the applicant must have been 'otherwise than for full valuable consideration' which was not restricted to contributions supplied under a contract but extended to any contribution provided for full consideration.[2] Third, it had to be shown that the deceased had demonstrated an undertaking or assumption of responsibility for the applicant.[3] This requirement was held not to have been satisfied on the facts of the case which indicated that the applicant was merely one of two people of independent means who had chosen to pool their individual resources to enable them to live together without either undertaking any responsibility for maintaining the other. The summons was accordingly struck out. The decision in *Re Beaumont*, was subsequently considered by the Court of Appeal in *Jelley v Iliffe*,[4] where a widower had been living with a widow in her house rent-free, for some eight years before her death. The parties had pooled their financial resources to pay living expenses and the widower had provided some furniture for the house, looked after the garden and done household jobs. The deceased widow, by her will, left all her property, including the house, to her children, which was consistent with an understanding she had had with them from whom he had acquired the house. The widower applied under the I(PFD)A 1975, s 1(1) for reasonable financial provision out of the deceased's estate on the ground that immediately before her death he was being maintained by her within s (1)(e) of the Act. The Court of Appeal held that the applicant satisfied the requirements of 'being maintained' in the I(PFD)A 1975, s 1(1)(e) as defined in s 1(3), applying *Re Beaumont*. Further that the fact of maintenance raised a presumption of 'assumed responsibility', and that it was not necessary to show a specific intention to this effect, not following *Re Beaumont*, on this point. In determining whether the deceased's contribution to the applicant's needs had been 'otherwise than for full valuable consideration' the court stated that a balance had to be struck between the benefits received, and those provided, by the applicant. On the facts of the case before them the Court of Appeal thought that the provision of rent-free accommodation was a significant contribution to a person's reasonable needs, particularly in the case of an old-age pensioner. Since it was not clear beyond doubt that the applicant's contribution had equalled or outweighed the benefit of the rent-free accommodation there was an arguable case and the issue was ordered to proceed to trial.

The Court of Appeal considered these cases in *Bishop v Plumley*[5] where the applicant was the cohabitee of the deceased, living with him as his wife and described as waiting on him 'hand and foot' and doing everything for him. She had enjoyed in return rent-free accommodation in a house that he had purchased with an inheritance. The court thought that there was no difficulty in finding that the deceased had made a substantial contribution towards her reasonable needs. The difficulty centred on whether she had provided full valuable consideration in return and thus disentitled herself from applying under paragraph (e). The court held that she had not, and this aspect of the case is more fully discussed in the next section.

In *Re B*[6] the Court of Appeal preferred the approach in *Jelley v Iliffe*[7] to the effect that the fact that one person has made a substantial contribution to another person's needs, in itself raised an inference of an assumption of responsibility for the latter.[8] On that basis a claim by a mother against the intestate estate of her deceased (disabled) daughter succeeded where the Court of Protection had made substantial inter vivos payments to her as her daughter's receiver for the maintenance of the daughter, out of which she also (as mother/carer) had benefited.[9]

1 [1980] Ch 444, [1980] 1 All ER 266.

2 On this requirement see also the confirmation of Sir Robert Megarry V-C's view by the Court of Appeal in *Jelley v Iliffe* [1981] Fam 128, [1981] 2 All ER 29. See also *Kourkgy v Lusher* (1981) 4 FLR 65 where the evidence established that the deceased had abandoned cohabitation and maintenance of the applicant some months before his death, and the claim failed. Likewise in *Layton v Martin* [1986] 2 FLR 227, [1986] Fam Law 212, a former mistress of the deceased whose five-year relationship with him ended two years before his death had no claim to any interest in his property, at law, equity, or under the 1975 Act.

3 That it is an essential ingredient in the qualification of a person entitled to make a claim as a dependant that the deceased assumed responsibility for his or her maintenance was approved by the Court of Appeal in *Jelley v Iliffe* [1981] Fam 128, [1981] 2 All ER 29, and more recently in *Baynes v Hedger* [2009] EWCA Civ 374, [2009] All ER (D) 50 (May). In *Jelley v Iliffe* and *Re B* [2000] 1 All ER 665 however, the Court of Appeal seem to have disagreed with Sir Robert Megarry V-C as to how such assumption might be demonstrated, and in both cases the mere fact of one person making a substantial contribution to another person's needs was said to raise an inference of an assumption by the former of responsibility for the latter. In *Baynes v Hedger* no assumption of responsibility was found in circumstances where the maintenance found was only partial, and where the facts showed that the deceased had sought to disclaim responsibility to the claimant in the last years of her life.

4 [1981] Fam 128, [1981] 1 All ER 29, provision of accommodation held to be a substantial benefit. Likewise in *Re Wilkinson, Neale v Newell* [1978] 1 All ER 221 (sister). See also *Graham v Murphy* [1997] 1 FLR 860; *Rees v Newbery and the Institute of Cancer Research* [1998] 1 FLR 1041 and *Wayling v Jones* [1995] 2 FLR 1029 (homosexual relationship). *Jelley v Iliffe* [1981] Fam 128, [1981] 2 All ER 29 has been considered in *Kourkgy v Lusher* (1981) 12 Fam Law 86 where a claim by a cohabitee failed, and applied in *Re Kirby* (1982) 11 Fam Law 210. See also *Malone v Harrison* [1979] 1 WLR 1353 on assumption of responsibility and computation of lump sum award; *Harrington v Gill* (1983) 4 FLR 265, cohabitant held entitled to a lump sum and also the deceased's house settled on her for life; *Williams v Roberts* [1984] Fam Law 210 and *Re Watson* [1999] 1 FLR 878 (ten years cohabitation).

5 [1991] 1 All ER 236, [1991] 1 WLR 582. It will be appreciated that this was a case, like many of those noted above, of an application by a cohabitee under the I(PFD)A 1975, s 1(1)(e), which would now be brought under s 1(1)(ba); See *Cyganik v Agulian* [2005] EWHC 444 (Ch), [2005] All ER (D) 400 (Mar), application by cohabitant, where the issue was whether the deceased was domiciled in England and Wales; see also *Witkowska v Kaminski* [2006] EWHC 1940 (Ch), [2006] 3 FCR 250.

6 [2000] 1 All ER 665; reversing Jonathan Parker J [1999] 2 All ER 425 who had dismissed the claim. The Court of Appeal emphasised that the 'assumption of responsibility' in the I(PFD)A 1975, s 3(4) was not part of the threshold requirements of s 1(1)(e) but was a factor to be taken into account, once the court was satisfied that the applicant had locus standi, in determining the merits of the claim and thus the exercise of the court's discretion. *Jelley v Iliffe* [1981] Fam 128, [1981] 2 All ER 29, was applied; *Re Beaumont, Martin v Midland Bank Trust Co Ltd* [1980] Ch 444, [1980] 1 All ER 266 was doubted. See also *Rees v Newbery and the Institute of Cancer Research* [1998] 1 FLR 1041 (immaterial that the maintenance of the applicant arose through a tenancy agreement).

7 *Jelley v Iliffe* [1981] Fam 128, [1981] 2 All ER 29.

8 In *Baynes v Hedger* [2008] 2 FLR 1805, on appeal [2009] EWCA Civ 374, [2009] All ER (D) 50 (May), a one-off outright gift of a house and establishment of a trust fund made many years before death did not demonstrate an assumption of responsibility, and nor did it demonstrate a continuing action of maintaining.

9 The daughter had been severely disabled at birth owing to medical negligence and an award of £250,000 had been made to her. This money was controlled by the Court of Protection which applied it for the benefit and maintenance of the daughter which inevitably also

benefited the mother who lived with and cared for the daughter. Thus the daughter had made a substantial provision in money or money's worth for the reasonable needs of the mother within the I(PFD)A 1975, s 1(1)(e) who could claim under that paragraph (as a dependant) against her daughter's estate.

III. THE DISCRETION

[105.21]

[Updated in footnote 1 for *Moore v Holdsworth* [2010] EWHC 683 (Ch), [2010] WTLR 1213. Updated in footnote 2 for *Barron v Woodhead* [2008] WTLR 1675, [2008] Fam Law 844.]

All applicants. With reference to all applicants the court, under the I(PFD)A 1975, s 3(1), has regard to:

(a) the financial resources and financial needs which the applicant has or is likely to have in the foreseeable future;[1]

(b) the financial resources and financial needs which any other applicant for an order under the I(PFD)A 1975, s 2 has or is likely to have in the foreseeable future;

(c) the financial resources and financial needs which any beneficiary of the estate of the deceased has or is likely to have in the foreseeable future.

(d) any obligations and responsibilities which the deceased has towards any applicant or towards any beneficiary of the estate of the deceased;

(e) the size and nature of the net estate of the deceased;

(f) any physical or mental disability of any applicant or any beneficiary of the estate of the deceased;

(g) any other matter, including the conduct of the applicant or any other person, which in the circumstances of the case the court may consider relevant.[2]

1 For a case on valuation see *Re Estate of Quilter (decd), Quilter v Quilter* [2003] EWHC 2986 (Ch), [2004] 1 EGLR 79. State benefits which may be available to a claimant are relevant, see *Moore v Holdsworth* [2010] EWHC 683 (Ch), [2010] WTLR 1213 where Kitchen J refused to order capital provision for a widow suffering from multiple sclerosis when the evidence showed that the local authority would fund her care package, subject to their right to seek payment from her if her assets exceeded a certain level, so that if capital provision was made a large part of it would ultimately be used up to pay for her care and other needs.

2 With respect to para (g), in *Stephanides v Cohen* [2002] EWHC 1869 (Fam), [2002] WTLR 1373, the relative conduct of a widow and a son was an important consideration in the making of an award under the 1975 Act. By contrast in *Re Waite (dec'd), Barron v Woodhead* [2008] WTLR 1675, [2008] Fam Law 844 a widower's alleged violence to the deceased was not relevant where he was likely to be homeless following the deceased's death and had been made bankrupt.

[105.26]

[Updated in footnote 3 for *Barron v Woodhead* [2008] WTLR 1675, [2008] Fam Law 844.]

Spouses or civil partners. Where the applicant is the spouse or the civil partner,[1] of the deceased the court will, under the I(PFD)A 1975, s 3(2), consider the following additional factors:

(a) the age of the applicant and the duration of the marriage or civil partnership;

(b) the contribution made by the applicant to the welfare of the family of the deceased, including any contribution made by looking after the home or caring for the family;

and, in the case of an application by a spouse or civil partner of the deceased, the court will also, unless at the date of the death a decree of judicial separation was in force and the separation was continuing, have regard to the provision which the applicant might reasonably have expected to receive if on the day on which the deceased died the marriage, instead of being terminated by death, had been terminated by a decree of divorce or by dissolution order of the civil partnership.

So far as matrimonial conduct is concerned the approach under the Act is analogous to that in the divorce court; Lord Denning MR in *Wachtel v Wachtel*[2] held that if the conduct of one spouse was 'both obvious and gross' so that it would be 'repugnant to anyone's sense of justice' to make an order against the other party, the court was free to decline an order. However, he went on, 'short of cases falling into this category, the court should not reduce its order for financial provision merely because of what was formerly regarded as guilt or blame'.[3]

1 As amended by the Civil Partnership Act 2004, s 71, Sch 4.

2 [1973] Fam 72; see also *Re Besterman* [1984] Ch 458, [1984] 2 All ER 656 where the fact that the wife was blameless was referred to: See also *Moody v Stevenson* [1992] Ch 486, sub nom *Re Moody, Moody v Stevenson* [1992] 2 All ER 524 and *Re Krubert* [1997] Ch 97.

3 *Wachtel v Wachtel* [1973] Fam 72 at 90. The Law Commission (Law Com no 61, p 11) expressed the hope that this standard would likewise apply for family provision. In *Re Waite (dec'd), Barron v Woodhead* [2008] WTLR 1675, [2008] Fam Law 844 a widower's alleged violence to the deceased was not relevant where he was likely to be homeless following the deceased's death and had been made bankrupt.

IV. THE ORDERS

[105.33]

[Updated in the text and footnote 3 for *Challinor v Challinor* [2009] EWHC (Ch), [2009] WTLR 1051.]

Transfers and settlement of property. 'An order for the transfer to the applicant of such property comprised in that estate as may be so specified'.[1]

> 'An order for the settlement for the benefit of the applicant of such property comprised in that estate as may be so specified'.[2]

These are extensions to the court's powers on family provision and are analogous to the powers contained in the Matrimonial Causes Act 1973, s 24, and thus consistent with the Law Commission's objective that the widow should be in no less advantageous position than the divorced wife. The powers have obvious relevance where the matrimonial home forms part of the estate but can be used with reference to any property. The power to transfer might be invoked where it is difficult or undesirable to realise an asset at that time in order to make a lump sum payment. The power to order a settlement might be exercised where an outright payment or transfer to the applicant might effect their entitlement to state benefits.[3] I(PFD)A 1975, s 2(1)(d) orders cannot be varied.[4]

1 I(PFD)A 1975, s 2(1)(c).
2 I(PFD)A 1975, s 2(1)(d); see *Harrington v Gill* (1983) 4 FLR 265, and *Moody v Stevenson* [1992] Ch 486, sub nom *Re Moody, Moody v Stevenson* [1992] 2 All ER 524.
3 See *Hanbury v Hanbury* [1999] 2 FLR 255 and *Challinor v Challinor* [2009] EWHC (Ch), [2009] WTLR 1051.
4 I(PFD)A 1975, s 6(9).

VOLUME 2

Precedents and statutes

PART A

Introductory note

Introductory note

I. GENERAL

(*a*) *Capacity and freedom from influence*

[200.4]

[Updated for the Law Society's April 2009 practice note.]

In any subsequent dispute the testator's solicitor may be called upon to give a statement as to the preparation of the will, and the circumstances in which it was executed, together with copies of any requested documents, to any interested party, and promptly when asked: see (1959) 56 Law Society's Gazette 619, *Re Moss, Larke v Nugus* [2000] WTLR 1033 (also reported sub nom *Larke v Nugus* in (1979) 123 Sol Jo 337), CA, and the Law Society's Disputed Wills practice note – 16 April 2009. If a solicitor, or indeed any other person, preparing a will takes any substantial interest under it he must see that the testator obtains independent advice (see *Re a Solicitor* [1975] QB 475, [1974] 3 All ER 853; *Tristram and Coote's Probate Practice* (30th edn) LexisNexis Butterworths, para 34.50; and the Solicitors Regulation Authority's 'Solicitors' Code of Conduct 2007', para 3.04).

(*c*) *Other points*

[200.28]

[Updated in para (d) for Human Fertilisation and Embryology Act 2008.]

Children, issue and other words descriptive of relationship. The rules of construction relating to references in wills and other instruments to children and issue and to any other terms used to denote a blood relationship have undergone major reform in recent years. For the development of the new statutory rules and the application of the former rules to existing instruments, reference should be made to Vol 1 (at paras **[72.1]**, **[74.1]** and **[75.1]** ff) and the statutes printed in Part G2 (at para **[245.1]** ff) and the notes thereto. The current position as regards the devolution of property on death, under a will made now, may be summarised as follows:

(a) ***Adoption.*** The governing statute is the Adoption and Children Act 2002 (ACA 2002), replacing with effect from 30 December 2005 the similar provisions of the Adoption Act 1976 (the relevant provisions of ACA 2002 are printed at paras **[245.92]–[245.101]** and discussed in Vol 1 at paras **[75.1]–[75.7]**). ACA 2002 provides that a child adopted under the Adoption Act 1976 or ACA 2002 or by any adoption recognised as valid by English law is to be treated for the purposes of the devolution of property, whether under a will or on an intestacy, as the legitimate child of his adoptive parent or parents (who can be same-sex couples). Effectively therefore any disability previously attaching to adopted status is removed. The one exception relates to property settled to devolve with a dignity or title of honour.

(b) ***Legitimation.*** The rights of persons who are legitimated by the subsequent marriage of their parents are governed by the Legitimacy Act 1976 (Part G, paras **[245.44]–[245.54]** and considered in Vol 1 at paras **[72.15]–[72.17]**) which provides that for succession purposes legitimated persons are to be treated as if born legitimate. There is a similar saving for property settled to devolve with a dignity or title of honour.

(c) ***Illegitimacy.*** The position is now governed by the Family Law Reform Act 1987 (FLRA 1987) (Part G, paras **[245.70]–[245.81]** and considered in Vol 1 at para **[72.14]**) which again effectively removes any disability to which persons who were either illegitimate or were claiming through illegitimate persons have in the past been subject, and in particular they are treated in the same way as legitimate children of the same parent when it comes to determining who is to benefit under a gift to, eg 'my children' or 'my nephews and nieces', unless a contrary intention is expressed. Again there is a saving for property settled to devolve with a dignity or title of honour. The FLRA 1987 replaces the FLRA 1969 and is wider in some respects than it (see para **[245.69]** for a summary of the main differences), although in the majority of cases where the meaning of a gift in a will is in issue the FLRA 1987 will have no different effect from that which the FLRA 1969 would have had.

(d) ***Artificial insemination and in vitro fertilisation.*** Recent medical developments have resulted in the enactment of special rules concerning the rights of succession of persons born in consequence of artificial insemination or other techniques designed to overcome infertility. These are now to be found in the Human Fertilisation and Embryology Acts of 1990 and 2008 (Part G, paras **[245.83]–[245.91]** and **[245.111]–[245.141]** and considered in Vol 1 at paras **[74.3]–[74.7]**). Where a woman carries a child as a result of the use of any of these techniques, the child is treated as her child in law and no other woman's; if she is married her husband will be treated as the father unless it is shown that he did not consent to the use of artificial insemination or other technique. The child will be treated as their legitimate offspring. If a woman who is not married has a child as a result of treatment regulated by these statutes, and with the consent of a man whose sperm has not been used to conceive the child and whom she has consented to have treated as the father, then he will be so treated (the rules for what constitutes consent for this purpose have been revised for treatment carried out on or after 6 April 2009). In the case of a child produced by surrogacy a parental order can, if certain conditions are fulfilled, be obtained under s 54 of the 2008 Act (see para **[245.133]** and SI 2010/985 at paras **[245.142]** ff). This treats the couple on whose behalf the surrogate mother bore the child as the parents of the child.

There is also, in relation to treatment carried out on or after 6 April 2009, parallel provision for same-sex female couples who have a child by means of treatment under the 1990 or 2008 Acts. The one who is not the mother is treated as a parent of the child if the couple have formed a civil partnership or the treatment is carried out with the appropriate consents. The provisions relating to children of same-sex female couples in a civil partnership will also apply to children of same-sex female couples in a marriage when the Marriage (Same Sex Couples) Act 2013 (see para **[245.149]** ff below) comes into force. For the purposes of succession to property it is provided that any enactment, deed, instrument or other document (whenever made) is to be construed in accordance with the rules summarised above with the consequence that a child born as a result of one of the techniques in question will be eligible under a will or on an intestacy as if he were the legitimate or (as the case may be) the illegitimate child of his 'parent' or 'parents'. Again there is a saving for property settled to devolve with a dignity or title of honour.

(e) ***Gender change.*** Under GRA 2004 (Part G, paras **[245.102]** ff and considered in Vol 1 at para **[81.1]**) a change of gender in accordance with that Act has effect for all legal purposes (except under a will or other instrument made before 4 April 2005). This is capable of changing the effect of any gift by will where the designation of the donee or donees is gender specific.

(f) ***Same sex marriage.*** When the Marriage (Same Sex Couples) Act 2013 (see para **[245.149]** ff below) is brought into force, words such as 'spouse', 'husband', 'wife', 'widow' and 'widower' will include parties or former parties to same sex marriages in documents made after the Act comes into force. The main significance will probably be for the membership of classes of beneficiaries who are objects of a discretion, where it is common to define the class as the descendants of a named person or persons and their spouses etc.

[200.29]

[Updated for Human Fertilisation and Embryology Act 2008.]

The present position is thus that for all practical purposes children who are adopted, legitimated or illegitimate, and children who are born to 'parents' as a consequence of the medical techniques just mentioned, are treated for succession purposes on an equal footing with legitimate children. In the case of testamentary succession this is subject to any contrary intention being expressed in the particular will. The earlier law on the rights of adopted, legitimated or illegitimate children (Part G, para **[245.1]** ff) remains relevant to the administration of estates or will trusts where the testator died or, in cases involving succession by illegitimate persons, made his will before the law on one or more of the above topics was changed, and to making an appointment under a special power of appointment where the power was created by a will or other instrument to which the earlier law applied (see B13 at para **[213.1]** ff). Where illegitimate persons are involved, the earlier law remains relevant (irrespective of the date of death of the testator) to wills made before the FLRA 1987 came into force on 4 April 1988 (see

FLRA 1987, s 19(7): Part G, para **[245.72]**), and, more importantly, to wills made before its predecessor the FLRA 1969 came into force on 1 January 1970 (see FLRA 1969, s 15(8): Part G, para **[245.39]**). It should be noted that a codicil which confirms a will made before one or both of these Family Law Reform Acts came into force does not by the fact of doing so cause the will to be treated as made after that or those Acts came into force (see the Preliminary Note to Part D at para **[237.8]**). By contrast, the rules in the Human Fertilisation and Embryology Acts 1990 and 2008, and SI 2010/985, referred to at para **[200.28]**, sub-para (d) apply to any instrument, whenever made, and this includes all wills irrespective of their date or the date of death of the testator.

[200.30]
Drafting wills using words descriptive of relationship. The statutory rules just mentioned, so far as they relate to adopted or legitimated children, or ones born as a result of the use of the medical techniques referred to above, will normally reflect what the testator would have wished anyway. This will not always be the case for the statutory rules relating to illegitimate children. The draftsman will need to bear in mind the new statutory rules, particularly those relating to the rights of illegitimate children, when taking instructions for a will. A married man with legitimate children may possibly have one or more illegitimate children as well, and not intend them to benefit to the same extent as his legitimate children, or at all. However, a gift to 'my children' without more will include the illegitimate children. Since it is now conclusively established that a solicitor taking instructions for a will owes a duty of care to take all usual steps to ensure that persons intended to benefit do in fact benefit and can be liable in damages to a disappointed beneficiary if he fails to discharge that duty (see *White v Jones* [1995] 2 AC 207, [1995] 1 All ER 691, HL; see also para **[200.46]**), the draftsman cannot leave the matter to chance. One way of dealing with the problem is to identify the children in the will by name, but this may not be convenient if the client is capable of having further children. Another possible course is to limit the gift to the children of the marriage. But the safest course (though not a very appealing one) is to enquire specifically of the client whether he has any illegitimate children and if he has (or may have) whether he wishes to exclude them, and, if he has and does, to exclude them expressly or exclude the Family Law Reform Acts from applying. For the latter purpose, we recommend the use of words such as 'Words descriptive of relationship shall be construed in all respects as if the Family Law Reform Act 1969, s 15 and the Family Law Reform Act 1987 had not been enacted'. A reference to the FLRA 1969 should be retained; since the FLRA 1987 repeals the FLRA 1969, s 15, such a provision which referred to the FLRA 1987 alone could be construed as a direction that the gift should be read as subject to the FLRA 1969. After the Marriage (Same Sex Couples) Act 2013 comes into force (see para **[245.149]** ff below), some testators who have made provision of any kind for beneficiaries who are defined as persons married or formerly married to other persons referred to in the will may want to add that Act to the list of statutes excluded from applying.

[200.35A]

[Paras [200.35A]–[200.35H] added to discuss the consequences of Perpetuities and Accumulations Act 2009 for will drafting.]

The Perpetuities and Accumulations Act 2009 (PAA 2009). The PAA 2009 (Part G, para **[246.174]** ff) has made fundamental changes to the law of perpetuities and of accumulations, in relation to testamentary and other dispositions made on or after 6 April 2010. It should in particular be noted that PAA 2009 does not apply to a will or codicil made before 6 April 2010 even if the testator dies on or after that date (subject to the possibility of republication by a codicil made on or after that date, see **[200.35G]**). See Vol 1, Chapter 94 for the perpetuity rules, and Vol 1 para **[95.A1]** for the accumulations rules. From the point of view of the drafting of wills after 5 April 2010, with which this introductory note is concerned, the main points are that a compulsory 125 year perpetuity period (PAA 2009, s 5) combined with 'wait and see' (PAA 2009, s 7) applies to all dispositions, and there are no restrictions on accumulation, apart from the perpetuity rule, except in the case of charitable trusts (PAA 2009, ss 13, 14). It is not necessary, and it is not advisable, to make express provision in wills as to the perpetuity period applicable to the will. No harm can be done by including an express declaration of a 125 year perpetuity period, but an express declaration of any other period would be of no effect and would risk giving a misleading impression to future administrators of the trust who are not fully aware of the post-2009 Act state of the law.

[200.35B]

The PAA 2009 perpetuity rules and trusts for persons in succession. Under PAA 1964 the perpetuity period applicable to a disposition was a fixed period of years (not exceeding 80) only if it was expressly declared to be. If there was no such express declaration, the common law period of a life in being plus 21 years, though with the added assistance of 'wait-and-see' in possibly non-compliant cases, would apply. Under PAA 2009 a perpetuity period of a life in being plus 21-years is not available; the period is 125 years from the date of the disposition in all cases. This means that if the draftsman of a trust of a form such as, eg, 'life interest to A, remainder to such of the children of A as attain the age of 21 years' wishes to make it certain from the outset that the interests will vest within the perpetuity period he would need to provide expressly that the interests of the children of A vest on them attaining the age of 21 or their being living but under that age at the expiry of 125 years from the date of the disposition. Similarly, if there is to be a power to pay or apply capital in favour of A, in order to achieve certainty of vesting from the outset the power would have to be exercisable during the life of A or until the earlier expiry of 125 years from the date of the disposition. Such provisions may, of course, eventually turn out to be needed in practice, if techniques for slowing the ageing process are discovered and become widely available. Unless and until that happens, however, including perpetuity restrictions in life interest and remainder, trusts will seem most eccentric to that minority of testators who read their wills before signing them, and will contribute to the negative public image of the legal professions as being out of touch with reality. Because of the 'wait-and-see' rules it is not necessary for the validity of trusts and powers of this kind to be drafted so that it is clear from the outset that they must vest within the perpetuity period, so long as it is possible that they might vest within it. It was the better practice when drafting trusts to which PAA 1964 applied to ensure that they were perpetuity rule-compliant from the outset, without relying on 'wait and see', but under PAA 1964 it was, as mentioned above, possible to draft life interest and remainder trusts which were compliant from the outset without resorting to express perpetuity restrictions. Now that PAA 2009 has replaced PAA 1964, a change of professional practice to relying on 'wait and see' when drafting trusts of the conventional life interest and remainder form would seem to be appropriate and defensible. We have therefore not introduced express perpetuity restrictions in the precedents for this type of trust in this work unless there is some real prospect of the trust continuing for 125 years. In practice, under the current IHT regime for trusts, it is not sensible to have fixed interest trusts other than in relation to a surviving spouse or civil partner (see paras **[200.128]**, **[200.129]**, **[200.131]**, and **[200.132]**), and so most trusts intended to endure for any length of time will be discretionary or partly discretionary ones where there is no embarrassment about providing restrictions on vesting so as to comply with the perpetuity rules.

[200.35C]
The PAA 2009 perpetuity rule and discretionary trusts. The compulsory perpetuity period of 125 years from the date of the disposition fits discretionary trusts particularly well. Such trusts typically run for a fixed period of years from the date of the disposition. The differences made by PAA 2009 are that the trust period can be any period up to 125 years, and that it is no longer necessary or advisable to state that the period in question is the perpetuity period applicable to the disposition (see para **[200.35A]**). Unless there is a strong compelling reason to provide a shorter period, a full 125 year period is recommended for new discretionary trusts as providing maximum flexibility, provided that there are full powers to bring the trust to an end at an earlier date.

[200.35D]
The rule against perpetuities under PAA 2009 and testamentary options or testamentary gifts of the grant of legal estates. Another innovation of PAA 2009 is that the rule against perpetuities is confined to applying to interest under trusts and executory bequests of personalty. It does not apply to future rights or interests arising from commercial transactions entered into after 5 April 2010 (see Vol 1, para **[95.40A]** for the details). Whether testamentary options, or directions in wills, eg, that a beneficiary should be granted a lease, are subject to the rule against perpetuities is not entirely clear. The practical position is that it is very unlikely that a situation will arise where this is an important issue. 125 years plus wait and see should be enough for any testamentary provision of this kind, if it is the case that the rule against perpetuities applies, and where the will directs the executors to execute a grant of an option or grant of a lease, once they have done so the instrument in question will fairly clearly fall outside the rule. In relation to options granted after 5 April 2010 to acquire land, the former 21-year compulsory perpetuity period for land options under PAA 1964, s 9 does not

apply. If the rule against perpetuities does apply to any testamentary options in wills made after that date, the full 125 year period under PAA 2009 is applicable.

[200.35E]

Accumulation post PAA 2009 and discretionary trusts. PAA 2009 abolishes, in relation to testamentary and other dispositions made on or after 6 April 2010 (other than charitable trusts), the restrictions on accumulation of income which originated with the Accumulations Act 1800, and which were latterly contained in LPA 1925, ss 164 and 166 and PAA 1964, s 13. This leaves the rule against perpetuities as the only restriction on the period for which income can be accumulated. However, as with the new perpetuities law, the new law on accumulation does not apply to wills or codicils made before 6 April 2010 of persons who die on or after that date (subject to the possibility of republication by a codicil made on or after that date—see **[200.35G]**). Discretionary trusts in wills being made on or after that date can include powers to accumulate income continuing throughout the trust period (provided that it does not exceed 125 years). This is of interest for fully discretionary trusts (see, eg Form B18.1 at para **[218.33]**) and trusts for the disabled (see paras **[226.4]** and **[226.6]**). Where the will creates a charitable trust the trustees can only be given power to accumulate income, or be directed to accumulate income, for a period of 21 years (PAA 2009, s 14(3), (4)).

[200.35F]

Accumulation post PAA 2009 and trusts for minors and young adults. Four years after the abolition of the special category of accumulation and maintenance trust for IHT purposes, a substantial aid to the drafting of such trusts comes along in the form of the abolition of restrictions on accumulation. Where there is a trust of capital vesting at an age greater than 18, the accumulation and maintenance trusts of TA 1925, s 31 can be adapted to continue until the vesting age (see for an example Form **B18.12** at para **[218.80]**). This will be a useful and sensible course to adopt in relation to age 18-to-25 trusts for bereaved minors, and generally in relation to trusts of capital for minors and young adults. The only qualification of this is that there could be an advantage in enabling the trustees to confer an interest in possession in advance of the vesting age where this would be an advantage from an income tax point of view (see para **[218.29]** ff for the income tax disadvantages of discretionary trusts). A power of advancement exercisable over the whole of a presumptive share would enable the trustees to do this, or there could be a specific power to substitute a different age from the age of vesting of capital as the age at which an interest in possession is attained.

[200.35G]

PAA 2009 and codicils. References in PAA 2009 to wills include codicils (s 20(7)). As already mentioned above, PAA 2009 will not apply to a will made before 6 April 2010 even if the testator dies on or after that date. Where a codicil is made on or after 6 April 2010 to a will made before that date, it seems that the codicil, by virtue of the doctrine of republication, is likely to cause the PAA 2009 to apply to the will even if there is no reference to perpetuities or accumulations, and even if the changes made by the codicil have nothing to do with the provisions of the will to which the perpetuity and accumulations rules are relevant, unless a contrary intention is expressed (see Vol 1, para **[22.3]**). If the will contains continuing trusts of any sort, and in particular where what is the perpetuity or accumulation period could make a difference to the beneficial interests, it will be better to declare explicitly that PAA 2009 is to apply (or that it is not to apply) in order to save argument. In such cases it will anyway be advisable to consider whether the trusts of the will should be revised to take advantage of the longer perpetuity and accumulation periods available under PAA 2009. See, further, para **[237.8]**.

[200.35H]
PAA 2009 and special powers of appointment or application of capital. As a matter of general principle, an appointment or application of capital under a special power is subject to the same perpetuity period and accumulation restrictions (if any) as the instrument which created the power. If the will or other instrument which created the power took effect before 6 April 2010, the relevant pre-PAA 2009 law of perpetuities and accumulations will apply to any exercise of the power. If the will or other instrument creating the power is made and takes effect on or after 6 April 2010, PAA 2009 applies to any exercise of the power, and the available perpetuity and accumulation periods are 125 years from the date on which the instrument creating the power took effect. 'Took effect' in this context in relation to a will means the date on which the testator died: see PAA 2009, s 20(6). As explained in more detail in vol 1 para **[94.50]**, there is a question whether PAA 2009, s 15(1) means that the Act applies to an exercise of a special power where the power was created by a will made before 6 April 2010, but the testator died on or after that date. It is possible that this is so, but it runs counter to the general principle mentioned in the first sentence of this paragraph. The cautious draftsman will assume that the previous law applies unless and until the point becomes clarified.

[200.36]
Rules of apportionment. The rules of apportionment laid down by the Apportionment Act 1870, and the rules of apportionment between capital and income known as the rules in *Howe v Earl of Dartmouth* (1802) 7 Ves 137, *Re Earl of Chesterfield's Trust* (1883) 24 Ch D 643 and *Allhusen v Whittell* (1867) LR 4 Eq 295 are widely regarded as an administrative inconvenience, especially in the case of smaller estates, and are frequently excluded. For a more detailed discussion of these rules, see B14 at paras **[214.35]–[214.38]**, **[214.43]** and **[214.44]**. In relation to the wills of persons dying on or after 1 October 2013, the Trusts (Capital and Income) Act 2013, s 1 (see para **[246.203]**) excludes apportionment under the 1870 Act and the equitable rules just mentioned unless a contrary intention is expressed. For precedents for excluding apportionment, which may still be useful in jurisdictions other than England and Wales, see Forms B14.1 to B14.3 at paras **[214.10]–[214.12]**, B14.10 at para **[214.19]**, B14.24 to B14.27 at paras **[214.39]–[214.42]** and B14.28 to B14.30 at paras **[214.45]–[214.47]**.

[200.40]

[Updated for Finance Acts 2008 and 2010.]

Capital gains tax rates. Until 5 April 2008, capital gains realised by individuals were charged to capital gains tax as if they were income, and capital gains realised by settlements and estates of deceased persons in the course of administration were charged to capital gains tax at the income tax trust rate, in 2007–08 40 per cent: TCGA 1992, s 4, ITA 2007, s 9. However, with effect from 6 April 2008 the rate of capital gains tax was 18 per cent for individuals, estates of deceased persons, and trusts alike, and the former difference between individual and trust rates of capital gains tax temporarily disappeared. However, for disposals on or after 23 June 2010 the rate was increased to 28 per cent for trusts and estates and for higher rate taxpayers, with it remaining at 18 per cent for standard rate taxpayers whose income and capital gains together do not reach the threshold of the higher rate of income tax. These tax rates are applied to the gains after deduction of annual exemption, which is more generous for individuals, and for estates in administration (until the end of the first two complete tax years after the deceased's death), than for settlements. Trust capital gains can obtain the more generous capital gains tax annual exemption attributable to a beneficiary where that beneficiary is a disabled person and the trust is such that it qualifies for special treatment under TCGA 1992, Sch 1, para 1 (see para **[226.6]** ff).

[200.41]

[Updated for the reissue of Simon's Taxes and changes in the trust rate of income tax.]

Income tax. Different forms of disposition have different income tax consequences. Where a beneficiary is entitled to the income of an asset or a fund of assets, or to a fixed proportion or amount of such income (whether by virtue of an absolute or limited interest), that income will be taxed as his income (see *Simon's Taxes* **C4.203**, **C4.501**, **C4.503**), although income of a deceased person's residuary estate in the course of administration is only taxed as the beneficiary's when it is distributed to him, and what remains undistributed is taxed as his when the administration is completed (see *Simon's Taxes,* **C4.116–127**). Income which is accumulated or which is to be distributed under the exercise of a discretion is charged to income tax at the trust rate, currently (in 20013–14) 45 per cent, but can come to be treated for income tax purposes as the income of a beneficiary after it has been distributed to him: see B18 at paras **[218.29]** and **[218.30]** and *Simon's Taxes* **C4.506**. However, discretionary trusts have the income tax disadvantage as compared with interest in possession trusts that if there is dividend income which is then distributed to a beneficiary the tax credit on the dividend does not carry through to the beneficiary: see para **[218.31]**. Undistributed trust income may be taxed at the personal income tax rate or rates of a beneficiary where that beneficiary is a bereaved minor or disabled person and the trust is such that it qualifies for special treatment under FA 2005, ss 23–43 (see paras **[217.4]**, **[226.9]** ff).

[200.44]

Execution. The formal requirements for the due execution of an English will are set out in Vol 1 at paras **[10.1]–[12.17]**. A testator who executes a will without a solicitor being present should be informed of these requirements in detail. He should also be warned that neither a witness to a will nor the spouse or civil partner of such witness can in general take a benefit under the will. Such gifts will only be saved by the Wills Act 1968 (Part G, para **[244.84]** ff) if such attestation is superfluous. To be valid, a will does not in general have to be dated (*Corbett v Newey* [1998] Ch 57, [1996] 2 All ER 914, CA), but it is preferable and usual for a will to be dated by the testator when it is executed, and if wills are undated it may be difficult to determine which is the last will and accordingly entitled to probate. However, there is one circumstance where dating is a legal requirement, namely where there is an appointment by will of a guardian—to be valid it must be dated: see Vol 1, para **[28.5]** and the ChA 1989, s 5(5), (Part G, para **[244.116]**). Where husband and wife or civil partners make wills together, it is worth checking that they are signing or have signed their own wills and not each other's: see *Marley v Rawlings* [2012] WTLR 639 and Vol 1, para **[6.1]**.

II. INHERITANCE TAX

(*a*) *Main characteristics*

[200.73]

[Updated for the March 2013 Budget.]

Tax rates. There is a single tax-rate scale which applies in full to the estate on death and to lifetime transfers made within three years before death. It currently (in the tax year 2013–14) consists of a nil rate for the first £325,000 and a single rate of 40 per cent once the nil-rate band is exceeded. It is currently the government's intention that the nil-rate band will remain at the same level at least until April 2018 (HMRC post-Budget Tax Information and Impact Note 20 March 2013 'Inheritance tax—nil-rate band'). This is subject to nil-rate band transfer for spouses and civil partners effective from 9 October 2007: see para **[200.75]**. The rate of IHT on lifetime transfers is a percentage of a full charge where the period between the transfer and the transferor's death is more than three years but fewer than seven years, the percentage being reduced for every year beyond three years that the transferor has survived (IHTA 1984, s 7). Transfers which are immediately chargeable (eg gifts into a settlement) are charged to tax at half full rates initially, but if the transferor dies within seven years the tax charge is recalculated, taking into account among other things the date of the transferor's death, any loss of business or agricultural relief by virtue of the disposal of business or agricultural property before the transferor's death (see the IHTA 1984, ss 113A, 113B, 124A, and 124B), and the tax rates prevailing at the transferor's death. If the tax so recalculated exceeds the tax already paid, the excess then becomes payable: IHTA 1984, s 7(2), (4), and (5). See para **[200.74]**.

[200.75]

[Updated for Finance Act 2008, s 10 and Sch 4.]

Nil-rate band transfer. This was announced by the Chancellor of the Exchequer in the Pre-Budget Report of 9 October 2007, to apply with effect from that date, and enacted by Finance Act 2008, s 10, Sch 4 inserting new IHTA 1984, ss 8A–8C. It allows the estate of anyone who dies after 8 October 2007 who was the survivor of a marriage or civil partnership to make use of nil rate band which was not used on the death of the predeceasing spouse or civil partner, irrespective of when the predeceasing spouse or civil partner died. It will be unused where the chargeable amount of the first to die's estate is zero or less than the nil-rate band at the time of his or her death, whether because all or part was exempt or because his or her estate was worth less than the nil-rate band (for the exemptions see paras **[200.84]** ff). The amount of transferable nil-rate band is calculated as follows, where A is the first to die of a married couple or civil partnership, and B is the second to die:

(1) Work out the maximum which could have been transferred on the death of A at a nil tax rate. This maximum is not reduced where the value of the assets owned by A at death was less than the then nil-rate band (see IHTA 1984, s 8A(2), definition of 'M'). This maximum is thus the amount of the nil-rate band under the rate table in force at the date of A's death, minus the aggregate of any lifetime chargeable transfers made or deemed to have been made by A in the seven years preceding his or her death, but increased by the previous application of these provisions if A died after 8 October 2007 and had had a previous spouse or civil partner who died without making full use of the nil-rate band. In the latter case the lack of a claim for nil-rate band transfer by A's personal representatives or anyone else within the permitted period (e g because A's estate was given to B or was too small for such a claim to make any difference) does not prevent a claim being made in respect of it as part of a claim for nil-rate band transfer on B's death, provided that it will not alter the amount of IHT payable on A's death (IHTA 1984, s 8B(2)).

(2) Then calculate the value actually transferred by the chargeable transfer taking effect on A's death, i e the value of the part of A's estate which has not on A's death gone to B, or a charity or other exempt recipient, or on IPDI trusts for B (for the exemptions see paras **[200.84]** ff). Where relevant this could include, for example, settled property in which A had an interest in possession or property subject to reservation in relation to A at death.

(3) Then deduct the amount arrived at under (2) above from the amount arrived at under (1) above. If the difference is a positive figure, there is available transferable nil-rate band. If the difference is zero or a negative quantity, there is none and the calculation stops here (see IHTA 1984, s 8A(2)).

(4) If stage (3) above shows that there is transferable nil-rate band, arrive at the percentage of the nil-rate band not used. The amount arrived at

under (3) above is divided by the nil-rate band in the rate table in force at the death of A, and the result is multiplied by a hundred (see IHTA 1984, s 8A(4)).

(5) Subject to (6)–(9) below, the nil-rate band in the rate table in force at the death of B is then increased by the percentage arrived at under (4) above when it comes to calculating the IHT on B's estate (see IHTA 1984, s 8A(3)).

(6) If the above calculations result in an increase in the nil-rate band in relation to B's estate on death of more than 100 per cent, the increase is limited to 100 per cent. This could occur where B had had one or more predeceased spouses or civil partners other than A who failed to make full use of their nil-rate band, or where A died after 8 October 2007 and had an enhanced nil-rate band as a result of a previous application of these rules (see IHTA 1984, s 8A(5), (6)).

(7) A claim for nil-rate band transfer will have to be made (see IHTA 1984, s 8A(3) and s 8B). It may be made by B's personal representatives within two years from the end of the month in which B died, or, if it ends later, within three months of them first acting as B's personal representatives. HMRC has power in individual cases to allow a longer period. If the personal representatives do not make a claim, anyone else liable for the IHT on B's death may do so within a period allowed in individual cases by HMRC. The burden will be on the taxpayer to show that the dispositions on A's death did not make full use of the available nil-rate band. It will be important to retain relevant records, particularly where A died intestate, or was a joint tenant of property, or left a will which did not leave all A's estate to B, or had an interest in possession in settled property. Estate accounts, any IHT assessments, and any deeds of variation, disclaimers, or appointments within two years of A's death made out of discretionary trusts created by A's will, particularly need to be retained so as to be available to B's personal representatives.

(8) If in relation to A's death there were deferred tax charges, under the rules for heritage property, non-agricultural woodlands, or alternatively secured pensions, there are rules in IHTA 1984, s 8C, and in amendments to IHTA 1984, 151BA, to make sure that either the deferred tax charge is taken into account in determining if and to what extent there is transferable nil-rate band, or that any transferable nil-rate band is taken into account in determining the amount of the deferred tax charge.

(9) If A has died not only before 9 October 2007 but also before 18 March 1986, ie the date when IHT replaced capital transfer tax, the rules are subject to modification in Finance Act 2008, Sch 4, para 10 so as to refer to the relevant earlier taxes (ie capital transfer tax or estate duty).

These rules eliminate the need for nil-rate band discretionary trusts in the majority of cases. For discussion of circumstances where such trusts might still be useful see para **[200.130]**. They also make survivorship clauses undesirable in relation to gifts by will to spouses or civil partners (see paras **[224.7]**–**[224.9]**).

[200.77]

[Updated for FA 2013, s 176, Sch 36.]

Deduction of liabilities on death. Liabilities of the deceased are deductible in determining his taxable estate on death for IHT purposes, so far as they were incurred for consideration in money or money's worth or imposed by law (IHTA 1984, s 5(5)), unless they fall within one or more of the following exceptions:

(1) there is a right of reimbursement reasonably likely to be obtained (IHTA 1984, s 162(1));
(2) the liability was incurred on or after 18 March 1986 and the consideration for it was property deriving from the deceased or consideration provided by someone who at any time before the deceased's death had had property deriving from the deceased (FA 1986 s 103(1)–(6));
(3) it is a liability connected with insurance made on or after 1 July 1986, where all or any of the sum assured is not part of the deceased's estate (FA 1986, s 103(7));
(4) where the deceased died on or after 17 July 2013 and the liability is non-deductible under IHTA 1984, s 162A (inserted by FA 2013, Sch 36) as having financed the acquisition, repair or enhancement of excluded property (for excluded property see para **[200.89]**);
(5) where the deceased died on or after 17 July 2013 and the liability is non-deductible under IHTA 1984, s 175A (inserted by FA 2013, Sch 36) because it is not discharged out of the deceased's estate or out of excluded property owned by the deceased. However, where there is a commercial reason for postponing discharge of the liability, it may still be deductible, particularly if it is a liability incurred in an arm's length transaction (see IHTA 1984, s 175A(2) and (3)).

Thus a liability incurred for no consideration, such as a deed of covenant, is not deductible for IHT purposes. If the deceased was entitled to a beneficiary-taxed interest in possession in settled property, but his free estate is insolvent, the excess of his liabilities over the assets of his free estate cannot then be deducted from the settled property in diminution of the IHT chargeable on the settled property on the deceased's death: *St Barbe Green v IRC* [2005] EWHC 14 (Ch), [2005] STC 288. Reasonable funeral expenses are deductible (IHTA 1984, s 172) and the cost of a tombstone or gravestone (Inland Revenue Statement of Practice SP 7/87). The administration expenses are not deductible, save that the expenses of administering or realising foreign property may be deductible if attributable to the location of the property and subject to a limit of five per cent of the value of the property (IHTA 1984, s 173), and the part of the estate spent on administration expenses apparently escapes being charged to IHT so far as the expenses are paid out of exempt residue (see para **[200.116]** below). Even if a liability is deductible, it may be subject to a rule requiring it to be deducted from particular assets: see para **[200.78]** below.

[200.78]

[Updated for FA 2013, s 176, Sch 36.]

Deduction of liabilities from particular assets is required as follows:

(1) Where the deceased died on or after 17 July 2013, and the liability was incurred on or after 6 April 2013 and financed the acquisition, repair or enhancement of 'relievable property'. Relievable property means in this context property qualifying for IHT business relief (see para **[205.4]** ff below), property qualifying for IHT agricultural relief (see para **[234.1]** ff below) or property entitled to IHT woodlands relief (see para **[234.14]** below). In such a case the liability must be deducted so far as possible from the relievable property which it financed before the amount of the relevant relief is determined. See IHTA 1984, s 162B inserted by FA 2013 Sch 36.

(2) Subject to IHTA 1984, s 162B requiring deduction from relievable property, liabilities which are incumbrances on property are deducted first from that property (IHTA 1984, s 162(4)).

(3) Also subject to IHTA 1984, s 162B requiring deduction from relievable property, liabilities to persons outside the UK which do not fall to be discharged in the UK and are not charged on property in the UK are deducted so far as possible from property outside the UK (IHTA 1984, s 162(5)).

[200.83]

[Updated for Finance Act 2008 s 10 and Sch 4, and Finance Act 2012, s 209 and Sch 33.]

Post-death rearrangement. It is often desired by the beneficiaries to alter the dispositions taking effect on the testator's death, sometimes to increase or alter the benefit taken by a particular beneficiary, sometimes to make better use of exemptions or reliefs, sometimes so as to pass assets on to the next generation. It is often possible to rearrange the devolution of the estate within two years of the testator's death so that the rearrangement is treated for IHT purposes as if done by the deceased, so that, for example, a rearrangement which gives more property to the deceased's surviving spouse obtains a corresponding increase in the amount of the estate which is exempt (see paras **[200.84]** ff below for the spouse exemption), or to increase the amount of nil-rate band transfer (see IHTA 1984, s 8A and para **[200.75]**), or to create or increase a charitable gift in order to obtain the lower rate on the chargeable part of the estate (see **[200.91A]** ff). The main methods of making such rearrangements are disclaimers or instruments of variation under the IHTA 1984, s 142 (see F3 at paras **[241.1]** ff) and distributions out of discretionary trusts created by will in accordance with the IHTA 1984, s 144 (see C3 at paras **[225.83]** ff). There are also distribution in accordance with the deceased's wishes of personal property in accordance with the IHTA 1984, s 143 (see B4 at paras **[204.9]** and **[204.10]**) and court orders (including certain kinds of agreed order) under the I(PFD)A 1975 (see the I(PFD)A, s 19: Part G, para **[247.25]**; and the IHTA 1984, s 146; see also Vol 1, para **[105.51]**).

(*b*) *Exemptions and reliefs relevant to testamentary dispositions*

[200.85]

[Updated for FA 2013, ss 177, 178.]

The extent of the IHT spouse or civil partnership exemption is restricted if the transferor, but not the transferor's spouse or civil partner, is domiciled in the UK, for which see IHTA 1984, s 18(2). Domicile in the UK for this purpose includes deemed domicile under IHTA 1984, s 267 (see para **[200.89]** below). In some cases there is a greater amount of exemption under a relevant double tax treaty. The limit under IHTA 1984, s 18(2) for transfers in these circumstances was £55,000 for transfers for 6 April 2013, but with effect from the latter date it is an amount equal to the nil-rate band for the time being (IHTA 1984, s 18(2) and (2A) as amended and inserted by FA 2013, s 178). The limit is on the cumulative total which can be exempt, so that, for example, if A is domiciled in the UK and makes a gift to his wife B who is not so domiciled, the gift will be exempt only to the extent that it does not exceed the difference between the current exemption limit and the total of all previous exempt transfers from A to B made since they were married. There is no seven-year cut-off point for the aggregation of previous transfers, and previous exempt transfers are taken into the aggregation even if they were made in circumstances that the limit did not apply to them, e g because made when A and B both had the same domicile.

Also, with effect from 6 April 2013, it is possible for the transferee spouse or civil partner who is domiciled outside the UK to elect to be treated as domiciled in the UK so as to avoid the limit on the exemption: IHTA 1984, ss 267ZA and 267ZB inserted by FA 2013, s 177. This can come at a cost where it causes transfers by the transferee to be brought into IHT charge. The election can be retrospective for up to seven years commencing with a date no earlier than 6 April 2013, and can in some circumstances be made by the personal representatives of the spouse or civil partner who was domiciled outside the UK.

[200.86]

[Updated for Finance Act 2008, s 10 and Sch 4.]

The introduction of nil-rate band transfer between spouses and civil partners (see para **[200.75]**) has the effect of reversing much standard tax-planning advice. Previously, spouses and civil partners were advised to try to make sure that the first to die would at death own sufficient assets to make use of all of his or her nil-rate band, and that the first to die should create a nil-rate band discretionary trust in his or her will (see para **[218.16]** ff for nil-rate band discretionary trusts). The transfer rules make the first of these completely unnecessary (see para **[200.75]**, sub-para (1)), and in most cases the sensible advice will be to rely on nil-rate band transfer and not create a nil-rate band discretionary trust by the will of the first to die. For the circumstances in which a nil-rate band discretionary trust might still be appropriate, see para **[200.130]**.

[200.87]

[Updated for FA 2012, s 209 and Sch 33 and FA 2013, Sch 21.]

Gifts to charities, registered community amateur sports clubs, political parties, housing associations, or for national purposes, and gifts to maintenance funds for historic buildings. There is exemption for all of these: IHTA 1984, ss 23–25 and 27. A political party has to have attained a specified level of success in the most recent general election for a gift to it to qualify for exemption: IHTA 1984, s 24(2). 'Gifts for national purposes' for the purposes of the exemption means gifts to any of the institutions (such as national museums and galleries, universities, local authorities and government departments) specified in the IHTA 1984, Sch 3: IHTA 1984, s 25(1). For charitable gifts, see B12, and for a gift by will to provide a maintenance fund, see Form C13.2 at para **[235.18]**. For the reduction in IHT rate obtainable for the chargeable part of an estate by making a testamentary gift or gifts to charity or registered sports clubs, see para **[200.91A]** ff. Registered community amateur sports clubs are ones registered with HMRC as such (Corporation Tax Act 2010, s 658 ff: IHTA 1984, s 23(7)). FA 2013, s 46 and Sch 21 amend the qualifying conditions for these, and may have the consequence, when the amendments come into force (on a date to be fixed by statutory instrument), that some of them who are currently registered will lose their registered status, with the consequence that gifts to them will no longer be exempt.

[200.89]

[Updated for FA 2013, s 177.]

Gifts made by persons with a foreign domicile. Property situated outside the UK and beneficially owned absolutely by someone with a foreign domicile (the rules are quite different for settled property, for which see the IHTA 1984, s 48(3)) is 'excluded property' (IHTA 1984, s 6(1)), which does not form part of that person's estate for the purposes of the charge to IHT on death: IHTA 1984, s 5(1). It must always be remembered that under the IHTA 1984, s 267 certain persons with a foreign domicile are treated as having a UK domicile for IHT purposes. In particular, anyone now giving up his UK domicile has to have a foreign domicile and be a foreign resident (for income tax purposes) for three years before he loses UK domicile for IHT purposes, and anyone with a foreign domicile is treated as having a UK domicile once they have been income tax resident in the UK for 17 out of 20 tax years, or for 16 out of 19 completed tax years in the case of anyone who is income tax resident in the current tax year. With effect from 6 April 2013, someone with a foreign domicile may be treated as having a UK domicile as a result of electing to be so treated under IHTA 1984, s 267ZA (see para **[200.85]** above).

[200.90]

Persons with a foreign domicile but deemed to have a UK domicile under the IHTA 1984, s 267 or s 267ZA are, however, helped by the IHTA 1984, ss 6(2) and 48(4)–(7). By virtue of those provisions, exempt government securities are 'excluded property' while beneficially owned by someone not domiciled or ordinarily resident in the UK and IHTA 1984, ss 267 and 267ZA do not apply for the purposes of that paragraph: IHTA 1984, ss 267(2) and 267ZA(5). There is an additional exception for persons domiciled in the Channel Islands or the Isle of Man who are entitled to certain types of government bonds or rights under certificated contractual savings schemes: IHTA 1984, s 6(3). The deemed domicile provisions are excluded in this case also: IHTA 1984, ss 267(2) and 267ZA(5).

For the advantages of creating will trusts where the testator is domiciled outside the UK see C14 at paras **[236.1]** ff.

[200.91A]

[Paras [200.91A]–[200.91F] describe the lower IHT rate under FA 2012, Sch 33 where a proportion is given to charity or registered clubs.]

The lower rate where a proportion is given to charity or registered clubs. FA 2012, s 209 and Sch 33 insert a new Sch 1A into IHTA 1984, which provides a lower (36 per cent) rate of IHT on any taxable 'component' of a deceased person's estate where 10 per cent or more of the 'baseline amount' for that component is given to charity or registered amateur sports clubs by a gift falling within IHTA 1984, s 23 (for which see paras **[200.87]**. and **[212.2]**). IHTA 1984, Sch 1A has effect in relation to the estates of persons dying on or after 6 April 2012 (FA 2012, Sch 33, para 10(1)). HMRC provide a new section of the IHT Manual on the lower rate (IHTM 45001 ff), and a reduced rate calculator at http://hmrc.gov.uk/tools/iht-reduced-rate/calculator.htm. The calculator is for working out whether a legacy is sufficient for there to be a component of the estate which qualifies for the reduced rate, or calculating the minimum amount which has to go to charity for a component to so qualify. For drafting gifts by will so as to qualify for the lower rate, see paras **[212.2A]** and **[212.4A]**, and for deeds of variation increasing or making charitable gifts to qualify for the lower rate, see paras **[241.15A]** and **[241.31]**.

The lower rate is only available in respect of transfers of value occurring on death, and is not available against deferred IHT charges which become payable under conditional exemption for heritage property, relief for woodlands, and relief for maintenance funds for historic buildings (FA 2012, Sch 33, paras 4–6 and 8).

[200.91B]

The lower rate of IHT—components of the estate. The three possible types of component of a deceased person's estate which are capable of qualifying for the lower rate in the absence of merger with another component are as follows (IHTA 1984, Sch 1A, para 3):

(1) 'the survivorship component': all or any severable shares of jointly held property which accrue to the other joint tenant or tenants under the *ius accrescendi* (or similar rights in Scottish or non-UK law);
(2) 'the settled property component': all or any settled property in which the deceased had one or more 'beneficiary-taxed' interests in possession falling within IHTA 1984, s 49(1), i e pre-22 March 2006 interests in possession, immediate post-death interests, disabled persons' interests, or transitional serial interests (see para **[200.92]**);
(3) 'the general component': all property in the estate other than property

in the survivorship component, property in the settled property component, or property subject to a reservation within the meaning of FA 1986, s 102. This will be the free estate disposable by will.

There is one other possible type of component; namely, property subject to a reservation within the meaning of FA 1986, s 102. This component cannot by itself qualify for the lower rate, but can do so by means of a merger with another component: see para **[200.91D]**.

[200.91C]

The lower rate of IHT—the baseline amount and the donated amount. If the deceased's estate contains more than one of the components referred to in para **[200.91B]** (other than property subject to a reservation), each is first looked at separately. If there is a part of any such component which is exempt under IHTA 1984, s 23 ('the donated amount') and which constitutes 10 per cent or more of the 'baseline amount' for that component, the lower rate applies to the chargeable part of that component (IHTA 1984, Sch 1A, paras 2 and 4). The baseline amount is the sum of: first, the part of the component which is exempt under IHTA 1984, s 23, and, secondly, the chargeable part of the component after the component's appropriate proportion of the available nil-rate band has been deducted from it (IHTA 1984, Sch 1A, para 5). The available nil-rate band (IHTA 1984, Sch 1A, para 5 Step 2) is the current amount of it in the rate table after deduction of any of it which has been used up on lifetime gifts, but increased by any transferable nil-rate band under IHTA 1984, s 8A (for which see para **[200.75]**).The available nil-rate band is shared among the chargeable parts of the components of the estate rateably according to value. It therefore turns out not to be a straightforward 10 per cent of the component or of the chargeable part of it which is the determining factor. If there is only one component of the deceased's estate (which is not property subject to a reservation) then the foregoing calculation is carried out on the estate and is concluded at this point. As mentioned in para **[200.91A]**, HMRC provide a calculator for working out whether a component of an estate qualifies for the reduced rate.

[200.91D]

The lower rate of IHT—merger of components. There is a second possible stage, which is that there can be an election, by notice in writing within two years of the deceased person's death, by the 'appropriate persons' (see para **[200.91F]**, to have one or more components, which may include property subject to a reservation, merged for the purposes of the calculation (IHTA 1984, Sch 1A, para 7). This enables a charitable gift or gift to registered sports clubs which exceeds the threshold for the component to which it belongs to benefit the components with which its component is merged. The 10 per cent threshold then has to be reached by the charitable gift or gifts in the merged components, relative to the combined value of the merged components, for the reduced rate to apply to the merged components. It seems from the wording of the merger provisions that if the election is made, and the combined components turn out not to qualify for the reduced rate of IHT, the right to the reduced rate is lost in relation to the component which by itself qualified for it, in the absence of a valid withdrawal of the election.

[200.91E]

The lower rate of IHT—application of partial exemption rules. Where the lower rate is or may be applicable, the partial exemption rules (see para **[200.112]** ff) must be applied subject to the two modifications described below for the purpose of establishing whether the lower rate applies. These are both modifications which make it easier to qualify for the lower rate.

The first modification of the partial exemption rules is that grossing up of specific gifts which do not bear their own IHT is to be done at the lower rate of 36 per cent (IHTA 1984, Sch 1A, para 6(1)). If calculation on that basis fails to show an entitlement to the lower rate, the calculations will have to be done again grossing up such gifts at 40 per cent. The HMRC website provides a grossing up calculator at 36 per cent.

The other modification is that, when working out whether the lower rate applies, the rules for partial exemption where there is business or agricultural relief in IHTA 1984, s 39A (see para **[200.117]** ff) are not to be applied to a specific gift of property which is exempt under IHTA 1984, s 23, for the purposes of calculating the 'donated amount', though it is still to be so applied in calculating the baseline amount and determining the extent of the chargeable part of the estate (IHTA 1984, Sch 1A, para 6(2)). This disapplication of s 39A means that where there is a specific gift of property to charity or registered clubs it is taken at its full unrelieved value for the purpose of determining the donated amount when determining whether the lower rate applies. It is relevant to cases where there is a specific gift of relieved property to charity or registered clubs, or, what is likely to be more common, where an estate includes relieved property which is not specifically given and there is a specific gift to charity, either of a cash amount or of specific property which is not relieved property.

[200.91F]

The lower rate of IHT—electing for merger or out of the lower rate. In addition to the merger election described in para **[200.91D]**, there is also the option of electing out of the lower rate (IHTA 1984, Sch 1A, para 8(1)). This is for cases where the administrative costs of working out and negotiating the reduced rate might exceed the amount of IHT which might be saved; for example, where there is a gift to charity of an asset of uncertain value, and in respect of which the value does not have to be ascertained if the lower rate is not claimed.

There is also a right to withdraw a merger election or an election out of the lower rate (IHTA 1984, Sch 1A, para 9(2)).

The persons who need to make an election to merge components are the 'appropriate persons' in relation to all the components to be merged (IHTA 1984, Sch 1A, para 7(6)), and the same persons need to participate in any withdrawal of the election (IHTA 1984, Sch 1A, para 9(2)). The persons to elect to opt out of the reduced rate, or withdraw the election to opt out, are the 'appropriate persons' in relation to the component or components in respect of which the opt-out or the withdrawal of an election is made (IHTA 1984, Sch 1A, para 8(2)).

The 'appropriate persons' in relation to each component are as follows (IHTA 1984, Sch 1A, para 7(7)). In relation to the general component they are all the personal representatives, unless there are none, in which case they are all the persons liable for the IHT on that component. In relation to any survivorship component they are all the persons to whom the property passes on the deceased's death, or their personal representatives. In relation to any settled property component they are all the trustees of the settled property comprised in the component, and in relation to property subject to a reservation they are all those in whom the property is vested when the election is made.

Elections have to be made in writing within two years of the deceased's death, though once made they can be withdrawn within the two-year period plus an extra month (IHTA 1984, Sch 1A, para 9).

Officers of the HMRC have a discretion to extend the time for making elections or withdrawing them (IHTA 1984, Sch 1A, para 9(3)). HMRC's IHT Manual says that the circumstances for allowing a late claim are the same as those for a late claim to nil-rate band transfer (IHTM45044). These are such matters as destruction by fire, serious illness or disruption of postal services (IHTM43009). It is to be regretted that the IHT Manual does not mention another circumstance which might be thought to justify allowing a late election (and which is not relevant to nil-rate band transfer), namely where agreeing or establishing the value of assets of the estate takes more than two years through no fault of the executors or trustees.

(*c*) *Will trusts*

[200.99]

[Updated for Perpetuities and Accumulations Act 2009 and FA 2013, Sch 44.]

Beneficiary-taxed interests in possession – disabled persons' interests. Disabled persons for this purpose are persons mentally incapable of managing their affairs, or in receipt of, or qualified to receive, attendance allowance (persons of 65 or over), or in receipt of, or qualified to receive, disability living allowance with the care component at the highest or middle rate (persons under 65). For cases where property is transferred into settlement on or after 8 April 2013 (so generally where a testator dies on or after 8 April 2013) they include in addition persons in receipt of (or qualified to receive) personal independence payment, an increased disablement pension, constant attendance allowance or armed forces independence payment, see IHTA 1984, s 89(4), (4A) (as amended and inserted by FA 2013, Sch 44, para 6(4),(5)) and s 89B(2) (as substituted by FA 2013, Sch 44, para 8(2)), incorporating into the inheritance tax legislation the definition of disabled person from FA 2005, Sch 1A. The term 'disabled person's interest' is defined in IHTA 1984, s 89B (as amended by FA 2013, Sch 44, paras 8, 10). It includes two types of interest which are relevant in the drafting of wills. The first is an actual interest in possession in settled property to which a disabled person is beneficially entitled, and the second is a non-interest in possession trust falling within IHTA 1984, s 89 which is treated as being an interest in possession trust.

(1) The requirements for an actual interest in possession to be a disabled person's interest have been made more stringent following amendments made by FA 2013. So where property has been transferred into a settlement before 8 April 2013 (so generally where a testator has died

before 8 April 2013 establishing a trust by his will) an interest in possession arising under the trust will be a disabled person's interest simply if the person entitled to it was disabled at the time of the transfer (ie the testator's death), see IHTA 1989, s 89B(1)(c), (2) (before amendment by FA 2013, Sch 44, paras 10(1), 8(2)). However, where property is transferred into a settlement on or after 8 April 2013 (so generally where a testator dies on or after 8 April 2013 establishing a trust by his will) an interest in possession arising under the trust will be a disabled person's interest only if the person entitled to it is disabled and if the trusts secure that if any settled property is applied during the disabled person's life for the benefit of a beneficiary, it is applied for the benefit of the disabled person, see IHTA 1989, s 89B(1)(c) (amended by FA 2013, Sch 44, para 10(1)). In this case, it seems that the relevant time for a person to qualify as disabled if his interest is to be disabled person's interest, is the date when the interest arises, rather than the date when property was transferred into settlement (as was previously the case) (see the new definition of 'disabled person' in IHTA 1984, s 89B(2) (as substituted by FA 2013, Sch 44, para 8(2)) which does not import into the definition the requirement that the person be disabled at the time of transfer into settlement as was previously the case (and as continues under IHTA 1984, s 89(4) for a non-interest in possession trust for a disabled person). Although the position is not entirely clear, it seems likely that his interest would continue to be a disabled person's interest even if he ceased to be disabled during the continuance of his interest. Another point to notice with regard to the new definition of disabled person's interest, is that the requirement that capital be applicable only for the benefit of the disabled person is tempered by the provision that certain powers are not incompatible with it, ie powers that enable the trustees to apply otherwise than for the benefit of the disabled person amounts (whether consisting of income or capital, or both) not exceeding an annual limit which is currently set at the lower of £3,000 and 3 per cent of the maximum value of the settled property during the tax year in question, and powers of advancement conferred by the TA 1925, s 32 (or equivalent Northern Ireland legislation), even where modified so as to be applicable to the whole of a presumptive or vested share of capital instead of one half (or powers to the like effect) (IHTA 1989, s 89C (inserted by FA 2013, Sch 44, para 10(2)). Still, the consent of the disabled person will be required to any exercise of a power of advancement since they will have a 'prior life or other interest' within the TA 1925, s 32(1), proviso (c), so that in practice such powers will not be exercisable where the disabled beneficiary is disabled by reason of mental incapacity.

(2) The requirements for a non-interest in possession trust to fall within IHTA 1984, s 89 so that the disabled person is treated as having an interest in possession in the property subject to it have also been changed, as a result of amendments made by FA 2013, s 216, Sch 44, para 6. For details of the requirements, both before and after amendment, see **[226.3]** and **[226.4]**.

Both these types of interest in possession (i e the actual interest in possession of (1) above and the deemed interest in possession of (2) above) are beneficiary-taxed. See IHTA 1984, ss 49(1A)(b), 89, 89B (as amended by FA 2013, Sch 44, paras 6, 8,10). See, further, Part C4 at paras **[226.1]** ff. Trusts for disabled persons can also obtain a measure of income tax and capital gains tax relief under FA 2005, ss 23–45, and now the qualifying requirements which the trusts have to satisfy to obtain the relief are similar to those relating to the IHT special treatment: see Part C4, paras **[226.3]** ff below. There is uprating of acquisition value on the death of the disabled person for capital gains tax purposes (see para **[200.39]**) where he has an actual interest in possession which is beneficiary-taxed, but not if he is deemed to have a beneficiary-taxed interest in possession under IHTA 1984, s 89.

[200.100]

[Updated for Finance Act 2008.]

Beneficiary-taxed interests in possession – transitional provisions. In addition to the general categories of beneficiary-taxed interest in possession described above, there are two transitional categories of interest in possession which remain beneficiary-taxed. These are interests in possession which commenced before 22 March 2006, and 'transitional serial interests'. The latter term comprises three sub-categories: interests in possession which follow on from a pre-22 March 2006 interest in possession in the same property and commence after 21 March 2006 but before 6 October 2008 (IHTA 1984, s 49C); a person's interest in possession under a pre-22 March 2006 settlement which commences on the death after 5 October 2008 of the spouse or civil partner of that person, where the deceased spouse or civil partner had been entitled to an interest in possession which had commenced before 22 March 2006 and had been in the same property (IHTA 1984, s 49D); certain successive interests in life insurance policies which were settled before 22 March 2006 (IHTA 1984, s 49E). These are not interests which can be created by a will disposing of free estate, but the rules concerning them can be relevant to the preparation of a will. Where a testator has an interest in possession in settled property it is necessary for estimating the likely IHT position on his death to know whether his interest is a beneficiary-taxed one. If it is, there is then the question of whether it will be fully taxable as part of the testator's estate on death and thus affect the rate of tax on the testator's free estate, and, if it potentially will be so taxable, whether anything can be done about it. For example, if the testator has a special power of appointment over the settled property it may be possible for him to make an appointment in favour of his spouse or civil partner. If the testator has an interest in possession which commenced before 22 March 2006 the appointment of an interest in possession to the surviving spouse or civil partner could cause the settled property to be exempt on the testator's death (by virtue of IHTA 1984, s 49D), whereas if the testator has a transitional serial interest it will be necessary to appoint an absolute interest to the surviving spouse or civil partner in order to obtain the exemption.

[200.108]

[Updated for FA 2013, Sch 44.]

Trusts for bereaved minors. As mentioned in para **[200.107]**, a trust can only fall within an IHTA 1984, s 71A trust if one of the beneficiary's parents has died, and if the trust (if created by will) is created by the will of a parent of the child. Section 71A has (as appears below) been amended by FA 2013, Sch 44, para 2 with respect to property transferred into settlement on or after 8 April 2013 (so generally where a parent dies on or after 8 April 2013). The main requirement as to the form taken by such a trust, for IHTA 1984, s 71A to apply, is that the beneficiary will become absolutely entitled to the income and capital on or before attaining the age of 18. The trusts must also be such that the income arising before the beneficiary attains 18 is either income to which the beneficiary is entitled as it arises, ie it is held on an interest in possession trust for the beneficiary, or it is subject to a power to apply the income for the benefit of the beneficiary (and there is no power to apply it for anyone else) and the rest of the income is accumulated and held on trust for the beneficiary absolutely on attaining 18. Note the following:

(1) If the beneficiary has an interest in possession as from the testator's death, the trust will nevertheless fall within s 71A rather than be an IPDI trust (IHTA 1984, s 49A(4)(a)). However, a bare trust for a minor does not fall within s 71A, not being settled property (see para **[200.110]**), and a disabled person's interest (see para **[200.99]**) does not fall within s 71A either (s 71A(1)).

(2) Powers over capital must (subject as appears in sub paragraph (4) below) be limited to a power to apply capital for the benefit of the beneficiary. However, it is expressly provided that the possession by the trustees of the power of advancement under Trustee Act 1925, s 32, or a similar express power, even if expanded to be exercisable over more than half of the beneficiary's prospective entitlement, does not prevent the section from applying: s 71A(4). This, together with the provision that an application of capital for the benefit of a beneficiary is not an occasion of IHT charge (s 71B(2)(c)), means that it is possible in an appropriate case to defer vesting beyond 18 by an exercise of a power of advancement before the beneficiary attains that age, provided that the exercise is genuinely for the benefit of the beneficiary, at an acceptable cost in terms of IHT – there is no IHT charge on the exercise of power, but the relevant property or 18-to-25 trust regimes will apply thereafter: see, further, para **[224.24]**.

(3) The compatibility with s 71A trusts of a Trustee Act 1925, s 32 power applying to the whole of a presumptive share, as just described, is thus made clear. Prior to tax year 2013–14, its compatibility with trusts for the vulnerable within FA 2005, ss 23–45 for income tax and capital gains tax purposes was uncertain, but now amendments to FA 2005, s 35(4) by FA 2013, Sch 44, para 16(3) have made clear that it is compatible, at least for tax year 2013–14 and onwards (see para **[217.3]**).

(4) Where property is transferred into settlement on or after 8 April 2013 (so generally where a testator dies on or after 8 April 2013), the

trustees may additionally have powers enabling them to apply otherwise than for the benefit of the bereaved minor amounts (whether consisting of income or capital, or both) not exceeding an annual limit which is currently set at the lower of £3,000 and 3 per cent of the maximum value of the settled property during the tax year in question (IHTA 1984, s 71A(4)(za), (4B)–(4E), inserted by FA 2013, Sch 44, para 2(3), (4)). Amounts so applied will not occasion an IHT charge (s 71B(2A), (2B) as inserted by FA 2013, Sch 44, para 3). Such powers are also compatible in tax year 2013–14 and onwards with trusts for the vulnerable within FA 2005, ss 23–45 (see FA 2005, s 35(4) by FA 2013, Sch 44, para 16(3)).

(5) HMRC accept that IHTA 1984, s 71A can apply to a class gift where each beneficiary has a presumptive undivided share of an entire fund, and that it can apply to some undivided shares but not to others: *STEP/CIOT/HMRC April 2007,* questions 26 and 27.

(6) It might be thought that where there is, for example, a class gift to the children of the testator, the individual presumptive shares have to be looked at separately to see if IHTA 1984, s 71A applies. This would mean that for the trusts to fall within s 71A, the prospective share to which each beneficiary will become entitled if he attains the age of 18 must be fixed from the outset, and that a trust will not fall within s 71A if there is power to vary the shares to be taken by each beneficiary before they attain the age of 18. However, HMRC have stated, without explaining how they derive this from the wording of s 71A, that they accept that it is compatible with s 71A to have a class gift where the shares ultimately taken by the beneficiaries may be varied as between or among beneficiaries who are for the time being living and under the age of 18, provided that all the beneficiaries retain continuously some presumptive share, however small (*S 71A etc guidance, June 2007,* para 1). Thus it is HMRC's opinion, first, that for s 71A to apply, the trusts must be such that a beneficiary's share of capital will be irrevocably determined no later than attaining the age of 18 and, secondly, that s 71A will cease to apply if a power to vary shares is exercised revocably so as to reduce the presumptive share of one of several beneficiaries to nil in circumstances where that beneficiary could have a presumptive share restored to him on a revocation of that exercise of the power. On the other hand, HMRC say that the mere existence of an unexercised power that can be exercised in this way does not prevent s 71A from applying.

(7) As regards the income of each share, the choice is between TA 1925, s 31 applying unamended, or interest in possession treatment of the income during the minority. The latter has the advantage that the income will be subject to income tax as the income of the minor beneficiary rather than under the discretionary trust income regime (see B18 at paras **[218.29]** and **[218.32]** for the latter).

(8) HMRC accept that a trust within s 71A can be created by the exercise of a special power of appointment created by the testator's will, but not by exercise of a general power (*STEP/CIOT/HMRC April 2007,* question 19). An example would be where a testator's will gives his surviving spouse a life interest and confers on the trustees a special

power of appointment exercisable for the benefit of the testator's issue, and that power is exercised by the trustees to create a trust which satisfies the s 71A preconditions.

(9) If s 71A applies, there is no IHT on the fund during the child's minority or on the child attaining his or her majority and becoming entitled to the capital, in the same way as formerly under IHTA 1984, s 71. If a 'vulnerable person election' can be made (see (3) above) and is made (FA 2005, ss 24, 37 – see para **[217.2]** below), the trustees' capital gains and undistributed income will be taxed as the beneficiary's (FA 2005, ss 25–33): see para **[217.2]**.

(10) If an IPDI comes to an end during the life of the person entitled to it (typically an IPDI given to the testator's surviving spouse), to be followed by a s 71A trust under the same settlement, the resulting deemed transfer of value on the termination of the IPDI is potentially exempt: see IHTA 1984, s 3A(1A)(c)(iii), (3B), and para **[200.128]**.

(11) One advantage of a s 71A trust is that capital gains tax holdover relief is available on the property vesting in the beneficiary at or before attaining the age of 18: TCGA 1992, s 260(2)(da) as inserted by FA 2006. However, if the underlying property is land and the s 71A trust is a class gift for, for example, three children of the testator of different ages, none of the beneficiaries will become absolutely entitled to any of the trust property for capital gains tax purposes until the youngest attains the age of 18 (assuming all the land is retained until then and none of it is appropriated to an individual share). In such a situation there would only be holdover relief on the share of the youngest (unless business assets holdover relief is available under TCGA 1992, s 165). If this is a cause for concern a relevant property trust or even a bare trust may be more appropriate.

[200.109]

[Updated for Perpetuities and Accumulations Act 2009 and FA 2013, Sch 44.]

Age 18-to-25 trusts for a bereaved minor. These are trusts within IHTA 1984, s 71D, which like s 71A has been amended by FA 2013, Sch 44, with respect to property transferred into settlement on or after 8 April 2013 (so generally where a parent dies on or after 8 April 2013). Apart from two important differences, the conditions for a trust to be within s 71D are the same as for trusts within s 71A, including the requirements that a parent of the beneficiary must have died, that (in the case of a trust created by a will) the trust must be established under the will of a deceased parent of the beneficiary or beneficiaries, and that it is not a trust for a disabled person within the rules referred to in para **[200.99]**. The main difference in the requirements for s 71D from those for s 71A is that the trusts should provide for absolute vesting of the capital and unapplied income no later than the age of 25, as opposed to the age of 18 in the case of s 71A trusts. The points made about IHTA 1984, s 71A trusts in sub-paras (2), (4)–(6) and (8) of para **[200.108]** apply equally, mutatis mutandis, to s 71D trusts. The corresponding provision ensuring compatibility of s 71D applying with a Trustee Act 1925, s 32 power being exercisable, including being exercisable over the whole of a presumptive share, is in IHTA 1984, s 71D(7), and the provision ensuring compatibility of s 71D (where property is transferred into settlement on or after 8 April 2013) with the trustees having powers enabling them to apply otherwise than for the benefit of the deceased's child amounts not exceeding an annual limit, is in s 71D(7)(za), (7B)–(7E), inserted by FA 2013, Sch 44, para 4(4), (5). The HMRC view of acceptable variability of the shares referred to in para **[200.108]**, sub-para (6), where a trust is intended to be within s 71D, is of course that a beneficiary's share must become fixed irrevocably no later than attaining the age of 25. The second, more technical difference, between the preconditions for s 71D to apply and those for s 71A, is that if an under-25 beneficiary has an interest in possession commencing at the testator's death (and the trusts would otherwise fall within s 71D) it is an IPDI trust not a s 71D trust (s 71D(5)(c)). There are three main differences of s 71D from s 71A in its tax consequences, as follows:

(1) A s 71D trust does not fall within FA 2005, ss 23–45, ie the special income tax and capital gains tax treatment for trusts for bereaved minors, for which see para **[217.4]**).
(2) The property in a s 71D trust will be subject to an IHT charge on the property vesting in the s 71D beneficiary, but only if absolute vesting occurs after the beneficiary has attained the age of 18. Where this happens, the property is subject to a 'relevant property' IHT exit charge, is not subject to the periodic charge, and the exit charge is calculated on the basis of the property having been relevant property only since the later to occur of the death of the testator or beneficiary attaining the age of 18 (s 71F).
(3) If an IPDI comes to an end during the life of the person entitled to it to be succeeded by a s 71D trust, the deemed transfer of value on the coming to an end of the IPDI is not potentially exempt.

As regards the income, the choice is between TA, 1925, s 31 applying unamended so that the beneficiary gets an interest in possession at 18, or extending the TA 1925, s 31 treatment of the income beyond the age of 18. It is strongly recommended that in all s 71D trusts the accumulation and maintenance trusts of income of TA 1925, s 31 are expressly extended to continue until the beneficiary attains the age of 25 (in the case of a will made on or after 6 April 2010 there are no restrictions on accumulation apart from the rule against perpetuities—see para **[200.35F]**). This is to avoid the possibility of it accidentally turning out to be an IPDI trust as a result of the testator dying when the beneficiary is between the ages of 18 and 25 in circumstances where s 31 applies without amendment. For extended accumulation and maintenance trusts see B18 at paras **[218.74]** ff, and Form C2.1, cl 8 at para **[224.36]**. Capital gains tax holdover relief is available on the property vesting in the beneficiary if it does so on or before he or she attains the age of 18 (TCGA 1992, s 260(2)(db) as inserted by FA 2006) or over 18 (TCGA 1992, s 260(2)(a)). The problem for the availability of holdover relief where the underlying property is land and the beneficial shares vest at different times, referred to in para **[200.108]** sub-para (10), is equally relevant to s 71D trusts.

[200.110]

[Updated for FA 2013, Sch 44.]

Bare trusts. A bare trust created by will, ie where a trustee holds property on trust for someone absolutely, is of little practical difference from an outright gift where the recipient is an adult who does not suffer from a mental disability. The possibility of creating by testamentary gift a bare trust for someone who is still a minor, however, is a possibility of increased interest after the FA 2006 changes to IHT. HMRC accept that the trust property is not 'settled property' for IHT purposes, and that this is so whether or not Trustee Act 1925, s 31 has been excluded (*STEP/CIOT/HMRC April 2007*, question 33). The practical effect of a bare trust for a minor is not very different from an IHTA 1984, s 71A trust for a bereaved minor (see para **[200.108]** for the latter). The main difference is that on the death of the minor beneficiary of a bare trust under the age of 18 the trust property will pass under the intestacy rules, and be subject to IHT on his or her death, while under a s 71A trust the trust property can devolve under the trusts of the will and will not be subject to IHT on the beneficiary's death. Also, where there is a class of minor beneficiaries, there can be no flexibility as to the shares taken by each in the case of a bare trust, while some limited flexibility is permitted, according to HMRC, in the case of a s 71A trust (see para **[200.108]**, sub-para (5)). A further difference in respect of property transferred into settlement on or after 8 April 2013 (so generally where a testator dies on or after 8 April 2013), is that the trustees may, compatibly with a 71A trust, have powers enabling them to apply otherwise than for the benefit of the minor beneficiary amounts (whether consisting of income or capital, or both) not exceeding an annual limit which is currently set at the lower of £3,000 and 3 per cent of the maximum value of the settled property during the tax year in question (IHTA 1984, s 71A(4)(za), (4B)–(4E), inserted by FA 2013, Sch 44, para 2(3), (4)). Such powers would not be compatible with a bare trust. The fact that the property passes under the intestacy rules has the disadvantage that if there is a surviving parent or parents the property is likely to devolve on him, her or them, but this disadvantage could perhaps be avoided where there is a class of beneficiaries, by making them entitled to the trust property as joint tenants (provided a least one survives the age of 18). The IHT charge on death will not be a disadvantage if the property is worth less than the nil-rate band at the beneficiary's death. A bare trust for a minor is the nearest to a s 71A trust which can be created in a will of a person who is not a parent of the intended beneficiary. If a will gives someone an IPDI (see para **[200.108]**), and that comes to an end during that person's life in favour of a bare trust for a minor, the deemed transfer of value on the coming to an end of the IPDI can be a potentially exempt transfer. For income tax and capital gains tax purposes the property subject to a bare trust arising under a will is the beneficiary's. The problem relating to s 71A trusts for the availability of holdover relief where the underlying property is land and the beneficial shares vest at different times, referred to in para **[200.108]**, sub-para (10), would not apply to a bare trust. A bare trust for a minor could and should include power for the trustees to apply income and capital for the benefit of the beneficiary, typically by Trustee Act 1925, ss 31 and 32 applying, preferably with s 32 applying to the whole of the beneficiary's entitlement.

(*g*) *Trusts in dispositions by will – usefulness, the alternatives, and tax consequences*

[200.132]

[Updated for Perpetuities and Accumulations Act 2009.]

Trusts for minor children, grandchildren, nieces, nephews etc. Where what is wanted is a trust for the testator's own minor children or stepchildren there are, in addition to the possibilities discussed in para **[200.131]**, the options of a s 71A or a s 71D trust: see paras **[200.108]** and **[200.109]** above for the requirements and advantages, and para **[200.128]** for the possibility of potential exemption where a s 71A trust succeeds an IPDI. If the testator is a parent or step-parent of the prospective beneficiaries but does not want vesting of capital in the beneficiaries by the age of 25, or he is not a parent or step-parent of the prospective beneficiaries, there are the possibilities of IPDIs (see para **[200.98]**), or a relevant property trust (see para **[218.8]** ff). For the comparative merits of IPDI and relevant property trusts see para **[200.131]**. Another option in the opposite direction is a bare trust: see para **[200.110]**. Where an IPDI is provided for a person under 18, or a s 71A trust is created with an interest in possession in the income while a beneficiary is under the age of 18, the beneficiary will become entitled to call for the current income from the age of 18, and on attaining that age to call for any income which has arisen during the minority which has not been applied for his or her benefit. If an IPDI is being provided for someone who may be a minor at the testator's death, remember to modify TA 1925, s 31 so that he or she will be absolutely entitled to the income as it arises while he or she is a minor: see Form C2.1, cl 8 at para **[224.36]**, for an example. TA 1925, s 31 unmodified makes contingent on attaining 18 the right to the income arising during the minority which is not applied for the beneficiary's benefit, and so prevents there being an interest in possession. Bare trusts, on the other hand (see para **[200.110]**), do not require express modification of s 31 in this manner because s 31 provides that unapplied income during the minority is added to capital if the beneficiary dies under the age or 18, and the beneficiary is entitled to the capital in any event. Where a trust of capital vesting contingently on attaining a specified age greater than 18 is being created for a minor or minors which will not fall within IHTA 1984, ss 71A or 71D, and where it is intended that the relevant property rather than the IPDI regime should apply, it is recommended that the accumulation and maintenance trusts of income of TA 1925, s 31 are expressly extended to continue until the age of vesting (the restrictions on accumulation for less than the perpetuity having been abolished for wills made on or after 6 April 2010—see para **[200.35F]**). This is to avoid the possibility of it accidentally turning out to be an IPDI trust as a result of the testator dying when the beneficiary is between the ages of 18 and the vesting age in circumstances where s 31 applies without amendment. For extended accumulation and maintenance trusts see B18 at paras **[218.74]** ff, and Form C2.1, cl 8 at para **[224.36]**.

(*h*) *Review of existing wills after FA 2006 and the Pre-Budget Report of 9 October 2007*

[200.136]

[Updated for FA 2013, Sch 44.]

Trusts for minor children and young persons. This is the category of testamentary provision which is most affected by FA 2006. Wills which were made before 22 March 2006 which contain trusts for minor children drafted with the former IHTA 1984, s 71 (accumulation and maintenance trusts) in mind will in many cases have different tax consequences from those originally contemplated when the will was made. How different will depend on the terms of the trust and what has happened by the time of the death of the testator. The main possibilities are as follows:

(1) The existing will contains a simple accumulation and maintenance trust where the beneficiaries are the children of the testator, capital vests in equal or other fixed shares at the age of 18, and Trustee Act 1925, s 31 applies to the income. It will fall within IHTA 1984, s 71A (see para **[200.108]**) and the tax consequences are much as originally contemplated. A codicil or new will is not needed.

(2) The existing will contains a simple accumulation and maintenance trust where the beneficiaries are the children of the testator, capital vests in equal or other fixed shares at the age of 25, and Trustee Act 1925, s 31 applies to the income. It falls within IHTA 1984, s 71D (see para **[200.109]**). The tax consequences are not as originally contemplated in that, in relation to the share of any beneficiary who has not attained the age of 25 before the testator's death, there will be an IHT charge on capital vesting at an age greater than 18 (see para **[200.109]**). Such IHT charge will in most cases be modest, and a price worth paying for postponement of vesting where such postponement is found to be appropriate. Further, if, as will often be the case, there is a full power of advancement, or similar power (typically the Trustee Act 1925, s 32 power expanded expressly apply to the whole of a presumptive share), the potential IHT charge can be avoided or substantially mitigated by the exercise of the power within two years of the testator's death to make the beneficiary absolutely entitled. Such a power may also be exercisable so as to create a short-term IPDI trust (IHTA 1984, s 144 would enable this – see para **[200.133]**). Review of such a will is not a pressing matter, but the testator could consider the alternative of IPDI trusts if the will was reviewed for other reasons.

(3) The existing will contains simple accumulation and maintenance trusts of the kinds described in (1) or (2) above of this paragraph, but the testator is not a parent of the beneficiaries, or he or she is but there is some element in the trust which prevents IHTA 1984, s 71A or 71D from applying. In this case the settled property will fall within the relevant property rules to the extent that the beneficiary or beneficiaries interested in it are under the age of vesting of capital at the testator's death, subject to one point. If the trusts are such that a beneficiary attains an interest in possession in his presumptive share before attaining the age of vesting of capital, and by the time of the

testator's death a beneficiary has attained the age at which an interest in possession is attained but not attained the age of vesting of capital, the position is as described under (4) below of this paragraph. As regards the whole or part of the fund which is relevant property at the death of the testator, if there is a sufficient power of advancement or similar power of the kind referred to under (2) above, the property can be converted into being subject to a bare trust or an IPDI trust by exercise of the power within two years of the testator's death. Review of the will would be appropriate if the trusts lack such a power and the potential beneficiaries are in their infancy, particularly if the fund could turn out to be substantial, or if there is a serious risk of part or all the fund being subject to interest in possession trusts at death. See (4) below for this last point.

(4) The existing will contains accumulation and maintenance trusts of the more complex kind, where there are initial accumulation and maintenance trusts, followed by interests in possession. Where the trust is of the testator's free estate (ie not created in exercise of a special power of appointment exercisable by will over a fund subject to an existing settlement) the FA 2006 rules can have a capricious effect. So far as the fund subject to this trust is held on trust for a beneficiary or beneficiaries who have by the time of the death of the testator attained the age at which an interest in possession commences, it will be subject to IPDIs and so beneficiary-taxed. So far as the fund is held for a beneficiary or beneficiaries who have not attained that age, it will be relevant property. It will continue to be relevant property after that beneficiary or those beneficiaries attain interests in possession, unless they become entitled to interests in possession within the period of two years following the testator's death, in which case they will become entitled to IPDIs by virtue of IHTA 1984, s 144. Thus different members of a class of beneficiaries may find that their funds are subject to quite different IHT treatment, depending on how old they are at the testator's death. For a comparison of relevant property and IPDI trusts see para **[200.131]**. However, it will be possible (if there are wide enough powers conferred on the trustees) to convert the relevant property to IPDIs within two years of the testator's death. IPDIs will have the tax treatment which was contemplated by the testator when he made the will, except where powers were conferred with the specific purpose of enabling the shares taken by different beneficiaries to be varied after interests in possession are attained (see **[200.131]** (5) for the disadvantages of varying beneficiary-taxed shares post FA 2006). Review of such a will is called for, therefore, if the powers are not adequate for conversion of relevant property to IPDI property, or variability of shares after interests in possession are obtained is particularly important to the testator. In the latter case the substitution of a fully discretionary trust should be considered.

(5) The existing will contains accumulation and maintenance trusts of any of the kinds mentioned above, in exercise of a power of appointment under an existing settlement. If the power is a general power (ie broadly, one which can be exercised in favour of anybody, including the testator's own estate), the position will be as set out above, since for

this purpose a general power over property is equivalent to ownership. Where it is the exercise of a special power of appointment under an existing settlement, IPDIs cannot be created and the trust property will be wholly relevant property from the testator's death, irrespective of the ages of beneficiaries and whether they have interests in possession (unless any such interest in possession is a disabled person's interest, see **[200.99]**). Although this is not the tax treatment intended by the testator, IPDIs are not available, and IHTA 1984, ss 71A, 71D, 142 and 144 cannot apply. If the appointment were reviewed, the only alternative with a different IHT outcome would be to appoint absolute interests. Review of the will could be carried out, but is not a high priority so long as the trustees of the settlement will have power to distribute the trust property absolutely soon after the testator's death. This is because the relevant property exit charge would be small or nil if such a distribution were done promptly (where the settled property is beneficiary-taxed property before the death), or very little increased (where the settled property is relevant property before the death), as compared with an absolute appointment taking effect on the death.

PART B

Clauses in wills

Commencement of will

[201.5A]

[Added for EU Regulation No 650/2012.]

Wills choosing English law to govern succession to the testator's estate as a whole. EU Regulation No 650/2012 on Succession applies in all EU states except the UK, the Republic of Ireland and Denmark, in relation to deaths on or after 17 August 2015. Despite the UK not being bound by it, it is relevant to the will of any UK national who owns property in any state which is subject to the Regulation, and who is hoping to survive until 17 August 2015, because it enables a choice of succession law, provided that the person making the choice is a national (at the time of making the will, or at his or her death) of the state whose law is chosen: see para **[24.2]** and the extracts from the Regulation at para **[248.1]** ff. It probably remains a good idea to make a separate will in accordance with the law of the territory where the property is situated, but to provide in it and any other will a declaration in accordance with Article 22 of the Regulation that English law is chosen as the law of succession. This will be recognised in the courts of any state subject to the Regulation. The choice of English law under Article 22 of the Regulation is of the domestic English law of succession, not including the English conflict of laws rules (see Article 34 at para **[248.18]**). Where someone who dies on or after 17 August 2015 has validly chosen English law under Article 22, but the English conflict of laws rules would apply the law of an EU state subject to the Regulation, either because the deceased had immovable property there, or was domiciled there, the question will arise as to whether English law will accept the renvoi back to English domestic law. The better view is that the English courts will accept the renvoi and apply the English domestic law of succession to the entire estate, including immovable property situated in the state concerned: see *Re Ross*[1] for a decision to this effect on analogous facts. For a declaration that English law shall apply to the succession as a whole, see the suggested formula in Form B1.7A at para **[201.12A]**.

1 [1930] 1 Ch 377.

[201.11]

[Updated in footnote 2 for EU Regulation No 650/2012.]

Form B1.6: Commencement of will of testator with UK and foreign property confining the will to UK property[1]

I [*testator*] of [*address*] hereby make this my will which shall affect only my property of every kind in the United Kingdom of Great Britain and

Northern Ireland and no other part of my property of any kind. I hereby revoke all former testamentary dispositions made by me to the extent that and so far only as they affect my property of every kind in the United Kingdom of Great Britain and Northern Ireland. I declare that I am domiciled in England and that the proper law of this my will shall be the law of England and Wales[2].

1 Where a testator is possessed of property outside the United Kingdom and is able to dispose of such property and the greater part thereof to persons residing outside that area, there are obvious advantages in arranging for the distribution of such estate in the country outside the United Kingdom so far as possible in order to avoid the difficulties and expense of transferring such sums from one country to another. This is also true in the case of property situated in a dominion or colony, and it can often be appropriate to make separate and entirely independent wills with respect to the property in the United Kingdom and that situated outside the United Kingdom. Probate of a will granted in England does not extend to such property (*Re Murray's Goods* [1896] P 65), unless some of it is brought to England (*Stubbings v Clunies-Ross* (1911) 27 TLR 361). For the converse case of probate granted in a British possession, or by a British court in a foreign country, see the Colonial Probates Act 1892; and as to a limited colonial grant, see *Re Smith's Goods* [1904] P 114. (See generally as to probate *Tristram and Coote's Probate Practice* (30th edn).) See also *In the Estate of Vickers* (2001–02) 4 ITELR 584, discussed in the note to para **[18.8]**. See also C14 at para **[236.1]** ff.

2 Such a declaration as to domicile will not be conclusive as to domicile at the date of death, nor indeed to domicile at the date of the declaration (see para **[236.10]**, n 1). The declaration will probably not constitute a choice of English law to govern the succession as a whole for the purposes of EU Regulation No 650/2012, Article 22 because it is a will confined to property in the UK. The declaration that English law is to apply only applies to property in the UK, not to the succession as a whole. For a declaration that English law shall apply to the succession as a whole, see Form B1.7A at para **[201.12A]**, and see also paras **[24.2]** and **[201.5A]**.

[201.12]

[Updated in footnote 1 for EU Regulation No 650/2012.]

Form B1.7: Commencement of concurrent will of testator with UK and foreign property confining the will to UK property[1]

I [*testator*] of [*address*] hereby revoke all testamentary dispositions made by me prior to the date hereof and hereby declare that this will and another will of even date herewith together constitute my last will. This will shall affect only my property of every kind in the United Kingdom of Great Britain and Northern Ireland and no other part of my property of any kind. [*or* This will shall not affect my property of any kind in the United States of America [*or as the case may be*] which I have disposed of by the said will of even date herewith.]

1 Care must be taken that the will dealing with the foreign property should be properly executed to pass all kinds of property according to the law of the foreign country, and for this purpose a lawyer of the foreign country should be consulted. In some cases, e g the United States, it is necessary to consider the law of the particular State in which the property is situated. Though an English will may by its words imply that foreign property is excluded, yet those words may be inserted because the testator believes he has otherwise effectively disposed of such property. If that other disposition has failed, the foreign property will pass under the English will: *Re Duke of Wellington, Glentanar v Wellington* [1948] Ch 118, [1947] 2 All ER 854. For a declaration choosing English law to govern the succession as a whole for the purposes of EU Regulation, No 650/2012 see Form B1.7A at para **[201.12A]**, and see also paras **[24.2]** and **[201.5A]**.

[201.12A]

[Added for EU Regulation No 650/2012.]

Form B1.7A: Commencement of concurrent will of testator with UK property and foreign property in an EU state other than the Republic of Ireland or Denmark, confining the will to UK property but choosing English law as the governing law of succession[1]

I [*testator*] of [*address*] hereby revoke all testamentary dispositions made by me prior to the date hereof and hereby declare that this will and another will of even date herewith together constitute my last will. This will shall affect only my property of every kind in the United Kingdom of Great Britain and Northern Ireland and no other part of my property of any kind in France [*or as the case may be*] which I have disposed of by the said will of even date herewith. I hereby declare that at the date hereof I have British nationality, and that I choose the law of England and Wales to govern my succession as a whole, to the intent that the law of England and Wales should be the applicable law of succession in relation to all my property wherever situated for the purposes of English law, and of EU Regulation Number 650/2012 and in particular Article 22 (choice of law) of such Regulation.

1 Care must be taken that the will dealing with the foreign property should be properly executed to pass all kinds of property according to the law of the foreign country, and for this purpose a lawyer of the foreign country should be consulted. For the EU Regulation, see paras **[24.2]** and **[201.5A]**. For the text of Article 22, choice of law, see para **[248.9]**. A similar declaration should appear in the foreign will.

Miscellaneous declarations and desires sometimes included in wills

GENERAL NOTE

Disposal of body

[202.4]

[Updated in footnote 1 for *Ghai v Newcastle City Council* [2010] EWCA Civ 59, *Lewisham Hospital NHS Trust v Hamuth* [2007] WTLR 309 and *Hartshorne v Gardner* [2008] 2 FLR 1681.]

Form B2.2: Expressions of desire as to cremation

A. I desire that my body may be cremated [in the crematorium at ——] and my ashes deposited at —— [or scattered on consecrated ground at ——][1] *or*

B. [*If the testator desires a more elaborate form of words, the following may be suggested:*] I desire that my trustees shall dispose of my remains by the cleansing fires of cremation and that my ashes shall be spread upon the garden of remembrance at ——[2] *or*

C. I direct that my body shall not be cremated.[3]

1 As to the law relating to cremation, see Vol 1, para **[7.33]**. Cremation must take place in a 'building' (and it has been held that Hindu cremation on a funeral pyre in the open air is possible on the basis of a broad construction of the term: *Ghai v Newcastle City Council (Ramgharia Gurdwara, Hitchin and another intervening)* [2010] EWCA Civ 59 reversing [2009] EWHC 978 (Admin), [2009] All ER (D) 68 (May)). Written directions for cremation are not essential, see also n 3 infra. The Cremation Society of Great Britain, Second Floor Brecon House, 16/16A Albion Place, Maidstone, Kent, ME14 5DZ; tel: (01622) 688 292, issue a printed form of this direction, which, when completed, they undertake to register in their records; and they endeavour to give effect to the expressed desire. The printed form is in duplicate, one part for registration with the society and the other to be handed to the executor or selected relative. The Cremation Society has a website at www.cremation.org.uk.

As to disposal of the body or ashes, disputes sometimes arise, as in *Fessi v Whitmore* [1999] 1 FLR 767, *Lewisham Hospital NHS Trust v Hamuth* [2007] WTLR 309 and *Hartshorne v Gardner* [2008] 2 FLR 1681 and *Burrows v HM Coroner for Preston* [2008] 2 FLR 1225.

2 This wording is based upon an actual will.

3 It is no longer unlawful to cremate a body where such a direction has been given, and whether cremation takes place is solely in the discretion of the deceased's executors or nearest relative, who are apparently free to disregard the deceased's wishes: see Vol 1, para **[7.33]**, n 4.

[202.18]

Maintenance of graves

Note. There are several methods of providing for the upkeep of a tomb or grave, none of them wholly satisfactory (See also Vol 1, para **[9.29]**).

[202.19]

[Updated for Perpetuities and Accumulations Act 2009.]

Gifts for maintenance of graves are not charitable. A gift for the maintenance of a grave or family tomb (not being part of the fabric of a church) is not charitable, but such gift may be valid as a private trust if it does not infringe the rule against perpetuities: see *Pirbright v Salwey* [1896] WN 86, followed in *Re Hooper, Parker v Ward* [1932] 1 Ch 38. It is therefore possible to leave a legacy on trust to apply the income for the maintenance of a grave during a perpetuity period, as in Form B2.8 at para **[202.31]**. The disadvantage of a gift in this form is that it is of limited duration and that while it is lawful for the trustees to give effect to the trust, there is no beneficiary to enforce it and its efficacy therefore depends upon the goodwill and conscientiousness of the trustees. Doubts have been expressed as to whether it is possible to provide for such a gift to take effect for one of the perpetuity periods permitted by the Perpetuities and Accumulations Act 1964 (PAA 1964) because of the terms of s 15(4) of the PAA 1964. The authors take the view that s 15(4) does not prevent the 80-year perpetuity period from being employed in trusts such as these in Form B2.8 at para **[202.31]**. The application of these perpetuity periods is not affected by Perpetuities and Accumulations Act 2009 (PAA 2009): see PAA 2009, s 18.

[202.28]

[Updated for Perpetuities and Accumulations Act 2009.]

Perpetual gifts from charity to charity are permissible. An alternative method of providing for the maintenance of a particular grave, which is embodied in Form B2.12 at para **[202.35]**, is also based on the law of charity but, unlike the provision contained in Form B2.9 at para **[202.32]**, is available wherever the grave is situated. The particular formula derives from the decision in *Re Tyler, Tyler v Tyler* [1891] 3 Ch 252, CA and involves: (i) an initial gift of property to a charity to be held on trust to apply the income in perpetuity either for its general purposes or for a particular charitable purpose administered by the selected charity; (ii) a condition requiring the charity to maintain the particular grave; and (iii) a gift over to a second charity on breach of that condition. The perpetuity rule does not apply to a gift from one charity to another, though it does apply where the gift over is from a charity to an individual (*Re Davies, Lloyd v Cardigan County Council* [1915] 1 Ch 543; *Re Talbot, Jubb v Sheard* [1933] Ch 895), or where the gift over is from an individual to a charity (*Worthing Corpn v Heather* [1906] 2 Ch 532). It must be noticed that the first gift must not be for the maintenance of the grave, as an indefinite gift for such a purpose will be invalid even though the first donee is a charity: see *Re Elliott, Lloyds Bank Ltd v Burton-on-Trent Hospital Management Committee* [1952] Ch 217, [1952] 1 All ER 145. In relation to Wills made on or after 6 April 2010 this rule is preserved by the PAA 2009, s 2(2) and (3), see Part G, para **[246.176]**. Where the gift over is not to a charity it must be limited to take effect only within the perpetuity period, and, if the trust fails after the perpetuity period, the gift will automatically fall into residue. The perpetuity period in such a case is not the period of 125 years provided by the PAA 2009, ss 5(1), 15(1)(a) (see Part A **[200.35A]** and Part G, para **[246.189]**) because PAA 2009 does not affect the perpetuity rules as applied to non-charitable purpose trusts: see the PAA 2009, s 18. The efficacy of a gift in this form depends on the willingness of the second donee to enforce the condition. It is therefore advisable that the second donee should be a body having a permanent existence which is likely to be interested in ensuring that the grave is maintained. However, it should be noted that the decision of *Tyler v Tyler* was not followed by the High Court of Australia in *RSPCA of NSW v Benevolent Society of New South Wales* (1960) 102 CLR 629 where the non-charitable conditions imposed upon a charity to which property was left were considered to be part of the trust and the dominant purpose of the gift.

[202.37]

[Updated for Perpetuities and Accumulations Act 2009.]

Form B2.13: Gift for the maintenance and upkeep of an animal

I give to my trustees the sum of £—— upon trust to invest the same and to apply the income therefrom for the upkeep and maintenance of my [dog *or other animal, describing it*] for the period of [twenty-one years[1]] from the date of my death if my said [dog] shall so long live and after the death of my said [dog] or after the expiration of the said period of twenty-one years whichever shall first happen the said sum shall fall into and form part of my residuary estate.

1 The period need not be confined to 21 years, provided that it does not exceed perpetuity limits, see **[202.19]**.

B3

Appointment of executors, trustees and guardians

PRELIMINARY NOTE ON EXECUTORS AND TRUSTEES

Guardians

[203.48]

[Updated for Human Fertilisation and Embryology Act 2008.]

(a) Children with two parents with parental responsibility. This category comprises children of a marriage, children whom the law deems to be the children of both the parties to a marriage or civil partnership, and children whose parents are not and have not been married to each other but whose fathers or other parents have acquired parental responsibility (for which see Vol 1, para **[28.2]**). Children deemed to be children of both parties to a marriage or civil partnership include children legitimated by the subsequent marriage or civil partnership of their parents, adopted by a married couple or civil partnership, conceived by artificial insemination or in vitro fertilisation, or the subject of a parental order after being born to a surrogate mother, in circumstances that they are treated as the child of both parties (ChA 1989, s 2(1) and (3): Part G, para **[244.113]**; HFEA 1990, ss 27 to 29, Part G, paras **[245.85]**–**[245.87]**, HFEA 2008, ss 33–55, and SI 2010/985, Part G, paras **[245.111]** ff).

[203.49]

[Updated for Human Fertilisation and Embryology Act 2008.]

An appointment of a guardian by the father of a child born out of wedlock will only be valid if it is made after he has acquired parental responsibility for the child, which he can do by agreement with the mother or a court order (see Vol 1, paras **[28.2]** and **[28.4]**), by having been registered as the father on the birth certificate where the registration was on or after 1 December 2003 (see para **[203.50]**), or by marrying the mother, which will have the effect that the child will be deemed to be the child of the marriage with both parents having parental responsibility (ChA 1989, s 2(1) and (3): Part G, para **[244.113]**; and FLRA 1987, s 1(2) and (3): Part G, para **[245.70]**). Where a same sex female couple who have not formed a civil partnership have a child by means of assisted reproduction where the treatment was on or after 6 April 2009, with the woman who is not the mother being treated as a parent of the child under HFEA 2008, s 43 (see Vol 1, para **[74.5]** and Part G, para **[245.122]**), the woman who is not the mother will acquire parental responsibility in similar circumstances to those in which the father of a child born out of wedlock would. An appointment made by a father or parent before he or she has acquired parental responsibility will be of no effect even if he or she subsequently acquires it. It should be remembered that if a father or parent does not have parental responsibility, and he or she and the mother do decide to make a parental responsibility agreement the father or parent will not acquire parental responsibility unless and until the agreement has been made in the prescribed form and has been registered with the Principal Registry of the Family Division of the High Court (see Vol 1, para **[28.2]**).

[203.50]

[Updated for Human Fertilisation and Embryology Act 2008.]

In addition to agreement (a 'parental responsibility agreement') or the court (on his or her application) ordering that he or she shall have parental responsibility for a child, the father or parent of a child (not married to or a civil partner of the mother) may acquire parental responsibility for a child if he or she becomes registered as the child's father or parent. See ChA 1989, s 4, as amended by the Adoption and Children Act 2002 with effect from 1 December 2003 (opposite sex couples) and ChA 1989, s 4ZA inserted by HFEA 2008, Sch 6, para 27 with effect from 6 April 2009 (same sex couples). See Vol 1, para **[28.1]**. Under the ChA 1989, as amended by the Adoption and Children Act 2002, a person married to, or in a civil partnership with, a child's parent may acquire parental responsibility for a stepchild by agreement or by order declaring that he shall have parental responsibility for the child. See ChA 1989, s 4A, as inserted by the Adoption and Children Act 2002 with effect from 30 December 2005. However, ChA 1989 and Adoption and Children Act 2002 draw a distinction between a parent and a step-parent. The latter is not a parent and so cannot appoint a guardian under ChA 1989.

B5

Gifts and other provisions relating to business property

PRELIMINARY NOTE

Business assets and inheritance tax—general points

[205.8]

[Updated for *McCall (PRs of Maclean) v HMRC* [2009] STC 990, *Lockyer (PRs of Pawson) v HMRC* [2013] STC 976, and *Trustees of David Zetland Settlement v HMRC* [2013] UKFTT 284 (TC).]

Types of business qualifying for business relief. Subject to the exceptions mentioned below, any trade or profession can qualify for inheritance tax business relief, either where it (or a partnership share of it) is directly owned by the testator, or where it is carried on by an unquoted company in which he has shares or a quoted company which he controls. The exceptions to this are for businesses of dealing in securities, stocks or shares, or land or buildings, or making or holding investments (IHTA 1984, s 105(3)), but that itself is subject to exceptions for UK discount houses, and market makers on the stock exchange, the London International Financial Futures and Options Exchange, or in regulated markets in the European Economic Area outside the UK: IHTA 1984, s 105(4), (7), SI 1992/3181 and SI 2012/2903. The Special Commissioners have held that ownership and management of land let to tenants is making or holding investments within the above exception and does not qualify for business relief, and this approach was approved by the High Court in *Weston v IRC* [2000] STC 1064 (see for the now numerous cases in this area *Foster's Inheritance Tax*, G1.12). In *McCall (PRs of Maclean) v HMRC* [2009] STC 990 the Northern Ireland Court of Appeal upheld the decision of the Special Commissioner that ownership and management of land let on seasonal grazing agreements was a business of holding investments and so not entitled to the relief. Relief has also been denied on these grounds for a property used for holiday lettings (*Lockyer (PRs of Pawson) v HMRC* [2013] STC 976), and a property let to commercial tenants (*Trustees of David Zetland Settlement v HMRC* [2013] UKFTT 284 (TC)). In both cases some services were provided, but not enough to tip the balance away from them being businesses of holding investments. There is no territorial limit on the location of the business, and it can be anywhere in the world (whereas agricultural relief can apply only to land in the European Economic Area and in relation to events before 23 April 2003 was confined to land in the UK, Channel Islands, or Isle of Man—see para **[234.2]**). The assets of a farming business other than the agricultural land itself can only qualify for business relief not agricultural relief, as the latter relief is confined to land and buildings etc attached to land. See para **[205.15]** below and C12 at para **[234.8]** for what happens when both reliefs might apply to agricultural land.

[205.10]

[Updated for FA 2013 Sch 36.]

Secured liabilities. Section 162(4) of the IHTA 1984 provides that a liability which is an incumbrance on any property shall, so far as possible, be taken to reduce the value of that property. Liabilities incurred for the purposes of a business will be taken into account in valuing it (or the company or partnership shares which it underlies) whether or not charged on the business assets, but s 162(4) could reduce relief further where borrowing for some purpose unconnected with the business is charged on business property. IHTA 1984, s 162(4) is, however, subject to IHTA 1984, s 162B, for which see para **[205.10A]** below.

[205.10A]

[Updated for FA 2013 Sch 36.]

Liabilities incurred on or after 6 April 2013 which financed business property. IHTA 1984, s 162B (inserted by FA 2013, Sch 36) provides that liabilities incurred on or after 6 April 2013 which are attributable to financing, directly or indirectly, the acquisition, maintenance, or enhancement of the value of, business property must be deducted first from that business property before determining the amount of business relief. This is so even if the liability is charged on property other than the business property. The effect of this is to prevent such liabilities from being deducted from property other than the business property, and can make a considerable difference to the amount of IHT payable on death where the testator has substantial liabilities of this type. Where a pre-6 April 2013 liability which financed business property is refinanced by new borrowing on or after that date which is used to pay off the previous loan, it is likely that the new borrowing will fall within s 162B.

Sole traders

[205.23]

[Updated for *Re Nelson Dance Family Settlement* [2009] STC 802.]

In relation to capital gains tax retirement relief, it was an established rule that an asset used in a business is not 'a business': see, e g *McGregor v Adcock* [1977] STC 206, *Pepper v Daffurn* [1993] STC 466, and *Jarmin v Rawlings* [1994] STC 1005. It was generally thought that the same principle would apply to IHT business relief, but in *Re Nelson Dance Family Settlement* [2009] STC 802 the High Court, upholding the Special Commissioner, held that it does not. It was thus held that a lifetime gift by a sole trader of a single asset used in a business carried on immediately before the gift was made did qualify for business relief. This is a less significant point in relation to inheritance tax on death, because if a person is in business as a sole trader at his death the entire business will be included in his deemed transfer of value on death, and if he has already ceased to trade and retained an asset of the former business the relief clearly will not apply. However, there is a question whether, in relation to inheritance tax on death where the estate is partially exempt, the *Nelson Dance* decision is relevant to the application of the IHTA 1984, s 39A (business or agricultural relief and partial exemption). In the absence of clarification on this point in litigation or an expression of opinion by HMRC, specific gifts by will of individual assets of the business should be avoided where there are exempt gifts: see the Preliminary Note to C11 at para **[233.6]**.

[205.73]

[Updated for Perpetuities and Accumulations Act 2009.]

Form B5.16: Power to trustees to carry on business where the will contains a general trust for conversion[1]

I declare that notwithstanding the trust for sale hereinbefore contained[2] it shall be lawful for my trustees to carry on [with a view to selling the same as a going concern] the business of a —— carried on by me at ——[3] and that in carrying on the said business they shall be free from the control or interference of any person or persons beneficially entitled under this my will and may employ in it any capital of my residuary estate.

1 See the Note at para **[205.25]**. Trustees carrying on a business under such a power are in a fiduciary relationship to the beneficiaries and cannot set up a competing business on their own account without severing all connection with the trust (*Re Thomson, Thomson v Allen* [1930] 1 Ch 203).

2 If a power to postpone sale is conferred the trustees would have an implied power to continue the business in the meantime: *Re Crowther, Midgley v Crowther* [1895] 2 Ch 56. But it is preferable to make express provision.

3 Under a direction to carry on the testator's business, the trustees or executors are entitled to the free use of the business premises and the fixed plant and machinery therein so long as they are entitled under the will to carry on the business (*Re Cameron, Nixon v Cameron* (1884) 26 Ch D 19). The trustees will be entitled to set aside sums for depreciation of assets and a reserve fund: *Re Crabtree, Thomas v Crabtree* (1911) 106 LT 49; *Re Robertson* [1953] 2 SCR 1.

B7

Gifts of leasehold land

PRELIMINARY NOTE

[207.21]

[Updated for Perpetuities and Accumulations Act 2009.]

Form B7.7: Contingent gift of leaseholds

I give my leasehold house known as —— unto my trustees upon trust for my niece [A] if and when she attains the age of twenty-five years.[1]

1 A contingent or future specific devise or bequest carries the intermediate income (subject to the provisions as to accumulations contained in the Act) from the death of the testator, except so far as the income is otherwise *expressly* disposed of (LPA 1925, s 175: Part G, para **[244.54]**). During the minority of the beneficiary, the income will be available for maintenance; if the beneficiary on attaining eighteen has not yet obtained a vested interest, the whole income will be payable to the beneficiary until he attains a vested interest, or dies, or his interest is otherwise defeated (TA 1925, s 31, as amended by the FLRA 1969, s 1(3) and Sch 1, Pt 1: Part G, para **[246.28]**).

[207.25]

[Updated in text and footnotes for Perpetuities and Accumulations Act 2009.]

Form B7.11: Gift of leaseholds upon trust out of the rents and profits to form sinking fund[1]

I give all my leasehold lands to my trustees upon the trusts and with the directions following:

(1) In the first place to pay out of the rents and profits thereof the rents payable in respect of the leases under which the same are held and perform and observe the lessees' covenants therein contained.

(2) In the next place to raise out of the said rents and profits any such annual sum (either for the premium or premiums in respect of a policy or policies of insurance to be effected by my trustees or by way of investment in their names and accumulation during any period[2]) as shall be sufficient in their opinion to provide at the expiration of the respective leases for which I hold the said leasehold lands a capital sum of £—— and to apply the annual sum so raised in paying the premiums for keeping on foot such policy or policies of insurance or by way of investment in the names of my trustees and accumulation accordingly.

(3) Subject thereto to stand possessed of my said leasehold lands and the rents and profits thereof upon trust etc [*set out the trusts of the surplus rents and profits*].

(4) My trustees shall invest the said sum of £—— as and when received or provided as aforesaid in manner herein mentioned and shall stand possessed thereof and of the investments for the time being representing the same and the income thereof upon the like trusts and subject to the like provisions in all respects as are hereinbefore declared and contained concerning my said leasehold lands and the rents and profits thereof so far as the same trusts and provisions may then be subsisting and capable of taking effect.

1 See para **[207.6]**. A clause of this kind could have adverse inheritance tax consequences in that it could be said that as part of the income of the trust property is to be accumulated there will be no interest in possession in at least a part of it, and possibly the whole, since the amount of income is decided by the trustees in their discretion. However, if the capital sum for which the trustees are to make provision at the expiry of the leases is no greater than the value of the leases as at the testator's death, so that the provision is merely one which directs the trustees to meet depreciation and not to increase the capital value of the trust assets, it may be that this can properly be regarded as an administrative provision rather than a dispositive provision, so that there will be an interest in possession in the whole: see *Miller v IRC* [1987] STC 108.

2 For wills made on or after 6 April 2010, there are no statutory restrictions on accumulation in respect of non-charitable trusts, see the PAA 2009, ss 13, 15(1)(a) (Part G, para **[246.187]**). This clause seems to be valid for any accumulation and certainly in so far as it provides for keeping up a policy however long its provisions continue: *Re Gardiner, Gardiner v Smith* [1901] 1 Ch 697.

[207.26]

[Updated in text and footnotes for Perpetuities and Accumulations Act 2009.]

Form B7.12: Alternative provision for sinking fund to replace leasehold value[1]

I give all my leasehold lands unto my trustees upon the trusts and with the directions following:

(1) Upon trust in the first place to pay out of the rents and profits thereof the rents payable in respect of the leases under which the same are held and to perform and observe the lessees' covenants therein contained and subject thereto to set aside out of the rents and profits of each such leasehold in each year such a sum and for such period as hereinafter directed.

(2) Subject as aforesaid my trustees shall stand possessed of the said leasehold lands and the rents and profits thereof upon trust [*set out the trusts of the leaseholds and the rents and profits*].

(3) The sum so to be set aside (as a sinking fund to secure the replacement of the wasting value of each leasehold) out of the net rents and profits of each leasehold in each year shall be calculated by dividing the net rents and profits of the year by one more than the number of complete years which at the date of my death the lease of that property has to run.

(4) In respect of each such leasehold the said annual sums deducted or set aside as aforesaid shall be invested as one fund and shall be accumulated by investing the income thereof as an accretion to that fund.

(5) Such accumulations shall cease upon the expiration of such lease while still held by my trustees or upon the sale of the leasehold in respect of which the said fund is being set aside and accumulated.

(6) Thereafter the fund so formed and the future income thereof shall be held by my trustees upon the same trusts (save for the setting aside of a sum out of income) as the leasehold itself is being held by my trustees or would be held if it had not expired or been sold, as the case may be, so far as the same trusts and provisions may then be subsisting and capable of taking effect.

(7) And I specially declare that the fund so set aside and accumulated in respect of a leasehold shall be primarily liable for all claims for dilapidations and breaches of covenant if such leasehold shall be still held by my trustees at the date of expiration of the lease thereof.[2]

1 See para **[207.25]**, n 1. This form is preferable in that the sum to be set aside is expressly to form a sinking fund to meet depreciation, and so is arguably an administrative provision rather than a dispositive provision. But if it should be thought to be a dispositive provision rather than an administrative provision, since the amount to be accumulated is determined by a formula, there is less risk of the clause causing there to be no interest in possession in the entire property.

2 A direction to set aside annual sums out of rents to secure replacement was not within the Thellusson Act, whether the sums be expended in keeping up a policy or in actual investment; neither was the direction to accumulate the income of the sums invested, see *Re Gardiner, Gardiner v Smith* [1901] 1 Ch 697, and *Re Hurlbatt, Hurlbatt v Hurlbatt* [1910] 2 Ch 553, at any rate as long as it was made bona fide for replacement, and not for the purpose of evading the Act. The same principle applies to a reserve fund where the executors are empowered to carry on a business: *Re Crabtree* (1911) 106 LT 49; *Re Robertson* [1953] 2 SCR 1. Sections 164 ff of the LPA 1925 (Part G, para **[246.66]** ff) (which replaced the Thellusson Act), did not appear to alter the position. For wills made on or after 6 April 2010, there are no longer any statutory restrictions on accumulation in respect of non-charitable trusts: see the PAA 2009, ss 13, 15(1)(a) (Part G, para **[246.187]**). For the taxation of accumulated income see the note to B18 at para **[218.30]**.

Rights of residence

The statutory right of occupation under a trust of land

[208.7]

[Updated for *Creasey v Sole* [2013] WTLR 931]

Land available for occupation. There are two main requirements of the TLATA 1996, s 12 (Part G, para **[246.115]**) for a beneficiary to have the right to occupy trust land. First, he must be beneficially entitled to an interest in possession in it, a separate topic discussed at paras **[208.12]** and **[208.13]**. Secondly, either the purposes of the trust must include making the land available for occupation by the beneficiary (or beneficiaries of a class of which he is a member or of beneficiaries in general) (TLATA 1996, s 12(1)(a)), or the land must be held by the trustees so as to be so available: TLATA 1996, s 12(1)(b). Could s 12(1)(a) apply solely by virtue of the will or settlement conferring a standard-form administrative power to permit occupation by beneficiaries? The words in brackets in s 12(1)(a) suggest that this may be so, but it seems peculiar that the existence of express powers of this kind in the will or settlement could confer such a right when those powers duplicate powers which are conferred on all trustees of land by statute. Does s 12(1)(b) confer a right of occupation of any land held by the trustees which is for the time being vacant (subject to suitability, etc under the TLATA 1996, s 12(2)), or must the trustees make some decision or take some action to make it available first? We feel that the latter view would produce a more sensible result, but the position is unclear, and it is certainly possible that any beneficiary with an interest in possession can claim the right to occupy land which is for the time being vacant (again subject to suitability, etc within s 12(2)). This can be illustrated by the example of a residuary estate consisting of residential properties let to tenants, with the testator's widow having a life interest, and the purposes of the trust within s 12(1)(a) not including making land available for her occupation. A tenant of a residential property departs, leaving it vacant. Does the life tenant then have a right of occupation of that property, ie is it one which is held by the trustees so as to be available for occupation by her within s 12(1)(b), or does it only become so held if the trustees decide eg not to re-let and to repair it and offer it to the widow as a residence? In *Creasey v Sole* [2013] WTLR 931 at para 121 it was held that land given by will to the testator's six children in equal shares was not available for occupation by one of those six children.

[208.9]

[Updated for *French v Barcham* [2008] 1 WLR 1124.]

Two or more beneficiaries. A more complicated difficulty arises where there are beneficiaries with similar concurrent interests but only some of whom for the time being have interests in possession. This is best illustrated by an example. Suppose that there is a trust of a farm for a class of four minor beneficiaries, who get vested interests in capital and income in equal shares at the age of 25 and attain interests in possession in their respective presumptive shares at the age of 18 under the Trustee Act 1925, s 31 by virtue of becoming entitled to be paid the current income of those shares (see para **[208.12]** as to whether this is an interest in possession in the land). The trustees farm the land themselves, employing a manager. The eldest of the beneficiaries then attains 18. Suppose that the TLATA 1996, s 12(1)(a) or (b) applies, either because a purpose of the trust is occupation by beneficiaries, or because (contrary to the tentative view expressed at para **[208.7]**) s 12(1)(b) is satisfied by the mere fact of there being vacant land in the trust. He then becomes a beneficiary entitled to occupy the land under the TLATA 1996, s 12 and cannot be prevented from doing so, subject only to the possible arguments that the land is not 'available' or not 'suitable' for occupation by him (TLATA 1996, s 12(2)) and to the right of the trustees to impose reasonable conditions on him in relation to his occupation: TLATA 1996, s 13(3) and (5). The trustees cannot exclude a beneficiary under the power in s 13(1) unless there are at least two beneficiaries with interests in possession, and then they cannot exclude all of them. It seems likely that 'reasonable conditions' would include requiring him to take over the farming business, including its liabilities, in particular the trustees' existing contractual liabilities to the farm manager and any borrowing secured on the land: TLATA 1996, s 13(5)(b). This may be impossible for the beneficiary to satisfy but if he is able to do so the difficult question then arises as to whether he can be required to pay compensation for the benefit of the beneficiaries who are still under 18. Section 13(6) of the TLATA 1996 (under which the trustees can require a beneficiary who is in occupation to make compensation arrangements in favour of beneficiaries who are not) only applies where there are two or more beneficiaries with interests in possession, and it has no application to this example of one of a class of beneficiaries having an interest in possession while the others do not. There is thus a lack of specific express provision for such a case. However, the question then arises whether the trustees can impose compensatory provisions on the occupying beneficiary for the benefit of the other three beneficiaries under the general power to impose reasonable conditions in the TLATA 1996, s 13(3). The appropriate condition would be that an appropriate rent for three-quarters of the value of the land be paid to the trustees to be treated as income of the three-quarters of the fund still subject to accumulation and maintenance trusts. The occupying beneficiary might try to say that a condition as to compensation of this kind can only be imposed to compensate other beneficiaries *who have a right of occupation under the Act which they are not able to exercise* (and this idea is supported by the TLATA 1996, s 15(2)). However, the trustees could reply that it is only fair to require compensation in circumstances where other beneficiaries have an interest in the property which would, in the absence of such compensation, bring them no benefit, but which would bring them an income benefit if the property was yielding income. They now have the support of the High Court decision *French v Barcham* [2008] 1 WLR 1124, where it was held that TLATA 1996 ss 12–15 are not an exhaustive regime for compensation for exclusion of a beneficiary from occupation of property held subject to a trust of land, and thus that a beneficiary with no right of occupation (in the particular case a trustee in bankruptcy) could claim equitable compensation from a beneficiary with a right occupation.

[208.10]

[Updated for *French v Barcham* [2008] 1 WLR 1124 and *Creasey v Sole* [2013] WTLR 931.]

Sub-trusts. Another somewhat unexpected result arises where there is a sub-trust of a beneficial interest, again best illustrated by an example. Suppose that a husband H and his wife W own a house as tenants in common. H dies, leaving his half share to his executors and trustees to hold it on trust for their daughter D for life. It seems from the TLATA 1996, ss 12(1) and 22(1), (2) (Part G, paras **[246.115]** and **[246.125]** respectively) that W has a right of occupation of the house under s 12 and D and H's will trustees do not have such a right: see '*Trustees with a Part Interest in Land: The impact of the Trusts of Land and Appointment of Trustees Act 1996*', Chris Jarman, [2007] PCB 263. This is because s 22(1) provides that 'beneficiary' in relation to a trust means any person who *under the trust* (emphasis supplied) has an interest in property subject to the trust, which seems to exclude D from being a beneficiary under the trust of the house for the purposes of the TLATA 1996, s 12(1), and because, while s 22(1) provides that 'beneficiary' includes trustees of a sub-trust, s 22(2) provides that beneficiaries who are beneficially entitled do not include such trustees, with the consequence that the trustees of H's will do not have a right of occupation which they can allow D to use. This is now confirmed by *Creasey v Sole* [2013] WTLR 931 at paras 125–129, where it was also suggested that an undivided half share is unavailable or unsuitable for occupation because it cannot be physically occupied. As in the example at para **[208.9]**, there is a question as to whether the trustees of the house could require W to pay compensation to the trustees of H's will for D's benefit, as a reasonable condition within the TLATA 1996, s 13(3) in relation to W's continued occupation of the house or under the general law. The arguments for and against are the same as in the example given at para **[208.9]**, with the balance tipping in favour of compensation being payable as a result of the High Court decision *French v Barcham* [2008] 1 WLR 1124.

[208.15]

[Updated for *French v Barcham* [2008] 1 WLR 1124.]

Tax aspects—trusts for children and the right of occupation. The questions discussed in the *Tax Journal* articles mentioned at para **[208.14]** do not include whether the existence of the rights and powers under the TLATA 1996, ss 12 and 13 could prejudice the application of the IHTA 1984, s 71 to accumulation and maintenance trusts. For deaths on and after 22 March

2006, it is no longer possible to create trusts which fall within IHTA 1984, s 71 and such trusts as were previously in existence will cease to attract special treatment under s 71 from 6 April 2008 (see Part A, para **[200.107]**) and further discussion of this issue is no longer necessary.

Reverting to the children's trust example discussed at para **[208.9]**, above, there is unlikely to be difficulty in relation to the more limited types of interest for young children which replace s 71. If the testator declares a trust of land for his young children which falls within IHTA 1984, s 71A (trusts for bereaved minors) or 71D (age 18-to-25 trusts), the situation discussed in para **[208.9]** would not cause those sections to cease to apply (see Part A, paras **[200.108]** and **[200.109]** for these kinds of trust). Where there are trusts under which the children take IPDIs, the problem discussed in para **[208.9]** does not arise because the beneficiaries would all simultaneously have interests in possession at all relevant times.

Where the situation discussed in para **[208.9]** could cause trouble is where there is a trust for a class of children of the kind that used to fall within IHTA 1984, s 71 but which does not fall within ss 71A or 71D because, typically, the children attain interests in possession on or before attaining the age of 25, but the trusts are such that they become entitled to capital either at a greater age, or not necessarily at all because they get life interests with remainders over (possibly combined with a power to pay capital to them). This type of trust has the problem (see para **[217.2]** below) that it will be a matter of chance whether at the testator's death it is an IPDI trust or a relevant property trust, or partly one and partly the other, depending on whether any or all of the beneficiaries have attained the age at which they become entitled to interests in possession by the time of the testator's death. There is the further complication that if one or more of the beneficiaries attain interests in possession in the period of two years after the testator's death, IHTA 1984, s 144 may have the effect of turning the interests in possession retrospectively into IPDIs (see Part A, para **[200.133]**). The situation discussed in para **[208.9]** might have been thought to have the disastrous effect that the eldest of several beneficiaries has an interest in possession in the entire property which is an IPDI, and is then in stages divested of the interest in appropriate parts of the property as the other beneficiaries attain the age at which interests in possession commence. Each time his interest is divested in relation to part of the fund it would be an occasion of immediate inheritance tax charge as a deemed lifetime (non-potentially exempt) transfer by him (see Part A, para **[200.71]**). However, now that it has been held in *French v Barcham* [2008] 1 WLR 1124, that TLATA 1996 ss 12–15 are not an exhaustive regime for compensation for exclusion of a beneficiary from occupation of property held subject to a trust of land, and thus that a beneficiary with no right of occupation can claim equitable compensation from a beneficiary with a right occupation, this is unlikely to be the correct analysis. Those with IPDIs probably have interests in possession only in their respective shares of the property, being subject to an obligation to compensate those who are out of occupation.

[208.16]

[Updated for *French v Barcham* [2008] 1 WLR 1124.]

Tax aspects—sub-trusts. The sub-trust example discussed at para **[208.10]**, i.e. the house owned as to half by W and as to half by H's will trustees holding it on trust for D for life, is discussed in the *Tax Journal* articles mentioned at para **[208.14]**, on the assumption that W cannot be required to make compensation payments for the benefit of D. HMRC accepts (see the *Tax Journal*, 30 January 1997, p 19 and 6 February 1997, p 19) that no taxable benefit flows from D to W in that example. There is a further question whether in these circumstances W has an interest in possession for inheritance tax purposes in H's former half of it with the result that it is subject to inheritance tax as part of W's estate on her death as well as her own absolute share. HMRC's answer that W is entitled to occupy the property pursuant to her statutory right as tenant in common and beneficiary of the trust of land, and is not, therefore, in receipt of a benefit from either the trustees of H's will or D, would seem to imply that W's taxable interest continues to be limited to half the property only. The decision in *French v Barcham* [2008] 1 WLR 1124 (see **[208.15]**) implies that this is correct on the basis that W is under an equitable obligation to pay compensation for the benefit of D.

[208.17]

[Updated for FA 2013, Sch 44.]

Interests in possession for inheritance tax purposes. The property subject to an interest in possession arising under a will of someone dying after 21 March 2006 will be taxed as relevant property unless the interest in possession is an IPDI (or a disabled person's interest): see Part A, paras **[200.92]**, **[200.98]** and **[200.99]**. As mentioned at paras **[208.12]** and **[208.13]**, the meaning of 'interest in possession' is not necessarily the same in the TLATA 1996 as it is in the IHTA 1984. It is thus possible that a beneficiary might have a right of occupation under the TLATA 1996 by virtue of an interest which is an interest in possession for the purposes of the TLATA 1996, but which is not an interest in possession for inheritance tax purposes, whether taxed as such or not. For example, it is possible that an interest such as that which was the subject matter of *Pearson v IRC* [1981] AC 753, [1980] 2 All ER 479, [1980] STC 318, which was there held not to be an interest in possession for inheritance tax purposes (ie a right to the income of settled property subject to a trustees' power to accumulate the income), constitutes an interest in possession for the purposes of the TLATA 1996, s 12 where land is held on trusts of that kind. It is then possible that if a beneficiary takes up occupation by virtue of an interest of this type he becomes entitled to an interest in possession for inheritance tax purposes. However, it is no longer necessarily the case that an interest in possession in property arising under TLATA 1996 in the ways discussed in the main work will cause the property to be taxed as part of the estate of the person entitled to the interest on his or her death. A beneficiary under a discretionary trust who is permitted to occupy the land in exercise of a trustees' power might then have an interest in possession for inheritance tax purposes – although this is unlikely – (see para **[200.95]**), but would not have an interest in possession such as to give him a right of occupation under the TLATA 1996.

Giving rights of residence by will

[208.19]

[Warning added at the end about 'free of tax' provisions.]

Main features of a trust to provide a residence. These should, we suggest, be the following—

(1) An interest in possession in the property, either a life or similar interest or one ending when ceasing to reside in the property—see para **[208.21]**. Although the TLATA 1996 confers the right of residence on any beneficiary with an interest in possession, it does not impose any restrictions on the circumstances in which an interest in possession may come to an end.
(2) No trust for sale (see Part A, paras **[200.55]** and **[200.56]**). Also unnecessary and probably redundant in an interest in possession trust are a power to permit occupation, because the beneficiary will have a statutory right of occupation (see para **[208.5]** ff), or power to impose conditions as to repair, insurance, etc by the beneficiary (because that is provided for by the TLATA 1996, s 13(3), (5): Part G, para **[246.116]**). A power to permit occupation by a beneficiary and impose conditions on the beneficiary as to repair, insurance, etc should be included in a discretionary trust.
(3) An expression of intention that the trust is to provide a residence for the beneficiary, where the main trust does not make that clear, so as to make plain that the statutory right of occupation applies: TLATA 1996, s 12(1)(a) (Part G, para **[246.115]**; see also para **[208.7]**).
(4) No exclusion of the duty of trustees to consult beneficiaries who have an interest in possession in trust land about the exercise of powers or duties in relation to the land under the TLATA 1996, s 11 (Part G, para **[246.114]**; see also para **[220.58]**).
(5) The rights of the beneficiary can be further enhanced by providing that the trustees' powers of sale, and possibly other powers or discretions as well, may only be exercised with the consent of the beneficiary: the TLATA 1996, s 8(2) (Part G, para **[246.110]**) expressly contemplates that the statutory powers of management may be subject to consents. Where the interest in possession ceases on giving up residence in the property, consideration should be given to whether the requirement of consent should cease at the same time: see para **[208.21]**. If it becomes necessary for the trustees to sell the property against the wishes of the beneficiary, e g because of serious disrepair or, where the property is leasehold, failure to observe the lessee's covenants, then the trustees may apply to the court for an order under the TLATA 1996, s 14, in particular s 14(2)(a) (Part G, para **[246.117]**; see also Part A, para **[200.62]**). It is no longer the case that making sale of land subject to a beneficiary's consent causes the same consent to be required for the exercise of other powers over the land (see para **[220.62]**) and express

provision must be made in relation to all powers or discretions which it is intended to make subject to a requirement of consent.

(6) The testator can also express a wish that the trustees should delegate all their powers of management of the land to the beneficiary under the TLATA 1996, s 9 (Part G, para **[246.111]**; see also para **[220.54]** ff). An expression of wishes rather than a direction is appropriate because it appears that trustees cannot be obliged to exercise the power.

(7) Where the beneficiary's rights cease on giving up residence, it is preferable if the trusts provide for sale of one residence and purchase another with the proceeds.

(8) Avoid the use of 'free of tax' provisions if the property is in the UK and/or the gift will be exempt on the testator's death, particularly if the property has an ultimate destination other than falling into the residuary estate: see para **[208.34A]**.

Other aspects

[208.30]

[Updated for FA 2013, Sch 44.]

Taxation. A beneficiary with a life interest in a property or its proceeds of sale will clearly have an interest in possession but if that arises under the will of someone dying after 21 March 2006, it does not necessarily have to be a beneficiary-taxed (see Part A, para **[200.92]** for this term) interest in possession for inheritance tax purposes. If the interest commences at the testator's death (occurring after 21 March 2006) it will be an IPDI within IHTA 1984, s 49A (see Part A, para **[200.98]**), and therefore a beneficiary-taxed interest. If it starts at a later date, unless it does so in circumstances that IHTA 1984, s 144 turns it into an IPDI (see Part A, para **[200.133]**), or it is a disabled person's interest within the meaning of IHTA 1984, s 89(1)(c) (see Part A, para **[200.99]**), it will be subject to inheritance tax under the 'relevant property' rules which formerly applied only to non-interest in possession property. The same will almost certainly be true where the beneficiary is entitled to reside in the property but has no larger beneficial interest. Where the trusts are discretionary, or are fixed trusts in favour of persons other than the beneficiary, and the beneficiary occupies the property by virtue of the trustees' exercise of a power to permit him or her to reside there, it is likely that this will also give the beneficiary an interest in possession in the property which may be a beneficiary taxed interest in possession for inheritance tax purposes, and HMRC are likely to so regard it: see *Foster's Inheritance Tax*, E1.47 and Part A, para **[200.95]**.

[208.34]

[Updated for FA 2010 s 8.]

Another inheritance tax problem for residences is the effectiveness of the nil rate band-using strategy of husband and wife owning the matrimonial home as tenants in common, and the first to die leaving his or her share of the home to a non-exempt beneficiary or beneficiaries such as their children, on the basis or with the intention that the surviving spouse will go on living there. An outright gift to the children is probably effective to keep the first to die's share out of the taxable estate of the survivor, but at the cost of the survivor being at risk of the children seeking an order for sale. However, writing protection from this risk for the survivor into the trusts is likely to cause the survivor to have an interest in possession in the first to die's share. For example, the arrangement of this kind in Form B8.10 (at para **[208.48]**) was held to have this effect in *IRC v Lloyd's Private Banking* [1998] STC 559, High Court (see n 1 to para **[208.48]**). Another arrangement which might work is to give the child or children a life interest or interests in the share of the first to die, because the TLATA 1996, ss 12 and 13 seem to have the effect that the surviving spouse has security of exclusive possession of the property while having, it is hoped, a taxable interest in only half the property: see paras **[208.10]** and **[208.16]**. The latter scheme is untested and the Inland Revenue have not expressed views on it. The most popular method of late, and one which has the considerable advantage of having been accepted as effective, at least in some form, by the Inland Revenue, is a nil rate band discretionary trust fund under the first to die's will where the trust fund is constituted by a personal obligation of the surviving spouse or by a charge on the first to die's share of the matrimonial home: see para **[218.19]** ff. Following the introduction, on 9 October 2007, of new rules providing for the transfer of unused nil-rate band (see para **[200.75]**), these schemes will largely be unnecessary.

The new inheritance tax rules under FA 2006 make inclusion of parts or shares of a private residence in a nil-rate band discretionary trust easier. This is because it is now possible to have an interest in possession in property and have the property within the relevant property charging regime: see paras **[208.31]** ff above. A possible strategy will be to appropriate an undivided share of the first to die's share of the property to the nil-rate band discretionary trust fund after two years have elapsed from the death: see paras **[218.19]**–**[218.22]** below.

There are some Special Commissioner cases on whether occupation rights gave an interest in possession and, if so, to what extent: see *Woodhall v IRC* [2000] STC (SCD) 558, *Faulkner v IRC* [2001] STC (SCD) 112, *Cook v IRC* [2002] STC (SCD) 318, *Oakley v IRC* [2005] STC (SCD) 343, and *Judge v Revenue and Customs Comrs* [2005] STC (SCD) 863 (see para **[208.33]** above).

The nil-rate inheritance tax band for 2007–8 was £300,000: see FA 2005, s 98. For 2008–9 it was £312,000, and from 2009–10 it has been £325,000: see FA 2006, s 155 and FA 2010 s 8. The government intends to introduce legislation to continue it at the same level until April 2018 (TIINS 20 March 2013, *Simon's Weekly Tax Intelligence*. 28 March 2013, p 978).

[208.34A]

[Added to draw attention to an IHT pitfall.]

Avoid free of tax provisions or use them with care. A specific gift of land in the UK is free of inheritance tax unless the contrary is stated (IHTA 1984 s 211; see para **[214.55]** ff). If such a gift is subject to an IPDI for the testator's spouse or civil partner it is anyway exempt from inheritance tax (see paras **[200.84]** and **[200.98]**). Accordingly, the words 'free of tax' are better avoided unless there is some specific reason for needing them, such as that the property is outside the UK (see **[214.59]** ff). If free of tax wording is inadvertently attached to a gift to provide a residence of the kind of which examples are provided here, and there is a gift in remainder after the occupant has died or ceased to reside which is to, eg, a named person or persons, rather than a direction that the property falls into the residuary estate, there is the following possible hazard. The person or persons with the remainder interest in the property might argue, from the fact that the words 'free of tax' are otherwise redundant, that the inheritance tax on the death of the occupant of the property should be paid out of the residuary estate. This could hold up the administration of the estate for years and cause particular difficulty if the residuary estate has already been distributed. See also **[214.66]**.

[208.43]

[Correction of cross-references to the clauses in B8.1 which might be incorporated.]

Form B8.6: Gift of residence for wife for life with the intention that she reside there—fuller form, providing for the possibility of a change of house by the testator before his death or by the trustees after his death[1]

(1) I give my [interest in the] freehold dwellinghouse known as ———, or (if the same shall be sold or otherwise disposed of before my death) the estate or interest owned by me at my death in my then dwellinghouse or my then principal dwellinghouse (if I have more than one),[2] to my trustees free of all sums charged or otherwise secured thereon at my death (which sums shall be paid out of my residuary estate) to hold the same and the assets from time to time representing the same on trust for [my wife] during her life and subject to [my wife's] said interest on trust as part of my residuary estate.

(2) It is a purpose of the foregoing trust to provide a home for [my wife] so long as she so desires[3] and I declare that my trustees shall not be liable for lack of insurance repair or payment of outgoings of any home occupied by her under the foregoing trust or for not taking steps to enforce any reasonable conditions imposed by my trustees on [my wife] in relation to her occupation of any such home.[4]

(3) In addition to their statutory powers of investment and acquisition of assets my trustees may acquire [land or buildings outside the United Kingdom or] any undivided share (whether in co-ownership with [my wife] or any other person) in land or buildings [in the United Kingdom or elsewhere] for any purpose including provision of a home for [my wife], and may apply capital in the improvement or repair of any land or buildings for the time being subject to the foregoing trust.[5]

[(4) My trustees shall have the same powers and [my wife] shall have the same rights in relation to any property subject to this clause which is situated outside England and Wales as they would have if it were situated in England and Wales.][6]

(5) All the powers of my trustees may be exercised by them in favour of or for the benefit of [my wife] even though she is one of my trustees, and at any time when she is not one of my trustees her consent shall still be required to any exercise of the trustees' powers of sale purchase or leasing in relation to any land or buildings or interest therein subject to this clause.[7]

[Other provisions of Form B8.1 at para **[208.38]** which could be added here are: sub-cl (4), (5) (6)(c), (d), and (8)(b). Take in administrative powers and provisions as appropriate (see para **[208.36]**), such as Form B20.20 (borrowing) at para **[220.69]**, Form B21.12 (trustee indemnity) at para **[221.16]** and Form B21.37 (trustee power to charge) at para **[221.49]**.]

1 This Form shows the TLATA 1996 at its best. The removal of the need for a trust for sale (see para **[200.55]**), the statutory right of occupation (see para **[208.5]** ff) and the wide administrative powers given to trustees of land (see para **[220.49]** ff), reduce the amount of express provision needed and enable clauses of this kind to be more concise and comprehensible. The right of residence can also be made to terminate on, eg remarriage or the formation of a civil partnership although this is not recommended because the wife will have limited security and may bring a claim under the Inheritance (Provision for Family and Dependants) Act 1975 (see Vol 1 at **[105.1]** ff). Under this clause, if the house is sold and the beneficiary goes to live with a relative or in rented accommodation, she will be entitled to the income of the proceeds of sale as invested. Because this Form gives the widow an interest in possession (the right of residence will be an IPDI, see paras **[200.98]** and **[200.31]**) in the property from the testator's death, the gift should be exempt from inheritance tax on the testator's death as a gift to a spouse, unless at the testator's death the testator is domiciled in the UK, his wife is not, and the £55,000 limit for exempt gifts in such circumstances is exceeded: see Part A, para **[200.85]**. If the house is outside the UK (or might be replaced by a property outside the UK), the inclusion of a provision freeing the gift from foreign death duties should be considered. If the form is being adapted for use for someone other than the testator's spouse, or the testator is domiciled in the UK but his spouse is not (so that the gift will not necessarily be wholly exempt from inheritance tax—see Part A, para **[200.85]**), and the inheritance tax on the gift might not be borne by residue in the absence of express provision to that effect (eg the property is or might be outside the UK or the gift is an exercise of a general power of appointment over settled property: see the Preliminary Note to B14 at para **[214.60]**) a provision freeing the gift from inheritance tax should also be considered. In order to adapt the form to take account of civil partnerships formed pursuant to CPA 2004, substitute 'civil partner' for 'wife' and amend 'she' to 'he' as appropriate.

2 If the testator might have more than one property at his death, Form B8.1, sub-cl (2) (at para **[208.38]**) would provide more comprehensively for this eventuality. The words 'interest in the' in the first line, in square brackets, are to be left in or omitted depending on whether the testator owns an undivided share of the property or the whole of it at the time of making the will.

3 This should be sufficient to confer the statutory right of occupation on the beneficiary under the TLATA 1996, s 12(1)(a) (Part G, para **[246.144]**): see para **[208.7]**.

4 In the interests of economy there is no expression of wishes as to the conditions to be imposed on the beneficiary, but such could be included as in Form B8.1, sub-cl (4) at para **[208.38]**. See also nn 5 and 6 to that subclause.

5 These are all thought to be applications of capital money which are not authorised by the TLATA 1996 or the TrA 2000 (see para **[220.52]** ff and Form B8.1, nn 9 and 10 at para **[208.38]**. This subclause can be omitted in whole or in part if there are provisions elsewhere in the will to the same effect which apply to this clause. See note 6 concerning the words in square brackets other than 'my wife'. The statutory powers of acquisition of assets are now in the TrA 2000, ss 3 and 8 (Part G, paras **[246.135]** and **[246.140]**; see also para **[220.11]** ff).

6 The statutory rights and powers under the TLATA 1996, s 6(1) (Part G, para **[246.108]** and see para **[220.49]**) only apply to land in England and Wales: TLATA 1996, s 27(3) (Part G, para **[246.130]**). If land in Scotland or Northern Ireland is acquired under the statutory power to do so in the TrA 2000, s 8(1) (Part G, para **[246.140]**), they have the same statutory powers of management in relation to that land (TrA 2000, s 8(3)), but this will not apply to land in Scotland or Northern Ireland acquired under an express power or comprised in the testator's estate at his death. This subclause may be omitted if there is no likelihood of the beneficiary wanting to live outside England and Wales, and if it is omitted the words in square brackets other than 'my wife' in the preceding subclause should also be omitted.

7 The TLATA 1996, s 8(2) enables exercise of the trustees' powers over land to be made subject to consents. The repeal of the LPA 1925, s 28(1) (see para **[200.60]**) means that a requirement of consent to a sale is no longer applied by statute to other powers.

[208.44]

[Further discussion of 'free of inheritance tax' in footnote 2.]

Form B8.7: Clause in will of widow or widower providing residence and furniture for children [1]

If any of my children are under [18]/[21] when I die then I give to my trustees free of [inheritance tax foreign death duties and][2] all sums of money charged or otherwise secured thereon at my death (which sums shall be paid out of my residuary estate) my freehold house known as [description] or other the house which I may own as my [principal] residence at the date of my death together with all my household furniture and household effects therein to hold such house furniture and effects and the assets from time to time representing the same ('the Fund') upon the following trusts and in accordance with the following provisions—

(a) my trustees shall hold the Fund in trust for such of my children as [are under the age [18]/[21] at my death and][3] shall attain the age of 25 years if more than one in equal shares;

(b) all of my children who have a vested or presumptive share under the foregoing trust shall be entitled to reside in the said house or any house representing the same free of charge and to use the said furniture and effects;[4]

(c) my trustees may allow such other persons as they think fit to reside in the house free of charge with any of my children who are for the time being residing there;

(d) my trustees shall keep the said house and the furniture and effects in good repair and insured comprehensively and to their full value and ensure that the rates and other outgoings are paid and the money required to discharge these obligations shall be found out of the income (or if that is insufficient then out of the capital) of the share or shares of my residuary estate in which the children who are residing in the house have for the time being a vested or contingent interest.

1 This clause contemplates a situation in which the testator's spouse is dead and in which he wishes to make express provision for his house to be used by his children while they are under 18 or 21. If the spouse is still alive the clause can be worded so as to take effect only if the spouse predeceases the testator, but it is not suitable for use in the event of the spouse surviving the testator. If the selected specified age is 18, the trust should be a trust for bereaved minors (see para **[200.108]**), and if the specified age is 21 (or another age between 18 and 25), the trust should be an age 18-to-25 trust (see para **[200.109]**).

The express right of occupation and the right of occupation under the TLATA 1996, s 12 (see para **[208.5]** ff) mean that the beneficiaries will have interests in possession for inheritance tax purposes (see para **[200.93]** ff). If the house is sold and the fund becomes one of investments, interests in possession in the more usual sense of being entitled to a share of the income (if any) will be attained at 18 (see the Note on maintenance in B18 at para **[218.50]**), this being a trust which carries the intermediate income: LPA 1925, s 175 (Part G, para **[244.54]**).

If full powers over residue are given to the trustees (e g as in Form C2.1 at para **[224.20]**), the trustees could allow the children to reside in the house. The main use of this clause will be where the trusts of residue are unsuitable for this purpose, the testator wishes to give priority to provision of a house, or there is a wide disparity in the ages of his children and it is desired to make this provision for younger children only (see n 3 infra).

The clause must, of course, be made consistent with the rest of the will. In particular, sub-cl (d) should be varied if necessary.

2 The words 'free of inheritance tax' will be unnecessary and should be avoided if the house is in the UK (see para **[208.34A]** and B14 at para **[214.55]** ff). Although this is not a life interest trust, there could be some inheritance tax on the property vesting in the children at the age of 25, and the presence of free of tax wording might cause the children to argue that that tax is paid out of residue (i e in a case where residue goes to someone else).

3 Clearly if the ages of the testator's children are widely separated the eldest will attain an absolute interest well before the younger ones cease to need the house to live in. These parts in square brackets can be used to cut down the membership of the class of children interested under this clause, and so postpone absolute vesting, but of course they also have the effect of excluding the older children from participating in the capital.

4 The reason for this subclause is that without it interests in possession would probably only arise at 18 (see note 1), with the consequence that the children over 18 would apparently have a statutory right of occupation under the TLATA 1996, s 12 (see para **[208.5]** ff) while those under 18 would not. This also means that those who are over 18 should not be able to argue that their statutory rights give them a right to occupy to the exclusion of those who are under 18 and do not have the statutory right to occupy. There might be difficulties about the interaction of the express and statutory rights of occupation, but it is submitted that this provision will give those under 18 interests in possession within the meaning of TLATA 1996, s 12.

Miscellaneous

[208.48]

[Note on 'free of inhertance tax' added.]

Form B8.11: Gift of the testator's interest as tenant in common in a house, the gift being postponed to allow the other tenants in common to continue to reside in the house[1]

I give all my share as beneficial tenant in common in the freehold property known as [*description of property*] and all other (if any) my interest therein[2] to my trustees to hold the same upon and subject to the following trusts and provisions—

(a) while any one or more of the following persons namely [*names of the other tenants in common*] remain alive and desire to reside in the property (and provided that the property is kept in good repair and insured comprehensively and to its full value with insurers approved by my trustees (their interest being noted on the policy) at no cost to my trustees and that my trustees are kept indemnified against all rates taxes and other outgoings in respect of the property) my trustees shall not make any objection to such residence and shall not disturb or restrict it in any way and shall not take any steps to enforce the trust for sale on which the property is held or to realise my share therein or to obtain any rents or profits from the property.

(b) subject as aforesaid my trustees shall hold the same as to both capital and income upon trust absolutely for [*name*].

1 Several people sometimes contribute to the purchase of a house as tenants in common, with the intention that all of them shall be allowed to live there for as long as they wish. Their rights in this respect may of course be defined in an agreement made between them at the time of purchase or at some later date. Failing this, however, it is necessary to include some suitable provision in their wills, and the clause which follows may be found appropriate for this purpose. From an inheritance tax point of view a provision of this kind is a 'settlement' (see the IHTA 1984, s 43(2)(a)) under which the testator's co-tenants in common may attain immediate post-death interests in possession: see *IRC v Lloyd's Private Banking Ltd* [1998] STC 559, High Court. This may not matter if their estates will be too small to attract

inheritance tax charges on their deaths. Alternatively, if the co-owners are of commensurate age and hold in equal shares, an inter-vivos mutual agreement that there shall be no sale until they all die or cease to reside ought for each co-owner to be a restriction on dealing with his share incurred for full consideration, and which would minimise the incidence of inheritance tax. For trustees' powers in relation to undivided shares, see the TA 1925, s 24 (Part G, para **[246.22]**).

2 For the difficulties which might be caused by 'free of inheritance tax' wording in this form see para **[208.34A]**.

B9

Testamentary options

PRELIMINARY NOTE

[209.5]

[Updated for Perpetuities and Accumulations Act 2009.]

Drafting testamentary options. In drafting options the draftsman should bear the following points in mind:

(1) Although an option which does not specify a particular time for its exercise is valid, it is clearly desirable in the interests of a speedy and efficient administration for a time limit to be imposed. The Perpetuities and Accumulations Act 1964, s 9(2) (Part G, para **[246.82]**) imposes a maximum time limit of 21 years for options relating to land but a period of a month or so is all that will ordinarily be required. For wills made on or after 6 April 2010, the perpetuity period is 125 years (and there is no other period): see the Perpetuities and Accumulations Act 2009, ss 5(1), 15(1)(a) (Part A **[200.35A]** and Part G, para **[246.189]**). Following the coming into force of the PAA 2009 it is uncertain whether or to what extent the rule against perpetuities applies to testamentary options, whatever the nature of the property. Insofar as the rule applies the period is 125 years although there will still be 'wait and see' under the PAA 2009, s 7 (Part G, para **[246.181]**). However, since the issue with testamentary options is the need to provide an option period that is short enough to permit administration to proceed if the option is not exercised, the draftsman should not be troubled by uncertainty as to the application of the rule against perpetuities. At the same time an option can be exercised only if the donee is aware of its existence. A time limit computed by reference to the death or the grant of probate may work unfairly if the donee is left in ignorance of his rights until too late. Older authority is to the effect that, in the context of testamentary options, time limits are enforced strictly: the rule being that equity will not enlarge the time specified in the will (see *Master v Willoughby* (1705) 2 Bro Parl Cas 244). With the exception of cases of fraud and, perhaps, laches, the older cases tend to hold that this is so even if blame for the failure to exercise the option within time can be laid at the door of the personal representatives: *Dawson v Dawson* (1837) 8 Sim 346. Thus, in *Re Avard Deceased, Hook v Parker* [1948] Ch 43, a decision of Roxburgh J, an option had to be exercised within three months of the death of a life tenant. An attempt to exercise the

option out of time failed. One method of reconciling the objectives of efficiency and fairness is to impose a primary duty on the trustees to give notice of the option to the donee and to compute the time for its exercise from the service of the notice. Forms B9.1 and B9.2 at paras **[209.6]** and **[209.7]** contain options in this form.

Recently, however, two first instance decisions have sought to bypass the strict rule as to time as described above by construing the will in such a way as to conclude that time is not of the essence in the exercise of testamentary options. These are *Allardyce v Roebuck* [2004] EWHC 1538 (Ch), [2004] 3 All ER 754 and *Re Bowles Deceased* [2003] EWHC 253 (Ch), [2003] Ch 422, both of which are discussed in Vol 1 at **[92.4]**. The problem may, therefore, be less acute if tackled by a more flexible court.

(2) Where options are granted to purchase property at a valuation rather than at a fixed price, it is essential to ensure that the gift contains adequate machinery for having the price determined. Thus, an option to purchase property at the value agreed with the district valuer for probate purposes will not be capable of operating in accordance with its terms if the district valuer declines to agree the value of the property, eg because the estate is exempt from inheritance tax: *Re Malpass, Lloyds Bank plc v Malpass* [1985] Ch 42 (where, however, Megarry V-C gave effect to the option by directing an inquiry as to the value of the property to which the district valuer could have been expected to agree for probate purposes). It is also important to ensure that the time limit imposed for exercise of the option is not inconsistent with the mechanism devised for valuation: there is little point in requiring that an option be exercised within three months of death at the value agreed with the District Valuer if that value is unlikely to be fixed until much later. Care should also be taken to ensure that the testator owns the whole of the property concerned and, if not, that there is a proper mechanism for determining the value of his interest: *Dutton v Dutton* [2001] WTLR 553.

(3) Where an option is given to purchase property at a valuation, the testator may wish also to give the donee the right to resile from the option should the price be higher than expected by him. Subclause (e)(v) of Form B9.3 at para **[209.8]** can be used or adapted for this purpose.

(4) It is inadvisable to confer options to purchase foreign property, particularly immovable property and possibly also shares in a foreign company, without first taking the advice of a local lawyer. It may be preferable for the testator to execute a will in accordance with the local law disposing of such property: see generally the Preliminary Note to C14 at paras **[236.1]** ff.

(5) Where an option is given to purchase business property and the property attracts an inheritance tax liability, eg because it qualifies only for 50 per cent relief or because there are 'excepted assets' which reduce the value to which the relief applies (as to which, see the Preliminary Note to B5 at para **[205.9]**) and the right to pay by instalments is available (see under 'Payment of inheritance tax by instalments' at paras **[205.17]**–**[205.20]**) the right to pay by instalments

will cease when a sale of the property pursuant to an exercise of the option takes place. This could cause particular difficulty where the option is to purchase at below market value as it is not clear that the option to pay by instalments will continue to be available in relation to that proportion of the market value which is effectively given to the option-holder.

(6) Where an estate is partially exempt from inheritance tax, eg because part of it is given to the testator's spouse, it is not clear whether the gift by will of an option to purchase business or agricultural property qualifying for relief will constitute a specific gift of that property for the purposes of the IHTA 1984, s 39A so as to attract all the relief attributable to the property. If it does not, the relief will be apportioned with a resultant reduction in the size of the exempt estate: see generally the Preliminary Note to C11 at para **[233.1]** ff.

[209.8]

[Updated in footnote 1 for Perpetuities and Accumulations Act 2009.]

Form B9.3: Devise of freehold property conditional upon the donee conferring a right of pre-emption on another person[1]

(a) Subject to the condition imposed by subclause (b) of this clause (if it arises under the provisions of that subclause) I give my freehold property known as, etc [and registered, etc] (in this clause called the property) absolutely to [*name*] of, etc [(hereinafter called the donee)] *or* if he predeceases me then to [*name*] of, etc (and such one of these two persons as becomes entitled (subject as aforesaid) to the property on my death is in this clause called the donee)].

(b) If [*name*] of, etc (in this clause called the option holder) survives me then the gift made by subclause (a) of this clause shall be conditional upon the donee entering into an agreement with the option holder by deed signed by him or on behalf of each of them and embodying the terms set out in subclause (e) of this clause (the cost of its preparation and stamping to be paid out of my residuary estate) and if the donee refuses to accept this condition then the gift of the property to the donee shall not take effect and I give the same instead absolutely to the option holder [*or*, [*name*] of, etc] [*or*, it shall fall instead into my residuary estate].

(c) My trustees shall within six months of my death give written notice to the donee of the contents of this clause and (unless in the meantime the donee has indicated his refusal to accept the condition imposed by subclause (b)) shall as soon as possible thereafter prepare an assent to vest the property in the donee and given written notice of its preparation to the donee informing him that they will deliver the assent or authorise its delivery duly executed to the donee or to the donee's agent if at the same time the donee will deliver to the option holder or to the option holder's agent the agreement referred to in subclause (b) of this clause duly executed by the donee and if the donee does not comply with the terms of such latter notice within two months of its receipt (he being given a reasonable opportunity to do so) then he shall be deemed to have refused to accept the condition imposed by subclause (b) of this clause.

(d) My trustees shall accumulate the income of the said property until the earliest to occur of the donee's acceptance of the property on the foregoing terms the donee's rejection of the same (including any deemed refusal under the foregoing subclause) or the expiry of the period of two years less one day from my death and shall hold such accumulations on trust for the donee if he accepts the property as aforesaid and otherwise [upon trust for [the option holder] [*name of alternative donee*] [as an accretion to my residuary estate].[2]

(e) The agreement referred to in subclause (b) of this clause shall embody the following terms:

(i) That it shall remain binding and effective until the end of the period of 21 years from my death or until the death of the option holder (whichever shall happen first).

(ii) That if the donee dies and the option holder within two months of the death gives written notice (in this clause called the option notice) to the donee's personal representatives of the option holder's desire to purchase the property then the terms set out in paragraphs (iv) and (v) of this subclause shall take effect.

(iii) That if the donee desires to dispose (whether by sale letting gift or otherwise) in his lifetime of the property or any part of it he shall give written notice of such desire to the option holder and if the option holder within two months of the receipt of such notice gives written notice (in this clause called the option notice) to the donee of the option holder's desire to purchase the property then the terms set out in paragraphs (iv) and (v) of this subclause shall take effect.

(iv) That if the option holder serves the option notice within the time prescribed by paragraphs (ii) or (iii) (as the case may be) of this clause then the option holder and the donee (or the donee's personal representatives) shall attempt to reach agreement on the value of the property in the open market and with vacant possession at the time of the service of the option notice and if such agreement has not been reached within one month from the service of the option notice then an independent surveyor shall be appointed to make a valuation binding on both parties and at their joint expense such appointment to be made by agreement between the parties or in default of agreement by the President for the time being of the Royal Institution of Chartered Surveyors to whom application may be made by either party.

(v) That once such valuation has been agreed or made in the manner stated and communicated to both parties the option holder shall have one month in which to decide whether he wants to proceed with his intended purchase of the property at that valuation and if within that month he serves written notice on the donee (or his personal representatives) of his desire to proceed then he shall be entitled on paying the amount of the valuation to the donee (or his personal representatives) to a conveyance of the property free from all incumbrances (except for any exceptions reservations and restrictive or other covenants and conditions to which it is already subject at the date of my death) and the option holder shall not be entitled to any abstract of title but shall accept such title as the donee has (or his personal representatives have) to the property save that it shall be vested in him free from incumbrances (except as stated) that the title deeds shall be handed to him and that the donee (or his personal representatives) shall supply him with such other evidence required to perfect the title (if any) as he (or they) may be able to provide.

(vi) That if the option holder does not serve the option notice within the time prescribed by paragraphs (ii) or (iii) of this subclause or if having done so he does not serve written notice within the time prescribed by and under the provisions of paragraph (v) of his desire to proceed with the purchase then the donee (or his personal representatives) may deal with or dispose of the property free in all respects from the rights of the option holder and the option holder shall forthwith effect the cancellation of any entry which he may have made under the provisions of the Land Charges Act 1972 the Land Registration Act 2002 (or any enactments amending or replacing them) in respect of his rights under the agreement.

(vii) That whilst the option holder has rights under the agreement the donee (or his personal representatives) shall keep the property in repair and insured comprehensively and to its full value (and with the option holder's interest noted on the policy) in some insurance office of repute and shall produce to the option holder on demand the insurance policy and the receipt for the last premium.

(viii) That the rights of the option holder under the agreement are personal to him and are not exercisable by his personal representatives.

(ix) That for the purposes of all the foregoing provisions time shall be of the essence of the contract.

1 Testators sometimes desire to make a gift of property to one donee but to ensure that if he wants to dispose of it he shall offer it first to some specified third party. The form which follows provides one method of carrying out such a desire. An advantage of requiring the donee to enter into an agreement with the third party lies in the fact that the third party can then register a class C (iv) land charge against the donee (or make an entry on the Register in the case of registered land) and thus safeguard his rights. As to the limitation to 21 years at subclause e(i), see the note at **[209.5]**. It is assumed that the property will not be mortgaged on the testator's death: if it may be, special provision should be made (e g that any mortgage shall be discharged out of residue).

2 See para **[209.6]**, n 6 and the Note in C3 at para **[225.83]** ff. As to length of option period, see para (1) of the Preliminary Note at para **[209.5]**.

B10

Pecuniary legacies

[210.37]

[Updated for Perpetuities and Accumulations Act 2009.]

Form B10.23: Legacy to minor to be applied in maintenance[1]

I give to [*name*] the sum of £—— free of inheritance tax[2] and I declare that if the said [*name*] shall be under the age of eighteen years at my death my trustees may apply the same or any part thereof for the maintenance education advancement or benefit of the said [*name*] in such manner as they think proper or pay the same or any part thereof to the guardian for the time being of the said [*name*] without being responsible to see to the application thereof.

I direct that the said legacy shall carry interest at the rate of —— per cent per annum from the date of my death until the said sum shall be paid or invested and that section 31 of the Trustee Act 1925 shall apply to such interest and to the income of the said legacy when invested.

1 The statutory powers of maintenance and advancement (the TA 1925, s 31 being the statutory power of maintenance out of income, and trust to accumulate the surplus, relating to property held for a minor) are set out in Part G at para **[246.29]**. For wills made on or after 6 April 2010, there are no statutory restrictions on accumulation in respect of non-charitable trusts: see the PAA 2009, ss 13, 15(1)(a) (Part G, para **[246.189]**). By amending the the age of majority in TA 1925, s 31 the period in which income is accumulated can also be increased. The power herein contained is wider than the statutory power of advancement. As to when a legacy to a minor carries interest from the death of the testator, see Vol 1, paras **[32.18]–[32.27]**, but, if it is intended that it should, it is better to avoid all question by saying so in express terms. A legacy to provide education carries interest from the testator's death: *Re Selby-Walker, Public Trustee v Selby-Walker* [1949] 2 All ER 178. We recommend, at any rate when such a legacy is of any size, that it carry income from the death of the testator, so that there is no argument that there is an occasion of inheritance tax charge at the point when the legacy begins to carry income with it. See also para **[210.46]**, n 1. It now means that a person with parental responsibility for the minor could call for the legacy on the minor's behalf, see para **[210.33]**. If a testator does not want this to happen, the form below, which does not give the minor an absolute and indefeasible entitlement to the legacy prior to the age of eighteen, is to be preferred.

2 See paras **[210.3]**, **[210.4]** and **[210.9]**, n 1.

[210.39]

[Updated for Perpetuities and Accumulations Act 2009.]

Form B10.25: Legacy of a capital sum for the education of children[1]

I give to my trustees the sum of £—— free of inheritance tax[2] upon trust to invest the same on any investments hereby authorised with power to vary and transpose the same and to hold such investments and the income thereof upon the following trusts:

(a) Upon trust to apply the income thereof at the sole discretion of my trustees for the education of my children who shall be under the age of [thirty] years or any one or more of them to the exclusion of the other or others in such shares as my trustees shall in their absolute discretion deem proper.

(b) Upon trust in the event of the income of the said fund not proving sufficient for the purposes of the education of my said children to raise so much as in the absolute discretion of my trustees they shall deem necessary of the capital of the said fund and apply the same as aforesaid for the education of my said children.[3]

(c) My trustees shall invest any surplus income from the fund in investments hereby authorised to be held as augmentations of the said fund[4].

(d) Without prejudice to their absolute discretion in the matter it is my desire that my trustees shall provide for the education of my said children at the following schools colleges or institutions ——.

(e) In addition to providing for the education in schools colleges or institutions my trustees may provide out of the said fund for my said children such books of reference or of an educational nature and all such instruments and other things as may be reasonably required for purposes of such education and as my trustees in their absolute discretion think fit and in so far as my trustees in the exercise of such discretion think advisable and may apply the fund for securing any of the said children to become articled for the purpose of any profession or to be received as a pupil of any professional practitioner.

(f) When all my children then surviving shall have attained the age of [thirty] years or all have died under that age the said fund or so much thereof as has not been expended in the execution of the foregoing trusts shall fall into and form part of my residuary estate.

1 IHTA 1984. For deaths on and after 22 March 2006 it is no longer possible to create trusts which have the inheritance tax benefits of IHTA 1984, s 71, for which this Form was designed (see para **[200.107]**). The settled property subject to the trusts of this form falls within the inheritance tax charging regime for relevant property (see para **[200.92]**) and so if the legacy is sizable it would be worthwhile considering a fully discretionary trust.

2 See paras **[210.3]**, **[210.4]** and **[210.9]**, n 1.

3 Any capital so applied would be deemed to be income of the beneficiary concerned: see *Cunard's Trustees v IRC* [1946] 1 All ER 159.

4 For wills made on or after 6 April 2010, there are no statutory restrictions on accumulation in respect of non-charitable trusts: see the PAA 2009, ss 13, 15(1)(a) (Part G, para **[246.189]**). It is no longer necessary to provide (as in the 9th edition) that surplus income must be held as a part of residue after the period of 21 years.

[210.47]

[Updated for Perpetuities and Accumulations Act 2009.]

Form B10.33: Legacy contingent on attaining eighteen or twenty-one carrying interest[1]

I give to my trustees the sum of £—— free of inheritance tax[2] upon trust to invest the same in any investments authorised by law for the investment of trust moneys with power from time to time to vary such investments and to hold the said sum and the investments representing the same and the income therefrom in trust for [*minor*] if he shall attain the age of [eighteen] [twenty-one] years but if the said [minor] shall die under that age [*gift over or direction that the sum and the investments and any accumulations of income shall fall into residue*].

1 The direction to set apart the sum given will cause the legacy to carry interest and the provisions of the TA 1925, s 31 (Part G, para **[246.29]**), will apply to it: see *Re Raine, Tyerman v Stansfield* [1929] 1 Ch 716. When a legacy is payable at a certain age, but is, in terms, contingent, the legacy becomes vested when there is a direction to pay the interest in the meantime to the person to whom the legacy is given; and not less so when there is superadded a direction that the trustees shall pay the whole or such part of the interest as they shall think fit: *Re Parker, Barker v Barker* (1880) 16 Ch D 44, at 45, 46, approved in *Re Williams, Williams v Williams* [1907] 1 Ch 180 at 183. The effect, therefore, of an express gift of the income would be to make the legacy vest at the testator's death, with a result very different from that intended by the above clause.

For wills made on or after 6 April 2010, there are no statutory restrictions on accumulation in respect of non-charitable trusts: see the PAA 2009, ss 13, 15(1)(a) (Part G, para **[246.189]**). See **[210.49]** n 2.

See generally Vol 1, para **[32.1]** ff.

2 See paras **[210.3]**, **[210.4]** and **[210.9]**, n 1.

[210.49]

[Updated for Perpetuities and Accumulations Act 2009.]

Form B10.35: Legacy contingent on attaining twenty-five or marrying, relying on the statutory powers of maintenance

I give to [*name*] if he [she] shall attain the age of twenty-five years [or marry under that age] the sum of £—— free of inheritance tax[1] with interest thereon from my death at the rate of £—— per cent per annum until the same be set apart or invested. And I declare that if the said [*name*] shall die under the age of twenty-five years [and a spinster] the said legacy and all unapplied accumulations of the income thereof and the investments then representing the said legacy and the said accumulations shall fall into and form part of my residuary estate.[2]

1 See paras **[210.3]**, **[210.4]** and **[210.9]**, n 1.

2 The statutory power of maintenance will apply. For wills made on or after 6 April 2010, there are no statutory restrictions on accumulation in respect of non-charitable trusts: see the PAA 2009, ss 13, 15(1)(a) (Part G, para **[246.189]**). After the age of eighteen the legatee will be entitled to payment of the full income both of the legacy and of the past accumulations of income (the TA 1925, s 31, as amended: Part G, para **[246.29]**; see also B18 at paras **[218.43]**–**[218.79]**). PAA 2009, ss 13, 15(1)(a) means that the TA 1925, s 31 need not now have this effect. Instead, accumulation of income can go on for a much longer period.

Where there is no gift over, a gift at 25 with a trust or direction to apply income for maintenance is a vested and not a contingent gift (*Re Gossling, Gossling v Elcock* [1903]

1 Ch 448), even if the direction is to apply such part only of the income as the trustees think fit (*Fox v Fox* (1875) LR 19 Eq 286; *Re Parker, Barker v Barker* (1880) 16 Ch D 44; *Re Ussher, Foster v Ussher* [1922] 2 Ch 321).

In a gift to A when he shall attain the age (or at the age) of twenty-five, the attainment of that age may be a part of the description of the legatee, so that the gift is contingent on his attaining the age: *Re Francis, Francis v Francis* [1905] 2 Ch 295; *Re Astor, Astor v Astor* [1922] 1 Ch 364; see also Vol 1, para **[93.6]**. If the gift is a pecuniary legacy it only carries interest if directed to be set apart as in this precedent.

Nil-rate band legacies

[210.72]

[Updated in footnote 1 for inheritance tax nil-rate band changes brought about by FA 2010.]

Form B10.51: Nil-rate band legacy[1]

If the gift of my residuary estate to [my wife, civil partner *or other exempt person, eg a charity*] shall take effect[2] I give to such of my children [*name*] [*name*] and [*name*] who shall survive me if more than one in equal shares absolutely a legacy of the maximum sum of money which can in the circumstances subsisting at my death be given by this clause without any liability being incurred for the payment of inheritance tax on or by reason of my death. And in particular but without prejudice to the generality of the foregoing the circumstances to be taken into account for the foregoing purpose shall include any chargeable transfers made by me during my lifetime (or events treated as such for inheritance tax purposes) the dispositions taking effect under this my will (apart from this present clause) or under any codicil hereto and any property treated as if it were part of my estate immediately before my death for inheritance tax purposes [provided that if such maximum sum exceeds [one-third] of the probate value of my estate (disregarding for this purpose any business [or agricultural] relief applicable thereto) then the amount of the foregoing legacy shall be equal to [one-third] of the said probate value] *or* [provided that if such maximum sum shall exceed [£325,000] I give instead of such maximum sum the said sum of [£325,000]].[3]

1 Where a testator's estate is likely to exceed the inheritance tax threshold, and his residuary estate will be exempt from inheritance tax because he is leaving it to an exempt person, for example, his spouse or civil partner, he may wish to leave to non-exempt persons, such as his children, the maximum amount which he can leave without incurring any inheritance tax liability. This clause makes provision for this. See Part A, paras **[200.84]–[200.91]** on this topic generally, the Note to B18 at para **[218.16]** ff and Form B18.2 at para **[218.32]** for nil-rate band discretionary trusts.

2 The gift should be made conditional upon the testator's residuary estate being exempt from inheritance tax because in the event of the testator's taxable estate exceeding the available nil-rate inheritance tax band, nothing will be payable according to the formula.

3 The IHT nil-rate band has been frozen at £325,000 until 5 April 2015: see FA 2010, s 8. Where the testator's residuary estate may include property with the benefit of business or agricultural property relief, in particular property qualifying for such relief at the rate of 100 per cent, the maximum sum of money which could pass under this clause could exceed by a very considerable amount the sum which is the inheritance tax threshold, and leave the surviving spouse with less, perhaps much less, than the testator intends (see para **[233.9]**). The testator would be well advised to place a limit on the amount of the legacy in these circumstances, as provided here. For business relief see the Preliminary Notes to B5 at para **[205.1]** ff, C11 at paras **[233.1]–[233.13]** and for agricultural relief, see the Preliminary Note to C12 at paras **[234.1]** ff.

B11

Annuities

[211.11]

[Updated in footnote 5 for Perpetuities and Accumulations Act 2009.]

Form B11.4: Gifts of annuity of such sum as after deduction of income tax at the basic rate for the time being will amount to a stated sum to be varied with reference to the Index of Retail Prices[1]

I give to my wife [*name*][2] for her life an annuity of such sum as after deduction of income tax at the basic rate for the time being in force will amount to the clear[3] sum of £—— or such other clear sum as may be substituted therefor as hereinafter provided such annuity to be paid in monthly instalments and the first payment to be made one month after my death.

As to such annuity I hereby declare and direct as follows:

(i) The amount thereof shall be increased or decreased by dividing the sum of £—— by the index figure in the Index of Retail Prices for the month in which my will is executed and (having made allowance for any rebasing of the Index which may have happened in the meantime) multiplying it by the index figure in that Index for the month in which my death occurs.

(ii) Any rebate allowance or repayment of income tax which may be allowed or made to my said wife [shall enure for her benefit] or [shall be accounted for by my said wife to my trustees].

(iii) My trustees [shall]/[may] provide for the payment thereof by setting apart and appropriating in respect thereof such part of my residuary estate as shall in their opinion be sufficient by the income thereof to pay such annuity (hereinafter called the annuity fund). My trustees shall have absolute discretion in assessing the amount so to be set apart having regard to any possible increase in the said Index and shall not be liable for any loss incurred by the annuitant by reason of the annuity fund subsequently proving insufficient.[4]

(iv) When such appropriation has been made the annuity shall be wholly charged on the annuity fund in exoneration of the rest of my estate but the capital of such fund may be resorted to in case at any time the income thereof is insufficient to pay the annuity.

(v) In so far as the income from the annuity fund shall in any year exceed the sum required to pay the annuity my trustees shall accumulate the same during the lifetime of my said wife[5] by investing the same in any investments hereby authorised as my trustees shall think fit. Such accumulations and the interest or income thereof shall be held by my trustees to make up any deficiency of the annuity in any subsequent year and in so far as they are not so required they shall form an accretion to the annuity fund and on the determination of the said annuity shall with the annuity fund fall into and form part of my residuary estate.[6]

For the purposes hereof the Index of Retail Prices shall mean the Index of Retail Prices published by HM Stationery Office or any official publication substituted therefor and in the event of any change after the date hereof in the reference base used to compile the said Index the figure taken to be that at which the said Index stands after such change shall be the figure at which the said Index would have stood if the reference base current at the date hereof had been retained.

1 The Index of Retail Prices is published monthly in the Department of Employment Gazette. The current index was introduced in 1956 and replaced earlier indexes to which it can be linked back (see Industrial Relations Handbook and a publication of the Stationery Office 'Method of Construction and Calculation of the Index of Retail Prices').
2 In order to adapt the form to take account of civil partnerships formed pursuant to CPA 2004, substitute 'civil partner' for 'wife' and substitute 'his' for 'her' where appropriate.
3 See para **[211.8]**, n 3.
4 In economic conditions of high inflation and a tendency of most investments to fail to maintain their value in real terms, the use of this form is likely to present the trustees with considerable difficulty in deciding what size fund is appropriate, and a discretion not to do so may be preferred. In such economic conditions there is a serious risk of a large proportion of the estate being used up to meet an annuity in this form, with much capital being paid out, and charged to income tax, as income.
5 For wills made on or after 6 April 2010, there are no statutory restrictions on accumulation in respect of non-charitable trusts, so accumulation will be permitted throughout the life of the wife and need not be limited to the period of 21 years: see the PAA 2009, ss 13, 15(1)(a) (Part G, para **[246.189]**).
6 As to the right to 'hold up' income to meet future annuity instalments, see *Re Berkeley, Inglis v Countess Berkeley* [1968] Ch 744, [1968] 3 All ER 364, CA and see generally Vol 1, para **[33.25]**. This subclause will mean that there is no interest in possession in the part of the annuity fund not treated as subject to the annuitant's interest in possession for inheritance tax purposes (see para **[211.3]**), and that that part will be subject to the 'discretionary trust' inheritance charging regime described in the Note to B18 at para **[218.1]** ff.

[211.23]

[Updated for FA 2013, Sch 44.]

Form B11.16: Gift of an annuity to a trustee in trust for a mentally disabled daughter[1]

I give to [*trustee*] during the life of my daughter [*name*][2] an annuity of £—— free of all inheritance tax[3] to be paid by equal quarterly payments the first whereof shall be made three months after my death and I authorise my trustees either to purchase from some insurance society of good repute an annuity of the above amount[4] or set apart and appropriate so much of my residuary estate (hereinafter called 'the annuity fund') as shall in their opinion be sufficient by means of the income thereof to pay such annuity and I direct as follows:

(1) When the annuity shall have been provided for in either of the ways aforesaid the rest of my estate shall be exonerated from payment

thereof and my trustees shall have recourse only to the annuity or the annuity fund to pay such annuity.

(2) The capital of the annuity fund (if any) may be resorted to in case at any time the income thereof is insufficient to pay the said annuity.

(3) On the cesser of the said annuity the annuity fund (if any) shall revert to my residuary estate and any surplus income arising in any year from the annuity fund shall be applied as income of my residuary estate.

(4)

(a) The said [*trustee*] shall stand possessed of the said annuity of £—— upon trust to pay or apply the same for the maintenance or benefit of my said daughter [*name*] including the payment of all expenses of and incidental to the provision of a home for and the care and maintenance of my said daughter [*name*] and the said [*trustee*] shall have full and uncontrolled discretion with respect to the application of the said annuity and if and so long as my said daughter shall reside with the said [*trustee*] [he] *or* [she] shall be entitled to retain for [his] *or* [her] own benefit out of the said annuity the sum of £—— by way of rent in respect thereof.[5]

(b) If at the date of the death of my said daughter there shall be any moneys resulting from any unapplied part of such annuity the same shall [fall as capital into my residuary estate]/[be paid by the said [*trustee*] to the treasurer for the time being of the —— Home for Incurables [*address*] whose receipt shall be a good discharge].

1 It is thought that this gives the annuitant an interest in possession for inheritance tax purposes which, because arising immediately on the death of the testator, will be an IPDI (see Part A at para **[200.98]**). If it does not do so, the annuitant, if incapable of administering her property or managing her affairs within the meaning of the Mental Health Act 1983 (as amended) (see Vol1 para **[4.12]**) at the date of the testator's death (or otherwise qualifying as a 'disabled person' at that time, see para **[226.4]** sub-para (i)), will be deemed to have an interest in possession under the IHTA 1984, s 89 (as amended by FA 2013, Sch 44, para 6). For a commentary on trusts for disabled persons, see C4 para **[226.3]** ff. and Part A, para **[200.99]**.

2 It may be important to name the daughter referred to in order to take account of GRA 2004 although in this context the point is unlikely. See Vol 1 at para **[81.1]**.

3 See para **[211.5]**, sub-para (i).

4 For a possible inheritance tax disadvantage of the exercise of this power see para **[211.6]**.

5 Compare Form B18.4 at para **[218.34]**.

B12

Charitable gifts

PRELIMINARY NOTE

[212.1]

[Updated for Charities Act 2006 commencement and Charities Act 2011.]

For a statement of the general law relating to charities see Vol 1, paras **[102.1]–[103.21]**. See the Note in B2 at para **[202.28]** ff for charitable gifts for the maintenance of graves. Many of the changes made by the Charities Act 2006 are now in force, and it and the earlier legislation have been consolidated into the Charities Act 2011 with effect from 14 March 2012: see paras **[102.2]**, **[102.3]**, **[103.9]**. Although the charitable status of some entities which were previously charities may be affected, the changes originally made by the Charities Act 2006 are unlikely to affect the making of testamentary gifts to charities described in this Chapter. The provisions of it as regards charities which merge have been construed by the court so as to be largely ineffective: see para **[212.2]**.

[212.2]

[Updated for Perpetuities and Accumulations Act 2009 and Finance Act 2010. Updated for Charities Act 2006, s 44, Charities Act 2011 and *Berry v IBS-STL (UK) Ltd* [2012] EWHC 666 (Ch), [2012] WTLR 1421.]

Property given to charities is wholly exempt from IHT: Inheritance Tax Act 1984 (IHTA 1984), s 23. For the purposes of this exemption property is given to charities if it becomes the property of charities or is held on trust for charitable purposes only (IHTA 1984, s 23(6)(a)). It is thought that originally, like the exemption for charities from income tax, the inheritance tax exemption was confined to charities established in the UK (see the income tax case of *Camille and Henry Dreyfus Foundation v IRC* [1956] AC 39, [1955] 3 All ER 97), but this has been changed by FA 2010 in order to comply with European law (see below). Gifts to certain institutions, e g the British Museum, the National Gallery and the National Trust are wholly exempt: IHTA 1984, s 25 and Sch 3. Gifts to political parties may in certain circumstances enjoy a similar exemption: IHTA 1984, s 24. Gifts to housing associations may also be exempt: IHTA 1984, s 24A. Gifts to amateur sports clubs falling within the definition in Corporation Tax Act 2010, Part 13, Chapter 9, which have been registered with HMRC, can also be exempt from IHT under IHTA 1984, s 23 (see IHTA 1984, s 23(1), (5A), (7)). For HMRC's treatment of charitable gifts for IHT purposes, see HMRC's Inheritance Tax Manual at IHTM11101.

Finance Act 2010, s 30, Sch 6 Parts 1 and 4 changes the law on the meaning of 'charity' for the purposes of IHT, with effect from 1 April 2012 (SI 2012/736). The meaning of 'charity' is expanded to include institutions in other Member States of the European Union and Iceland and Norway (see FA 2010, Sch 6, para 2(3) and SI 2010/1904), but narrowed so as to apply only to bodies of persons or trusts which not only have charitable purposes but also satisfy certain conditions as to registration and having managers who are 'fit and proper persons'. This raises the possibility that some gifts by will to named charities could fail to qualify for the IHT charity exemption because the recipient or recipients have charitable purposes but do not comply with these additional conditions. It is unlikely that there will be any problem about gifts to named charities where the donees are major national charities. Where there could be a problem is gifts to named small local charities. However, a gift to a charity which is on the Charity Commission's Register (which can be searched online – see below) or has been approved by HMRC Charities will usually be accepted by HMRC as being within the exemption. If the will gives property to the testator's executors or trustees to be held on a charitable discretionary trust, that qualifies for the exemption under IHTA 1984, s 23(6)(a) as property held on trust for charitable purposes only, and is not subject to the conditions as to registration etc imposed by FA 2010, Sch 6 (which relate to direct gifts to charities). In the case of a testator who wishes to make a gift to a charity outside the UK but in the EEA it may be difficult to be certain that the charity will qualify for the exemption.

Many charitable gifts are concerned with quite small charities in which the testator has taken an active interest. It is with such charities that practical difficulties may occur: that is, that they have very little organisation and it may be difficult to find someone who can give a proper receipt for the legacy. It is wise in such cases to provide not only that the receipt of the treasurer or other proper officer shall be a full discharge, but to go further and say that the receipt of the person who professes to be the proper officer shall be such a discharge. In all cases it is important for those drawing the will to ascertain the precise name of the charity which the testator intends to benefit, for, on the one hand, there are many with very similar names and, on the other hand, testators commonly speak of a charity by a name which is quite different from its proper name. Failure to give the charity's correct name may result in the gift going to the wrong charity or even failing altogether. At the very least a misdescription of a charity can lead to delay and expense in the administration of the estate, and often greater expense than the value of the gift itself. Now that most charities can be registered the name should be checked with the Charity Commission and there is no excuse for failing to do so. The Charity Commission's Register of Charities can be consulted online at www.charity-commission.gov.uk (England and Wales) and www.o-scr.org.uk (Scotland) to find the correct name and address of any registered charity which a testator wishes to benefit. Some charities are exempt from registration. In such cases what needs to be found out is whether the charity is recognised by HMRC as qualifying for charity tax exemptions.

[212.2ZA]

[Updated for Berry v IBS-STL (UK) Ltd [2012] WTLR 1421 and Charities Act 2011.]

Charities which merge or disappear between will-making and death. Charities Act 2006 (CA 2006), s 44 with effect from 28 November 2007, now re-enacted as Charities Act 2011 (CA 2011), s 311, makes provision for the problem where a charitable institution, to which a gift is made by will, merges with one or more other charities before the death of the testator. CA 2011, s 311 (see Vol 1, para **[103.9]**) provides that if a merger of charities has been registered in the register of charity mergers, a gift which is expressed as a gift to a pre-merger charity takes effect as a gift to the post-merger institution into which it has merged. However, in the case of *Berry v IBS-STL (UK) Ltd* [2012] EWHC 666 (Ch), [2012] WTLR 1421, a testatrix had given her residuary estate to such of six named charities as were in existence at the date of her death, and one of them had merged with another charity before her death. It was held that the provision in the will did not express a gift to the merged charity, because the gift was only to such of the named charities as existed at her death, and the merged charity no longer existed at the time of the testator's death. Accordingly, the provision now re-enacted as CA 2011, s 311 did not apply. On the other hand, the judge in that case did express the view that s 311 would apply to a share of residue directed to be held on trust for a charity, as well as to a direct gift of a sum of money or other property to a charity (para [8] of the judgment).The will contained a provision very similar to Form B12.29 at para **[212.31]**, and the executors were held to be able to distribute the share at their discretion to a similar charity. Clauses like that in Form B12.29 still can be worth including despite CA 2011, s 311. This is particularly so where a charitable gift is contingent on the recipient being in existence at the testator's death, as in the *Berry v IBS-STL* case. Even where it is not so contingent, it is possible that the recipient might never have existed, or might have been wound up rather than merged.

[212.2ZB]

[Updated for Perpetuities and Accumulations Act 2009.]

Accumulation of income. For wills made on or after 6 April 2010, there are no statutory restrictions on accumulation in respect of non-charitable trusts, so accumulation will be permitted throughout the trust period: see the PAA 2009, ss 13, 15(1)(a) (Part G, para **[246.189]**). However, to the extent that a will provides for property to be held on trust for charitable purposes, if the will imposes or confers on the trustees a duty or power to accumulate income, and apart from this section the duty or power would last beyond the end of the statutory period of 21 years starting with the first day when the income must or may be accumulated (as the case may be), it ceases to have effect at the end of that period: PAA 2009, s 14(1), (3)–(5) (Part G, para **[246.188]**). There is an exception where the provision is made by a court or the Charity Commission for England and Wales: PAA 2009, s 14(2) (Part G, para **[246.188]**). If a duty or power ceases to have effect by reason of the above the income to which the duty or power would otherwise have applied must go to the person who would have been entitled to it if there had been no duty or power to accumulate, or be applied for the purposes for which it would have had to be applied if there had been no such duty or power: PAA 2009, s 14(6) (Part G, para **[246.188]**).

[212.2A]

[Added for the IHT reduced rate under IHTA 1984, Sch 1A, inserted by Finance 2012.]

Drafting charitable gifts so as to qualify for the lower (36%) IHT rate on the chargeable part of the estate. For the qualifying conditions for the lower rate, see para **[200.91A]** ff, available in relation to the estates of persons dying on or after 6 April 2012. As explained in para **[200.91C]**, the charitable gifts have to be equal to or more than a threshold amount which is 10 per cent of a 'baseline amount' which is not necessarily the same as the estate itself. A 'formula' clause suitable for inclusion in a will, to ensure that a donated amount reaches the 10 per cent threshold, appears in HMRC's Inheritance Tax Manual (at IHTM45008), which is much the same as a draft produced by STEP, and see Form B12.2A at para **[212.4A]**. This makes a gift of a sum equal to a specified percentage of the baseline amount for the relevant component of the estate, which in relation to a will is the general component (for the other components see para **[200.91B]**). The formula has the difficulty that calculating the resulting amount of the charitable legacy in an estate with more than one component, and which also has available nil-rate band, is not straightforward. The nil-rate band has to be allocated among components according to the relative sizes of the chargeable parts of each component, while the chargeable part and thus the baseline amount of the general component will vary with the amount of the charitable legacy (see IHTA 1984, Sch 1A, para 5 step 2 and para **[200.91C]**). To alleviate this problem, HMRC's website's reduced rate calculator at http://hmrc.gov.uk/tools/iht-reduced-rate/calculator.htm will calculate the minimum amount of a given component which needs to go to charity so as to qualify for the reduced rate, in a case where there is more than one component. For someone who wants to give no more than the minimum to qualify for the lower rate, a 'formula' gift of this type is likely to be the best option. If he wishes to give more than the minimum, and does so by specifying a percentage of the baseline amount greater than 10 per cent, the HMRC reduced rate calculator will not calculate the size of the charitable gift and doing so without its assistance will be hard work if the estate has more than one component. If the testator wishes to be more generous than the minimum, it will make life easier for the executors if the gift is of a specific sum of money, or a specific percentage of the gross amount of the component, subject to the alternative of it being 10 per cent of the baseline amount for that component if that turns out to be a greater amount. See Form B12.2A at para **[212.4A]**.

[212.4]

[Updated for Charities Act 2011, and the grammar of the final sentence improved.]

Form B12.2: Gifts of shares of residue to individual and charitable institutions

My trustees shall hold my residuary estate and the income thereof upon trust as to:

(a) a one third share for my son [*name*][1] for his own use and benefit absolutely;

(b) a one third share for the charity known as [*name and address of charity*] for its general purposes (the receipt of the person who professes to be the treasurer or other proper officer for the time being of the charity to be sufficient discharge to my trustees); and

(c) a one third share for such charitable institution or institutions in England [which have amongst their objects the relief of those in need by reason of youth, age, ill-health, disability, financial hardship or other disadvantage][2] as my trustees may in their absolute discretion within the period of one year from my death select and if more than one in such proportions as my trustees may think proper (the receipt of the person who professes to be the treasurer or other proper officer for the time being of any selected charitable institution to be sufficient discharge to my trustees) and in default of or subject to any such selection for the aforesaid charity [*name of charity*] for its general purposes.

And I hereby declare that in determining the said one third shares of my residuary estate my trustees shall divide my residuary estate into three shares without making any allowance for the inheritance tax payable by reason of my death and attributable to my residuary estate and then shall reduce such share as is not exempt from inheritance tax by the inheritance tax attributable thereto.[3]

1 Following the commencement of GRA 2004 on 4 April 2005, it may be important to name the son referred to. See Vol 1 at para **[81.1]**.

2 See Charities Act 2011, s 3(1)(j) for this new head of charity, which was first introduced in Charities Act 2006 as an updated version of the traditional category of 'the relief of aged and infirm persons'.

3 Where shares of residue will not be exempt from inheritance tax, a declaration such as this should be included to avoid complicated calculations, see para **[214.72]**.

[212.4A]

[Added for the IHT reduced rate under IHTA 1984, Sch 1A, inserted by Finance 2012.]

Form B12.2A: Gifts of shares of residue to individuals and charitable institutions so as to qualify for the reduced IHT rate on the chargeable part of the estate

My trustees shall hold my residuary estate and the income thereof as follows:

(a) they shall hold whichever shall be the greater of[1]:

  (i) such a sum from my residuary estate as shall constitute a donated amount equal to ten per cent (10%) of the baseline amount in relation to the general component[2] of my estate; and 'donated amount', 'baseline amount' and 'general component' for this purpose have the same meanings as in Inheritance Tax Act 1984, Schedule 1A; or

  (ii) [fifteen] per cent ([15]%) of my residuary estate;

upon trust for [*name of charity*];

(b) subject as aforesaid, my trustees shall hold my residuary estate and the income thereof upon trust for my son [*name*] and my daughter [*name*][3] in equal shares absolutely Provided that if the foregoing trust for my said son or my said daughter fails for any reason then what would have been his or her share thereunder shall be held in trust for all or any his or her children and remoter issue living at or after my death who attain the age of 18 years in equal shares per stirpes but so that no issue shall take whose parent attains a vested interest under the foregoing trust.

And I hereby declare that in determining the said percentage share of my residuary estate my trustees shall determine such share without making any allowance for the inheritance tax payable by reason of my death and attributable to my residuary estate and then shall reduce the part which is not exempt from inheritance tax by the inheritance tax attributable thereto.[4]

1 For the reasons for putting the gift in this way rather than simply giving a higher percentage than ten per cent, see para **[212.2A]**.

2 If there may be more than one component and it is desired to give enough to charity to get the reduced rate for other components, substitute for 'the general component' here 'the aggregate of the general, [survivorship], [settled property] components [reservation of benefit property]' with an appropriately placed 'and', and add appropriate terms to the list of terms having the same meaning as in IHTA 1984, Sch 1A. For the components see para **[200.91B]** and for merger of components see para **[200.91D]**.

3 Following the commencement of GRA 2004 on 4 April 2005, it may be important to name the son and daughter referred to. See Vol 1 at para **[81.1]**. If these beneficiaries are not the testator's issue, so that WA 1837, s 33 would not apply, a substitutional provision such as that included here is recommended.

4 Where part of residue will not be exempt from inheritance tax, a declaration such as this should be included to avoid complicated calculations, see para **[214.72]**.

[212.5]

[Updated in footnote 1 for the IHT reduced rate under IHTA 1984, Sch 1A, inserted by Finance 2012.]

Form B12.3: Gift of a share of residue upon trust for charitable objects to be selected by trustees[1]

(1) My trustees shall hold one equal [fourth] part of my residuary estate and the income thereof upon trust to apply the same for such charitable institutions or such other charitable objects in England as my trustees may in their absolute discretion select and to pay such share and income to or for such institutions or objects if more than one in such proportions as my trustees may think proper and I declare that the receipt of the [person who professes to be the][2] treasurer or other proper officer for the time being of any such charity shall be an effectual discharge to my trustees in respect of any sum (whether of capital or income) allocated under this gift.

(2) I express the wish without imposing any binding trust or obligation that my trustees should distribute the whole of the said equal [fourth] part of my residuary estate and the income thereof within the period of two years from my death [and until such distribution is complete my trustees shall have power to invest all moneys liable to be invested in any property of whatever description or location as if they were a sole beneficial owner of such moneys].[3]

(3) The fractional shares of my residuary estate shall be determined by dividing my residuary estate into the fractional shares set out above without

making any allowance for the inheritance tax payable by reason of my death and attributable to my residuary estate and then reducing such shares as are not exempt from inheritance tax by the inheritance tax attributable thereto.[4]

1 This form will be suitable where it is envisaged that the distribution will take place shortly after the testator's death. For a long-term discretionary trust, see Form C13.1 at para **[235.2]**. Care must be taken as to the description of the objects to be benefited in a gift such as this. It is clear that a gift for 'charitable objects' is good. A gift for 'charitable and benevolent objects' has also been held to be good (*Re Best, Jarvis v Birmingham Corpn* [1904] 2 Ch 354). On the other hand, a gift for 'charitable or benevolent objects' will be void for uncertainty (*Hunter v A-G* [1899] AC 309; *Re Horrocks, Taylor v Kershaw* [1939] P 198, [1939] 1 All ER 579; *Chichester Diocesan Fund and Board of Finance Inc v Simpson* [1944] AC 341, [1944] 2 All ER 60); but 'a gift for charitable or religious purposes' is good (*Re Ward, Public Trustee v Ward* [1941] Ch 308, [1941] 2 All ER 125, CA); the Charitable Trusts (Validation) Act 1954 validated certain existing charitable trusts that would otherwise have been void but did not have an effect on trusts created thereafter. See generally Vol 1, para **[102.23]**.

There is a prima facie presumption that every power given to a trustee, even one involving the exercise of a very wide discretion such as the above is vested in them virtue officii and accordingly passes with the office to the holders for the time being thereof (*Re Smith, Eastick v Smith* [1904] 1 Ch 139). If, therefore, the testator desires that the power of selection is only to be exercised by the individuals named as trustees special provision must be made. A testator may leave the selection of charity beneficiaries to trustees: see *A-G v National Provincial Bank* [1924] AC 262, [1923] All ER Rep 123 at 264 and 126 respectively.

For an alternative formulation of the amount of the charitable gift which makes it not less than the minimum to qualify for the reduced rate under IHTA 1984, Sch 1A on the chargeable part, see Form B12.2A at para **[212.4A]**.

2 To avoid practical difficulties in obtaining a receipt it is wise to include these words.

3 These words could be left out, because they are no broader than the general power of investment by which personal representatives can now make any kind of investment which they could make if they were absolutely entitled to the assets of the estate: TrA 2000, ss 3 and 35 (Part G, paras **[246.135]** and **[246.167]**).

4 If other shares of residue will not be exempt from inheritance tax, a declaration such as this should be included to avoid complicated calculations, see para **[214.72]**.

[212.6]

[Updated for Charities Act 2011.]

Form B12.4: Gift of residue upon a charitable trust[1]

I give my residuary estate (hereinafter called 'the trust fund') to my trustees to hold the same upon the following trusts with and subject to the following powers and provisions:

(1) In this clause 'charity' shall have the same meaning as under the Charities Act 2011 and 'charities' has a corresponding meaning.[2]

(2) My trustees shall pay the income of the trust fund to such charity or charities if more than one in such shares and in such manner generally as my trustees shall in their absolute discretion think fit provided that until the expiration of the period of 21 years from my death my trustees shall have power to accumulate the whole or any part of such income by investing the same and the resulting income thereof in any manner hereby authorised so that any accumulations so made shall form an accretion to the capital from which such income arose for all purposes.

(3) Notwithstanding the foregoing trust of income my trustees shall have power at any time or times to pay transfer or apply the whole or any part or parts of the capital of the trust fund to or for the benefit

of such charity or charities in such shares if more than one and in such manner generally as my trustees shall in their absolute discretion think fit.

(4) I express the wish without imposing any trust or legal obligation that my trustees should consider the purpose of the relief of poor persons resident in the county of – and charities which have amongst their objects the relief of such persons as the principal beneficiaries of the trust fund and the income thereof.

(5) The receipt of the person who professes to be the treasurer or other proper officer for the time being of any charity shall be sufficient discharge to my trustees.[3]

1 See also Form C13.1 at para **[235.2]**. The will should include suitable investment powers for the trustees as this trust may continue for some time.

2 Under Charities Act 2011, s 1 Charity is defined as an institution which is established for charitable purposes only, and falls to be subject to the control of the High Court in the exercise of its jurisdiction with respect to charities and the term 'Charitable purpose' is defined for the first time. See Vol 1, at para **[102.3]**.

3 To avoid practical difficulties in obtaining a receipt it is wise to include these words.

[212.31]

[Updated for *Berry v IBS-STL (UK) Ltd* [2012] EWHC 666 (Ch), [2012] WTLR 1421.]

Form B12.29: General provision against lapse of charitable gifts—subject to Charities Act 2011, s 311[1]

If any institution society trust or body of persons (incorporated or unincorporated) which is intended to be the recipient or beneficiary of any gift made by me herein or in any codicil hereto [and which is referred to hereby or by such codicil as a charity or charitable[2]] shall be found never to have existed or to have ceased to exist or to have been amalgamated with another institution society or body of persons before my death and such gift does not take effect as a gift to some other institution trust or body of persons by virtue of section 311 of the Charities Act 2011 then the benefit intended to be given under such gift shall be paid transferred or applied to such charitable institutions societies or bodies of persons established in the United Kingdom of Great Britain and Northern Ireland or for such charitable purposes in the said United Kingdom and if more than one in such shares as my trustees in their absolute discretion think fit and I express the wish without imposing any trust or obligation that in carrying out the foregoing trust my trustees should seek to benefit a charity or charities as close as possible in purpose to those of the institution society or body of persons intended to be benefited by my said original gift.

1 The purpose of this is to fill the gap in a case where a charitable gift fails. It will be of wider scope in a case where a charitable gift or gifts are contingent on the recipient being in existence at the date of the testator's death, because in such a case Charities Act 2011, s 311 will not apply if the intended recipient has merged with another charity before the testator's death: see *Berry v IBS-STL (UK) Ltd* [2012] EWHC 666 (Ch), [2012] WTLR 1421 and para **[212.2ZA]**. This clause will not prevent the gift going to a charity which is in insolvent liquidation at the death of the testator but which has yet to be formally dissolved. See Form B12.30 below for a form intended to prevent a gift taking effect to a charity which is the subject of a winding-up order at the testator's death.

2 Some draftsmen may prefer to add these words, as otherwise a gift to any institution, even though not intended as a charitable gift, will be caught. But if such words are included, care must be taken to describe expressly all intended charitable objects as charities.

[212.32]

[Added as a consequence of *Berry v IBS-STL (UK) Ltd* [2012] EWHC 666 (Ch), [2012] WTLR 1421.]

Form B12.30: Overriding provision in the event of non-existence or change in the recipients of charitable gifts[1]

Notwithstanding the other provisions of this my will and notwithstanding the provisions of section 311 of the Charities Act 2011, if any institution society trust or body of persons (incorporated or unincorporated) which is intended to be the recipient of any gift made by me herein[2] [and which is referred to hereby as a charity or charitable[3]] shall be found never to have existed or to have ceased to exist or to have been amalgamated with another institution society or body of persons or to have changed its name or charitable purposes or to have become subject to a winding-up order or to have been struck off the register of charities kept by the Charity Commission before my death then the benefit intended to be given under such gift shall be paid transferred or applied to such charitable institutions societies or bodies of persons established in the United Kingdom of Great Britain and Northern Ireland or for such charitable purposes in the said United Kingdom and if more than one in such shares as my trustees in their absolute discretion think fit and I express the wish without imposing any trust or obligation that in carrying out the foregoing trust my trustees should seek to benefit a charity or charities as close as possible in purpose to those of the institution society or body of persons intended to be benefited by my said original gift.

1 This overrides the terms of the charitable gifts themselves where an event such as a change of name or a winding-up order has occurred which would not as a matter of the general law cause the gift to fail, and also overrides Charities Act 2011, s 311. The latter would anyway be prevented from applying where a charitable gift is contingent on the recipient being in existence at the testator's death: *Berry v IBS-STL (UK) Ltd* [2012] EWHC 666 (Ch), [2012] WTLR 1421. See, further, para **[212.2ZA]**.

2 Because this clause may in some circumstances override the terms of individual gifts, there is no reference at this point to gifts made by a codicil. If there are charitable gifts in a codicil where this clause appears in the will, the codicil needs expressly to refer to, repeat, or incorporate this clause by reference, if the charitable gifts in the codicil are to be subject to it.

3 See footnote 2 to para **[212.31]** above.

B13

Exercises of special powers of appointment

Perpetuities

[213.7]

[Updated for Perpetuities and Accumulations Act 2009.]

The perpetuity period applicable to the interests created under a special power of appointment is the perpetuity period applicable to the instrument creating the special power. So when exercising a special power of appointment, care must be taken to ensure that the interests which it creates vest in interest within the perpetuity period applicable to the instrument creating the power (subject to what is said in para **[200.35B]** about drafting certain trusts to which PAA 2009 applies). This is particularly important where the instrument creating the special power of appointment took effect before 16 July 1964 because in this case there is no 'wait and see' rule which might save an otherwise perpetuitous appointment by enabling it to be treated as valid until it is apparent that the interests must vest, if at all, outside the perpetuity period. The 'wait and see' rule as introduced by Perpetuities and Accumulations Act 1964 only applies in relation to instruments creating a power which took effect on or after 16 July 1964, see the Perpetuities and Accumulations Act 1964 (PAA 1964), ss 3 and 15(5) (Part G, paras **[246.76]** and **[246.88]**). In some cases, instruments creating a special power of appointment will expressly define the applicable perpetuity period, for example, in the case of instruments taking effect on or after 16 July 1964 but before 6 April 2010 a period of 80 years or less may have been selected as provided by the PAA 1964, s 1(1), (Part G, para **[246.74]**), in which case the interests created by any exercise of the power should be made to vest within that period. In relation to powers created by wills or other instruments made on or after 6 April 2010, the perpetuity period is 125 years (and there is no other period): see the PAA 2009, ss 5(1), 15(1)(a) (Part A **[200.35A]** ff and Part G, para **[246.179]**). The position is uncertain as to whether PAA 2009 applies to an exercise of a special power created by a will which was made before 6 April 2010 of someone who dies on or after it: see the PAA 2009, s 15(1)(b) and para **[200.35H]**. In wills or other instruments made on or after 6 April 2010 it is not necessary to specify that the perpetuity period is 125 years: PAA 2009, s 5(2) (Part G, para **[246.179]**). This will now be the perpetuity period (commencing with the date of the instrument creating the power, or the testator's death in the case of a will) when drafting an appointment in exercise of a power arising under a will or other instrument made on or after 6 April 2010: see the PAA 2009, s 6(2) (Part G, para

[246.180]). An appointment under such a power should preferably be expressly limited so that all interests vest (in interest if not in possession) and all powers are exercised within the 125-year period although the will or other instrument creating the power may now be silent as to the period. We should add that if this is not done in an appointment, there will still be 'wait and see' under the PAA 2009, s 7 (Part G, para **[246.181]**), but it is better practice to draft trusts of which it is clear from the outset that they will vest within the relevant perpetuity period at any rate where there is a real possibility of the trusts continuing to the end of the period: see para **[200.35B]** for circumstances in which relying on wait and see could be appropriate. If there is no express perpetuity period in a pre-6 April 2010 instrument creating the power the period of a life or lives in being plus 21 years should be used. For perpetuities generally see Vol 1, para **[94.1]** ff and for perpetuities in relation to powers of appointment see para **[94.41]** ff.

Accumulations

[213.8]

[Updated for Perpetuities and Accumulations Act 2009.]

If a power created by a will or other instrument made before 6 April 2010 expressly or impliedly authorises the appointment of a trust or power of accumulation, excessive accumulations should not be directed, i e accumulation for a longer period than that authorised by law and by the instrument creating the power. The periods of accumulation permitted by law are contained in the Law of Property Act 1925 (LPA 1925), s 164 (Part G, para **[246.56]**) and (for instruments taking effect on or after 16 July 1964) the PAA 1964, s 13 (Part G, para **[246.86]**). The instrument creating the power will sometimes expressly incorporate one of these periods of accumulation prescribed by LPA 1925, s 164 or PAA 1964, s 13, otherwise it is a matter of construction of the instrument as a whole whether a period has been selected and which period it is. These periods, only one of which may apply in respect of any disposition, are in addition to any accumulations pursuant to the TA 1925, s 31 (Part G, para **[246.29]**), see the LPA 1925, s 165 (Part G, para **[246.57]**). For accumulations generally see Vol 1, para **[95.1]** ff. For powers created by wills or other instruments made on or after 6 April 2010, there are no statutory restrictions on accumulation in respect of non-charitable trusts, so a power or trust to accumulate income during any or all of the perpetuity period will (subject to any restrictions imposed by the will or other instrument) be valid: see the PAA 2009, ss 13, 15(1)(a) (Part G, para **[246.187]** and **[246.189]**) and paras **[200.35E]** and **[200.35F]**. It is important to appreciate when exercising a power of appointment that if the power was created by a testamentary or other instrument which took effect before 6 April 2010 the pre-PAA 2009 law of accumulations applies. In the case of a power created by a will which was made before 6 April 2010, but where the testator died on or after that date, there is uncertainty as to whether PAA 2009 applies (see para **[200.35H]**). In such a case the cautious draftsman should assume that the pre-PAA 2009 restrictions will apply, unless and until the point is clarified.

Some Tax Considerations

[213.9]

[Updated for Perpetuities and Accumulations Act 2009 and FA 2013, Sch 44.]

Very often a person with a special power of appointment will have a beneficiary-taxed interest in possession in the property over which the power is exercisable (see Part A, paras **[200.92]** ff), and so on his death the value of the property will be treated as forming part of his estate for inheritance tax purposes. Therefore, if the appointor's interest in possession commenced before 22 March 2006 and his or her spouse or civil partner is an object of the power, it may be advantageous if an interest in possession (a life or lesser interest) is appointed to the spouse or civil partner so that the inheritance tax spouse exemption will be available on the appointor's death. The interest given to the spouse or civil partner will be a transitional serial interest under IHTA 1984, s 49D which receives beneficiary-taxed treatment for inheritance tax purposes (see para **[200.100]**). The partial exemption rules of the Inheritance Tax Act 1984 (IHTA 1984), ss 36 to 42, for charging tax on death where the deemed transfer of value on death is partly exempt and partly chargeable will apply separately to such property from the appointor's free estate: IHTA 1984, s 40. If the spouse or civil partner is a disabled person within IHTA 1984, s 89B(2) or s 89(4) (as substituted by FA 2013, Sch 44, paras 8(2), 6(4)), an appointment of an interest in possession or discretionary trusts for him or her may also qualify for the exemption as a disabled person's interest (para **[200.99]**), in a case where IHTA 1984, s 49D would not apply. However, if the circumstances are such that an interest in possession appointed to the appointor's spouse or civil partner would not qualify for beneficiary-taxed treatment as a transitional serial interest or disabled person's interest, only an absolute appointment will attract the spouse/civil partner exemption. An interest in possession will not be an IPDI where it is created in exercise of a special power as the settlement is not being created by the appointor's will: see IHTA 1984, s 49A and para **[200.98]**.

[213.10]

[Updated for Perpetuities and Accumulations Act 2009.]

Under the terms of a settlement (whether made by will or lifetime disposition), the settlor or the settlor's spouse or civil partner may have a beneficiary-taxed interest in possession (see Part A, para **[200.92]** ff) in the settled property and a special power of appointment in respect of the settled property. If he exercises his special power to create continuing trusts (assuming they are authorised by the power) to take effect immediately after his interest in possession, he will be regarded, for the purposes of the charging rules for relevant property (for which see paras **[218.8]**–**[218.15]**) as the settlor of a new settlement at the time when his interest in possession ceases (except in the unusual case of him being the settlor and the appointment being of a beneficiary-taxed interest in possession for his spouse or civil partner). See IHTA 1984, s 80, but also IHTA 1984, s 61(2)) which provides that for the purposes of calculating the ten year anniversary for the periodic charge to inheritance tax, the settlement should be regarded as having commenced when the property first became settled. In circumstances where s 80 applies, for the relevant property to qualify after the cessation of the interest in possession as excluded property under the IHTA 1984, s 48(3)(a), or for the exemption in s 65(8) from an inheritance tax exit charge when relevant property becomes invested in exempt government securities, the condition as to the domicile of the settlor outside the UK at the time of his settlement must be satisfied both by the original settlor and his spouse or civil partner at the times when their respective settlements were made or deemed to be made, see the IHTA 1984, s 82. (See *Foster's Inheritance Tax*, E4.52, for a more detailed treatment of the IHTA 1984, s 80, and its consequences.)

[213.12]

[Updated in footnote 5 for Perpetuities and Accumulations Act 2009.]

Form B13.1: Appointment by widow of her husband's residuary estate among children and issue

In exercise of the power of appointment conferred on me by [the will of my late husband[1] who died on —— which was proved *etc*] to appoint the capital and income of my late husband's[1] residuary estate [to or for the benefit of our children and issue in such shares and with such trusts powers and provisions for their respective benefit exercisable at the discretion of any person or persons as I shall appoint[2]] I hereby direct that the trustees of the will of my said husband[1,3] shall after my death stand possessed of my late husband's[1] residuary estate upon trust to divide the same into three equal parts and hold the same upon the trusts and with and subject to the powers and provisions following:

(1) As to one equal third part and the income thereof upon trust for such of the children of my late son [*name*][4] as shall survive me and attain the age of twenty-one if more than one in equal shares absolutely provided that if any of such children shall predecease me or survive me but die without having attained the age of twenty-one leaving a child or children living at my death or born thereafter such child or children shall take if more than one equally between them the share which his her or their parent would have taken if he or she had survived me and attained the age of twenty-one[5];

(2) As to one equal third part and the income thereof upon trust for my daughter [*name*][4] absolutely;

(3) As to the remaining one equal third part upon trust to pay the income thereof to my son [*name*][4] for his life[6] and subject thereto as to both capital and income for such of his children living at my death or born thereafter who shall attain the age of twenty-one if more than one in equal shares absolutely[7];

(4) If the foregoing trusts herein declared of any equal third part of my late husband's residuary estate shall fail then each such part (together with any part or parts which may accrue thereto under this present provision) shall accrue to the other part or parts hereby appointed the trusts whereof shall not at the date of such accrual have failed;

(5) The powers of section 32 of the Trustee Act 1925 shall apply to the

foregoing trusts [as if the words 'one half of' were omitted from proviso (a) to subsection (1) thereof[8]].

1 In order to adapt the form to take account of civil partnerships formed pursuant to CPA 2004, substitute 'civil partner' for 'husband' throughout. The references to children and issue might still be relevant but the form will otherwise require significant amendment to suit the requirements of civil partners.

2 The terms of this power are based on the power considered in *Re Hunter's Will Trusts, Gilk v Harris* [1963] Ch 372, [1962] 3 All ER 1050. They were held not to authorise the creation of an immediate discretionary trust for a class of appointees.

3 In exercising a special power of appointment the appointor should not (unless the power expressly or impliedly authorises it, see *Re Redgate, Marsh v Redgate* [1903] 1 Ch 356) appoint the settled funds to the trustees of the appointor's will. Under such an appointment the trustees of the settled property in respect of which the power is exercised are not bound to transfer the settled funds to the trustees of the will, but ought to carry out and execute the appointor's directions themselves (see *Busk v Aldam* (1874) LR 19 Eq 16; *Scotney v Lomer* (1886) 31 Ch D 380; *Re Tyssen, Knight-Bruce v Butterworth* [1894] 1 Ch 56; *Re Mackenzie, Bain v Mackenzie* [1916] 1 Ch 125).

4 Following the commencement of GRA 2004 on 4 April 2005, it is important to name the sons and daughter referred to. See Vol 1 at para **[81.1]**.

5 The appropriateness of this provision depends upon when the husband's will was made. If the husband's will was made before 6 April 2010 and he died before then no perpetuity period was defined in the husband's will, the common law perpetuity period will apply. Since the power is conferred by the husband's will which would only have come into force on his death his widow and the children of the marriage will be lives in being for the purposes of the common law rule against perpetuities. Therefore appointments to the children which vest in interest during their lifetimes will be valid, as will be appointments to their children which vest on the death of the widow or at or before they attain 21, and to the children of such a child who predeceases the widow or dies under 21 so long as there is no contingency such as the attainment of a specified age. If, on the other hand, the husband's will was made on or after 6 April 2010 the statutory perpetuity period of 125 years will apply: see the PAA 2009, ss 5(1), 15(1)(a) (Part G, para **[246.180]** and **[246.189]**); but see also **[213.7]**. Whilst a restriction to the common law period as in this subclause will not invalidate the trust, a higher age of vesting could be adopted without making any difference to the perpetuity position. This is because, without an express restriction that makes all interests vest (in interest if not in possession) and all powers exerciseable within the 125-year period from the husband's death, the vailidity is by virtue of 'wait and see' under the PAA 2009, s 7 (Part G, para **[246.181]**). See also **[200.35B]** and **[200.35H]**.

6 The terms of the power as recited would not permit an appointment of the income on protective trusts because the discretionary trust of income arising after any forfeiture would be an improper delegation of the power. It is not clear whether a power to pay or apply capital to a life tenant would be permitted.

7 See n 5 above.

8 The incorporation of the statutory power of advancement of the TA 1925, s 32 (Part G, para **[246.30]**) to pay one half of a beneficiary's presumptive share for his advancement or benefit, will not be an improper delegation, and it is thought that in the case of the terms of the recited power it will not be an improper delegation to extend the power to be exercisable in respect of the whole of a beneficiary's presumptive share.

[213.13]

[Updated for Perpetuities and Accumulations Act 2009.]

Form B13.2: Appointment by woman of fund in which she has a life interest in unequal shares, one child's share appointed direct to his own children, another's settled on him for life, the others appointed absolutely[1]

In exercise of the power of appointment conferred on me by [the will of my late father who died on —— which was proved etc] to appoint the capital and income of his residuary estate in which I have a life interest [to all or any one or more exclusively of the others or other of my issue at such times and if more than one in such shares with such provisions for maintenance education and advancement and otherwise at the discretion of any person and with such gifts over and generally in such manner for the benefit of my issue or some or one of them as I shall appoint[2]] I hereby direct that the trustees of the will of my late father[3] shall after my death stand possessed of my late father's residuary estate upon trust to divide the same into five equal parts and hold the same upon the trusts and with and subject to the powers and provisions following:

(1) As to two equal fifth parts upon trust to pay the income thereof to my daughter [*name*][4] for her life and subject thereto as to both capital and income for such of her children living at my death or born thereafter before the vesting day (as defined in my late father's will)[5] who shall attain the age of twenty-one or shall be living on the vesting day if earlier if more than one in equal shares absolutely.

(2) As to one equal fifth part and the income thereof upon trust for such of the children of my daughter [*name*][4] living at my death or born thereafter before the vesting day who shall attain the age of twenty-one or shall be living on the vesting day (as defined in my late father's will)[6] if earlier if more than one in equal shares absolutely.

(3) As to one equal fifth part and the income thereof upon trust for my son [*name*][4] absolutely.

(4) As to the remaining one equal fifth part and the income thereof upon trust for my son [*name*][4] absolutely.

(5) The powers and provisions of section 32 of the Trustee Act 1925 shall apply to the foregoing trusts as if the words 'one half of' were omitted from proviso (a) to subsection (1) thereof.

(6) I declare that in the foregoing subclauses of this present clause the terms 'child' and 'children' shall have the same meanings as they have in my late father's will.[7]

(7) The administrative powers and provisions of clauses —— of my late father's will shall continue to apply to my late father's residuary estate so far as consistent with the beneficial interests hereby appointed and the trustees of my late father's will shall have the following additional powers:[8]

    (i) power to invest trust moneys in any property of whatever description or location as if they were a sole beneficial owner of such moneys;

    (ii) power to borrow money with or without giving security and on such terms as to interest repayment and otherwise for any purpose connected with the trusts hereby appointed and no lender from whom the trustees borrow money in purported exercise of this power shall be concerned to enquire as to the propriety amount or purpose of any such borrowing.

1 For the purposes of this form it is assumed that the appointor's father died before 16 July 1964 and before the birth of any of the appointor's children. Therefore, the interests created must be certain to vest within the common law perpetuity period because there will be no 'wait and see' rule to save an otherwise perpetuitous appointment, see para **[213.7]**. For the case where the death occurred on or after 16 July 1964 or the will was made on or after 6 April 2010 see **[213.7]**.

2 The terms of this power are based on the power considered in *Re Rank's Settlement Trusts, Newton v Rollo* [1979] 1 WLR 1242.
3 See para **[213.12]**, n 2.
4 Following the commencement of GRA 2004 on 4 April 2005, it is important to name the sons and daughters referred to. See Vol 1 at para **[81.1]**.
5 It is assumed that the appointor's father's will contains an express perpetuity restriction, with a defined vesting day 21 years from the death of the last survivor of the appointor and Royal lives. If it is not defined then, on the assumption referred to at n 1, the common law period of a life or lives in being plus 21 years will apply, so that if the appointor's grandchildren's interests were expressed to vest at the latest on the expiry of the period of 21 years from the death of the appointor there would be no perpetuity problem. For an alternative approach where the father's will was made on or after 6 April 2010, see Form B13.1 n 5 at **[213.12]**.
6 See n 5, above.
7 See para **[213.7]**.
8 In *Re Rank's Settlement Trusts, Newton v Rollo,* above, the terms of the power were held to authorise the creation of additional administrative powers.

B14

Residue

ADMINISTRATION TRUSTS

[214.2]

[Updated for the Trusts (Capital and Income) Act 2013.]

Trust for sale and conversion or power of sale. It is now (ie from the commencement of the TLATA 1996 on 1 January 1997) no longer necessary or important to provide a trust for sale and conversion in administration trusts of residue, because it is no longer the case that the Settled Land Act 1925 will apply to land comprised in residue in the event of residue being subject to trusts for persons in succession, subject to a contingency, etc: see paras **[200.51]** and **[200.52]**). If there is land in residue which is held on trust it will be a 'trust of land' within the TLATA 1996, and it makes little or no difference whether or not there is a trust for sale: see para **[200.54]**). We recommend that, in general, trusts for sale are not provided (see paras **[200.55]** and **[200.56]**). We do, however, recommend the express provision of a power of sale if there is no provision of a trust for sale, even though there are wide powers of sale conferred by the Administration of Estates Act 1925 (AEA 1925), ss 39 and 40 (Part G, paras **[246.48]** and **[246.49]**) and the TLATA 1996, s 6(1) (Part G, para **[246.91]**) for the purposes of the administration. This is because once the administration is over the trustees of the will are not given by the general law any general power of sale over residuary personalty (see para **[220.23]**), and it is an unusual residuary estate which does not contain some personalty, and because it is not clear to what extent s 39 of the AEA 1925 confers power to sell assets situated outside England and Wales, particularly land. For examples of administration trusts without a trust for sale, see Form B14.1 at para **[214.10]**, and the statutory administration trust for intestates' estates in the AEA 1925, s 33(1), as substituted by the TLATA 1996, Sch 2, para 5(2) which provides that the estate shall be held in trust by the personal representatives with the power to sell it (Part G, para **[244.58]**). For circumstances in which a trust for sale may still be appropriate see Part A, para **[200.56]** and Form B15.8 at para **[215.8]** for an example of use of a trust for sale to maximise the chances of an early sale. It seems that if all residuary realty and personalty are together disposed of, made subject to a power of sale and charged with payment of debts and testamentary expenses, this will still create a mixed fund from which the debts and testamentary expenses are payable generally rather than from an undisposed of share (ie the statutory order of application of assets under the AEA 1925, Sch I, Pt II is still varied to that extent): see *Allan v Gott*

(1872) 7 Ch App 439 and para **[214.6]**. The provision of a power of sale rather than a trust for sale, together with an indication of intention that the time of sale should be within the trustees' discretion, may have had the effect that the rule in *Howe v Dartmouth* did not apply in wills coming into effect before 1 October 2013: see para **[214.38]**. For the position on and after that date, see para **[249.2A]** below.

The Law of Property Act 1925 (LPA 1925), s 25(3) used to provide that a power to retain or sell land was to be treated as a trust for sale with power to postpone sale. This is now repealed with effect from 1 January 1997 by the TLATA 1996, Sch 4.

[214.2A]

[Inserted to take account of the Trusts (Capital and Income) Act 2013.]

Exclusion of apportionment rules. In relation to 'new trusts', ie trusts created or arising after 1 October 2013 (including trusts created or arising on or after that date under powers conferred before that date), the presumption under s 2 of the Apportionment Act 1870 that income is to be apportioned on a time basis and the equitable rules of apportionment known as the rule in *Howe v Dartmouth* (both branches), the rule in *Re Earl of Chesterfield's Trusts*, and the rule in *Allhusen v Whittell* (for which see Vol 1, paras **[38.17]** ff and Vol 2, para **[214.35]** ff) are disapplied subject to any contrary intention in the trust instrument or the power under which the trust is created: s 1(1), (2) and (4) of the Trusts (Capital and Income) Act 2013: see generally paras **[246.202]** ff. We recommend that express exclusion of these apportionment rules is omitted from new wills which are subject to the law of England and Wales, although no harm is likely to arise from continuing to exclude them expressly. The main reason for not including express exclusion is that it saves words, paper, and effort, and is one less provision which needs to be explained to testators with enquiring minds who take the trouble to read their own wills.

The Trusts (Capital and Income) Act 2013 does not exclude the rules in *Re Bird* [1901] 1 Ch 916 and *Re Atkinson* [1904] 2 Ch 160 from applying. These rules, for which see Vol 1, para **[38.28]**, are concerned with what happens when there is a shortfall in what is received by way of principal and interest from a debt or security. They operate in a sensible manner, and excluding them would leave a serious problem of how to deal with what is received in the rare case where such a shortfall occurs.

Forms B14.1 and B14.2 are set out below in an amended form which no longer contains express exclusion of the apportionment rules. In the cases of Forms B14.3, B14.4, and B14.10, it should be borne in mind that the express exclusions of the various apportionment rules is unnecessary, and may be deleted, when and if any of those forms is incorporated in a will governed by the law of England and Wales made after 1 October 2013.

[214.10]

[Updated for the Trusts (Capital and Income) Act 2013.]

Form B14.1: Administration trust without a trust for sale

NOTE

For reasons mentioned at paras **[214.1]** and **[214.2]** it is no longer necessary for the administration trusts of residue to contain a trust for sale and conversion, and we recommend that they do not do so unless there is some specific reason for including a trust for sale. It is particularly appropriate not to provide one where there are life interest or other trusts which may continue for some time after the testator's death, and even more so where occupation of land by beneficiaries is contemplated. Where the gift of residue is into immediate and absolute fractional shares a trust for sale is arguably still appropriate: see Form B15.8 at para **[215.8]**.

If there is no trust for sale it is still appropriate to include an express power of sale, because the general law confers no general power to sell personalty (there is a power to sell it for purposes of administration under the AEA 1925, s 39 and a power to sell it in order to invest in investments authorised by the Trustee Act 2000 (TrA 2000)). The administration trust of an intestate's estate under the AEA 1925, s 33(1) has been amended by the TLATA 1996, Sch 2, para 5(2) so as to provide a power, not a trust, to sell: it is printed as so amended in Part G at para **[244.58]**.

The form below does not expressly exclude the rules in *Howe v Dartmouth* and *Re Chesterfield's Trusts*, or statutory apportionment. This is because in relation to 'new trusts', ie trusts created or arising after 1 October 2013, the presumption under s 2 of the Apportionment Act 1870 that income is to be apportioned on a time basis and the equitable rules of apportionment known as the rule in *Howe v Dartmouth* (both branches), the rule in *Re Earl of Chesterfield's Trusts* and the rule in *Allhusen v Whittell* are disapplied subject to any contrary intention in the trust instrument or the power under which the trust is created: s 1(1), (2) and (4) of the Trusts (Capital and Income) Act 2013. See generally paras **[214.2A]**, **[214.38]**, **[214.43]**, and **[246.202]** ff. This Form provides a discretion as to the burden of liabilities as between capital and income to take the place of the rule in *Allhusen v Whittell*. It contains no directions as to the incidence of inheritance tax (except in so far as inheritance tax is a testamentary expense).

For a direction as to inheritance tax see eg Form C3.1, cl 5 at para **[225.15]**.

FORM

(1) I give all my property not hereby or by any codicil hereto otherwise effectively disposed of [(including any entailed or other property over which I shall have at my death a general power of disposition by will)][1] to my trustees upon trust with power at their discretion to sell all or any of it when they think fit.[2]

(2) My trustees shall pay my funeral and testamentary expenses my debts and any legacies given by this will or any codicil hereto out of such property or its proceeds of sale and shall have a discretion as to how such payments shall be borne as between capital and income.[3]

(3) Subject as aforesaid my trustees shall invest all money comprised in such property or arising from its sale in any of the investments hereby authorised with power to change such investments into any others hereby authorised and the said property and the assets from time to time representing the same (hereinafter called 'my residuary estate') shall be held on the trusts hereinafter declared.

1 Subject to any express contrary intention property subject to a general power will be carried by a residuary gift under the WA 1837, s 27 (Part G, para **[244.27]**), but in the case of entailed property the will must refer to the property, or the instrument under which it was acquired, or entailed property generally for the statutory power of disposition to be exercised: LPA 1925, s 176(1) (Part G, para **[244.53]**). Although no new entails can be created on or after 1 January 1997 (see para **[200.53]**), entails created before that date can continue to exist and, if they do, the statutory power of disposition of them by will continues to be available.

2 This wording could be made even more concise, such as 'My trustees shall have power to sell all or any of such property'. One reason for using the slightly more elaborate wording in this Form used to be that it follows the wording which was held in *Re Pitcairn* [1896] 2 Ch 199 to prevent the rule in *Howe v Dartmouth* from applying, though this is no longer necessary for new trusts. See further, para **[214.2A]**.

3 The words from 'and shall have' give the trustees a discretion over the burden of debts and testamentary expenses as between capital and income. See paras **[214.43]** and **[214.44]**..

[214.11]

[Updated for the Trusts (Capital and Income) Act 2013.]

Form B14.2: Administration trust without a trust for sale, concise form[1]

(1) My trustees shall hold all my property not hereby or by any codicil hereto otherwise effectively disposed of [(including any entailed or other property over which I shall have at my death a general power of disposition by will)][2] and the assets from time to time representing the same ('my residuary estate') upon the trusts and with the powers set out below.

(2) In the administration of my estate and the execution of the trusts hereof or of any codicil hereto my trustees shall have power to sell the assets comprised in my estate as and when they think fit and shall have a discretion as to how expenses debts and legacies shall be borne as between capital and income.

1 This form omits any direction as to incidence of debts, administration expenses and legacies and leaves the incidence of them to statute. For the statutory order see paras **[214.4]**–**[214.9]**. It also omits any exclusion of apportionment rules in reliance on Trusts (Capital and Income) Act 2013: see para **[214.2A]**.

2 See para **[214.10]**, n 1.

EXCLUSION OF APPORTIONMENT BETWEEN CAPITAL AND INCOME (RULES IN *HOWE V EARL OF DARTMOUTH* AND *RE CHESTERFIELD'S TRUSTS*)

[214.34A]

[Inserted concerning the Trusts (Capital and Income) Act 2013.]

Wills made on or after 1 October 2013. In relation to 'new trusts', i e trusts created or arising after 1 October 2013 (including trusts created or arising on or after that date under powers conferred before that date), the equitable rules of apportionment known as the rule in *Howe v Dartmouth* (both branches), and the rule in *Re Earl of Chesterfield's Trusts*, are disapplied subject to any contrary intention in the trust instrument or the power under which the trust is created: s 1(1), (2) and (4) of the Trusts (Capital and Income) Act 2013: see generally paras **[246.202]** ff. Paragraphs **[214.35]**–**[214.42]** must be read subject to this, and express exclusion of these rules is no longer desirable or necessary: see para **[214.2A]**.

EXCLUSION OF RULE FOR APPORTIONMENT OF LIABILITIES BETWEEN CAPITAL AND INCOME (RULE IN *ALLHUSEN V WHITTELL*)

[214.42A]

[Inserted concerning the Trusts (Capital and Income) Act 2013.]

Wills made on or after 1 October 2013. In relation to 'new trusts', ie trusts created or arising after 1 October 2013 (including trusts created or arising on or after that date under powers conferred before that date), the equitable rule of apportionment known as the rule in *Allhusen v Whittell* is disapplied subject to any contrary intention in the trust instrument or the power under which the trust is created: s 1(1), (2) and (4) of the Trusts (Capital and Income) Act 2013: see generally paras **[246.202]** ff. Paragraphs **[214.43]**–**[214.47]** must be read subject to this, and express exclusion of this rule is no longer desirable or necessary: see para **[214.2A]**.

EXCLUSION OF TIME APPORTIONMENT

[214.47A]

[Inserted concerning the Trusts (Capital and Income) Act 2013.]

Wills made on or after 1 October 2013. In relation to 'new trusts', ie trusts created or arising after 1 October 2013 (including trusts created or arising on or after that date under powers conferred before that date), the presumption under s 2 of the Apportionment Act 1870 that income is to be apportioned on a time basis is disapplied subject to any contrary intention in the trust instrument or the power under which the trust is created: s 1(1), (2) and (4) of the Trusts (Capital and Income) Act 2013: see generally paras **[246.202]** ff. Paragraphs **[214.48]**–**[214.54]** must be read subject to this, and express exclusion of time apportionment is no longer desirable or necessary: see para **[214.2A]**.

[214.50]

The AA 1870 is applicable on the death of the testator (see below), the death of a life tenant, and when there is a gift to a class of minor beneficiaries to which the Trustee Act 1925, s 31 (Part G, para **[246.26]**) applies and the class increases or decreases by birth or death (*Re Joel's Will Trusts, Rogerson v Brudenell-Bruce* [1967] Ch 14, [1966] 2 All ER 482). It does not apply in relation to the forfeiture of a protective life interest (*Re Jenkins, Williams v Jenkins* [1915] 1 Ch 46) or on the commencement or determination of any discretionary trust of income (*Weir's Settlement Trusts* [1971] Ch 145 at 167).

The Apportionment Act 1834 (AA 1834) was superseded, but not repealed, by the AA 1870. The AA 1834 was, however, repealed by the Statute Law (Repeals) Act 1977 (c 18), s 1(1), Sch 1, Pt XVI.

B16

Life interests

PRELIMINARY NOTE

[216.4]

[Updated for the Perpetuities and Accumulations Act 2009.]

Perpetuities. When drafting the trusts which are to take effect following a life interest, care must be taken that they do not infringe the rule against perpetuities. The rule, simply stated, is that every future interest in property must vest in interest (not necessarily in possession) within a perpetuity period allowed by law. For wills made on after 6 April 2010 there is, by virtue of the Perpetuities and Accumulations Act 2009 (PAA 2009), ss 1, 5, 15(1)(a), a mandatory perpetuity period of 125 years (see Part G, paras **[246.175]**, **[246.179]**, **[246.189]**, and see para **[96.6]**). For wills made before 6 April 2010 it was possible to select either a statutory perpetuity period of 80 years (or less): see the Perpetuities and Accumulations Act 1964 (PAA 1964), s 1 (Part G, para **[246.74]**), or the common law perpetuity period of a life or lives in being plus 21 years. The measuring life or lives could be, or could include, lives which had no connection with the trusts created, for example, those descendants of George V living at the testator's death, but then they would have to have been expressly specified in the will as measuring lives. However, the more common and often more appropriate measuring lives were of those persons connected with the trusts. In this case it was not always necessary to specify expressly that those persons are the measuring lives. For example, a gift to such of the testator's grandchildren who attain the age of 21 and survive the testator's widow did not infringe the rule against perpetuities because the grandchildren's interests would necessarily vest within 21 years of the death of the last survivor of the testator's widow and children.

[216.5]

[Updated for the Perpetuities and Accumulations Act 2009.]

Wait and see rule. Although it is better if all interests created by will are certain to, or are expressly stated to, vest within the perpetuity period, the 'wait and see' rule (introduced by the PAA 1964 in 1964 and carried over with modification to the PAA 2009) has meant that if it is not certain when a disposition takes effect that all of the interests will vest within a perpetuity period then one can wait and see if the interest does in fact vest within an available perpetuity period (Part G, paras **[246.76]**, **[246.181]**, and see para

[94.17]). (Before 1964 this lack of certainty was fatal to the interests which might not necessarily vest). For a fuller account of perpetuities, see para **[200.35A]** ff, and Vol 1, para **[94.1]** ff.

[216.8]

[Updated for the Perpetuities and Accumulations Act 2009.]

Form B16.1: Statutory protective trusts, varied by allowing accumulation after a forfeiture has occurred[1]

Note. It is possible for a life interest subject to the statutory protective trusts to be an immediate post-death interest (see IHTA 1984, s 88(4)(b)(i) and para **[200.104]** above), although it is unlikely that HMRC would accept that where the protective trusts are varied as in this Form, the relief of IHTA 1984, s 88 will apply. Nevertheless, for deaths on or after 22 March 2006 and pending any forfeiture, the life interest in this Form should be an immediate post-death interest if it takes effect immediately on the testator's death (or is subject only to a survivorship condition permitted by IHTA 1984, s 92: see paras **[219.6]**–**[219.7]**), and is not, for example, postponed to another interest (see para **[216.2]** above). If it is not afforded relief under IHTA 1984, s 88 its termination may occasion an IHT charge under IHTA 1984, s 52(1) which would be immediately chargeable, and since the termination of an immediate post-death interest on or after 22 March 2006 will be deemed to be a gift of the underlying settled property for the purposes of FA 1986, s 102, and since the life tenant may continue to benefit under the protective trusts, the gift with reservation rules could apply: see FA 1986, s 102ZA and para **[200.76]** above. Accordingly, a testator wishing to establish a protective life interest which is an immediate post-death interest is probably best advised to rely on statutory protective trusts without any amendment so that relief under IHTA 1984, s 88 will apply. However, where the protected life interest would not qualify as an immediate post-death interest (eg. because it takes effect on the termination of an immediate post-death interest) and the underlying settled property would be within the IHT charging regime anyway, this Form would not have these disadvantageous IHT consequences.

I declare that the income hereinbefore directed to be held upon trust for or to be paid to the said [*name*] for life shall not vest absolutely in the said [*name*] but shall be held by my trustees [*or* I declare that the annuity hereinbefore bequeathed to the said [*name*] shall not vest in the said [*name*] absolutely but shall be received and held by my trustees] upon the statutory protective trusts (subject to the variations hereinafter mentioned) for the benefit of the said [*name*] for the period of his [*her*] life.[2]

Provided however that in each year during which my trustees under the said statutory trusts have a discretion as to the application of the said income [annuity] my trustees shall from time to time determine in their uncontrolled discretion how much (if any part at all) of the income of the current year they will apply under the statutory trusts and the said trusts shall apply to the amount so determined and my trustees shall accumulate the balance of the said income [annuity] in the way of compound interest by investing the same and the resulting income thereof[3] but with power for my trustees in their uncontrolled discretion to determine from time to time during the said period during which they have a discretion as to the application of the said income [annuity] that any part of the past accumulations shall be income of the current year and be applicable accordingly at the discretion of my trustees, and I declare that after the death of the said [*name*] the said accumulations or the balance thereof shall be an accretion to the capital of the property from which such accumulations arose and be one fund with such capital for all purposes and shall be held by my trustees upon trust accordingly [*in the case of an annuity*, fall into the capital of my residuary estate and be distributed accordingly].[4]

1 See the TA 1925, s 33 (Part G, para **[246.31]**), which provides a statutory method of effecting a 'protected life interest'. The section contemplates that the whole of the yearly income (or annuity) must be applied every year, and does not provide for any accumulations (*Re Gourju's Will Trusts* [1943] Ch 24, [1942] 2 All ER 605; compare *Re Mellor, Alvarez v Dodgson* [1922] 1 Ch 312, [1922] All ER Rep 735; *Re Peel, Tattersall v Peel* [1936] Ch 161).

2 For wills made before 6 April 2010, protective trusts for an individual living at the testator's death raised no perpetuity issue as that individual was a life in being for the purposes of the common law perpetuity period, so that any discretionary trust arising on any forfeiture during the individual's lifetime would not last beyond a permissible perpetuity period. For wills made on or after 6 April 2010 however a mandatory perpetuity period of 125 years applies, see the PAA 2009, ss 5(1), 15(1)(a) (Part G, paras **[246.179]**, **[246.189]**, and see para **[94.6]**). Nevertheless, given the 'wait and see' provision of the PAA 2009, s 7 (Part G, para **[246.181]** and see para **[94.17]**), and the practical certainty that an individual living at the testator's death will not survive a further 125 years, no perpetuity problem should arise if this form is used in a will made on or after 6 April 2010.

3 For wills made on or after 6 April 2010, income arising in respect of non-charitable trusts may be accumulated throughout the perpetuity period of 125 years which will apply to those trusts: see the PAA 2009, s 13 (Part G, para **[246.187]**, and see para **[95.0]**). Since it is a practical certainty that the testator's widow will not survive more than 125 years, this form authorises accumulation throughout her lifetime without limiting it to 125 years.

4 Although these variations of the trusts set out in the TA 1925, s 33 (Part G, para **[246.31]**) preserve its basic scheme, it seems that HMRC will not be prepared to accept these forms as 'to the like effect' for the purposes of IHT relief under the IHTA 1984, s 88 which disregards a forfeiture of an immediate post-death interest for IHT purposes (for which see Part A, para **[200.104]**). Therefore, the occasion of the forfeiture of the life interest (if it is an immediate post-death interest) when such discretionary trusts take effect will be a chargeable transfer for IHT purposes under the IHTA 1984, ss 2(1) and 52(1), and a gift of the underlying settled property for the purposes of FA 1986, s 102. For some guidance on what trusts might be like to those of the TA 1925, s 33 (Part G, para **[246.31]**), see *Re Wallace's Settlements, Fane v Wallace* [1968] 2 All ER 209, [1968] 1 WLR 711. See also Form C3.2, cl 4(4) at para **[225.32]** and *Foster's Inheritance Tax*, E6.21.

[216.9]

[Updated for the Perpetuities and Accumulations Act 2009.]

Form B16.2: Protective income trusts for woman for life[1]

Note. It is possible for a life interest subject to the statutory protective trusts to be an immediate post-death interest (see IHTA 1984, s 88(4)(b)(i) and para **[200.104]** above), although it is unlikely that HMRC would accept that where the protective trusts are varied as in either of the alternative Forms below, the relief of IHTA 1984, s 88 will apply. Nevertheless, for deaths on or after 22 March 2006 and pending any forfeiture, the life interest in either of the alternative Forms should be an immediate post-death interest if it takes effect immediately on the testator's death (or is subject only to a survivorship condition permitted by IHTA 1984, s 92: see paras **[219.6]**–**[219.7]**), and is not, for example, postponed to another interest (see para **[216.2]** above). If it is not afforded relief under IHTA 1984, s 88 its termination may occasion an IHT charge under IHTA 1984, s 52(1) which would be immediately chargeable, and since the termination of an immediate post-death interest on or after 22 March 2006 will be deemed to be a gift of the underlying settled property for the purposes of FA 1986, s 102, and since the life tenant may continue to benefit under the protective trusts, the gift with reservation rules could apply: see FA 1986, s 102ZA and para **[200.76]** above. Accordingly, a testator wishing to establish a protective life interest which is an immediate post-death interest is probably best advised to rely on statutory protective trusts without any amendment so that relief under IHTA 1984, s 88 will apply. However, where the protected life interest would not qualify as an immediate post-death interest (eg. because it takes effect on the termination of an immediate post-death interest) and the underlying settled property would be within the IHT charging regime anyway, neither of these Forms would have these disadvantageous IHT consequences.

(A) USING THE STATUTORY PROTECTIVE TRUSTS

My trustees shall hold the income of [my residuary estate] upon protective trusts for the benefit of [*name*] during her life provided that the discretionary trusts by statute implied to arise after the failure or determination during the life of the said [*name*] of the trust to pay such income to her shall be varied as follows:[2]

(i) My trustees may in their discretion apply any income accrued but unapplied in any previous year for the purposes of such discretionary trusts in any subsequent year.

(ii) After the death of any object of such discretionary trusts my trustees may in their discretion while [*name*] is still living within three years of the date of such death apply any income which accrued in his or her lifetime in or towards the discharge of any liability incurred by or on behalf of any such object which my trustees may think fit to satisfy.

(iii) Notwithstanding the protective trusts hereinbefore declared and without determining her life interest thereunder the said [*name*] may by deed or deeds but with the consent of my trustees therein expressed (which consent my trustees shall have absolute power to give or withhold) assign any part or parts not exceeding in the whole one half of the income of [my residuary estate] to any her child children or issue[3] who shall at the date of such assignment have attained the age of [eighteen] [twenty-one] years or have married or shall marry within one month after such assignment.[4]

(iv) Further and notwithstanding the protective trusts hereinbefore declared and without determining the life interest thereunder of the said [*name*] my trustees shall have power at any time or times during the lifetime of the said [*name*] either before or after her life interest shall have failed or determined to pay or apply the whole or any part or parts of the capital of [my residuary estate] to or for the benefit of the said [*name*].

(v) My trustees shall have power at any time or times before the life interest of the said [*name*] shall have failed or determined by deed or deeds to declare that they shall henceforth hold the income of [my residuary estate] or any part or share thereof upon trust to pay the same to the said [*name*] during her life and not upon protective trusts for her benefit.

(B) ALTERNATIVE FORM—WITHOUT USING REFERENCE TO THE STATUTORY PROTECTIVE TRUSTS[5]

My trustees shall pay the income of [my residuary estate] to the said [*name*] during her life unless or until some act or event shall have happened or shall happen whereby the said income or any part thereof if belonging absolutely to her would become vested in or charged in favour of some other person.[6] And in the event of the failure or determination during her life of the trust last above declared in her favour my trustees shall during the remainder of her life[7] pay or apply such income unto or for or towards the personal support maintenance and education of the said [*name*] [her husband] and her issue[8] for the time being and the person who if she were dead would for the time being be interested in [my residuary estate] or such one or more to the exclusion of the others or other of such objects of this discretionary trust in such manner and if more than one in such shares as my trustees shall think proper with power while [*name*] is still living within three years after the death of any object of such discretionary trust to apply any income which accrued in his or her lifetime in or towards the discharge of any liability incurred by or on behalf of any such object which my trustees shall think fit to satisfy.

[*Add sub-cls* (*iii*), (*iv*) *and* (*v*) *of alternative* Form (A) *above*.]

1 Although these variations of the trusts set out in the TA 1925, s 33 (Part G, para **[246.31]**) preserve its basic scheme, it seems that HMRC will not be prepared to accept these forms as 'to the like effect' for the purposes of IHT relief under IHTA 1984, s 88 which disregards a forfeiture of an immediate post-death interest for IHT purposes (for which see Part A, para **[200.104]**). Therefore, the occasion of the forfeiture of the life interest (if it is an immediate post-death interest) when such discretionary trusts take effect will be a chargeable transfer for IHT purposes under IHTA 1984, ss 2(1) and 52(1). Further, since the termination of an immediate post-death interest on or after 22 March 2006 will be deemed to be a gift of the underlying settled property for the purposes of FA 1986, s 102. For some guidance on what trusts might be like to those of the TA 1925, s 33 (Part G, para **[246.31]**); see *Re Wallace's Settlements, Fane v Wallace* [1968] 2 All ER 209, [1968] 1 WLR 711. See also Form C3.2, cl 4(4) at para **[225.32]** and *Foster's Inheritance Tax*, E6.21.

2 For wills made before 6 April 2010, protective trusts for an individual living at the testator's death raised no perpetuity issue as that individual was a life in being for the purposes of the common law perpetuity period, so that any discretionary trust arising on any forfeiture during the individual's lifetime would not last beyond a permissible perpetuity period. For wills made on or after 6 April 2010 however a mandatory perpetuity period of 125 years applies, see the PAA 2009, ss 5(1), 15(1)(a) (Part G, paras **[246.179]**, **[246.189]**, and see para **[94.6]**). Nevertheless, given the 'wait and see' provision of the PAA 2009, s 7 (Part G, para **[246.181]** and see para **[94.17]**), and the practical certainty that an individual living at the testator's death will not survive a further 125 years, no perpetuity problem should arise if this form is used in a will made on or after 6 April 2010.

3 These words prima facie include illegitimate children or issue: see Part A, paras **[200.28]** and **[200.29]**.

4 This provision will enable a settlement to be made on the marriage of a child of the protected life tenant.

5 See n 3 to Form B16.1 at para **[216.8]**. The differences between the trusts of this clause and those of the TA 1925, s 33 (Part G, para **[246.31]**) are the same as the differences between those of the preceding Form (A) and s 33 with the additional variation that the remainderman is an object of the discretionary trust of income even if the principal beneficiary has a spouse or civil partner or issue living (compare s 33(1)(ii)(b)).

6 Singular includes plural and vice versa, and person a corporation (LPA 1925, s 61: Part G, para **[246.54]**). See on this clause, *Re Pilkington's Will Trusts, Pilkington v Harrison* [1937] Ch 574, [1937] 3 All ER 213.

7 See n 2, above.

8 See n 3, above.

[216.13]

[Updated for the Perpetuities and Accumulations Act 2009.]

Form B16.6: Trust for wife during widowhood subject to an obligation to maintain children

In trust to pay the income thereof to my wife during her widowhood she thereout maintaining and educating my sons while under the age of twenty-five years and my unmarried daughters[1] but my wife so long as she maintains and educates my children to the satisfaction of my trustees shall not be liable to account for the said income.[2]

1 For wills made before 6 April 2010, a direction to a widow to maintain another raised no perpetuity issue as both the widow and that other were lives in being for the purposes of the common law perpetuity period, so that the direction would not last beyond a permissible perpetuity period. For wills made on or after 6 April 2010 however a mandatory perpetuity period of 125 years applies, see the PAA 2009, ss 5(1), 15(1)(a) (Part G, paras **[246.179]**, **[246.189]**, and para **[94.6]**). Nevertheless, given the 'wait and see' provision of the PAA 2009, s 7 (Part G, para **[246.181]** and see para **[94.17]**), and the practical certainty that an individual living at the testator's death will not survive a further 125 years, no perpetuity problem should arise if this form is used in a will made on or after 6 April 2010.

2 *Re Booth, Booth v Booth* [1894] 2 Ch 282; *Re G (Infants)* [1899] 1 Ch 719; *Comiskey v Bowring-Hanbury* [1905] AC 84; *Re Ramsay, Thorpe v Ramsay* [1917] 2 Ch 64. This form imposes an obligation, and is not merely a precatory direction. If no obligation is to be imposed, this should be expressly stated as in the next following form. If the income in question is the income of a legacy, the legacy will carry interest from the testator's death where the primary object is maintenance (*Re Ramsay, Thorpe v Ramsay*), but not otherwise (*Re Crane, Adams v Crane* [1908] 1 Ch 379). For the purposes of IHT the wife will not have an interest in possession and so if the trust takes effect immediately on the testator's death it will not create an immediate post-death interest and the underlying settled property will be relevant property for IHT purposes (see para **[218.8]** ff).If this is not desired it will be safer to use the next following form instead.

[216.16]

[Updated for the Perpetuities and Accumulations Act 2009.]

Form B16.9: Trust of income for several persons for life giving a general testamentary power of disposition to the survivor[1]

In trust to pay the income thereof to my three daughters [*names*] and the survivors and survivor of them during their or her respective lives or life and after the death of such survivor in trust as to both the capital and income of the trust fund for such persons and in such manner as such survivor shall by will or codicil appoint [*add gift over in default of appointment as desired*].[2]

1 For deaths on or after 22 March 2006, the initial life interest each daughter takes should be an immediate post-death interest if it takes effect immediately on the testator's death (or is subject only to a survivorship condition permitted by IHTA 1984, s 92: see paras **[219.6]**–**[219.7]**), and is not, for example, postponed to another interest (see para **[216.2]** above). However, the further life interest a survivor acquires on the death of any of them, will not be an immediate post-death interest so that the settled property subject to it may then fall within the IHT charging regime for relevant property (see para **[218.8]** ff above).

2 It is not unusual to make the ultimate gift to the last survivor absolutely but the result of giving him a general testamentary power of appointment is much the same as he can dispose of it as his property. If this form was used in a will made before 6 April 2010, the daughters will have been lives in being for the purposes of the common law perpetuity period, so that the general power would necessarily be exercised (if at all) within a permissible perpetuity period. For wills made on or after 6 April 2010 however a mandatory perpetuity period of 125 years applies, see the PAA 2009, ss 5(1), 15(1)(a) (Part G, paras **[246.179]**, **[246.189]**, and see para **[94.6]**). Nevertheless, given the 'wait and see' provision of the PAA 2009, s 7(5), (6) (Part G, para **[246.181]** and see para **[94.17]**), and the practical certainty that no individual living at the testator's death will survive more than 125 years so that a general power of appointment given to her will in practice be exercised (if at all) within 125 years, no perpetuity problem should arise if this form is used in a will made on or after 6 April 2010.

[216.19]

[Updated for the Perpetuities and Accumulations Act 2009.]

Form B16.12: Trust for wife for life and then to unmarried daughters for life[1]

My trustees shall hold my [residuary estate] upon the following trusts:

(i) Upon trust to pay the income thereof to my wife [*name*] during her life.

(ii) If both my daughters [*name*] and [*name*] shall be living and unmarried at the death of my said wife[2] to pay the income thereof to my said daughters in equal shares either for the period of their joint lives or until the marriage of either of them whichever period shall be the shorter and on the death or marriage of one of my said daughters to pay the income of the appropriated fund hereinafter defined to my surviving or unmarried daughter (as the case may be) until her death or marriage.

(iii) If only one of my said daughters shall survive my said wife and shall at the death of my said wife be unmarried then to pay the income of the appropriated fund to such unmarried daughter until her death or marriage.

(iv) The appropriated fund hereinbefore mentioned shall be a fund set aside either at the death of my wife or at the death or on the marriage of the first of my said daughters to die or marry as the case may be and shall consist of investments sufficient at the time when such fund shall be set aside to produce the gross yearly sum before deduction of income tax of £——.[3]

(v) Subject to the above provisions and subject as hereinafter provided to hold [my residuary estate] in trust both as to capital and income in trust for all my children [who shall attain the age of eighteen] in equal shares.[4] Provided that if any child of mine has died or shall die in my lifetime leaving issue living at my death such issue shall stand in the place of such deceased child and take per stirpes and equally between them if more than one the share of [my residuary estate] which such deceased child of mine would have taken if he or she had survived me and had attained a vested interest but so that no issue shall take whose parent is alive and capable of taking under this provision of my will.

(vi) So long as either of my said daughters remain unmarried such unmarried daughters shall not take any share or interest in the income of [my residuary estate] without bringing her share of the income of the appropriated fund into hotchpot and accounting for the same.

1 For deaths on or after 22 March 2006, the life interest for the wife should be an immediate post-death interest if it takes effect immediately on the testator's death (or is subject only to a survivorship condition permitted by IHTA 1984, s 92: see paras **[219.6]**–**[219.7]**), and is not, for example, postponed to another interest (see para **[216.2]** above). However, the subsequent life interests for the daughters, will not be immediate post-death interests (unless the wife has predeceased the testator so her life interest has not taken effect) so that unless they, or any of them are disabled person's interests (see para **[200.99]** above), the settled property subject to it may then fall within the IHT charging regime for relevant property (see para **[218.8]** ff above).

2 This clause assumes that the wife survives the husband, but if at this point and at corresponding points later in the clause, the words 'at the death of my said wife' are replaced by the words 'at the death of the survivor of myself and my said wife,' the clause will be applicable to the case where the wife predeceases the testator. There seems little reason to doubt that, as the clause stands, if the wife's interest fails, the later interests will be accelerated. If this form was used for wills made before 6 April 2010, the wife and daughters will have been lives in being for the purposes of the common law perpetuity period, so that the interests of the daughters would necessarily vest within a permissible perpetuity period. For wills made on or after 6 April 2010 however a mandatory perpetuity period of 125 years applies, see the PAA 2009, ss 5(1), 15(1)(a) (Part G, paras **[246.179]**, **[246.189]**, and see para **[94.6]**). Nevertheless, given the 'wait and see' provision of the PAA 2009, s 7 (Part G, para **[246.181]** and see para **[94.17]**), and the practical certainty that no individual living at the testator's death will survive more than 125 years, so that the daughters' interests will in practice vest within 125 years, no perpetuity problem should arise if this form is used in a will made on or after 6 April 2010.

3 The unmarried daughter may not be entitled to much in the way of rebates or allowances, and it seems that a gross sum will be as convenient as any.

4 This trust for the testator's children should be a trust for bereaved minors if it comes into possession while the children are under 18 (see para **[200.108]** above).

[216.20]

[Updated for the Perpetuities and Accumulations Act 2009.]

Form B16.13: Trust for wife for life and then to children as she shall appoint, with hotchpot provision[1]

(i) Upon trust to pay the income thereof [of my residuary estate] to my wife for her life[2] and subject thereto.

(ii) Upon trust as to both capital and income for all or any one or more of my children and remoter issue in such shares and subject to such powers provisions and generally in such manner as my said wife shall by deed or will appoint[3] and subject to any such appointment upon trust for all my children living at my death if more than one in equal shares as tenants in common.

(iii) Any child who or whose issue takes any interest under the foregoing provision in default of appointment shall not take such interest in default of appointment without bringing into hotchpot any share or shares appointed to him or her or his or her issue and accounting for the same unless the appointment shall direct to the contrary.

1 This is a very short form and makes no provision under the trusts in default of appointment for children who die in the testator's lifetime leaving issue although the power of appointment can be exercised in favour of such issue. For a longer form, see Form B17.4 at para **[217.12]** and for a form with a wider power of appointment, see Forms B16.14 at para **[216.21]**. Illegitimate children will be eligible: see Part A, paras **[200.28]** and **[200.29]**.

2 For deaths on or after 22 March 2006, the life interest for the wife should be an immediate post-death interest if it takes effect immediately on the testator's death (or is subject only to a survivorship condition permitted by IHTA 1984, s 92: see paras **[219.6]**–**[219.7]**), and is not, for example, postponed to another interest (see para **[216.2]** above).

3 The wife could use this special power to appoint trusts for the testator's children which could qualify as trusts for bereaved minors or age 18–25 trusts (see para **[200.108]** ff above). If this form was used for a will made before 6 April 2010, the wife will have been a life in being for the purposes of the common law perpetuity period, so that the special power of appointment would necessarily be exercised (if at all) within a permissible perpetuity period. For wills made on or after 6 April 2010 however a mandatory perpetuity period of 125 years applies, see the PAA 2009, ss 5(1), 15(1)(a) (Part G, paras **[246.179]**, **[246.189]**, and see para **[94.6]**). Nevertheless, given the 'wait and see' provision of the PAA 2009, s 7(3), (4) (Part G, para **[246.181]** and see para **[94.17]**), and the practical certainty that no individual living at the testator's death will survive more than 125 years so that a special power of

appointment given to her will in practice be exercised (if at all) within 125 years, no perpetuity problem should arise if this form is used in a will made on or after 6 April 2010.

[216.21]

[Updated for the Perpetuities and Accumulations Act 2009.]

Form B16.14: Trust for wife for life and then to issue upon such trusts as she shall appoint[1]

(i) Upon trust to pay the income thereof of [my residuary estate] to my wife for her life[2] and subject thereto.

(ii) Upon trust as to both capital and income for all or any one or more of my children and remoter issue for such interests at such ages or times in such shares and with and subject to such powers and discretions exercisable over capital or income by any person or persons as my wife shall by deed or will (without transgressing the rules against perpetuities) appoint.[3]

(iii) In default of and subject to any such appointment in trust for all my children living at my death if more than one in equal shares as tenants in common provided that if any child of mine shall have died in my lifetime whether before or after the date hereof leaving issue living at my death such issue shall take by substitution and if more than one in equal shares per stirpes the share of my residuary estate that such deceased child of mine would have taken in default or subject to any appointment as aforesaid had he or she survived me but so that no issue shall take whose parent is alive at my death and so capable of taking.

1 This form authorises the testator's widow to appoint new trusts, including discretionary trusts, for the benefit of the testator's issue.

2 For deaths on or after 22 March 2006, the life interest for the wife should be an immediate post-death interest if it takes effect immediately on the testator's death (or is subject only to a survivorship condition permitted by IHTA 1984, s 92: see paras **[219.6]–[219.7]**), and is not, for example, postponed to another interest (see para **[216.2]** above).

3 The wife could use this special power to appoint trusts for the testator's children which could qualify as trusts for bereaved minors or age 18-to-25 trusts (see para **[200.108]** ff above). If this form was used for a will made before 6 April 2010, the wife will have been a life in being for the purposes of the common law perpetuity period, so that the special power of appointment would necessarily be exercised (if at all) within a permissible perpetuity period. For wills made on or after 6 April 2010 however a mandatory perpetuity period of 125 years applies, see the PAA 2009, ss 5(1), 15(1)(a) (Part G, paras **[246.179]**, **[246.189]**, and see para **[94.6]**). Nevertheless, given the 'wait and see' provision of the PAA 2009, s 7(3), (4) (Part G, para **[246.181]** and see para **[94.17]**), and the practical certainty that no individual living at the testator's death will survive more than 125 years so that a special power of appointment given to her will in practice be exercised (if at all) within 125 years, no perpetuity problem should arise if this form is used in a will made on or after 6 April 2010.

[216.22]

[Updated for the Perpetuities and Accumulations Act 2009.]

Form B16.15: Trust for wife during widowhood, then to son for life with remainder to his children[1]

(i) Upon trust to pay the income of [my residuary estate] to my wife during her widowhood.

(ii) After the death or remarriage of my wife my trustees shall hold my residuary estate upon trust to pay the income thereof to my son [*name*] during his life and subject thereto upon trust in equal shares for all the children of my said son who shall attain the age of [eighteen] [twenty-one] years or marry thereunder[2].

1 For deaths on or after 22 March 2006, the life interest for the wife should be an immediate post-death interest if it takes effect immediately on the testator's death (or is subject only to a survivorship condition permitted by IHTA 1984, s 92: see paras **[219.6]**–**[219.7]**), and is not, for example, postponed to another interest (see para **[216.2]** above). The son's successive life interest will not be an immediate post-death interest (unless the wife has predeceased the testator so her life interest has not taken effect), and unless it is a disabled person's interest (see para **[200.99]** above), the settled property then subject to it will fall within the IHT charging regime for relevant property and remain there during the subsistence of any trusts for the son's children. If the widow's life interest determines on her remarriage this may occasion an IHT charge under IHTA 1984, s 52(1), and this will be immediately chargeable unless the son's successive life interest is a disabled person's interest.

2 If this form was used for a will made before 6 April 2010, the son will have been a life in being for the purposes of the common law perpetuity period, so that the interests of his children will necessarily vest within a permissible perpetuity period. For wills made on or after 6 April 2010 however a mandatory perpetuity period of 125 years applies, see the PAA 2009, ss 5(1), 15(1)(a) (Part G, paras **[246.179]**, **[246.189]**, and see para **[94.6]**). Nevertheless, given the 'wait and see' provision of the PAA 2009, s 7 (Part G, para **[246.181]** and see para **[94.17]**), and the practical certainty that all grandchildren of the testator will attain the age of 21 within 125 years of his death, no perpetuity problem should arise if this form is used in a will made on or after 6 April 2010.

[216.23]

[Updated for the Perpetuities and Accumulations Act 2009.]

Form B16.16: Trust for wife for life and then to children for life with substitution of their issue[1]

My trustees shall hold my residuary estate and the income thereof upon the following trusts:

(a) Upon trust to pay the income thereof to my wife if she shall survive me during her life and subject thereto.

(b) Upon trust to divide my residuary estate into equal shares the number of such shares being equal to the number of my children living at the death of the survivor of myself and my said wife together with the number of my children who have died (whether before or after the date hereof) prior to such date as aforesaid leaving issue living at such date. Such shares to be held upon the trusts and subject to the powers and provisions hereinafter contained.

(c) In the case of each such living child of mine one share shall be held upon the following trusts:

  (i) upon trust to pay the income thereof to such child during his or her life [*or* upon protective trusts for such child's benefit during his or her life] and after the death of such child.

  (ii) upon trust to pay the said income to any wife or husband of such child of mine who shall survive him or her during the residue of such wife's or husband's life.

  (iii) upon trust as to both the capital and income of such share for all or such one or more exclusively of the others or other of the children or remoter issue of such child of mine at such times and if more than one in such shares and with such provisions for maintenance advancement and otherwise for the benefit of such children or remoter issue or some or one of them at the discretion of my trustees or any other persons and generally in such manner in all respects as such children of mine shall by deed revocable or irrevocable or by will or codicil appoint.[2] And subject to any such appointment.

(iv) upon trust for the child or children of such child of mine who attain the age of [eighteen] [twenty-one] years or being female attain that age or marry under that age and if more than one in equal shares.

(v) provided always that no child of such child of mine who or whose issue shall take any part of such share by virtue of any appointment by such child of mine under the power aforesaid shall unless such child of mine so direct share in the unappointed part of such share without bringing the part so appointed into hotchpot and accounting therefor.

(d) In the case of the issue of each such deceased child of mine one share shall be held upon the following trusts: upon trust in equal shares (if more than one) for all or any of the children or child of such deceased child of mine living at the date of the death of the survivor of myself and my said wife who attain the age of [eighteen] [twenty-one] years or marry under that age and for all or any of the issue living at the date aforesaid who attain the age of [eighteen] [twenty-one] years or marry under that age of any child (who dies before the aforesaid date leaving issue living at the aforesaid date) of such child of mine such issue to take through all degrees according to their stocks in equal shares (if more than one) the share which their parent would have taken if living at the aforesaid date and so that no issue shall take whose parent is living at the aforesaid date and so capable of taking.[3]

(e) If the trusts of any such share as aforesaid shall fail by reason of no person attaining a vested interest therein then I direct that subject to the trusts powers and provisions herein contained or which may be applicable thereto by statute the said share and any share or shares which may accrue thereto by virtue of this present proviso shall be held by my trustees as an accretion to the other share or shares (and equally if more than one) the trusts whereof shall not at the date of such accruer have failed as aforesaid and upon the trusts powers and provisions applicable thereto herein contained or such of them as at the date of such accruer shall be capable of taking effect.

1 For deaths on or after 22 March 2006, the life interest for the wife should be an immediate post-death interest if it takes effect immediately on the testator's death (or is subject only to a survivorship condition permitted by IHTA 1984, s 92: see paras **[219.6]**–**[219.7]**), and is not, for example, postponed to another interest (see para **[216.2]** above). The children's successive life interests will not be immediate post-death interests (unless the wife has predeceased the testator so her life interest has not taken effect), and unless they are disabled person's interests (see para **[200.99]** above), the settled property then subject to it will fall within the IHT charging regime for relevant property and remain there during the subsistence of the subsequent trusts.

2 A joint power of appointment can be given to a daughter and her husband. At common law a power of appointment could not be given to the husband alone if he survived (*Re Abbott,*

Peacock v Frigout [1893] 1 Ch 54), because such husband might be a person not born in the testator's lifetime, but would now be saved, at least partially, by the 'wait and see' provisions introduced by the PAA 1964, s 3 (Part G, para **[246.76]**) (for wills made before 6 April 2010), and continued in the PAA 2009, s 7 (Part G, para **[246.181]**) (for wills made on or after 6 April 2010).

3 Compare the AEA 1925, s 47(1) (Part G, para **[244.63]**). If this form was used for a will made before 6 April 2010, the testator's widow and children will have been lives in being for the purposes of the common law perpetuity period, so that all the interests will necessarily vest within a permissible perpetuity period. For wills made on or after 6 April 2010 however a mandatory perpetuity period of 125 years applies, see the PAA 2009, ss 5(1), 15(1)(a) (Part G, paras **[246.179]**, **[246.189]**, and see para **[94.6]**). Nevertheless, given the 'wait and see' provision of the PAA 2009, s 7 (Part G, para **[246.181]** and see para **[94.17]**), and the practical certainty that the interests will vest within 125 years of the testator's death, no perpetuity problem should arise if this form is used in a will made on or after 6 April 2010.

[216.25]

[Updated for the Perpetuities and Accumulations Act 2009.]

Form B16.18: Clause directing trustees to resort to the capital of residue in order to make up income to a minimum amount[1]

I direct that if in any year the net income from [my residuary estate] in the hands of my widow she retaining all rebates allowances and repayments for her own benefit which shall be included in the computation of the said net income does not amount to £—— then my trustees shall [at the written request of my widow] resort to the capital of my residuary estate to make good the deficiency.[2]

1 This clause directs trustees to make up income to a specified amount. It is thought that the total sum paid to the beneficiary is liable to income tax, see *Cunard's Trustees v IRC* [1946] 1 All ER 159, and HMRC have said they will treat payments out of capital as the income of the beneficiary where, by the terms of the trust instrument, payments out of capital are required to be made, or may be made, in order to supplement income to a fixed amount or a certain defined level, see the Trusts, Settlements and Estates Manual, TSEM 3757. See n 1 to Form B16.20 at para **[216.27]**.

2 If this form was used for a will made before 6 April 2010, the wife will have been a life in being for the purposes of the common law perpetuity period, so that this direction will necessarily have been confined within a permissible perpetuity period. For wills made on or after 6 April 2010 however a mandatory perpetuity period of 125 years applies, see the PAA 2009, ss 5(1), 15(1)(a) (Part G, paras **[246.179]**, **[246.189]**, and see para **[94.6]**). Nevertheless, given the 'wait and see' provision of the PAA 2009, s 7 (Part G, para **[246.181]** and see para **[94.17]**), and the practical certainty that the testator's widow will not survive more than 125 years from the testator's death, no perpetuity problem should arise if this form is used in a will made on or after 6 April 2010.

[216.26]

[Updated for the Perpetuities and Accumulations Act 2009.]

Form B16.19: Clause empowering trustees to resort to capital[1]

My trustees may at the written request of my widow at any time or times raise any sum or sums [(not exceeding £—— in any one year and not exceeding £—— in all)] out of the capital of my residuary estate and pay such sum or sums to or for the absolute benefit of my widow in addition to the income of my residuary estate hereinbefore given to her but in any such case my trustees shall have an absolute discretion whether or not they will raise such sums notwithstanding the written request of my said widow.[2]

1 This form gives trustees power to resort to capital to make up income, rather than, as in the immediately preceding form, directing them to do so to make up income to a specified sum. The trustees must be satisfied that the raising of such sums is for the benefit of the wife or for that of the children whom the wife is supporting: *Re Powles, Little v Powles* [1954] 1 All ER 516, [1954] 1 WLR 336. It is not clear whether sums paid to the beneficiary will be liable to income tax, see n 1 to Form B16.20 at para **[216.27]**.

2 If this form was used for a will made before 6 April 2010, the wife will have been a life in being for the purposes of the common law perpetuity period, so that this power will necessarily have been confined within a permissible perpetuity period. For wills made on or after 6 April 2010 however a mandatory perpetuity period of 125 years applies, see the PAA 2009, ss 5(1), 15(1)(a) (Part G, paras **[246.179]**, **[246.189]**, and see para **[94.6]**). Nevertheless, given the 'wait and see' provision of the PAA 2009, s 7 (Part G, para **[246.181]** and see para **[94.17]**), and the practical certainty that the testator's widow will not survive more than 125 years from the testator's death, no perpetuity problem should arise if this form is used in a will made on or after 6 April 2010.

[216.27]

[Updated for the Perpetuities and Accumulations Act 2009.]

Form B16.20: Clause empowering trustees to lend capital money to make up income of a share of residue to a stated amount[1]

I direct that if in any year during the lifetime of the said [*beneficiary*] the income of the share of residue hereinbefore bequeathed to the said [*beneficiary*] [*or* for the benefit of the said [*beneficiary*] and [her]/[his] children [and issue]] shall after deduction therefrom of income tax at the basic rate for the time being in force but without taking into account rebates allowances or repayments of tax be less than £—— my trustees may in their absolute discretion out of the capital of the said residue lend to the said [*beneficiary*] upon her [his] written undertaking that such moneys shall be recoverable and that interest shall be paid thereon as hereinafter stated the difference between the net income of the said share of residue and the sum of £—— provided that the said [*beneficiary*] shall not be called upon by my trustees to repay any such moneys during [her]/[his] lifetime but that they shall be recoverable only after [her]/[his] death from [her]/[his] estate and provided that in arriving at the sum to be borrowed the interest on any previous loan shall not be taken into consideration.[2]

[*Add rate and terms of payment of interest.*]

1 Form B16.18 at para **[216.25]** directs trustees to make up income to a stated amount by resorting to capital, and B16.19 at para **[216.26]** gives a power to trustees to make up income by resorting to capital. If an arrangement such as that of Form 16.18 is adopted (that is, directing a resort to the capital of the residuary estate) it is thought that the total sum paid to the beneficiary is liable to income tax, see *Cunard's Trustees v IRC* [1946] 1 All ER 159, and HMRC have said they will treat payments out of capital as the income of the beneficiary where, by the terms of the trust instrument, payments out of capital are required to be made, or may be made, in order to supplement income to a fixed amount or a certain defined level, see the Trusts, Settlements and Estates Manual, TSEM 3757. It is less clear that this result follows if Form 16.19 is adopted, but it is possible that it does. It would seem that this result may be avoided by giving the trustees a right to recover the sums advanced from the beneficiary so advanced: see *Williamson v Ough* [1936] AC 384, HL.

2 If this form was used for a will made before 6 April 2010, the named beneficiary will have been a life in being for the purposes of the common law perpetuity period, so that this direction will necessarily have been confined within a permissible perpetuity period. For wills made on or after 6 April 2010 however a mandatory perpetuity period of 125 years applies, see the PAA 2009, ss 5(1), 15(1)(a) (Part G, paras **[246.179]**, **[246.189]**, and see para **[94.6]**). Nevertheless, given the 'wait and see' provision of the PAA 2009, s 7 (Part G, para

[246.181] and see para [94.17]), and the practical certainty that the named beneficiary will not survive more than 125 years from the testator's death, no perpetuity problem should arise if this form is used in a will made on or after 6 April 2010.

[216.29]

[Updated for the Family Provision (Intestate Succession) Order 2009]

Form B16.22: Gift of residue incorporating intestacy provisions[1]

I devise and bequeath all the residue of my property to my trustees upon the same trusts and powers both as to the sale investment and administration thereof and as to the beneficial interests therein as if I had died intestate in respect thereof.

1 Subject to appointing executors and making some specific legacies, a person may wish his estate to pass as on an intestacy, or be prepared for this to happen if a will has to be made urgently. For the provisions which apply on an intestacy see the AEA 1925, ss 33 and 47 (Part G, paras **[244.60]** and **[244.63]**). If a testator leaves a spouse or civil partner and issue, the spouse or civil partner takes the personal chattels, a net sum which for a death on or after 1 February 2009 is £250,000 (see the Family Provision (Intestate Succession) Order 2009, SI 2009/135) with interest currently at 6 per cent from the date of death, and a life interest in half the residue. Subject to the interest of the widow or civil partner, the issue take the residue with stirpital substitution throughout. For deaths on or after 22 March 2006, the life interest for a widow or civil partner under the intestacy provisions should be an immediate post-death interest, and the statutory trusts for the minor children of the testator should be a trust for bereaved minors within IHTA 1984, s 71A (see para **[200.108]** above).

[216.30]

[Updated for the Perpetuities and Accumulations Act 2009.]

Form B16.23: Settlement of child's share of residuary estate[1]

My trustees shall hold my residuary estate upon trust for such of my children who shall survive me if more than one in equal shares. Provided that the share of my residuary estate of all such children who shall survive me shall not vest absolutely in such child but shall be retained by my trustees and held upon the following trusts:

(1) To pay the income from such share to such child for life and such child shall have power by will or codicil to appoint to any spouse or civil partner who shall survive him or her a life or less interest in such income[2] [And so that if and so long as such child is under the age of 18 years my trustees may pay or otherwise apply for or towards the maintenance education or benefit of such child the whole or such part or parts of the income of such share as my trustees in their absolute discretion think fit and shall retain the balance of such income upon trust for such child absolutely but my trustees may at any time or times while such child is under the age of 18 years pay or apply such retained income as if it were income arising in the then current year and section 31 of the Trustee Act 1925 shall not apply to such share].[3]

(2) From and after the death of such child [and subject to any such appointment as aforesaid to a surviving spouse or civil partner] such share and the income thereof shall be held upon such trusts for such one or more of his or her children and remoter issue as he or she

may by deed with or without power of revocation and new appointment or by will or codicil appoint.

(3) In default of any such appointment and so far as any such appointment shall not extend such share shall be held upon trust for all the children or any child of such child of mine who [being male] — shall attain the age of [eighteen] [twenty-one] years or [being female shall attain that age or] previously marry or form a civil partnership and if more than one equally as tenants in common. Provided that no child of any such child of mine shall take any part of my child's share in default of appointment under this present trust without bringing into hotchpot any part of the share of my child which he or she may have appointed in favour of such child or of any of such child's issue under the power in that behalf hereinbefore contained unless my child making the appointment shall direct to the contrary.

(4) If the share of my child or any part thereof shall not vest absolutely in some person or persons under the foregoing trusts then after the death of my child his or her share or the part thereof which shall not so vest shall (subject to the trusts powers and provisions hereby or by statute vested in my trustees in respect of the income or the capital thereof and to every exercise of the same by my trustees) be held in trust for such persons or person as he or she shall by will or codicil appoint and in default of any such appointment in trust for the statutory beneficiaries entitled as if he or she had died intestate without ever having married or formed a civil partnership and without leaving a parent and such share had formed part of his or her estate.

(5) If at the date when such child of mine attains the age of [fifty] years he or she shall never have had a child or if at the said date all the children he or she shall then have had shall have died without attaining a vested interest in his or her share or if subsequently to the said date all the children he or she shall have had shall die without any of them attaining such a vested interest as aforesaid then my trustees may at any time or times after the date when such child of mine attains the age of fifty years or the subsequent date when his or her last surviving child shall die without attaining such a vested interest as aforesaid as the case may be and during the life of such child of mine transfer the whole or any part or parts of his or her share in its then actual state of investment to such child of mine absolutely freed and discharged from the trusts powers and provisions hereof.[4]

1 If this clause is used it will be advisable to add a clause expressly authorising the executors or trustees to appropriate; see Form B20.24 at para **[220.77]**. As to the construction of the words children and issue, see Part A, paras **[200.28]** and **[200.29]**. For deaths on or after 22 March 2006, the initial life interest each child takes should be an immediate post-death interest if it takes effect immediately on the testator's death (or is subject only to a survivorship condition permitted by IHTA 1984, s 92: see paras **[219.6]**–**[219.7]**), and is not, for example, postponed to another interest. However, a further life interest appointed to a spouse (or civil partner) under the power of sub-clause (1) of the Form will not be an immediate post-death interest, and unless it is a disabled person's interest within IHTA 1984, s 89B (see para **[200.99]** above), the settled property subject to it will then fall within

the IHT charging regime for relevant property and remain there during the subsistence of any further trusts which are not disabled person's interests (see para **[200.107]** above).

If this form was used for a will made before 6 April 2010, the testator's children will have been lives in being for the purposes of the common law perpetuity period, so that the powers of appointment given to the children would necessarily be exercised (if at all) within a permissible perpetuity period, and the trusts taking effect in remainder to the life interests and in default of appointment would necessarily vest within a permissible perpetuity period. For wills made on or after 6 April 2010 however a mandatory perpetuity period of 125 years applies, see the PAA 2009, ss 5(1), 15(1)(a) (Part G, paras **[246.179]**, **[246.189]**, and see para **[94.6]**). Nevertheless, given the 'wait and see' provision of the PAA 2009, s 7 (Part G, para **[246.181]** and see para **[94.17]**), and the practical certainty that the powers of appointment will be exercised (if at all) and the remainder interests will vest within 125 years of the testator's death, no perpetuity problem should arise if this form is used in a will made on or after 6 April 2010.

2 Such an appointment would fail if a divorce (or dissolution of a civil partnership) takes place, since a divorced spouse cannot be a spouse (and a former civil partner cannot be a civil partner) who survives a named person: *Re Kettlewell, Jones v Kettlewell* (1907) 98 LT 23; *Re Williams' Settlement, Greenwell v Humphries* [1929] 2 Ch 361, [1929] All ER Rep 632; *Re Slaughter, Trustees Corpn Ltd v Slaughter* [1945] Ch 355, [1945] 2 All ER 214; *Re Allan, Allan v Midland Bank Executor and Trustee Co Ltd* [1954] Ch 295, [1954] 1 All ER 646.

3 This provision should be included where the testator may have a minor child living at his death, and he wishes such child to have a life interest which will be an immediate post-death interest within IHTA 1984, s 49A (see para **[216.2]** above). TA 1925, s 31 needs to be excluded because the trust of accumulations under the TA 1925, s 31 (Part G, para **[246.29]**) which applies where a minor beneficiary has a life interest is such as to give the minor beneficiary a contingent interest in such accumulations. The purpose of this substitution for s 31 is to cause the income which is not applied for the child's benefit during his minority to be held on trust absolutely for the child, so as to confer an interest in possession for IHT purposes. An infant cannot be paid income to which he is entitled (see Vol 1, para **[9.39]**) but it is thought that he or she has an interest in possession in income if it would form part of his estate if he or she died under the age of 18 (and unmarried and without a civil partner).

4 See n 3 to Form B16.24 at para **[216.31]**.

[216.31]

[Updated for the Perpetuities and Accumulations Act 2009.]

Form B16.24: Provision directing payment of capital to a female life tenant having no likelihood of children, where she has herself a general power of appointment in default of children[1]

If at the date when [*name*] [any daughter of mine] attains the age of [50] years she shall never have had a child[2] or if at the said date all the children[1] she shall then have had shall have died without attaining a vested interest in the [*property*] [*share of my residuary estate*] of which [she] [such daughter] is life tenant hereunder or if subsequently to the said date all the children [she] [such daughter] shall have had shall die without any of them attaining such a vested interest as aforesaid then my trustees shall at the date when the said [*name*] [such daughter] attains the age of [50] years or upon the subsequent date when the last surviving child of the said [*name*] [such daughter] shall die without attaining such a vested interest as aforesaid as the case may be transfer such [*property*] [*share*] as aforesaid in its then actual state of investment to the said [*name*] [such daughter] freed and discharged [from any life interest in the whole or a part thereof to which any husband of the said [*name*] [such daughter] who might survive her would or might have become entitled after her death whether under any appointment actually then made or otherwise and] from every [other] trust or power to take effect after her death under the trusts hereinbefore contained.[3]

1 If this form was used for a will made before 6 April 2010, a daughter of the testator will have been a life in being for the purposes of the common law perpetuity period, so that this direction will necessarily have been confined within a permissible perpetuity period. For wills made on or after 6 April 2010 however a mandatory perpetuity period of 125 years applies, see the PAA 2009, ss 5(1), 15(1)(a), (Part G, paras **[246.179]**, **[246.189]**, and see para **[94.6]**). Nevertheless, given the 'wait and see' provision of the PAA 2009, s 7 (Part G, para **[246.181]** and see para **[94.17]**), and the practical certainty that the daughter will not survive more than 125 years from the testator's death, no perpetuity problem should arise if this form is used in a will made on or after 6 April 2010.

2 Including an illegitimate child unless a contrary intention is shown: see Part A, paras **[200.28]** and **[200.29]**.

3 This precedent is for use when a female life tenant is entitled, in default of children attaining a vested interest, to a general power of appointment, or where in similar circumstances the property would otherwise go direct to her next of kin on her death. Any appointment to a surviving husband made under a power is overridden. It has been suggested that, where there is no longer any prospect of children, it is better that the life tenant should be able to break the trust even to the disadvantage of a husband who may survive her rather than that the money should go to (possibly) distant relatives. As to when the court used to presume a woman to be past childbearing, see *Re Whichelow, Bradshaw v Orpen* [1953] 2 All ER 1558, [1954] 1 WLR 5; *Allen v Crane* [1953] ALR 959, St R Qd 95; *Re Pettifor's Will Trusts* [1966] Ch 257, [1966] 1 All ER 913; and *Re Westminster Bank Ltd's Declaration of Trust* [1963] 2 All ER 400n, [1963] 1 WLR 820; see also the PAA 1964, s 2(1)(a) (Part G, para **[246.75]**) for the presumption in the context of the rule against perpetuities. These authorities can no longer be relied on: see para **[221.34]**, n 1. For this form in the context of a set of beneficial trusts see Form B 16.23 at para **[216.30]**.

Settled Legacies

[216.32]

[Updated for the Perpetuities and Accumulations Act 2009.]

Form B16.25: Settled legacy—concise form[1]

(i) I give to my trustees the sum of £—— [free of IHT and foreign death duties[1]] upon trust to invest the same in any investments hereby authorised or authorised by law for the investment of trust funds with power to vary the same and to hold the same in trust to pay the income therefrom to A. during his life.

(ii) Subject thereto as to both capital and income for all or any the children or child[2] of A. who attain the age of [eighteen] [twenty-one] years or marry under that age and if more than one in equal shares.[3]

[(iii) I hereby declare that the administrative provisions of this my will relating to residue shall apply to this legacy].

[*If it is desired to impose protective trusts, substitute the following in clause* (*i*) *above*: and to hold the income of the same upon protective trusts for the benefit of A. during his life.[4]]

1 For deaths on or after 22 March 2006, the initial life interest of A should be an immediate post-death interest if it takes effect immediately on the testator's death (or is subject only to a survivorship condition permitted by IHTA 1984, s 92: see paras **[219.6]–[219.7]**), and is not, for example, postponed to another interest (see para **[216.2]** above). If the property remains on trust after A's death, the settled property will then fall within the IHT charging regime for relevant property (see para **[218.8]** ff above), unless A's children are also the testator's children in which case if the selected age of contingency for the children's

remainder trust is 18, it should be a trust for bereaved minors (see para **[200.108]** above), and if the specified age is 21 (or another age between 18 and 25), the trust should be an age 18-to-25 trust (see para **[200.109]** above).

2 See paras **[210.3]**, **[210.4]** and **[214.64]** for IHT and pecuniary legacies. These words are unnecessary if there is a general direction covering inheritance such as Forms B14.33 at para **[214.76]** or B14.34 at para **[214.77]** or the legacy will be payable wholly out of UK free estate.

3 Illegitimate and legitimated children will now be included; see Part A, paras **[200.28]** and **[200.29]**. If this form was used for a will made before 6 April 2010, the named beneficiary will have been a life in being for the purposes of the common law perpetuity period, so that his children's interests will necessarily vest within a permissible perpetuity period. For wills made on or after 6 April 2010 however a mandatory perpetuity period of 125 years applies, see the PAA 2009, ss 5(1), 15(1)(a) (Part G, paras **[246.179]**, **[246.189]**, and see para **[94.6]**). Nevertheless, given the 'wait and see' provision of the PAA 2009, s 7 (Part G, para **[246.181]** and see para **[94.17]**), and the practical certainty that the interests will vest within 125 years of the testator's death, no perpetuity problem should arise if this form is used in a will made on or after 6 April 2010.

4 Where the income was given until marriage and upon marriage settled on the beneficiary and her children and in fact the beneficiary never married, the capital on the death of the beneficiary fell into residue: *Re Henry Will Trust, Mussett v Smith* [1953] 1 All ER 531, [1953] 1 WLR 376.

5 For the IHT treatment of protective trusts, see Part A, para **[200.104]**. For TA 1925, s 33, which defines protective trusts, see Part G, para **[246.31]**.

[216.33]

[Updated for the Perpetuities and Accumulations Act 2009.]

Form B16.26: Settled legacy—full form

I. FORM INCORPORATING STATUTORY WILL FORM[1]

I give to [*legatee*] the sum of £—— [free of IHT and foreign death duties[2]] and I declare that Form 7 of the Statutory Will Forms 1925 is incorporated in this my will and shall apply to this legacy [subject to the following modification, *add any necessary modification*].

II. FORM SETTING OUT THE TRUSTS[3]

I give to my trustees the sum of £—— [free of IHT and foreign death duties] upon trust to invest the same in any investments hereby authorised [*or* authorised by law for the investment of trust funds] with power to vary and transpose the same and to hold such investments and the income thereof:

(a) Upon trust to pay the income of the said investments to A. during his life and after his death;

[*or, if the life interest is to be protected:*

(a) Upon trust to hold the income of the said investments on protective trusts for A. during his life[4]];

(b) Upon trust if the said A. shall so direct by will to pay the income of the said investments or such part thereof as the said A. shall so direct to any wife [or civil partner] of the said A. who shall survive him during the residue of her life or for such less period as the said A. shall so direct and subject thereto;

(c) Upon trust as to both capital and income of the said investments for all or such one or more exclusively of the others or other of the children or remoter issue[5] of the said A. at such time and if more than one in such shares and with such provisions for maintenance advancement and otherwise for the benefit of such children or issues[5] or some or one of them at the discretion of my trustees or any other persons and generally in such manner in all respects as the said. A. shall by deed revocable or irrevocable or by will or codicil appoint And in default of and subject to any such appointment;

(d) Upon trust for all or any the children or child[5] of the said A. who shall attain the age of [eighteen] [twenty-one] years or marry under that age if more than one in equal shares as tenants in common;

(e) Provided always that no child of the said A. who or whose issue shall take by virtue of any appointment under the aforesaid power any share of the said investments shall unless the said A. so direct share in the unappointed part of the said investments without bringing the share so appointed into hotchpot and accounting therefor;

(f) If there shall be no child of the said A. who under the trust in default of appointment hereinbefore contained shall attain a vested interest in the said investments then the said investments and the income thereof and all accumulations of income shall be held upon trust for such persons and purposes and generally in such manner as the said A. shall by deed revocable or irrevocable by will or codicil appoint and subject to any such appointment;

(g) Upon trust for the next of kin of the said A. ascertained according to and in the shares provided by the law relating to intestacy as if the said A. had died intestate and a bachelor;

[(h) I hereby declare that the administrative provisions of this my will relating to residue shall apply to this legacy.]

1 For Form 7 see Part E, para **[238.13]**.

2 See n 1 to Form B16.25 at para **[216.32]**.

3 For deaths on or after 22 March 2006, the initial life interest of A should be an immediate post-death interest if it takes effect immediately on the testator's death (or is subject only to a survivorship condition permitted by IHTA 1984, s 92: see paras **[219.6]**–**[219.7]**), and is not, for example, postponed to another interest (see para **[216.1]** above). This is the case even if the protective trust option is chosen (see IHTA 1984, s 88(4)(b)(i) and para **[200.104]** above). A further life interest appointed to a spouse (or civil partner) under the power of sub-clause (b) of the Form will not be an immediate post-death interest, and unless it is a disabled person's interest within IHTA 1984, s 89B (see para **[200.99]** above), spouse or civil partner exemption will not be available on A's death, and the settled property subject to it will then fall within the IHT charging regime for relevant property (see para **[218.8]** ff above).

If this form was used for a will made before 6 April 2010, the named beneficiary will have been a life in being for the purposes of the common law perpetuity period, so that the powers of appointment would necessarily be exercised (if at all) within a permissible perpetuity period, and the trusts taking effect in remainder to the life interest and in default of appointment would necessarily vest within a permissible perpetuity period. For wills made on or after 6 April 2010 however a mandatory perpetuity period of 125 years applies, see the PAA 2009, ss 5(1), 15(1)(a) (Part G, paras **[246.179]**, **[246.189]**, and see para **[94.6]**). Nevertheless, given the 'wait and see' provision of the PAA 2009, s 7 (Part G, para **[246.181]** and see para **[94.17]**), and the practical certainty that the powers of appointment will be exercised (if at all) and the remainder interests will vest within 125 years of the testator's death, no perpetuity problem should arise if this form is used in a will made on or after 6 April 2010.

4 See n 4 to Form B16.25 at para **[216.32]**.

5 Including an illegitimate child unless a contrary intention is shown: see Part A, paras **[200.28]** and **[200.29]**.

Ancillary provisions

[216.34]

[Updated for the Perpetuities and Accumulations Act 2009.]

Form B16.27: Trust for accumulation of income[1]

[Subject to the payment of the said annuity to my wife [*name*]] my trustees shall accumulate for the period of my wife's life the [surplus] income of my residuary estate by investing the same and the income therefrom in any investments hereby authorised with power to vary such investments as my trustees shall think until the death of my wife and shall then hold the accumulated fund as capital of my residuary estate but so that no part of such fund shall be invested in the purchase of land.

1 For wills made on or after 6 April 2010, income arising in respect of non-charitable trusts may be accumulated throughout the perpetuity period of 125 years which will apply to those trusts: see the PAA 2009, ss 13, 15(1)(a), Part G, paras **[246.187]**, **[246.189]**, and para **[95.0]** above). Since it is a practical certainty that the testator's widow will not survive more than 125 years, this form authorises accumulation throughout her lifetime without limiting it to 125 years. This clause assumes that the income of the residuary estate is more than sufficient to maintain the widow and children and provides for the accumulation of the surplus income in order to provide more capital for the children.

For the taxation of accumulated income see paras **[218.29]**–**[218.36]**.

This clause could be unsatisfactory for IHT reasons. Part of the residuary estate will be treated as subject to the annuitant's interest in possession which could be an immediate post-death interest if it takes immediate effect on the testator's death (see the Preliminary Note to B11 at para **[211.1]** ff) and the remainder will be taxed as relevant property (see para **[218.8]** ff).

B17

Trusts for children

PRELIMINARY NOTE

[217.1]

[Updated for FA 2013, Sch 44.]

Trusts for bereaved minors and age 18-to-25 trusts within IHTA 1984, ss 71A and 71D. The former provision for accumulation and maintenance trusts for children contained in IHTA 1984, s 71 cannot apply to trusts created or coming into possession after 21 March 2006. In relation to trusts coming into effect after 21 March 2006, including wills of persons dying after that date, there are two much more limited categories of trust for minor children which receive advantageous treatment for IHT purposes: under IHTA 1984, ss 71A ('trusts for bereaved minors') and 71D ('age 18-to-25 trusts') (both sections have been amended by FA 2013, Sch 44, with respect to property transferred into settlement on or after 8 April 2013, so generally where a parent dies on or after 8 April 2013). For either section to apply, at least one of the beneficiary's parents must have died, and a trust in a will can only fall within either section if it is established under *the will of a parent of the child.* Parents for this purpose extend to step-parents and anyone who at his or her death has parental responsibility for the child: see s 71H. The s 71D trust is essentially a variant on the s 71A trust which permits a higher vesting age, at the cost of possibly incurring an IHT charge of probably modest proportions.

For a fuller account of these two forms of testamentary trust, see the Notes to paras **[200.108]**–**[200.109]** above. For a summary of the available types of testamentary trusts for minors see para **[224.24]**, and for examples of immediate post-death interest and relevant property trusts for minors in Forms C2.2 at **[224.42]** ff and C2.6 at **[224.102]** ff.

[217.3]

[Updated for income tax and capital gains tax rate changes.]

Income tax and capital gains tax. The income tax rate applicable to trusts for tax years 2010–11 to 2012–2013 was 50 per cent, (42.5 per cent for dividends) and is 45 per cent for 2013–2014. The rate of capital gains tax on trusts was 18 per cent for the period 6 April 2010 to 22 June 2010 and 28 per cent from 23 June 2010. In the case of a 'trust for the vulnerable' within FA 2005, ss 23–45, income and gains are taxed as if they were the principal beneficiary's: see the Notes to para **[217.4]** and Part C4 below. This may produce a significant income tax advantage, and now that the rates of capital gains tax for trusts and individuals are once again different (they were the same, ie. 18 per cent, for the period 6 April 2008 to 22 June 2010), it may once again produce a significant capital gains tax advantage.

[217.4]

[Updated for FA 2013, Sch 44.]

Trusts for the vulnerable. A type of trust for minor children with special tax treatment is created by FA 2005, ss 23–45 (amended by FA 2013, Sch 44, para 16, with effect for the tax year 2013–14 and subsequent years). This is a 'trust for the vulnerable' for a 'relevant minor', which broadly corresponds with the trust for a bereaved minor discussed in the Note to para **[217.1]** above, and more nearly (though still not exactly) following amendment by FA 2013, Sch 44, para 16. This type of trust enables the trustees and beneficiary to elect for the income and capital gains to be taxed as if the trust assets and income were the property of the relevant minor instead of being taxed at the trust rates. This note and the form set out below concentrate on the aspects of the rules which fall within the scope of *Williams on Wills*, namely the drafting of trusts which qualify for this special treatment. The details of what the special treatment is and how it is obtained will be found in HMRC's Trusts, Settlements and Estates Manual, TSEM 3400 et seq, (although at the time of writing this guidance has not been updated to take into account changes made by FA 2013, Sch 44, para 16), and *Tolley's Income Tax 2013–14,* paras 68.19–68.21.

For the purposes of FA 2005, ss 23–45, a relevant minor is a child under the age of 18 who has at least one deceased parent (s 39). Creating a qualifying 'trust for the vulnerable' is thus a possibility for a testator who has minor children to consider when deciding what provisions to include in his will to take effect in the event of him dying while one or more of them are still minors. It is important to note that where it is a question of creating by will a 'trust for the vulnerable' for a 'relevant minor' within FA 2005, ss 23–45, it can only be done by the will of a parent of the relevant minor, and other relatives are not able to do so (see s 35(2)(a)).

For a trust fund held for a minor child to be able to qualify for this special treatment it has to be one under which he will become absolutely entitled to the trust property and its income at the age of 18, and also to any income of the property which has been accumulated before that time (s 35(3)(a)). As regards the trusts while the relevant minor is under 18, there is one condition as to the trusts of capital and one as to the trusts of income. The capital condition is that while the relevant minor is living and under 18 there must be no power to apply capital other than for the benefit of the relevant minor (s 35(3)(b)). The income condition is that while the relevant minor is living and under 18 either he must be entitled to the income (if any) as it arises or if any such income is applied for the benefit of a beneficiary, it is applied for the benefit of the relevant minor (s 35(3)(c) as amended by FA 2013, Sch 44, para 16(2), amending the language, but not the purport of s 35(3)(c)). In other words, a trust of capital and income for a relevant minor contingently on attaining the age of 18, to which TA 1925, s 31 applied, would qualify.

It is expressly provided for tax year 2013–14 and onwards, that the application of the statutory power of advancement (the Trustee Act 1925, s 32 or the Northern Irish equivalent), including where it is extended to be exercisable in respect of the whole of a presumptive share of capital, or an express power of advancement to like effect, does not prevent the trusts from being qualifying trusts (FA 2005, s 35(4)(b)–(f) as substituted by FA 2013, Sch 44, para 16(3) for tax year 2013–14 and onwards). For tax years prior to 2013–14 it was provided only that an unextended statutory power of advancement (or similar power) would be compatible. This was inconvenient and inconsistent with the requirements of a trust for a bereaved minor which enabled an extended statutory power of advancement to be included (see para **[217.1]** above). The requirements of the two types of trust regarding powers of advancement have now been brought into line. Additionally, the fact that trustees might have powers to apply annually up to £3,000 (or 3 per cent of the value of the trust fund) otherwise than for the benefit of the minor, will not prevent a trust from qualifying for 'vulnerable beneficiary' treatment (FA 2005, s 35(4)(a) as substituted by FA 2013, Sch 44, para 16(3) for tax year 2013–14 and onwards), just as such powers will not prevent a trust from qualifying as a bereaved minor trust.

FA 2005, s 36 makes clear that trusts can qualify for the special treatment if they relate to part rather than the whole of an asset, provided that the part of the asset and its income are sufficiently identifiable to be able to determine whether it is held on qualifying trusts. It seems likely that a trust of an undivided fractional or percentage share of an asset or fund of assets and of the income of that share would have sufficiently definite subject-matter for it to be possible for the qualifying conditions to apply. HMRC's guidance on this topic is not very clear. They certainly consider that there may be a problem if the minor is entitled to a fractional share of income, that is an undivided part of the income of an asset, but do not expressly deal with the case where a minor's entitlement is to the underlying fractional share of an asset, and so the income arising from that fractional share, see Trusts, Settlements and Estates Manual, TSEM 3440. The main practical point here is to make sure that there is a power of appropriation without any consents being required, so that if there turns out to be a difficulty about obtaining the special tax treatment for an undivided share of a fund, specific assets can be appropriated to the trust for the relevant minor in order to obtain the special treatment.

Although the requirements for a trust to qualify for the special capital gains tax and income tax treatment for trusts for the vulnerable under FA 2005, ss 23–45 are now closer to the requirements for IHTA 1984, s 71A (trusts for bereaved minors), they are still narrower. IHTA 1984, s 71A can apply collectively to a class of minors without individual members of the class being certain of becoming entitled to any specific part or share of the fund, whereas the property held for the benefit of the relevant minor in a vulnerable beneficiary trust must be ring fenced for that minor (see Trusts, Settlements and Estates Manual, TSEM 3437). This makes sense given the particular type of tax treatment afforded to such trusts.

Although the intestacy trusts are expressly declared to qualify as trusts for the vulnerable for a relevant minor (FA 2005, s 35(1)(a)), when drafting will trusts intended to fall within FA 2005, ss 23–45, it will not be sufficient to copy out the statutory trusts in the AEA 1925. This is because marriage under the age of 18 is an alternative contingency under the intestacy trusts but is not a permitted alternative contingency in the case of express trusts appearing in a will: compare IHTA 1984, s 71A(3)(a) with FA 2005, s 35(3)(a). In this respect also trusts for vulnerable minors appear to differ from a trust for bereaved minors. For a precedent for a trust for vulnerable minors, see Form B17.1 under para **[217.9]** below.

[217.5]

[Updated for Rainbird v Smith [2013] WTLR 1609.]

Substitution. When trusts for the testator's children or remoter issue are being drafted it should be remembered that the new s 33 of the Wills Act 1837 (WA 1837) (substituted by the AJA 1982, s 19: Part G, para **[244.36]**) provides a statutory substitution clause in some circumstances, even in relation to class gifts: see Vol 1, para **[47.14]** ff. The substitutional provisions of s 33 for class gifts are of such uncertain application to the more common kinds of class gift that we recommend that express provision is made for substitution, or that s 33 is expressly excluded. It was held in *Rainbird v Smith* [2012] EWHC 4276 (Ch), [2013] WTLR 1609 that there was an intention contrary to s 33 applying where there was a gift to the testator's daughters as should survive the testator if more than one in equal shares. Also, the statutory substitution can only apply where a child or remoter descendant of the testator predeceases him, and will not operate to substitute issue of someone who survives the testator but dies before attaining some age upon the attaining of which the gift is contingent. Express substitutional clauses can and should be made to apply in whatever circumstances a primary gift fails.

One feature of the provisions relating to trusts for bereaved minors within IHTA 1984, s 71A, or age 18-to-25 trusts within IHTA 1984, s 71D, contained in a will which should be noted is that they only apply to *children* of the deceased parent. If, therefore, the trusts include a substitutional proviso in favour of the children of a child dying under the age of 18 and the proviso takes effect, the property or share of property which then devolves on the deceased parent's grandchildren will become 'relevant property' for IHT purposes, though without any charge to tax on the death of the child where that occurs after the testator's death: IHTA 1984, s 71B(2)(b). The same is true in relation to age 18-to-25 trusts for children of the testator where a child dies under 18: s 71E(2)(b). If the child attains the age of 18, the property will become liable to tax under ss 71E and 71F in the same manner as if it were relevant property (with no possibility of a periodic charge, however). If the child thereafter dies before attaining 25, there will be in addition an exit charge in respect of such property under s 71F, save where the death occurs within two years of the testator's death: s 144(1)(a).

[217.6]

[Updated for the Perpetuities and Accumulations Act 2009.]

Perpetuities. When drafting trusts for children and issue care must be taken that they do not infringe the rule against perpetuities, see the Preliminary Note to B16 at paras **[216.2]** and **[216.3]** and for a fuller account of perpetuities, see para **[200.35A]** ff and Vol 1, para **[94.1]** ff. It should be noted that for wills made on or after 6 April 2010, there is, by virtue of the Perpetuities and Accumulations Act 2009, ss 1, 5, 15(1)(a), a mandatory perpetuity period of 125 years.

[217.9]

[Updated for FA 2013, Sch 44.]

Form B17.1: Trust for the minor children of the testator at age 18 falling within Inheritance Tax Act 1984, s 71A (trusts for bereaved minors) and Finance Act 2005, ss 23–45 (special income tax and capital gains tax treatment for trusts for the vulnerable)[1]

(1) My trustees shall hold [my residuary estate][2] upon trust for such of my children as are living at my death and attain the age of 18 years if more than one in equal shares absolutely.

(2) If for any reason any child of mine does not attain a vested interest under the foregoing trust and there are descendants of his or hers who are living at my death (or the death of such child of mine if later) and who attain the age of 18 years such descendants shall take in equal shares per stirpes the share such child of mine would have taken if he had attained a vested interest and so that no descendant shall take whose parent attains a vested interest under the foregoing trust.

(3) The foregoing trusts shall carry the intermediate income and section 31 of the Trustee Act 1925 shall apply thereto.

(4) Section 32 of the Trustee Act 1925 (relating to payment or application of capital) shall apply to the foregoing trust as if the words 'one-half of' were omitted from sub-section (1)(a) thereof. [3]

(5) My trustees shall have power at their absolute discretion to appropriate specific assets to or towards the vested or presumptive share under the foregoing trusts of any child or remoter descendant of mine and on the basis of such evidence of values or advice as to values as they think fit.[4]

1 See the notes to paras **[217.1]–[217.4]** above.

2 An earlier definition of the trust fund is assumed, which could be a pecuniary legacy or a specific gift or residue or a share of residue, and which should be defined as including the assets from time to time representing whatever is initially given.

3 An extended statutory power of advancement is compatible with bereaved minor trusts (IHTA 1984, s 71A(4)) and also, for tax year 2013–14 and subsequent years, trusts within the Finance Act 2005, ss 23–45 (FA 2005, s 35(4)(b)–(f) as substituted by FA 2013, Sch 44, para 16(3)). See the note under para **[217.4]** above.

4 See the note under para **[217.4]** above as to the advisability of including this power of appropriation.

[217.12]

[Updated for the Perpetuities and Accumulations Act 2009.]

Form B17.4: Trust for children or issue as life tenant shall appoint: variation where there is a joint power of appointment[1]

In trust for all or such one or more exclusively of the others or other of the children or remoter issue[2] of the said —— [and ——] at such time and if more than one in such shares and with such provisions for maintenance advancement and otherwise for the benefit of such children or issue or some or one of them at the discretion of my trustees or any other persons and with such gifts over and generally in such manner as the said —— [and —— shall by deed revocable or irrevocable jointly appoint and in default of and subject to any such appointment as the survivor of them] shall by deed revocable or irrevocable or by will or codicil appoint and subject to any such appointment in trust for the child or children of the said —— [and ——] who shall attain the age of [eighteen] [twenty-one] years or [being female] previously marry and if more than one in equal shares as tenants in common provided that if any child of the said —— [and ——] dies in the lifetime of —— [*or* before the death of the survivor of —— and ——] leaving issue living at the death of [the survivor of —— and] —— then such issue if and when they attain the age of [eighteen] [twenty-one] years or marry thereunder shall take by substitution and if more than one in equal shares per stirpes the share of my residuary estate which such child would have taken had he or she survived [the survivor of —— and] —— but so that no issue shall take whose parent is alive and so capable of taking.[3]

Any child who or whose issue take any interest under the foregoing provision in default of appointment shall not take such interest in default of appointment without bringing into hotchpot any share or shares appointed to him or her or his or her issue and accounting for the same unless the appointment shall direct to the contrary.

1 Though it may be more common to give the capital of the residue to children equally, it is certainly a wise precaution, where there is a life interest given to a wife, that she should be given a power of appointment, for this enables the division of the estate to be considered at the last possible moment. By this means those who have prospered or married well may be given less than those who have suffered misfortune and all inequalities of fortune may be compensated for to a great extent. Class gifts – The 'rules of convenience' are fully stated in Vol 1 at para [66.1] ff.

2 Illegitimate children and issue will be objects of the power: see Vol 1, para **[72.14]**.

3 If this form was used for a will made before 6 April 2010, a named life tenant will have been a life in being for the purposes of the common law perpetuity period, so that the power of appointment would necessarily be exercised (if at all) within a permissible perpetuity period, and the trusts taking effect in remainder and in default of appointment would necessarily vest within a permissible perpetuity period. For wills made on or after 6 April 2010 however a mandatory perpetuity period of 125 years applies, see the PAA 2009, ss 5(1), 15(1)(a) (Part G, paras **[246.179]**, **[246.189]**, and see para **[94.6]**). Nevertheless, given the 'wait and see' provision of the PAA 2009, s 7 (Part G, para **[246.181]** and see para **[94.17]**), and the practical certainty that the power of appointment will be exercised (if at all) and the remainder interests will vest within 125 years of the testator's death, no perpetuity problem should arise if this form is used in a will made on or after 6 April 2010.

[217.15]

[Updated for the Perpetuities and Accumulations Act 2009.]

Form B17.7: Trust for children at twenty-one by settling each child's share and giving trustees power to pay or apply capital in favour of life tenant[1]

In trust for my children[2] living at my death who attain the age of twenty-one years or marry thereunder if more than one in equal shares.

Provided that the share of my residuary trust fund so given to every child of mine who shall survive me and attain twenty-one years or marry shall not vest absolutely in such child but shall be retained by my trustees upon the following trusts:

(i) The income of such share shall be paid to such child during his or her life.

(ii) Provided that my trustees shall have power in their absolute discretion from time to time during the life of such child after such child shall have attained the age of twenty-one years to pay transfer or apply to or for the benefit of such child the whole or any part or parts of the capital of such share freed and discharged from the trusts and powers hereof.

(iii) Subject as aforesaid such share and the income thereof shall be held upon trust for such one or more of his or her issue[3] immediate or remote as he or she may by deed with or without power of revocation and new appointment or by will or codicil appoint.

(iv) In default of such appointment and in so far as any such appointment shall not extend and subject to the foregoing trusts and powers such share shall be held for all the children or the child of such child of mine who attain the age of twenty-one years or marry thereunder if more than one as tenants in common in equal shares provided that no such child shall take in default of appointment without bringing into hotchpot any part of such share my child may have appointed in his or her favour or in favour of his or her issue under the power in that behalf hereinbefore contained unless my child making such appointment shall direct to the contrary.[4]

1 This may seem an involved provision but its purpose is to protect a child from becoming entitled to capital at too young an age. The settled property subject a trust in this form will be relevant property for IHT purposes and thus liable to periodic and exit charges, or else beneficiary-taxed, if the trusts come into possession on the testator's death and the children have attained interests in possession at the time of the testator's death or within two years of it: see para **[217.2]** above.

2 Illegitimate and legitimated children will be eligible: see Part A, para **[200.28]**.

3 Illegitimate issue may take: see Part A, para **[200.28]**.

4 If this form was used for a will made before 6 April 2010, a child of the testator will have been a life in being for the purposes of the common law perpetuity period, so that the powers to pay or apply capital and of appointment would necessarily be exercised (if at all) within a permissible perpetuity period, and the trusts taking effect in remainder and in default of appointment would necessarily vest within a permissible perpetuity period. For wills made on or after 6 April 2010 however a mandatory perpetuity period of 125 years applies, see the PAA 2009, ss 5(1), 15(1)(a) (Part G, paras **[246.179]**, **[246.189]**, and see para **[94.6]**). Nevertheless, given the 'wait and see' provision of the PAA 2009, s 7 (Part G, para **[246.181]** and see para **[94.17]**), and the practical certainty that the powers to pay or apply capital and of appointment will be exercised (if at all) and the remainder interests will vest within 125 years of the testator's death, no perpetuity problem should arise if this form is used in a will made on or after 6 April 2010.

[217.16]

[Updated for the Perpetuities and Accumulations Act 2009.]

Form B17.8: Trust for children of a person who takes no life interest

In trust for all the children[1] of [*name*] [whenever born during the lifetime of [*name of parent*][2]] who attain the age of [eighteen] [twenty-one] years [or being female marry under that age] if more than one in equal shares as tenants in common.[3]

1 It is not envisaged that the trust in this form will be for the testator's children, so the settled property subject to it will be relevant property for IHT purposes and thus liable to periodic and exit charges, or else beneficiary-taxed if the trusts come into possession on the testator's death and the children have attained interests in possession at the time of the testator's death or within two years of it: see para **[217.2]** above. See n 2 to Form B17.4 at para **[217.12]**. Illegitimate issue may take: see Part A, para **[200.29]**.

2 See Vol 1, para **[66.1]** ff, on gifts to a class. If the gift is to children of a person who is not life tenant and the class is definitely extended to *all* his children, distribution will be delayed until his death, for until then the number cannot be ascertained. Where there is a life interest, words such as 'born or to be born' are referred to birth before the death of the life tenant and do not further extend the class (*Mogg v Mogg* (1815) 1 Mer 654), and so with 'all and every the children' (*Andrews v Partington* (1791) 3 Bro CC 401). If the class is to remain open indefinitely there should be a power of advancement exercisable over the whole of a presumptive share (see Form B18.20 at para **[218.105]**), so that the trusts can be terminated when it becomes reasonably certain that no more members of the class will be born.

3 If this form was used for a will made before 6 April 2010, the named parent will have been a life in being for the purposes of the common law perpetuity period, so that the interests of his children will necessarily vest within a permissible perpetuity period. For wills made on or after 6 April 2010 however a mandatory perpetuity period of 125 years applies, see the PAA 2009, ss 5(1), 15(1)(a) (Part G, paras **[246.179]**, **[246.189]**, and see para **[94.6]**). Nevertheless, given the 'wait and see' provision of the PAA 2009, s 7 (Part G, para **[246.181]** and see para **[94.17]**), and the practical certainty that the interests will vest within 125 years of the testator's death, no perpetuity problem should arise if this form is used in a will made on or after 6 April 2010.

[217.18]

[Updated for the Perpetuities and Accumulations Act 2009.]

Form B17.10: Trust for children of another, including children dying in testator's lifetime leaving issue[1]

In trust for the children of [*name*] living at my death or born afterwards who attain the age of [eighteen] [twenty-one] years or die under that age leaving issue and any children of the said [*name*] who may have died in my lifetime whether before or after the date hereof leaving issue living at my death or then en ventre but born afterwards if more than one in equal shares as tenants in common but so that the share of any child of the said [*name*] dying in my lifetime shall pass to his or her personal representatives as part of such child's estate and as if such child had survived me.[2]

1 The settled property subject a trust in this form will be relevant property for IHT purposes and thus liable to periodic and exit charges, or else beneficiary-taxed if the trusts come into possession on the testator's death and the children have attained interests in possession at the time of the testator's death or within two years of it: see para **[217.2]** above. Illegitimate issue may take: see Part A, para **[200.28]**.

2 See n 2 to Form B17.7 at para **[217.15]**. If this form was used for a will made before 6 April 2010, the named parent will have been a life in being for the purposes of the common law perpetuity period, so that the interests of his children (and remoter issue) will necessarily vest within a permissible perpetuity period. For wills made on or after 6 April 2010 however

a mandatory perpetuity period of 125 years applies, see the PAA 2009, ss 5(1), 15(1)(a) (Part G, paras **[246.179]**, **[246.189]**, and see para **[94.6]**). Nevertheless, given the 'wait and see' provision of the PAA 2009, s 7 (Part G, para **[246.181]** and see para **[94.17]**), and the practical certainty that the interests will vest within 125 years of the testator's death, no perpetuity problem should arise if this form is used in a will made on or after 6 April 2010.

[217.22]

[Updated for the Perpetuities and Accumulations Act 2009.]

Form B17.14: Remainder trust for children and issue of deceased children of life tenant at eighteen or twenty-one or on previous marriage[1]

In trust in equal shares (if more than one) for all or any the children or child of [*life tenant*] living at the date of the death of the survivor of myself and the said [*life tenant*] who attain the age of [eighteen] [twenty-one] years or marry under that age and for all or any of the issue living at the said date who attain the age of [eighteen] [twenty-one] years or marry under that age of any child of the said [*life tenant*] who dies before the said date or is already dead leaving issue living at the said date such issue to take through all degrees according to their stocks in equal shares (if more than one) the share which their parent would have taken if living at the said date and so that no issue shall take whose parent is living at the said date and so capable of taking.[2]

1 Illegitimate children and issue as well as children and issue adopted at any time will prima facie be eligible; see Part A, para **[200.28]**. If the life tenant dies or surrenders his or her interest before the interests of any of the children or issue have attained absolute interests this trust will only qualify for favoured IHT treatment under IHTA 1984, s 71A or 71D in relation to any beneficiaries who are children or stepchildren of the testator. See para **[217.1]** above.

2 If this form was used for a will made before 6 April 2010, a named life tenant will have been a life in being for the purposes of the common law perpetuity period, so that the interests of his children (or remoter issue) would necessarily vest within a permissible perpetuity period. For wills made on or after 6 April 2010 however a mandatory perpetuity period of 125 years applies, see the PAA 2009, ss 5(1), 15(1)(a) (Part G, paras **[246.179]**, **[246.189]**, and see para **[94.6]**). Nevertheless, given the 'wait and see' provision of the PAA 2009, s 7 (Part G, para **[246.181]** and see para **[94.17]**), and the practical certainty that the interests will vest within 125 years of the testator's death, no perpetuity problem should arise if this form is used in a will made on or after 6 April 2010.

[217.24]

[Updated for the Perpetuities and Accumulations Act 2009.]

Form B17.16: Trust for children of another person who attain twenty-five within the limits of the rule against perpetuities[1]

In trust for the children of [*name*] born in my lifetime or after my death[2] who before the expiration of the period of [one hundred and twenty-five years][3] from my death attain the age of twenty-five years or marry under that age or are living but under the said age and unmarried at the expiration of such period if more than one in equal shares as tenants in common.[4]

1 As to the construction of children and issue see Part A, para **[200.28]**.

2 The words 'after my death' extend the trust to children whenever born.

3 For wills made on or after 6 April 2010, the perpetuity period is 125 years (and no other period): see the PAA 2009, ss 5(1), 15(1)(a) (Part G, para **[246.179]**, **[246.189]**). So this form adopts a period of 125 years within which the interests must vest, though a shorter period

could be specified, ie. such period as is estimated will cover the named individual's child-bearing or begetting years plus 25 years.

4 The settled property subject to a trust in this form will be relevant property for IHT purposes and thus liable to periodic and exit charges, or else beneficiary-taxed if the trusts come into possession on the testator's death and the children have attained interests in possession at the time of the testator's death or within two years of it: see para **[217.2]** above.

[217.32]

[Updated for the Perpetuities and Accumulations Act 2009.]

Form B17.24: Trust for children other than a child who becomes entitled to settled estates[1]

In trust for the children of [*name*] who attain the age of [eighteen] [twenty-one] years or being female marry under that age if more than one in equal shares as tenants in common (other than and except any son or sons of the said [*name*] who on or before attaining the age of [eighteen] [twenty-one] years or any daughter or daughters of the said [*name*] who on or before attaining that age or marrying shall become entitled as tenant in tail [*or* in tail male] in possession or in remainder immediately expectant upon the determination of a life interest in possession to the —— Estates settled by etc *or* devised by etc)[2] and if there shall be no child (other than and except as aforesaid) who shall attain the age of [eighteen] [twenty-one] years or being female shall marry under that age then in trust for such of the excepted children as attain the age of [eighteen] [twenty-one] years or being female marry under that age if more than one in equal shares.[3]

1 If this form is used, and the age of vesting is greater than 18 years, accumulation and maintenance trusts of income should continue until the age of vesting (which is possible for wills made on or after 6 April 2010, see PAA 2009, s 13, 15(1)(a) (Part G, para **[246.187]**, **[246.189]**), otherwise there could be the termination of an immediate post-death interest which would be treated as a chargeable transfer for IHT purposes (under the IHTA 1984, ss 2 and 52(1)) where one of the beneficiaries comes to be within the exception after becoming entitled to an immediate post-death interest in his presumptive share. See Forms B18.11 to B18.13 at paras **[218.77]**–**[218.79]** for extended accumulation and maintenance provisions. See also B18 at paras **[218.72]**–**[218.76]** on the advantages of extended accumulation and maintenance provisions. As the beneficiaries are not children of the testator, IHTA 1984, ss 71A or 71D cannot apply to the trusts, and the funds will either be relevant property, absolute property, or immediate post-death interest property depending on the ages of the beneficiaries at the testator's death and whether TA 1925, s 31(1) (see para **[246.29]**) applies modified or unmodified.

2 Although no new entails can be created after 1 January 1997 (see paras **[200.52]** and **[200.53]**, entails created before that date can continue to exist.

3 If this form was used for a will made before 6 April 2010, the named parent will have been a life in being for the purposes of the common law perpetuity period, so that the interests of his children would necessarily vest within a permissible perpetuity period. For wills made on or after 6 April 2010 however a mandatory perpetuity period of 125 years applies, see the PAA 2009, ss 5(1), 15(1)(a) (Part G, paras **[246.179]**, **[246.189]**, and see para **[94.6]**). Nevertheless, given the 'wait and see' provision of the PAA 2009, s 7 (Part G, para **[246.181]** and see para **[94.17]**), and the practical certainty that the interests will vest within 125 years of the testator's death, no perpetuity problem should arise if this form is used in a will made on or after 6 April 2010.

[217.35]

[Updated for the Perpetuities and Accumulations Act 2009.]

Form B17.27: Trust after life interest to a wife for nephews and nieces as wife shall appoint, and in default of appointment equally[1]

In trust for all or any one or more exclusively of the others or other of my nephews and nieces children of my [deceased] brothers or sisters in such shares and generally in such manner as my wife shall by deed revocable or irrevocable or by will or codicil appoint and subject to any such appointment in trust for all my said nephews or nieces living at my death [*or* the death of my wife] if more than one in equal shares as tenants in common.[2]

1 Nephews and nieces should always be carefully defined otherwise relations by marriage or even great-nephews and great-nieces may make a claim. As to the meaning of nephews and nieces, see Vol 1, para **[71.5]**.

2 If this form was used for a will made before 6 April 2010, the testator's widow will have been a life in being for the purposes of the common law perpetuity period, so that the power of appointment would necessarily be exercised (if at all) within a permissible perpetuity period, and the trusts taking effect in default of appointment would necessarily vest within a permissible perpetuity period. For wills made on or after 6 April 2010 however a mandatory perpetuity period of 125 years applies, see the PAA 2009, ss 5(1), 15(1)(a) (Part G, paras **[246.179]**, **[246.189]**, and see para **[94.6]**). Nevertheless, given the 'wait and see' provision of the PAA 2009, s 7 (Part G, para **[246.187]** and see para **[94.17]**), and the practical certainty that the power of appointment will be exercised (if at all) and the interests will vest within 125 years of the testator's death, no perpetuity problem should arise if this form is used in a will made on or after 6 April 2010.

B18

Discretionary trusts and powers

DISCRETIONARY TRUSTS

[218.16]

[Updated for the transferable nil-rate band.]

Nil-rate band discretionary trusts. The inheritance tax nil-rate band is now (in tax year 2013–2014) £325,000, and is intended by the government to remain so until 2017–2018. If a testator leaves his entire estate to his spouse or civil partner in the event of the spouse or civil partner surviving him, and at the time of his death has not made any lifetime gifts in the previous seven years, he will not have used any of his nil-rate band in the event of his spouse or civil partner surviving him. Prior to new rules introduced on 9 October 2007, this would have wasted his nil-rate band. He could have left up to his available nil-rate band to non-exempt recipients, e g his children, without any inheritance tax being payable. However, he may not have wanted to leave an amount up to the nil-rate band direct to the children in the event of his dying survived by his spouse or civil partner if such survivor would or might need access to the income or even the capital of the whole of the testator's estate after his death. So, a testator who wished to enable his spouse or civil partner to be able to benefit from his entire estate and its income if need be, but who nevertheless wished to provide for a nil-rate band's worth of his estate to devolve on e g his children, without it being charged to inheritance tax as part of the spouse's or civil partner's estate, often did so by means of a discretionary trust. On and from 9 October 2007 new rules provide that to the extent that a testator does not fully utilise his nil-rate band allowance, a nil-rate band carry forward allowance will be available to his spouse or civil partner in addition to her own nil-rate band allowance: see para **[200.75]** above. Therefore, the device of the nil-rate band discretionary trust will no longer figure as such an essential tool of inheritance tax planning. Nevertheless, there will be instances where it may still be appropriate to incorporate a nil-rate band discretionary trust in a will. For example, if a testator has assets which are predicted to increase more in value than the nil-rate band, it may be advantageous for inheritance tax purposes if a nil-rate band trust is incorporated in his will with power for the executors to appropriate those assets to the value of the nil-rate band to the trust. Another possibility is that a nil-rate band discretionary trust may be desirable for non-fiscal reasons, eg. to make income and capital immediately available to beneficiaries other than the testator's spouse or civil partner, or to keep assets out of the surviving spouse's or civil partner's estate if, for example, it is possible that she may be declared bankrupt, or perhaps require long-term care when her own assets would be taken into account in determining her entitlement to local authority funding, but assets in a discretionary trust may not.

[218.22]

[Updated for SDLT rate change on 1 January 2010.]

Another reason for using the charge scheme—SDLT. Where, nevertheless, a nil-rate band discretionary trust is to be constituted by a debt or charge, the charge scheme is to be preferred to the debt scheme, because if properly implemented HMRC's view is that it will not give rise to stamp duty land tax, whereas a debt scheme will (at least if the value charged against the residential property exceeds the nil-rate threshold for residential property which is £125,000 on and from 1 January 2010). HMRC's views appeared in *Modernising Stamp Duty on land and buildings in the UK*: *Practitioners' Newsletter*, Issue 4 (7 December 2004). They cite the commonest examples of such transactions and their stamp duty land tax consequences as follows:

- The legacy trustees accept the surviving spouse's promise to pay in satisfaction of the pecuniary legacy and in consideration of that promise land is transferred to the surviving spouse. The promise to pay is chargeable consideration for stamp duty land tax purposes.
- The legacy trustees accept the personal representatives' promise to pay in satisfaction of the pecuniary legacy and land is transferred to the surviving spouse in consideration of the spouse accepting liability for the promise. The acceptance of liability for the promise is chargeable consideration for stamp duty land tax purposes. The amount of chargeable consideration is the amount promised (not exceeding the market value of the land transferred).
- Land is transferred to the surviving spouse and the spouse charges the property with payment of the amount of the pecuniary legacy. The legacy trustees accept this charge in satisfaction of the pecuniary legacy. The charge is money' s worth and so is chargeable consideration for stamp duty land tax purposes.
- The personal representatives charge land with the payment of the pecuniary legacy. The personal representatives and legacy trustees also agree that the trustees have no right to enforce payment of the amount of the legacy personally against the owner of the land for the time being. The legacy trustees accept this charge in satisfaction of the legacy. The property is transferred to the surviving spouse subject to the charge. There is no chargeable consideration for stamp duty land tax purposes provided that there is no change in the rights or liabilities of any person in relation to the debt secured by the charge.

[218.27]

[Updated for capital gains tax changes.]

Capital gains tax and discretionary trusts. Prior to 6 April 2008, the rates of capital gains tax for an individual were arrived at by adding the capital gains made in a tax year to his or her income and charging them in effect to income tax. By contrast, capital gains tax on the gains of a settlement prior to 6 April 2008 was charged at the income tax trust rate under the Income Tax Act 2007, s 9(1) (formerly known as the rate applicable to trusts under Income and Corporation Taxes Act 1988 (ICTA 1988), s 686), 40 per cent in the tax year 2007–08 (see the Taxation of Chargeable Gains Act 1992 (TCGA 1992), s 4(1AA)(a)). The realisation of a chargeable gain on the sale of assets held in a discretionary trust before 6 April 2008 thus involved paying more capital gains tax than would be paid if the assets were owned absolutely by an individual who, after taking into the account the chargeable gain, was not a higher rate tax payer. From 6 April 2008 until 22 June 2010 there was a flat rate of capital gains tax applicable across the board, including individuals and trusts, of 18 per cent (without indexation relief or taper relief): TCGA 1992, s 4 as substituted by Finance Act 2008, s 8. However, from 23 June 2010 trusts and higher rate taxpayers pay capital gains tax on gains accruing on or after that date at the rate of 28 per cent, whereas non-higher rate taxpayers continue to pay capital gains tax at 18 per cent. Therefore, a trust may once again pay more capital gains tax than at least some taxpayers.

[218.30]

[Updated for HMRC v Peter Clay Trust [2009] STC 469.
Updated for income tax rate changes.]

The Income Tax Act 2007, s 479(4) (formerly ICTA 1988, s 686(1)) provides that income which is not UK company dividend income is to be taxed on the trustees at 'the trust rate' (50 per cent for tax years 2010–11 to 2012–2013 and 45 per cent for 2013–2014). The income caught by the section includes inter alia income which falls to be accumulated and income which is payable to a beneficiary under a discretion (whether or not there is power to accumulate) (see the Income Tax Act 2007, s 480(1), (2)). Income applicable under the TA 1925, s 31 (Part G, para **[246.29]**) during the minority of a beneficiary would fall within this definition. Various categories of income are excluded from the operation of s 479(4) (although not from basic rate tax), of which it is sufficient to mention income applied in defraying trust expenses which are properly chargeable to income (or would be so chargeable but for some express provision of the trust): a restrictive interpretation of these words was adopted by the House of Lords in *Carver v Duncan* [1985] 2 All ER 645. What is so chargeable to income is expenditure exclusively for the benefit of the income beneficiaries, though this can be an apportioned part of a fee, even a fixed fee, in respect of work some of which was exclusively for income beneficiaries and some of which also benefited capital: see *HMRC v Peter Clay Trust* [2009] STC 469. The Income Tax Act 2007, ss 493–494 (formerly ICTA 1988, s 687) provide that income paid to a beneficiary as income is to be treated as income net of the trust rate. The trustees are responsible for the payment of the amount of such tax subject to set off of the 'tax pool' which will include the income tax already paid to HMRC. A beneficiary who receives income under a discretion and who pays tax at a rate below the trust rate or who has unused personal reliefs available to him may be able to recover some part of the tax paid by the trustees in respect of such income. The ultimate burden of tax on income to which these sections apply is thus unaffected as long as such income is distributed as income, but if, for example, income is accumulated and subsequently distributed in the form of capital there can be no recovery of any part of the tax paid in respect of such accumulations. Thus accumulation of discretionary trust income (excluding UK company dividends), as opposed to distributing it, is often fiscally unattractive.

[218.31]

[Updated for income tax rate changes.]

If the trust includes UK company dividend income, however, the rules which came into force from 1999–2000 mean that accumulation of such income will generally be preferable to distribution of it, where it is subject to a discretionary trust, and that a beneficiary having an interest in possession is preferable to it being subject to a discretionary or accumulation trust. A dividend from a UK company comes with a tax credit (currently 1/9 of the amount distributed), and under the Income Tax Act 2007, ss 9(2), 479(3) (formerly ICTA 1988, s 686), tax on such income is charged on the trustees at the dividend trust rate (formerly the Schedule F trust rate) (42.5 per cent for tax years 2010–11 to 2012–13 and 37.5 per cent for 2013–14). If the trustees distribute the dividend income, they are deemed to make a payment grossed up at the normal trust rate (50 per cent for tax years 2010–11 to 2012–13 and 45 per cent for 2013–14), and are liable under Income Tax Act 2007, ss 493–494 (formerly ICTA 1988, s 687) to tax on this grossed up amount. The tax credit on the dividends does not, however, go into the 'tax pool' to reduce this liability, so the trustees are only able to set off the tax actually paid by them under Income Tax Act 2007, s 479. The beneficiary who receives the dividend income is liable for tax on that payment at his own income tax rate, but with the benefit of a credit for the amount paid by the trustees, so he is entitled to a tax repayment or liable for further tax, as appropriate. The overall effect of the rules is that if a discretionary trust is to invest in UK company shares it will probably be better for the income produced thereby to be accumulated, rather than distributed, and for capital payments or loans to be made to the beneficiaries rather than income distributions. Another possibility is to appoint an interest in possession, so that the income and the tax credit is the beneficiary's. The 2006 changes to IHT on trusts means that it is possible to have an interest in possession for income tax purposes while retaining 'relevant property' IHT status, provided, in the case of a will trust, that the interest in possession commences more than two years after the testator's death (see, further, para **[200.126]** sub-para (2)).

[218.32]

[Updated for income tax rate changes.]

For 2005–06 and onwards there is a new special trust tax rate which applies to the first £1000 for 2010–11 which would otherwise be chargeable to tax at the trust rate or the dividend trust rate: see the Income Tax Act 2007, s 491 (formerly TA 1988, s 686D). Such income is instead chargeable to income tax at the basic rate, the lower rate or the dividend ordinary rate, depending on the nature of the income (Income Tax Act 2007, s 491(3), formerly TA 1988, s 686(3)).

[218.33]

[Updated for the Perpetuities and Accumulations Act 2009.]

Form B18.1: Discretionary trust for the testator's family

(1) In this clause:

(i) 'the trust period' means the period starting with the date of my death and ending 125 years afterwards;[1]

(ii) 'the beneficiaries' means [*here set out the persons comprising the class of beneficiaries. An example would be*: my wife my sister [*name*] and all the children and remoter issue of myself or of my said sister who may be born before the end of the trust period together with any spouse civil partner widow widower or surviving civil partner of any such children or remoter issue (and so that the expressions 'widow', 'widower' and 'surviving civil partner' shall include a widow widower or surviving civil partner who has married or formed a civil partnership)].

(2) My trustees shall hold the capital and income of the trust fund upon trust for all or such one or more of the beneficiaries at such ages or times in such shares and upon such trusts for the benefit of all or any one or more of the beneficiaries as my trustees (being at least two in number or a [trust] corporation)[2] may by deed or deeds[3] revocable or irrevocable at any time or times during the trust period appoint and in making any such appointment my trustees shall have powers as full as those which they could possess if they were the absolute beneficial owner of the trust fund and in particular (but without prejudice to the generality of the foregoing words) may:

(i) appoint new trustees of the whole or any part or parts of the trust fund and provide for the remuneration of any who may be professional or corporate trustees;

(ii) create or delegate powers and discretions over capital or income (including powers of further delegation) whether of a dispositive or administrative nature;

Provided that:

(a) no appointment shall be capable of being made and no revocable appointment shall be capable of being revoked after the expiration of the trust period;

(b) no appointment shall prejudice or affect any prior payment transfer or application of income or capital hereunder;

(c) any appointment under the foregoing power may be made subject and without prejudice to any existing interests trusts or powers;

(d) any such appointment may be made of income without any appointment of capital; and

(e) my trustees (being at least two in number or a [trust][4] corporation) may at any time or times during the trust period by deed or deeds extinguish, or release or restrict the foregoing power in any manner and to any extent.[5]

(3) In default of and subject to and until any appointment made under the provisions of the preceding subclause:

(i) during the trust period my trustees shall pay or apply the income of the trust fund to or for the maintenance or support or otherwise for the benefit of all or any one or more of the beneficiaries as my trustees may in their absolute discretion think fit; provided that my trustees may if they in their absolute discretion think fit accumulate such income or any part of it by way of compound interest by investing the same and its resulting income in any way authorised by this will and if they do so they shall hold such accumulations as part of the capital of the trust fund but may nonetheless in any future year during the trust period apply them or any part of them as if they were arising in that year[6];

(ii) upon the expiry of the trust period my trustees shall hold the trust fund as to both capital and income absolutely for [*here insert the dispositions to take effect at the end of the trust period in default of previous appointment. For example*: such of the beneficiaries as are then living and if more than one in equal shares.

or

such of my children and remoter issue as are then living and if more than one in equal shares according to their stocks and so that no issue shall take whose parent is still alive and so capable of taking].

(4) [As Form B18.32 at para **[218.118]**.][7]

1 For wills made on or after 6 April 2010, the perpetuity period is 125 years (and no other period): see the PAA 2009, ss 5(1), 15(1)(a) (Part G, paras **[246.179]**, **[246.189]**) and see para **[94.6]**. So this form adopts a trust period of 125 years. A shorter trust period could be specified if the testator does not wish the trust to last that long, although the perpetuity period will still be 125 years. It is not necessary to specify, in addition to the specification as to the length of the trust period, that the perpetuity period is 125 years: PAA 2009, s 5(2). This contrasts with the situation under the former law where if the common law perpetuity period was not relied upon it was necessary to specify that the perpetuity period was 80 years, or fewer, see the PAA 1964, s 1(1). The 125 year perpetuity period commencing with the death of the testator will be the perpetuity period when drafting an appointment in exercise of the power of sub-clause (2), whether the trust period selected is 125 years (as in this form) or a shorter period: see the PAA 2009, s 6(2) (Part G, para **[246.180]**). Accordingly, an appointment under the power should be expressly limited so that all interests vest (in interest if not in possession) and all powers are exercised within the 125 year period. We should add that if this is not done in an appointment, there will still be 'wait and see' under the PAA 2009, s 7 (Part G, para **[246.181]**), but it is better practice to draft trusts of which it is clear from the outset that they will vest within the relevant perpetuity period.

2 For the meaning of trust corporation see the Preliminary Note to B3 at para **[203.28]**. If a foreign corporate trustee might be appointed, the word 'trust' should be omitted.

3 For precedents, see Forms F4.1 to F4.4 at paras **[242.7]–[242.11]**.

4 See n 2, above.

5 A power conferred on trustees in that capacity cannot be released by them unless they have express power to do so: see Vol 1, para **[40.10]**.

6 For wills made on or after 6 April 2010, there are no statutory restrictions on accumulation in respect of non-charitable trusts, so accumulation will be permitted throughout the trust period: see the PAA 2009, ss 13, 15(1)(a) (Part G, para **[246.187]**, **[246.189]**) and see para **[95.0]**.

7 This will enable the trustees to exercise their powers and discretions in favour of one of their number.

[218.34]

[Updated for the Perpetuities and Accumulations Act 2009 and FA 2013, Sch 44.]

Form B18.2: Legacy equal to inheritance tax threshold to be held on discretionary trusts[1]

(1) In this clause the following expressions have the following meanings—

(a) 'the trust legacy' means the legacy by this clause bequeathed to my legacy trustees and the assets for the time being representing the same;

(b) 'the beneficiaries' means and includes [my wife [*name*]] and my children and remoter issue;[2]

(c) 'the trust period' means the period commencing on my death and expiring 125 years afterwards;[3] and

(d) 'my legacy trustees' means [*name*] of [*address*] and [*name*] of [*address*] or other the trustee or trustees for the time being of the trust legacy].[4]

(2) If [my wife] shall survive me[5] then I bequeath to my legacy trustees free of inheritance tax and foreign death duties[6] a legacy of [£325,000][7] *or* [the maximum sum of money (if any) which can in the circumstances subsisting at my death be given by this clause without any liability being incurred for the payment of inheritance tax on or by reason of my death. And in particular but without prejudice to the generality of the foregoing the circumstances to be taken into account for the foregoing purpose shall include any chargeable transfers made by me during my lifetime (or events treated as such for inheritance tax purposes) the dispositions taking effect under this Will (apart from this present clause) or under any codicil hereto and any property treated as if it were part of my estate immediately before my death for inheritance tax purposes].[8]

(3) My legacy trustees shall hold the trust legacy and the income thereof upon such trusts for the benefit of all or any one or more exclusively of the others or other of the beneficiaries and if more than one in such shares and with such trusts and powers [(including trusts and powers conferring a discretion as to the distribution of capital or income exercisable by my legacy trustees or by any other person or persons)][9] and with such provisions generally as my legacy trustees (not being fewer than two in number or being a corporation) shall by any deed or deeds revocable or irrevocable appoint provided that no appointment shall be made and no revocable appointment shall be revoked after the expiration of the trust period.

[(4) At any time or times during the trust period my legacy trustees (not being fewer than two in number or being a corporation) may raise the whole or any part or parts of the trust legacy and pay or apply the same to or for the advancement or benefit of any of the beneficiaries for the time being living in such manner as they think fit.][10]

(5) Subject to any exercise of the foregoing power[s] my legacy trustees shall during the trust period hold the trust legacy upon trust to pay or apply the income thereof to or for the maintenance education or benefit of all or any one or more of the beneficiaries for the time being living in such shares if more than one and generally in such manner as they think fit provided that my legacy trustees may during the trust period[11] accumulate the whole

or any part of the income of the trust legacy by investing the same and the resulting income thereof in any of the investments hereby authorised and any accumulations of income so made shall form part of the capital of the trust legacy for all purposes.

(6) Subject to any exercise of the foregoing powers the trust legacy and the income thereof shall be held at the expiration of the trust period in trust absolutely for such of my children and remoter issue as shall then be living in equal shares per stirpes.

(7) Any capital or income of the trust legacy not otherwise disposed of by this clause shall be held in trust for such of my children as survive me if more than one in equal shares absolutely.

(8) Any of my trustees or my legacy trustees may exercise any power or discretion hereby or by law conferred notwithstanding that he or she has a direct or indirect personal interest in the mode or result of such exercise.[12]

(9) Instead of the trust legacy being satisfied by the payment of cash or by the appropriation of property—[13]

(a) my trustees may charge (with or without there being any personal liability of any person or persons) any property which is (or but for this clause would be) comprised in [my residuary estate] with payment of a sum of money equal to or less than the amount of the trust legacy to my legacy trustees and my legacy trustees shall accept such charge for such sum as the whole or a part (as the case may be) of the trust legacy; and

(b) my trustees may require my legacy trustees to accept in satisfaction of all or part of the trust legacy a binding promise of payment (secured or unsecured) made personally by [my wife] or by my trustees as trustees of [my residuary estate] which debt shall be payable on demand and my legacy trustees shall accept such debt as the whole or a part (as the case may be) of the trust legacy.

(10) The following shall apply in relation to the powers in the last preceding subclause—

(a) my trustees may require to be included such terms if any as they think fit in relation to a charge under subclause (9)(a) above or a debt under subclause (9)(b) above including terms as to interest (if any) and terms linking the debt or sum charged to the Retail Prices Index or otherwise providing for its amount to vary with the passage of time according to a formula provided that the debt or sum charged shall be payable to my legacy trustees on demand and the charge shall be enforceable by my legacy trustees at any time;

(b) my legacy trustees may leave the charge or debt outstanding for as long as they think fit and refrain from exercising their rights in relation to it and waive the payment of all or any part of any interest due in respect of it and may accept any substitute debt or charge undertaken or created by any person;

(c) my trustees may assent to the vesting of [my residuary estate] subject to an outstanding obligation to pay or satisfy the trust legacy and my legacy trustees may appoint new trustees in exercise of the statutory power to do so before the trust legacy has been paid or satisfied;[14]

(d) my legacy trustees and my trustees shall not be liable if [my wife] is or becomes unable to pay the debt or any security is or becomes inadequate or for any other loss or disadvantage which may occur as a result of their exercising or choosing not to exercise any of the foregoing powers; and

(e) the foregoing powers are in addition to any other powers given by this will or any codicil or by the general law and the foregoing powers may be exercised even though my trustees and my legacy trustees are the same persons or [my wife] is among either or both sets of trustees provided that such powers shall not be exercisable by a sole trustee who is [my wife].

(11) My trustees may constitute the trust legacy wholly or partly by appropriating to it at their discretion any property or proportionate share of any property and for this purpose may take such advice as to the value of the said property or proportionate share as they think fit.[15]

(12) Where the trust legacy is for the time being wholly or partly constituted by a proportionate share of a dwellinghouse or other property my legacy trustees shall have all the powers of an absolute owner in relation to such share and property and in particular may at their discretion join with the other proprietor or proprietors of such property:

(i) to permit a beneficiary under the trusts of the trust legacy to have the use or enjoyment of the property in kind on such terms as my legacy trustees think fit; or

(ii) to effect or enable a sale of the property and the purchase of another property in the same or similar co-ownership with the trust legacy constituted by a proportionate share thereof.

1 See paras **[218.16]–[218.23]** for the purpose of this form, and whether or not it is still advisable following the introduction on 9 October 2007 of nil-rate band transfer. It may be adapted for use where the testator may leave a husband or civil partner. It is to go with a gift of the rest of the testator's estate to his spouse or civil partner, either absolutely or for life (or another interest in possession, but in either case such that the spouse or civil partner has an immediate post-death interest or a disabled person's interest: see paras **[200.98]–[200.99]** above). See Forms C3.4 at para **[225.57]** and C3.5 at para **[225.68]** for forms of complete wills incorporating a disposition of this type.

2 The definition of the discretionary class may need to be enlarged or adapted in individual cases. See also n 2 to Form C3.6 at para **[225.100]**.

3 For wills made on or after 6 April 2010, the perpetuity period is 125 years (and no other period): see the PAA 2009, ss 5(1), 15(1)(a) (Part G, paras **[246.179]**, **[246.189]**) and see para **[94.6]**. So this form adopts a trust period of 125 years. A shorter trust period could be specified if the testator does not wish the trust to last that long, although the perpetuity period will still be 125 years.

4 The main circumstances in which there should be separate trustees of the legacy are where a charge scheme might be entered into, in which case the testator's spouse or civil partner should not be one of the executors and trustees but could be a trustee of the legacy, or where the testator's spouse or civil partner is or might be sole executor and a debt scheme might be entered into, or where there is a life interest trust of residue for the surviving spouse or civil partner. See para **[218.22]**.

5 This form assumes an exempt gift of residue to the testator's spouse or civil partner, or a gift of it on an interest in possession trust for the spouse or civil partner (e g a life interest) such that the spouse or civil partner has an immediate post-death interest or a disabled person's interest: see paras **[200.98]–[200.99]** above, so that the estate is wholly or mostly exempt apart from this gift. This gift of a nil-rate band fund on discretionary trusts should not be subject to a condition that the spouse or civil partner survives the testator by a certain period (and note that an omnibus commorientes clause such as Form B19.2 at para **[219.15]**

could have this effect). This is because the IHTA 1984, s 92 may not apply to such a survivorship condition, since the condition would not be as to the survival of the beneficiary under the nil-rate fund, as the section appears to require; see para **[219.8]**.

6 See the Preliminary Note to B14 at para **[214.35]** ff for the reasons for having these words if the testator has any foreign assets. It can be better to make this gift *subject* to tax. Making the gift subject to inheritance tax will, in the event of this gift taking the non-exempt estate over the inheritance tax threshold (eg because of changes in the law or the testator having made lifetime gifts during the seven years preceding his death), cause the size of the chargeable estate to be less than it would be if the gift was free of inheritance tax: see B14 at para **[214.74]**.

7 The current threshold is £325,000 until 5 April 2015. If a legacy of £325,000 is settled on discretionary trusts and if, as in this form, all other benefits devolve on the spouse, no inheritance tax will be payable on the testator's death unless lifetime transfers fall to be taken into account or there is property treated as part of the testator's estate for inheritance tax purposes such as property subject to a reservation (see Part A, para **[200.76]**), or settled property in which he had an interest in possession within the IHTA 1984, s 49(1).

8 The formula in square brackets is designed to ensure that the amount of the discretionary legacy does not exceed the inheritance tax threshold where other non-exempt gifts are made or where lifetime chargeable transfers fall to be taken into account on the death. Where a legacy subject to a discretionary trust is included in a will where the residuary gift will not be exempt from inheritance tax (see paras **[218.24]** and **[218.25]**), the second alternative formula for defining the amount of the settled legacy should not be used. This is because the amount of inheritance tax payable on the estate will be the same whatever the size of the legacy. The probable result of using the second alternative formula where none of the residue was exempt would be that if the taxable estate were within the nil-rate band and no inheritance tax was payable, the legacy would use up the entire residue, and that if any inheritance tax were payable on the estate the legacy would be nil. We suggest that where there is no exempt residue either a specified cash sum should be settled on discretionary trusts, or residue should be left on discretionary trusts with the idea that an appointment falling within the IHTA 1984, s 144 (for which see the Note in C3 at para **[225.83]** ff) can be made if the discretionary trust fund turns out after the testator's death to be larger than is appropriate.

9 The words in square brackets authorise the creation of discretionary powers, eg powers to advance capital to a life tenant, which may not otherwise be valid: see Vol 1, para **[40.5]**.

10 A power to pay or apply capital, being exercisable in a less formal manner than a power of appointment, may be a useful power to confer. It is essential that its exercise is adequately evidenced.

11 For wills made on or after 6 April 2010, there are no statutory restrictions on accumulation in respect of non-charitable trusts, so accumulation will be permitted throughout the trust period: see the PAA 2009, ss 13, 15(1)(a) (Part G, paras **[246.187]**, **[246.189]**) and see para **[95.0]**.

12 This will enable the trustees to exercise their powers and discretions in favour of one of their number.

13 These powers and the provisions of the next subclause are included so as to enable a debt or charge scheme to be used as a means of avoiding the surviving spouse or civil partner having an interest in possession in the trust fund subject to the trusts of this clause, where there are insufficient assets other than the matrimonial home with which to constitute that trust fund. See paras **[218.19]–[218.22]**.

14 The purpose of this is so that new trustees of the residuary estate can be appointed before a charge is entered into, in a case where the surviving spouse is one of the personal representatives or the personal representatives and the trustees of the discretionary legacy are the same persons, and to make clear that new or additional trustees of the discretionary trust legacy can be appointed before the legacy is constituted as a debt from the surviving spouse or civil partner where the surviving spouse or civil partner is the sole trustee of it: see para **[218.22]** for the reasons for avoiding these states of affairs.

15 If post-21 March 2006 a beneficiary is permitted to occupy a property owned by a discretionary trust, whereas this may give that beneficiary an interest in possession, it will not necessarily be the type of interest in possession which will cause the property to be treated as part of his or her estate for inheritance tax purposes. Only an interest in possession which is an immediate post-death interest, a disabled person's interest, or a transitional serial interest (see paras **[200.98]–[200.100]** above) will have this result. In the

context of a discretionary trust established by will, if a permission to occupy is given within two years of the testator's death, and this gives rise to an interest in possession this may be back-dated to the testator's death under IHTA 1984, s 144, so that it would be an immediate post-death interest and result in the property being treated as part of the beneficiary's estate for inheritance tax purposes: see para **[225.83]** ff. But if the permission is not granted until after the second anniversary of the testator's death, and the beneficiary to whom it is granted is not a disabled person within the meaning of IHTA 1984, s 89B(2) (as substituted by FA 2013, Sch 44, para 8(2)) at (where the testator died before 8 April 2013) the testator's death or (where the testator on or after 8 April 2013) at the date of the grant, so that her interest is not a disabled person's interest within IHTA 1984, s 89B (as amended by FA 2013, Sch 44, paras 8, 10) (see para **[200.99]** above), it should not result in the property being treated as part of the beneficiary's estate for inheritance tax purposes. Therefore, an express power to appropriate property or a share of property may be given to trustees to exercise in appropriate circumstances, and sub-clauses (11) and (12) contain such a power and associated provisions.

[218.35]

[Updated for the Perpetuities and Accumulations Act 2009.]

Form B18.3: Devise to beneficiary on discretionary trusts[1]

I devise my freehold land at —— in the county of —— known as —— to my trustees upon trust to sell the same and to hold the rents and profits until sale after payment thereout of all outgoings usually chargeable against income and the net income from the proceeds of sale in trust for [*name*] during [his]/[her] life provided always that at any time or times instead of paying any such rents and profits or income accruing during the life of the said [*name*] to [him]/[her] my trustees may apply any such rents and profits or income for or towards the personal support maintenance and education of the said [*name*] or [his]/[her] issue for the time being or such one or more to the exclusion of the others or other of such objects of this discretionary power in such manner and if more than one in such shares as my trustees shall think proper with power within three years after the death of any object of such discretionary power to apply any income which accrued in his or her lifetime in or towards the discharge of any liability incurred by or on behalf of any such object which my trustees shall think fit to satisfy, and after the death of the said [*name*] [*gift over to remainderman or as the beneficiary shall appoint*].[2]

1 This form may be appropriate as an alternative to a protected life interest, (see e g Forms B16.1 to B16.3 at paras **[216.6]–[216.8]** and Form B18.7 at para **[218.39]**) where a testator feels that the object of his bounty may be at risk of bankruptcy, divorce or some other calamity when it would be advantageous for the trustees to be able to divert income from the beneficiary to, e g persons dependent upon him. The trust for sale is not strictly necessary in the light of the TLATA 1996 (see para **[200.48]** ff), but since the purpose of the form is to provide the beneficiary with an income rather than a place to live, it may be appropriate. The trusts of this clause, which give the beneficiary a life interest subject to power for the trustees to divert the income elsewhere, are of a type which does not confer an interest in possession on the main beneficiary for inheritance tax purposes; see *Pearson v IRC* [1981] AC 753; see generally Part A, paras **[200.93]–[200.97]**. However, it is possible that she would have an interest in possession for the purposes of the TLATA 1996, so that unless the land devised was unavailable (e g let) or unsuitable (e g business premises) for her occupation, she might have a right to occupy the land under the TLATA 1996, s 12 (Part G, para **[246.115]**; see also para **[208.5]** ff). Therefore, if the testator wishes to avoid this, a full discretionary trust form should be used, e g Form B18.1 at para **[218.33]**.

For the taxation of the income and capital gains of discretionary trusts, see paras **[218.27]–[218.32]**.

2 If this form was used for a will made before 6 April 2010, the named beneficiary will have been a life in being for the purposes of the common law perpetuity period, so that the powers over income would necessarily be exercised (if at all) within a permissible perpetuity period. For wills made on or after 6 April 2010 however a mandatory perpetuity period of 125 years applies, see the PAA 2009, ss 5(1), 15(1)(a) (Part G, paras **[246.179]**, **[246.189]**, and see para **[94.6]**). Nevertheless, given the 'wait and see' provision of the PAA 2009, s 7 (Part G, para **[246.181]** and see para **[95.17]**), and the practical certainty that the named beneficiary will not live for more than 125 years from the testator's death, no perpetuity problem should arise if this form is used in a will made on or after 6 April 2010.

[218.36]

[Updated for the Perpetuities and Accumulations Act 2009 and FA 2013, Sch 44.]

Form B18.4: Trusts for a disabled person[1]

If my said son A (hereinafter called 'A') shall be living and be a disabled person within the meaning of the Inheritance Tax Act 1984, s 89[2] at the time of my death the said [share of my residuary estate] directed to be held upon trust for him as aforesaid (hereinafter called 'the share') shall not vest absolutely in A but shall be retained by my trustees and held upon the following trusts and with and subject to the following powers:

(1) My trustees shall have power at their absolute discretion to pay or apply the whole or any part or proportion of the income of the share to or for the benefit of A during his life.[3]

(2) My trustees shall while A is living[4] accumulate the income of the share which shall not be paid or applied for the benefit of A as aforesaid as an accretion to the capital of the share but shall have power to pay or apply such accumulations during the life of A as if the same were income of the then current year.

(3) Notwithstanding the foregoing trust and power my trustees shall have power during the life of A to pay or apply the whole or any part or parts of the capital of the share to or for the benefit of A.

(4) Subject to the foregoing trusts and to any or every exercise of the foregoing powers my trustees shall hold the share or such part thereof as shall not have been paid or applied as aforesaid and the income thereof upon trust for [such of my children other than A and remoter issue (including any issue of A) as shall be living at the death of A in equal shares per stirpes so that no issue shall take whose parent is living at the death of A and capable of taking]/[all or any my grandchildren or grandchild whenever born during the lifetime of the last of my children to die who shall attain the age of 18 years if more than one in equal shares].

(5) Section 32 of the Trustee Act 1925 (relating to the payment or application of capital) shall apply in all respects as if the words 'one-half of' had been omitted from proviso (a) of subsection (1) thereof.

1 This form is intended to satisfy the conditions laid down in the IHTA 1984, s 89 and is for use in a will executed on or after 8 April 2013 (see the Preliminary Note to C4 at paras **[226.3]** ff). It assumes that the testator has made a gift in an earlier clause of the will to his disabled son, and that it is an absolute gift conditional only on surviving the testator. The trusts of the clause only come into operation if the disabled son 'A' is still disabled within the meaning of s 84(4) (as substituted by FA 2013, Sch 44, para 6(4)) at the testator's death because it seems that the section will only apply if he is disabled at the time of the testator's

death. During A's life current income is only paid for his benefit at the discretion of the trustees and is otherwise accumulated (so as to comply with s 89(1) (as amended by FA 2013, Sch 44, para 6), but he will be deemed for inheritance tax purposes to have an interest in possession which qualifies as a disabled person's interest which means that the underlying capital will be treated as part of his estate for inheritance tax purposes (IHTA 1984, ss 49(1A)(b), 89(2), 89B(1)(a)). Subclause (4) confers a power to apply capital but only for the benefit of A so as to comply with s 89(1)(b) (as substituted by FA 2013, Sch 44, para 6(2)).

Subclause (6) provides for the statutory power of advancement to apply with modification to be applicable to the whole of a presumptive share. An extended statutory power of advancement is now compatible with trusts falling within IHTA 1984, s 89 (as amended by FA 2013, Sch 44, para 6) (see para **[226.4]** sub-para (v)).

This form should also qualify as a trust for the benefit of a 'vulnerable beneficiary' (FA 2005, s 34(4) and see para **[226.9]** ff). A trust so qualifying allows a claim for special tax treatment bringing the trustees' income and capital gains tax liability into line with what the vulnerable beneficiary's liability would have been if he or she had received the income directly or had realised the trust gains (see FA 2005, ss 23–45 and para **[226.9]**).

2 A disabled person may be someone: (i) incapable by reason of mental disorder within the meaning of the Mental Health Act 1983 (as amended) of administering his property or managing his affairs; (ii) in receipt of (or qualified to receive) an attendance allowance under the Social Security Contributions and Benefits Act 1992, s 64 or the Social Security Contributions and Benefits (Northern Ireland) Act 1992, s 64; (iii) in receipt of (or qualified to receive) a disability living allowance under the Social Security Contributions and Benefits Act 1992, s 71 or the Social Security Contributions and Benefits (Northern Ireland) Act 1992, s 71, by virtue of entitlement to the care component at the highest or middle rate (IHTA 1984, s 89(4)); or (iv) in receipt of (or qualified to receive) personal independence payment, an increased disablement pension, constant attendance allowance or armed forces independence payment: see IHTA 1984, s 89(4), (4A) (as amended and inserted by FA 2013, Sch 44, para 6(4),(5)).

3 For wills made on or after 6 April 2010 a mandatory perpetuity period of 125 years applies, see the PAA 2009, ss 5(1), 15(1)(a) (Part G, paras **[246.179]**, **[246.189]**, and see para **[94.6]**). Given the 'wait and see' provision of the PAA 2009, s 7 (Part G, para **[246.181]** and see para **[94.17]**), and the practical certainty that the named beneficiary will not live for more than 125 years from the testator's death, no perpetuity problem should arise if this form is used in a will made on or after 6 April 2010.

4 For wills made on or after 6 April 2010, there are no statutory restrictions on accumulation in respect of non-charitable trusts: see the PAA 2009, ss 13, 15(1)(a) (Part G, paras **[246.187]**, **[246.189]**) and see para **[95.0]**.

POWERS

[218.37]

[Updated for the Perpetuities and Accumulations Act 2009 and FA 2013, Sch 44.]

Form B18.5: Power to daughter to appoint life interest in a settled share to her husband[1]

Provided always and I hereby declare that notwithstanding the trusts hereinbefore contained my said daughter [*name*] shall have power[2] by deed revocable or irrevocable or by will or codicil to appoint to any husband who may survive her for the residue of his life or for any less period [the whole or] any part [not exceeding one-half] of the income of my said daughter's share[3] or the income of any asset or assets comprised in such share or of any part or share of such share [not exceeding one-half of the value at the date of such deed will or codicil of such share (all values for this purpose to be determined conclusively by my trustees)] and she may if she thinks fit appoint protective trusts of such income for his benefit during his life or any less period.

1 Such a power may be less desirable than previously, at least from an inheritance tax perspective, on and after 22 March 2006. Where the daughter is entitled to a life interest which arises after 22 March 2006 and is an immediate post-death interest, any interest in possession appointed to her husband will not attract the spouse exemption from inheritance tax unless it qualifies as a disabled person's interest (see para **[200.99]** above). This would be the only relevant type of interest in possession which would have the result of treating her husband as beneficially entitled to the underlying trust property for inheritance tax purposes under IHTA 1984, s 49(1), (1A)(b) thus enabling the spouse exemption to be claimed. Unless the husband has a disabled person's interest, the underlying trust property will then fall into the relevant property regime. A testator may still, however, wish to confer such a power for the benefit of the daughter's husband. For an alternative form see Form 18.8 at para **[218.40]**.

2 If this power is only to be effectually exercised in default of children or issue attaining a vested interest, insert here: 'in case no child or other issue of such daughter shall attain a vested interest in such daughter's share.'

If this form was used for a will made before 6 April 2010, the daughter will have been a life in being for the purposes of the common law perpetuity period, so that the power of appointment would necessarily be exercised (if at all) within a permissible perpetuity period. For wills made on or after 6 April 2010 however a mandatory perpetuity period of 125 years applies, see the PAA 2009, ss 15(1)(a) (Part G, paras **[246.179]**, **[246.189]**, and see para **[94.6]**). Nevertheless, given the 'wait and see' provision of the PAA 2009, s 7 (Part G, para **[246.181]** and see para **[94.17]**), and the practical certainty that the power of appointment will be exercised (if at all) within 125 years of the testator's death, no perpetuity problem should arise if this form is used in a will made on or after 6 April 2010.

3 It is assumed that the fund is divided into shares, each of which is settled on a child of the testator with remainder to his or her own children. For examples see Forms C2.6 at para **[224.95]** and C7.4 at para **[229.37]**.

[218.39]

[Updated for the Perpetuities and Accumulations Act 2009.]

Form B18.7: Protective life interest with a power to raise and pay capital[1]

I give to my trustees the sum of £—— free of inheritance tax payable on my death [*or* the residue of my property both real and personal wherever situate being or arising] as to the income thereof upon protective trusts for the benefit of A during his life and my trustees shall until the failure or determination of the trust of income in favour of the said A have the further power at their absolute discretion and without being liable in any way to account for the exercise of such discretion to raise and pay to the said A for his own absolute use and benefit at any time or times as my trustees shall determine [the whole or any part or parts of] [any sum or sums not exceeding on any one occasion £—— clear of expenses out of] the capital of the said fund [*or* residue] and my trustees shall hold any part of the said fund [residue] not so transferred to the said A during his lifetime as the said A shall by will or codicil appoint and in default of and subject to any such appointment [*set out trusts in remainder*] and I direct that my trustees shall on no account be liable or responsible for making any such payment whether of income or capital to the said A after the failure or determination of his said determinable life interest unless or until they shall have received express notice of the act or event causing such failure or determination.[2]

1 The effect of this clause is that trustees can pay sums out of capital to the beneficiary and this may prove a very useful provision where the beneficiary has only a life interest whether protected or not. Care should be taken not to exercise the power in such manner as to encourage HMRC to claim that the capital advanced is liable to tax as income in the beneficiary's hands, e g by making advances of regular amounts at regular intervals to pay

everyday living expenses. In *Stevenson v Wishart* [1987] STC 266 recurring payments of large sums out of trust capital for a discretionary beneficiary's nursing-home expenses were held not to be income, but the decision leaves open the question whether it is possible that recurring payments of capital made by trustees under a power of the kind in this Form could be taxed as income if they were intended to defray ordinary living expenses. HMRC will treat payments out of capital as the income of the beneficiary where, by the terms of the trust instrument, payments out of capital are required to be made, or may be made, in order to supplement income to a fixed amount or a certain defined level. See the *Trusts, Settlements and Estates Manual*, TSEM 3757. It is possible for a life interest subject to the statutory protective trusts to be an immediate post-death interest (see IHTA 1984, s 88(4)(b)(i) and para **[200.104]** above), and the exercise of a power to pay capital to a life tenant with an immediate post-death interest does not involve a charge to inheritance tax: see Part A, para **[200.96]** and the IHTA 1984, s 53(2), (2A). For a shorter form of power to pay or apply capital for the benefit of a life tenant see Form B18.8 at para **[218.40]** and for a form by reference to the statutory power of advancement see Form B18.22 at para **[218.107]**.

2 If this form was used for a will made before 6 April 2010, the named beneficiary will have been a life in being for the purposes of the common law perpetuity period, so that the powers to pay capital and of appointment would necessarily be exercised (if at all) within, and any discretionary trust arising on any forfeiture of the life interest would not last beyond, a permissible perpetuity period. For wills made on or after 6 April 2010 however a mandatory perpetuity period of 125 years applies, see the PAA 2009, ss 5(1), 15(1)(a) (Part G, paras **[246.179]**, **[246.189]**, and see para **[94.6]**). Nevertheless, given the 'wait and see' provision of the PAA 2009, s 7 (Part G, para **[246.181]** and see para **[94.17]**), and the practical certainty that the named beneficiary will not survive more than 125 years from the testator's death, no perpetuity problem should arise if this form is used in a will made on or after 6 April 2010.

[218.40]

[Updated for the Perpetuities and Accumulations Act 2009 and FA 2013, Sch 44.]

Form B18.8: Life interest subject to trustees' power to pay or apply capital to or for the benefit of the life tenant, with remainders to the life tenant's children subject to powers of the life tenant to appoint a life interest to his spouse and to appoint capital among his issue[1]

(1) My trustees shall hold [the trust fund] on trust to pay the income thereof to [my son] during his life;[2]

(2) provided that my trustees shall have power in their absolute discretion from time to time during the life of [my son] to pay transfer or apply the whole or any part or parts of the capital of [the trust fund] in which [my son] has for the time being an interest in possession (within the meaning of Part III of the Inheritance Tax Act 1984)[3] to or for the benefit of [my son] in such manner as they shall in their absolute discretion think fit;[4]

(3) subject to the foregoing trust and any or every exercise of the foregoing power my trustees shall hold [the trust fund] and the income thereof upon such trusts in such shares or proportions and with and subject to such powers and provisions (which may include discretionary trusts or powers or administrative powers or provisions) for the benefit of all or such one or more of [my son's] children and remoter issue as [he] may by deed (revocable or irrevocable) or by will or codicil appoint;

(4) in default of and subject to any such appointment and subject to the foregoing trusts and any or every exercise of the foregoing powers my trustees shall hold [the trust fund] and the income thereof upon trust for the child or children of [my son] who shall attain the age of 21 years if more than one in equal shares;

(5) notwithstanding the foregoing trusts and powers for the benefit of the issue of [my son] he shall have power by deed (revocable or irrevocable) or by will or codicil to appoint to any wife of his who may survive him as his widow a life or lesser interest (or a life or lesser interest on protective trusts) in the whole or any part or parts of [the trust fund] and the foregoing trusts for [my son's] children and any or every exercise of the foregoing power for the benefit of his issue shall take effect subject to such life or lesser interest;[5]

(6) [*As* Form B18.32 *at para* **[218.118]**].[6]

1 If this form was used for a will made before 6 April 2010, the testator's son will have been a life in being for the purposes of the common law perpetuity period, so that the powers to pay capital and of appointment would necessarily be exercised (if at all) within a permissible perpetuity period, and the trusts taking effect in remainder and in default of appointment would necessarily vest within a permissible perpetuity period. For wills made on or after 6 April 2010 however a mandatory perpetuity period of 125 years applies, see the PAA 2009, ss 5(1), 15(1)(a) (Part G, paras **[246.179]**, **[246.189]**, and see para **[94.6]**). Nevertheless, given the 'wait and see' provision of the PAA 2009, s 7 (Part G, para **[246.181]** and see para **[94.17]**), and the practical certainty that the powers will be exercised (if at all) and the remainder interests will vest within 125 years of the testator's death, no perpetuity problem should arise if this form is used in a will made on or after 6 April 2010.

2 For deaths on or after 22 March 2006, the son's life interest should be an immediate post-death interest if it takes effect immediately on the testator's death (or is subject only to a survivorship condition permitted by IHTA 1984, s 92, see paras **[219.6]**–**[219.7]**), and is not, for example, postponed to another interest (see para **[216.1]** above). If after his death the property remains in trust, it will fall within the inheritance tax charging regime for relevant property (see the Note to para **[200.92]** above).

3 The point of restricting the power to property in which the life tenant has an interest in possession is that if his life interest is terminated by him, e g surrendering or assigning it in favour of the remaindermen, the power will automatically cease to be exercisable.

4 See n 1 to Form B18.7 at para **[218.39]**. This power would authorise lending capital to or for the benefit of the life tenant in an appropriate case (*Re Kershaw's Trusts* (1868) LR 6 Eq 322), although an express power to lend such as Form B18.27 at para **[218.113]** could usefully be incorporated. The case law on the scope of the statutory power of advancement, discussed at paras **[218.87]**–**[218.103]** is also relevant to an express power of this kind.

5 Where the son becomes entitled to his interest in possession on or after 22 March 2006, any interest in possession appointed to his spouse will only attract the spouse exemption from inheritance tax if it is also a disabled person's interest (see para **[200.99]** above). This would be the only relevant type of interest in possession which would have the result of treating his spouse or civil partner as beneficially entitled to the underlying for inheritance tax purposes under IHTA 1984, s 49(1), (1A)(b) thus enabling the spouse exemption to be claimed.

6 This will enable the trustees to exercise their power to pay or apply capital to the life tenant and the statutory power of advancement (for which see paras **[218.87]**–**[218.103]**) in favour of one of their number.

[218.41]

[Updated for the Perpetuities and Accumulations Act 2009.]

Form B18.9: Power to pay, to children who have life interests, increasing proportions of capital as they grow older[1]

Notwithstanding the trust hereinbefore declared my trustees may in the exercise of their absolute discretion as they think fit on or after the attainment of the age of [25] years by any child of mine pay transfer or apply to or for the benefit of such child one third or any less part of the share of such child and on or after the attainment of the age of [30] years by any child of mine pay transfer or apply to or for the benefit of such child a further third or any less part of the share of such child and on or after the attainment of the age of [35] years by any child of mine pay transfer or apply to or for the benefit of such child the whole or any part or parts of the share (or such of the same as has not previously been so paid transferred or applied) of such child [and I express the wish but without restricting my trustees' discretion in any way that each of my children shall receive all the capital of his share by the time he attains the age of 35 years].

1 This form presupposes a trust for the testator's children in shares which are settled on them for life with remainders to their own children. For a form of complete will containing a clause of this kind see Form C8.6 at para **[230.81]**.

If this form was used for a will made before 6 April 2010, a child of the testator will have been a life in being for the purposes of the common law perpetuity period, so that the powers to pay capital would necessarily be exercised (if at all) within a permissible perpetuity period. For wills made on or after 6 April 2010 however a mandatory perpetuity period of 125 years applies, see the PAA 2009, ss 5(1), 15(1)(a) (Part G, paras **[246.179]**, **[246.189]**, and see para **[94.6]**). Nevertheless, given the 'wait and see' provision of the PAA 2009, s 7 (Part G, para **[246.181]** and see para **[94.17]**), and the practical certainty that the powers will be exercised (if at all) within 125 years of the testator's death, no perpetuity problem should arise if this form is used in a will made on or after 6 April 2010.

[218.42]

[Updated for the Perpetuities and Accumulations Act 2009.]

Form B18.10: Power to trustees to vary trusts of child's settled share[1]

Provided always and I hereby declare that my trustees shall have power during the lifetime of any child of mine by any deed or deeds to vary all or any of the trusts in this my will contained concerning the share of residue whether original or accruing hereby bequeathed to such child and to settle the whole or any part of such share upon such trusts for the benefit of such child and his or her spouse and his children or issue or any of them in such manner and form and with such provisions stipulations and agreements as my trustees may think proper including discretionary trusts and powers and administrative powers and provisions as my trustees think fit.

1 If this form was used for a will made before 6 April 2010, a child of the testator will have been a life in being for the purposes of the common law perpetuity period, so that the power would necessarily be exercised (if at all) within a permissible perpetuity period. For wills made on or after 6 April 2010 however a mandatory perpetuity period of 125 years applies, see the PAA 2009, ss 5(1), 15(1)(a) (Part G, paras **[246.179]**, **[246.189]**, and see para **[94.6]**). Nevertheless, given the 'wait and see' provision of the PAA 2009, s 7 (Part G, para **[246.181]** and see para **[94.17]**), and the practical certainty that the power will be exercised (if at all) within 125 years of the testator's death, no perpetuity problem should arise if this form is used in a will made on or after 6 April 2010.

MAINTENANCE

[218.67]

[Updated for income tax rate changes.]

(n) Income tax. It should be remembered that income which is to be accumulated or which is payable at the discretion of the trustees or any other person in so far as it is not used to defray trust expenses is taxable in the hands of the trustees at the trust rate applicable to trusts (50 per cent in tax years 2010–2011 to 2012–13 and 45 per cent for 2013–14), (unless it is UK company dividend income when it is taxable at the dividend trust rate, 42.5 per cent in tax years 2010–2011 to 2012–13 and 37.5 per cent in 2013–14): Income Tax Act 2007, s 479 (formerly ICTA 1988, s 686). This provision will apply to express discretionary and accumulation trusts, but it will also apply in cases where the maintenance and accumulation provisions of the TA 1925, s 31 apply, ie until the beneficiary has attained full age. Income applied for the benefit of a beneficiary under a power will be treated as such beneficiary's income for tax purposes and he or she may be able to recover some part of the tax already paid by the trustees: Income Tax Act 2007, ss 493–494 (formerly ICTA 1988, s 687). See also paras **[218.29]**–**[218.32]**.

[218.71]

[Updated for the Perpetuities and Accumulations Act 2009.]

(q) Section 31 and the permitted periods of accumulation. It seems that accumulation under the TA 1925, s 31 during a minority is always valid. For wills made on or after 6 April 2010 this is because PAA 2009 provides that there are no statutory restrictions on accumulation in respect of non-charitable trusts: see PAA 2009, ss 13, 15(1)(a) (Part G, paras **[246.187]**, **[246.189]**, and see **[95.0]**). For wills made before 6 April 2010 when there are such restrictions, this is because irrespective of whether a permitted accumulation period is available under the LPA 1925, s 164 (Part G, para **[246.56]**) or the PAA 1964, s 13 (Part G, para **[246.86]**) the accumulation is directed by statute. Section 165 of the LPA 1925 (Part G, para **[246.57]**) provides (in relation to wills made before 6 April 2010) that where accumulations of surplus income are made during a minority under any statutory power (or under the general law), the period for which such accumulations are permitted to be made is not to be taken into account in determining the periods for which accumulations are permitted to be made by the LPA 1925, s 164 (which is treated by the PAA 1964, s 13 as including those added by that section), and accordingly an express trust for accumulation in a will made before 6 April 2010 for any other permitted period will not be invalidated by reason of accumulations also having been made during a minority under a statutory power (or the general law). It is not easy to work out exactly what the LPA 1925, s 165 is providing, and there is very little authority on it. The reference to a statutory power is a reference to the provisions for accumulation under the TA 1925, s 31; although the latter are strictly speaking a *trust* to accumulate, they are ancillary to the statutory power of maintenance (see *Re Turner's Will Trusts, District Bank Ltd v Turner* [1937] Ch 15).

[218.72]

[Updated for the Perpetuities and Accumulations Act 2009.]

For wills made before 6 April 2010, only one of the permitted periods of accumulation under the LPA 1925, s 164 is available in relation to any particular disposition, and it is a matter of construction of the instrument making the disposition to determine which period has seemingly been chosen: see eg *Jagger v Jagger* (1883) 25 Ch D 729; *Re Watt's Will Trusts, Watt v Watt* [1936] 2 All ER 1555, 1562, and *Re Ransome* [1957] Ch 348,

361. A possible interpretation is therefore that the LPA 1925, s 165 means no more than that a will or other disposition made before 6 April 2010 is not deprived of choice of accumulation period by providing trusts to which accumulation under the TA 1925, s 31 applies; for example, providing trusts to which s 31 applies does not amount to a selection of the duration of minorities of persons who would be entitled to the income if of full age (the period permitted by the LPA 1925, s 164(1)(d): Part G, para **[246.42]**), and the 21-year accumulation period could still be used.

[218.73]

[Updated for the Perpetuities and Accumulations Act 2009.]

There is a more radical interpretation of the LPA 1925, s 165, which is that for a will made before 6 April 2010 it permits accumulation under the TA 1925, s 31 cumulatively with accumulation under the relevant period under s 164. This argument is really only of interest in relation to the 21-year period under s 165(1)(b) (or the PAA 1964, s 13(1)(a)); it would mean that the accumulation period was suspended during a period of accumulation under the TA 1925, s 31, but started again where it left off once the accumulation under s 31 had finished. If this was correct it would be possible for accumulation for a beneficiary to continue until he reached the age of 25 outside the period of 21 years from the testator's death, unless and until there had been accumulation other than under the TA 1925, s 31 for a total of 21 years, and this was the interpretation apparently accepted by Astbury J in *Re Maber* [1928] Ch 88 at 93, although it was not necessary for his decision in that case. This seems too good to be true, and it would have the inconvenient consequence that the 21-year period would apply differently to different parts of the same trust fund where there was a trust for eg the children of a named person. It is, however, an interpretation which cannot be completely ruled out on the wording of the LPA 1925, ss 164 and 165, and if right would have the advantage of avoiding the often adverse consequences of provisions which go beyond the permitted accumulation periods (see Vol 1, paras **[95.8]** and **[95.13]**). For wills made on or after 6 April 2010 it is not an issue because PAA 2009 provides that there are no statutory restrictions on accumulation in respect of non-charitable trusts: see PAA 2009, ss 13, 15(1)(a) (Part G, para **[246.187]**, **[246.189]**, and see **[95.0]**).

[218.74]

[Updated for the Perpetuities and Accumulations Act 2009.]

(r) Extended accumulation and maintenance provisions. The accumulation and maintenance provisions of the TA 1925, s 31, as amended by the FLRA 1969 (Part G, para **[246.29]**), only apply during the minority of a beneficiary, that is, until the age of 18. Thus if there is a gift of capital to members of a class contingently on attaining 25 (for example as in an age 18-to-25 trust, see para **[200.109]** above), and s 31 applies, each member of the class will be entitled to be paid the income of his presumptive share on attaining the age of 18, and will have an interest in possession in his presumptive share from that time. Where an age 18-to-25 trust is proposed, it may be desired to extend accumulation and maintenance provisions so as to continue beyond 18, to 25. This may be desirable for personal considerations (it is often felt that 18 is too early an age to start receiving a sometimes substantial income), but it may also be desirable to avoid the children having immediate post-death interests (see para **[200.98]** above) from the testator's death, which they would do if they were over 18 at his death (and under 25) and TA 1925, s 31 applied to give them interests in possession from his death. This is because although the income condition of IHTA 1984, s 71D(6)(c) (ie. that pending a beneficiary's attainment of an absolute interest, the beneficiary must be entitled to all the income arising from the settled property, or no income may be applied for the benefit of any other person) may be satisfied where the beneficiary has an interest in possession, if the beneficiary has an interest in possession immediately from the testator's death (or it arises within two years of death, see para **[200.136]**) it will be an immediate post-death interest, which will prevent the underlying trust property being subject to an age 18-to-25 trust, see IHTA 1984, s 71D(5)(c)(ii). Whereas an immediate post-death interest would have the advantage that no inheritance tax would be payable when the beneficiary attained an absolute vested interest at (or under) 25 (see IHTA 1984, s 53(2)), it would have the disadvantage that capital gains tax hold-over relief would not be available in respect of any gain on the trustees' deemed disposal under TCGA 1992, s 71. Conversely, if the property was subject to an age 18-to-25 trust, then there would be an occasion of inheritance tax exit charge when the beneficiary attained an absolute vested interest at (or under) 25 (see IHTA 1984, s 71E(1)(a)), but capital gains tax holdover relief would be available under TCGA 1992, s 260(2)(a). Since any inheritance tax exit charge may be nil or small, an age 18-to-25 trust could therefore have an advantage over an immediate post-death interest.

[218.75]

[Updated for the Perpetuities and Accumulations Act 2009.]

If extended accumulation and maintenance provisions were included in a will made before 6 April 2010, one of the accumulation periods permitted by the LPA 1925, s 164 would have had to have been used. The period of 21 years from the death of the testator was normally the most appropriate: see paras **[218.71]**–**[218.73]** for its relationship with accumulation under TA 1925, s 31. If it was certain that all the beneficiaries would be over the age of 4 at the testator's death, the 21-year accumulation period would continue until all had attained 25 and accumulation and maintenance provisions could continue to that age. If the class was to consist only of persons living at the testator's death, accumulation and maintenance provisions could be made to continue until the age of 21.

[218.76]

[Updated for the Perpetuities and Accumulations Act 2009.]

For wills made on or after 6 April 2010, PAA 2009 provides that there are no statutory restrictions on accumulation in respect of non-charitable trusts: see PAA 2009, ss 13, 15(1)(a) (Part G, paras **[246.187]**, **[246.189]**, and see **[95.0]**). Therefore accumulation can be authorised for whatever period is appropriate, eg. if an age 18-to-25 trust is intended, until each child of the testator attains 25. See Form B18.12 at para **[218.80]**.

[218.80]

[Updated for the Perpetuities and Accumulations Act 2009.]

Form B18.12: Statutory maintenance and accumulation to continue to the age of twenty-five[1]

Section 31 of the Trustee Act 1925 shall apply to the foregoing trust provided that in relation to the presumptive share of any of [*beneficiaries*] the said section 31 shall have effect as if the age of majority were the age of twenty five years (the expressions 'infant' 'infancy' and 'minority' therein being construed accordingly) and as if there were substituted the words 'twenty five years' for the words 'eighteen years' wherever the same occur in the said section 31.

1 See paras **[218.74]–[218.78]**. This form may be used in a will made on or after 6 April 2010 since PAA 2009 provides there are no statutory restrictions on accumulation in respect of non-charitable trusts contained in a such a will: see the PAA 2009, ss 13, 15(1)(a) (Part G, paras **[246.187]**, **[246.189]**, and see **[95.0]**). The idea behind this clause is to allow maintenance and accumulation to continue until a beneficiary attains 25. This Form should be compatible with age 18-to-25 trusts within IHTA 1984, s 71D (see para **[200.109]** above).

[218.81]

[Updated for the Perpetuities and Accumulations Act 2009.]

Form B18.13: Statutory maintenance and accumulation to continue until capital vests[1]

Section 31 of the Trustee Act 1925 shall apply to the foregoing trusts Provided that in relation to the presumptive share of any beneficiary the said section 31 shall have effect as if the age of majority were the age at which such beneficiary shall become absolutely entitled to such presumptive share under the foregoing trusts (the expressions 'infant' 'infancy' and 'minority' therein being construed accordingly) and as if there were substituted such age for the words 'eighteen years' wherever the same occur in the said section 31 (as amended as aforesaid).

1 See paras **[218.74]–[218.78]**. This form may be used in a will made on or after 6 April 2010 since PAA 2009 provides there are no statutory restrictions on accumulation in respect of non-charitable trusts contained in a such a will: see the PAA 2009, ss 13, 15(1)(a) (Part G, paras **[246.187]**, **[246.189]**, and see **[95.0]**). The idea behind this clause is to allow maintenance and accumulation to continue until a beneficiary becomes absolutely entitled to capital, whenever that may be.

[218.84]

[Updated for the Perpetuities and Accumulations Act 2009.]

Form B18.16: Maintenance of a class; applicable to shares in income as well as in capital[1]

With regard to maintenance I direct as follows:

(1) Subject to any prior interests in the income hereinafter mentioned my trustees shall receive such part of the income arising from [my residuary estate] as is for the time being attributable to the shares or presumptive or prospective shares in my residuary estate or in the income thereof of such of [my children] [the children of the said [*name*]] as for the time being are under the age of [eighteen]

[twenty-one] years and they may pay or apply the whole or so much thereof as they in their discretion think fit for or towards the maintenance education or benefit of such children for the time being under the said age of [eighteen] [twenty-one] years as a class and if my trustees think fit unequally as between such children and shall not be bound to consider whether or not there is any other income applicable for the same purposes or whether or not there is any person bound by law to provide for the maintenance or education of such children or any of them.

(2) My trustees may pay the whole or any part of the said income to the parent or guardian or guardians of any of such children or to any such children if of the age of sixteen years or more without seeing to the application thereof and shall accumulate the surplus (if any) of the said income in each year by investing the same and the resulting income thereof in manner hereby authorised and subject to sub-clause (3) below my trustees may at any time apply such accumulations as if the same were income of the current year.

(3) When and so often as any child of [mine] [the said [*name*]] attains the age of [eighteen] [twenty-one] years a share in the then existing accumulations corresponding to the share of my residuary estate to which or to the income of which such child shall then be entitled shall be transferred to the capital of such last-mentioned share and be dealt with accordingly and so that if any share in which or in the income of which any of the said children shall for the time being have a vested interest shall be increased by any event which may happen a share in the accumulations which exist at the date of such event proportionate to the increase in such share shall be transferred to the capital of such share and be dealt with accordingly.[2]

1 For consideration of this type of provision which can be used where a testator has left property to a class of beneficiaries in specified shares and whether it is compatible with IHTA 1984, s 71A or s 71D see paras **[218.69]** and **[218.70]**. For wills made before 6 April 2010, the age of twenty-one should only have been chosen as the relevant age if all the children in question would have been in existence by the time of the testator's death: see further n 2 to Form B18.17 at para **[218.85]**. For wills made on or after 6 April 2010 however, PAA 2009 provides that there are no statutory restrictions on accumulation in respect of non-charitable trusts so that the age of twenty-one may be chosen in such a will: see the PAA 2009, ss 13, 15(1)(a) (Part G, paras **[246.187]**, **[246.189]**, and see **[95.0]**).

2 Paragraph (3) contemplates a division and transfer of the accumulations from time to time as and when any child becomes absolutely entitled.

Under the usual form of maintenance clause (including the statutory clause: TA 1925, s 31 (Part G, para **[246.29]**)) trustees ought to keep the accumulated income of each child's share distinct.

[218.85]

[Updated for the Perpetuities and Accumulations Act 2009.]

Form B18.17: Another clause providing for maintenance out of a common fund[1]

With regard to maintenance I direct as follows:

(1) Subject to any prior interests in the income hereinafter mentioned my trustees shall receive the income arising from my residuary estate or from so much thereof as shall not for the time being have become

subject to an absolute interest or an interest in possession of any child[2] [of mine] [of the said [*name*]] under the trusts hereinbefore contained and may pay or apply such income or so much thereof as my trustees shall think fit for the maintenance education or benefit of such [of my children] [children of the said [*name*]] as shall for the time being be under the age of [eighteen] [twenty-one] years or any one or more exclusively of the others or other of such children in such proportions at such time and in such manner in all respects as my trustees shall in their sole discretion think proper with liberty to my trustees to pay the whole or any part of the said income to the guardian or guardians of any of the said children for the purposes aforesaid without seeing to the application thereof; and

(2) My trustees shall invest the surplus (if any) of the said income in investments of the nature hereby authorised and shall accumulate the same at compound interest by investing the resulting income thereof as an accretion thereto and shall hold such accumulations as accretions to the capital of the whole part or parts of my residuary estate from which they arose and as one fund therewith for all purposes.[3]

1 For consideration of this type of clause in relation to IHTA 1984, s 71A and 71D, see paras **[218.69]** and **[218.70]**.

2 For a will made before 6 April 2010, if the class would not have closed at the death, e g because the gift was to the children of a person who may still be living at the testator's death, the age contingency specified throughout the clause should have been 18 not 21. Otherwise the accumulation provision in sub-cl (2) may be invalid: see the LPA 1925, s 164(1)(d) (Part G, para **[246.56]**) restricting the power to accumulate to the minority (which ends at 18) of any beneficiary otherwise entitled to income. For wills made on or after 6 April 2010 however PAA 2009 provides that there are no statutory restrictions on accumulation in respect of non-charitable trusts so that the age of 21 may be chosen in such a will: see the PAA 2009, ss 13, 15(1)(a) (Part G, paras **[246.187]**, **[246.189]**, and see **[95.0]**).

3 For fear of possible inheritance tax difficulties as regards the application of IHTA 1984, s 71A and 71Dff, there is no power to apply accumulations as income of the current year. We recommend that a power of advancement over the whole of a presumptive share is added to make up for this.

[218.86]

[Updated for the Perpetuities and Accumulations Act 2009.]

Form B18.18: Maintenance clause; simple express trusts[1]

(1) Subject and without prejudice to any prior interest or charge affecting the income hereinafter mentioned, I empower my trustees during the minority [or minority and spinsterhood as the case may be] of any child [of mine] [*or* grandchild of mine] [*or* of the said [*name*]] to apply the whole or such part as my trustees shall think fit of the income of the expectant or presumptive share[2] of such child [*or* grandchild] for or towards his or her maintenance education or benefit with power to pay the same to the parent or to the guardian or guardians of such child [*or* grandchild] for the purposes aforesaid without seeing to the application thereof.[3]

(2) My trustees may exercise the power aforesaid whether or not there is any other fund or income available for any of the aforesaid purposes and whether or not there is any person bound by law to provide for such maintenance or education.

(3) The surplus income shall be accumulated by investing the same and the resulting income thereof in any investments of the kind hereby authorised and such accumulations shall be added to the property or to the share therein from which the same was derived and shall devolve therewith so as to follow the destination of such property or share but my trustees shall be entitled at any time to apply any part of such accumulations for any of the purposes aforesaid as if the same were income arising in the then current year.

1 This form may be useful where the will may have to be acted on abroad, or where it is desired to express an ordinary maintenance clause in a will rather than to let the statutory clause apply. Further, it is a form which can be readily adapted to provide express accumulation and maintenance trusts to a higher age than 18. If, for example, it is desired to have these to the age of 21 for the testator's children, substitute for the words 'during the minority … of any child of mine' the words 'while any child of mine has not attained the age of 21 years'. This Form would be compatible with trusts for bereaved minors within IHTA 1984, s 71A (see para **[200.108]** above) or age 18-to-25 trusts within IHTA 1984, s 71D (see para **[200.109]** above).

It excludes the necessity of applying only a portion of the income where the trustees have notice of other available income (TA 1925, s 31: Part G, para **[246.29]**). In the Canadian case of *Re Larsen's Will* (1968) 66 WWR 358 a clause in similar terms was held wide enough to authorise the purchase by the trustees of an annuity for a beneficiary in need.

2 Where a woman was entitled to a share on birth of issue and, being over 50 years of age, had no children, the court refused to hold that she was past childbearing, and she was, therefore, entitled to an expectant or presumptive share and to maintenance under an express maintenance clause: *Re Allen* [1953] ALR 959, St R Qd 95.

3 Giving a person power to maintain the minor out of income will not make the gift to the minor vested, if it is otherwise contingent: *Re Rogers, Lloyds Bank Ltd v Lory* [1944] Ch 297, [1944] 2 All ER 1.

ADVANCEMENT

[218.89]

[Updated for FA 2013, Sch 44.]

(b) Extent of power. The amount which may be raised and applied is not to exceed one-half of the presumptive or vested share or interest of the person to be advanced; the amount advanced is to be brought into account if the person is or becomes absolutely entitled to a share in the property; but the advancement may be made notwithstanding that his interest is liable to be defeated by the exercise of a power of appointment, or to be diminished by an increase of the class to which he belongs. It will not therefore be necessary to make an absolute appointment to a person in order that he may be advanced; and again, if the class be merely the children of A, and A's wife dies, the whole class can be advanced up to the limit, notwithstanding that A might marry again and have a second family. We recommend that the power is always made exercisable over the whole of a presumptive share (see eg Form B18.20 at para **[218.105]**). An extended power of advancement exercisable over the whole of a beneficiary's presumptive share, is compatible with trusts for bereaved minors within IHTA 1984, s 71A (see para **[200.108]** above) and age 18-to-25 trusts within IHTA 1984, s 71D (see para **[200.109]** above), and for tax year 2013–14 and subsequent years, vulnerable person trusts within FA 2005, ss 25–33 (FA 2005, s 35(4)(b)–(f) as substituted by FA 2013, Sch 44, para 16(3) and see para **[217.4]**).

Provisions for failure of primary trusts

SUBSTITUTION CLAUSES

[219.18]

[Updated for the Perpetuities and Accumulations Act 2009.]

Form B19.5: Substitution clause limited to children of deceased children[1]

Provided that if any of my said children is already dead or shall predecease me or shall die after my death without attaining the age of [eighteen] [twenty-one] [thirty] years leaving a child or children who shall attain the age of [eighteen] [twenty-one] years or marry thereunder such child or children shall take by substitution and if more than one in equal shares the share of my residuary estate [the trust fund] which his her or their parent would have taken if he or she had survived me and attained a vested interest.[2]

1 As to the construction of children and issue see Vol 1, Chs 71 to 76.
2 If this form was used for a will made before 6 April 2010, all the interests would necessarily vest within the common law perpetuity period of a life or lives in being plus twenty-one years. For wills made on or after 6 April 2010, a mandatory perpetuity period of 125 years applies, see the PAA 2009, ss 5(1), 15(1)(a) (Part G, paras **[246.179]**, **[246.189]**, and see para **[94.6]**), within which these interests would also necessarily vest.

[219.19]

[Updated for the Perpetuities and Accumulations Act 2009.]

Form B19.6: Trust for testator's children at twenty-five with substitution of issue of a child who predeceases the testator and further substitution of children on death after the testator's death without attaining a vested interest[1, 2]

(1) My trustees shall hold [my residuary estate] in trust for such of my children as shall be living at my death and attain the age of [25] years if more than one in equal shares.

(2) Provided that if any of my children is already dead or predeceases me the share of [my residuary estate] to which such child would be entitled if he or she survived me and attained a vested interest shall be held in trust for such of his or her children and remoter issue (if any) as shall be living at my death and attain the age of [21] years in equal shares per stirpes and so that no issue shall take whose parent is living at my death and capable of taking.

(3) Provided further that if any child of mine or any remoter issue of mine presumptively entitled under the foregoing proviso is living at or after my death but dies without attaining a vested interest under the foregoing

trusts the share of [my residuary estate] to which such child or issue of mine would be entitled if he or she lived to attain such a vested interest shall be held in trust for such of his children (if any) as attain the age of 21 years or marry under that age if more than one in equal shares.[3]

1 As to the construction of children and issue see Vol 1, Chs 71 to 76.

2 The initial trusts of Clause (1) for the testator's children should qualify as age 18-to-25 trusts within IHTA 1984, s 71D if the age of vesting is 25 (see para **[200.109]** above), although if the children's trust came into possession immediately following the testator's death, and is not postponed to any other interest, and any child is over the age of 18 but under the specified age, and entitled to an interest possession by virtue of TA 1925, s 31(1)(ii) (see para **[246.29]**), he or she would have an immediate post-death interest. If and when the trusts of Clauses (2) or (3) come into effect, the property subject to them would fall within the inheritance tax charging regime for relevant property (see the Note to para **[200.92]** above).

3 If this form was used for a will made before 6 April 2010, all the interests would necessarily vest within the common law perpetuity period of a life or lives in being plus twenty-one years. For wills made on or after 6 April 2010, a mandatory perpetuity period of 125 years applies, see the PAA 2009, ss 5(1), 15(1)(a) (Part G, paras **[246.179]**, **[246.189]**, and see para **[94.6]**), within which these interests would also necessarily vest.

[219.28]

[Updated for the Perpetuities and Accumulations Act 2009.]

Form B19.15: General form of gift over on failure of the trusts of residue[1]

If [any share or shares of] my residuary estate shall not vest absolutely in some person or persons under the preceding trusts, then [such undisposed of share or shares of] my residuary estate shall (subject to the trusts powers and provisions hereby or by statute vested in my trustees in respect of the income or capital thereof and to every exercise of the same by my trustees) be held by my trustees [for such person or persons as *some previous beneficiary*] shall by will or codicil appoint and in default of such appointment] in trust for my brothers and sisters living at my death and the children of any then deceased brother or sister of mine who attain the age of [eighteen] [twenty-one] years or marry thereunder if more than one in equal shares as tenants in common but so that the children of any such deceased brother or sister shall take between them as tenants in common only the share their parent would have taken had he or she survived me.[2]

1 This form assumes that the residue is given to the testator's immediate family. It may readily be adapted to cases where the testator has no brothers or sisters and wishes to benefit more remote relatives or strangers.

As to the construction of words denoting a blood relationship see Vol 1, paras **[71.1]**–**[71.5]**.

2 If this form was used for a will made before 6 April 2010, all the interests would necessarily vest within the common law perpetuity period of a life or lives in being plus twenty-one years. For wills made on or after 6 April 2010, a mandatory perpetuity period of 125 years applies, see the PAA 2009, ss 5(1), 15(1)(a) (Part G, paras **[246.179]**, **[246.189]**, and see para **[94.6]**), within which these interests would also necessarily vest.

B20

Administrative powers and provisions

GENERAL PRELIMINARY NOTE

[220.8]

[Updated for FA 2013, Sch 44.]

In the case of trusts intended to fall within the Inheritance Tax Act 1984 (IHTA 1984), s 71A or 71D, ie. trusts for bereaved minors and age 18-to-25 trusts (see paras **[200.108]–[200.109]** above) the requirements are more stringent and even more care must be taken to see that there are no administrative powers which prevent the conditions for such trusts from applying. It will be appreciated that a power to pay expenses not properly attributable to capital (or not properly attributable to the settled property in question), whether or not it is actually exercised, could prevent the beneficiaries becoming entitled to that capital on or before attaining either 18 or 25 (as the case may be)—ie it could prevent the trusts from satisfying s 71A(3)(a) or s 71D(6)(a). Further, the same would be the consequence of the existence of a power to permit enjoyment in kind of trust assets which was capable of being exercised in favour of persons other than the beneficiaries. Similarly, a power that permitted the income to be applied in some way other than to or for the benefit of the beneficiaries or accumulation would prejudice the application of s 71A(3)(c) or 71D(6)(c), except in cases of trusts arising under wills of testators who die on or after 8 April 2013, where such applications (together with similar applications of capital) do not exceed an annual limit which is currently set at the lower of £3,000 and 3 per cent of the maximum value of the settled property during the tax year in question (IHTA 1984, s 71A(4)(za), (4B)–(4E), inserted by FA 2013, Sch 44, para 2(3), (4)).

PRELIMINARY NOTE ON INVESTMENT POWERS

Investment powers

[220.40]

[Updated for the Financial Services and Markets Act 2000.]

Form B20.1: Power of investment confined to fixed interest investments quoted shares and legal estates in land[1]

Trust moneys may be invested in any of the following (and the statutory general power of investment and power to acquire land shall not apply)—

(a) the public stocks funds or government securities of the United Kingdom of Great Britain and Northern Ireland or any member state of the British Commonwealth or any member state of the European Union or any province or state having a separate local legislature and forming part of any of the foregoing;
(b) bonds stocks debentures or other securities of any municipal or local body or authority in the British Commonwealth or the European Union;
(c) the units of any authorised unit trust scheme for the time being authorised under the Financial Services and Markets Act 2000;
(d) the shares or deposits of any building society within the meaning of the Building Societies Act 1986 registered in the United Kingdom;
(e) in any investments of whatsoever nature which at the date of purchase are or on allotment will be listed on the Stock Exchange or on any of the stock exchanges of New York, Montreal, Paris, Frankfurt, Amsterdam, Milan, Madrid, Zurich, Tokyo, Hong Kong or Johannesburg;
(f) in the acquisition of freehold and leasehold legal estates (including legal mortgages or charges) in land situate in the United Kingdom including land for occupation by a beneficiary [pursuant to the power hereinafter contained][2] provided that—
    (i) leasehold estates in land shall be purchased only if at the date of the purchase the unexpired term exceeds fifty years,
    (ii) in relation to land in Scotland what may be acquired under the foregoing power is the estate or interest of the proprietor of the dominum utile or, in the case of land not held on feudal tenure, the estate or interest of the owner, or (subject to proviso (a) above) a tenancy, and
    (iii) 'land' includes buildings and rights over land.[3]

1 This is narrower than the statutory powers of investment (for which see paras **[220.12]** and **[220.17]**), for the cautious testator. It is intended to cover the main types of fixed interest investment, quoted shares, and legal estates in land other than leases of 50 years or less unexpired. In practice these are probably all that prudent trustees with a fund of cash to invest, maintaining a balance of income and capital growth, would want to invest in, but it could turn out to be unduly restrictive. Where a testator is inclined towards something of this sort, it might be better to put it as an expression of wishes rather than a restriction on the trustees' powers. For the power to restrict or exclude the statutory powers of investment see the TrA 2000, ss 6(1) and 9 (Part G, paras **[246.138]** and **[246.141]**). For the non-excludable requirements of the TrA 2000, ss 4 and 5 as to having regard to the standard investment criteria and obtaining advice see paras **[220.13]** and **[220.14]**. The power permits investment in mortgages secured on UK land, whereas the statutory powers under the TrA 2000, s 3 (see para **[220.16]**) permit investment in mortgages secured on land anywhere.

2 The cautious draftsman will include this restriction for IHT reasons: see para **[220.4]** ff and the Note in B18 at paras **[218.67]** and **[218.68]**. For a power to permit beneficiaries to occupy or enjoy in kind trust assets, see Form B18.17 at para **[218.83]**.

3 This is based on the TrA 2000, s 8 (see para **[220.17]** and Part G, para **[246.140]**), but subject to the restriction (deriving from the more traditional investment clauses) that leasehold land with 50 or less years to run should not be acquired.

[220.48]

[Updated for the Perpetuities and Accumulations Act 2009.]

Form B20.9: Clause as to bonus shares[1]

If my trustees shall by virtue of any shareholding in any company for the time being held by my trustees upon the trusts hereof and listed on a stock exchange become entitled to any shares or stocks or securities distributed as dividend such that in the opinion of my trustees the capital value of the shares in respect of which the dividend is distributed is diminished by more than 10 per cent (comparing with their listed value immediately before and immediately after they became listed ex dividend but leaving out of account so far as possible any other factors influencing value other than the holdings becoming ex dividend) my trustees may apportion such whole or part of the said bonus shares stocks or securities to capital as in their opinion shall be just and reasonable.

1 For clauses negativing rules of apportionment generally, see Forms B14.24 to B14.29 at paras **[214.39]–[214.46]**. This clause is intended to deal with a case where a substantial dividend based on accumulated profits or capital profits of the company over a long period is declared in the form of distribution of shares in a subsidiary in order to achieve a demerger or a reduction in capital. The law seems to be that if it is a direct demerger the shares distributed will be income, but if it is an indirect one they are capital: see *Sinclair v Lee* [1993] Ch 497, sub nom *Re Lee, Sinclair v Lee* [1993] 3 All ER 926. Thus what is in substance a capital split or repayment is treated under the general law in some situations as a distribution which constitutes income, and where this involves a substantial diminution of the capital value of the original holding this is unfair on the capital beneficiaries and a windfall to the income beneficiaries. There are objections to using this clause, however. First, its effects for IHT purposes in relation to fixed interest trusts or bereaved minor or age 18-to-25 trusts are unclear and such effects may be adverse–treating what would otherwise be income as capital might affect the intended IHT status of the trusts (but *Miller v IRC* [1987] STC 108, for which see n 1 to para **[220.61]** gives some support to the view that the intended IHT status would not be prejudiced). Secondly, for wills made before 6 April 2010, a clause in this form may involve an unlawful direction to accumulate after the expiration of the relevant accumulation period. However, for wills made on or after 6 April 2010, there are no statutory restrictions on accumulation: see the PAA 2009, ss 13, 15(1)(a) (Part G, paras **[246.187]**, **[246.189]**) and see para **[95.0]**.

[220.61]

[Updated for the Perpetuities and Accumulations Act 2009.]

Form B20.12: Treatment of mining rent and royalties and proceeds of timber[1]

(1) All the rent or royalties from any mining lease or licence of land held by my trustees shall be treated as income and none shall be apportioned to capital.[2]

(2) The net proceeds of sale of any timber which is cut and sold from any land held by my trustees shall be treated wholly as income.[3]

1 This form makes clear that mineral rents and royalties and the proceeds of sale of timber are to be treated wholly as income. Before 1 January 1997, the SLA 1925, ss 47 (mineral rents) and 66 (timber), which apportion these between capital and income, applied to land held on trust for sale by virtue of the LPA 1925, s 28(2) (subject to express provision in the trust instrument). The LPA 1925, s 28(2) was repealed by the TLATA 1996, and these provisions of the SLA 1925 do not apply to trusts of land within the meaning of the TLATA 1996 (see Part A, para **[200.51]** for this term). It is uncertain whether the non-application of these provisions means that the former rule of the general law that the whole of mineral rents and proceeds of timber are capital (see nn 2 and 3) are revived, or

whether the wide power of management of land in the TLATA 1996, s 6(1) (see para **[220.49]**) has the effect that mineral rents and royalties and the sale proceeds of timber are income, or at any rate that it is within the trustees' powers to treat them as such. In this state of uncertainty, where trust property may include mining leases or saleable timber it will save argument to include provision of this kind. The other possible ways of dealing with the problem are to give the trustees a discretion to apportion some to capital, or to provide that a fixed proportion is apportioned to capital. Both these options risk treating what is really income as capital, and prejudicing the existence of an interest in possession (and in particular an immediate post-death interest, see para **[200.198]** above) for IHT purposes or the application of the IHTA 1984, s 71A (trusts for bereaved minors, see para **[200.120]** above) or s 71D (age 18-to-25 trusts, see para **[200.121]** above), but a discretionary power would probably not have this effect, although it would have the problem that the trustees would have very little guidance as to how to exercise it. In *Miller v IRC* [1987] STC 108 it was held by the Court of Session that a power of the trustees to set aside income for meeting depreciation of the capital value of trust assets, or for any other reason the trustees thought advisable or necessary, was an administrative power which did not prevent the liferentrix from having an interest in possession for IHT purposes. For wills made before 6 April 2010, when statutory restrictions on accumulation apply in respect of non-charitable trusts, there is an express exception from the rules against excessive accumulations for the accumulation of the proceeds of timber or wood (LPA 1925, s 164(2)(iii): Part G, para **[246.44]**), but no similar provision for mineral rents, so treating the latter as capital when they were really income might be a breach of the rules against accumulations. For wills made on or after 6 April 2010 though, there are no statutory restrictions on accumulation: see the PAA 2009, ss 13, 15(1)(a) (Part G, paras **[246.187]**, **[246.189]**) and see para **[95.0]**.

2 Under the general law, before statutory intervention originally by the Settled Land Act 1882, mineral rents counted as capital if the tenant for life was impeachable for waste: *Re Ridge, Hellard v Moody* (1885) 31 Ch D 504 at 508. Under the SLA 1925, s 47 if the tenant for life is impeachable for waste, three-quarters of the rents are capitalised and he is entitled to a quarter, and if he if he is not so impeachable, one-quarter is capital. This could be varied by express provision, and it has been common to exclude this provision in settled land settlements and provide that the entire rents are income. Without express provision, someone with a life interest in the proceeds of sale under a trust for sale had the same rights to income as a tenant for life impeachable for waste (*Re Ridge, Hellard v Moody*), so that the capitalisation was of three-quarters of the mineral rents.

3 Under the general law, before statutory intervention originally by the Settled Land Act 1882, the proceeds of sale of timber counted as capital if the tenant for life was impeachable for waste: *Honeywood v Honeywood* (1874) LR 18 Eq 306. Under the SLA 1925, s 66 if the tenant for life is impeachable for waste three-quarters of the net proceeds of timber are capitalised. 'Timber' in this context is oak, ash and elm of the age of 20 years or more but not so old as not to have useable timber (*Honeywood v Honeywood*), but this can be varied by local custom. As mentioned in n 1, the SLA 1925, s 66 does not apply to trusts of land within the meaning of the TLATA 1996, and there is uncertainty as to whether or not proceeds of timber should be capitalised in the absence of express provision.

B21

Trustees and executors

CONDUCT OF TRUSTEESHIP

[221.29]

[Updated in footnote for Charities Act 2011.]

Form B21.25: Direction that opinion of majority of trustees is to prevail[1]

I declare that should any difference of opinion at any time exist between the trustees for the time being of this my will in relation to the commission or omission of any act or otherwise howsoever in the execution of the trusts of this my will or any codicil hereto the opinion of the majority of such trustees shall prevail and shall do so even if any one or more of such trustees may be personally interested or concerned in the matter in dispute or question provided that at least one trustee in the majority has no such personal interest.

1 Trustees other than trustees of a charity cannot without this special provision act by a majority: *Blacket v Blizard* (1829) 9 B & C 851; *Luke v South Kensington Hotel Co* (1879) 11 Ch D 121; *Re Roth, Goldberger v Roth* (1896) 74 LT 50; *Astbury v Astbury* [1898] 2 Ch 111. As to charity trustees, see *Re Whiteley, Bishop of London v Whiteley* [1910] 1 Ch 600; and the Charities Act 2011, s 333 re-enacting Charities Act 1993, s 82.

[221.34]

[Updated for Human Fertilisation and Embryology Act 2008.]

Form B21.30: Power to distribute on assumption that no further children

My trustees shall have power at their absolute discretion to distribute income or capital of my estate or of any fund deriving from it on the assumption that a woman who has attained the age of 55 years will have no further children and if they exercise this power my trustees shall not be liable for the assumption turning out to be incorrect (without prejudice to any beneficiary's right to trace trust assets against any other beneficiary).[1]

1 Existing authority that trustees can distribute on the assumption that a woman of 55 is past the age of childbearing (see Vol 1, paras **[66.3]** and **[216.29]**) can no longer be relied on, because advances in medical science mean that a woman who has passed the menopause could still have a child by means of in vitro fertilisation using donated eggs, and because if this were to happen she would be treated as the mother of the child for all purposes, including gifts by will, by virtue of the HFEA 1990, ss 27 and 29 (Part G, paras **[245.85]** and **[245.87]**) or, in relation to treatment on or after 6 April 2009, HFEA 2008, ss 33–53 (Part G, paras **[245.112]** ff.) It is still possible to apply to the court for liberty to distribute on the basis of evidence that a particular person having another child is impossible or very unlikely (see *Re Levy Estate Trust* [2000] CLY, para 5263 and *Re Cassidy* [1979] VR 369). There is a

statutory presumption that a woman over 55 will not adopt a child: see the AA 1976, s 42(5) (Part G, para **[245.60]**). Provision as in this clause is not usually needed if the beneficial trusts, powers and provisions themselves confer powers, such as a wide power of appointment or powers of advancement over the whole of a presumptive share, which would enable a trust fund to be appointed absolutely or distributed absolutely without waiting to see if more members of a class are born.

PART C

Complete wills

Wills for use in emergency

[223.10]

[Updated in text and footnote 3 for Perpetuities and Accumulations Act 2009.]

Form C1.9: Gift of estate on discretionary trusts for family[1]

I [*name*] of [*address*] revoke all former testamentary dispositions and declare this to be my last will.

1. I appoint [*name*] of [*address*] and [*name*] of [*address*] (hereinafter called 'my trustees' which expression shall include the trustees for the time being of this will) to be the executors and trustees of this will.

2. Subject to the payment thereout of my debts and my funeral and testamentary expenses my trustees shall hold all my estate both real and personal upon the trusts and with and subject to the powers and provisions hereinafter declared and contained.

3. (1) In this clause—

(a) 'the beneficiaries' means and includes
- (i) my [wife/husband/civil partner] [*name*]
- (ii) my children and remoter issue
- (iii) the spouse civil partner widow widower or surviving civil partner of any of my children and remoter issue;[2]

(b) 'the trust period' means the period of 125 years immediately following my death.[3]

(2) My trustees shall have the following powers exercisable at any time and from time to time during the trust period:

(a) Power by deed or deeds to appoint that they shall hold the whole or any part or parts of my estate upon trust for all or such one or more of the discretionary beneficiaries and if more than one in such shares and with such trusts and powers (including trusts and powers conferring a discretion as to the disposition of capital or income) and provisions (including provisions for the accumulation of income during any period or periods permitted by law) as my trustees think fit.[4]

(b) Power to pay or apply the whole or any part or parts of my estate to or for the advancement support or benefit of all or any one or more of the discretionary beneficiaries in such manner as my trustees think fit.[5]

(3) Subject to any exercise of the foregoing powers my trustees shall hold my estate during the trust period upon trust to pay or apply the income thereof to or for the maintenance education support or benefit of all or any

one or more of the discretionary beneficiaries for the time being living and if more than one in such shares and generally in such manner as my trustees shall think fit and shall hold the capital of my estate at the expiration of the trust period upon trust for such of my children and remoter issue then living and if more than one in equal shares per stirpes each child of mine being treated as a head of stock.

(4) The power to appoint capital conferred by subclause (2) hereof shall be exercisable whether or not a grant of administration has been obtained and whether or not the administration of my estate is complete.[6]

(5) The powers to appoint and apply capital and the discretion as to the distribution of income conferred by subclauses (2) and (3) hereof shall be exercisable notwithstanding that any of my trustees has a personal interest in such exercise provided that there are not fewer than two trustees and that at least one of them has no such personal interest.[7]

4. In relation to my estate my trustees shall have all the powers of management and investment of a sole beneficial owner.[8]

5. The power of appointing trustees of this will shall be vested in my [wife/husband/civil partner] during [her/his] life.

6. Any of my trustees being a professional or business person may be paid reasonable remuneration for services provided by him as personal representative or trustee.[9]

AS WITNESS my hand this —— day of —— 20——

SIGNED by the [testator/testatrix] in our presence and then by us in [his/hers][2]	}	[*Signature of testator/testatrix*]

[*Signatures, addresses and descriptions of two witnesses*]

1 This form is intended for use by a testator who is uncertain as to the ultimate disposition of his estate and is content to leave the decision to his trustees.

2 The composition of the discretionary class will vary according to the circumstances of the individual testator.

3 This is the longest period which can be specified under the PAA 1964, s 1, the text of which appears in Part G, para **[246.74]**. For wills made on or after 6 April 2010, the perpetuity period is 125 years (and no other period): see the PAA 2009, ss 5(1), 15(1)(a). See Part A **[200.35A]** and Part G, para **[246.179]**). This form and others in this volume also adopts a trust period of 125 years although a shorter trust period could be specified if the testator does not wish the trust to last that long. The perpetuity period, however, will still be 125 years and it is not necessary to specify, in addition to the specification as to the length of the trust period, that the perpetuity period is 125 years: PAA 2009, s 5(2) (Part G, para **[246.179]**). This contrasts with the situation under the former law where, if the common law perpetuity period was not relied upon, it was necessary to specify that the perpetuity period was 80 years, or fewer, see PAA 1964, s 1(1). The 125-year perpetuity period commencing with the death of the testator will be the perpetuity period when drafting an appointment in exercise of the power of sub-clause (2), whether the trust period selected is 125 years (as in this form) or a shorter period: see the PAA 2009, s 6(2) (Part G, para **[246.180]**). Accordingly, an appointment under the power needs to be expressly limited so that all interests vest (in interest if not in possession) and all powers are exercised within the 125-year period. We should add that if this is not done in an appointment, there will still be 'wait and see' under the PAA 2009, s 7 (Part G, para **[246.181]**), but it is better practice to draft trusts of which it is clear from the outset that they will vest within the relevant perpetuity period.

4 This is a wide power of appointment which expressly authorises the creation of discretions as to the disposition of capital and income.

5 A power to apply capital is a useful adjunct which can be exercised without any formality.
6 Although not strictly necessary, this provision may be useful in cases where a speedy appointment is required, e g an appointment within two years of the death complying with the IHTA 1984, s 144 (see para **[225.83]** ff), in view of arguments which HMRC has been known to advance to the effect that no appointment can be made before the completion of the administration. It should be remembered that for the technical reason discussed in the note to C3.6 (para **[225.85]**) an appointment or application of capital within three months of the testator's death will not attract the operation of s 144.
7 Since family trustees may well be appointed, a provision in this form is desirable.
8 This clause confers wide powers of investment and management. For administrative powers generally see B20 at para **[220.11]**.
9 See n 4 to Form C1.8 at para **[223.9]**.

C2

Wills for married couples (or civil partners) with young children

PRELIMINARY NOTE

[224.14]

[Updated for Human Fertilisation and Embryology Act 2008.]

One method of excluding *illegitimate* children of one or other party to the marriage from taking under a gift is to exclude the statutory rules of construction which include illegitimate persons in words descriptive of relationship (see Part A, paras **[200.28]**–**[200.33]** and Vol 1, para **[72.14]**). This will not be sufficient where there are children who are intended to be excluded from the gift who are children of another marriage of one of the spouses. In Forms C2.1 (at para **[224.27]**) and C2.2 (at para **[224.42]**) where the primary gift of residue is an absolute gift to the surviving spouse, optional words are included in the alternative gift which restrict the donees of the gift to the children of the marriage (see paras **[224.35]** and **[224.50]**). If such words are included, any illegitimate children of the testator or testatrix, or children by some other marriage, will be excluded, but the gift will include legitimated children of the marriage (see the Legitimacy Act 1976, s 5(3): Part G, para **[245.48]**), adopted children of the marriage (see the Adoption Act 1976, s 39(1), Part G, para **[245.58]**, and the Adoption and Children Act 2002, s 67, Part G, para **[245.93]**), children of the marriage born as a result of in vitro fertilisation or artificial insemination with the husband's consent, and children born through surrogacy where there is a parental order in favour of both spouses (see the Human Fertilisation and Embryology Act 1990, s 28(2) and 29(1), (3): Part G, paras **[245.86]** and **[245.87]**; Human Fertilisation and Embryology Act 2008, ss 35, 48(1) and (5) and 54; SI 2010/985: Part G, paras **[245.114]**, **[245.127]**, **[245.133]** and **[245.142]** ff). On these topics see also Vol 1, paras **[72.15]**–**[72.18]**, **[74.5]**–**[74.7]**, and **[75.1]**–**[75.9]** respectively.

[224.24]
Trusts for the testator's children and IHT. For deaths on and after 22 March 2006, there are five different IHT regimes which might apply to trusts for the testator's children established by will. These are (and see also para **[200.125]** ff)—

(a) Trusts for bereaved minors within IHTA 1984, s 71A. The main characteristics of such trusts are described in para **[200.108]** above, but they are essentially trusts under which the testator's children (or stepchildren, or children for whom the testator has parental responsibility) will be fully entitled to the assets in the trust at age 18. For parental responsibility see Vol 1, para **[28.2]**, and for the meaning of step-parent where there is a civil partnership see para **[224.35]**, n 1. The main IHT advantages of such trusts are threefold: firstly, property subject to such trusts will be exempt from the relevant property regime; secondly, the lifetime termination of an IPDI (eg. for the surviving spouse) in favour of such trusts will be a potentially exempt transfer (see IHTA 1984, s 3A(3B)); and thirdly, there will be no IHT charges when a beneficiary becomes absolutely entitled to the settled property or dies under the age of 18, or on its being paid or applied for the advancement or benefit of a beneficiary (see IHTA 1984, s 71B(2)). There is also a capital gains tax advantage in that when assets are paid out of the trusts and the trustees are deemed under TCGA 1992, s 71 to make a disposal of them at market value, hold-over relief may be available under TCGA 1992, s 260(2)(da). The obvious disadvantage of trusts for bereaved minors is the fact that the children must become absolutely entitled to capital at a young age (ie. 18), however since TA 1925, s 32, extended to enable the whole of a beneficiary's share to be applied for his or her benefit, is compatible with a trust for bereaved minors (see IHTA 1984, s 71A(4)), it may be possible if shortly before the 18th birthday of a particular beneficiary the trustees consider him or her to be too immature to handle large sums of money, for them to exercise this power to prolong the trusts, eg. by postponing the beneficiary's entitlement to a later age. Such an exercise would not trigger any IHT by reason of IHTA 1984, s 71B(2)(c), although the settled property would then fall within the IHT relevant property regime. Forms C2.1, C2.3 and C2.5 below provide options to include trusts for bereaved minors.

(b) Age 18-to-25 trusts within IHTA 1984, s 71D. The main characteristics of such trusts are described in para **[200.109]** above, but they are essentially trusts under which the testator's children (or stepchildren, or children for whom the testator has parental responsibility) will be fully entitled to the assets in the trust at age 25. For parental responsibility see Vol 1, para **[28.2]**, and for the meaning of step-parent where there is a civil partnership see para **[224.35]**, n 1. The main merit of these trusts over trusts for bereaved minors is that they permit postponement of absolute vesting of capital, albeit at a (usually modest) cost in IHT. Property subject to them will be exempt from the relevant property regime and there will be no IHT charges when a beneficiary becomes absolutely entitled to the settled property under the age of 18, or dies under the age of 18, or on the property being paid or applied for the advancement or benefit of a beneficiary under the age of 18 (see IHTA 1984, s 71E(2)), but if the property remains settled after a beneficiary reaches 18, an IHT charge would arise on his or her absolute entitlement after that date, on his or her death, and on any application of capital for his or her benefit, up to a maximum of 4.2% (on present rates of IHT): see IHTA 1984, s 71E(1), (2). There is a capital gains tax advantage in such trusts in that when assets are paid out and the trustees are deemed under TCGA 1992, s 71 to make a disposal of them at market value, hold-over relief should be available under TCGA 1992, s 260(2)(d) (if there is also an IHT charge) or s 260(2)(db) (if there is not). Forms C2.1, C2.3 and C2.5 below provide options to include age 18-to-25 trusts. It is appropriate to continue accumulation and maintenance trusts beyond the age of 18 and so far as possible to ensure that the trusts do not take effect as IPDI trusts on the testator's death, see para **[224.25]**.

(c) IPDIs within IHTA 1984, s 49A. These are described at para **[200.98]** above, but are essentially interests in possession which take immediate effect on the testator's death (subject only to a permissible survivorship clause under IHTA 1984, s 92). They cannot therefore arise in succession to a life interest for the testator's spouse. Where the surviving spouse or civil partner is given a life interest in the estate of the first to die, and subject to that both wills give the children interests in possession in both estates, after the death of the survivor the same trusts will give rise to relevant property IHT treatment for the estate of the first to die, and IPDI treatment for the estate of the second to die. Where the surviving spouse is given a life interest, therefore, it is probably better to provide relevant property trusts for the children if s 71A or 71D trusts are not wanted or available. An IPDI can be coupled with a power for the trustees to pay or apply capital to or for the benefit of the beneficiary of the interest, and even a provision for absolute entitlement to capital at a specified age. While the beneficiary is a minor, TA 1925, s 31 must be excluded or amended so that the beneficiary is treated as having an interest in possession (see for example, clause 8.2 of Form C2.2 below where TA 1925, s 31 is excluded), but while the beneficiary is a minor income may still be applied for his maintenance or other benefit and any not so applied may be accumulated, When the beneficiary attains 18, he would be entitled to those accumulations as of right. The essential advantage of such trusts over trusts for bereaved minors and age 18-to-25 trusts is that the beneficiaries do not have to become absolutely entitled to capital at an early age, whilst at the same time the property is outside the relevant property regime. Whether it is a significant advantage to be outside the relevant property regime is debatable and may depend on the value of the property concerned, since although there will be no IHT charge when the beneficiary becomes entitled to capital (by reason of IHTA 1984, s 53(2)), no hold-over relief would be available to postpone a capital gains tax charge on such an event, and there could be an IHT charge on the beneficiary's death since the underlying trust property would be treated as comprised in the beneficiary's estate for IHT purposes (under IHTA 1984, s 49(1), (1A)(a)). See also paras **[200.131]** ff. Form C2.2 below includes IPDIs for the testator's children.

(d) The relevant property regime (see para **[200.92]** above). This regime will, broadly speaking, cover any trusts which do not fall within the above categories. So, for example, it would cover discretionary trusts where trustees have wide discretions over income and capital, and also more rigid trusts which do not fall within any of the above categories because, for example, the age of vesting is too high, or the trustees have overriding powers over capital. The flexibility which wide discretionary trusts provide may mean that it is worth being within the relevant property regime (even if the value of the property concerned is such that periodic and exit charges will give rise to actual tax charges). Form C2.6 below includes wide discretionary trusts for the testator's children and remoter issue.

(e) A bare trust. This produces a result similar to a IHTA 1984, s 71A trust, but not identical: see para **[200.110]**. Where the testator is a parent of the beneficiary or beneficiaries, a s 71A trust is an available option and will probably seem a better choice than a bare trust. A bare trust is an option of more interest to a testator who is not a parent of the beneficiary or beneficiaries, and therefore does not have the option of a s 71A trust.

[224.25]

[Updated in text for Perpetuities and Accumulations Act 2009.]

Haphazard IHT status—relevant property trusts and age 18-to-25 trusts which may turn out to be IPDIs. Something to avoid is a trust which is haphazard as to whether it will be an IPDI or relevant property trust, for IHT purposes, depending on the ages of the beneficiaries at the death of the testator. An obvious example is a type of trust which used to be drafted to fall within IHTA 1984, s 71, which begins with an accumulation and maintenance trust and then gives the beneficiaries interests in possession for their lives commencing at a specified age or time. The share of a beneficiary who, by the time of the death of the testator or within two years after his death, attains the age at which his or her interest in possession starts, will get IPDI treatment, and the share of any beneficiary who is still under that age by at least two years after the death of the testator will get relevant property treatment. See also para **[200.136]**, (4). In the interests of fairness and certainty, trusts should either be wholly IPDI trusts, with the beneficiaries having interests in possession with effect from the testator's death even while they are under the age of 18 (see Form 18.15, para **[218.81]** for an example of a relevant modification of Trustee Act 1925, s 31), or wholly relevant property trusts, to achieve which any interest in possession should only commence after at least two years have elapsed from the testator's death: see para **[200.133]**. Where a trust of capital vesting contingently on attaining a specified age greater than 18 is being created for a minor or minors which will not fall within s 71D, and, where it is intended that the relevant property rather than the IDPI regime should apply, it is recommended that the accumulation and maintenance trusts of income of TA 1925, s 31 are expressly extended to continue until the beneficiary attains the age of vesting: see Form C2.1, cl 8 at para **[224.36]** for an example. This will make sure that the trust will have IHT relevant property status if the beneficiary is under the age of vesting at the testator's death, irrespective of what that age is. Without such extended accumulation and maintenance trusts, so that a beneficiary becomes entitled under TA 1925, s 31 to be paid the current income at the age of 18, he would have an IPDI if he is between the ages of 18 and the vesting age at the death of the testator. The same point arises, with the same solution, where an IHTA 1984, s 71D trust is being created: see para **[200.109]**. For extended accumulation and maintenance trusts see also B18 at paras **[218.74]** ff.

[224.26]

[Updated in text for Perpetuities and Accumulations Act 2009 and FA 2013, Sch 44.]

Trusts for the testator's children and income tax and capital gains tax. As well as there being special IHT regimes which may be applicable to trusts for the testator's children, there is also a special income tax and capital gains tax regime. For tax years 2004–05 onwards there is a special tax treatment available for 'qualifying trusts' for 'vulnerable beneficiaries', who include infants, at least one of whose parents has died. A trust so qualifying allows a claim for tax treatment bringing the trustees' income and capital gains tax liability into line with what the vulnerable beneficiary's liability would have been if he or she had received the income directly or had realised the trust gains (see FA 2005, ss 23–45 and para **[217.4]** above). The trusts for children in forms C2.1, C2.3 and C2.5 may, for tax year 2013–14 and subsequent years, be qualifying trusts for these purposes if the age contingency of attaining 18 is included (and deletions as specified in the footnotes are made).The statutory power of advancement is incorporated with the usual modification of enabling the whole of a beneficiary's presumptive share of capital, and not merely one half, to be paid or applied for his or her advancement or benefit (see, for example, Form C2.1, clause 8(2), para **[224.36]**). For tax year 2013–14 and subsequent years, this will be compatible with trusts within the Finance Act 2005, ss 23–45 (FA 2005, s 35(4)(b)–(f) as substituted by FA 2013, Sch 44, para 16(3)): see para **[217.4]** above. Without resorting to FA 2005, ss 23–45, it is possible to obtain treatment of the income for income tax purposes as the minor beneficiary's, as opposed to it being subject to the trust rate under ITA 2007, ss 479–483, by giving the beneficiary an interest in possession while under the age of 18. This is compatible with the trust falling within IHTA 1984, s 71A: see IHTA 1984, ss 49A(4) and 71A(1)(c)(i). The special capital gains tax treatment under FA 2005, ss 23–45 is considered at para **[217.4]** above.

[224.34]

[Updated for Trusts (Capital and Income) Act 2013]

ADMINISTRATION TRUSTS OF RESIDUE

6. (1) I give all my property not hereby or by any codicil hereto otherwise effectively disposed of [(including any entailed or other property over which I shall have at my death a general power of disposition by will)][1] to my trustees to hold on the trusts set out below with power to sell all or any of it.[2]

(2) My trustees shall pay my funeral and testamentary expenses[3] and debts and any legacies given by this will or any codicil hereto out of such property or its proceeds and shall have a discretion as to how such payments shall be borne as between capital and income.[4]

(3) Subject as above my trustees shall hold such property and the assets from time to time representing the same (hereinafter called 'my residuary

estate') on the trusts set out below and shall invest all money comprised in such property or arising from its sale in any of the investments hereby authorised with power to change such investments into any others hereby authorised.[5]

1 Subject to any express contrary intention property subject to a general power will be carried by a residuary gift under the WA 1837, s 27 (Part G, para **[244.29]**), but in the case of entailed property the will must refer to the property, or the instrument under which it was acquired, or entailed property generally for the statutory power of disposition to be exercised: LPA 1925, s 176(1), (Part G, para **[244.55]**). Although no new entails can be created on or after 1 January 1997 (see paras **[200.52]** and **[200.53]**), entails created before that date can continue to exist and, if they do, the statutory power of disposition of them by will continues to be available.

2 This serves to create a mixed fund of residuary realty and personalty (see para **[214.64]** for the significance of this).

3 Testamentary expenses will include IHT on UK free estate, including real property: IHTA 1984, s 211(1) (Part G, para **[246.100]** and see the Preliminary Note to B14 at paras **[214.55]–[214.63]**). Accordingly, even if specific gifts or pecuniary legacies are intended to be free of IHT, it will not be necessary to make express provision for the incidence of IHT, unless (in the case of a specific gift) the gift is of property of a kind which bears its own tax, or (in the case of a pecuniary legacy) the legacy is payable out of property (usually residue) which includes property of a kind which bears its own tax. The main relevant categories of property bearing its own tax are foreign property and property which is settled property immediately before the testator's death: see the Preliminary Note to B14 at paras **[214.55]–[214.63]** (settled property can be disposed of under a will where it is subject to a general testamentary power of appointment or is entailed—see n 1 above).

4 The rule in *Allhusen v Whittell* (1867) LR 4 Eq 295 (see Vol 1, para **[38.26]** and para **[214.43]**) is excluded by statute: see para **[214.2A]** and the Trusts (Capital and Income) Act 2013 (para **[246.200]** ff. In its absence there could be a question as to whether income can be used to pay liabilities, and this wording makes it clear that the executors have a discretion in the matter. A direction to pay the liabilities out of capital can have the unsatisfactory consequences referred to at para **[214.44]**.

5 It is no longer necessary to include wording which excludes the rules of equitable apportionment or the Apportionment Act 1870: see para **[214.2A]** and the Trusts (Capital and Income) Act 2013 (para **[246.200]** ff.

[224.35]

[Updated for Perpetuities and Accumulations Act 2009 and for FA 2013, Sch 44.]

BENEFICIAL TRUSTS FOR ISSUE

7. My trustees shall hold my residuary estate and the income thereof upon trust for such of my children [by my [wife/husband]][1] as shall survive me and attain the age of [18/25] years[2] and if more than one in equal shares provided that if any such child shall not attain a vested interest under the foregoing trust then any children or remoter descendants of him or her living at or born after my death who shall attain the age of [18/25] years or shall be living but under that age at the expiry of 125 years from my death[3] shall take and if more than one equally through all degrees according to their stocks the share of my residuary estate which such child of mine would have taken if he or she had attained a vested interest and so that no child or remoter descendant of a child of mine shall take whose parent attains a vested interest and section 33 of the Wills Act 1837 shall not apply to the foregoing trusts[4].

1 These words ensure that the alternative gifts in the wills of both spouses are identical in terms of whom they benefit, in circumstances where one spouse has children who are not children of the other spouse, and it is desired to exclude them. See, further, the Preliminary

Note on reciprocal wills and the ultimate destination of property at paras **[224.13]**–**[224.15]** and for forms for use where one spouse has children who are not children of the marriage and wishes to benefit them by his or her will see C5 at para **[227.1]** ff. If there are intended beneficiaries under this trust who are the children of one spouse but not of the other, or if this Form is being adapted for use by civil partners either or both of whom have children, the children could be identified as 'my children and the children of my [wife/husband/civil partner] as shall be living at my death'. In this case it needs to be made clear whether or not children of the other spouse or civil partner born after the testator's death are excluded, and it should be borne in mind that inclusion of the children of both would include illegitimate children who might be forgotten or not known about. A testator can create trusts within IHTA 1984, ss 71A or 71D for his or her stepchildren (IHTA 1984, s 71H), and in the case of a testator who is in a civil partnership this includes children of the other civil partner (IHTA 1984, s 272, definition of 'stepchild', and CPA 2004, s 246).

2 If the age contingency of attaining 18 is included, and the trusts for children come into possession while they are still infants, these trusts should be trusts for bereaved minors within IHTA 1984, s 71A and so exempt from the IHT relevant property regime (see para **[224.24]** above). They will also, for tax year 2013–14 and subsequent years, be 'qualifying trusts' for the benefit of 'vulnerable beneficiaries' for income tax purposes under FA 2005, ss 23–45. The statutory power of advancement is incorporated in clause 8 with the usual modification of enabling the whole of a beneficiary's presumptive share of capital, and not merely one half, to be paid or applied for his or her advancement or benefit, but for tax year 2013–14 and subsequent years, this will be compatible with trusts within the Finance Act 2005, ss 23–45 (FA 2005, s 35(4)(b)–(f) as substituted by FA 2013, Sch 44, para 16(3)): see para **[217.4]** above. If the age contingency selected is 25 and the trusts for children come into possession while they are under 25 these trusts should be age 18-to-25 trusts within IHTA 1984, s 71D and so exempt from the IHT relevant property regime although an IHT charge will arise on a beneficiary becoming absolutely entitled to capital when over the age of 18 (see paras **[200.109]** and **[224.24]** above). If the age contingency selected is 25, the trusts would not also be 'qualifying trusts' for the benefit of 'vulnerable beneficiaries' within FA 2005, ss 23–45 (see para **[217.4]** above).

3 This clause previously contained a substitution clause for children only. The perpetuity rule reasons for doing this have ceased to apply (see below), and including descendants remoter than children has the advantage that if either testator lives to an advanced age without changing his or her will and outliving a child and a child of that child, the latter's descendants can still take. For wills made on or after 6 April 2010, the perpetuity period is 125 years (and there is no other period): see the PAA 2009, ss 5(1), 15(1)(a) (Part A **[200.35]** and Part G, para **[246.179]**). The substitution clause was previously in favour of children only, and the age contingency in this clause was no more than attaining the age of 21, so as not to infringe the common law rule against perpetuities. For wills made on or after 6 April 2010 the age of vesting makes no difference to the perpetuity position. It is still preferablet if all interests vest within the perpetuity period. We should add that if this is not so, there will still be 'wait and see' under the PAA 2009, s 7 (Part G, para **[246.181]**). If this trust for children or remoter descendants takes effect, the property subject to it would be within the IHT relevant property regime, except so far as they are entitled to interest in possession by the time of the death of the testator, in which case the property will be subject to an IPDI or IPDIs (see paras **[200.125]** ff, **[224.24]**).

4 The contingencies imposed on this gift and the substitutional provisions probably exclude WA 1837, s 33 (see para **[47.18]**), but it can save argument to make this clear.

[224.36]

[Updated for Perpetuities and Accumulations Act 2009 and for FA 2013, Sch 44.]

MAINTENANCE, ACCUMULATION AND ADVANCEMENT

Either

[8. (1) Section 31 of the Trustee Act 1925 (relating to accumulation and maintenance) shall apply in relation to the trusts hereby or by any codicil hereto declared as if:

(a) in paragraph (i) of subsection (1) of the said section the words 'as the trustees think fit' were substituted for the words 'as may in all the circumstances be reasonable'; and
(b) the proviso to the said subsection (1) were omitted].[1]

[Provided that in relation to any presumptive share of my residuary estate of any child of mine [by my [wife/husband]][2]] the said section 31 (amended as aforesaid) shall have effect as if the age of majority were the age of 25 years (and so that the expressions 'infancy', 'minority' and 'infant' and all references to the age of eighteen years in the said Section 31 shall be construed accordingly).][3]

Or

[8. (1) The income of the presumptive share of my residuary estate of any beneficiary which arises while he or she is living and under the age of 18 years shall be held on trust for him or her absolutely and indefeasibly and section 31 of the Trustee Act 1925 shall not apply to such income Provided that my trustees may pay or apply all or any part or parts of such income for his or her benefit at any time or times during his or her minority.][4]

(2) Section 32 of the Trustee Act 1925 (relating to advancement) shall apply in relation to the said trusts as if the words 'one half of' were omitted from proviso (a) to subsection (1) thereof.[5]

(3) Whenever my trustees shall have an obligation or discretion under the provisions of this will or any codicil hereto or under the general law to apply income or capital for the benefit of a minor beneficiary they may either pay the same without liability to account to his or her parent guardian or any other adult person with whom such beneficiary may be residing or to such beneficiary himself or herself if of the age of 16 years or more and so that the receipt of such parent guardian or other person or of such minor beneficiary shall be a full and sufficient discharge to my trustees for the income or capital so applied.[6]

1 Where the primary trust in clause 7, para **[224.35]**, has a vesting age of 18, either include this subclause (1), without the proviso, or include the alternative subclause below which confers an interest in possession (for which see further n 4 below). Where the primary trust in clause 7, para **[224.35]**, has a vesting age of 25, include this subclause together with the proviso (for which see further n 3 below).

2 This reference needs to be to the same persons as the beneficiaries under the primary trust in clause 7: see **[224.35]** and n 1 to it.

3 This proviso is for inclusion where the age contingency for the alternative gift for the testator's children in clause 7, para **[224.35]**, is the age of 25. For wills made on or after 6 April 2010, there are no statutory restrictions on accumulation in respect of non-charitable trusts, so accumulation will be permitted throughout the trust period: see the PAA 2009, s 13, 15(1)(a) (Part G, para **[246.189]**). It is no longer necessary, therefore, to introduce a restriction in order to comply with the rule against excessive accumulations as was previously the case: see the form of this clause as set out in the 9th Edition.

4 A trust can fall within IHTA 1984, s 71A even if the beneficiary has an interest in possession while under 18 (see paras **[200.108]**, **[224.24]**). If the first alternative subclause (1) is included, the income of a beneficiary's share while he or she is under 18 will be subject to the trust rate under ITA 2007, ss 479–483 (see para **[224.26]**), whereas if this second alternative is included the income will be subject to income tax as the beneficiary's. The disadvantage of this is that if he or she dies under the age of 18 the income will devolve under the intestacy rules as they apply to him or her instead of devolving with the capital.

5 This should be included whichever sub-cl (1) is chosen. The extended power is compatible with trusts for bereaved minors within IHTA 1984, s 71A (see para **[200.108]** above) and age

18-to-25 trusts within IHTA 1984, s 71D (see para **[200.109]** above), and for tax year 2013–14 and subsequent years, trusts within the Finance Act 2005, ss 23–45 (FA 2005, s 35(4)(b)–(f) as substituted by FA 2013, Sch 44, para 16(3)): see para **[217.4]**.

6 This should be included whichever subclause (1) is chosen. A parent (with parental responsibility) and a guardian of a minor are empowered by the ChA 1989, s 3(3) (Part G, para **[244.114]**) to give a good receipt for the minor's property: see Vol 1, para **[9.41]**. The power in this subclause is wider in that it authorises the payment of income or capital to a parent who does not have parental responsibility, any adult with whom the minor is residing, and the minor himself or herself if 16 or over.

[224.65]

[Updated for Perpetuities and Accumulations Act 2009 and for FA 2013, Sch 44.]

REMAINDER TRUSTS FOR CHILDREN AND ISSUE[1]

Either

[6. Subject to the trust and to any exercise of the power aforesaid my trustees shall hold my residuary estate upon trust for such of my children [by my [wife/husband]][2] as shall survive me and attain the age of [18/25][3] years and if more than one [in such shares as my trustees shall from time to time by deed or deeds revocable or irrevocable appoint in accordance with the provisions below and in default of such appointment][4] in equal shares Provided that if any such child shall die in my lifetime or having survived me shall die before attaining a vested interest leaving a child or children living at or born after my death who shall attain the age of [18/21][5] years such last-mentioned child or children shall take if more than one equally between them the share of my residuary estate to which their deceased parent would have become entitled had he or she lived to attain a vested interest [and provided further that no appointment under the power aforesaid shall be made and no appointment shall be revoked so as to

(i) diminish or increase the share (or the accumulations of income forming part of the share) of a child who at the date of such appointment or revocation has reached the age of [18/25] years;

(ii) diminish or increase the share (or the accumulations of income forming part of the share) devolving on his or her child or children of a child who has died under the age of [18/25] years; or

(iii) give a share (or accumulations of income forming part of the share) to a child who at the date of such appointment has been excluded from benefit as a result of an exercise of the power][6].]

Or

[6. (1) Subject to the trust and to any exercise of the power aforesaid my trustees shall hold my residuary estate and the income thereof upon trust for such of my children and remoter issue and if more than one in such shares and with such trusts powers and provisions (including trusts and powers conferring on any person or persons a discretion as to the disposition of capital or income and including provisions for the accumulation of income during any period permitted by law)[7] as my [wife/husband] shall by any deed or deeds revocable or irrevocable or by will or codicil appoint.

(2) Subject to and in default of any such appointment my trustees shall hold my residuary estate upon trust for such of my children [by my

[wife/husband]][8] as survive me and attain the age of 18 years[9] and if more than one in equal shares provided that:

(a) if [any child of mine]/[any child of mine by my [wife/husband]][10] shall die in my lifetime or having survived me shall die before attaining a vested interest leaving a child or children surviving me or born after my death who shall attain the age of [18/21][11] years such last-mentioned child or children shall take if more than one equally between them the share of my residuary estate to which such deceased child of mine would have become entitled had he or she lived to attain a vested interest; and

(b) no person who or whose issue shall take an interest in any part or share of my residuary estate under any such appointment as aforesaid shall participate in the unappointed part without bringing into account the appointed part or share and accounting for the same accordingly.]

1 Alternative clauses are set out, the first giving the children fixed interests, the second conferring an overriding power of appointment amongst issue on the spouse. Under neither alternative are the interests of the children contingent on surviving the life tenant, so that the interest of a child who survives the testator and attains the vesting age (if any) but predeceases the life tenant will vest in his or her personal representatives as part of his or her estate on death.

2 These words will ensure that the ultimate remainders in the wills of both spouses are identical in terms of whom they benefit, in circumstances where one spouse has children who are not children of the other spouse and who are not intended to benefit. See, further, the Preliminary Note on reciprocal wills and the ultimate destination of property at paras **[224.13]**–**[224.15]** and for forms for use where one or both spouses have children who are not children of the marriage, and who are intended to benefit, see C5 at para **[227.1]** ff. If there are intended beneficiaries under this trust who are the children of one spouse but not of the other, or if this Form is being adapted for use by civil partners either or both of whom have children, see para **[224.35]**, n 1.

3 If the age contingency of attaining 18 is included, and the trusts for children come into possession while they are still infants, these trusts should be trusts for bereaved minors within IHTA 1984, s 71A and so exempt from the IHT relevant property regime (see para **[224.24]** above). (See the following footnote for a possible advantage in the trusts for the children being bereaved minor trusts in the event of the surviving spouse wishing to release her life interest during her life). They may also, for tax year 2013–14 and subsequent years, be 'qualifying trusts' for the benefit of 'vulnerable beneficiaries', for income tax and capital gains tax purposes within FA 2005, ss 23–45 (at least if the power to vary shares is not included, see note 4 below). The statutory power of advancement is incorporated in clause 8 with the usual modification of enabling the whole of a beneficiary's presumptive share of capital, and not merely one half, to be paid or applied for his or her advancement or benefit, but for tax year 2013–14 and subsequent years, this will be compatible with trusts within the Finance Act 2005, ss 23–45 (FA 2005, s 35(4)(b)–(f) as substituted by FA 2013, Sch 44, para 16(3)): see para **[217.4]** above. If the age contingency selected is 25 and the trusts for children come into possession while they are under 25 these trusts should be age 18-to-25 trusts within IHTA 1984, s 71D and so exempt from the IHT relevant property regime although an IHT charge will arise on a beneficiary becoming absolutely entitled to capital when over the age of 18 (see para **[224.24]** above). If the age contingency selected is 25, the trusts would not also be 'qualifying trusts' for the benefit of 'vulnerable beneficiaries' (see para **[217.4]** above).

4 HMRC have confirmed that they consider that a power to vary shares may be compatible with trusts for bereaved minors and age 18-to-25 trusts, so long as the share of a child who has attained 18 or 25 (as the case may be), or has died leaving children on whom his share devolves cannot be varied, and also so long as a child who has been excluded from benefit on an exercise of the power cannot be reinstated as a beneficiary: see paras **[200.108]** and

[200.109]. It will not though be compatible with 'qualifying trusts' for the benefit of 'vulnerable beneficiaries', for income tax and capital gains tax purposes within FA 2005, ss 23–45: see para **[217.4]** above.

5 For wills made on or after 6 April 2010, the perpetuity period is 125 years (and there is no other period): see the PAA 2009, ss 5(1), 15(1)(a) (Part A **[200.35A]** and Part G, para **[246.179]**). The age contingency for the grandchildren in this clause need not, therefore, be limited to 21 years (a limit included so as not to infringe the common law rule against perpetuities). This restriction on the age contingency to 21 is no longer necessary although it is still important that all interests vest within the perpetuity period. We should add that if this is not done, there will still be 'wait and see' under the PAA 2009, s 7 (Part G, para **[246.181]**).

6 Include this proviso if the power for the trustees to vary the shares of the children is included. See n 4 above.

7 For wills made on or after 6 April 2010, there are no statutory restrictions on accumulation in respect of non-charitable trusts, so accumulation will be permitted throughout the trust period: see the PAA 2009, s 13, 15(1)(a) (Part G, para **[246.189]**).

8 As the age of contingency is 18, if these trusts for children come into possession following the surviving spouse's death while they are still infants, they should be trusts for bereaved minors within IHTA 1984, s 71A and so exempt from the IHT relevant property regime (see para **[224.24]** above). If the surviving spouse were to surrender her life interest (wholly or partially) during her lifetime while the children were under the age of 18, and release her power of appointment, so that the trusts for the children were accelerated, potential exemption from IHT should be available under IHTA 1984, s 3A(3B) because the accelerated trusts will be trusts for bereaved minors (see para **[200.128]** above). So as to avoid the surviving spouse being deemed to make a gift with reservation for IHT purposes under FA 1986, s 102ZA, (see para **[200.76]** above), which would nullify the IHT effectiveness of the early surrender of her life interest, it will be important that she is not capable of benefiting in the future from the property in which she surrenders her life interest. So, for example, her surrender should be coupled with an assignment of any interest she may have in the settled property in which she surrenders her life interest in the event of none of the children attaining the age of 18 (eg. as on a partial intestacy of the testator).

9 See n 8 above. Even if this trust is restricted in this way it is not necessary to impose the same restriction on the objects of the power in the preceding clause.

10 The second of these alternatives is appropriate where the primary trust is confined to the children of the marriage.

11 See n 5 above.

[224.66]

[Updated for Perpetuities and Accumulations Act 2009 and for FA 2013, Sch 44.]

MAINTENANCE, ACCUMULATION AND ADVANCEMENT

7. Section 31 of the Trustee Act 1925 (relating to accumulation and maintenance) shall apply in relation to the trusts hereby or by any codicil hereto declared as if:

(a) in paragraph (i) of subsection (1) of the said section the words 'as the trustees think fit' were substituted for the words 'as may in all the circumstances be reasonable'; and

(b) the proviso to the said subsection (1) were omitted[1]

[Provided that in relation to any presumptive share of my residuary estate of any child of mine the said section 31 (amended as aforesaid) shall have effect as if the age of majority were the age of 25 years (and so that the expressions 'infancy', 'minority' and 'infant' and all references to the age of eighteen years in the said Section 31 shall be construed accordingly).][2]

(2) Section 32 of the Trustee Act 1925 (relating to advancement) shall apply in relation to the said trusts as if the words 'one half of' were omitted from proviso (a) to subsection (1) thereof.[3]

(3) Whenever my trustees shall have an obligation or discretion under the provisions of this will or any codicil hereto or under the general law to apply income or capital for the benefit of a minor beneficiary they may either pay the same without liability to account to his or her parent guardian or any other adult person with whom such beneficiary may be residing or to such beneficiary himself or herself if of the age of 16 years or more and so that the receipt of such parent guardian or other person or of such minor beneficiary shall be a full and sufficient discharge to my trustees for the income or capital so applied.[4]

1 Where the contingency for the testator's children is attaining the age of 18 there is the alternative possibility of the beneficiaries having interests in possession and during their minorities. See the second alternative clause 8(1) in para **[224.36]** and n 4 thereto. However, combining this with the shares being variable is not recommended, because it is capable of causing considerable confusion about who is entitled to what income if the shares are varied.

2 This proviso is for inclusion where the age contingency for the testator's children in the first alternative clause 6 is the age of 25. For wills made on or after 6 April 2010, there are no statutory restrictions on accumulation in respect of non-charitable trusts, so accumulation will be permitted throughout the trust period: see the PAA 2009, s 13, 15(1)(a) (Part G, para **[246.189]**). It is no longer necessary, therefore, to introduce a restriction in order to comply with the rule against excessive accumulations as was previously the case: see the form of this clause as set out in the 9th Edition.

3 The extended power is compatible with trusts for bereaved minors within IHTA 1984, s 71A (see para **[200.108]** above) and age 18-to-25 trusts within IHTA 1984, s 71D (see para **[200.109]** above), and for tax year 2013–14 and subsequent years, trusts within the Finance Act 2005, ss 23–45 (FA 2005, s 35(4)(b)–(f) as substituted by FA 2013, Sch 44, para 16(3)): see para **[217.4]**.

4 A parent (with parental responsibility) and a guardian of a minor are empowered by the ChA 1989, s 3(3) (Part G, para **[244.114]**) to give a good receipt for the minor's property: see Vol 1, para **[9.41]**. The power in this subclause is wider in that it authorises the payment of income or capital to a parent who does not have parental responsibility, any adult with whom the minor is residing, and the minor himself or herself if 16 or over.

[224.80]

[Updated in text and footnote 1 for Perpetuities and Accumulations Act 2009.]

MAINTENANCE, ACCUMULATION AND ADVANCEMENT

6. (1) Section 31 of the Trustee Act 1925 (relating to accumulation and maintenance) shall apply in relation to the trusts hereby or by any codicil hereto declared as if:

(a) in paragraph (i) of subsection (1) of the said section the words 'as the trustees think fit' were substituted for the words 'as may in all the circumstances be reasonable'; and

(b) the proviso to the said subsection (1) were omitted

Provided that in relation to the presumptive share of any property of any child of mine living at my death the said section 31 (amended as aforesaid) shall have effect as if the age of majority were the age of 21 years (and so that the expressions 'infancy', 'minority' and 'infant' and all references to the age of eighteen years in the said Section 31 shall be construed accordingly).[1]

(2) Section 32 of the Trustee Act 1925 (relating to advancement) shall apply in relation to the said trusts as if the words 'one half of' were omitted from proviso (a) to subsection (1) thereof.[2]

(3) Whenever my trustees shall have an obligation or discretion under the provisions of this will or any codicil hereto or under the general law to apply income or capital for the benefit of a minor beneficiary they may either pay the same without liability to account to his or her parent guardian or any other adult person with whom such beneficiary may be residing or to such beneficiary himself or herself if of the age of 16 years or more and so that the receipt of such parent guardian or other person or of such minor beneficiary shall be a full and sufficient discharge to my trustees for the income or capital so applied.[3]

1 For wills made on or after 6 April 2010, there are no statutory restrictions on accumulation in respect of non-charitable trusts, so accumulation will be permitted throughout the trust period: see the PAA 2009, s 13, 15(1)(a) (Part G, para **[246.189]**). It is no longer necessary, therefore, to introduce a restriction to the age of 21 years in order to comply with the rule against excessive accumulations as was previously the case: see the form of this clause as set out in the 9th Edition. Thus, a greater age could be included in this provision.

2 The extended power is compatible with age 18-to-25 trusts within IHTA 1984, s 71D (see para **[200.109]** above).

3 A parent (with parental responsibility) and a guardian of a minor are empowered by the ChA 1989, s 3(3) (Part G, para **[244.114]**) to give a good receipt for the minor's property: see Vol 1, para **[9.41]**. The power in this subclause is wider in that it authorises the payment of income or capital to a parent who does not have parental responsibility, any adult with whom the minor is residing, and the minor himself or herself if 16 or over.

[224.95]

[Updated for Perpetuities and Accumulations Act 2009 and for FA 2013, Sch 44.]

BENEFICIAL TRUSTS OF RESIDUE

8. My trustees shall hold my residuary estate upon the following trusts:
   (a) if my wife shall survive me[1] my trustees shall pay the income of my residuary estate to my wife during her [life/widowhood];[2]
   (b) provided that my trustees shall have power in their absolute discretion from time to time so long as my wife is entitled to be paid the income of all or any part of the capital of my residuary estate (or would be so entitled if such capital yielded income) to pay transfer or apply the whole or any part or parts of such capital[3] to her or for her benefit in such manner as they shall in their absolute discretion think fit;
   (c) subject as aforesaid my trustees shall hold my residuary estate in trust as to both capital and income in equal shares if more than one for all my children[4] who attain the age of [18/25] years[5] [or marry under that age][6] provided that:
      (i) if any such child of mine shall have died in my lifetime whether before or after the date of this my will leaving issue living at my death who attain the age of [18/21][7] years [or marry under that age] then such issue shall take if more than one in equal shares per stirpes the share of my residuary estate which their deceased parent would have taken had he or she survived me and attained a vested interest but so that no issue shall take whose parent is alive at my death and so capable of taking;
      (ii) if any such child of mine shall survive me but shall die before attaining a vested interest under the foregoing trust leaving a child or children who attain the age of [18/21][7] years or marry

under that age then such child or children shall take by substitution if more than one in equal shares the share of my residuary estate which such child of mine would have taken if he or she had attained a vested interest;[8]

(d) subject as aforesaid my trustees shall hold my residuary estate in trust as to both capital and income for [the children of my sister [*name*] in equal shares] absolutely.

1 If a survivorship clause is wanted the words 'for the period of one month' (or other period up to six months) can be added at this point. See the Preliminary Note on survivorship conditions at paras **[224.5]–[224.10]** for the reasons for not including a survivorship clause as between husband and wife or civil partners. If there is a survivorship condition in this subclause, one should also be included in cl 5 above: see cl 5, n 2 at para **[224.92]**.

2 The wife's interest in possession, whether it be for life or widowhood, will be an IPDI within IHTA 1984, s 49A, so spouse exemption from IHT should be available (see para **[200.84]** above). Post-21 March 2006, the provision for automatic termination of an IPDI on events such as remarriage is probably not advisable because potential exemption from IHT will only be available if the termination results in another person acquiring an absolute interest or a disabled person's interest, or causes the settled property to become subject to a trust for bereaved minors (see paras **[200.71]**, **[200.128]**). Therefore, if the testator wishes his spouse's interest to be only an interest during her widowhood it may be advisable if the age contingency in the trusts for children (in sub-cl (c)) is 18 so that the trusts for children will either be trusts for bereaved minors (if the children are under 18 at the time the spouse remarries), or absolute interests (if they are over 18), and either way potential exemption should be available. Further, so as to avoid the surviving spouse being deemed to make a gift with reservation for IHT purposes under FA 1986, s 102ZA, (see para **[200.76]** above), which would nullify the IHT effectiveness of the termination of her life interest being a potentially exempt transfer, it will be important that she is not capable of benefiting in the future from the residuary estate (for example on a partial intestacy of the testator in the event of the testator's issue not attaining vested interests), therefore an ultimate default trust should be included, as in sub-clause (d).

If this form is being adapted for use by a civil partner with children, and the testator wishes his civil partner's interest to terminate on his forming another civil partnership (or marrying), the interest should be expressed to last during the civil partner's life 'or only until he forms a civil partnership or marries'.

3 There are two reasons for restricting the power to being exercisable only over capital in which the wife has an interest in possession: first, to ensure that the power is not exercisable if there is a divorce and the primary trust fails; and second, to ensure that the power ceases to be exercisable if the wife assigns or surrenders her life interest. See the Preliminary Note at paras **[224.16]–[224.23]**.

4 This trust is not confined to being in favour of the children of the marriage. See the Preliminary Note on reciprocal wills and the ultimate destination of property at paras **[224.13]–[224.15]**.

5 If the age contingency of attaining 18 is included, and the trusts for children come into possession while they are still infants, these trusts should be trusts for bereaved minors within IHTA 1984, s 71A and so exempt from the IHT relevant property regime (see para **[224.24]** above).They may also, for tax year 2013–14 and subsequent years, be 'qualifying trusts' for the benefit of 'vulnerable beneficiaries' within FA 2005, ss 23–45 (at least if the alternative contingency of marriage under the age of 18 is not included, see para **[217.4]** above). The statutory power of advancement is incorporated in clause 9 with the usual modification of enabling the whole of a beneficiary's presumptive share of capital, and not merely one half, to be paid or applied for his or her advancement or benefit, but for tax year 2013–14 and subsequent years, this will be compatible with trusts within the Finance Act 2005, ss 23–45 (FA 2005, s 35(4)(b)–(f) as substituted by FA 2013, Sch 44, para 16(3)): see para **[217.4]** above. If the age contingency selected is 25 and the trusts for children come into possession while they are under 25, these trusts should be age 18-to-25 trusts within IHTA 1984, s 71D and so exempt from the IHT relevant property regime, although an IHT charge will arise on a beneficiary becoming absolutely entitled to capital when over the age

of 18 (see para **[224.24]** above). If the age contingency selected is 25 the trusts would not also be 'qualifying trusts' for the benefit of 'vulnerable beneficiaries' (see para **[217.4]** above).

6 This form follows the rules of intestate succession and makes no difference between sons and daughters as regards marriage under the vesting age: AEA 1925, s 47(1)(i) (Part G, para **[244.63]**). Where it is desired to make a distinction between sons and daughters, the words 'or marry under that age' should be changed to 'or being daughters attain that age or marry under that age' on each occasion where it occurs. Do not, however, include this contingency at all if it is intended that the trusts should fall within the Finance Act 2005, ss 23–45: see para **[217.4]** above.

7 For wills made on or after 6 April 2010, the perpetuity period is 125 years (and there is no other period): see the PAA 2009, ss 5(1), 15(1)(a) (Part A **[200.35A]** and Part G, para **[246.179]**). The age contingency for the grandchildren in this clause need not, therefore, be limited to 21 years (a limit included so as not to infringe the common law rule against perpetuities). This restriction on the age contingency to a maximum of 21 years is no longer necessary although it is still important that all interests vest within the perpetuity period. We should add that if this is not done, there will still be 'wait and see' under the PAA 2009, s 7 (Part G, para **[246.181]**).

8 Clause 8(c) combines two different sorts of substitution, the substitution of issue remoter than children being only relevant to cases where the testator's child has predeceased the testator, since a child could not leave issue remoter than his own children if he died under the vesting age. If either substitutional provision takes effect, the property subject to it would be within the IHT relevant property regime, and any termination of the spouse's life interest on her remarriage in relation to it would be an immediately chargeable transfer.For a slightly more comprehensive clause on the same lines, see Form B19.6 at para **[219.19]**.

[224.96]

[Updated for Perpetuities and Accumulations Act 2009 and for FA 2013, Sch 44.]

MAINTENANCE, ACCUMULATION AND ADVANCEMENT

9. Section 31 of the Trustee Act 1925 (relating to accumulation and maintenance) shall apply in relation to the trusts hereby or by any codicil hereto declared as if:

(a) in paragraph (i) of subsection (1) of the said section the words 'as the trustees think fit' were substituted for the words 'as may in all the circumstances be reasonable'; and

(b) the proviso to the said subsection (1) were omitted.

[Provided that in relation to any presumptive share of my residuary estate of any child of mine the said section 31 (amended as aforesaid) shall have effect as if the age of majority were the age of 25 years (and so that the expressions 'infancy', 'minority' and 'infant' and all references to the age of eighteen years in the said Section 31 shall be construed accordingly).][1]

(2) Section 32 of the Trustee Act 1925 (relating to advancement) shall apply in relation to the said trusts as if the words 'one half of' were omitted from proviso (a) to subsection (1) thereof.[2]

(3) Whenever my trustees shall have an obligation or discretion under the provisions of this will or any codicil hereto or under the general law to apply income or capital for the benefit of a minor beneficiary they may either pay the same without liability to account to his or her parent guardian or any other adult person with whom such beneficiary may be residing or to such beneficiary himself or herself if of the age of 16 years or more and so that the receipt of such parent guardian or other person or of such minor beneficiary shall be a full and sufficient discharge to my trustees for the income or capital so applied.[3]

1 This proviso is for inclusion where the age contingency for the testator's children in clause 8(c) is the age of 25. For wills made on or after 6 April 2010, there are no statutory restrictions on accumulation in respect of non-charitable trusts, so accumulation will be permitted throughout the trust period: see the PAA 2009, s 13, 15(1)(a) (Part G, para **[246.189]**). It is no longer necessary, therefore, to introduce a restriction in order to comply with the rule against excessive accumulations as was previously the case: see the form of this clause as set out in the 9th Edition.

2 The extended power is compatible with trusts for bereaved minors within IHTA 1984, s 71A (see para **[200.108]** above) and age 18-to-25 trusts within IHTA 1984, s 71D (see para **[200.109]** above), and for tax year 2013–14 and subsequent years, trusts within the Finance Act 2005, ss 23–45 (FA 2005, s 35(4)(b)–(f) as substituted by FA 2013, Sch 44, para 16(3)): see para **[217.4]**.

3 A parent (with parental responsibility) and a guardian of a minor are empowered by the ChA 1989, s 3(3) (Part G, para **[244.114]**) to give a good receipt for the minor's property: see Vol 1, para **[9.41]**. The power in this subclause is wider in that it authorises the payment of income or capital to a parent who does not have parental responsibility, any adult with whom the minor is residing, and the minor himself or herself if 16 or over.

[224.112]

[Updated for Perpetuities and Accumulations Act 2009 and Marriage (Same Sex Couples) Act 2013.]

DISCRETIONARY TRUSTS

9.(1) In this clause the following expressions have the following meanings, namely:

(a) 'the trust fund' means the property directed to be held on the trusts of this clause and the assets for the time being representing the same;

(b) 'the discretionary beneficiaries' means my children and remoter issue and the spouses civil partners widows widowers and surviving civil partners of my children and remoter issue[1] [and (subject to clause 8(2)(b) above) my wife].[2]

(c) 'the trust period' means the period of 125 years commencing on my death;

(2) My trustees shall hold the trust fund and the income thereof upon trust for all or such one or more of the discretionary beneficiaries at such ages or times in such shares and upon such trusts for the benefit of the discretionary beneficiaries as my trustees (being at least two in number) may by deed or deeds revocable or irrevocable executed at any time or times during the trust period appoint and in making any such appointment my trustees shall have powers as full as those which they would possess if they were an absolute beneficial owner of the trust fund and in particular (but without prejudice to the generality of the foregoing words) my trustees may in any exercise of the foregoing power as they in their absolute discretion think fit:

(a) delegate give or impose to or upon themselves or any other person or persons and in relation to any trust or disposition any discretionary powers or discretionary trusts conditions limitations restrictions or provisions including powers of further delegation or powers to create further discretionary trusts or powers;[3]

(b) create trusts or powers for the accumulation of income;[4]

(c) appoint or create administrative powers or provisions of whatever nature;

Provided that:

(i) no such appointment shall invalidate any payment transfer or application of capital or income previously made under any of the trusts or powers herein elsewhere contained;

(ii) every interest limited under any exercise of such power shall vest in interest (if at all) not later than the expiration of the trust period;

(iii) any appointment may if my trustees think fit be made subject and without prejudice to any existing interest or interests in possession or to any other existing interests trusts or powers;[5]

(iv) any such appointment may be made in respect of income alone without any appointment of capital; and

(v) any such revocable appointment shall (so far as then unrevoked) cease to be revocable on the expiration of the trust period.

(3) In default of and subject to any exercise of the foregoing power my trustees (being at least two in number) may at their discretion at any time or times during the trust period pay transfer or apply the whole or any part or parts of the trust fund to or for the benefit of all or any one or more of the discretionary beneficiaries for the time being living in such manner as my trustees think fit.[6]

(4) Subject to any or every exercise of the foregoing powers my trustees shall during the trust period hold the trust fund upon trust to pay or apply the income thereof to or for the maintenance education or benefit of all or any one or more of the discretionary beneficiaries for the time being living in such shares if more than one and generally in such manner as they think fit provided that my trustees may accumulate[7] the whole or any part of the income of the trust fund by investing the same and the resulting income thereof in any of the investments hereby authorised and any accumulations of income so made shall form part of the capital of the trust fund for all purposes.

(5) Subject to the foregoing trust and any or every exercise of the foregoing powers my trustees shall hold the trust fund and the income thereof at the expiration of the trust period in trust absolutely for such of my children and remoter issue as shall then be living in equal shares per stirpes so that no child or remoter issue shall take as share whose parent is then living and capable of taking.

(6) Any capital or income of the trust fund not otherwise disposed of by this clause shall be held in trust for such of my children as shall survive me if more than one in equal shares.

1 The definition of the discretionary class may need to be enlarged or adapted in individual cases, for example if issue of the spouse who are not issue of the testator are intended to be capable of benefiting. If the testator does not wish to include civil partners of his issue in the discretionary class, he will probably also want to exclude persons in same sex marriages with his issue. The Marriage (Same Sex Couples) Act 2013 (see paras **[245.149]** ff) has been passed but not yet brought into force.

2 The surviving spouse is entitled to the income and can have capital paid to her or for her benefit under the power in clause 8 (2)(a), and so it is not essential for her to be a member of the class of discretionary beneficiaries from the point of view of providing her with access to income or capital. The reason for including her in this class is that it provides greater flexibility as to what can be achieved in exercise of the power of appointment. The danger of including her is that the need to remove her from the class may be overlooked if her life interest is terminated during her life: see para **[224.111]**, n 3.

3 These words authorise the creation of discretionary powers, e g powers to advance capital to a life tenant, which might not otherwise be valid: see Vol 1, para **[40.5]**.

4 For wills made on or after 6 April 2010, there are no statutory restrictions on accumulation in respect of non-charitable trusts, so accumulation will be permitted throughout the trust period: see the PAA 2009, s 13, 15(1)(a) (Part G, para **[246.189]**)

5 This confirms that the trustees could make an appointment in remainder expectant upon the surviving spouse's life interest, and so in effect vary the remainder capital trusts, without causing her IPDI to come to an end (see para **[200.98]**). Trusts for bereaved minors can arise by appointment under a will (see paras **[200.108]**, **[200.128]** above), so if circumstances were appropriate it would be possible for the trustees to appoint a trust for bereaved minors in relation to a part, say, of the residuary estate, and then terminate the surviving spouse's IPDI in that part by way of potentially exempt transfer (see para **[200.108]** above).

6 A power to apply capital, being exercisable in a less formal manner, may be useful. But it is essential that its exercise should be adequately evidenced.

7 See note 4 above.

C3

Wills for married couples (or civil partners) with adult children

Form C3.1: Reciprocal wills giving nil-rate band legacy to children and residue to spouse with default gift to children in equal/unequal shares

[225.13]

[Updated in footnote 1 for Finance Act 2010. Updated in footnote 6 and in the text for Perpetuities and Accumulations Act 2009.]

GIFT OF NIL RATE BAND LEGACY TO CHILDREN[1]

3. (1) If my [wife/husband] shall survive me[2] then I give to my trustees a pecuniary legacy of the maximum sum (if any) [not exceeding £——][3] which can in the circumstances subsisting at my death be given by this clause without any liability being incurred for the payment of inheritance tax on or by reason of my death and in particular (without prejudice to the generality of the foregoing) for the purpose of determining the amount of such maximum sum the circumstances to be taken into account shall include all chargeable transfers made by me during my life (or events treated as such for inheritance tax purposes) so far as relevant for the computation of inheritance tax on my death the dispositions taking effect under this will (apart from this clause) or under any codicil hereto and any property treated as if it were part of my estate for inheritance tax purposes].

EITHER[4]

(2) My trustees shall hold the said legacy upon trust for such of my children [*name*] [*name*] and [*name*][5] as shall survive me and if more than one in equal shares Provided that if any of my said children shall predecease me leaving a child or children surviving me [who shall attain the age of [18/21/25] years[6]] such last-mentioned child or children shall take and if more than one equally between them the share of the said legacy which such deceased child of mine would have taken had he or she survived me.

OR

(2) My trustees shall hold the said legacy upon trust to divide the same into [10] equal parts and shall hold:

(a) [5] of such parts upon trust for [my son] [name];
(b) a further [3] of such parts upon trust for [my daughter] [*name*]; and

(c) the remaining [2] of such parts upon trust for [my daughter] [*name*][7] Provided that:

(i) if any of my said children shall predecease me leaving a child or children living at my death [who shall attain the age of [18/21/25] years[8]] such last-mentioned child or children shall take and if more than one equally between them the share of the said legacy which such deceased child of mine would have taken had he or she survived me;

(ii) if the trusts of any share of the said legacy shall fail because a child of mine predeceases me without leaving a child who attains a vested interest under paragraph (i) of this proviso then such share (and any share which may have accrued thereto hereunder) shall accrue to the other shares or share of the said legacy the trusts of which have not failed and if more than one [in equal shares]/[in the proportions which such shares bear to each other].

(3) The said legacy shall carry interest at the yearly rate of 6 per cent from my death until the same shall be paid or satisfied or set apart and invested and section 31 of the Trustee Act 1925 (as hereinafter modified) shall apply thereto.[9]

1 Subclause (1) of this clause gives a legacy of a sum determined in accordance with a formula which represents the maximum sum which can be given without incurring a liability for IHT. The current IHT threshold is £325,000. The government has announced that the rate will remain £325,000 at least until 2017–18: see the Budget TIIN 20 March 2013 'Inheritance Tax—Nil-Rate Band', *Simon's Weekly Tax Intelligence* 28 March 2013, p 978. The formula for ascertaining the amount of the legacy is intended to ensure that the amount of the discretionary legacy does not exceed the IHT threshold where other non-exempt gifts are made by the will, or where there are non-exempt lifetime chargeable transfers or property treated as part of the testator's estate to be taken into account on the death. It also adjusts the legacy to any future increases in the nil-rate band where the IHT threshold is increased after the will has been made.

2 This precondition is imposed to avoid unnecessary duplication of gifts (ie this one and the residuary gift) in the event of the spouse not surviving the testator.

3 In view of the uncertainty about the nil-rate band in the next few years it would be advisable to set a cash limit on the amount of this gift. See para **[225.9]**. Another reason for setting a cash limit on it is where the testator has business or agricultural property: see the Preliminary Note to C11 at paras **[233.8]–[233.10]**.

4 The alternative forms give the legacy to the children either in equal or unequal shares, with substitutional provisions for the children of a predeceasing child. Similar alternatives are provided in the gift of residue which takes effect if the spouse does not survive the testator.

5 See the Preliminary Note on reciprocal wills and the ultimate destination of property at para **[225.7]**.

6 In this clause the grandchildren are all lives in being at the testator's death which was important for the common law perpetuity rule. For wills made on or after 6 April 2010, the perpetuity period is 125 years (and there is no other period): see the PAA 2009, ss 5(1), 15(1)(a) (Part A **[200.35A]** and Part G, para **[246.179]**). The clause could, therefore, be redrawn to extend to grandchildren born after the testator's death without infringing the rule against perpetuities. If the gift to them is subject to an age contingency, and any of them have not satisfied it at the testator's death, but the substitutional trust takes effect, the property subject to it will be within the IHT charging regime for relevant property, unless they are entitled to interests in possession by the time of the testator's death and thus have IPDIs (see paras **[200.92]**, **[224.25]** above).

7 See the Preliminary Note on reciprocal wills and the ultimate destination of property at para **[225.7]**.

8 See n 6 above.

9 There is a contingency in the substitutional provision in proviso (i) to sub-cl (2) of this clause. A contingent legacy does not ordinarily carry the intermediate income, but one of the exceptions to this is where the legacy is directed to be set apart, invested and held on trust (see Vol 1, para **[32.15]**). This clause directs the trustees to hold the legacy on trust, and that may be sufficient to carry the intermediate income, but sub-cl (3) makes the position clear.

[225.14]

[Updated for Trusts (Capital and Income) Act 2013.]

ADMINISTRATION TRUSTS OF RESIDUE

4. (1) I give all my property not hereby or by any codicil hereto otherwise effectively disposed of [(including any entailed or other property over which I shall have at my death a general power of disposition by will)][1] to my trustees to hold on the trusts set out below with power to sell all or any of it.[2]

(2) My trustees shall pay my funeral and testamentary expenses[3] and debts and any legacies given by this will or any codicil hereto out of such property or its proceeds and shall have a discretion as to how such payments shall be borne as between capital and income.[4]

(3) Subject as above my trustees shall hold such property and the assets from time to time representing the same (hereinafter called 'my residuary estate') on the trusts set out below and shall invest all money comprised in such property or arising from its sale in any of the investments hereby authorised with power to change such investments into any others hereby authorised.[5]

1 See Form C2.1, cl 6, n 1 at para **[224.34]**.
2 See Form C2.1, cl 6, n 2 at para **[224.34]**.
3 See Form C2.1, cl 6, n 3 at para **[224.34]**.
4 See Form C2.1, cl 6, n 4 at para **[224.34]**.
5 See Form C2.1, cl 6, n 5 at para **[224.34]**.

[225.16]

[Updated in text and footnote 3 for Perpetuities and Accumulations Act 2009.]

BENEFICIAL TRUSTS OF RESIDUE[1]

6. (1) My trustees shall hold my residuary estate upon trust for my [wife/husband] if [she/he] shall survive me.

EITHER

[(2) If my [wife/husband] fails to survive me my trustees shall hold my residuary estate upon trust for such of my children [*name*] [*name*] and [*name*][2] as shall survive me and if more than one in equal shares Provided that if any of my said children shall predecease me leaving a child or children surviving me [who shall attain the age of [18/21/25] years[3]] such last-mentioned child or children shall take and if more than one equally between them the share of my residuary estate which such deceased child of mine would have taken had he or she survived me.]

OR

[(2) If my [wife/husband] fails to survive me my trustees shall hold my residuary estate upon trust to divide the same into [10] equal parts and shall hold:

(a) [5] of such parts upon trust for [my son] [*name*];

(b) a further [3] of such parts upon trust for [my daughter] [*name*]; and

(c) the remaining [2] of such parts upon trust for [my daughter] [*name*];[4]

provided that:

(i) if any of my said children predeceases me leaving a child or children living at my death [who shall attain the age of [18/21/25] years[5]] such last-mentioned child or children shall take and if more than one equally between them the share of my residuary estate which such deceased child of mine would have taken had he or she survived me;

(ii) if the trusts of any share of my residuary estate shall fail because a child of mine predeceases me without leaving a child who attains a vested interest under paragraph (i) of this proviso then such share (and any share which may have accrued thereto hereunder) shall accrue to the other shares or share of the said legacy the trusts of which have not failed and if more than one [in equal shares]/[in the proportions which such shares bear to each other].

1 Residue devolves on the other spouse, if surviving. If the other spouse does not survive the testator, residue is given to the children. Two alternatives are given for the trust for the children; the alternatives correspond with the alternatives in the legacy contained in cl 3(2) of this form at para **[225.13]**.

2 See the Preliminary Note on reciprocal wills and the ultimate destination of property at para **[225.7]**.

3 In this clause the grandchildren are all lives in being at the testator's death which was important for the common law perpetuity rule. For wills made on or after 6 April 2010, the perpetuity period is 125 years (and there is no other period): see the PAA 2009, ss 5(1), 15(1)(a) (Part A **[200.35A]** and Part G, para **[246.179]**). The clause could, therefore, be redrawn to extend to grandchildren born after the testator's death without infringing the rule against perpetuities. If the gift to them is subject to an age contingency, and any of them have not satisfied it at the testator's death, but the substitutional trust takes effect, the property subject to it will be within the IHT charging regime for relevant property, unless they are entitled to interests in possession by the time of the testator's death and thus have IPDIs (see paras **[200.92]**, **[224.25]** above).

4 See the Preliminary Note on reciprocal wills and the ultimate destination of property at para **[225.7]**.

5 See n 3 above.

Form C3.2: Reciprocal wills with nil-rate band legacy on trust for the children, residue on trust for spouse for life and then on trust for the children, son taking a life interest and daughter a protected life interest

[225.32]

[Updated in text and footnote 6 for Perpetuities and Accumulations Act 2009 and FA 2013, Sch 44.]

GIFT OF NIL-RATE BAND LEGACY ON TRUST FOR CHILDREN[1]

4. (1) If my [wife/husband] shall survive me[2] then I give to my trustees a pecuniary legacy of the maximum sum (if any) [not exceeding £——][3] which

can in the circumstances subsisting at my death be given by this clause without any liability being incurred for the payment of inheritance tax on or by reason of my death and in particular (without prejudice to the generality of the foregoing) for the purpose of determining the amount of such maximum sum the circumstances to be taken into account shall include all chargeable transfers made by me during my life (or events treated as such for inheritance tax purposes) so far as relevant for the computation of inheritance tax on my death the dispositions taking effect under this will (apart from this clause) or under any codicil hereto and any property treated as if it were part of my estate for inheritance tax purposes.

(2) My trustees shall hold the said legacy upon trust to invest the same in any investments hereby authorised with power to vary the same and shall hold the same and the assets from time to time representing the same (hereinafter called 'the trust legacy') upon trust to divide the same into two equal shares hereinafter respectively called 'my son's share' and 'my daughter's share'.

(3) My trustees shall hold my son's share upon the following trusts:

(a) my trustees shall pay the income of my son's share to my son [*name*] ('my son') during his life;[4]

(b) provided that my trustees shall have power in their absolute discretion from time to time during my son's life to pay transfer or apply the whole or any part or parts of my son's share to him or for his benefit in such manner as they shall in their absolute discretion think fit;

(c) subject as aforesaid my son shall have power at any time by deed or deeds revocable or irrevocable or by will or codicil to appoint to any wife who may survive him as his widow (including power to appoint to a named wife contingently on her surviving him as his widow) an interest in the income of the whole or any part or parts of my son's share for the residue of her life or for any lesser period;[5]

[(d) subject as aforesaid my trustees shall hold my son's share upon such trusts for the benefit of all or such one or more exclusive of the others or other of my son's children and remoter issue if more than one in such shares and with such trusts and powers for their respective benefit (including trusts and powers conferring a discretion as to the disposition of capital or income by whomsoever exercisable) and such provisions (including provisions for the accumulation of income during any period permitted by law and administrative provisions of whatever nature) as my son may by any deed revocable or irrevocable or by will or codicil appoint;]

[(d)/(e)] subject as aforesaid my trustees shall hold my son's share upon trust for such of the children of my son as shall attain the age of [18/21][6] years if more than one in equal shares;

[(e)/(f)] subject as aforesaid my trustees shall hold my son's share as an accretion to my daughter's share and as one fund therewith for all purposes.

(4) My trustees shall hold my daughter's share upon the following trusts:

(a) my trustees shall hold my daughter's share upon protective trusts[7] for the benefit of my daughter [*name*] ('my daughter') during her life provided that none of my trustees shall be liable for paying to my daughter the income of my daughter's share accruing after the forfeiture of her protected life interest unless such trustee shall have express notice of the act thing or event giving rise to the forfeiture; [8]

(b) Provided further that my trustees shall have power in their absolute discretion from time to time during my daughter's life to pay transfer or apply the whole or any part or parts of my daughter's share to her or for her benefit in such manner as they shall in their absolute discretion think fit and whether or not any forfeiture of her foregoing protective life interest shall have occurred;

(c) subject as aforesaid my daughter shall have power at any time by deed or deeds revocable or irrevocable or by will or codicil to appoint to any husband who may survive her as her widower (including power to appoint to a named husband contingently on him surviving her as her widower) an interest in the income of the whole or any part or parts of my daughter's share for the residue of his life or for any lesser period;[9]

[(d) subject as aforesaid my trustees shall hold my daughter's share upon such trusts for the benefit of all or such one or more exclusive of the others or other of my daughter's children and remoter issue if more than one in such shares and with such trusts and powers for their respective benefit (including trusts and powers conferring a discretion as to the disposition of capital or income by whomsoever exercisable) and such provisions (including provisions for the accumulation of income during any period permitted by law and administrative provisions of whatever nature) as my daughter may by any deed revocable or irrevocable or by will or codicil appoint;]

[(d)/(e)] subject as aforesaid my trustees shall hold my daughter's share upon trust for such of the children of my daughter as shall attain the age of [18/21][10] years if more than one in equal shares;

[(e)/(f)] subject as aforesaid my trustees shall hold my daughter's share as an accretion to my son's share and as one fund therewith for all purposes.

(5) The trusts hereinbefore declared of the capital of my son's share and my daughter's share shall carry the intermediate income (so far as not disposed of under any trust having priority thereto) and section 31 of the Trustee Act 1925 (as hereinafter modified) shall apply thereto.

(6) Section 32 of the Trustee Act 1925 (as hereinafter modified) shall apply in relation to the said trusts.

1 See Form C3.1, cl 3, n 1 at para **[225.13]**.
2 See Form C3.1, cl 3, n 2 at para **[225.13]**.
3 See Form C3.1, cl 3, n 3 at para **[225.13]**.
4 The son's life interest should be an IPDI within IHTA 1984, s 49A (see paras **[200.98]** and **[216.1]** above), so the property subject to it should be outside of the relevant property regime for IHT purposes. But if he appoints an interest in possession to his spouse or civil partner under sub-clause (c) it will only attract the spouse or civil partner exemption from IHT if it is also a disabled person's interest (see para **[200.99]** above). This would be the only relevant type of interest in possession which would have the result of treating his spouse or civil partner as beneficially entitled to the underlying settled property for IHT purposes under IHTA 1984, s 49(1), (1A)(b) thus enabling the spouse or civil partner exemption to be claimed. During the subsistence of the spouse's or civil partner's interest in possession (unless it is a disabled person's interest) and any continuing trusts for his children whether

appointed or taking effect in default, the property would fall within the IHT charging regime for relevant property (see para **[200.92]** above).

5 This power will have the practical advantage of enabling the son to make provision for his widow, but will have no IHT advantage unless the interest appointed is a disabled person's interest (see n 4 above).

6 For wills made on or after 6 April 2010, the perpetuity period is 125 years (and there is no other period): see the PAA 2009, ss 5(1), 15(1)(a) (Part A **[200.35A]** and Part G, para **[246.179]**). The age contingency in this clause was included so as not to infringe the common law rule against perpetuities. For wills made prior to 6 April 2010, if there was no express perpetuity period in the instrument creating the power the period of a life or lives in being plus 21 years ought to have been used. Thus, the grandchildren would not necessarily be alive at the testator's death and it was therefore important to restrict the age contingency to 21 so as not to infringe the common law rule against perpetuities. For wills made on or after 6 April 2010 this restriction on the age contingency to 21 is not necessary although it is still important that all interests vest within the perpetuity period. We should add that if this is not done, there will still be 'wait and see' under the PAA 2009, s 7 (Part G, para **[246.181]**).

7 The statutory protective trusts are set out in the TA 1925, s 33 (Part G, para **[246.31]**). The daughter's protected life interest should be an IPDI within IHTA 1984, s 49A (see para **[200.98]** above), so the property subject to it should be outside the relevant property regime for IHT purposes. It would remain so even if she forfeited her life interest, see IHTA 1984, s 88 (amended by FA 2006, Sch 20, para 24), see para **[200.104]**. But if she appoints an interest in possession to her spouse or civil partner under sub-clause (c) it will only attract the spouse or civil partner exemption from IHT if it is also a disabled person's interest (see para **[200.99]** above). This would be the only relevant type of interest in possession which would have the result of treating his spouse or civil partner as beneficially entitled to the underlying for IHT purposes under IHTA 1984, s 49(1), (1A)(b) thus enabling the spouse or civil partner exemption to be claimed. During the subsistence of the spouse's or civil partner's interest in possession (unless it is a disabled person's interest) and any continuing trusts for her children whether appointed or taking effect in default, the property would fall within the IHT charging regime for relevant property (see para **[200.92]** above).

8 The proviso to this subclause will protect an innocent trustee who continues to pay income to the protected life tenant after the forfeiture of her interest unless he has express notice of the event giving rise to the forfeiture.

9 This power will have the practical advantage of enabling the daughter to make provision for her widower, but will have no IHT advantage unless the interest appointed is a disabled person's interest (see n 7 above).

10 See n 6 above.

[225.35]

[Updated for FA 2013, Sch 44.]

BENEFICIAL TRUSTS OF RESIDUE

7. (1) My trustees shall hold my residuary estate upon trust to pay the income thereof to my [wife/husband] during [her/his] life.[1]

(2) Provided that my trustees shall have power in their absolute discretion from time to time so long as my [wife/husband] is entitled to be paid the income of all or any part of the capital of my residuary estate (or would be so entitled if such capital yielded income) to pay transfer or apply the whole or any part or parts of such capital[2] to [her/him] or for [her/his] benefit in such manner as they shall in their absolute discretion think fit.

(3) Subject as aforesaid my trustees shall divide my residuary estate into two equal shares (hereinafter respectively called 'my son's residuary share' and 'my daughter's residuary share') and shall hold my son's residuary share upon the trusts and with and subject to the powers and provisions hereinbefore declared in respect of my son's share of the trust legacy and shall hold

my daughter's residuary share upon the trusts and with and subject to the powers and provisions hereinbefore declared in respect of my daughter's share of the trust legacy.[3]

(4) The powers to pay transfer or apply capital of my son's residuary share to or for the benefit of my son and of my daughter's residuary share to or for the benefit of my daughter hereinbefore (by reference) declared shall be exercisable during the life of my [wife/husband] [with [her/his] written consent][4] and for this purpose my trustees shall have power during the life of my [wife/husband] to appropriate my residuary estate to or between my son's residuary share and my daughter's residuary share wholly or partially and in any manner they think fit.

1 The surviving spouse's life interest will be an IPDI within IHTA 1984, s 49A, so spouse exemption from IHT should be available (see paras **[200.84]**, **[200.98]**, **[216.1]** above).

2 There are two reasons for restricting the power to capital in which the spouse has an interest in possession: first, to ensure that the power is not exercisable if there is a divorce and the primary trust fails and, secondly, to ensure that the power ceases to be exercisable if the spouse assigns or surrenders his or her life interest. It is important that this power should cease to be exercisable in such an event because the termination of an IPDI on or after 22 March 2006 will be deemed to be a gift of the underlying settled property for the purposes of FA 1986, s 102, so that unless the beneficiary of the IPDI is excluded altogether from benefit after the termination, the gift with reservation rules could apply, see FA 1986, s 102ZA, (see para **[200.76]** above). On the possibility of divorce see the Preliminary Note to C2 at para **[224.16]–[224.23]**.

3 If the testator is not survived by his spouse, and the remainder trusts for the children take effect immediately on his death, then the IHT consequences will be as in the notes to Clauses 4(3) and 4(4) above. But if the spouse survives, and they take effect in remainder to the spouse's life interest, the property subject to the remainder trusts will be within the IHT charging regime for relevant property even during the childrens' life interests since they will not be IPDIs (and unless they meet certain conditions, including the child being disabled, they will not be disabled persons' interests (see para **[200.99]** above)) (see para **[225.25]** above).

4 Including these words will give the surviving spouse protection against losing the benefit of any of the fund against his or her will. The disadvantage of including them is that the surviving spouse will be the settlor of the income for income tax purposes if the power is exercised. The latter is probably not a serious disadvantage, as this only has adverse consequences where a 'settlor' retains a possibility of benefit or where he or she settles property on his or her minor children. This form is for use where the children are adult.

Form C3.3: Will dividing residue between spouse and issue

[225.51]

[Updated in text and footnote 8 for Perpetuities and Accumulations Act 2009.]

BENEFICIAL TRUSTS OF RESIDUE

6. (1) My trustees shall hold one equal half share of my residuary estate upon trust for my [wife/husband] absolutely.[1]

(2) Subject as aforesaid my trustees shall hold my residuary estate[2] upon trust to divide the same into two equal shares (hereinafter respectively called 'my son's children's share' and 'my daughter's share').

(3) My trustees shall hold my son's children's share upon trust for such of the children of my son [(whenever born)][3] as shall be living on the vesting day (as hereinafter defined)[4] or shall earlier attain the age of [18/21/25] years[5] and if more than one in equal shares provided that:

(a) if any child of my son shall predecease me or having survived me shall die before attaining a vested interest under the foregoing trust leaving a child or children surviving me or born after my death who shall be living on the vesting day or shall earlier attain the age of [18/21/25] years such last-mentioned child or children shall take if more than one equally between them the share of my son's children's share which such deceased child of my son would have taken had he or she lived to attain a vested interest therein;

(b) if there shall be no child or grandchild of my son who shall live to attain a vested interest under the foregoing trusts my trustees shall hold my son's children's share upon trust for my son absolutely.[6]

(4) My trustees shall hold my daughter's share upon trust for my daughter absolutely provided that if my daughter shall predecease me my trustees shall hold my daughter's share upon trust for such of her children as shall survive me and attain the age of [18/21/25] years and if more than one in equal shares.[7]

(5) The foregoing trusts shall carry the intermediate income of my residuary estate and section 31 of the Trustee Act 1925 (as hereinafter modified) shall apply thereto.

(6) Section 32 of the Trustee Act 1925 (as hereinafter modified) shall apply in relation to my residuary estate.

(7) If the trusts of either of my son's children's share or my daughter's share shall fail or determine the same shall accrue to and be held upon the trusts affecting the other such share or such thereof as are still subsisting and capable of taking effect at the date of such accruer.

(8) In this clause the expression 'the vesting day' means the day on which shall expire the period of 125 years less three days immediately following my death[8].

(9) I declare that if the foregoing trust for my [wife/husband] shall take effect then the half share of my residuary estate to be held in trust for [her/him] shall be ascertained by equal division of my residuary estate inclusive of any inheritance tax payable by reason of my death and attributable to my son's children's share and my daughter's children's share (which shall be borne exclusively by the latter two shares).[9]

1 For the reasons for not including survivorship conditions as between husband and wife or civil partners see **[224.6]–[224.9]**.

2 The gift of the residuary estate contained in this subclause will carry the wife's share if she fails to survive or the gift to her fails as a result of a divorce. See the Note on the possibility of divorce (or dissolution of civil partnership) to C2.1 at paras **[224.16]–[224.23]**.

3 If included, the words in brackets will exclude the rule in *Andrews v Partington* and the class of eligible children will not be closed when the first child attains the specified age: *Re Edmondson's Will Trusts* [1972] 1 All ER 444, [1972] 1 WLR 183, CA. However, the trustees will be able to advance the entire presumptive share of any child in exercise of the power of advancement under the TA 1925, s 32 as extended to the whole of a presumptive share under cl 7 at para **[225.52]**.

4 See sub-cl (9) for the definition of 'the vesting day'.

5 Since an ultimate vesting provision is incorporated, any age may be specified.

6 If the trusts for the children (or grandchildren) of the testator's son come into possession while they are under the specified vesting age, the trusts will be subject to the IHT relevant property regime (see paras **[200.92]**, **[224.24]** above). This is subject to the point that if interests in possession commence before the vesting of capital, and any child of the testator's son attains the age at which interests in possession commence (without also attaining the age of vesting of capital) before the testator dies or within two years after his death, the share held for such child will be subject to an IPDI and beneficiary-taxed: see

paras **[218.74]**, **[224.25]**. The same could apply to the share of a grandchild of the testator's son who takes an interest under the substitution clause by reason of his or her parent predeceasing the testator, but not to a grandchild of the testator's son who takes by substitution as a consequence of the death after the death of the testator of his or her parent before attaining the vesting age. To avoid so far as possible an accidental IPDI, extend accumulation and maintenance trusts to the maximum: see para **[225.52]**, n 1.

7 If the trusts for the daughter's children come into possession while they are under the specified vesting age, the trusts will be subject to the IHT relevant property regime (see paras **[200.92]**, **[224.24]**), subject to the same IPDI possibility as described in n 6 above.

8 For wills made on or after 6 April 2010, the perpetuity period is 125 years (and there is no other period): see the PAA 2009, ss 5(1), 15(1)(a) (Part A **[200.35A]** and Part G, para **[246.179]**). There is no longer any good reason to define the vesting day by reference to any other period.

9 See the Preliminary Note to B14 at para **[214.72]** for the reasons for making provision of this type in relation to residuary estates which are partially exempt from IHT.

[225.52]

[Updated in text and footnote 1 for Perpetuities and Accumulations Act 2009.]

MAINTENANCE, ACCUMULATION AND ADVANCEMENT

7. (1) Section 31 of the Trustee Act 1925 (relating to accumulation and maintenance) shall apply in relation to the trusts hereby or by any codicil hereto declared as if:

(a) in paragraph (i) of subsection (1) of the said section the words 'as the trustees think fit' were substituted for the words 'as may in all the circumstances be reasonable'; and

(b) the proviso to the said subsection (1) were omitted

[Provided that in relation to any presumptive share of my residuary estate of any person living at my death the said section 31 (amended as aforesaid) shall have effect as if the age of majority were the age of [21/25] years (and so that the expressions 'infancy', 'minority' and 'infant' and all references to the age of eighteen years in the said Section 31 shall be construed accordingly).][1]

(2) Section 32 of the Trustee Act 1925 (relating to advancement) shall apply in relation to the said trusts as if the words 'one half of' were omitted from proviso (a) to subsection (1) thereof

(3) Whenever my trustees shall have an obligation or discretion under the provisions of this will or any codicil hereto or under the general law to apply income or capital for the benefit of a minor beneficiary they may either pay the same without liability to account to his or her parent guardian or any other adult person with whom such beneficiary may be residing or to such beneficiary himself or herself if of the age of 16 years or more and so that the receipt of such parent guardian or other person or of such minor beneficiary shall be a full and sufficient discharge to my trustees for the income or capital so applied.[2]

1 For wills made on or after 6 April 2010, there are no statutory restrictions on accumulation in respect of non-charitable trusts, so accumulation will be permitted throughout the trust period: see the PAA 2009, s 13, 15(1)(a) (Part G, para **[246.187]**). It is no longer necessary, therefore, to introduce a restriction in order to comply with the rule against excessive accumulations as was previously the case: see the form of this clause as set out in the 9th Edition. If the testator dies when a beneficiary is under the vesting age, the fund held for that beneficiary will be subject to the IHT relevant property regime rather than the IPDI regime (see para **[225.51]** n 7). Relevant property treatment will often be preferable to IPDI

treatment (see paras **[200.131]**, **[200.132]**, **[224.24]**), and, where IPDI treatment seems to be preferable in the circumstances prevailing after the testator's death it will be possible to convert the trust retrospectively to an IPDI trust by exercise of the power of advancement within two years of the testator's death in reliance on IHTA 1984, s 144 (see para **[225.119]** ff). Conversion from an IPDI trust to a relevant property one would involve an IHT lifetime chargeable transfer by the beneficiary unless it can be achieved by a deed of variation within IHTA 1984, s 142. However, if it is desired to have IPDI treatment for these trusts, Trustee Act 1925, s 31 should be excluded, using a clause such as the second alternative clause 8(1) in Form C2.1, para **[224.36]**.

2 A parent (with parental responsibility) and a guardian of a minor are empowered by the ChA 1989, s 3(3) (Part G, para **[244.114]**) to give a good receipt for the minor's property: see Vol 1, para **[9.41]**. The power in this subclause is wider in that it authorises the payment of income or capital to a parent who does not have parental responsibility, any adult with whom the minor is residing, and the minor himself or herself if 16 or over.

Form C3.4: Reciprocal wills containing nil-rate band legacy on discretionary trusts with gift of residue to spouse

[225.60]

[Updated for Perpetuities and Accumulations Act 2009 and for FA 2013, Sch 44.]

GIFT OF NIL-RATE BAND LEGACY ON DISCRETIONARY TRUSTS[1]

2. (1) If my [wife/husband] shall survive me[2] then I give to my legacy trustees (hereafter defined) a pecuniary legacy of the maximum sum (if any)[3] which can in the circumstances subsisting at my death be given by this clause without any liability being incurred for the payment of inheritance tax on or by reason of my death and in particular (without prejudice to the generality of the foregoing) for the purpose of determining the amount of such maximum sum the circumstances to be taken into account shall include all chargeable transfers made by me during my life (or events treated as such for inheritance tax purposes) so far as relevant for the computation of inheritance tax on my death the dispositions taking effect under this will (apart from this clause) or under any codicil hereto and any property treated as if it were part of my estate for inheritance tax purposes.

(2) In this clause the following expressions have the following meanings, namely:

(a) 'the trust legacy' means the legacy by this clause bequeathed to my legacy trustees and the assets for the time being representing the same;

(b) 'my legacy trustees' means and includes [*name*] of [*address*] and [*name*] of [*address*] or other the trustee or trustees for the time being of the trust legacy[4];

(c) 'the beneficiaries' means and includes my [wife/husband] and my children and remoter issue;[5]

(d) 'the trust period' means the period commencing on my death and expiring 125 years less three days thereafter.[6]

(3) My legacy trustees shall hold the trust legacy and the income thereof upon trust for all or such one or more of the beneficiaries at such ages or times in such shares and upon such trusts for the benefit of the beneficiaries as my legacy trustees (being at least two in number [or a trust corporation][7]) may by deed or deeds revocable or irrevocable executed at any time or times during the trust period appoint and in making any such appointment my

legacy trustees shall have powers as full as those which they would possess if they were an absolute beneficial owner of the trust legacy and in particular (but without prejudice to the generality of the foregoing words) my legacy trustees may in any exercise of the foregoing power as they in their absolute discretion think fit:

(a) delegate give or impose to or upon themselves or any other person or persons and in relation to any trust or disposition any discretionary powers or discretionary trusts conditions limitations restrictions or provisions including powers of further delegation or powers to create further discretionary trusts or powers;[8]

(b) create trusts or powers for the accumulation of income;

(c) appoint or create administrative powers or provisions of whatever nature;

Provided that:

(i) no such appointment shall invalidate any payment transfer or application of capital or income previously made under any of the trusts or powers herein elsewhere contained;

(ii) every interest limited under any exercise of such power shall vest in interest (if at all) not later than the expiration of the trust period;

(iii) any such appointment may be made in respect of income alone without any appointment of capital; and

(iv) any such revocable appointment shall (so far as then unrevoked) cease to be revocable on the expiration of the trust period.

(4) In default of and subject to any exercise of the foregoing power my legacy trustees (being at least two in number [or a trust corporation][9]) may at their discretion at any time or times during the trust period pay transfer or apply the whole or any part or parts of the trust legacy to or for the benefit of all or any one or more of the beneficiaries for the time being living in such manner as my legacy trustees think fit.[10]

(5) Subject to any or every exercise of the foregoing powers my legacy trustees shall during the trust period hold the trust legacy upon trust to pay or apply the income thereof to or for the maintenance education or benefit of all or any one or more of the beneficiaries for the time being living in such shares if more than one and generally in such manner as they think fit provided that my legacy trustees may accumulate the whole or any part of the income of the trust legacy by investing the same and the resulting income thereof in any of the investments hereby authorised and any accumulations of income so made shall form part of the capital of the trust legacy for all purposes.

(6) Subject to the foregoing trust and any or every exercise of the foregoing powers my legacy trustees shall hold the trust legacy and the income thereof at the expiration of the trust period in trust absolutely for such of my children and remoter issue as shall then be living in equal shares per stirpes.

(7) Any capital or income of the trust legacy not otherwise disposed of by this clause shall be held in trust for such of my children as shall survive me if more than one in equal shares

(8) Instead of the trust legacy being satisfied by the payment of cash or by the appropriation of property:[11]

(a) my trustees may charge (with or without there being any personal liability of any person or persons) any property which is (or but for this clause would be) comprised in my residuary estate with payment of a sum of money equal to or less than the amount of the trust legacy to my legacy trustees and my legacy trustees shall accept such charge for such sum as the whole or a part (as the case may be) of the trust legacy; and

(b) my trustees may require my legacy trustees to accept in satisfaction of all or part of the trust legacy a binding promise of payment (secured or unsecured) made personally by my wife or by my trustees as trustees of my residuary estate which debt shall be payable on demand and my legacy trustees shall accept such debt as the whole or a part (as the case may be) of the trust legacy.

(9) The following shall apply in relation to the powers in the last preceding subclause:

(a) my trustees may require to be included such terms if any as they think fit in relation to a charge under subclause (8)(a) above or a debt under subclause (8)(b) above including terms as to interest (if any) and terms linking the debt or sum charged to the Retail Prices Index or otherwise providing for its amount to vary with the passage of time according to a formula provided that the debt or sum charged shall be payable to my legacy trustees on demand and the charge shall be enforceable by my legacy trustees at any time;

(b) my legacy trustees may leave the charge or debt outstanding for as long as they think fit and refrain from exercising their rights in relation to it and waive the payment of all or any part of any interest due in respect of it and may accept any substitute debt or charge undertaken or created by any person;

(c) my trustees may assent to the vesting of my residuary estate subject to an outstanding obligation to pay or satisfy the trust legacy and my legacy trustees may appoint new trustees in exercise of the statutory power to do so before the trust legacy has been paid or satisfied;[12]

(d) my legacy trustees and my trustees shall not be liable if my wife is or becomes unable to pay the debt or any security is or becomes inadequate or for any other loss or disadvantage which may occur as a result of their exercising or choosing not to exercise any of the foregoing powers; and

(e) the foregoing powers are in addition to any other powers given by this will or any codicil or by the general law and the foregoing powers may be exercised even though my trustees and my legacy trustees are the same persons or my wife is among either or both sets of trustees provided that such powers shall not be exercisable by a sole trustee who is my wife.

(10) My trustees may constitute the trust legacy wholly or partly by appropriating to it at their discretion any property or proportionate share of

any property and for this purpose may take such advice as to the value of the said property or proportionate share as they think fit.[13]

(11) Where the trust legacy is for the time being wholly or partly constituted by a proportionate share of a dwellinghouse or other property my legacy trustees shall have all the powers of an absolute owner in relation to such share and property and in particular may at their discretion join with the other proprietor or proprietors of such property:

(i) to permit a beneficiary under the trusts of the trust legacy to have the use or enjoyment of the property in kind on such terms as my legacy trustees think fit; or

(ii) to effect or enable a sale of the property and the purchase of another property in the same or similar co-ownership with the trust legacy constituted by a proportionate share thereof.

1 See Form C3.1, cl 3, n 1 at para **[225.13]**. This trust will be subject to the IHT relevant property regime, for which see **[218.8]** ff. For nil-rate band discretionary trusts see para **[218.16]** ff.

2 See Form C3.1, cl 3, n 2 at para **[225.13]**.

3 At this point in this formula in Form C3.1, cl 3, at para **[225.13]** a maximum limit is imposed for the reasons given in n 3 at para **[225.13]**. It is not appropriate to do so here. In Form C3.1 the nil-rate band legacy is given outright to the children, whereas here the surviving spouse is a beneficiary under the discretionary trust imposed on the nil-rate band legacy. Also, any excess over what turns out to be an acceptable size for the nil-rate band legacy could be appointed absolutely to the surviving spouse within two years of the testator's death and be treated as an exempt gift to the surviving spouse as a result of the application of IHTA 1984, s 144 (see paras **[225.83]**–**[225.91]**).

4 The main reasons for having separate trustees of the legacy are where a charge scheme might be entered into, in which case the testator's spouse should not be one of the executors and trustees but could be a trustee of the legacy, or where a debt scheme might be entered into and the testator's spouse might be sole executor: see para **[218.22]** above.

5 The definition of the discretionary class may need to be enlarged or adapted in individual cases.

6 For wills made on or after 6 April 2010, the perpetuity period is 125 years (and there is no other period): see the PAA 2009, ss 5(1), 15(1)(a) (Part A **[200.35A]** and Part G, para **[246.179]**). There is no longer any good reason to define the trust period by reference to any other period. The trust period is longer than may be needed in most cases, but gives considerable flexibility.

7 These words should be included if a trust corporation is to be an executor, or if there is a possibility that a trust corporation might subsequently be appointed a trustee. In either case express provision for the remuneration of a trust corporation so acting (not included in this form) may be added; see eg Forms B3.11 to B3.14 at paras **[203.28]**–**[203.31]** and Form B21.40 at para **[221.52]**. If express provision is not made, then the TrA 2000, s 29 authorises a trust corporation to receive reasonable remuneration (Part G, para **[246.161]**). Nonetheless, if a particular trust corporation is being appointed executor it should be ascertained whether it is content to receive only statutory remuneration or whether it requires express provision for its charges which may be in excess of those which might be authorised by statute. If it is desired to make it possible for a foreign corporation to be appointed as sole trustee, it will also be necessary to amend these words to '(being not fewer than two in number or a corporation)' and to vary the statutory power of appointment of new trustees as in Form B21.36 at para **[221.41]**.

8 These words authorise the creation of discretionary powers, eg powers to advance capital to a life tenant, which might not otherwise be valid: see Vol 1, para **[40.5]**.

9 See n 7 above.

10 A power to apply capital, being exercisable in a less formal manner, may be useful. But it is essential that its exercise should be adequately evidenced.

11 These powers and provisions are included so as to enable a debt or charge scheme to be used as a means of avoiding the surviving spouse having an interest in possession in the trust

fund subject to the trusts of this clause, where there are insufficient assets other than the matrimonial home with which to constitute that trust fund. See para **[218.19]** ff.

12 The purpose of this is so that new trustees of the residuary estate can be appointed before a charge is entered into, in a case where the surviving spouse is one of the personal representatives or the personal representatives and the trustees of the discretionary legacy are the same persons, and to make clear that new or additional trustees of the discretionary trust legacy can be appointed before the legacy is constituted as a debt from the surviving spouse where the surviving spouse is the sole trustee: see para **[218.22]** for the reasons for avoiding these states of affairs.

13 If post-21 March 2006 a beneficiary is permitted to occupy a property owned by a discretionary trust, whereas this may give that beneficiary an interest in possession, it will not necessarily be the type of interest in possession which will cause the property to be treated as part of his or her estate for IHT purposes. Only an interest in possession which is an IPDI, a disabled person's interest, or a transitional serial interest (see paras **[200.98]–[200.100]** above) will have this result. In the context of a discretionary trust established by will, if a permission to occupy is given within two years of the testator's death, and this gives rise to an interest in possession this may be backdated to the testator's death under IHTA 1984, s 144, so that it would be an IPDI and result in the property being treated as part of the beneficiary's estate for IHT purposes: see para **[225.83]** ff. But if the permission is not granted until after the second anniversary of the testator's death, and the beneficiary to whom it is granted is not a disabled person within the meaning of IHTA 1984, s 89B(2) (as substituted by FA 2013, Sch 44, para 8(2)) at (where the testator died before 8 April 2013) the testator's death or (where the testator on or after 8 April 2013) at the date of the grant, so that her interest is not a disabled person's interest within IHTA 1984, s 89B (as amended by FA 2013, Sch 44, paras 8, 10) (see para **[200.99]** above), it should not result in the property being treated as part of the beneficiary's estate for IHT purposes. Therefore, an express power to appropriate property or a share of property may be given to trustees to exercise in appropriate circumstances, and sub-clauses (10) and (11) contain such a power and associated provisions.

[225.62]

[Updated in text and footnote 3 for Perpetuities and Accumulations Act 2009.]

BENEFICIAL TRUSTS OF RESIDUE

4. (1) My trustees shall hold my residuary estate upon trust for my [wife/husband] [*name*] absolutely if [she/he] shall survive me.[1]

(2) If my [wife/husband] shall predecease me my trustees shall hold my residuary estate upon trust for such of my children [by my [wife/husband]][2] as shall survive me if more than one in equal shares, provided that if any of my [said][3] children shall predecease me leaving a child or children surviving me [who shall attain the age of [18/21/25] years][4] such last-mentioned child or children shall take if more than one equally between them the share of my residuary estate which such deceased child of mine would have taken had he or she survived me.

(3) The foregoing trusts shall carry the intermediate income of my residuary estate and section 31 of the Trustee Act 1925 (as hereinafter modified) shall apply thereto.

(4) Section 32 of the Trustee Act 1925 (as hereinafter modified) shall apply in relation to my residuary estate.

1 A survivorship condition is neither necessary nor advisable. See the Preliminary Note on survivorship conditions at para **[225.4]**.

2 These words ensure that the alternative gifts for the children in the wills of both spouses are identical in terms of whom they benefit, in circumstances where one spouse has children who are not children of the other spouse. See, further, the Preliminary Note to C2 on reciprocal wills and the ultimate destination of property at paras **[224.9]–[224.11]**. For forms

for use where one spouse has children who are not children of the marriage and wishes to benefit them by his or her will see C5 at para **[227.2]** ff.

3 For wills made on or after 6 April 2010, the perpetuity period is 125 years (and there is no other period): see the PAA 2009, ss 5(1), 15(1)(a) (Part A **[200.35A]** and Part G, para **[246.179]**). The age contingency in this clause was included so as not to infringe the common law rule against perpetuities. For wills made prior to 6 April 2010, if there was no express perpetuity period in the instrument creating the power the period of a life or lives in being plus 21 years ought to have been used. Thus, the grandchildren would not necessarily be alive at the testator's death and it was therefore important to restrict the age contingency to 21 so as not to infringe the common law rule against perpetuities. For wills made on or after 6 April 2010 this restriction on the age contingency to 21 is not necessary although it is still important that all interests vest within the perpetuity period. We should add that if this is not done, there will still be 'wait and see' under the PAA 2009, s 7 (Part G, para **[246.181]**). If the gift to them is subject to an age contingency, and any of them have not satisfied it at the testator's death, but the substitutional trust takes effect, the property subject to it will be within the IHT charging regime for relevant property or the IPDI regime (see para **[225.51]** n 7 above).

4 To be included if the trust is confined to the children of the marriage.

[225.63]

[Updated in text and footnote 6 for Perpetuities and Accumulations Act 2009.]

MAINTENANCE, ACCUMULATION AND ADVANCEMENT

5. (1) Section 31 of the Trustee Act 1925 (relating to accumulation and maintenance) shall apply in relation to the trusts hereby or by any codicil hereto declared as if:

(a) in paragraph (i) of subsection (1) of the said section the words 'as the trustees think fit' were substituted for the words 'as may in all the circumstances be reasonable'; and

(b) the proviso to the said subsection (1) were omitted

[Provided that in relation to any presumptive share of my residuary estate of any grandchild of mine living at my death the said section 31 (amended as aforesaid) shall have effect as if the age of majority were the age of [21/25] years (and so that the expressions 'infancy', 'minority' and 'infant' and all references to the age of eighteen years in the said Section 31 shall be construed accordingly).][1]

(2) Section 32 of the Trustee Act 1925 (relating to advancement) shall apply in relation to the said trusts as if the words 'one half of' were omitted from proviso (a) to subsection (1) thereof.

(3) Whenever my trustees or my legacy trustees shall have an obligation or discretion under the provisions of this will or any codicil hereto, or under the general law, to apply income or capital for the benefit of a minor beneficiary, they may either pay the same without liability to account to his or her parent, guardian or any other adult person with whom such beneficiary may be residing, or to such beneficiary himself or herself if of the age of 16 years or more and so that the receipt of such parent, guardian or other person or of such minor beneficiary shall be a full and sufficient discharge to my trustees or my legacy trustees (as the case may be) for the income or capital so applied.[2]

1 For wills made on or after 6 April 2010, there are no statutory restrictions on accumulation in respect of non-charitable trusts, so accumulation will be permitted throughout the trust period: see the PAA 2009, ss 13, 15(1)(a) (Part G, para **[246.187]**). It is no longer necessary,

therefore, to introduce a restriction in order to comply with the rule against excessive accumulations as was previously the case: see the form of this clause as set out in the 9th Edition.

2 A parent (with parental responsibility) and a guardian of a minor are empowered by the ChA 1989, s 3(3) (Part G, para **[244.114]**) to give a good receipt for the minor's property: see Vol 1, para **[9.41]**. The power in this subclause is wider, in that it authorises the payment of income or capital to a parent who does not have parental responsibility, any adult with whom the minor is residing, and the minor himself or herself if aged 16 or over.

Form C3.5: Reciprocal wills giving nil-rate band legacy on discretionary trusts and settling residue on protective trusts for spouse for life, with overriding trustees' powers over capital, and discretionary trusts for issue after the surviving spouse's death

[225.75]

[Updated in text for Perpetuities and Accumulations Act 2009.]

BENEFICIAL TRUSTS OF RESIDUE

6. (1) My trustees shall hold my residuary estate upon protective trusts[1] for the benefit of my [wife/husband] during [her/his] life provided that none of my trustees shall be liable for continuing to pay the income of my residuary estate to my [wife/husband] after [she/he] has done or attempted to do or has suffered any act or thing or an event has occurred which has caused [her/his] interest to determine unless such trustee has had actual notice of such act thing or event.[2]

(2) Subject as aforesaid my trustees shall hold my residuary estate upon trust until the vesting day (defined below) to pay the income thereof to or for the maintenance education or benefit of all or any one or more of the discretionary beneficiaries (defined below) for the time being living in such shares if more than one and generally in such manner as they think fit provided that my trustees may accumulate the whole or any part of the income of my residuary estate by investing the same and the resulting income thereof in any of the investments hereby authorised and any accumulations of income so made shall form part of the capital of my residuary estate for all purposes.[3]

(3) Subject to the foregoing my trustees shall hold my residuary estate and the income thereof in trust absolutely for such of my children and remoter issue as shall be living on the vesting day (defined below) in equal shares per stirpes so that no child or remoter issue shall take a share whose parent is then living and capable of taking.

(4) Any capital or income of my residuary estate not otherwise disposed of by this clause shall be held in trust for such of my children as shall survive me if more than one in equal shares.

1 The statutory protective trusts are set out in the TA 1925, s 33 (Part G, para **[246.31]**). Provided that no forfeiture has occurred before the testator's death, the spouse will be treated as having an IPDI for IHT purposes even if there is a forfeiture and the discretionary income trust arises: see the IHTA 1984, s 88 (amended by FA 2006, Sch 20 para 24), and Part A, paras **[200.20]**, **[200.104]**. No power to advance capital to the spouse is included in this clause in view of the wide overriding powers of appointment and application contained in cl 7. If the surviving spouse becomes bankrupt before the death of the testator, with the consequence that the interest in possession is forfeit with effect from the testator's death, it is arguable that IHTA 1984, s 88 would not have the effect of treating the surviving spouse as having an IPDI. This would mean that there would be no spouse

exemption in relation to the residuary estate. If there is a risk that the surviving spouse might become bankrupt before the testator's death, and it is felt to be more important to obtain the spouse exemption from IHT than to keep all the income out of the clutches of the trustee in bankruptcy, add the following words at the end of the subclause "and provided further that section 33 of the Trustee Act 1925 shall have effect in relation to the foregoing trust as if in subsection (1)(i) thereof there were substituted the words 'after the commencement of the trust period' for the words 'whether before or after the termination of any prior interest'".

2 The proviso is included in order to protect the trustees who may well be ignorant of the events giving rise to a forfeiture.

3 Under these remainder trusts the residuary estate will fall within the IHT charging regime for relevant property after the death of the surviving spouse (see paras **[200.92]**, **[200.131]**, **[218.18]**). However similar the trusts of this fund and those of the nil-rate band legacy are, under the will of the first to die, the two funds are likely to have to remain separately identifiable for IHT charging purposes because this fund will be treated as a separate settlement made by the surviving spouse: see IHTA 1984, s 80.

[225.76]

[Updated in text and footnote 2 for Perpetuities and Accumulations Act 2009.]

OVERRIDING POWERS TO APPOINT AND APPLY CAPITAL

7. (1) In this clause and clause 6 above the following expressions have the following meanings:

- (a) the expression 'the discretionary beneficiaries' means and includes:
  - (i) my [wife/husband];
  - (ii) my children and remoter issue whether living at my death or born thereafter;
  - (iii) any spouse civil partner widow widower or surviving civil partner of any of my said children or remoter issue (and 'widow' 'widower' and 'surviving civil partner' shall include a widow widower or surviving civil partner who has married or formed a civil partnership);[1]
- (b) 'the vesting day' means the day on which shall expire the period of 125 years less three days immediately following my death[2].

(2) Notwithstanding and in derogation of the foregoing trusts my trustees (being not fewer than two in number [or a trust corporation][3]) may [with the consent in writing of my [wife/husband] during [her/his] life and otherwise at their discretion][4] exercise any of the following powers:

- (a) power at any time or times and from time to time before the vesting day by deed or deeds revocable or irrevocable to appoint the whole or any part or parts of my residuary estate and the income thereof upon such trusts and with and subject to such powers and provisions for the benefit of all or such one or more exclusive of the others or other of the discretionary beneficiaries as my trustees may in their absolute discretion think fit and my trustees may in exercise of the foregoing power:
  - (i) delegate or create powers or discretions over capital or income including powers of further delegation or powers to create further powers or discretions over capital or income;
  - (ii) create powers or trusts for the accumulation of income;
  - (iii) provide for the total or partial exclusion from benefit of any person or persons or class of persons;

(iv) create administrative powers or provisions of whatever nature;
(v) appoint income alone without any appointment of capital;
(vi) make any appointment having effect subject to and without prejudice to any pre-existing interest or interests in possession or to any other pre-existing interests trusts or powers;[5]

Provided that:

(1) no such appointment shall invalidate any payment transfer or application of capital or income previously made or any entitlement to income which has already accrued under any of the trusts or powers herein elsewhere contained;
(2) every interest limited under any exercise of such power shall vest in interest (if at all) not later than the vesting day; and
(3) any such revocable appointment shall (so far as then unrevoked) cease to be revocable on the vesting day;

(b) subject to any previous exercise of the foregoing power of appointment, power at any time or times and from time to time before the vesting day in their absolute discretion to pay transfer or apply the whole or any part or parts of my residuary estate to or for the benefit of all or any one or more exclusive of the others or other of the discretionary beneficiaries if more than one in such shares and generally in such manner as my trustees shall think fit;

(c) power at any time or times and from time to time before the vesting day by deed or deeds to release or restrict all or any of the powers contained in the present subclause (including this present power) either in whole or in part and in any manner they think fit.

1 The definition of the class will need to be framed so as to fit the particular circumstances of the testator.

2 For wills made on or after 6 April 2010, the perpetuity period is 125 years (and there is no other period): see the PAA 2009, ss 5(1), 15(1)(a) (Part A **[200.35A]** and Part G, para **[246.179]**). There is no longer any good reason to define the vesting day by reference to any other period.

3 See Form C3.4, cl 2, n 7 at para **[225.60]**.

4 These words are inserted for the spouse's protection, but have the disadvantage that any appointment or application of capital with his or her consent which cuts short his or her income interest may make him or her settlor of such income for tax purposes. As it is assumed that the children are grown up, being a settlor for income tax purposes will only be a disadvantage if an appointment or application of capital is being made under which the spouse will retain a possibility of benefit. If an appointment is made to terminate the spouse's IPDI (other than in favour of the spouse absolutely) it is important that the spouse cannot benefit thereafter (whether under the appointed trusts, on a failure of the appointed trusts, on a revocation of the appointed trusts, or at all) since the termination of an IPDI on or after 22 March 2006 will be deemed to be a gift of the underlying settled property for the purposes of FA 1986, s 102, so that unless the spouse is excluded altogether from benefit after the termination, the gift with reservation rules could apply, see FA 1986, s 102ZA, (see para **[200.76]** above). A termination of the spouse's IPDI, other than in favour of absolute interests, a trust for bereaved minors or a disabled person's interest (when potential exemption should be available) will generally be a chargeable transfer.

5 This confirms that the trustees could make an appointment in remainder expectant upon the surviving spouse's life interest, and so in effect vary the remainder capital trusts, without causing the spouse's IPDI to come to an end (see para **[200.98]**).

Note on two-year discretionary trusts (IHTA 1984, s 144)

[225.83]

NOTE

Section 144. On and after 22 March 2006, IHTA 1984, s 144 provides as follows:

(1) Subsection (2) below applies where property comprised in a person's estate immediately before his death is settled by his will and, within the period of two years after his death and before any interest in possession has subsisted in the property, there occurs—
- (a) an event on which tax would (apart from subsection (2) below) be chargeable under any provision, other than section 64 or 79, of Chapter III of Part III of this Act, or
- (b) an event on which tax would be so chargeable but for section 75 or 76 above or paragraph 16(1) of Schedule 4 to this Act.

(1A) Where the testator dies on or after 22nd March 2006, subsection (1) above shall have effect as if the reference to any interest in possession were a reference to any interest in possession that is—
- (a) an immediate post-death interest, or
- (b) a disabled person's interest.

(2) Where this subsection applies by virtue of an event within paragraph (a) of subsection (1) above, tax shall not be charged under the provision in question on that event; and in every case in which this subsection applies in relation to an event, this Act shall have effect as if the will had provided that on the testator's death the property should be held as it is held after the event.

(3) Subsection (4) below applies where—
- (a) a person dies on or after 22nd March 2006,
- (b) property comprised in the person's estate immediately before his death is settled by his will, and
- (c) within the period of two years after his death, but before an immediate post-death interest or a disabled person's interest has subsisted in the property, there occurs an event that involves causing the property to be held on trusts that would, if they had in fact been established by the testator's will, have resulted in—
  - (i) an immediate post-death interest subsisting in the property, or
  - (ii) section 71A or 71D above applying to the property.

(4) Where this subsection applies by virtue of an event—
- (a) this Act shall have effect as if the will had provided that on the testator's death the property should be held as it is held after the event, but
- (b) tax shall not be charged on that event under any provision of Chapter 3 of Part 3 of this Act.

(5) Subsection (4) above also applies where—
- (a) a person dies before 22nd March 2006,
- (b) property comprised in the person's estate immediately before his death is settled by his will,
- (c) an event occurs—
  - (i) on or after 22nd March 2006, and
  - (ii) within the period of two years after the testator's death,

that involves causing the property to be held on trusts within subsection (6) below,
- (d) no immediate post-death interest, and no disabled person's interest, subsisted in the property at any time in the period beginning with the testator's death and ending immediately before the event, and
- (e) no other interest in possession subsisted in the property at any time in the period beginning with the testator's death and ending immediately before 22nd March 2006.

(6) Trusts are within this subsection if they would, had they in fact been established by the testator's will and had the testator died at the time of the event mentioned in subsection (5)(c) above, have resulted in—
- (a) an immediate post-death interest subsisting in the property, or
- (b) section 71A or 71D above applying to the property.

Section 144 thus applies (inter alia) where discretionary trusts are created by will, and an appointment or distribution is made out of the property held on those trusts within two years of the testator's death (provided, in certain cases described below, that it is not made within three months after his death). Section 144 operates not only to relieve the appointment or distribution from any IHT charge which might otherwise arise, but also to treat the distribution or appointment as a disposition made by the testator's will. The second of these effects is very much more important than the first, because any IHT charge on property leaving a discretionary trust within two years of its commencement is unlikely to be very great (see the Note in B18 at paras **[218.8]**–**[218.18]**). The main importance of an appointment or distribution falling within s 144(1) is either that it makes an exemption from IHT on the testator's death applicable (e g spouse or civil partner exemption, charitable exemption), or that it changes the IHT status of settled property from being relevant property to being, eg, beneficiary-taxed (see para **[200.92]**) or a trust for a bereaved minor (see para **[200.108]**). See also para **[242.4]** for the operation of section 144. For s 144 and gifts of business and agricultural property see **[223.10A]**.

[225.86]

[Updated for FA 2013, Sch 44.]

Where s 144 applies – IPDIs. As mentioned above, the occasions when an appointment from relevant property will give rise to an exit charge are much reduced as a result of the changes made by FA 2006 (see **[200.92]**). So, for example, an appointment of an interest in possession out of relevant property will not give rise to an exit charge unless the interest is a disabled person's interest (see para **[200.99]** above). Therefore, if s 144(1) were the only relieving provision in s 144, it would not be possible post-21 March 2006 to obtain the spouse or civil partner exemption by way of an appointment of an interest in possession to the testator's spouse or civil partner, unless the interest in possession qualified as a disabled person's interest (see para **[200.99]** above). Accordingly subsections (3)–(6) of s 144 (inserted by FA 2006) provide that where an appointment of trusts is made within two years of the testator's death, and it is such that if those trusts had been included in the testator's will they would have resulted in an IPDI (on the hypothesis, in the case of a testator dying before 22 March 2006, that he died at the date of the appointment), those trusts will be treated by virtue of subsection (4) of s 144 as having had effect from the testator's death. This means that, for example, if property is appointed within two years of the testator's death to the testator's spouse for life, out of a discretionary trust created by the testator's will, the spouse exemption will apply to that property as at the testator's death. It should be noted that s 144(3)–(6), in contrast to s 144(1) and (2) (see para **[225.85]**), can apply to an appointment made within three months of the testator's death. For further discussion of the interaction between the IPDI rules and IHTA 1984, s 144, and the problems of creating or avoiding creating an IPDI in the two years following a testator's death, see para **[200.133]**. See also para **[242.4]**.

[225.90]

[Updated in text for Perpetuities and Accumulations Act 2009.]

Advantages of testamentary discretionary trusts invoking s 144. Wills taking advantage of the IHTA 1984, s 144 are popular, and Form C3.6 is a precedent for one. It provides a useful method of allowing for changes in circumstances which might occur between the testator's will and his death. Varying the dispositions of the deceased is easier if it can be done by a distribution or appointment falling under s 144 rather than by a variation or disclaimer under s 142 (for which see Note to F3 at paras **[241.1]**–**[241.21]**); it will usually require the agreement of fewer people, and there is no problem where minors or unborns are benefited by the will. Also, there is no question of anyone other than the deceased being the 'settlor' for income tax or capital gains tax purposes. (For the position where there is a variation by an instrument in writing within the IHTA 1984, s 142, see Note to F3 at paras **[241.11]**, **[241.17]** and **[241.19]**.) The discretionary trust is of the residuary estate. Note that if there is property which qualifies for IHT business or agricultural relief it is important (in wills of spouses or civil partners) for the discretionary trust to be of a specific gift of such property: see para **[233.10A]**. Ensuring that the testator is the settlor (and the only settlor) for capital gains tax purposes can be a particularly important point for a testator with a foreign domicile. This is because under an instrument of variation creating a settlement, the beneficiary of an absolute gift under the testator's will who makes the instrument will be the settlor for capital gains tax purposes (see

TCGA 1992, s 68C(2) with effect in respect of variations made on or after 6 April 2006), and accordingly the settled property will be subject to the rules for offshore settlements with a UK domiciled settlor where it is administered abroad and the beneficiary settlor under the instrument of variation has a UK domicile, even if the testator had a foreign domicile (see F3 at para **[241.17]**). Where there is no foreign element, and a deed of variation is made by a beneficiary which puts an absolute interest into a settlement, the capital gains on the settled property will be taxed as the beneficiary's if he retains an interest under the trusts. However, since 5 April 2008 this has not mattered, because of the change to a uniform flat rate of capital gains tax of 18 per cent, though it may start mattering again if progressive rates of capital gains tax are reintroduced.

[225.92]

[Updated for Perpetuities and Accumulations Act 2009.]

Form C3.6: Will providing two-year discretionary trust

Note. This form creates a two-year discretionary trust with wide powers to appoint new trusts and to pay or apply capital, with a discretionary trust of income pending exercise of the powers or the earlier expiry of two years from the testator's death. Just before the end of the two-year period fixed trusts come into operation if there has been no exercise of the powers, and the coming into operation of these trusts in these circumstances will fall within s 144 of the IHTA 1984. The fixed trusts are an absolute gift to the testator's spouse if surviving, and otherwise to the children. Different or more elaborate default trusts could be substituted, depending on what mixture of exempt and non-exempt gifts is desired, and whom the testator wishes to benefit in the event of no exercise of the powers being made. If the testator wants to have a long-term discretionary trust as the default arrangement then a form such as C6.2 (see para **[228.19]**) would be more appropriate. However, the powers in Form C3.6 would enable the trustees to create a long-term discretionary trust if they wished to do so. If the testator wants trusts in default of appointment under which the beneficiary or beneficiaries have IPDIs, those trusts should commence just before the end of two years from the testator's death, and if the testator wants interest in possession trusts which get IHT relevant property treatment the trusts should start after the end of two years from the testator's death: see paras **[200.131]**, **[200.133]**. As well as considering what is to happen if the powers are not exercised, the testator should also leave a clear written expression of his wishes (but without imposing any trust or obligation) as to how he would like the powers exercised. If the testator has business or agricultural assets which he wants to put into a s 144 trust they should not be included in a discretionary trust of the residuary estate as in this form, but should be the subject matter of a specific gift: see para **[233.10A]**.

This Form C3.6 may be adapted for use for civil partners, the words 'my wife/husband' being replaced with 'my civil partner' throughout. Care should be taken to identify correctly in each will the children who are to benefit.

[225.100]

[Updated for Perpetuities and Accumulations Act 2009.]

DEFINITIONS

3. (1) In this clause the following expressions shall have the following meanings, namely:

(a) 'the discretionary period' shall mean the period beginning immediately after [the end of the period of three months from] the day of my death and ending with the day before the second anniversary of my death;[1]

(b) the expression 'the beneficiaries' shall mean [*here set out the class of beneficiaries. An example would be:* my [wife/husband] [*name*] the children and remoter issue of my parents [*names*] and the children and remoter issue of my [wife's/husband's] parents [*names*] the spouses and former spouses of any of the foregoing and any other person or persons who may during the discretionary period upon the nomination of my [wife/husband] or of any such children and remoter issue be appointed by my trustees at their absolute discretion by deed to be a member or members of the class of beneficiaries].[2]

1 The powers are only exercisable during this period. Under IHTA 1984, s 144, IPDIs, trusts for bereaved minors or age 18-to-25 trusts may be appointed at any time in the two-year period after the testator's death to have the benefits of s 144, but if absolute interests are to be appointed, it is not possible to make an appointment or distribution which falls within the IHTA 1984, s 144 within three months of the testator's death (see para **[225.85]** for the non-application of s 144 to such an appointment). The words in square brackets might be included therefore to prevent this point being overlooked in the case of an absolute appointment, although as seen it will not be necessary to so restrict the appointment period in relation to the appointment of IPDIs, trusts for bereaved minors or age 18-to-25 trusts. The period expires the day before the second anniversary of the testator's death, so that the default trust in cl 3(5) comes into operation on the second anniversary and thus commences within the two-year period from the testator's death and complies with the requirements of the IHTA 1984, s 144. It is important to note that the last day for exercising the powers will be the day *before* the second anniversary of the death.

2 A power of nomination in this form is thought to be valid (cf *Blausten v IRC* [1972] Ch 256, [1972] 1 All ER 41 and *Re Manisty's Settlement* [1974] Ch 17, [1973] 2 All ER 1203), and its inclusion gives maximum flexibility to the appointments which can be made: see para **[225.91]**. It would apparently be possible to have a very wide hybrid or intermediate fiduciary power with a class of objects of virtually everyone: see *Re Hay's Settlement Trusts, Greig v McGregor* [1981] 3 All ER 786, [1982] 1 WLR 202, *Re Beatty's Will Trusts* [1990] 3 All ER 844, [1990] 1 WLR 1503, and Vol 1, para **[39.31]**. Further, in *Re Beatty's Will Trusts,* this particular form, as it appeared in the 6th edition of this work (as Form C10.2 on pp 1473–1477 of that edition), was referred to by Hoffmann J as an example of a will containing wide discretionary powers and trusts which was not, in his judgment, invalid as a delegation of the testator's powers of testamentary disposition.

[225.101]

[Updated in text and footnote 4 for Perpetuities and Accumulations Act 2009.]

POWER OF APPOINTMENT

(2) My trustees shall hold the capital and income of my residuary estate upon trust for all or such one or more of the beneficiaries at such ages or times in such shares and upon such trusts for the benefit of the beneficiaries as my trustees[1] may by irrevocable[2] deed or deeds executed at any time or times during the discretionary period[3] appoint and in making any such appointment my trustees shall have powers as full as those which they would possess if they were an absolute beneficial owner of my residuary estate and in particular (but without prejudice to the generality of the foregoing words) my trustees may in any exercise of the foregoing power as they in their absolute discretion think fit:

(a) delegate give or impose to or upon themselves or any other person or persons and in relation to any trust or disposition any discretionary powers or discretionary trusts conditions limitations restrictions or provisions including powers of further delegation or powers to create further powers or discretions;
(b) create trusts or powers for the accumulation of income;[4]
(c) create administrative powers or provisions of whatever nature;
(d) make provision for the burden of any testamentary expenses taxes or

debts payable out of my estate as between different assets funds shares or interests in any manner and to any extent as my trustees think fit;

Provided that:

(i) no such appointment shall invalidate any payment transfer or application of capital or income previously made under any of the trusts or powers herein elsewhere contained;

(ii) the foregoing power shall be exercisable by my trustees at any time during the discretionary period[5] and any exercise thereof shall have immediate effect for all purposes notwithstanding that at the date of exercise there shall have been no grant of probate or administration in respect of the property over which the said power shall be exercised or the administration of my estate shall not have been completed in respect of such property or any other property comprised in my estate;

(iii) the persons who may exercise the foregoing power before any such grant as aforesaid are the persons hereinbefore named as my executors other than any of them who shall have died [or whose appointment as my executor shall have ceased to have effect][6] or who shall have renounced probate of my will.[7]

1 There should be no restrictions on the character or number of the trustees for this purpose, as it is not entirely certain that the statutory power to appoint new trustees can be exercised while the estate is in the course of administration; an alternative, where such restrictions are thought necessary, would be to have express powers to appoint new trustees of the power during the administration of the estate.

2 There seems to be little point in the trustees being able to revoke an appointment since the exercise of any power of revocation would have to be limited to the two-year period, and if s 144 applied to a revocable appointment when made (eg one appointing an interest in possession to the surviving spouse), its application to that appointment would not be altered by subsequent revocation of the appointment.

3 See n 1 to sub-cl (1)(a) of this clause at para **[225.100]**.

4 For wills made on or after 6 April 2010, there are no statutory restrictions on accumulation in respect of non-charitable trusts, so accumulation will be permitted throughout the trust period: see the PAA 2009, s 13, 15(1)(a) (Part G, para **[246.187]**). See B18 at paras **[218.72]**–**[218.76]**.

5 See n 1 to sub-cl (1)(a) of this clause at para **[225.100]**.

6 These words could be included if the testator's spouse is a named executor. If there is a subsequent divorce the provisions appointing executors and conferring powers of appointment will have effect as if the spouse had died: WA 1837, s 18A (Part G, para **[244.18]**) and see the Preliminary Note to C2 at paras **[224.12]**–**[224.19]**. Section 18A would probably apply to this proviso in the absence of these words but they make the position clear. Similar provisions apply on the dissolution of a civil partnership, see Part G, para **[244.20]**.

7 This proviso is included to make clear that an appointment may be made before probate is applied for, and by whom, so that where it is decided to appoint some or all of the estate to an exempt beneficiary, such as the testator's spouse or charity, the benefit of the relevant exemption can be claimed when it comes to paying the IHT due as a condition of obtaining a grant of probate.

C4

Wills providing for someone with a disability

[Updated for FA 2013, Sch 44.]

Cross References

See also Forms B11.16 (at para **[211.23]**) and B18.4 (at para **[218.34]**). For protective trusts see Forms C3.2 (at para **[225.23]** ff) and C3.5 (at para **[225.68]** ff).

PRELIMINARY NOTE

[226.1]
The main factors relevant to a will providing for someone suffering from a severe physical or mental disability will usually be the following:

(i) the needs of the disabled person;
(ii) where the disabled person is not capable of managing his or her own affairs, avoiding the necessity for the appointment of a deputy under MCA 2005 so far as possible (deputies under MCA 2005 replaced receivers under the Mental Health Act 1983 with effect from 1 October 2007);
(iii) minimising the adverse impact of IHT, income tax and capital gains tax, so far as compatible with other objectives;
(iv) trying to ensure that the benefit provided by the will does provide some genuine additional advantage to the disabled person, and does not simply cause a corresponding reduction in means-tested state benefits, thus leaving him or her no better off.

A discretionary trust will usually be the best solution, at any rate where the disabled person is incapable of managing his own affairs, although it may have income tax disadvantages (see para **[226.8]**). In particular it will avoid the need for a deputy (at any rate as regards the trust property and its income), and is the best that can be done to provide for the disabled person but at the same time to avoid the trust property being taken into account for state benefit purposes (see para **[226.2]**). Further, the testator has a choice as to what IHT charging rules will apply, ie whether the trust fund is taxed as a fully discretionary trust under IHTA 1984, Part III or as a beneficiary-taxed interest in possession trust under the special provisions of IHTA 1984, s 89 for discretionary trusts for a disabled person (see paras **[226.3]** ff). The other main possibilities are:

(i) an interest in possession trust, which may be better from the point of view of income tax (see para **[226.7]**) but disadvantageous in that the income will be taken into account in assessing means-tested benefit and a deputy might be needed to look after the income;
(ii) a gift to the disabled person himself, where he is physically disabled but capable of managing his affairs—the main question here is the effect on state benefits, where he is in receipt of them;
(iii) gifts of all the testator's property to other children or relatives of the testator in the hope or on the understanding that they will make provision for the disabled person when it is needed;
(iv) a gift to a charity for the disabled in the hope or on the understanding that it will provide assistance to the disabled person—some charities for the disabled have schemes along these lines and enquiries should be made of the charities relevant to the disabled person's disability;
(v) a discretionary charitable trust under which donations to charities which may help the disabled person can be made.

Any of (iii) to (v) will avoid the risk that the property given by the will of the testator will be taken into account as part of the disabled person's means when means-tested benefits are assessed, but of course run the risk that no benefit at all will reach the disabled person from the testator's gift. They also run the risk that proceedings under the I(PFD)A 1975 will be brought on behalf of the disabled person against the testator's estate.

[226.2]

State benefits. The benefits which may be available to a disabled person are many and complex, and frequently changing, and the details of them are outside the scope of this work. The main means-tested state benefit is income support, and the rules for assessing means for this purpose at the moment disregard income and capital available under a discretionary trust except so far as it is actually paid to or applied for the benefit of the disabled person. Where a disabled person has an interest in possession under a trust, the income to which he is entitled will be taken into account for these purposes. Increasingly the care of disabled persons is the responsibility of local authorities under the Community Care policy. Local authorities are entitled to take into account the resources of a person to whom they provide services in fixing the level of charge for them. There are no general rules as to whether, and, if so, how, discretionary trust income or capital will be taken into account by local authorities, but there would seem to be a better chance that the income and capital of a trust will not be taken into account, at any rate so long as not paid to or applied for the benefit of the disabled person, when it is only applicable under a discretion than when the disabled person has an entitlement under fixed trusts. However, there are many possibilities as to the type of discretionary trust. If there are wide and unrestricted powers over a substantial amount of capital exercisable in favour of the disabled person, the fund is more likely to be taken into account by the local authority (or under any future change of rules for state benefits) than if the powers over capital are more restricted (or non-existent); similarly, a fund which is tailored to the disabled person's circumstances (eg the trusts come to an end when he dies, or the trustees are directed to have regard primarily to his interests when deciding whether to exercise their powers) is more likely to be taken into account than one which is not.

[226.3]
IHT treatment of trusts for the disabled. A choice of IHT regime is available in relation to a discretionary trust for a disabled person, ie between taxation as a beneficiary-taxed interest in possession trust or taxation as a 'relevant property' discretionary trust (the relative merits of these two options are considered at para **[226.5]**). This is because settled property subject to a discretionary trust which satisfies certain conditions in relation to a disabled person is treated for IHT purposes, by virtue of IHTA 1984, s 89, as if the disabled person has an interest in possession in it (s 89(2)), and because, post-21 March 2006, settled property subject to a disabled person's deemed interest in possession still gets beneficiary-taxed treatment (IHTA 1984, s 89(1)(A) and s 49(1A)(b)). The conditions of s 89 which must be met for a trust to receive this treatment are now different depending on the date of the testator's death and the date of execution of his will (or codicil) under which the trust in question arises. So:

(i) where the testator died before 8 April 2013 (so that property is treated as becoming comprised in the trust before 8 April 2013), the trust in his will or codicil (which will necessarily have been executed before 8 April 2013) will be within s 89 if it complies with the conditions of s 89 before amendment by FA 2013, ie 'the old conditions';
(ii) where the testator dies on or after 8 April 2013 (so that property is treated as becoming comprised in the trust on or after 8 April 2013) and where his will (or codicil) is executed before 8 April 2013 (including where it is confirmed by codicil on or after 8 April 2013), the trust will be within s 89 if it complies with 'the old conditions'. Section 89 will, however, nevertheless apply in these circumstances if the trust happens to comply with the conditions of s 89 as amended by FA 2013, Sch 44, para 6, ie 'the new conditions'; and
(iii) where the testator dies on or after 8 April 2013 (so that property is treated as becoming comprised in the trust on or after 8 April 2013) and where his will (or codicil) is executed on or after 8 April 2013, the trust should comply with the new conditions.

(See FA 2013, Sch 44, paras 9 and 20).

It is, however, additionally provided that a trust arising under a will (or codicil) made on or after 8 April 2013 and complying with the old conditions will be within s 89 if its provisions are in the same terms as a trust contained in a will (or codicil) executed by the same testator before that date (see FA 2013, Sch 44, paras 9(2) and 20(1)(b)(ii)). This provision is no doubt to ensure that a trust is not deprived of the benefit of s 89 by inadvertence, such as where a testator has made a will before 8 April 2013 containing a s 89 trust, then makes a new will on or after that date changing some of the provisions, but not the s 89 trust which is simply repeated in the same terms. In such a case HMRC would no doubt wish to have evidence that the trust of the new will does indeed replicate the terms of a trust contained in a previous will. If the previous will (or a copy of it) is retained then this should be sufficient.

Still, where a testator is making a will (or codicil) on or after 8 April 2013, which is to contain a trust intended to comply with s 89, we would recommend that it complies with the new conditions even if the testator has previously made a will (or codicil) containing a trust complying with the old conditions,

The new conditions of s 89 (ie after amendment by FA 2013, Sch 44, para 6) are that the property is held on trusts:

(i) under which, during the life of a disabled person, no interest in possession subsists (s 89(1)(a)), and
(ii) which secure that, if any of the settled property or income arising from it is applied during the disabled person's life for the benefit of a beneficiary, it is applied for his benefit (s 89(1)(b) amended by FA 2013, Sch 44, para 6(2)).

The old conditions of s 89 (ie before amendment by FA 2013, Sch 44, para 6) are that the property is held on trusts:

(i) under which, during the life of a disabled person, no interest in possession subsists (s 89(1)(a)), and
(ii) which secure that not less than half the settled property which is applied during the disabled person's life is applied for his benefit (s 89(1)(b) before it was amended by FA 2013).

Although the first condition of the new and old conditions ostensibly remains the same, the second condition of the new conditions impacts upon the first, making the first condition of the new conditions substantially different from the first condition of the old conditions, as will appear below.

As already mentioned, the consequence of a trust for a disabled person complying with s 89 (whether by reason of satisfaction of the old conditions or the new conditions) is that the disabled person is treated as having a 'disabled person's interest' (see IHTA 1984, ss 89(2) and 89B(1)(a)). It is therefore a beneficiary-taxed interest, that is, one where the settled property is treated for IHT purposes as if it were the property of the beneficiary (see paras **[200.84]** and **[200.90]**). This means that a lifetime settlement within s 89 for a disabled person can obtain potential exemption, but in the case of a settlement for a disabled person in a will the case is less overwhelming for creating a beneficiary-taxed interest, because the fund going into the settlement is nevertheless subject to IHT on the testator's death, and a relevant property settlement for a disabled person can have the advantages discussed in para **[226.5]**.

[226.4]

Commentary on IHTA 1984, s 89. We have the following points concerning s 89, where either the new conditions or the old conditions would be in point:

(i) A disabled person for the purposes of s 89 is:

(a) a person who is incapable of administering his property or managing his affairs by reason of mental disorder within the Mental Health Act 1983 (MeHA 1983). A mental disorder within the MeHA 1983 is defined as any disorder or disability of the mind (see MeHA 1983, s 1(2) as substituted by the Mental Health Act 2007, s 1(1), (2) on and from 3 November 2008). Prior to that, 'mental disorder' was defined as mental illness, arrested or incomplete development of mind, psychopathic disorder, and any other disorder or disability of mind;

(b) a person in receipt of attendance allowance under the Social Security Contributions and Benefits Act 1992, s 64 (or the equivalent Northern Ireland legislation). Attendance allowance is for persons of 65 or more who are so severely disabled physically or mentally that they require frequent attendance in connection with bodily functions, or continual supervision to avoid substantial danger to themselves or others either by day or by night (Social Security Contributions and Benefits Act 1992, s 64, and see *Cockburn v Chief Adjudication Officer; Secretary of State for Social Security v Fairey* [1997] 3 All ER 844, [1997] 1 WLR 799, HL);

(c) a person in receipt of a disability living allowance under the Social Security Contributions and Benefits Act 1992, s 71 (or the equivalent Northern Ireland legislation) by virtue of entitlement to the care component at the highest or middle rate. Disability living allowance is similar to attendance allowance but is for persons under 65;

and in addition where property is transferred into settlement on or after 22 March 2006, so generally where a testator dies on or after 22 March 2006:

(d) a person who would be in receipt of one of the allowances of (b) or (c) above but for certain specified reasons, such as being non-UK resident, living in a care home or being in hospital for renal dialysis;

and in addition where property is transferred into settlement on or after 8 April 2013, so generally where a testator dies on or after 8 April 2013:

(e) a person in receipt of personal independence payment under the Welfare Reform Act (or the equivalent Northern Ireland legislation) by virtue of entitlement to the daily living component. This payment is gradually replacing disability living allowance from 8 April 2013;
(f) a person in receipt of an increased disablement pension under the Social Security Contributions and Benefits Act 1992, s 104 (or the equivalent Northern Ireland legislation);
(g) a person in receipt of constant attendance allowance under article 14 of the Personal Injuries (Civilians) Scheme 1983 (SI 1983/686), or article 8 of the Naval, Military and Air Forces etc (Disablement and Death) Service Pensions Order 2006 (SI 2006/606);
(h) a person in receipt of armed forces independence payment under a scheme established under section 1 of the Armed Forces (Pensions and Compensation) Act 2004 (or who would be in such receipt but for residing in the Royal Hospital, Chelsea); or
(i) a person who would be in receipt of an allowance, pension or payment within (e) to (g) but for certain specified reasons, such as being non-UK resident, living in a care home or being in hospital for renal dialysis.

See IHTA 1984, s 89(4), (4A) as amended and inserted by FA 2013, Sch 44, para 6(4), (5), incorporating the definition of 'disabled person' from FA 2005, Sch 1A for transfers into settlement on or after 8 April 2013, thus extending the meaning from persons within (a) to (d) above to include persons within (e) to (i) above.

(ii) IHTA 1984, s 89 applies to property settled by will where the disabled person was disabled (within any of the meanings described in (i) above) 'when the property was transferred into settlement' (see s 89(4)), ie at the time of the testator's death. Thus where a testator makes provision in the form required by s 89 for the benefit of a person who counts as disabled at the date of the will but who ceases to do so before the testator's death, s 89 will not apply. On the other hand where the beneficiary is a 'disabled person' within s 89 at the testator's death, and s 89 applies to funds given on trust for his benefit by the testator's will, if he subsequently ceases to count as disabled as defined in s 89, the section will nevertheless continue to apply to the funds.

We have the following points where the new conditions of Section 89 would be in point, which are relevant generally where a testator is making a will (or codicil) on or after 8 April 2013 which is to contain a trust intended to comply with Section 89:

(iii) IHTA 1984, s 89 will only apply to property settled by the will (or codicil) if the trusts are such that during the life of the disabled person no interest in possession subsists in that property (see s 89(1)(a)) and if they further secure that if any of the income of the property is applied during the disabled person's life for the benefit of a beneficiary, it is applied for the disabled person's benefit (see s 89(1)(b) as substituted by FA 2013, Sch 44, para 6(2)). This means that during the disabled person's life (and subject to having powers within (v)(a) below) the trustees should have only two options as to what to do with the income, either to apply it for the disabled person's benefit, or accumulate it as an addition to capital. Thus there might either be a trust to accumulate income during the disabled person's life, but subject to a power for the trustees to apply it for the disabled person's benefit, or a trust to apply it for the disabled person's benefit, but subject to a power to accumulate. (Now that the restrictions on accumulation of income have been abolished for wills made on or after 6 April 2009 – PAA 2009, ss 13 and 15, for which see Volume 1, para **[95.A1]** –accumulation can, in practice, be directed or authorised throughout the disabled person's life.) Either way, no interest in possession would subsist in the property since the disabled person would have no right to income as it arose, and any income not accumulated would be applicable for the benefit of the disabled person only.

(iv) In addition to the requirement that any income applied during the disabled person's life for a beneficiary's benefit must be applied for the disabled person's benefit, is the requirement that any capital applied during the disabled person's life for a beneficiary's benefit must be applied for the disabled person's benefit (see s 89(1)(b) as substituted by FA 2013, Sch 44, para 6(2)). This requirement may not though be as restrictive as might at first appear given the further provisions specified in (v) below.

(v) The requirements that any income or capital applied during the disabled person's life be applied for the disabled person's benefit are tempered by IHTA 1984, s 89(3) (as substituted by FA 2013, Sch 44, para 6(3)) which provides that trusts shall not be treated as falling outside the section by reason only of:

(a) the trustees having powers that enable them to apply otherwise than for the benefit of the disabled person amounts (whether consisting of income or capital, or both) not exceeding an annual limit which is currently set at the lower of £3,000 and 3 per cent of the maximum value of the settled property during the tax year in question (s 89(3)(a), (3A)-(3E));

(b) the powers of advancement conferred by the Trustee Act 1925 (TA 1925), s 32 (or the Trustee Act (Northern Ireland) 1958, s 33), even where modified so as to be applicable to the whole of a presumptive or vested share of capital (instead of one half as provided in the TA 1925, s 32(1), proviso (a)) (s 89(3)(b)–(e)); and

(c) the trustees having powers to the like effect of those specified in (b) above (s 89(3)(f)).

If the statutory power of advancement applies (unmodified or modified), and there are discretionary trusts of income, it is possible that the disabled person would not be someone having a 'prior life or other interest' within the TA 1925, s 32(1), proviso (c) so as to make his consent a prerequisite to any exercise of the power: see *Re Beckett's Settlement, Re Beckett, Eden v Von Stutterheim* [1940] Ch 279 and **B18** at para **[218.90]**. In that case it was held that the objects of a discretionary trust did not have a 'prior life or other interest' such that their consent was required. There were though a large number and it was considered that it could not have been the intention to fetter the discretion of the trustees with regard to advancement by imposing on them the obligation to obtain the consent of all the persons, many of them perhaps infants and unable to give their consent, who were interested under the terms of the discretionary trust. Still, the decision was essentially that the object of a discretion did not have a 'prior life or other interest' within the meaning of TA 1925, s 32(1), proviso (c) so whether there are numerous objects or only one should not make a difference. On the face of it therefore, the powers of (b) and (c) above could operate to enable the whole of the capital of a disabled person's trust to be applied for the benefit of remaindermen to the exclusion of the disabled person, notwithstanding the requirement that any capital applied during the disabled person's life for a beneficiary's benefit must be applied for the disabled person's benefit. It is not clear whether this result was intended.

(vi) A point arises about the requirement of IHTA 1984, s 89(1)(a) that there should be no interest in possession. If it really is a requirement that there must be no possibility of an interest in possession arising during the life of the disabled person, it could be argued that if s 89 is to apply there must be no powers which can be exercised so as to create an interest in possession. A power which can be of particular utility in trusts of this type is the power to permit the disabled person to occupy a residence comprised in the trust fund, or to have the use of furniture or equipment acquired by the trustees as part of the trust fund. The exercise of such powers so as, eg to provide the disabled person with a permanent residence, could have the effect of conferring an interest in possession (see Part A, para **[200.121]**). Therefore, it could be argued, if it is to be certain that a set of trusts comes within s 89, it is necessary to avoid conferring powers of this kind. However, this would be so inconvenient, and it would be such a bizarre consequence given that an actual interest in possession for a disabled person may get the same IHT treatment (see para **[200.84]**), that it is in our view better to include such powers (unless it is clear that the particular disabled person could not be benefited by the exercise of such powers), and hope that HMRC do not regard the existence of such powers as incompatible with s 89 applying (we know of no published views of HMRC concerning this point). There should be power to restrict such powers so that they can be appropriately cut down if it becomes apparent that HMRC do regard them as preventing s 89 from applying.

(vii) What is said in (vi) above applies equally to powers of appointment or powers to pay or apply capital, which are powers which clearly enable the creation of interests in possession unless specifically restricted so as not to be so exercisable. There is the practical difference that it would not usually be as inconvenient to prohibit the creation of an interest in possession during the life of the disabled person under an exercise of a power of appointment or a power to pay or apply capital than it would be to prohibit the creation of an interest in possession under an exercise of a power to permit occupation or enjoyment in kind of land or other trust assets. However, if HMRC accept that the existence of a power to create an interest in possession by allowing occupation or use of trust property is compatible with IHTA 1984, s 89, then they should also accept that the existence of a power of appointment or payment or application of capital which enables the creation of an interest in possession is also so compatible. We recommend the inclusion of a power to restrict any power of appointment or power to pay or apply capital, which can be used to bring the trusts within IHTA 1984, s 89 should it become apparent that HMRC regard the existence of a power to create an interest in possession as incompatible with the application of s 89.

We have the following points where the old conditions of s 89 would be in point, so generally where a testator has made a will (or codicil) before 8 April 2013 containing a trust intended to comply with s 89 (including where he makes a new (or codicil) on or after 8 April 2013 simply repeating the trust contained in the earlier will (or codicil)):

(viii) IHTA 1984, s 89 will only apply to property settled by such a will (or codicil) if the trusts are such that during the life of the disabled person no interest in possession subsists in that property (see s 89(1)(a)). This is not subject to the requirement of the new conditions that income can only be applied for the benefit of the disabled person. So it follows that if there is a discretionary trust of income, the entire income could in theory be applied for the benefit of persons other than the disabled person without jeopardising the application of s 89.

(ix) In addition to the requirement that no interest in possession subsists during the disabled person's lifetime, is the requirement that the trusts secure that not less than half the settled property which is applied during the disabled person's life is applied for his benefit (s 89(1)(b) before substitution by FA 2013, Sch 44, para 6(2)).

(x) IHTA 1984, s 89(3) (before amendment by FA 2013, Sch 44, para 6(3)), provides that trusts shall not be treated as falling outside the section by reason only of the powers of advancement conferred by the TA 1925, s 32 (or the Trustee Act (Northern Ireland) 1958, s 33). However, this is a reference to the statutory power as it stands, and not the statutory power as modified in any way. It would, it seems, not be compatible with IHTA 1984, s 89 (before amendment) for the statutory power of advancement to be made applicable to the whole of a presumptive or vested share (instead of one half as provided in the TA 1925, s 32(1), proviso (a)). If the statutory power applies, and there are discretionary trusts of income, it is likely that the disabled person would not be someone having a 'prior life or other interest' within the TA 1925, s 32(1), proviso (c) so as to make his consent a prerequisite to any exercise of the power: see (v) above.

(xi) The same points arise about the requirement of IHTA 1984, s 89(1)(a)) that there should be no interest in possession as arise at (vi) and (vii) above.

[226.5]

Relative advantages of the different IHT regimes. The provision which became IHTA 1984, s 89 originated under capital transfer tax when discretionary trusts were subject to much more onerous tax charges than interest in possession ones. The general rules for capital transfer tax and its successor IHT on settled property have since then been transformed out of recognition, and it is not always an advantage for trusts to fall within IHTA 1984, s 89 where the trusts in question are being created by will. If a trust is being created by lifetime gift, a s 89 trust has the advantage that potential exemption will be available (see paras **[200.71]** and **[200.84]**), but where it is being created by will the IHT charge on the testator's estate will be the same whether the trust is a relevant property trust or a s 89 trust, unless the disabled person is the testator's spouse or civil partner. Probably the main situations, when making a will, where s 89 trusts have a clear tax advantage over relevant property trusts are where the disabled beneficiary is the testator's spouse or civil partner, because the spouse or civil partner exemption will apply on the testator's death, or where the fund will go to charity on the death of the disabled person, so that it will be exempt from IHT on the disabled person's death. Otherwise, the balance of advantage will vary from case to case, depending on factors such as the size of the fund, the expectation of life of the disabled beneficiary, and the likely availability of liquid assets with which to pay periodic charges if it is a relevant property trust. Further, particularly following the amendments made to IHTA 1984, s 89 by FA 2013, Sch 44, para 6, it will be a key consideration whether the testator wishes to benefit other non-disabled persons from the trust. If he does, then it might be better to create a full discretionary trust within the relevant property charging regime. If IHTA 1984, s 89 applies to settled property, it treats the property as subject to an interest in possession to which the relevant disabled person is beneficially entitled and this interest in possession (if arising on or after 22 March 2006) will be a disabled person's interest which means that the underlying capital will be treated as part of the disabled person's estate for inheritance tax purposes (ss 49(1A)(b), 89(2), 89B(1)(a)). This will mean that there should be no occasions of IHT charge during the disabled person's life, except where a payment or application of capital is made in favour of other beneficiaries and so gives rise to a deemed transfer of value by the disabled person (see Part A, para **[200.87]**). Payment of capital to the disabled person will be free of IHT charge (IHTA 1984, s 53(2)), and the application of capital for his direct benefit will probably be treated in the same way (although s 53(2) does not expressly include this). The periodic and exit charges applicable to discretionary trusts (see IHTA 1984, Pt III, Ch III and B18 at paras **[218.8]** and **[218.9]**) will not apply. However, the deemed interest in possession also means that on the death of the disabled person the settled property will be charged to IHT as part of his 'estate'. This will not be disadvantageous if, as will often be the case, his 'estate' including the trust fund is unlikely to exceed the IHT threshold. For a fund substantially in excess of the IHT threshold a relevant property discretionary trust not falling within IHTA 1984, s 89 would probably be more lightly taxed under the IHT rules as they stand at the moment, unless the disabled person lives for a very long time after the testator's death; it will bear periodic charges and exit charges under IHTA 1984, Pt III, Ch III at a modest rate (see B18 at paras **[218.8]** and **[218.9]**) and will not be taxed as part of the disabled person's estate. Such a trust can also be available without restriction to benefit other members of the family. However, although the IHT legislation taxes relevant property trusts lightly at the moment, this could change (and on 3 May 2013, HMRC published a consultation in this regard, 'Inheritance tax: simplifying charges on trusts – the next stage'). On the other hand, a relevant property trust can be converted free of IHT charge to a s 89 trust within two years after the testator's death in reliance on IHTA 1984, s 144 (see para **[225.83]** ff), but conversion in the opposite direction in that period is likely to be difficult or impossible, and if it can be done it could involve an IHT charge. For trusts falling within IHTA 1984, s 89 (as amended by FA 2013, Sch 44, para 6), so for use in wills to be executed on or after 8 April 2013, see Form B18.4 (at para **[218.34]**) and Forms C4.1, C4.2 and C4.3 (at paras **[218.13]** ff). Form C4.3 (at para **[226.57]**) creates a trust within s 89 (as amended) for the testator's spouse, so as to obtain, on the testator's death, the IHT exemption for gifts to spouses.

[226.5A]
Disabled person's interest. The IHT regime makes specific provision for a further type of trust specifically for the disabled, and relevant to testamentary dispositions, and that is the type of disabled person's interest which is an actual interest in possession (rather than the deemed interest in possession arising under IHTA 1984, s 89): see IHTA 1984, ss 89B(1)(c) (as amended by FA 2013, Sch 44, para 10(1), and para **[200.99]**). The requirements for an actual interest in possession to be a disabled person's interest have been made more stringent following amendments made by FA 2013. So where property has been transferred into a settlement before 8 April 2013 (so generally where a testator has died before 8 April 2013 establishing a trust by his will), an interest in possession arising under the trust will be a disabled person's interest simply if the person entitled to it was disabled at the time of the transfer (ie the testator's death): see IHTA 1989, s 89B(1)(c), (2) (before amendment by FA 2013, Sch 44, paras 8(2), 10(1)). However, where property is transferred into a settlement on or after 8 April 2013 (so generally where a testator dies on or after 8 April 2013 establishing a trust by his will) an interest in possession arising under the trust will be a disabled person's interest only if the person entitled to it is disabled and if the trusts secure that if any settled property is applied during the disabled person's life for the benefit of a beneficiary, it is applied for the benefit of the disabled person: see IHTA 1989, s 89B(1)(c) (amended by FA 2013, Sch 44, para 10(1)). In this case it seems that the relevant time for a person to qualify as disabled, if his interest is to be disabled person's interest, is the date when the interest arises, rather than the date when property was transferred into settlement (as was previously the case), see the new definition of 'disabled person' in IHTA 1984 s 89B(2) (as substituted by FA 2013, Sch 44, para 8(2)) which does not import into the definition the requirement that the person be disabled at the time of transfer into settlement as was previously the case (and as continues under IHTA 1984, s 89(4) for a non-interest in possession trust for a disabled person). Although the position is not entirely clear, it seems likely that his interest would continue to be a disabled person's interest even if he ceased to be disabled during the continuance of his interest. The requirement that capital be applicable only for the benefit of the disabled person is tempered (as in the case of a disabled person's trust within s 89) by the provision that powers as in **[226.4]** sub-para (v) above, are compatible: see IHTA 1989, s 89C (inserted by FA 2013, Sch 44, para 10(2)). The IHT consequences of a

disabled person having an actual interest in possession which qualifies as a disabled person's interest are similar to those of a disabled person having a deemed interest in possession under IHTA 1984, s 89. A significant difference, however, is that the income belongs to the disabled person as it arises, and so is taxed as his, and also treated as his for state benefit purposes. In the context of wills, it will often be the case that an interest in possession granted to a disabled person would get beneficiary-taxed treatment in any event as an IPDI, ie if it arises (or is treated as arising under IHTA 1984, s 142 or 144) immediately on the death of the testator (see para **[200.98]**). In that case (and where he dies on or after 8 April 2013 when the conditions for a disabled person's interest are more stringent) it may be easier to rely on IPDI treatment. The interest in possession can then be subject to overriding powers in favour of beneficiaries other than the disabled person, which it could not be if it was to qualify as a disabled person's interest.

[226.6]
Capital gains tax annual exemption. By the TCGA 1992, Sch 1, para 1 (as amended by FA 2013, Sch 44, para 13), a trust which satisfies the new conditions of IHTA 1984, s 89 (as amended by FA 2013, Sch 44, para 6) (or indeed IHTA 1984, s 89B(1)(c) (as amended by FA 2013, Sch 44, para 10(1)) has the advantage of the full amount of capital gains tax annual exemption of capital gains in any year of assessment (currently £10,900 for the tax year 2013–14), as opposed to the reduced amount usually available to trustees. A trust which only satisfies the old conditions of IHTA 1984, s 89, and not the new conditions, will not have the advantage of the full amount of capital gains tax annual exemption but only the reduced amount usually available to trustees.

[226.7]
Capital gains tax rates. Capital gains tax has been charged at a flat rate of 28 per cent on trusts with effect on and from 23 June 2010. Previously to that, and from 5 April 2008, the rate for trusts had been 18 per cent, as it was for individuals. The pre-6 April 2008 position was that until 5 April 2008 the gains of a settlement (whether discretionary or subject to an interest in possession) were charged at the income tax rate applicable to trusts under ITA 2007, ss 9 and 479 ff (formerly the Income and Corporation Taxes Act 1988, ss 686, 687), latterly 40 per cent (TCGA 1992, s 4(1AA)(a)) (see Part A, paras **[200.40]** and **[200.41]**). There is, however, the possibility of a lower effective rate than 28 per cent if the trusts fall within FA 2005, ss 23–45 as a trust for the vulnerable, for which see para **[226.9]** ff below.

[226.8]
Income tax. Income tax will, generally, be charged at 'the trust rate' (currently 45 per cent for the tax year 2013–14 in respect of income over £1,000) unless there is an actual interest in possession (see Part A, para **[200.41]**). However, the tax on any of the income which is paid to or applied for the benefit of a beneficiary will be adjusted to that appropriate to the personal tax position of the beneficiary. For the rules specific to UK company dividend income arising to trustees of discretionary trusts, see Preliminary Note to B18 at para **[218.30]**. This is subject to the possibility of

a trust for a disabled person qualifying as a trust for the vulnerable within FA 2005, ss 23–45, and receiving more favourable income tax treatment, for which see para **[226.9]** ff below.

[226.9]

Trusts for the vulnerable for disabled persons. A further possible type of trust for disabled persons conferring a tax advantage is created by FA 2005, ss 23–45. This is a 'trust for the vulnerable' for a 'disabled person', which has the advantage that the trustees and beneficiary can elect for the income and capital gains to be taxed as the disabled person's instead of being taxed at the trust rates, which have been increased considerably in recent years (see para **[200.41]** above). This note and the form set out below concentrate on the aspects of these rules which fall within the scope of *Williams on Wills*, namely the drafting of trusts which qualify for this special treatment. The details of what the special treatment is and how it is obtained will be found in HMRC's Trusts, Settlements and Estates Manual, TSEM 3400 et seq (although at the time of writing this guidance has not been updated to take into account changes made by FA 2013, Sch 44, para 15) and *Tolley's Income Tax 2013–14,* paras 68.19– 68.21. The advantages of this special treatment are as follows:

(i) The income tax advantage is essentially that undistributed income is taxed as if it were the beneficiary's income. This is not quite as beneficial as might at first appear because if income is distributed the trustees still have to account for income tax at the trust rate (currently 45 per cent for tax year 2013–14) so far as not already paid on the income which is distributed, the beneficiary has to make a repayment claim if this is in excess of his liability, and there is still no carry-through to the beneficiary of the tax credit on dividends.
(ii) The capital gains tax advantage is that the trustees are, in effect, taxed on chargeable gains as if they had arisen to the beneficiary who may pay tax on all or some of the gains at a lower rate than the trustees. So, in tax year 2013–14 at 18 per cent if his total income and gains do not exceed the upper limit of the income tax basic rate band, rather than the 28 per cent trust rate.

The conditions for the above treatment from and including 2013–14 are similar to the new conditions for trusts within IHTA 1984, s 89 (as amended by FA 2013, Sch 44, para 6) (see paras **[226.3]**, **[226.4]**, sub-paras (iii)–(v)) and those for the full capital gains tax annual exemption (see para **[226.6]**). Previously (ie for tax year 2012–2013 and prior years), the conditions for trusts to be within FA 2005, ss 23–45 did not match the old conditions for trusts within IHTA 1984, s 89, so that whereas a trust might be within IHTA 1984, s 89, it would not necessarily be able to elect for the income and capital gains tax treatment of FA 2005, ss 23–45. It is a welcome change that the conditions for the various tax reliefs for trusts for the disabled have now been brought into line by amendments made by FA 2013, s 216, Sch 44. As already mentioned, there will usually be some tax advantage in a trust falling within FA 2005, ss 23–45, in the form of a lower rate of income tax on accumulated income, and a lower rate of capital gains tax. It may be noted, however, that a trust falling within FA 2005, ss 23–45 will also generally be a trust entitled to the higher annual exemption for capital gains tax (see para **[226.6]**) so that an election for FA 2005, ss 23–45 treatment will not necessarily give the trust an advantage of a higher annual exemption (unless perhaps the trust is one of two or more disabled person's trusts made by the same settlor/testator, in which case the annual exemption will be shared between the trusts: see TCGA 1992, Sch 1, para 1(3)–(5)). Forms C4.1, C4.2 and C4.3 (at paras **[218.13]** ff) contain trusts which are thought to fall within FA 2005, s 34 and IHTA 1984, s 89).

[226.10]
Trusts for the vulnerable—qualifying conditions. FA 2005, s 38 (as substituted by FA 2013, Sch 44, para 17) defines the disabled persons whose trusts can qualify for the special treatment under FA 2005, ss 23–45 for 2013–14 onwards as the same persons as those who qualify as disabled for the purposes of IHTA 1984, s 89: see para **[226.4]**, sub-para (i) above (regardless of when property passed into the trust). FA 2005, s 34 (as amended by FA 2013, Sch 44, para 15) defines the qualifying trusts for disabled persons. To be qualifying trusts for 2013–14 and onwards the property subject to them must satisfy two conditions, one relating to capital (see para **[226.11**) and the other relating to income (see para **[226.12]**). These conditions must be satisfied during the vulnerable person's lifetime or until the termination of the trusts if that occurs before his death (s 34(1)). It is not clear what sort of trust with a possibility or certainty of termination before the death of the disabled person is capable of being a qualifying trust. For example, would trusts which for the time being satisfy the income and capital conditions, but which are subject to an overriding power of the trustees to appoint different trusts which would not qualify, be for the time being qualifying trusts? This seems unlikely. It may be that such an arrangement fails to satisfy the capital condition on the basis that the overriding power is or could create a power of application within the meaning of s 34(2)(a) which falls outside it, or that 'until the termination of the trusts' in s 34(1)(b) means 'until the entire settlement terminates' rather than 'until the qualifying trust for the benefit of the disabled beneficiary terminates'. Another possibility is that 'until the termination of the trusts' in s 34(1) refers to the termination of the trusts for the benefit of the disabled beneficiary by the passing of time where the date of termination is predetermined, rather than by the occurrence of a contingency or the exercise of a power. Section 34(4) is probably intended to enable protective trusts for a disabled person to fall within these provisions, until a forfeiture occurs, where they otherwise would not. If so, and if it is the case that a protective trust could not be a qualifying trust before a forfeiture occurred in the absence of a provision such as 34(4), 'until the termination of the trusts' in s 34(1)(b) has a very restricted meaning.

[226.11]
Trusts for the vulnerable—qualifying condition as to trusts of capital. The condition relating to capital is that the trusts must secure that the only applications of capital which can be made are applications for the benefit of the disabled person (s 34(2)(a)). However, for tax year 2013–14 and onwards, the fact that the trustees have the powers specified in para **[226.4]**, sub-para (v) above, namely, power to apply annually up to £3,000 (or 3 per cent

of the value of the trust fund) otherwise than for the benefit of the disabled person, or the extended statutory power of advancement (TA 1925, s 32 or the Trustee Act (N Ireland) 1958, s 33) or a like power, will not prevent this condition from being satisfied (FA 2005, s 34(3), as substituted by FA 2013, Sch 44, para 15(3)). For years prior to 2013–14, it was only the unextended statutory power of advancement (or a like power subject to the same restrictions) which was compatible with the capital condition.

[226.12]

Trusts for the vulnerable—qualifying condition as to trusts of income. The income condition is that the trusts secure that the disabled person is entitled to all the income arising from the property (if any) or that if any such income is applied for the benefit of a beneficiary, it is applied for the benefit of the disabled person (FA 2005, s 34(2)(b), as amended by FA 2013, Sch 44, para 15(2), amending the language, but not the purport of s 34(2)(b)). So either the disabled person must have an interest in possession or, if not, there cannot be a discretion over income exercisable in favour of anyone other than the disabled person. For wills made on or after 6 April 2010, there are no statutory restrictions on accumulation in respect of non-charitable trusts, and so accumulation will be permitted throughout the trust period: see the PAA 2009, ss 13, 15(1)(a) (Part G, para **[187]**). Now that accumulation is possible throughout the trust period it is possible for the trust to provide that the trustees should either apply the income for the beneficiary's benefit or accumulate it during the whole of the trust period (or the life of the beneficiary) thus satisfying the condition without giving rise to an interest in possession.

[226.13]

Form C4.1: Reciprocal wills for husband and wife with a disabled child and other children; gift by first to die of entire estate to survivor subject to a nil-rate band discretionary trust, and a discretionary trust of residue on the death of the survivor

Note. This Form is for use in a will executed on or after 8 April 2013 if it is to contain the option of a trust which is to comply with IHTA 1984, s 89. When wills are being made to provide for a disabled child, there will often be uncertainty as to the future condition of the child, and there will usually be uncertainty about the future availability of and rules surrounding state benefits and local authority care, and the future incidence of taxation. Where the child is currently in the care of his parents, there is also the considerable uncertainty as to what will happen to him on the death of the second to die of his parents. Accordingly, this form for the wills of both husband and wife, leaves the decision as to what provision to make for the disabled child on the death of the second parent to die, to the executors' discretion.

[226.14]

On the death of the first to die. Under the will of the first of the spouses to die there is a nil-rate band discretionary trust under which the surviving spouse and the children, including the disabled child, are beneficiaries, and subject to that the residuary estate goes to the surviving spouse absolutely. This nil-rate band trust falls within the ordinary discretionary trust IHT charging rules, and does not fall within IHTA 1984, s 89. Because of nil-rate band transfer (see para **[200.74]**), the nil-rate band trust is not needed for IHT-saving reasons unless one of the special reasons discussed in para **[200.130]** applies, but it provides flexibility. The powers are wide enough to enable the trustees to turn it into a s 89 trust for the disabled child (or perhaps a s 89B(1)(c) trust, see **[226.5A]**), if that turns out to be a good idea, or they can appoint it to the surviving spouse absolutely or for life if a discretionary trust is not wanted and nil-rate band transfer seems a better use of the first to die's nil-rate band. For notes on nil-rate band discretionary trusts see B18 at paras **[218.16]–[218.18]**.

[226.15]

On the death of the survivor. Under the will of the survivor there are some pecuniary legacies and a gift of the estate on wide discretionary trusts and powers for a class which includes the disabled child and charity among the beneficiaries, with the idea that the trustees can appoint whatever seems to be the best arrangement at the time, and rely on IHTA 1984, s 144 (see C3 at paras **[225.83]–[225.91]**) where the appointment has IHT implications, particularly where property is distributed to charity or a wholly charitable trust is set up in relation to part of the fund (see below). If no exercise of their powers is made by the trustees during the two years after the testator's death, there are two alternatives as to the default trusts after the end of two years from the testator's death (ie the trusts taking effect in the absence of any exercise of the trustees' powers during those two years) according to whether sub-cls (4) and (5) of cl 10 (see para **[226.33]**) are included in the will or left out. If those subclauses are included, his disabled child will become the sole beneficiary of the trust during his lifetime (save for permissible applications of capital and income which may be made for other beneficiaries within the annual limit (see **[226.5]**, sub-para (v)(a)) and the trust will be brought within IHTA 1984, s 89 (as amended by FA 2013, Sch 44, para 6) (see para **[226.3]**). This is achieved by restricting the powers over capital and income after the end of the two-year period so that only the annual limit may be applied during the disabled child's life otherwise than for his benefit. If the existence of powers which authorise the trustees to create interests in possession during the disabled child's life does not prevent IHTA 1984, s 89 (as amended) from applying (see para **[226.4]**, sub-paras (vi) and (vii)), the inclusion of sub-cls (4) and (5) of cl 10 will mean that in default of any exercise of the trustees' powers during the two years following the testator's death s 89 (as amended) will apply and the disabled child will be treated for IHT purposes as entitled to an interest in possession (which is a disabled person's interest) in the whole of the residuary estate (see para **[226.5]**). Such trusts will also fall within FA 2005, ss 23–45 (trusts for the vulnerable) and qualify for full capital gains tax annual exemption under TCGA 1992, Sch 1, para 1 (see paras **[226.6]**, **[226.12]**). If sub-cls (4) and (5) of cl 10 are not included in the will, the trusts in default of exercise of the trustees' powers within the two-year period will be full discretionary trusts for all the testator's children and remoter issue etc, subject to IHT under the ordinary relevant property discretionary trust charging rules (IHTA 1984, Pt III, Ch III: see B18 at paras **[218.6]–[218.15]**). The trustees can appoint trusts falling within IHTA 1984, s 89 (as amended), FA 2005, ss 23–45 (trusts for the vulnerable) and qualifying for full capital gains tax annual exemption under TCGA 1992, Sch 1, para 1 (see paras **[226.6]**, **[226.12]**), but the trusts will not fall within them automatically.

[226.16]

Scope of powers and IHTA 1984, s 89. We mention in sub-paras (vi) and (vii) of para **[226.4]** the possibility that the existence of powers which allow the trustees to create an interest or interests in possession may not be compatible with IHTA 1984, s 89 (as amended by FA 2013, Sch 44, para 6) applying. We also mention that this would be extremely inconvenient and that there is no indication that HMRC take this view. Accordingly the provisions in this form intended to cause s 89 to apply (ie sub-cls (4) and (5) of cl 10 at para **[226.33]**) do not in terms restrict the trustees' powers so as to prevent the creation of interests in possession during the life of the disabled beneficiary. There is a general restriction on the administrative powers in cl 9(2)(iii) to the effect that those powers are not to prevent s 89 (as amended by FA 2013, Sch 44, para 6) from applying (see para **[224.31]**). Also, a power to release or restrict powers is included. If during the two years following the testator's death it is clear that HMRC do regard the existence of powers to create an interest or interests in possession during the disabled beneficiary's life as incompatible with s 89 (as amended), and it is desired that s 89 (as amended) should apply, an appropriate restriction could be imposed.

[226.17]

After the death of the disabled child. It should also be noted that in the absence of any exercise of the trustees' powers the discretionary trusts of the surviving spouse's residuary estate will continue well beyond the death of the disabled child (see the definition of 'the trust period' in cl 8(2)(b) and the discretionary trust of income in cl 8(4) at para **[226.30]**). This means that if sub-cls (4) and (5) of cl 10 are included in the will (see para **[226.16]**), and IHTA 1984, s 89 (as amended by FA 2013, Sch 44, para 6) applies during the life of the disabled child so as to treat him as having an interest in possession in the residuary estate, the IHT status of the trusts from the death of the disabled child until the end of the trust period will be discretionary trusts falling within IHTA 1984, Pt III, Ch III (see B18 at paras **[218.6]–[218.15]**), and there will be an exit charge on property which is distributed out of the estate after the disabled child's death (in addition to the IHT charge on the residuary estate as part of the disabled child's estate on his death). Under the rules as they stand at the moment this exit charge will be very small if it occurs a short time after the disabled child's death (see B18 at para **[218.11]**). However, it can be avoided altogether if an appointment is made before the disabled child's death of fixed trusts which take effect on his death. If it is found desirable to restrict the trustees' powers, either in order to get the trusts within IHTA 1984, s 89 (as amended) (see para **[226.4]**, sub-paras (vi) and (vii)), or to reduce the chances of the residuary estate being taken into account for state etc, benefit purposes (see para **[226.2]**), it should be done so far as possible so as to leave the trustees with flexible powers to determine what the trusts will be on or after the disabled child's death.

[226.18]

Charities as objects of the discretions. The discretionary beneficiaries under both the nil-rate band legacy trusts and the residuary trusts include charities. This means that not only are the trustees able to distribute income or capital to charities, but they are also able, by virtue of IHTA 1984, s 144 (see C3 at paras **[225.83]–[225.91]**), to obtain IHT charitable exemption on the death of the surviving spouse in relation to any of the surviving spouse's residuary estate distributed to particular charities during the period of two years from the testator's death, or appointed during that period on permanent and irrevocable discretionary trusts which have charities as the only objects. In relation to the nil-rate band legacy fund under the will of the first to die it will be possible to obtain charitable exemption from the exit charge where the circumstances are such that the fund has risen in value sufficiently to become taxable.

[226.19]

Power of advancement. Where trusts are being drafted so as to fall within IHTA 1984, s 89 (as amended by FA 2013, Sch 44, para 6), or so as to be capable of doing so, in a will drafted for execution on or after 8 April 2013, a statutory power of advancement may be included, even if it extended so as to be exercisable over the whole of a beneficiary's presumptive share of capital: see para **[226.4]**, sub-para (v)(b). There is though no express provision in this form for this.

[226.20]

Letters of wishes. These should be left by the testators, setting out their wishes with regard to the discretionary trusts, and expressed not to create any legally binding trust or obligation. It is particularly important that they should indicate what proportion of the estate of the second of them to die they would like to go into a fund to help the disabled child and what proportion they would like to go to the other children immediately. Where the estate is likely to be fairly small it will usually be intended that the non-disabled children will only receive significant benefit after the death of the disabled child.

[226.21]

For another example of a trust falling within IHTA 1984, s 89 (as amended by FA 2013, Sch 44, para 6) to be included in a will to be executed on or after 8 April 2013, see Form B18.4 at para **[218.34]**.

This form may be adapted for use for civil partners, the words 'my wife/husband' being replaced with 'my civil partner' throughout. Care should be taken to identify correctly in each will the children who are to benefit.

[226.22]

REVOCATION CLAUSE

I [*name*] of [*address*] revoke all former testamentary dispositions made by me and declare this to be my last will.[1]

1 There is no presumption that wills in similar form are mutual wills in the technical sense, but in view of the close tailoring of the two wills to each other, it would be appropriate to add a declaration excluding mutual wills as in the revocation clause of Form C2.1 at para **[224.28]**.

[226.23]

APPOINTMENT OF EXECUTORS AND TRUSTEES AND DEFINITION OF 'MY TRUSTEES'

1. I appoint [*name*] of [*address*] and [*name*] of [*address*][1] (hereinafter together called 'my trustees' which expression shall where the context so admits include my personal representatives for the time being and the trustees for the time being hereof) to be the executors and trustees of this will.

1 For reasons given in para **[218.22]** (4) the surviving spouse should not be a general executor if the charge scheme method of constituting the nil-rate band trust is to be used.

[226.24]

APPOINTMENT OF GUARDIANS[1]

2. If my [wife/husband] shall predecease me I appoint [*name*] of [*address*] [and [*name*] of [*address*]] to be the [guardian/guardians] of my children during their respective minorities.

1 For reasons given in the Note on appointment of guardians in B3 (at paras **[203.47]**–**[203.59]**) it is better to provide appointments of guardians which take effect only on the death of the survivor. It should be noted that the legal status of guardians will cease in relation to a mentally disabled child when he or she attains the age of 18. This clause should be omitted if the children are all already over the age of 18.

[226.25]

LEGACIES TO TAKE EFFECT ON THE DEATH OF THE SECOND TO DIE

3. If I survive my [wife/husband][1] I give the following pecuniary legacies free of tax:[2]

[(a) To my son [*name*][3] the sum of £——;
(b) To my daughter [*name*][4] the sum of £——;
(c) To [*name*] of [*address*] the sum of £——.]

1 The words in square brackets should be included where these are intended to be legacies which are given once only, on the death of the second of the spouses to die. It should be noted that where the words in square brackets are not included, and the nil-rate band utilising legacy below is expressed as a specified sum of money, the latter needs to be reduced by the total amount or value of the legacies given by this clause which are not exempt legacies, such as ones to the surviving spouse or to charity. For reciprocal wills containing legacies intended to take effect under only one of the wills where there is a survivorship condition in the main gift see Form C9.2 at para **[231.14]** ff.

It should be noted that if there is a divorce, these legacies will still take effect, and only take effect, on the death of the survivor of the former spouses, if they do not change their wills.

2 These pecuniary legacies are declared to be 'free of tax' to take account of the risk that they may be payable out of a residuary estate which includes property of a kind which bears its own IHT, such as property situated outside the UK, with the consequence that the legacies might without this declaration be liable to bear their own IHT so far as payable out of that property: see the Preliminary Note to B14 at paras **[214.59]**–**[214.60]**. The expression 'free of tax' is employed here in conjunction with the definition and direction as to payment in cl 6 of this form at para **[226.28]**.

3 Ie one of the non-disabled children of the testator.
4 See n 3 above.

[226.26]

GIFT OF NIL-RATE BAND LEGACY ON DISCRETIONARY TRUSTS

4.(1) In this clause the following expressions have the following meanings:

(a) 'the trust legacy' means the legacy by this clause bequeathed to my legacy trustees and the assets for the time being representing the same;

(b) 'the legacy beneficiaries' means:

(i) my [wife/husband];

(ii) my children and remoter issue;[1]

(iii) any spouse widow or widower of any of such children or remoter issue (and 'widow' and 'widower' shall include a widow or widower who has remarried);

(iv) any institution (whether corporate or not) which is established for charitable purposes only and is a charity under the law of England and Wales within the meaning of section 1(1) of the Charities Act 2011.[2]

(c) 'A' means my [son/daughter] A[3];

(d) 'the trust period' means the period of 125 years commencing on the date of my death;[4] and

(e) 'my legacy trustees' means [*name*] of [*address*] and [*name*] of [*address*][5] or other the trustee or trustees for the time being of the trust legacy.

(2) If my [wife/husband] shall survive me[6] then I bequeath to my legacy trustees free of tax a legacy of the maximum sum of money (if any) which can in the circumstances subsisting at my death be given by this clause without any liability being incurred for the payment of inheritance tax on or by reason of my death. And in particular but without prejudice to the generality of the foregoing the circumstances to be taken into account for the foregoing purpose shall include any chargeable transfers made by me during my lifetime (or events treated as such for inheritance tax purposes) the dispositions taking effect under this Will (apart from this present clause) or under any codicil hereto and any property treated as if it were part of my estate immediately before my death for inheritance tax purposes.

(3) My legacy trustees shall hold the trust legacy and the income thereof upon such trusts for the benefit of all or any one or more exclusively of the others or other of the legacy beneficiaries and if more than one in such shares and with such trusts and powers (which may include discretionary trusts or powers conferred on my legacy trustees or any other person or persons and may also include power to create further discretionary trusts or powers)[7] and with such provisions generally as my legacy trustees (not being fewer than two in number or being a corporation) shall by any deed or deeds revocable or irrevocable appoint provided that no appointment shall be made and no revocable appointment shall be revoked after the expiration of the trust period.

(4) At any time or times during the trust period my legacy trustees (not being fewer than two in number or being a corporation) may pay or apply

the whole or any part or parts of the trust legacy to or for the advancement or benefit of any of the legacy beneficiaries for the time being living in such manner as they think fit.[8]

(5) Subject to any exercise of the foregoing powers my legacy trustees shall during the trust period hold the trust legacy upon trust to pay or apply the income thereof to or for the maintenance education or benefit of all or any one or more of the legacy beneficiaries for the time being living in such shares if more than one and generally in such manner as they think fit provided that my legacy trustees may during the trust period accumulate the whole or any part of the income of the trust legacy by investing the same and the resulting income thereof in any of the investments hereby authorised and any accumulations of income so made shall form part of the capital of the trust legacy for all purposes.

(6) Subject to any exercise of the foregoing powers the trust legacy and the income thereof shall be held at the expiration of the trust period in trust absolutely for such of my grandchildren and remoter issue [who are issue of my children by my wife/husband][9] as shall then be living in equal shares per stirpes (with my children [by my wife/husband] as the heads of stock) so that no issue shall take whose parent is living at the expiration of the trust period and capable of taking[10].

(7) After the death of my [wife/husband] my trustees shall have power during the trust period in their absolute discretion to transfer the trust legacy or any part or parts thereof to the trustees of any fund held on any discretionary or other trusts arising under the will of my [wife/husband] which are wholly or partly for the benefit of any one or more of the legacy beneficiaries (whether or not persons other than the legacy beneficiaries may also be benefited) to be held as an accretion to such fund and as one fund therewith for all purposes provided that the foregoing power shall not be exercisable unless such transfer can be effected without infringing the rule against perpetuities as it affects the trust legacy.[11]

(8) Any capital or income of the trust legacy not otherwise disposed of by this clause shall be held in trust for such of my children other than A as survive me if more than one in equal shares absolutely.

(9) Instead of the trust legacy being satisfied by the payment of cash or by the appropriation of property:

(a) my trustees may charge (with or without there being any personal liability of any person or persons) any property which is (or but for this clause would be) comprised in my residuary estate with payment of a sum of money equal to or less than the amount of the trust legacy to my legacy trustees and my legacy trustees shall accept such charge for such sum as the whole or a part (as the case may be) of the trust legacy;

(b) my trustees may require my legacy trustees to accept in satisfaction of all or part of the trust legacy a binding promise of payment (secured or unsecured) made personally by my [wife/husband] or by my trustees as trustees of my residuary estate which debt shall be payable on demand and my legacy trustees shall accept such debt as the whole or a part (as the case may be) of the trust legacy; and

(c) without prejudice to the power of appropriation herein elsewhere contained my trustees may constitute the trust legacy wholly or partly by appropriating to it at their discretion any property or proportionate share of any property and for this purpose may take such advice as to the value of the said property or proportionate share as they think fit and where the trust legacy is for the time being wholly or partly constituted by a proportionate share of a dwelling-house or other property my legacy trustees shall have all the powers of an absolute owner in relation to such share and property and in particular may at their discretion join with the other proprietor or proprietors of such property:

(i) to permit a beneficiary under the trusts of the trust legacy to have the use or enjoyment of the property in kind on such terms as my trustees think fit; or

(ii) to effect or enable a sale of the property and the purchase of another property in the same or similar co-ownership with the trust legacy constituted by a proportionate share thereof.

(10) The following shall apply in relation to the powers in the last preceding subclause:

(a) my trustees may require to be included such terms if any as they think fit in relation to a charge under subclause (9)(a) above or a debt under subclause (9)(b) above including terms as to interest (if any) and linking the debt or sum charged to the Index of Retail Prices or otherwise providing for its amount to vary with the passage of time according to a formula provided that the debt or the sum of money secured by the charge shall be payable to my legacy trustees on demand and the charge shall be enforceable by my legacy trustees at any time;

(b) my legacy trustees may leave the charge or debt outstanding for as long as they think fit and refrain from exercising their rights in relation to it and waive the payment of all or any part of any interest due in respect of it and may accept any substitute debt or charge undertaken or created by any person;

(c) my trustees may assent to the vesting of my residuary estate subject to an outstanding obligation to pay or satisfy the trust legacy and my legacy trustees may appoint new trustees of the trust legacy in exercise of the statutory power to do so before the trust legacy has been paid or satisfied;

(d) my legacy trustees and my trustees shall not be liable if my [wife/husband] is or becomes unable to pay the debt or any security is or becomes inadequate or for any other loss or disadvantage which may occur as a result of their exercising or choosing not to exercise any of the foregoing powers; and

(e) the foregoing powers are in addition to any other powers given by this will or any codicil or by the general law and the foregoing powers may be exercised even though my trustees and my legacy trustees are the same persons or my [wife/husband] is among either or both sets of trustees provided that such powers shall not be exercisable by a sole trustee who is my [wife/husband].

(11) Clauses 9 to 14 inclusive below shall apply to the trusts of this clause as if references therein to my trustees were references to my legacy trustees.

1 Add 'by my wife/husband' if appropriate, here and in the trusts of residue in clause 8(2)(a)(i) in para **[226.30]**. See the Preliminary Note to C2 at paras **[224.13]**–**[224.15]**. It is desirable that the nil-rate band legacy in the will of the first to die is held on trusts as similar as possible to those of the residuary estate of the survivor, so that the two funds can be amalgamated after the death of the latter if they are both trusts falling within IHTA 1984, s 89.

2 Charities Act 2011, s 1(1) replaced Charities Act 2006, s 1(1), with effect from 14 March 2012, the latter having replaced Charities Act 1993, s 96(1) which had some verbal differences but was substantially the same. For the current definition see Vol 1, para **[102.3]**. If the disabled child is being cared for by some charitable body, it may be useful to have express power to make appointments in favour of that charity.

3 This is the disabled child, in order to exclude him or her from the fixed trusts which take effect if the discretionary trusts come to an end without the trustees' powers being exhaustively exercised (see subclause (8) of this clause).

4 For wills made on or after 6 April 2010, the perpetuity period is 125 years (and there is no other period): see the PAA 2009, ss 5(1), 15(1)(a) (Part A **[200.35A]** and Part G, para **[246.179]**). The nil-rate band legacy in the one will and the residuary estate in the other will have the same perpetuity period. This is particularly important for the amalgamation of the funds to be possible. See cl 4(7) of this form for the power to amalgamate them.

5 For reasons given in **[218.22]** (5) the legacy trustees and general trustees should not be exactly the same persons, though there could be overlap in case it turns out to be desired to use a charge scheme to constitute the trust fund.

6 This precondition is imposed to avoid unnecessary duplication of gifts (i e this one and the residuary gift) in the event of the spouse not surviving the testator. Survivorship conditions are no longer recommended as between spouses or civil partners (see para **[224.6]** ff). Even if it is preferred in general to continue to include survivorship conditions, this gift should not be made conditional on the spouse surviving the testator by a survivorship period: see the Preliminary Note to C3 at para **[225.4]**.

7 These words authorise the creation of discretionary trusts or powers which might not otherwise be valid: see Vol 1, para **[40.5]**.

8 A power to apply capital, being exercisable in a less formal manner, may be useful, but it is essential that its exercise should be adequately evidenced. It is an important power to include where a disabled person is a beneficiary, because it will authorise, e g payments to be made to persons or charities looking after or helping the disabled person, where such payments are beneficial to the disabled person. See the Note in B18 at para **[218.92]** ff for the wide scope of a power to apply property for a person's benefit. The reference to a trust corporation is for the reasons given in n 1 of para **[226.37]**.

9 See n 1 above.

10 Since the trust period will be 125 years from the testator's death, the beneficiaries do not include the testator's children.

11 In order to maximise the chances of this power being exercisable the trusts of the nil-rate band legacy and of the residue under the other spouse's will are made as similar as possible. It may be possible to amalgamate the funds if they are both subject to beneficiary-taxed deemed interests in possession of the same person, by virtue of IHTA 1984, s 89. If they are relevant property they will have to remain separately identifiable funds because they will have different settlors, different factors in their calculations of the tax rate on periodic charges and exit charges, and different dates of periodic charges.

[226.27]

ADMINISTRATION TRUSTS OF RESIDUE

5. (1) I give all my property not hereby or by any codicil hereto otherwise effectively disposed of [(including any entailed or other property over which I shall have at my death a general power of disposition by will)][1] to my

trustees to hold on the trusts set out below with power at their discretion to sell all or any of it as and when they think fit.[2]

(2) My trustees shall pay my funeral and testamentary expenses[3] and debts and any legacies given by this will or any codicil hereto out of such property or its proceeds and shall have a discretion as to how such payments shall be borne as between capital and income.[4]

(3) Subject as above my trustees shall hold such property and the assets from time to time representing the same (hereinafter called 'my residuary estate') on the trusts set out below and shall invest all money comprised in such property or arising from its sale in any of the investments hereby authorised with power to change such investments into any others hereby authorised.[5]

1 See Form C2.1, cl 6, n 1 at para **[224.34]**.
2 See Form C2.1, cl 6, n 2 at para **[224.34]**.
3 See Form C2.1, cl 6, n 3 at para **[224.34]**.
4 See Form C2.1, cl 6, n 4 at para **[224.34]**
5 Exclusion of the equitable rules of apportionment and the Apportionment Act 1870, which conventionally appears around here, is no longer needed in wills made on or after 1 October 2013: Trusts (Capital and Income) Act 2013 s 1. See paras **[246.200]**, **[246.201]**.

[226.28]

GIFTS MADE FREE OF TAX

6. Any specific gift or pecuniary or general legacy made by this will or any codicil hereto which is expressed to be 'free of tax' shall be free from the payment of any inheritance tax or foreign tax or duty payable on or by reason of my death to which such gift or legacy would otherwise be subject and such inheritance tax or foreign tax or duty shall be paid out of my residuary estate.[1]

1 Where specific gifts and pecuniary legacies are of, or wholly payable out of, free estate in the UK, the IHT on them will be a testamentary expense payable out of residue without any express provision, and it is only where there is foreign property or settled property being disposed of by the will that a gift which is intended to be free of tax needs to be expressly declared to be free of tax. See also the Note to B14 at paras **[214.59]–[214.60]**.

[226.29]

PRIMARY TRUST OF RESIDUE IN FAVOUR OF SPOUSE IF SURVIVING

7. If my [wife/husband] shall survive me[1] my trustees shall hold my residuary estate and the income thereof upon trust for [her/him] absolutely.

1 Residue devolves on the other spouse, if surviving. If the other spouse does not survive the testator, residue passes to wide discretionary trusts, see cl 8 at para **[226.25]**. It is not appropriate to incorporate a survivorship condition in the gift to the spouse: see the Notes on survivorship conditions in C2 at **[224.6]** ff and C3 at para **[225.4]**.

[226.30]

ALTERNATIVE GIFT OF RESIDUE ON DISCRETIONARY TRUSTS FOR CHILDREN AND ISSUE

8. (1) If my [wife/husband] shall not survive me[1] my trustees shall hold my residuary estate and the income thereof upon the trusts and with and subject to the powers and provisions hereinafter in this clause declared and contained.

(2) In this clause the following expressions have the following meanings namely:

(a) 'the residuary beneficiaries' means and includes:[2]

(i) my children and remoter issue;[3]

(ii) any spouse widow or widower of any of such children or remoter issue (and 'widow' and 'widower' shall include a widow or widower who has remarried);[4]

(iii) any institution (whether corporate or not) which is established for charitable purposes only and is a charity under the law of England and Wales within the meaning of section 1(1) of the Charities Act 2011;[5]

(b) 'the trust period' means the period commencing on the day of my death and expiring 125 years from the death of my [wife/husband];[6] and

(c) 'the relevant day' means the day falling two years less one day after my death.

(3) Subject as provided in clause 10 below[7] my trustees (being not less than two in number or a trust corporation except as hereinafter provided)[8] may at any time or times and from time to time during the trust period exercise either or both of the following powers namely:

(a) power at any time or times and from time to time by deed or deeds revocable or irrevocable to appoint the whole or any part or parts of my residuary estate upon trust for all or such one or more exclusive of the others or other of the residuary beneficiaries if more than one in such shares and either absolutely or at such age or time or respective ages or times and with such trusts and powers for their respective benefit and such provisions as my trustees may think fit and in making any such appointment my trustees shall have powers as full as those which they would possess if they were an absolute beneficial owner of my residuary estate and in particular (but without prejudice to the generality of the foregoing words) my trustees may in any exercise of the foregoing power as they in their absolute discretion think fit:

(i) to delegate give or impose to or upon themselves or any other person or persons any discretionary powers or discretionary trusts conditions limitations restrictions or provisions including powers of further delegation or powers to create further discretionary trusts or powers;

(ii) create powers or trusts for the accumulation of income during any period permitted by law;

(iii) create administrative powers or provisions of whatever nature;

Provided that:

(i) no such appointment shall invalidate any payment transfer or application of capital or income previously made under any of the trusts or powers herein elsewhere contained;

(ii) every interest limited under any exercise of such power shall vest in interest (if at all) not later than the expiration of the trust period;

(iii) any such appointment may be made in respect of income alone without any appointment of capital;
(iv) any such revocable appointment shall (so far as then unrevoked) cease to be revocable on the expiration of the trust period;
(v) in any appointment made before the relevant day (but not in any appointment made thereafter) my trustees may make provision for the burden of any testamentary expenses taxes or debts payable out of my estate as between different assets funds shares or interests in such manner and to such extent as my trustees think fit;
(vi) the foregoing power of appointment may be exercised notwithstanding that there shall have been no grant of probate or administration in respect of the property over which the said power shall be exercised or that the administration of my estate shall not have been completed in respect of such property or any other property comprised in my estate and so long as no such grant as aforesaid has been obtained the persons who may exercise the foregoing power are the persons hereinbefore named as my executors other than any of them who shall have died or whose appointment as my executor shall have ceased to have effect or who shall have renounced probate of my will;
(vii) the foregoing power of appointment may be exercised before the relevant day by a sole trustee who is not a trust corporation;[9]

(b) power (subject to any or every exercise of the foregoing power) at any time or times and from time to time in their absolute discretion to pay transfer or apply my residuary estate or any part or parts thereof to or for the benefit of all or any one or more exclusive of the others or other of the residuary beneficiaries for the time being in existence if more than one in such shares and generally in such manner as my trustees shall think fit provided that the foregoing power of payment transfer or application of capital may be exercised before the relevant day by a sole trustee who is not a trust corporation.[10]

(4) In default of and subject to any or every exercise of the foregoing powers my trustees shall hold my residuary estate during the trust period upon trust to pay or apply the income thereof to or for the maintenance education or benefit of all or any one or more of the residuary beneficiaries and if more than one in such shares and in such manner generally as my trustees think fit provided that during the trust period my trustees may accumulate all or any part or parts of such income by investing the same and the resulting income thereof in any investments hereby authorised and so that any accumulations so made shall form part of the capital of my residuary estate from which such income arose for all purposes.

(5) Subject as aforesaid my trustees shall hold my residuary estate and the income thereof at the expiration of the trust period upon trust for such of my grandchildren and remoter issue [who are issue of my children by my

wife/husband] as shall be then living in equal shares per stirpes (with my children [by my wife/husband] as the heads of stock).

(6) Any capital or income of my residuary estate not otherwise disposed of by this clause shall be held in trust for such of my children other than [*name*][11] as shall survive me and if more than one in equal shares.

1 Residue devolves on the other spouse, if surviving. If the other spouse does not survive the testator, residue is given on discretionary trusts for the children etc. It will be taxed as relevant property (see para **[218.8]** ff) unless it is brought within IHTA 1984, s 89 (as amended by FA 2013, Sch 44, para 6) by positive act of the trustees or by clause 10(4) (para **[226.33]**) operating. It is not appropriate to incorporate a survivorship condition in the gift to the spouse: see the Preliminary Notes on survivorship conditions in C2 at para **[224.6]** ff and C3 at para **[225.4]**.

2 For a wider class, including power to add to it, see Form C3.6, cl 3(1)(b) at para **[225.100]**.

3 See cl 4(1)(b)(ii), n 1 at para **[226.26]**.

4 Instructions must be taken on the composition of the class. In settlements created after 21 March 2006, the IHT reasons for including spouses etc in a discretionary class are much diminished, because appointing successive interests in possession to spouses or civil partners no longer, in general, gets the spouse or civil partner exemption (see **[200.84]**, **[200.98]**, **[200.99]**).

5 See cl 4(1), n 2 at para **[226.26]**. See also the Note to this form at para **[226.18]**.

6 For wills made on or after 6 April 2010, the perpetuity period is 125 years (and there is no other period): see the PAA 2009, ss 5(1), 15(1)(a) (Part A **[200.35A]** and Part G, para **[179]**). This trust period will necessarily be within the perpetuity period of 125 years starting on the testator's death. The whole 125 years is not used here, but rather a period matching that of the trust period of the will of the first spouse to die in view of the possibility of an amalgamation of the nil rate legacy from the will of the first spouse to die with residue of the second to die.

7 Clause 10 contains a power to release and restrict powers (cl 10(2) at para **[226.32]**) and an optional restriction intended to bring IHTA 1984, s 89 (as amended by FA 2013, Sch 44, para 6) into operation (cl 10(4) and (5) at para **[226.32]**).

8 See proviso (viii) to sub-cl (3)(a) and sub-cl (3)(b) of this clause, for the modification of this provision during the two years following the testator's death. For the appointment of a trust corporation see cl 14 at para **[226.37]** and the note thereto.

9 If it were required that there should be two trustees during the two years after the testator's death, difficulty could arise if the number of trustees was reduced to one and the administration of the estate was not complete, as it is not clear that the statutory power to appoint new trustees could be exercised in such circumstances.

10 See cl 4(4), n 8 at para **[226.26]** and, for the reasons for the proviso, see n 9 above.

11 Ie the name of the disabled child, whom it will probably be appropriate to exclude from this ultimate gift of capital.

[226.31]

ADMINISTRATIVE POWERS[1]

9. (1) In this clause where the context so admits:

(a) the expression 'land' includes buildings and estates interests or rights of any kind in or over land; and

(b) during the administration of my estate the expression 'beneficiary' includes any person who would be a beneficiary if such administration had been completed and the expression 'beneficially interested' and references to income of any asset being payable or capable of being paid to or for the benefit of a beneficiary shall be construed accordingly.

(2) None of the powers or provisions contained in subclause (3) below of this clause shall be capable of being exercised or operating in any manner

such that if such power or provision were capable of being so exercised or so operating the existence of the same would:

(i) prevent any person who would in the absence of such power or provision have been entitled to an interest in possession falling within section 49(1A) of the Inheritance Tax Act 1984 in any property from being entitled to such interest; or

(ii) prevent section 71A or 71D of the Inheritance Tax Act 1984 from applying to any property to which in the absence of such power or provision either section would have applied;[2] or

(iii) prevent any person who would in the absence of such power or provision have been treated as entitled to an interest in possession by virtue of section 89 of the Inheritance Tax Act 1984 in any property from being entitled to such interest.

(3) In the administration of my estate and the execution of the trusts hereof or of any codicil hereto my trustees shall (subject to clause 10 below) have the following powers in addition to those conferred by law but subject to the last foregoing subclause:

(a) power to invest moneys sell assets and change investments with the unrestricted freedom of choice and powers of disposition and acquisition of a sole beneficial owner with in particular power to make unsecured loans, acquire non-income yielding assets, and purchase land anywhere in the world or chattels for any purpose including occupation or enjoyment in kind by a beneficiary under the power set out below;[3]

(b) power to delegate all or any of their investment powers to a professional investment manager or managers whether individual or corporate and whether or not also a nominee holder of assets for my trustees (and who may be or include one or more of my trustees or the beneficiaries hereunder) upon such terms as to remuneration and otherwise (including terms authorising self-dealing or providing for the limitation of the liability of the investment manager or managers) as my trustees think fit and section 22 of the Trustee Act 2000 shall not apply;[4]

(c) power to vest or register any property in any person or persons whether individual or corporate and whether or not an investment manager to whom powers have been delegated under the foregoing power (and who may be or include one or more of my trustees or the beneficiaries hereunder) as nominee or nominees for my trustees upon such terms as to remuneration or otherwise (including terms authorising self-dealing or providing for the limitation of the liability of the nominee) as my trustees think fit and section 22 of the Trustee Act 2000 shall not apply;[5]

(d) power to borrow money with or without giving security and on such terms as to interest and repayment and otherwise as my trustees may think fit for any purpose connected with the administration of my estate or the trusts declared herein or in any codicil hereto (including investment) and no lender from whom my trustees borrow money in purported exercise of this power shall be concerned to enquire as to the propriety amount or purpose of any such borrowing;[6]

(e) power to lend money to a beneficiary to whom any of the income of such money is payable or to whom or for whose benefit any income of such money is capable of being paid or applied in exercise of a discretion (or who would be such a beneficiary if such money yielded income) and to do so at a full or concessionary rate of interest or interest free;[7]

(f) all the powers of an absolute owner in relation to any land (wherever situated) held by them;[8]

(g) power to apply capital held on the same trusts as any land (or which would be so held if the administration of my estate had been completed) in the improvement or adaptation of such land and to apply such capital or the income of such capital on the repair or maintenance of such land;[9]

(h) power to permit any beneficiary to have the beneficial occupation use or enjoyment in kind of any land or chattel or other tangible property on such terms as to repair insurance or payment of outgoings by the beneficiary or any other person or persons or otherwise howsoever as my trustees think fit including power for the benefit of a beneficiary to permit any other person or persons (whether beneficiaries or not) to occupy use or enjoy any of the types of asset aforesaid together with such beneficiary or otherwise. Provided that the foregoing power shall only be exercisable and such permission to occupy or enjoy in kind may only continue in the following circumstances:

(i) so long as any of the income of such land chattel or other tangible property is payable to such beneficiary or capable of being paid or applied to him or for his benefit in exercise of a discretion (or would be so payable or capable of being so paid or applied if such land chattel or other property yielded income);

(ii) in the case of land, so long as for the time being the occupation thereof is compatible with any statutory rights of occupation of any other beneficiary or beneficiaries;[10]

(i) power to exercise all the powers of appropriation (and other incidental powers) conferred by statute on a personal representative without the necessity of obtaining any consents and notwithstanding that one or more of my trustees may be beneficially interested in the exercise of such power.[11]

1 See Form C2.1, cl 9, n 1 at para **[224.37]**.
2 See Form C2.1, cl 9, n 2 at para **[224.37]**. This restriction is not needed so long as the trusts are discretionary, but it is included in case trusts of any of these kinds are created by the trustees in exercise of any of their powers.
3 See Form C2.1, cl 9, n 3 at para **[224.37]**.
4 See Form C2.1, cl 9, n 4 at para **[224.37]**.
5 See Form C2.1, cl 9, n 5 at para **[224.37]**.
6 See Form C2.1, cl 9, n 6 at para **[224.37]**.
7 See Form C2.1, cl 9, n 7 at para **[224.37]**.
8 See Form C2.1, cl 9, n 8 at para **[224.37]**.
9 See para **[220.52]** for the reasons for this provision.

10 See Form C2.1, cl 9, n 10 at para **[224.37]**. Express provision for occupation etc by persons other than a beneficiary is added to this subclause to make it clear that the trustees may, eg provide a residence for a disabled beneficiary and someone who is looking after him.

11 See Form C2.1, cl 9, n 11 at para **[224.37]**.

[226.32]

EXERCISE AND RELEASE OF POWERS

10. (1) In this clause:

(a) the expression 'the relevant day' has the same meaning as in clause 8 above of this will;

(b) the expression 'the trust period' has in relation to the trust legacy the same meaning as in clause 4 above of this will and has in relation to my residuary estate the same meaning as in clause 8 above of this will.

(2) My trustees shall have power at any time or times and from time to time during the trust period by deed or deeds to release or restrict all or any of the powers hereinbefore contained (whether dispositive or administrative) or this present power either in whole or in part and in any manner they think fit Provided that except in the case of any exercise of the foregoing power in respect of my residuary estate before the relevant day the trustees shall be at least two in number or a trust corporation.[1]

(3) Any power or discretion hereby or by law conferred on my trustees (including a power or discretion as to the disposition of capital or income) shall be exercisable notwithstanding that any of my trustees has a personal interest in such exercise [Provided that except in the case of any exercise of a power over my residuary estate before the relevant day[2] there are not fewer than two trustees and at least one of my trustees has no such personal interest].[3]

1 This power could be used to convert the trusts of the trust legacy into discretionary trusts falling within IHTA 1984, s 89 (as amended by FA 2013, Sch 44, para 6) (see para **[226.4]**, sub-paras (i) and (vii)), and also those of the residuary estate if sub-cls (4) and (5) of this clause are not included in the will. So, for example, it might be used to limit applications of capital and income for beneficiaries other than the disabled person to applications within the annual limit (currently the lower of £3,000 and the maximum value of the trust property) (see para **[226.4]**, sub-paras (v). It could also be used to narrow the trustees' powers over capital if it is found that extensive powers over capital exercisable in favour of the disabled child are having an adverse effect on state benefits or local authority provision for him or her, or to restrict their powers so that they cannot create an interest or interests in possession during the disabled child's life if that turns out to be necessary for HMRC to accept that IHTA 1984, s 89 (as amended) applies (see para **[226.4]**, sub-paras (vi) and (vii)), and it is desired that s 89 (as amended) should apply.

2 This restriction is only imposed after the initial two-year period from the testator's death because it could cause difficulty for exercise of the powers during the initial period.

3 The words in square brackets should be omitted if the executors and trustees will or might all be members of the testator's family.

[226.33]

RESTRICTION FOR THE PURPOSES OF IHTA 1984, S 89

[(4) If my [son/daughter] [*name of disabled child*] shall be living after the relevant day and shall have been at my death a disabled person within the meaning of that term in section 89 of the Inheritance Tax Act 1984 none of the discretions or powers hereinbefore contained shall be exercisable after the relevant day during the life of my said [son/daughter] so as to cause the aggregate amount of income and/or capital applied otherwise than for the benefit of my said [son/daughter] to exceed the annual limit for the time being within the meaning of section 89(3A) of the Inheritance Tax Act 1984 to the intent that section 89 of the Inheritance Tax Act 1984 shall apply to my residuary estate after the relevant day during the life of my said [son/daughter].[1]

(5) Provided that my trustees may by any deed or deeds executed before the relevant day declare that the foregoing subclause (4) of this clause shall not apply to the whole or any part or share of my residuary estate which may be specified in such deed and the operation of the foregoing subclause (4) shall be excluded or restricted accordingly.[2]]

1 This and the next subclause, if included, will restrict the exercise of the trustees' powers after the expiry of two years from the surviving spouse's death in a way which will convert the trusts into 'disabled trusts' within IHTA 1984, s 89 (as amended by FA 2013, Sch 44, para 6), provided that the disabled child is disabled within the meaning of s 89 at the testator's death (see para **[226.4]**, sub-para (i)), and provided that the existence of powers under which the trustees could create an interest in possession during the disabled child's life is compatible with s 89 (see para **[226.4]**, sub-paras (vi) and (vii) and cl 10(2), n 1 at para **[226.32]**). Since the restriction will come into effect no more than two years after the death, its doing so will not constitute a chargeable event and the disabled trusts will be deemed to have been a provision of the testator's will: IHTA 1984, s 144 (see C3 at paras **[225.83]**–**[225.91]**). The restriction applies to the powers in cl 9 as well as those in cl 8, as there are various powers in cl 9 which could be characterised as powers to apply capital, such as the power to permit enjoyment in kind in cl 9(h) and the power to lend in cl 9(e).

2 Subclause (5) enables the executors by deed executed within two years of the death to exclude the operation of sub-cl (4) in relation to the whole or any part of residue. If sub-cls (4) and (5) are omitted, or they are included but the power in sub-cl (5) is exercised, the residuary estate or the part to which the exercise of the power relates will continue to be held on full discretionary trusts without any restriction on the powers of appointment or application and will be subject to IHT periodic and exit charges under the relevant property regime in IHTA 1984, Pt III, Ch III (see B18 at paras **[218.8]** and **[218.9]**).

[226.34]

RECEIPTS ON BEHALF OF CHARITABLE INSTITUTIONS

11. The receipt of any person who professes to be the treasurer or other proper officer for the time being of any institution (whether corporate or not) shall be a sufficient discharge to my trustees in respect of any money or other asset which becomes payable or transferable to such institution under any exercise of any power or discretion herein contained.

[226.35]

TRUSTEE INDEMNITY

12. (1) My trustees shall not be liable for any act or default of any investment manager or nominee employed in good faith to manage or hold assets of my estate nor for any act or default of any person having the occupation use or enjoyment of property in kind nor for any depreciation wear and tear or damage to any such property while in the possession of any such person.[1]

[(2) Section 11(1) of the Trusts of Land and Appointment of Trustees Act 1996 (consultation with beneficiaries) shall not apply to the exercise by my trustees of their functions in relation to any land subject to the trusts of this my will].[2]

1 This makes it clear that the trustees are not liable for the defaults of others who may have possession or control of trust property, nor for the depreciation of property (such as chattels made available to a disabled beneficiary) which remain trust assets but are being enjoyed in kind. In respect of the defaults of an investment manager or nominee, this indemnity may be wider than that of the TrA 2000, s 23(1) (Part G, para **[246.155]**) which only exempts a trustee from liability for such defaults if he has complied with the statutory duty of care, a standard which may be higher than that of 'good faith'. Whereas it is clear that a wider indemnity such as this can apply where trustees have exercised an express power to appoint an investment manager or nominee, it is not clear that a wider indemnity can be conferred where trustees have exercised the statutory power (see n 4 to cl 8 at para **[224.37]** and Preliminary Note to B21 at para **[221.14]**). For a wider form of indemnity, see e g Form B21.12 at para **[221.16]**. If a paid trustee is to rely on this indemnity clause which may limit his liability in negligence in that it may absolve him from negligent failure to intervene to prevent loss, the testator should specifically be made aware of its meaning and effect (see para **[221.13]** above).

2 The TLATA 1996, s 11(1) which obliges trustees of land to consult beneficiaries of full age and beneficially entitled to an interest in possession, and so far as consistent with the general interest of the trust to give effect to the wishes of those beneficiaries or (in the event of a dispute) the majority by value, will not be relevant so long as the trusts are discretionary, but it may become so in the event that interest in possession trusts are created by the trustees in exercise of any of their powers. In that case the testator may wish to exclude it (Part G, para **[246.114]** and see Preliminary Note to B20 at para **[220.58]**).

[226.36]

PROFESSIONAL TRUSTEE CHARGING CLAUSE

13. Any of my trustees being a professional or business man may charge and be paid all usual professional and other proper charges for business transacted acts done advice given and time spent by him or his firm in connection with the administration of my estate or in connection with the trusts hereof including acts which a personal representative or trustee not being in any profession or business could have done personally[1].

1 In spite of the TrA 2000, s 29(2) (Part G, para **[246.161]**) giving certain professional trustees authority to charge for their services on or after 1 February 2001, an express remuneration clause entitling any professional or business person to charge may still be advisable: see B21 at para **[221.35]**.

[226.37]

APPOINTMENT OF A TRUST CORPORATION

14. A trust corporation (within the meaning of the Trustee Act 1925) may be appointed a trustee hereof (whether as a sole trustee or jointly with another trustee or trustees) and may charge for so acting in accordance with its published scale of charges at the time of its appointment or on such other basis as may be agreed between the trust corporation and the persons making the appointment.[1]

1 It may become necessary for a trust corporation to take on the trusteeship if suitable family members die or do not want to act. Further, it may be possible and appropriate to appoint a trust corporation which is connected with a charity for persons with the relevant disability. If express provision is not made for a corporate trustee's remuneration, then the TrA 2000,

s 29 authorises it to receive reasonable remuneration (Part G, para **[246.161]**). Nonetheless, an express charging clause such as this may be desirable since a particular trust corporation might not be prepared to act in return for the statutory remuneration.

[226.38]

TESTIMONIUM

IN WITNESS whereof I have hereunto set my hand this —— day of ——20——.

[226.39]

ATTESTATION CLAUSE

SIGNED by the above-named [testator/testatrix] as [his/her] last will in the presence of us both present at the same time who at [his/her] request and in [his/her] presence and in the presence of each other have signed our names below as witnesses: } [*Signature of testator/testatrix*]

[*Signatures, addresses and descriptions of two witnesses*]

[226.40]

Form C4.2: Reciprocal wills for husband and wife with grown-up children of whom one is disabled; gift by first to die of entire estate to survivor subject to a nil-rate band discretionary trust; on the death of the survivor a trust of residue for the children in equal shares with the disabled child's share settled on a trust satisfying the conditions of the Inheritance Tax Act 1984, s 89 (as amended) and being a 'trust for the vulnerable' within the Finance Act 2005, ss 23–45

Note. This Form is for use in a will executed on or after 8 April 2013 containing a trust which is to comply with IHTA 1984, s 89. Generally, such a trust must comply with the conditions of IHTA 1984, s 89, as amended by FA 2013, Sch 44, para 6 (see **[226.4]** ff above). This is a variant of Form C4.1 where the trusts of residue on the death of the surviving spouse are completely different. The residuary estate of the second to die is given to the children in equal shares with substitution of remoter descendants in the case of a child predeceasing the testator, and the share of the disabled child is settled on trusts which it is thought will fall within IHTA 1984, s 89 (as amended by FA 2013, Sch 44, para 6) and also FA 2005, s 34 (trusts for the vulnerable for disabled persons – see **[226.9]** ff above). It takes advantage of PAA 2009 (Part G, para **[246.174]** ff and see **[200.35A]** ff) to provide a combination of a discretion to apply income for the benefit of the disabled child during his life and a trust to accumulate the surplus during his life. The share of residue held for the disabled child should also fall within TCGA 1992, Sch 1, para 1, so as to qualify for a full capital gains tax annual exemption (see para **[226.6]** for this). It is not restricted to the 125-year perpetuity period, but relies on 'wait and see', for the reasons given in **[200.35B]**.

This form may be adapted for use for civil partners, the words 'my wife/husband' being replaced with 'my civil partner' throughout. Care should be taken to identify correctly in each will the children who are to benefit.

[226.41]

REVOCATION CLAUSE

I [*name*] of [*address*] revoke all former testamentary dispositions made by me and declare this to be my last will.

[226.42]

APPOINTMENT OF EXECUTORS AND TRUSTEES AND DEFINITION OF 'MY TRUSTEES'

1. [*As in cl 1 of* Form C4.1 *at para* **[226.23]**.]

[226.43]

APPOINTMENT OF GUARDIANS

2. [*As in cl 2 of* Form C4.1 *at para* **[226.24]**.]

[226.44]

LEGACIES TO TAKE EFFECT ON DEATH OF SECOND TO DIE

3. [*As in cl 3 of* Form C4.1 *at para* **[226.25]**.]

[226.45]

GIFT OF NIL-RATE BAND LEGACY ON DISCRETIONARY TRUSTS

4. [*As in cl 4 of* Form C4.1 *at para* **[226.26]**.]

[226.46]

ADMINISTRATION TRUSTS OF RESIDUE

5. [*As in cl 5 of* Form C4.1 *at para* **[226.27]**.]

[226.47]

GIFTS MADE FREE OF TAX

6. [*As in cl 6 of* Form C4.1 *at para* **[226.28]**.]

[226.48]

PRIMARY TRUST OF RESIDUE IN FAVOUR OF SPOUSE IF SURVIVING

7. If my [wife/husband] shall survive me my trustees shall hold my residuary estate and the income thereof upon trust for [her/him] absolutely.[1]

1 See para **[226.29]** n 1.

[226.49]

TRUST OF RESIDUE FOR CHILDREN AND ISSUE IF SPOUSE NOT SURVIVING

8. (1) If my [wife/husband] shall not survive me my trustees shall hold my residuary estate and the income thereof upon trust for such of my children as shall survive me if more than one in equal shares absolutely subject as provided below.

(2) If for any reason any child of mine does not attain a vested interest under the foregoing trust and there are children or remoter issue of his or hers who survive me and attain the age of 18 years such children and remoter issue shall take in equal shares per stirpes the share such child of

mine would have taken if he or she had attained a vested interest and so that no issue shall take whose parent attains a vested interest under the foregoing trust.

(3) If at the time of my death my said [son/daughter] A (hereinafter called 'A') shall be living and shall be a disabled person within the meaning of Schedule 1A of the Finance Act 2005, then the said share of my residuary estate directed to be held upon trust for [him/her] as aforesaid (hereinafter called 'the share') shall not vest absolutely in A but shall be retained by my trustees and held upon the following trusts and with and subject to the following powers:

(a) My trustees shall have power at their absolute discretion to pay transfer or apply the whole or any part or proportion of the income of the share to or for the benefit of A during [his/her] life.

(b) My trustees shall during the life of A accumulate the income of the share which shall not be paid or applied for the benefit of A as aforesaid as an accretion to the capital of the share but shall have power to pay or apply such accumulations during the life of A as if the same were income of the then current year.

(c) Notwithstanding the foregoing trusts and power my trustees shall have power at their absolute discretion during the life of A to pay or apply the whole or any part or parts of the capital of the share to or for the benefit of A.

(d) Subject to the foregoing trusts and to any or every exercise of the foregoing powers my trustees shall hold the share or such part thereof as shall not have been paid or applied as aforesaid and the income thereof upon trust absolutely for such of my children other than A and remoter issue (including any issue of A) as shall be living at the death of A in equal shares per stirpes so that no issue shall take whose parent is living at the death of A and capable of taking.

(e) Section 32 of the Trustee Act 1925 (relating to the payment or application of capital) shall apply in all respects as if the words 'one-half of' had been omitted from proviso (a) of subsection (1) thereof.[1]

1 An extended statutory power of advancement is now compatible with trusts falling within IHTA 1984, s 89 (as amended by FA 2013, Sch 44, para 6) and FA 2005, ss 23–45 (trusts for the vulnerable), and qualifying for full capital gains tax annual exemption under TCGA 1992, Sch 1, para 1 (see para **[226.4]**, sub-para (v), and paras **[226.11]** and **[226.6]**).

[226.50]

ADMINISTRATIVE POWERS

9. [*As in cl 9 of* Form C4.1 *at para* **[226.31]**.]

[226.51]

EXERCISE AND RELEASE OF POWERS

10. [*As in cl 10(1)–(3) of* Form C4.1 *at para* **[226.32]**.]

[226.52]

RECEIPTS ON BEHALF OF CHARITABLE INSTITUTIONS

11.[As in cl 11 of Form C4.1 at para [226.34].]

[226.53]

TRUSTEE INDEMNITY

12. [*As in cl 12 of* Form C4.1 *at para* **[226.35]**.]

[226.54]

PROFESSIONAL TRUSTEE CHARGING CLAUSE

13. [*As in cl 13 of* Form C4.1 *at para* **[226.36]**.]

[226.55]

APPOINTMENT OF A TRUST CORPORATION

14. [*As in cl 14 of* Form C4.1 *at para* **[226.37]**.]

[226.56]

TESTIMONIUM AND ATTESTATION CLAUSES

[*As in* Form C4.1 *at paras* **[226.38]** *and* **[226.39]**.]

[226.57]

Form C4.3: Will providing for spouse suffering from mental disorder

Note. This form is for use in a will executed on or after 8 April 2013 containing a trust which is to comply with IHTA 1984, s 89. Generally, such a trust must comply with the conditions of IHTA 1984, s 89 as amended by FA 2013, Sch 44, para 6 (see **[226.4]** above).This form incorporates a nil-rate band legacy on discretionary trusts under which the mentally disabled spouse is a beneficiary, and then settles residue on trusts for the benefit of the spouse which will be treated as conferring an interest in possession on the spouse which will be a disabled person's interest which gets beneficiary-taxed treatment (IHTA 1984, ss 49(1A)(b), 89B(1)(a), (c)). The estate is thus made fully available for the upkeep of the spouse while minimising the spouse's entitlement to assets, and making sure that no IHT is paid on the testator's death if the spouse survives the testator. It is no longer necessary to have a nil-rate band trust under the will of the first to die in order to avoid wasting the first to die's nil-rate band, except in the special circumstances discussed in para **[200.130]**. The main point of having such a trust in this case is that the nil-rate band trust fund is available for the benefit of the surviving spouse, but it is not subject to the restrictions required by IHTA 1984, s 89 and can thus be more freely used to benefit other beneficiaries if it is not needed for the support of the surviving spouse. If within the period of two years after the testator's death it is decided that the nil-rate band trust is not wanted, it can be appointed on appropriate trusts for the surviving spouse so that the estate is wholly exempt, in reliance on IHTA 1984, s 144 (see **[225.83]** ff).

This form may be adapted for use for civil partners, the words 'my wife/husband' being replaced with 'my civil partner' throughout. Care should be taken to identify correctly in each will the children who are to benefit.

[226.58]

REVOCATION CLAUSE

I [*name*] of [*address*] revoke all former testamentary dispositions made by me and declare this to be my last will.

[226.59]

APPOINTMENT OF EXECUTORS AND TRUSTEES AND DEFINITION OF 'MY TRUSTEES'

1. I appoint [*name*] of [*address*] and [*name*] of [*address*] (hereinafter together called 'my trustees' which expression shall where the context so admits include my personal representatives for the time being and the trustees for the time being hereof) to be the executors and trustees of this will.

[226.60]

BEQUEST OF PERSONAL CHATTELS[1]

2. (1) I give the following items free of tax:[2]

[(a) To my son [*name*] my father's signet ring;

(b) to my daughter [*name*] my mother's engagement ring;]

(2) If my [wife/husband] [*name*] ('my [wife/husband]') shall survive me then subject as aforesaid I give all my personal chattels as defined by section 55(1)(x) of the Administration of Estates Act 1925[3] to my trustees free of tax to hold the same upon trust as follows:

(a) my trustees shall have power during the life of my [wife/husband] to distribute the said chattels among the legacy beneficiaries (as defined in clause 3 below) or any one or more of them and in such manner as my trustees think fit;

(b) my trustees shall have power during the life of my [wife/husband] to sell any of the said chattels and to dispose of any thereof which are of little value to any person and in any manner (including power to dispose of the same for no consideration) as they think fit;

(c) subject to and in default of any distribution or disposal as aforesaid my trustees shall hold the said chattels and any proceeds of sale thereof on trust for my [wife/husband] during [her/his] life (and clauses 8 to 13 below shall apply to such chattels and proceeds of sale);

(d) subject as aforesaid my trustees shall hold the said chattels or their proceeds of sale as part of my residuary estate.[4]

1 If the testator's spouse survives the testator, it is not appropriate for the chattels to go to the spouse absolutely (because of the spouse's mental incapacity), nor is it appropriate for them to fall into the residuary estate as there are no powers to distribute the capital of the latter to persons other than the spouse (contrast the extensive powers over residue in Form C4.1, cl 8, at para **[226.30]**).

2 See Form C3.1, cl 2, n 2 at para **[225.12]**. The words 'free of tax' would only be of significance if the items given were outside the UK at the testator's death.

3 See Part G, para **[246.67]** for the wording of this definition, and for further discussion of the meaning of 'personal chattels' see Vol 1, para **[64.44]**.

4 With a disposition in this form, if the testator's spouse survives the testator, the IHT spouse exemption will apply to the chattels on the testator's death, and that will not be affected by subsequent distribution to other persons: neither of IHTA 1984, s 143 (see B4 at paras **[204.9]** and **[204.10]**) or s 144 (see C3 at paras **[225.83]**–**[225.91]**) will apply. A wider class of objects of the discretion could be introduced as in sub-cls (4) and (5) of Form B4.11 at para **[204.25]**.

If it is preferred to have a non-exempt gift of chattels, at any rate so far as they do not fall into the residuary estate, a short-term discretionary trust such as that in Form B4.11 at para **[204.25]** could be used; if it is used, Form B4.11 should perhaps be varied so that the trustees can add chattels to the residuary estate before the period of two years from death has ended, so that the size of the non-exempt estate apart from cl 3, and thus the size of the nil-rate band legacy given by cl 3, can be ascertained at an early date.

[226.61]

GIFT OF NIL-RATE BAND LEGACY ON DISCRETIONARY TRUSTS

3. [*As in cl 4 of* Form C4.1 *at para* **[226.26]**.]

[226.62]

ADMINISTRATION TRUSTS OF RESIDUE

4. [*As in cl 5 of* Form C4.1 *at para* **[226.27]**.]

[226.63]

GIFTS MADE FREE OF TAX

5. [*As in cl 6 of* Form C4.1 *at para* **[226.28]**.]

[226.64]

BENEFICIAL TRUSTS OF RESIDUE FOR SPOUSE[1]

6. During the life of my [wife/husband] my trustees shall hold my residuary estate and the income thereof upon the trusts following:

[EITHER]

[(a) My trustees shall pay or apply the income of my residuary estate for the maintenance or otherwise for the benefit of my [wife/husband] in such manner as they shall think fit]

[OR]

[(a) My trustees shall pay or apply the income of my residuary estate for the maintenance or otherwise for the benefit of my [wife/husband] provided that my trustees may accumulate the whole or any part of such income by investing the same and the resulting income thereof in any of the investments hereby authorised and the accumulations so made shall form part of the capital of my residuary estate for all purposes;

(b) Notwithstanding the foregoing trust my trustees (being not fewer than two in number or a trust corporation) may at any time or times and from time to time during the life of my [wife/husband] apply the whole or any part or parts of my residuary estate for [her/his] maintenance support or benefit in such manner as they think fit.

1 This clause contains alternative forms of provision for the benefit of the mentally disabled spouse in sub-cl (a), the first requiring the trustees to apply all the trust income for her or his benefit, and the second giving the trustees a discretion as to whether to, say, apply it, or to accumulate it. Whichever is selected is followed by a power in sub-cl (b), which enables the trustees to resort to capital for the spouse's maintenance.

The first version of sub-cl (a) would give rise to an actual interest in possession for IHT purposes which will be a disabled person's interest which gets beneficiary-taxed treatment

(IHTA 1984, ss 49(1A)(b), 89(1)(a)). If there is uncertainty as to whether the spouse will qualify as a disabled person within the definition in IHTA 1984, s 89(4)–(6), this will have the advantage that he or she will have an IPDI, qualifying for beneficiary-taxed treatment and thus spouse exemption, if the spouse does not qualify as a disabled person. It is thought that the second form of sub-cl (a) would (together with sub-cl (b)) be treated for IHT purposes as giving rise to a deemed interest in possession under IHTA 1984, s 89 (as amended by FA 2013, Sch 44, para 6). It is thought that either form of sub-cl (a) would qualify the trust as one for a vulnerable person within FA 2005, s 34 (see **[226.9]** ff above) and for the full capital gains tax annual allowance: see in particular the TCGA 1992, Sch 1, para 1(1)(b) and para **[226.6]**. On the other hand, the first version of sub-cl (a) could result in the whole of the income being taken into account as the spouse's in any means test for benefit purposes. See for the social security and fiscal implications of disabled trusts the Preliminary Note at para **[226.2]** ff.

[226.65]

REMAINDER TRUSTS FOR CHILDREN AND ISSUE

7. (1) Subject as aforesaid my trustees shall hold my residuary estate and the income thereof upon trust for such of my children as shall survive me and if more than one in equal shares absolutely.

(2) Provided that if any of my children shall predecease me leaving a child or children surviving me such last-mentioned child or children shall take and if more than one equally between them the share of my residuary estate which such deceased child of mine would have taken had he or she survived me.

(3) Section 32 of the Trustee Act 1925 (relating to advancement) shall apply as if the words 'one half of' were omitted from proviso (a) to subsection (1) thereof.[1]

1 An extended statutory power of advancement is compatible with trusts falling within IHTA 1984, s 89 (as amended by FA 2013, s 89B(1)(c), Sch 44, para 6) and FA 2005, ss 23–45 (trusts for the vulnerable), and qualifying for full capital gains tax annual exemption under TCGA 1992, Sch 1, para 1 (see para **[226.4]** sub-para (v), and paras **[226.11]** and **[226.6]**).

[226.66]

ADMINISTRATIVE POWERS

8. [*As in cl 9 of* Form C4.1 *at para* **[226.31]**, *amending '(subject to cl 10 below)' in the second line of cl 9(3) to '(subject to cl 9 below)'*.]

[226.67]

EXERCISE AND RELEASE OF POWERS

9. (1) My trustees (being not fewer than two in number or a trust corporation) shall have power at any time or times and from time to time during the life of my [wife/husband] by deed or deeds to release or restrict all or any of the powers hereinbefore contained (whether dispositive or administrative) or this present power either in whole or in part and in any manner they think fit.[1]

(2) Any power or discretion hereby or by law conferred on my trustees (including a power or discretion as to the disposition of capital or income) shall be exercisable notwithstanding that any of my trustees has a personal interest in such exercise [provided that at least one of my trustees has no such personal interest].[2]

1 The main reason for including such a power is in case any of the powers turn out to be regarded by HMRC as incompatible with IHTA 1984, s 89. For the main concern of this kind, see para **[226.4]**, sub-paras (vi) and (vii). It could also be useful where the alternative cl 6(a) at para **[226.64]**, including the proviso permitting accumulation of income, has been included in the will, and it is found that HMRC will not accept that IHTA 1984, s 89 applies (perhaps because the spouse does not qualify as a disabled person), but would accept that there would be an interest in possession if the power to accumulate were released; if the release were effected during the two years after the testator's death the spouse exemption might be obtained on the testator's death by virtue of IHTA 1984, s 144 (see C3 at paras **[225.83]–[225.91]**).

2 The words in square brackets should be omitted if the executors and trustees will or might all be members of the testator's family.

[226.68]

RECEIPTS ON BEHALF OF CHARITABLE INSTITUTIONS

10. [*As in cl 11 of* Form C4.1 *at para* **[226.34]**.]

[226.69]

TRUSTEE INDEMNITY

11. [*As in cl 12 of* Form C4.1 *at para* **[226.35]**.]

[226.70]

PROFESSIONAL TRUSTEE CHARGING CLAUSE

12. [*As in cl 13 of* Form C4.1 *at para* **[226.36]**.]

[226.71]

APPOINTMENT OF A TRUST CORPORATION

13. [*As in cl 14 of* Form C4.1 *at para* **[226.37]**.]

[*Testimonium and attestation clause as in* Form C4.1 *at paras* **[226.38]** and **[226.39]**.

C5

Wills where there is more than one family

Form C5.1: Will of twice-married testator who has adult children from his first marriage and minor children from his second and who owns the matrimonial home; nil-rate band discretionary trust, and gift of residue on trust for second wife for life with remainder to all the testator's children

[227.14]

[Updated in text and footnotes for Perpetuities and Accumulations Act 2009 and FA 2013, Sch 44.]

GIFT OF NIL-RATE BAND LEGACY ON DISCRETIONARY TRUSTS[1]

EITHER

5. (1) If my wife shall survive me[2] then I give to my legacy trustees (hereafter defined) a pecuniary legacy of the maximum sum (if any) which can in the circumstances subsisting at my death be given by this clause without any liability being incurred for the payment of inheritance tax on or by reason of my death and in particular (without prejudice to the generality of the foregoing) for the purpose of determining the amount of such maximum sum the circumstances to be taken into account shall include all chargeable transfers made by me during my life (or events treated as such for inheritance tax purposes) so far as relevant for the computation of inheritance tax on my death the dispositions taking effect under this will (apart from this clause) or under any codicil hereto and any property treated as if it were part of my estate for inheritance tax purposes [and furthermore in determining the foregoing maximum sum it shall be assumed that the nil-rate band maximum (within the meaning of Section 8A of the Inheritance Tax Act 1984) at the time of my death will be treated as increased for the purposes of the charge to inheritance tax on my death by any amount by which it would be treated as increased if a claim was made under that section and I direct my Trustees to make such a claim].[3]

OR

(1) If my wife shall survive me[4] then I give to my legacy trustees (hereafter defined) a pecuniary legacy of whichever is the less of:

(a) the amount by which the nil-rate band maximum (within the meaning of section 8A of the Inheritance Tax Act 1984) at the time of my death would be treated as increased for the purposes of the charge to inheritance tax on my death if a claim was made under that section; or

(b) the maximum sum (if any) which can in the circumstances subsisting at my death be given by this clause without any liability being incurred for the payment of inheritance tax on or by reason of my death and in particular (without prejudice to the generality of the foregoing) for the purpose of determining the amount of such maximum sum the circumstances to be taken into account shall include all chargeable transfers made by me during my life (or events treated as such for inheritance tax purposes) so far as relevant for the computation of inheritance tax on my death the dispositions taking effect under this will (apart from this clause) or under any codicil hereto and any property treated as if it were part of my estate for inheritance tax purposes and furthermore in determining such maximum sum it shall be assumed that the nil-rate band maximum (within the meaning of section 8A of the Inheritance Tax Act 1984) at the time of my death will be treated as increased for the purposes of the charge to inheritance tax on my death by any amount by which it would be treated as increased if a claim was made under that section and I direct my trustees to make such a claim.[5]

(2) In this clause the following expressions have the following meanings, namely:

(a) 'the income beneficiaries' means my wife and my children and remoter issue;

(b) 'the capital beneficiaries' means my children and remoter issue;

(c) 'my legacy trustees' means and includes [*name*] of [*address*] and [*name*] of [*address*] or other the trustee or trustees for the time being of the trust legacy[6];

(d) 'the trust period' means the period of 125 years commencing on my death.[7]

(3) My legacy trustees shall hold the said legacy upon trust to invest the same in any investments hereby authorised with power to vary the same and shall hold the said legacy and the assets from time to time representing the same (hereinafter called 'the trust legacy') and the income thereof upon trust for all or such one or more of the capital beneficiaries at such ages or times in such shares and upon such trusts for the benefit of the capital beneficiaries as my legacy trustees (being at least two in number [or a trust corporation][8]) may by deed or deeds revocable or irrevocable executed at any time or times during the trust period appoint and in making any such appointment my legacy trustees shall have powers as full as those which they would possess if they were an absolute beneficial owner of the trust legacy and in particular (but without prejudice to the generality of the foregoing words) my legacy trustees may in any exercise of the foregoing power as they in their absolute discretion think fit:

(a) delegate give or impose to or upon themselves or any other person or persons and in relation to any trust or disposition any discretionary powers or discretionary trusts conditions limitations restrictions or provisions including powers of further delegation or powers to create further discretionary trusts or powers;[9]

(b) create trusts or powers for the accumulation of income;[10]

(c) create administrative powers or provisions of whatever nature;

Provided that:

(i) no such appointment shall invalidate any payment transfer or application of capital or income previously made under any of the trusts or powers herein elsewhere contained;

(ii) every interest limited under any exercise of such power shall vest in interest (if at all) not later than the expiration of the trust period;

(iii) any such appointment may be made in respect of income alone without any appointment of capital; and

(iv) any such revocable appointment shall (so far as then unrevoked) cease to be revocable on the expiration of the trust period.

(4) In default of and subject to any exercise of the foregoing power my legacy trustees (being at least two in number [or a trust corporation][11]) may at their discretion at any time or times during the trust period pay transfer or apply to or for the benefit of all or any one or more of the capital beneficiaries for the time being living the whole or any part or parts of the trust legacy in any manner they in their absolute discretion think fit.[12]

(5) Subject to any or every exercise of the foregoing powers my legacy trustees shall during the trust period hold the trust legacy upon trust to pay or apply the income thereof to or for the maintenance education or benefit of all or any one or more of the income beneficiaries for the time being living in such shares if more than one and generally in such manner as they think fit provided that my legacy trustees may accumulate the whole or any part of the income of the trust legacy by investing the same and the resulting income thereof in any of the investments hereby authorised and any accumulations of income so made shall form part of the capital of the trust legacy from which such income arose for all purposes [provided that my legacy trustees shall have power during the trust period to pay or apply such accumulations of income as if they were income of the current year].[13]

(6) Subject to the foregoing trust and any or every exercise of the foregoing powers my legacy trustees shall hold the trust legacy and the income thereof at the expiration of the trust period in trust absolutely for such of my children and remoter issue as shall then be living in equal shares per stirpes so that no child or issue of mine shall take a share if his or her parent is living at the expiration of the trust period and so capable of taking.

(7) Any capital or income of the trust legacy not otherwise disposed of by this clause shall be held in trust for such of my children as shall survive me if more than one in equal shares absolutely.

(8) Instead of the trust legacy being satisfied by the payment of cash or by the appropriation of property[14]:

(a) my trustees may charge (with or without there being any personal liability of any person or persons) any property which is (or but for this clause would be) comprised in my residuary estate with payment of a sum of money equal to or less than the amount of the trust legacy to my legacy trustees and my legacy trustees shall accept such charge for such sum as the whole or a part (as the case may be) of the trust legacy; and

(b) my trustees may require my legacy trustees to accept in satisfaction of all or part of the trust legacy a binding promise of payment (secured or unsecured) made personally by my wife or by my trustees as trustees of my residuary estate which debt shall be payable on demand and my legacy trustees shall accept such debt as the whole or a part (as the case may be) of the trust legacy.

(9) The following shall apply in relation to the powers in the last preceding subclause:

(a) my trustees may require to be included such terms if any as they think fit in relation to a charge under subclause (8)(a) above or a debt under subclause (8)(b) above including terms as to interest (if any) and terms linking the debt or sum charged to the Retail Prices Index or otherwise providing for its amount to vary with the passage of time according to a formula provided that the debt or sum charged shall be payable to my legacy trustees on demand and the charge shall be enforceable by my legacy trustees at any time;

(b) my legacy trustees may leave the charge or debt outstanding for as long as they think fit and refrain from exercising their rights in relation to it and waive the payment of all or any part of any interest due in respect of it and may accept any substitute debt or charge undertaken or created by any person;

(c) my trustees may assent to the vesting of my residuary estate subject to an outstanding obligation to pay or satisfy the trust legacy and my legacy trustees may appoint new trustees in exercise of the statutory power to do so before the trust legacy has been paid or satisfied;[15]

(d) my legacy trustees and my trustees shall not be liable if my wife is or becomes unable to pay the debt or any security is or becomes inadequate or for any other loss or disadvantage which may occur as a result of their exercising or choosing not to exercise any of the foregoing powers; and

(e) the foregoing powers are in addition to any other powers given by this will or any codicil or by the general law and the foregoing powers may be exercised even though my trustees and my legacy trustees are the same persons or my wife is among either or both sets of trustees provided that such powers shall not be exercisable by a sole trustee who is my wife.

(10) My trustees may constitute the trust legacy wholly or partly by appropriating to it at their discretion any property or proportionate share of any property and for this purpose may take such advice as to the value of the said property or proportionate share as they think fit.[16]

(11) Where the trust legacy is for the time being wholly or partly constituted by a proportionate share of a dwellinghouse or other property my legacy trustees shall have all the powers of an absolute owner in relation to such share and property and in particular may at their discretion join with the other proprietor or proprietors of such property:

(i) to permit an income beneficiary under the trusts of the trust legacy to have the use or enjoyment of the property in kind on such terms as my legacy trustees think fit; or

(ii) to effect or enable a sale of the property and the purchase of another property in the same or similar co-ownership with the trust legacy constituted by a proportionate share thereof.

(12) The powers and provisions of clauses 10 to 13 inclusive hereof shall apply to the trust legacy with references therein to 'my trustees' being treated as references to 'my legacy trustees'.

1 See Form C3.1, cl 3, n 1 at para **[225.13]**. For a discussion of nil-rate band discretionary trusts, see B18 at paras **[218.16]–[218.32]**. For the possible reasons for including a nil-rate band discretionary trust in a will of this type see para **[227.8]**. This trust will be subject to the IHT relevant property regime, for which see **[218.8]** ff.

The trusts of this legacy are such that the widow is an object of the discretionary trust of income, but capital can only be appointed, paid or applied for the benefit of the children and remoter issue. If the testator dies while the children of the second marriage are still minors the capital can be used to pay for their education or support, which will relieve the widow of expense she would otherwise incur.

If the testator prefers the trusts to include powers to appoint, pay or apply capital in favour of the widow, Form C3.4, cl 2 at para **[225.60]** could be substituted.

2 See Form C3.1, cl 3, n 2 at para **[225.13]**.

3 This sub-cl without the words at the end in square brackets is for use where the testator does not have a potential enhanced nil-rate band under the nil-rate band carry-forward rules (i e his previous marriage ended in divorce), but he has other reasons for including a nil-rate band discretionary trust (see paras **[200.130]** and **[227.8]**). The provision at the end in square brackets should be added if the testator does have a potential increased nil-rate band under the nil-rate band carry-forward rules (i e his previous marriage ended with the death of his previous wife, and she did not use all her nil-rate band), and he wishes the trust fund to be a legacy of the whole of his available nil-rate band. If the testator does have a potential increased nil-rate band under the nil-rate band carry-forward rules his current wife should make a will containing a nil-rate band discretionary trust to take effect if she dies first, to avoid waste of the nil-rate band in the event of her doing so.

4 See Form C3.1, cl 3, n 2 at para **[225.13]**.

5 This second alternative sub-cl (1) is for the case where the testator does have a potential increased nil-rate band under the nil-rate band carry-forward rules (i e his previous marriage ended with the death of his previous wife, and she did not use all her nil-rate band), but he wishes the trust fund to be a legacy which is limited to the amount by which his available nil-rate band is potentially increased under the carry-forward rules. This would leave his basic nil-rate band to be carried forward and used on his current wife's death. If the testator does have a potential increased nil-rate band under the nil-rate band carry-forward rules his current wife should make a will containing a nil-rate band discretionary trust to take effect if she dies first, to avoid waste of nil-rate band in the event of her doing so.

6 The main reasons for having separate trustees of the legacy are where a charge scheme might be entered into, in which case the testator's spouse should not be one of the executors and trustees but could be a trustee of the legacy, or where a debt scheme might be entered into and the testator's spouse might be sole executor: see para **[218.22]** above.

7 For wills made on or after 6 April 2010, the perpetuity period is 125 years (and there is no other period): see the PAA 2009, ss 5(1), 15(1)(a) (Part A **[200.35A]** and Part G, para **[246.179]**).Using the perpetuity period as the trust period gives a trust period that is longer than may be needed in most cases, but gives considerable flexibility. In particular, if both parents were to die while the children of the second marriage were still minors, the whole of this fund would continue to be available for their support at the discretion of the trustees.

8 These words in square brackets should be included if a trust corporation is to be an executor, or there is a possibility that a trust corporation might subsequently be appointed a trustee. In either case express provision for the remuneration of a trust corporation so acting (not included in this form) should be added: see, e g Forms B3.13 to B3.16 at paras **[203.32]–[203.35]**, Form B21.40 **[221.52]** and Form C4.1, cl 1 at para **[226.18]**.

9 These words authorise the creation of discretionary powers which might not otherwise be valid: see Vol 1, para **[40.5]**.
10 For wills made on or after 6 April 2010, there are no statutory restrictions on accumulation in respect of non-charitable trusts, so accumulation will be permitted throughout the trust period: see the PAA 2009, ss 13, 15(1)(a) (Part G, para **[246.187]**).
11 See n 8 above.
12 Such a power to apply capital could be used to apply cash for the benefit of the children of the second marriage quickly and informally, e g paying fees for education or direct to the educational institution. However, it is essential that its exercise should be adequately evidenced.
13 The addition of these words will enable accumulated income to be paid or applied for the benefit of the wife; if they are omitted, any income which has been accumulated will form part of capital for all purposes and be unavailable for the wife.
14 These powers and provisions are included so as to enable a debt or charge scheme to be used as a means of avoiding the surviving spouse having an IPDI in the trust fund subject to the trusts of this clause, where there are insufficient assets other than the matrimonial home with which to constitute that trust fund. See para **[218.19]** ff and also n 16 below. As the wife is given a life interest, it is a charge scheme rather than a debt scheme which will be appropriate.
15 The purpose of this is so that new trustees of the residuary estate can be appointed before a charge is entered into, in a case where the surviving spouse is one of the personal representatives or the personal representatives and the trustees of the discretionary legacy are the same persons, and to make clear that new or additional trustees of the discretionary trust legacy can be appointed before the legacy is constituted as a debt from the surviving spouse where the surviving spouse is the sole trustee: see para **[218.22]** for the reasons for avoiding these states of affairs.
16 If post-21 March 2006 a beneficiary is permitted to occupy a property owned by a discretionary trust, whereas this may give that beneficiary an interest in possession, it will not necessarily be the type of interest in possession which will cause the property to be treated as part of his or her estate for IHT purposes. Only an interest in possession which is an IPDI, a disabled person's interest, or a transitional serial interest (see paras **[200.98]**–**[200.100]** above) will have this result. In the context of a discretionary trust established by will, if a permission to occupy is given within two years of the testator's death, and this gives rise to an interest in possession this may be backdated to the testator's death under IHTA 1984, s 144, so that it would be an IPDI and result in the property being treated as part of the beneficiary's estate for IHT purposes: see para **[225.83]** ff. But if the permission is not granted until after the second anniversary of the testator's death, and the beneficiary to whom it is granted is not a disabled person within the meaning of IHTA 1984, s 89B(2) (as substituted by FA 2013, Sch 44, para 8(2)) at (where the testator died before 8 April 2013) the testator's death or (where the testator on or after 8 April 2013) at the date of the grant, so that her interest is not a disabled person's interest within IHTA 1984, s 89B (as amended by FA 2013, Sch 44, paras 8, 10) (see para **[200.99]** above), it should not result in the property being treated as part of the beneficiary's estate for IHT purposes. Therefore, an express power to appropriate property or a share of property may be given to trustees to exercise in appropriate circumstances, and sub-cll (10) and (11) contain such a power and associated provisions.

[227.15]

[Updated for Trusts (Capital and Income) Act 2013.]

ADMINISTRATION TRUSTS OF RESIDUE

6. (1) I give all my property not hereby or by any codicil hereto otherwise effectively disposed of [(including any entailed or other property over which I shall have at my death a general power of disposition by will)][1] to my trustees to hold on the trusts set out below with power to sell all or any of it.[2]

(2) My trustees shall pay my funeral and testamentary expenses[3] and debts and any legacies given by this will or any codicil hereto out of such

property or its proceeds and shall have a discretion as to how such payments shall be borne as between capital and income.[4]

(3) Subject as above my trustees shall hold such property and the assets from time to time representing the same (hereinafter called 'my residuary estate') on the trusts set out below and shall invest all money comprised in such property or arising from its sale in any of the investments hereby authorised with power to change such investments into any others hereby authorised.[5]

1 See Form C2.1, cl 6, n 1 at para **[224.34]**.
2 See Form C2.1, cl 6, n 2 at para **[224.34]**.
3 See Form C2.1, cl 6, n 3 at para **[224.34]**.
4 See Form C2.1, cl 6, n 4 at para **[224.34]**.
5 See Form C2.1, cl 6, n 5 at para **[224.34]**.

[227.17]

[Updated in text and footnote 6 for Perpetuities and Accumulations Act 2009.]

BENEFICIAL TRUSTS OF RESIDUE

8. (1) My trustees shall hold my residuary estate upon trust to pay the income thereof to my wife during her life.[1]

[(2) Notwithstanding the foregoing trust my trustees (being not fewer than two in number [or a trust corporation][2] may at any time and from time to time during the life of my wife pay transfer or apply any part or parts not exceeding in the aggregate [one quarter]/[one half][3] of my residuary estate to or for the benefit of my wife in such manner as they think fit provided that the foregoing power shall only be exercisable over capital of which the income is for the time being payable to my wife (or would be payable if such capital yielded income).][4]

(3) Subject as aforesaid my trustees shall hold my residuary estate and the income thereof upon trust for such of my children as shall survive me and in the case of those who are then under the age of [18/25] years as shall attain that age[5] and if more than one in equal shares provided that if any child of mine shall predecease me or having survived me shall fail to attain the age of [18/25] years leaving a child or children surviving me or born after my death who shall attain the age of [18/21] years such last-mentioned child or children shall take if more than one equally between them the share of my residuary estate which such deceased child of mine would have taken had he or she lived to attain a vested interest.[6]

1 The life interest for the surviving spouse will be an IPDI within IHTA 1984, s 49A (see para **[200.98]**), so spouse exemption from IHT should be available. For the reasons for not including survivorship condition see the Preliminary Note on survivorship conditions at paras **[224.5]** ff and Form C2.1, cl 4, n 1 at para **[224.31]**.
2 See n 8 to cl 5(3) of this form at para **[227.14]**.
3 One of these should be deleted, or both deleted and some other fraction substituted.
4 There are two reasons for restricting the exercise of the power to capital in which the widow has an interest in possession: first, to ensure that the power is not exercisable if there is a divorce and the life interest given by the previous subclause lapses (see the Preliminary Note to C2, at para **[224.16]]–[224.23]**ff); and secondly, to ensure that the power ceases to be exercisable if the wife assigns or surrenders her life interest. It is important that this power should cease to be exercisable in such an event because the termination of an IPDI on or after 22 March 2006 will be deemed to be a gift of the underlying settled property for the

purposes of FA 1986, s 102, so that unless the beneficiary of the IPDI is excluded altogether from benefit after the termination, the gift with reservation rules could apply, see FA 1986, s 102ZA, (see para **[200.76]** above).

This entire clause can be omitted if the testator does not wish there to be any power to pay the widow capital. On the other hand, if he wants this power to apply to the whole of the residuary estate, a provision such as cl 7(2) of Form C3.2 at para **[225.35]** could be substituted.

5 The choice here is between a vesting age of 18, which will mean that it is a trust for bereaved minors within IHTA 1984, s 71A (see para **[200.108]**), or a vesting age of 25, which will mean that it is an age 18-to-25 trust within IHTA 1984, s 71D (see para **[200.109]**). A s 71A trust would have the advantage that the termination of the widow's life interest during her life in favour of such a trust would be potentially exempt: see paras **[200.108]** and **[200.128]**. If a greater vesting age, or life interests, are desired, the choice is between IPDI trusts or relevant property trusts (see paras **[200.98]**, **[200.126]**, **[200.132]**). If trusts of this type but with an element of flexibility are desired cl 6 of C2.3 at para **[224.65]** could be adapted. If 25 is adopted as the vesting age, the accumulation and maintenance trusts of income under TA 1925, s 31 should be extended beyond the age of 18: see the proviso to cl 10(1) of this form at para **[227.18]**.

6 For wills made on or after 6 April 2010, the perpetuity period is 125 years (and there is no other period): see the PAA 2009, ss 5(1), 15(1)(a) (Part A **[200.35A]** and Part G, para **[246.179]**). The age contingency for the grandchildren in this clause need not, therefore, be limited to 21 years (a limit included so as not to infringe the common law rule against perpetuities). This restriction on the age contingency to a maximum of 21 years is no longer necessary although it is still important that all interests vest within the perpetuity period. We should add that if this is not done, there will still be 'wait and see' under the PAA 2009, s 7 (Part G, para **[246.181]**). Any settled property which becomes subject to this substitutional proviso will fall within the IHT charging regime for relevant property (see para **[218.8]** ff) if the relevant grandchildren are under the age of vesting at the death of the later to die of the testator and his wife, unless the testator dies after his wife, the age of vesting is 21, and a substituted grandchild has an IPDI as a result of being over 18 (and thus entitled to an interest in possession by virtue of TA 1925, s 31) but under 21 at or within two years after the testator's death (see para **[224.25]**). The possibility of a grandchild becoming entitled to an IPDI can be avoided by extending the accumulation and maintenance trusts of TA 1925, s 31 to the age of 21 for grandchildren.

[227.18]

[Updated in text and footnote 2 for Perpetuities and Accumulations Act 2009.]

MAINTENANCE, ACCUMULATION AND ADVANCEMENT[1]

9. (1) Section 31 of the Trustee Act 1925 (relating to accumulation and maintenance) shall apply in relation to the trusts hereby or by any codicil hereto declared as if:

(a) in paragraph (i) of subsection (1) of the said section the words 'as the trustees think fit' were substituted for the words 'as may in all the circumstances be reasonable'; and

(b) the proviso to the said subsection (1) were omitted;

[Provided that in relation to any presumptive share of my residuary estate of any child of mine the said section 31 (amended as aforesaid) shall have effect as if the age of majority were the age of 25 years (and so that the expressions 'infancy', 'minority' and 'infant' and all references to the age of eighteen years in the said Section 31 shall be construed accordingly)][2].

(2) Section 32 of the Trustee Act 1925 (relating to advancement) shall apply in relation to the said trusts as if the words 'one half of' were omitted from proviso (a) to subsection (1) thereof.[3]

(3) Whenever my trustees shall have an obligation or discretion under the provisions of this will or any codicil hereto or under the general law to

apply income or capital for the benefit of a minor beneficiary they may either pay the same without liability to account to his or her parent guardian or any other adult person with whom such beneficiary may be residing or to such beneficiary himself or herself if of the age of 16 years or more and so that the receipt of such parent guardian or other person or of such minor beneficiary shall be a full and sufficient discharge to my trustees for the income or capital so applied.[4]

1 For alternative provisions see the forms in B18 at paras **[218.79]–[218.108]**.

2 This proviso is for inclusion where the vesting age in the gift to children in cl 8(3) is the age of 25. For wills made on or after 6 April 2010, there are no statutory restrictions on accumulation in respect of non-charitable trusts, so accumulation will be permitted throughout the trust period: see the PAA 2009, ss 13, 15(1)(a) (Part G, para **[246.187]**). It is no longer necessary, therefore, to introduce a restriction in order to comply with the rule against excessive accumulations as was previously the case: see the form of this clause as set out in the 9th Edition.

3 The extended power is compatible with trusts for bereaved minors within IHTA 1984, s 71A (see para **[200.108]** above) and age 18-to-25 trusts within IHTA 1984, s 71D (see para **[200.109]** above).

4 A parent (with parental responsibility) and a guardian of a minor are empowered by the ChA 1989, s 3(3) (Part G, para **[244.114]**) to give a good receipt for the minor's property: see Vol 1, para **[9.41]**. The power in this subclause is wider in that it authorises the payment of income or capital to a parent who does not have parental responsibility, any adult with whom the minor is residing, and the minor himself or herself if 16 or over.

Form C5.2: Reciprocal wills of spouses both having adult children by previous marriages (but none by their own), the first to die making a nil-rate band gift to his or her own children and giving the survivor a life interest in residue with remainder to his or her own children, and the survivor leaving his or her estate to his or her own children

[227.29]

[Updated in text and footnote 3 for Perpetuities and Accumulations Act 2009.]

GIFT OF NIL RATE BAND LEGACY TO CHILDREN[1]

3. (1) If my [wife/husband] shall survive me[2] then I give a legacy of the sum hereinafter specified to such of my children [*name*] [*name*] and [*name*] as survive me and if more than one in equal shares provided that if any of my said children shall predecease me leaving issue living at my death who shall attain the age of [18/21/25] years[3] such issue shall take and if more than one in equal shares per stirpes the share of the legacy hereby given which such deceased child of mine would have taken had he or she survived me but so that no issue shall take whose parent (being such issue as aforesaid) is living at my death.

[(2) The amount of the legacy hereby given shall be the maximum sum (if any)) [not exceeding £——][4] which can in the circumstances subsisting at my death be given by this clause without any liability being incurred for the payment of inheritance tax on or by reason of my death. And in particular (without prejudice to the generality of the foregoing) for the purpose of determining the amount of such maximum sum the circumstances to be taken into account shall include all chargeable transfers made by me during my life (or events treated as such for inheritance tax purposes) so far as relevant for the computation of inheritance tax on my death the dispositions taking effect under this will (apart from this clause) or under any codicil hereto and any property treated as if it were part of my estate for inheritance tax purposes.[5]

[(3)/(2)] The legacy hereby given shall carry interest at the yearly rate of [6 per cent] from my death until paid or satisfied and section 31 of the Trustee Act 1925 (as hereinafter modified) shall apply thereto.[6]

[[4)/(3)] Section 32 of the Trustee Act 1925 (as hereinafter modified) shall apply in relation to the foregoing trusts.

1 A legacy in favour of the children can be included if the estate is of sufficient value and the testators wish their own children not to have to wait to receive anything until both testators are dead. If the surviving spouse might need access to the income or capital of the legacy, a discretionary legacy such as that contained in Form C3.4, cl 2, (at para **[225.60]**), or Form C5.1, cl 5, (at para **[227.14]**) (which has more restricted powers to benefit the surviving spouse) could be substituted, or this clause can be omitted and nil-rate band carry-forward relied on to use the first to die's nil-rate band: see para **[227.25]**. For the continuing possible uses of nil-rate band gifts see paras **[200.130]**, **[227.8]** and for nil-rate band discretionary trusts see the Note in B18 at paras **[218.16]–[218.32]**.

As regards the formula used to determine the amount, see Form C3.1, cl 3, n 1 at para **[225.13]** and Form C3.4, cl 2, n 1 at para **[225.60]**.

2 This precondition is imposed to avoid unnecessary duplication of gifts (ie this one and the residuary gift), and to avoid difficulties as to the effect where the amount of the legacy is determined by a formula, in the event of the spouse not surviving the testator. This gift should not be made conditional on the spouse surviving the testator by a survivorship period: see the Preliminary Note to C3 at para **[225.4]**.

3 For wills made on or after 6 April 2010, the perpetuity period is 125 years (and there is no other period): see the PAA 2009, ss 5(1), 15(1)(a) (Part A **[200.35A]** and Part G, para **[246.179]**). The age contingency for the grandchildren or remoter issue did not have to be limited to 21 years (a limit included so as not to infringe the common law rule against perpetuities) because they would all be lives in being at the testator's death for common law perpetuity purposes. It is still important that all interests vest within the perpetuity period the greater the vesting age, the greater is the risk that a descendant of the testator will die under the vesting age after the testator's death leaving issue—persons in the latter category will not take an interest. We should add that if this is not done, there will still be 'wait and see' under the PAA 2009, s 7 (Part G, para **[246.181]**). If the substitutional gift is subject to an age contingency, and any of the substituted beneficiaries have not satisfied it at the testator's death, but the substitutional trust takes effect, the property subject to it will be within the inheritance tax charging regime for relevant property (see para **[218.8]**). The possibility of substituted issue of the second of the testators to die becoming entitled to IPDIs (see paras **[200.92]**, **[224.25]** above) is avoided by the extended accumulation and maintenance trusts of income provided in cl 6(1) of this form at para **[227.32]**.

4 In view of the possible large increases in the nil-rate band in the next few years it would be advisable to set a cash limit on the amount of this gift. See para **[225.9]**. Another reason for setting a cash limit on it is where the testator has business or agricultural property: see the Preliminary Note to C11 at paras **[233.8]–[233.10]**.

5 See Form C3.1, cl 3, n 1 at para **[225.13]**.

6 There is a contingency in the substitutional proviso to sub-cl (1) of this clause. A contingent legacy does not ordinarily carry the intermediate income, a factor which might have the unwelcome inheritance tax consequence that the surviving spouse has an interest in possession in the capital out of which the legacy is payable from the testator's death until the time when the legacy becomes payable. Subclause (3) is introduced to ensure that the legacy does carry the intermediate income.

[227.32]

[Updated in text and footnote 2 for Perpetuities and Accumulations Act 2009.]

MAINTENANCE, ACCUMULATION AND ADVANCEMENT

6. (1) Section 31 of the Trustee Act 1925 (relating to accumulation and maintenance) shall apply in relation to the trusts hereby or by any codicil hereto declared as if:

(a) in paragraph (i) of subsection (1) of the said section the words 'as the trustees think fit' were substituted for the words 'as may in all the circumstances be reasonable'; and

(b) the proviso to the said subsection (1) were omitted;

[Provided that in relation to any presumptive share of my residuary estate of any grandchild or remoter issue of mine the said section 31 (amended as aforesaid) shall have effect as if the age of majority were the age of [21/25][1] years (and so that the expressions 'infancy', 'minority' and 'infant' and all references to the age of eighteen years in the said Section 31 shall be construed accordingly)][2].

(2) [*As in cl 9(2) of* Form C5.1 *at para* **[227.18]**.]

(3) [*As in cl 9(3) of* Form C5.1 *at para* **[227.18]**.]

1 The age here should be that which is the age of vesting in the substitution clauses in cll 3(1) and 5(3) of this form (paras **[227.29]** and **[227.31]**). If it is 18, this proviso is not needed.

2 This proviso is for inclusion where the vesting age in the substitutional gifts to grandchildren and remoter issue in cll 3(1) and 5(3) is greater than 18. For wills made on or after 6 April 2010, there are no statutory restrictions on accumulation in respect of non-charitable trusts, so accumulation will be permitted throughout the trust period: see the PAA 2009, ss 13, 15(1)(a) (Part G, para **[246.187]**). It is no longer necessary, therefore, to introduce a restriction in order to comply with the rule against excessive accumulations as was previously the case: see the form of this clause as set out in the 9th Edition. The effect of extending this period is to avoid any of these beneficiaries having accidental IPDIs. See C2, para **[224.25]** and para **[224.36]** n 3.

Form C5.4: Will of married man with adult children making provision for an illegitimate child who is a minor by means of a settled legacy

[227.54]

[Updated in text and footnotes for Perpetuities and Accumulations Act 2009.]

SETTLED LEGACY FOR ILLEGITIMATE CHILD[1]

3. (1) I give free of tax[2] a pecuniary legacy of £—— to [*name*] of [*address*] and [*name*] of [*address*].

(2) In this clause 'the legacy fund trustees' means and includes the said named persons or other the trustees or trustee for the time being of the legacy fund as hereinafter defined and pending the payment or transfer of the legacy fund as hereinafter defined shall also include my trustees.

(3) The said legacy shall carry interest from the date of my death at the rate of [4] per cent per annum until paid set aside or satisfied by appropriation.

(4) The legacy fund trustees shall hold the said legacy upon trust to invest the same in any investments hereby authorised with power to vary the same and shall hold the said legacy and the investments from time to time

representing the same (in this clause together called 'the legacy fund') and the income thereof upon the trusts set out below.

(5) The legacy fund trustees shall hold the legacy fund and the income thereof upon trust for my [son/daughter] [*name of illegitimate child*] (hereinafter called 'the beneficiary') absolutely if [he/she] shall attain the age of 25[3] years provided that if [he/she] shall die before the said age of 25 years leaving a child or children [him/her] surviving who shall attain the age of 21 years such child or children shall take the legacy fund absolutely and if more than one equally between them.[4]

(6) The foregoing trusts shall carry the intermediate income of the legacy fund and section 31 of the Trustee Act 1925 (as hereinafter modified) shall apply thereto [provided that in relation to the beneficiary and his interest in the legacy fund the said section 31 (amended as aforesaid) shall have effect as if the age of majority were the age of 25 years (and so that the expressions 'infancy', 'minority' and 'infant' and all references to the age of eighteen years in the said Section 31 shall be construed accordingly)][5].

(7) Section 32 of the Trustee Act 1925 (as hereinafter modified shall apply to the foregoing trusts.

(8) Subject as aforesaid the legacy fund shall [fall into my residuary estate].

(9) The following provisions shall have effect with regard to the legacy fund trustees:

(a) if the said [*name of trustee appointed in subclause (1)*] shall die in my lifetime or shall refuse or be unable to act as a legacy fund trustee then I appoint [*name*] of [*address*] to be such a trustee in his place;

(b) if the said [*name of other trustee appointed in subclause (1)*] shall die in my lifetime or shall refuse or be unable to act as an original legacy fund trustee then I appoint [*name*] of [*address*] to be such a trustee in his place;

(c) if one of the persons appointed by name as an original trustee of the legacy fund in subclause (1) of this clause and the person appointed in his or her place under the foregoing provisions of this subclause shall both die in my lifetime or refuse or be unable to act as such a trustee then any other person appointed by name as an original trustee of the legacy fund by subclause (1) of this clause or the foregoing provisions of this subclause (as the case may be) may nominate additional trustees of the legacy fund;

(d) if all the persons hereinbefore appointed by name as original trustees shall die in my lifetime or shall refuse or be unable to act as such trustees then [*name*] of [*address*] [or failing [him/her] my trustees] may nominate additional trustees of the legacy fund;

(e) subject as aforesaid the power of appointing new trustees of the legacy fund [shall be vested in [the said] [*name*] of [*address*] during [his/her] life and otherwise] shall be the statutory power.[6]

1 In deciding what the amount of the legacy should be the testator needs to consider the level of support he is currently providing for the child, and what level of provision will be sufficient to avoid a claim being made under the Inheritance (Provision for Family and Dependants) Act 1975. He may need to make codicils from time to time to increase the legacy for inflation or to take account of changed circumstances. It could be tied to the

inheritance tax threshold, as in Form C5.2, cl 3(2) at para **[227.29]**, but that could work capriciously and would not be a level of provision fixed by reference to the child's circumstances.

2 See Form C3.1, cl 2, n 2 at para **[225.17]**.

3 If the testator dies while the beneficiary is living and under the age of 25, the trust will be an age 18-to-25 trust within IHTA 1984, s 71D (see para **[200.109]** above). A possible alternative would be to substitute 18 as the age of vesting thus creating a trust for a bereaved minor within IHTA 1984, s 71A (see para **[200.108]** above).

4 A further alternative would be to provide a life interest with power to pay or apply capital to or for the benefit of the child; Form C2.2, cls 7 and 8 at paras **[224.50]** and **[224.51]** could be adapted for this purpose. It could either be a relevant property or an IPDI trust. For wills made on or after 6 April 2010, the perpetuity period is 125 years (and there is no other period): see the PAA 2009, ss 5(1), 15(1)(a) (Part A **[200.35A]** and Part G, para **[246.179]**). The age contingency for the grandchildren in this clause need not, therefore, be limited to 21 years (a limit included so as not to infringe the common law rule against perpetuities). This restriction on the age contingency of the grandchildren to a maximum of 21 years is no longer necessary although it is still important that all interests vest within the perpetuity period. We should add that if this is not done, there will still be 'wait and see' under the PAA 2009, s 7 (Part G, para **[246.181]**).

5 For wills made on or after 6 April 2010, there are no statutory restrictions on accumulation in respect of non-charitable trusts, so accumulation will be permitted throughout the trust period: see the PAA 2009, ss 13, 15(1)(a) (Part G, para **[246.187]**). It is no longer necessary, therefore, to introduce a restriction in order to comply with the rule against excessive accumulations as was previously the case: see the form of this clause as set out in the 9th Edition. Advantage may be taken of this to extend the provisions for maintenance and accumulation contained in the TA 1925, s 31 to the vesting age. For further discussion of the extension of accumulation and maintenance trusts in this way, and alternative forms for doing so, see B18 at paras **[218.74]–[218.78]**. It is a particularly good idea to extend accumulation and maintenance trusts of income in relation to a trust intended to be within IHTA 1984, s 71D (see para **[200.109]** above), as it ensures that IHTA 1984, s 71D will apply, if the beneficiary is under 25 at the testator's death, irrespective of the age of the beneficiary at the time of the testator's death: see para **[224.25]**.

6 The reason for these rather elaborate provisions is that the executors and the testator's immediate family may not be the most appropriate people to decide who should be trustees of this fund if the nominated persons do not take office. Further, the testator may not wish the child's mother to have too much influence on the trusteeship or administration of this fund. Accordingly, this subclause provides for alternative trustees to be nominated, and for someone to be nominated to decide who should be trustees in the absence of any of the named persons taking office. These provisions are mostly concerned with who will be the trustees in the first place; once the separate trustees are constituted they will appoint their own successors under the statutory power, unless someone is nominated to exercise it in sub-cl (9)(e).

Wills for unmarried couples with children

Form C6.1: Reciprocal wills of couple living together who have young children and who are planning to marry

[228.12]

[Updated for Trusts (Capital and Income) Act 2013.]

ADMINISTRATION TRUSTS OF RESIDUE

6. (1) I give all my property not hereby or by any codicil hereto otherwise effectively disposed of [(including any entailed or other property over which I shall have at my death a general power of disposition by will)][1] to my trustees to hold on the trusts set out below with power to sell all or any of it.[2]

(2) My trustees shall pay my funeral and testamentary expenses[3] and debts and any legacies given by this will or any codicil hereto out of such property or its proceeds and shall have a discretion as to how such payments shall be borne as between capital and income.[4]

(3) Subject as above my trustees shall hold such property and the assets from time to time representing the same (hereinafter called 'my residuary estate') on the trusts set out below and shall invest all money comprised in such property or arising from its sale in any of the investments hereby authorised with power to change such investments into any others hereby authorised.[5]

1 See Form C2.1, cl 6, n 1 at para **[224.34]**.
2 See Form C2.1, cl 6, n 2 at para **[224.34]**.
3 See Form C2.1, cl 6, n 3 at para **[224.34]**.
4 See Form C2.1, cl 6, n 4 at para **[224.34]**.
5 See Form C2.1, cl 6, n 5 at para **[224.34]**.

[228.13]

[Updated in text and footnotes for Perpetuities and Accumulations Act 2009.]

BENEFICIAL TRUSTS OF RESIDUE

7. (1) My trustees shall hold my residuary estate upon trust for such of my children by the said [*name of intended spouse*] as survive me and attain the age of [18/25] years[1] and if more than one in equal shares provided that if any such child of mine shall predecease me or having survived me shall die before attaining the age aforesaid leaving a child or children living at or born after my death who shall attain the age of [18/21] years[2] such last-mentioned child or children shall take if more than one equally between them the share

of my residuary estate to which such deceased child of mine would have become entitled had he or she lived to attain a vested interest.

(2) The foregoing trusts shall carry the intermediate income of my residuary estate and section 31 of the Trustee Act 1925 (as hereinafter modified) shall apply thereto accordingly [provided that in relation to any presumptive share of my residuary estate of any child of mine by the said [*name of intended spouse*][2] the said section 31 (as modified as aforesaid) shall have effect as if the age of majority were the age of 25 years (and so that the expressions 'infancy', 'minority' and 'infant' and all references to the age of eighteen years in the said Section 31 shall be construed accordingly)][3].

(3) Section 32 of the Trustee Act 1925 (as hereinafter modified) shall apply in relation to my residuary estate.

[(4) Subject as aforesaid my trustees shall hold my residuary estate and the income thereof [for [*name*] absolutely]/[for such charitable purposes as my trustees may declare]].

1 The age contingency does not have to be restricted to 21. The choice here is between a vesting age of 18, which will mean that it is a trust for bereaved minors within IHTA 1984, s 71A (see para **[200.108]**), or a vesting age of 25, which will mean that it is an age 18-to-25 trust within IHTA 1984, s 71D (see para **[200.109]**). If a greater vesting age, or life interests, are desired, the choice is between IPDI trusts or relevant property trusts (see paras **[200.98]**, **[200.126]**, **[200.132]**).

2 For wills made on or after 6 April 2010, the perpetuity period is 125 years (and there is no other period): see the PAA 2009, ss 5(1), 15(1)(a) (Part A **[200.35A]** and Part G, para **[246.179]**). The age contingency for the grandchildren in this clause need not, therefore, be limited to 21 years (a limit included so as not to infringe the common law rule against perpetuities). This restriction on the age contingency to a maximum of 21 years is no longer necessary although it is still important that all interests vest within the perpetuity period. We should add that if this is not done, there will still be 'wait and see' under the PAA 2009, s 7 (Part G, para **[246.181]**). Any settled property which becomes subject to this substitutional proviso will fall within the IHT charging regime for relevant property (see para **[218.8]** ff) unless the age of vesting is 21 and a substituted grandchild has an IPDI as a result of being over 18 (and thus entitled to an interest in possession by virtue of TA 1925, s 31) but under 21 at or within two years after the testator's death (see para **[224.25]**). The possibility of a grandchild becoming entitled to an IPDI can be avoided by having a second proviso to subclause (2) of this clause extending the accumulation and maintenance trusts of TA 1925, s 31 to the age of 21 for grandchildren.

3 For wills made on or after 6 April 2010, there are no statutory restrictions on accumulation in respect of non-charitable trusts, so accumulation will be permitted throughout the trust period: see the PAA 2009, ss 13, 15(1)(a) (Part G, para **[246.187]**). It is no longer necessary, therefore, to introduce a restriction in order to comply with the rule against excessive accumulations as was previously the case: see the form of this clause as set out in the 9th Edition. This proviso should be included if the age of vesting is 25. It will ensure that the trusts for the children are within the age 18-to-25 trust regime of IHTA 1984, s 71D for beneficiaries under the age of 25 at the testator's death irrespective of the age they have attained by that time (see para **[224.25]**).

[228.19]

[Updated for capital gains tax changes.]

Form C6.2: Reciprocal wills of couple living together who have children, leaving residue on discretionary trusts

Note. Where a couple are unmarried there is no spouse exemption, and the IHT on the death of the first to die is the same whether his will creates a discretionary trust or gives an absolute interest or interest in possession to the survivor. A discretionary trust can thus be an appropriate option and this form provides an example of one. The main point of a discretionary trust would be to give greater flexibility and to avoid what in some circumstances might be a heavy IHT charge arising on the survivor's death in respect of property given to the survivor absolutely or for an interest in possession from the estate of the first to die. At the same time IHT on discretionary trusts is not too onerous a burden at the moment and for a fund of a size not exceeding the IHT threshold it can be nil (see B18 at paras **[218.8]–[218.20]**).

A discretionary trust would enable some or all of the income to be paid to the survivor without the latter having an interest in possession in the property subject to the trust, and thus without that property being treated as part of his or her estate for IHT purposes, and would enable income to be paid directly for the benefit of a child and treated as the child's for income tax purposes. Where the income is distributed in exercise of a discretion or accumulated the burdensome income tax provisions for such income under ITA 2007, ss 9, 479–483, 493–498, will apply, which bear particularly heavily on dividend income (see para **[218.29]–[218.32]**), but the post-21 March 2006 IHT rules mean that once two years have elapsed from the testator's death it will be possible to appoint interests in possession to beneficiaries to obtain the more favourable income tax treatment of this type of trust while retaining IHT 'relevant property' status (see para **[200.126]** (2)). The rate of capital gains tax on property subject to a trust is a flat rate of 28 per cent from 23 June 2010: see para **[200.40]** and B18 at paras **[218.26]** and **[218.27]**.

A further consequence of the post-21 March 2006 IHT rules is that tangible property, such as a dwellinghouse used as a residence, or an interest in it, can be included in a discretionary trust even though the actual enjoyment of such items may constitute an interest in possession for IHT purposes: see Part A, paras **[200.92]**, **[200.95]**, **[200.126]** (2). If such property is to retain IHT relevant property status when included in the property settled by a will, it is important to avoid creating an interest in possession in it during the first two years after the death of the testator: see para **[200.133]**. If the testators own their principal residence, or any other property, as joint tenants, it will be essential to sever the joint tenancy if they desire the first to die's interest in such residence or other property to become subject to the discretionary trust under the will of the first to die. Chattels, however, unless they particularly valuable, are not suitable for inclusion in a trust, because the expense and difficulty of identifying and keeping track of them is usually out of all proportion to their value. Accordingly in this form these are given absolutely to the survivor.

[228.28]

[Updated in text and footnotes for Perpetuities and Accumulations Act 2009.]

DISCRETIONARY TRUSTS OF RESIDUE[1]

7. (1) In this clause the following expressions have the following meanings namely:

(a) 'the beneficiaries' means and includes:

(i) the said [*name of partner*];

(ii) my children and remoter issue whenever born;

[(iii) the children and remoter issue whenever born of [*name of partner*]];[2]

(iv) the spouses widows and widowers of any of the said children or remoter issue (and 'widow' and 'widower' shall include a widow or widower who has remarried);

(v) any other person or persons or charitable institution or institutions (whether corporate or not) who may be added to the class of beneficiaries under the power for that purpose hereinafter contained; and

(vi) any other persons who become beneficiaries under subclause (2) below of this clause;

(b) 'the trust period' means the period of 125 years immediately following my death; and [3]

(c) 'the relevant day' means the day falling two years less one day after my death.[4]

(2) If at any time during the trust period the said [*name of partner*] shall have died and there shall be no living child or remoter issue of mine then the beneficiaries shall also include:

(a) the children and remoter issue of each of my grandparents;
(b) the children and remoter issue of each of the grandparents of the said [*name of partner*]; and
(c) any institution (whether corporate or not) which is established for purposes which are exclusively charitable.[5]

(3) My trustees (being not less than two in number or a trust corporation except as hereinafter provided)[6] may at any time or times and from time to time during the trust period exercise any of the following powers, namely:

(a) power at any time or times and from time to time by deed or deeds[7] revocable or irrevocable to appoint the whole or any part or parts of my residuary estate upon trust for all or such one or more exclusive of the others or other of the beneficiaries if more than one in such shares and either absolutely or at such age or time or respective ages or times and with such trusts and powers for their respective benefit and such provisions as my trustees may think fit and in making any such appointment my trustees shall have powers as full as those which they would possess if they were an absolute beneficial owner of my residuary estate and in particular (but without prejudice to the generality of the foregoing words) my trustees may in any exercise of the foregoing power as they in their absolute discretion think fit:
   (i) delegate give or impose to or upon themselves or any other person or persons any discretionary powers or discretionary trusts conditions limitations restrictions or provisions including powers of further delegation or powers to create further discretionary trusts or powers;[8]
   (ii) create powers or trusts for the accumulation of income during any period permitted by law;
   (iii) create administrative powers or provisions of whatever nature;

   Provided that:
   (i) no such appointment shall invalidate any payment transfer or application of capital or income previously made under any of the trusts or powers herein elsewhere contained;
   (ii) every interest limited under any exercise of such power shall vest in interest (if at all) not later than the expiration of the trust period;
   (iii) any such appointment may be made in respect of income alone without any appointment of capital;
   (iv) any such revocable appointment shall (so far as then unrevoked) cease to be revocable on the expiration of the trust period;
   (v) any such appointment may make provision for the burden of any testamentary expenses taxes or debts payable out of my estate as between different assets funds shares or interests in such manner and to such extent as my trustees think fit;

(vi) the foregoing power of appointment may be exercised notwithstanding that there shall have been no grant of probate or administration in respect of the property over which the said power shall be exercised or that the administration of my estate shall not have been completed in respect of such property or any other property comprised in my estate and so long as no such grant as aforesaid has been obtained the persons who may exercise the foregoing power are the persons hereinbefore named as my executors other than any of them who shall have died or whose appointment as my executor shall have ceased to have effect or who shall have renounced probate of my will;[9]

(vii) the foregoing power of appointment may be exercised before the relevant day by a sole trustee who is not a trust corporation;[10]

(b) power (subject to any or every exercise of the foregoing power) at any time or times and from time to time in their absolute discretion to pay transfer or apply my residuary estate or any part or parts thereof to or for the benefit of all or any one or more exclusive of the others or other of the beneficiaries for the time being in existence if more than one in such shares and generally in such manner as my trustees shall think fit provided that the foregoing power of payment transfer or application of capital may be exercised before the relevant day by a sole trustee who is not a trust corporation;[11]

(c) power at any time or times and from time to time to appoint at their absolute discretion by deed any person or persons or charitable institution or institutions (whether corporate or not) to be a member or members of the class of beneficiaries upon the nomination of the said [*name of partner*] or of any children or remoter issue of mine [or of [*name of partner*]][12] who are for the time being over the age of 16 years; provided that:

(i) the foregoing power may be exercised before the relevant day by a sole trustee who is not a trust corporation; and

(ii) proviso (vi) (exercise of power before probate or completion of the administration of my estate) to the power of appointment in subclause (3)(a) above shall apply to this power as if the references in it to the said power of appointment were references to this power and as if references to property comprised in my residuary estate were references to the whole of my residuary estate;[13]

(d) power at any time or times and from time to time by deed or deeds to release or restrict all or any of the foregoing powers or this present power either in whole or in part and in any manner they think fit provided that the foregoing power may be exercised before the relevant day by a sole trustee who is not a trust corporation.

(4) In default of and subject to any or every exercise of the foregoing powers my trustees shall hold my residuary estate during the trust period upon trust to pay or apply the income thereof to or for the maintenance education or benefit of all or any one or more of the beneficiaries and if

more than one in such shares and in such manner generally as my trustees think fit; provided that my trustees may accumulate[14] all or any part or parts of such income by investing the same and the resulting income thereof in any investments hereby authorised and so that any accumulations so made shall form part of the capital of my residuary estate (or the part thereof from which such income arose) for all purposes.

(5) Subject as aforesaid my trustees shall hold my residuary estate and the income thereof at the expiration of the trust period upon trust for such of my grandchildren and remoter issue as shall be then living in equal shares per stirpes.

(6) Any capital or income of my residuary estate not otherwise disposed of by this clause shall be held in trust for such of my children as shall survive me and if more than one in equal shares.

1 Because it may be important to be able to make appointments or distributions within two years of death falling within the ITA 1984, s 144 (see C3 at paras **[225.83]–[225.91]**), various provisions are included to facilitate such appointments. However, in contrast with Form C3.6, cl 3 at paras **[225.100]–[225.104]** (which is formulated with s 144 in mind), in this form the discretionary trusts and powers continue for a full perpetuity period of 125 years and do not cease at the end of two years from the testator's death.

2 This should be included where either partner has children by someone other than the current partner.

3 This is the longest period which can be specified under the PAA 1964, s 1, the text of which appears in Part G, para **[246.74]**. For wills made on or after 6 April 2010, the perpetuity period is 125 years (and no other period): see the PAA 2009, ss 5(1), 15(1)(a). See Part A **[200.35A]** and Part G, para **[246.179]**). This form and others in this volume also adopts a trust period of 125 years although a shorter trust period could be specified if the testator does not wish the trust to last that long. The perpetuity period, however, will still be 125 years and it is not necessary to specify, in addition to the specification as to the length of the trust period, that the perpetuity period is 125 years: PAA 2009, s 5(2) (Part G, para **[246.179]**). This contrasts with the situation under the former law where, if the common law perpetuity period was not relied upon, it was necessary to specify that the perpetuity period was 80 years, or fewer, see the PAA 1964, s 1(1). The 125 year perpetuity period commencing with the death of the testator will be the perpetuity period when drafting an appointment in exercise of the power of sub-clause (2), whether the trust period selected is 125 years (as in this form) or a shorter period: see the PAA 2009, s 6(2) (Part G, para **[246.180]**). Accordingly, an appointment under the power needs to be expressly limited so that all interests vest (in interest if not in possession) and all powers are exercised within the 125 year period. We should add that if this is not done in an appointment, there will still be 'wait and see' under the PAA 2009, s 7 (Part G, para **[246.181]**), but it is better practice to draft trusts of which it is clear from the outset that they will vest within the relevant perpetuity period.

4 This definition relates to some short-term measures to make it easier for appointments within the ITA 1984, s 144 to be made.

5 If the primary beneficiaries die out, this will enables the trustees to distribute the estate to more distant relations or charity, and avoids an intestacy, or the class of beneficiaries being reduced to consisting only of the widows and widowers of issue.

6 See proviso (vii) to subclause (3)(a) and subclauses (3)(b), (c) and (d) of this clause for the modification of this provision during the two years following the testator's death, so as to make it easier for appointments within the ITA 1984, s 144 to be made.

7 For precedents of appointments see the forms in F4 at paras **[242.7]–[242.16]**.

8 These words authorise the creation of discretionary trusts or powers which might not otherwise be valid: see Vol 1, para **[40.5]**.

9 This is included so as to make it easier to make an appointment within the ITA 1984, s 144 at an early stage. The main reason for such a provision, i e to make exempt appointments before applying for a grant of probate (see C3 at paras **[225.83]–[225.91]**), is not likely to apply in relation to wills in this form, however, because of the lack of a spouse exemption.

10 This is included with the ITA 1984, s 144 (see C3 at paras **[225.83]–[225.91]**) in mind. If it were required that there should be two trustees during the two years after the testator's death, difficulty could arise if the number of trustees were reduced to one and the administration of the estate was not complete, as it is not clear that the statutory power to appoint new trustees could be exercised in such circumstances.

11 For the reasons for the proviso, see n 10 above. A power to apply capital is a useful alternative to a power of appointment, because fewer formalities are needed for its exercise, and because it permits a wide range of applications for a person's benefit such as lending him money, paying his debts, etc: see B18 at paras **[218.94]–[218.98]** for the scope of a power of this type. It is important that the exercise of such a power should be adequately evidenced.

12 To be included where either partner has children by someone other than the current partner.

13 See Form C3.6, cl 3(1)(b), n 2 at para **[225.100]**. In wills of this type for unmarried couples with children, it is a particularly good idea to include a power to add to the class of beneficiaries such as this subclause, as it will be a means of adding, e g unmarried partners of the testator's issue, or children of uncertain paternity, to the class of beneficiaries. The power to add charities would enable transfers to charity to be made so as to obtain IHT charitable gift exemption on the testator's death where the transfer fell within the ITA 1984, s 144 (for which see C3 at paras **[225.83]–[225.91]**), and the second proviso enables charity to be added to the class of beneficiaries before probate is obtained. For the purpose of the first proviso see subclause 3(a)(vii), n 10 above.

14 For wills made on or after 6 April 2010, there are no statutory restrictions on accumulation in respect of non-charitable trusts, so accumulation will be permitted throughout the trust period: see the PAA 2009, ss 13, 15(1)(a) (Part G, para **[246.187]**).

Form C6.3: Will of man separated (but not judicially separated) from wife and living with another woman, where divorce proceedings are contemplated

[228.37]

[Updated in text and footnote 4 for Perpetuities and Accumulations Act 2009.]

GIFT OF INTEREST IN DWELLINGHOUSE ON TRUSTS PERMITTING WIFE TO OCCUPY DWELLINGHOUSE FOR LIFE OR DURING WIDOWHOOD[1]

3. (1) I give to my trustees all my interest in the dwellinghouse situate at [*address*] which is now occupied by my wife and which is vested in us both as beneficial tenants in common in equal shares to hold the same upon the trusts hereinafter declared.

(2) So long as my wife [shall not remarry and] shall desire to occupy the said dwellinghouse my trustees shall permit her to have the use and enjoyment thereof and shall not seek to bring about a sale of the same or take any step to prevent my wife from having the beneficial use and occupation thereof.

(3) Subject as aforesaid[2] my trustees shall hold the said interest and the assets for the time being representing the same (hereinafter called 'the trust fund') upon trust for such of my children as shall survive me and attain the age of 25 years[3] and if more than one in equal shares; provided that if any of my children shall not live to attain a vested interest under the foregoing trust leaving a child or children living at or born after my death who shall attain the age of 21 years[4] such last-mentioned child or children shall take and if more than one equally between them the share of the trust fund which his her or their parent would have taken had he or she lived to attain a vested interest.

(4) The foregoing trusts shall carry the intermediate income of the trust fund and section 31 of the Trustee Act 1925 (as hereinafter modified) shall apply thereto.

(5) Section 32 of the Trustee Act 1925 (as hereinafter modified) shall apply in relation to the said trusts.

[(6) I declare that I have made no further provision for my wife on the grounds that if she survives me as my widow she will become entitled to a widow's pension and that she is otherwise adequately provided for].[5]

1 This gift confers a residence right on the wife which will lapse on divorce. It will create a trust of an undivided share in land, which will be a trust of land within the TLATA 1996 (see the LPA 1925, s 205(1)(ix), as amended by the TLATA 1996, s 23(2) and Sch 4: Part G, para **[246.74]**). It is assumed that the testator has severed any joint tenancy to which the matrimonial home is subject. See the Note to this form at para **[228.33]**. It is thought that the wife will have an IPDI in the half share of the house and that the spouse exemption will apply (see paras **[200.84]**, **[200.95]** and **[200.98]**).

2 The gift in favour of the children will be accelerated on the dissolution of the marriage: see the WA 1837, s 18A (Part G, para **[244.18]**).

3 See Form C6.1, cl 7, n 1, at para **[228.13]**. See also the extended accumulation and maintenance provision in cl 6(1) of this form at para **[228.40]**, and Form C6.1, cl 7, n 3, at para **[228.13]**.

4 For wills made on or after 6 April 2010, the perpetuity period is 125 years (and there is no other period): see the PAA 2009, ss 5(1), 15(1)(a) (Part A **[200.35A]** and Part G, para **[246.179]**). The age contingency for the grandchildren in this clause need not, therefore, be limited to 21 years (a limit included so as not to infringe the common law rule against perpetuities). This restriction on the age contingency to a maximum of 21 years is no longer necessary although it is still important that all interests vest within the perpetuity period. We should add that if this is not done, there will still be 'wait and see' under the PAA 2009, s 7 (Part G, para **[246.181]**).See Form C6.1, cl 7, n 2, at para **[228.13]**.

5 A declaration in this form may possibly be useful in the event that the husband dies before the marriage is dissolved and the wife makes a claim under the I(PFD)A 1975 (Part G, para **[247.1]** ff and discussed in Vol 1 at para **[105.1]** ff).

[228.39]

[Updated in text and footnote 3 for Perpetuities and Accumulations Act 2009.]

BENEFICIAL TRUSTS OF RESIDUE

5. (1) My trustees shall hold my residuary estate and the income thereof upon trust for [*name of partner*] if she survives me [by the period of one month][1] absolutely.

(2) If the said [*name of partner*] shall not survive me then my trustees shall hold my residuary estate upon trust for such of my children as shall survive me and attain the age of 25 years[2] and if more than one in equal shares provided that if any of my children shall not live to attain a vested interest under the foregoing trust leaving a child or children living at or born after my death who shall attain the age of [18/21] years[3] such last-mentioned child or children shall take and if more than one equally between then the share of my residuary estate which his her or their parent would have taken had he or she lived to attain a vested interest.

(3) The foregoing trust shall carry the intermediate income of my residuary estate and section 31 of the Trustee Act 1925 (as hereinafter modified) shall apply thereto.

(4) Section 32 of the Trustee Act 1925 (as hereinafter modified) shall apply in relation to the said trusts.

1 The words in square brackets will ensure that if the testator and partner die in a common accident or within the period of one month of each other, the residuary estate will devolve directly on the children. If the period does not exceed six months, the gift to the children will be treated (by IHTA 1984, s 92) for IHT purposes as having taken effect, on the

testator's death. Survivorship conditions can have a useful function in relation to a non-exempt (from IHT) gift, but not in relation to a gift to a spouse or civil partner: see the Preliminary Note to C2 at paras **[224.6]–[224.10]**.

2 See Form C6.1, cl 7, n 1, at para **[228.13]**. See also the extended accumulation and maintenance provision in cl 6(1) of this form at para **[228.40]**, and Form C6.1, cl 7, n 3, at para **[228.13]**.

3 For wills made on or after 6 April 2010, the perpetuity period is 125 years (and there is no other period): see the PAA 2009, ss 5(1), 15(1)(a) (Part A **[200.35A]** and Part G, para **[246.179]**). The age contingency for the grandchildren in this clause need not, therefore, be limited to 21 years (a limit included so as not to infringe the common law rule against perpetuities). This restriction on the age contingency to a maximum of 21 years is no longer necessary although it is still important that all interests vest within the perpetuity period. We should add that if this is not done, there will still be 'wait and see' under the PAA 2009, s 7 (Part G, para **[246.181]**).See Form C6.1, cl 7, n 2, at para **[228.13]**.

[228.40]

[Updated in text and footnote 1 for Perpetuities and Accumulations Act 2009.]

MAINTENANCE, ACCUMULATION AND ADVANCEMENT

6. (1) Section 31 of the Trustee Act 1925 (relating to accumulation and maintenance) shall apply in relation to the trusts hereby or by any codicil hereto declared as if:

(a) in paragraph (i) of subsection (1) of the said section the words 'as the trustees think fit' were substituted for the words 'as may in all the circumstances be reasonable'; and

(b) the proviso to the said subsection (1) were omitted,

provided that in relation to any presumptive share or shares of any child of mine under any such trust or trusts the said section 31 (amended as aforesaid) shall have effect as if the age of majority were the age of 25 years (and so that the expressions 'infancy', 'minority' and 'infant' and all references to the age of 18 years in the said Section 31 shall be construed accordingly).[1]

(2) [*As in cl 8(2) of* Form C6.1 *at para* **[228.14]**.]

(3) [*As in cl 8(3) of* Form C6.1 *at para* **[228.14]**.]

1 For wills made on or after 6 April 2010, there are no statutory restrictions on accumulation in respect of non-charitable trusts, so accumulation will be permitted throughout the trust period: see the PAA 2009, ss 13, 15(1)(a) (Part G, para **[246.187]**). It is no longer necessary, therefore, to introduce a restriction in order to comply with the rule against excessive accumulations as was previously the case: see the form of this clause as set out in the 9th Edition. See Form C6.1, cl 7, n 3, at para **[228.13]**.

C7

Wills for sole parents with young children

Form C7.1: Will of mother giving entire estate to her minor child

[229.6]

[Updated for Trusts (Capital and Income) Act 2013.]

ADMINISTRATION TRUSTS OF RESIDUE

3. (1) I give all my property not hereby or by any codicil hereto otherwise effectively disposed of [(including any entailed or other property over which I shall have at my death a general power of disposition by will)][1] to my trustees to hold on the trusts set out below with power to sell all or any of it.[2]

(2) My trustees shall pay my funeral and testamentary expenses[3] and debts and any legacies given by this will or any codicil hereto out of such property or its proceeds and shall have a discretion as to how such payments shall be borne as between capital and income.[4]

(3) Subject as above my trustees shall hold such property and the assets from time to time representing the same (hereinafter called 'my residuary estate') on the trusts set out below and shall invest all money comprised in such property or arising from its sale in any of the investments hereby authorised with power to change such investments into any others hereby authorised.[5]

1 See para **[224.34]**, n 1.
2 See para **[224.34]**, n 2.
3 See para **[224.34]**, n 3.
4 See para **[224.34]**, n 4.
5 See para **[224.34]**, n 5.

[229.7]

[Updated for the Perpetuities and Accumulations Act 2009.]

BENEFICIAL TRUSTS OF ESTATE

4. (1) My trustees shall hold my residuary estate upon trust for my said [son/daughter] if [he/she] shall attain the age of 25 years[1] absolutely provided that if [he/she] shall predecease me or having survived me die before attaining the said age leaving a child or children [him/ her] surviving who attain the age of 21 years[2] such last mentioned child or children shall take my residuary estate and if more than one in equal shares.

(2) The foregoing trusts shall carry the intermediate income of my residuary estate and section 31 of the Trustee Act 1925 (as hereinafter

modified) shall apply thereto provided that in relation to my said [son/daughter] the said section 31 (amended as aforesaid) shall take effect for all purposes as if the age of majority were the age of 25 years[3] and so that all references in the said section 31 to 'infancy' 'minority' and 'infant' and all references therein to the age of eighteen years shall be construed accordingly.

(3) Section 32 of the Trustee Act 1925 (as hereinafter modified) shall apply in relation to my residuary estate.

(4) My trustees may exercise their powers to apply income or capital for the benefit of my said [son/daughter] by paying or transferring the same to [his/her] guardian for the time being.[4]

(5) Subject as aforesaid my trustees shall hold my residuary estate upon trust for such of my brothers and sisters [*name*] [*name*] [*name*] and [*name*] as survive me and if more than one in equal shares.

1 A child of the testator will necessarily reach the age of 25 within 125 years of the testator's death, which period of 125 years will be the perpetuity period for wills made on or after 6 April 2010, see the PAA 2009, ss 5(1), 15(1)(a) (Part G, paras **[246.179]**, **[246.189]** and see para **[94.6]**). If the vesting age is 25 or less the trust will fall within one of the favoured categories: the choice here is between a vesting age of 18, which will mean that it is a trust for a bereaved minor within IHTA 1984, s 71A (see para **[200.108]**), or a vesting age of 25, which will mean that it is an age 18-to-25 trust within IHTA 1984, s 71D (see para **[200.109]**). If a greater vesting age, or a life interest, is desired, the choice is between a relevant property trust or an IPDI trust (see paras **[200.98]**, **[200.126]** and **[200.132]**). If 25 is adopted as the vesting age, the accumulation and maintenance trusts of income under TA 1925, s 31 can be extended beyond the age of 18 as in sub-cl (2).

2 If this form was used for a will made before 6 April 2010, the testator's child will be a life in being for the purposes of the common law perpetuity period, so that the interests of his children will necessarily vest within a permissible perpetuity period. For wills made on or after 6 April 2010 however a mandatory perpetuity period of 125 years applies, see the PAA 2009, ss 5(1), 15(1)(a) (Part G, paras **[246.179]**, **[246.189]**, and see para **[94.6]**). Nevertheless, given the 'wait and see' provision of the PAA 2009, s 7 (Part G, para **[246.181]** and see para **[94.17]**), and the practical certainty that the interests will vest within 125 years of the testator's death, no perpetuity problem should arise if this form is used in a will made on or after 6 April 2010. Any settled property which becomes subject to this substitutional proviso will fall within the IHT charging regime for relevant property (see para **[218.8]** ff) if the substituted grandchildren are under the age of vesting at the death of the testator, unless the age of vesting is 21 and a substituted grandchild has an IPDI as a result of being over 18 (and thus entitled to an interest in possession by virtue of TA 1925, s 31) but under 21 at or within two years after the testator's death (see para **[224.25]**). The possibility of a grandchild becoming entitled to an IPDI can be avoided by extending the accumulation and maintenance trusts of TA 1925, s 31 to the age of 21 for grandchildren. If the fund is likely to be below the IHT threshold, the IHT classification of this trust is not important.

3 For wills made on or after 6 April 2010, it is possible to extend the statutory provisions for maintenance and accumulation to any age which may be attained during the period of 125 years following the testator's death, see PAA 2009, ss 13, 15(1)(a), (Part G, paras **[246.187]**, **[246.189]**). See the note on extended accumulation and maintenance provisions in B18 at paras **[218.74]**–**[218.78]**. The age at which accumulation and maintenance trusts of income cease should not be greater than 25 where (as will usually be the case) it is desired that the IHTA 1984, s 71D should apply: see Part A, para **[200.109]**. On the other hand, it is recommended, in relation to trusts of this type where capital vests contingently on attaining a specified age, that accumulation and maintenance trusts should be extended in this way to the maximum possible age (not more than the vesting age) to prevent the beneficiary having an IPDI in consequence of attaining the age at which the accumulation and maintenance trusts cease by the time of the testator's death or within two years after it (see para **[224.25]**).

4 It is not strictly necessary to include a power to pay income or capital to a guardian in view of the ChA 1989, s 3(3) (Part G, para **[244.114]**) which authorises any person with 'parental responsibility' in respect of a child to receive or recover property which the child is entitled to receive or recover, but it does no harm to include an express power.

Form C7.2: Will of mother appointing sister sole executrix and guardian of children and giving entire estate to her if accepting office, with alternative gift to children

[229.21]

[Updated for the Perpetuities and Accumulations Act 2009.]

BENEFICIAL TRUSTS OF ESTATE

7. (1) My trustees shall hold my residuary estate upon trust for such of my children as shall survive me and attain the age of 25 years[1] and if more than one in equal shares provided that if any of my children shall predecease me or survive me and die under the said age leaving a child or children living at or after my death who shall attain the age of 21 years[2] such last-mentioned child or children shall take and if more than one equally between them the share of my residuary estate which such deceased child of mine would have taken had he or she survived me.

(2) The foregoing trusts shall carry the intermediate income of my residuary estate and section 31 of the Trustee Act 1925 (as hereinafter modified) shall apply thereto provided that in relation to the presumptive share of my residuary estate of any child of mine the said section shall take effect for all purposes as if the age of majority were the age of 25 years and so that all references in the said section 31 to 'infancy' 'minority' and 'infant' and all references therein to the age of eighteen years shall be construed accordingly.[3]

(3) Section 32 of the Trustee Act 1925 (as hereinafter modified) shall apply in relation to my residuary estate.

(4) My trustees may exercise their powers to apply income or capital for the benefit of any of my said children by paying or transferring the same to [his/her] guardian for the time being.[4]

(5) Subject as aforesaid my trustees shall hold my residuary estate upon trust for such of my brothers and sisters [*name*] [*name*] [*name*] and [*name*] as survive me if more than one in equal shares.

1 See Form C7.1, cl 4(1), n 1 at para **[229.7]**.
2 See Form C7.1, cl 4(1), n 2 at para **[229.7]**.
3 See Form C7.1, cl 4(2), n 3 at para **[229.7]**.
4 See Form C7.1, cl 4(4), n 4 at para **[229.7]**.

Form C7.4: Will of widow or widower settling residue on children equally for life with remainder to their children

[229.46]

[Updated for the Perpetuities and Accumulations Act 2009.]

SETTLEMENT OF CHILD'S SHARE OF RESIDUE[1]

8. The share of my residuary estate to which any child of mine shall become entitled under the last foregoing clause hereof shall not vest absolutely in such child ('the beneficiary') but shall be retained by my trustees and held upon the following trusts:

EITHER

(1) The income of such share ('the share') shall be held upon the following trusts during the beneficiary's life (and section 31 of the Trustee Act 1925 shall not apply to it):

(a) for the purposes of this subclause 'the discretionary period' means the period commencing at my death and ending on the third anniversary thereof or if earlier on the death of the beneficiary provided that if the beneficiary is living and under the age of 18 years at such third anniversary then 'the discretionary period' means the period commencing at my death and expiring on the beneficiary's 18th birthday or his or her earlier death;

(b) my trustees shall have power to pay to the beneficiary or to his or her parent or guardian or apply for the benefit of the beneficiary the whole or such part (if any) of the income of the share arising during the discretionary period as my trustees in their absolute discretion think fit and my trustees shall accumulate the income of the share arising during the discretionary period which is not so paid or applied as an accretion to the capital of the share but with power to apply such accumulations as income of the current year;

(c) subject as aforesaid my trustees shall hold the share upon trust to pay the income thereof to the beneficiary during his or her life;[2]

OR

(1) my trustees shall hold such share ('the share') upon trust to pay the income thereof to the beneficiary during his or her life provided that any income of the share which arises while the beneficiary is living and under the age of 18 years shall be held on trust for him or her absolutely and indefeasibly and section 31 of the Trustee Act 1925 shall not apply to such income but provided further that my trustees may pay or apply all or any part or parts of such income for his or her benefit at any time or times during his or her minority];[3]

(2) subject as aforesaid my trustees shall hold the share upon trust for such of the children of the beneficiary as shall attain the age of [18/21] years and if more than one in equal shares absolutely;[4]

(3) the trust declared by subclause (2) above shall carry the intermediate income of such share and section 31 of the Trustee Act 1925 (as hereinafter modified) shall apply thereto;

(4) section 32 of the Trustee Act 1925 (as hereinafter modified) shall apply in relation to the trust declared by subclause (2) above;

(5) notwithstanding the trusts aforesaid so long as the beneficiary is entitled to be paid the income of all or any part of the capital of the share (or would be so entitled if such capital yielded income)[5] my trustees shall have power in their absolute discretion from time to time to pay transfer or apply the whole or any part or parts of such capital to or for the benefit of such child in such manner as they shall in their absolute discretion think fit;[6]

(6) subject as aforesaid the share and any other share of my residuary estate which may have accrued thereto hereunder (or so much

thereof as shall not have been paid or applied under any of the powers applicable thereto hereunder) shall go and accrue to the other shares or share of my residuary estate the trusts of which are at the date of such accruer subsisting and capable of taking effect;

(7) subject as aforesaid my trustees shall hold the share upon trust for [the beneficiary or his or her estate absolutely].

1 See the note at the beginning of this form at para **[229.37]**. The life interest trust is either subject to the relevant property regime or provides an IPDI within IHTA 1984, s 49A (see the Note to para **[200.98]** above) according to whichever version of sub-cl (1) is chosen: see nn 2 and 3 to this clause.

2 If this version of sub-cl (1) is used the trusts for the children will fall within the IHT relevant property regime (for which see para **[218.8]** ff). The initial non-interest in possession period needs to be more than two years for the reasons given in para **[200.133]**. Three years is adopted for drafting convenience but it could be a shorter period exceeding two years.

3 If this version of sub-cl (1) is used the children's interests will be IPDIs and therefore will fall within the IHT beneficiary-taxed regime (for which see paras **[200.92]**, **[200.98]**).

4 If this form was used for a will made before 6 April 2010, the testator's child will be a life in being for the purposes of the common law perpetuity period, so that the interests of his children will necessarily vest within a permissible perpetuity period. For wills made on or after 6 April 2010 however a mandatory perpetuity period of 125 years applies, see the PAA 2009, ss 5(1), 15(1)(a) (Part G, para **[246.179]**, **[246.189]**, and see para **[94.6]**). Nevertheless, given the 'wait and see' provision of the PAA 2009, s 7 (Part G, para **[246.181]** and see para **[94.17]**), and the practical certainty that the interests will vest within 125 years of the testator's death, no perpetuity problem should arise if this form is used in a will made on or after 6 April 2010. If any grandchild becomes entitled under this sub-clause while still under the vesting age his or her share will fall within the IHT charging regime for relevant property (see paras **[200.92]**, **[218.8]** ff) irrespective of whether during the testator's child's lifetime it was a relevant property or IPDI trust.

5 See Form C2.2, cl 8(6), n 4 at para **[224.51]**.

6 If this form was used for a will made before 6 April 2010, the child will have been a life in being for the purposes of the common law perpetuity period, so that this power will necessarily have been confined within a permissible perpetuity period. For wills made on or after 6 April 2010 however a mandatory perpetuity period of 125 years applies, see the PAA 2009, ss 5(1), 15(1)(a) (Part G, paras **[246.179]**, **[246.189]**, and see para **[94.6]**). Nevertheless, given the 'wait and see' provision of the PAA 2009, s 7 (Part G, para **[246.181]** and see para **[94.17]**), and the practical certainty that the testator's child will not survive more than 125 years from the testator's death, no perpetuity problem should arise if this form is used in a will made on or after 6 April 2010.

Wills for sole parents with adult children

PRELIMINARY NOTE

[230.1]

[Updated for the transferable nil-rate band.]

These forms are entitled forms for widows or widowers, but they are suitable for other sole parents. The forms in C7 for sole parents with young children concentrate on providing for the children, but where a sole parent's children are grown up there are wider possibilities as to the form which testamentary dispositions may take. In particular, there is the possibility of making 'generation skipping' provision for grandchildren, which has the advantages set out in Part A, para **[200.125]**. When making provision for infant grandchildren by way of trust, the choice lies among: immediate post-death interests in possession (see para **[200.98]**), relevant property trusts (see para **[200.108]**), or bare trusts (see para **[200.110]**). For further discussion of these options see paras **[200.131]** and **[200.132]**. The former IHT-privileged category of accumulation and maintenance trusts within IHTA 1984, s 71 for minors and young persons has been abolished by FA 2006 for trusts created after 21 March 2006, and in particular for trusts created by the wills of persons dying after that date. The FA 2006 created two much more limited categories of IHT-privileged trust for minors, namely trusts for bereaved minors falling within IHTA 1984, s 71A, and 18-to-25 trusts falling within IHTA 1984, s 71D, but such trusts can only be created by testamentary provision by the will of a parent or step-parent of the beneficiary or beneficiaries, or by a person with parental responsibility for the beneficiary or beneficiaries (see paras **[200.107]**) and **[200.108]**). Therefore, a grandparent cannot create such trusts for his or her grandchildren.

Where the testator is a widow, widower or surviving civil partner, she or he may have the benefit of nil-rate band carry-forward which allows the estate of anyone who dies after 8 October 2007 who was the survivor of a marriage or civil partnership to make use of nil-rate band which was not used on the death of the predeceasing spouse or civil partner, irrespective of when the predeceasing spouse or civil partner died, see para **[200.75]**.

Form C8.1: Will of widow or widower leaving residue to children absolutely

[230.7]

[Updated for Trusts (Capital and Income) Act 2013.]

ADMINISTRATION TRUSTS OF RESIDUE

4. (1) I give all my property not hereby or by any codicil hereto otherwise effectively disposed of [(including any entailed or other property over which

I shall have at my death a general power of disposition by will)][1] to my trustees to hold on the trusts set out below with power to sell all or any of it.[2]

(2) My trustees shall pay my funeral and testamentary expenses[3] and debts and any legacies given by this will or any codicil hereto out of such property or its proceeds and shall have a discretion as to how such payments shall be borne as between capital and income.[4]

(3) Subject as above my trustees shall hold such property and the assets from time to time representing the same (hereinafter called 'my residuary estate') on the trusts set out below and shall invest all money comprised in such property or arising from its sale in any of the investments hereby authorised with power to change such investments into any others hereby authorised.[5]

1 Subject to any express contrary intention, property subject to a general power will be carried by a residuary gift under the WA 1837, s 27 (Part G, para **[244.29]**), but in the case of entailed property the will must refer to the property, or the instrument under which it was acquired, or entailed property generally for the statutory power of disposition to be exercised: LPA 1925, s 176(1), (Part G, para **[244.55]**). Although no new entails can be created on or after 1 January 1997 (see para **[200.53]**), entails created before that date can continue to exist and, if they do, the statutory power of disposition of them by will continues to be available.

2 This serves to create a mixed fund of residuary realty and personalty (see para **[214.64]** for the significance of this).

3 Testamentary expenses will include IHT on UK free estate, including real property: IHTA 1984, s 211(1) (Part G, para **[246.100]**; see also the Note to B14 at paras **[214.55]**–**[214.63]**). Accordingly, even if specific gifts or pecuniary legacies are intended to be free of IHT, it will not be necessary to make express provision for the incidence of IHT unless (in the case of a specific gift) the gift is of property of a kind which bears its own tax, or (in the case of a pecuniary legacy) the legacy is payable out of property (usually residue) which includes property of a kind which bears its own tax. The main relevant categories of property bearing its own tax are foreign property and property which is settled property immediately before the testator's death: see the Note to B14 at paras **[214.55]**–**[214.63]** (settled property can be disposed of under a will where it is subject to a general testamentary power of appointment or is entailed—see n 1 above).

4 The rule in *Allhusen v Whittell* (1867) LR 4 Eq 295 (see Vol 1, paras **[38.26]** and **[214.43]**) is now excluded by statute: see para **[214.2A]** and the Trusts (Capital and Income) Act 2013 (para **[246.202]** ff). In its absence there could be a question as to whether income can be used to pay liabilities, and this wording makes it clear that the executors have a discretion in the matter. A direction to pay the liabilities out of capital can have the unsatisfactory consequences referred to at para **[214.44]**.

5 It is no longer necessary to include wording which excludes the rules of equitable apportionment or the Apportionment Act 1870: see para **[214.2A]** and the Trusts (Capital and Income) Act 2013 (para **[246.202]** ff).

[230.9]

[Updated for the Perpetuities and Accumulations Act 2009.]

BENEFICIAL TRUSTS OF RESIDUE

6. (1) My trustees shall hold my residuary estate upon trust for such of my children [*name*] [*name*] and [*name*][1] as shall survive me and if more than one in equal shares.

(2) Provided that if any of my said children shall predecease me leaving issue me surviving who shall attain the age of 18 years[2] such issue shall take and if more than one in equal shares through all degrees according to their stocks the share of my residuary estate which such deceased child of mine

would have taken had he or she survived me and so that no issue shall take whose parent (being such issue as aforesaid) survives me and attains the said age.[3]

(3) The trusts declared by the foregoing sub-clause shall carry the intermediate income of my residuary estate and section 31 of the Trustee Act 1925 (as hereinafter modified) shall apply thereto.

(4) Section 32 of the Trustee Act 1925 (as hereinafter modified) shall apply in relation to the said trusts.

(5) Subject as aforesaid my trustees shall hold my residuary estate and the income thereof upon trust for [such of my nephews and nieces [*name*] [*name*] [*name*] and [*name*]] as shall survive me if more than one in equal shares provided that if any of my said [nephews and nieces] shall predecease me leaving issue me surviving who shall attain the age of 18 years[4] such issue shall take and if more than one in equal shares through all degrees according to their stocks the share of my residuary estate which such deceased [nephew or niece] of mine would have taken had he or she survived me and so that no issue shall take whose parent (being such issue as aforesaid) survives me and attains the said age.[5]

(6) Subject as aforesaid my trustees shall hold my residuary estate and the income thereof upon trust for [such charitable purposes or institutions (whether corporate or not) having exclusively charitable purposes and in such proportions as they think fit].

1 Identifying the children who are intended to take by name will have the effect of excluding any other children, e g illegitimate children, who might otherwise be able to claim an interest.

2 Since the eligible issue are all ascertained at the testator's death, they will necessarily reach the age of 18 within 125 years of the testator's death, which period of 125 years will be the perpetuity period for wills made on or after 6 April 2010, see the PAA 2009, ss 5(1), 15(1)(a) (Part G, paras **[246.179]**, **[246.189]**, and see para **[94.6]**). The vesting age for their interests need not therefore be limited to 18, and could be any other age which they will necessarily attain within 125 years. However, the requirement in relation to all substituted issue that they be living at the testator's death means that where, for example, a child of the testator predeceases him, leaving a child who survives the testator but dies under the vesting age leaving a child of his who was born after the death of the testator, the latter will not take a share. The greater the age of vesting, the greater is the risk of this happening. An alternative which avoids this risk is for there to be no age contingency, so that the shares of the substituted beneficiaries vest absolutely at the testator's death even if they are under the age of 18: see cl 8 of Form C3.7 at para **[225.119]** for an example. If on the other hand it is preferred to take this risk and have an age of vesting greater than 18, then the accumulation and maintenance trusts of income in Trustee Act 1925, s 31 should be extended so far as possible to the vesting age: see cl 4(3) of Form C11.1 at para **[233.19]**.

The IHT consequences are that if there is an age contingency (and there are extended accumulation and maintenance trusts of income where that age is greater than 18), and the testator dies when the substitution clause has taken effect and any substituted beneficiary is under the age of vesting, the IHT relevant property rules (see para **[218.8]** ff) will apply until the age of vesting is reached. If there is no age contingency, the share of any substituted beneficiary who is under 18 at the time of the testator's death will be held on a bare trust for that beneficiary (see para **[200.110]**). The contingent gift to grandchildren cannot take effect as a trust for bereaved minors or an age 18-to-25 trust (see paras **[200.98]** and **[200.99]**).

3 The wording of the substitutional proviso is based on the wording of the statutory trusts contained in the AEA 1925, s 47(1)(i) (Part G, para **[244.63]**). A substitutional proviso which is limited to children may be more appropriate to the testator's family circumstances, in which case Form C4.2, cl 7(2) at para **[226.43]** may be adopted instead.

4 See n 2 above.

5 See n 3 above.

Form C8.2: Will of widow or widower dividing residue between son and daughter, son's share being settled on protective trusts for his benefit and daughter's share being either given to her absolutely or settled on trusts for her benefit

[230.17]

[Updated for the Perpetuities and Accumulations Act 2009.]

As regards the daughter's share this form includes two options. Under the first she takes the share absolutely if surviving with a substitutional proviso for her children (or for her issue generally). Under the second her share is settled on conventional trusts giving her a life interest which would qualify as an IPDI (see Part A, para **[200.98]**), a power to appoint a life interest to a widower, a power of appointment amongst her issue and a default trust for her children (with substitution of issue). A power for the trustees to apply capital for her benefit is also included, and if she has no issue at or after attaining the age of 50 she has a general power to appoint her share by deed. If she dies at any time without issue she has a general testamentary power of appointment.

If this form was used for a will made before 6 April 2010, the testator's son and daughter and other issue living at his death will have been lives in being for the purposes of the common law perpetuity period, so that all the interests would vest, and the powers of appointment and application of capital would necessarily be exercised (if at all) within a permissible perpetuity period. For wills made on or after 6 April 2010 however a mandatory perpetuity period of 125 years applies, see the PAA 2009, ss 5(1), 15(1)(a) (Part G, paras **[246.179], [246.189],** and see para **[94.6]**). Nevertheless, given the 'wait and see' provision of the PAA 2009, s 7 (Part G, para **[246.181]** and see para **[94.17]**), and the practical certainty that the interests will vest and the powers will be exercised (if at all) within 125 years of the testator's death, no perpetuity problem should arise if this form is used in a will made on or after 6 April 2010.

Form C8.3: Will of widow or widower leaving one share of residue on trust for the children absolutely and the other share subjected to immediate post-death interests for the grandchildren

[230.38]

[Updated for the Perpetuities and Accumulations Act 2009.]

SETTLEMENT OF GRANDCHILDREN'S SHARES OF GRANDCHILDREN'S FUND[1]

8. The share of the grandchildren's fund to which any grandchild of mine shall become entitled under the last foregoing clause hereof shall not vest in such grandchild but shall be retained by my trustees and held upon the following trusts:

(1) my trustees shall hold such share (hereinafter called 'the settled share') upon trust to pay the income thereof to such grandchild (hereinafter called 'the primary beneficiary') for life;

(2) if and so long as the primary beneficiary is under the age of 18 years my trustees may pay or otherwise apply for or towards the maintenance education or benefit of the primary beneficiary the whole or

such part or parts of the income of the settled share as my trustees in their absolute discretion think fit and shall retain the balance of such income upon trust for the primary beneficiary absolutely but my trustees may at any time or times while the primary beneficiary is living and under the age of 18 years pay or apply such retained income as if it were income arising in the then current year and section 31 of the Trustee Act 1925 shall not apply to the settled share;[1]

(3) I declare that the purpose and intent of sub-clauses (1) and (2) above of this clause is that the primary beneficiary shall from my death have an interest in possession (within the meaning of Part III of the Inheritance Tax Act 1984) in the settled share during his or her life and even if and while such primary beneficiary is a minor;

(4) subject as aforesaid my trustees shall hold the settled share upon trust for all or any of the children or child of the primary beneficiary and if more than one in equal shares;[2]

(5) the provisions of section 32 of the Trustee Act 1925 (as hereinafter modified) shall apply in relation to the settled share;

(6) notwithstanding the trusts aforesaid so long as the primary beneficiary is entitled to be paid the income of all or any part of the capital of the settled share (or would be so entitled if such capital yielded income)[3] my trustees shall have power in their absolute discretion from time to time to pay transfer or apply the whole or any part or parts of such capital to or for the benefit of the primary beneficiary in such manner as they shall in their absolute discretion think fit[4];

(7) subject as above the settled share (or so much as has not been applied under any of the above powers) shall accrue to the share or shares of the other primary beneficiaries (and if more than one in the proportion which such other shares bear to one another) the trusts of which have not at the date of accruer failed or determined (otherwise than by absolute vesting) and shall form one fund with such other share or shares for all purposes and if there is no such share at the date of such accruer it shall be held upon trust for the estate of the primary beneficiary absolutely.

1 See para **[218.53]** ff for the trusts of accumulations under the TA 1925, s 31 (Part G, para **[246.29]**) which unless varied or excluded are such as usually to give minor beneficiaries a contingent interest in such accumulations, even if they have a vested interest in the income. The purpose of this substitution for s 31 is to cause the income which is not applied for the primary beneficiary's benefit during his minority to be held on trust absolutely for the primary beneficiary, so as to confer an interest in possession for IHT purposes. An infant cannot be paid income to which he is entitled (see Vol 1, para **[9.39]**) but it is thought that he or she has an interest in possession in income if it would form part of his estate if he or she died under the age of 18 (and unmarried and without a civil partner). Such interest in possession will be an IPDI within IHTA 1984, s 49A (see paras **[200.98]** and **[224.24]** ff above).

2 The remainder interests are absolute. This is essentially in the interests of keeping it simple, on the footing that the capital will probably be distributed to the primary beneficiaries during their lifetimes. If this form was used for a will made before 6 April 2010, the primary beneficiary will have been a life in being for the purposes of the common law perpetuity period, so that the interests of his children would necessarily vest within a permissible perpetuity period. For wills made on or after 6 April 2010 however a mandatory perpetuity

period of 125 years applies, see the PAA 2009, ss 5(1), 15(1)(a) (Part G, paras **[246.179]**, **[246.189]**, and see para **[94.6]**). Nevertheless, given the 'wait and see' provision of the PAA 2009, s 7 (Part G, para **[246.181]** and see para **[94.17]**), and the practical certainty that the interests will vest within 125 years of the testator's death, no perpetuity ugproblem should arise if this form is used in a will made on or after 6 April 2010.

3 The reason for restricting the power in this way is to ensure that if the principal beneficiary releases his life interest in favour of the remainderman this power automatically ceases to apply.

4 If this form was used for a will made before 6 April 2010, the primary beneficiary will have been a life in being for the purposes of the common law perpetuity period, so that this power will necessarily have been confined within a permissible perpetuity period. For wills made on or after 6 April 2010 however a mandatory perpetuity period of 125 years applies, see the PAA 2009, ss 5(1), 15(1)(a) (Part G, paras **[246.179]**, **[246.189]**, and see para **[94.6]**). Nevertheless, given the 'wait and see' provision of the PAA 2009, s 7 (Part G, para **[246.181]** and see para **[94.17]**), and the practical certainty that the primary beneficiary will not survive more than 125 years from the testator's death, no perpetuity problem should arise if this form is used in a will made on or after 6 April 2010.

[230.45]

[Updated for the Perpetuities and Accumulations Act 2009 and the change in capital gains tax rate for 2010–2011.]

Form C8.4: Will of grandparent incorporating discretionary trusts of residue for grandchildren

NOTE

Note. This form is primarily for a testator who wishes to benefit not just his grandchildren living at his death, but also grandchildren (and remoter issue) who might be born after his death. The form it takes is a discretionary trust which provides wide flexibility for residue to be utilised for the benefit of the grandchildren (and remoter issue). Discretionary trusts have the advantage that the individual beneficiaries do not automatically become entitled to capital at any age, and can be protected against any tendency they may develop to dissipate capital.

If considered appropriate at the time of the testator's death, appointments could be made from the discretionary trust within two years taking advantage of IHTA 1984, s 144, see paras **[225.83]**–**[225.91]**. For example, absolute interests might be appointed to grandchildren then living who were considered responsible and able to handle capital sums, or perhaps IPDIs might be appointed to living grandchildren to keep part of the residue out of the IHT relevant property regime. However, if it is expected that more grandchildren will be born, at least part of residue could be retained on full discretionary trusts for them.

Residue settled on discretionary trusts will be subject to the IHT relevant property rules (see para **[218.8]** ff). The capital gains tax rate for a discretionary trust is a flat rate (28 per cent for 23 June 2010 to 5 April 2011): TCGA 1992, s 4; see also Part A, paras **[200.39]** and **[200.40]**.

[230.52]

[Updated for the Perpetuities and Accumulations Act 2009.]

DEFINITIONS

6. (1) In this clause the following expressions shall have the following meanings, namely:

(a) 'the discretionary period' shall mean the period beginning immediately after the day of my death and ending with the day before the one hundred and twenty-fifth anniversary of my death[1];

(b) the expression 'the beneficiaries' shall mean my grandchildren and remoter issue Provided that if at any time no grandchild shall be living but a child or children of mine shall be living 'the beneficiaries' shall at that time include my children.[2]

1 For wills made on or after 6 April 2010, the perpetuity period is 125 years (and no other period): see the PAA 2009, ss 5(1), 15(1)(a) (Part G, paras **[246.179]**, **[246.189]**) and see para **[94.6]**. So this form adopts a discretionary period of 125 years. A shorter period could be specified if the testator does not wish the trust to last that long, although the perpetuity period will still be 125 years. It is not necessary to specify, in addition to the specification as to the length of the discretionary period, that the perpetuity period is 125 years: PAA 2009, s 5(2). This contrasts with the situation under the former law where if the common law perpetuity period was not relied upon it was necessary to specify that the perpetuity period was 80 years, or fewer, see the PAA 1964, s 1(1).

2 Since it is assumed that the testator wishes principally to make provision for his grandchildren, they are the prime beneficiaries. But if at any time he should have no grandchildren living, this definition of 'beneficiaries' enables his children to benefit.

[230.55]

[Updated for the Perpetuities and Accumulations Act 2009.]

DISCRETIONARY TRUST OF INCOME AND POWER TO ACCUMULATE

(4) In default of and subject to any exercise of the foregoing powers the income of my residuary estate shall during the discretionary period be held by my trustees on trust to pay or apply the same to or for the benefit of any one or more of the beneficiaries for the time being living as my trustees may in their discretion think fit provided that my trustees shall have power at their absolute discretion to accumulate the whole or any part or parts of such income as an accretion to my residuary estate for all purposes[1].

1 For wills made on or after 6 April 2010, there are no statutory restrictions on accumulation in respect of non-charitable trusts, so accumulation will be permitted throughout the trust period: see the PAA 2009, s 13, 15(1)(a) (Part G, para **[246.187]**, **[246.189]**) and see para **[95.0]**.

[230.62]

Form C8.5: Will of widow leaving her house to a daughter who is looking after her and residue to grandchildren on bare trusts

REVOCATION CLAUSE

I [*name*] of [*address*] hereby revoke all former testamentary dispositions made by me and declare this to be my last will.

[230.65]

[Definition of net proceeds of sale added.]

GIFT OF DWELLINGHOUSE OR ITS VALUE TO DAUGHTER[1]

3. (1) I give my freehold dwellinghouse known as [*address*] or (if it is sold during my lifetime) any other dwellinghouse which I may own at my death and which was purchased for use by me as my principal residence[2] to my said

daughter [*name*] [free of all sums charged thereon or otherwise secured thereon at my death (which sums shall be paid out of my residuary estate)][3] [and] [free of tax].[4]

(2) If the foregoing gift shall fail by reason of the sale during my lifetime of the last dwellinghouse owned by me and used or intended to be used by me as my principal residence then I give to my said daughter free of tax[5] a pecuniary legacy equal in value to the net proceeds (as defined below) of such dwellinghouse.

(3) For the foregoing purpose the net proceeds are the proceeds of sale after deduction of all costs incurred in finding a buyer, negotiating and entering into a contract of sale, and completing the sale, and also after deducting any capital gains tax or other taxes paid by or on behalf of me in consequence of the sale [and after deducting any sums charged on the dwellinghouse and discharged from the proceeds]/[but not deducting any sums charged on the dwellinghouse and discharged from the proceeds].[6]

1 This clause contains a gift not only of the dwellinghouse owned by the testatrix at the date of the will but of any dwellinghouse substituted for it and caters for the possibility of the testatrix having no home, e g because she has gone into a nursing home and has sold her house, by giving the daughter a legacy in lieu.

2 This form of words should ensure that the daughter takes any house purchased as a substitute residence even though it has ceased to be used as such by the testatrix, e g because she has gone into a home.

3 Without these words the gift will be subject to any sums charged on the property at the testator's death: AEA 1925 s 35 (see para **[246.62]**). The testator needs to decide whether or not the gift is subject to any sums charged on the property, and the draftsman needs to make sure that this subclause and the definition of the net proceeds of sale in subclause (3) give effect to the testator's intention.

4 The IHT on land in the UK is a testamentary expense (see B14 at para **[214.55]**) and strictly speaking, these words are only needed if the residence is outside the UK or might be replaced by one which is. If the testator is already living outside the UK there are special factors to consider, such as foreign laws of succession: see further C14 at paras **[236.1]**–**[236.8]**. See Form C8.1, cl 5 at para **[230.8]** incorporated as cl 5 of this form, for the definition of 'free of tax'.

Where there are specific gifts or pecuniary legacies elsewhere in the will which are declared to be 'free of tax', it would be a good idea to include those words here as well, even if the residence is in the UK, to avoid any suggestion that, because of the absence of those words here when they are included elsewhere, this gift is intended to be subject to tax.

5 There are stronger reasons for including these words in relation to a pecuniary legacy than there are for land: see the note to Form C8.1, cl 2 at para **[230.5]**.

6 See footnote 3 above, and delete the first alternative if the gift in subclause (1) is not subject to sums charged on the dwellinghouse, and delete the second alternative if the gift in subclause (1) is subject to such sums.

[230.73]

[Updated for the Perpetuities and Accumulations Act 2009.]

Form C8.6: Will of widow or widower settling residue on trusts for children with progressive powers to pay them capital at different ages

Note. In this form residue is settled in equal shares on the children for life with remainders over in favour of their children, the trustees being given power to apply each child's share for the benefit of such child which is initially fairly restricted but which increases in scope as the child gets older and which finally authorises the application of the entire share. If the testator or testatrix would prefer to include an unrestricted power, Form

C2.2, cl 8(e) (at para **[224.44]**) could be substituted for cl 7(g) of this form. The children's life interests will be IPDIs, see para **[200.98]**.

If this form was used for a will made before 6 April 2010, the testator's children will have been lives in being for the purposes of the common law perpetuity period, so that all the interests would vest, and the powers of appointment and application of capital would necessarily be exercised (if at all) within a permissible perpetuity period. For wills made on or after 6 April 2010 however a mandatory perpetuity period of 125 years applies, see the PAA 2009, ss 5(1), 15(1)(a) (Part G, paras **[246.179]**, **[246.189]**, and see para **[94.6]**). Nevertheless, given the 'wait and see' provision of the PAA 2009, s 7 (Part G, para **[246.181]** and see para **[94.17]**), and the practical certainty that the interests will vest and the powers will be exercised (if at all) within 125 years of the testator's death, no perpetuity problem should arise if this form is used in a will made on or after 6 April 2010.

C9

Wills for members of childless households

PRELIMINARY NOTE

[231.5]

[Updated for the transferable nil-rate band and the reduced rate of IHT on the chargeable part of the estate under IHTA 1984, Sch 33 where sufficient is given to charity.]

Inheritance tax. Members of childless households are less likely to be concerned about IHT saving than testators with children, and the forms in this section contain no devices designed to achieve any saving of IHT apart from some survivorship contingencies (for which see below). Nil-rate band transfer, effective on and from 9 October 2007 (see para **[200.75]**), means that the first to die of a married couple or civil partners making an exempt gift to the survivor of all his or her estate is a sound IHT-minimising strategy in most cases. In cases where it might still be appropriate for a married person or civil partner to make a non-exempt gift so as to make use of their nil-rate band (for which see para **[200.130]**), reference should be made to the Preliminary Note to C3 at paras **[225.1]**–**[225.8]** and Form C5.1, cl 5 at para **[227.14]**. The main IHT-saving step which might be taken in cases of couples who are neither married or in a civil partnership is to provide a discretionary trust of the estate of the first to die. If it is desired to take such an IHT-saving step, see Form C6.2 and the Note thereto at para **[228.19]** ff.

Another IHT-saving opportunity is now provided by IHTA 1984 Sch 1A, inserted by FA 2012, Sch 33, whereby a reduced rate of IHT on the chargeable part of an estate can be obtained where a certain proportion of the estate goes to charity. See para **[200.91A]** ff for the qualifying conditions, and Form B12.2A at para **[212.4A]** for a precedent.

[231.14]

[Updated for the transferable nil-rate band.]

Form C9.2: Reciprocal wills for husband and wife or civil partners, each giving his or her entire estate to the other contingently on surviving him or her by a specified period, and providing in the alternative pecuniary legacies, a specific gift and a gift of residue in favour of the nephews and nieces of both testators in equal or other specified proportions

Note. This form is intended for use by a childless married couple or childless civil partners who wish the survivor to have the entire estate of both, but who each have their own relatives whom they ultimately wish to benefit after the death of both. Nil-rate band transfer, effective on and from 9 October 2007 (see **[200.75]**), means that the first to die of a married couple or civil partners making an exempt gift to the survivor of all his or her estate is a sound IHT-minimising strategy in most cases. In cases where it might still be appropriate for either to make a non-exempt gift so as to make use of their nil-rate band (for which see **[200.130]**), a legacy of an amount equal to the nil- rate band and settled on trusts under which the survivor is eligible to benefit could be used. Form C3.4 (at para **[225.60]**), cl 2 of which contains a legacy of this description, could readily be adapted for use in such a case.

This form divides up the survivor's residue between the two families, while Form C9.3 provides a legacy (on the survivor's death) equal to the value of the first to die's estate in favour of the latter's relatives. For discussion of the relative merits of the two forms see the Preliminary Note at para **[231.2]**. For further points on gifts as in this form, see the Note to Form C5.3 at paras **[227.35]**–**[227.45]**.

This form could also be used for a couple who are not married to each other or not in a civil partnership. The name of the other person should be substituted for 'my [wife/husband/civil partner]' throughout.

[231.22]

[Updated for Trusts (Capital and Income) Act 2013.]

ADMINISTRATION TRUSTS OF RESIDUE

7. (1) I give all my property not hereby or by any codicil hereto otherwise effectively disposed of [(including any entailed or other property over which I shall have at my death a general power of disposition by will)][1] to my trustees to hold on the trusts set out below with power to sell all or any of it.[2]

(2) My trustees shall pay my funeral and testamentary expenses[3] and debts and any legacies given by this will or any codicil hereto out of such property or its proceeds and shall have a discretion as to how such payments shall be borne as between capital and income.[4]

(3) Subject as above my trustees shall hold such property and the assets from time to time representing the same (hereinafter called 'my residuary estate') on the trusts set out below and shall invest all money comprised in such property or arising from its sale in any of the investments hereby authorised with power to change such investments into any others hereby authorised.[5]

1 See para **[230.7]**, n 1.
2 See para **[230.7]**, n 2.
3 See para **[230.7]**, n 3.
4 See para **[230.7]**, n 4.
5 See para **[230.7]**, n 5.

[231.42]

[Updated for the transferable nil-rate band.]

Form C9.4: Reciprocal wills for couple each giving the other a life interest in residue with legacies payable on the death of the survivor and different ultimate trusts of their respective estates

Note. This form deals with the problem outlined in the Preliminary Note of childless couples wishing to provide for each other while ensuring that their respective estates ultimately pass to their own relatives by settling residue on the survivor for life rather than making an outright gift of it. It is drafted for married couples or civil partners but may be adapted for others.

The home will usually be a major item of property owned by the couple; the purpose of putting the residuary estate of the first to die in trust for his or her relatives may be frustrated if his or her interest in the house passes to the other absolutely under a joint tenancy. *It is essential when preparing wills of this type to examine the title to the home carefully to see how it is held*; if it is owned by the testators as joint tenants beneficially the parties must be asked whether they wish the interest in the home of the first of them to die to be settled on trust under his or her will. If so, they must be advised to effect a severance, and, if not, a careful record should be made and retained of their intention that the joint tenancy should continue. Notwithstanding well reported authorities on the point, many cases of negligent will-drafting continue to arise as a result of a failure to take the elementary precaution of ensuring an unwanted joint tenancy is severed.

If a will of this type is being made for a married couple or civil partners who are concerned about the utilisation of the nil-rate band of the first to die, Form C3.2, cl 4 at para **[225.32]**, or Form C3.4, cl 2 at para **[225.60]** could be adapted for the purpose. With the introduction of nil-rate band transfer, effective on and from 9 October 2007 (see para **[200.75]**), this will be less of a concern than it was previously. For cases where it may still be a concern, see para **[200.130]**.

[231.47]

[Updated for the Perpetuities and Accumulations Act 2009.]

BENEFICIAL TRUSTS OF RESIDUE

4. (1) My trustees shall hold my residuary estate upon trust to pay the income thereof to my [wife/husband/civil partner] during [her/his] life[1] [provided that so long as my [wife/husband/civil partner] is entitled to be paid the income of all or any part of the capital of my residuary estate (or would be so entitled if it yielded income)[2] my trustees shall have power from time to time to pay transfer or apply the whole or any part or parts of such capital to or for the support or benefit of my [wife/husband/civil partner] as they shall in their absolute discretion think fit].[3]

(2) Subject to the trust [and to any exercise of the power] aforesaid my trustees shall hold my residuary estate upon trust on the later to occur of my death or the death of my [wife/husband/civil partner] to pay to the following persons [if then living][4] pecuniary legacies free of all inheritance tax and foreign death duties payable on or by reason of my death or the death of my [wife/husband/civil partner][5] (and with interest thereon at the yearly rate of 6 per cent from the later to occur of my death or the death of my [wife/husband/civil partner]) of the amounts hereinafter respectively mentioned namely:

(a) to [*name*] of [*address*] the sum of ——;
(b) to [*name*] of [address] the sum of ——;
(c) to [the Vicar and Churchwardens of the Parish of ——] the sum of £—— for such charitable purposes in the said Parish as they think fit.

(3) Subject as aforesaid my trustees shall hold my residuary estate and the income thereof upon trust for such of my nephews and nieces [*name*] [*name*] [*name*] and [*name*][6] as shall survive me and if more than one in equal shares absolutely provided that if any of my said nephews or nieces shall predecease me leaving a child or children surviving me such child or children shall take and if more than one equally between them the share of my residuary estate which such deceased nephew or niece would have taken had he or she lived to attain a vested interest.[7]

1 The life interest for the survivor will be an IPDI within IHTA 1984, s 49A (see para **[200.98]**), so where the survivor is a surviving spouse or civil partner, exemption from IHT should be available.

2 For the reasons for limiting the power in this way see the Preliminary Note to C2 at paras **[224.17]–[224.19]**.

3 For a provision of this type which limits the amount which can be paid or applied to or for the benefit of the beneficiary see Form C5.2, cl 5(2) at para **[227.27]**. If this form was used for a will made before 6 April 2010, the life tenant will have been a life in being for the purposes of the common law perpetuity period, so that this power will necessarily have been confined within a permissible perpetuity period. For wills made on or after 6 April 2010 however a mandatory perpetuity period of 125 years applies, see the PAA 2009, ss 5(1), 15(1)(a) (Part G, paras **[246.79]**, **[246.189]**, and see para **[94.6]**). Nevertheless, given the 'wait and see' provision of the PAA 2009, s 7 (Part G, para **[246.181]** and see para **[94.17]**), and the practical certainty that the life tenant will not survive more than 125 years from the testator's death, no perpetuity problem should arise if this form is used in a will made on or after 6 April 2010.

4 If the provisions of cl 4(1) fail by reason of divorce or dissolution of civil partnership, the remainder trusts will have effect as if the spouse or civil partner had died on the date of the decree: see the WA 1837, ss 18A, 18C (Part G, para **[244.18]**, **[244.20]**) and the Preliminary Note to C2 at paras **[224.17]**–**[224.19]**. If this contingency is included in a will made on or after 6 April 2010 then there is the risk that these gifts of pecuniary legacies could fail, since they will not necessarily vest within 125 years of the testator's death. However, given the 'wait and see' provision of the PAA 2009, s 7 (Part G, para **[246.181]** and see para **[94.17]**), and the practical certainty that they will so vest, this risk must be very small.

5 If the testator's spouse or civil partner survives the testator, the legacies are likely to be subject to a rateable share of the IHT arising on the spouse's or civil partner's death in the absence of an express direction to the contrary: see *Foster's Inheritance Tax*, K2.03.

6 As to the desirability of identifying nephews and nieces (or other relatives) see the Preliminary Note to this section at para **[231.9]**. The persons named at this point will be different persons in each will, and persons other than nephews and nieces can readily be substituted.

7 Trusts in favour of children other than the testator's own children, e g children of nephews and nieces as here, cannot be trusts for bereaved minors or age 18-to-25 trusts. See the notes to paras **[200.151]** and **[200.152]**. Therefore to avoid property held for such children being within the relevant property regime, the substitutional trust for the children of nephews and nieces does not include any age contingency, and if the trust takes effect it will take effect in favour of minor children absolutely.

C10

Wills for childless individuals

PRELIMINARY NOTE

[232.1]

[Updated for the reduced rate of IHT on the chargeable part of the estate under IHTA 1984, Sch 1A where sufficient is given to charity.]

The forms in this section provide a selection of alternative dispositions for childless individuals. These forms are in many respects similar to those in C7 and C8 for sole parents. One significant difference, however, is that in the case of wills of parents in favour of their own children, the class will necessarily close on the parent's death. In the case of an uncle or aunt, especially one who is relatively young, this is not necessarily so and, unless special provision is made, after-born nephews and nieces may be excluded from benefit. If the estate is substantial and includes landed estates, reference should be made to Form C13.2 at para **[235.18]** ff.

Another difference is that trusts in favour of children other than a testator's own children, cannot be trusts for bereaved minors or age 18-to-25 trusts. See the notes to paras **[200.151]** and **[200.152]**. Therefore if property is to be held on trust for children other than the testator's own, the children will have either IPDIs within IHTA 1984, s 49A (see para **[200.98]**), or the property will be within the IHT relevant property regime.

One tax planning possibility to bear in mind is generation skipping. Gifts direct to the youngest available generation could save significant amounts of IHT in the long run (see Part A, paras **[200.88]** and **[200.91]**). Form C10.1 is an example of a will which gives each sibling's share direct to his or her children if he or she has any at the testator's death.

Another IHT-saving opportunity is now provided by IHTA 1984, Sch 1A, inserted by FA 2012, Sch 33, whereby a reduced rate of IHT on the chargeable part of an estate can be obtained where a certain proportion of the estate goes to charity. See para **[200.91A]** ff for the qualifying conditions, and Form B12.2A at para **[212.4A]** for a precedent.

Where it is desired to assist older generations, particularly where it is desired to benefit the elderly, a discretionary trust could save IHT. Form C10.2 at paras **[232.15]–[232.26]** is an example of this strategy.

[232.2]

Form C10.1: Will of young person dividing his or her estate equally between his or her siblings but making a gift of the share of a sibling with living children direct to such children

[232.7]

[Updated for Trusts (Capital and Income) Act 2013.]

ADMINISTRATION TRUSTS OF RESIDUE

4. (1) I give all my property not hereby or by any codicil hereto otherwise effectively disposed of [(including any entailed or other property over which I shall have at my death a general power of disposition by will)][1] to my trustees to hold on the trusts set out below with power to sell all or any of it.[2]

(2) My trustees shall pay my funeral and testamentary expenses[3] and debts and any legacies given by this will or any codicil hereto out of such property or its proceeds and shall have a discretion as to how such payments shall be borne as between capital and income.[4]

(3) Subject as above my trustees shall hold such property and the assets from time to time representing the same (hereinafter called 'my residuary estate') on the trusts set out below and shall invest all money comprised in such property or arising from its sale in any of the investments hereby authorised with power to change such investments into any others hereby authorised.[5]

1 See para **[230.7]**, n 1.
2 See para **[230.7]**, n 2.
3 See para **[230.7]**, n 3.
4 See para **[230.7]**, n 4.
5 See para **[230.7]**, n 5.

Form C10.2: Will of young person creating discretionary trust of residue for his or her parents and brothers and sisters and their issue

[232.22]

[Updated for the Perpetuities and Accumulations Act 2009.]

DISCRETIONARY TRUSTS OF RESIDUE

6. (1) My trustees shall hold my residuary estate and the income thereof upon the trusts and with and subject to the powers and provisions hereinafter declared and contained.

(2) In this clause the following expressions have the following meanings, namely:

(a) 'the residuary beneficiaries' means and includes:[1]

(i) my parents [*name*] and [*name*] [and my grandparents [*names of surviving grandparents*]];

(ii) my brothers and sisters [*name*] [*name*] [*name*] [*name*] and [*name*] and their respective children and remoter issue;

(iii) any spouse civil partner widow widower or surviving civil partner of any of my said brothers and sisters or their respective children or remoter issue (including any widow widower or surviving civil partner who has married or formed a civil partnership);

(b) 'the trust period' means the period commencing on the day of my death and expiring on the one hundred and twenty-fifth anniversary thereof; [2]

(3) Subject as hereinafter provided my trustees (being not fewer than two in number or being a trust corporation)[3] may at any time or times and from time to time during the trust period (and whether before or after the grant of probate and regardless of whether the administration of my estate is complete) exercise either or both of the following powers namely:

(a) power at any time or times and from time to time by deed or deeds revocable or irrevocable to appoint the whole or any part or parts of my residuary estate upon trust for all or such one or more exclusive of the others or other of the residuary beneficiaries if more than one in such shares and either absolutely or at such age or time or respective ages or times and with such trusts and powers for their respective benefit and such provisions as my trustees think fit and in making any such appointment my trustees shall have powers as full as those which they would possess if they were an absolute beneficial owner of my residuary estate and in particular (but without prejudice to the generality of the foregoing words) my trustees may in any exercise of the foregoing power:

   (i) delegate give or impose to or upon themselves or any other person or persons any discretionary powers or discretionary trusts conditions limitations restrictions or provisions including powers of further delegation or powers of further creation of discretionary trusts or powers;

   (ii) create powers or trusts for the accumulation of income during any period permitted by law;

   (iii) create administrative powers or provisions of whatever nature;

   Provided that:

   (i) no such appointment shall invalidate any payment transfer or application of capital or income previously made under any of the trusts or powers herein elsewhere contained;

   (ii) every interest limited under any exercise of such power shall vest in interest (if at all) not later than the expiration of the trust period;

   (iii) any such appointment may be made in respect of income alone without any appointment of capital; and

   (iv) any such revocable appointment shall (so far as then unrevoked) cease to be revocable on the expiration of the trust period;

(b) power (subject to any or every exercise of the foregoing power) at any time or times and from time to time in their absolute discretion to pay transfer or apply my residuary estate or any part or parts thereof to or for the benefit of all or any one or more exclusive of the others or other of the residuary beneficiaries for the time being in existence if more than one in such shares and generally in such manner as my trustees think fit.

(4) In default of and subject to any or every exercise of the foregoing powers my trustees shall hold my residuary estate during the trust period upon trust to pay or apply the income thereof to or for the maintenance education or benefit of all or any one or more of the residuary beneficiaries and if more than one in such shares and in such manner generally as my trustees think fit provided that my trustees may accumulate all or any part or parts of such income by investing the same and the resulting income thereof in any investments hereby authorised and so that any accumulations so made shall form part of the capital of my residuary estate (or the part thereof from which such income arose) for all purposes[4].

(5) Subject as aforesaid my trustees shall hold my residuary estate and the income thereof at the expiration of the trust period upon trust for such of the residuary beneficiaries as shall be then living in equal shares per capita.

(6) Any capital or income of my residuary estate not otherwise disposed of by this clause shall be held in trust for such of my brothers and sisters as shall survive me and if more than one in equal shares.

1 For an alternative definition, including power to add people to the class, see Form C3.6, cl 3(1)(b) at para **[225.100]** or Form C6.2, cl 7(1)(a) and (3)(c) at para **[228.28]**.

2 For wills made on or after 6 April 2010, the perpetuity period is 125 years (and no other period): see the PAA 2009, ss 5(1), 15(1)(a) (Part G, paras **[246.179]**, **[246.189]**) and see para **[94.6]**. So this form adopts a trust period of 125 years. It is not necessary to specify, in addition to the specification as to the length of the trust period, that the perpetuity period is 125 years, see the PAA 2009, s 5(2). This contrasts with the situation under the former law where if the common law perpetuity period was not relied upon it was necessary to specify that the perpetuity period was 80 years, or fewer, see PAA 1964, s 1(1).

3 For more elaborate provisions permitting the exercise of powers by a sole trustee during the two-year period following the death see Form C4.1, cl 8 at para **[226.25]**, see also the Note to this form at para **[232.15]**.

4 For wills made on or after 6 April 2010, there are no statutory restrictions on accumulation in respect of non-charitable trusts, so accumulation will be permitted throughout the trust period: see the PAA 2009, s 13, 15(1)(a) (Part G, para **[246.187]**, **[246.189]**) and see para **[95.0]**.

Form C10.4: Will of older childless person settling residue in equal shares on brothers and sisters (or nephews and nieces) for life with remainders for their children

[232.39]

[Updated for the Perpetuities and Accumulations Act 2009.]

Note. This form is a variant of the preceding form and differs in that the interests of the brothers and sisters (or nephews and nieces) are settled on them for life with power (if desired) to advance the capital of each beneficiary's share to or for the benefit of such beneficiary. The life interests should qualify as IPDIs (see para **[200.98]** above). If any of the brothers and sisters (or nephews and nieces) have children an element of generation skipping might be considered appropriate, in which case Form C10.1 at paras **[232.4]**–**[232.14]** could be used or adapted.

If this form was used for a will made before 6 April 2010, the testator's brothers and sisters (or nephews and nieces) living at his death will have been lives in being for the purposes of the common law perpetuity period, so that all the interests would vest, and the powers of appointment and application of capital would necessarily be exercised (if at all) within a permissible perpetuity period. For wills made on or after 6 April 2010 however a mandatory perpetuity period of 125 years applies, see the PAA 2009, ss 5(1), 15(1)(a) (Part G, paras **[246.179]**, **[246.189]**, and see para **[94.6]**). Nevertheless, given the 'wait and see' provision of the PAA 2009, s 7 (Part G, para **[246.181]** and see para **[94.17]**), and the practical certainty that the interests will vest and the powers will be exercised (if at all) within 125 years of the testator's death, no perpetuity problem should arise if this form is used in a will made on or after 6 April 2010.

Form C10.5: Will of unmarried childless person in favour of unmarried sister for life with remainders over to brothers and sisters or their issue

[232.58]

[Updated for the Perpetuities and Accumulations Act 2009.]

BENEFICIAL TRUSTS OF RESIDUE

6. (1) My trustees shall hold my residuary estate upon trust to pay the income thereof to my said sister [*name of unmarried sister*] during her life[1] [provided that my trustees (being not fewer than two in number or being a trust corporation) may at any time or times and from time to time during the life of my said sister pay transfer or apply the capital of the whole or any part or parts of my residuary estate to or for the support or benefit of my said sister in such manner as they think fit].[2]

(2) Subject as aforesaid my trustees shall hold my residuary estate and the income thereof upon trust in equal shares for such of my brothers and sisters [*name*] [*name*] and [*name*][3] as shall be living at the later to occur of my death and the death of my said sister [*name of unmarried sister given the life interest under subclause* (*1*)] ('the vesting date')[4] and the issue living at the vesting date of such of my said brothers and sisters as shall be dead at the vesting date such issue to take if more than one in equal shares per stirpes the share which such deceased brother or sister of mine would have taken had he or she lived to attain a vested interest and so that no issue shall take whose parent lives to attain a vested interest.[5]

(3) The foregoing trusts shall carry the intermediate income of such share and section 31 of the Trustee Act 1925 (as hereinafter modified) shall apply thereto.

(4) Section 32 of the Trustee Act 1925 (as hereinafter modified) shall apply in relation to the foregoing trusts.

1 This life interest will be an IPDI within IHTA 1984, s 49A (see para **[200.98]**).

2 For a power of this type which is limited to being exercisable only over part of the capital see Form C5.1, cl 9(2) at para **[227.13]**. If this form was used for a will made before 6 April 2010, the life tenant will have been a life in being for the purposes of the common law perpetuity period, so that this power will necessarily have been confined within a permissible perpetuity period. For wills made on or after 6 April 2010 however a mandatory perpetuity period of 125 years applies, see the PAA 2009, ss 5(1), 15(1)(a) (Part G, paras **[246.179]**, **[246.189]** and see para **[94.6]**). Nevertheless, given the 'wait and see' provision of the PAA 2009, s 7 (Part G, para **[246.181]** and see para **[94.17]**), and the practical certainty that the life tenant will not survive more than 125 years from the testator's death, no perpetuity problem should arise if this form is used in a will made on or after 6 April 2010.

3 The names here will not include the unmarried sister who gets a life interest under the preceding subclause.

4 If this form was used for a will made before 6 April 2010, the testator's sister will have been a life in being for the purposes of the common law perpetuity period, so that the vesting date would necessarily be within a permissible perpetuity period. For wills made on or after 6 April 2010 however, a mandatory perpetuity period of 125 years applies, see the PAA

2009, ss 5(1), 15(1)(a) (Part G, paras **[246.179]**, **[246.189]**, and see para **[94.6]**). Nevertheless, given the 'wait and see' provision of the PAA 2009, s 7 (Part G, para **[246.181]** and see para **[94.17]**), and the practical certainty that the vesting date will be within 125 years of the testator's death, no perpetuity problem should arise if this form is used in a will made on or after 6 April 2010.

5 It is assumed that the unmarried sister who is given a life interest has no children. If she did have any children this clause would need modifying to enable them to be capable of benefiting under it. Trusts in favour of children other than the testator's own children cannot be trusts for bereaved minors or age 18-to-25 trusts. See the notes to paras **[200.107]** and **[200.108]**. Therefore to avoid property held for such children being within the IHT relevant property regime, the substitutional trust for issue does not include any age contingency, and if the trust takes effect it will take effect in favour of minor children absolutely.

Form C10.6: Will of childless individual giving charitable and other legacies, with a specific gift of a house and residue given on trust for nephews and nieces for life with remainders for their children

[232.73]

[Updated for the Perpetuities and Accumulations Act 2009.]

SETTLEMENT OF SHARES

9. The share of my residuary estate to which any nephew or niece of mine shall become entitled under the last foregoing clause hereof shall not vest in such nephew or niece absolutely but shall be retained by my trustees and held upon the trusts following namely (such nephew or niece hereinafter being referred to as 'the beneficiary'):

(a) my trustees shall hold such share upon trust to pay the income thereof to the beneficiary during his or her life [provided that if and so long as the beneficiary is under the age of 18 years my trustees may pay or otherwise apply for or towards the maintenance education or benefit of the beneficiary the whole or such part or parts of the income of such share as my trustees in their absolute discretion think fit and shall retain the balance of such income upon trust for the beneficiary absolutely but my trustees may at any time or times while the beneficiary is living and under the age of 18 years pay or apply such retained income as if it were income arising in the then current year and section 31 of the Trustee Act 1925 shall not apply to the settled share][1];

(b) provided that my trustees shall have power in their absolute discretion from time to time during the beneficiary's life and before the vesting day to pay transfer or apply the whole or any part or parts of such share to him or for his benefit in such manner as they shall in their absolute discretion think fit;

(c) subject as aforesaid the beneficiary shall have power at any time before the vesting day by deed or deeds revocable or irrevocable or by will or codicil to appoint to any spouse [or civil partner] who may survive him or her as his or her widow or widower [or surviving civil partner] in the event of his or her death before the vesting day (including power to appoint to a named spouse [or civil partner] contingently on such named spouse [or civil partner] surviving him or her as his or her widow or widower [or surviving civil partner] in such event) an interest in the income of the whole or any part or parts of such share for the residue of such spouse's [or civil partner's] life or for any less period;[2]

(d) subject as aforesaid if the beneficiary shall die before the vesting day my trustees shall hold such share upon trust as to both capital and income for all or such one or more exclusively of the others or other of the children and remoter issue of the beneficiary at such time or times and if more than one in such shares and with such trusts powers and provisions (including trusts and powers conferring on any person or persons a discretion as to the disposition of capital or income or provisions for the accumulation of income during any period permitted by law or administrative powers of whatever description) as the beneficiary shall before the vesting day by deed or deeds revocable or irrevocable or by will or codicil appoint;

(e) subject as aforesaid my trustees shall hold such share upon trust as to both capital and income for all or any the children or child of the beneficiary born before the vesting day and if more than one in equal shares [provided that no child of the beneficiary who or whose issue shall take any part of such share by virtue of any appointment under the foregoing power shall be entitled to participate in the unappointed part of such share without bringing the part so appointed into hotchpot and accounting for the same accordingly (except to the extent that there is a contrary direction in such appointment)];

(f) the trust declared by paragraph (e) above shall carry the intermediate income of such share and section 31 of the Trustee Act 1925 (as hereinafter modified) shall apply thereto;

(g) section 32 of the Trustee Act 1925 (as hereinafter modified) shall apply in relation to such share;

(h) subject as aforesaid if the beneficiary shall die before the vesting day my trustees shall hold such share upon trust as to both capital and income for such persons or purposes as the beneficiary shall by will or codicil appoint and subject to any such appointment;

(i) subject as aforesaid my trustees shall hold such share upon trust for the next of kin of the beneficiary living at his or her death or the earlier occurrence of the vesting day ascertained as if the beneficiary had died intestate without having married;

(j) in this clause 'the vesting day' means whichever of the following days shall be the earlier:

 (i) the day on which shall expire 21 years less three days after the death of the last survivor of such of my said nephews and nieces as shall be living at my death; and

 (ii) the day on which shall expire 125 years less three days after my death[3].

1 This proviso must be included if any of the beneficiaries may be minors at the time of the testator's death, and if it is intended that their life interests should qualify as IPDIs. This is because unless TA 1925, s 31 (Part G, para **[246.29]**) is excluded, as here, or varied, it will give minor beneficiaries with a life interest only a contingent interest in accumulations made under TA 1925, s 31. The purpose of this substitution for s 31 is to cause the income which is not applied for the beneficiary's benefit during his minority to be held on trust absolutely for the beneficiary, so as to confer an interest in possession for IHT purposes. A minor cannot be paid income to which he is entitled (see Vol 1, para **[9.39]**) but it is thought that he

or she has an interest in possession in income if it would form part of his estate if he or she died under the age of 18 (and unmarried and without a civil partner). Such interest in possession will be an IPDI within IHTA 1984, s 49A (see paras **[200.98]** and **[224.24]** ff above).

2 A life interest for a spouse or civil partner appointed in exercise of this power will not (after 21 March 2006) enable IHT exemption for gifts to a spouse or civil partner to be claimed in relation to the share, but it may still be desired that a beneficiary should have the ability to make this provision for a spouse or civil partner.

3 For wills made on or after 6 April 2010, the perpetuity period is 125 years (and no other period): see the PAA 2009, ss 5(1), 15(1)(a) (Part G, paras **[246.179]**, **[246.189]**) and see para **[94.6]**. So this form limits the vesting day to a day within that period.

C11

Wills disposing of business property

Allocation of business and agricultural relief between the exempt and non-exempt parts of an estate

[233.6]

[Updated in sub-para (1) for *Re Nelson Dance Family Settlement* [2009] STC 802.]

What is a specific gift for the purposes of the Inheritance Tax Act 1984, s 39A. As stated above, a testator's estate will get maximum benefit from business relief or agricultural relief if there is a specific gift to a non-exempt beneficiary *of* 'relevant business property' (ie property qualifying for business relief) or *of* 'agricultural property' (see para **[234.2]** for the meaning of this expression). 'Specific gift' is defined in IHTA 1984, s 42(1) (which applies to s 39A, among other sections of the Act) to mean any gift other than a gift of residue or a share of residue, but this does not determine what is a specific gift *of* a particular kind of property. The only other provision with any relevance to its meaning is s 39A(6) mentioned at para **[233.4]**—gifts payable out of business or agricultural property are not for the purposes of s 39A specific gifts of that property.

It is our view that a specific gift will only qualify as a specific gift of relevant business property or agricultural property for the purposes of IHTA 1984, s 39A(2) if the property comprised in the gift and going to the beneficiary, considered in isolation from the rest of the estate, is relevant business property or agricultural property. If this is correct, the following points should be noted—

(1) When a business is carried on by the testator as sole proprietor and the business as a whole qualifies for business relief on his death as 'a business' (see B5 at para **[205.22]**), a specific gift of an individual asset of that business by itself will on this view not be a specific gift of relevant business property (see B5 at para **[205.23]** for the distinction between a business and individual business assets). Whether business relief is available in respect of a business on a testator's death depends on the circumstances immediately before his death, not on the dispositions made by his will, and so it is thought that the business relief attributable to this individual asset comprised in a specific gift will not be lost completely in a case such as this, but will be divided rateably between the exempt and non-exempt parts of the estate instead of being concentrated on the specific gift. There is a question whether the decision of the High Court in *Re Nelson Dance Family Settlement*

[2009] STC 802, that a lifetime gift of an individual asset used in a business carried on immediately before the gift was made could qualify for business relief, has any relevance to the interpretation of IHTA 1984, s 39A(2). The reasoning in *Nelson Dance* is based very much on the definition of a transfer of value as being the diminution in the value of the transferor's estate, and there is considerable doubt as to whether it has any relevance to the meaning of 'specific gifts of relevant business property' in s 39A(2). In the absence of encouragement from the courts or HMRC to believe otherwise, it should be assumed that a specific gift by will of an individual asset of a business will not be a specific gift of relevant business property.

(2) A similar point would arise in relation to a specific gift of a farm building or farm house, where the farm land itself was the subject of another gift. As stated in the Preliminary Note to C12 at paras **[234.2]** and **[234.3]**, buildings and farmhouses only qualify as agricultural property if they are combined with agricultural land and are of a character appropriate to it: IHTA 1984, s 115(2). Again, it is thought that a farm house or building given by a specific gift which did not also include the farm land would still qualify for agricultural relief on the testator's death, but that the relief attributable to the farmhouse would be apportioned rateably between the non-exempt and exempt parts of the estate because the house by itself is not 'agricultural property' for the purposes of IHTA 1984, s 39A(2).

(3) In the rare cases of controlling holdings of unquoted voting securities qualifying for 100 per cent business relief or controlling holdings of quoted shares or securities qualifying for 50 per cent business relief (IHTA 1984, ss 104(1) and 105(1)(b) and (cc)), the type of problem described above does not seem to arise where, for example, a testator makes a specific gift of part only of his holding. Shares or securities in either category qualify for the relief even if they do not by themselves give control, provided that they contribute to the testator's control of the company together with other shares or securities owned by him: see IHTA 1984, s 105(1)(b) and (cc).

(4) There is also a question as to whether a gift of relevant business property or agricultural property to one person, subject to a testamentary option for another to purchase it, is a specific gift of that property for the purposes of IHTA 1984, s 39A. It might be argued that it is not a gift of such property to the person to whom the primary gift is made, because he may end up with cash instead of the property, and that the option holder is not the recipient of a *gift* of such property (or not wholly—it depends on the price) and anyway might not exercise the option and receive the business (or agricultural) property. Such an arrangement is at its most provocative to HMRC where the property entitled to relief is given to a non-exempt beneficiary subject to an option given to the testator's spouse or civil partner to purchase it. However, whether or not it is an exempt beneficiary who is given the option is not strictly relevant to the legal merits of the argument. The attitude of HMRC to this point is not known, and in the absence of a clear indication that HMRC accept such arrangements as specific gifts

of the business or agricultural property within IHTA 1984, s 39A(2) they are better avoided if possible; see para **[233.7]** for alternatives.

Non-exempt gifts on the death of the first to die (of spouses or civil partners) and business or agricultural property

[233.10A]

[New paragraph added.]

IHTA 1984 s 144 (two-year discretionary trusts) and business or agricultural property—the importance of it being a specific gift. This is something to bear in mind in wills of spouses or civil partners or any other dispositions where there may be partial exemption and business or agricultural relief. If it is intended to have discretionary trusts to take advantage of IHTA 1984 s 144 (see **[225.83]** ff), any business or agricultural property should be the subject of a specific gift on to discretionary trusts, and not be part of a residuary gift on to discretionary trusts. This is because under IHTA 1984 s 39A (see para **[233.2]** ff), in a partially exempt estate, the full amount of the business or agricultural relief only attaches to the business or agricultural property if there is a specific gift of it. Section 144 cannot be used to make business or agricultural assets in residue the deemed subject-matter of a deemed specific gift taking effect on the death of the testator, where what is desired is that those assets continue to be held long-term on discretionary or other relevant property trusts. Section 144 only applies where property loses its relevant property status.

Where there are liabilities which financed business or agricultural property

[233.12A]

[New paragraph re liabilities and FA 2013 Sch 36.]

Liabilities incurred on or after 6 April 2013 which financed business (or agricultural) property. As mentioned in para **[205.10A]**, IHTA 1984, s 162B (inserted by FA 2013, Sch 36) provides that any liability incurred on or after 6 April 2013 which is attributable to financing, directly or indirectly, the acquisition, maintenance, or enhancement of the value of, business property or agricultural property (and qualifying for IHT business or agricultural relief) must be deducted first from the property it financed before determining the amount of IHT business or agricultural relief. This is so even if the liability is charged on property other than the business or agricultural property. Where a pre-6 April 2013 liability which financed business or agricultural property is refinanced by new borrowing on or after that date which is used to pay off the previous loan, it is likely that the new borrowing will fall within s 162B. The significance of this for will drafting is that if the testator has any liabilities falling into this category, and wishes to make a non-exempt specific gift of the relevant business or agricultural property, s 162B needs to be taken into account in estimating the IHT consequences of the intended pattern of disposition. It may be that, for example, the liability as well as the IHT payable as a result of the liability not being deductible from unrelieved assets would be too much to throw onto residue, and that, for example, the specific gift should be burdened with the liability.

Form C11.1: Will settling private company shares entitled to business relief and optional 'top up' legacy on a nil-rate band discretionary trust, with residue given to wife with alternative gift to issue

[233.14]

[Cross-reference to the new para [233.10A] added].

One further point about creating a discretionary trust of this sort in cases where the testator's spouse survives the testator is that if the shares do turn out to be subject to more IHT than expected the liability can be reduced by making an appointment falling within IHTA 1984, s 144 (see C3 at para **[225.83]** ff) of some or all of the shares to the surviving spouse within two years of the testator's death, so as to increase the amount of the testator's estate to which the exemption for gifts to spouses applies. For a particular advantage of this type of disposition over including the business assets in a discretionary trust of residue see **[233.10A]**. A further feature of this form, (at para **[233.17]**, cl 2(1)(b)), is an optional 'top up' legacy, for use where the circumstances are such that it is appropriate to make use of the testator's nil-rate band as well as the business relief, if the testator's spouse survives the testator and the taxable value of the shares is less than the amount of nil-rate band available on the testator's death (see para **[233.9]** for the circumstances where this may be appropriate). For further discussion of this type of disposition see the Preliminary Note at para **[233.9]** and the Note on nil-rate band discretionary trusts in B18 at para **[218.16]** ff. The legacy is defined by a formula so as to be the maximum which can be given without an IHT charge arising on the testator's death. It is intended to ensure that the amount of the discretionary trust fund does not exceed the IHT threshold where other non-exempt gifts are made by the will, or where there are non-exempt lifetime chargeable transfers or other property treated as part of the testator's estate which have to be taken into account in determining the IHT charge on the testator's estate on death. However, in view of the presence of business relief it may be necessary or appropriate to impose an upper cash limit on the gift to prevent the entire estate going into the discretionary trust: see the Preliminary Note at para **[233.9]** and the words in square brackets in cl 2(1)(b) of this form at para **[233.17]** which are commented on in n 4 to that paragraph.

[233.17]

[Updated for Perpetuities and Accumulations Act 2009.]

GIFT OF SHARES AND NIL-RATE BAND LEGACY ON DISCRETIONARY TRUSTS[1]

2.

EITHER

(1) [If my wife shall survive me and the trust for her of my residuary estate hereinafter contained shall take effect][2] I give to my trustees all the [25p] ordinary shares in [Will Williams & Company Limited] (hereinafter called 'the company') which I shall own at my death subject to payment thereout of any IHT payable by reason of my death which is attributable thereto (after allowing for any reduction in value for inheritance tax purposes which is attributed thereto).[3]

OR

(1) [If my wife shall survive me and the trust for her of my residuary estate hereinafter contained shall take effect][4] I give to my trustees the following—

(a) all the [25p] ordinary shares in [Will Williams & Company Limited] (hereinafter called 'the company') which I shall own at my death subject to payment thereout of any IHT payable by reason of my death which is attributable thereto (after allowing for any reduction in value for inheritance tax purposes which is attributed thereto);[5] and

(b) the maximum sum (if any) [not exceeding £—][6] which can in the circumstances subsisting at my death be given by virtue of this subclause (b) without any liability being incurred for the payment of inheritance tax on or by reason of my death; and in particular (without prejudice to the generality of the foregoing) for the purpose of determining the amount of such maximum sum the circumstances to be taken into account shall include all chargeable transfers made by me during my life (or events treated as such for inheritance tax purposes) so far as relevant for the computation of inheritance tax on my death the dispositions taking effect under this will (apart from this subclause) or under any codicil hereto and any property treated as if it were part of my estate for inheritance tax purposes[7] [and furthermore in determining the foregoing maximum sum it shall be assumed that the nil-rate band maximum (within the meaning of Section 8A of the Inheritance Tax Act 1984) at the time of my death will be treated as increased for the purposes of the charge to inheritance tax on my death by any amount by which it would be treated as increased if a claim was made under that section and I direct my Trustees to make such a claim][8] [provided that the foregoing gift of a sum of money contained in this subclause (b) shall not have effect if my wife shall predecease me or the trust for her of my residuary estate hereinafter contained shall fail for any other reason].[9]

(2) In this clause the following expressions have the following meanings namely:

(a) 'the relevant beneficiaries' means and includes my wife my children and remoter descendants (whether living at my death or born thereafter) and the spouses civil partners widows widowers and former civil partners (including those who have entered into a subsequent marriage or civil partnership) of my children and remoter descendants;[10]

(b) 'the trust period' means the period of 125 years less three days commencing on the date of my death;[11]

(3) My trustees may at their absolute discretion sell or retain the said shares for as long as they think fit and shall invest [the said legacy (if any) and][12] the proceeds of sale of the said shares when and if sold in any investments hereby authorised with power to vary the same and shall hold the said shares [and the said legacy][13] and the assets from time to time representing the same (hereinafter called 'the trust fund') and the income thereof upon the trusts and with and subject to the powers and provisions hereinafter declared and contained.

(4) My trustees shall hold the trust fund and the income thereof upon trust for all or such one or more of the relevant beneficiaries at such ages or times in such shares and upon such trusts for the benefit of the relevant beneficiaries as my trustees (being at least two in number or a trust corporation) may by deed or deeds revocable or irrevocable executed at any

time or times during the trust period appoint and in making any such appointment my trustees shall have powers as full as those which they would possess if they were an absolute beneficial owner of the trust fund and in particular (but without prejudice to the generality of the foregoing words) my trustees may in any exercise of the foregoing power as they in their absolute discretion think fit:

(a) delegate give or impose to or upon themselves or any other person or persons and in relation to any trust or disposition any discretionary powers or discretionary trusts including powers of further delegation or powers to create further discretionary trusts or powers;[14]

(b) create trusts or powers for the accumulation of income;

(c) create administrative powers or provisions of whatever nature;

Provided that:

(i) no such appointment shall invalidate any payment transfer or application of capital or income previously made under any of the trusts or powers herein elsewhere contained;

(ii) every interest limited under any exercise of such power shall vest in interest (if at all) not later than the expiration of the trust period;

(iii) any such appointment may be made in respect of income alone without any appointment of capital; and

(iv) any such revocable appointment shall (so far as then unrevoked) cease to be revocable at the expiration of the trust period.

(5) In default of and subject to any exercise of the foregoing power my trustees (being at least two in number or a trust corporation) may at their discretion at any time or times during the trust period pay transfer or apply the whole or any part or parts of the trust fund to or for the benefit of all or any one or more exclusive of the others or other of the relevant beneficiaries for the time being living if more than one in such shares and generally in such manner as my trustees shall think fit.[15]

(6) Subject to any or every exercise of the foregoing powers my trustees shall during the trust period hold the trust fund upon trust to pay or apply the income thereof to or for the maintenance education or benefit of all or any one or more of the relevant beneficiaries for the time being living in such shares if more than one and generally in such manner as they think fit provided that my trustees may during the trust period accumulate[16] the whole or any part of the income of the trust fund by investing the same and the resulting income thereof in any of the investments hereby authorised and any accumulations of income so made shall form part of the capital of the trust fund (or the part thereof from which such income arose) for all purposes.

(7) Subject to the foregoing trust and to any or every exercise of the foregoing powers my trustees shall hold the trust fund and the income thereof at the expiration of the trust period in trust absolutely for such of my descendants as shall then be living in equal shares per stirpes.

(8) Any capital or income of the trust fund not otherwise disposed of by this clause shall be held in trust for such of my children as shall survive me if more than one in equal shares absolutely.[17]

1 See the Note to this form at paras **[233.13]** and **[233.14]**.

2 Where the main or only objective of the discretionary trust is to make use of the business relief on the shares and the testator's nil-rate band if the testator's spouse survives the testator and becomes entitled to the residuary estate (see the Note to this form at para **[233.13]**), it is appropriate to impose this precondition. However, where an objective of the discretionary trust is to keep the holding together irrespective of whether the spouse becomes entitled to residue (see the Note to this form at para **[233.13]**), these words should be omitted.

3 Making the gift subject to IHT will, in the event of the testator's spouse surviving the testator and the gift of the shares giving rise to an IHT charge (see B5 at para **[205.51]** for possible reasons why this should happen), cause the size of the chargeable estate to be less than it would be if the gift was free of IHT: see B14 at para **[214.74]**. Without these words the gift of the shares will be free of IHT if they are located in the UK: see B14 at para **[214.55]** ff.

Where this gift is to take effect even if the testator's spouse does not survive the testator (see the last preceding note), it may be preferable for this gift to be free of IHT in those circumstances, which can be achieved by making the direction that the gift is subject to tax contingent on the spouse surviving the testator and becoming entitled to the residuary estate.

This first alternative version of sub-cl (1) is for use where the top up additional legacy is not wanted.

4 See n 2 above. If these words are omitted, the proviso to sub-cl (1)(b) should be included (see n 9 below).

5 See the first two paragraphs of n 3 above. This second alternative version of sub-cl (1) is for use where the top up additional legacy is wanted. See para **[200.130]** for the circumstances where such provision is still worth making despite nil-rate band carry-forward.

6 If the shares given by sub-cl (a) are entitled to 100 per cent business relief (see B5 at para **[205.29]** ff for 100 per cent relief on shares), and the testator has made no lifetime gifts within the seven years preceding his death, and there is no property outside his free estate which is taxable as part of his estate on his death, this legacy will be equal at least to the nil-rate band. Further, for reasons given in the Preliminary Note at para **[233.9]**, if there are other assets of the estate qualifying for business or agricultural relief then the cash legacy could exceed the nil-rate band or even, in an extreme case, use up the entire estate. In either case the testator might prefer to limit the amount of this legacy, as in these words in square brackets, so that his spouse gets some assets absolutely under the gift of residue.

However, the spouse is not excluded from benefit where the trusts of the legacy are, as in this form, discretionary trusts under which the spouse is a beneficiary. If the testator does not mind the possibility that the benefit to his spouse under the will might be solely that of being an object of a discretionary trust, he can take maximum advantage of the IHT reliefs if no upper limit is imposed on the legacy. It is much more important to impose an upper limit of this kind where the trusts of the legacy are such that the spouse is excluded from benefit, as in Form C11.2, cl 2 at para **[233.29]**.

7 See the Preliminary Note at para **[233.9]** and the Note to this form at para **[233.14]**.

8 These words should be included where the testator potentially has an increased nil-rate band on death under the nil-rate band carry-forward rules (see para **[200.75]**) by reason of a previous marriage or civil partnership which ended in the death of the other party, and where the other party did not make full use of his or her nil-rate band in the dispositions taking effect on his or her death. Persons in this situation have a particularly strong IHT-planning reason for providing a nil-rate band discretionary trust in their wills to take effect in the event of their being survived by the current spouse or civil partner: see para **[200.130]**.

9 See n 4 above. This proviso should be included if the condition as to the wife's survival is omitted from the opening words of this alternative sub-cl (1) so that the discretionary trust of the shares takes effect even if the spouse predeceases the testator (for reasons given in the Note to this form at para **[233.13]**, sub-para (3)).

10 The definition of the discretionary class may need to be enlarged or adapted in individual cases. For wider classes, and power to add to the class of beneficiaries, see Form C3.6. cl 3(1)(b) at para **[225.100]**, Form C4.1, cl 8(2)(a) at para **[226.26]**, Form C6.2, cls 7(1)(a), (2) and (3)(c) at para **[228.28]**.
11 For the perpetuity period for wills made on or after 6 April 2010, which no longer needs to be declared by the trust instrument, see para **[200.35A]** ff.
12 These words in square brackets should be omitted if the first alternative sub-cl (1) is adopted.
13 See n 11 above.
14 These words authorise the creation of discretionary trusts and powers which otherwise might not be within the scope of the power: see Vol 1, para **[40.5]**.
15 A power to apply capital, being exercisable in a less formal manner, may be useful. But it is essential that its exercise should be adequately evidenced.
16 For accumulation of income under wills made on or after 6 April 2010 see para **[200.35E]**.
17 If it may be necessary to resort to an appropriation of part of a principal private residence, or a debt or charge scheme, to satisfy the top up legacy then separate trustees of the legacy should be provided as in Form C5.1, cl 5, at para **[227.14]**, and the appropriate administrative powers added as in sub-cll (8)–(11) of that clause.

[233.18]

[Updated for Trusts (Capital and Income) Act 2013.]

ADMINISTRATION TRUSTS OF RESIDUE

3. (1) I give all my property not hereby or by any codicil hereto otherwise effectively disposed of [(including any entailed or other property over which I shall have at my death a general power of disposition by will)][1] to my trustees to hold on the trusts set out below with power to sell all or any of it.[2]

(2) My trustees shall pay my funeral and testamentary expenses[3] and debts and any legacies given by this will or any codicil hereto out of such property or its proceeds and shall have a discretion as to how such payments shall be borne as between capital and income.[4]

(3) Subject as above my trustees shall hold such property and the assets from time to time representing the same (hereinafter called 'my residuary estate') on the trusts set out below and shall invest all money comprised in such property or arising from its sale in any of the investments hereby authorised with power to change such investments into any others hereby authorised.[5]

1 See para **[230.7]**, n 1.
2 See para **[230.7]**, n 2.
3 See para **[230.7]**, n 3.
4 See para **[230.7]**, n 4.
5 See para **[230.7]**, n 5.

[233.19]

[Updated for Perpetuities and Accumulations Act 2009.]

BENEFICIAL TRUSTS OF RESIDUE

4. (1) My trustees shall hold my residuary estate upon trust for my wife absolutely if she shall survive me.

(2) If my wife shall predecease me my trustees shall hold my residuary estate upon trust for such of my children [by my wife][1] as shall survive me if more than one in equal shares[2] provided that if any of my children [by my wife][3] shall predecease me leaving a child or children surviving me who shall

attain the age of [18/21/25/30] years such last-mentioned child or children shall take if more than one the share of my residuary estate which such deceased child of mine would have taken had he or she survived me.[4]

(3) The foregoing trusts for grandchildren of mine shall carry the intermediate income of my residuary estate and section 31 of the Trustee Act 1925 (as hereinafter modified) shall apply thereto [as if the age of majority were the age of [21/25/30][5] years (so that the expressions 'infancy', 'minority' and 'infant' and all references to the age of eighteen years in the said Section 31 shall be construed accordingly)].[6]

(4) Section 32 of the Trustee Act 1925 (as hereinafter modified) shall apply in relation to my residuary estate.

1 These words are for inclusion where the testator has children other than children of the marriage who are not intended to benefit. An alternative, for where there will not be any more children of the marriage, is to make the gift to named children. See further the Preliminary Note to C2 on reciprocal wills and the ultimate destination of property at para **[224.13]** ff. For forms for use where one spouse has children who are not children of the marriage and wishes to benefit them by his or her will see C5 at para **[227.1]** ff.

2 It is assumed that the children are all adult and so there is no age contingency.

3 To be included if the trust is confined to the children of the marriage. See n 1 above.

4 The substitutional gift to grandchildren, if it takes effect and a grandchild is under the age of vesting at the testator's death, will fall within the IHT relevant property regime (for which see para **[218.8]** ff). If the age of vesting is greater than 18, the extended accumulation and maintenance trusts of income clause 5(1)(c) will make sure that the trust will fall within the relevant property rules whatever the age of a substituted grandchild if under the age of vesting at the testator's death, avoiding the possibility of the trust operating as an IPDI trust in the event of a substituted grandchild having attained the age of 18 but not the age of vesting of capital at the testator's death (see para **[224.25]**). The alternative possibility is to provide for substituted minor grandchildren to have interests in possession during their minorities so that the trust operates as an IPDI one: for such a provision see for example Form C2.1, second alternative cl 8(1), at para **[224.36]**.

5 This should be the same as the age of vesting in sub-cl (2).

6 This proviso is for inclusion if the age of vesting in sub-cl (2) is greater than 18. See n 4 above. See para **[200.35F]** for extended accumulation provisions in wills made on or after 6 April 2010 and so falling within PAA 2009. They are no longer confined to the period of 21 years from the testator's death.

Form C11.2: Reciprocal wills for husband and wife who have recently acquired share capital of private trading company, the first to die making a direct gift of the shares to the children and otherwise leaving estate to the survivor

[233.29]

[Updated for Perpetuities and Accumulations Act 2009.]

GIFT TO CHILDREN OF PRIVATE COMPANY SHARES[1]

2. (1) In this clause 'the relevant shares' means the [25p] ordinary shares in [Will Williams & Company Limited] owned by me at the date of this my will.

(2) If my [wife/husband] shall survive me[2] and if by the time of my death I shall have owned the relevant shares for a continuous period of two years[3] then I give [all]/[100][4] of the relevant shares subject to payment thereout of any inheritance tax payable by reason of my death which is attributable

thereto (after allowing for any reduction in value for inheritance tax purposes which is attributed thereto)[5] to my trustees to hold the same on the trusts set out below.

(3) My trustees may at their absolute discretion sell or retain the said shares for as long as they think fit and shall invest the proceeds of sale of the said shares when and if sold in any investments hereby authorised with power to vary the same and shall hold the said shares and the assets from time to time representing the same (hereinafter called 'the trust fund') and the income thereof upon the trusts and with and subject to the powers and provisions hereinafter declared and contained.

(4) My trustees shall hold the trust fund and the income thereof upon trust for such of my children [*name*] [*name*] and [*name*][6] as shall survive me and if more than one in equal shares provided that if any of my said children shall predecease me leaving a child or children surviving me who shall attain the age of [18/21/25/30] years[7] such last-mentioned child or children shall take and if more than one equally between them the share of the trust fund which such deceased child of mine would have taken had he or she survived me.

(5) The foregoing trusts for grandchildren of mine shall carry the intermediate income of the trust fund and section 31 of the Trustee Act 1925 (as hereinafter modified) shall apply thereto [as if the age of majority were the age of [21/25/30][8] years (so that the expressions 'infancy', 'minority' and 'infant' and all references to the age of eighteen years in the said Section 31 shall be construed accordingly)].[9]

(6) Section 32 of the Trustee Act 1925 (as hereinafter modified) shall apply in relation to the trust fund.

1 See the Note above, for the importance of reviewing the terms of this gift if more of the same shares are acquired, or there is any relevant change in the company or its share capital. It may be preferred to have a discretionary trust of the property given by this clause, such as in Form C11.1, cl 2 at para **[233.17]**. It might also be desired to have a top up nil-rate band pecuniary legacy as in the second alternative sub-cl (1) of that clause.

2 The objective of this gift is to make use of the business relief on the shares if the testator's spouse survives the testator (see the Note to this form at para **[233.26]**), and this precondition is imposed to avoid unnecessary duplication of gifts (ie this one and the residuary gift) in the event of the spouse not surviving the testator. If the residuary gift to the spouse fails through divorce, there will be such duplication, but the trusts taking effect will be the same.

3 If the shares do not qualify for business relief by the time of the testator's death it is better for them to pass to the surviving spouse under the exempt residuary gift in the hope that the combined period of ownership of the testator and surviving spouse (taken into account together under IHTA 1984, s 108) will be sufficient for business relief to apply on the death of the spouse.

4 Delete one alternative, and if 'all' is deleted, amend the number of shares as appropriate. It is a matter for decision how much of the holding should be the subject of a non-exempt gift on the first death, and how much of it should go to the surviving spouse, depending on factors such as whether the shares may be entitled to business relief in the hands of the surviving spouse, what other resources the surviving spouse will have, and whether he or she will be working for the company (see also para **[233.11]**). If there is business or agricultural relief applicable which depends on control of the company (see paras **[205.5]**, **[205.6]** and **[234.6]** for the categories of relief depending on control) and the spouses between them have control of it, that will favour giving sufficient to the surviving spouse for him or her to maintain control.

5 Making the gift subject to IHT will, in the event of the gift of the shares giving rise to an IHT charge (see B5 at para **[205.51]** for possible reasons why this should happen), cause the

size of the chargeable estate to be less than it would be if the gift was free of IHT: see B14 at para **[214.74]**. Without these words the gift of the shares will be free of IHT if they are located in the UK: see B14 at para **[214.59]**.

6 See the Preliminary Note to C2 on reciprocal wills and the ultimate destination of property at paras **[224.13]–[224.15]**.

7 See Form C11.1, cl 4(2), n 4 at para **[233.19]**.

8 This should be the same as the age of vesting in sub-cl (4).

9 See Form C11.1, cl 4(3), n 6 at para **[233.19]**.

[233.31]

[Updated for Perpetuities and Accumulations Act 2009.]

BENEFICIAL TRUSTS OF RESIDUE

4. (1) My trustees shall hold my residuary estate upon trust for my [wife/husband] absolutely if [she/he] shall survive me.

(2) If my [wife/husband] shall predecease me my trustees shall hold my residuary estate upon trust for such of my children [*name*] [*name*] and [*name*][1] as shall survive me if more than one in equal shares provided that if any of my said children shall predecease me leaving a child or children surviving me who shall attain the age of [18/21/25/30][2] years such last-mentioned child or children shall take if more than one the share of my residuary estate which such deceased child of mine would have taken had he or she survived me.

(3) The foregoing trusts for grandchildren of mine shall carry the intermediate income of my residuary estate and section 31 of the Trustee Act 1925 (as hereinafter modified) shall apply thereto [as if the age of majority were the age of [21/25/30][3] years (so that the expressions 'infancy', 'minority' and 'infant' and all references to the age of eighteen years in the said Section 31 shall be construed accordingly)].[4]

(4) Section 32 of the Trustee Act 1925 (as hereinafter modified) shall apply in relation to my residuary estate.

1 See the Preliminary Note to C2 on reciprocal wills and the ultimate destination of property at paras **[224.13]–[224.15]**.

2 See Form C11.1, cl 4(2), n 4 at para **[233.19]**.

3 This should be the same as the age of vesting in sub-cl (2).

4 See Form C11.1, cl 4(3), n 6 at para **[233.19]**.

Form C11.3: Will giving business carried on as sole trader or in partnership to sons, and legacies to daughters, with residue to wife for life with remainder to children with substitution clause and hotchpot of specific gifts

[233.45]

[Updated for Perpetuities and Accumulations Act 2009.]

BENEFICIAL TRUSTS OF RESIDUE

7. (1) My trustees shall hold my residuary estate upon trust to pay the income thereof to my wife during her life.[1]

(2) Provided that my trustees shall have power in their absolute discretion from time to time so long as my wife is entitled to be paid the income of all or any part of the capital of my residuary estate (or would be so entitled if such capital yielded income) to pay transfer or apply the whole or any part

or parts of such capital[2] to her or for her benefit in such manner as they shall in their absolute discretion think fit.

(3) Subject as aforesaid my trustees shall hold my residuary estate upon such trusts for the benefit of all or such one or more exclusive of the others or other of my children and remoter issue if more than one in such shares and with such trusts and powers for their respective benefit (including trusts and powers conferring a discretion as to the disposition of capital and income by whomsoever exercisable) and such provisions (including provisions for the accumulation of income during any period permitted by law and administrative provisions of whatever nature) as my trustees may during the life of my wife by any deed revocable during the life of my wife or irrevocable appoint provided that my trustees may at any time or times and from time to time during the life of my wife by deed or deeds release or restrict the foregoing power either in whole or in part and in any manner they think fit.[3]

(4) Subject as aforesaid my trustees shall hold my residuary estate upon trust for such of my children [*name*] [*name*] [*name*] and [*name*] as shall survive me if more than one in the shares set out below Provided that if any of my said children shall predecease me leaving a child or children surviving me who shall attain the age of [18/21/25/30] years[4] such last-mentioned child or children shall take and if more than one equally between them the share of my residuary estate which such deceased child of mine would have taken had he or she survived me.

(5) The shares referred to in the last foregoing subclause shall be equal shares provided that—

(a) any child of mine who is or has been entitled to a gift under clause 2 or 3 above shall bring the same into hotchpot as part of his or her share (net of inheritance tax) of my residuary estate and account for the same accordingly;[5]

(b) the value or amount of any gift brought into hotchpot as aforesaid shall be the net value or amount thereof (after deduction of any inheritance tax or other liabilities to which it is subject) at my death[6] and for this purpose my trustees may as soon as practical after my death (whether or not my wife's foregoing life interest takes effect) at the expense of my residuary estate obtain a professional valuation of whatever is taken by either of my said sons under clause 2 above and any such valuation shall be binding on all parties;[7] and

(c) for the avoidance of doubt I declare that if any gift to a child of mine directed to be brought into hotchpot as aforesaid exceeds the value of what would be that child's share if the property comprised in such gift formed part of my residuary estate then he or she shall not be under any obligation to make any repayment or transfer of any part of such gift to my residuary estate or to the other persons interested in my residuary estate and my residuary estate shall be divided among the other persons interested as if that child of mine was not entitled to a share thereof.[8]

(6) The foregoing trusts for grandchildren of mine shall carry the intermediate income of my residuary estate and section 31 of the Trustee Act 1925 (as hereinafter modified) shall apply thereto [as if the age of majority were

the age of [21/25/30][9] years (so that the expressions 'infancy', 'minority' and 'infant' and all references to the age of eighteen years in the said Section 31 shall be construed accordingly)].[10]

(7) Section 32 of the Trustee Act 1925 (as hereinafter modified) shall apply in relation to my residuary estate.

1 The gift of residue to the testator's spouse for life is an IPDI to which the spouse exemption can apply (see paras **[200.84]**, **[200.98]**).

2 There are two reasons for restricting the power to capital in which the wife has an interest in possession: first, to ensure that the power is not exercisable if there is a divorce and the primary trust lapses (see the Preliminary Note to C2 on the possibility of divorce at paras **[224.16]**–**[224.23]**); and, second, to ensure that the power ceases to be exercisable if the wife assigns or surrenders her life interest (for an example of the possible importance of the latter point see *IRC v Cookson* [1977] 2 All ER 331, [1977] 1 WLR 962). For the reasons for not expressly restricting exercise of the power to the perpetuity period of 125 years under PAA 2009 see para **[200.35B]**.

3 This enables account to be taken of events occurring during the widow's life, such as the death of children of the testator, high inflation, or a major increase in the value of the business given to the sons. See cl 8 at para **[233.46]** for an expression of wishes as to how this power should be exercised, and the Note at para **[233.36]**. For the reasons for not expressly restricting exercise of the power to the perpetuity period of 125 years under PAA 2009 see para **[200.35B]**.

4 See Form C11.1, cl 4(2), n 4 at para **[233.19]**.

5 It should be noted that the specific gifts do not have substitution clauses, and the testator's children's interests vest on the testator's death both under the specific gifts and the trusts of residue, so that these hotchpot provisions do not need to refer to the position of substituted beneficiaries. There is no hotchpot of interests appointed under the power of appointment.

6 This could clearly be very unfair, particularly if the testator's wife's life interest has taken effect and there has been significant inflation since the testator's death. However, it is not practical to make provision for all the things which might happen between the testator's and the wife's death; instead the arrangements can be varied by exercise of the power of appointment if the trustees can agree during the testator's widow's lifetime on how they should be varied.

7 It is not advisable to provide for the value to be that agreed with the Inland Revenue for probate purposes because if the business property given by cl 2 is subject to 100 per cent business relief, or it is not but the gifts in cls 2 and 3 are clearly within the testator's nil-rate band, the Inland Revenue will not wish to engage in negotiations over the value.

8 This is implicit in a direction for hotchpot, but this is not always readily appreciated and it can save disappointment and argument if it is spelt out expressly.

9 This should be the same as the age of vesting in sub-cl (4).

10 See Form C11.1, cl 4(3), n 6 at para **[233.19]** above.

C12

Wills disposing of farms and farming businesses

PRELIMINARY NOTE

IHT agricultural relief

[234.2]

[Updated for FA 2009, s 122.]

Meaning of agricultural property. This is defined by IHTA 1984, s 115(2) as agricultural land or pasture and as including woodland and any building used in connection with the intensive rearing of livestock or fish if such woodland or building is occupied with agricultural land or pasture and such occupation is ancillary to that of the land or pasture; the definition also includes such cottages, farm buildings and farmhouses and land occupied with them as are of a character appropriate to the property. Other assets which are included expressly or as a matter of Revenue practice are stud farms (IHTA 1984, s 115(4)), milk quota when given or devolving on death with the land, ponds, land used for short-rotation coppice (IHTA 1984, as amended by Finance Act 1995, s 145), set aside land, and land in a wildlife habitat scheme (IHTA 1984, as amended by the Finance Act 1997, s 124C). It used to be the case that in order to qualify for relief, agricultural property must be situated in the UK, the Channel Islands or the Isle of Man (IHTA 1984, s 115(5)). However, this restriction has turned out to be a breach of EU, EEC, and EEA law, and FA 2009, s 122 amends IHTA 1984, s 115(5) so as to make agricultural relief available in relation to agricultural property outside the UK which is in the European Economic Area (EEA) at the time of the event giving rise to an IHT charge, retrospectively to 23 April 2003 as well as for the future. The EEA currently consists of the members of the EU plus Norway, Iceland, and Liechtenstein. Where the property is outside the UK, Channel Islands and Isle of Man, the agricultural value qualifying for the relief is that which the property would have if it were subject to provisions equivalent in effect to a perpetual covenant confining its use to agriculture (IHTA 1984, s 115(3) as amended by FA 2009, s 122(2)).

[234.3]

[Updated for *Atkinson v HMRC* [2012] STC 289 and *Hanson v HMRC* [2012] UKFTT 95 (TC), [2012] SFTD 705.]

The inclusion of houses and buildings. The Interpretation Act 1978 defines 'land' to include buildings so far as no contrary intention is expressed, and it applies to IHTA 1984. However, it has been held that the express reference in the IHTA 1984, s 115(2) to cottages, farm buildings and farmhouses of a character appropriate to the property excludes the general definition from applying, so that a house used for agricultural purposes but not owned together with agricultural land did not qualify for relief. The appropriate principles for determining whether a farmhouse is of a character appropriate to the agricultural property were summarised as follows:

'… first, one should consider whether the house is appropriate by reference to its size, content and layout, with the farm buildings and the particular area of farmland being farmed …; secondly, one should consider whether the house is proportionate in size and nature to the requirements of the farming activities conducted on the agricultural land or pasture in question …; thirdly that although one cannot describe a farmhouse which satisfies the "character appropriate" test one knows one when one sees it …; fourthly, one should ask whether the educated rural layman would regard the property as a house with land or a farm …; and, finally, one should consider the historical dimension and ask how long the house in question has been associated with the agricultural property and whether there was a history of agricultural production …' (see *Lloyds TSB (personal representatives of Antrobus decd) v IRC* [2002] STC (SCD) 468 at para 48)

The inclusion of farmhouses is an important aspect of the relief; it enables a farmhouse which was occupied by the deceased (or by the transferor in the case of a lifetime transfer) as his residence to qualify for agricultural relief when it could never qualify for business relief, and such a house can represent a significant part of the value of agricultural property. Particularly in the case of substantial houses, it is important to consider the nature of the building in the context of the agricultural property generally. In *Arnander v Customs and Excise Comrs* [2006] STC (SCD) 800 the Special Commissioner held that a seven bedroom Grade 2* listed manor house, owned together with 110 acres of agricultural land failed to attract relief on three grounds: it was not a 'farmhouse', nor 'of a character appropriate to the farmland', nor was it 'occupied for the purposes of agriculture' because the owners had employed a contractor to farm for them because they were too ill to do so themselves.

The following points should be borne in mind:

(1) Severance of the agricultural land from the house, eg by making a lifetime gift of the farmland without the house, is to be avoided where possible because it will cause the relief to cease to be available in relation to the house. It has been held by the Upper Tribunal in *Hanson v HMRC* [2013] UKUT 224 (TCC), affirming [2012] UKFTT 95 (TC), [2012] SFTD 705 that a farmhouse can qualify as agricultural property if it is in the same occupation as agricultural land in relation to which it satisfies the 'character appropriate' test, even though that agricultural land was not in the deceased's ownership at his death.
(2) If the amount of agricultural land is perhaps on the low side in relation to the house for the house to qualify for the relief, buying some extra adjacent land could be a worthwhile investment (it would still have to be occupied for two years or owned for seven years before it counted—see below).

(3) When it comes to making a will, a non-exempt gift of the farmhouse and an exempt gift of the farmland is not a good idea because the house by itself is not agricultural property—a non-exempt gift of the land and an exempt gift of the house would be better, and a non-exempt gift of both even better (from an IHT point of view). See the Preliminary Note to C11 at paras **[233.2]–[233.6]**.

(4) The farmhouse will not qualify for the relief unless it is occupied by someone engaged in agriculture for the required period (see para **[234.4]**). In *Harrold v IRC* [1996] STC (SCD) 195, the Special Commissioners held that the relief did not apply to a farmhouse which was unoccupied and awaiting renovation. A similar problem arises where the farmer has retired, as in *Arnander v HMRC* [2006] STC (SCD) 800. In *HMRC v Atkinson* [2012] STC 289 reversing [2012] UKFTT 95 (TC), [2010] UKFTT 108 (TC) the tax Tribunals had to consider a case where the farm was owned by the deceased and let to a family partnership in which he was a partner. The farm included a bungalow in which the deceased had lived in until he became ill some four years before his death. The rest of his life was spent initially in a hospital and later in a care home. Throughout the deceased's illness and until his death no one lived in the bungalow which remained furnished and contained his belongings. He visited the bungalow from time to time, participated in decisions about the farming business, and remained one of the partners until his death. It was held by the Upper Tribunal, reversing the decision of the First-tier Tribunal, that the bungalow was not occupied for the purposes of agriculture by the time of the deceased's death, and had not been for four years, ie from when it ceased to be possible for the deceased to return to live in the bungalow.

(5) The relief is restricted to the agricultural value (see para **[234.7]**). Houses which are restricted to agricultural use (for planning purposes) often sell at a discount from the value they would have without the restriction. HMRC have taken to arguing that part of the value of any farmhouse which is not so restricted, typically a third of its value, is not entitled to the relief. They had a victory on this point in *Lloyds TSB Private Banking Plc v Peter Twiddy (Inland Revenue Capital Taxes)*, Lands Tribunal 10/10/2005, where the Lands Tribunal held that the agricultural value qualifying for agricultural relief of a farmhouse was 30 per cent below market value because it was an historic building in an attractive location which had the effect of uplifting its market value beyond what it would be if restricted to occupation for agriculture.

[234.9]

[Cross reference to the new para [233.10A] added.]

Agricultural relief and partially exempt estates. Like business relief, agricultural relief operates so as to reduce the value transferred by the transfer on death before exemptions are taken into account. Section 39A of the IHTA 1984, introduced by Finance Act 1986, s 105, applies where there is agricultural relief on assets comprised in a partially exempt estate (see the Preliminary Note to C11 at paras **[233.2]–[233.7]**). Accordingly, where a farmer owning qualifying agricultural property wishes to make provision for a wife and children, he would be well-advised to consider making a specific gift of agricultural property to the children and the balance of the estate to the spouse. This is likely to be considerably cheaper in fiscal terms than the other way round: see the Preliminary Note to C11 at paras **[233.6]–[233.10]**. If he wants to leave his agricultural property on discretionary trusts, with a view to the executors deciding on the most advantageous course of action in the two years following his death in reliance on IHTA 1984, s 144, he should still make a specific gift of it onto discretionary trusts, rather than including it in a residuary gift on discretionary trusts, for the reason given in para **[233.10A]**. On the other hand, as mentioned at para **[234.5]**, if agricultural property does not qualify for relief because it has not been owned or occupied by the transferor for either of the periods mentioned in the IHTA 1984, s 117, a gift of the property to the testator's spouse could enable the spouse to take advantage of the testator's period of ownership or occupation.

Other aspects

[234.13A]

[New paragraph concerning FA 2013, Sch 36.]

Liabilities. IHTA 1984, s 162B (inserted by FA 2013, Sch 36) provides that any liability incurred on or after 6 April 2013 which is attributable to financing, directly or indirectly, the acquisition, maintenance, or enhancement of the value of, business property or agricultural property (and qualifying for IHT business or agricultural relief) must be deducted first from the property it financed before determining the amount of IHT business or agricultural relief. See, further, paras **[205.10A]** and **[233.12A]**.

[234.14]

[Updated for FA 2009, s 122 and FA 2013, Sch 36.]

Woodlands. Woodlands which are not ancillary to agricultural land and which do not therefore qualify for agricultural relief may qualify for the separate relief which is available under the IHTA 1984, Part V, Chapter III for woodlands which have been beneficially owned for five years or acquired by gift: see generally *Foster's Inheritance Tax*, G4. The relief takes the form of a deferment of the charge to IHT on death until the woodlands are sold or given away by inter vivos transfer other than to the donor's spouse. This relief resembles the conditional exemption for works of art etc under the IHTA 1984, ss 30–34 but it is not strictly an exemption within the meaning of the Act, but a right to elect to have the woodlands left out of account in determining the chargeable transfer made on death: see ss 126(1)(a) and 130(1)(a). Since anyone who inherits woodlands which qualify for this relief will himself be qualified for the relief on his death however soon it may occur (see s 125(1)), there are less strong reasons than in the case of business assets or agricultural property for testators avoiding gifts of woodlands which qualify for relief to their spouses. It is advisable for specific gifts of woodlands to be made subject to IHT attributable thereto and payable on the testator's death for the reasons given in B14 at para **[214.67]**. It used to be the case that in order to qualify for the relief, woodlands must be situated in the UK (IHTA 1984, s 125(1)(a)). However, this restriction has turned out to be a breach of EU, EEC, and EEA law, and FA 2009, s 122 contains provision for non-agricultural woodlands relief to be available in relation to land outside the UK which is in the EEA (see para **[234.2]** for this) retrospectively to 23 April 2003 as well as for the future. IHTA 1984, s 162B (inserted by FA 2013, Sch 36) provides that any liability incurred on or after 6 April 2013 which is attributable to financing, directly or indirectly, the acquisition, planting, maintenance, or enhancement of the value of, woodland (and qualifying for IHT woodlands relief) must be deducted first from the value of the woodland it financed before determining the amount of the IHT relief. For the restrictions on deducting liabilities incurred to finance business or agricultural property which have the same essential elements as this restriction, see paras **[205.10A]** and **[233.12A]**.

[234.17]

Form C12.1: Will of widower giving estate equally between his children, one son being given an option to purchase the farming assets

[234.22]

[Updated for Trusts (Capital and Income) Act 2013.]

ADMINISTRATION TRUSTS OF RESIDUE

4. (1) I give all my property not hereby or by any codicil hereto otherwise effectively disposed of [(including any entailed or other property over which I shall have at my death a general power of disposition by will)][1] to my trustees to hold on the trusts set out below with power to sell all or any of it.[2]

(2) My trustees shall pay my funeral and testamentary expenses[3] and debts and any legacies given by this will or any codicil hereto out of such property or its proceeds and shall have a discretion as to how such payments shall be borne as between capital and income.[4]

(3) Subject as above my trustees shall hold such property and the assets from time to time representing the same (hereinafter called 'my residuary estate') on the trusts set out below and shall invest all money comprised in such property or arising from its sale in any of the investments hereby authorised with power to change such investments into any others hereby authorised.[5]

1 See n 1 to cl 4 of Form C8.1 at para **[230.7]**.
2 See n 2 to cl 4 of Form C8.1 at para **[230.7]**.
3 See n 3 to cl 4 of Form C8.1 at para **[230.7]**.
4 See n 4 to cl 4 of Form C8.1 at para **[230.7]**.
5 See n 5 to cl 4 of Form C8.1 at para **[230.7]**.

[234.24]

[Updated for Perpetuities and Accumulations Act 2009.]

BENEFICIAL TRUSTS OF RESIDUE

6. (1) My trustees shall hold my residuary estate upon trust for such of my children AB CD and EF as shall survive me and if more than one in equal shares.

(2) Provided that if any of my said children shall fail to attain a vested interest under the foregoing trust and there are issue of such child of mine living at or after my death who shall attain the age of [18/21/25] years[1] such issue shall take through all degrees according to their stocks in equal shares if more than one the share of my residuary estate which such child of mine would have taken had he or she attained a vested interest and so that no issue shall take whose parent (being issue of such child of mine) attains a vested interest.[2]

(3) The trusts declared by the foregoing subclause shall carry the intermediate income of my residuary estate and section 31 of the Trustee Act 1925 (as hereinafter modified) shall apply thereto [as if the age of majority were the age of [21/25][3] years (so that the expressions 'infancy', 'minority' and 'infant' and all references to the age of eighteen years in the said Section 31 shall be construed accordingly)].[4]

(4) Section 32 of the Trustee Act 1925 (as hereinafter modified) shall apply in relation to the said trusts.

1 One of these ages should be selected. The IHT consequences are that if there is an age contingency (and there are extended accumulation and maintenance trusts of income where that age is greater than 18), and the testator dies when the substitution clause has taken effect and any substituted beneficiary is under the age of vesting, the IHT relevant property rules (see para **[218.8]** ff) will apply until the age of vesting is reached. If there is no age contingency, the share of any substituted beneficiary who is under 18 at the time of the testator's death will be held on a bare trust for that beneficiary (see para **[200.110]**). The contingent gift to grandchildren cannot take effect as a trust for bereaved minors or an age 18-to-25 trust (see paras **[200.98]**, **[200.99]**). If the accumulation and maintenance trusts of Trustee Act 1925, s 31 stand unmodified, but vesting is contingent on attaining an age greater than 18, and a substituted beneficiary is over the age of 18 and under the vesting age at the death of the testator, he will be entitled to an IPDI (see para **[200.98]**).

2 The wording of the substitutional proviso is partly based on the wording of the statutory trusts contained in the AEA 1925, s 47(1)(i) (Part G, para **[244.63]**). A substitutional proviso which is limited to children may be more appropriate to the testator's family circumstances in which case cl 7(2) of Form C4.3 at para **[226.65]** may be adopted instead.

3 This should be the same as the age of vesting in sub-cl (2).

4 This part in square brackets is for inclusion if the age of vesting in sub-cl (2) is greater than 18. See n 1 above. See para **[200.35F]** for extended accumulation provisions in wills made on or after 6 April 2010 and so falling within PAA 2009.

[234.31]

Form C12.2: Will of farmer leaving legacies to his daughters, a right of residence in a farm cottage to his wife, and residue to his son if farming at his death, with residue given to the children in equal shares if he is not

[234.36]

[Updated for Perpetuities and Accumulations Act 2009.]

PECUNIARY LEGACIES FOR DAUGHTERS

4. (1) If the gift of the whole of my residuary estate in favour of my son set out below shall take effect I give to each of my said daughters who shall survive me free of tax[1] the sum of [£50,000].

(2) Provided that if either of my said daughters shall predecease me leaving a child or children surviving me who shall attain the age of 18 years[2] such last-mentioned child or children shall take and if more than one equally between them the legacy which such deceased daughter of mine would have taken had she survived me.

(3) My trustees shall have power to assent to the vesting of the assets comprised in my residuary estate (as defined below) in my son before the foregoing legacies are paid or satisfied in full or at all and whether or not they have so assented my trustees may agree with my son any terms they think fit for deferment of the payment of the said legacies for up to [10] years from my death and my trustees may accept any security they think fit (or no security at all)[3] shall not be obliged to require interest to be paid at a full market rate or at all on any outstanding legacies and shall not be liable for any default of AB or any other adverse consequences of leaving payment of such legacies outstanding.[4]

1 The pecuniary legacies are declared to be 'free of tax' in case the residuary estate out of which they are payable includes property of a kind which bears its own tax, such as foreign property or settled property, with the consequence that without this express provision the legacies might, at least to some extent, have to bear their own tax. See B14 at paras **[214.55]–[214.60]**. The definition of 'free of tax' will be in cl 6 of this form. There is no IHT advantage in making the legacies subject to tax because residue is not exempt (contrast cl 4 of Form C11.3 at para **[233.42]**).

2 If the age of vesting is greater than 18 years, there is more risk of a grandchild dying after the death of the testator under the age of vesting and leaving children who do not benefit. If on the other hand it is preferred to have an age of vesting greater than 18, then the accumulation and maintenance trusts of income in Trustee Act 1925, s 31 should be extended to the vesting age: see cl 4(3) of Form C11.1 at para **[233.19]**. For the IHT consequences see Form C12.1, cl 6, n 1, at para **[234.24]**.

3 If the legacies are charged on the agricultural assets it will reduce the agricultural relief in the event of the son's death: see para **[234.10]**.

4 These powers are conferred expressly in case there are minors interested in one or both of the legacies or the daughters may not be willing to leave the legacies outstanding unless obliged to do so. If the farmland is subjected to a charge to secure the payment of the legacies in regular instalments over a fixed period there is a risk that this will cause the farmland to be settled property for IHT purposes (IHTA 1984, s 43(2)(c)) and that, if no interest is paid on the legacies, it might be argued that the son then has an interest in possession in the entire property which is partially terminated on the payment of any instalment of the legacies (see Part A, para **[200.102]** for the IHT consequences of the termination of an interest in possession). It will be better either to have a personal covenant, or a charge for payment of a single sum on a particular date.

C13

Wills for owners of substantial property

PRELIMINARY NOTE

[235.2]

Form C13.1: Will of owner of substantial property with no immediate family containing specific gift of controlling shareholding in family company on trusts for the employees and leaving residue on charitable trusts

[235.7]

[Updated for the Perpetuities and Accumulations Act 2009.]

GIFT OF COMPANY SHARES TO SEPARATE TRUSTEES ON EMPLOYEE TRUSTS

4. (1) I give free of tax[1] to [*name*] [and] [*name*] [and [*name*]][2] all my shares in my family company known as [*name of company*][3] to hold on the trusts and with and subject to the powers and provisions hereinafter declared and contained.

(2) In this clause the following expressions have the following meanings—

(a) 'the company' means the said [*name of company*];

(b) 'the company fund trustees' means the said [*name*] [and] the said [*name*] [and the said [*name*]] and the [survivors or] survivor of them or other the trustees or trustee for the time being of the company fund;[4]

(c) 'the company fund' means the shares in the company hereby given to the company fund trustees and the assets from time to time representing the same;

(d) 'excluded person' means any person referred to in paragraphs (a) to (d) of subsection (4) of section 28 of the Inheritance Tax Act 1984 on the footing that—

(i) the company referred to in paragraph (a) of the said subsection is the company as hereinbefore defined,

(ii) the settlement referred to in paragraph (b) of the said subsection is the disposition on trust contained in this present clause,

(iii) the transfer of value referred to in paragraph (c) of the said subsection is that which is deemed to occur immediately before my death for inheritance tax purposes, and

(iv) the said paragraphs shall be construed and applied subject to and in accordance with all other statutory provisions to which they are subject or which contain definitions relevant to their interpretation.[5]

(e) 'the employees'[6] means and includes all persons who at any time after my death have either held office with or been employed (in whatever capacity) by the company (whether or not such person continues to hold office with or be employed by the company) and 'employee' means any one of the employees;

(f) 'dependants'[7] means in relation to any employee or deceased employee—
   (i) the spouse widow or widower of such employee,
   (ii) any child of such employee during his or her minority,
   (iii) any other person whom the company fund trustees may consider to be a dependant of such employee;

(g) 'the beneficiaries'[8] means and includes—
   (i) the employees,
   (ii) the dependants of any employee or deceased employee;

   Provided that no excluded person shall be a beneficiary and any person who becomes an excluded person shall forthwith cease to be a beneficiary;

(h) 'the trust period' means the period of 125 years immediately following my death.[9]

(3) During the trust period the company fund trustees shall pay or apply the income of the company fund to or for the maintenance education support or benefit of all or such one or more exclusively of the others or other of the beneficiaries for the time being in existence and if more than one in such shares and generally in such manner [or for such charitable purposes generally][10] as the company fund trustees shall in their absolute discretion think fit Provided that during the trust period[11] the company fund trustees may accumulate the whole or any part or parts of the income of the company fund by investing the same and the resulting income thereof in any of the investments hereby authorised and any accumulations so made shall form part of the capital of the company fund for all purposes.

(4) Notwithstanding the trust aforesaid the company fund trustees may at any time or times and from time to time during the trust period pay or apply the whole or any part or parts of the capital of the company fund to or for the advancement or benefit of all or any one or more exclusively of the others or other of the beneficiaries for the time being in existence and if more than one in such shares and in such manner generally [or for such charitable purposes generally][12] as the company fund trustees may in their absolute discretion think fit.

(5) Subject to the trusts and to any exercise of the powers aforesaid the company fund trustees shall hold the company fund and the income thereof upon trust for such charitable purposes generally[13] as they may in their absolute discretion think fit.

(6) The administrative powers and provisions contained in clause 9 hereof shall apply in relation to the company fund and the income thereof as if references therein to 'my trustees' were references to 'the company fund trustees' and references therein to 'my estate' were references to 'the company fund'.

1 See the notes to cls 2 and 3 at paras **[235.5]** and **[235.6]**. If the shares in the company confer control, the gift should be exempt from IHT: see the Note to this form at para **[235.2]**.

2 It may be convenient to appoint separate trustees of the company fund.
3 If the shares in the company confer control, the gift should be exempt from IHT: see the Note to this form at para **[235.2]**.
4 See n 2, above.
5 The excluded categories are essentially participators in the company entitled to five per cent or more of the share capital. It is not very satisfactory to use referential drafting of this kind, but the elaboration of the statutory provisions is such that it is not practical to attempt to reproduce them in full: see the IHTA 1984, ss 13(5), 28(4) to (7), and 102 and the Income and Corporation Taxes Act 1988, ss 414 to 417.
6 The definitions of 'the employees' and 'the beneficiaries' are based on the provisions of the IHTA 1984, ss 86(1) and (3)(a) and 28(1), (4) and (5).
7 The definition of 'dependants' is based on the IHTA 1984, s 86(1)(b).
8 See nn 6 and 7, above.
9 For wills made on or after 6 April 2010, the perpetuity period is 125 years (and no other period): see the PAA 2009, ss 5(1), 15(1)(a) (Part G, paras **[246.179]**, **[246.189]**) and see para **[94.6]**. So this form adopts a trust period of 125 years. A shorter trust period could be specified if the testator does not wish the trust to last that long, although the perpetuity period will still be 125 years. It is not necessary to specify, in addition to the specification as to the length of the trust period, that the perpetuity period is 125 years: PAA 2009, s 5(2). This contrasts with the situation under the former law where in order to rely on a period of years in gross in lieu of the common law perpetuity period it was necessary to specify that the perpetuity period was 80 years, or fewer, see the PAA 1964, s 1(1).
10 It is permissible to include charitable objects without prejudicing the exempt status of the trusts: see the IHTA 1984, s 86(3) and the Note to this form at para **[235.2]**. If a power to benefit charity is not required the words in square brackets should be omitted.
11 For wills made on or after 6 April 2010, there are no statutory restrictions on accumulation in respect of non-charitable trusts, so accumulation will be permitted throughout the trust period: see the PAA 2009, ss 13, 15(1)(a) (Part G, paras **[246.187]**, **[246.189]**) and see para **[95.0]**.
12 See n 11, above.
13 See n 11, above. A trust for charitable purposes is a convenient ultimate trust.

[235.8]

[Updated footnote references.]

GIFT OF FAMILY SEAT

5. I give free of tax[1] the mansion house and grounds known as [*name of house*] and situate in the Parish of [ ] in the County of [ ] and the contents thereof to my nephew [*name*] in fee simple and absolutely.

1 See the notes to to cls 2 and 3 of this form at paras **[235.5]** and **[235.6]**.

[235.9]

[Updated for Trusts (Capital and Income) Act 2013.]

ADMINISTRATION TRUSTS OF RESIDUE[1]

6. (1) I give all my property not hereby or by any codicil hereto otherwise effectively disposed of [(including any entailed or other property over which I shall have at my death a general power of disposition by will)] to my trustees to hold on the trusts set out below with power to sell all or any of it.

(2) My trustees shall pay my funeral and testamentary expenses and debts and any legacies given by this will or any codicil hereto out of such property or its proceeds and shall have a discretion as to how such payments shall be borne as between capital and income.

(3) Subject as above my trustees shall hold such property and the assets from time to time representing the same (hereinafter called 'my residuary

estate') on the trusts set out below and shall invest all money comprised in such property or arising from its sale in any of the investments hereby authorised with power to change such investments into any others hereby authorised.

1 See the notes to the administration trusts contained in Form C8.1, cl 4 at para **[230.7]**.

[235.11]

[Updated for the Perpetuities and Accumulations Act 2009 and Charities Act 2011.]

CHARITABLE TRUSTS OF RESIDUE

8. (1) The charity hereby constituted shall be known as '[*name of charity*]'.

(2) In this clause the following expressions have the following meanings namely—

- (a) 'charitable purposes' means purposes which are exclusively charitable under the law of England and Wales;
- (b) 'charity' means any institution (whether corporate or unincorporated) established for charitable purposes only and 'charities' has a corresponding meaning [1]; and
- (c) 'the accumulation period' means the period of 21 years immediately following my death.

(3) My trustees shall hold my residuary estate upon trust to apply the income thereof[2] for such charitable purposes connected with [*here state nature of desired charitable purposes: eg* the relief of poverty *or* the promotion of research for the public benefit into the causes and treatment of diabetes][3] [and for such charitable purposes generally][4] as my trustees may from time to time determine provided that my trustees may at any time or times during the accumulation period accumulate the whole or any part or parts of the income of my residuary estate by investing the same and the resulting income thereof in any of the investments hereby authorised and any accumulations so made shall form part of the capital of my residuary estate for all purposes.[5]

[(4) My trustees may at any time and from time to time resort to the whole or any part or parts of the capital of my residuary estate and apply the same as if it were income.][6]

(5) In the administration of the charity hereby constituted my trustees shall have the following powers (in addition to those conferred by clause 9 below)—

- (a) power either themselves to apply the income [or capital][7] for the purposes hereby declared or for that purpose to pay the same to any other charity or charities having similar objects;
- (b) power to do all such things as may in the opinion of my trustees be conducive to the promotion of the charitable objects hereby declared;
- (c) power by deed to extend restrict vary or modify the trusts powers and provisions relating to my residuary estate in any manner whatever provided that the foregoing power shall not be exercisable so as to cause or permit any of my residuary estate or the income thereof to be payable or applicable otherwise than for charitable purposes;

(d) power to create a new charitable body (whether corporate or unincorporated) having exclusively charitable objects identical with or similar to the objects hereby declared and to confer on such body such administrative and other powers as my trustees think fit and as shall be consistent with charitable status and to transfer to such body the whole or any part of my residuary estate for the promotion of its objects.

1 Charities Act 2011, s 1(1) replacing Charities Act 2006, s 1(1) with effect from 14 March 2012 has a definition of a charity which does not differ in substance from that in the previous legislation (ie Charities Act 1993, s 96(1)), but its definition of charitable purposes in s 2 differs from the preceding law in various respects, most notably by imposing a general requirement of public benefit (see Charities Act 2011, ss 2–4 and para **[102.3]**). If the residue given on charitable trusts constitutes at least 10 per cent of the 'baseline amount', the reduced rate of 36 per cent IHT will be available on the chargeable part of the estate. See para **[200.91A]** ff.

2 The primary (and only) trust is to apply the income of residue for charitable purposes, but power is conferred by cl 8(4) to resort to capital. A perpetual income trust for charitable purposes is valid: *Re Levy* [1960] Ch 346, [1960] 1 All ER 42. If the testator wishes to create such a trust, the power to resort to capital should be omitted.

3 Care should be taken to ensure that the charitable purposes are adequately described.

4 It is wise to include charitable purposes generally in case the specific purposes are defectively described or there is some development which makes it desirable to modify the original purposes.

5 The proviso confers a power to accumulate income for 21 years. Although the restrictions on accumulating income have been abolished for wills made on or after 6 April 2010 in respect of private non-charitable trusts, restrictions remain for charitable trusts: see the PAA 2009, ss 14, 15(1)(a) (Part G, paras **[246.188]**, **[246.189]**) and see para **[95.0]**.

The exemption from income tax for charity income is only available in relation to income of the appropriate kind which is 'applied' for charitable purposes: see the Income Tax Act 2007, ss 507–564. It is therefore preferable, where trustees accumulate income of funds held on charitable trusts, that they should do so with some specific charitable objective in view. It is probable that income which is accumulated as a general accretion to the funds of a charity counts as 'applied' for charitable purposes and qualifies for this exemption, but it is not absolutely certain: see *IRC v Helen Slater Charitable Trust Ltd* [1982] Ch 49, [1981] 3 All ER 98.

6 See n 2, above.

7 If sub-cl (4) is not included, the words in square brackets should be omitted.

[235.18]

Form C13.2: Will of a bachelor landowner settling the principal family estate together with a share of residue on one nephew and his issue, creating a maintenance fund for the upkeep of the mansion house and settled chattels and settling substantial legacies on two nieces and their issue

[235.20]

[Updated for the Perpetuities and Accumulations Act 2009.]

INTERPRETATION CLAUSE

2. [(1)] I declare that in the interpretation of this will the following words and expressions have the following meanings, namely—

(a) 'my trustees' means and includes my personal representatives for the time being and the trustees or trustee for the time being hereof whether original or substituted and if there shall at any time be no such trustees shall (where the context permits) include the persons empowered by statute to exercise or perform any power or trust hereby or by statute conferred upon my trustees and willing or bound to exercise or perform the same;

(b) 'the mansion house' means the mansion house at present occupied by me known as —— together with the outbuildings and appurtenances thereto belonging;

(c) 'the settled chattels' means the pictures items of furniture objets d'art and other chattels located at the mansion house which are listed in an inventory prepared by Messrs —— and dated ——;

(d) 'the principal estate' means and includes:

(i) the mansion house,

(ii) the settled chattels,

(iii) my agricultural estate known as the —— estate situate at —— in the County of —— together with all other real and leasehold property and other interests in land in the said County to which I may be entitled at the time of my death,

(iv) the share of my residuary estate hereinafter bequeathed to my trustees as part of the principal estate, and

(v) the assets from time to time representing the premises respectively;[1]

(e) 'the maintenance fund' means the sum of [£2,000,000] hereinafter bequeathed for the maintenance repair and preservation of the heritage property and the investments for the time being representing the same;

(f) 'the [W] trust fund' shall mean the sum of [£500,000] hereinafter settled on my niece [MW] and her issue and the investments for the time being representing the same;

(g) 'the [L] trust fund' shall mean the like sum of [£500,000] hereinafter settled on my niece [VL] and her issue and the investments for the time being representing the same;

(h) 'the vesting day' shall mean the day on which shall expire the period of 125 years immediately following my death.

[(2) This will shall be read and construed as if section 15 of the Family Law Reform Act 1969 [the Children Act 1975/the Legitimacy Act 1976/the Adoption Act 1976], the Family Law Reform Act 1987 and the Human Fertilisation and Embryology Act 1990 had not been enacted.][2]

1 The clauses disposing of the principal estate are only appropriate to land in England and Wales.

2 References to children and issue will now, in the absence of a contrary intention, be read as including references to illegitimate, adopted and legitimated persons by virtue of the enactments mentioned in this paragraph: (Part G, paras **[245.39]**, **[245.48]**, **[245.60]**, **[245.72]** and **[245.77]** and Vol 1, paras **[72.10]**–**[72.18]** and **[74.3]**–**[74.7]**). If a testator also wishes to exclude the operation of GRA 2004 a reference to the Act should be included in this sub-clause. Although the Act, unlike the other statutes referred to in the sub-clause, does not expressly provide that for the purpose of construing a will or settlement or other disposition of property its provisions may be excluded, it is thought that a provision, such as sub-clause 2(2), which provides that a will is to be construed without reference to the provisions of the Act is perfectly valid. In a will of this type the testator may desire to exclude the statutory rules of construction (or some of them) in which case this paragraph should be included and adapted as appropriate.

[235.22]

[Updated for the Perpetuities and Accumulations Act 2009.]

BEQUEST OF LEGACY ON TRUST[1]

4. I bequeath to my trustees free of tax[2] the sum of [£500,000] with interest thereon from the date of my death until the appropriation thereof or of investments thereto at the basic rate payable for the time being on funds in court[3] upon trust to invest the said sum in or upon any of the investments hereinafter authorised and to hold such investments and the investments for the time being representing the same (hereinafter called 'the [W] trust fund') upon the following trusts, namely—

(a) the income of the [W] trust fund and the said interest payable from the date of my death shall be held [upon trust to pay the same to]/[upon protective trusts[4] for the benefit of] my niece [MW] wife of [JW] during her life;

(b) after the death of the said [MW] the [W] trust fund shall be held in trust for such one or more of the children and remoter issue of the said [MW] upon with and subject to such trusts powers and provisions (including trusts and powers conferring a discretion as to the disposition of capital and income or provisions for the accumulation of income during any period permitted by law) as the said [MW] may by deed or deeds with or without power of revocation and new appointment or by will or codicil appoint;

(c) in default of any such appointment and subject to any partial appointment the [W] trust fund shall be held in trust for all the children or any the child of the said [MW] who have attained or shall attain the age of 18 years as tenants in common equally provided always that no child of the said [MW] shall take any part or share of and in the [W] trust fund in default of appointment without bringing into hotchpot any part or share therein which may have been appointed to him or her or to his or her issue;[5]

(d) in default of any child or remoter issue of the said [MW] living to attain a vested interest in the whole of the [W] trust fund the same shall upon her decease be held in trust for such person or persons as she shall by will or codicil appoint and in default of any such appointment and subject to any partial appointment;[6]

(e) in trust for her next of kin[7] living at her death [*alternatively* for the persons or person who would have been her statutory next-of-kin if she had died intestate possessed thereof domiciled in England and a spinster [and without a parent] and (if more than one) in the same shares as those in which they would have been entitled to her estate];

(f) provided nevertheless that notwithstanding and in priority to the preceding trusts it shall be lawful for the said [MW] by will or codicil to appoint that the income of [any part not exceeding [two-thirds] of] the [W] trust fund shall be paid to any husband who may survive her during his life or for any less period or determinable upon the happening of any event;[8]

(g) the foregoing trusts shall carry the intermediate income of the [W] trust fund and the provisions of section 31 of the Trustee Act 1925 (as hereinafter modified) shall apply thereto;

(h) section 32 of the Trustee Act 1925 (as hereinafter modified) shall apply in relation to the [W] trust fund.

1 If this form was used for a will made before 6 April 2010, the named beneficiary MW will have been a life in being for the purposes of the common law perpetuity period, so that the powers of appointment would necessarily be exercised (if at all) within a permissible perpetuity period, and the trusts taking effect in remainder to the life interest and in default of appointment would necessarily vest within a permissible perpetuity period. For wills made on or after 6 April 2010 however a mandatory perpetuity period of 125 years applies, see the PAA 2009, ss 5(1), 15(1)(a) (Part G, paras **[246.179]**, **[246.189]**) and see para **[96.6]**. Nevertheless, given the 'wait and see' provision of the PAA 2009, s 7 (Part G, para **[246.181]** and see para **[94.17]**), and the practical certainty that the powers of appointment will be exercised (if at all) and the remainder interests will vest within 125 years of the testator's death, no perpetuity problem should arise if this form is used in a will made on or after 6 April 2010.

2 See notes to cls 2 and 7 of Form C13.1 at paras **[235.5]** and **[235.10]**. Where a legacy given free of IHT is settled, the freedom from the tax should extend only to tax payable upon or by reason of the death of the testator himself. Otherwise there is a danger that future taxes (e g IHT payable on the deaths of the tenants for life) may be thrown upon residue, a result which would render the administration of the residue impossibly difficult (see such cases as *Re Stoddart, Bird v Grainger* [1916] 2 Ch 444; *Re Eve, Hall v Eve* [1917] 1 Ch 562; *Re Kennedy, Corbould v Kennedy* [1917] 1 Ch 9).

3 See Civil Procedure Rules, Part 40, *Practice Direction – Accounts, Inquiries etc* para 15.

4 The protective life interest given to the niece will be a beneficiary-taxed IPDI unless she becomes bankrupt before the testator's death (see para **[225.75]**, n 1). She will continue to be treated as entitled to an IPDI if a forfeiture occurs after the testator's death (see para **[200.104]**).The trusts for her children will then fall within the IHT relevant property regime (see para **[218.8]** ff) until absolute vesting occurs if they have not attained the age of vesting by the time of the niece's death.

5 The trusts for her children will fall within the IHT relevant property regime (see para **[218.8]** ff) until absolute vesting occurs if they have not attained the age of vesting by the time of the later to occur of the testator's death or the niece's death.

6 For a clause allowing the fund to be paid to a female tenant for life who is past the age of childbearing, where the trusts are similar to these, see Form B16.24 at para **[216.31]** and for a form enabling her to take over the trust fund in these circumstances, see the second alternative cl 6(3) of Form C8.2 at para **[230.24]**.

7 See Vol 1, para **[77.1]** and see the AEA 1925, ss 46 to 50, (Part G, paras **[244.62]**–**[244.67]**).

8 The property subject to any interest appointed by the niece to her husband under this power will be subject to the IHT relevant property rules and so the exemption for transfers between spouses will not apply to this property on the death of the niece (see paras **[200.84]**, **[200.92]**).

[235.23]

[Updated for the Perpetuities and Accumulations Act 2009.]

BEQUEST OF LEGACY ON TRUSTS BY REFERENCE TO PRIOR LEGACY

5. I bequeath free of tax[1] to my trustees the further sum of [£500,000] with interest thereon at the rate of [six] per cent per annum[2] from the date of my death until the appropriation thereof or of investments thereto upon trust to invest the same upon any of the investments hereinafter authorised and to hold such investments and the investments for the time being representing the same (hereinafter called 'the [L] trust fund') and the said interest upon with and subject to similar trusts powers and provisions as are hereinbefore contained in relation to the [W] trust fund but substituting throughout the name of my niece [VL] for that of my said niece [MW] and the expression the [L] trust fund for the expression the [W] trust fund.

1 See the notes to clauses 2 and 7 of Form C13.1 at paras **[235.5]** and **[235.10]**.

2 See n 2 to cl 4 of this form at para **[235.22]**.

[235.24]

[Updated for the Perpetuities and Accumulations Act 2009.]

SETTLED DEVISE OF PRINCIPAL ESTATE

6. I devise and bequeath the principal estate [free of tax]/[subject to payment thereout of any inheritance tax attributable thereto (making due allowance for any reduction in value for inheritance tax purposes which is attributed thereto)][1] unto my trustees upon the following trusts—

(a) upon trust for my nephew [JE the elder] the son of my late sister [SE] during his life with remainder;
(b) upon trust for [JE the younger] his only son living at the date of this my will during his life with remainder;
(c) upon trust for the first son of the said [JE the younger] to attain the age of 21 years[2] absolutely with remainder;
(d) upon trust for the first daughter of the said [JE the younger] to attain the age of 21 years absolutely with remainder;
(e) upon trust for the first future-born son of the said [JE the elder] to attain the age of 21 years absolutely with remainder;
(f) upon trust for [ME] the only daughter living at the date of this my will of the said [JE the elder] during her life with remainder;
(g) upon trust for the first son of the said [ME] to attain the age of 21 years absolutely with remainder;
(h) upon trust for the first daughter of the said [ME] to attain the age of 21 years absolutely with remainder;
(i) upon trust for the first future-born daughter of the said [JE the elder] to attain the age of 21 years absolutely with remainder;
(j) upon trust for my own right heirs absolutely.[3]

1 This gift will be free of IHT unless the contrary is stated: see the Preliminary Note to B14 at paras **[214.55]–[214.58]**, although if it is intended to be free of tax it will be advisable to say so specifically at this point because other gifts are expressed to be free of tax, and the absence of any direction as to the burden of IHT in relation to this gift might give rise to doubt as to what was intended in this respect. If it is a substantial agricultural estate, in hand or let on tenancies commencing after 31 August 1995, it may be wholly entitled to 100 per cent agricultural relief: see the Preliminary Note to C12 at paras **[234.1]–[234.10]**.

However, there may be a likelihood or a risk that this gift will not be wholly free from IHT, and, if so, it may be appropriate to make it bear its own IHT. The IHT would be likely to be payable by instalments, and by interest-free instalments in relation to land on which there is an agricultural relief (see the Preliminary Note to B5 at paras **[205.17]–[205.20]**). It would enable the administration of the residuary estate to be speeded up if the executors did not have to retain any of it against the payment of the instalments of IHT on this estate. A share of the residuary estate is added to this gift which might be used to pay the tax.

2 If this form was used for a will made before 6 April 2010, JE the younger and the other named parents of children attaining 21 will have been lives in being for the purposes of the common law perpetuity period, so that the interests of their children would necessarily vest within a permissible perpetuity period. For wills made on or after 6 April 2010 however a mandatory perpetuity period of 125 years applies, see the PAA 2009, ss 5(1), 15(1)(a) (Part G, para **[246.179], [246.189]**) and see para **[94.6]**. Nevertheless, given the 'wait and see' provision of the PAA 2009, s 7 (Part G, para **[246.181]** and see para **[94.17]**), and the practical certainty that any children of the named parents will attain 21 within 125 years of the testator's death, no perpetuity problem should arise if this form is used in a will made on or after 6 April 2010.

3 It is assumed in the above clause that at the date of the will there are living only two children, i e one son and one daughter of the testator's nephew. For the effect of a gift to a person's right heirs, see Vol 1, para **[78.1]** ff. The IHT consequences of this clause are that the person who in the circumstances prevailing at the testator's death gets a life interest from his death will have a beneficiary-taxed IPDI (see para **[200.98]**). If his or her interest is succeeded by a further life interest or interests the property subject will fall into the IHT relevant property regime. A discretionary trust with a letter of wishes might save IHT (see para **[235.1]**), but the wishes might not be respected.

[235.25]

[Updated for the Perpetuities and Accumulations Act 2009.]

CLAUSE CUTTING DOWN ABSOLUTE INTERESTS TO LIFE INTERESTS

7. I declare that every child of the said [JE the elder] or of the said [JE the younger] or of the said [ME] who shall be hereafter born[1] in my lifetime shall instead of taking an interest in the capital of the principal estate under the foregoing trusts take a life interest only therein with remainder to his or her first son to attain the age of 21 years absolutely or in default of such son for his or her first daughter to attain the age of 21 years absolutely. [2]

1 A child en ventre sa mère at the testator's death and born afterwards would not, it seems, come within this clause: see *Villar v Gilbey* [1907] AC 139, HL.

2 If this form was used for a will made before 6 April 2010, the children born in the testator's lifetime will have been lives in being for the purposes of the common law perpetuity period, so that the interests of their children would necessarily vest within a permissible perpetuity period. For wills made on or after 6 April 2010 however a mandatory perpetuity period of 125 years applies, see the PAA 2009, ss 5(1), 15(1)(a) (Part G, paras **[246.179]**, **[246.189]**) and see para **[94.6]**. Nevertheless, given the 'wait and see' provision of the PAA 2009, s 7 (Part G, para **[246.181]** and see para **[94.17]**), and the practical certainty that any children of theirs will attain 21 within 125 years of the testator's death, no perpetuity problem should arise if this form is used in a will made on or after 6 April 2010

[235.28]

[Updated for the Perpetuities and Accumulations Act 2009.]

GIFT OF MAINTENANCE FUND

10. (1) In this clause the following expressions have the following meanings, namely—

(a) 'the heritage trustees' means such persons as my trustees may appoint and the Commissioners for Her Majesty's Revenue and Customs may approve pursuant to paragraph 2(1)(b) of Schedule 4;[1]

(b) 'the maintenance fund' means the fund so defined in subclause (2) hereof;

(c) 'the vesting day' means the day on which the principal estate shall vest in a beneficiary absolutely under the trusts declared by clause 6 hereof;[2]

(d) 'the heritage period' means the period commencing on my death and expiring on the later to occur of the following two events:

  (i) the sixth anniversary of the day immediately following my death,[3] and

  (ii) the vesting day[4];

(e) 'the Act' means the Inheritance Tax Act 1984;

(f) 'Schedule 3' and 'Schedule 4' mean Schedule 3 and Schedule 4 respectively to the Act;

(g) 'the heritage property' means so much of the mansion house and the settled chattels as shall for the time being from time to time during the heritage period be qualifying property[5] within the meaning of paragraph 3(2) of Schedule 4;

(h) 'the heritage bodies' means and includes:
  (i) the bodies mentioned in Schedule 3,[6] and
  (ii) any body established for exclusively charitable purposes which is a qualifying charity within the meaning of paragraph 3(4) of Schedule 4.[7]

(2) For the purpose of maintaining repairing and preserving the heritage property I bequeath to the heritage trustees free of tax[8] the sum of [£2,000,000] with interest thereon from the date of my death until the appropriation thereof or of investments thereto at the basic rate payable for the time being on funds in court[9] upon trust to invest the said sum in or upon any of the investments hereinafter authorised and to hold such investments and the investments for the time being representing the same (hereinafter called 'the maintenance fund') upon the trusts hereinafter declared and contained And for the purpose aforesaid my trustees shall as soon as reasonably possible after my death and in any event within two years of my death[10] apply to the Commissioners for Her Majesty's Revenue and Customs[11] for a direction under paragraph 1 of Schedule 4 in relation to the bequest hereby made Provided that if no such direction shall be given the bequest made by this clause shall be null and void and the said sum of [£2,000,000] shall be deemed to have devolved on my death free of tax[12] as part of my principal estate.

(3) The heritage trustees shall stand possessed of the maintenance fund and the income thereof upon the trusts and with and subject to the powers and provisions following:

(a) the heritage trustees shall stand possessed of the maintenance fund upon trust during the heritage period to apply all or so much of the income thereof (including all income thereof accruing after my death) as may be required for the maintenance repair or preservation of or making provision for public access to the heritage property (by whomsoever the same may from time to time be owned and on whatever trusts the same may from time to time be held) or for defraying the expenses of the heritage trustees in relation to the maintenance fund;

(b) if at any time or times during the heritage period the income of the maintenance fund or some part thereof for any reason cannot be applied in accordance with paragraph (a) hereof the heritage trustees shall pay the same to all or any one or more of the heritage bodies and if more than one in such shares as the heritage trustees in their absolute discretion shall think fit;

(c) notwithstanding the foregoing trusts the heritage trustees shall have power during the heritageperiod to accumulate the whole or any part or parts of the income of the maintenance fund by investing the same and the resulting income thereof in any of the investments hereby authorised and so that all such accumulations of income shall be held as a separate fund which shall be applied (as to both capital and income) at any time or times and from time to time during the heritage period and in any event not later than the expiration of the heritage period as if the same were income of the maintenance fund applicable under paragraphs (a) and (b) hereof;[13]

(d) notwithstanding the trusts and any exercise of the power aforesaid the trustees shall have power at any time or times and from time to time during the heritage period to raise any sum or sums [not exceeding in the aggregate the sum of £[500,000]] out of the capital of the maintenance fund (not for this purpose including any accumulations of income) and apply the same for any of the purposes for which income is applicable under paragraph (a) hereof;

Provided always that the heritage trustees shall have power by deed to modify the foregoing trusts to such extent as may be necessary to secure the approval of the Commissioners for Her Majesty's Revenue and Customs pursuant to paragraph 2(1)(a)(i) of Schedule 4.[14]

(4) For so long after the sixth anniversary of the day immediately following my death as the vesting day has not occurred the heritage trustees shall have power by deed or deeds to declare that as from the date of any such deed all or any part of the maintenance fund shall cease to be held on the trusts and with and subject to the powers set out in subclause (2) above and so that thereafter during the remainder of the heritage period the maintenance fund or such part thereof shall be held upon the trusts and with and subject to the powers and provisions applicable to the principal estate and as one fund therewith for all purposes.[15]

(5) Subject as aforesaid the heritage trustees shall hold the maintenance fund upon the trusts and with and subject to the powers and provisions as are hereinbefore declared of and concerning the principal estate and as one fund therewith for all purposes.

(6) The powers conferred on my trustees by this clause may be exercised before as well as after obtaining a grant of probate of this will and notwithstanding that the administration of my estate is not complete.[16]

1 The trustees must be approved by HMRC and must include a trust corporation, a solicitor, an accountant or a member of such professional body as they may allow in the case of the property concerned: IHTA 1984, Sch 4, para 2(1)(b).

The legislation refers to the Treasury but the Treasury's functions under Schedule 4 were transferred to the Revenue (now HMRC) by the Finance Act 1985, s 95.

2 As appears above, it is a practical certainty that the trusts of Clause 6 will vest within the mandatory perpetuity period of 125 years which applies for wills made on or after 6 April 2010, see the PAA 2009, ss 5(1), 15(1)(a) (Part G, paras **[246.179]**, **[246.189]**) and see para **[94.6]**).

3 The minimum duration required for the trusts of a maintenance fund is six years: IHTA 1984, Sch 4, para 3(1)(a).

4 The heritage period is defined so as to last for six years or until the principal estate vests in a beneficiary absolutely under cl 6, whichever is the longer. During this period the maintenance fund will not form part of the taxable estate of a beneficiary unless the power conferred by sub-cl (3) is exercised.

5 Property is qualifying property if designated under the IHTA 1984, s 31 and if the requisite undertaking is given under s 30 (if conditional exemption is claimed) or under Sch 4, para 3(3) (if not).

6 The bodies mentioned in IHTA 1984, Sch 3 are national heritage bodies such as the National Gallery and the British Museum.

7 A charity is a qualifying charity if it exists wholly or mainly for maintaining, repairing or preserving heritage property: IHTA 1984, Sch 4, para 3(4).

8 This 'free of tax' formula is not strictly necessary as the gift will qualify as an exempt transfer under IHTA 1984, s 27 if the Revenue give a direction: IHTA 1984, Sch 4, para 1.
9 This is the rate of interest currently payable on legacies in an administration by the court: Civil Procedure Rules, Part 40, *Practice Direction – Accounts, Inquiries etc*, para 15.
10 The claim should ordinarily be made within two years: IHTA 1984, s 27(1A).
11 See n 1, above.
12 See Form C13.1, cl 2, n 1 at para **[235.5]**.
13 For wills made on or after 6 April 2010, there are no statutory restrictions on accumulation in respect of non-charitable trusts, so accumulation will be permitted throughout the heritage period: see the PAA 2009, s 13, 15(1)(a) (Part G, paras **[246.187]**, **[246.189]**) and see para **[95.0]**. Although income accruing during the heritage period may be accumulated, it must be applied for heritage purposes: IHTA 1984, Sch 4, para 3(1)(c).
14 This power is inserted in case the Revenue insist on a modification of the trusts as a condition of giving a direction pursuant to the IHTA 1984, Sch 4, para 1.
15 This power enables the heritage trustees to determine the trusts after the minimum six-year period. The exercise of the power will trigger a tax charge under the IHTA 1984, Sch 4, Pt II.
16 The trustees are probably entitled to exercise their powers before the grant of probate and before the administration is complete, but this provision removes any doubt on the point.

C14

Wills with a foreign element

PRELIMINARY NOTE

[236.1]

[Updated for new edition of Cheshire, North and Fawcett's *Private International Law*.]

Domicile. The forms in this work are for use by testators who have an English domicile. Catering for the needs of testators with a foreign domicile is a specialised topic and gives rise to fiscal and other considerations on which specialist advice, including the advice of foreign lawyers, will usually be required. However, some of the general considerations affecting testators with a foreign domicile are mentioned below, even though forms for wills with a foreign proper law, which are normally appropriate for testators with a foreign domicile, are outside the scope of this work. Domicile is itself a rather technical topic. For a discussion of the concept generally, see Vol 1, paras **[23.2]–[23.5]**, and for a more extended discussion reference should be made to Cheshire, North and Fawcett's *Private International Law* (14th edn), pp 153 ff and Dicey, Morris and Collins, *The Conflict of Laws* (14th edn), Vol 1, pp 130 ff.

[236.3]

[Updated for FA 2013, Sch 36.]

Persons with a foreign domicile. As mentioned above, forms which cater for testators who do not have a UK domicile are outside the scope of this work, but we would mention the following general points. Property situated outside the UK is 'excluded property' for IHT purposes if an individual domiciled outside the UK (and not deemed to be domiciled in the UK under IHTA 1984, s 267: see para **[236.2]**) is beneficially entitled to it: IHTA 1984, s 6(1). It should be noted that since 17 July 2013 a new anti-avoidance provision disallows as deductions for IHT purposes any liabilities attributable to financing, directly or indirectly, the acquisition of, or maintenance or enhancement of the value of, excluded property, subject to some limited exceptions (IHTA 1984, s 162A, inserted by FA 2013, Sch 36). This applies to transfers or deemed transfers on or after 17 July 2013, irrespective of when the liabilities were incurred. Settled property situated outside the UK which was settled by a settlor or testator who was not domiciled in the UK (or deemed to be so: see above) at the date of the settlement or death is also 'excluded property': s 48(3). Broadly speaking 'excluded property' escapes IHT altogether and settled property which is 'excluded property' will escape tax regardless of the domicile and residence of the beneficiaries. It would therefore be quite possible for an individual who is not domiciled in the UK (and not deemed to be so domiciled under IHTA 1984, s 267: see para **[236.2]**), even if he lives in the UK, to make a will leaving his foreign estate on discretionary trusts for beneficiaries who live in the UK which avoid future IHT charges. So long as the property remains situated outside the UK it will escape the periodic and exit charges which would otherwise apply (see B18 at paras **[218.8]**–**[218.15]** for these). The changes made to IHT by FA 2006 have introduced a new hazard for testators with a foreign domicile in that any continuing trust following an IPDI given to a testator's spouse or civil partner will be a relevant property trust, and will, by virtue of IHTA 1984, ss 80 and 82, be treated for the purposes of the relevant property rules, including the rules for determining whether the settled property is excluded property, as if the property were settled by the surviving spouse or civil partner on his or her death. This means that even if if the testator has a non-UK domicile at his or her death, the settled property will not be capable of being excluded property after the death of the surviving spouse or civil partner if the latter is domiciled (or deemed by IHTA 1984, s 267 to be domiciled) in the UK on his or her death. A testator with a non-UK actual and fiscal domicile, at any rate if he has substantial property outside the UK, will usually be advised to make appropriate arrangements, either by way of inter vivos settlement or by will, which are governed by foreign law rather than to incorporate such arrangements in his English will. (If he were to make a will in English form it might possibly prejudice his status as a non-UK domiciliary.) A non UK-domiciled testator may of course own property in the UK which will be liable to IHT in the normal way and may wish to make a will in English form disposing of such property. If so, he should use a commencement, such as that contained in Form B1.6 at para **[201.11]**, limiting the operation of his English will to his UK assets.

[236.4]

[Updated for Finance Act 2006 Sch 20 and Finance Act 2013, ss 177, 178.]

Spouses with different domiciles. Since the abolition of the wife's dependent domicile by the Domicile and Matrimonial Proceedings Act 1973, s 1 spouses have been able to have different domiciles from each other. If a case arises where one spouse or civil partner has a UK domicile and the other has a foreign domicile, the unlimited IHT exemption for inter-spouse or inter-civil partner transfers will apply only to transfers by the non-domiciled spouse or civil partner to the UK-domiciled spouse or civil partner. Transfers in the opposite direction are only exempt up to a cash limit on the cumulative total of such transfers. The limit under IHTA 1984, s 18(2) for transfers in these circumstances was £55,000 for transfers before 6 April 2013, but with effect from the latter date it is an amount equal to the nil-rate band for the time being (IHTA 1984, s 18(2) and (2A) as amended and inserted by FA 2013, s 178).Lifetime transfers under which the non-domiciled spouse or civil partner takes an absolute interest will qualify as potentially exempt transfers and will fall out of charge if the donor spouse or civil partner survives the transfer by seven years. There is sometimes a relevant double taxation convention which provides for a more generous exemption in some circumstances: see e g the Convention with the USA of 19 October 1978 (SI 1979/1454), art 8(4). There is also effective from 6 April 2013 an option for the transferee spouse or civil partner who is domiciled outside the UK to elect to be treated as domiciled in the UK so as to avoid the limit on the exemption: IHTA 1984, ss 267ZA and 267ZB inserted by FA 2013, s 177. See, further, para **[200.85]**.

[236.5A]
The EU Regulation No 650/2012. For this see para **[24.2]** and the extracts from the Regulation at para **[248.1]** ff. It will only apply to the estates of persons dying on or after 17 August 2015. It applies to all EU states except the UK, Republic of Ireland, and Denmark. Although the UK is not subject to it, where a UK citizen owns property, especially immovable property, in an EU country to which the Regulation applies, he or she can choose English domestic law of succession to apply to his estate (Art 22 of the Regulation, set out at para **[248.9]**). This will be recognised in the courts of the state where the property is situated, and probably also by the English courts (see para **[201.5A]**).

[236.9]

[Updated for EU Regulation No 650/2012.]

Form C14.1: Will of English-domiciled testator/testatrix owning property in England and in foreign country, appointing separate executors to administer foreign property with direction to remit the proceeds of the foreign estate to the English executors

Note. This form caters for the English-domiciled testator/testatrix whose dependants live in England but who owns property of significant value in a foreign jurisdiction as well as property in England (or elsewhere in the UK). It may well be difficult for English executors to exercise effective control and supervision over the administration of the foreign estate. This form caters for this difficulty by providing for the appointment of separate local executors to administer the foreign estate and remit the proceeds to the English executors. Such a device would normally be appropriate when the foreign estate is situate in a common law jurisdiction which recognises the office of executor, but it may not be suitable in other cases. The advice of lawyers practising in the particular jurisdiction should be taken. In the case of federal states, e g the United States, Canada and Australia, the relevant jurisdiction may be an individual state or province rather than the federal state itself. Where the foreign estate is situated in an EU state subject to EU Regulation 650/2012 (operating for deaths on or after 17 August 2015), it will be possible to choose English law to govern the succession: see paras **[24.2]** and **[201.5A]**. A declaration in accordance with the Regulation is included as an alternative in Clause 1 of this Form at para **[236.10]**.

In this form the gifts to the testator's children are in favour of all his children without being confined to children of the marriage or named children. See the Preliminary Note to C2 at para **[224.14]** for the significance of this point.

This form can be adapted for use by civil partners, substituting 'civil partner' for 'wife/husband'. References to children or other ultimate beneficiaries will have to be adapted according to circumstances.

[236.10]

[Updated for new edition of Cheshire, North and Fawcett's *Private International Law* and EU Regulation No 650/2012.]

REVOCATION CLAUSE AND DECLARATION OF DOMICILE AND CHOICE OF LAW

I [*name*] of [*address*] hereby revoke all former dispositions made by me and declare this to be my last will And I further declare that my domicile is English[1], my nationality British and that [I choose the law of England to govern my succession as a whole, to the intent that the law of England should be the applicable law of succession in relation to all my property wherever situated for the purposes of English law, and of EU Regulation Number 650/2012 and in particular Article 22 (choice of law) of such Regulation]/ [my will is to be construed and to take effect according to English law][2] [I also declare that all sums of money herein mentioned are stated and payable in sterling].[3]

1 A declaration by a testator to the above effect may be useful when, owing to the testator's birth or residence or the nature and location of his business interests, a reasonable doubt may arise as to his true domicile. Domicile is not, however, a mere question of intention, and such a declaration, if contradicted or unsupported by the actual facts, is inoperative: *Re Steer* (1858) 3 H & N 594; *Brunel v Brunel* (1871) LR 12 Eq 298; *Doucet v Geoghegan* (1878) 9 Ch D 441; *Bradford v Young* (1885) 29 Ch D 617; *Winans v A-G* [1904] AC 287; *Re Liddell-Grainger's Will Trusts, Dormer v Liddell-Grainger* [1936] 3 All ER 173. As to domicile generally see Cheshire, North and Fawcett's *Private International Law* (14th edn), pp 153 ff and Dicey, Morris and Collins, *The Conflict of Laws* (14th edn), Vol 1, pp 130 ff, especially at pp 142–143 with regard to the effect of declarations of this sort.

2 The general rule is that in the absence of any contrary indication the construction of a will of movables is governed by the law of the testator's domicile (*Re Cunnington, Healing v Webb* [1924] 1 Ch 68); it seems that the construction of a will of immovable property is also prima facie governed by the law of the domicile but subject to the constraints imposed by the local law: Dicey & Morris, *The Conflict of Laws* (14th edn), Vol 2, p 1255. This declaration resolves any possible doubt on this point in favour of English law. It should be noted, however, that at the moment the operation of such a declaration is confined to construction. The material or essential validity of any disposition of immovable property, e g the application of forced heirship rules, will depend on the local law: Dicey & Morris, op cit, Vol 2, pp 1251–1253. The EU Regulation No 650/2012, however, in relation to the estates of persons dying on or after 17 August 2015, will allow English law to be chosen by a UK national to govern the succession to all his or her property situated in states subject to the Regulation. Accordingly, for testators expecting to live until then, with property in an EU state subject to the Regulation, a declaration choosing English law for the purposes of the Regulation has been included as an alternative. See, further, paras **[24.2]**, **[201.5A]**, **[236.5A]** and **[248.9]**.

3 References to currency in a will are prima facie to be construed in accordance with the law of the domicile: Dicey & Morris, *The Conflict of Laws* (14th edn), Vol 2, pp 1255–1257. Even so, difficulties can arise where a legacy expressed in 'pounds' is given to a beneficiary resident in a foreign jurisdiction that also denotes its money in 'pounds'. It is safer to make the position clear if legacies to non-residents are to be included.

[236.16]

[Updated for Trusts (Capital and Income) Act 2013.]

ADMINISTRATION TRUSTS OF RESIDUE

6. (1) I give all my property not hereby or by any codicil hereto otherwise effectively disposed of [(including any entailed or other property over which

I shall have at my death a general power of disposition by will)][1] to my trustees to hold on the trusts set out below with power to sell all or any of it.[2]

(2) My trustees shall pay my funeral and testamentary expenses[3] and debts and any legacies given by this will or any codicil hereto out of such property or its proceeds and shall have a discretion as to how such payments shall be borne as between capital and income.[4]

(3) Subject as above my trustees shall hold such property and the assets from time to time representing the same (hereinafter called 'my residuary estate') on the trusts set out below and shall invest all money comprised in such property or arising from its sale in any of the investments hereby authorised with power to change such investments into any others hereby authorised.[5]

1 See para **[230.7]**, n 1.
2 See para **[230.7]**, n 2.
3 See para **[230.7]**, n 3.
4 See para **[230.7]**, n 4.
5 See para **[230.7]**, n 5.

[236.18]

[Updated for the Perpetuities and Accumulations Act 2009.]

BENEFICIAL TRUSTS OF RESIDUE

8. My trustees shall hold my residuary estate:
   (a) upon trust to pay the income thereof to my [wife/husband] during [her/his] life;[1]
   (b) Provided that my trustees shall have power in their absolute discretion from time to time so long as my [wife/husband] is entitled to be paid the income of all or any part of the capital of my residuary estate (or would be so entitled if such capital yielded income) to pay transfer or apply the whole or any part or parts of such capital[2] to [her/him] or for [her/his] benefit in such manner as they shall in their absolute discretion think fit;
   (c) subject as aforesaid upon trust as to both capital and income for all or such one or more exclusively of the others or other of my children or remoter issue at such times and if more than one in such shares and with such trusts and powers (including trusts and powers conferring a power or discretion on my trustees or any other person or persons as to the disposition of capital or income) and such provisions (including provisions for the accumulation of income during any period permitted by law and including administrative provisions of whatever nature) and generally in such manner as my [wife/husband] shall by deed revocable or irrevocable or by will or codicil appoint;[3]
   (d) subject as aforesaid upon trust for such of my children[4] as survive me if more than one in equal shares;
   (e) Provided always that if any child of mine dies (or has already died) in my lifetime leaving a child or children living at my death who attain the age of 18 years such child or children shall take if more

than one equally between them the share which his her or their parent would have taken had such parent survived me;[5]

(f) Provided further that no child of mine who or whose children shall take by virtue of any such appointment as aforesaid shall unless my [wife/husband] so directs share in the unappointed part of my residuary estate without bringing the part appointed into hotchpot and accounting therefor;

(g) subject as aforesaid upon trust for the children of my deceased brother [*name*] living at my death and the children then living of any then deceased child of my said brother who whether children or children of children attain the age of 18 years in equal shares if more than one but so that the children of any then deceased child of my said brother shall take (if more than one equally between them) only the share which their parent would have taken had such parent lived to attain a vested interest;[6] and

(h) subject as aforesaid upon the trusts upon which the same would be held at my death if I had died possessed thereof intestate domiciled in England and Wales and without having married or had issue.[7]

1 The surviving spouse's interest will be a beneficiary-taxed IPDI which will qualify for the spouse exemption: see paras **[200.84]** and **[200.98]**.

2 There are two reasons for restricting the power to capital in which the spouse has an interest in possession: first, to ensure that the power is not exercisable if there is a divorce and the primary trust fails; and second, to ensure that the power ceases to be exercisable if the spouse assigns or surrenders his or her life interest. See the Note to C2 at paras **[224.16]–[224.23]**. It is particularly important for her to cease to be the object of this power if she assigns or surrenders her life interest because it will be a deemed gift of the settled property for gift with reservation purposes: see para **[200.76]**.

3 Any continuing trusts to follow the spouse's IPDI which are appointed under this power will be subject to the relevant property IHT regime unless there is a disabled person's interest: see paras **[200.92]** and **[218.8]** ff. If this form was used for a will made before 6 April 2010, the surviving spouse will have been a life in being for the purposes of the common law perpetuity period, so that the power of appointment would necessarily be exercised (if at all) within a permissible perpetuity period. For wills made on or after 6 April 2010 however a mandatory perpetuity period of 125 years applies, see the PAA 2009, ss 5(1), 15(1)(a) (Part G, paras **[246.179], [246.189]**) and see para **[94.6]**. Nevertheless, given the 'wait and see' provision of the PAA 2009, s 7 (Part G, para **[246.181]** and see para **[94.17]**), and the practical certainty that the power of appointment will be exercised (if at all) within 125 years of the testator's death, no perpetuity problem should arise if this form is used in a will made on or after 6 April 2010.

4 See the Note to this form at para **[236.9]**.

5 If this trust takes effect in possession, whether immediately on the death of the testator or after the death of the spouse, at a time when any of the grandchildren are under the age of 18, the shares of those grandchildren will be subject to the relevant property IHT regime unless there is a disabled person's interest: see paras **[200.92]** and **[218.8]** ff.

6 See n 5 above.

7 In some cases it may be appropriate to ascertain the class of next-of-kin at some other time, e g the death of the spouse if surviving, so as to confine the gift to the kin then living. There is no objection to so doing: see *Hutchinson v National Refuges for Homeless and Destitute Children* [1920] AC 795, [1920] All ER Rep 701.

[236.24]

[Updated for EU Regulation No 650/2012.]

Form C14.2: Reciprocal wills of English-domiciled couple who own foreign holiday home and who intend to execute foreign wills giving the home to their son on the death of the survivor, leaving their estates to each other with the survivor making a tax-free gift of holiday home to the son (with a tax-free legacy equal to the amount of the IHT on the home in the event that the foreign wills are executed), giving the daughter a compensating legacy and leaving residue to the son and daughter equally

Note. The ownership of foreign holiday homes is becoming increasingly common. This form is intended to cater for a couple who own such a home and intend that it should devolve on the death of the survivor on one of their children. Clients in the position of such a couple should be advised to take the advice of a local lawyer with a view to making wills in local form. (It is particularly important in the case of immovable property to establish whether there are any relevant forced heirship rules under the local law and whether English law would give effect to them where the property is owned by an English domiciliary.) This form contemplates that local wills will in due course be made revoking and replacing the specific gift of the house, but provides in the meantime for a specific free of tax gift of the holiday home to the son. (Foreign property prima facie bears its own IHT, and for most purposes also bears any foreign estate or inheritance taxes on it: see the Preliminary Note at para **[236.6]**.) The free of tax gift of the home will be revoked by the foreign wills when they are made and the form provides in that event for the gift to the son of a tax-free legacy of the amount of the IHT and any local taxes which would otherwise be payable by him.

Where the foreign estate is situated in an EU state subject to EU Regulation 650/2012 (operating for deaths on or after 17 August 2015), this will and the foreign will should include a choice of English law to govern the succession. See paras **[24.2]** and **[201.5A]**. A declaration in accordance with the Regulation is included in Clause 1 of this Form at para **[236.25]**.

This form can be adapted for use by civil partners, substituting 'civil partner' for 'wife/ husband'. References to children or other ultimate beneficiaries will have to be adapted according to circumstances.

[236.25]

[Updated for EU Regulation No 650/2012.]

REVOCATION CLAUSE AND CHOICE OF LAW

I [*name*] of [*address*] hereby revoke all former testamentary dispositions made by me and declare this to be my last will. I declare that my nationality is British and that I choose the law of England to govern my succession as a whole, to the intent that the law of England should be the applicable law of succession in relation to all my property wherever situated for the purposes of English law, and of EU Regulation Number 650/2012 and in particular Article 22 (choice of law) of such Regulation.

[236.39]

[Updated for EU Regulation No 650/2012.]

Form C14.3: Reciprocal wills of English-domiciled couple who own foreign holiday home and who have already executed foreign wills giving the home to their son on the death of the survivor, leaving their estates to each other with the survivor leaving a tax-free legacy to the son equal to the amount of the IHT on the holiday home, giving the daughter a compensating legacy and leaving residue to the son and daughter equally

Note. The form corresponds closely with Form C14.2, the difference being that this form is intended for use after foreign wills making gifts of the foreign holiday home (and its contents) have been executed. It is assumed that there is no relevant restriction on the power to dispose of the property under the local law, and that the wills made under the local law are ones whereby the husband and wife each gives his or her interest in the property (and contents) to the other, subject to the same survivorship condition (if any) as in this will, and in the alternative gives it to their son if the gift to the other does not take effect. This form is thus for wills which do not deal with the foreign holiday home and no specific gift of the holiday home is included, but the will of the survivor gives a tax-free legacy to the son of an amount equal to the IHT and any local taxes payable in respect of the holiday home if the gift of it in the foreign will to the son takes effect.

The holiday home is excluded from this will only to the extent that it is effectually disposed of under the foreign will, and so if the foreign will fails for some reason, this will will be effective to dispose of it.

Where the foreign estate is situated in an EU state subject to EU Regulation 650/2012 (operating for deaths on or after 17 August 2015), this will and the foreign will should include a choice of English law to govern the succession. See paras **[24.2]** and **[201.5A]**. A declaration in accordance with the Regulation is included in Clause 1 of this Form at para **[236.40]**.

This form can be adapted for use by civil partners, substituting 'civil partner' for 'wife/husband'. References to children or other ultimate beneficiaries will have to be adapted according to circumstances.

[236.40]

[Updated for EU Regulation No 650/2012.]

REVOCATION CLAUSE AND CHOICE OF LAW

I [*name*] of [*address*] hereby revoke all former testamentary dispositions made by me save for my will made according to the law of [*name of foreign country*] dated [*date*] (hereinafter called 'my foreign will') and declare this to be my last will in respect of all movable and immovable property of mine which is situate anywhere in the world at the time of my death except for the property disposed of by my foreign will. I declare that my nationality is British and that I choose the law of England to govern my succession as a whole, to the intent that the law of England should be the applicable law of succession in relation to all my property wherever situated for the purposes of English law, and of EU Regulation Number 650/2012 and in particular Article 22 (choice of law) of such Regulation.

PART D

Codicils

D

Codicils

PRELIMINARY NOTE

[237.2]

[Updated for the Perpetuities and Accumulations Act 2009.]

Changes in the law since the date of a will may necessitate or make desirable changes to the provisions of the will. For instance, the changes made to the rules against perpetuities and accumulations by the Perpetuities and Accumulations Act 2009 (see paras **[94.6]** ff, and paras **[95.0]** ff), in particular the new extended perpetuity period and the abolition of the rule restricting accumulations, may make changes desirable where a testator has included continuing trusts in his will. Or the changes to the IHT treatment of trusts by the Finance Act 2006, Sch 20 may require wills to be reconsidered and amended. For example, for deaths on and after 22 March 2006, it is no longer possible to create trusts which have the IHT benefits of IHTA 1984, s 71, (see para **[200.119]** above), although it is still possible to create trusts for the testator's children which have certain IHT benefits, namely trusts for bereaved minors within IHTA 1984, s 71A, (see para **[200.108]** above), and age 18-to-25 trusts within IHTA 1984, s 71D, (see para **[200.109]** above). Further, although an interest in possession taking immediate effect on death on or after 22 March 2006 ('an immediate post-death interest' within IHTA 1984, s 49A, (see para **[200.98]** above)) will still have the result of treating the beneficiary of it as beneficially entitled to the underlying settled property, a subsequent interest in possession will not (unless it is a disabled person's interest within IHTA 1984, s 89B, (see para **[200.99]** above). Therefore, where a will contains trusts for children, or successive interests in possession they should be reviewed to ensure they achieve maximum IHT efficiency consistent with the testator's objectives. Although if changes to any trusts contained in the will are required as a result of this legislation, it may be preferable to make a new will rather than to try and incorporate them in a codicil.

[237.8]

[Updated for the Perpetuities and Accumulations Act 2009.]

New statutory rules affecting wills or the interpretation of them sometimes apply according to the date of death of the testator, and sometimes according to the date of making the will. Two important statutory provisions which only apply to wills made after they came into force are the Family Law

Reform Act 1969 (FLRA 1969), s 15 and the Family Law Reform Act 1987 (FLRA 1987), s 1, extending the rights of illegitimate persons so that, among other things, a gift to a person or persons defined by relationship to someone else is presumed to include illegitimate persons (see Vol 1, paras **[72.10]–[72.14]**, and Part A, paras **[200.28]–[200.32]**, and the statutes are set out in Part G, paras **[245.37]** ff and **[245.69]** ff). However, each of these statutory provisions also provides that the subsequent confirmation of a will which was made before the statute came into force, by a codicil made after it came into force, does not have the effect of treating the will as made after it came into force (FLRA 1969, s 15(8): Part G, para **[245.39]** and FLRA 1987, s 19(7): Part G, para **[245.72]**). As a result, the confirmation of a will made before the FLRA 1987 came into force (on 4 April 1988), by a codicil made on or after 4 April 1988, will not by itself cause the construction of the will to be governed by the 1987 Act; if the will was made after 1969 it will continue to be governed by the FLRA 1969 (see FLRA 1987, Sch 3, para 9: Part G, para **[245.80]**), although the practical consequences of this are quite likely to be the same as they would be if the will was governed by the FLRA 1987, and if it was made before 1970 it will continue to be governed by the common law rules whereby illegitimate persons were presumed to be excluded in the absence of words to the contrary. To avoid possible uncertainties of construction where a codicil is being made to a pre-4 April 1988 will, particularly where it is a pre-1 January 1970 will, it is recommended that express provision should be made either excluding the statutory rule or rules introduced since the will was made, or else making them applicable (see further Part A, para **[200.30]**): see cl 3 of Form D1 at para **[237.11]** for an example.

By contrast, it seems to be the case that the main provisions of the Perpetuities and Accumulations Act 2009 (PAA 2009) which generally apply only to wills made on or after 6 April 2010, see the PAA 2009, s 15(1)(a) (Part G, para **[246.189]**), will apply to a will made before 6 April 2010 but confirmed by a codicil made on or after 6 April 2010. This is because the PAA 2009 contains no provision such as that found in the FLRA 1969 or the FLRA 1987 excluding the general rule that the effect of the confirmation of a will by a codicil is to bring the dispositions of the will down to the date of the codicil, see Vol 1, para **[20.4]** (effect of confirmation of wills by codicils). In the absence of such a provision, the general rule would seem to apply. Accordingly, where a will made before 6 April 2010 is confirmed by a codicil made on or after 6 April 2010, the new rules of PAA 2009 would seem to apply to any trusts declared in the will. In particular, a mandatory 125 year perpetuity period will apply, and accumulations of income (arising under non-charitable trusts) may be made throughout that period (see paras **[94.6]** ff, paras **[94.6]** ff, paras **[95.0]** ff). Generally though, this should not cause any problems if the original trusts are not updated by the codicil. If an 80 year trust period has been chosen, or a 21 year accumulation period, these periods will remain valid. Even where a common law period of lives in being plus 21 years has been relied upon, this should not in practice cause difficulties since it will be unlikely in the extreme that interests vesting within the common law period would not vest within 125 years, and a varied version of the 'wait and see' rule is carried over from PAA 1964 to PAA 2009, see the PAA 2009, s 7 (Part G, para **[246.181]**, paras **[94.17]** ff).

Nevertheless, where a codicil is being prepared after 5 April 2010 for a will made before 6 April 2010 and the will contains trusts, and in particular trusts relying on a common law perpetuity period, consideration should be given to whether these trusts, and in particular the trust period, should be amended in the light of the fact that a mandatory 125 year perpetuity period will apply as a result of the codicil confirming the will (see paras **[94.6]** ff).

Even if amendments to the trust and accumulation periods are not strictly required, a testator who has made his will pre-6 April 2010 may wish to take the opportunity of updating his will so as to extend the period during which the trusts may last and the period during which income may be accumulated. Whereas it will usually be better if a new will is executed, an example of a codicil containing such amendments is given below, see Form D21A at para **[237.31A]**.

[237.10]

[Updated for Human Fertilisation and Embryology Act 2008.]

The statutory rules of construction relating to adopted persons which have had effect from 1 January 1976 (they were introduced by the Children Act 1975, consolidated into the Adoption Act 1976 as from 1 January 1988, and re-enacted in the Adoption of Children Act 2002, Pt 1, Ch 4, which came into force on 30 December 2005 (see Part H, Additional Statutes, para **[245.96]**, below), apply to the will of a person dying on or after 1 January 1976 regardless of the date of execution of the will, so that a confirmation of a codicil can make no difference (see Vol 1, para **[75.4]** and, see ACA 2002, s 73(4), Sch 4, para 18, Part H, Additional Statutes, paras **[245.100]** and **[245.102]**, below. See also Chapter 75, above). The position is the same as regards the rules of construction relating to legitimated children contained in the Legitimacy Act 1976 (see Vol 1, para **[72.16]** and the Legitimacy Act 1976, s 10(3): Part G, para **[245.51]**). The Human Fertilisation and Embryology Act 1990 (HFEA 1990), ss 27 to 29, which came into force on 1 August 1991, and HFEA 2008, ss 33 to 53 which replaced the 1990 Act provisions from 6 April 2009, and make provision for who is to be treated as father, mother or parent of a child produced by means (such as artificial insemination or in vitro fertilisation) regulated by the Act, seems to apply to dispositions made before or after the Act so that a post-Act confirmation of a pre-Act instrument will not bring these provisions into play; they will already apply (see Vol 1, para **[74.6]** and the HFEA 1990, s 29(3): Part G, para **[245.87]**). For the law relating to codicils generally, see Vol 1, para **[20.1]** ff.

[237.30]

[Updated for the nil-rate inheritance tax band.]

Form D20: Codicil increasing the amount of a legacy to the current inheritance tax nil-rate band[1]

I [*testator*] of [*address*] declare this to be a [first] codicil to my will which is dated the —— day of ——.

RECITAL OF LEGACY

Whereas by my said will I have bequeathed to [*name*] a legacy of £—— which was the upper limit of the nil-rate inheritance tax band at the date of my said will and that upper limit has since increased to £——.

INCREASE OF LEGACY

1. Now I hereby increase the said legacy of £—— to the said [*name*] to the said sum of £——.

CONFIRMATION

2. In all other respects I hereby confirm my said will.[2]

[*Testimonium and attestation clause as in* Form D1 *at para* **[237.11]**.]

1 For nil-rate band legacies see Part A, para **[200.101]**, the Preliminary Note to B18 at para **[218.16]** ff and Form B10.51 at para **[210.72]**. The nil-rate IHT band until 5 April 2015 is £325,000. The introduction from 9 October 2007 of nil-rate band transfer (see para **[200.75]** above) may lead a testator to rethink altogether the strategy of including a nil-rate band gift in his will, (see para **[237.3]** above).

2 See Preliminary Note at paras **[237.7]–[237.10]** and cl 3 of Form D1 at para **[237.11]**.

[237.31]

[Updated for the nil-rate inheritance tax band.]

Form D21: Codicil imposing an actual value limit on a formula nil-rate band legacy to the testator's children[1]

I [*testator*] of [*address*] declare this to be a [first] codicil to my will which is dated the —— day of ——.

RECITAL OF NIL-RATE BAND LEGACY

Whereas by clause —— of my said will I have bequeathed to my children in equal shares a legacy equivalent to the maximum sum of money which can in the circumstances subsisting at my death be given by the said clause without any liability being incurred for the payment of inheritance tax on or by reason of my death.[2]

LIMIT ON LEGACY

1. Now I hereby declare that in the event that the said maximum sum of money exceeds the sum of £—— the said legacy to my children shall be the said sum of £——.

CONFIRMATION

2. In all other respects I hereby confirm my said will.[3]

[*Testimonium and attestation clause as in* Form D1 *at para* **[237.11]**.]

1 A testator whose estate will include property with the benefit of business or agricultural property relief may wish to place a limit on a nil-rate legacy because the availability of such relief may cause the nil-rate legacy to exceed the upper limit of the nil-rate IHT band at the date of the testator's death. See the Preliminary Note to C11 at paras **[233.8]–[233.10]**. A limit may be particularly desirable where the bulk of the testator's estate comprises business property with the benefit of 100 per cent relief because then a nil-rate legacy without a limit might include most of the estate. Generally speaking, and particularly where part of the testator's estate may be exempt from IHT (eg. by reason of the spouse or civil partner exemption), it will be wise for IHT purposes if property with the benefit of business or

agricultural property relief is the subject of a specific chargeable gift so that full advantage is taken of the business or agricultural property relief.

2 The IHT nil-rate band until 5 April 2015 is £325,000. The introduction from 9 October 2007 of nil-rate band transfer (see para **[200.75]** above) may lead a testator to rethink altogether the strategy of including a nil-rate band gift in his will, (see para **[237.3]** above).

3 See Preliminary Note at paras **[237.7]**–**[237.10]** and cl 3 of Form D1 at para **[237.11]**.

[237.31A]

[Updated for the Perpetuities and Accumulations Act 2009.]

Form D21A: Codicil changing the trust period and the accumulation period applicable to the trusts of a will[1]

I [*testator*] of [*address*] declare this to be a [first] codicil to my will which is dated the —— day of ——.

I hereby confirm my said will save only that all references to 'the trust period' shall be read as references to the period of 125 years from my death and all references to 'the accumulation period' shall similarly be read as references to the period of 125 years from my death.[2]

[*Testimonium and attestation clause as in* Form D1 *at para* **[237.11]**.]

1 In the light of the Perpetuities and Accumulations Act 2009 (see para **[237.8]**), a testator who has made his will before 6 April 2010 may wish to take the opportunity of updating it so as to extend the period during which the trusts may last and the period during which income may be accumulated. Great care must be taken when making such changes by codicil to ensure that the trusts, as altered, will be valid and workable.

2 It is assumed that the will has a defined 'trust period' (eg. 80 years) and a defined 'accumulation period', e g 21 years, so that the codicil simply changes the meanings of these terms. If the will also includes a declaration that the perpetuity period is to be 80 years (or some lesser period), the declaration will have no effect and the period will be 125 years, see the PAA 2009, s 5(2) (Para G, para **[246.179]**).

PART E

Statutory Will Forms 1925

E

Statutory Will Forms 1925

[238.6]

[Updated for the Perpetuities and Accumulations Act 2009.]

It should be noted that the statutory forms have not been amended to take account of the Family Law Reform Act 1969 (FLRA 1969), the Inheritance Tax Act 1984 (IHTA 1984), the Trusts of Land and Appointment of Trustees Act 1996 (TLATA 1996), the Civil Partnership Act 2004 (CPA 2004), or the Perpetuities and Accumulations Act 2009 (PAA 2009). Accordingly while reference to persons of 'full age' in Form 3 are now to be construed as references to persons who have attained the age of 18 years, the express references to the age of 21 years contained in the beneficial trusts set out in Forms 9 and 10 remain unchanged. The administration trusts set out in Form 8 continue to refer to 'duties' but this term is deemed to include a reference to IHT: see IHTA 1984, Sch 6, para 1 and Finance Act 1986, s 100(1)(b). A trust for sale and conversion as appears in Form E8 at para **[238.14]** is in general no longer necessary in administration trusts as a result of the TLATA 1996: see para **[214.1]** ff. Furthermore, the trusts of Forms E7 and E9, at paras **[238.13]**, **[238.15]**, are drafted by reference to a common law perpetuity period of lives in being plus 21 years which is not a valid perpetuity period for wills made on or after 5 April 2010 for which there is a mandatory perpetuity period of 125 years by virtue of the PAA 2009, ss 5(1), 15(1)(a) (Part G, paras **[246.179]**, **[246.189]**, and see para **[94.6]**). Whereas it is not ideal to use forms based on pre-PAA 2009 perpetuity periods, in practice it should not cause difficulties since it will be unlikely in the extreme that interests vesting within the common law period would not vest within 125 years, and a varied version of the 'wait and see' rule is carried over from PAA 1964 to PAA 2009, see the PAA 2009, s 7 (Part G, para **[246.181]**).

Forms which may only be applied by specific reference

[238.13]

[Updated for the Perpetuities and Accumulations Act 2009.]

Form E7: Statutory Will Forms 1925, Form 7: Trusts of a settled legacy[1]

Any legacy of money or investments to which this clause is applied shall be subject to the following provisions:

(1) The trustees shall stand possessed of the legacy upon trust to invest the same in their names or under their control in any authorised

investments, with power, at the like discretion, to vary the investments thereof for others of a like nature.

(2) The trustees shall stand possessed of the legacy, and of the investments representing the same and all statutory accumulations, if any, of income thereof, hereinafter included in the description of such legacy upon trust to pay the income thereof to the legatee during the life of the legatee.

(3) After the death of the legatee, the capital and income of the legacy shall be held—

In trust for all or any one or more exclusively of the other or others, of the issue[2] of the legatee, whether children or remoter descendants, at such time, and if more than one in such shares, with such provisions for maintenance, education, advancement, and otherwise, at the discretion of any person or persons, and with such gifts over, and generally in such manner, for the benefit of such issue, or some or one of them, as the legatee shall, by deed, revocable or irrevocable, or by will appoint; but so that, under any appointment, a child shall not, otherwise than by way of advancement, take a vested interest, except upon attaining the age of twenty-one years or upon marriage.

And in default of and until and subject to any such appointment—

In trust for all or any the children or child[2] of the legatee, who attain the age of twenty-one years, or marry under that age, and if more than one in equal shares.

(4) Any child of the legatee, who, or whose issue, takes any part of the legacy under any appointment by the legatee, shall not, in the absence of any direction by the legatee to the contrary, take any share in the unappointed part without bringing the share or shares appointed to him or his issue into hotchpot and accounting for the same accordingly.

(5) If the legatee shall not have any child who, under the trusts in default of appointment hereinbefore contained, attains a vested interest in the legacy, then, subject to the trusts and powers hereinbefore expressed in favour of the legatee and his issue, the legacy and the income thereof and all statutory accumulations, if any, of income shall fall into and form part of my residuary personal estate.

(6) The legatee may, notwithstanding any of the trusts hereinbefore expressed concerning his legacy, from time to time or at any time by deed, revocable or irrevocable, or by will, appoint to or for the benefit of any spouse who may survive the legatee, during the residue of the life of such spouse or for any less period (and subject or not to any conditions, and with such gifts over, and discretionary or other trusts for the benefit of the spouse and issue of the legatee, as the legatee may think fit), all or any part of the annual income of the legacy of the legatee, or of so much thereof as shall not before the death of the legatee, have been paid or applied under any power affecting the same.

And, upon any such appointment, the trusts and powers limited to take effect after the death of the legatee, shall take effect subject to the interest limited by any such appointment:

Provided that the power last aforesaid, to appoint by deed, shall not be exercisable by a woman while under coverture.

1 This form settles any legacy directed to be subject to it upon trust for the legatee for life, and after his death for his issue as he should appoint, and in default of appointment for his children at 21. It is drafted by reference to the common law perpetuity period, so that all interests will vest within 21 years of the death of the legatee. The common law perpetuity period is not, though, a valid perpetuity period for wills made on or after 5 April 2010 for which there is a mandatory perpetuity period of 125 years by virtue of the PAA 2009, ss 5(1), 15(1)(a) (Part G, paras **[246.179]**, **[246.189]**, and see para **[94.6]**). Nevertheless, if this Form is used, it is unlikely that it will cause difficulties in practice since it will be unlikely in the extreme that interests vesting within the common law period will not vest within 125 years, and a varied version of the 'wait and see' rule is carried over from PAA 1964 to PAA 2009, see the PAA 2009, s 7 (Part G, para **[246.181]**). If the legacy takes effect immediately on death (or subject only to a survivorship condition permitted by IHTA 1984, s 92: see paras **[219.6]**–**[219.7]**) and the legatee is not an infant it will be an immediate post-death interest within IHTA 1984, s 49A (see para **[200.98]** above and para **[216.1]** above). If the testator is the parent of the life tenant's children, the default remainder trust for the children will not be a trust for bereaved minors within IHTA 1984, s 71A (see para **[200.108]** above), but should be an age 18-to-25 trust within IHTA 1984, s 71D to the extent that any of the children are under 21 on the date it takes effect (see para **[200.109]** above) (unless it has taken effect immediately on the testator's death, and any child was over the age of 18 but under the age of 21, and immediately entitled to an interest possession by virtue of TA 1925, s 31(1)(ii), so that he or she would have an immediate post-death interest). Any life interest appointed to a spouse of the legatee under the power of Clause (6) will not be an immediate post-death interest within IHTA 1984, s 49A (see para **[200.98]** above and para **[216.1]** above).

2 Unless excluded, the statutory rules of construction, whereby references to children and issue include references to illegitimate, legitimated and adopted persons (Part G, Section 2, para **[245.1]**), will apply. For a form in which the statutory rules are excluded see Form C13.2, cl 2(f) at para **[235.18]**.

[238.15]

[Updated for the Perpetuities and Accumulations Act 2009.]

Form E9: Statutory Will Forms 1925, Form 9: Trusts for spouse for life, with power to appoint to issue and gift over to them[1]

Any property disposed of by my will (otherwise than in exercise of a special power) to which this clause is applied[2] shall be subject to the following provisions:

(1) The property (including the investments for the time being representing the same) shall be held upon trust to pay the income thereof to my spouse for life.

(2) After the death of my spouse, the capital and income of the property shall be held—

(i) In trust for all or any one or more, exclusively of the other or others, of my issue, whether children or remoter descendants,[3] at such time, and if more than one in such shares, with such provisions for maintenance, education, advancement and otherwise, at the discretion of any person or persons, and with such gifts over, and generally in such manner, for the benefit of such issue, or some or one of them, as my spouse shall, by deed, revocable or irrevocable, or by will, appoint; but so that, under any appointment, a child shall not, otherwise than by way of advancement, take a vested interest, except upon attaining the age of twenty-one years or upon marriage.

(ii) And in default of and until and subject to any such appointment in trust, in equal shares if more than one, for all or any of my children or child[3] who survive me and attain the age of twenty-one years[4] or marry under that age, and for all or any of the issue[3] living at my death who attain the age of twenty-one years[4] or marry under that age or any child of mine who predeceases me, such issue to take through all degrees, according to their stocks, in equal shares if more than one, the share or shares which his or their parent would have taken if living at my death and so that no issue shall take whose parent is living at my death and so capable of taking.

(3) Any person who, or whose issue, takes any part of the property, under any appointment by my spouse, shall not, in the absence of any direction by my spouse to the contrary, take any share in the unappointed part, without bringing the shares appointed to such person or his issue into hotchpot, and accounting for the same accordingly.

1 This form settles any property directed to be subject to it upon trust for the surviving spouse for life, and after her death for the testator's issue as the surviving spouse should appoint, and in default of appointment for the testator's children at 21 or earlier marriage. It is drafted by reference to the common law perpetuity period, so that all interests will vest within 21 years of the death of the spouse. The common law perpetuity period is not, though, a valid perpetuity period for wills made on or after 5 April 2010 for which there is a mandatory perpetuity period of 125 years by virtue of the PAA 2009, ss 5(1), 15(1)(a) (Part G, paras **[246.179]**, **[246.189]**, and see para **[94.6]**). Nevertheless, if this Form is used, it is unlikely that it will cause difficulties in practice since it will be unlikely in the extreme that interests vesting within the common law period will not vest within 125 years, and a varied version of the 'wait and see' rule is carried over from PAA 1964 to PAA 2009, see the PAA 2009, s 7 (Part G, para **[246.182]**). If the spouse's life interest takes effect immediately on death (or subject only to a survivorship condition permitted by IHTA 1984, s 92: see paras **[219.6]**–**[219.7]**) it will be an immediate post-death interest within IHTA 1984, s 49A so spouse exemption from inheritance tax should be available, see para **[216.1]** above. The default remainder trust for the children will not be a trust for bereaved minors within IHTA 1984, s 71A (see para **[200.108]** above), but should be an age 18-to-25 trust within IHTA 1984, s 71D to the extent that any of the children are under 21 on the date it takes effect (see para **[200.109]** above) (unless it has taken effect immediately on the testator's death, and any child was over the age of 18 but under the age of 21, and immediately entitled to an interest possession by virtue of TA 1925, s 31(1)(ii) (see para **[246.29]**), so that he or she would have an immediate post-death interest). The spouse could appoint trusts for the testator's children which would be within IHTA 1984, s 71A (see para **[200.108]** above) if they took effect while the children were under the age of 18.

2 These provisions will commonly be applied to residue.

3 See para **[238.13]**, n 1, above.

4 The reference to 21 years in this and the following form are unaffected by the FLRA 1969.

[238.16]

[Updated for the Perpetuities and Accumulations Act 2009.]

Form E10: Statutory Will Forms 1925, Form 10: Trusts for spouse and issue, without a power of appointment[1]

Any property disposed of by my will (otherwise than in exercise of a special power) to which this clause is applied shall be subject to the following provisions:

(1) The property (including the investments for the time being representing the same) shall be held upon trust to pay the income thereof to my spouse for life.

(2) After the death of my spouse the capital and income of the property shall be held in trust, in equal shares if more than one, for all or any of my children or child,[2] who survive me and attain the age of twenty-one years[3] or marry under that age, and for all or any of the issue[2] living at my death, who attain the age of twenty-one years[1] or marry under that age, of any child of mine who predeceases me, such issue to take through all degrees, according to their stocks, in equal shares, if more than one, the share or shares which his or their parent would have taken if living at my death; and so that no issue shall take whose parent is living at my death and so capable of taking.

1 This form settles any property directed to be subject to it upon trust for the surviving spouse for life, and after her death for the testator's children at 21 or earlier marriage. All interests will vest within 21 years of the death of the testator, so necessarily within the mandatory perpetuity period of 125 years which applies to wills made on or after 6 April 2010 by virtue of the PAA 2009, ss 5(1), 15(1)(a) (Part G, paras **[246.179]**, **[246.189]**, and see para **[94.6]**). If the spouse's life interest takes effect immediately on death (or subject only to a survivorship condition permitted by IHTA 1984, s 92: see paras **[219.6]**–**[219.7]**) it will be an immediate post-death interest within IHTA 1984, s 49A, so spouse exemption from inheritance tax should be available, see para **[216.1]** above. The remainder trust for the children will not be a trust for bereaved minors within IHTA 1984, s 71A (see para **[200.120]** above), but should be an age 18-to-25 trust within IHTA 1984, s 71D to the extent that any of the children are under 21 on the date it takes effect (see para **[200.121]** above) (unless it has taken effect immediately on the testator's death, and any child was over the age of 18 but under the age of 21, and immediately entitled to an interest possession by virtue of TA 1925, s 31(1)(ii), so that he or she would have an immediate post-death interest).

2 See para **[238.13]**, n 1.

3 See para **[238.15]**, n 3.

PART F

Non-testamentary instruments

F1

Renunciation of probate and disclaimer of trusteeships

PRELIMINARY NOTE

[239.1]

[Updated for *Kershaw v Micklethwaite* [2010] EWHC 506 (Ch).]

An executor appointed by the will of a deceased person who has not intermeddled with the estate may either reserve his position, in which case powers will be reserved to him to prove the will at a later stage if he so wishes, or he may renounce probate. The renunciation should be in writing and should be filed in court. A renunciation can be withdrawn but, if it has been filed, not without the leave of the court. See generally as to renunciation Vol 1, para **[25.13]**.

A renunciation of probate by an executor who is also appointed a trustee is not conclusive evidence that the trusteeship is renounced as well (see Vol 1, para **[27.4]**, n 8). He should therefore expressly disclaim the trusteeship, and a separate document is convenient because a renunciation of probate has to be filed with the court. A deed of disclaimer of the trusteeship will also be appropriate where someone appointed trustee but not executor wishes to disclaim. Where someone appointed a sole executor is willing to be executor but not trustee, he should take out probate and appoint new trustees in his place, when the administration is complete, under the statutory power in Trustee Act 1925 (TA 1925), s 36 (Part G, para **[246.34]**). See Form F1.4 at para **[239.5]**. If none of the named executors proves the will or accepts office as trustee of it the administrators will become trustees of the will on completion of the administration and among all the other usual powers of trustees will be able to appoint new trustees under the statutory power: see *Re Cockburn's Will Trusts, Cockburn v Lewis* [1957] Ch 438, [1957] 2 All ER 522.

Section 50 of the Administration of Justice Act 1985 confers jurisdiction on the High Court to appoint a new personal representative in substitution of some or all of the existing ones, or, if there are two or more of them, terminate the appointment of one or more, but not all, of the personal representatives. The Court is not empowered to increase the number of personal representatives. Application can be made by a personal representative or a beneficiary, and so an application under this section is a means whereby a personal representative can apply to be relieved of his office after he has obtained a grant. It is also a means by which a beneficiary can obtain the removal of a personal representative against his will, though only where the personal representative's continuance in office would prevent the proper administration of the estate or would not be in the interests of the beneficiaries, see *Kershaw v Micklethwaite* [2010] EWHC 506 (Ch).

A personal representative who is substituted under this section is an executor (except for the purposes of any chain of representation) if he is appointed to act together with executors, and otherwise is an administrator.

F3

Disclaimers and variations of beneficial interests

PRELIMINARY NOTE

[241.3]

[Updated for *Wills v Gibbs* [2008] STC 808 and Finance Act 2012, Sch 33.]

Notice of intention for IHTA 1984, s 142 to apply, and the requirement of informing any charity which is benefited. Since the effect of the IHTA 1984, s 142 is to treat a disposition made by a beneficiary as one made by the deceased, it can result in additional IHT becoming payable where an exempt beneficiary, such as the deceased's wife, assigns her interest. The personal representatives might not have enough assets left in their possession with which to pay the extra tax, and anyway s 142 not applying could be more advantageous in some circumstances (such as where the deceased has fully utilised his available nil-rate IHT band and the wife makes a substantial gift out of the deceased's assets). Section 142(2), (2A) therefore provides that for the section to apply to an instrument varying the deceased's dispositions, the instrument of variation must contain a statement, made by all the 'relevant persons', to the effect that they intend s 142(1) to apply to the variation. The 'relevant persons' are defined as the person or persons making the instrument, and where the variation results in additional tax being payable, the personal representatives. Personal representatives may, however, decline to join in such a statement if they have no or insufficient assets to discharge the additional tax. These requirements for a statement of intention were introduced for variations made after 31 July 2002 and replace the former requirement for an election to be made within six months of execution of the instrument of variation. If additional tax is payable as a result of the variation, there is an obligation on the relevant persons to deliver a copy of the instrument of variation to HMRC, and notify them of the amount of additional tax within six months: see IHTA 1984, s 218A, inserted by FA 2002, s 120(2), (4). Otherwise there is no obligation, as previously, to report the instrument.

If it is desired that some dispositions should be made to which s 142 applies, and some to which it does not, they could be made by separate instruments, with the one containing the appropriate statement, and the other not. It should also be noted that s 142(2) does not apply to *disclaimers* within s 142(1), and that the application of s 142 to disclaimers is thus automatic (unless they are made orally—in which case s 142 does not apply at all), so a statement within s 142(2) is not required, although it may be desirable for the sake of clarity. Where the deceased's surviving spouse makes an instrument of variation under which he or she assigns (to a non-exempt beneficiary) a specific gift or legacy which does not bear its own IHT, the persons interested in residue, out of which any extra tax will be paid, cannot, it seems, prevent a statement of intention under s 142(2) being made. A statement of intention under s 142(2), once made, cannot be revoked.

If it is intended that TCGA 1992, s 62(6) should apply to an instrument of variation (see para **[241.17]**), it must similarly contain a statement by the persons making the instrument that they intend s 62(6) to apply: see TCGA 1992, s 62(7) as substituted by FA 2002, s 52 with effect for instruments made after 31 July 2002. Note that there is no requirement for the personal representatives to join in this statement if they are not making the instrument.

For an example of a statement of intention within IHTA 1984, s 142(2) and TCGA 1992, s 62(7), see para **[241.25]**, below.

If the statement of intention is omitted, once the deed has been made it is too late to get the deed within s 142 unless rectification can be obtained. For a case where the statement of intention for the purposes of s 142(2) was omitted accidentally from a deed of variation, and the omission remedied by way of rectification, see *Wills v Gibbs* [2008] STC 808. It was held, following *Jervis v Howle and Talke Colliery* [1937] Ch 67, to be sufficient evidence of intention that the maker of the deed intended the deed to come within s 142, though he was not aware of the specific need for a statement of that intention in the deed.

If the deceased died on or after 6 April 2012, and an instrument of variation relating to his or her estate benefits a charity, the instrument will only fall within IHTA 1984, s 142 if it can be demonstrated to the satisfaction of HMRC that the charity has been notified of the existence of the instrument: see IHTA 1984, s 142(3A) and (3B) inserted by FA 2012, Sch 33, para 9. This additional requirement is imposed in anticipation of an increase in instruments of variation benefiting charities in order to take advantage of IHTA 1984, Sch 1A (inserted by FA 2012, Sch 33), which in relation to deaths on or after 6 April 2012 reduces the rate of IHT where a certain proportion of the estate goes to charity (see, further, paras **[200.91A]**, **[212.2A]**, and Form B12.2A at para **[212.4A]** and Form F3.11 at para **[241.32]**).

[241.5]

[Updated for *Wells* (*PRs of Glowacki*) *v HMRC* [2008] STC (SCD) 188.]

Meaning of 'estate' for the purposes of section 142. Section 142(1) is expressly confined to variations or disclaimers relating to the property comprised in a deceased person's estate immediately before his death, which at first glance means the aggregate of all property to which that person was beneficially entitled other than excluded property (see IHTA 1984, s 5(1)). However, s 142(5) gives a special meaning to 'estate' for the purposes of s 142(1), by providing that it includes excluded property. It also provides that it does not include property in which the deceased had an interest in possession immediately before his death. This means that the only relieving provision where someone wishes not to receive an interest in settled property which falls into possession on the death of a life tenant is s 93 of the IHTA 1984, which applies only to a disclaimer made otherwise than for a consideration in money or money's worth. Section 142(5) also provides that 'estate' for s 142(1) purposes does not include property which was treated as comprised in the deceased's estate at death because it was property subject to a reservation within FA 1986, s 102 (see para **[200.76]**).

It should also be noted that s 142 can apply to assets passing on a person's death, other than property which was settled property immediately before the death, which do not pass under that person's will, such as nominated savings bank accounts and interests in joint tenancies. For a form of variation of the disposition of a deceased's interest under a joint tenancy, see Form F3.5 at para **[241.26]**.

A deed of variation within IHTA 1984, s 142 cannot take assets out of the death estate, and in particular cannot give rise to a deemed lifetime gift, treated as made by the deceased before his death, of an asset of the deceased's estate at his death, but can only substitute, for the dispositions taking effect on death, other dispositions deemed to take effect on death of the assets which were comprised in the deceased's estate for the purposes of s 142(1): see *Wells (PRs of Glowacki) v HMRC* [2008] STC (SCD) 188.

[241.7]

[Updated for *Lau v HMRC*.]

Consideration. Section 142(3) of the IHTA 1984 provides that s 142(1) does not apply to a variation or disclaimer made for any consideration in money or money's worth, other than consideration consisting of the making in respect of another of the deceased's dispositions of a variation or disclaimer to which s 142(1) applies. One particular point to watch in relation to this provision is that if the donee under an instrument of variation agrees to pay the costs of the instrument that could be consideration which takes the instrument outside s 142(1). For further points relating to this provision see paras **[241.13]** and **[241.14]**. For an example of a disclaimer failing to fall within s 142 because done for a consideration see the Special Commissioner case of *Lau v HMRC* [2009] STC (SCD) 352. It was a disclaimer by the testator's son of a non-exempt specific gift so as to fall into exempt residue (given to the testator's widow), where the disclaimer was done on the basis of an assurance that the widow would make an equivalent lifetime gift back to the son.

[241.16]

[Updated for the Estates of Deceased Persons (Forfeiture Rule and Law of Succession) Act 2011 ('EDP(FRLS)A 2011').]

Disclaimers. If a disclaimer is contemplated the following points should be borne in mind:

(i) The law relating to disclaimers is technical and obscure. While some of its salient features are noted below, reference should be made to *Ing on*

Bona Vacantia at pp 207 ff and *Halsbury's Laws of England*, 4th edn Reissue, Vol 50, paras **[390]**–**[392]** at pp 284–286, for a fuller treatment. See also Vol 1, para **[46.1]** ff.

(ii) The disclaimer does not strictly speaking operate as a disposition of property. As was said in an old case, a man 'cannot have an estate put into him in spite of his teeth'. Thus a disclaimer will not divest a gift in favour of the disclaiming beneficiary, but will prevent it from vesting in him. Acceptance of a gift or any part of it is inconsistent with an intention to renounce or disclaim it. The right to disclaim a gift is therefore extinguished as soon as any benefit has been received thereunder: see eg *Re Wimperis, Wicken v Wilson* [1914] 1 Ch 502. While it is usually possible to disclaim one testamentary gift without disclaiming another, this will not be permissible where such right is impliedly excluded. This will often be the case where gifts of onerous property and unencumbered property are made to the same person. Nor is it permissible to disclaim part only of a single gift. In *Re Joel, Rogerson v Joel* [1943] Ch 311, [1943] 2 All ER 263, CA, a gift of a leasehold house 'together with its contents' was in fact held to be a single gift and the legatee was accordingly held not to be entitled to disclaim the onerous leasehold whilst accepting the contents of the house.

(iii) Since, as we have already seen, disclaimers operate not to divest a gift but to prevent it from vesting, there is no requirement of form. A disclaimer even of an interest in land may thus be effected by informal writing, by conduct or even orally. But to be effective for the purposes of s 142 of the IHTA 1984 the disclaimer must be in writing. (IHTA 1984, s 142(1) applies automatically to a written disclaimer so long as it is made within two years of death and for no extraneous consideration, so a statement within s 142(2) is not required. See para **[241.3]**, above.) In general a disclaimer may also be retracted where nobody has altered his position on the faith of it. This right is not thought to be available where the disclaimer is by deed: see *Ing*, above at pp 209–210. In the interests of certainty it seems preferable for a disclaimer to be effected by deed.

(iv) It has sometimes been argued that it is not possible to disclaim an interest arising under an intestacy on the grounds that such interest is conferred by statute: see eg Sir William Goodhart QC's article 'Disclaimer of Interests on Intestacy?' in 40 *Conveyancer* at p 292. This would be an inconvenient restriction and, as Sir William himself points out, is inconsistent with the actual decision of Walton J in *Re Scott, Widdows v Friends of the Clergy Corpn* [1975] 2 All ER 1033, [1975] 1 WLR 1260, though the point was not in fact argued in that case.

(v) It is essential to give careful thought to what dispositions will take effect on a disclaimer being made. For example, sometimes a disclaimer of a life interest will accelerate the remainder interests, and sometimes it will give rise to a partial intestacy, depending on the nature of the remainder trusts; see Vol 1, para **[48.4]** ff. A disclaimer of a specific gift will usually cause the property to fall into residue. *Re Scott* discusses the effect of a disclaimer of certain interests arising under the intestacy rules, but the difficult problem as to the effect of a disclaimer by a child of a deceased intestate of his interest in that intestate's estate where that child himself has issue seems now to have been answered by the Court of Appeal in *Re DWS* [2001] Ch 568, [2001] 1 All ER 97, though the effect of that decision has been reversed by EDP(FRLS)A 2011 in relation to deaths on or after 1 February 2012 (the commencement date fixed by SI 2011/2913). What was decided in *Re DWS* was that no issue could take if the parent was living at the death of the intestate; that if a surviving parent was prevented from taking by disclaimer or disqualification, the intestate's estate should pass not to the surviving parent's child, but to others. EDP(FRLS)A 2011 has inserted a new AEA 1925, s 46A, in relation to the estates of intestates dying on or after 1 February 2012, under which for both forfeiture and disclaimer purposes the disqualified or disclaiming person is treated as having predeceased the intestate for the purposes of the intestacy rules. See para **[48.8]** and the text of AEA 1925, s 46A at para **[244.62A]**,

(vi) It is important to note, however, that EDP(FRLS)A 2011 does not apply where there is disclaimer of an interest under a will, except where there is statutory substitution under WA 1837, s 33. See paras **[9.17]** and **[48.8]**, and WA 1837, s 33A, inserted by EDP(FRLS)A 2011, s 12, and set out at para **[244.36A]**. Therefore, a will does not necessarily take effect as if a person disclaiming an interest under it has predeceased the testator, and careful thought is needed as to the consequences where a disclaimer is contemplated. If in doubt, use an instrument of variation instead, if possible.

[241.18]

[Updated for Finance Act 2008, ss 99, 100, Sch 32.]

Stamp duty and stamp duty land tax. Stamp duty on deeds of variation is now a muddle; it has almost been superseded but not quite in all circumstances. The subject is best approached historically. An instrument within the IHTA 1984, s 142, other than a disclaimer, used to attract ad valorem stamp duty as a voluntary disposition to the extent of the bounty passing thereunder: cf *Thorn v IRC* [1976] 2 All ER 622, [1976] 1 WLR 915. The charge to ad valorem stamp duty on voluntary dispositions was abolished as was the charge to ad valorem duty on instruments varying the dispositions of the estate of a deceased person where such instruments would formerly have attracted duty as conveyances on sale, provided that such instruments were executed within two years of the death: Finance Act 1985, ss 82(1) and 84(1). There remained the fixed duties (50p until 30 September 1999, then £5) but the fixed duty and the need for adjudication was avoided if the instrument was certified to be an instrument falling within category L or category M of the Schedule to the Stamp Duty (Exempt Instruments) Regulations 1987. Then, from 1 December 2003, stamp duty was largely replaced by stamp duty land tax (SDLT). FA 2003, s 125 provided that stamp duty under FA 1999, Sch 13 was, from the commencement of SDLT only, to be charged in respect of instruments relating to stock or marketable securities. However, in addition to the fixed duties on such instruments, the £5 duty on deeds of variation which would otherwise be chargeable as conveyances on sale remained (FA 1985, s 84(8)), as did the requirements of adjudication for deeds of variation and gifts (FA 1985, ss 82(5) and 84(9)), unless there was a certificate under the 1987 Regulations. A certificate that an instrument falls within category L or category M of the Schedule to the Stamp Duty (Exempt Instruments) Regulations 1987 should no longer have been necessary in order to avoid paying a fixed stamp duty, apart from the case of an instrument varying the disposition of stock or marketable securities, or an instrument which would be a conveyance or transfer on sale (ie a variation made in consideration of another variation in relation to the same estate where the latter constituted dutiable consideration). The requirement of adjudication apparently remained. In response to the introduction of stamp duty land tax, HMRC specifically amended its Inheritance Tax Manual IHTM 35060 on 10 April 2006, but to instruct its staff that where an instrument has not been duly stamped, or does not contain the appropriate exemption certificate within categories L or M in the schedule to the Regulations, they should apply the following procedure:

(a) any communication to the effect that IHTA 1984, s 142 applies must contain a caveat in such terms as 'provided the document is duly stamped and adjudicated, or the appropriate exemption certificate under the Stamp Duty/Exempt Instruments Regulations 1987 is attached';
(b) if the parties are relying on the instrument to reduce the liability to IHT, they must insist that the document is stamped, or the exemption certificate is attached, before giving effect to the terms of the instrument; but
(c) in other cases, having raised the caveat above, the matter need not be pursued further.

This guidance does not appear limited to variations affecting stock or marketable securities, although previously in their Customer Newsletters of April 2004 and August 2004, HMRC had indicated that an exemption certificate would only be required where both the deed effected a variation of stocks or shares, and unusually the deed acted as the transfer. This guidance also dates from before FA 2008, for which see below.

FA 2008 then abolished, for instruments executed on or after 13 March 2008, the remaining fixed duties and adjudication requirements, in particular in relation to gifts and deeds of variation relating to stock or marketable securities, except in relation to instruments effecting 'land transactions' (FA 2008, ss 99, 100, Sch 32, paras 1, 2, 3, and 10). Land transactions here are any acquisition of an estate, interest, right or power in or over land in the UK other than a security interest, licence, tenancy at will, franchise advowson or manor (FA 2008, s 99, Sch 32, para 22(2), FA 2003, ss 43 and 48(1)–(3)). Accordingly, it apparently remains the case that a deed of variation needs still to be certified under the Stamp Duty (Exempt Instruments) Regulations 1987 to avoid the need for adjudication and, in the case of one involving stampable consideration, the £5 duty, where it involves the acquisition of an estate, interest etc in or over land. However, it may be that deeds of variation relating to unadministered residuary estate will not fall into this category, even where there is land in the residuary estate, because of the nature of an interest in unadministered residue: see Vol 1, para **[38.16]**.

Stamp duty land tax is essentially a tax on land transactions, charging ad valorem tax on the consideration given for the acquisition of an interest in land (see para **[220.72]**, above). Generally, s 142 variations in respect of land or interests in land will not give rise to a liability because they will not be made for consideration. But where they are so made (ie in consideration of the variation of other dispositions in the same estate) they will be exempt from stamp duty land tax by reason of FA 2003, Sch 3, para 4(1), (2), which provides that a transaction following a person's death that varies a disposition (whether effected by will, under the law relating to intestacy or otherwise) of property of which the deceased was competent to dispose is exempt from charge if:

(1) the transaction is carried out within the period of two years after a person's death; and
(2) no consideration in money or money's worth other than the making of a variation of another such disposition is given for it.

This exemption applies whether or not the administration of the estate is complete or the property has been distributed in accordance with the original dispositions (FA 2003, Sch 3, para 4(3)). It is not clear though, whether this exemption covers a variation involving a deceased's severable share of assets held on a joint tenancy since the same is not generally property *of which the deceased was competent to dispose*. The exemption from SDLT means that no SDLT return is required (FA 2003, ss 76, 77).

[241.19]

[Updated for HMRC's Trusts Settlements and Estates Manual TSEM 1840.]

Income tax. There is no income tax provision exactly corresponding to the IHTA 1984, s 142, and an instrument within s 142 will not generally be treated as a disposition by the deceased for the purposes of income tax. Rather, legislation has confirmed that the settlor for income tax purposes of a settlement created by variation is the person who made the variation, at least where that person would, in the absence of the variation, have been entitled to the varied property absolutely. ITA 2007, s 472 provides that where a disposition of property following a person's death is varied and becomes settled property in consequence of the variation (and would not, but for the variation, have become settled property), and TCGA 1992, s 62 (6) applies in respect of the variation, the person who is to be treated as having made the settlement and provided the property for the purposes of the settlement is:

(a) a person who immediately before the variation was entitled to the property, or to property from which it derives, absolutely as legatee;
(b) a person who would have become entitled to the property, or to property from which it derives, absolutely as legatee but for the variation;
(c) a person who immediately before the variation would have been entitled to the property, or to property from which it derives, absolutely as legatee but for being an infant or other person under a disability; and
(d) a person who would, but for the variation, have become entitled to the property, or to property from which it derives, absolutely as legatee if he had not been an infant or other person under a disability.

The main implication of this is that where an instrument of variation settles property on trust it will be a settlement of which the maker of the instrument is the settlor for income tax purposes. Accordingly, if the maker of the instrument retains a beneficial interest (eg he is a beneficiary under a discretionary trust), the income of the relevant property will be subject to income tax as his income under ITTOIA 2005, s 624 and, even if he is not a beneficiary, if his minor children are beneficiaries income which is applied for them will be taxed as his under ITTOIA 2005, s 629.

However, it is thought that the HMRC view is that a disclaimer does not constitute a 'settlement' for income tax purposes, and it is notable that ITA 2007, s 472 refers only to variations and not disclaimers, and see HMRC's Trusts Settlements and Estates Manual TSEM 1840. Thus if it is possible for a beneficiary under a deceased person's estate to achieve a desired result by a disclaimer rather than an instrument of variation, and that desired result would have adverse consequences under the provisions for charging income tax on settlors of settlements (for example, a parent wants to dispose of a life interest in favour of his minor children who are interested in remainder), a disclaimer would have the advantage that he would not be treated as the settlor.

However, if the varied property would have been settled property even apart from the variation (eg. if property is settled by the deceased's will upon trust for his widow for life, remainder to his son, and the widow and son agree a variation to create new trusts for the son's children) the settlor for income tax purposes is to be regarded as the deceased. More specifically, ITA 2007, s 473 provides that where property was or would have become comprised in a settlement which arose on the deceased person's death, but in consequence of the variation the property, or property derived from it, becomes comprised in another settlement, the deceased shall be treated as having made the other settlement.

An instrument of variation may have some further retrospective effect for income tax purposes, if the instrument relates to a residuary estate which is still in the course of administration when the instrument is made. Where this is the case, and there is any income of that residuary estate which has already accrued to the personal representatives before the date of the transfer, and which has not been distributed by them to any beneficiaries, then the Income and Corporation Taxes Act 1988, ss 695 to 701 (as amended by Finance Act 1995, Sch 18) have the effect that someone with an interest (absolute or limited) in a residuary estate still in the course of administration is able to transfer the right to such income so that the income is charged to income tax as the income of the person to whom the income is transferred. The essential scheme is, broadly, that any income of the estate which is distributed to a beneficiary while the estate is being administered is taxed as the income of that beneficiary, and any income which is still undistributed at the point when the administration is completed is taxed as the income of the person who is then entitled to it. These new rules can apply in relation to the estate of a person who died before 6 April 1995, if the administration of his estate had not been completed before that date. Accordingly, it can now be worthwhile from an income tax point of view to include in an instrument of variation, which disposes of the present or future right to income or capital of a residuary estate in the course of administration, a disposition of the right to undistributed income of the residuary estate which has accrued before the variation, if the personal income tax rates of the recipient of the income will be lower than those of the maker of the instrument.

FA 2004, Sch 15 introduced a new income tax charge for tax years 2005–6 onwards upon a taxpayer's occupation of land where he has previously disposed of an interest in that land, or for his use of chattels where he has previously disposed of an interest in them (FA 2004, Sch 15, paras 3, 6). It also deems intangible property in a settlor-interested settlement to produce an income at a prescribed rate, taxable on the settlor (FA 2004, Sch 15, para 8). However, any disposition made by a person ('the chargeable person') in relation to an interest in the estate of another person is to be disregarded for the purposes of Sch 15 if by virtue of IHTA 1984, s 17, the disposition is not treated for the purposes of IHT as a transfer of value by the chargeable person. IHTA 1984, s 17 prevents a variation or disclaimer within s 142(1) being a transfer of value. So, for example, where the devisee of a dwelling-house varies its disposition by a s 142 variation, perhaps transferring it to a discretionary trust, while continuing to occupy it as part of a debt or charge scheme (see para **[218.19]**), he will not be treated as making a transfer of value by virtue of IHTA 1984, s 17, so he will not have disposed of it for the purposes of FA 2004, Sch 15 and so no income tax charge tax charge can arise in respect of his continued occupation. Similarly, where the legatee of shares in a private company with a policy of not declaring dividends settles them on discretionary trusts of which he is a beneficiary by a s 142 variation, an income cannot be deemed under FA 2004, Sch 15, para 8 as for the purposes of Sch 15 he has not settled them as required by para 8(2).

[241.27]

[Updated for the nil-rate inheritance tax band 2010–2015.]

Form F3.6: Deed of variation creating a nil-rate band non-exempt legacy where entire estate given to the deceased's widow[1]

THIS DEED OF VARIATION is made the [*date*] BETWEEN [*name*] of [*address*] ('the Widow') of the first part [*name*] of [*address*] and [*name*] of [*address*] ('the Children') of the second part and [*name*] of [*address*] and [*name*] of [*address*] ('the Trustees') of the third part.

Whereas:

(A) By his last Will ('the Will') dated [*date*] [*name*] late of [*address*] ('the Testator') appointed the Trustees as executors and trustees.

(B) The Testator died on [*date*][2] [and on the [*date*] the Will was proved by the Trustees in the —— Probate Registry].[3]

(C) By Clause —— of the Will the Testator gave his residuary estate ('the Residuary Estate') to the Trustees to hold the same upon trust for the Widow absolutely.

(D) The Widow desires to vary the disposition of the Residuary Estate effected by the Will so as to benefit the Children in the manner appearing below.

NOW THIS DEED WITNESSES as follows:

1. By way of variation of the above-recited disposition of the Residuary Estate of the Testator effected by the Will the Widow the

Children and the Trustees hereby agree and declare that the Will shall have effect and the estate of the Testator shall be administered as if the Testator had given by the Will a pecuniary legacy of [£325,000][4] to the Children in equal shares absolutely subject to payment of any inheritance tax payable in respect of the Testator's death and attributable thereto.[5]

2. Subject as aforesaid the provisions of the Will shall continue to have effect.
3. The parties to this deed hereby certify that this instrument falls within category M in the Schedule to the Stamp Duty (Exempt Instruments) Regulations 1987.[6]
4. The parties to this deed declare that they intend that the provisions of [Section 142(1) of the Inheritance Tax Act 1984] [and] [Section 62(6) of the Taxation of Chargeable Gains Act 1992] shall apply to the variations made by this deed, to the intent that such variations shall be treated as if they were made by the Deceased for the purposes of [inheritance tax] [and] [capital gains tax].[7]

In witness etc[8]

1 This, at least prior to 9 October 2007, has perhaps been one of the commonest types of deed of variation. It makes use of the deceased's nil-rate band where it is wholly or largely unused as a result of all or most of the estate being given to his widow. Following the introduction on 9 October 2007 of nil-rate band transfer it may no longer be so popular (see para **[200.75]** above). For nil-rate band gifts see Part A, para **[200.101]** and for nil-rate band discretionary trusts see the Note in B18 at para **[218.16]–[218.18]**.

2 The deed must be made within two years of the death if IHTA 1984, s 142(1) is to apply: see the Preliminary Note at paras **[241.1]** and **[241.3]**.

3 An instrument of variation can be made before probate is granted: see the Preliminary Note at para **[241.1]**.

4 This is the IHT threshold in relation to a death during tax years 2009–10 to 2014–15. For 2008–9 it was £312,000. The legacy should be reduced from the amount of the nil-rate band at the deceased's death by any lifetime transfers of value made in the seven years before the deceased's death which are chargeable, by any non-exempt specific gifts or pecuniary legacies contained in the will, and by any other property which is chargeable to IHT as part of the deceased's estate on death. A formula can be used if there is uncertainty about the correct amount of the legacy: see cl 1 of Form F3.8 at para **[241.29]**.

5 These words are worth including if there is the slightest doubt as to whether there might be an IHT liability, and do no harm if there is not. See the Preliminary Note at para **[241.12]** and the Preliminary Note to B14 at para **[214.74]**.

6 This exemption certificate will be necessary to avoid a £5 fixed duty if the variation relates to stock or marketable securities, but may also be advisable where it does not in view of HMRC pronouncements. See the Preliminary Note at para **[241.18]**.

7 If IHTA 1984, s 142(1) and TCGA 1992, s 62(6) are to apply, the instrument of variation must contain a statement to that effect. See also the Preliminary Note at para **[241.3]**. If IHTA 1984, s 142(1) is to apply, the Children will be deemed to have taken the nil-rate band legacy on the testator's death for all IHT purposes, and there will be no nil-rate band carry forward allowance (see para **[200.75]** above). If IHTA 1984, s 142 is not to apply, the widow will make a potentially exempt transfer, and the testator's unused nil-rate band will be carried forward.

8 For execution, see Form F3.3 at para **[241.24]**.

[241.28]

[Updated for the nil-rate inheritance tax band.]

Form F3.7: Deed of variation conferring a short-term interest in possession on a surviving spouse[1]

THIS DEED OF VARIATION is made the [*date*] BETWEEN [*name*] of [*address*] and [*name*] of [*address*] ('the Children') of the first part [*name*] of [*address*] ('the Widow') of the second part and [*name*] of [*address*] and [*name*] of [*address*] ('the Trustees') of the third part.

Whereas:

(A) By his last Will ('the Will') dated [*date*] [*name*] late of [*address*] ('the Testator') appointed the Trustees as executors and trustees.

(B) The Testator died on the [*date*][2] [and on the [*date*] the Will was duly proved by the Trustees].[3]

(C) By Clause —— of the Will the Testator gave his residuary estate ('the Residuary Estate') to the Trustees to hold the same upon trust for the Children in equal shares absolutely.

(D) The Children desire to vary the disposition of the Residuary Estate effected by Clause —— of the Will in the manner appearing below.

NOW THIS DEED made in pursuance of the said desire and by way of variation of the disposition of the Residuary Estate effected by Clause —— of the Will WITNESSES as follows:

1. The parties to this deed hereby agree and declare that the Will shall have effect and be deemed to have had effect as from the death of the Testator and the Testator's estate shall be administered as if in lieu of the above-recited direction to the Trustees to hold the Residuary Estate upon trust for the Children in equal shares absolutely the Will had contained[—

   (1) a legacy to the Children in equal shares absolutely of [£325,000][4] and a direction that any inheritance tax attributable to such legacy by reason of the death of the Testator should be borne by the Children in equal shares absolutely in exoneration of the Residuary Estate of the Testator;[5] and

   (2)][6] a direction to the Trustees to hold the Residuary Estate [(subject to the above-mentioned legacy)] upon trust to pay its income to the Widow for the period of her life or for a period expiring on the [*date*][7] (whichever shall be the shorter period) and subject thereto to hold the Residuary Estate (subject to the above-mentioned legacy) and its income upon trust for the Children in equal shares absolutely.

2. [*Stamp duty certificate as cl 3 of* Form F3.6 *at para* **[241.27]**.]
3. [*Statement of intention as cl 4 of* Form F3.6 *at para* **[241.27]**.]

In witness etc[8].

1 This form is designed to pass a testator's estate to non-exempt persons, but at least to the extent that it exceeds the testator's available nil-rate band, channelled through the estate of the surviving spouse by giving him or her a short-term interest in possession so that the spouse exemption may be claimed on the testator's death. (If the deceased died on or after 22 March 2006 the short-term interest in possession should be an immediate post-death interest within IHTA 1984, s 49A, (see para **[200.98]** above)). Upon the termination of the

interest in possession, when the remainder gifts for non-exempt persons take effect, the surviving spouse should be treated as making a potentially exempt transfer which should escape a charge to IHT if the surviving spouse survives it for seven years. See Preliminary Note at para **[241.13]**. Since exemption from IHT is available in the same way between civil partners as it is between married couples (see para **[241.13]** above), this deed may be adapted to give a short-term interest in possession to a surviving civil partner.

2 The deed must be made within two years of the death if IHTA 1984, s 142(1) is to apply: see the Preliminary Note at paras **[241.1]** and **[241.3]**.

3 An instrument of variation can be made before probate is granted: see the Preliminary Note at para **[241.10]**.

4 See n 4 to cl 1 of Form F3.6 at para **[241.27]**.

5 See n 5 to cl 1 of Form F3.6 at para **[241.27]**.

6 Since the introduction on 9 October 2007 nil-rate band transfer (see para **[200.75]** above), it may be preferable from an IHT point of view for a nil-rate band legacy not to be carved out, and for the surviving spouse to take a short-term interest in possession in the whole of residue, thus preserving the transferable nil-rate band.

7 This date should be after the date of the deed of variation and after the expiry of the two-year period from the death of the testator, see Preliminary Note at para **[241.13]**.

8 For execution, see Form F3.3 at para **[241.24]**.

[241.30]

[Updated for the Perpetuities and Accumulations Act 2009 and FA 2013, Sch 44.]

Form F3.9 Deed of variation of trusts of a will settling a life interest on discretionary trusts without disturbing remainders[1]

THIS DEED OF VARIATION is made the [*date*] BETWEEN [*name*] of [*address*] ('the Life Tenant') of the one part and [*name*] of [*address*] and [*name*] of [*address*] ('the Trustees') of the other part.

Whereas:

(A) By his last Will ('the Will') dated [*date*] [*name*] late of [*address*] ('the Testator') appointed the Trustees as executors and trustees.

(B) The Testator died on the [*date*][2] [and on the [*date*] the Will was duly proved by the Trustees].[3]

(C) By Clause —— of the Will the Testator gave his residuary estate ('the Residuary Estate') to the Trustees to hold the same upon trust to pay its income to the Life Tenant for his life and subject thereto upon trust for such of the children of the Life Tenant who should attain the age of 21 and be living at his death in equal shares absolutely with a substitutional trust for the children of any such child who should die before attaining a vested interest.

(D) The Life Tenant desires to vary the disposition of the Residuary Estate effected by Clause —— of the Will for the benefit of his children and remoter issue (who together with the Life Tenant are 'the Beneficiaries')[4] in the manner appearing below.

NOW THIS DEED WITNESSES as follows:

1. By way of variation of the above-recited disposition of the Residuary Estate of the Testator made by Clause —— of the Will the Life Tenant HEREBY ASSIGNS his life interest in the Residuary Estate (which life interest shall include the net income of the Residuary Estate which shall have arisen between the Testator's death and the date of this Deed)[5] unto the Trustees to hold the same as follows—

   (1) The Trustees shall hold the income of the Residuary Estate arisen or arising during the life of the Life Tenant upon trust

to pay or apply the same to or for the benefit of all or such one or more exclusively of the others or other of the Beneficiaries and if more than one in such shares and in such manner generally as the Trustees shall in their absolute discretion think fit provided that the Trustees shall have power to accumulate the whole or any part of such income[6] by investing the same and the resulting income in any manner authorised by the Will so that any accumulations shall be held as an accretion to the Residuary Estate but subject to a power exercisable by the Trustees at any time during the life of the Life Tenant to pay or apply any such accumulations or any part of them as if they were income of the Residuary Estate arising in the then current year.

(2) Notwithstanding the foregoing the Trustees shall have power by any deed or deeds revocable or irrevocable from time to time during the life of the Life Tenant to appoint that all or any part or parts of the income of the Residuary Estate during the remainder of the life of Life Tenant or any less period shall be held upon with and subject to such trusts powers and provisions (including discretionary trusts or powers) in favour or for the benefit of all or such one or more exclusively of the others or other of the Beneficiaries if more than one in such shares and in such manner generally as the Trustees shall in their absolute discretion think fit Provided that no exercise of the said power shall invalidate any prior payment application or accumulation of income hereunder.[7]

2. Nothing contained in thus deed shall effect the devolution under the Will of the Residuary Estate on and following the death of the Life Tenant.
3. [*Stamp duty certificate as cl 3 of* Form F3.6 *at para* **[241.27]**.]
4. [*Statement of intention as cl 4 of* Form F3.6 *at para* **[241.27]**.]

In witness etc[8].

1 It can happen that a will leaves property upon trust for a life tenant for life, with remainder to individuals who are minors or whose identity cannot be finally ascertained until the death of the life tenant. This form allows a life tenant to remove property from his estate for IHT purposes by settling his life interest on discretionary trusts, with the remainder trusts taking effect on his death being unaffected. For the IHT charging regime for settlements without a qualifying interest in possession see B18 at para **[218.8]** ff. If the testator died before 8 April 2013 and the life tenant is elderly or infirm, check that he or she was not at the testator's death qualified under the IHTA 1984, s 89(4) as the principal beneficiary under a disabled trust for IHT purposes (see para **[226.3]** ff). If so, the trusts might fall within the IHTA 1984, s 89 so that he or she is treated as retaining an interest in possession. This could be avoided by a variation which amends the powers over capital in such a way that s 89 does not apply, but if the remaindermen are minors or unborns this may only be achievable by applying to the court under the Variation of Trusts Act 1958. If though the testator died on or after 8 April 2013, the new conditions of IHTA 1984, s 89 (amended by FA 2013, Sch 44, para 6) should mean that the above trust cannot qualify as a disabled trust for IHT purposes (see para **[226.3]** ff).

Note also that HMRC will apparently not regard a variation varying or disposing of a life interest as effective for IHT purposes if the deed of variation is made after the life tenant's death: see *IHT Newsletter* December 2001, p 5 (but a disclaimer by the life tenant's personal representatives could in their view be effective). See Note at para **[241.14]**.

2 The deed must be made within two years of the death if IHTA 1984, s 142(1) is to apply: see the Preliminary Note at paras **[241.1]** and **[241.3]**.

3 An instrument of variation can be made before probate is granted: see the Preliminary Note at para **[241.10]**.

4 If the life tenant is to be an object of the discretionary trust, provided that a statement of intention is made that IHTA 1984, s 142(1) should apply to the variation, the life tenant's assignment should not be a gift subject to a reservation: see the Preliminary Note at para **[241.9]**.

It is not entirely clear what the effect of a statement of intention that the TCGA 1992, s 62(6) should apply would be for determining who the settlor is. Prior to the enactment of TCGA 1992, s 68C it was thought that whether or not TCGA 1992, s 62(6) applied, the deceased would be treated as the settlor of the capital of the residuary estate, and the life tenant as the settlor of the income arising during his lifetime, so that by being an object of the discretionary trust of income, any chargeable gains in respect of any accumulations of income would be taxed as the life tenant's as such accumulations would be property originating from him: see TCGA 1992, ss 77 and 79(2). However, TCGA 1992, s 68C now provides rules for who the settlor is in respect of variations made on or after 6 April 2006 (see Preliminary Note at para **[241.17]**). It is not entirely clear though how they operate in relation to variations such as the present where the will establishes a settlement, and the effect of the variation is to vary only the trust of income. It is submitted that the position is the same as it was thought to be before these rules were introduced. This is because either the rules do not apply in the precise circumstances of the case, so that one must determine who the settlor is under normal capital gains tax principles (as before), or because the rules apply separately to the income and the capital, and TCGA, 1992 s 68C(2) applies to treat the life tenant as the settlor of the income, and TCGA 1992, s 68C(5) or (6) applies to treat the deceased as settlor in relation to the capital. For income tax purposes the income would be treated as the life tenant's by reason of his being an object of the trust and the person who settled the income on the discretionary trusts: see Preliminary Note at para **[241.19]**.

5 If the deed is made before the administration is compete, this would be effective to transfer any undistributed income, for income tax purposes, from the life tenant to the discretionary trusts: see the Preliminary Note at para **[241.19]**.

6 For an instrument limiting property in trust, such as a deed of variation, made on or after 6 April 2010, there are no statutory restrictions on accumulation in respect of non-charitable trusts, so accumulation will be permitted throughout the lifetime of the former life tenant (so long as he does not survive 125 years): see the PAA 2009, s 13, 15(1)(a) (Part G, paras **[246.187]**, **[246.189]**).

7 This power would permit the trustees to appoint an interest in possession to any of the beneficiaries. This might be desirable for income tax purposes.

8 For execution, see Form F3.3 at para **[241.24]**.

[241.31]

[Added for the IHT reduced rate under IHTA 1984, Sch 1A, inserted by Finance 2012.]

Form F3.11 Deed of variation of trusts of residuary estate increasing a charitable gift so as to qualify for the reduced IHT rate on the chargeable part of the estate[1]

THIS DEED OF VARIATION is made the [*date*] BETWEEN [*name*] of [*address*], [*name*] of [*address*], [*name*] of [*address*] and [*name*] of [*address*] ('the Relevant Beneficiaries') of the one part and [*name*] of [*address*] and [*name*] of [*address*] ('the Trustees') of the other part.

Whereas:

(A) By his last Will ('the Will') dated [*date*] [*name*] late of [*address*] ('the Testator') appointed the Trustees as executors and trustees.

(B) The Testator died on the [*date*][2] [and on the [*date*] the Will was duly proved by the Trustees].[3]

(C) By Clause —— of the Will the Testator gave his residuary estate ('the Residuary Estate') to the Trustees to hold the same upon trust for the Relevant Beneficiaries and [*name of charity*] in equal shares

(D) The Relevant Beneficiaries desire to vary the disposition of the Residuary Estate effected by Clause —— of the Will so as to increase the amount given to [*name of charity*] in the manner appearing below.

NOW THIS DEED WITNESSES as follows:

1. By way of variation of the above-recited disposition of the Residuary Estate of the Testator made by Clause —— of the Will, the Relevant Beneficiaries and the Trustees hereby agree and declare that the Will shall have effect and the Testator's estate shall be administered by the Trustees as if there had been inserted at the end of the said Clause —— a proviso that if the share of the Residuary Estate held on trust for [*name of charity*] is less in amount or value than ten per cent (10 %) of the baseline amount in relation to the general component[4] of the Testator's estate, then the share of the Residuary Estate held on trust for [*name of charity*] shall be increased so as to be equal to ten per cent (10 %) of the baseline amount in relation to the general component of the Testator's estate, and the other shares of the Residuary Estate shall be reduced accordingly so that such of the Residuary Estate as is not held on trust for [*name of charity*] is held on trust for the Relevant Beneficiaries in equal shares[5].
2. In Clause 1 above 'baseline amount' and 'general component' have the same meanings as in Inheritance Tax Act 1984, Schedule 1A.
3. [*Stamp duty certificate as cl 3 of* Form F3.6 *at para* **[241.27]**.]
4. [*Statement of intention as cl 4 of* Form F3.6 *at para* **[241.27]**.]

In witness etc[6].

1 For the reduced rate of IHT where a person who dies on or after 6 April 2012 has left ten per cent or more of the 'baseline amount' to charity, see paras **[200.91A]** ff and **[212.2A]**. It will sometimes be the case that the amount given to charity by a testator falls short of qualifying for the reduced rate by a narrow margin, and that increasing the charitable gift so as to qualify for the reduced rate would save more in IHT than the amount which would be lost to the non-charity beneficiaries by increasing the gift.

Note that an instrument of variation which gives assets to charity will only fall within IHTA 1984, s 142 if the charity is notified of the instrument's existence (IHTA 1984 s 142(3A) and (3B) inserted by FA 2012, Sch 33, para 9). If the charity is a party to the instrument, it will be obvious from the instrument that it has been notified. This Form assumes that the charity will not be a party. It is not necessary for the charity to be a party where its entitlement under the will is not affected, and in many cases it may be more convenient not to ask the charity to join in making the instrument.

2 The deed must be made within two years of the death if IHTA 1984, s 142(1) is to apply: see the Preliminary Note at paras **[241.1]** and **[241.3]**.

3 An instrument of variation can be made before probate is granted: see the Preliminary Note at para **[241.10]**.

4 See para **[200.91B]** for the components of the estate, and see footnote 2 to Form B12.2A at para **[212.4A]** for the possibility of increasing the charitable gift so as to enable more than one component to qualify for the reduced rate of IHT.

5 If the values of the assets of the estate at death are known or agreed with HMRC then this clause can be simplified considerably by putting a cash figure on the increased gift to the charity. The formula as in this clause is for cases where HMRC's agreement of all relevant values (or of, eg, claims for exemption, reliefs, or nil-rate band transfer) is not yet forthcoming, or where assets such as a house may yet be sold and the sale price substituted

for the probate value. The formula here assumes that the only charitable gift in the will is the share of residue. If there are, eg, specific gifts to charity as well, they need to be taken into account in this formula.

6 For execution, see Form F3.3 at para **[241.24]**.

F4

Exercises of dispositive powers created by wills

PRELIMINARY NOTE

[242.1]

[Updated for the Perpetuities and Accumulations Act 2009.]

When exercising a special power of appointment, care must be taken that the exercise is authorised by the terms of the power. For example, it can only be exercised for the benefit of the named objects of the power; trusts and powers should not be delegated (by eg the appointment of discretionary trusts and dispositive powers) unless the power authorises such delegation; the interests which it creates must vest within the perpetuity period applicable to the instrument creating the power; and excessive accumulations of income must not be directed or authorised. Where the will creating the power was made on or after 6 April 2010 the perpetuity period is 125 years from the testator's death and no other, and there are no restrictions on accumulation apart from the rule against perpetuities (Perpetuities and Accumulations Act 2009 (PAA 2009): Part G, para **[246.175]**, and see paras **[200.35A]** ff and Vol 1 chapters 94 and 95). It is uncertain whether PAA 2009 applies to the exercise of a special power created by a will which was made before 6 April 2010 of someone who dies on or after it: see the PAA 2009, s 15(1)(b) (Part G, para **[246.175]**) and para **[200.35H]**. In such a case the cautious draftsman should assume that the pre PAA 2009 restrictions will apply, unless and until the point is clarified. If the power requires, as powers of appointment usually do, an appointment by deed then a deed is necessary for the appointment to be valid. For some observations on these points in relation to exercises of special powers of appointment by will (which will apply with any necessary modifications to appointments made by an inter vivos instrument), see B13 at **[213.1]** ff (and for a fuller treatment of the exercise of special powers of appointment, see Vol 1, paras **[39.1]** and **[40.1]** ff).

One obvious, though important, difference between the exercise of a dispositive power by will or codicil, and the exercise of such a power by an inter vivos instrument such as a deed, is that an appointment by deed takes effect immediately following the execution of the deed whereas an appointment by will only takes effect upon the death of the appointor. Accordingly, an exercise by will can be revoked or altered at any time before the death of the appointor and before the appointment has taken effect. An appointment by deed, however, will have effect according to its terms unless and until it is made expressly revocable and is in fact revoked.

Some examples of the exercise of powers of advancement are also provided here (in Forms F4.8 and F4.9 at paras **[242.17]–[242.19]**). By powers of advancement we mean the statutory power of advancement (Trustee Act 1925, s 32: Part G, para **[246.30]**), or express powers in the same essential form, ie powers to pay or apply capital to or for the benefit of one or more persons, or the like. Such a power is, like a power of appointment, subject to the rule against perpetuities in such a way that interests created in exercise of the power need to vest within a perpetuity period calculated from the creation of the power (*Pilkington v IRC* [1964] AC 612, [1962] 3 All ER 622), but the rules as to what may be done in exercise of such a power may be more liberal and rather different from those surrounding a power of appointment: see B18 at para **[218.85]** ff. Also, it is usually the case that a power of advancement is not subject to the formal requirements for its exercise to which a power of appointment is commonly subject.

[242.7]

[Updated for the nil-rate inheritance tax band 2010–2011.]

Form F4.1: Appointment from discretionary trust within two years of testator's death[1]

THIS DEED OF APPOINTMENT is made the [*date*] by [*name*] of [*address*] and [*name*] of [*address*] ('the Trustees').

Whereas:

(A) By his last Will ('the Will') dated [*date*] [*name*] late of [*address*] ('the Testator') appointed the Trustees to be the executors and trustees of the Will.

(B) The Testator died on the [*date*][2] and on the [*date*] the Will was duly proved by the Trustees.[3]

(C) By Clause —— of the Will the Testator directed the Trustees to hold the capital and income of his residuary estate ('the residuary estate') upon trust for all or such one or more of the beneficiaries ('the beneficiaries') at such ages or times in such shares and upon such trusts for the benefit of the beneficiaries as the Trustees should by irrevocable deed or deeds executed at any time or times during the discretionary period (as defined in the Will) appoint.

(D) The discretionary period was defined by Clause —— of the Will to mean the period beginning immediately after the end of the period of three months from the day of the Testator's death and ending with the day before the second anniversary of his death.

(E) The beneficiaries as defined in the Will include [*name*] who is the widow of the Testator and [*name*] and [*name*] who are the children of the Testator.

(F) The Trustees desire to exercise their above-mentioned power of appointment for the benefit of the said [*name*] [*name*] and [*name*] in the manner appearing below.

NOW THIS DEED WITNESSES that the Trustees in exercise of their above-mentioned power of appointment and each and every other power them enabling HEREBY IRREVOCABLY APPOINT that the residuary estate shall be held upon the following trusts:

(1) upon trust as to [£325,000] for the said children of the Testator [*name*] and [*name*] in equal shares absolutely [Provided that any inheritance tax attributable thereto and payable in respect of the death of the Testator should be borne by the said [*name*] and [*name*] in equal shares absolutely];[4] and

(2) subject as aforesaid upon trust for the said widow of the Testator [*name*] absolutely.

IN WITNESS whereof the Trustees have executed these presents as their deed the day and year first above written.[5]

SIGNED and delivered as a deed by the said [*name*] in the presence of— } [*Signature of trustee*]

[*Signature, address and description of witness*]

[*The foregoing from 'SIGNED' to be repeated for each trustee*]

1 This form is designed to take advantage of IHTA 1984, s 144. For a form of will which envisages such an appointment, see Form C3.6 at para **[225.92]** ff, and for notes on s 144 see C3 at para **[225.83]** ff and the Preliminary Note at para **[242.4]**, and the Preliminary Note at **[242.5]** on the capital gains tax consequences of an absolute appointment. The recitals of the terms of the will in this form are based on Form C3.6.

Provided that the appointment fulfils the conditions of s 144, there will be no exit charge under the IHTA 1984, s 65 on the appointment and the appointment will be treated as having effect from the deceased's death.

A type of appointment such as this, if the sum appointed to the testator's children is within the testator's available nil-rate band, has, at least prior to 9 October 2007, been one of the commonest types of appointment to take advantage of IHTA 1984, s 144, since if made within two years of death (and not within three months), it makes use of the deceased's nil-rate band. Following the introduction on 9 October 2007 of rules to carry forward unused nil-rate band allowance it may no longer be so popular, and it may be preferred to make an appointment to the testator's spouse because to the extent that the testator's nil-rate band is unused, it will be carried forward (see para **[200.75]** above).

2 To take advantage of the IHTA 1984, s 144, the appointment must be made not more than two years after the testator's death, but not within the first three months after his death: see the Preliminary Note at para **[242.4]**. Where the testator died before 22 March 2006, the relevant provisions, are IHTA 1984, s 144(1), (2), and where he dies on or after 22 March 2006 they are IHTA 1984, s 144(1), (1A), (2).

3 Whether or not the power of appointment may be exercised before the will has been proved, or before the executors have become trustees will depend upon the terms of the will. HMRC once took the view that executors could not exercise a power of appointment until the property which was to be appointed was vested in them as trustees, but they now seem to accept that a power may be exercised by executors if on the true construction of the will they have authority to exercise it in that capacity, for example, where a will expressly confers the power on them in their capacity as executors as well as trustees, or appoints the individuals who actually exercise the power as executors and trustees, referring to them in the will as 'my trustees' with the power being given to 'my trustees'.

4 So as to avoid IHT in respect of the death of the testator, the sum appointed should not be more than the maximum which non-exempt persons can take without any liability being incurred for IHT on or by reason of the testator's death, taking into account the testator's lifetime chargeable transfers, property treated as his for IHT purposes at the time of his death and the dispositions taking effect under his will and under the deed of appointment. In case this appointment should happen to push the testator's chargeable estate above the IHT threshold at the time of his death, for example, on its subsequently being discovered that the testator had made a lifetime chargeable transfer, a direction that any IHT should be borne by the appointees should result in less IHT being payable than if the legacy was free

of tax: see the Preliminary Note at para **[242.4]**. £325,000 is the IHT threshold in relation to a death during tax years 2009–10 and 2010–11.

5 The requirements of the Law of Property (Miscellaneous Provisions) Act 1989, s 1, for the making of a deed are that it is clear on its face that it is intended by the parties to it to be a deed, that it is signed by each party in the presence of a witness who attests the signature (two witnesses if someone signs for a party), and that it is delivered as a deed by each party or someone authorised to do so on his behalf. Sealing is not necessary.

[242.12]

[Updated for the Perpetuities and Accumulations Act 2009 and FA 2013, Sch 44.]

Form F4.5: Appointment of immediate post-death interests in residue for the testator's grandchildren

NOTE

This form presupposes that the testator has settled his residuary estate upon trusts for his grandchildren, which trusts bring residue within the IHT relevant property regime. For example, he may have settled residue upon usual form discretionary trusts, or (having died on or after 22 March 2006) upon trust for his grandchildren contingently upon attaining a specified age without any of them having attained that specified age at his death or being entitled to an interest in possession from his death (which interest in possession would be an immediate post-death interest, (see para **[200.98]** above)). The appointment will confer interests in possession on his grandchildren (even if any of them are minors), so that provided the appointment is made within two years of the testator's death, they will be treated as having immediate post-death interests by virtue of IHTA 1984, s 144(3)–(6), and there will be no IHT charge. If an appointment in this form was not made until after the expiry of two years from the testator's death, IHTA 1984, s 144 would not apply to backdate the appointed interests in possession to the testator's death, so they would not be immediate post-death interests and (unless any of the interests in possession qualified as disabled person's interests within IHTA 1984, s 89B (see para **[200.99]** above)) the residuary estate would remain within the relevant property regime for IHT purposes.

If the administration of the estate is complete at the time of the appointment, then whether or not there is a deemed disposal by the trustees of the property in question under the TCGA 1992, s 71 when new trusts are appointed depends upon whether the trust property moves to a new and separate settlement. If the power which is exercised does not authorise the trustees to remove the property from the original settlement, there will be no deemed disposal. If it does so authorise them, an Inland Revenue Statement of Practice, SP 7/84, 11 October 1984, states that there will be no deemed disposal where the appointed trusts are non-exhaustive or revocable, and that it is unlikely that a deemed disposal will occur when the duties with regard to the appointed assets fall to the trustees of the original settlement in their capacity as such. The trusts of this appointment are revocable, and also the trustees of the appointed assets are the trustees of the will, so that it is probable that no disposal can be deemed to have been made.

THIS DEED OF APPOINTMENT is made the —— day of —— BY [*names and addresses of trustees*] ('the Trustees' which expression shall include the trustees for the time being of the Will defined below) and is

SUPPLEMENTAL To the Will ('the Will') dated —— of [*name of testator*] ('the Testator') who died on —— and whose said will was on —— duly proved by the Trustees (being the executors named in the Will)

Whereas:

(1) By Clause [*insert number of relevant clause*] of the Will the Testator gave the Trustees power during the trust period (as defined in the Will)[1] to appoint that his residuary estate be held upon such trusts for all or such one or more of his grandchildren and remoter issue at such ages or times in such shares and upon such trusts and with such powers for their benefit as the Trustees should think fit[2]

(2) The Testator left [six] grandchildren surviving him

(3) The Trustees desire by this deed to exercise the power of appointment given them by Clause [*insert number of relevant clause*] of the Will.

NOW THIS DEED WITNESSETH as follows:

1. The Trustees in exercise of their said power of appointment under the Will hereby appoint (subject to the power of revocation below) that the Testator's residuary estate shall be held upon trust for the Testator's grandchildren living at his death in equal shares but the share of the residuary estate to which a grandchild shall become entitled shall not vest in such grandchild but shall be retained by the Trustees and held upon the following trusts:

(a) the Trustees shall hold such share ('the settled share') upon trust to pay the income of the settled share [(including income which has arisen before the date of this deed and since the Testator's death)][3] to such grandchild ('the grandchild') for life;

(b) if and so long as the grandchild is under the age of 18 years the Trustees may pay or otherwise apply for or towards the maintenance education or benefit of the grandchild the whole or such part or parts of the income of the settled share as the Trustees in their absolute discretion think fit and shall retain the balance of such income upon trust for the grandchild absolutely but the Trustees may at any time or times while the grandchild is living and under the age of 18 years pay or apply such retained income as if it were income arising in the then current year and section 31 of the Trustee Act 1925 shall not apply to the settled share;[4]

(c) subject as above the Trustees shall hold the settled share upon trust for the children or child of the grandchild born during the trust period and if more than one in equal shares absolutely;[5]

(d) the provisions of section 32 of the Trustee Act 1925 shall apply in relation to the settled share as if the words 'one half of' were omitted from proviso (a) to subsection (1);

(e) notwithstanding the above trusts during the trust period and so long as the grandchild is entitled to be paid the income of all or any part of the capital of the settled share (or would be so entitled if such capital yielded income) the trustees shall have power in their absolute discretion from time to time to pay transfer or apply the whole or any part or parts of such capital to or for the benefit of the grandchild in such manner as they shall in their absolute discretion think fit; and

(f) subject as above the settled share (or so much as has not been applied under any of the above powers) shall accrue to the share or shares of the other grandchildren (and if more than one equally) the trusts of which have not at the date of accruer failed or determined (otherwise than by absolute vesting) to form one fund with such other share or shares for all purposes.

2. The administrative provisions of the will which are contained in Clauses [*set out here relevant clauses*] thereof shall apply to the trusts declared by this deed [save only for the following modifications [*set out any modifications which may be desired*].[6]

3. Provided always that the Trustees shall have power by deed or deeds executed during the trust period to revoke this deed in whole or in part Provided that no such revocation shall prejudice any person's entitlement to an interest in possession (within the meaning of Part III of the Inheritance Tax Act 1984) in any part of the Testator's residuary estate up to the time of such revocation nor invalidate any prior payment transfer or application of capital.

In witness.[7]

1 If the will was made before 6 April 2010 then the trust period should have been defined by reference to the PAA 1964 which enabled a maximum 80 year perpetuity period to be selected, or else the common law period of a life or lives in being plus 21 years. However. if the will was made (or confirmed by codicil made) on or after 6 April 2010 a mandatory 125 year perpetuity period will apply to the trusts of the will. In either case, the perpetuity period applicable to the will will apply to the trusts created in exercise of the power of appointment so that all appointed interests must vest in interest within that perpetuity period (see para **[242.1]** above).

2 The precise terms of the power of appointment of the actual will must be considered carefully.

3 If the appointment is made within two years of the testator's death, and it is hoped to rely on the backdating effect of IHTA 1984, s 144, (and particularly where the testator died on or after 22 March 2006), the appointment should cover not only income arising in respect of residue following the date of the appointment, but also income arising since the testator's death, see the Preliminary Note at para **[242.4]**). Where residue is subject to usual form discretionary trusts under the terms of the testator's will, the trustees will have a discretion over income as well as capital so it should be possible for an appointment to cover income which has already arisen.

4 See para **[218.51]** for the trusts of accumulations under the TA 1925, s 31 (Part G, para **[246.29]**) which unless varied or excluded are such as usually to give minor beneficiaries a contingent interest in such accumulations, even if they have a vested interest in the income. The purpose of this substitution for s 31 is to cause the income which is not applied for the grandchild's benefit during his minority to be held on trust absolutely for the grandchild, so as to confer an interest in possession for IHT purposes. An infant cannot be paid income to which he is entitled (see Vol 1, para **[9.39]**) but it is thought that he or she has an interest in possession in income if it would form part of his estate if he or she died under the age of 18 (and unmarried and without a civil partner). Such an interest in possession will be an immediate post-death interest within IHTA 1984, s 49A (see para **[200.98]** above and para **[216.1]** above).

5 Although this gives the children of a grandchild absolute interests, these interests are in fact defeasible by exercise of the power of revocation contained below, so if and when they take effect on the termination of a grandchild's life interest, the settled share would become relevant property for IHT purposes (see para **[200.92]**).

6 Care should be taken to ensure that none of the administrative powers of the will is incompatible with an interest in possession.
7 For execution, see Form F4.1 at para **[242.7]**.

[242.13]

[Updated for FA 2013, Sch 44.]

Form F4.6: Appointment from discretionary trust of investments to a bereaved minor trust or age 18–25 trust

NOTE

This form, like Form F4.4 above, presupposes that the trust property is still in the form of investments and that these are being appointed in specie amongst beneficiaries who are children of the testator. The appointment is not to those beneficiaries absolutely, but on continuing trusts. Since the appointees are children of the testator, a bereaved minor trust or age 18–25 trust may be appointed. If the selected age of contingency is 18, the trust appointed should be a trust for bereaved minors (see para **[200.108]** above), and if the specified age is 25, the trust should be an age 18–25 trust (see para **[200.109]** above). Although there is a question as to whether a trust for a bereaved minor or an age 18–25 trust can arise under the exercise of a special power of appointment rather than under the words of the will itself, it seems to the writers that such trusts can arise provided the appointment does not create a new and separate settlement (and HMRC seem to share this opinion) (see para **[200.107]** above). The same question arises with respect to trusts for the vulnerable within the Finance Act 2005, ss 23–45 (see para **[217.4]**), but given the identical statutory wording that the trusts be 'established under the will of a deceased parent' (IHTA 1984, ss 71A(2)(a), 71D(2)(a), and FA 2005, s 35(2)(a)), the answer is presumably the same (although HMRC's views on FA 2005, s 35(2)(a) specifically are not known). If the appointment is made within two years of the testator's death (whether the death occurred before or after 22 March 2006), there will be no IHT charge and the appointment will be backdated to the testator's death for IHT purposes (see IHTA 1984, s 144(3)–(6)). If the appointment is made more than two years after death, IHTA 1984, s 144 cannot apply, and there would be an exit charge under IHTA 1984, s 65 since trusts for bereaved minors and age 18-to-25 trusts are expressly excluded from the relevant property regime (see paras **[218.92]**).

If the same form were used for an appointment to children who were not children of the testator, the settled property appointed would remain subject to the IHT charging regime for relevant property, and even if the appointment is made within two years of the testator's death, IHTA 1984, s 144 has no backdating effect (see para **[200.107]** above). In any event there would be no exit charge under IHTA 1984, s 65 (see paras **[218.8]**–**[218.14]**) on the appointment. If it is the intention to avoid the relevant property regime, then an appointment to an infant (not being a child or stepchild of the testator) would have to be made to that infant absolutely.

As to whether or not there is a deemed disposal by the trustees of the property in question under the TCGA 1992, s 71 when new trusts are appointed, see the Note above. The trusts of this appointment are non-exhaustive, and the trustees of the appointed assets are the trustees of the will, so that it is probable that no disposal can be deemed to have been made.

[242.14]

[Updated for the Perpetuities and Accumulations Act 2009 and FA 2013, Sch 44.]

THIS DEED OF APPOINTMENT is made the —— day of —— BY [*names and addresses of trustees*] ('the Trustees') and is SUPPLEMENTAL TO the Will ('the Will') dated —— of [*name of testator*] ('the Testator') who died on —— and whose said will was on —— duly proved by [*names of executors*] the executors named in the Will

Whereas:

(1) The Testator left [three] minor children surviving namely [*name*] who was born on [*date*] [*name*] who was born on [*date*] and [*name*] who was born on [*date*]

(2) The property now subject to the trusts of the Will consists of the investments [and cash] set out in the schedule to this deed ('the Appointed Property')

(3) The trustees desire by this deed to exercise the power of appointment given them by Clause [*insert number of relevant clause*] of the Will.

NOW THIS DEED WITNESSETH as follows:

1. The Trustees in exercise of their said power of appointment under the Will hereby irrevocably appoint the Appointed Property upon the following trusts:

   (a)

   (i) Upon trust as to both capital and income for such of the Testator's children as shall attain the age of [18]/[25][1] years and if more than one in equal shares absolutely.

   (ii) The above trust shall carry the intermediate income [(including income which has arisen before the date of this deed and since the Testator's death)][2] and Section 31 of the Trustee Act 1925 (relating to accumulation and maintenance) shall apply [in relation to a child of the Testator in all respects as if the age of majority were the age of 25 years (and so that the expressions 'infancy', 'minority' and 'infant' and all references to the age of eighteen years in the Section shall be construed accordingly)]/[in relation to a child of the Testator in all respects as if the age of majority were the age of 25 years or such lesser age as that child will attain (if living) on his birthday immediately preceding the expiry of twenty one years from the date of the Testator's death (and so that the expressions 'infancy', 'minority' and 'infant' and all references to the age of eighteen years in the Section shall be construed accordingly)].[3]

   (iii) Section 32 of the Trustee Act 1925 (relating to advancement) shall apply in relation to the above trust as if the words 'one half of' were omitted from proviso (a) to subsection (1).[4]

   (b) Provided that if any of the Testator's children dies before attaining a vested interest but leaving a child or children living at his death then such child or children shall take absolutely and if more than one in equal shares so much of the Appointed Property as that person would have taken had he attained a vested interest.[5]

2. The administrative provisions of the will which are contained in Clauses [*set out here relevant clauses*] thereof shall apply to the trusts declared by this deed [save only for the following modifications [*set out any modifications which may be desired*].[6]

In witness.[7]

THE SCHEDULE

[*The schedule is to contain all the trust property which is being appointed*]

1 If the specified age is 18, the trust appointed should be a trust for bereaved minors (see para **[200.108]** above) (and may be a trust within the Finance Act 2005, ss 23–45: see the Note above), and if the specified age is 25, the trust should be an age 18–25 trust (see para **[200.109]** above).

2 If the appointment is made within two years of the testator's death, and it is hoped to rely on the backdating effect of IHTA 1984, s 144, (and particularly where the testator died on or after 22 March 2006), the appointment should cover not only income arising in respect of the appointed property following the date of the appointment, but also income arising since the testator's death, see the Preliminary Note at para **[242.4]**). Where the appointed property is subject to usual form discretionary trusts under the terms of the testator's will, the trustees will have a discretion over income as well as capital so it should be possible for an appointment to cover income which has already arisen.

3 Inclusion of either of these modifications to TA 1925, s 31 (see para **[246.29]**) should be considered if an age 18-to-25 trust is intended. Its effect will be to enable the income of each child's presumptive share to be accumulated for as long as possible. If the will containing the power of appointment which is to be exercised was made on or after 6 April 2010, then there are no longer statutory restrictions on the accumulation of income arising in respect of non-charitable trusts, see the PAA 2009, ss 13, 15(1)(a) (Part G, para **[246.187]**, **[246.189]** and see para **[95.0]**). Therefore, the first option of extending accumulation until each child attains 25 can be used. If, however, the will was made before 6 April 2010 then the restrictions of LPA 1926, ss 164–166 and PAA 1964, s 13 apply to the will (and any appointment made under it), so the second option should be used, restricting accumulation to 21 years from the testator's death, or until the child attains 25 if sooner. So if all of the testator's children are aged at least 4 at the testator's death, accumulation of income will be possible until each attains 25. If the appointment is made within two years of the testator's death (so that IHTA 1984, s 144 would apply) and it is wished to create an age 18-to-25 trust rather than an immediate post-death interest, it will be important to extend accumulation if any of the testator's children have attained the age 18 at the testator's death. If Trustee Act 1925, s 31 applied unmodified, a child over 18 would be entitled to income absolutely (by virtue of TA 1925, s 31(1)(ii)) and the backdating effect of IHTA 1984, s 144(4) would be to treat that child as having an immediate post-death interest from the testator's death. It is not absolutely clear what the position would be if the child in question was under 18 at the date of the testator's death, but over the age of 18 at the date of the appointment, i e whether the effect of the child having an interest in possession from the date of the appointment would be sufficient to treat him as having an interest in possession from the testator's death, so it is suggested that if an age 18-to-25 trust is intended in these circumstances, TA 1925, s 31 should apply as modified by this clause.

4 The extended statutory power of advancement is compatible with a trust for bereaved minors and an age 18-to-25 trust, see IHTA 1984, ss 71A(4)(b), 71D(7)(b), and for tax year 2013–14 and subsequent years, trusts within the Finance Act 2005, ss 23–45 (FA 2005, s 35(4)(b)–(f) as substituted by FA 2013, Sch 44, para 16(3)): see para **[217.4]**.

5 Children of a child of the testator who does not reach the age of contingency will take their deceased parent's share of the appointed property absolutely. It is not possible to create a trust for bereaved minors or age 18-to-25 trust for persons other than the testator's children (or stepchildren or those for whom he has parental responsibility).

6 Care should be taken to ensure that none of the administrative powers of the will is incompatible with a trust for bereaved minors or an age 18-to-25 trust.
7 For execution, see Form F4.1 at para **[242.7]**.

[242.15]

[Updated for FA 2013, Sch 44 and Trusts (Capital and Income) Act 2013.]

Form F4.7: Appointment of a trust for bereaved minors terminating an immediate post-death interest

NOTE

This appointment partially terminates a surviving spouse's immediate post-death interest (see para **[200.98]** above) and appoints a trust for bereaved minors within IHTA 1984, s 71A for the testator's children (see para **[200.108]** above) so that the life tenant will be treated as having made a potentially exempt transfer: IHTA 1984, s 3A (1A)(a), (b), (c)(iii), (3B) and (7) and s 52. This is one of the few occasions when the termination of an immediate post-death interest in favour of continuing trusts will be a potentially exempt transfer. As well as the termination of a post-21 March 2006 immediate post-death interest in favour of a trust for bereaved minors being a potentially exempt transfer, it seems to be the case that the termination, in favour of a trust for bereaved minors, of an interest in possession which was subsisting before 22 March 2006 and which satisfies the conditions of an immediate post-death interest (see IHTA 1984, s 49A) will be a potentially exempt transfer. This is because the definition of immediate post-death interest is not confined to interests in possession arising on or after 22 March 2006, although generally the importance of an interest being an immediate post-death interest will be where it arises on or after 22 March 2006 (see IHTA 1984, s 49(1A)(a)).

As noted at **[242.15]** above, there is a question as to whether a trust for a bereaved minor (and, indeed, a trust for the vulnerable within the Finance Act 2005, ss 23–45 (see para **[217.4]**)) can arise under the exercise of a special power of appointment. It seems to the writers though that they can.

Following the termination of an immediate post-death interest on or after 22 March 2006, it is vital for IHT purposes that the beneficiary of the immediate post-death interest is excluded from all possibility of future benefit from the property in which the interest subsisted. This is because the termination of an immediate post-death interest on and after 22 March 2006 will be treated as a gift of the underlying settled property by the beneficiary for the purposes of the gift with reservation rules of FA 1986, s 102 (see FA 1986, s 102ZA). The appointment below therefore appoints exhaustive trusts so as to remove the possibility of the life tenant's interest in possession being revived on a failure of the appointed trusts and is irrevocable so that again there is no possibility of a revival of her interest. It is also irrevocable since otherwise the appointed trusts would not qualify as trusts for bereaved minors. Although the appointed trusts are exhaustive and irrevocable, the trustees of the appointed trusts are expressed to be the trustees of the will, and the administrative powers and provisions of the will will continue to apply, so it is not thought that the appointment would be the occasion of a deemed disposal by the trustees under the TCGA 1992, s 71, (see Note to Form F4.4 at para **[242.10]**).

It is assumed that the will provides life interest trusts for the testator's widow subject to an overriding power of appointment.

The exclusion of statutory apportionment has been deleted because it is taken care of by Trusts (Capital and Income) Act 2013: see paras **[214.2A]** and **[246.200]** ff.

[242.16]

[Updated for FA 2013, Sch 44 and Trusts (Capital and Income) Act 2013.]

THIS DEED OF APPOINTMENT is made the [*date*] BY [*name*] of [*address*] and [*name*] of [*address*] ('the Trustees' which expression shall where the context so admits include the trustee or trustees for the time being of the Will defined below).

Whereas:

(A) This deed is supplemental to the Will ('the Will') dated the [*date*] of [*name*] ('the Testator') who died on the [*date*] and which was duly proved by [*names of executors*] the executors named in the Will on the [*date*] in the [*name*] Probate Registry.

(B) By Clauses —— to —— of the Will the trustees of the Will were directed to hold the Testator's residuary estate ('the residuary estate') upon trust to pay its income to the Testator's widow [*name*] ('the Life Tenant') and subject to that upon certain trusts and subject to certain powers for the benefit of the Testator's children and remoter issue.

(C) By Clause —— of the Will notwithstanding and in derogation of the above-recited trusts and powers the Trustees (being not fewer than two in number or a trust corporation) have power at any time or times and from time to time before the vesting day (as defined in the Will) by any deed or deeds revocable or irrevocable to appoint any part or share of the residuary estate (up to the whole) upon trust for all or such one or more exclusive of the others or other of the discretionary beneficiaries (as defined in the Will and called 'the discretionary beneficiaries') if more than one in such shares and either absolutely or at such age or time or respective ages or times and with such trusts and powers for their respective benefit and such provisions as the Trustees think fit and the Trustees may in exercise of the foregoing power (inter alia) delegate or create powers or discretions over capital or income or appoint administrative powers or provisions but subject to a proviso that (inter alia) every interest limited under any exercise of the foregoing power shall vest in interest (if at all) not later than the vesting day.

(D) The Trustees are the present trustees of the Will and the residuary estate now consists of the assets specified in the Schedule hereto.

(E) The discretionary beneficiaries include the children and remoter issue of the Testator living at his death or born thereafter.

(F) There are now living [two] minor children of the Testator namely [*name*] who was born on the [*date*] and [*name*] who was born on the [*date*].[1]

(G) The Trustees desire to exercise their above-mentioned power of appointment for the benefit of the grandchildren and remoter issue of the Testator in the manner appearing below.

NOW THIS DEED WITNESSETH as follows:

1. The Trustees in exercise of their above-mentioned power of appointment and each and every other power them enabling HEREBY IRREVOCABLY APPOINT that the residuary estate and its income shall be held upon the following trusts (to the intent and so that the interest of the Life Tenant shall cease) and with and subject to the following powers:
   (1) The Trustees shall hold the residuary estate Upon Trust for such of the children of the Testator as shall attain the age of eighteen years if both in equal shares absolutely Provided always that if any of such children shall die without having attained the age of eighteen years leaving a child or children him or her surviving such child or children shall take if more than one equally between them the share of the residuary estate which their parent would have taken if he or she had lived to attain the age of eighteen years.[1]
   (2) Subject as above the Trustees shall hold the residuary estate upon trust for the Testator's children in equal shares absolutely.
   (3) The above trusts shall carry the intermediate income of the residuary estate and section 31 of the Trustee Act 1925 (relating to maintenance and accumulation) shall accordingly apply [as modified by the Will]/[as if the proviso to subsection (1) had been omitted].[2]
   (4) The powers in section 32 of the Trustee Act 1925 (relating to the payment or application of capital) shall apply to the above trusts [as modified by the Will]/[as if the words 'one-half of' were omitted from proviso (a) to subsection (1)].[3]
2. For the avoidance of doubt it is hereby declared that the powers and provisions of Clauses —— to —— of the Will shall continue to apply to the residuary estate.[4]

In witness etc[5]

THE SCHEDULE

[*List of assets comprised in Trust Fund*]

1 It must be unlikely that this substitutional trust will take effect (ie. that an individual will die under 18 leaving a child or children), but if it does the children of a deceased child will take their deceased parent's share of the residuary estate absolutely. It is not possible to create a trust for bereaved minors or age 18-to-25 trust for persons other than the testator's children (or stepchildren or those for whom he has parental responsibility).

2 If the will has already modified TA 1925, s 31 in an appropriate way, use the first optional words.

3 If the will has already modified TA 1925, s 32 in an appropriate way, use the first optional words. The extended statutory power of advancement is compatible with a trust for bereaved minors, see IHTA 1984, s 71A(4)(b), and for tax year 2013–14 and subsequent years, trusts within the Finance Act 2005, ss 23–45 (FA 2005, s 35(4)(b)–(f) as substituted by FA 2013, Sch 44, para 16(3)): see para **[217.4]**.

4 The administrative powers of the will will continue to apply. Care should be taken to ensure that none of them is incompatible with a trust for bereaved minors. The power of appointment recited is, however, wide enough for further administrative provisions to be included in the appointment.

5 For execution, see Form F4.1 at para **[242.7]**.

Miscellaneous documents giving effect to legacies

[243.4]

[Updated for the nil-rate inheritance tax band 2010–2011.]

Form F5.3: Deed of promise to give effect to a nil-rate band debt scheme[1]

Note: Even following the introduction of the nil-rate band carry forward allowance (see para **[200.75]** above), it may still be desirable in certain instances to keep in place a nil-rate band discretionary trust established by a testator's will and to constitute it by a debt or charge, see para **[243.1]** above.

Where a promise is given to satisfy a pecuniary legacy, as in this Form, and as a result the promisor takes land (or an interest in land) which would otherwise have been used to satisfy the legacy, HMRC's view is that the promise is chargeable consideration for stamp duty land tax purposes so there could be a liability to stamp duty land tax. See paras **[218.19]**–**[218.22]** above, and para **[220.72]** above. Such a liability might be avoided if a charge was taken instead of a promise, as in Form F5.4.

THIS DEED is made the [*date*] BETWEEN (1) [*name of surviving spouse or civil partner*] of [*address*] ('the Promisor') (2) [*name of executor*] of [*address*] and [*name of executor*] of [*address*] ('the Executors') and (3) [*name of Legacy Trustee*] of [*address*] and [*name of Legacy Trustee*] of [*address*] ('the Legacy Trustees')[2]

SUPPLEMENTAL to the will ('the Will') dated [*date*] of [*name of testator*] ('the Testator') who died on [*date*] and which was proved by the Executors on [*date*] in the [*name*] Registry

Whereas—

(A) By clause + of the Will the Testator gave to the Legacy Trustees a pecuniary legacy determined according to a formula ('the Trust Legacy') to hold the same upon the trusts there set out.

(B) In the events which have happened the amount of the Trust Legacy is [£325,000].[3]

(C) By clause + of the Will the Executors were given power instead of satisfying the Trust Legacy by the payment of cash or the appropriation of property to require the Legacy Trustees to accept a binding promise of payment made personally by the Promisor which shall be repayable on demand.[4]

(D) The Executors have decided to satisfy the Trust Legacy by exercising such power to require the Legacy Trustees to accept a binding promise of payment of [£325,000] [linked to the Index of Retail Prices] made personally by the Promisor and the Promisor has agreed to make such promise.

NOW THIS DEED WITNESSETH:

1. The Promisor promises to pay on demand[5] to the Legacy Trustees the sum of [£325,000] [or (if greater) the sum determined under the following clause].

[2. The sum determined under this clause shall be the sum produced by dividing the sum of [£325,000] by the index figure in the Index of Retail Prices for the month in which this deed is executed and (having made allowance for any rebasing of the Index which may have happened in the meantime) multiplying it by the index figure in that Index for the month in which repayment is made. (For these purposes the Index of Retail Prices shall mean the Index of Retail Prices published by HM Stationery Office or any official publication substituted for it and in the event of any change after the date of this deed in the reference base used to compile the said Index the figure taken to be that at which the said Index stands after such change shall be the figure at which the said Index would have stood if the reference base current at the date of this deed had been retained.)]

[3. If a partial repayment is made, such repayment shall be treated as representing such part of the sum of [£325,000] as produces the amount of such partial repayment by the above method.]

[2.]/[4.] The Legacy Trustees declare that they hold the foregoing debt and all moneys payable thereunder upon the trusts declared by the Will in respect of the Trust Legacy.

IN WITNESS whereof the parties hereto have executed these presents as their deed the day and year first above written.[6]

SIGNED and delivered as a deed by the said [*name*] in the presence of— } [*Signature*]

[*Signature, address and description of witness*]

[*The foregoing from 'SIGNED' to be repeated for each party*]

1 This form is for use where a testator has given residue to his spouse or civil partner absolutely, made a nil-rate band gift onto discretionary trusts in his will, made provision for his executors to require the trustees of those trusts to accept a promise of payment from the surviving spouse or civil partner in satisfaction of the gift, as in Forms B18.2 or C3.4 at paras **[218.32]** and **[225.57]** ff, and the executors and surviving spouse or civil partner have agreed to satisfy the gift in this way. For an explanation of the scheme, see paras **[218.19]**–**[218.22]**.

2 The Legacy Trustees will have been appointed by the will and should include at least one person who is not the surviving spouse or civil partner: see para **[218.22]**, sub-para (3).

3 This is the IHT threshold in relation to a death during tax years 2009–10 and 2010–11. For 2008–09 it was £312,000. Insert the amount of the legacy ascertained in accordance with the terms of the will.

4 It is important that the loan is repayable on demand so as to assist the argument that an interest in possession is not created: see paras **[218.19]** and **[218.20]**.

5 See n 4 above.

6 The requirements of the Law of Property (Miscellaneous Provisions) Act 1989, s 1 for the making of a deed are that it is clear on its face that it is intended by the parties to it to be a

deed, that it is signed by each party in the presence of a witness who attests the signature (two witnesses if someone signs for a party), and that it is delivered as a deed by each party or someone authorised to do so on his behalf. Sealing is not necessary.

[243.5]

[Updated for the nil-rate inheritance tax band.]

Form F5.4: Deed of charge to give effect to a nil-rate band charge scheme[1]

Note:

Even following the introduction of the nil-rate band carry forward allowance (see para **[200.75]** above), it may still be desirable in certain instances to keep in place a nil-rate band discretionary trust established by a testator's will and to constitute it by a debt or charge, see para **[243.1]** above.

THIS DEED is made the [*date*] BETWEEN (1) [*name of executor*] of [*address*] and [*name of executor*] of [*address*] ('the Executors')[2] and (2) [*name of Legacy Trustee*] of [*address*] and [*name of Legacy Trustee*] of [*address*] ('the Legacy Trustees')

SUPPLEMENTAL to the will ('the Will') dated [*date*] of [*name*] ('the Testator') who died on [*date*] and which was proved by the Executors on [*date*] in the [*name*] Registry

Whereas—

(A) By clause + of the Will the Testator gave to the Legacy Trustees a pecuniary legacy determined according to a formula ('the Trust Legacy') to hold the same upon the trusts there set out.

(B) In the events which have happened the amount of the Trust Legacy is [£325,000].[3]

(C) By clause + of the Will the Executors were given power instead of satisfying the Trust Legacy by the payment of cash or the appropriation of property to charge property comprised in the Testator's residuary estate (or but for clause + would be comprised) with payment of a sum of money equal to or less than the amount of the Trust Legacy.

(D) There is comprised in the Testator's residuary estate (or but for clause + would be comprised) [a one-half beneficial share in the property known as [*description*] ('the Beneficial Share')].

(E) The Executors have decided to satisfy the Trust Legacy by exercising such power to charge [the Beneficial Share] with payment to the Legacy Trustees on demand of the sum of [£325,000] [linked to the Index of Retail Prices] enforceable by the Legacy Trustees at any time (without there being any personal liability of any person).[4]

NOW THIS DEED WITNESSETH:

1. The Executors HEREBY CHARGE [the Beneficial Share] with payment to the Legacy Trustees on demand of the sum of [£325,000] [or (if greater) the sum calculated under the following clause] and such charge is to be enforceable by the Legacy Trustees at any time.[5]

[2. The sum determined under this clause shall be the sum produced by dividing the sum of [£325,000] by the index figure in the Index of Retail Prices for the month in which this deed is executed and (having made allowance for any re-basing of the Index which may have happened in the meantime) multiplying it by the index figure in that Index for the month in which repayment is made. (For these purposes the Index of Retail Prices shall mean the Index of Retail Prices published by HM Stationery Office or any official publication substituted for it and in the event of any change after the date of this deed in the reference base used to compile the said Index the figure taken to be that at which the said Index stands after such change shall be the figure at which the said Index would have stood if the reference base current at the date of this deed had been retained.)]

[3. If a partial repayment is made, such repayment shall be treated as representing such part of the sum of [£325,000] as produces the amount of such partial repayment by the above method.]

[2]/[4] The Legacy Trustees accept the above charge in [full]/[partial] satisfaction of the Trust Legacy and declare that they hold the foregoing charge and all moneys received thereunder upon the trusts declared by the Will in respect of the Trust Legacy and agree that the Legacy Trustees shall have no right to enforce payment of the amount charged personally against the owner or owners for the time being of the Beneficial Share.

IN WITNESS whereof the parties hereto have executed these presents as their deed the day and year first above written.[6]

SIGNED and delivered as a deed by the said [*name*] in the presence of— } [*Signature*]

[*Signature, address and description of witness*]
[*The foregoing from 'SIGNED' to be repeated for each party*]

1 This form is for use where a testator has made a nil-rate band gift onto discretionary trusts in his will, made provision for his executors to charge property comprised in his estate with payment of a sum of money in satisfaction of the gift, as in Forms B18.2, C3.4, or C3.5 at paras **[218.32]**, **[225.57]** ff and **[225.68]** ff, and the executors have decided to satisfy the gift in this way. For an explanation of the scheme, see paras **[218.19]**–**[218.22]** and for reasons for using the charge scheme rather than the debt scheme (as in Form F5.3 at para **[243.4]**), see also para **[218.21]**.

2 The surviving spouse or civil partner should preferably not be one of the executors in circumstances where FA 1986, s 103 might apply, and the executors and legacy trustees should not be exactly the same persons, see para **[218.22]**, sub-paras (4) and (5).

3 This is the IHT threshold until 5 April 2015. Insert the amount of the legacy ascertained in accordance with the terms of the will.

4 It is important that the charge is enforceable on demand so as to assist the argument that an interest in possession is not created, see paras **[218.19]**–**[218.20]**.

5 See n 4 above.

6 The requirements of the Law of Property (Miscellaneous Provisions) Act 1989, s 1 for the making of a deed are that it is clear on its face that it is intended by the parties to it to be a deed, that it is signed by each party in the presence of a witness who attests the signature (two witnesses if someone signs for a party), and that it is delivered as a deed by each party or someone authorised to do so on his behalf. Sealing is not necessary.

PART G

Legislation

Contents

REGULATION (EU) 650/2012

SECTION 1

Wills and intestacy

WILLS ACT 1837

(7 Will 4 & 1 Vict c 26)

[3 July 1837]

[244.35A]

Note to sections 33 and 33A. Section 33 provides that where a will makes a gift to child or remoter descendant of the testator and the intended beneficiary predeceases the testator leaving issue living at the testator's death, the issue take the gift by substitution. Section 33A was introduced by the Estates of Deceased Persons (Forfeiture Rule and Law of Succession) Act 2011 in relation to persons dying on or after 1 February 2012 so as to negative the effect of *Re DWS decd* [2001] Ch 568, [2001] 1 All ER 97, CA, by extending the operation of the substitutional gift to the issue of an intended beneficiary who survives the testator but is disqualified from taking by reason of the forfeiture rule or because he has disclaimed the gift. A minor consequential amendment is also made to section 33(3). See generally Vol 1, para **[47.15]**.

Deaths on or after 1 January 1983

[244.36]
33. Gifts to children or other issue who leave issue living at the testator's death shall not lapse.— (1) Where—

- (a) a will contains a devise or bequest to a child or remoter descendant of the testator; and
- (b) the intended beneficiary dies before the testator, leaving issue; and
- (c) issue of the intended beneficiary are living at the testator's death,

then, unless a contrary intention appears by the will, the devise or bequest shall take effect as a devise or bequest to the issue living at the testator's death.
(2) Where—

- (a) a will contains a devise or bequest to a class of persons consisting of children or remoter descendants of the testator; and
- (b) a member of the class dies before the testator, leaving issue; and
- (c) issue of that member are living at the testator's death,

then, unless a contrary intention appears by the will, the devise or bequest shall take effect as if the class included the issue of its deceased member living at the testator's death.
(3) Issue shall take under this section through all degrees, according to their stock, in equal shares if more than one, any gift or share which their parent would have taken and so that [(subject to section 33A)][1] no issue shall take whose parent is living at the testator's death and so capable of taking.
(4) For the purposes of this section—

(a) the illegitimacy of any person is to be disregarded; and
(b) a person conceived before the testator's death and born living thereafter is to be taken to have been living at the testator's death.[2]

1 Words in square brackets inserted by the Estates of Deceased Persons (Forfeiture Rule and Law of Succession) Act 2011, s 2(1), (3) with effect from 1 February 2012: Estates of Deceased Persons (Forfeiture Rule and Law of Succession) Act 2011 (Commencement) Order 2011, SI 2011/2903, art 2.
2 Section 33, as printed here, was substituted by the AJA 1982, s 19 in relation to the wills of persons dying on or after 1 January 1983. By virtue of sub-s (4)(a), references to 'child' and 'issue' include illegitimate children and issue and by virtue of the Adoption and Children Act 2002 (paras **[245.91]** ff below), replacing the Adoption Act 1976, s 39 (para **[245.58]** below), also include adopted children and issue.

[244.36A]

[33A Disclaimer or forfeiture of gift (1) This section applies where a will contains a devise or bequest to a person who—

(a) disclaims it, or
(b) has been precluded by the forfeiture rule from acquiring it.

(2) The person is, unless a contrary intention appears by the will, to be treated for the purposes of this Act as having died immediately before the testator.
(3) But in a case within subsection (1)(b), subsection (2) does not affect the power conferred by section 2 of the Forfeiture Act 1982 (power of court to modify the forfeiture rule).
(4) In this section "forfeiture rule" has the same meaning as in the Forfeiture Act 1982.][1]

1 Section 33A inserted by the Estates of Deceased Persons (Forfeiture Rule and Law of Succession) Act 2011, s 2(1) (3) with effect from 1 February 2012: Estates of Deceased Persons (Forfeiture Rule and Law of Succession) Act 2011 (Commencement) Order 2011, SI 2011/2903, art 2.

ADMINISTRATION OF ESTATES ACT 1925

(15 & 16 Geo 5 c 23)

[9 April 1925]

[244.59]

Note. This Act came into force on 1 January 1926 (s 58(2) (repealed)).

PART IV
DISTRIBUTION OF RESIDUARY ESTATE

* * * * *

[244.61]

Note to sections 46 to 49. Sections 46 to 49 of this Act were extensively amended in relation to deaths occurring on or after 1 January 1953 by the Intestates' Estates Act 1952.

They were further amended in relation to deaths on or after 1 January 1967 by the Family Provision Act 1966 (FPA 1966), s 1, and further minor amendments were made by the Administration of Justice Act 1977 (AJA 1977), s 28.

Further amendments as respects intestates dying on or after 1 January 1996 were effected by the Law Reform (Succession) Act 1995, s 1 and are noted to the provisions concerned.

In relation to the estates of persons dying on or after 1 January 1970 and before 4 April 1988 Part IV of the AEA 1925 takes effect subject to the FLRA 1969, s 14 (para **[245.38]** below) and in relation to deaths on or after 4 April 1988 subject to the FLRA 1987, ss 1 and 18 (paras **[245.70]**–**[245.71]** below).

With effect from 5 December 2005 extensive amendments are made to Pt IV of AEA 1925, particularly ss 46 and 47, by CPA 2004, ss 71 and 263(2), Sch 4, paras 7–12 and Civil Partnership Act 2004 (Commencement No 2) Order 2005, SI 2005/3175.

Two more recent amendments should be noted. First, in relation to the spouses or civil partners of persons dying intestate on or after 1 February 2009 the amounts of the fixed net sums payable under paras (2) and (3) of the Table in AEA 1925, s 46(1)(i) are increased from £125,000 to £250,000 and from £200,000 to £450,000 respectively: Family Provision (Intestate Succession) Order 2009, SI 2009/135. Secondly, the basis on which the life interest of a surviving spouse or civil partner is capitalised under s 47A is adjusted in cases where the election to do so is made on or after 1 February 2009 to take account of changed social and economic circumstances by the substitution of new tables to the Intestate Succession (Interest and Capitalisation) Order 1977: Intestate Succession (Interest and Capitalisation) (Amendment) Order 2008, SI 2008/3162: see paras **[244.90]** ff below.

The most recent amendment is the introduction of a new section 46A by the Estates of Deceased Persons (Forfeiture Rule and Law of Succession) Act 2011 in relation to persons dying on or after 1 February 2012. Section 46A negatives the effect of *Re DWS decd* [2001] Ch 568, [2001] 1 All ER 97, CA, by treating a person who would have been entitled to an interest in the estate of a person who dies intestate but disclaims the interest or is disqualified from taking by reason of the forfeiture rule as having predeceased the intestate, subject in the latter case to the jurisdiction of the court under the Forfeiture Act 1982 to modify the rule. The 2011 Act also introduces a new subsection (4A) in section 47 so as to ensure that the statutory trusts take effect in accordance with the new rule contained in section 46A and new subsections (4B), (4C) and (4D) to permit the child of a person dying under the age of 18 without having married or formed a civil partnership with the other parent to inherit. See generally Vol 1, paras **[104.8]**, **[104.9]**.

[244.62]

46 Succession to real and personal estate on intestacy (1) The residuary estate of an intestate shall be distributed in the manner or be held on the trusts mentioned in this section, namely:—

[(i) If the intestate leaves a [spouse or civil partner][1], then in accordance with the following Table:

TABLE

If the intestate—

(1) leaves—

(a) no issue, and (b) no parent, or brother or sister of the whole blood, or issue of a brother or sister of the whole blood	the residuary estate shall be held in trust for the surviving [spouse or civil partner][1] absolutely.

(2) leaves issue (whether or not persons mentioned in sub-paragraph (b) above also survive)	the surviving [spouse or civil partner][1] shall take the personal chattels absolutely and, in addition, the residuary estate of the intestate (other than the personal chattels) shall stand charged with the payment of a [fixed net sum][2], free of death duties and costs, to the surviving [spouse or civil partner][1] with interest thereon from the date of the death ... [at such rate as the Lord Chancellor may specify by order][3] until paid or appropriated, and, subject to providing for that sum and the interest thereon, the residuary estate (other than the personal chattels) shall be held— (a) as to one half upon trust for the surviving [spouse or civil partner][1] during his or her life, and, subject to such life interest, on the statutory trusts for the issue of the intestate, and (b) as to the other half, on the statutory trusts for the issue of the intestate.
(3) leaves one or more of the following, that is to say, a parent, a brother or sister of the whole blood, or issue of a brother or sister of the whole blood, but leaves no issue	the surviving [spouse or civil partner][1] shall take the personal chattels absolutely and, in addition, the residuary estate of the intestate (other than the personal chattels) shall stand charged with the payment of a [fixed net sum][4], free of death duties and costs, to the surviving [spouse or civil partner][1] with interest thereon from the date of the death ... [at such rate as the Lord Chancellor may specify by order][5] until paid or appropriated, and, subject to providing for that sum and the interest thereon, the residuary estate (other than the personal chattels) shall be held— (a) as to one half in trust for the surviving [spouse or civil partner][1] absolutely, and (b) as to the other half— (i) where the intestate leaves one parent or both parents (whether or not brothers or sisters of the intestate or their issue also survive) in trust for the parent absolutely or, as the case may be, for the two parents in equal shares absolutely (ii) where the intestate leaves no parent, on the statutory trusts for the brothers and sisters of the whole blood of the intestate.]

[The fixed net sums referred to in paragraphs (2) and (3) of this Table shall be of the amounts provided by or under section 1 of the Family Provision Act 1966]

(ii) If the intestate leaves issue but no [spouse or civil partner][1], the residuary estate of the intestate shall be held on the statutory trusts for the issue of the intestate;

(iii) If the intestate leaves no [spouse or civil partner][1] and no issue but both parents, then ... the residuary estate of the intestate shall be held in trust for the father and mother in equal shares absolutely;

(iv) If the intestate leaves no [spouse or civil partner][1] and no issue but one parent, then ... the residuary estate of the intestate shall be held in trust for the surviving father or mother absolutely;

(v) If the intestate leaves no [spouse or civil partner][1] and no issue and no] parent, then ... the residuary estate of the intestate shall be held in trust for the following persons living at the death of the intestate, and in the following order and manner, namely:—

First, on the statutory trusts for the brothers and sisters of the whole blood of the intestate; but if no person takes an absolutely vested interest under such trusts; then

Second, on the statutory trusts for the brothers and sisters of the half blood of the intestate; but if no person takes an absolutely vested interest under such trusts; then

Third, for the grandparents of the intestate and, if more than one survive the intestate, in equal shares; but if there is no member of this class; then

Fourth, on the statutory trusts for the uncles and aunts of the intestate (being brothers or sisters of the whole blood of a parent of the intestate); but if no person takes an absolutely vested interest under such trusts; then

Fifth, on the statutory trusts for the uncles and aunts of the intestate (being brothers or sisters of the half blood of a parent of the intestate) ...

(vi) In default of any person taking an absolute interest under the foregoing provisions, the residuary estate of the intestate shall belong to the Crown or to the Duchy of Lancaster or to the Duke of Cornwall for the time being, as the case may be, as bona vacantia, and in lieu of any right to escheat.

The Crown or the said Duchy or the said Duke may (without prejudice to the powers reserved by section 9 of the Civil List Act 1910, or any other powers), out of the whole or any part of the property devolving on them respectively, provide, in accordance with the existing practice, for dependents, whether kindred or not, of the intestate, and other persons for whom the intestate might reasonably have been expected to make provision.

[(1A) The power to make orders under subsection (1) above shall be exercisable by statutory instrument subject to annulment in pursuance of a resolution of either House of Parliament; and any such order may be varied or revoked by a subsequent order made under the power.][6]

(2) A husband and wife shall for all purposes of distribution or division under the foregoing provisions of this section be treated as two persons.

[(2A) Where the intestate's [spouse or civil partner][1] survived the intestate but died before the end of the period of 28 days beginning with the day on which the intestate died, this section shall have effect as respects the intestate as if the [spouse or civil partner][1] had not survived the intestate.][7]

[(3) Where the intestate and the intestate's [spouse or civil partner][1] have died in circumstances rendering it uncertain which of them survived the other and the intestate's [spouse or civil partner][1] is by virtue of section one hundred and eighty-four of the Law of Property Act 1925, deemed to have survived the intestate, this section shall, nevertheless, have effect as respects the intestate as if the [spouse or civil partner][1] had not survived the intestate.

(4) The interest payable on [the fixed net sum][8] payable to a surviving [spouse or civil partner][1] shall be primarily payable out of income.][9]

1 The words 'spouse or civil partner' are substituted throughout s 46 for the words 'husband or wife' by CPA 2004, ss 71 and 263(2). Sch 4, para 7.

2 Words in square brackets substituted by the Family Provisions Act 1966, s 1(2), in relation to persons dying on or after 1 January 1967, for the words 'net sum of five thousand pounds'. The Lord Chancellor has power under s 1(3), (4) of that Act to vary this fixed net sum by statutory instrument. This 'fixed net sum' was £8,750 where the date of death was prior to 1 July 1972 (FPA 1966, s 1(1)) but is £15,000 where the death occurred on or after that date and before 15 March 1977 (Family Provision (Intestate Succession) Order 1972, SI 1972/916); £25,000 where the death occurred on or after the latter date and before 1 March 1981 (Family Provision (Intestate Succession) Order 1977, SI 1977/415); £40,000 where the death occurred on or after 1 March 1981 (the Family Provision (Intestate Succession) Order 1981, SI 1981/255); £75,000 where the death occurred on or after 1 June 1987 (the Family Provision (Intestate Succession) Order 1987, SI 1987/799); £125,000 where the death occurred on or after 1 December 1993 (the Family Provision (Intestate Succession) Order 1993, SI 1993/2906); and £250,000 where the death occurred on or after 1 February 2009 (the Family Provision (Intestate Succession) Order 2009, SI 2009/135).

3 Words omitted were repealed by SL(R)A 1981. Words in square brackets substituted by AJA 1977, s 28(1) for the rate of per cent per annum. The rate of interest was 7 per cent per annum from 15 September 1977 to 30 September 1983 and from 1 October 1983 is 6 per cent per annum: see the Intestate Succession (Interest and Capitalisation) Order 1977 (SI 1977/1491), art 2, as amended by SI 1983/1374 (see para **[244.92]** below).

4 Words in square brackets substituted by FPA 1966, s 1(2), in relation to persons dying on or after 1 January 1967, for the words 'net sum of twenty thousand pounds'. The Lord Chancellor has power under s 1(3), (4) to vary this fixed net sum by statutory instrument. This fixed net sum was £30,000 where the death occurred before 1 July 1972, £40,000 for deaths on or after that date and before 15 March 1977, £55,000 for deaths on or after the latter date and before 1 March 1981, and is £85,000 for deaths on or after 1 March 1981 and before 1 June 1987, £125,000 for deaths on or after 1 June 1987 and before 1 December 1993, and is £200,000 for deaths on or after 1 December 1993 and before 1 February 2009; and is £450,000 for deaths on or after 1 February 2009. The relevant statutory instruments are the same as those relating to the fixed net sum under para (2) of the Table; see n 2.

5 The words omitted were repealed by SL(R)A 1981. See n 3 for the rates of interest.

6 Sub-s (1A): inserted by AJA 1977, s 28(1).

7 Sub-s (2A): inserted by LR(S)A 1995, s 1(1), as respects an intestate dying on or after 1 January 1996.

8 Words in square brackets substituted by FPA 1966, s 1(2), in relation to persons dying on or after 1 January 1967, for the words 'net sum of five thousand pounds or, as the case may be, twenty thousand pounds'. As to the fixed net sum and the rate of interest, see nn 2 and 3 above.

9 Sub-ss (3) and (4) inserted by the Intestates' Estates Act 1952, s 1(4) and subsequently amended: see nn 1 and 8 above.

[244.62A]

[46A Disclaimer or forfeiture on intestacy (1) This section applies where a person—

(a) is entitled in accordance with section 46 to an interest in the residuary estate of an intestate but disclaims it, or

(b) would have been so entitled had the person not been precluded by the forfeiture rule from acquiring it.

(2) The person is to be treated for the purposes of this Part as having died immediately before the intestate.

(3) But in a case within subsection (1)(b), subsection (2) does not affect the power conferred by section 2 of the Forfeiture Act 1982 (power of court to modify the forfeiture rule).

(4) In this section "forfeiture rule" has the same meaning as in the Forfeiture Act 1982.][1]

1 Section 46A inserted by the Estates of Deceased Persons (Forfeiture Rule and Law of Succession) Act 2011, s 1(1), (2) with effect from 1 February 2012: Estates of Deceased Persons (Forfeiture Rule and Law of Succession) Act 2011 (Commencement) Order 2011, SI 2011/2903, art 2.

[244.63]

47 Statutory trusts in favour of issue and other classes of relatives of intestate (1) Where under this Part of this Act the residuary estate of an intestate, or any part thereof, is directed to be held on the statutory trusts for the issue of the intestate, the same shall be held upon the following trusts, namely:—

(i) In trust, in equal shares if more than one, for all or any the children or child of the intestate, living at the death of the intestate, who attain the age of eighteen years[1] or marry under that age [or form a civil partnership under that age][2], and for all or any of the issue living at the death of the intestate who attain the age of eighteen years[2] or marry[, or form a civil partnership,] under that age of any child of the intestate who predeceases the intestate, such issue to take through all degrees, according to their stocks, in equal shares if more than one, the share which their parent would have taken if living at the death of the intestate, and so that [(subject to section 46A)][3] no issue shall take whose parent is living at the death of the intestate and so capable of taking;

(ii) The statutory power of advancement, and the statutory provisions which relate to maintenance and accumulation of surplus income, shall apply, but when an infant marries [, or forms a civil partnership,][2] such infant shall be entitled to give valid receipts for the income of the infant's share or interest;

[*(iii) Where the property held on the statutory trusts for issue is divisible into shares, then any money or property which, by way of advancement or on the marriage of a child of the intestate, has been paid to such child by the intestate or settled by the intestate for the benefit of such child (including any life or less interest and including property covenanted to be paid or settled) shall, subject to any contrary intention expressed or appearing from the circumstances of the case, be taken as being so paid or settled in or towards satisfaction of the share of such child or the share which such child would have taken if living at the death of the intestate, and shall be brought into account, at a valuation (the value to be reckoned as at the death of the intestate), in accordance with the requirements of the personal representatives;*][4]

(iv) The personal representatives may permit any infant contingently interested to have the use and enjoyment of any personal chattels in such manner and subject to such conditions (if any) as the personal representatives may consider reasonable, and without being liable to account for any consequential loss.

(2) If the trusts in favour of the issue of the intestate fail by reason of no child or other issue attaining an absolutely vested interest—

(a) the residuary estate of the intestate and the income thereof and all statutory accumulations, if any, of the income thereof, or so much thereof as may not have been paid or applied under any power affecting the same, shall go, devolve and be held under the provisions of this Part of this Act as if the intestate had died without leaving issue living at the death of the intestate;

(b) references in this Part of this Act to the intestate 'leaving no issue' shall be construed as 'leaving no issue who attain an absolutely vested interest';

(c) references in this Part of this Act to the intestate 'leaving issue' or 'leaving a child or other issue' shall be construed as 'leaving issue who attain an absolutely vested interest.'

(3) Where under this Part of this Act the residuary estate of an intestate or any part thereof is directed to be held on the statutory trusts for any class of relatives of the intestate, other than issue of the intestate, the same shall be held on trusts corresponding to the statutory trusts for the issue of the intestate (other than the provision for bringing any money or property into account) as if such trusts (other than as aforesaid) were repeated with the substitution of references to the members or member of that class for references to the children or child of the intestate.

[(4) References in paragraph (i) of subsection (1) of the last foregoing section to the intestate leaving, or not leaving, a member of the class consisting of brothers or sisters of the whole blood of the intestate and issue of brothers or sisters of the whole blood of the intestate shall be construed as references to the intestate leaving, or not leaving, a member of that class who attains an absolutely vested interest.]

[(4A) Subsections (2) and (4) are subject to section 46A.][5]

[(4B) Subsections (4C) and (4D) apply if a beneficiary under the statutory trusts—

(a) fails to attain an absolutely vested interest because the beneficiary dies without having reached 18 and without having married or formed a civil partnership, and

(b) dies leaving issue.

(4C) The beneficiary is to be treated for the purposes of this Part as having died immediately before the intestate.

(4D) The residuary estate (together with the income from it and any statutory accumulations of income from it) or so much of it as has not been paid or applied under a power affecting it is to devolve accordingly.][6]
[(5) Repealed by the Family Provision Act 1966, ss 9, 10, Sch 2.]

1 In relation to intestates dying before the FLRA 1969 came into force on 1 January 1970, the age was 21 years.
2 The references in square brackets in sub-s (1)(i)(ii) to the formation of a civil partnership inserted with effect from 5 December by the Civil Partnership Act 2004, ss 71 and 263(2), Sch 4, para 8 and Civil Partnership Act 2004 (Commencement) Order 2005, SI 2005/3175.
3 Words in square brackets in section 47(1)(i) inserted by the Estates of Deceased Persons (Forfeiture Rule and Law of Succession) Act 2011, s 1(1) (3) with effect from 1 February 2012: Estates of Deceased Persons (Forfeiture Rule and Law of Succession) Act 2011 (Commencement) Order 2011, SI 2011/2903, art 2.
4 Sub-s(1)(iii) repealed by LR(S)A 1995, ss 1(2)(a), 5, Schedule as respects persons dying intestate on or after 1 January 1996.
5 Subsection (4A) inserted by the Estates of Deceased Persons (Forfeiture Rule and Law of Succession) Act 2011, s 1(1) (4) with effect from 1 February 2012: Estates of Deceased Persons (Forfeiture Rule and Law of Succession) Act 2011 (Commencement) Order 2011, SI 2011/2903, art 2.
6 Subsections (4B), (4C) and 4(D) inserted by the Estates of Deceased Persons (Forfeiture Rule and Law of Succession) Act 2011, s 3 with effect from 1 February 2012: Estates of Deceased Persons (Forfeiture Rule and Law of Succession) Act 2011 (Commencement) Order 2011, SI 2011/2903, art 2.

INTESTATE SUCCESSION (INTEREST AND CAPITALISATION) ORDER 1977

SI 1977/1491

[244.90]

Note. This Order was made on 4 September 1977 by the Lord Chancellor under the AEA 1925, s 46(1)(i) (as substituted by the Intestates' Estates Act 1952, s 1, and as amended by the AJA 1977, s 28(1)) and s 47A(3A) of the 1925 Act (as inserted by the AJA 1977, s 28(3)). The Order came into force on 15 September 1977: see article 1(1). Article 2 of the Order originally increased the rate of interest payable on the statutory legacy until paid or appropriated from 4 per cent pa to 7 per cent pa or, in the case of persons dying before 1 January 1953, to 8 per cent, pa). Article 2 was amended by the Intestate Succession (Interest and Capitalisation) Order 1983, SI 1983/1374 so as to reduce the rate to 6 per cent per annum with effect from 1 October 1983. This last rate of interest has not since been altered.

Article 3 and the Schedule sets out the formula for calculating the value of the life interest of the surviving spouse of an intestate who elects to capitalise his or her life interest. With effect from 1 February 2009 the Schedule and its tables have been replaced with a new schedule and new tables designed to take account of increases in life expectancy and decreases in the yields on Government Stocks.

The 1977 Order is printed below as amended by the Intestate Succession (Interest and Capitalisation) Order 1983, SI 1983/1374, the Civil Partnership Act 2004 (Amendments to Subordinate Legislation) Order 2005, SI 2005/2114 and the Intestate Succession (Interest and Capitalisation) (Amendment) Order 2009, SI 2009/3162.

The Schedule to the 1977 Order and the replacement Schedule together with their respective tables are printed at paras **[244.129B]** ff below.

[244.91]

1. Citation and Interpretation.— (1) This Order may be cited as the Intestate Succession (Interest and Capitalisation) Order 1977 and shall come into operation on 15th September 1977.

(2) The Interpretation Act 1889 shall apply to the interpretation of this Order as it applies to the interpretation of an Act of Parliament.

[244.92]

2. Interest on Statutory Legacy. For the purposes of section 46(1)(i) of the Administration of Estates Act 1925, as it applies both in respect of persons dying before 1953 and in respect of persons dying after 1952, the specified rate of interest shall be [6] per cent per annum.[1]

1 The figure in square brackets was substituted by SI 1983/1374 with effect from 1 October 1983: see para **[244.90]** above.

[244.93]

3. Capitalisation of Life Interests.— (1) Where after the coming into operation of this Order an election is exercised in accordance with subsection (6) or (7) of section 47A of the Administration of Estates Act 1925, the capital value of the life interest of the surviving spouse [or civil partner][1] shall be reckoned in accordance with the following provisions of this article.

(2) There shall be ascertained, by reference to the index compiled by the Financial Times, The Institute of Actuaries and the Faculty of Actuaries, the gross redemption yield[1] on fifteen-year Government Stocks[1] at the date on which the election was exercised or, if the index was not compiled on that date, by reference to the index on the last date before that date on which it was compiled; and the column which corresponds to that yield in whichever of the Tables set out in the Schedule hereto is applicable to the sex of the surviving spouse [or civil partner][1] shall be the appropriate column for the purposes of paragraph (3) of this article.[2]

(3) The capital value for the purposes of paragraph (1) of this article is the produce of the part of the residuary estate (whether or not yielding income) in respect of which the election was exercised and the multiplier shown in the appropriate column opposite the age which the surviving spouse [or civil partner][1] had attained at the date on which the election was exercised.[1]

1 Words in square brackets in sub-ss (1), (2) and (3) inserted with effect from 5 December 2005 by Civil Partnership Act 2004, s 259 and Civil Partnership Act 2004 (Amendments to Subordinate Legislation) Order 2005, SI 2005/2114, arts 1, 2(6), Sch 6, para1(1), (2).

2 As originally in force art 3(2) referred to 'the *average* gross redemption yield on *medium coupon* fifteen-year Government Stocks'. With effect from 1 February 2009 article 3(2) is amended by the Intestate Succession (Interest and Capitalisation) Order 2008, SI 2008/3162, arts 1, 2(1) by omitting the words 'average' and 'medium coupon' to reflect changes since 1977 in the way that the yields on United Kingdom Government stocks are calculated. 'Medium coupon' yields are no longer produced; however, the yield figures for 15-year United Kingdom Government Stocks are published as 'FTSE UK Gilt Indices' on the website of the Financial Times.

[244.93A]

SCHEDULE

[The schedule and replacement schedule to this Order which contain the tables referred to in article 3 are printed at paras **[244.129B]** ff below.]

CHILDREN ACT 1989

(1989 c 41)

[16 November 1989]

[244.112]

Note. The Children Act 1989 (ChA 1989) was brought into force on 14 October 1991 (SI 1991/828). The Act as amended contains comprehensive provisions or the welfare of children, including their guardianship. The powers to appoint guardians are now contained in s 5. A parent with 'parental responsibility' (a term defined by s 3) has power under s 5(3) to appoint an individual to be the child's guardian after his or her death and a guardian is given the like power by s 5(4). The power may be exercised by will or any other writing, subject to the requirement that it be dated and either signed by the person making the appointment or signed at his direction before witnesses; see s 5(5). Sections 2 to 4 prescribe the circumstances in which a parent is deemed to have the parental responsibility which is a prerequisite to the exercise of the power to appoint guardians. Section 4 has been amended with effect from 1 December 2003 by the Adoption and Children Act 2002, s 111. The amendments extend parental responsibility for illegitimate children to fathers registered on the birth certificate, where registration occurs on or after the commencement day. Adoption and children Act 2002, s 112 added with effect from 30 December 2005 a new s 4A providing for the acquisition of parental responsibility by step-parents. Section 6 sets out the circumstances in which the appointment of a guardian may be revoked or disclaimed. One additional important feature of the ChA 1989 is that s 3(3) extends to a parent (and now a step-parent) with parental responsibility the right to call for and deal with all property belonging to his minor child, a right which was formerly available under the Guardianship Act 1973, s 7 only to a guardian.

With effect from 6 April 2009 the ChA 1989 is amended by HFEA 2008 to cater for cases where a child is born as a result of one of the procedures regulated by HFEA 1990 and 2008 and the mother has agreed that another woman who is not her civil partner is to be treated as the other parent. In such cases the ChA 1989 is amended so as to extend parental responsibility to that other parent in appropriate circumstances.

For a more detailed account of these provisions, and for their practical implications for will drafting, see Vol 1, para **[28.1]** ff and para **[203.47]** ff above.

PART I
INTRODUCTORY

* * * * *

[244.113]

2. Parental responsibility for children.— (1) Where a child's father and mother were married to each other at the time of his birth, they shall each have parental responsibility for the child.

[(1A) Where a child—

(a) has a parent by virtue of section 42 of the Human Fertilisation and Embryology Act 2008; or

(b) has a parent by virtue of section 43 of that Act and is a person to whom section 1(3) of the Family Law Reform Act 1987 applies, the child's mother and the other parent shall each have parental responsibility for the child.][1]

(2) Where a child's father and mother were not married to each other at the time of his birth—

(a) the mother shall have parental responsibility for the child;

(b) the father shall not have parental responsibility for the child, unless he acquires it in accordance with the provisions of this Act.

[(2A) Where a child has a parent by virtue of section 43 of the Human Fertilisation and Embryology Act 2008 and is not a person to whom section 1(3) of the Family Law Reform Act 1987 applies—

(a) the mother shall have parental responsibility for the child;
(b) the other parent shall have parental responsibility for the child if she has acquired it (and has not ceased to have it) in accordance with the provisions of this Act.][2]

(3) References in this Act to a child whose father and mother were, or (as the case may be) were not, married to each other at the time of his birth must be read with section 1 of the Family Law Reform Act 1987 (which extends their meaning).
(4) The rule of law that a father is the natural guardian of his legitimate child is abolished.
(5) More than one person may have parental responsibility for the same child at the same time.
(6) A person who has parental responsibility for a child at any time shall not cease to have that responsibility solely because some other person subsequently acquires parental responsibility for the child.
(7) Where more than one person has parental responsibility for a child, each of them may act alone and without the other (or others) in meeting that responsibility; but nothing in this Part shall be taken to affect the operation of any enactment which requires the consent of more than one person in a matter affecting the child.
(8) The fact that a person has parental responsibility for a child shall not entitle him to act in any way which would be incompatible with any order made with respect to the child under this Act.
(9) A person who has parental responsibility for a child may not surrender or transfer any part of that responsibility to another but may arrange for some or all of it to be met by one or more persons acting on his behalf.
(10) The person with whom any such arrangement is made may himself be a person who already has parental responsibility for the child concerned.
(11) The making of any such arrangement shall not affect any liability of the person making it which may arise from any failure to meet any part of his parental responsibility for the child concerned.

1 Subsection (1A) inserted with effect from 6 April 2009 for certain purposes and from 1 September 2009 for all remaining purposes by the Human Fertilisation and Embryology Act 2008, s 56, Sch 6, para 26(1), (2) and the Human Fertilisation and Embryology Act 2008 (Commencement No 1 and Transitional Provisions) Order 2009, SI 2009/479, art 6(1)(e), (f), (2).
2 Subsection (2A) inserted with effect from 6 April 2009 for certain purposes and from 1 September 2009 for all remaining purposes by the Human Fertilisation and Embryology Act 2008, s 56, Sch 6, para 26(1), (3) and the Human Fertilisation and Embryology Act 2008 (Commencement No 1 and Transitional Provisions) Order 2009, SI 2009/479, art 6(1)(e), (f), (2).

[244.115A]

[4ZA Acquisition of parental responsibility by second female parent

(1) Where a child has a parent by virtue of section 43 of the Human Fertilisation and Embryology Act 2008 and is not a person to whom section 1(3) of the Family Law Reform Act 1987 applies, that parent shall acquire parental responsibility for the child if—

- (a) she becomes registered as a parent of the child under any of the enactments specified in subsection (2);
- (b) she and the child's mother make an agreement providing for her to have parental responsibility for the child; or
- (c) the court, on her application, orders that she shall have parental responsibility for the child.

(2) The enactments referred to in subsection (1)(a) are—

- (a) paragraphs (a), (b) and (c) of section 10(1B) and of section 10A(1B) of the Births and Deaths Registration Act 1953;
- (b) paragraphs (a), (b) and (d) of section 18B(1) and sections 18B(3)(a) and 20(1)(a) of the Registration of Births, Deaths and Marriages (Scotland) Act 1965; and
- (c) sub-paragraphs (a), (b) and (c) of Article 14ZA(3) of the Births and Deaths Registration (Northern Ireland) Order 1976.

(3) The Secretary of State may by order amend subsection (2) so as to add further enactments to the list in that subsection.
(4) An agreement under subsection (1)(b) is also a 'parental responsibility agreement', and section 4(2) applies in relation to such an agreement as it applies in relation to parental responsibility agreements under section 4.
(5) A person who has acquired parental responsibility under subsection (1) shall cease to have that responsibility only if the court so orders.
(6) The court may make an order under subsection (5) on the application—

- (a) of any person who has parental responsibility for the child; or
- (b) with the leave of the court, of the child himself, subject, in the case of parental responsibility acquired under subsection (1)(c), to section 12(4).

(7) The court may only grant leave under subsection (6)(b) if it is satisfied that the child has sufficient understanding to make theproposed application.][1]

1 Section 2ZA inserted with effect from 6 April 2009 for certain purposes and from 1 September 2009 for all remaining purposes by the Human Fertilisation and Embryology Act 2008, s 56, Sch 6, para 27 and the Human Fertilisation and Embryology Act 2008 (Commencement No 1 and Transitional Provisions) Order 2009, SI 2009/479, art 6(1)(e), (f), (2).

PART XII
MISCELLANEOUS AND GENERAL

* * * * *

GENERAL

* * * * *

[244.119]
105. Interpretation.— (1) In this Act—

* * * * *

'child' means … a person under the age of eighteen;

* * * * *

'guardian of a child' means a guardian (other than a guardian of the estate of a child) appointed in accordance with the provisions of section 5;

* * * * *

['parental responsibility' has the meaning given in section 3;
'parental responsibility agreement' has the meaning given in [sections 4(1)[, 4ZA(4)] and 4A(2)][1];
'prescribed' means prescribed by regulations made under this Act;

* * * * *

'residence order' has the meaning given by section 8(1);

* * * * *

(2) References in this Act to a child whose father and mother were, or (as the case may be) were not, married to each other at the time of his birth must be read with section 1 of the Family Law Reform Act 1987 (which extends the meaning of such references).

1 Words in outer set of square brackets substituted with effect from 30 December 2005 by the Adoption and Children Act 2002, ss 139, 148, Sch 3, para 70(c) (with Sch 4, paras 6–8) and the Adoption and Children Act 2002 (Commencement No 9) Order 2005, SI 2005/2213, art 2(o) and reference in inner set of square brackets inserted with effect from 6 April 2009 by the Human Fertilisation and Embryology Act 2008, s 56, Sch 6, para 31 and the Human Fertilisation and Embryology Act 2008 (Commencement No 1 and Transitional Provisions) Order 2009, SI 2009/479, art 6(1)(e), (f).

INTESTATE SUCCESSION (INTEREST AND CAPITALISATION) ORDER 1977

SI 1977/1491

SCHEDULE

[244.129A]

Note. The schedules and tables below form part of the Intestate Succession (Interest and Capitalisation) Order 1977 which is printed at paras **[244.90]** ff above. The schedule set out in para **[244.129B]** below formed part of the original 1977 Order and in the case of an election to capitalise a life interest made under the AEA 1925, s 47A on or after 15 September 1977 (when the 1977 Order came into force) the capital value of the life interest was reckoned under art 3 in accordance with the tables contained in the Schedule. Article 3 of the 1977 Order was slightly amended (it is printed as amended in para **[244.93]** above) and the Schedule to the Order replaced with the Schedule to the Intestate Succession (Interest and Capitalisation) (Amendment) Order 2008, SI 2008/3162, which is printed at para **[244.129C]** below. The 2008 Order came into force on 1 February 2009 and in the case of an election made on or after that date the capital value of the life interest is calculated in accordance with the new Schedule.

[244.129B]

Schedule
Table 1

Multiplier to be applied to the part of the residuary estate in respect of which the election is exercised to obtain the capital value of the life interest of a surviving husband [or a surviving male civil partner][1] when the average gross redemption yield on medium coupon fifteen-year Government Stocks is at the rate shown

Age Last Birthday of Husband [or a surviving male civil partner][2]	*Less than 8.50%*	*8.50% or between 8.50% and 9.50%*	*9.50% or between 9.50% and 10.50%*	*10.50% or between 10.50% and 11.50%*	*11.50% or between 11.50% and 12.50%*	*12.50% or between 12.50% and 13.50%*	*13.50% or between 13.50% and 14.50%*	*14.50% or between 14.50% and 15.50%*	*15.50% or more*
16	0.882	0.897	0.908	0.917	0.923	0.927	0.931	0.934	0.936
17	0.879	0.895	0.906	0.915	0.921	0.926	0.930	0.933	0.935
18	0.876	0.892	0.904	0.913	0.920	0.925	0.929	0.932	0.934
19	0.873	0.890	0.902	0.911	0.918	0.923	0.928	0.931	0.933
20	0.870	0.887	0.900	0.909	0.917	0.922	0.926	0.930	0.933
21	0.866	0.884	0.897	0.907	0.915	0.921	0.925	0.929	0.932
22	0.863	0.881	0.895	0.905	0.913	0.919	0.924	0.928	0.931
23	0.859	0.878	0.892	0.903	0.911	0.918	0.923	0.927	0.930
24	0.855	0.875	0.890	0.901	0.909	0.916	0.921	0.925	0.929
25	0.852	0.872	0.887	0.898	0.907	0.914	0.920	0.924	0.928

Age Last Birthday of Husband [or a surviving male civil partner][2]	*Less than 8.50%*	*8.50% or between 8.50% and 9.50%*	*9.50% or between 9.50% and 10.50%*	*10.50% or between 10.50% and 11.50%*	*11.50% or between 11.50% and 12.50%*	*12.50% or between 12.50% and 13.50%*	*13.50% or between 13.50% and 14.50%*	*14.50% or between 14.50% and 15.50%*	*15.50% or more*
26	0.847	0.868	0.884	0.896	0.905	0.912	0.918	0.923	0.926
27	0.843	0.864	0.880	0.893	0.903	0.910	0.916	0.921	0.925
28	0.838	0.860	0.877	0.890	0.900	0.908	0.914	0.919	0.923
29	0.834	0.856	0.873	0.887	0.897	0.905	0.912	0.917	0.922
30	0.828	0.851	0.869	0.883	0.894	0.903	0.910	0.915	0.920
31	0.823	0.847	0.865	0.879	0.891	0.900	0.907	0.913	0.918
32	0.818	0.842	0.861	0.876	0.887	0.897	0.904	0.911	0.916
33	0.812	0.837	0.856	0.871	0.884	0.893	0.901	0.908	0.913
34	0.806	0.831	0.851	0.867	0.880	0.890	0.898	0.905	0.911
35	0.799	0.825	0.846	0.862	0.875	0.886	0.895	0.902	0.908
36	0.792	0.819	0.840	0.857	0.871	0.882	0.891	0.899	0.905
37	0.785	0.813	0.834	0.852	0.866	0.878	0.887	0.895	0.902
38	0.778	0.806	0.828	0.846	0.861	0.873	0.883	0.891	0.898
39	0.771	0.799	0.822	0.840	0.856	0.868	0.879	0.887	0.894
40	0.763	0.792	0.815	0.834	0.850	0.863	0.874	0.883	0.890
41	0.755	0.784	0.808	0.828	0.844	0.857	0.869	0.878	0.886
42	0.746	0.776	0.801	0.821	0.838	0.852	0.863	0.873	0.881

Age Last Birthday of Husband [or a surviving male civil partner][2]	*Less than 8.50%*	*8.50% or between 8.50% and 9.50%*	*9.50% or between 9.50% and 10.50%*	*10.50% or between 10.50% and 11.50%*	*11.50% or between 11.50% and 12.50%*	*12.50% or between 12.50% and 13.50%*	*13.50% or between 13.50% and 14.50%*	*14.50% or between 14.50% and 15.50%*	*15.50% or more*
43	0.737	0.768	0.793	0.814	0.831	0.845	0.857	0.868	0.876
44	0.728	0.759	0.785	0.806	0.824	0.839	0.851	0.862	0.871
45	0.719	0.750	0.776	0.798	0.816	0.832	0.845	0.856	0.866
46	0.709	0.741	0.768	0.790	0.809	0.825	0.838	0.850	0.860
47	0.699	0.731	0.758	0.781	0.801	0.817	0.831	0.843	0.853
48	0.688	0.721	0.749	0.772	0.792	0.809	0.823	0.836	0.847
49	0.678	0.711	0.739	0.763	0.783	0.800	0.815	0.828	0.839
50	0.666	0.700	0.729	0.753	0.774	0.791	0.807	0.820	0.832
51	0.655	0.689	0.718	0.743	0.764	0.782	0.798	0.812	0.824
52	0.643	0.678	0.707	0.732	0.754	0.772	0.789	0.803	0.815
53	0.631	0.666	0.695	0.721	0.743	0.762	0.779	0.794	0.807
54	0.619	0.654	0.684	0.710	0.732	0.752	0.769	0.784	0.797
55	0.606	0.641	0.671	0.698	0.721	0.741	0.758	0.774	0.787
56	0.594	0.628	0.659	0.685	0.709	0.729	0.747	0.763	0.777
57	0.580	0.615	0.646	0.673	0.696	0.717	0.735	0.752	0.766
58	0.567	0.602	0.633	0.660	0.683	0.705	0.723	0.740	0.755
59	0.553	0.588	0.619	0.646	0.670	0.692	0.711	0.728	0.743

Age Last Birthday of Husband [or a surviving male civil partner][2]	*Less than 8.50%*	*8.50% or between 8.50% and 9.50%*	*9.50% or between 9.50% and 10.50%*	*10.50% or between 10.50% and 11.50%*	*11.50% or between 11.50% and 12.50%*	*12.50% or between 12.50% and 13.50%*	*13.50% or between 13.50% and 14.50%*	*14.50% or between 14.50% and 15.50%*	*15.50% or more*
60	0.539	0.574	0.605	0.632	0.657	0.678	0.698	0.715	0.731
61	0.525	0.560	0.590	0.618	0.642	0.664	0.684	0.702	0.718
62	0.510	0.545	0.576	0.603	0.628	0.650	0.670	0.688	0.704
63	0.496	0.530	0.561	0.588	0.613	0.636	0.656	0.674	0.691
64	0.481	0.515	0.546	0.573	0.598	0.621	0.641	0.659	0.676
65	0.466	0.500	0.530	0.558	0.583	0.605	0.626	0.644	0.661
66	0.451	0.485	0.515	0.542	0.567	0.590	0.610	0.629	0.646
67	0.436	0.469	0.499	0.526	0.551	0.574	0.594	0.613	0.631
68	0.421	0.454	0.483	0.510	0.535	0.557	0.578	0.597	0.615
69	0.407	0.438	0.467	0.494	0.518	0.541	0.562	0.581	0.598
70	0.392	0.423	0.452	0.478	0.502	0.524	0.545	0.564	0.582
71	0.377	0.407	0.436	0.462	0.485	0.508	0.528	0.547	0.565
72	0.362	0.392	0.420	0.445	0.469	0.491	0.511	0.530	0.548
73	0.348	0.377	0.404	0.429	0.452	0.474	0.494	0.513	0.531
74	0.333	0.362	0.388	0.413	0.436	0.457	0.477	0.496	0.513
75	0.319	0.347	0.373	0.397	0.419	0.441	0.460	0.479	0.496
76	0.305	0.332	0.357	0.381	0.403	0.424	0.443	0.461	0.479

Age Last Birthday of Husband [or a surviving male civil partner][2]	*Less than 8.50%*	*8.50% or between 8.50% and 9.50%*	*9.50% or between 9.50% and 10.50%*	*10.50% or between 10.50% and 11.50%*	*11.50% or between 11.50% and 12.50%*	*12.50% or between 12.50% and 13.50%*	*13.50% or between 13.50% and 14.50%*	*14.50% or between 14.50% and 15.50%*	*15.50% or more*
77	0.292	0.318	0.342	0.365	0.387	0.407	0.426	0.444	0.461
78	0.278	0.304	0.328	0.350	0.371	0.391	0.410	0.427	0.444
79	0.265	0.290	0.313	0.335	0.355	0.375	0.393	0.410	0.427
80	0.253	0.277	0.299	0.320	0.340	0.359	0.377	0.394	0.410
81	0.241	0.264	0.285	0.306	0.325	0.343	0.361	0.377	0.393
82	0.229	0.251	0.272	0.292	0.310	0.328	0.345	0.361	0.377
83	0.218	0.239	0.259	0.278	0.296	0.313	0.330	0.346	0.361
84	0.207	0.227	0.246	0.265	0.282	0.299	0.315	0.331	0.345
85	0.196	0.216	0.234	0.252	0.269	0.285	0.301	0.316	0.330
86	0.186	0.205	0.223	0.240	0.256	0.272	0.287	0.302	0.315
87	0.177	0.195	0.212	0.228	0.244	0.259	0.274	0.288	0.301
88	0.168	0.185	0.201	0.217	0.232	0.247	0.261	0.275	0.288
89	0.159	0.176	0.191	0.207	0.221	0.235	0.249	0.262	0.275
90	0.151	0.167	0.182	0.197	0.211	0.224	0.237	0.250	0.262
91	0.144	0.159	0.173	0.187	0.201	0.214	0.227	0.239	0.251
92	0.137	0.151	0.165	0.179	0.192	0.205	0.217	0.229	0.240
93	0.130	0.144	0.158	0.171	0.183	0.196	0.208	0.219	0.230

Age Last Birthday of Husband [or a surviving male civil partner][2]	*Less than 8.50%*	*8.50% or between 8.50% and 9.50%*	*9.50% or between 9.50% and 10.50%*	*10.50% or between 10.50% and 11.50%*	*11.50% or between 11.50% and 12.50%*	*12.50% or between 12.50% and 13.50%*	*13.50% or between 13.50% and 14.50%*	*14.50% or between 14.50% and 15.50%*	*15.50% or more*
94	0.124	0.138	0.151	0.163	0.175	0.187	0.199	0.210	0.221
95	0.119	0.132	0.144	0.156	0.168	0.179	0.190	0.201	0.212
96	0.113	0.126	0.138	0.149	0.161	0.172	0.182	0.193	0.203
97	0.108	0.120	0.132	0.143	0.154	0.164	0.175	0.185	0.195
98	0.103	0.115	0.126	0.137	0.147	0.157	0.167	0.177	0.187
99	0.098	0.109	0.119	0.130	0.140	0.150	0.159	0.169	0.178
100 and over	0.093	0.103	0.112	0.123	0.133	0.143	0.151	0.161	0.169

1 Words in square brackets in main heading inserted with effect from 5 December 2005 by Civil Partnership Act 2004, s 259 and Civil Partnership Act 2004 (Amendments to Subordinate Legislation) Order 2005, SI 2005/2114, arts 1, 2(6), Sch 6, para1(1), (3)(a).

2 Words in square brackets in first column heading inserted with effect from 5 December 2005 by Civil Partnership Act 2004, s 259 and Civil Partnership Act 2004 (Amendments to Subordinate Legislation) Order 2005, SI 2005/2114, arts 1, 2(6), Sch 6, para1(1), (3)(b).

[244.129C]

Table 2

Multiplier to be applied to the part or the residuary estate in respect of which the election is exercised to obtain the capital value of the life interest of a surviving wife [or a surviving female civil partner][1], when the average gross redemption yield on medium coupon fifteen-year Government Stocks is at the rate shown.

Age Last Birthday of Wife [or a surviving female civil partner][2]	*Less than 8.50%*	*8.50% or between 8.50% and 9.50%*	*9.50% or between 9.50% and 10.50%*	*10.50% or between 10.50% and 11.50%*	*11.50% or between 11.50% and 12.50%*	*12.50% or between 12.50% and 13.50%*	*13.50% or between 13.50% and 14.50%*	*14.50% or between 14.50% and 15.50%*	*15.50% or more*
16	0.892	0.905	0.915	0.922	0.927	0.930	0.933	0.936	0.937
17	0.889	0.903	0.913	0.920	0.925	0.929	0.933	0.935	0.937
18	0.887	0.901	0.911	0.919	0.924	0.929	0.932	0.934	0.936
19	0.884	0.899	0.910	0.917	0.923	0.928	0.931	0.934	0.936
20	0.882	0.897	0.908	0.916	0.922	0.927	0.930	0.933	0.935
21	0.879	0.895	0.906	0.915	0.921	0.926	0.929	0.932	0.934
22	0.877	0.893	0.904	0.913	0.920	0.925	0.928	0.931	0.934
23	0.874	0.890	0.902	0.911	0.918	0.923	0.927	0.931	0.933
24	0.871	0.888	0.900	0.910	0.917	0.922	0.926	0.930	0.932
25	0.868	0.885	0.898	0.908	0.915	0.921	0.925	0.929	0.932

Age Last Birthday of Wife [or a surviving female civil partner][2]	*Less than 8.50%*	*8.50% or between 8.50% and 9.50%*	*9.50% or between 9.50% and 10.50%*	*10.50% or between 10.50% and 11.50%*	*11.50% or between 11.50% and 12.50%*	*12.50% or between 12.50% and 13.50%*	*13.50% or between 13.50% and 14.50%*	*14.50% or between 14.50% and 15.50%*	*15.50% or more*
26	0.864	0.882	0.896	0.906	0.914	0.920	0.924	0.928	0.931
27	0.861	0.879	0.893	0.904	0.912	0.918	0.923	0.927	0.930
28	0.857	0.876	0.891	0.901	0.910	0.916	0.921	0.925	0.929
29	0.853	0.873	0.888	0.899	0.908	0.915	0.920	0.924	0.928
30	0.849	0.869	0.885	0.896	0.906	0.913	0.918	0.923	0.926
31	0.845	0.866	0.882	0.894	0.903	0.911	0.916	0.921	0.925
32	0.840	0.862	0.878	0.891	0.901	0.908	0.914	0.919	0.923
33	0.836	0.858	0.875	0.888	0.898	0.906	0.912	0.918	0.922
34	0.831	0.853	0.871	0.884	0.895	0.903	0.910	0.916	0.920
35	0.826	0.849	0.867	0.881	0.892	0.901	0.908	0.913	0.918
36	0.820	0.844	0.863	0.877	0.889	0.898	0.905	0.911	0.916
37	0.815	0.839	0.858	0.873	0.885	0.895	0.902	0.909	0.914
38	0.809	0.834	0.853	0.869	0.881	0.891	0.899	0.906	0.911
39	0.803	0.828	0.848	0.864	0.877	0.888	0.896	0.903	0.909
40	0.796	0.822	0.843	0.860	0.873	0.884	0.893	0.900	0.906
41	0.790	0.816	0.838	0.855	0.869	0.880	0.889	0.897	0.903
42	0.783	0.810	0.832	0.850	0.864	0.876	0.885	0.893	0.900

Age Last Birthday of Wife [or a surviving female civil partner][2]	*Less than 8.50%*	*8.50% or between 8.50% and 9.50%*	*9.50% or between 9.50% and 10.50%*	*10.50% or between 10.50% and 11.50%*	*11.50% or between 11.50% and 12.50%*	*12.50% or between 12.50% and 13.50%*	*13.50% or between 13.50% and 14.50%*	*14.50% or between 14.50% and 15.50%*	*15.50% or more*
43	0.775	0.803	0.826	0.844	0.859	0.871	0.881	0.889	0.896
44	0.768	0.796	0.820	0.838	0.854	0.866	0.877	0.885	0.893
45	0.760	0.789	0.813	0.832	0.848	0.861	0.872	0.881	0.889
46	0.752	0.782	0.806	0.826	0.842	0.856	0.867	0.876	0.885
47	0.744	0.774	0.799	0.819	0.836	0.850	0.862	0.872	0.880
48	0.735	0.766	0.791	0.812	0.829	0.844	0.856	0.866	0.875
49	0.726	0.757	0.783	0.804	0.822	0.837	0.850	0.861	0.870
50	0.716	0.748	0.775	0.797	0.815	0.831	0.844	0.855	0.865
51	0.707	0.739	0.766	0.788	0.807	0.823	0.837	0.849	0.859
52	0.697	0.729	0.757	0.780	0.799	0.816	0.830	0.842	0.853
53	0.686	0.719	0.747	0.771	0.791	0.808	0.822	0.835	0.846
54	0.676	0.709	0.737	0.761	0.782	0.799	0.814	0.827	0.839
55	0.664	0.698	0.727	0.751	0.772	0.790	0.806	0.820	0.831
56	0.653	0.687	0.716	0.741	0.763	0.781	0.797	0.811	0.823
57	0.641	0.676	0.705	0.730	0.752	0.771	0.788	0.802	0.815
58	0.629	0.664	0.693	0.719	0.741	0.761	0.778	0.793	0.806
59	0.616	0.651	0.681	0.707	0.730	0.750	0.767	0.783	0.796

Age Last Birthday of Wife [or a surviving female civil partner][2]	*Less than 8.50%*	*8.50% or between 8.50% and 9.50%*	*9.50% or between 9.50% and 10.50%*	*10.50% or between 10.50% and 11.50%*	*11.50% or between 11.50% and 12.50%*	*12.50% or between 12.50% and 13.50%*	*13.50% or between 13.50% and 14.50%*	*14.50% or between 14.50% and 15.50%*	*15.50% or more*
60	0.603	0.638	0.669	0.695	0.718	0.739	0.757	0.772	0.786
61	0.590	0.625	0.656	0.683	0.706	0.727	0.745	0.761	0.776
62	0.577	0.612	0.643	0.670	0.693	0.715	0.733	0.750	0.764
63	0.563	0.598	0.629	0.656	0.680	0.702	0.721	0.738	0.753
64	0.549	0.584	0.615	0.642	0.667	0.688	0.708	0.725	0.740
65	0.534	0.569	0.600	0.628	0.653	0.674	0.694	0.712	0.728
66	0.520	0.555	0.586	0.613	0.638	0.660	0.680	0.698	0.714
67	0.505	0.540	0.570	0.598	0.623	0.645	0.666	0.684	0.700
68	0.490	0.524	0.555	0.583	0.608	0.630	0.651	0.669	0.686
69	0.475	0.509	0.539	0.567	0.592	0.615	0.635	0.654	0.671
70	0.459	0.493	0.523	0.551	0.576	0.599	0.619	0.638	0.655
71	0.444	0.477	0.507	0.535	0.560	0.582	0.603	0.622	0.640
72	0.428	0.461	0.491	0.518	0.543	0.566	0.586	0.606	0.623
73	0.413	0.445	0.475	0.501	0.526	0.549	0.570	0.589	0.606
74	0.398	0.429	0.458	0.485	0.509	0.532	0.552	0.572	0.589
75	0.382	0.413	0.442	0.468	0.492	0.514	0.535	0.554	0.572
76	0.367	0.397	0.425	0.451	0.475	0.497	0.517	0.536	0.554

Age Last Birthday of Wife [or a surviving female civil partner][2]	*Less than 8.50%*	*8.50% or between 8.50% and 9.50%*	*9.50% or between 9.50% and 10.50%*	*10.50% or between 10.50% and 11.50%*	*11.50% or between 11.50% and 12.50%*	*12.50% or between 12.50% and 13.50%*	*13.50% or between 13.50% and 14.50%*	*14.50% or between 14.50% and 15.50%*	*15.50% or more*
77	0.352	0.381	0.408	0.434	0.457	0.479	0.499	0.518	0.536
78	0.337	0.365	0.392	0.417	0.440	0.461	0.482	0.500	0.518
79	0.322	0.350	0.376	0.400	0.423	0.444	0.464	0.482	0.500
80	0.307	0.334	0.360	0.383	0.406	0.426	0.446	0.464	0.482
81	0.293	0.319	0.344	0.367	0.389	0.409	0.428	0.446	0.463
82	0.279	0.304	0.328	0.351	0.372	0.392	0.410	0.428	0.445
83	0.265	0.290	0.313	0.335	0.355	0.375	0.393	0.410	0.427
84	0.252	0.276	0.298	0.319	0.339	0.358	0.376	0.393	0.409
85	0.239	0.262	0.284	0.304	0.323	0.342	0.359	0.376	0.392
86	0.227	0.249	0.269	0.289	0.308	0.326	0.343	0.359	0.374
87	0.215	0.236	0.256	0.275	0.293	0.310	0.327	0.342	0.357
88	0.204	0.224	0.243	0.261	0.279	0.295	0.311	0.327	0.341
89	0.193	0.212	0.230	0.248	0.265	0.281	0.296	0.311	0.325
90	0.182	0.201	0.218	0.235	0.251	0.267	0.282	0.296	0.310
91	0.173	0.190	0.207	0.223	0.239	0.254	0.268	0.282	0.296
92	0.164	0.180	0.197	0.212	0.227	0.242	0.256	0.269	0.282
93	0.155	0.171	0.187	0.202	0.216	0.230	0.243	0.256	0.269

Age Last Birthday of Wife [or a surviving female civil partner][2]	*Less than 8.50%*	*8.50% or between 8.50% and 9.50%*	*9.50% or between 9.50% and 10.50%*	*10.50% or between 10.50% and 11.50%*	*11.50% or between 11.50% and 12.50%*	*12.50% or between 12.50% and 13.50%*	*13.50% or between 13.50% and 14.50%*	*14.50% or between 14.50% and 15.50%*	*15.50% or more*
94	0.147	0.162	0.177	0.192	0.205	0.219	0.232	0.244	0.256
95	0.139	0.154	0.168	0.182	0.195	0.208	0.221	0.233	0.244
96	0.132	0.146	0.159	0.173	0.185	0.198	0.210	0.222	0.233
97	0.125	0.138	0.151	0.164	0.176	0.188	0.199	0.211	0.222
98	0.118	0.130	0.143	0.155	0.167	0.178	0.189	0.200	0.210
99	0.110	0.122	0.134	0.146	0.157	0.168	0.178	0.189	0.199
100 and over	0.102	0.114	0.125	0.137	0.147	0.158	0.167	0.178	0.188

1 Words in square brackets in main heading inserted with effect from 5 December 2005 by Civil Partnership Act 2004, s 259 and Civil Partnership Act 2004 (Amendments to Subordinate Legislation) Order 2005, SI 2005/2114, arts 1, 2(6), Sch 6, para1(1), (4)(a).

2 Words in square brackets in first column heading inserted with effect from 5 December 2005 by Civil Partnership Act 2004, s 259 and Civil Partnership Act 2004 (Amendments to Subordinate Legislation) Order 2005, SI 2005/2114, arts 1, 2(6), Sch 6, para1(1), (4)(b).

[244.129D]

Table 1

Multiplier to be applied to the part of the residuary estate in respect of which the election is exercised to obtain the capital value of the life interest of a surviving husband or a surviving male civil partner when the gross redemption yield on fifteen-year Government Stocks is at the rate shown

Age last birthday of hus-band or male civil partner	*Less than 2.5%*	*2.5% or between 2.5% and 3.5%*	*3.5% or between 3.5% and 4.5%*	*4.5% or between 4.5% and 5.5%*	*5.5% or between 5.5% and 6.5%*	*6.5% or between 6.5% and 7.5%*	*7.5% or between 7.5% and 8.5%*	*8.5% or between 8.5% and 9.5%*	*9.5% or between 9.5% and 10.5%*	*10.5% or between 10.5% and 11.5%*	*11.5% or more*
16	0.630	0.761	0.836	0.881	0.907	0.922	0.932	0.938	0.942	0.944	0.946
17	0.625	0.756	0.833	0.878	0.905	0.921	0.931	0.937	0.941	0.944	0.945
18	0.620	0.752	0.829	0.875	0.903	0.920	0.930	0.936	0.941	0.943	0.945
19	0.615	0.747	0.825	0.872	0.901	0.918	0.929	0.936	0.940	0.943	0.945
20	0.610	0.743	0.822	0.870	0.899	0.917	0.928	0.935	0.939	0.942	0.945
21	0.604	0.738	0.818	0.867	0.896	0.915	0.927	0.934	0.939	0.942	0.944
22	0.599	0.733	0.814	0.863	0.894	0.913	0.925	0.933	0.938	0.941	0.944
23	0.594	0.728	0.809	0.860	0.891	0.911	0.924	0.932	0.937	0.941	0.943
24	0.588	0.723	0.805	0.857	0.889	0.909	0.922	0.931	0.936	0.940	0.943
25	0.582	0.717	0.801	0.853	0.886	0.907	0.921	0.930	0.936	0.940	0.942
26	0.577	0.712	0.796	0.849	0.883	0.905	0.919	0.928	0.935	0.939	0.942

Age last birthday of husband or male civil partner	*Less than 2.5%*	*2.5% or between 2.5% and 3.5%*	*3.5% or between 3.5% and 4.5%*	*4.5% or between 4.5% and 5.5%*	*5.5% or between 5.5% and 6.5%*	*6.5% or between 6.5% and 7.5%*	*7.5% or between 7.5% and 8.5%*	*8.5% or between 8.5% and 9.5%*	*9.5% or between 9.5% and 10.5%*	*10.5% or between 10.5% and 11.5%*	*11.5% or more*
27	0.571	0.706	0.791	0.846	0.880	0.903	0.917	0.927	0.934	0.938	0.941
28	0.565	0.701	0.786	0.842	0.877	0.900	0.915	0.926	0.932	0.937	0.940
29	0.559	0.695	0.781	0.837	0.874	0.898	0.913	0.924	0.931	0.936	0.940
30	0.553	0.689	0.776	0.833	0.870	0.895	0.911	0.922	0.930	0.935	0.939
31	0.546	0.683	0.771	0.829	0.867	0.892	0.909	0.920	0.928	0.934	0.938
32	0.540	0.676	0.765	0.824	0.863	0.889	0.907	0.918	0.927	0.933	0.937
33	0.533	0.670	0.759	0.819	0.859	0.886	0.904	0.916	0.925	0.931	0.936
34	0.527	0.663	0.753	0.814	0.854	0.882	0.901	0.914	0.923	0.930	0.935
35	0.520	0.657	0.747	0.809	0.850	0.879	0.898	0.912	0.922	0.928	0.933
36	0.514	0.650	0.741	0.803	0.845	0.875	0.895	0.909	0.919	0.927	0.932
37	0.507	0.643	0.734	0.798	0.841	0.871	0.892	0.907	0.917	0.925	0.931
38	0.500	0.636	0.728	0.792	0.836	0.867	0.888	0.904	0.915	0.923	0.929
39	0.493	0.628	0.721	0.785	0.830	0.862	0.885	0.901	0.912	0.921	0.927
40	0.485	0.621	0.714	0.779	0.825	0.858	0.881	0.897	0.910	0.918	0.925
41	0.478	0.613	0.706	0.773	0.819	0.853	0.877	0.894	0.907	0.916	0.923
42	0.471	0.605	0.699	0.766	0.813	0.847	0.872	0.890	0.903	0.913	0.921
43	0.463	0.597	0.691	0.759	0.807	0.842	0.867	0.886	0.900	0.910	0.918
44	0.456	0.589	0.683	0.751	0.800	0.836	0.863	0.882	0.896	0.907	0.916

Age last birthday of husband or male civil partner	*Less than 2.5%*	*2.5% or between 2.5% and 3.5%*	*3.5% or between 3.5% and 4.5%*	*4.5% or between 4.5% and 5.5%*	*5.5% or between 5.5% and 6.5%*	*6.5% or between 6.5% and 7.5%*	*7.5% or between 7.5% and 8.5%*	*8.5% or between 8.5% and 9.5%*	*9.5% or between 9.5% and 10.5%*	*10.5% or between 10.5% and 11.5%*	*11.5% or more*
45	0.448	0.580	0.675	0.744	0.794	0.830	0.857	0.877	0.893	0.904	0.913
46	0.440	0.572	0.666	0.736	0.786	0.824	0.852	0.873	0.888	0.900	0.910
47	0.432	0.563	0.658	0.728	0.779	0.817	0.846	0.868	0.884	0.896	0.906
48	0.424	0.554	0.649	0.719	0.771	0.811	0.840	0.862	0.879	0.892	0.903
49	0.416	0.545	0.640	0.711	0.763	0.803	0.834	0.856	0.874	0.888	0.899
50	0.408	0.536	0.630	0.702	0.755	0.796	0.827	0.850	0.869	0.883	0.895
51	0.400	0.526	0.621	0.692	0.746	0.788	0.820	0.844	0.863	0.878	0.890
52	0.392	0.517	0.611	0.683	0.738	0.780	0.812	0.837	0.857	0.873	0.885
53	0.383	0.507	0.601	0.673	0.728	0.771	0.804	0.830	0.851	0.867	0.880
54	0.375	0.497	0.591	0.663	0.719	0.762	0.796	0.823	0.844	0.861	0.875
55	0.366	0.487	0.580	0.653	0.709	0.753	0.788	0.815	0.837	0.855	0.869
56	0.357	0.477	0.569	0.642	0.698	0.743	0.779	0.807	0.829	0.848	0.863
57	0.349	0.467	0.558	0.631	0.688	0.733	0.769	0.798	0.821	0.840	0.856
58	0.340	0.456	0.547	0.620	0.677	0.723	0.759	0.789	0.813	0.833	0.849
59	0.331	0.445	0.536	0.608	0.665	0.712	0.749	0.779	0.804	0.824	0.841
60	0.322	0.435	0.524	0.596	0.654	0.701	0.738	0.769	0.795	0.816	0.833
61	0.313	0.424	0.512	0.584	0.641	0.689	0.727	0.759	0.785	0.806	0.825
62	0.304	0.413	0.500	0.571	0.629	0.677	0.716	0.748	0.774	0.797	0.815

Age last birthday of husband or male civil partner	*Less than 2.5%*	*2.5% or between 2.5% and 3.5%*	*3.5% or between 3.5% and 4.5%*	*4.5% or between 4.5% and 5.5%*	*5.5% or between 5.5% and 6.5%*	*6.5% or between 6.5% and 7.5%*	*7.5% or between 7.5% and 8.5%*	*8.5% or between 8.5% and 9.5%*	*9.5% or between 9.5% and 10.5%*	*10.5% or between 10.5% and 11.5%*	*11.5% or more*
63	0.295	0.401	0.488	0.558	0.616	0.664	0.704	0.736	0.764	0.786	0.806
64	0.286	0.390	0.475	0.545	0.603	0.651	0.691	0.724	0.752	0.776	0.796
65	0.277	0.379	0.462	0.532	0.590	0.638	0.678	0.712	0.740	0.765	0.785
66	0.268	0.367	0.450	0.519	0.576	0.624	0.665	0.699	0.728	0.753	0.774
67	0.259	0.356	0.437	0.505	0.562	0.610	0.651	0.685	0.715	0.740	0.762
68	0.250	0.344	0.424	0.491	0.547	0.596	0.637	0.671	0.701	0.727	0.750
69	0.240	0.333	0.410	0.476	0.533	0.581	0.622	0.657	0.687	0.714	0.737
70	0.231	0.321	0.397	0.462	0.517	0.565	0.606	0.642	0.673	0.699	0.723
71	0.222	0.309	0.383	0.447	0.502	0.549	0.590	0.626	0.657	0.684	0.708
72	0.213	0.297	0.369	0.432	0.486	0.533	0.574	0.610	0.641	0.669	0.693
73	0.204	0.285	0.355	0.417	0.470	0.516	0.557	0.593	0.624	0.652	0.677
74	0.195	0.273	0.341	0.401	0.453	0.499	0.540	0.575	0.607	0.635	0.660
75	0.186	0.261	0.327	0.385	0.436	0.482	0.522	0.557	0.589	0.617	0.642
76	0.177	0.249	0.313	0.370	0.419	0.464	0.503	0.539	0.570	0.598	0.624
77	0.168	0.237	0.299	0.354	0.402	0.446	0.485	0.519	0.551	0.579	0.604
78	0.159	0.225	0.284	0.337	0.385	0.427	0.465	0.500	0.531	0.559	0.585
79	0.150	0.214	0.270	0.321	0.367	0.409	0.446	0.480	0.510	0.538	0.564
80	0.142	0.202	0.256	0.305	0.349	0.390	0.426	0.459	0.490	0.517	0.543

Age last birthday of husband or male civil partner	*Less than 2.5%*	*2.5% or between 2.5% and 3.5%*	*3.5% or between 3.5% and 4.5%*	*4.5% or between 4.5% and 5.5%*	*5.5% or between 5.5% and 6.5%*	*6.5% or between 6.5% and 7.5%*	*7.5% or between 7.5% and 8.5%*	*8.5% or between 8.5% and 9.5%*	*9.5% or between 9.5% and 10.5%*	*10.5% or between 10.5% and 11.5%*	*11.5% or more*
81	0.133	0.191	0.242	0.289	0.332	0.371	0.406	0.439	0.468	0.496	0.521
82	0.125	0.179	0.228	0.273	0.314	0.352	0.386	0.418	0.447	0.473	0.498
83	0.117	0.168	0.215	0.257	0.297	0.333	0.366	0.397	0.425	0.451	0.475
84	0.109	0.157	0.201	0.242	0.279	0.314	0.346	0.376	0.403	0.429	0.453
85	0.102	0.147	0.188	0.227	0.262	0.296	0.326	0.355	0.381	0.406	0.429
86	0.095	0.137	0.176	0.212	0.246	0.278	0.307	0.334	0.360	0.384	0.406
87	0.088	0.127	0.164	0.198	0.230	0.260	0.288	0.314	0.339	0.362	0.384
88	0.081	0.118	0.152	0.185	0.215	0.243	0.270	0.295	0.318	0.340	0.362
89	0.075	0.110	0.142	0.172	0.200	0.227	0.252	0.276	0.299	0.320	0.340
90	0.070	0.102	0.132	0.160	0.187	0.212	0.236	0.259	0.280	0.301	0.320
91	0.065	0.094	0.122	0.149	0.174	0.198	0.221	0.242	0.263	0.282	0.301
92	0.060	0.088	0.114	0.139	0.162	0.185	0.207	0.227	0.247	0.265	0.283
93	0.056	0.082	0.106	0.130	0.152	0.173	0.194	0.213	0.231	0.249	0.266
94	0.052	0.076	0.099	0.121	0.142	0.162	0.181	0.200	0.217	0.234	0.251
95	0.048	0.071	0.092	0.113	0.133	0.152	0.170	0.188	0.204	0.221	0.236
96	0.045	0.066	0.086	0.106	0.124	0.143	0.160	0.176	0.192	0.208	0.223
97	0.042	0.062	0.081	0.099	0.117	0.134	0.150	0.166	0.181	0.196	0.210
98	0.039	0.058	0.075	0.093	0.109	0.125	0.141	0.156	0.170	0.184	0.198

Age last birthday of husband or male civil partner	*Less than 2.5%*	*2.5% or between 2.5% and 3.5%*	*3.5% or between 3.5% and 4.5%*	*4.5% or between 4.5% and 5.5%*	*5.5% or between 5.5% and 6.5%*	*6.5% or between 6.5% and 7.5%*	*7.5% or between 7.5% and 8.5%*	*8.5% or between 8.5% and 9.5%*	*9.5% or between 9.5% and 10.5%*	*10.5% or between 10.5% and 11.5%*	*11.5% or more*
99	0.037	0.054	0.071	0.087	0.102	0.118	0.132	0.146	0.160	0.173	0.186
100 and over	0.034	0.050	0.066	0.081	0.096	0.110	0.124	0.137	0.150	0.163	0.175

[244.129E]

Table 2

Multiplier to be applied to the part of the residuary estate in respect of which the election is exercised to obtain the capital value of the life interest of a surviving wife or a surviving female civil partner when the gross redemption yield on fifteen-year Government Stocks is at the rate shown

Age last birthday of wife or female civil partner	*Less than 2.5%*	*2.5% or between 2.5% and 3.5%*	*3.5% or between 3.5% and 4.5%*	*4.5% or between 4.5% and 5.5%*	*5.5% or between 5.5% and 6.5%*	*6.5% or between 6.5% and 7.5%*	*7.5% or between 7.5% and 8.5%*	*8.5% or between 8.5% and 9.5%*	*9.5% or between 9.5% and 10.5%*	*10.5% or between 10.5% and 11.5%*	*11.5% or more*
16	0.650	0.779	0.851	0.892	0.916	0.929	0.937	0.942	0.944	0.946	0.947
17	0.645	0.775	0.848	0.890	0.914	0.928	0.936	0.941	0.944	0.946	0.947
18	0.640	0.771	0.845	0.888	0.912	0.927	0.936	0.941	0.944	0.946	0.947
19	0.636	0.767	0.842	0.885	0.911	0.926	0.935	0.940	0.944	0.946	0.947
20	0.631	0.762	0.838	0.883	0.909	0.925	0.934	0.940	0.943	0.945	0.947
21	0.626	0.758	0.835	0.880	0.907	0.923	0.933	0.939	0.943	0.945	0.947
22	0.621	0.753	0.831	0.878	0.905	0.922	0.932	0.938	0.942	0.945	0.946
23	0.615	0.749	0.828	0.875	0.903	0.921	0.931	0.938	0.942	0.944	0.946
24	0.610	0.744	0.824	0.872	0.901	0.919	0.930	0.937	0.941	0.944	0.946
25	0.605	0.739	0.820	0.869	0.899	0.917	0.929	0.936	0.941	0.944	0.946

Age last birthday of wife or female civil partner	*Less than 2.5%*	*2.5% or between 2.5% and 3.5%*	*3.5% or between 3.5% and 4.5%*	*4.5% or between 4.5% and 5.5%*	*5.5% or between 5.5% and 6.5%*	*6.5% or between 6.5% and 7.5%*	*7.5% or between 7.5% and 8.5%*	*8.5% or between 8.5% and 9.5%*	*9.5% or between 9.5% and 10.5%*	*10.5% or between 10.5% and 11.5%*	*11.5% or more*
26	0.599	0.734	0.816	0.866	0.897	0.916	0.928	0.935	0.940	0.943	0.945
27	0.594	0.729	0.812	0.863	0.894	0.914	0.926	0.934	0.939	0.943	0.945
28	0.588	0.724	0.807	0.859	0.892	0.912	0.925	0.933	0.939	0.942	0.945
29	0.582	0.719	0.803	0.856	0.889	0.910	0.924	0.932	0.938	0.942	0.944
30	0.577	0.713	0.798	0.852	0.886	0.908	0.922	0.931	0.937	0.941	0.944
31	0.571	0.708	0.794	0.848	0.883	0.906	0.920	0.930	0.936	0.940	0.943
32	0.565	0.702	0.789	0.844	0.880	0.903	0.919	0.929	0.935	0.940	0.943
33	0.559	0.696	0.784	0.840	0.877	0.901	0.917	0.927	0.934	0.939	0.942
34	0.552	0.690	0.778	0.836	0.874	0.898	0.915	0.926	0.933	0.938	0.941
35	0.546	0.684	0.773	0.832	0.870	0.896	0.913	0.924	0.932	0.937	0.941
36	0.540	0.678	0.767	0.827	0.866	0.893	0.910	0.922	0.930	0.936	0.940
37	0.533	0.671	0.762	0.822	0.862	0.890	0.908	0.920	0.929	0.935	0.939
38	0.527	0.664	0.756	0.817	0.858	0.886	0.905	0.918	0.927	0.934	0.938
39	0.520	0.658	0.750	0.812	0.854	0.883	0.902	0.916	0.926	0.932	0.937
40	0.513	0.651	0.743	0.807	0.849	0.879	0.900	0.914	0.924	0.931	0.936
41	0.506	0.644	0.737	0.801	0.845	0.875	0.896	0.911	0.922	0.929	0.935
42	0.499	0.636	0.730	0.795	0.840	0.871	0.893	0.909	0.920	0.927	0.933

Age last birth-day of wife or female civil partner	*Less than 2.5%*	*2.5% or between 2.5% and 3.5%*	*3.5% or between 3.5% and 4.5%*	*4.5% or between 4.5% and 5.5%*	*5.5% or between 5.5% and 6.5%*	*6.5% or between 6.5% and 7.5%*	*7.5% or between 7.5% and 8.5%*	*8.5% or between 8.5% and 9.5%*	*9.5% or between 9.5% and 10.5%*	*10.5% or between 10.5% and 11.5%*	*11.5% or more*
43	0.492	0.629	0.723	0.789	0.835	0.867	0.890	0.906	0.917	0.926	0.932
44	0.485	0.621	0.716	0.783	0.829	0.862	0.886	0.903	0.915	0.924	0.930
45	0.477	0.613	0.708	0.776	0.823	0.858	0.882	0.899	0.912	0.921	0.928
46	0.470	0.605	0.701	0.769	0.817	0.852	0.878	0.896	0.909	0.919	0.926
47	0.462	0.597	0.693	0.762	0.811	0.847	0.873	0.892	0.906	0.916	0.924
48	0.454	0.589	0.685	0.754	0.805	0.841	0.868	0.888	0.902	0.913	0.922
49	0.447	0.580	0.676	0.747	0.798	0.835	0.863	0.883	0.899	0.910	0.919
50	0.439	0.572	0.668	0.739	0.791	0.829	0.858	0.879	0.895	0.907	0.916
51	0.431	0.563	0.659	0.730	0.783	0.823	0.852	0.874	0.891	0.903	0.913
52	0.422	0.553	0.650	0.722	0.775	0.816	0.846	0.868	0.886	0.899	0.910
53	0.414	0.544	0.640	0.713	0.767	0.808	0.839	0.863	0.881	0.895	0.906
54	0.406	0.534	0.631	0.703	0.758	0.800	0.832	0.857	0.876	0.890	0.902
55	0.397	0.525	0.620	0.694	0.749	0.792	0.825	0.850	0.870	0.885	0.897
56	0.388	0.515	0.610	0.684	0.740	0.784	0.817	0.843	0.864	0.880	0.893
57	0.379	0.504	0.600	0.673	0.730	0.775	0.809	0.836	0.857	0.874	0.888
58	0.371	0.494	0.589	0.663	0.720	0.765	0.800	0.828	0.850	0.868	0.882
59	0.361	0.483	0.577	0.652	0.709	0.755	0.791	0.820	0.843	0.861	0.876

Age last birth-day of wife or female civil partner	*Less than 2.5%*	*2.5% or between 2.5% and 3.5%*	*3.5% or between 3.5% and 4.5%*	*4.5% or between 4.5% and 5.5%*	*5.5% or between 5.5% and 6.5%*	*6.5% or between 6.5% and 7.5%*	*7.5% or between 7.5% and 8.5%*	*8.5% or between 8.5% and 9.5%*	*9.5% or between 9.5% and 10.5%*	*10.5% or between 10.5% and 11.5%*	*11.5% or more*
60	0.352	0.472	0.566	0.640	0.698	0.745	0.782	0.811	0.835	0.854	0.869
61	0.343	0.461	0.554	0.628	0.687	0.734	0.771	0.802	0.826	0.846	0.862
62	0.334	0.450	0.542	0.616	0.675	0.722	0.761	0.792	0.817	0.837	0.854
63	0.324	0.438	0.529	0.603	0.662	0.710	0.749	0.781	0.807	0.828	0.846
64	0.315	0.427	0.517	0.590	0.649	0.698	0.737	0.770	0.797	0.819	0.837
65	0.305	0.415	0.504	0.577	0.636	0.685	0.725	0.758	0.786	0.808	0.828
66	0.295	0.403	0.490	0.563	0.622	0.671	0.712	0.746	0.774	0.797	0.817
67	0.286	0.391	0.477	0.549	0.608	0.657	0.698	0.732	0.761	0.786	0.806
68	0.276	0.378	0.463	0.534	0.593	0.642	0.684	0.719	0.748	0.773	0.795
69	0.266	0.366	0.449	0.519	0.578	0.627	0.669	0.704	0.734	0.760	0.782
70	0.256	0.353	0.435	0.504	0.562	0.611	0.653	0.689	0.720	0.746	0.769
71	0.246	0.340	0.420	0.488	0.545	0.595	0.637	0.673	0.704	0.731	0.754
72	0.236	0.327	0.405	0.472	0.529	0.578	0.620	0.656	0.688	0.715	0.739
73	0.226	0.314	0.390	0.455	0.512	0.560	0.602	0.639	0.671	0.698	0.723
74	0.216	0.301	0.375	0.439	0.494	0.542	0.584	0.621	0.653	0.681	0.706
75	0.206	0.288	0.359	0.422	0.476	0.524	0.565	0.602	0.634	0.662	0.688
76	0.196	0.275	0.344	0.404	0.457	0.504	0.546	0.582	0.614	0.643	0.669

Age last birth-day of wife or female civil partner	*Less than 2.5%*	*2.5% or between 2.5% and 3.5%*	*3.5% or between 3.5% and 4.5%*	*4.5% or between 4.5% and 5.5%*	*5.5% or between 5.5% and 6.5%*	*6.5% or between 6.5% and 7.5%*	*7.5% or between 7.5% and 8.5%*	*8.5% or between 8.5% and 9.5%*	*9.5% or between 9.5% and 10.5%*	*10.5% or between 10.5% and 11.5%*	*11.5% or more*
77	0.186	0.262	0.328	0.387	0.439	0.485	0.526	0.562	0.594	0.623	0.649
78	0.176	0.248	0.312	0.369	0.420	0.465	0.505	0.541	0.573	0.602	0.628
79	0.166	0.235	0.296	0.351	0.400	0.444	0.484	0.519	0.551	0.580	0.606
80	0.156	0.222	0.281	0.334	0.381	0.424	0.462	0.497	0.529	0.557	0.583
81	0.147	0.209	0.265	0.316	0.361	0.403	0.440	0.474	0.506	0.534	0.560
82	0.138	0.197	0.250	0.298	0.342	0.382	0.418	0.451	0.482	0.510	0.536
83	0.129	0.184	0.234	0.280	0.322	0.361	0.396	0.428	0.458	0.485	0.511
84	0.120	0.172	0.219	0.263	0.303	0.340	0.374	0.405	0.434	0.461	0.486
85	0.111	0.160	0.205	0.246	0.284	0.320	0.352	0.382	0.410	0.436	0.460
86	0.103	0.149	0.191	0.230	0.266	0.299	0.330	0.359	0.386	0.411	0.435
87	0.095	0.138	0.177	0.214	0.248	0.280	0.309	0.337	0.363	0.387	0.410
88	0.088	0.127	0.164	0.198	0.230	0.261	0.289	0.315	0.340	0.363	0.385
89	0.081	0.118	0.152	0.184	0.214	0.242	0.269	0.294	0.318	0.340	0.361
90	0.075	0.109	0.140	0.170	0.199	0.225	0.251	0.274	0.297	0.318	0.338
91	0.069	0.100	0.130	0.158	0.184	0.210	0.233	0.256	0.277	0.297	0.317
92	0.063	0.093	0.120	0.146	0.171	0.195	0.217	0.238	0.259	0.278	0.297
93	0.059	0.086	0.111	0.136	0.159	0.181	0.202	0.222	0.242	0.260	0.278

Age last birth-day of wife or female civil partner	*Less than 2.5%*	*2.5% or between 2.5% and 3.5%*	*3.5% or between 3.5% and 4.5%*	*4.5% or between 4.5% and 5.5%*	*5.5% or between 5.5% and 6.5%*	*6.5% or between 6.5% and 7.5%*	*7.5% or between 7.5% and 8.5%*	*8.5% or between 8.5% and 9.5%*	*9.5% or between 9.5% and 10.5%*	*10.5% or between 10.5% and 11.5%*	*11.5% or more*
94	0.054	0.079	0.103	0.126	0.148	0.169	0.189	0.207	0.226	0.243	0.260
95	0.050	0.073	0.096	0.117	0.137	0.157	0.176	0.194	0.211	0.228	0.244
96	0.046	0.068	0.089	0.109	0.128	0.146	0.164	0.181	0.197	0.213	0.228
97	0.043	0.063	0.083	0.101	0.119	0.137	0.153	0.169	0.185	0.200	0.214
98	0.040	0.059	0.077	0.094	0.111	0.127	0.143	0.158	0.173	0.187	0.201
99	0.037	0.055	0.071	0.088	0.104	0.119	0.134	0.148	0.162	0.175	0.188
100 and over	0.034	0.051	0.066	0.082	0.097	0.111	0.125	0.138	0.152	0.164	0.177

CIVIL PARTNERSHIP ACT 2004

(2004 c)

[18 November 2004]

[244.130]

Note. This Act, which came into force on 5 December 2005, gives legal recognition to same-sex relationships by permitting two persons of the same sex to register their relationship as a civil partnership and by conferring on civil partnership effectively the same status as marriage. The provisions of the Act relating to the formation, dissolution and annulment of civil partnerships are beyond the scope of this work, but the Act modifies the law of relating to wills, intestate succession and family provision. These changes are effected principally by amending existing legislation, notably WA 1837, AEA 1925 and I(PFD)A 1975. These amendments are noted elsewhere. The Act also contains express provisions concerning succession which are set out below.

PART 1
INTRODUCTION

[244.131]

1 Civil partnership (1) A civil partnership is a relationship between two people of the same sex ('civil partners')—

- (a) which is formed when they register as civil partners of each other—
  - (i) in England or Wales (under Part 2),
  - (ii) in Scotland (under Part 3),
  - (iii) in Northern Ireland (under Part 4), or
  - (iv) outside the United Kingdom under an Order in Council made under Chapter 1 of Part 5 (registration at British consulates etc or by armed forces personnel), or
- (b) which they are treated under Chapter 2 of Part 5 as having formed (at the time determined under that Chapter) by virtue of having registered an overseas relationship.

(2) Subsection (1) is subject to the provisions of this Act under or by virtue of which a civil partnership is void.

(3) A civil partnership ends only

- [(a)] on death, dissolution or annulment,
- [(b) in the case of a civil partnership formed as mentioned in subsection (1)(a)(i) or (iv), on the conversion of the civil partnership into a marriage under section 9 of the Marriage (Same Sex Couples) Act 2013.][1]

(4) The references in subsection (3) to dissolution and annulment are to dissolution and annulment having effect under or recognised in accordance with this Act.

(5) [*Not reproduced here.*]

1 Subsection (3) is amended from a date to be appointed by the Marriage (Same Sex Couples) Act 2013, s17(4), 21(3) and Sch 7, Pt 2, paras 33, 34, No date has yet been appointed.

SECTION 2

Succession rights and adoption, legitimation, illegitimacy, change of gender and same sex marriage

[245.1]

Note. This Section may appear at first glance to be a rag-bag of topics, but they are topics which have in common that they are all statutory provisions which can affect the interpretation of words in wills and other dispositive instruments which are descriptive of relationships, such as 'child', 'daughter' or 'wife'.

First, this Section reproduces in chronological order all the statutory provisions which have governed and now govern the property rights of adopted, legitimated, and illegitimate children under dispositions of property and the rules of intestate succession. They also of course govern the rights of such children's parents and other relatives. We have omitted the Adoption of Children Act 1949, the relevant provisions of which were replaced retrospectively from the same commencement date by the Adoption Act 1950, and the provisions of the Children Act 1975 concerning the effects of legitimation and adoption which were replaced, again with retrospective effect from the same commencement date, by the Legitimacy Act 1976 (LA 1976) and the Adoption Act 1976 (AA 1976).

The main effect of these statutes has been to reverse the common law presumptions as to the meaning of words descriptive of family relationships in dispositions of property, such as wills or settlements (for these presumptions see Vol 1, paras **[72.1]** and **[75.1]** ff) and to enlarge the categories of issue who can take under the intestacy rules. With exceptions relating to children born as a result of procedures authorised by the Human Fertilisation and Embryology Act (HFEA) 1990 and HFEA 2008, each change in the law has only applied to dispositions made after the change in the law has taken effect, and so the repealed statutes included here continue to be relevant to dispositions made when they were in force. The exceptions are to be found inHFEA 1990), s 29(3), HFEA 2008 s 48(5), and SI 2010/985, Sch 1 at paras **[245.87]**, **[245.127]**, and **[245.147]** below.

At common law references to children were presumed to be references to legitimate children, i e children born in lawful wedlock, and references to other relationships were likewise confined to persons who were legitimate and who claimed descent or kinship exclusively through persons who were legitimate. Not only were illegitimate persons excluded but also persons who were adopted or legitimated. Statute has made progressive inroads on the austerity of the common law rule. As regards adopted and legitimated children this process culminated in the Children Act 1975 which provided that in relation to instruments made on or after 1 January 1976 (including the wills whenever made of persons dying on or after that date) references to children (or persons related in any other way) were to be deemed in the absence of a contrary intention to include references to adopted and legitimated children (or persons who were adopted or legitimated and claimed descent or kinship through adopted or legitimated persons) and to be deemed to do so whether the adoption or legitimation occurred before or after the date of the instrument or death. The relevant provisions of the Children Act 1975 are not reproduced in this section as they were replaced (with effect from the same commencement date) by the identical provisions of the LA 1976 and the AA 1976.

As regards illegitimate persons the process of development culminated in the comprehensive provisions contained in the Family Law Reform Act 1987 (FLRA 1987) which provides that in relation to instruments made on or after the commencement of the Act (which in the case of wills means wills actually made and not merely confirmed by codicil on or after that time) references to children (or other relatives) are to be deemed to include illegitimate children (or persons claiming kinship through illegitimate persons). This Act (which replaced the more limited provisions of the Family Law Reform Act 1969 (FLRA 1969) was brought into force on 4 April 1988. (For the background to the Act see the Law Commission's Second Report on Illegitimacy, October 1986 (Law Com No 157, Cmnd 9913).)

Mention should also be made of the HFEA 1990 which made special provision in relation to persons born as a result of artificial insemination, in vitro fertilisation or other artificial means and for succession rights to be conferred on such persons. This Act was amended by the Human Fertilisation and Embryology (Deceased Fathers) Act 2003 and further amended by the Human Fertilisation and Embryology Act 2008 which replaces the succession provisions in the earlier legislation in relation to children born as a result of treatment received on or after 6 April 2009.

In relation to older instruments, however, the former rules of construction which have now been superseded by statute may still be relevant. This section therefore reproduces all the relevant statutory provisions.

For an account of the law governing the property rights of adopted, legitimated and illegimate children see Vol 1, paras **[72.1]** ff and **[75.1]** ff.

This section also contains relevant parts of the Gender Recognition Act 2004 (paras **[245.102]** ff below) which was brought into force on 4 April 2005 and the Marriage (Same Sex Couples) Act 2013 (paras **[245.149]** ff below) which has yet to be brought into force. The Gender Recognition Act 2004 makes provision for changes of gender to be legally recognised. The Marriage (Same Sex Couples) Act 2013 legalises same sex marriages and permits the conversion of civil partnerships into marriages. Both Acts can affect succession rights, by affecting the meaning of words of relationship: see Notes at paras **[245.103]** and **[245.149]** below.

LEGITIMACY ACT 1976

(1976 c 31)

[22 July 1976]

[245.43]

Note. This Act currently governs the property rights of legitimated children. In effect, the Act protects the rights of legitimated children by treating them as if they had been born legitimate. The rules of construction reflecting this policy are contained in s 5 (para **[245.48]**) and apply to instruments made on or after 1 January 1976, replacing the corresponding rules introduced by the Children Act 1975 from the same commencement date. The new rules apply to a will made before 1 January 1976 if the testator dies on or after that date and apply whether the legitimation takes place before or after the death. The Act has been amended by AA 1976 and FLRA 1987 and more recently by HFEA 2008 to cater for the legitimation of the children of same-sex couples who subsequently form a civil partnership. The relevant provisions of the Act as so amended are printed below.

[245.45A]

[2A Legitimation by subsequent civil partnership of parents. Subject to the following provisions of this Act, where—

(a) a person ('the child') has a parent ('the female parent') by virtue of section 43 of the Human Fertilisation and Embryology Act 2008 (treatment provided to woman who agrees that second woman to be parent),

(b) at the time of the child's birth, the female parent and the child's mother are not civil partners of each other,

(c) the female parent and the child's mother subsequently enter into a civil partnership, and

(d) the female parent is at the date of the formation of the civil partnership domiciled in England and Wales,

the civil partnership shall render the child, if living, legitimate from the date of the formation of the civil partnership.][1]

1 Section 2A inserted with effect from 6 April 2009 for certain purposes and from 1 September 2009 for remaining purposes by the Human Fertilisation and Embryology Act 2008, s 56, Sch 6, para 16 and the Human Fertilisation and Embryology Act 2008 (Commencement No 1 and Transitional Provisions) Order 2009, SI 2009/479, art 6(1)(e), (f), (2).

[245.46]

3. Legitimation by extraneous law. [(1)][1] Subject to the following provisions of this Act, where the parents of an illegitimate person marry one another and the father of the illegitimate person is not at the time of the marriage domiciled in England and Wales but is domiciled in a country by the law of which the illegitimate person became legitimated by virtue of such subsequent marriage, that person, if living, shall in England and Wales be recognised as having been so legitimated from the date of the marriage notwithstanding that, at the time of his birth, his father was domiciled in a country the law of which did not permit legitimation by subsequent marriage.

[(2) Subject to the following provisions of this Act, where—

(a) a person ('the child') has a parent ('the female parent') by virtue of section 43 of the Human Fertilisation and Embryology Act 2008 (treatment provided to woman who agrees that second woman to be parent),

(b) at the time of the child's birth, the female parent and the child's mother are not civil partners of each other,

(c) the female parent and the child's mother subsequently enter into a civil partnership, and

(d) the female parent is not at the time of the formation of the civil partnership domiciled in England and Wales but is domiciled in a country by the law of which the child became legitimated by virtue of the civil partnership,

the child, if living, shall in England and Wales be recognised as having been so legitimated from the date of the formation of the civil partnership notwithstanding that, at the time of the child's birth, the female parent was domiciled in a country the law of which did not permit legitimation by subsequent civil partnership.][1]

1 The existing section was renumbered sub-s (1) and sub-s (2) was added with effect from 6 April 2009 for certain purposes and from 1 September 2009 for remaining purposes by the Human Fertilisation and Embryology Act 2008, s 56, Sch 6, para 17 and the Human Fertilisation and Embryology Act 2008 (Commencement No 1 and Transitional Provisions) Order 2009, SI 2009/479, art 6(1)(e), (f), (2).

[245.51]

10. Interpretation.— (1) In this Act, except where the context otherwise requires—

'disposition' includes the conferring of a power of appointment and any other disposition of an interest in or right over property;

'existing', in relation to an instrument, means one made before 1st January 1976;

'legitimated person' means a person legitimated or recognised as legitimated—

(a) under section 2[, 2A][1] or 3 above;

(b) under section 1 or 8 of the Legitimacy Act 1926; or

(c) except in section 8, by legitimation (whether or not by virtue of the subsequent marriage of his parents) recognised by the law of England and Wales and effected under the law of any other country;

and cognate expressions shall be construed accordingly;

'power of appointment' includes any discretionary power to transfer a beneficial interest in property without the furnishing of valuable consideration;

'void marriage' means a marriage, not being voidable only, in respect of which the High Court has or had jurisdiction to grant a decree of nullity, or would have or would have had such jurisdiction if the parties were domiciled in England and Wales.

(2) For the purposes of this Act 'legitimated person' includes, where the context admits, a person legitimated, or recognised as legitimated, before the passing of the Children Act 1975.

(3) For the purpose of this Act, except where the context otherwise requires—

(a) the death of the testator is the date at which a will or codicil is to be regarded as made;

(b) an oral disposition of property shall be deemed to be contained in an instrument made when the disposition was made.

(4) It is hereby declared that references in this Act to dispositions of property include references to a disposition by the creation of an entailed interest.

(5) Except in so far as the context otherwise requires, any reference in this Act to an enactment shall be construed as a reference to that enactment as amended by or under any other enactment, including this Act.

1 Reference to the new s 2A in para (a) of the definition of 'legitimated person' in sub-s (1) was inserted with effect from 6 April 2009 for certain purposes and from 1 September 2009 for remaining purposes by the Human Fertilisation and Embryology Act 2008, s 56, Sch 6, para 17 and the Human Fertilisation and Embryology Act 2008 (Commencement No 1 and Transitional Provisions) Order 2009, SI 2009/479, art 6(1)(e), (f), (2).

FAMILY LAW REFORM ACT 1987

(1987 c 42)

[15 May 1987]

[245.69]

Note. This Act implements a number of Law Commission recommendations for the removal of the legal disadvantages attaching to illegitimacy. The general principle established by s 1 is embodied in the rule of construction set out in sub-s (1) thereof that both in the 1987 Act itself and in all enactments passed and instruments made after the coming into force of the section, references to any relationship between two persons shall, in the absence of a contrary intention, be construed without regard to whether or not the parents of either of them have or had been married to each other at any time. Subsections (2) and (3) exclude the primary rule of construction in relation to any person who is treated as legitimate by statute or who is legitimated or adopted or is otherwise treated in law as legitimate. This qualification of the primary rule of construction preserves the rights of these categories of person, who are otherwise catered for under the general law or under existing legislation (i e the LA 1976 and the AA 1976). Section 1 was brought into force on 4 April 1988 by the Family Law Reform Act 1987 (Commencement No 1) Order 1988 (SI 1988/425).

Part II of the 1987 Act amended, inter alia, the Guardianship of Minors Act 1971, ss 3 and 4; as from 1 April 1989 (SI 1989/382). These provisions were themselves replaced by the ChA 1989, ss 5 and 6, as from 14 October 1991 (ss 5(1) to (10), (13) and 6) and 1 February 1992 (s 5(11), (12)) (SI 1991/828, as amended by SI 1991/1990), which are the provisions currently in force (see paras **[244.116]** ff above).

Part III of the 1987 Act is concerned with property rights. Section 18 (which replaced the more limited provisions of the Family Law Reform Act 1969, s 14) expressly extends the general principle established by s 1 to the rules of intestate succession as they apply to the estates of persons dying after the coming into force of that section. Section 18(2) provides that for the purposes of the intestacy rules an illegitimate person (not being a person treated as legitimate or a legitimated or adopted person) is to be presumed not to have been survived by his father or any person related to him only through his father, unless the contrary is shown. (Compare the more limited presumption contained in s 14(4) of the 1969 Act: para **[245.38]** above). Section 19 (which replaced s 15 of the 1969 Act: para **[245.39]** above) makes more detailed provision for the application of the general principle to inter vivos dispositions and wills and codicils made on or after the date on which that section comes into force. It should be noted that s 19(7) (like s 15(8) of the 1969 Act) provides that a will or codicil made before that date is not to be treated as made on or after that date by reason only that it is confirmed by a codicil made on or after that date. However, the 1987 Act differs from the 1969 Act in the following respects:—

(i) Unlike s 15 of the 1969 Act, it applies to words creating an entailed interest unless a contrary intention appears (see s 19(2) of the 1987 Act, and compare s 15(2) of the 1969 Act). However, like s 15 of the 1969 Act, it does not apply to property limited to devolve with a dignity or title of honour (s 19(4) of the 1987 Act, s 15(5) of the 1969 Act).

(ii) Section 15(1) of the 1969 Act would not have applied if the only illegitimacy causing difficulty was that of the person from whom the relationship had to be traced, e g 'the uncles of R', where R, but not his father, mother or uncles, was illegitimate. The 1987 Act (see in particular s 1(1)) applies to such a case. However, in this type of case the common law presumption that words of relationship were confined to legitimate relations would usually have been displaced because the gift could only have any meaning if the presumption were to be displaced.

(iii) Section 15 of the 1969 Act only applied to references to a relationship where it had the effect of benefiting or rendering capable of benefit someone who was either himself illegitimate or claimed to be related through a person who was illegitimate (s 15(2)); there is no such restriction in the 1987 Act. Thus the descendants of a named monarch for the purposes of a royal lives perpetuity period, in a post-3 April 1988 disposition, will include illegitimate descendants if no contrary intention is shown. To avoid the risk of uncertainty in such a perpetuity period the 1987 Act should be excluded in relation to it. Another example to which the 1987 Act applies but s 15 of the 1969 Act would not have so applied is 'issue' in the precondition of a conditional gift such as 'If X shall predecease me leaving issue', where the gift does not confer any benefit on the issue of X (see e g Form B19.11 at para **[219.24]**).

(iv) Unlike s 15 of the 1969 Act, the general principle embodied in s 1 of the 1987 Act applies in relation to the construction of statutes and statutory instruments passed or made after the coming into force of the section. (See also the corresponding provision added to the Interpretion Act 1978, Sch 1.) Previously specific provision was often made in statutes to cater for illegitimate children. This will no longer be necessary.

Section 20 repeals (without replacing) s 17 of the 1969 Act (para **[245.41]** above) which enabled personal representatives and trustees to distribute property without having ascertained whether or not illegitimate persons were entitled to the property or a share of it under ss 14, 15 or 16 of the 1969 Act (paras **[245.38]–[245.40]** above). It should be noted the repeal takes effect in relation to all distributions made after the date on which s 20 of the 1987 Act comes into force, including distributions out of the estates of persons dying before that date and of trust property settled before that date. In all such cases personal representatives and trustees will need to protect themselves by giving notice by advertisement pursuant to the Trustee Act 1925 (TA 1925), s 27 (para **[246.25]** below); see *Re Aldhous* [1955] 2 All ER 80, [1955] 1 WLR 459. The provisions of Pt III of the 1987 Act were bought into force on 4 April 1988 at the same time as s 1 (SI 1988/425).

The 1987 Act also effects certain minor and consequential amendments to other statutory provisions, in particular the TA 1925, s 33 and the AEA 1925, s 50: see paras **[246.31]** below and **[244.67]** above.

The 1987 Act has been amended by the ACA 2002 and more recently by the HFEA 2008 so as to cater for the position of a child born as a result of in vitro fertilisation or other procedure regulated by the 1990 Act where the mother agrees that another woman who is not her civil partner shall be treated as the other parent. The relevant provisions of the 1987 Act as amended are printed below.

PART I
GENERAL PRINCIPLE

[245.70]
1. General principle.— (1) In this Act and enactments passed and instruments made after the coming into force of this section, references (however expressed) to any relationship between two persons shall, unless the contrary intention appears, be construed without regard to whether or not the father and mother of either of them, or the father and mother of any person through whom the relationship is deduced, have or had been married to each other at any time.

(2) In this Act and enactments passed after the coming into force of this section, unless the contrary intention appears—

(a) references to a person whose father and mother were married to each other at the time of his birth include; and

(b) references to a person whose father and mother were not married to each other at the time of his birth do not include,

references to any person to whom subsection (3) below applies, and cognate references shall be construed accordingly.

(3) This subsection applies to any person who—

(a) is treated as legitimate by virtue of section 1 of the Legitimacy Act 1976;

(b) is a legitimated person within the meaning of section 10 of that Act;

[(ba) has a parent by virtue of section 42 of the Human Fertilisation and Embryology Act 2008 (which relates to treatment provided to a woman who is at the time of treatment a party to a civil partnership or, in certain circumstances, a void civil partnership);

(bb) has a parent by virtue of section 43 of that Act (which relates to treatment provided to woman who agrees that second woman to be parent) who—

(i) is the civil partner of the child's mother at the time of the child's birth, or

(ii) was the civil partner of the child's mother at any time during the period beginning with the time mentioned in section 43(b) of that Act and ending with the child's birth;][1]

[(c) is an adopted child within the meaning of the Adoption and Children Act 2002][2]; or

(d) is otherwise treated in law as legitimate.

(4) For the purpose of construing references falling within subsection (2) above, the time of a person's birth shall be taken to include any time during the period beginning with—

(a) the insemination resulting in his birth; or

(b) where there was no such insemination, his conception,

and (in either case) ending with his birth.

[(5) A child whose parents are parties to a void civil partnership shall, subject to subsection (6), be treated as falling within subsection (3)(bb) if at the time when the parties registered as civil partners of each other both or either of the parties reasonably believed that the civil partnership was valid.

(6) Subsection (5) applies only where the woman who is a parent by virtue of section 43 was domiciled in England and Wales at the time of the birth or, if she died before the birth, was so domiciled immediately before her death.

(7) Subsection (5) applies even though the belief that the civil partnership was valid was due to a mistake as to law.

(8) It shall be presumed for the purposes of subsection (5), unless the contrary is shown, that one of the parties to a void civil partnership reasonably believed at the time of the formation of the civil partnership that the civil partnership was valid.][3]

1 Paragraphs (ba) and (bb) of sub-s (3) were inserted with effect from 6 April 2009 by the Human Fertilisation and Embryology Act 2008, s 56, Sch 6, para 24(1), (2) and the Human Fertilisation and Embryology Act 2008 (Commencement No 1 and Transitional Provisions) Order 2009, SI 2009/479, art 6(1)(d), (f).

2 Paragraph (c) of sub-s (3) substituted with effect from 30 December 2005: ACA 2002, s 139(1), Sch 3, paras 50 and 51 and Adoption and Children Act 2002 (Commencement No 9) Order 2005, SI 2005/2213, art 2(o).

3 Subsections (5) to (8) were inserted with effect from 6 April 2009 by the Human Fertilisation and Embryology Act 2008, s 56, Sch 6, para 24(1), (3) and the Human Fertilisation and Embryology Act 2008 (Commencement No 1 and Transitional Provisions) Order 2009, SI 2009/479, art 6(1)(d), (f).

PART III
PROPERTY RIGHTS

[245.71]

18. Succession on intestacy.— (1) In Part IV of the Administration of Estates Act 1925 (which deals with the distribution of the estate of an intestate), references (however expressed) to any relationship between two persons shall be construed in accordance with section 1 above.

(2) For the purposes of subsection (1) above and that Part of that Act, a person whose father and mother were not married to each other at the time of his birth shall be presumed not to have been survived by his father, or by any person related to him only through his father, unless the contrary is shown.

[(2A) In the case of a person who has a parent by virtue of section 43 of the Human Fertilisation and Embryology Act 2008 (treatment provided to woman who agrees that second woman to be parent), the second and third references in subsection (2) to the person's father are to be read as references to the woman who is a parent of the person by virtue of that section.][1]

(3) In [section 50(1) of the Administration of Estates Act 1925][2] (which relates to the construction of documents), the reference to Part IV of that Act, or to the foregoing provisions of that Part, shall in relation to an instrument inter vivos made, or a will or codicil coming into operation, after the coming into force of this section (but not in relation to instruments inter vivos made or wills or codicils coming into operation earlier) be construed as including references to this section.

(4) This section does not affect any rights under the intestacy of a person dying before the coming into force of this section.

1 Subsection (2A) inserted with effect from 6 April 2009 by the Human Fertilisation and Embryology Act 2008, s 56, Sch 6, para 25(1), (2) and the Human Fertilisation and Embryology Act 2008 (Commencement No 1 and Transitional Provisions) Order 2009, SI 2009/479, art 6(1)(d), (f).

2 Words in brackets in sub-s (3) substituted for 'section 50(1) of that Act' with effect from 6 April 2009 by the Human Fertilisation and Embryology Act 2008, s 56, Sch 6, para 25(1), (3) and the Human Fertilisation and Embryology Act 2008 (Commencement No 1 and Transitional Provisions) Order 2009, SI 2009/479, art 6(1)(d), (f).

HUMAN FERTILISATION AND EMBRYOLOGY ACT 1990

(1990 c 37)

[1 November 1990]

[245.82]

Note. This Act introduces a new system of control for the treatment of infertility and for research involving human embryos. It also contains provisions identifying the persons who are to be treated in law as the father (if any) and mother of persons coming into existence as a consequence of artificial insemination or other techniques to deal with infertility that are regulated by the Act (ss 27 and 28). These provisions will affect the construction of wills and other dispositions (even if made before the commencement of the relevant provision), and the operation of the intestacy rules (s 29(3)). There is also provision (s 30) for the courts to make orders, inter alia applying the adoption legislation, in cases of surrogate motherhood. Sections 1, 2, 27 to 29 came into force on 1 August 1991 (SI 1991/1400), and the ancillary provisions in ss 47 to 49 came into force on or before that date. Section 30 was brought into force on dates in 1994 (SI 1994/1776). The Act was slightly amended by the Adoption and Children Act 2002 and was further amended with effect from 1 December 2003 by the Human Fertilisation and Embryology (Deceased Fathers) Act 2003. The 1990 and 2003 Acts have recently been superseded by the Human Fertilisation and Embryology Act 2008 and the provisions of s 29 (which relate to status and succession) have been superseded as regards children born as a result of treatment received on or after 6 April 2009 by the provisions of Part 2 of the 2008 Act. Section 30 of the 1990 Act ceased to have effect on 6 April 2010 when the provisions of ss 54 and 55 of the 2008 Act (relating to parental orders) were brought into force. The relevant sections of the 1990 Act are printed as amended below. The Parental Orders (Human Fertilisation and Embryology) Regulations 1994 (SI 1994/2767) made under s 30(9) are set out at paras **[245.91A]** ff below. These were replaced with effect from 6 April 2010 by the Human Fertilisation and Embryology (Parental Orders) Regulations 2010 (SI 2010/985) made under s 55 of the 2008 Act (see paras **[245.142]** ff below).

PRINCIPAL TERMS USED

[245.83]

1. Meaning of 'embryo', 'gamete' and associated expressions.— [(1) In this Act, except where otherwise stated—

(a) embryo means a live human embryo where fertilisation is complete, and
(b) references to an embryo include an egg in the process of fertilisation,

and, for this purpose, fertilisation is not complete until the appearance of a two cell zygote.][1]
[(1) In this Act (except in section 4A[2] or in the term 'human admixed embryo')—

(a) embryo means a live human embryo and does not include a human admixed embryo (as defined by section 4A(6)), and
(b) references to an embryo include an egg that is in the process of fertilisation or is undergoing any other process capable of resulting in an embryo.][3]

(2) This Act, so far as it governs bringing about the creation of an embryo, applies only to bringing about the creation of an embryo outside the human body; and in this Act—

[(a) references to embryos the creation of which was brought about *in vitro* (in their application to those where fertilisation is complete) are to those where fertilisation began outside the human body whether or not it was completed there, and][4]
[(a) references to embryos the creation of which was brought about in vitro (in their application to those where fertilisation or any other process by which an embryo is created is complete) are to those where fertilisation or any other process by which the embryo was created began outside the human body whether or not it was completed there, and][5]
(b) references to embryos taken from a woman do not include embryos whose creation was brought about *in vitro*.

(3) This Act, so far as it governs the keeping or use of an embryo, applies only to keeping or using an embryo outside the human body.
[(4) References in this Act to gametes, eggs or sperm, except where otherwise stated, are to live human gametes, eggs or sperm but references below in this Act to gametes or eggs do not include eggs in the process of fertilisation.][6]
[(4) In this Act (except in section 4A)—

(a) references to eggs are to live human eggs, including cells of the female germ line at any stage of maturity, but (except in subsection (1)(b)) not including eggs that are in the process of fertilisation or are undergoing any other process capable of resulting in an embryo,
(b) references to sperm are to live human sperm, including cells of the male germ line at any stage of maturity, and
(c) references to gametes are to be read accordingly.][7]

[(5) For the purposes of this Act, sperm is to be treated as partner-donated if the donor of the sperm and the recipient of the sperm declare that they have an intimate physical relationship.][8]

[(6) If it appears to the Secretary of State necessary or desirable to do so in the light of developments in science or medicine, regulations may provide that in this Act (except in section 4A) 'embryo', 'eggs', 'sperm' or 'gametes' includes things specified in the regulations which would not otherwise fall within the definition.
(7) Regulations made by virtue of subsection (6) may not provide for anything containing any nuclear or mitochondrial DNA that is not human to be treated as an embryo or as eggs, sperm or gametes.][9]

1 Subsection (1) is to be replaced by the Human Fertilisation and Embryology Act 2008, s 1(1), (2) with the subsection next following from a date to be appointed. No date has yet been appointed.
2 Section 4A, which is to be inserted in the 1990 Act by s 4 of the 2008 Act from a date which has not yet been appointed, contains certain prohibitions on the use of genetic material not of human origin.
3 See note 1 above.
4 Paragraph (a) of sub-s (2) is to be replaced by the Human Fertilisation and Embryology Act 2008, s 1(1), (3) with the paragraph next following from a date to be appointed. No date has yet been appointed.
5 See note 4 above.
6 Subsection (4) is to be replaced by the Human Fertilisation and Embryology Act 2008, s 1(1), (4) with the subsection next following from a date to be appointed. No date has yet been appointed.
7 See note 6 above.
8 Subsection (5) is to be inserted with effect from 5 July 2007 by regs 1(2), 3 and 4 of the Human Fertilisation and Embryology (Quality and Safety) Regulations 2007, SI 2007/1522, which were made under powers conferred by the European Communities Act 1972, s 2(2) to give effect to Directive 2004/23/EC of the European Parliament and of the Council of 31 March 2004 and Commission Directives 2006/17/EC and 2006/86/EC.
9 Subsections (6) and (7) are to be replaced by the Human Fertilisation and Embryology Act 2008, s 1(1), (5) from a date to be appointed. No date has yet been appointed. The term 'nuclear DNA' is defined by s 2 of the Act and the term 'mitochondrial DNA' is defined by s 35A of the Human Fertilisation and Embryology Act 1990 as inserted by s 26 of the 2008 Act.

STATUS

[245.85]
27. Meaning of 'mother'[1].— (1) The woman who is carrying or has carried a child as a result of the placing in her of an embryo or of sperm and eggs, and no other woman, is to be treated as the mother of the child.
(2) Subsection (1) above does not apply to any child to the extent that the child is treated by virtue of adoption as not being the [woman's child][2].
(3) Subsection (1) above applies whether the woman was in the United Kingdom or elsewhere at the time of the placing in her of the embryo or the sperm and eggs.

1 This section has been superseded in so far as it relates to children carried by women as a result of the placing in them of embryos or of sperm and eggs on or after 6 April 2009, the date on which ss 33–38 of HFEA 2008 came into force: see s 57(2) and Human Fertilisation and Embryology Act 2008 (Commencement No 1 and Transitional Provisions) Order 2009, SI 2009/479, art 6(1)(b). But the section continues to apply to children carried by women as a result of these procedures prior to that date.
2 Words substituted in sub-s (2) with effect from 30 December 2005: ACA 2002, s 139(1), Sch 3, paras 76 and 77 and Adoption and Children Act 2002 (Commencement No 9) Order 2005, SI 2005/2213, art 2(o).

[245.86]
28. Meaning of 'father'[1].— (1) [Subject to subsections (5A) to (5I) below,][2] This section applies in the case of a child who is being or has been carried by a woman as the result of the placing in her of an embryo or of sperm and eggs or her artificial insemination.
(2) If—

(a) at the time of the placing in her of the embryo or the sperm and eggs or of her insemination, the woman was a party to a marriage, and
(b) the creation of the embryo carried by her was not brought about with the sperm of the other party to the marriage,

then, subject to subsection (5) below, the other party to the marriage shall be treated as the father of the child unless it is shown that he did not consent to the placing in her of the embryo or the sperm and eggs or to her insemination (as the case may be).
(3) If no man is treated, by virtue of subsection (2) above, as the father of the child but—

(a) the embryo or the sperm and eggs were placed in the woman, or she was artificially inseminated, in the course of treatment services provided for her and a man together by a person to whom a licence applies, and
(b) the creation of the embryo carried by her was not brought about with the sperm of that man,

then, subject to subsection (5) below, that man shall be treated as the father of the child.
(4) Where a person is treated as the father of the child by virtue of subsection (2) or (3) above, no other person is to be treated as the father of the child.
(5) Subsections (2) and (3) above do not apply—

(a) in relation to England and Wales and Northern Ireland, to any child who, by virtue of the rules of common law, is treated as the legitimate child of the parties to a marriage,
(b) (*applies to Scotland only*), or
(c) to any child to the extent that the child is treated by virtue of adoption as not being the child of any person other than the adopter or adopters [man's child][3].

[(5A) If—

(a) a child has been carried by a woman as the result of the placing in her of an embryo or of sperm and eggs or her artificial insemination,
(b) the creation of the embryo carried by her was brought about by using the sperm of a man after his death, or the creation of the embryo was brought about using the sperm of a man before his death but the embryo was placed in the woman after his death,
(c) the woman was a party to a marriage with the man immediately before his death,

(d) the man consented in writing (and did not withdraw the consent)—
(i) to the use of his sperm after his death which brought about the creation of the embryo carried by the woman or (as the case may be) to the placing in the woman after his death of the embryo which was brought about using his sperm before his death, and
(ii) to being treated for the purpose mentioned in subsection (5I) below as the father of any resulting child,
(e) the woman has elected in writing not later than the end of the period of 42 days from the day on which the child was born for the man to be treated for the purpose mentioned in subsection (5I) below as the father of the child, and
(f) no-one else is to be treated as the father of the child by virtue of subsection (2) or (3) above or by virtue of adoption or the child being treated as mentioned in paragraph (a) or (b) of subsection (5) above,

then the man shall be treated for the purpose mentioned in subsection (5I) below as the father of the child.

(5B) If—

(a) a child has been carried by a woman as the result of the placing in her of an embryo or of sperm and eggs or her artificial insemination,
(b) the creation of the embryo carried by her was brought about by using the sperm of a man after his death, or the creation of the embryo was brought about using the sperm of a man before his death but the embryo was placed in the woman after his death,
(c) the woman was not a party to a marriage with the man immediately before his death but treatment services were being provided for the woman and the man together before his death either by a person to whom a licence applies or outside the United Kingdom,
(d) the man consented in writing (and did not withdraw the consent)—
(i) to the use of his sperm after his death which brought about the creation of the embryo carried by the woman or (as the case may be) to the placing in the woman after his death of the embryo which was brought about using his sperm before his death, and
(ii) to being treated for the purpose mentioned in subsection (5I) below as the father of any resulting child,
(e) the woman has elected in writing not later than the end of the period of 42 days from the day on which the child was born for the man to be treated for the purpose mentioned in subsection (5I) below as the father of the child, and
(f) no-one else is to be treated as the father of the child by virtue of subsection (2) or (3) above or by virtue of adoption or the child being treated as mentioned in paragraph (a) or (b) of subsection (5) above,

then the man shall be treated for the purpose mentioned in subsection (5I) below as the father of the child.

(5C) If—

(a) a child has been carried by a woman as the result of the placing in her of an embryo,
(b) the embryo was created at a time when the woman was a party to a marriage,
(c) the creation of the embryo was not brought about with the sperm of the other party to the marriage,
(d) the other party to the marriage died before the placing of the embryo in the woman,
(e) the other party to the marriage consented in writing (and did not withdraw the consent)—
  (i) to the placing of the embryo in the woman after his death, and
  (ii) to being treated for the purpose mentioned in subsection (5I) below as the father of any resulting child,
(f) the woman has elected in writing not later than the end of the period of 42 days from the day on which the child was born for the other party to the marriage to be treated for the purpose mentioned in subsection (5I) below as the father of the child, and
(g) no-one else is to be treated as the father of the child by virtue of subsection (2) or (3) above or by virtue of adoption or the child being treated as mentioned in paragraph (a) or (b) of subsection (5) above,

then the other party to the marriage shall be treated for the purpose mentioned in subsection (5I) below as the father of the child.

(5D) If—

(a) a child has been carried by a woman as the result of the placing in her of an embryo,
(b) the embryo was not created at a time when the woman was a party to a marriage but was created in the course of treatment services provided for the woman and a man together either by a person to whom a licence applies or outside the United Kingdom,
(c) the creation of the embryo was not brought about with the sperm of that man,
(d) the man died before the placing of the embryo in the woman,
(e) the man consented in writing (and did not withdraw the consent)—
  (i) to the placing of the embryo in the woman after his death, and
  (ii) to being treated for the purpose mentioned in subsection (5I) below as the father of any resulting child,
(f) the woman has elected in writing not later than the end of the period of 42 days from the day on which the child was born for the man to be treated for the purpose mentioned in subsection (5I) below as the father of the child, and
(g) no-one else is to be treated as the father of the child by virtue of subsection (2) or (3) above or by virtue of adoption or the child being treated as mentioned in paragraph (a) or (b) of subsection (5) above,

then the man shall be treated for the purpose mentioned in subsection (5I) below as the father of the child.
(5E) (*Applies to Scotland only*).
(5F) The requirement under subsection (5A), (5B), (5C) or (5D) above as to the making of an election (which requires an election to be made either on or before the day on which the child was born or within the period of 42 or, as the case may be, 21 days from that day) shall nevertheless be treated as satisfied if the required election is made after the end of that period but with the consent of the Registrar General under subsection (5G) below.
(5G) The Registrar General may at any time consent to the making of an election after the end of the period mentioned in subsection (5F) above if, on an application made to him in accordance with such requirements as he may specify, he is satisfied that there is a compelling reason for giving his consent to the making of such an election.
(5H) In subsections (5F) and (5G) above 'the Registrar General' means the Registrar General for England and Wales, the Registrar General of Births, Deaths and Marriages for Scotland or (as the case may be) the Registrar General for Northern Ireland.
(5I) The purpose referred to in subsections (5A) to (5D) above is the purpose of enabling the man's particulars to be entered as the particulars of the child's father in (as the case may be) a register of livebirths or still-births kept under the Births and Deaths Registration Act 1953 or the Births and Deaths Registration (Northern Ireland) Order 1976 or a register of births or still-births kept under the Registration of Births, Deaths and Marriages (Scotland) Act 1965.][4]
(6) Where—

- (a) the sperm of a man who had given such consent as is required by paragraph 5 of Schedule 3 to this Act was used for a purpose for which such consent was required, or
- (b) the sperm of a man, or any embryo the creation of which was brought about with his sperm, was used after his death,

he is not[, subject to subsections (5A) and (5B) above,][5] to be treated as the father of the child.
(7) The references in subsection (2) above [and subsections (5A) to (5D) above][6] to the parties to a marriage at the time there referred to—

- (a) are to the parties to a marriage subsisting at that time, unless a judicial separation was then in force, but
- (b) include the parties to a void marriage if either or both of them reasonably believed at that time that the marriage was valid; and for the purposes of this subsection it shall be presumed, unless the contrary is shown, that one of them reasonably believed at that time that the marriage was valid.

(8) This section applies whether the woman was in the United Kingdom or elsewhere at the time of the placing in her of the embryo or the sperm and eggs or her artificial insemination.
(9) In subsection (7)(a) above, 'judicial separation' includes a legal separation obtained in a country outside the British Islands and recognised in the United Kingdom.

1 This section has been superseded in so far as it relates to children carried by women as a result of the placing in them of embryos or of sperm and eggs on or after 6 April 2009, the date on which ss 33–38 of HFEA 2008 came into force: see s 57(2) and Human Fertilisation and Embryology Act 2008 (Commencement No 1 and Transitional Provisions) Order 2009, SI 2009/479, art 6(1)(b). But the section continues to apply to children carried by women as a result of these procedures prior to that date.

2 Words in square brackets in sub-s (1) inserted with effect from 1 December 2003 by Human Fertilisation and Embryology (Deceased Fathers) Act 2003, s 2(1), Sch, para 13 and Human Fertilisation and Embryology (Deceased Fathers) Act 2003 (Commencement) Order 2003, SI 2003/3095, art 2.

3 Words substituted in sub-s (5) with effect from 30 December 2005: ACA 2002, s 139(1), Sch 3, paras 76 and 78 and Adoption and Children Act 2002 (Commencement No 9) Order 2005, SI 2005/2213, art 2(o).

4 Subsections (5A)–(5I) inserted with effect from 1 December 2003 by Human Fertilisation and Embryology (Deceased Fathers) Act 2003, s 1(1) and Human Fertilisation and Embryology (Deceased Fathers) Act 2003 (Commencement) Order 2003, SI 2003/3095, art 2.

5 Words in square brackets in sub-s (6) inserted with effect from 1 December 2003 by Human Fertilisation and Embryology (Deceased Fathers) Act 2003, s 2(1), Sch, para 14 and Human Fertilisation and Embryology (Deceased Fathers) Act 2003 (Commencement) Order 2003, SI 2003/3095, art 2.

6 Words in square brackets in sub-s (7) inserted with effect from 1 December 2003 by Human Fertilisation and Embryology (Deceased Fathers) Act 2003, s 2(1), Sch, para 15 and Human Fertilisation and Embryology (Deceased Fathers) Act 2003 (Commencement) Order 2003, SI 2003/3095, art 2.

[245.87]

29. Effect of sections 27 and 28[1].— (1) Where by virtue of section 27 or 28 of this Act a person is to be treated as the mother or father of a child, that person is to be treated in law as the mother or, as the case may be, father of the child for all purposes.

(2) Where by virtue of section 27 or 28 of this Act a person is not to be treated as the mother or father of a child, that person is to be treated in law as not being the mother or, as the case may be, father of the child for any purpose.

(3) Where subsection (1) or (2) above has effect, references to any relationship between two people in any enactment, deed or other instrument or document (whenever passed or made) are to be read accordingly.

[(3A) Subsections (1) to (3) above do not apply in relation to the treatment in law of a deceased man in a case to which section 28(5A), (5B), (5C) or (5D) of this Act applies.

(3B) Where subsection (5A), (5B), (5C) or (5D) of section 28 of this Act applies, the deceased man—

(a) is to be treated in law as the father of the child for the purpose referred to in that subsection, but

(b) is to be treated in law as not being the father of the child for any other purpose.

(3C) Where subsection (3B) above has effect, references to any relationship between two people in any enactment, deed or other instrument or document (whenever passed or made) are to be read accordingly.

(3D) In subsection (3C) above 'enactment' includes an enactment comprised in, or in an instrument made under, an Act of the Scottish Parliament or Northern Ireland legislation.][2]

(4) In relation to England and Wales and Northern Ireland, nothing in the provisions of section 27(1) or 28(2) to (4) [or (5A) to (5I)][3], read with this section, affects—

(a) the succession to any dignity or title of honour or renders any person capable of succeeding to or transmitting a right to succeed to any such dignity or title, or

(b) the devolution of any property limited (expressly or not) to devolve (as nearly as the law permits) along with any dignity or title of honour.

(5) (*Applies to Scotland only.*)

1 This section has been superseded in so far as it relates to children carried by women as a result of the placing in them of embryos or of sperm and eggs on or after 6 April 2009, the date on which ss 33–38 of HFEA 2008 came into force: see s 57(2) and Human Fertilisation and Embryology Act 2008 (Commencement No 1 and Transitional Provisions) Order 2009, SI 2009/479, art 6(1)(b). But the section continues to apply to children carried by women as a result of these procedures prior to that date.

2 Subsections (3A)–(3D) inserted with effect from 1 December 2003 by Human Fertilisation and Embryology (Deceased Fathers) Act 2003, s 1(2) and Human Fertilisation and Embryology (Deceased Fathers) Act 2003 (Commencement) Order 2003, SI 2003/3095, art 2.

3 Words in square brackets in sub-s (4) inserted with effect from 1 December 2003 by Human Fertilisation and Embryology (Deceased Fathers) Act 2003, s 2(1), Sch, para 16 and Human Fertilisation and Embryology (Deceased Fathers) Act 2003 (Commencement) Order 2003, SI 2003/3095, art 2.

[245.88]

30. Parental orders in favour of gamete donors[1].— (1) The court may make an order providing for a child to be treated in law as the child of the parties to a marriage (referred to in this section as 'the husband' and 'the wife') if—

(a) the child has been carried by a woman other than the wife as the result of the placing in her of an embryo or sperm and eggs or her artificial insemination,

(b) the gametes of the husband or the wife, or both, were used to bring about the creation of the embryo, and

(c) the conditions in subsections (2) to (7) below are satisfied.

(2) The husband and the wife must apply for the order within six months of the birth of the child or, in the case of a child born before the coming into force of this Act, within six months of such coming into force.

(3) At the time of the application and of the making of the order—

(a) the child's home must be with the husband and the wife, and

(b) the husband or the wife, of both of them, must be domiciled in a part of the United Kingdom or in the Channel Islands or the Isle of Man.

(4) At the time of the making of the order both the husband and the wife must have attained the age of eighteen.

(5) The court must be satisfied that both the father of the child (including a person who is the father by virtue of section 28 of this Act), where he is not the husband, and the woman who carried the child have freely, and with full understanding of what is involved, agreed unconditionally to the making of the order.
(6) Subsection (5) above does not require the agreement of a person who cannot be found or is incapable of giving agreement and the agreement of the woman who carried the child is ineffective for the purposes of that subsection if given by her less than six weeks after the child's birth.
(7) The court must be satisfied that no money or other benefit (other than for expenses reasonably incurred) has been given or received by the husband or the wife for or in consideration of—

(a) the making of the order,
(b) any agreement required by subsection (5) above,
(c) the handing over of the child to the husband and the wife, or
(d) the making of any arrangements with a view to the making of the order, unless authorised by the court.

(8) For the purposes of an application under this section—

(a) in relation to England and Wales, section 92(7) to (10) of, and Part I of Schedule 11 to, the Children Act 1989 (jurisdiction of courts) shall apply for the purposes of this section to determine the meaning of 'the court' as they apply for the purposes of that Act and proceedings on the application shall be 'family proceedings' for the purposes of that Act,
(b) (*applies to Scotland only*), and
(c) in relation to Northern Ireland, 'the court' means the High Court or any county court within whose division the child is.

(9) Regulations may provide—

(a) for any provision of the enactments about adoption to have effect, with such modifications (if any) as may be specified in the regulations, in relation to orders under this section, and applications for such orders, as it has effect in relation to adoption, and applications for adoption orders, and
(b) for references in any enactment[2] to adoption, an adopted child or an adoptive relationship to be read (respectively) as references to the effect of an order under this section, a child to whom such an order applies and a relationship arising by virtue of the enactments about adoption, as applied by the regulations, and for similar expressions in connection with adoption to be read accordingly,

and the regulations may include such incidental or supplemental provision as appears to the Secretary of State necessary or desirable in consequence of any provision made by virtue of paragraph (a) or (b) above.
(10) In this section 'the enactments about adoption' means the [Adoption and Children Act 2002][3], the Adoption (Scotland) Act 1978 and the Adoption (Northern Ireland) Order 1987.

(11) Subsection (1)(a) above applies whether the woman was in the United Kingdom or elsewhere at the time of the placing in her of the embryo or the sperm and eggs or her artificial insemination.

1 This section ceased to have effect on 6 April 2010 (when the provisions of ss 54 and 55 of the Human Fertilisation and Embryology Act 2008 came into force) and was repealed: Human Fertilisation and Embryology Act 2008, ss 57(3), 66, 68(2), Sch 8, Pt 1 and Human Fertilisation and Embryology Act 2008 (Commencement No 3) Order 2010 (SI 2010/987). Orders made under this section prior to that date will continue to have effect: see s 57(4) of the 2008 Act.

2 References to 'any enactment' in this paragraph are to be read with effect from 1 December 2003 as including a reference to any enactment contained in s 28(5A) to (5I) of this Act: Human Fertilisation and Embryology (Deceased Fathers) Act 2003, s 2(1), Sch, para 17 and SI 2003/3095, art 2.

3 Words substituted in sub-s (10) with effect from 30 December 2005: ACA 2002, s 139(1), Sch 3, paras 76 and 79 and Adoption and Children Act 2002 (Commencement No 9) Order 2005, SI 2005/2213, art 2(o).

PARENTAL ORDERS (HUMAN FERTILISATION AND EMBRYOLOGY) REGULATIONS 1994

(SI 1994/2767)

[245.91A]

Note. These Regulations, made under s 30(9) of the Human Fertilisation and Embryology Act 1990 (now wholly superseded by the Human Fertilisation and Embryology Act 2008 printed at paras **[245.111]** ff below), define the property rights of a child in respect of whom a parental order has been made under s 30. These rights are defined by reference to the Adoption Act 1976 with appropriate modifications. The new rule of construction is that such a child is treated (subject to any contrary indication) as the child of the person or persons who have obtained the parental order. This rule applies to the construction of any instrument save 'an existing instrument', ie an instrument made at any time before 1 January 1976. These Regulations were replaced with effect from 6 April 2010 by the Human Fertilisation and Embryology (Parental Orders) Regulations 2010 (printed at paras **[245.142]** ff below) but continue to apply in relation to any order made before that date **[245.91B]**.

[245.91B]

1. Citation, commencement, interpretation and extent.— (1) These Regulations may be cited as the Parental Orders (Human Fertilisation and Embryology) Regulations 1994 and shall come into force on 1st November 1994.

(2) In these Regulations unless the context otherwise requires—

'the 1990 Act' means the Human Fertilisation and Embryology Act 1990;

'the 1976 Act' means the Adoption Act 1976 and references to sections are to sections of the 1976 Act;

'the Order' means the Adoption (Northern Ireland) Order 1987 and references to articles are to articles of the Order;

'parental order' means an order under section 30 of the 1990 Act (parental orders in favour of gamete donors) providing for a child to be treated in law as a child of the parties to a marriage.

(3) These Regulations extend to England and Wales and Northern Ireland.

[245.91C]

2. Application of Adoption Act 1976 provisions with modifications to parental orders and applications for such orders The provisions of the 1976 Act set out in column 1 of Schedule 1 to these Regulations shall have effect with the modifications (if any) set out in column 2 of that Schedule in relation to parental orders made in England and Wales and applications for such orders, as they have effect in relation to adoption and applications for adoption orders.

* * * * *

SCHEDULE 1
APPLICATION OF ADOPTION ACT 1976 PROVISIONS WITH MODIFICATIONS TO PARENTAL ORDERS AND APPLICATIONS FOR SUCH ORDERS

Regulation 2

[245.91D]

Column 1	***Column 2***	
Provisions of the 1976 Act	*Modifications*	
Applications by Gamete Donors for a parental order		
(b) Section 12(1) to (3) (adoption orders)	(i)	As if for the words 'an adoption order' on each occasion they appear there were substituted the words 'a parental order';
	(ii)	as if in subsection (1) for the word 'adopters' there were substituted the words 'husband and wife' and as if for the words 'an authorised' there were substituted the word 'the'.
Effect of a parental order		
2. Section 39(1)(a), (2), (4) and (6) (status conferred by adoption)	(i)	As if for the words 'an adopted child' there were substituted, on each occasion they appear, the words 'a child who is the subject of a parental order';
	(ii)	as if in section 39(1)(a) the words 'where the adopters are a married couple,' were omitted and for the words 'child of the marriage' there were substituted the words 'child of the marriage of the husband and wife';

Column 1	Column 2	
Provisions of the 1976 Act	*Modifications*	
	(iii)	as if in section 39(2) for the word 'adopters' there were substituted the words 'persons who obtain the parental order' and the words 'or adopter' and the words 'subject to subsection (3),' were omitted;
	(iv)	as if in section 39(6) for the word 'adoption' there were substituted the words 'the making of the parental order' and the words 'Subject to the provisions of this Part,' and ', or after 31st December 1975, whichever is the later' were omitted.
Interpretation of certain events consequent upon the making of a parental order		
3.—(a) Section 42 (rules of construction for instruments concerning property)	(i)	As if in section 42(2) for the words 'section 39(1)' there were substituted the words 'section 39(1)(a) as applied with modifications by regulation 2 of and paragraph 2 of Schedule 1 to the Parental Orders (Human Fertilisation and Embryology) Regulations 1994';
	(ii)	as if in section 42(2), for the words 'of the adoptive parent or parents' there were substituted the words 'in respect of whom the husband and wife have obtained a parental order';
	(iii)	as if in section 42(2)(a) for the words 'adopted child' there were substituted the words 'child the subject of the parental order' and for the word 'adoption' there were substituted the words 'the parental order';
	(iv)	as if in section 42(2)(b) for the words 'adopted' there were substituted the words 'in respect of whom parental orders were made';
	(v)	as if in section 42(4) for the word 'adoption' there were substituted the words 'making of the parental order' and for the words 'adopted child' there were substituted the words 'child the subject of the parental order';

Column 1	***Column 2***
Provisions of the 1976 Act	*Modifications*
	(vi) as if in section 42(5) for the word 'adopt' there were substituted the words 'obtain a parental order in respect of ' and as if after the words in section 42(4) ' section 39(2)' and, in section 42(5) 'section 39', there were inserted the words 'as applied with modifications by regulation 2 of and paragraph 2 of Schedule 1 to the Parental Orders (Human Fertilisation and Embryology) Regulations 1994'.
(b) Section 44 (property devolving with peerages etc)	As if for the words 'an adoption' on each occasion they appear there were substituted the words 'the making of a parental order'.
(c) Section 45 (protection of trustees and personal representatives)	As if in section 45(1) for the words 'adoption has been effected' there were substituted the words 'parental order has been made'.
(d) Section 46 (meaning of 'disposition')	(i) As if for the words 'this Part' on each occasion they appear and in section 46(5) the words 'the Part', there were substituted the words 'sections 39, 42, 44, 45 and 47 as applied with modifications by regulation 2 of and paragraphs 2 and 3(a), (b), (c) and (e) respectively of Schedule 1 to the Parental Orders (Human Fertilisation and Embryology) Regulations 1994'; and
	(ii) as if in section 46(2) for the word 'applies' there were substituted the word 'apply'.

Column 1	***Column 2***	
Provisions of the 1976 Act	*Modifications*	
(e) Section 47 (miscellaneous enactments)	(i)	As if for subsection (1) there were substituted the words '(1) Section 39(2) as applied with modifications by regulation 2 of and paragraph 2 of Schedule 1 to the Parental Orders (Human Fertilisation and Embryology) Regulations 1994 does not apply so as to prevent a child who is the subject of a parental order from continuing to be treated as the child of a person who was in law the child's mother or father before the order was made, for the purposes of the table of kindred and affinity in Schedule 1 to the Marriage Act 1949 and of Sections 10 and 11 (incest) of the Sexual Offences Act 1956; and
	(ii)	as if in subsection (2) for the words 'Section 39' there were substituted the words 'Section 39 as applied with modifications by regulation 2 of and paragraph 2 of Schedule 1 to the Parental Orders (Human Fertilisation and Embryology) Regulations 1994'.
Orders, rules and regulations		
6. Section 67(1), (2), (5) and (6) (orders, rules and regulations)	(i)	As if after the words 'this Act' on each occasion they appear, there were inserted the words 'as applied with modifications by regulation 2 of and Schedule 1 to the Parental Orders (Human Fertilisation and Embryology) Regulations 1994';
	(ii)	as if in section 67(2) the words ', except section 3(1),' were omitted; and
	(iii)	as if in section 67(6) after the words 'paragraph 1(1)' there were inserted the words 'as applied with modifications by regulation 2 of and paragraphs 4(b) and 8(a) respectively of Schedule 1 to the Parental Orders (Human Fertilisation and Embryology) Regulations 1994'.
Interpretation		
7. Section 72(1) (interpretation)	(i)	As if after the definition of 'guardian' there were inserted the words ' "husband and wife" means, in relation to the provisions of this Act as they have effect in relation to parental orders and applications for such orders, the husband and wife as defined in section 30 of the Human Fertilisation and Embryology Act 1990;'; and

Column 1	***Column 2***
Provisions of the 1976 Act	*Modifications*
	(ii) as if after the definition of 'parent' there were inserted the words ' "parental order" means an order under section 30 of the Human Fertilisation and Embryology Act 1990;'.

HUMAN FERTILISATION AND EMBRYOLOGY (DECEASED FATHERS) ACT 2003

(2003 c 24)

[18th September 2003]

[245.102A]

Note. This Act, like the Human Fertilisation and Embryology Act 1990, has now ceased to have effect: see the Introductory Note to the 1990 Act at para **[245.82]** above. The 2003 Act made provision about the circumstances in which, and the extent to which, a man was to be treated in law as the father of a child where the child had been born as a result of fertility treatment of the nature specified in the 1990 Act which was undertaken after the man's death. Sections 1 and 2 and the Schedule made amendments to the 1990 Act, the relevant provisions of which are printed as so amended at paras **[245.83]** ff above. Section 3 of the 2003 Act which is set out below provided that (with certain qualifications) those amendments were to have retrospective effect.

[245.102B]

3 Retrospective, transitional and transitory provision.— (1) This Act shall (in addition to any case where the sperm or embryo is used on or after the coming into force of section 1) apply to any case where the sperm of a man, or any embryo the creation of which was brought about with the sperm of a man, was used on or after 1st August 1991 and before the coming into force of that section.

(2) Where the child concerned was born before the coming into force of section 1 of this Act, section 28(5A) or (as the case may be) (5B) of the Human Fertilisation and Embryology Act 1990 (c. 37) shall have effect as if for paragraph (e) there were substituted—

'(e) the woman has elected in writing not later than the end of the period of six months beginning with the coming into force of this subsection for the man to be treated for the purpose mentioned in subsection (5I) below as the father of the child,'.

(3) Where the child concerned was born before the coming into force of section 1 of this Act, section 28(5C) of the Act of 1990 shall have effect as if for paragraph (f) there were substituted—

'(f) the woman has elected in writing not later than the end of the period of six months beginning with the coming into force of this subsection for the other party to the marriage to be treated for the purpose mentioned in subsection (5I) below as the father of the child,'.

(4) Where the child concerned was born before the coming into force of section 1 of this Act, section 28(5D) of the Act of 1990 shall have effect as if for paragraph (f) there were substituted—

'(f) the woman has elected in writing not later than the end of the period of six months beginning with the coming into force of this subsection for the man to be treated for the purpose mentioned in subsection (5I) below as the father of the child,'.

(5) Where the child concerned was born before the coming into force of section 1 of this Act, section 28 of the Act of 1990 shall have effect as if—

(a) subsection (5E) were omitted; and
(b) in subsection (5F) for the words from '(which requires' to 'that day)' there were substituted '(which requires an election to be made not later than the end of a period of six months)'.

(6) Where the man who might be treated as the father of the child died before the passing of this Act—

(a) subsections (5A) and (5B) of section 28 of the Act of 1990 shall have effect as if paragraph (d) of each subsection were omitted;
(b) subsections (5C) and (5D) of that section of that Act shall have effect as if paragraph (e) of each subsection were omitted ...

* * * * *

GENDER RECOGNITION ACT 2004

(2004 c 7)

[1st July 2004]

[245.103]

Note. This Act, which came into force on 4 April 2005 (Gender Recognition Act 2004 (Commencement) Order 2005, SI 2005/54), recognises sex changes by permitting a person who is at least 18 years of age to apply for a gender recognition certificate. If granted, the applicant will be treated as having 'the acquired gender' for all purposes, including succession. The construction of wills or other instruments made before the commencement date is unaffected by the grant of a gender recognition certificate. Otherwise the grant of a certificate has retrospective effect subject to any order which a court may make on the application of a person who is adversely affected. The significance of the Act for the law of wills is that, for example, the beneficiaries under a gift to 'my daughters' in a will made after the commencement date would include any sons whose gender has changed in a manner recognised under the Act.

HUMAN FERTILISATION AND EMBRYOLOGY ACT 2008

(2008 c 22)

[13th November 2003]

[245.111]

Note. This Act makes further and more comprehensive provision for the control of the treatment of infertility and research involving human embryos and the use of genetic material not of human origin and, in Part 2, for the identification of the persons who are to be treated as the 'mother', 'father' or 'parent' of a child who is born as a result of assisted reproduction. Part 2 largely supersedes the corresponding provisions the Human Fertilisation and Embryology Act 1990 (or will do so when fully brought into force) but only in relation to a children carried by women as a result of treatment received after the commencement of the relevant provisions on 6 April 2009. But the 2008 Act does not repeal the 1990 Act which continues to apply in relation to children born as a result of treatment received before that date. The Human Fertilisation and Embryology (Parental Orders) Regulations 2010 (SI 2010/985), which were made under s 55 of the Act and came into force on 6 April 2010, are printed at paras **[245.142]** ff below.

PART 2
PARENTHOOD IN CASES INVOLVING ASSISTED REPRODUCTION

Meaning of 'mother'

[245.112]
33 Meaning of 'mother'.— (1) The woman who is carrying or has carried a child as a result of the placing in her of an embryo or of sperm and eggs, and no other woman, is to be treated as the mother of the child.
(2) Subsection (1) does not apply to any child to the extent that the child is treated by virtue of adoption as not being the woman's child.
(3) Subsection (1) applies whether the woman was in the United Kingdom or elsewhere at the time of the placing in her of the embryo or the sperm and eggs.

Application of sections 35 to 47

[245.113]
34 Application of sections 35 to 47.— (1) Sections 35 to 47 apply, in the case of a child who is being or has been carried by a woman (referred to in those sections as 'W') as a result of the placing in her of an embryo or of sperm and eggs or her artificial insemination, to determine who is to be treated as the other parent of the child.
(2) Subsection (1) has effect subject to the provisions of sections 39, 40 and 46 limiting the purposes for which a person is treated as the child's other parent by virtue of those sections.

Meaning of 'father'

[245.114]
35 Woman married [to a man][1] at time of treatment.— (1) If—

(a) at the time of the placing in her of the embryo or of the sperm and eggs or of her artificial insemination, W was a party to a marriage [with a man],[1] and

(b) the creation of the embryo carried by her was not brought about with the sperm of the other party to the marriage,

then, subject to section 38(2) to (4), the other party to the marriage is to be treated as the father of the child unless it is shown that he did not consent to the placing in her of the embryo or the sperm and eggs or to her artificial insemination (as the case may be).

(2) This section applies whether W was in the United Kingdom or elsewhere at the time mentioned in subsection (1)(a).

1 Words inserted in section title and in subsection (1)(a) from a date to be appointed by the Marriage (Same Sex Couples) Act 2013, s17(4), 21(3) and Sch 7, Pt 2, paras 37, 38, No date has yet been appointed.

[245.115]

36 Treatment provided to woman where agreed fatherhood conditions apply. If no man is treated by virtue of section 35 as the father of the child and no woman is treated by virtue of section 42 as a parent of the child but—

(a) the embryo or the sperm and eggs were placed in W, or W was artificially inseminated, in the course of treatment services provided in the United Kingdom by a person to whom a licence applies,

(b) at the time when the embryo or the sperm and eggs were placed in W, or W was artificially inseminated, the agreed fatherhood conditions (as set out in section 37) were satisfied in relation to a man, in relation to treatment provided to W under the licence,

(c) the man remained alive at that time, and

(d) the creation of the embryo carried by W was not brought about with the man's sperm,

then, subject to section 38(2) to (4), the man is to be treated as the father of the child.

[245.116]

37 The agreed fatherhood conditions.— (1) The agreed fatherhood conditions referred to in section 36(b) are met in relation to a man ('M') in relation to treatment provided to W under a licence if, but only if,—

(a) M has given the person responsible a notice stating that he consents to being treated as the father of any child resulting from treatment provided to W under the licence,

(b) W has given the person responsible a notice stating that she consents to M being so treated,

(c) neither M nor W has, since giving notice under paragraph (a) or (b), given the person responsible notice of the withdrawal of M's or W's consent to M being so treated,

(d) W has not, since the giving of the notice under paragraph (b), given the person responsible—

 (i) a further notice under that paragraph stating that she consents to another man being treated as the father of any resulting child, or

 (ii) a notice under section 44(1)(b) stating that she consents to a woman being treated as a parent of any resulting child, and

(e) W and M are not within prohibited degrees of relationship in relation to each other.

(2) A notice under subsection (1)(a), (b) or (c) must be in writing and must be signed by the person giving it.
(3) A notice under subsection (1)(a), (b) or (c) by a person ('S') who is unable to sign because of illness, injury or physical disability is to be taken to comply with the requirement of subsection (2) as to signature if it is signed at the direction of S, in the presence of S and in the presence of at least one witness who attests the signature.

[245.117]
38 Further provision relating to sections 35 and 36.— (1) Where a person is to be treated as the father of the child by virtue of section 35 or 36, no other person is to be treated as the father of the child.
(2) In England and Wales and Northern Ireland, sections 35 and 36 do not affect any presumption, applying by virtue of the rules of common law, that a child is the legitimate child of the parties to a marriage.
(3) In Scotland, sections 35 and 36 do not apply in relation to any child who, by virtue of any enactment or other rule of law, is treated as the child of the parties to a marriage.
(4) Sections 35 and 36 do not apply to any child to the extent that the child is treated by virtue of adoption as not being the man's child.

[245.118]
39 Use of sperm, or transfer of embryo, after death of man providing sperm.— (1) If—
(a) the child has been carried by W as a result of the placing in her of an embryo or of sperm and eggs or her artificial insemination,
(b) the creation of the embryo carried by W was brought about by using the sperm of a man after his death, or the creation of the embryo was brought about using the sperm of a man before his death but the embryo was placed in W after his death,
(c) the man consented in writing (and did not withdraw the consent)—
  (i) to the use of his sperm after his death which brought about the creation of the embryo carried by W or (as the case may be) to the placing in W after his death of the embryo which was brought about using his sperm before his death, and
  (ii) to being treated for the purpose mentioned in subsection (3) as the father of any resulting child,
(d) W has elected in writing not later than the end of the period of 42 days from the day on which the child was born for the man to be treated for the purpose mentioned in subsection (3) as the father of the child, and
(e) no-one else is to be treated—
  (i) as the father of the child by virtue of section 35 or 36 or by virtue of section 38(2) or (3), or
  (ii) as a parent of the child by virtue of section 42 or 43 or by virtue of adoption,

then the man is to be treated for the purpose mentioned in subsection (3) as the father of the child.

(2) Subsection (1) applies whether W was in the United Kingdom or elsewhere at the time of the placing in her of the embryo or of the sperm and eggs or of her artificial insemination.
(3) The purpose referred to in subsection (1) is the purpose of enabling the man's particulars to be entered as the particulars of the child's father in a relevant register of births.
(4) In the application of this section to Scotland, for any reference to a period of 42 days there is substituted a reference to a period of 21 days.

[245.119]
40 Embryo transferred after death of husband etc who did not provide sperm.— (1) If—

- (a) the child has been carried by W as a result of the placing in her of an embryo,
- (b) the embryo was created at a time when W was a party to a marriage [with a man],[1]
- (c) the creation of the embryo was not brought about with the sperm of the other party to the marriage,
- (d) the other party to the marriage died before the placing of the embryo in W,
- (e) the other party to the marriage consented in writing (and did not withdraw the consent)—
  - (i) to the placing of the embryo in W after his death, and
  - (ii) to being treated for the purpose mentioned in subsection (4) as the father of any resulting child,
- (f) W has elected in writing not later than the end of the period of 42 days from the day on which the child was born for the man to be treated for the purpose mentioned in subsection (4) as the father of the child, and
- (g) no-one else is to be treated—
  - (i) as the father of the child by virtue of section 35 or 36 or by virtue of section 38(2) or (3), or
  - (ii) as a parent of the child by virtue of section 42 or 43 or by virtue of adoption,

then the man is to be treated for the purpose mentioned in subsection (4) as the father of the child.
(2) If—

- (a) the child has been carried by W as a result of the placing in her of an embryo,
- (b) the embryo was not created at a time when W was a party to a marriage or a civil partnership but was created in the course of treatment services provided to W in the United Kingdom by a person to whom a licence applies,
- (c) a man consented in writing (and did not withdraw the consent)—
  - (i) to the placing of the embryo in W after his death, and
  - (ii) to being treated for the purpose mentioned in subsection (4) as the father of any resulting child,
- (d) the creation of the embryo was not brought about with the sperm of that man,

(e) the man died before the placing of the embryo in W,
(f) immediately before the man's death, the agreed fatherhood conditions set out in section 37 were met in relation to the man in relation to treatment proposed to be provided to W in the United Kingdom by a person to whom a licence applies,
(g) W has elected in writing not later than the end of the period of 42 days from the day on which the child was born for the man to be treated for the purpose mentioned in subsection (4) as the father of the child, and
(h) no-one else is to be treated—
  (i) as the father of the child by virtue of section 35 or 36 or by virtue of section 38(2) or (3), or
  (ii) as a parent of the child by virtue of section 42 or 43 or by virtue of adoption,

then the man is to be treated for the purpose mentioned in subsection (4) as the father of the child.
(3) Subsections (1) and (2) apply whether W was in the United Kingdom or elsewhere at the time of the placing in her of the embryo.
(4) The purpose referred to in subsections (1) and (2) is the purpose of enabling the man's particulars to be entered as the particulars of the child's father in a relevant register of births.
(5) In the application of this section to Scotland, for any reference to a period of 42 days there is substituted a reference to a period of 21 days.

1 Words inserted in subsection (1)(b) from a date to be appointed by the Marriage (Same Sex Couples) Act 2013, s17(4), 21(3) and Sch 7, Pt 2, paras 37, 38, No date has yet been appointed.

[245.120]
41 Persons not to be treated as father.— (1) Where the sperm of a man who had given such consent as is required by paragraph 5 of Schedule 3 to the 1990 Act (consent to use of gametes for purposes of treatment services or non-medical fertility services) was used for a purpose for which such consent was required, he is not to be treated as the father of the child.
(2) Where the sperm of a man, or an embryo the creation of which was brought about with his sperm, was used after his death, he is not, subject to section 39, to be treated as the father of the child.
(3) Subsection (2) applies whether W was in the United Kingdom or elsewhere at the time of the placing in her of the embryo or of the sperm and eggs or of her artificial insemination.

Cases in which woman to be other parent

[245.121]
42 Woman in civil partnership [or marriage to a woman][1] at time of treatment.— (1) If at the time of the placing in her of the embryo or the sperm and eggs or of her artificial insemination, W was a party to a civil partnership [or marriage with another woman],[1] then subject to section 45(2) to (4), the other party to the civil partnership [or marriage][2] is to

be treated as a parent of the child unless it is shown that she did not consent to the placing in W of the embryo or the sperm and eggs or to her artificial insemination (as the case may be).
(2) This section applies whether W was in the United Kingdom or elsewhere at the time mentioned in subsection (1).

1 Words inserted in section title and in subsection (1) from a date to be appointed by the Marriage (Same Sex Couples) Act 2013, s17(4), 21(3) and Sch 7, Pt 2, paras 37, 38, No date has yet been appointed.
2 Words 'or marriage' inserted from a date to be appointed by the Marriage (Same Sex Couples) Act 2013, s17(4), 21(3) and Sch 7, Pt 2, paras 37, 38, No date has yet been appointed.

[245.122]
43 Treatment provided to woman who agrees that second woman to be parent. If no man is treated by virtue of section 35 as the father of the child and no woman is treated by virtue of section 42 as a parent of the child but—

- (a) the embryo or the sperm and eggs were placed in W, or W was artificially inseminated, in the course of treatment services provided in the United Kingdom by a person to whom a licence applies,
- (b) at the time when the embryo or the sperm and eggs were placed in W, or W was artificially inseminated, the agreed female parenthood conditions (as set out in section 44) were met in relation to another woman, in relation to treatment provided to W under that licence, and
- (c) the other woman remained alive at that time,

then, subject to section 45(2) to (4), the other woman is to be treated as a parent of the child.

[245.123]
44 The agreed female parenthood conditions.— (1) The agreed female parenthood conditions referred to in section 43(b) are met in relation to another woman ('P') in relation to treatment provided to W under a licence if, but only if,—

- (a) P has given the person responsible a notice stating that P consents to P being treated as a parent of any child resulting from treatment provided to W under the licence,
- (b) W has given the person responsible a notice stating that W agrees to P being so treated,
- (c) neither W nor P has, since giving notice under paragraph (a) or (b), given the person responsible notice of the withdrawal of P's or W's consent to P being so treated,
- (d) W has not, since the giving of the notice under paragraph (b), given the person responsible—
  - (i) a further notice under that paragraph stating that W consents to a woman other than P being treated as a parent of any resulting child, or
  - (ii) a notice under section 37(1)(b) stating that W consents to a man being treated as the father of any resulting child, and

(e) W and P are not within prohibited degrees of relationship in relation to each other.

(2) A notice under subsection (1)(a), (b) or (c) must be in writing and must be signed by the person giving it.
(3) A notice under subsection (1)(a), (b) or (c) by a person ('S') who is unable to sign because of illness, injury or physical disability is to be taken to comply with the requirement of subsection (2) as to signature if it is signed at the direction of S, in the presence of S and in the presence of at least one witness who attests the signature.

[245.124]
45 Further provision relating to sections 42 and 43.— (1) Where a woman is treated by virtue of section 42 or 43 as a parent of the child, no man is to be treated as the father of the child.
(2) In England and Wales and Northern Ireland, sections 42 and 43 do not affect any presumption, applying by virtue of the rules of common law, that a child is the legitimate child of the parties to a marriage.
(3) In Scotland, sections 42 and 43 do not apply in relation to any child who, by virtue of any enactment or other rule of law, is treated as the child of the parties to a marriage.
(4) Sections 42 and 43 do not apply to any child to the extent that the child is treated by virtue of adoption as not being the woman's child.

[245.125]
46 Embryo transferred after death of civil partner [or wife][1] or intended female parent.— (1) If—

(a) the child has been carried by W as the result of the placing in her of an embryo,
(b) the embryo was created at a time when W was a party to a civil partnership [or marriage with another woman],[1]
(c) the other party to the civil partnership [or marriage][2] died before the placing of the embryo in W,
(d) the other party to the civil partnership [or marriage][2] consented in writing (and did not withdraw the consent)—
  (i) to the placing of the embryo in W after the death of the other party, and
  (ii) to being treated for the purpose mentioned in subsection (4) as the parent of any resulting child,
(e) W has elected in writing not later than the end of the period of 42 days from the day on which the child was born for the other party to the civil partnership [or marriage][2] to be treated for the purpose mentioned in subsection (4) as the parent of the child, and
(f) no one else is to be treated—
  (i) as the father of the child by virtue of section 35 or 36 or by virtue of section 45(2) or (3), or
  (ii) as a parent of the child by virtue of section 42 or 43 or by virtue of adoption,

then the other party to the civil partnership [or marriage][2] is to be treated for the purpose mentioned in subsection (4) as a parent of the child.

(2) If—

(a) the child has been carried by W as the result of the placing in her of an embryo,
(b) the embryo was not created at a time when W was a party to a marriage or a civil partnership, but was created in the course of treatment services provided to W in the United Kingdom by a person to whom a licence applies,
(c) another woman consented in writing (and did not withdraw the consent)—
  (i) to the placing of the embryo in W after the death of the other woman, and
  (ii) to being treated for the purpose mentioned in subsection (4) as the parent of any resulting child,
(d) the other woman died before the placing of the embryo in W,
(e) immediately before the other woman's death, the agreed female parenthood conditions set out in section 44 were met in relation to the other woman in relation to treatment proposed to be provided to W in the United Kingdom by a person to whom a licence applies,
(f) W has elected in writing not later than the end of the period of 42 days from the day on which the child was born for the other woman to be treated for the purpose mentioned in subsection (4) as the parent of the child, and
(g) no one else is to be treated—
  (i) as the father of the child by virtue of section 35 or 36 or by virtue of section 45(2) or (3), or
  (ii) as a parent of the child by virtue of section 42 or 43 or by virtue of adoption,

then the other woman is to be treated for the purpose mentioned in subsection (4) as a parent of the child.
(3) Subsections (1) and (2) apply whether W was in the United Kingdom or elsewhere at the time of the placing in her of the embryo.
(4) The purpose referred to in subsections (1) and (2) is the purpose of enabling the deceased woman's particulars to be entered as the particulars of the child's other parent in a relevant register of births.
(5) In the application of subsections (1) and (2) to Scotland, for any reference to a period of 42 days there is substituted a reference to a period of 21 days.

1 Words inserted in section title and in subsection (1)(b) from a date to be appointed by the Marriage (Same Sex Couples) Act 2013, s17(4), 21(3) and Sch 7, Pt 2, paras 37, 38, No date has yet been appointed.
2 In subsection (1) words 'or marriage' in square brackets inserted in each place they appear from a date to be appointed by the Marriage (Same Sex Couples) Act 2013, s17(4), 21(3) and Sch 7, Pt 2, paras 37, 38, No date has yet been appointed.

[245.126]
47 Woman not to be other parent merely because of egg donation. A woman is not to be treated as the parent of a child whom she is not carrying and has not carried, except where she is so treated—

(a) by virtue of section 42 or 43, or

(b) by virtue of section 46 (for the purpose mentioned in subsection (4) of that section), or
(c) by virtue of adoption.

Effect of sections 33 to 47

[245.127]
48 Effect of sections 33 to 47.— (1) Where by virtue of section 33, 35, 36, 42 or 43 a person is to be treated as the mother, father or parent of a child, that person is to be treated in law as the mother, father or parent (as the case may be) of the child for all purposes.
(2) Where by virtue of section 33, 38, 41, 45 or 47 a person is not to be treated as a parent of the child, that person is to be treated in law as not being a parent of the child for any purpose.
(3) Where section 39(1) or 40(1) or (2) applies, the deceased man—

(a) is to be treated in law as the father of the child for the purpose mentioned in section 39(3) or 40(4), but
(b) is to be treated in law as not being the father of the child for any other purpose.

(4) Where section 46(1) or (2) applies, the deceased woman—

(a) is to be treated in law as a parent of the child for the purpose mentioned in section 46(4), but
(b) is to be treated in law as not being a parent of the child for any other purpose.

(5) Where any of subsections (1) to (4) has effect, references to any relationship between two people in any enactment, deed or other instrument or document (whenever passed or made) are to be read accordingly.
(6) In relation to England and Wales and Northern Ireland, a child who—

(a) has a parent by virtue of section 42, or
(b) has a parent by virtue of section 43 who is at any time during the period beginning with the time mentioned in section 43(b) and ending with the time of the child's birth a party to a civil partnership with the child's mother,

is the legitimate child of the child's parents.
(7) In relation to England and Wales and Northern Ireland, nothing in the provisions of section 33(1) or sections 35 to 47, read with this section—

(a) affects the succession to any dignity or title of honour or renders any person capable of succeeding to or transmitting a right to succeed to any such dignity or title, or
(b) affects the devolution of any property limited (expressly or not) to devolve (as nearly as the law permits) along with any dignity or title of honour.

(8) In relation to Scotland—

(a) those provisions do not apply to any title, coat of arms, honour or dignity transmissible on the death of its holder or affect the succession to any such title, coat of arms or dignity or its devolution, and

(b) where the terms of any deed provide that any property or interest in property is to devolve along with a title, coat of arms, honour or dignity, nothing in those provisions is to prevent that property or interest from so devolving.

References to parties to marriage or civil partnership

[245.128]

49 Meaning of references to parties to a marriage.— (1) The references in sections 35 to 47 to the parties to a marriage at any time there referred to—

(a) are to the parties to a marriage subsisting at that time, unless a judicial separation was then in force, but

(b) include the parties to a void marriage if either or both of them reasonably believed at that time that the marriage was valid; and for the purposes of those sections it is to be presumed, unless the contrary is shown, that one of them reasonably believed at that time that the marriage was valid.

(2) In subsection (1)(a) 'judicial separation' includes a legal separation obtained in a country outside the British Islands and recognised in the United Kingdom.

[245.129]

50 Meaning of references to parties to a civil partnership.— (1) The references in sections 35 to 47 to the parties to a civil partnership at any time there referred to—

(a) are to the parties to a civil partnership subsisting at that time, unless a separation order was then in force, but

(b) include the parties to a void civil partnership if either or both of them reasonably believed at that time that the civil partnership was valid; and for the purposes of those sections it is to be presumed, unless the contrary is shown, that one of them reasonably believed at that time that the civil partnership was valid.

(2) The reference in section 48(6)(b) to a civil partnership includes a reference to a void civil partnership if either or both of the parties reasonably believed at the time when they registered as civil partners of each other that the civil partnership was valid; and for this purpose it is to be presumed, unless the contrary is shown, that one of them reasonably believed at that time that the civil partnership was valid.

(3) In subsection (1)(a), 'separation order' means—

(a) a separation order under section 37(1)(d) or 161(1)(d) of the Civil Partnership Act 2004 (c 33),

(b) a decree of separation under section 120(2) of that Act, or

(c) a legal separation obtained in a country outside the United Kingdom and recognised in the United Kingdom.

Further provision about registration by virtue of section 39, 40 or 46

[245.130]
51 Meaning of 'relevant register of births'. For the purposes of this Part a 'relevant register of births', in relation to a birth, is whichever of the following is relevant—

(a) a register of live-births or still-births kept under the Births and Deaths Registration Act 1953 (c 20),
(b) a register of births or still-births kept under the Registration of Births, Deaths and Marriages (Scotland) Act 1965 (c 49), or
(c) a register of live-births or still-births kept under the Births and Deaths Registration (Northern Ireland) Order 1976 (SI 1976/1041 (NI 14)).

[245.131]
52 Late election by mother with consent of Registrar General.— (1) The requirement under section 39(1), 40(1) or (2) or 46(1) or (2) as to the making of an election (which requires an election to be made either on or before the day on which the child was born or within the period of 42 or, as the case may be, 21 days from that day) is nevertheless to be treated as satisfied if the required election is made after the end of that period but with the consent of the Registrar General under subsection (2).
(2) The Registrar General may at any time consent to the making of an election after the end of the period mentioned in subsection (1) if, on an application made to him in accordance with such requirements as he may specify, he is satisfied that there is a compelling reason for giving his consent to the making of such an election.
(3) In this section 'the Registrar General' means the Registrar General for England and Wales, the Registrar General of Births, Deaths and Marriages for Scotland or (as the case may be) the Registrar General for Northern Ireland.

Interpretation of references to father etc where woman is other parent

[245.132]
53 Interpretation of references to father etc.— (1) Subsections (2) and (3) have effect, subject to subsections (4) and (6), for the interpretation of any enactment, deed or any other instrument or document (whenever passed or made).
(2) Any reference (however expressed) to the father of a child who has a parent by virtue of section 42 or 43 is to be read as a reference to the woman who is a parent of the child by virtue of that section.
(3) Any reference (however expressed) to evidence of paternity is, in relation to a woman who is a parent by virtue of section 42 or 43, to be read as a reference to evidence of parentage.
(4) This section does not affect the interpretation of the enactments specified in subsection (5) (which make express provision for the case where a child has a parent by virtue of section 42 or 43).
(5) Those enactments are—

(a) the Legitimacy Act (Northern Ireland) 1928 (c 5 (NI)),
(b) the Schedule to the Population (Statistics) Act 1938 (c 12),
(c) the Births and Deaths Registration Act 1953 (c 20),
(d) the Registration of Births, Deaths and Marriages (Special Provisions) Act 1957 (c 58),
(e) Part 2 of the Registration of Births, Deaths and Marriages (Scotland) Act 1965 (c 49),
(f) the Congenital Disabilities (Civil Liability) Act 1976 (c 28),
(g) the Legitimacy Act 1976 (c 31),
(h) the Births and Deaths Registration (Northern Ireland) Order 1976 (SI 1976/1041 (NI 14)),
(i) the British Nationality Act 1981 (c 61),
(j) the Family Law Reform Act 1987 (c 42),
(k) Parts 1 and 2 of the Children Act 1989 (c 41),
(l) Part 1 of the Children (Scotland) Act 1995 (c 36),
(m) section 1 of the Criminal Law (Consolidation) (Scotland) Act 1995 (c 39), and
(n) Parts 2, 3 and 14 of the Children (Northern Ireland) Order 1995 (SI 1995/755 (NI 2)).

(6) This section does not affect the interpretation of references that fall to be read in accordance with section 1(2)(a) or (b) of the Family Law Reform Act 1987 or Article 155(2)(a) or (b) of the Children (Northern Ireland) Order 1995 (references to a person whose father and mother were, or were not, married to each other at the time of the person's birth).

Parental orders

[245.133]
54 Parental orders.— (1) On an application made by two people ('the applicants'), the court may make an order providing for a child to be treated in law as the child of the applicants if—

(a) the child has been carried by a woman who is not one of the applicants, as a result of the placing in her of an embryo or sperm and eggs or her artificial insemination,
(b) the gametes of at least one of the applicants were used to bring about the creation of the embryo, and
(c) the conditions in subsections (2) to (8) are satisfied.

(2) The applicants must be—

(a) husband and wife,
(b) civil partners of each other, or
(c) two persons who are living as partners in an enduring family relationship and are not within prohibited degrees of relationship in relation to each other.

(3) Except in a case falling within subsection (11), the applicants must apply for the order during the period of 6 months beginning with the day on which the child is born.
(4) At the time of the application and the making of the order—

(a) the child's home must be with the applicants, and
(b) either or both of the applicants must be domiciled in the United Kingdom or in the Channel Islands or the Isle of Man.

(5) At the time of the making of the order both the applicants must have attained the age of 18.
(6) The court must be satisfied that both—

(a) the woman who carried the child, and
(b) any other person who is a parent of the child but is not one of the applicants (including any man who is the father by virtue of section 35 or 36 or any woman who is a parent by virtue of section 42 or 43),

have freely, and with full understanding of what is involved, agreed unconditionally to the making of the order.
(7) Subsection (6) does not require the agreement of a person who cannot be found or is incapable of giving agreement; and the agreement of the woman who carried the child is ineffective for the purpose of that subsection if given by her less than six weeks after the child's birth.
(8) The court must be satisfied that no money or other benefit (other than for expenses reasonably incurred) has been given or received by either of the applicants for or in consideration of—

(a) the making of the order,
(b) any agreement required by subsection (6),
(c) the handing over of the child to the applicants, or
(d) the making of arrangements with a view to the making of the order,

unless authorised by the court.
(9) For the purposes of an application under this section—

(a) in relation to England and Wales, section 92(7) to (10) of, and Part 1 of Schedule 11 to, the Children Act 1989 (c 41) (jurisdiction of courts) apply for the purposes of this section to determine the meaning of 'the court' as they apply for the purposes of that Act and proceedings on the application are to be 'family proceedings' for the purposes of that Act,
(b) in relation to Scotland, 'the court' means the Court of Session or the sheriff court of the sheriffdom within which the child is, and
(c) in relation to Northern Ireland, 'the court' means the High Court or any county court within whose division the child is.

(10) Subsection (1)(a) applies whether the woman was in the United Kingdom or elsewhere at the time of the placing in her of the embryo or the sperm and eggs or her artificial insemination.
(11) An application which—

(a) relates to a child born before the coming into force of this section, and
(b) is made by two persons who, throughout the period applicable under subsection (2) of section 30 of the 1990 Act, were not eligible to apply for an order under that section in relation to the child as husband and wife,

may be made within the period of six months beginning with the day on which this section comes into force.

[245.134]
55 Parental orders: supplementary provision.— (1) The Secretary of State may by regulations provide—

(a) for any provision of the enactments about adoption to have effect, with such modifications (if any) as may be specified in the regulations, in relation to orders under section 54, and applications for such orders, as it has effect in relation to adoption, and applications for adoption orders, and
(b) for references in any enactment to adoption, an adopted child or an adoptive relationship to be read (respectively) as references to the effect of an order under section 54, a child to whom such an order applies and a relationship arising by virtue of the enactments about adoption, as applied by the regulations, and for similar expressions in connection with adoption to be read accordingly.

(2) The regulations may include such incidental or supplemental provision as appears to the Secretary of State to be necessary or desirable in consequence of any provision made by virtue of subsection (1)(a) or (b).
(3) In this section 'the enactments about adoption' means—

(a) the Adoption (Scotland) Act 1978 (c 28),
(b) the Adoption and Children Act 2002 (c 38),
(c) the Adoption and Children (Scotland) Act 2007 (asp 4), and
(d) the Adoption (Northern Ireland) Order 1987 (SI 1987/2203 (NI 22)).

Amendments of enactments

[245.135]
56 Amendments relating to parenthood in cases involving assisted reproduction. Schedule 6 contains amendments related to the provisions of this Part.

General

[245.136]
57 Repeals and transitional provision relating to Part 2.— (1) Sections 33 to 48 have effect only in relation to children carried by women as a result of the placing in them of embryos or of sperm and eggs, or their artificial insemination (as the case may be), after the commencement of those sections.
(2) Sections 27 to 29 of the 1990 Act (which relate to status) do not have effect in relation to children carried by women as a result of the placing in them of embryos or of sperm and eggs, or their artificial insemination (as the case may be), after the commencement of sections 33 to 48.

(3) Section 30 of the 1990 Act (parental orders in favour of gamete donors) ceases to have effect.
(4) Subsection (3) does not affect the validity of any order made under section 30 of the 1990 Act before the coming into force of that subsection.

[245.137]
58 Interpretation of Part 2.— (1) In this Part 'enactment' means an enactment contained in, or in an instrument made under—

(a) an Act of Parliament,
(b) an Act of the Scottish Parliament,
(c) a Measure or Act of the National Assembly for Wales, or
(d) Northern Ireland legislation.

(2) For the purposes of this Part, two persons are within prohibited degrees of relationship if one is the other's parent, grandparent, sister, brother, aunt or uncle; and in this subsection references to relationships—

(a) are to relationships of the full blood or half blood or, in the case of an adopted person, such of those relationships as would subsist but for adoption, and
(b) include the relationship of a child with his adoptive, or former adoptive, parents,

but do not include any other adoptive relationships.
(3) Other expressions used in this Part and in the 1990 Act have the same meaning in this Part as in that Act.

PART 3
MISCELLANEOUS AND GENERAL

* * * * *

General

* * * * *

[245.138]
63 Meaning of 'the 1990 Act'. In this Act, 'the 1990 Act' means the Human Fertilisation and Embryology Act 1990 (c 37).

* * * * *

[245.139]
67 Extent (1) Subject to the following provisions, this Act extends to England and Wales, Scotland and Northern Ireland.
(2) Any amendment or repeal made by this Act has the same extent as the enactment to which it relates (ignoring extent by virtue of an Order in Council).[1]

1 The remaining subsections are not relevant.

[245.140]

68 Commencement.— (1) The following provisions of this Act come into force on the day on which this Act is passed—

sections 61 to 64;

section 67, this section and section 69.

(2) The remaining provisions of this Act come into force in accordance with provision made by the Secretary of State by order.[1]

1 The provisions of ss 33 to 53, 56 (for certain purposes), 57(1), (2) and 58 were brought into force on 6 April 2009 by the Human Fertilisation and Embryology Act 2008 (Commencement No 1 and Transitional Provisions) Order 2009, SI 2009/479, art 6(1)(a), (b), (c), and (f). Section 55 was brought into force on 6 April 2009 as was s 54 (but only for the purpose of enabling regulations to be made under s 55): Human Fertilisation and Embryology Act 2008 (Commencement No 2 and Transitional Provisions) and (Commencement No 1 Amendment) Order 2009, SI 2009/2232. Section 54 was fully brought into force on 6 April 2010: Human Fertilisation and Embryology Act 2008 (Commencement No 3) Order 2010, SI 2010/987. The regulations made under s 55, printed at paras **[245.142]** ff below, came into effect on the same day.

[245.141]

69 Short title. This Act may be cited as the Human Fertilisation and Embryology Act 2008.

* * * * *

HUMAN FERTILISATION AND EMBRYOLOGY (PARENTAL ORDERS) REGULATIONS 2010

SI 2010/985

[245.142]

Note. These Regulations, made under s 55 of the Human Fertilisation and Embryology Act 2008, define the property rights of a child in respect of whom a parental order has been made under s 54. These rights are defined by reference to the Adoption and Children Act 2002 with appropriate modifications. The rule of construction introduced by these Regulations is similar to the rule of construction introduced by the Parental Orders (Human Fertilisation and Embryology) Regulations 1994 made under s 30 of the Human Fertilisation and Embryology Act 1990 (see paras [245.91A] ff above); a child in respect of whom a parental order has been made under s 54 is treated (subject to any contrary indication) as the child of the person or persons who have obtained the order. However, there is one important distinction. Under the 2010 Regulations ss 67(6) and 69(1) 2002 Act are modified by omitting the reference to Schedule 4 to the Act; this has the consequence that 'an existing instrument', i e an instrument made at any time before 1 January 1976, is not excluded from the operation of the new rule and a child in respect of whom a parental order is made under s 54 of the 2008 Act will be treated as the child of the person or persons who have obtained the order in any instrument whenever made; cf s 29(3) of the 1990 Act and s 48(5) of the 2008 Act.

[245.143]

1. Citation, commencement, extent and interpretation (1) These Regulations may be cited as the Human Fertilisation and Embryology (Parental Orders) Regulations 2010 and shall come into force on 6th April 2010.

(2) Any provision of these Regulations which applies or modifies an enactment has the same extent as the enactment to which it relates.

(3) Subject to paragraph (2), these Regulations extend to England and Wales, Scotland and Northern Ireland.
(4) In these Regulations—

'the 2002 Act' means the Adoption and Children Act 2002;
'the 2007 Act' means the Adoption and Children (Scotland) Act 2007;
'the 2008 Act' means the Human Fertilisation and Embryology Act 2008; and
'the 1987 Order' means the Adoption (Northern Ireland) Order 1987.

(5) In these Regulations, and in any provision that is applied with modifications by regulation 2, 3 or 4 and Schedule 1, 2 or 3, 'parental order' means an order under section 54 of the 2008 Act (parental orders) and, for the purposes of the provisions specified in paragraph (6), also includes an order under section 30 of the Human Fertilisation and Embryology Act 1990 (parental orders).
(6) The provisions referred to in paragraph (5) are—

(a) sections 60, 77 to 82 of, and Schedule 1 to, the 2002 Act, as applied with modifications by regulation 2 and Schedule 1;
(b) Articles 50 to 54 of, and Schedule 2 to, the 1987 Order, as applied with modifications by regulation 3 and Schedule 2;
(c) sections 53 to 57 of, and Schedule 1 to, the 2007 Act, as applied with modifications by regulation 4 and Schedule 3; and
(d) paragraphs 1, 13, 17, 18 and 20 of Schedule 4 to these Regulations.

[245.144]
2. Application of certain provisions of the 2002 Act subject to modifications
The provisions of the 2002 Act set out in column 1 of Schedule 1 have effect in relation to parental orders made in England and Wales and applications for such orders as they have effect in relation to adoption orders and applications for such orders, subject to the modifications set out in column 2 of that Schedule.

[245.145] [Regulations 3 and 4 apply to Northern Ireland and Scotland.]

[245.146]
5. References in enactments to be read as references to parental orders etc
In the enactments mentioned in column 1 of Schedule 4, the references mentioned in column 2 of that Schedule (which relate to adoption, adopted children or an adoptive relationship) are to be read as provided for in column 2.

* * * * *

SCHEDULE 1
APPLICATION OF ADOPTION AND CHILDREN ACT 2002 PROVISIONS WITH MODIFICATIONS TO PARENTAL ORDERS AND APPLICATIONS FOR SUCH ORDERS

Regulation 2

[245.147]

Column 1	*Column 2*	
Provisions of the 2002 Act	*Modifications*	
* * * * *		
Section 67(1) to (3), (5) and (6) (status conferred by adoption)	(i)	As if for the words 'an adopted person' on each occasion they appear there were substituted 'a person who is the subject of a parental order';
	(ii)	as if for the words 'adopters or adopter' on each occasion they appear there were substituted 'persons who obtained the order';
	(iii)	as if in section 67(2) the words from 'and, if adopted by' to 'section 51(2),' were omitted;
	(iv)	as if in section 67(2) for 'the couple in question' there were substituted 'those persons';
	(v)	as if section 67(3)(a) were omitted;
	(vi)	as if in section 67(3)(b) the words 'in any other case,' and 'subject to subsection (4)' were omitted;
	(vii)	as if in section 67(5) for 'adoption' there were substituted 'parental order';
	(viii)	as if in section 67(6) for 'and Schedule 4' there were substituted 'as applied with modifications by regulation 2 of and Schedule 1 to the Parental Order Regulations'; and
	(ix)	as if in section 67(6) for the word 'adoption' on each occasion it appears there were substituted 'making of the parental order'.
Section 68(3) (adoptive relatives)	As if in section 68(3) for the words from 'adoptive mother' onwards there were substituted 'mother and father of a child who is the subject of a parental order obtained by two persons of the same sex is to be read as a reference to the child's parents'.	
Section 69 (rules of interpretation for instruments concerning property)	(i)	As if in section 69(1) the words 'and to Schedule 4' were omitted;

Column 1	***Column 2***
Provisions of the 2002 Act	*Modifications*
* * * * *	
	(ii) as if in section 69(2) after 'and (2)' there were inserted 'as applied with modifications by regulation 2 of and Schedule 1 to the Parental Order Regulations';
	(iii) as if in section 69(2) for 'adoptive parent or parents' there were substituted 'persons who obtained the parental order';
	(iv) as if in section 69(2)(a) for 'adopted person' there were substituted 'person who is the subject of the parental order' and for 'adoption' there were substituted 'the parental order';
	(v) as if in section 69(2)(b) for 'adopted' there were substituted 'who are the subject of parental orders';
	(vi) as if in section 69(3) after 'subsection (2)' and in section 69(4) after 'Section 67(3)' and in section 69(5)(b) after 'section 67', there were inserted 'as applied with modifications by regulation 2 of and Schedule 1 to the Parental Order Regulations';
	(vii) as if in section 69(4) for 'adopted person' there were substituted 'person who is the subject of a parental order' and for 'adoption' there were substituted 'parental order is made';
	(viii) as if in section 69(5)(a) for 'adopt' there were substituted 'apply for a parental order in respect of'; and
	(ix) as if in section 69(5)(b) for the words from 'as her child' to 'the instrument' there were substituted 'for the purposes of the instrument as her child or as the child of the person with whom she obtained the order'.
Section 71 (property devolving with peerages etc)	(i) As if for the words 'an adoption' on each occasion they appear there were substituted 'a parental order'; and
	(ii) as if in section 71(3) after 'Subsection (2)' there were inserted 'as applied with modifications by regulation 2 of and Schedule 1 to the Parental Order Regulations'.
Section 72(1) (protection of trustees and personal representatives)	As if in section 72(1) for 'adoption' there were substituted 'parental order' and for 'effected' there were substituted 'made'.

Column 1	*Column 2*
Provisions of the 2002 Act	*Modifications*
* * * * *	
Section 73 (meaning of disposition)	As if in section 73(3) after the words 'This Chapter' there were inserted 'as applied with modifications by regulation 2 of and Schedule 1 to the Parental Order Regulations'.
* * * * *	

SCHEDULE 4
REFERENCES IN ENACTMENTS TO BE READ AS REFERENCES TO PARENTAL ORDERS ETC

Regulation 5

[245.148]

Column 1	*Column 2*
* * * * *	
13 Sections 27(2) (meaning of mother) and 28(5)(c) (meaning of father) of the Human Fertilisation and Embryology Act 1990	The references to adoption are to be read as including references to a parental order.
* * * * *	
20 Sections 33(2) (meaning of mother) and 38(4) (further provision relating to sections 35 and 36) of the 2008 Act	The references to adoption are to be read as including a reference to a parental order.

MARRIAGE (SAME SEX COUPLES) ACT 2013
2013 c 30

[17th July 2013]

[245.149]

Note. This Act, which legalises same sex marriages and also permits the conversion of civil partnerships into marriages with retrospective effect, also contains consequential provisions concerning the construction of statutes and documents. The general principle set out in section 11 is that in English law marriage has the same effect in relation to a same sex marriage as it does to an opposite sex marriage. This principle affects the construction of statutes (see Schedule 3) and private legal instruments (see Schedule 4) other than instruments made before the coming into force of section 11 (para 1(1) of Schedule 4). The instruments so excluded would include a will made before that time of a testator dying after that time. The principle embodied in section 11 is not absolute. Part 2 of Schedule 4 provides that the common law presumption that a child born to a woman during her marriage is also the child of her husband is not to apply in the case of a marriage between two women. The principle is also subject to the limiting provisions specified in Part 7 of Schedule 4. Section 17 confers wide powers by statutory instrument to make transitional and consequential provision which will doubtless be exercised so as to establish new and more detailed rules of construction The Act has not yet been brought into force and no statutory instruments have yet been made. The potential importance of the Act for the law of wills is that references in wills made after the commencement date to spouses, husbands, wives, widows and widowers, are likely to include parties or former parties to same sex marriages in the absence of the expression of a contrary intention.

PART 1

MARRIAGE OF SAME SEX COUPLES IN ENGLAND AND WALES

EXTENSION OF MARRIAGE

[245.150]
1. Extension of marriage to same sex couples (1) Marriage of same sex couples is lawful.

* * * * *

OTHER PROVISIONS RELATING TO MARRIAGES OF SAME SEX COUPLES

[245.151]
9. Conversion of civil partnership into marriage (1) The parties to an England and Wales civil partnership may convert their civil partnership into a marriage under a procedure established by regulations made by the Secretary of State.

* * * * *

(6) Where a civil partnership is converted into a marriage under this section—

(a) the civil partnership ends on the conversion, and
(b) the resulting marriage is to be treated as having subsisted since the date the civil partnership was formed.

* * * * *

EFFECT OF EXTENSION OF MARRIAGE

[245.152]
11. Effect of extension of marriage (1) In the law of England and Wales, marriage has the same effect in relation to same sex couples as it has in relation to opposite sex couples.

(2) The law of England and Wales (including all England and Wales legislation whenever passed or made) has effect in accordance with subsection (1).
(3) Schedule 3 (interpretation of legislation) has effect.
(4) Schedule 4 (effect of extension of marriage: further provision) has effect.
(5) For provision about limitations on the effects of sub-sections (1) and (2) and Schedule 3, see Part 7 of Schedule 4.

* * * * *

PART 3

FINAL PROVISIONS

[245.153]
17. Transitional and consequential provision (1) The Secretary of State or Lord Chancellor may, by order, make such transitional, transitory or saving provision as the Secretary of State or Lord Chancellor considers appropriate in connection with the coming into force of any provision of this Act.
(2) The Secretary of State or Lord Chancellor may, by order, make such provision as the Secretary of State or Lord Chancellor considers appropriate in consequence of this Act.
(3) The provision that may be made by an order under subsection (1) or (2) includes provision amending UK legislation.
(4) Schedule 7 (transitional and consequential provision etc) has effect.

* * * * *

[245.154]
20. Extent (1) This Act extends to England and Wales.

* * * * *

[245.155]
21. Short title and commencement (1) This Act may be cited as the Marriage (Same Sex Couples) Act 2013.
(2) This section and sections 15 and 16 come into force on the day on which this Act is passed.
(3) Subject to that, this Act comes into force on such day as the Secretary of State may by order appoint; and different days may be appointed for different purposes.

* * * * *

SCHEDULE 3
INTERPRETATION OF LEGISLATION

Section 11

PART 1

EXISTING ENGLAND AND WALES LEGISLATION

[245.156]
1. **Interpretation of existing England and Wales legislation** (1) In existing England and Wales legislation—

(a) a reference to marriage is to be read as including a reference to marriage of a same sex couple;
(b) a reference to a married couple is to be read as including a reference to a married same sex couple; and
(c) a reference to a person who is married is to be read as including a reference to a person who is married to a person of the same sex.

(2) Where sub-paragraph (1) requires a reference to be read in a particular way, any related reference (such as a reference to a marriage that has ended, or a reference to a person whose marriage has ended) is to be read accordingly.
(3) For the purposes of sub-paragraphs (1) and (2) it does not matter how a reference is expressed.

* * * * *

4. **General** This Part of this Schedule does not limit section 11(1) or (2).

PART 2

NEW ENGLAND AND WALES LEGISLATION

[245.157] 5—(1) This paragraph applies to provision made by—

(a) this Act and any subordinate legislation made under it, or
(b) new England and Wales legislation,

including any such provision which amends existing England and Wales legislation.
(2) The following expressions have the meanings given—

(a) 'husband' includes a man who is married to another man;
(b) 'wife' includes a woman who is married to another woman;
(c) 'widower' includes a man whose marriage to another man ended with the other man's death;
(d) 'widow' includes a woman whose marriage to another woman ended with the other woman's death;

and related expressions are to be construed accordingly.
(3) A reference to marriage of same sex couples is a reference to—

(a) marriage between two men, and
(b) marriage between two women.

(4) A reference to a marriage of a same sex couple is a reference to—

(a) a marriage between two men, or
(b) a marriage between two women.

(5) A reference to a same sex couple who are not married but are living together as a married couple is a reference to—

(a) two men who are not married but are living together as a married couple, or
(b) two women who are not married but are living together as a married couple.

(6) This Part of this Schedule does not limit section 11(1) or (2).

SCHEDULE 4
EFFECT OF EXTENSION OF MARRIAGE: FURTHER PROVISION

Section 11

PART 1
PRIVATE LEGAL INSTRUMENTS

[245.158]
1. Existing instruments (1) Section 11 does not alter the effect of any private legal instrument made before that section comes into force.
(2) In this paragraph 'private legal instrument' includes—

(a) a will,
(b) an instrument (including a private Act) which settles property,
(c) an instrument (including a private Act) which provides for the use, disposal or devolution of property, and
(d) an instrument (including a private Act) which—
  (i) establishes a body, or
  (ii) regulates the purposes and administration of a body,

(whether the body is incorporated or not and whether it is charitable or not);

but (with the exception of the kinds of private Act mentioned above) it does not include England and Wales legislation.

* * * * *

PART 2
PRESUMPTION ON BIRTH OF CHILD TO MARRIED WOMAN

[245.159]
2. Common law presumption (1) Section 11 does not extend the common law presumption that a child born to a woman during her marriage is also the child of her husband.

(2) Accordingly, where a child is born to a woman during her marriage to another woman, that presumption is of no relevance to the question of who the child's parents are.

* * * * *

PART 7
PROVISIONS WHICH LIMIT EQUIVALENCE OF ALL MARRIAGES ETC

[245.160]
27. Contrary provision (1) The relevant enactments are subject to—

(a) the preceding provisions of this Schedule, and
(b) any order under sub-paragraph (3).

(2) The relevant enactments are subject to any other contrary provision made by—

(a) the other provisions of this Act,
(b) any other subordinate legislation made under this Act, and
(c) any new England and Wales legislation,

including any such contrary provision contained in amendments of existing England and Wales legislation.
(3) The Secretary of State may by order—

(a) provide that a relevant enactment has effect subject to provision made by the order, or
(b) specify cases in which a relevant enactment does not apply.

(4) In this paragraph 'relevant enactment' means—

(a) section 11(1) and (2) and Schedule 3 (equivalence of all marriages in law), or
(b) section 9(6)(b) (marriage arising from conversion of civil partnership treated as having subsisted from formation of civil partnership).

* * * * *

SCHEDULE 7
TRANSITIONAL AND CONSEQUENTIAL PROVISION ETC

Section 17 * * * * *

PART 2

MINOR AND CONSEQUENTIAL AMENDMENTS

[245.161] [Paragraphs 31 to 36 and 37 to 41 make amendments to the Civil Partnership Act 2004 and Human Fertilisation and Embryology Act 2008 which so far as relevant are noted above.]

SECTION 3

Miscellaneous provisions relevant to the drafting of wills

[246.1]

Note. This section does not contain a comprehensive collection of conveyancing statutes, but a selection of statutes which a will draftsman may often have to consider. It includes statutes relating to beneficial interests, administrative powers conferred on personal representatives and trustees and powers to appoint new trustees and trustees' investment powers.

APPORTIONMENT ACT 1870

(33 & 34 Vict c 35)

[1 August 1870]

[246.1A]

Note. At common law rent and other periodical payments were not generally in the absence of a direction to the contrary apportionable on a time basis as between life tenant and remainderman. This rule was partly modified by the Apportionment Act 1834. The 1834 Act was superseded (though not formally abolished) by the more comprehensive provisions of the Apportionment Act 1870 and was only repealed in 1977 by the Statute Law (Repeals) Act 1977 (c 18), s1(1), Sch 1, Pt XVI. Section 2 of the 1870 Act, which enacted the general rule that income was apportionable on a time basis has now been disapplied by section 1(1), (4) and (5) of the Trusts (Capital and Income) Act 2013 (see paras **[246.202]** ff below) in relation to any 'new trust', i e any trust created or arising on or after the day on which the section came into force (including a trust created or arising under a power conferred before that day). The section was brought into force on 1 October 2013: Trusts (Capital and Income) Act 2013 (Commencement No 1) Order 2013 (SI 2013/676). Section 2 of the 1870 Act will continue to apply to trusts created or arising before 1 October 2013.

[246.2]

1. Short title. This Act may be cited for all purposes as 'The Apportionment Act, 1870.'

[246.3]

2. Rents, etc to be apportionable in respect of time.[1] … All rents, annuities, dividends, and other periodical payments in the nature of income (whether reserved or made payable under an instrument in writing or otherwise) shall, like interest on money lent, be considered as accruing from day to day, and shall be apportionable in respect of time accordingly.[2]

1 Subject to any contrary indication, this section is disapplied in relation to any trust created or arising on or after 1 October 2013 (including a trust created or arising under a power

conferred before that date), but continues to apply to trusts coming into operation before that date: see the Introductory Note at para **[246.1A]** above and see paras **[246.202]** ff below.

2 The words omitted from this section were repealed by the Statute Law Revision (No 2) Act 1893.

* * * * *

LAW OF PROPERTY ACT 1925

(15 & 16 Geo 5 c 20)

[9 April 1925] * * * * *

PART VII
PERPETUITIES AND ACCUMULATIONS

* * * * *

ACCUMULATIONS

[246.56]

164. General restrictions on accumulation of income.—[1] (1) No person may by any instrument or otherwise settle or dispose of any property in such manner that the income thereof shall, save as hereinafter mentioned, be wholly or partially accumulated for any longer period than one of the following, namely:—

(a) the life of the grantor or settlor; or
(b) a term of twenty-one years from the death of the grantor, settlor or testator; or
(c) the duration of the minority or respective minorities of any person or persons living or en ventre sa mere at the death of the grantor, settlor or testator; or
(d) the duration of the minority or respective minorities only of any person or persons who under the limitations of the instrument directing the accumulations would, for the time being, if of full age, be entitled to the income directed to be accumulated.

In every case where any accumulation is directed otherwise than as aforesaid, the direction shall (save as hereinafter mentioned) be void; and the income of the property directed to be accumulated shall, so long as the same is directed to be accumulated contrary to this section, go to and be received by the person or persons who would have been entitled thereto if such accumulation had not been directed.

(2) This section does not extend to any provision—

(i) for payment of the debts of any grantor, settlor, testator or other person;
(ii) for raising portions for—
    (a) any child, children or remoter issue of any grantor, settlor or testator; or

(b) any child, children or remoter issue of a person taking any interest under any settlement or other disposition directing the accumulations or to whom any interest is thereby limited;

(iii) respecting the accumulation of the produce of timber or wood;

and accordingly such provisions may be made as if no statutory restrictions on accumulation of income had been imposed.
(3) The restrictions imposed by this section apply to instruments made on or after the twenty-eighth day of July, eighteen hundred, but in the case of wills only where the testator was living and of testamentary capacity after the end of one year from that date.

1 Sections 164 to 166 of the Law of Property Act 1925 together with section 13 of the Perpetuities and Accumulations Act 1964 are repealed with effect from 6 April 2010 but not in relation to instruments taking effect before that date: Perpetuities and Accumulations Act 2009, ss 15, 21, Sch: see paras **[246.174]** ff below.

[246.57]
165. Qualification of restrictions on accumulation.[1] Where accumulations of surplus income are made during a minority under any statutory power or under the general law, the period for which such accumulations are made is not (whether the trust was created or the accumulations were made before or after the commencement of this Act) to be taken into account in determining the periods for which accumulations are permitted to be made by the last preceding section, and accordingly an express trust for accumulation for any other permitted period shall not be deemed to have been invalidated or become invalid, by reason of accumulations also having been made as aforesaid during such minority.

1 Sections 164 to 166 of the Law of Property Act 1925 together with section 13 of the Perpetuities and Accumulations Act 1964 are repealed with effect from 6 April 2010 but not in relation to instruments taking effect before that date: Perpetuities and Accumulations Act 2009, ss 15, 21, Sch: see paras **[246.174]** ff below.

[246.58]
166. Restriction on accumulation for the purchase of land.—[1] (1) No person may settle or dispose of any property in such manner that the income thereof shall be wholly or partially accumulated for the purchase of land only, for any longer period than the duration of the minority or respective minorities of any person or persons who, under the limitations of the instrument directing the accumulation, would for the time being, if of full age, be entitled to the income so directed to be accumulated.
(2) This section does not, nor do the enactments which it replaces, apply to accumulations to be held as capital money for the purposes of the Settled Land Act 1925 or the enactments replaced by that Act, whether or not the accumulations are primarily liable to be laid out in the purchase of land.
(3) This section applies to settlements and dispositions made after the twenty-seventh day of June eighteen hundred and ninety-two.

* * * * *

1 Sections 164 to 166 of the Law of Property Act 1925 together with section 13 of the Perpetuities and Accumulations Act 1964 are repealed with effect from 6 April 2010 but not

in relation to instruments taking effect before that date: Perpetuities and Accumulations Act 2009, ss 15, 21, Sch: see paras **[246.174]** ff below.

PERPETUITIES AND ACCUMULATIONS ACT 1964

(1964 c 55)

[16 July 1964]

* * * * *

ACCUMULATIONS

[246.86]
13. Amendment of s 164 of Law of Property Act 1925.—[1] (1) The periods for which accumulations of income under a settlement or other disposition are permitted by section 164 of the Law of Property Act 1925 shall include—

(a) a term of twenty-one years from the date of the making of the disposition and
(b) the duration of the minority or respective minorities of any person or persons in being at that date.

(2) It is hereby declared that the restrictions imposed by the said section 164 apply in relation to a power to accumulate income whether or not there is a duty to exercise that power, and that they apply whether or not the power to accumulate extends to income produced by the investment of income previously accumulated.

1 This section together with sections 164 to 166 of the Law of Property Act 1925 are repealed with effect from 6 April 2010 but not in relation to instruments taking effect before that date: Perpetuities and Accumulations Act 2009, ss 15, 21, Sch: see paras **[246.174]** ff below.

* * * * *

SUPPLEMENTAL

[246.88]
15. Short title, interpretation and extent.— (1) This Act may be cited as the Perpetuities and Accumulations Act 1964.
(2) In this Act—
'disposition' includes the conferring of a power of appointment and any other disposition of an interest in or right over property, and references to the interest disposed of shall be construed accordingly;
'in being' means living or en ventre sa mere;
'power of appointment' includes any discretionary power to transfer a beneficial interest in property without the furnishing of valuable consideration;
'will' includes a codicil;
and for the purposes of this Act a disposition contained in a will shall be deemed to be made at the death of the testator.

(3) For the purposes of this Act a person shall be treated as a member of a class if in his case all the conditions identifying a member of the class are satisfied, and shall be treated as a potential member if in his case some only of those conditions are satisfied but there is a possibility that the remainder will in time be satisfied.
(4) Nothing in this Act shall affect the operation of the rule of law rendering void for remoteness certain dispositions under which property is limited to be applied for purposes other than the benefit of any person or class of persons in cases where the property may be so applied after the end of the perpetuity period.
(5) The foregoing sections of this Act shall apply (except as provided in section 8(2) above) only in relation to instruments taking effect after the commencement of this Act, and in the case of an instrument made in the exercise of a special power of appointment shall apply only where the instrument creating the power takes effect after that commencement;
Provided that section 7 above shall apply in all cases for construing the foregoing reference to a special power of appointment.
[(5A) The foregoing sections of this Act shall not apply in relation to an instrument taking effect on or after the day appointed under section 22(2) of the Perpetuities and Accumulations Act 2009 (commencement), but this shall not prevent those sections applying in relation to an instrument so taking effect if—

(a) it is a will executed before that day, or
(b) it is an instrument made in the exercise of a special power of appointment, and the instrument creating the power took effect before that day.

(5B) Subsection (5A) above shall not affect the operation of sections 4(6) and 11(2) above.] [1]
(6) This Act shall apply in relation to a disposition made otherwise than by an instrument as if the disposition had been contained in an instrument taking effect when the disposition was made.
(7) This Act binds the Crown.

1 Subss (5A) and (5B) inserted with effect from 6 April 2010 by the Perpetuities and Accumulations Act 2009, s 16: see para **[246.190]** below.

PERPETUITIES AND ACCUMULATIONS ACT 2009

(2009 c 18)

[12 November 2009]

[246.174]

Note. This Act was brought into force on 6 April 2010. The main changes effected by the Act are the following. First, the rule against perpetuities will now apply only to what may be termed "family" interests, principally successive interests arising under trusts; it will not apply to "commercial" interests, e.g. options for the purchase of land or easements, and will be disapplied in relation to all forms of pension scheme, though not to nominations or the exercise of powers under such schemes. Secondly, the perpetuity period will be 125 years and it will not be possible to specify any other period. Thirdly, the existing statutory restrictions on accumulations are abolished save in relation to charities in respect of which special rules apply. These changes are prospective only. Settlements made before 6 April 2010 and appointments made on or after that date under settlements made before that date will continue to be governed by the former law. For a more detailed account of the new rules see Vol 1, Chapter 94 and Vol 2, paras **[200.35A]–[200.35H]** above.

APPLICATION OF RULE AGAINST PERPETUITIES

[246.175]

1. Application of the rule (1) The rule against perpetuities applies (and applies only) as provided by this section.

(2) If an instrument limits property in trust so as to create successive estates or interests the rule applies to each of the estates or interests.

(3) If an instrument limits property in trust so as to create an estate or interest which is subject to a condition precedent and which is not one of successive estates or interests, the rule applies to the estate or interest.

(4) If an instrument limits property in trust so as to create an estate or interest subject to a condition subsequent the rule applies to—

(a) any right of re-entry exercisable if the condition is broken, or
(b) any equivalent right exercisable in the case of property other than land if the condition is broken.

(5) If an instrument which is a will limits personal property so as to create successive interests under the doctrine of executory bequests, the rule applies to each of the interests.

(6) If an instrument creates a power of appointment the rule applies to the power.

(7) For the purposes of subsection (2) an estate or interest includes an estate or interest—

(a) which arises under a right of reverter on the determination of a determinable fee simple, or
(b) which arises under a resulting trust on the determination of a determinable interest.

(8) This section has effect subject to the exceptions made by section 2 and to any exceptions made under section 3.

(9) [*This subsection amends the Law of Property Act 1925, s 4*(*3*) (*rights of entry affecting legal estate*).]

[246.176]
2. Exceptions to rule's application (1) This section contains exceptions to the application of the rule against perpetuities.
(2) The rule does not apply to an estate or interest created so as to vest in a charity on the occurrence of an event if immediately before the occurrence an estate or interest in the property concerned is vested in another charity.
(3) The rule does not apply to a right exercisable by a charity on the occurrence of an event if immediately before the occurrence an estate or interest in the property concerned is vested in another charity.
(4) The rule does not apply to an interest or right arising under a relevant pension scheme.
(5) The exception in subsection (4) does not apply if the interest or right arises under—

(a) an instrument nominating benefits under the scheme, or
(b) an instrument made in the exercise of a power of advancement arising under the scheme.

[246.177]
3. Power to specify exceptions (1) The Lord Chancellor may by order provide that the rule against perpetuities is not to apply—

(a) in cases of a specified description, or
(b) if specified conditions are fulfilled.

(2) Different descriptions and conditions may be specified for different purposes.
(3) Any order under this section may include such supplementary, incidental, consequential or transitional provisions as appear to the Lord Chancellor to be necessary or expedient.
(4) In this section "specified" means specified in the order.
(5) The power to make an order under this section is exercisable by statutory instrument.
(6) A statutory instrument containing an order under this section may not be made unless a draft of the instrument has been laid before and approved by a resolution of each House of Parliament.

[246.178]
4. Abolition of existing exceptions These provisions cease to have effect—

(a) section 121(6) of the Law of Property Act 1925 (c. 20) (rule against perpetuities not to apply to certain powers and remedies);
(b) section 162 of that Act (declaration that rule does not apply in certain cases);
(c) section 163 of the Pension Schemes Act 1993 (c. 48) (rule not to apply to trusts and dispositions concerning certain pension schemes).

PERPETUITY PERIOD

[246.179]
5. Perpetuity period (1) The perpetuity period is 125 years (and no other period).

(2) Subsection (1) applies whether or not the instrument referred to in section 1(2) to (6) specifies a perpetuity period; and a specification of a perpetuity period in that instrument is ineffective.

PERPETUITIES: MISCELLANEOUS

[246.180]

6. Start of perpetuity period (1) The perpetuity period starts when the instrument referred to in section 1(2) to (6) takes effect; but this is subject to subsections (2) and (3).

(2) If section 1(2), (3) or (4) applies and the instrument is made in the exercise of a special power of appointment the perpetuity period starts when the instrument creating the power takes effect; but this is subject to subsection (3).

(3) If section 1(2), (3) or (4) applies and—

- (a) the instrument nominates benefits under a relevant pension scheme, or
- (b) the instrument is made in the exercise of a power of advancement arising under a relevant pension scheme,

the perpetuity period starts when the member concerned became a member of the scheme.

(4) The member concerned is the member in respect of whose interest in the scheme the instrument is made.

[246.181]

7. Wait and see rule (1) Subsection (2) applies if (apart from this section and section 8) an estate or interest would be void on the ground that it might not become vested until too remote a time.

(2) In such a case—

- (a) until such time (if any) as it becomes established that the vesting must occur (if at all) after the end of the perpetuity period the estate or interest must be treated as if it were not subject to the rule against perpetuities, and
- (b) if it becomes so established, that does not affect the validity of anything previously done (whether by way of advancement, application of intermediate income or otherwise) in relation to the estate or interest.

(3) Subsection (4) applies if (apart from this section) any of the following would be void on the ground that it might be exercised at too remote a time—

- (a) a right of re-entry exercisable if a condition subsequent is broken;
- (b) an equivalent right exercisable in the case of property other than land if a condition subsequent is broken;
- (c) a special power of appointment.

(4) In such a case—

- (a) the right or power must be treated as regards any exercise of it within the perpetuity period as if it were not subject to the rule against perpetuities, and

(b) the right or power must be treated as void for remoteness only if and so far as it is not fully exercised within the perpetuity period.

(5) Subsection (6) applies if (apart from this section) a general power of appointment would be void on the ground that it might not become exercisable until too remote a time.
(6) Until such time (if any) as it becomes established that the power will not be exercisable within the perpetuity period, it must be treated as if it were not subject to the rule against perpetuities.

[246.182]
8. Exclusion of class members to avoid remoteness (1) This section applies if—

(a) it is apparent at the time an instrument takes effect or becomes apparent at a later time that (apart from this section) the inclusion of certain persons as members of a class would cause an estate or interest to be treated as void for remoteness, and
(b) those persons are potential members of the class or unborn persons who at birth would become members or potential members of the class.

(2) From the time it is or becomes so apparent those persons must be treated for all the purposes of the instrument as excluded from the class unless their exclusion would exhaust the class.
(3) If this section applies in relation to an estate or interest to which section 7 applies, this section does not affect the validity of anything previously done (whether by way of advancement, application of intermediate income or otherwise) in relation to the estate or interest.
(4) For the purposes of this section—

(a) a person is a member of a class if in that person's case all the conditions identifying a member of the class are satisfied, and
(b) a person is a potential member of a class if in that person's case some only of those conditions are satisfied but there is a possibility that the remainder will in time be satisfied.

[246.183]
9. Saving and acceleration of expectant interests (1) An estate or interest is not void for remoteness by reason only that it is ulterior to and dependent on an estate or interest which is so void.
(2) The vesting of an estate or interest is not prevented from being accelerated on the failure of a prior estate or interest by reason only that the failure arises because of remoteness.

[246.184]
10. Determinable interests becoming absolute (1) If an estate arising under a right of reverter on the determination of a determinable fee simple is void for remoteness the determinable fee simple becomes absolute.
(2) If an interest arising under a resulting trust on the determination of a determinable interest is void for remoteness the determinable interest becomes absolute.

[246.185]
11. Powers of appointment (1) Subsection (2) applies to a power of appointment exercisable otherwise than by will (whether or not it is also exercisable by will).
(2) For the purposes of the rule against perpetuities the power is a special power unless—

(a) the instrument creating it expresses it to be exercisable by one person only, and
(b) at all times during its currency when that person is of full age and capacity it could be exercised by that person so as immediately to transfer to that person the whole of the interest governed by the power without the consent of any other person or compliance with any other condition (ignoring a formal condition relating only to the mode of exercise of the power).

(3) Subsection (4) applies to a power of appointment exercisable by will (whether or not it is also exercisable otherwise than by will).
(4) For the purposes of the rule against perpetuities the power is a special power unless—

(a) the instrument creating it expresses it to be exercisable by one person only, and
(b) that person could exercise it so as to transfer to that person's personal representatives the whole of the estate or interest to which it relates.

(5) Subsection (6) applies to a power of appointment exercisable by will or otherwise.
(6) If for the purposes of the rule against perpetuities the power would be a special power under one but not both of subsections (2) and (4), for the purposes of the rule it is a special power.

[246.186]
12. Pre-commencement instruments: period difficult to ascertain (1) If—

(a) an instrument specifies for the purposes of property limited in trust a perpetuity period by reference to the lives of persons in being when the instrument takes effect,
(b) the trustees believe that it is difficult or not reasonably practicable for them to ascertain whether the lives have ended and therefore whether the perpetuity period has ended, and
(c) they execute a deed stating that they so believe and that subsection (2) is to apply to the instrument,

that subsection applies to the instrument.
(2) If this subsection applies to an instrument—

(a) the instrument has effect as if it specified a perpetuity period of 100 years (and no other period);
(b) the rule against perpetuities has effect as if the only perpetuity period applicable to the instrument were 100 years;
(c) sections 6 to 11 of this Act are to be treated as if they applied (and always applied) in relation to the instrument;

(d) sections 1 to 12 of the Perpetuities and Accumulations Act 1964 (c. 55) are to be treated as if they did not apply (and never applied) in relation to the instrument.

(3) A deed executed under this section cannot be revoked.

ACCUMULATIONS

[246.187]
13. Abolition of restrictions These provisions cease to have effect—

(a) sections 164 to 166 of the Law of Property Act 1925 (c. 20) (which impose restrictions on accumulating income, subject to qualifications);
(b) section 13 of the Perpetuities and Accumulations Act 1964 (which amends section 164 of the 1925 Act).

[246.188]
14. Restriction on accumulation for charitable trusts (1) This section applies to an instrument to the extent that it provides for property to be held on trust for charitable purposes.
(2) But it does not apply where the provision is made by a court or the Charity Commission for England and Wales.
(3) If the instrument imposes or confers on the trustees a duty or power to accumulate income, and apart from this section the duty or power would last beyond the end of the statutory period, it ceases to have effect at the end of that period unless subsection (5) applies.
(4) The statutory period is a period of 21 years starting with the first day when the income must or may be accumulated (as the case may be).
(5) This subsection applies if the instrument provides for the duty or power to cease to have effect—

(a) on the death of the settlor, or
(b) on the death of one of the settlors, determined by name or by the order of their deaths.

(6) If a duty or power ceases to have effect under this section the income to which the duty or power would have applied apart from this section must—

(a) go to the person who would have been entitled to it if there had been no duty or power to accumulate, or
(b) be applied for the purposes for which it would have had to be applied if there had been no such duty or power.

(7) This section applies whether or not the duty or power to accumulate extends to income produced by the investment of income previously accumulated.

APPLICATION OF STATUTORY PROVISIONS

[246.189]
15. Application of this Act (1) Sections 1, 2, 4 to 11, 13 and 14 apply in relation to an instrument taking effect on or after the commencement day, except that—

(a) those sections do not apply in relation to a will executed before that day, and
(b) those sections apply in relation to an instrument made in the exercise of a special power of appointment only if the instrument creating the power takes effect on or after that day.

(2) Section 12 applies (except as provided by subsection (3)) in relation to—

(a) a will executed before the commencement day (whether or not it takes effect before that day);
(b) an instrument, other than a will, taking effect before that day.

(3) Section 12 does not apply if—

(a) the terms of the trust were exhausted before the commencement day, or
(b) before that day the property became held on trust for charitable purposes by way of a final disposition of the property.

(4) The commencement day is the day appointed under section 22(2).

[246.190]
16. Limitation of 1964 Act to existing instruments
[*Amends the Perpetuities and Accumulations Act 1964, s 15* (*which makes provision as to the instruments to which that Act applies*) *by inserting with effect from 6 April 2010 new subsections* (*5A*) *and* (*5B*).]

GENERAL

[246.191]
17. The Crown (1) This Act does not extend the application of the rule against perpetuities in relation to the Crown.
(2) Subject to that, this Act binds the Crown.

[246.192]
18. Rule as to duration not affected
This Act does not affect the rule of law which limits the duration of non-charitable purpose trusts.

[246.193]
19. Provision made otherwise than by instrument
If provision is made in relation to property otherwise than by an instrument, this Act applies as if the provision were contained in an instrument taking effect on the making of the provision.

[246.194]
20. Interpretation (1) For the purposes of this Act this section contains provisions relating to the interpretation of these expressions—

(a) power of appointment, general power of appointment and special power of appointment;

(b) relevant pension scheme;
(c) taking effect (in relation to a will);
(d) will.

(2) A power of appointment includes—

(a) a discretionary power to create a beneficial interest in property without the provision of valuable consideration;
(b) a discretionary power to transfer a beneficial interest in property without the provision of valuable consideration.

(3) Section 11 applies to interpret references to a general or special power of appointment.
(4) Each of these is a relevant pension scheme—

(a) an occupational pension scheme;
(b) a personal pension scheme;
(c) a public service pension scheme.

(5) The expressions in subsection (4)(a) to (c) have the meanings given by sections 1 and 181(1) of the Pension Schemes Act 1993 (c. 48).
(6) An instrument which is a will takes effect at the testator's death.
(7) A reference to a will includes a reference to a codicil.

[246.195]
21. Repeals
The enactments mentioned in the Schedule are repealed to the extent specified, but subject to the provision at the end of the Schedule.

[246.196]
22. Commencement (1) This section and sections 23 and 24 come into force on the day on which this Act is passed.
(2) The other provisions of this Act come into force on such day as the Lord Chancellor may appoint by order made by statutory instrument.

[246.197]
23. Extent
This Act extends to England and Wales only.

[246.198]
24. Short title
This Act may be cited as the Perpetuities and Accumulations Act 2009.

SCHEDULE

Section 21

REPEALS

[246.199]

Short title and chapter	*Extent of repeal*
Law of Property Act 1925	In section 4(3), the words from "but" to the end. Section 121(6). Section 162. Sections 164 to 166.
Perpetuities and Accumulations Act 1964 (c. 55)	Section 13.
Pension Schemes Act 1993 (c. 48)	Section 163.

These repeals have effect in accordance with section 15 of this Act.

[246.200]

CHARITIES ACT 2011

(2011 c 25)
[27 May 1993]

SCHEDULE 7
CONSEQUENTIAL AMENDMENTS

PART 1

GENERAL AMENDMENTS

* * * * *

APPLICATION OF CERTAIN ENACTMENTS TO TRUST CORPORATIONS

[246.201]
3. (1) In the definition of 'trust corporation' contained in the provisions listed in sub-paragraph (2) the reference to a corporation appointed by the court in any particular case to be a trustee includes a reference to a corporation appointed by the Commission under this Act to be a trustee.
(2) The provisions are—

(a) section 117(1)(xxx) of the Settled Land Act 1925,
(b) paragraph 18 of section 68(1) of the Trustee Act 1925,
(c) section 205(xxviii) of the law of Property Act 1925,
(d) section 55(1)(xxvi) of the Administration of Estates Act 1925, and

(e) section 128 of the Senior Courts Act 1981,

(3) This paragraph is to be treated as always having had effect.

(4) In sub-paragraph (2), the reference to section 128 of the Senior Courts Act 1981 is to be read—

(a) in relation to any time before 1 January 1982, as a reference to section 175(1) of the Supreme Court of Judicature (Consolidation) Act 1925, and

(b) in relation to any time on or after that date but before the day on which paragraph 1(2) of Schedule 11 to the Constitutional Reform Act 2005 came into force, as a reference to section 128 of the Supreme Court Act 1986.[1]

1 This re-enacts and replaces Charities Act 1993, s 35 with effect from 14 March 2012, with only verbal changes. Section 175(1) of the Supreme Court (Consolidation) Act 1925 was repealed by the Supreme Court Act 1981, s 152(4), Sch 7 and replaced by s 128 of that Act, and the Supreme Court Act 1981 was renamed the Senior Courts Act 1981 by the Constitutional Reform Act 2005.

[246.202]

TRUSTS (CAPITAL AND INCOME) ACT 2013

(2013 c 1)

[31 January 2013]

Note. This Act effects important changes affecting the administration of trusts and estates. Section 1 provides for the disapplication of certain rules of apportionment. Section 1(1) disapplies the statutory presumption under the Apportionment Act 1870 requiring the apportionment of income by reference to the period or periods over which it has accrued. For a fuller account of this change see Vol 1, para **[246.1A]** above.

Section 1(2) disapplies certain of the equitable rules of apportionment requiring adjustments as between capital and income. (As to these rules generally, see paras **[38.17]** ff.) The particular rules disapplied in section 1(2) are (a) the first branch of the rule in *Howe v Earl of Dartmouth* (which requires that in the absence of a direction to sell unauthorised investments of a wasting or hazardous nature must nevertheless be converted and reinvested), (b) the second branch of the rule in *Howe v Earl of Dartmouth* (which requires that pending the conversion of such unauthorised investments the life tenant should be credited with interest on the value of the unconverted property, traditionally at the rate of 4% per annum), (c) the rule in *Re Earl of Chesterfield's Trusts* (which requires that on the conversion of future or reversionary property a calculation should be made of the sum which, if invested at the testator's death at 4% interest accumulating with yearly rests, would amount to the net sum received on the sale of the reversionary property and the balance by which the net proceeds of sale exceeds that sum should be paid to the income beneficiary) and (d) the rule in *Allhusen v Whittell* (which requires that where successive interests in residue are given the life tenant must account to capital for the income attributable to that part of residue which is subsequently required for the payment of debts and legacies). These rules have in practice often been expressly excluded, but this will no longer be necessary. The disapplication of these rules applies to any 'new trust', ie any trust created or arising on or after 1 October 2013 (the day on which section 1 was brought into force). including a trust created or arising under a power conferred before that day. The disapplication of these rules is subject to any contrary intention.

It should be noted that the equitable rules known as the rules in *Re Bird* and *Re Atkinson* (which apply when a debt or security comprised in a settled fund or estate is insufficient to discharge the principal and arrears of interest due) are not disapplied by section 1. For the rules of equitable apportionment generally, see Vol 1, paras **[38.13]** ff. Sections 2 and 3 cure an anomaly in the classification of dividends received by shareholders as the result of a demerger.

In the case of a direct demerger, i e a demerger which involves the transfer by the main company of part of its business to a new subsidiary and the declaration of a dividend which is satisfied by the distribution to the shareholders of the share capital of the new subsidiary, the share capital so distributed was classified as income: *Bouch v Sproule* (1877) LR 12 App Cas 385. This meant that if shares in the main company formed part of the capital fund subject to a settlement, that asset would as a consequence of the demerger be converted into income. However, it was later held in *Sinclair v Lee* [1993] Ch 497 that in the case of an indirect demerger, i e a demerger involving the transfer of the shares in the new subsidiary to a new holding company and the distribution to the shareholders of the shares in the new holding company, the shares so distributed constituted capital. Section 2 cures this anomaly by treating all corporate distributions which are tax-exempt under section 1076, 1077 or 1078 of the Corporation Tax Act 2010 as capital. Section 3 empowers trustees, if they are satisfied that but for the tax-exempt distribution there would have been an income distribution, to make a compensatory distribution of capital to the income beneficiary.

Sections 1 to 3 were brought into force on 1 October 2013: Trusts (Capital and Income) Act 2013 (Commencement No 1) Order 2013 (SI 2013/676).

[246.203]

1. Disapplication of apportionment etc. rules (1) Any entitlement to income under a new trust is to income as it arises (and accordingly section 2 of the Apportionment Act 1870, which provides for income to accrue from day to day, does not apply in relation to the trust).

(2) The following do not apply in relation to a new trust—

(a) the first part of the rule in *Howe v Earl of Dartmouth* (which requires certain residuary personal estate to be sold);

(b) the second part of that rule (which withholds from a life tenant income arising from certain investments and compensates the life tenant with payments of interest);

(c) the rule known as the rule in *Re Earl of Chesterfield's Trusts* (which requires the proceeds of the conversion of certain investments to be apportioned between capital and income);

(d) the rule known as the rule in *Allhusen v Whittell* (which requires a contribution to be made from income for the purpose of paying a deceased person's debts, legacies and annuities).

(3) Trustees have power to sell any property which (but for subsection (2)(a)) they would have been under a duty to sell.

(4) Subsections (1) to (3) have effect subject to any contrary intention that appears—

(a) in any trust instrument of the trust; and

(b) in any power under which the trust is created or arises.

(5) In this section 'new trust' means a trust created or arising on or after the day on which this section comes into force (and includes a trust created or arising on or after that day under a power conferred before that day).

[246.204]

2. Classification of certain corporate distributions as capital (1) A receipt consisting of a tax-exempt corporate distribution is to be treated for the purposes of any trust to which this section applies as a receipt of capital (even if it would otherwise be treated for those purposes as a receipt of income).

(2) Subsection (1) has effect subject to any contrary intention that appears—

- (a) in any trust instrument of the trust; and
- (b) in any power under which the trust is created or arises.

(3) The following are tax-exempt corporate distributions for the purposes of this section and section 3—

- (a) a distribution that is an exempt distribution by virtue of section 1076, 1077 or 1078 of the Corporation Tax Act 2010; and
- (b) any other distribution of assets (in any form) by a body corporate, where the distribution is of a description by an order made by the Secretary of State by statutory instrument.

(4) An order under subsection (3)(b) may specify a description of distribution only if neither income tax nor capital gains tax is chargeable in respect of a distribution of that description.
(5) A statutory instrument containing an order under subsection (3)(b) is subject to annulment in pursuance of a resolution of either House of Parliament.
(6) This section applies to any trust, whether created or arising before or after this section comes into force.

[246.205]
3. Power to compensate income beneficiary (1) This section applies in any case where—

- (a) by virtue of section 2 a tax-exempt corporate distribution made by a body corporate is treated for the purposes of a trust to which that section applies as a receipt of capital; and
- (b) the trustees are satisfied that it is likely that, but for the distribution, there would have been a receipt from the body corporate that would have been a receipt of income for the purposes of the trust.

(2) The trustees may make a payment out of the capital funds of the trust, or transfer any property of the trust, to an income beneficiary for the purpose set out in subsection (3) (and any such payment or transfer is to be treated as a payment or transfer of capital).
(3) The purpose is placing the income beneficiary (so far as practicable) in the position in which the trustees consider that the beneficiary would have been had there been a receipt of income mentioned in subsection (1)(b).
(4) In this section 'income beneficiary', in relation to a trust, means a person entitled to income arising under the trust, or for whose benefit such income may be applied.

* * * * *

[246.206]
5. Crown application, extent and commencement (1) Sections 1 to 3 bind the Crown.
(2) This Act extends to England and Wales only.

(3) This section and section 6 come into force on the day on which this Act is passed, but otherwise this Act comes into force on such day as the Secretary of State may by order made by statutory instrument appoint.
(4) An order under subsection (3) may—

- (a) appoint different days for different purposes;
- (b) make such provisions as the Secretary of State considers necessary or expedient for transitory, transitional or saving purposes in connection with the coming into force of any provision of this Act.

[246.207]
6. Short title This Act may be cited as the Trusts (Capital and Income) Act 2013.

SECTION 5

European succession legislation

REGULATION (EU) NO 650/2012
OF THE EUROPEAN PARLIAMENT AND OF THE COUNCIL

[248.1]

Note. On 4 July 2012 the European Parliament and Council adopted a Regulation harmonising certain aspects of the law of succession of Member States of the European Union which was published in the Official Journal on 27 July 2012. The Regulation will apply to the succession to persons dying on or after 17 August 2015. The Regulation does not extend to the United Kingdom and Ireland which opted out or to Denmark which did not take part in its adoption.

Although the Regulation does not bind the United Kingdom, some of its provisions may affect the devolution of the estates of English testators who are either resident or own property in a Continental country and the form of their wills. Those provisions which may have some relevance are set out below. One of the principal features of the Regulation is the adoption of habitual residence as the common connecting factor. This term is not defined, but Recitals (23)–(25) which are set out below (in paras **[248.2]**–**[248.4]**) contain clear indications as to how the term should be construed. Article 1 which defines the scope of the Regulation and certain of the definitions in Article 3 are included (in paras **[248.5]** and **[248.6]**) as is the major part Chapter III (in paras **[248.7]**–**[248.21]**) which deals with the applicable law. Article 83 which appears in Chapter VII (General and final provisions) and contains transitional provisions is also included (in para **[248.22]**). Chapters II, IV, V and VI which respectively contain provisions relating to jurisdiction, the recognition and enforcement of decisions, authentic instruments and court settlements and the European Certificate of Succession are omitted. From a will draftsman's point of view the important provision is Article 22 (see para **[248.9]**) permitting a choice of law in certain circumstances. See also paras **[24.2]** and **[201.5A]**, and the suggested form of declaration under Article 22 in Form B1.7A at para **[201.5A]**.

RECITALS

* * * * *

[248.2] (23) In view of the increasing mobility of citizens and in order to ensure the proper administration of justice within the Union and to ensure that a genuine connecting factor exists between the succession and the Member State in which jurisdiction is exercised, this Regulation should provide that the general connecting factor for the purposes of determining both jurisdiction and the applicable law should be the habitual residence of the deceased at the time of death. In order to determine the habitual residence, the authority dealing with the succession should make an overall assessment of the circumstances of the life of the deceased during the years preceding his death and at the time of his death, taking account of all relevant factual elements, in particular the duration and regularity of the deceased's presence in the State concerned and the conditions and reasons for that presence. The habitual residence thus determined should reveal a close and stable connection with the State concerned taking into account the specific aims of this Regulation.

[248.3] (24) In certain cases, determining the deceased's habitual residence may prove complex. Such a case may arise, in particular, where the deceased for professional or economic reasons had gone to live abroad to work there, sometimes for a long time, but had maintained a close and stable connection with his State of origin. In such a case, the deceased could, depending on the circumstances of the case, be considered still to have his habitual residence in his State of origin in which the centre of interests of his family and his social life was located. Other complex cases may arise where the deceased lived in several States alternately or travelled from one State to another without settling permanently in any of them. If the deceased was a national of one of those States or had all his main assets in one of those States, his nationality or the location of those assets could be a special factor in the overall assessment of all the factual circumstances.

[248.4] (25) With regard to the determination of the law applicable to the succession the authority dealing with the succession may in exceptional cases – where, for instance, the deceased had moved to the State of his habitual residence fairly recently before his death and all the circumstances of the case indicate that he was manifestly more closely connected with another State – arrive at the conclusion that the law applicable to the succession should not be the law of the State of the habitual residence of the deceased but rather the law of the State with which the deceased was manifestly more closely connected. That manifestly closest connection should, however, not be resorted to as a subsidiary connecting factor whenever the determination of the habitual residence of the deceased at the time of death proves complex.

* * * * *

CHAPTER I
SCOPE AND DEFINITIONS

[248.5]

Article 1
Scope 1. This Regulation shall apply to succession to the estates of deceased persons. It shall not apply to revenue, customs or administrative matters.

2. The following shall be excluded from the scope of this Regulation:

(a) the status of natural persons, as well as family relationships and relationships deemed by the law applicable to such relationships to have comparable effects;

(b) the legal capacity of natural persons, without prejudice to point (c) of Article 23(2) and to Article 26;

(c) questions relating to the disappearance, absence or presumed death of a natural person;
(d) questions relating to matrimonial property regimes and property regimes of relationships deemed by the law applicable to such relationships to have comparable effects to marriage;
(e) maintenance obligations other than those arising by reason of death;
(f) the formal validity of dispositions of property upon death made orally;
(g) property rights, interests and assets created or transferred otherwise than by succession, for instance by way of gifts, joint ownership with a right of survivorship, pension plans, insurance contracts and arrangements of a similar nature, without prejudice to point (i) of Article 23(2);
(h) questions governed by the law of companies and other bodies, corporate or unincorporated, such as clauses in the memoranda of association and articles of association of companies and other bodies, corporate or unincorporated, which determine what will happen to the shares upon the death of the members;
(i) the dissolution, extinction and merger of companies and other bodies, corporate or unincorporated;
(j) the creation, administration and dissolution of trusts;
(k) the nature of rights *in rem*; and
(l) any recording in a register of rights in immovable or movable property, including the legal requirements for such recording, and the effects of recording or failing to record such rights in a register.

* * * * *

[248.6]

Article 3
Definitions 1. For the purposes of this Regulation:

(a) "succession" means succession to the estate of a deceased person and covers all forms of transfer of assets, rights and obligations by reason of death, whether by way of a voluntary transfer under a disposition of property upon death or a transfer through intestate succession;
(b) "agreement as to succession" means an agreement, including an agreement resulting from mutual wills, which, with or without consideration, creates, modifies or terminates rights to the future estate or estates of one or more persons party to the agreement;
(c) "joint will" means a will drawn up in one instrument by two or more persons;
(d) "disposition of property upon death" means a will, a joint will or an agreement as to succession.

* * * * *

CHAPTER III
APPLICABLE LAW

[248.7]

Article 20

Universal application Any law specified by this Regulation shall be applied whether or not it is the law of a Member State.

[248.8]

Article 21

General rule 1. Unless otherwise provided for in this Regulation, the law applicable to the succession as a whole shall be the law of the State in which the deceased had his habitual residence at the time of death.
2. Where, by way of exception, it is clear from all the circumstances of the case that, at the time of death, the deceased was manifestly more closely connected with a State other than the State whose law would be applicable under paragraph 1, the law applicable to the succession shall be the law of that other State.

[248.9]

Article 22

Choice of law 1. A person may choose as the law to govern his succession as a whole the law of the State whose nationality he possesses at the time of making the choice or at the time of death.
A person possessing multiple nationalities may choose the law of any of the States whose nationality he possesses at the time of making the choice or at the time of death.
2. The choice shall be made expressly in a declaration in the form of a disposition of property upon death or shall be demonstrated by the terms of such a disposition.
3. The substantive validity of the act whereby the choice of law was made shall be governed by the chosen law.
4. Any modification or revocation of the choice of law shall meet the requirements as to form for the modification or revocation of a disposition of property upon death.

[248.10]

Article 23

The scope of the applicable law 1. The law determined pursuant to Article 21 or Article 22 shall govern the succession as a whole.

2. That law shall govern in particular:

(a) the causes, time and place of the opening of the succession;
(b) the determination of the beneficiaries, of their respective shares and of the obligations which may be imposed on them by the deceased, and the determination of other succession rights, including the succession rights of the surviving spouse or partner;
(c) the capacity to inherit;
(d) disinheritance and disqualification by conduct;
(e) the transfer to the heirs and, as the case may be, to the legatees of the assets, rights and obligations forming part of the estate, including the conditions and effects of the acceptance or waiver of the succession or of a legacy;
(f) the powers of the heirs, the executors of the wills and other administrators of the estate, in particular as regards the sale of property and the payment of creditors, without prejudice to the powers referred to in Article 29(2) and (3);
(g) liability for the debts under the succession;
(h) the disposable part of the estate, the reserved shares and other restrictions on the disposal of property upon death as well as claims which persons close to the deceased may have against the estate or the heirs;
(i) any obligation to restore or account for gifts, advancements or legacies when determining the shares of the different beneficiaries; and
(j) the sharing-out of the estate.

[248.11]

Article 24
Dispositions of property upon death other than agreements as to succession
1. A disposition of property upon death other than an agreement as to succession shall be governed, as regards its admissibility and substantive validity, by the law which, under this Regulation, would have been applicable to the succession of the person who made the disposition if he had died on the day on which the disposition was made.
2. Notwithstanding paragraph 1, a person may choose as the law to govern his disposition of property upon death, as regards its admissibility and substantive validity, the law which that person could have chosen in accordance with Article 22 on the conditions set out therein.
3. Paragraph 1 shall apply, as appropriate, to the modification or revocation of a disposition of property upon death other than an agreement as to succession. In the event of a choice of law in accordance with paragraph 2, the modification or revocation shall be governed by the chosen law.

[248.12]

Article 25
Agreements as to succession 1. An agreement as to succession regarding the succession of one person shall be governed, as regards its admissibility, its substantive validity and its binding effects between the parties, including the

conditions for its dissolution, by the law which, under this Regulation, would have been applicable to the succession of that person if he had died on the day on which the agreement was concluded.

2. An agreement as to succession regarding the succession of several persons shall be admissible only if it is admissible under all the laws which, under this Regulation, would have governed the succession of all the persons involved if they had died on the day on which the agreement was concluded. An agreement as to succession which is admissible pursuant to the first subparagraph shall be governed, as regards its substantive validity and its binding effects between the parties, including the conditions for its dissolution, by the law, from among those referred to in the first subparagraph, with which it has the closest connection.

3. Notwithstanding paragraphs 1 and 2, the parties may choose as the law to govern their agreement as to succession, as regards its admissibility, its substantive validity and its binding effects between the parties, including the conditions for its dissolution, the law which the person or one of the persons whose estate is involved could have chosen in accordance with Article 22 on the conditions set out therein.

[248.13]

Article 26

Substantive validity of dispositions of property upon death 1. For the purposes of Articles 24 and 25 the following elements shall pertain to substantive validity:

(a) the capacity of the person making the disposition of property upon death to make such a disposition;
(b) the particular causes which bar the person making the disposition from disposing in favour of certain persons or which bar a person from receiving succession property from the person making the disposition;
(c) the admissibility of representation for the purposes of making a disposition of property upon death;
(d) the interpretation of the disposition;
(e) fraud, duress, mistake and any other questions relating to the consent or intention of the person making the disposition.

2. Where a person has the capacity to make a disposition of property upon death under the law applicable pursuant to Article 24 or Article 25, a subsequent change of the law applicable shall not affect his capacity to modify or revoke such a disposition.

[248.14]

Article 27

Formal validity of dispositions of property upon death made in writing 1. A disposition of property upon death made in writing shall be valid as regards form if its form complies with the law:

(a) of the State in which the disposition was made or the agreement as to succession concluded;

(b) of a State whose nationality the testator or at least one of the persons whose succession is concerned by an agreement as to succession possessed, either at the time when the disposition was made or the agreement concluded, or at the time of death;

(c) of a State in which the testator or at least one of the persons whose succession is concerned by an agreement as to succession had his domicile, either at the time when the disposition was made or the agreement concluded, or at the time of death;

(d) of the State in which the testator or at least one of the persons whose succession is concerned by an agreement as to succession had his habitual residence, either at the time when the disposition was made or the agreement concluded, or at the time of death; or

(e) in so far as immovable property is concerned, of the State in which that property is located.

The determination of the question whether or not the testator or any person whose succession is concerned by the agreement as to succession had his domicile in a particular State shall be governed by the law of that State.

2. Paragraph 1 shall also apply to dispositions of property upon death modifying or revoking an earlier disposition. The modification or revocation shall also be valid as regards form if it complies with any one of the laws according to the terms of which, under paragraph 1, the disposition of property upon death which has been modified or revoked was valid.

3. For the purposes of this Article, any provision of law which limits the permitted forms of dispositions of property upon death by reference to the age, nationality or other personal conditions of the testator or of the persons whose succession is concerned by an agreement as to succession shall be deemed to pertain to matters of form. The same rule shall apply to the qualifications to be possessed by any witnesses required for the validity of a disposition of property upon death.

[248.15]

Article 28

Validity as to form of a declaration concerning acceptance or waiver A declaration concerning the acceptance or waiver of the succession, of a legacy or of a reserved share, or a declaration designed to limit the liability of the person making the declaration, shall be valid as to form where it meets the requirements of:

(a) the law applicable to the succession pursuant to Article 21 or Article 22, or

(b) the law of the State in which the person making the declaration has his habitual residence.

* * * * *

[248.16]

Article 31

Adaptation of rights *in rem* Where a person invokes a right *in rem* to which he is entitled under the law applicable to the succession and the law of the Member State in which the right is invoked does not know the right *in rem* in question, that right shall, if necessary and to the extent possible, be adapted to the closest equivalent right *in rem* under the law of that State, taking into account the aims and the interests pursued by the specific right *in rem* and the effects attached to it.

[248.17]

Article 32

Commorientes Where two or more persons whose successions are governed by different laws die in circumstances in which it is uncertain in what order their deaths occurred, and where those laws provide differently for that situation or make no provision for it at all, none of the deceased persons shall have any rights to the succession of the other or others.

[248.18]

Article 33

Estate without a claimant To the extent that, under the law applicable to the succession pursuant to this Regulation, there is no heir or legatee for any assets under a disposition of property upon death and no natural person is an heir by operation of law, the application of the law so determined shall not preclude the right of a Member State or of an entity appointed for that purpose by that Member State to appropriate under its own law the assets of the estate located on its territory, provided that the creditors are entitled to seek satisfaction of their claims out of the assets of the estate as a whole.

[248.19]

Article 34

Renvoi 1. The application of the law of any third State specified by this Regulation shall mean the application of the rules of law in force in that State, including its rules of private international law in so far as those rules make a *renvoi*:

(a) to the law of a Member State; or
(b) to the law of another third State which would apply its own law.

2. No *renvoi* shall apply with respect to the laws referred to in Article 21(2), Article 22, Article 27, point (b) of Article 28 and Article 30.

[248.20]

Article 35

Public policy (ordre public) The application of a provision of the law of any State specified by this Regulation may be refused only if such application is manifestly incompatible with the public policy (*ordre public*) of the forum.

[248.21]

Article 36

States with more than one legal system – territorial conflicts of laws

1. Where the law specified by this Regulation is that of a State which comprises several territorial units each of which has its own rules in respect of succession, the internal conflict-of-law rules of that State shall determine the relevant territorial unit whose rules of law are to apply.

2. In the absence of such internal conflict-of-laws rules:

(a) any reference to the law of the State referred to in paragraph 1 shall, for the purposes of determining the law applicable pursuant to provisions referring to the habitual residence of the deceased, be construed as referring to the law of the territorial unit in which the deceased had his habitual residence at the time of his death;

(b) any reference to the law of the State referred to in paragraph 1 shall, for the purposes of determining the law applicable pursuant to provisions referring to the nationality of the deceased, be construed as referring to the law of the territorial unit with which the deceased had the closest connection;

(c) any reference to the law of the State referred to in paragraph 1 shall, for the purposes of determining the law applicable pursuant to any other provisions referring to other elements as connecting factors, be construed as referring to the law of the territorial unit in which the relevant element is located.

3. Notwithstanding paragraph 2, any reference to the law of the State referred to in paragraph 1 shall, for the purposes of determining the relevant law pursuant to Article 27, in the absence of internal conflict-of-laws rules in that State, be construed as referring to the law of the territorial unit with which the testator or the persons whose succession is concerned by the agreement as to succession had the closest connection.

[248.22]

Article 37

States with more than one legal system – inter-personal conflicts of laws In relation to a State which has two or more systems of law or sets of rules applicable to different categories of persons in respect of succession, any reference to the law of that State shall be construed as referring to the system of law or set of rules determined by the rules in force in that State. In the absence of such rules, the system of law or the set of rules with which the deceased had the closest connection shall apply.

* * * * *

CHAPTER VII
GENERAL AND FINAL PROVISIONS

* * * * *

[248.23]

Article 83

Transitional provisions 1. This Regulation shall apply to the succession of persons who die on or after 17 August 2015.

2. Where the deceased had chosen the law applicable to his succession prior to 17 August 2015, that choice shall be valid if it meets the conditions laid down in Chapter III or if it is valid in application of the rules of private international law in force, at the time the choice was made, in the State in which the deceased had his habitual residence or in any of the States whose nationality he possessed.

3. A disposition of property upon death made prior to 17 August 2015 shall be admissible and valid in substantive terms and as regards form if it meets the conditions laid down in Chapter III or if it is admissible and valid in substantive terms and as regards form in application of the rules of private international law in force, at the time the disposition was made, in the State in which the deceased had his habitual residence or in any of the States whose nationality he possessed or in the Member State of the authority dealing with the succession.

4. If a disposition of property upon death was made prior to 17 August 2015 in accordance with the law which the deceased could have chosen in accordance with this Regulation, that law shall be deemed to have been chosen as the law applicable to the succession.

* * * * *